# Lecture Notes in Computer Science    16358

Founding Editors

Gerhard Goos
Juris Hartmanis

## Editorial Board Members

The series Lecture Notes in Computer Science (LNCS), including its subseries Lecture Notes in Artificial Intelligence (LNAI) and Lecture Notes in Bioinformatics (LNBI), has established itself as a medium for the publication of new developments in computer science and information technology research, teaching, and education.

LNCS enjoys close cooperation with the computer science R & D community, the series counts many renowned academics among its volume editors and paper authors, and collaborates with prestigious societies. Its mission is to serve this international community by providing an invaluable service, mainly focused on the publication of conference and workshop proceedings and postproceedings. LNCS commenced publication in 1973.

Sushmita Mitra · Sriparna Saha ·
Bijaya Ketan Panigrahi · Sudeep Sarkar ·
Santanu Chaudhury
Editors

# Pattern Recognition and Machine Intelligence

11th International Conference, PReMI 2025
Delhi, India, December 11–14, 2025
Proceedings, Part II

 Springer

*Editors*
Sushmita Mitra
Indian Statistical Institute
Kolkata, West Bengal, India

Bijaya Ketan Panigrahi
Indian Institute of Technology Delhi
New Delhi, Delhi, India

Santanu Chaudhury
IIT Delhi
New Delhi, Delhi, India

Sriparna Saha
Indian Institute of Technology Patna
Bihta, Bihar, India

Sudeep Sarkar
University of South Florida
Tampa, FL, USA

ISSN 0302-9743     ISSN 1611-3349  (electronic)
Lecture Notes in Computer Science
ISBN 978-3-032-18479-5     ISBN 978-3-032-18480-1  (eBook)
https://doi.org/10.1007/978-3-032-18480-1

# Preface

Machine learning and pattern recognition play a pivotal role in today's data-driven world by enabling systems to automatically identify trends, make predictions, and adapt to complex real-world situations. Applications include critical domains such as industrial automation, healthcare, finance, and education. It is our pleasure to present the proceedings of PReMI 2025, the 11th International Conference on Pattern Recognition and Machine Intelligence, which took place from 11–14 December 2025 at the Indian Institute of Technology Delhi, India. The conference was organized by the Department of Electrical Engineering, Indian Institute of Technology Delhi (IIT Delhi), in collaboration with the Machine Intelligence Unit (MIU), Indian Statistical Institute (ISI), Kolkata. The goal of PReMI 2025, similar to its earlier editions, was to provide an international platform for presentation of high-quality novel research contributions in pattern recognition, machine intelligence, and related fields, while fostering a meaningful exchange of ideas among researchers, industry professionals, and students.

The birth of this conference can be traced to 2004, when a group of enthusiastic volunteers from MIU, under the able stewardship of Sankar K. Pal, deliberated on holding the first edition of PReMI in 2005 at ISI Kolkata. The path was difficult and strewn with obstacles. But they succeeded. Thereafter, the conference has been organized every alternate year around the country, as well as in international destinations such as Moscow and Warsaw. The 2009 edition was held in IIT Delhi with the late C. A. Murthy playing a stellar role in its success. We recalled the past with great pleasure as we held the eleventh version in 2025, once again in Delhi.

This year the conference was structured primarily into the following tracks, namely, Artificial Intelligence, Bioinformatics, Computer Vision, Cyber-physical systems, Data Science, Document Understanding, Edge AI, Evolutionary Computation, Health Analytics, Image Processing, Medical Imaging, Natural Language Processing, Pattern Recognition, Quantum AI, Signal Processing, Soft Computing/Computational Intelligence, Speech and Audio Processing, Swarm Intelligence, Video Processing, AR-VR, and Haptics. We received a total of 427 submissions across all tracks. After a rigorous and careful review process, a total of 154 papers were accepted for inclusion in these proceedings (an acceptance rate of approximately 36%). Each submission received an average of three reviews in a single-blind review framework. To complement the main program, a number of workshops and tutorials were held on 11 December. Tutorials were on emerging topics such as Foundations of Diffusion Models for Visual Content Generation, Developmental Neuroscience-Inspired Machine Learning, Generative Learning with Causal Awareness: Methods and Real-World Applications, Pattern Recognition to Action: Deep RL for LLMs and Robots, and Scalable Tensor Decomposition and Applications. Several workshops were also integrated into the conference schedule, providing focused discussion on timely sub-areas of interest. The topics of the workshops included

- AI in Spatial Computing: AR/VR, Metaverse
- AI4SG: AI for Social Good

- TinyML & Neuromorphic Computing for Edge Intelligence
- Quantum Computing and Machine Learning (QCML)
- Machine Intelligence in Quality Assessment of Biomedical Data
- Graph Reasoning Unleashed: GNNs in LLMs, High-Order Inference, and Healthcare
- Brain Creativity and Decay, Intelligent Biomarkers Related to Aging and Diseases (AI4CD)
- Multilingual Document Digitization for Indian Languages: Standards, Tools, and Trends
- Opthalmic AI
- Rare Earth Metals & AI

A doctoral symposium was also organized as a part of the conference program. This symposium was an exclusive event for PhD students who were enrolled at the time of the conference. The primary goal of the doctoral symposium was to provide a forum for in-depth research discussions and to foster a mentoring and peer network for the participants. It offered a unique opportunity for doctoral students to showcase their doctoral research contributions in different topics within the broader areas of interest to PReMI 2025. Additionally, a Diversity and Inclusion track was organized within the framework of PReMI 2025.

We were honored to host Jayaram K. Udupa (University of Pennsylvania, USA), Mohan Kankanhalli (National University of Singapore, Singapore), Subbarao Kambhampati (Fulton School Of Engineering, Arizona State University, USA), Ragini Verma (DICIPHR, USA), Baba C. Vemuri (University of Florida, USA), Danilo Pietro Pau (STMicroelectronics, Italy), Ashutosh Garg (CEO and Co-founder of Eightfold.ai), and Arpita Patra (IISC, Bangalore), as keynote speakers, whose talks significantly enriched the technical discourse.

We express our heartfelt gratitude to all those who made PReMI 2025 possible: the honorary chairs, general chairs, organizing committee, area chairs, program committee and reviewers, workshop and tutorial chairs, publication chairs, diversity chair, industry chairs, publicity, startup innovation and doctoral symposium chairs, authors, participants, and volunteers. Special thanks to the authors for their dedication, and to the reviewers for their critical insights and timely efforts.

We are pleased to convey our sincere gratitude to Springer LNCS for their continued support in the preparation of this volume of the prestigious PReMI 2025. Particular mention must be made of Springer for their continuous guidance in the process. We also extend our appreciation to all individuals who took on the significant responsibilities associated with secretarial tasks. Finally, our heartfelt thanks go to everyone who contributed to managing and hosting the PReMI 2025 review process on the METEOR platform.

We hope that the contents of this volume will serve as a valuable resource and source of inspiration, promoting cross-disciplinary interactions and driving future advances in pattern recognition, machine intelligence, and related domains.

December 2025

Sushmita Mitra<br>Sriparna Saha<br>Bijaya Ketan Panigrahi

# Organization

## Patron

| | |
|---|---|
| Rangan Banerjee | Indian Institute of Technology Delhi, India |

## Honorary Chairs

| | |
|---|---|
| Sankar K. Pal | Indian Statistical Institute Kolkata, India |
| Andrej Skowron | University of Warsaw, Poland |

## General Chairs

| | |
|---|---|
| Santanu Chaudhury | Indian Institute of Technology Delhi, India |
| Sudeep Sarkar | University of South Florida, USA |

## Program Chairs

| | |
|---|---|
| Sushmita Mitra | Indian Statistical Institute Kolkata, India |
| Sriparna Saha | Indian Institute of Technology Patna, India |
| B. K. Panigrahi | Indian Institute of Technology Delhi, India |

## Area Chairs

| | |
|---|---|
| Kolin Paul | Indian Institute of Technology Delhi, India |
| Sudeshna Sarkar | Indian Institute of Technology Kharagpur, India |
| Aruna Tiwari | Indian Institute of Technology Indore, India |
| M. Tanveer | Indian Institute of Technology Indore, India |
| Sukhendu Das | Indian Institute of Technology Madras, India |
| Asif Ekbal | Indian Institute of Technology Patna, India |
| Amit Sethi | Indian Institute of Technology Bombay, India |
| Debarka Sengupta | Indraprastha Institute of Information Technology Delhi, India |
| Monika Aggarwal | Indian Institute of Technology Delhi, India |
| Utpal Garain | Indian Statistical Institute Kolkata, India |

| | |
|---|---|
| Soma Biswas | Indian Institute of Science Bengaluru, India |
| Nishchal Verma | Indian Institute of Technology Kanpur, India |
| Umapada Pal | Indian Statistical Institute Kolkata, India |
| Partha Pratim Das | Ashoka University, India |
| Nitin V. George | Indian Institute of Technology Gandhinagar, India |
| Badri Narayan Subudhi | Indian Institute of Technology Jammu, India |
| Arun Kumar | Indian Institute of Technology Delhi, India |
| Pinaki Roy Chowdhury | Defence Research and Development Organisation, India |
| Gaurav Bhatnagar | Indian Institute of Technology Jodhpur, India |
| Susmita Sur-Kolay | Ashoka University, India |
| Deepak Fulwani | Indian Institute of Technology Jodhpur, India |
| Subhashish Chaudhury | Indian Institute of Technology Bombay, India |

## Organizing Chairs

| | |
|---|---|
| Tapan K. Gandhi | Indian Institute of Technology Delhi, India |
| S. Indu | Delhi Technological University, India |

## Industry Chairs

| | |
|---|---|
| Arpan Pal | TCS, India |
| Kaushik Saha | Indian Institute of Technology Delhi, India |

## Diversity Chair

| | |
|---|---|
| Lipika Dey | Ashoka University, India |

## Publication Chairs

| | |
|---|---|
| Sanjukta Roy | Indian Statistical Institute Kolkata, India |
| Ayesha Choudhary | Jawaharlal Nehru University, India |

## Tutorial Chairs

| | |
|---|---|
| Malay Bhattacharya | Indian Statistical Institute Kolkata, India |
| Monidipa Das | IISER Kolkata, India |

## Startup Innovation Chair

Manoj Kumar                         STM Electronics, India

## Workshop Chairs

Sandeep Kumar                       Indian Institute of Technology Delhi, India
Amrit Singh Bedi                    University of Florida, USA

## Publicity Chairs

Somnath Dey                         Indian Institute of Technology Indore, India
Saurabh Das                         Indian Institute of Technology Indore, India

## Doctoral Symposium Chair

Chetan S. Ralekar                   Indian Institute of Technology Roorkee, India

## International Liaison

Dominik Ślęzak                      University of Warsaw, Poland
Sergei O. Kuznetsov                 HSE Moscow, Russia

## Volunteer Committee

Rohan Kirti                         Indian Institute of Technology Patna, India
Sofia Jamil                         Indian Institute of Technology Patna, India
Riddhasree Bhattacharyya            Indian Statistical Institute Kolkata, India
Surochita Pal                       SRM University, India
Chhavi Dhiman                       Delhi Technological University, India
N. Jayanthi                         Delhi Technological University, India
Shobha Sharma                       Indian Institute of Technology Delhi, India
Shruti Aggarwal                     Delhi Technological University, India
Siddhant Ujjain                     Indian Institute of Technology Delhi, India
Prakash Mishra                      Indian Institute of Technology Delhi, India
Sapna Mishra                        Indian Institute of Technology Delhi, India

| | |
|---|---|
| Neha Sharma | Delhi Technological University, India |
| Amit Bhongade | Harvard Medical School, USA |
| Lakshay | Indian Institute of Technology Delhi, India |

## Additional Reviewers

| | |
|---|---|
| Abhay Alok | Surochita Pal |
| Hemant Patil | Riddhasree Bhattacharyya |
| Utpal Sikdar | Subham Raj |
| Sumit Mishra | Tanmoy Kanti Halder |
| Shweta | Pranab Sahoo |
| Sayantan Maitra | Anushree Bablani |
| Naveen Saini | Pratik Dutta |
| Pratik Dutta | Shally Gupta |
| Tulika Saha | Tej Singh |
| Sugata Banerji | Mohd. Aquib |
| Dipanjyoti Paul | Nabamita Deb |
| Santosh Mishra | Ankit Yadav |
| Chanchal Suman | Akshay Mool |
| Nikhilanand Arya | Rakesh Chander Joshi |
| Apoorva Singh | Aatreya Sengupta |
| Krishanu Maity | Angshuman Jana |
| Nitish Kumar | Sibani Panigrahi |
| Sarmistha Das | Shweta Gupta |
| Biswajit Chatterjee | Abhishek Mukhopadhyay |
| Rohan Kirti | Upasana Tripathi |
| Gautam Kumar | Sapna Mishra |
| Ashutosh Kumar Sinha | Rohit Misra |
| Medhasree Ghosh | Amit Bhongade |
| Anmol Kumar | Pushpraj Singh Chauhan |
| Debasish Das | Abdul Quadir |
| Utsav Nareti | Mushir Akhtar |
| Priya Kumari | Ranjeet Kumar Rout |
| Swagata Mukherjee | Abdur Rahaman |
| Sofia Jamil | Shouvik Chakraborty |
| Md. Tauseef Alam | Anil Kumar |
| Prakash Mishra | Sunidhi Singh |
| Shobha Sharma | Monika Singh |
| Shruti Aggarwal | Nitin Yadav |
| Sapna S. Mishra | Navpreet |
| Chhavi Dhiman | Bam Bahadur Sinha |
| N. Jayanthi | Vivek Soren |
| Siddhant Ujjain | Sajad Ahmad Rather |
| Neha Sharma | Deepak Sethi |

Harivinod N.
Jyotismita Talukdar
Rupam Bhattacharya
Subrata Sinha
Ajay Kaushik
Roli Kushwaha
Sumit Dutta
Sumantara Dutta
Shobhanjana Kalita
Agniva Banerjee
Debanjan Sadhya
Rijul Soans
Mohd Shamsh Tabarej
Aparajita Khan
Paramartha Dutta
Vasudha Bhatnagar
Chiranjib Sur
Saptadipa Mazumder
Kamakshi Rautela
Shikha Singhal
Hima Bindu
Gaurav Kumar
Anupma Sharma
Aman Jolly
Kishore Babu Nampalle
Shailendra Raghuwanshi
Aashania Antil
Narendra Kumar
Pushpendra Kumara
Munnu Sonkar
Lipika Dey
S. Indu
Muskan Agarwal
Palak Handa
Vineet Srivastava
Chaithra
Archana B. Saxena
Ram Prakash Sharma
Dhruv Sharma
Reshma Rastogi
Santosh Singh Rathore
Geethanjali Kher
Anubhab Maity
Hirak Mazaumdar
Diya Saha

Manjira Sinha
Deepti Sharma
Pabitra Mitra
Jhalak Dutta
Bagesh Kumar
Upasana Talukdar
Sourav Dutta
M. Srivani
Arun Bhadwal
Deepshikha Aggarwal
Mukesh Sahu
Ram Prakash Sharma
Sunil Singh
Shyamali Mitra
Ashutosh Pandey
Akhila P.
Angshuman Jana
Arshpreet Kaur
Vikram Singh
Gaurav Kumar
Mrinmoy Bhattacharjee
Shreyas Nagoor
Vishakha Pareek
Athira Krishnan
Nandadulal Jana
Swalpa Kumar Roy
Ashis Kumar Dhara
Shramana Dey
Pallabi Dutta
Pranay Adak
Shovan Barma
Vipin Venugopal
Saptarsi Goswami
Palash Ghosal
Ritik Mishra
Monidipa Das
Anup Nandy
Anuradha Kumari
Mainak Ghosh
Haider Banka
Sunita Sarkar
Rupam Sah
Gaurav Bhatnagar
Sneha Ayushi
Hardik Sharma

Ramesh Moorthy  
Santosh Satapathy  
Bharat Richhariya  
Puneet Kumar  
Vivek Yelleti  
Deepu Vijayasenan  
Deepak Mishra  
Mohit  
Sudestna Nahak  
Sourabh Yadav  
Somnath Mukhopadhyay  
Hari Chandana Pichhika  
Anjum  
Alok Kumar Tiwari  
Nihal  
Rajendra Pamula  
Vazim Ibrahim  
Ahana Patra  
Kuldip Katiyar  
Sourish Sarkar  
Sayan Chatterjee  
M. Tanveer  
Joseph  
Debanga Raj Neog  
Ankit Shukla  
Vishnu Bharadwaj Parkala  
Vishakha Pareek  
Kushagra Agrawal  
Nishtha Tomar  
Chiranjoy Chattopadhyay  
Md. Abdul Aziz Al Aman  
Himanshu Agarwal  
Rishabh  
Manisha Verma  
Amitesh Singh Rajput  
Manisha Verma  
Ashirbad Samantaray  
Kishore Babu Nampalle  
Palak Handa  
Akoramurthy B.  
Vivek Vijay  
Debarshi Kumar Sanyal  
Mayank Garg  
P. Radha Krishna  
Subhasis Banerjee  

Zahir Khan  
Mohammad Wassaf Ali  
Divyansh Bhatia  
Sanoj Kumar  
Kapil Ahuja  
Vishwambhar Pathak  
Pranay Yadav  
Anand Jha  
Manisha Manjramkar  
Soumen Paul  
Hemraj Kumawat  
Jagdeesh K.  
Imran Ansari  
Shalini Tomar  
Priyanka Jain  
Pabitra Pal  
Shivakumara Palaiahnakote  
Nishkal Prakash  
Reshma Rastogi  
J. Panda  
Binod Kumar  
Ananya Bonjyotsna  
Chandra Sudip  
Arpita Sarkar  
Abhirup Banerjee  
Siddhartha Bhattacharyya  
Paul Anshuman  
Jana Nanda Dulal  
Parag Chaudhuri  
Sonal Dixit  
Debaditya Barman  
Borra Tarun  
Debaditya Barman  
R. Dhanalakshmi  
M. K. Bhuyan  
Kamal Kumar  
John Paul Martin  
Saurabh J. Shigwan  
Shuvo Saha Roy  
Dhruba K. Bhattacharyya  
Swalpa K. Roy  
Prajna Prajna  
Anirban Mukhopadhyay  
Jayadeva  
Basabi Chakraborty

Niteesh Sahni
M. Jayanthi
Shyam Rajput
Rupam Bhattacharyya
Rayanoothala Praneetha Sree
Sharat Chandran
Sumantra Dutta Roy
Kiran Talele
Geeta Sikka
Neeti Kashyap
Amit Chatterjee
Bhabatosh Chanda
Avinash Ratre
Tamilselvi
Ajai Kumar Gautam
Kavita Bhatt
Nisarg Trivedi

Kaustubh Wade
Ramineni Rohith
Debopam Ghosh
Saroj Pandit
Daksh Patel
Monika Singh
Prasanth Sambarkar
Anukul Pandey
Sachin Taran
Lavi Tanwar
Satyabama
Varun Sangwan
Manjeet Chillar
Pankaj Dahiya
Srikanth Panigrahi
Rahul Thakur

# Keynote Talks

# Hybrid Intelligence: A Symbiotic Union of Natural Intelligence and AI to Advance Medical Image Analysis

Jayaram K. Udupa

Professor of Radiologic Science in Radiology at University of Pennsylvania

**Abstract.** In the medical field, "knowledge" has been accumulated over centuries through human cognitive processes about human body as a system, as such there is always a common reference for all aspects of the system. As an example, any image of the human body has an underlying anatomy that is common to all human bodies, unlike in general computer vision, where there is no concept of a common underlying "anatomy of the scene" to be analyzed. We refer to this knowledge, which is facilitated through millions of years of human evolution, as Natural Intelligence (NI). NI excels in its ability to perform global tasks such as recognizing the whereabouts of an object in the image but fails miserably in local tasks such as detailed quantitative local scrutiny of the object. Conversely, AI excels in most local tasks but still fares poorly in global tasks. Efforts to overcome this bottleneck have spanned the entire period of development of deep networks beginning from fully convolutional networks to U-Net and its variations, dilated convolutional networks, attention mechanisms, and recently transformer and self-attention mechanisms, all through AI. We refer to this dichotomy between NI and AI as Recognition-Delineation paradigm or RD paradigm. Exploiting this RD paradigm, in this talk I will demonstrate how we may form a symbiotic union of NI and AI, called Hybrid Intelligence (HI), where NI and AI help each other to overcome their respective shortcomings, leading to an HI methodology which is superior to both. I will present examples of this mutualism and HI methods under two applications – image segmentation for radiation therapy planning and disease prognostication for incisional hernia prediction.

Author Biography: Jayaram K. Udupa PhD, FIEEE, FAIMBE, LFIEEE. He obtained his PhD in computer science from the Indian Institute of Science, Bangalore, in 1976, directly after his B.Eng degree, with a gold medal for best thesis. He joined the Medical Image Processing Group (MIPG) which was founded in 1976 in the Department of Computer Science, State University of New York, Buffalo, in 1978, as an Assistant Professor. The whole group moved to the Department of Radiology, University of Pennsylvania, Philadelphia, in 1981, where he has headed and nurtured the group since 1982 and has been a tenured professor since 1994. Recognizing the pre-eminence and the numerous contributions of Udupa and MIPG, the premier journal IEEE Transactions on Medical Imaging published an invited paper describing the history, development, and contributions of MIPG in 2002. Since his first published journal paper in 1974 on character recognition, he has made numerous contributions spanning almost the entire period of existence of the area of 3D image processing, 3D visualization, 3D image analysis, and their body-wide medical applications, and is widely considered one of the founding members of this field. He published the first MRI brain image analysis paper with the Nobel Laureate Paul Lauterbur when Lauterbur was producing the earliest MRI images known. He developed the first known software package for 3D image processing and visualization (3DVIEWNIX 6, which was considered one of the 10 best systems developed during the early 1990's, and CAVASS 7 are recent examples in its lineage) and widely distributed them with source code since 1980 before the term "open source" was coined. In recent years, he introduced the concept and methodology of Hybrid Intelligence combining the complementary strengths of AI and natural human intelligence. To date he has secured $25M grant funding as a PI/Co-PI from NIH, NSF, and DoD, given 303 invited lectures world-wide, published two books, 246 peer-reviewed journal papers, and 320 peer-reviewed full conference papers, and mentored 90 PhD students/post-doctoral fellows. His research interests include: computer vision theory; algorithms, advanced AI and hybrid intelligence methodologies, and their body-wide medical applications.

# Towards Trustworthy Multimodal Models

Mohan Kankanhalli

Director of NUS Artificial Intelligence Institute (NAII)

**Abstract.** Large Language Models and Vision Language Models have seen dramatic improvements in capability over the last three years. Despite their continually improving performance on a variety of benchmarks, there are still some fundamental trust issues that hinder the wide- scale real-world deployment of these powerful multimodal models. This talk will present some of the recent work done in our group at NUS that highlight these issues. We will cover the areas of hallucinations, bias and jail break attacks. We will end the talk by detailing some of the challenges and the open research questions in the field.

Author Biography: Prof. Mohan Kankanhalli is Provost's Chair Professor of Computer Science at the National University of Singapore (NUS), where he is the Founding Director of the NUS AI Institute. He is also the Deputy Executive Chairman of AI Singapore, which is Singapore's National AI R&D Program. He has held senior leadership roles as the Dean of NUS School of Computing and Vice Provost of Graduate Education for NUS. He obtained his BTech from IIT Kharagpur and MS and PhD from the Rensselaer Polytechnic Institute. Mohan's research interests are in Multimodal Computing, Computer Vision, and Trustworthy AI. Mohan was a member of World Economic Forum's 2023-2024 Global Future Council on Artificial Intelligence. He is currently a member of ACM's Global Technology Policy Council. He is a Fellow of IEEE, IAPR and ACM.

# (How) Do LLMs Reason?

Subbarao Kambhampati

Professor at Fulton School of Engineering, Arizona State University

**Abstract.** Large Language Models, auto-regressively trained on the digital footprints of humanity, have shown impressive abilities in generating coherent text completions for a vast variety of prompts. While they excelled from the beginning in producing completions in appropriate style, factuality and reasoning/planning abilities remained their Achilles heel (premature claims notwithstanding). More recently a breed of approaches dubbed "reasoning models" (LRMs). These approaches leverage two broad and largely independent ideas: (i) test-time inference – which involves getting the base LLMs do more work than simply providing the most likely completion, including using them in generate and test approaches such as LLM-Modulo (that pair LLM generation with a bank of verifiers) and (ii) post-training methods–which go beyond simple auto-regressive training on web corpora by collecting, filtering and training on derivational traces (that are often anthropomorphically referred to as "chains of thought" and "reasoning traces"), and modifying the base LLM with it using supervised fine tuning or reinforcement learning methods. Their success on benchmarks notwithstanding, there are significant questions and misunderstandings about these methods–including whether they can provide correctness guarantees, whether they do adaptive computation, whether the intermediate tokens they generate can be viewed as reasoning traces in any meaningful sense, and whether they are costly Rube Goldberg reasoning machines that incrementally compile verifier signal into the generator or truly the start of a golden era of general purpose System 1+2 AI systems. Drawing from our ongoing work in planning, I will present a broad perspective on these approaches and their promise and limitations.

Author Biography: Subbarao Kambhampati is a professor of computer science at Arizona State University. Kambhampati studies fundamental problems in planning and decision making, motivated in particular by the challenges of human-aware AI systems. He is a fellow of Association for the Advancement of Artificial Intelligence, American Association for the Advancement of Science, and Association for Computing machinery, and a recent recipient of the AAAI Patrick H. Winston Outstanding Educator award. He served as the president of the Association for the Advancement of Artificial Intelligence, a trustee of the International Joint Conference on Artificial Intelligence, the chair of AAAS Section T (Information, Communication and Computation), and a founding board member of Partnership on AI. Kambhampati's research as well as his views on the progress and societal impacts of AI have been featured in multiple national and international media outlets.

# Geometry Aware Equivariant Deep Learning
# with Applications


Baba C. Vemuri

Distinguished Professor, Wilson and Marie Collins Professor of Engineering at the
University of Florida



**Abstract.** Developing deep neural networks (DNNs) for manifold-valued data
sets has gained significant interest of late in the deep learning research community.
Manifold-valued data abound many fields of Engineering and Sciences including
but not limited to, Medical Imaging, Computer Vision, Robotics, etc., for example, diffusion Magnetic Resonance Imaging (dMRI) data, shape (landmarks) data,
directional data, covariance matrices, GPS data and others. In this talk, a new
theory and supporting architecture for DNNs tailored for manifold-valued data
inputs dubbed, ManifoldNet, will be presented. Analogous to vector spaces where
convolutions are equivalent to computing weighted means, manifold-valued data
convolutions will be defined using the weighted Frechet Mean (wFM). To this
end, a provably convergent recursive algorithm for computation of the wFM of the
given data is presented, where the weights are to be learned. Further, the proposed
wFM operator is provably equivariant to the natural group actions ad- mitted by
the data manifold and achieves a contraction mapping. A novel network architecture to realize the ManifoldNet will be detailed during the talk. Experiments
showcasing the performance of the ManifoldNet on regression and classification
problems in Neuroimaging will be presented. Finally, if time permits, a generalization of the ManifoldNet to accommodate higher order manifold-valued
convolutions will be briefly discussed.


Author Biography: Baba C. Vemuri received the PhD in Electrical and Computer Engineering from the University of Texas at Austin. Currently, he is a Distinguished University Professor in the Department of Computer and Information Sciences and Engineering
and holds the Wilson and Marie Collins professorship of Engineering at the University
of Florida. He holds affiliate appointments in the Department of Statistics, Mathematics,
ECE and BME at the University of Florida. His research interests include Geometric Deep Learning, Geometric Statistics, Medical Image Computing, Computer Vision,
Machine Learning and Information Geometry. For the last several years, his research
work has primarily focused on statistical analysis of manifold-valued data with applications to Medical Image Computing and Computer Vision. Along this theme, he has been
developing algorithms for the recursive computation of statistics on Riemannian manifolds pertinent to manifold-valued data sets e.g., diffusion magnetic resonance images
(dMRI), manifold of linear subspaces (Grassmann manifold) etc. His research team has
developed novel methods for 3D image segmentation, unimodal and multimodal image
(rigid+nonrigid) registration, nonrigid registration of 3D point sets, metric learning, dictionary learning and large margin classifiers. He has published over 200 fully refereed

articles in journals and conference proceedings. He received the US National Science Foundation Research Initiation Award (NSF RIA) in 1988 and the Whitaker Foundation Award in 1994. He has received, several best paper awards at various International Conferences (including 3 times best poster presentation award at the biennial International Conf. on Information Processing in Medical Imaging - IPMI'01,'05 and '21), the IEEE Edward J McCluskey Technical Achievement Award (2017) for, "pioneering and sustaining contributions to Computer Vision and Medical Image Analysis." He is a Fellow of the IEEE (2001) and the ACM (2009). In 2015, he was awarded the Doctoral Dissertation Mentorship Award from the Herbert Wertheim College of Engineering at UFL

# Beyond TinyML, Time for Generative Edge AI

Danilo Pietro Pau

Technical Director, IEEE, AAIA and ST Fellow

**Abstract.** Following seminal research on fixed function machine learning since 2006 by G. Hinton and others, the industry offered centralized cloud services in 2017 following the "unlimited hardware assets proposition". Next in 2018 a large community of semiconductor industries has been aggregated around the ambitions of TinyML "under 1 mW" proposition which successfully headed, nowadays, to many edge products proliferation by solving their heterogeneity challenges. In the meanwhile, research by I. Goodfellow and others with tireless enthusiasm continued to develop ultra hyper parametrized artificial intelligence, toward trillion weights, workloads which only few cloud companies can afford today, and which are a sever threat for the planet's resources. Therefore, TinyML community following a call to action, evolved into EdgeAI thus embracing the challenge to bring back Generative AI workloads to the edge for the benefit of the daily users. This proposition includes a path to bring into edge language models, reasoning capabilities. Convincing case studies such as multimodal visual question and answering for intelligent edge camera and conversational human machine interface start to build a foundation of edge applications on multi-processing units and in some cases also advanced micro controllers. At the same time, the low power TinyML ambition is evolving into energy efficiency, which open up new opportunities for the research ambitions such as in memory computing, new transistor architecture and material which will revolutionize the industry across the board in the attempt to match human brain efficiency.

Author Biography: Danilo Pietro Pau is an accomplished expert in System R&D with over three decades of tenure at STMicroelectronics, Danilo Pietro Pau holds an impressive academic and professional portfolio, positioning them among top Italian scientists. Their Google Scholar metrics include an h-index of 31 and an i10-index of 93. They are a prolific inventor and author, holding 109 inventions, 80 EU and 72 US patents, and having produced 248 scientific publications, 113 ISO/IEC/MPEG documents, and delivering 153 invited talks. Graduating in Electronic Engineering from Politecnico di Milano in 1992, his technical expertise spans decades, encompassing early HD-MAC decoding, MPEG video memory reduction, H.264 video processing, and graphics standards like OpenVG/OpenGL-ES. A key focus since 2016 has been computer vision and tiny AI, with contributions integrated into major STMicroelectronics platforms like ST EdgeAI Core Technology and the ST EdgeAI Developer Cloud. His significant contributions to the field are recognized through multiple prestigious fellowships, including being elevated to IEEE Fellow in 2019, AAIA Fellow in 2022, and becoming an invited member of the National Academy of Artificial Intelligence (NAAI) and an IEEE Industry Distinguished Lecturer in 2025. Danilo have held numerous leadership roles in professional bodies such as the IEEE and the TinyML Foundation, where he chaired the TinyML on Device Learning group and co-founded AutoTinyML. Active in preserving the history of technology, Danilo curated three IEEE Milestones, including "Multiple Silicon Technologies on a chip, 1985" and "MPEG Multimedia Integrated Circuits, 1984–1993". Danilo's innovative work has been recognized with multiple corporate and industry awards, such as the Finmeccanica Innovation Award and several STMicroelectronics STAR awards. Danilo continues to cooperate widely with academics and researchers, driven by a strong commitment to innovation and scientific community involvement for example on Generative EdgeAI by chairing the working group under the auspicious of EdgeAI Foundation.

# Digital Twins: A Path to Personal Language Models

Ashutosh Garg

Co-founder and CEO, Eightfold AI

**Abstract.** Today's AI systems are increasingly capable - yet fundamentally impersonal. Large Language Models (LLMs) generate fluent responses, but they do not truly know the individuals they serve: their skills, their aspirations, how they learn, or what guidance they most need. Without context, personalization is shallow. This talk explores how Digital Twins - dynamic, continuously learning representations of each individual's knowledge, experience, and growth - form the foundation of personal language models that can reason and act on our behalf. Built from real-world interactions in work and learning environments, a Digital Twin can capture not only skills and accomplishments but intent, preferences, and latent potential. When paired with agentic LLMs, these Twins unlock new capabilities: career copilots that evolve with the worker, adaptive learning assistants that teach the next skill at the right time, and knowledge systems that preserve expertise rather than losing it when people transition roles. However, realizing this vision requires breakthroughs in secure data governance, model alignment, explainability, and individual consent. There are critical questions to address: How do we ensure personal models remain private and portable? Can we guarantee fairness and avoid reinforcing historical bias? How do we measure growth, not just past achievements? Drawing from deployments across nations and global enterprises, this talk presents both the promise and the technical challenges of moving beyond generic LLMs to AI that truly understands each of us. By building Digital Twins responsibly, we can unlock a future where every person has a continuously learning model - a partner in productivity and a pathway to opportunity.

Author Biography: Ashutosh Garg is the Co-Founder and CEO of Eightfold AI and Co-Founder of Viven, an AI company building digital twins for the enterprise. A two-time unicorn founder, he was recognized by the U.S. State Department as one of the ten immigrant founders who have created two unicorns. In 2024, Ashutosh received the IIT Distinguished Alumni Award. A prolific researcher and inventor, he has published 35+ peer-reviewed papers, authored three books, and been awarded 50+ patents. His work has received 10,000+ citations, and he has been featured in The New York Times and invited to the White House to discuss the future of AI. Prior to founding Eightfold, Ashutosh worked on core machine learning and search infrastructure at Google and conducted research at IBM. He holds a B.Tech from IIT Delhi and a Ph.D. in Computer Science from the University of Illinois at Urbana–Champaign.

# AI for Clinically Meaningful Research: Building a Quantitative Brain Health Ecosystem

Ragini Verma

Professor in DiCIPHR, Department of Radiology and Professor of Neurosurgery, University of Pennsylvania

**Abstract.** Neuroimaging has entered an era where datasets are large but fragmented, rich but noisy, and clinically under-leveraged. Traditional analysis pipelines struggle with multimodal integration, site variability, missing data, and weak links to patient outcomes, leading to findings that are statistically impressive but clinically irrelevant. Additionally, datasets are expanding, through national health initiatives, academic collaborations, and increasing MRI access, but they remain fragmented, heterogeneous, and difficult to translate into clinical utility. This talk presents a pathway for using AI to build a quantitative brain health ecosystem that is scalable, equitable, and clinically meaningful. The talk will highlight four pillars that make such an ecosystem possible:

1. Normative modeling and reference ranges that convert population variability into individualized deviation maps.
2. Distributed and privacy-preserving analytics that integrate multi-site MRI data without data transfer, allow hospitals and research centers to contribute to large-scale neuroimaging science without sharing raw data, enabling scalable science across global cohorts.
3. AI-driven summary indices that turn complex MRI features into actionable markers of brain microstructure, connectivity, and aging, yielding interpretable markers of brain integrity and recovery, usable in routine radiology and neurology practice.
4. Mechanistic and translational alignment, ensuring AI findings reflect real biology, link to clinical outcomes, and support decision-making in disorders like TBI, tumors, and developmental conditions.

Examples across traumatic brain injury and other neurological disorders will illustrate how AI transforms raw imaging into clinically meaningful, patient-specific insight, laying the groundwork for a truly quantitative brain health ecosystem.

Author Biography: Ragini Verma, PhD, is Professor of Radiology at the University of Pennsylvania, a Distinguished Investigator of the Academy for Radiology; Biomedical Imaging Research, and a Fellow of the American Institute for Medical and Biological Engineering (AIMBE). She directs the DiCIPHR Lab (Diffusion & Connectomics in Precision Healthcare Research), where her team develops and applies advanced neuroimaging methods to illuminate brain structure, connectivity, and pathology—paving the way for precision medicine and translational science. Her research spans diffusion

MRI, connectomics, and multimodal data integration, with a particular focus on brain tumors, traumatic brain injury, and developmental disorders. Dr. Verma has pioneered methods for modeling the tumor microenvironment using diffusion tensor imaging and free-water correction and has developed clinically translated tools for surgical planning. She is also advancing frameworks for distributed data analysis, normative brain health summaries, and AI-driven large-scale data integration to enable precision neuroimaging. Through her leadership of multi-site consortia, she remains deeply committed to bridging discovery with clinical impact. Dr. Verma also serves as Associate Vice Chair for Translation and Commercialization in Penn Radiology. In this role, she is building a Translation Accelerator to connect academia, industry, and clinical practice, with the goal of speeding the adoption of imaging biomarkers into routine care, improving patient outcomes, and finding AI-based solutions for clinical needs.

# Secure Computation for Machine Learning

Arpita Patra

Professor of Computer Science at the Indian Institute of Science (IISc)

**Abstract.** Secure Computation is the standard-bearer and holy-grail problem in Cryptography that permits a collection of data-owners to compute a collaborative result, without any of them gaining any knowledge about the data provided by the other, except what is derivable from the result of the computation. In this talk, I will present a high-level overview of our recent contributions to privacy-preserving machine-learning computation built on advances in secure computation techniques.

Author Biography: Arpita Patra is a Professor in the Department of Computer ScienceAutomation (CSA), EECS Division, at the Indian Institute of Science (IISc) Bangalore, India. Together with her students, she is part of the Cryptography and Information Security (CrIS) Lab. At IISc, she is also associated with the Theoretical Computer Science Group at CSA, the Security Group at EECS, AI @ IISc, and the Robert Bosch Centre for Cyber-Physical Systems. She worked with Silence Laboratories as a visiting professor in the summer of 2024, and she served as a visiting faculty researcher at Google Research between August 2022 and July 2023. Before joining IISc, she spent three enriching years as a post-doctoral fellow at the University of Bristol, UK (hosted by Prof. Nigel Smart), ETH Zurich, Switzerland (hosted by Prof. Ueli Maurer), and Aarhus University, Denmark (hosted by Prof. Ivan Damgaard). She completed her PhD (with Prof. C. Pandu Rangan) and her Master of Science by Research (with Prof. Sukhendu Das) at IIT Madras. Born in a remote village in West Bengal, she graduated from Haldia Institute of Technology and completed her earlier schooling at Kumarpur Hateswar High School and Gobardhanpur Pramathanath Vidyayatan in West Bengal.

# Tribal Worldviews and Epistemic Plurality: Reimagining Ethical AI

Piyashi Dutta

Lead, Tribal Research and Knowledge Centre (TRKC), New Delhi

**Abstract.** At the center of contemporary debates on knowledge lies a persistent tension between image and reality, illustrating how polished narratives about who counts as a "knower" acquire legitimacy while the lived epistemologies of tribal and Global South communities are systematically marginalised. This disjuncture is neither accidental nor benign; it is a form of epistemic injustice in which these worldviews are dismissed as anecdotal, unscientific, or peripheral to modern knowledge production. The talk will foreground epistemic plurality as an urgent intellectual and ethical project. Tribal worldviews rooted in relationality, collective meaning-making, ecological reciprocity, and embodied knowledge demon strate that there exist multiple, rigorous ways of understanding the world. Indian tribal philosophies, grounded in interdependence rather than individualism and custodianship rather than ownership, exemplify what genuine epistemic plurality entails. Their exclusion distorts the global knowledge landscape and reinforces longstanding hierarchies of legitimacy and power. After mapping these questions of knowledge and epistemic justice will the talk shift to Artificial Intelligence, a domain often imagined as neutral and universal. By examining how AI systems inherit the biases and omissions of the societies that build them, the discussion argues that the absence of plural epistemologies results in technologies that are context-blind and detached from lived realities. Integrating tribal epistemes is therefore not symbolic but essential to imagining ethical, human-centred, and context-sensitive AI futures.

Author Biography: Piyashi Dutta is a sociologist and media educator with over a decade of experience exploring how communities think, remember, and create meaning. She holds a PhD in Sociology from Tezpur University and is a double gold medalist from her postgraduate programme at the same institution. She completed her doctoral research as an ICSSR doctoral fellow. She currently leads the Tribal Research and Knowledge Centre (TRKC), New Delhi, where her work brings together tribal studies, decolonising research methodologies, gender, and communication. Her research consistently interrogates the politics of knowledge production and foregrounds community epistemologies over extractive, archive-bound academic lenses. Her pioneering study of the whistling tradition (Jingrwai Iawbei) of the Khasi community in Kongthong, Meghalaya, remains the only systematic documentation of this extraordinary sonic practice. The research has drawn international attention, including coverage by the BBC. Dr. Dutta has published widely in Scopus-indexed journals, contributed to edited volumes with Routledge and Manipal University Press, and authored Stories of Resilience: Media Voices from the North-East — the first comprehensive report on media in Northeast India, produced with

CHRI Delhi and hosted by the People's Archive of Rural India (PARI). Piyashi believes knowledge can be gained by "travelling on foot, sitting by the hearth, listening more than speaking—and, when tired, being revived with a very good cup of coffee."

# Artificial Intelligence Technologies on Fast Track: Paradigm Shifts in the Global IPR Arena


Prabuddha Ganguli

CEO, Vision-IPR



**Abstract,** Artificial Intelligence (AI) is galloping on a fast track with its evolution from generative AI to AI Agents and now to Agentic AIs. Disruptive "Pole-vaulting" from "machine learning" involving pattern recognition and prediction to "machine wisdom" endowed with holistic understandingintegration, contextual awareness, judgment with foresight including ethical reasoning is bringing these AI Systems in proximity to their Human creators. The next phase is about "Human-AI Co-Wisdom" and "Collective Intelligence" Systems shifting from human-centric creativity to machine-augmented creations, with paradigm shifts in Intellectual Property Rights (IPR), demanding new definitions of ownership, originality, and protection.

AI Creations and/or AI mediated creations raises doubts on ownership criteria, thereby raising questions on inventorship, inventive-step, authorship, benchmarks in patents and copyright laws. Further, the distinction between human creativity and mere generation of ideas with augmented thinking using autonomous AI systems is increasingly becoming pours. This poses challenges to concepts of originality. AI models are trained exploiting a range of databases, some of which are proprietary, even though available in the open domain. The last few years have experienced AI related litigations in courts on infringements of patents and copyright, patent validity, "fair use"/"fair dealing" of databases protected by copyright or kept as trade secrets. The fragmented scenario of Agentic AIs now demands standards in open platforms to avoid "vendor lock-in".

The presentation will landscape the present scenario of the fast tracked AI technologies, the challenges they pose to the existing IPR Frameworks, approaches being adopted in various jurisdictions to enable interoperability and scalability of Agentic AI Systems, and evolving policy guidelines, to aid researches in designing their research projects for accelerated commercialisation.



Author Biography: Prabuddha Ganguli, a national of India, is presently Advisor of VISION-IPR in Mumbai. He obtained his M.Sc. in Chemistry from the Indian Institute of Technology (Kanpur), Ph.D. in Chemical Physics from the Tata Institute of Fundamental Research, Mumbai, and completed his Post Doctoral Research in Germany and Canada. He was a Visiting Scientist at the Bhabha Atomic Research Centre in 1981 before joining Hindustan Lever, Ltd. as a Research Scientist. Professor Ganguli began his career as a Research Scientist in Basic and Industrial Research and was subsequently involved in Technology Assessment, Forecasting and Transfer including Factory Management and Business Planning. From 1991 to 1996, he was the Head of Information Services and

Patents at the Hindustan Lever Research Centre. His last assignment at HLL involved corporate information risk and security management and knowledge management. He has now set up a consulting group 'VISION-IPR' to offer services in management of IPR, information security and knowledge management. He is a qualified and a leading Patent Attorney in India and an expert in IPR and Information Management.

# Policy Optimization and Large Language Models


Sunny Manchanda

Director, DRDO Young Scientist Laboratory – AI



**Abstract.** Policy optimization has emerged as a foundational paradigm for aligning, improving, and scaling the capabilities of large language models (LLMs). By treating language generation as a sequential decision-making process, policy optimization enables models to learn directly from human preferences, structured rewards, and iterative feedback. This talk will trace the evolution from classical RL-based approaches such as REINFORCE, PPO in RLHF to modern direct preference optimization methods (DPO, ORPO, KTO, GRPO) that simplify training while improving stability and sample efficiency. We will also examine how policy optimization is driving advances in reasoning—RLVR, and small-model controllers that coordinate larger LLMs.


Author Biography: Sunny Manchanda is the Director of the DRDO Young Scientist Laboratory for Artificial Intelligence (DYSL-AI), making him one of the youngest directors in DRDO. A Machine Learning researcher by training, he holds a Master's in Computer Science (AIData Sciences) from IIT Delhi. His work focuses on deep learning, computer vision, natural language processing, and AI-driven decision-making. He has authored several publications in reputed conferences like IEEE, AAAI, EMNLP, and WACV. With over a decade at DRDO, starting from the Netra AEW&C project, he now leads cutting-edge AI research for defence and civilian applications, while also actively engaging in outreach to inspire the next generation of innovators.

# Contents

## Evolutionary Computation



## Health Analytics

**Image Processing**



**Medical Imaging**

**Miscellaneous**



**Natural Language Processing**

**Pattern Recognition**

## Quantum AI



## Signal Processing



## Soft Computing/Computational Intelligence

## Speech and Audio Processing



## Swarm Intelligence

**Video Processing**

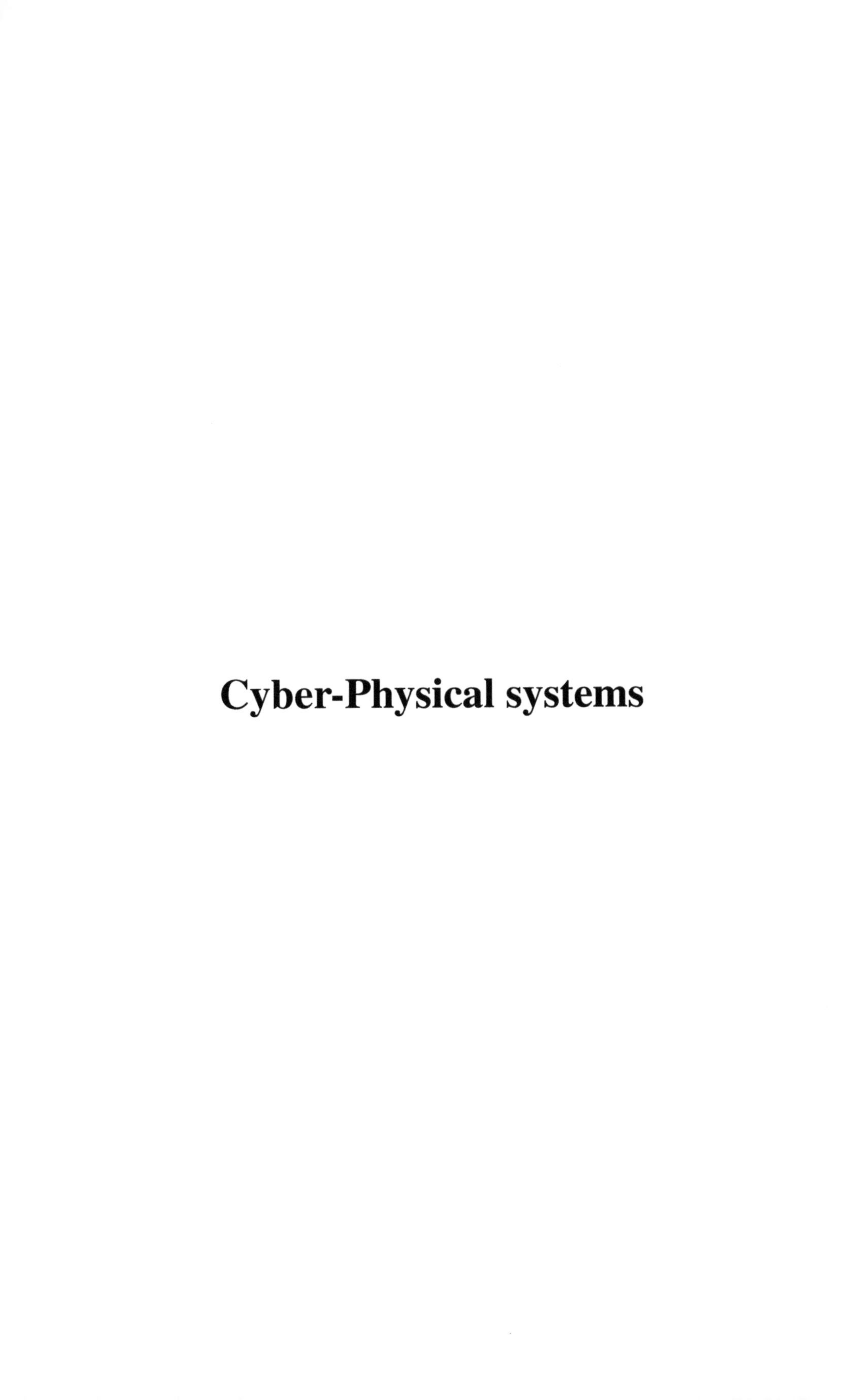

# Cyber-Physical systems

# Blockchain-Enabled Decentralized Spam Call Detection Framework Using ML Scoring

Subhobroto Sasmal[1], Ananya Bisoi[2], Sreyosh Majumder[3], Subhas Barman[4]([✉]), and Jhuma Dutta[4]

[1] Heritage Institute of Technology, Kolkata 700107, West Bengal, India
[2] Kalinga Institute of Industrial Technology, Bhubaneswar 751024, Odisha, India
[3] VIT-AP University, G-30, Inavolu, Beside AP Secretariat, Amaravati 522237, Andhra Pradesh, India
[4] Jalpaiguri Government Engineering College, Jalpaiguri 735102, West Bengal, India
{subhas.barman,jhuma.dutta}@cse.jgec.ac.in

**Abstract.** The proliferation of spam calls in telecommunications networks poses serious risks, including fraud and harassment. To protect users, we propose a hybrid framework that combines a machine learning-based spam detection mechanism with blockchain-secured logging to ensure accuracy, accountability, and trustworthiness in the results. The system uses Isolation Forest and Random Forest models, supported by rule-based heuristics, to analyse calling patterns and assign spam risk levels. Detection outcomes are stored securely using Ethereum smart contracts, while full metadata is stored off-chain via IPFS, with the content hash recorded on-chain to ensure traceability. Deployment using IPFS significantly reduces gas costs. The system achieves an average inference time of 0.24 s and processes over 151,000 records per hour, meeting real-time telecom needs. As real-world telecom datasets are sensitive and legally restricted, we evaluated the system on synthetic datasets generated to replicate spam-like activity. While this limits generalizability, results act as proof-of-concept, with accuracy (98.5%), recall (100%), and AUC (0.99) reflecting feasibility. The model is scalable, secure, and cost-efficient, offering a practical foundation for future use with anonymized real datasets.

**Keywords:** Spam detection · Machine learning · Smart contract · IPFS · Blockchain technology · Telecom security · Ethereum · Caller authentication

## 1 Introduction

Blockchain has become a key technology for secure and tamper-proof data handling across telecommunications, healthcare, and finance [3,4,6,7,16]. As mobile networks and digital services expand, ensuring reliable tower–user connections


S. Mitra et al. (Eds.): PReMI 2025, LNCS 16358, pp. 3–12, 2026.
https://doi.org/10.1007/978-3-032-18480-1_1

has become increasingly complex. The telecom sector alone contributed over USD 5.2 billion to global GDP in 2022 and is expected to exceed USD 2.5 trillion by 2030 [2,11,23]. However, with 5.5 billion users, telecom systems face serious threats like fraudulent calls, SIM scams, phishing, and unauthorized access to call records [10], while KYC and verification remain limited due to weak tower authentication [18,24], tamperable CDR storage [19,20], interoperability issues [5], blockchain latency [8,14,21], and compliance conflicts [19,20]. The FCC reports over 4 billion monthly robocalls in the US [9]. To address these challenges, we propose a decentralized spam detection framework integrating blockchain with adaptive machine learning. Prior studies show that blockchain reduces telecom fraud by 95% [18,24], enables secure roaming [12], and support real-time verification [5]. Our system authenticates users and classifies call metadata with Isolation Forest, Random Forest, and rules, records high-risk calls on Ethereum via smart contracts while storing full metadata in InterPlanetary File System (IPFS) with Content Identifier (CID) anchoring for low cost and data integrity. The system processes 151k records/hour throughput with 0.24s latency using Ganache and Web3.py, evaluated on synthetic datasets generated and labeled via ChatGPT, with metrics like precision, recall, and AUC. Prior work used blockchain [19,20,24] or ML approaches [2,8,21] for spam detection but is costly or siloed. Our contributions are threefold: (i) a hybrid ML pipeline with selective blockchain anchoring for real-time spam detection, (ii) a cost-efficient scheme storing metadata hashes on-chain with full records in IPFS, and (iii) a modular design supporting SS7 and VoIP for scalable telecom deployment.

## 2   Literature Survey

Telecom networks face increasing fraud, spoofing, and spam attacks. Traditional rule-based systems are reactive, offering limited real-time protection. Recent research explores Blockchain and machine learning (ML) to resolve these gaps. BBCA [24] and permissioned blockchains [21] enable secure identity verification. Paper [19] uses Ethereum smart contracts to protect call records but suffers from latency limitations which are mitigated by block-lattice storage [20]. Smart contracts support 5G roaming [12] and behavioral monitoring [26], and Polkadot parachains improve interoperability [5]. General Data Protection Regulation (GDPR) compliance is ensured via Attribute-Based Encryption [1,25]. Merkle trees [20], and federated learning [17] support enhanced scalability.

ML approaches detect spam using Random Forests, Decision Trees, and lightweight models [13,14,21], while TAGNN [22] identifies clusters of fraudulent activity. Paper [8] uses Natural Language Processing (NLP) to detect baiting and scams. Graph-based analysis with blockchain logging spots SIM fraud and robocalls [19,22].

Key research gaps and our contributions can be summarized as follows:

| Sl. No. | Research Gap | Our Contribution |
|---|---|---|
| 1 | Authentication and secure CDR storage are separate [19, 24] | Securely log authenticated calls on blockchain |
| 2 | Blockchain logging has high latency and storage overhead [20] | Selective logging of high-risk calls reduces cost and latency |
| 3 | ML-based detection is siloed from auth/storage layers [8, 14, 21] | Real-time spam detection integrated with call flow |
| 4 | Limited interoperability between telecom systems [5] | Supports both legacy SS7 and modern VoIP |
| 5 | Privacy compliance is inconsistent [20] | Lightweight design with periodic anchoring ensures GDPR alignment |

# 3   System Architecture and Design

The proposed system integrates blockchain technology into telecom operations to facilitate secure workflows, thereby enhancing security and transparency. It includes three modules: User Authentication, Core Operations, and Call Block Creation. Operators securely activate numbers (DB1) and register towers (DB2). During calls, the system validates metadata, checks for spam, and uploads flagged records to IPFS. The CID is stored on Ethereum and indexed in DB3. Spam detection uses rule-based scoring with Isolation Forest and Random Forest models. The `SpamDetector` trains on CDR features, while `OptimizedSpamInference` handles real-time prediction. Caller history and adaptive thresholds boost accuracy and local caching provides low-latency inference. The `BlockCreator` smart contract logs call metadata as IPFS CIDs. Its key functions—`createMeta`, `getCid`, and `totalMetas`—enable secure, decentralized and auditable call tracking. The system workflow and smart contract logic are illustrated in Fig. 1 and Fig. 2 respectively.

## 3.1   Privacy and Regulatory Compliance

Telecom datasets contain sensitive information (caller IDs, receiver IDs, call durations, etc.) and are strictly regulated under GDPR in the EU and Indian laws, including the Indian Telegraph Act, IT Act 2000, IT (Traffic Data) Rules 2009, and the Digital Personal Data Protection Act 2023. To comply, our framework applies data minimization to only essential features, pseudonymization by hashing caller and callee identifiers, and separates storage where only IPFS hashes are recorded on Ethereum. Lastly, high-risk calls are selectively anchored, and IPFS records are encrypted with access control, ensuring privacy protection while maintaining tamper-proof, auditable spam call records (Fig. 3).

# 4   Experimental Setup

The system integrates blockchain, IPFS, and hybrid machine learning to deliver scalable, tamper-resistant, real-time spam detection for telecom networks. A

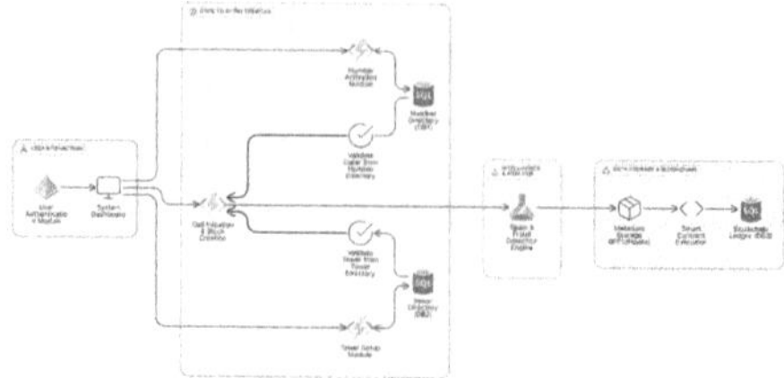

**Fig. 1.** Proposed blockchain-based telecom architecture

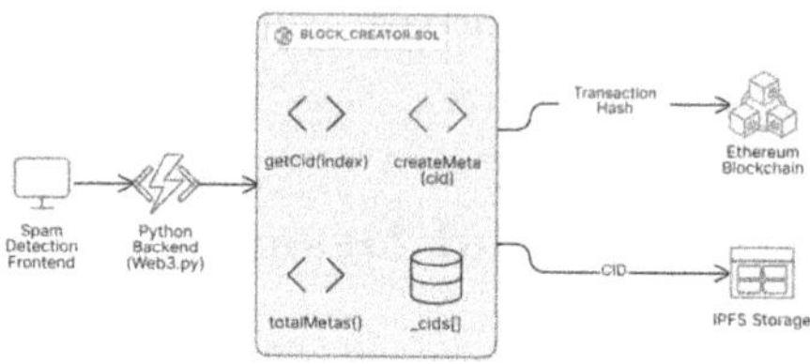

**Fig. 2.** Smart contract structure for call logging and IPFS integration

local Ethereum blockchain is simulated with Ganache, where Solidity contracts deployed via Remix log only the content hash (CID) of call records, while full metadata is stored on IPFS. For testing, we also built a version that stores everything on-chain, but it was not deployed due to cost constraints. A Flask backend bridges frontend, ML engine, and blockchain: as call metadata arrives, it triggers a pipeline combining Isolation Forest for anomaly detection, Random Forest for classification, and a rule-based layer using duration, volume, and diversity. A weighted score assigns Low–Severe Risk, with only the CID logged. The frontend supports call submission, risk visualization, and blockchain verification. The complete workflow—ML inference, IPFS upload, and blockchain anchoring—executes in under 2.6 s Fig. 4, with Pinata managing the decentralized storage.

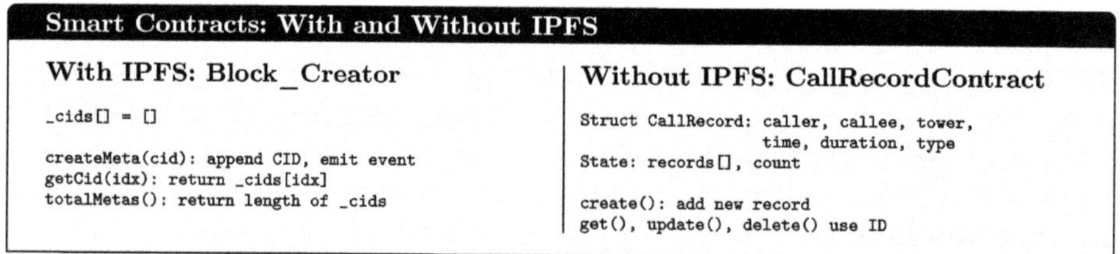

**Fig. 3.** Comparison of Smart Contract Logic: With and Without IPFS

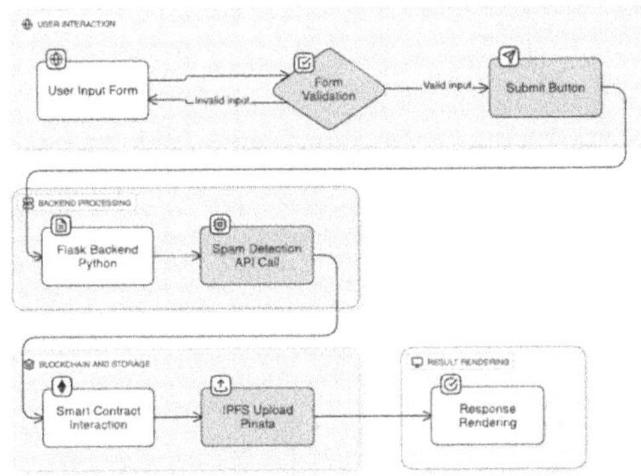

**Fig. 4.** Frontend workflow showing form submission, ML prediction, IPFS upload, blockchain logging and result display

# 5  Results and Discussion

The proposed spam detection framework was evaluated in a simulated telecom environment, with emphasis on gas efficiency, blockchain immutability, machine learning (ML) performance, latency, and throughput. The evaluation also included a baseline comparison with recent works to highlight design trade-offs and regulatory implications.

## 5.1  Gas Usage and Cost Estimation

This study compares two Ethereum smart contracts: `ipfs_hash_block` for storing IPFS hashes and `full_call_record_block` for full metadata. The IPFS approach is ∼2.75× cheaper to deploy and ∼2× more efficient in execution and transaction costs. Over time, gas usage stabilizes, favoring lightweight contracts for scalability. IPFS is ideal for scalable logging; full-record blocks offer richer audit trails at higher cost. The cost comparison is illustrated in Table 1 and Fig. 5.

**Table 1.** Gas, Transaction, and Execution Cost Comparison Across Phases

| Phase | ipfs_hash_block | | | full_call_record_block | | |
|---|---|---|---|---|---|---|
| | Gas | Tx | Exec | Gas | Tx | Exec |
| Deployment | 586,226 | 509,761 | 424,661 | 1,614,329 | 1,403,764 | 1,258,308 |
| First Call | 132,514 | 115,229 | 93,077 | 244,185 | 212,334 | 189,114 |
| Repeated Call | 112,849 | 98,129 | 75,977 | 224,520 | 195,234 | 172,014 |

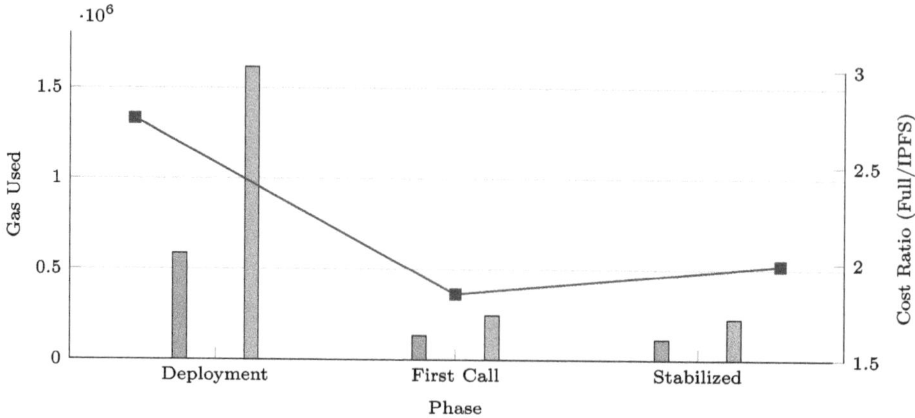

**Fig. 5.** Gas usage comparison for IPFS and Full Call Record Blocks across phases. Line shows Full/IPFS cost ratio.

## 5.2  Spam Detection, Evaluation, and Blockchain Consistency

Blockchain immutability is ensured via `parentHash`, `stateRoot`, and `transactionsRoot`, which cryptographically link blocks to expose any tampering. A hybrid Isolation Forest + Random Forest model, trained on synthetic CDRs, achieved approximately 98.5% accuracy, 100% recall, and AUC $\sim$0.99, as shown in Table 2 and Fig. 6. These results are promising but represent a *proof-of-concept benchmark*, since synthetic datasets lack real-world variability.

System performance remained efficient: end-to-end latency stayed below 2.6 s, with IPFS pinning as the primary contributor, while ML inference and blockchain logging added negligible delay, as illustrated in Fig. 7. Throughput consistently reached 146,000–151,000 records per hour, demonstrating scalability under simulated conditions (Fig. 8).

**Table 2.** Model Performance (synthetic dataset, proof-of-concept results)

| Dataset | Acc. | Prec. | Recall | AUC |
|---|---|---|---|---|
| spam_calls_3 | 98.52% | 83.33% | 100% | $\sim$0.99 |
| june_spam_calls | 98.40% | 86.21% | 100% | $\sim$0.99 |

## 5.3  Scalability and Comparisons

High Ethereum gas fees limit large-scale deployment, but Layer-2 solutions such as Polygon or Optimism reduce costs. Though IPFS adds retrieval delays, selectively logging high-risk calls maintains efficiency and compliance. As shown

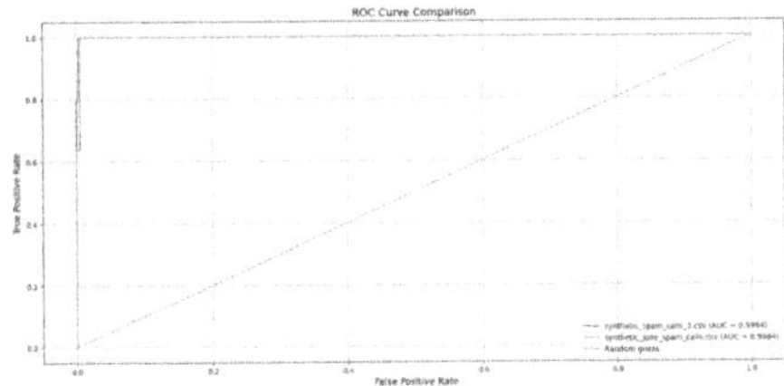

**Fig. 6.** ROC curve of hybrid spam detection model

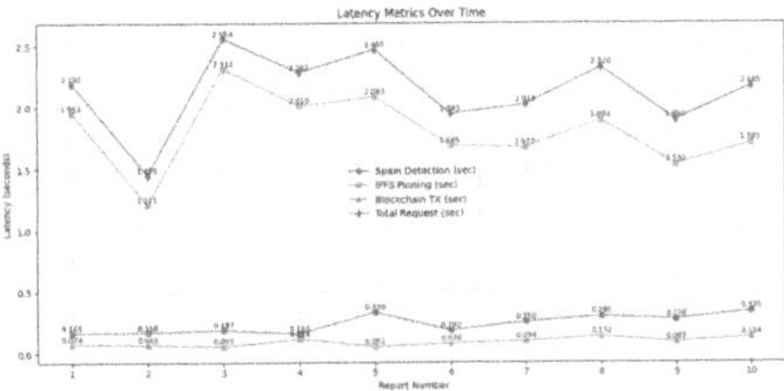

**Fig. 7.** Latency breakdown across pipeline

in Table 3, our framework outperforms ML-only models (AI-based UCTS: 95.2%, RoBERTa-MHARC: 98.10% F1) and blockchain-only methods (PDGNN: 88.13% F1), achieving >98.5% accuracy with tamper-proof, real-time, and law-compliant detection.

## 6   Conclusion and Future Work

This paper presents a hybrid spam call detection framework that integrates machine learning, blockchain, and IPFS to address telecommunications fraud. The system combines Isolation Forest for anomaly detection, Random Forest for classification, and rule-based heuristics to analyze calling patterns. Ethereum smart contracts ensure immutable and transparent logging, while IPFS provides

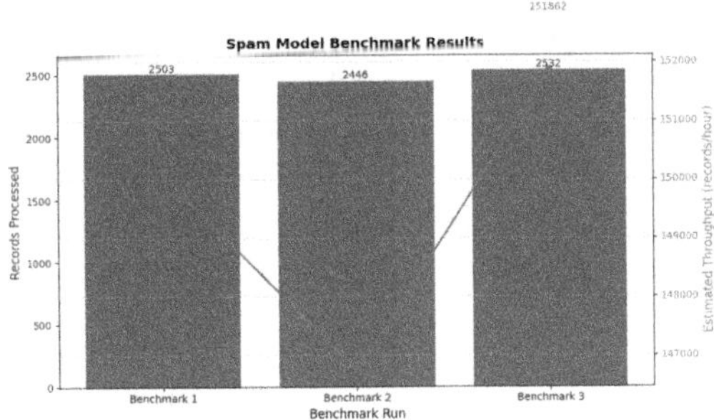

**Fig. 8.** Throughput Benchmark Results

**Table 3.** Baseline performance of spam detection approaches

| Approach | Core Method | Storage Strategy | Accuracy/Recall | Regulatory Alignment | Limitations |
|---|---|---|---|---|---|
| AI-based UCTS [20] | BERT + Machine Learning | Cloud-based | 95.2% | Privacy-compliant anonymization | Synthetic data, proof-of-concept stage |
| PDGNN [16] | Chebyshev-GCN + Subgraph Sampling | Lightweight network construction | 88.13% F1 (EthereumG1) | Blockchain transparency | Limited to Ethereum phishing, scalability constraints |
| RoBERTa-MHARC [15] | RoBERTa + Multi-head Attention + Residual Connections | Pre-trained embeddings | 97.65% F1 (FBS), 98.10% F1 (Custom dataset) | Data anonymization (PII masking) | Limited dataset diversity, high computational complexity |
| Random Forest (Telecom) [27] | Random Forest Classifier | CDR-based analysis | 99% (Training & Testing) | Privacy-preserving (no PII) | Focused on IRSF only, requires balanced datasets |
| Our work | Hybrid (Isolation Forest + Random Forest + Rules) | Selective IPFS + hash anchoring | ~98.5%/100%* | GDPR + Indian law alignment | Synthetic data; proof-of-concept |

a decentralized and cost-efficient storage layer, effectively reducing deployment costs by a factor of 2.75 and execution costs by a factor of 2 compared to conventional full on-chain methods.

Evaluation on synthetic datasets achieved approximately 98.5% accuracy, 100% recall, and AUC of 0.99, with average inference time of 0.24 s and throughput exceeding 151,000 records per hour. The modular architecture supports both SS7 and VoIP systems, while privacy mechanisms including pseudonymization and encrypted IPFS storage align with GDPR and India's DPDP Act 2023. However, reliance on synthetic datasets limits generalizability, as real telecom data remains restricted due to privacy regulations. The reported metrics represent proof-of-concept validation requiring empirical validation with genuine call detail records.

Future work will focus on collaboration with telecom operators to access anonymized real-world datasets for large-scale testing. Gas optimization through Layer-2 solutions like Polygon will enhance economic sustainability for large-scale deployment. Advanced ML techniques such as graph neural networks and federated learning offer opportunities for improved detection accuracy. Integration with existing infrastructure including STIR/SHAKEN protocols and expansion to SMS spam detection would provide comprehensive cross-channel protection. Overall, the proposed research lays a strong foundation for practical telecom security, demonstrating the viability of merging machine learning intelligence with blockchain's immutability to develop scalable, compliant, and real-world-ready solutions through collaboration among researchers, telecom providers, and regulators.

# References


1. Al-Farsi, S., Rathore, M.M., Bakiras, S.: Security of blockchain-based supply chain management systems: challenges and opportunities. Appl. Sci. **11**(12), 5585 (2021)
2. Ashfaq, T., et al.: A machine learning and blockchain based efficient fraud detection mechanism. Sensors **22**(19), 7162 (2022)
3. Barman, S., Chattopadhyay, S., Samanta, D.: A lightweight authentication protocol for a blockchain-based off-chain medical data access in multi-server environment. SN Comput. Sci. **5**, 292 (2024). https://doi.org/10.1007/s42979-024-02660-4
4. Barman, S., Chattopadhyay, S., Samanta, D., Barman, S.: A blockchain-based approach to secure electronic health records using fuzzy commitment scheme. Secur. Privacy **5**(4), e231 (2022). https://doi.org/10.1002/spy2.231
5. Bayraktar, S., Goren, S., Serif, T.: Blockchain interoperability for future telecoms (2025)
6. Dutta, J., Barman, S.: Smart contract and blockchain-based secured approach for storing and sharing electronic health records. Multimedia Tools Appl. **84**, 16883–16907 (2025). https://doi.org/10.1007/s11042-024-19714-7
7. Dutta, J., Barman, S., Sen, S., et al.: Easypay: a user-friendly blockchain-powered payment gateway. Clust. Comput. **27**, 10633–10652 (2024). https://doi.org/10.1007/s10586-024-04506-3
8. Fakieh, A., Akremi, A.: An effective blockchain-based defense model for organizations against vishing attacks. Appl. Sci. **12** (2022). https://doi.org/10.3390/app122413020
9. Federal Communications Commission: Stop unwanted robocalls and texts (2025). https://www.fcc.gov/consumers/guides/stop-unwanted-robocalls-and-texts. Accessed 2 Jul 2025; consumer guide with tips, complaint procedures, and regulatory details :contentReference[oaicite:1]index=1
10. GSMA: The Mobile Economy 2023. Technical report, GSMA Intelligence, London, England (2023). published March 2023. https://www.gsma.com/mobileeconomy/wp-content/uploads/2023/03/270223-The-Mobile-Economy-2023.pdf
11. GSMA: Mobile economy (2025). https://www.gsma.com/solutions-and-impact/connectivity-for-good/mobile-economy/. Accessed 2 Jul 2025. Provides global and regional insights including that mobile technologies generated $6.5 trillion (5.8% of GDP) in 2024 and that 5G supports over 7 billion connections: contentReference[oaicite:1]index=1
12. Hameed, K., Bajwa, I.S., Sarwar, N., Anwar, W., Mushtaq, Z., Rashid, T.: Integration of 5g and block-chain technologies in smart telemedicine using IoT. J. Healthcare Eng. **2021**(1), 8814364 (2021)
13. Kara, M., Aydın, M.A., Balık, H.H.: Bcvop2p: decentralized blockchain-based authentication scheme for secure voice communication. Intell. Autom. Soft Comput. **31**(3) (2022)
14. Kashir, M., Bashir, S.: Machine learning techniques for sim box fraud detection. 2019 International Conference on Communication Technologies (ComTech), pp. 4–8 (2019). https://api.semanticscholar.org/CorpusID:195222354
15. Li, J., Zhang, C., Jiang, L.: Innovative telecom fraud detection: A new dataset and an advanced model with Roberta and dual loss functions. Appl. Sci. **14**(24), 11628 (2024)
16. Li, P., Xie, Y., Xu, X., Zhou, J., Xuan, Q.: Phishing fraud detection on Ethereum using graph neural network. arXiv:2204.08194 (2022). https://doi.org/10.48550/arXiv.2204.08194

17. Liu, L., Tsai, W.T., Bhuiyan, M.Z.A., Peng, H., Liu, M.: Blockchain-enabled fraud discovery through abnormal smart contract detection on Ethereum. Futur. Gener. Comput. Syst. **128**, 158–166 (2022)
18. Numeracle, Inc.: Validating telephone calls by verifying entity identities using blockchains. International Patent WO2020190906A1 (2020). https://patents.google.com/patent/WO2020190906A1, published under the Patent Cooperation Treaty (PCT)
19. Ramachandran, A., Kantarcioglu, M.: Using blockchain and smart contracts for secure data provenance management. arXiv:abs/1709.10000 (2017). https://api.semanticscholar.org/CorpusID:27866756
20. Rani, T.K., Monika, S.: An intelligent unauthorized call tracking and fraud detection system. Int. J. Res. Publ. Rev. **6**(3), 4657–4659 (2025). https://doi.org/10.55248/gengpi.6.0325.1223
21. S., A., Pughazendi, N.: Spam call protection using machine learning. Int. J. Adv. Res. Innovative Ideas Educ. **10**(5), 708–712 (2024)
22. Singanamalla, S., et al.: Telechain: bridging telecom policy and blockchain practice. In: Proceedings of the 5th ACM SIGCAS/SIGCHI Conference on Computing and Sustainable Societies, pp. 280–299 (2022)
23. Size, P.M.: Share & trends analysis report by product (pe, pp, pu, pvc, pet, polystyrene, abs, pbt, ppo, epoxy polymers, lcp, pc, polyamide). By Application, By End Use, And Segment Forecasts **2030**, 31 (2022)
24. Tas, I.M., Baktir, S.: Blockchain-based caller-id authentication (BBCA): a novel solution to prevent spoofing attacks in VOIP/SIP networks. IEEE Access **12**, 60123–60137 (2024). https://doi.org/10.1109/ACCESS.2024.3393487
25. Wang, H., Song, Y.: Secure cloud-based EHR system using attribute-based cryptosystem and blockchain. J. Med. Syst. **42**, 1–9 (2018). https://api.semanticscholar.org/CorpusID:49568235
26. Wood, I., Kepkowski, M., Zinatullin, L., Darnley, T., Kaafar, D.: An analysis of scam baiting calls: identifying and extracting scam stages and scripts (2023). https://doi.org/10.48550/arXiv.2307.01965
27. Yehya, B.A., Salhab, N.: Telecommunications fraud machine learning-based detection. In: 2023 4th International Conference on Data Analytics for Business and Industry (ICDABI), pp. 656–661. IEEE (2023)

# A Parallel Cryptographic Hashing Technique for Securing Educational Credentials

Chanchal Saini$^{(\boxtimes)}$ [iD] and N. Poonguzhali [iD]

Jawaharlal Nehru University, New Delhi, India
`chanch91_scs@jnu.ac.in`, `poonguzhali@jnu.ac.in`

**Abstract.** As a fundamental cryptographic primitive, hash functions are widely used in various applications like digital signatures, blockchain, cloud storage etc. Most of the existing schemes are made for generalized purpose and not domain-specific. This paper present EduHash, a domain specific and parallel hash function optimized for more secure credential verification in blockchain based education system. By integrating a multi-round substitution-permutation network, tree based parallel compression and a keyed sponge construction, EduHash helps in accelerating the diffusion and enhances the avalanche effect without trading off with security. All these components helps in achieving resistance to collision, and domain-specific authentication. Experimental evaluation is done with 10,000 academic records showcasing strong avalanche behavior with 50.02% bit change, ideal bit distribution, high entropy, and statistical resistance against known cryptanalytic attacks. Comparative analysis shown EduHash performs competitively across key security metrics. The results suggest EduHash as a viable solution for scalable, tamper-resistant, and decentralized educational credential verification.

**Keywords:** Cryptographic Hash Function · Educational Credentials · Security Optimization · SHA-256 · Blockchain

## 1 Introduction

The current state of digital security is marked by rising threats such as data breaches and credential forgery, especially in education system [1–3]. Cryptography is essential to ensure data integrity, confidentiality, and trust in decentralized environments [4,5]. Cryptographic hash functions [6] are the fundamental building blocks in today's modern digital society which takes an input of arbitrary length and produce a fixed length output deterministically which is called hash or digest. A hash function ensures that even a small change in input will result in a completely different output, known as Avalanche Effect, while making it computationally infeasible to reverse the hash or find two different inputs producing the same output, known as preimage and collision resistance and these properties of hash function helps to secure data integrity.

© The Author(s), under exclusive license to Springer Nature Switzerland AG 2026
S. Mitra et al. (Eds.): PReMI 2025, LNCS 16358, pp. 13–21, 2026.
https://doi.org/10.1007/978-3-032-18480-1_2

Cryptographic hash function have undergone significant evolution since the 1970s. Traditional hash function like Secure Hash Algorithm (SHA-1 and SHA-2) have served the foundational role in digital signatures, certificates and blockchain structures. But as the data volumes grow and computational environment diversify, these traditional CHFs face various limitations in terms of speed, scalability, energy usage, etc. [7]. The very early Message Digest (MD) family, including MD2, MD4, and MD5, laid the foundation of Cryptographic Hash Function, but were eventually broken by advances in cryptanalysis [8]. The U.S. National Security Agency (NSA) introduced the Secure Hash Algorithm series, starting with SHA-0, SHA-1, followed by more secure SHA-2 family. The concern about the structural limitations of these function led to NIST SHA-3 competition from 2007 to 2012, which further introduced Keccak [9], the basis of SHA-3 standard, featuring a novel sponge construction. The focus of cryptographic hashing has shifted towards domain specific, parallelizable, and hardware efficient design optimized for blockchain, Internet of Things, and zero-knowledge proofs [4,9].

## 2  Related Works

In the context of education, where it is essential to verify learners' academic credentials securely and transparently, hash function helps in the creation of immutable digital fingerprints that can be stored on-chain without exposing the full data. According to Satoshi Nakamoto's work [1], hash functions are used in linking blockchain blocks and securing transactions histories. This basic principle is used in educational blockchain, where hash digests of academic credentials are recorded to facilitate non trustable verification mechanisms. As discussed by Ocheja et al. [2], and Wang et al. [3], blockchain based educational system relies on cryptographic hash function to ensure that students data are verifiable, tamper-evident, and interoperable to across institutions. Many systems use standard hash functions, especially SHA-256 and Keccak (SHA-3), to make sure academic works are authentic and cannot be denied later i.e. non-repudiation. Said et al. [10] presented a blockchain based educational qualifications management system where each certificate's metadata is hashed and then stored immutably on-chain to prevent forgery. Fartichou et al. [11] introduced BlockMEDC, a smart contract based used to hash and register Moroccan university certificates, providing publicly verifiable and fraud resistance credentialing. Tariq et al. [12] developed Cerberus, decentralized framework for degree authentication, where cryptographic hashes serves as unique, tamper-proof identifiers for each issued academic credential. Upadhyay et al. [7] performed a comparative study on the Avalanche effects of different hash functions and highlighted that while existing hash functions performed well generally, but when applied in constrained environments some suffer from computational inefficiency or weak avalanche behavior.

Yang et al. [4] introduced a multi-iterative parallel compression structure that boosts hashing speed by processing input blocks at the same time. Their work reduced internal collisions and improved the mixing properties of the internal state through multiple compression rounds. Similarly, Ayubi et al. [5] proposed a chaotic complex hash function based on non linear quadratic maps, enhancing the unpredictability and statistical randomness of the output which is important trait for resisting preimage and differential attacks. Alahmari eta al. [6] and Windarta et al. [9] also emphasize the importance of lightweight and application specific cryptographic hash functions that can offer security without burdening the computational resources of verifier or issue. Despite all these advancements, [13] most education specific blockchain applications rely on general purpose cryptographic primitive without tailoring unique requirements for academic workflow such as real time verification, cross institution credentials exchange. PublicEduChain [14] and Meta-learning framework [15], highlighted the trend towards student owned educational data and metaverse ready learning environment will demand more advanced cryptographic capabilities where hash function will not only serve as integrity checkers but also play roles in data access control, anonymization, smart contract decisions making.

## 3 Proposed System for Education Credential Hashing: EduHash

The proposed EduHash is a domain-specific cryptographic hash function optimized for securing credentials in blockchain-enabled educational infrastructures. It combines a multi-round Substitution-Permutation Network compression function, a tree-based parallel structure, and a keyed sponge construction to provide high security and institutional bindings. EduHash converts academic credentials into unique codes stored on a secure blockchain ledger. When verifying a certificate, it checks if the document's fingerprint matches the stored code. Unlike general-purpose hash functions like SHA2 and SHA3, EduHash targets educational data, including transcripts, degree certificates, and learner credentials. Optimized for parallelism, EduHash processes multiple credentials records simultaneously. Keyed hashing ties the output to a specific educational authority or institution, binding data integrity checks to the issuer's identity. This design enhances trust and authenticity in verified credentials through blockchain.

### 3.1 EduHash System Overview

The proposed EduHash operates in four sequential stages: data pre-processing, block-wise compression, tree-based parallel compression, and a keyed sponge finalization. The input block being processed in parallel, sent into a tree structure, and is finalized using a keyed sponge to generate a 256-bit output. This final hash can then be stored on a blockchain as a verifiable and immutable credential reference.

**Stage 1 Data Preparation:** The initial phase of EduHash pipeline, is responsible for transforming raw academic credential data into standardized and secure input format which is suitable for hashing. Academic records may come in different formats including JSON, XML or PDF. To ensure the consistency and robustness, heterogeneous data is serialized and processed before hashing.

**Stage 2 Compression Function (9-Round SPN).** The second stage involves the application of substitution -permutation network(SPN) based compression function to fixed size 256 bits. Each block of 512 bits is split into two halves, M1 and M2, each consisting of 256 bits. The compression function proceeds in five transformation. In each round, state undergoes multiple transformations to ensure sufficient diffusion and non-linearity as shown in Fig. 1. Each block is processed independently to generate intermediate digests. The SPN design includes S-box substitution, bit permutation, modular arithmetic, and round dependent transformation to ensure the non linear behavior and diffusion of input bits. This process is repeated 9 times to ensure that SPN compression function can generate significantly different output for a smallest change in input. This output of stage 2 is served as input for the next stage.

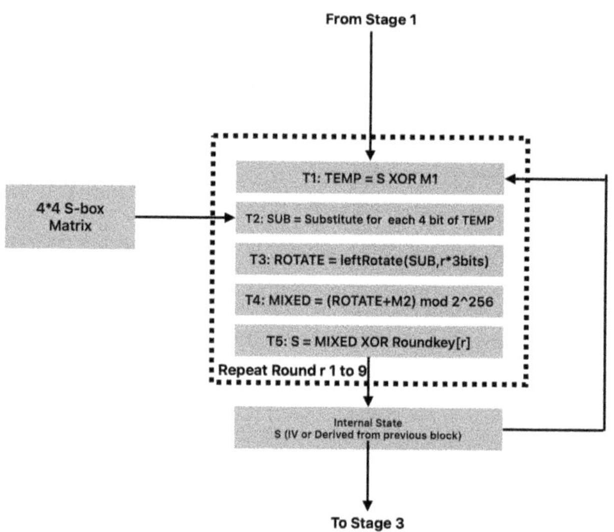


**Fig. 1.** Compression Function

**Stage 3 Tree-Based Compression.** The intermediate hashes from stage are paired and recursively hashed together using the same compression function, forming the next level of the tree. This process is repeated till a single root hash remains. Any modification to a single block will propagate upwards, changes the final digest, thereby ensuring integrity across the entire dataset, thus batch verification without the need to reprocess the entire dataset.

**Stage 4 Keyed Sponge Construction.** The output from stage 3 which is a single root digest, is feed to stage 4 where keyed sponge construction is applied to finalize the hash. This introduces domain specificity and additional security to the output. The sponge is initialized with a 512-bit internal state, divided into two segments: a 256-bit rate and a 256-bit capacity. The root digest and a secret key are XORed into the rate portion of the state. This binds the final hash of the issuer's identity, providing an authentication layer. The function then performs multiple rounds of permutation on the internal state using a cryptographic permutation function. Once the permutation rounds are complete, the first 256 bits of the sponge state are extracted as the final hash representing a secure, unique and domain bounded summary of original data. Adversaries cannot forge new hashes based on partial information because of the keyed sponge as it prevents length extension. The final output from the stage 4 is 256 bits block which can be sent to the blockchain for the specified purpose.

## 4 Performance Evaluation

The performance analysis of EduHash has been discussed from the perspective of security. A secure hash function is one which is collision resisted, uniformly distributed, and sensitive to slightest of change in input. This section will discuss the properties of EduHash: avalanche effect, bit distribution, random message test, collision resistance and statistical attack analysis. The proposed system is experimented on 10,000 academic records from Kaggle [16].

**Avalanche Effect.** A secure hash function has high avalanche performance to prevent attackers from predicting input message blocks and chaining variables based solely on the hash value. This vulnerability can lead to collisions. For each record in the file, a minimal appending was introduced, and the number of bit changes from the original hash value was counted. The resulting bit differences per record are shown in Fig. 2.

The proposed EduHash has an average bit difference of 128.05, resulting in an avalanche percentage of 50.02%. This confirms ideal diffusion, where even a small input change flips almost half of the output bits.

**Bit Distribution.** To evaluate bit distribution for EduHash, output of each record which is of 256 bit is aggregated and number of ones vs zeros per record were counted from a total of 2 Million+ hash bits. The overall distribution of one and zeros for the dataset is as shown in Fig. 3. The average for number of 1s per hash is 128.01 and average for number of 0s per hash is 127.9. This shows that bits are normally distributed which shows the excellent randomness present in EduHash.

**Hamming Distance.** Hamming Distance (HD) is the difference between two hash outputs when the input is changed and a good hash function causes 50% of the bits flipped (avalanche effect). A random record was selected from the data and a small change in input is done 8 times to find the hamming distance between the original hash output and changed hash output as shown in Table 1

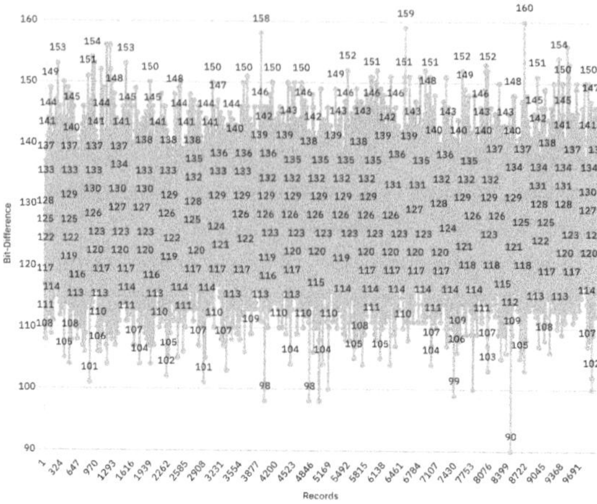

**Fig. 2.** Total number of bits change per record

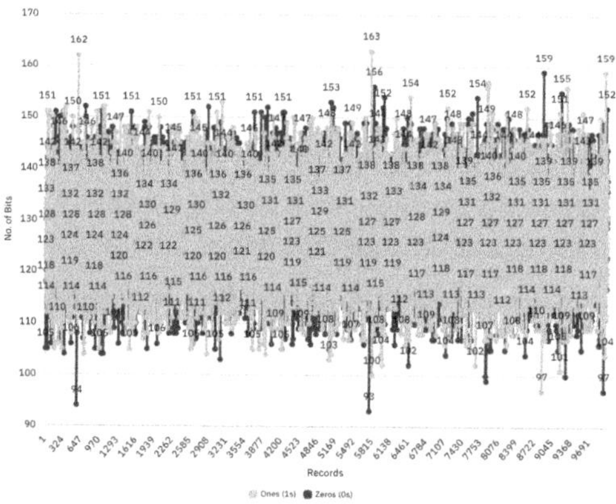

**Fig. 3.** Bit Distribution for 1's and 0's

**Table 1.** Hash values and hamming distances between original and eight different modified versions.

| Modified Version | Hash Value | HD |
|---|---|---|
| Origianal Hash | b54f1bc92742d36083669fc5d7a2835775436708129db929d1727069b6c1b052 | / |
| Mod 1 | 1af6d612e9fd2079d621cebb67da26af48bfca33a59b3781be4c52137eadce57 | 145 |
| Mod 2 | 47fd3a79cd3781e08ba7ea195aee0e69c6b3ac2506c3d6e8a7e0b65561ebd21d | 125 |
| Mod 3 | 82ff5e1fcdd932da58f712998aaf4705660fd36326c65ec712c67d83a1f662d9 | 134 |
| Mod 4 | 64c680afe4201ba1fb7eec30e4ec32dd6bc6453354c3d0b94a16091ddf518317 | 119 |
| Mod 5 | 299862fb601379d64ec4d9e3dedbbfcfa551f903ae99140290e1990759d1b71a | 119 |
| Mod 6 | 8bf0d0bb2bae2853ac67285a4386e45bc2ee8b6ab22ffcddd81b7892e5775e01 | 135 |
| Mod 7 | 25b4429da3f89e6e187872c4f65be6d758d79aeab7deb89243ac20026ce06f13 | 123 |
| Mod 8 | c27ea9e13ac8dafb626f23e006ad3927df580ad54a3083acaccf5f411db2ff49 | 131 |

This indicates the perfect avalanche behavior, showing that EduHash reacts sensitively to minor changes in input data.

**Collision Resistance.** A collision occurs when two different inputs produce same hash as output. In this experiment n number of different random records are checked and no collision was detected. This shows the strong collision resistance, which is crucial for applications like digital certificates and academic transcripts verification.

**Preimage and Second Preimage Resistance.** Preimage resistance ensures the impossibility to guess the original input given the hash output only. And the second preimage resistance ensures that even if attacker knows one input and its hash, they cannot find another input that gives the same hash. In the experiment for EduHash no preimage and second preimage was found showing that EduHash is secure for data authentication.

**Statistical Attack Analysis.** In cryptography, set of techniques used to evaluate hash functions for patterns or biases. Statistical attack analysis measures bit distribution, entropy, hamming distance, and chi-squares scores. Bit distribution and hamming distance show positive results. Entropy measures randomness; in hashing, it shows uniform bit distribution. For binary strings, entropy H is calculated using Shannon's entropy. EduHash has Entropy of 1 bit per bit, indicating excellent randomness and no biases. Chi-square test compares observed and expected frequencies of 0s and 1s in hash output. A low chi-square value indicates excellent uniformity. EduHash's chi-square score is 0.161002 and P-value is 0.688236, suggesting high uniformity. This confirms EduHash's strong randomness and statistical resilience against frequency-based cryptanalysis.

**Comparison to Hash Function.** A comparative analysis of four cryptographic hash functions SHA-256, SHA3-256, BLAKE2b and the proposed EduHash is presented in Fig. 4, across several security related metrics. EduHash demonstrated performance that is slightly better than the other algorithms. EduHash shows strong result in Avalanche effect and Hamming Distance, indicating robust

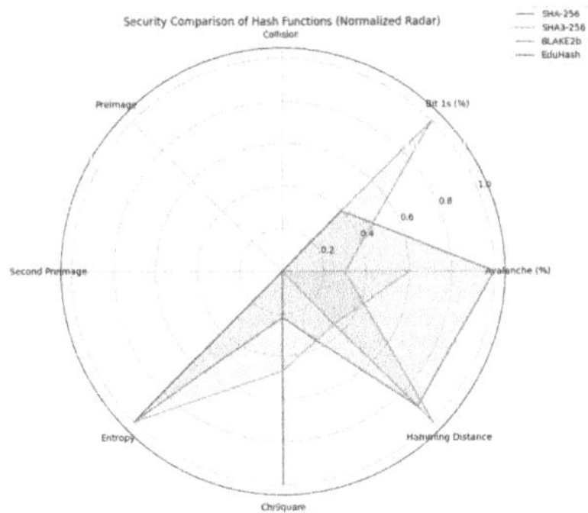


**Fig. 4.** XXX

diffusion and sensitivity to input changes. In metrics such as Entropy, Chi-Square, Pre-image, and Second Pre-image resistance, EduHash remain competitive showing no significant weakness. This visualization supports the fact that EduHash can be considered as a strong candidate for secure applications, particularly in education system or lightweight blockchain framework.

## 5   Conclusion

The proposed system Eduhash, a specialized cryptographic hash function proposed for secure, scalable credential verification in blockchain based education systems. By using the combination of substitution-permutation network, tree-based parallelism, and a keyed sponge construction, EduHash ensures data integrity, domain binding, and efficient processing. The architecture of EduHash is designed in such a way that it is suitable for both hardware and software implementations, and addressing real-world needs for trustworthy and decentralized academic records. These changes would make EduHash a better solution for issuing and verifying credentials in a decentralized and privacy-focused way within blockchain-based education systems.

## References


1. Nakamoto, S.: Bitcoin: A Peer-to-Peer Electronic Cash System. Cryptography Mailing list (2009). https://metzdowd.com
2. Ocheja, P., Agbo, F.J., Oyelere, S.S., Flanagan, B., Ogata, H.: Blockchain in education: a systematic review and practical case studies. IEEE Access **10**, 99525–99540 (2022). https://doi.org/10.1109/ACCESS.2022.3206791
3. Wang, X., Younas, M., Jiang, Y., Imran, M., Almusharraf, N.: Transforming education through blockchain: a systematic review of applications, projects, and challenges. IEEE Access **13**, 13264–13284 (2025). https://doi.org/10.1109/ACCESS.2024.3519350
4. Yang, Y., Zhang, X.: A novel hash function based on multi-iterative parallel structure. Wireless Pers. Commun. **127**, 1–18 (2022). https://doi.org/10.1007/s11277-022-09906-5
5. Ayubi, P., Setayeshi, S., Rahmani, A.: Chaotic complex hashing: a simple chaotic keyed hash function based on complex quadratic map. Chaos, Solitons Fractals **173**, 113647 (2023). https://doi.org/10.1016/j.chaos.2023.113647
6. Alahmari, S., Rajeyyagarai, S., Al-Turjman, F.: Davis mayer streebog cryptographic hash-based blockchain for secure transaction management using SDN in IIoT applications. J. Signal Process. Syst. **95** (2022). https://doi.org/10.1007/s11265-022-01825-9
7. Upadhyay, D., Gaikwad, N., Zaman, M., Sampalli, S.: Investigating the avalanche effect of various cryptographically secure hash functions and hash-based applications. IEEE Access. **10**, 112472–112486 (2022). https://doi.org/10.1109/ACCESS.2022.3215778
8. Yang, Y., Tian, X., Pei, P., He, X., Zhang, X.: Novel cryptographic hash function based on multiple compressive parallel structures. Soft. Comput. **26**, 1–16 (2022). https://doi.org/10.1007/s00500-022-07504-y

9. Windarta, S.M.T., Ramli, S., Pranggono, K., Gunawan, B., Teddy.: Lightweight cryptographic hash functions: design trends, comparative study, and future directions. IEEE Access. **10**, 82272–82294 (2022). https://doi.org/10.1109/ACCESS.2022.3195572
10. Said, S.H., Sinde, R.S., Kosia, E.M., Dida, M.A.: A comprehensive blockchain-based system for educational qualifications management and verification to counter forgery. IEEE Access **13**, 31562–31589 (2025). https://doi.org/10.1109/ACCESS.2025.3542545
11. Fartitchou, M., Lamaakal, I., Makkaoui, K.E., Allali, Z.E., Maleh, Y.: BlockMEDC: blockchain smart contracts system for securing Moroccan higher education digital certificates. IEEE Access **13**, 39152–39175 (2025). https://doi.org/10.1109/ACCESS.2025.3546177
12. Tariq, A., Binte Haq, H., Ali, S.T.: Cerberus: a blockchain-based accreditation and degree verification system. IEEE Trans. Comput. Soc. Syst. **10**(4), 1503–1514 (2023). https://doi.org/10.1109/TCSS.2022.3188453
13. Abdelsalam, M., Shokry, M., Idrees, A.M.: A proposed model for improving the reliability of online exam results using blockchain. IEEE Access **12**, 7719–7733 (2024). https://doi.org/10.1109/ACCESS.2023.3304995
14. Tanriverdí, M.: PublicEduChain: a framework for sharing student-owned educational data on public blockchain network. IEEE Access **12**, 51772–51785 (2024). https://doi.org/10.1109/ACCESS.2024.3385660
15. Golam, M., Ara Tuli, E., Naufal Alief, R., Kim, D.-S., Lee, J.-M.: Meta-learning: a digital learning management framework using blockchain for metaverses. IEEE Access **12**, 92774–92786 (2024). https://doi.org/10.1109/ACCESS.2024.3408878
16. https://www.kaggle.com/datasets/nadeemajeedch/students-performance-10000-clean-data-eda/data

# Designing Lightweight and Privacy-Preserving IDS Applying Federated Learning Technique


Aditya Kumar Singh, Arpita Srivastava, and Ditipriya Sinha[✉]

Department of Computer Science and Engineering, National Institute of Technology Patna, Patna, Bihar, India
ditipriyasinha87@gmail.com



**Abstract.** An Intrusion Detection System (IDS) plays an important role in securing the network from harmful cyber-attacks. In this paper, a novel framework is introduced that combines federated ensemble learning, unsupervised clustering, and advanced feature selection to develop a lightweight and privacy-preserving IDS. The proposed approach is evaluated on benchmark datasets such as NSL-KDD and UNSW-NB15. A Modified Shuffled Frog Leaping Algorithm (SFLA) is introduced for optimal feature selection, utilizing ensemble classifiers (MLP, Random Forest, and Xgboost) and a new fitness function that balances the False Alarm Rate (FAR) and F1-score. After feature selection, Fuzzy C-Means (FCM) clustering is applied to attack samples to form multiple clients for Horizontal Federated Learning (HFL). Each client trains locally while sharing only feature importance values for global aggregation, ensuring data privacy. Finally, a soft voting–based ensemble model is used for prediction. Accuracy rate of proposed model is 99.28% and 91.04% on the NSL-KDD and UNSW-NB15 datasets, respectively. Experimental results confirm that the proposed system effectively detects diverse attacks in a decentralized environment while maintaining high accuracy, low false alarm rate, and strong data privacy.

**Keywords:** Cyber-Security · IDS · SFLA; Fuzzy C-Means Clustering; Federated Learning (FL)


## 1 Introduction

After COVID-19, everyone moved online, increasing threats. IDS is vital for cybersecurity, monitoring networks to detect and prevent unauthorized access and malicious activities, protecting data. Many IDS face issues like false alarms, poor generalization, and difficulty detecting zero-day attacks, mainly due to poor feature selection. Feature selection, choosing Relevant features for intrusion detection, improves accuracy and reduces system load. Techniques include filter-based, wrapper-based, and evolutionary algorithms. SFLA, inspired by frog food search, is effective but faces challenges like premature convergence and low diversity. A Modified SFLA (MSFLA) with clustering, entropy-guided importance, ensemble fitness, adaptive evolution, and global shuffling addresses these problems. Key features include local selection, privacy preservation, global refinement, and ensemble prediction.



S. Mitra et al. (Eds.): PReMI 2025, LNCS 16358, pp. 22–36, 2026.
https://doi.org/10.1007/978-3-032-18480-1_3

HFL is used in the proposed IDS, with each client having identical features but different data samples. This setup suits distributed environments like corporate branches, IoT networks, or edge devices. Federated Deep Learning models (e.g., ANNs, CNNs, LSTMs) train by sharing gradients. Training is harder for tree-based models (e.g., Decision Tree (DT), Random Forest (RF)) since they are non-parametric and don't support direct gradient exchange. Nonetheless, tree-based classifiers are effective for IDS due to their interpretability, efficiency, and robustness to class imbalance, making them ideal for real-time intrusion detection and deployment.

**Key Contributions of the Proposed Framework:**

I. A modified SFLA employs clustering-based initialization, entropy scoring, and an ensemble fitness function for feature selection, enhancing intrusion detection, reducing false alarms, and creating a lightweight IDS model. Fuzzy C-Means clustering is used to realistically divide the attack data, where each cluster acts as an independent client.

II. The proposed IDS system implements Horizontal Federated Learning (HFL), where raw data is not shared, but only feature importance scores are exchanged with the server, thus maintaining data privacy.

III. A new feature aggregation strategy is designed that effectively integrates tree-based models into a federated learning setup without using gradients or sharing model parameters. An ensemble soft-voting mechanism is implemented on server side, which makes global predictions more robust and generalized across all clients.

The remainder of this paper is organized as follows: Sect. 2 reviews the literature, Sect. 3 details the Methodology, Sect. 4 presents the results and analysis, and finally, Sect. 5 summarizes the conclusion and future directions.


## 2  Literature Review

IDS are crucial in today's connected digital world. As IoT devices, edge computing, and multi-organization networks expand, traditional centralized IDS face issues with data privacy and communication overhead. Researchers are developing new optimization and privacy techniques to enhance IDS. Feature selection, vital in IDS research, often employs popular metaheuristic algorithms. Ghanbari and Heidari (2017) used Shuffled Frog Leaping Algorithm (SFLA) for Persian handwritten digit recognition, with better performance [1]. In [2], authors employed a modified Genetic Algorithm for feature selection in the IDS domain, altering the fitness function. Liu et al. (2022) proposed a more advanced version with dynamic step size and simulated annealing [3]. Authors in [4] introduce Fed-GA-CNN-IDS, a method for ICS intrusion detection using NAS with GA to develop lightweight CNN architectures for federated learning. Tested on Gas Pipeline, SWaT, and WADI datasets, it achieved similar or better accuracy with less model complexity compared to existing IDS. Federated Learning (FL) helps address privacy and data-sharing issues. In [5], author states that increasing demand for IoT devices calls for robust intrusion detection systems (IDS). AI-driven IDS like "Automated Separate Guided Attention Federated Graph Neural Network. Devine et al. (2025) have developed an FL-based secure IDS using a gradient obfuscation technique [6]. Rehman et al. (2024) have introduced FFL-IDS using fog computing against jamming attacks [7]. Khraisat et al. (2025) have developed a lightweight FL-IDS optimized for IoT devices [8]. This paper's approach uses HFL, sharing feature importance scores rather than raw data or model gradients, suitable for models like decision trees and random forests. Clustering also aids IDS research by dividing client data. The authors in [9] introduce FLOGA-AD, a novel federated anomaly detection framework for satellite networks using a genetic algorithm for client selection. The model combines a hybrid deep learning architecture with a Convolutional Vision Transformer for spatial features and LSTM for temporal modeling. Tested on the UNSW-NB15 and STIN datasets, FLOGA-AD improves performance by 3% and 5% over the deep federated framework DFL-TD. It ensures performance and privacy using Differential Privacy and Secure Aggregation during updates. Ensemble learning also contributes to IDS success. Sarhan et al. (2022) have proposed the HBFL framework, which uses a combination of blockchain and ensemble [10]. Several papers in the literature uses the metaheuristic algorithms for the feature selection in the IDS domain. The authors in [11] use two-phase metaheuristic algorithms. First, modified PSO selects a feature subset, then modified ACO finds the optimal subset in the second phase. The authors in [12] present a hybrid NIDS combining signature and anomaly detection, using modified grey wolf optimization for feature selection and an ensemble of tree models for known attacks. Many studies explored metaheuristic optimization, FL, clustering, and ensemble learning separately but not in a unified framework. All shortcomings were removed, and these techniques were integrated after modification.

# 3  Methodology

## 3.1  Proposed Framework

The overall proposed framework is categorized into five major sections such as (i) data preprocessing, (ii) data balancing, (iii) feature selection, (iv) data segregation and clustering, and (v) federated learning-based classification. The complete block diagram of the proposed framework is shown in Fig. 1.

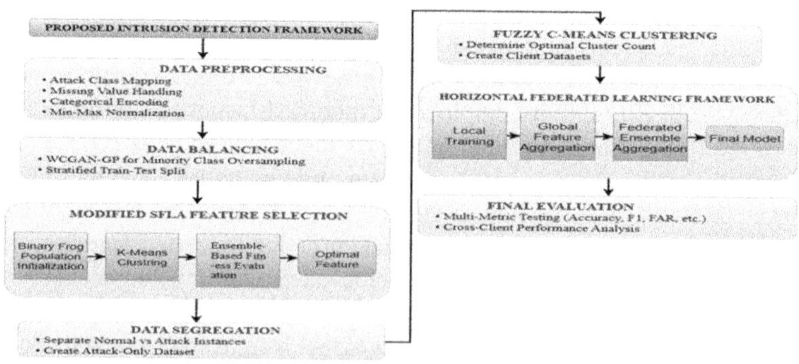


**Fig. 1.** Complete Block Diagram of Proposed Framework.

### 3.1.1 Data Preprocessing

Data preprocessing is essential for developing machine learning models, especially for Intrusion Detection Systems (IDS). It involves handling missing data, encoding categorical features, and scaling. Label encoding converts categorical features into numbers. Min-Max normalization scales numerical features in both datasets.

### 3.1.2 Data Balancing Using WCGAN-GP

Data balancing is crucial for class imbalance, where some classes have too many samples while others have too few. Wasserstein GAN with Gradient Penalty (WCGAN-GP) is used for this purpose, as shown in Fig. 2. Classes with fewer samples than a set threshold are minority, others are majority. The target count is set to the smallest majority class, and each minority class generates enough synthetic samples to reach it. WCGAN-GP generates these samples from noise vectors, creating data similar to the original minority class. The synthetic samples are added to the minority classes to create a balanced dataset.

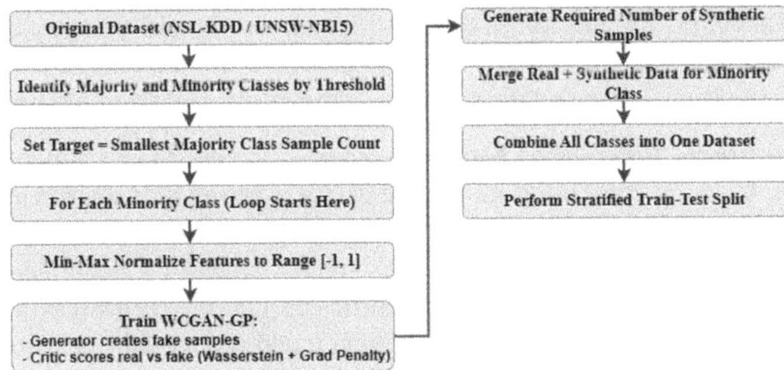


**Fig. 2.** WCGAN-GP Data Balancing Process.

### 3.1.3 Modified Shuffled Frog Leaping Algorithm (SFLA)-Based Feature Selection

During this phase, feature selection uses modified Shuffled Frog Leaping Algorithm on the balanced dataset. Key modifications to the classical SFLA to improve IDS feature selection are explained. Figure 3 shows the block diagram of the modified SFLA.

(i) *Frog Initialization:* The function that initializes the frog population also generates candidate solutions in binary format, with each frog representing a possible feature subset. An initial population is generated, with each frog encoded as a binary vector where each element indicates if a feature is selected (1) or not (0). This creates a binary matrix, each row a candidate solution. A simple fitness function evaluates the initial population by summing each binary vector, counting selected features. Let fi $\in 0,1$ $m$ be a binary vector for the i-th frog.

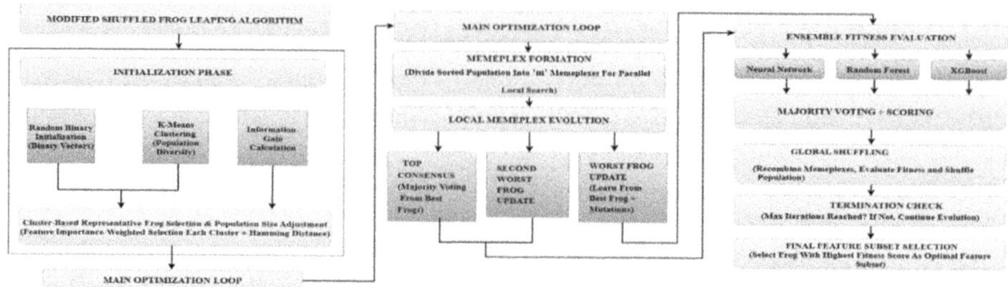

**Fig. 3.** Block Diagram of Modified SFLA.

$$Fitness(f_i) = \sum_{j=1}^{m} f_{i,j} \tag{1}$$

This counts number of 1s (active features) in binary vector. A K-Means Clustering groups binary populations and fitness values into clusters based on similarity, ensuring diverse solutions. Each frog is assigned to a cluster. An entropy-based metric evaluates feature relevance, prioritizing those that distinguish strong and weak solutions. Frogs with fitness above median are in one class; those below are in another. DT scores after training indicate each feature's informativeness regarding binarized fitness.

(ii) *Modified fitness function in feature selection:* A new fitness function evaluates feature subsets by combining multiple classifiers acting as a team (ensemble) that judges best subset. It produces a score based on prediction accuracy and number of false alerts. After prediction, two metrics are calculated: F1 Score and FAR. Final fitness score is a weighted mix of these metrics. Equation (2) ensures fitness function favors feature subsets that maximize accuracy and reduce false alarms, crucial for high-risk areas like intrusion detection. Frog with highest score represents an optimal or near-optimal feature set for classification.

$$\text{Fitness Score} = 0.7 \times \text{F1} + 0.3 \times (1 - \text{FAR}) \tag{2}$$

(iii) *Memeplex Shuffling:* SFLA enhances feature subset optimization through memeplex shuffling for local & global learning. It begins with a diverse frog population as binary vectors. Process involves multiple global iterations, each with local memeplex evolution and shuffling. Memeplexes merge after local updates, & frog fitness is re-evaluated. Best frog after iterations finds the final solution through cooperative learning, classifier evaluation, and memeplex exploration. Algorithm 1 describes this modified SFLA for feature selection.

---

**Algorithm 1.** Modified SFLA with Majority Voting.

---

**Require:** Feature matrix X, labels y, frogs P, memeplexes M, global iters G, local iters T, voting size K, penalty $\lambda$, threshold $\theta$
**Ensure:** Final selected mask f_best, selected features F_selected

| | |
|---|---|
| 1. | **procedure** |
| 2. | **begin** |
| 3. | **function** Fitness(f, X, y, $\lambda$): |
| 4. | Train MLP, RF, XGB on selected features |
| 5. | Predict and ensemble via majority voting |
| 6. | Compute: $\varphi(f) = \alpha \cdot F1 + (1 - \alpha) \cdot (1 - FAR) - \lambda \cdot \|f\|_1$ |
| 7. | **return** fitness score |
| 8. | **end function** |
| 9. | Initialize P frogs with diversity + clustering |
| 10. | Evaluate fitness for all frogs |
| 11. | **for** g = 1 to G: |
| 12. | Sort frogs and divide into M memeplexes |
| 13. | **for** each memeplex: |
| 14. | **for** t = 1 to T: |
| 15. | Select top-K frogs, compute consensus mask |
| 16. | Identify worst frog f_w |
| 17. | Update f_w towards consensus |
| 18. | Flip random bit in updated frog |
| 19. | **if** new fitness is better |
| 20. | replace f_w |
| 21. | **end if** |
| 22. | **end for** |
| 23. | **end for** |
| 24. | Recombine memeplexes and re-evaluate |
| 25. | **end for** |
| 26. | **if** any frog has fitness < $\theta$: |
| 27. | Select among them the one with max features |
| 28. | **end if** |
| 29. | **else:** |
| 30. | Select frog with best fitness |
| 31. | **end else** |
| 32. | **return** f_best, F_selected = {j | f_best[j] = 1} |
| 33. | **end** |
| 34. | **end procedure** |

---

### 3.1.4  Data Segregation and Fuzzy C-Means Clustering

A dataset is created with selected features; normal class rows are removed, leaving attack class rows for another attack-only dataset. Fuzzy C-Means clustering is applied to this attack dataset to mimic real-world federated setups. Optimal number of clusters is determined through metrics like the Xie-Beni index, partition coefficient, and silhouette score. Each cluster, acting as a client, represents a unique attack distribution, forming multiple client datasets with diverse attacks. Normal data is evenly shared among clients for fairness. If class imbalance exists, data balancing uses techniques like WCGAN-GP.

### 3.1.5   HFL Using Tree-Based Classifiers with Information Gain and Ensemble-Based Aggregation

This phase introduces a HFL framework that trains a global IDS model across multiple clients without sharing raw data. Clients use Fuzzy C-Means clustering, each having unique attack and normal data with identical features for compatibility.

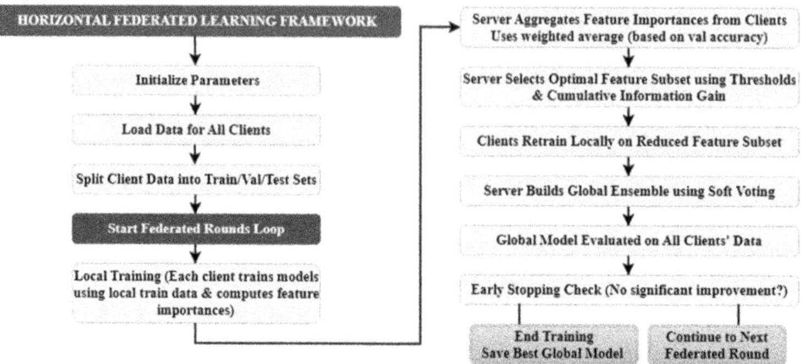


**Fig. 4.**  Block Diagram of HFL using Tree-Based Classifiers.

Each client trains a DT classifier on local data using an entropy criterion effective for imbalanced, non-IID data. Features are selected based on information gain, indicating importance in separating classes, with importance scores aggregated globally by the server, weighted by client validation accuracy. Different thresholds determine global feature selection, shared for retraining to enhance model generalization, speed convergence, reduce overfitting, and lower computation. Clients send validation and test predictions to the server, which builds a global ensemble through soft voting weighted by validation performance. Training stops if validation accuracy or F1-score shows no significant improvement over several rounds. Figure 4 shows the system diagram, and Algorithm 2 details the step-by-step process.

| **Algorithm 2.** Horizontal Federated Learning with Tree-Based Classifiers. |
|---|

**Input:**
    C: Set of clients $\{c_1, c_2, ..., c_n\}$ with local datasets $\{D_1, D_2, ..., D_n\}$
    F: Initial feature set $\{f_1, f_2, ..., f_m\}$
    T: Set of information gain thresholds $\{\tau_1, \tau_2, ..., \tau_k\}$
    $R_{max}$: Maximum communication rounds
    $\delta_{min}$: Minimum improvement threshold
    P: Patience for early stopping
**Output:**
    M*: Final global ensemble model
    F*: Optimized feature subset

```
1.    procedure Federated Training:
2.        begin
3.        Initialize F_current ← F, F_idx ← {1, 2, ..., m}
4.        r ← 1, acc_best ← 0, f1_best ← 0, no_improve ← 0
5.        While r ≤ R_max and no_improve < P:
6.            Local Training:
7.                For each client c_i ∈ C:
8.                    Train decision tree DT_i on D_i using F_current with entropy criterion
9.                    Compute feature importance I_i from DT_i
10.                   Evaluate validation accuracy acc_i on local validation set
11.               End for
12.           End Local Training
13.           Global Aggregation:
14.               Aggregate feature importances: I_agg ← Σ(w_i * I_i) where w_i = acc_i / Σ acc_i
15.           End Global Aggregation
16.           Feature Selection:
17.               For each threshold τ ∈ T:
18.                   Select features F_τ where cumulative I_agg ≤ τ
19.                   Evaluate average validation accuracy v_τ across clients using F_τ
20.               End for
21.               Select optimal F_current, F_idx with highest v_τ
22.           End Feature Selection
23.           Ensemble Construction:
24.               Create weighted ensemble M_r using {DT_1, ..., DT_n} with weights {w_1, ..., w_n}
25.           End Ensemble Construction
26.           Performance Evaluation:
27.               Compute average validation metrics acc_avg, f1_avg across clients
28.               If acc_avg > acc_best + δ_min or f1_avg > f1_best + δ_min:
29.                   Update M* ← M_r, F* ← F_current
30.                   acc_best ← acc_avg, f1_best ← f1_avg
31.                   no_improve ← 0
32.               End if
33.               Else:
34.                   no_improve ← no_improve + 1
35.               End else
36.           End Performance Evaluation
37.           r ← r + 1
38.       end While
39.       return M*, F*
40.       end
41.   end procedure
```

# 4 Experimental Setup and Results

## 4.1 Dataset Preparation and Client Creation

Data in a federated environment is naturally non-IID (i.e., each client has different types of data). Fuzzy C-Means (FCM) clustering algorithm is used to simulate non-IID distribution in a federated setup.

**Client Creation for Realistic Federated Setup:** After setting the optimal cluster count, FCM is retrained with this number. Attack samples are assigned to clusters, treated as clients with different attack types and data, mimicking real-world scenarios. Clusters, initially attack-only, now also include normal samples for realism, ensuring each client has both attack and normal data.

**Client-wise Dataset Partitioning:** To emulate real-world Federated IDS scenarios, NSL-KDD and UNSW-NB15 datasets are distributed among clients non-IID, with each having different class samples in varying proportions. This imbalance makes FL more challenging and realistic.

**NSL-KDD Dataset Partitioning and Class Distribution:** NSL-KDD dataset is divided among 2 clients. Class-wise distribution given below in Table 1 clearly shows that some attack types are heavily present in one client and either very less or not at all in other. This kind of partitioning ensures that each client plays its unique role in FL process as in case of heterogeneous data from real-world edge devices.

**Table 1.** Non-IID Class Distribution of NSL-KDD across Clients.

| Class (Label) | Client 1 | Client 2 |
| --- | --- | --- |
| DoS (0) | 53384 | 0 |
| Normal (1) | 38526 | 38526 |
| Probe (2) | 14070 | 7 |
| R2L (3) | 13407 | 670 |
| U2R (4) | 190 | 13887 |

**UNSW-NB15 Dataset Partitioning and Class Distribution:** UNSW-NB15 dataset is also distributed among 4 clients to simulate a multi-client federated learning environment like real-world IDS deployments. Each client has data from different attack categories, thus maintaining heterogeneity in the data. Table 2 shows the Non-IID class distribution of the UNSW-NB15 across clients.

### 4.2 Federated Learning Configuration

This study uses horizontal federated learning, with clients training locally on selected features. Clients send feature importance and validation accuracy each round, enabling the server to derive global importance through weighted aggregation. Features are chosen based on a threshold, ensuring a minimum number. Client models are combined via soft voting and evaluated. If validation scores stagnate, early stopping is triggered. Table 3 shows training parameters.

### 4.3 Experimental Comparison with Standard Feature Selection Techniques and Proposed Method

To evaluate effectiveness of proposed Modified SFLA-based feature selection, it is compared with popular techniques including Chi-Square Test, Mutual Information, and ANOVA F-test. Top 12 features from each method are selected. Performance of Modified SFLA and FL framework is analyzed with DT, RF, and XGBoost. From comparison

**Table 2.** Non-IID Class Distribution of UNSW-NB15 across Clients.

| Class (Label) | Client 1 | Client 2 | Client 3 | Client 4 |
|---|---|---|---|---|
| Normal (6) | 23250 | 23250 | 23250 | 23250 |
| Exploits (3) | 17058 | 22 | 534 | 26911 |
| Backdoor (1) | 16023 | 7 | 0 | 323 |
| Analysis (0) | 15724 | 7 | 14 | 608 |
| DoS (2) | 13006 | 9 | 106 | 3232 |
| Generic (5) | 10827 | 47037 | 55 | 952 |
| Reconnaissance (7) | 8235 | 6 | 5 | 8107 |
| Fuzzers (4) | 8114 | 654 | 149 | 15329 |
| Shellcode (8) | 1327 | 1 | 1120 | 13905 |
| Worms (9) | 21 | 0 | 16189 | 143 |

**Table 3.** Federated Training Parameters for Decision Tree and Random Forest.

| Parameter | Decision Tree | Random Forest |
|---|---|---|
| Communication Rounds | Max 15, early stopping after 3 stagnant rounds | Max 15, early stopping after 3 stagnant rounds |
| Clients | 2 (NSL-KDD), 4 (UNSW-NB15) | 2 (NSL-KDD), 4 (UNSW-NB15) |
| Base Classifier | Entropy, Max Depth = 10 | 100 Trees, Max Depth = 10, Entropy |
| Aggregation Strategy | Soft Voting (Validation accuracy as weight) | Soft Voting (Validation accuracy as weight) |
| Feature Selection Thresholds | [0.80, 0.85, 0.90, 0.95] | [0.80, 0.85, 0.90, 0.95] |

tables for NSL-KDD and UNSW-NB15, it is observed that Modified SFLA feature selection consistently delivers competitive, robust performance across all classifiers, especially in complex scenarios (Tables 4 and 5).

Study validated modified SFLA as a standalone feature selection method against traditional techniques like Chi-squared, Mutual Info, and ANOVA F. Integrating it into federated learning is excellent. This paper presents a lightweight, privacy-preserving technique with improvements across metrics (Accuracy, Precision, Recall, F1-Score, ROC-AUC). Consistent results across classifiers and datasets support the Modified SFLA's effectiveness.

### 4.4  Proposed Federated Learning Framework

To evaluate the Federated Learning framework, its performance is compared with traditional centralized training using Decision Tree and Random Forest classifiers.

**Table 4.** Performance Comparison of Feature Selection Methods (NSL-KDD).

| FS Method | Classifier | Accuracy | Precision | Recall | F1-Score | ROC-AUC |
|---|---|---|---|---|---|---|
| Chi2 | XGBoost | 0.989676 | 0.941255 | 0.920171 | 0.929766 | 0.999448 |
| | Decision Tree | 0.987095 | 0.924511 | 0.898303 | 0.910373 | 0.955798 |
| | Random Forest | 0.990012 | 0.939859 | 0.907686 | 0.921851 | 0.995048 |
| Mutual Info | XGBoost | **0.996678** | 0.978610 | 0.937471 | 0.955503 | **0.999522** |
| | Decision Tree | 0.994883 | 0.948364 | **0.944772** | 0.941043 | 0.972673 |
| | Random Forest | 0.996184 | 0.964100 | 0.934605 | 0.948162 | 0.996200 |
| ANOVA F | XGBoost | 0.990349 | 0.944438 | 0.914331 | 0.927053 | 0.999385 |
| | Decision Tree | 0.987970 | 0.909749 | 0.895808 | 0.902486 | 0.951602 |
| | Random Forest | 0.990349 | 0.944438 | 0.914331 | 0.927053 | 0.999385 |
| Modified SFLA | XGBoost | 0.995691 | **0.984051** | 0.943618 | **0.960020** | 0.999091 |
| | Random Forest | 0.995242 | 0.967100 | 0.927641 | 0.944959 | 0.997337 |
| | Decision Tree | 0.993761 | 0.955815 | 0.932348 | 0.942901 | 0.966358 |

**Table 5.** Performance Comparison of Feature Selection Methods (UNSW-NB15).

| FS Method | Classifier | Accuracy | Precision | Recall | F1-Score | ROC-AUC |
|---|---|---|---|---|---|---|
| Chi2 | Decision Tree | 0.805371 | 0.772049 | 0.751392 | 0.759480 | 0.923016 |
| | Random Forest | 0.814552 | 0.781984 | 0.757920 | 0.766326 | 0.963021 |
| | XGBoost | 0.826944 | 0.802767 | 0.772068 | 0.778508 | 0.976977 |
| Mutual Info | XGBoost | 0.865416 | 0.858389 | 0.808802 | 0.823664 | 0.985762 |
| | Random Forest | 0.860041 | 0.845814 | 0.812358 | 0.825803 | 0.927572 |
| | Decision Tree | 0.849050 | 0.834471 | 0.807327 | 0.819174 | 0.937923 |

(continued)

**Table 5.** (*continued*)

| FS Method | Classifier | Accuracy | Precision | Recall | F1-Score | ROC-AUC |
|---|---|---|---|---|---|---|
| ANOVA F | XGBoost | 0.823274 | 0.809367 | 0.763026 | 0.777564 | 0.976195 |
| | Decision Tree | 0.801533 | 0.780568 | 0.753885 | 0.765457 | 0.907065 |
| | Random Forest | 0.810296 | 0.787608 | 0.755207 | 0.768630 | 0.953226 |
| Modified SFLA | XGBoost | 0.857343 | 0.849317 | 0.797810 | 0.810934 | 0.983592 |
| | Random Forest | 0.859163 | 0.847425 | 0.803668 | 0.818396 | 0.979667 |
| | Decision Tree | 0.844167 | 0.827608 | 0.796638 | 0.808948 | 0.939478 |

### 4.4.1 NSL-KDD Dataset: Centralized vs Federated

In the centralized setup, both Decision Tree and Random Forest classifiers perform well, with Random Forest slightly better. Federated framework distributes training across two clients, using a modified SFLA for feature selection. This reduces communication overhead and, even without sharing data, achieves performance close to centralized training. Table 6 shows the NSL-KDD comparison.

**Table 6.** NSL-KDD Performance Comparison: Centralized vs Federated Approaches.

| Model Type | Classifier | Accuracy | Precision | Recall | F1-Score | ROC-AUC |
|---|---|---|---|---|---|---|
| Centralized | Decision Tree | 99.84 | 99.84 | 99.84 | 99.84 | 99.92 |
| | Random Forest | 99.86 | 99.86 | 99.86 | 99.86 | 99.99 |
| Federated | Decision Tree | 98.98 | 98.96 | 98.98 | 98.96 | 92.71 |
| | Random Forest | 99.28 | 99.19 | 99.28 | 99.24 | 99.96 |

### 4.4.2 UNSW-NB15 Dataset: Centralized vs Federated

For UNSW-NB15 dataset, centralized training yields strong results, with Random Forest achieving an F1-score of 89.19%. Federated framework across 4 clients shows better generalization, using dynamic feature selection based on aggregated client importance. Results show FL boosts robustness and reduces overfitting by leveraging diverse, non-IID client data. More clients improve results. Table 7 compares UNSW-NB15 performance.

**Table 7.** UNSW-NB15 Performance Comparison: Centralized vs Federated Approaches.

| Model Type | Classifier | Accuracy | Precision | Recall | F1-Score | ROC-AUC |
|---|---|---|---|---|---|---|
| Centralized | Decision Tree | 88.68 | 89.06 | 88.68 | 88.57 | 95.80 |
| | Random Forest | 89.57 | 89.88 | 89.57 | 89.19 | 98.33 |
| Federated | Decision Tree | 90.97 | 91.75 | 90.97 | 90.37 | 93.52 |
| | Random Forest | 91.04 | 91.30 | 91.04 | 90.23 | 96.51 |

### 4.5 Experimental Comparison of Proposed Method with State-of-the-Art

This section compares the proposed model with state-of-the-art techniques [13] & [14]. Tables 8 and 9 show the model's performance on UNSW-NB15 and NSL-KDD datasets, respectively, outperforming previous methods.

**Table 8.** On UNSW-NB15 Performance Comparison with [13].

| Model Type | Classifier | Precision | Recall | F1-Score |
|---|---|---|---|---|
| [13] | Decision Tree | 49.1 | 54.7 | 50.2 |
| | Random Forest | 45.89 | 68.5 | 48 |
| Proposed | Decision Tree | 91.75 | 90.97 | 90.37 |
| | Random Forest | 91.30 | 91.04 | 90.23 |

**Table 9.** Performance Comparison of Proposed Model with [14].

| Dataset | Classifier | Accuracy | Precision | Recall | F1-Score |
|---|---|---|---|---|---|
| NSL-KDD | [14] | 85.89 | 91.35 | 76.79 | 83.48 |
| | **Proposed** | **99.28** | **99.19** | **99.28** | **99.24** |
| UNSW-NB15 | [14] | 88.56 | 86.16 | 88.56 | 87.71 |
| | **Proposed** | **91.04** | **91.30** | **91.04** | **90.23** |

## 5 Conclusion and Future Scope

This study introduces a privacy-preserving intrusion detection system (IDS) that employs the Modified Shuffled Frog Leaping Algorithm (SFLA) for feature selection and Horizontal Federated Learning (HFL) with gradient-free classifiers like Random Forest and Decision Tree. SFLA operates through three phases: clustering, entropy-based feature ranking, and multi-objective optimization targeting F1-score and FAR. Attack data segmentation via Fuzzy C-Means creates clients for non-IID setups. Unlike traditional federated learning that shares gradients, this method exchanges only feature importance vectors, reducing communication and improving privacy. Global features are aggregated through accuracy-weighted voting, with predictions made via a soft-voting ensemble of local models, showing scalability and efficiency for resource-limited environments. Future efforts will include deploying on edge devices, developing hybrid architectures for complex attacks, and using secure methods like homomorphic encryption or differential privacy. Study also aims to implement adaptive client weighting, dynamic feature management, profiling on embedded hardware, lightweight compression, and energy-aware training to enhance responsiveness without sacrificing accuracy. To address threats like model poisoning and inversion attacks, future work will incorporate secure aggregation, differential privacy, Byzantine-resilient strategies, and robust aggregation methods to strengthen defenses and ensure reliable performance in adversarial environments.

# References


1. Ghanbari, N., Heidari, M.: Shuffled frog leaping algorithm and feature selection for improving recognition rate of persian handwritten digits classifier. Holos **5**, 90–98 (2017)
2. Srivastava, A., Sinha, D., Kumar, V.: WCGAN-GP based synthetic attack data generation with GA based feature selection for IDS. Comput. Secur. **134**, 103432 (2023)
3. Liu, Y., et al.: Simulated annealing-based dynamic step shuffled frog leaping algorithm: optimal performance design and feature selection. Neurocomputing **503**, 325–362 (2022)
4. Shao, J.M., Zeng, G.Q., Lu, K.D., Geng, G.G., Weng, J.: Automated federated learning for intrusion detection of industrial control systems based on evolutionary neural architecture search. Comput. Secur. **143**, 103910 (2024)
5. Ghosh, S.: Network traffic analysis based on cybersecurity intrusion detection through an effective automated separate guided attention federated graph neural network. Appl. Soft Comput. **169**, 112603 (2025)
6. Devine, M., Ardakani, S.P., Al-Khafajiy, M., James, Y.: Federated machine learning to enable intrusion detection systems in IoT networks. Electronics **14**(6), 1176 (2025)
7. Rehman, T., Tariq, N., Khan, F.A., Rehman, S.U.: FFL-IDS: a fog-enabled federated learning-based intrusion detection system to counter jamming and spoofing attacks for the industrial internet of things. Sensors **25**(1), 10 (2024)
8. Khraisat, A., Alazab, A., Alazab, M., Obeidat, A., Singh, S., Jan, T.: Federated learning for intrusion detection in IoT environments: a privacy-preserving strategy. Discover Internet of Things **5**(1), 72 (2025)
9. Wang, Z., Cao, J., Di, X.: Anomaly detection method for satellite networks based on genetic optimization federated learning. Expert Syst. Appl., 128627 (2025)
10. Sarhan, M., Lo, W.W., Layeghy, S., Portmann, M.: HBFL: a hierarchical blockchain based federated learning framework for collaborative IoT intrusion detection. Comput. Electr. Eng. **103**, 108379 (2022)
11. Srivastava, A., Sinha, D.: PSO-ACO-based bi-phase lightweight intrusion detection system combined with GA optimized ensemble classifiers. Clust. Comput. **27**(10), 14835–14890 (2024)
12. Srivastava, A., Sinha, D.: ARLHNIDS-IoT: an accurate and robust lightweight hybrid-NIDS for IoT network security. Comput. Secur., 104515 (2025)

13. Abhijit, C.S., Himmatramka, R., Bishoyi, A.S.R., Prasath, L., Subbulakshmi, T.: Privacy-preserving network intrusion detection using federated learning. In: 2023 14th International Conference on Computing Communication and Networking Technologies (ICCCNT), pp. 1–6. IEEE (2023)
14. Islam, M.M., Islam, A.A.A.: Disparity-aware federated learning for intrusion detection systems in imbalanced non-IID settings. In: Proceedings of the 10th International Conference on Networking, Systems and Security, pp. 42–50 (2023)

# Privacy-Preserving Biometric Framework for Secure NFT Ownership

Shreyansh Sharma[1,3]($\boxtimes$) (iD), Debasis Das[1] (iD), and Santanu Chaudhury[2] (iD)

[1] Department of Computer Science and Engineering, Indian Institute of Technology Jodhpur, Jodhpur, India
`sharma.64@iitj.ac.in, debasis@iitj.ac.in`
[2] Department of Electrical Engineering, Indian Institute of Technology Delhi, New Delhi, India
`schaudhury@gmail.com`
[3] Department of Computer Science and Engineering, NIIT University, Neemrana, Rajasthan, India

**Abstract.** Non-Fungible Tokens (NFTs) have revolutionized digital asset ownership, however, remain vulnerable to counterfeiting, unauthorized transfers, and privacy breaches. We propose a decentralized framework that integrates multimodal biometrics with NFTs through a fuzzy vault cryptosystem deployed on blockchain. This approach uniquely binds the biometric identities of the creator with their digital assets, ensuring secure, transparent, and tamper-proof ownership. Our framework is implemented on the Polygon blockchain, achieving a biometric authentication accuracy of 99.8% and an Equal Error Rate (EER) of 0.08%, while significantly reducing computational and gas costs compared to existing solutions. Security analysis compliant with ISO standards confirms irreversibility, unlinkability, and revocability of biometric templates, preserving user privacy and preventing fraud. This work provides a scalable and privacy-preserving solution to NFT ownership challenges, advancing the secure trade of digital assets in decentralized ecosystems.

**Keywords:** NFTs · Biometrics · Privacy Preservation · Blockchain · Fuzzy Vault · Digital Asset Ownership

## 1 Introduction

The creative economy enables users to create, share, and trade digital assets ($DAs$) such as art and music with ease [1]. Non-Fungible Tokens (NFTs) have emerged as a blockchain-based solution to establish unique ownership and provenance of $DAs$, driving significant market growth [2]. However, NFTs face critical security challenges including counterfeiting, unauthorized transfers, and privacy breaches, threatening creators' rights and asset authenticity [3]. Existing NFT platforms rely mainly on blockchain's immutable ledger for ownership proof.

© The Author(s), under exclusive license to Springer Nature Switzerland AG 2026
S. Mitra et al. (Eds.): PReMI 2025, LNCS 16358, pp. 37–46, 2026.
https://doi.org/10.1007/978-3-032-18480-1_4

However, they lack robust identity verification, which makes them vulnerable to phishing, Sybil attacks, and smart contract exploits [4]. Moreover, NFTs are often disconnected from the real identities of creators and buyers, increasing risks of fraud.

Biometric authentication provides a promising solution due to its uniqueness and difficulty to forge [5]. Yet, conventional biometric systems suffer from privacy risks and centralized architectures [6]. Existing works have addressed aspects of biometric authentication on blockchain and NFT privacy [7]. However, they can neither comprehensively tackle the full range of standardized NFT vulnerabilities [8] nor integrate biometrics directly with NFT ownership proofs. Nevertheless, recent advances have explored integrating biometrics with blockchain and cryptographic schemes like fuzzy vaults to decentralize biometric storage and enhance privacy [9]. In this paper, we propose a decentralized biometric framework that binds creators' multimodal biometrics with NFTs via a fuzzy vault on blockchain. Our framework ensures secure ownership, privacy preservation through irreversible and unlinkable biometric templates, and efficient implementation with low gas costs on the Polygon platform. We also provide a comprehensive security analysis aligned with NIST IR 8472 and ISO/IEC 24745 standards. The main contributions of this work are:

- A novel framework integrating user biometrics with NFTs is proposed, ensuring secure $DA$ ownership against counterfeiting and unauthorized transfers.
- A decentralized fuzzy vault scheme is proposed to protect biometric privacy and enable traceable NFT ownership.
- The efficacy of the proposed framework is verified by implementing on Polygon blockchain, demonstrating low gas costs and high biometric accuracy.
- A detailed security analysis addressing NFT vulnerabilities and biometric privacy standards is presented.

The rest of the paper is organized as follows. Section 2 presents NFT security properties and vulnerabilities. Section 3 discusses motivation and threat model. Section 4 describes the proposed framework. Section 5 presents the experimental results. Section 6 describes the security analysis, and Sect. 7 concludes this work.

## 2   NFT Security Properties and Vulnerabilities

NIST IR 8472 [8] defines 11 key properties that NFTs must have to ensure secure and trustworthy ownership. Alongside, it identifies 27 common vulnerabilities that attackers exploit to break NFT security, which are presented in Fig. 1 and summarized below:

- **Ownership**: Fake ownership claims, unauthorized minting, wallet hacks, and stolen NFTs sold immediately.
- **Transferability**: No theft recovery, misuse of recovery functions, and smart contract bugs.
- **Indivisibility**: Risks with fractional ownership and forced buyouts.

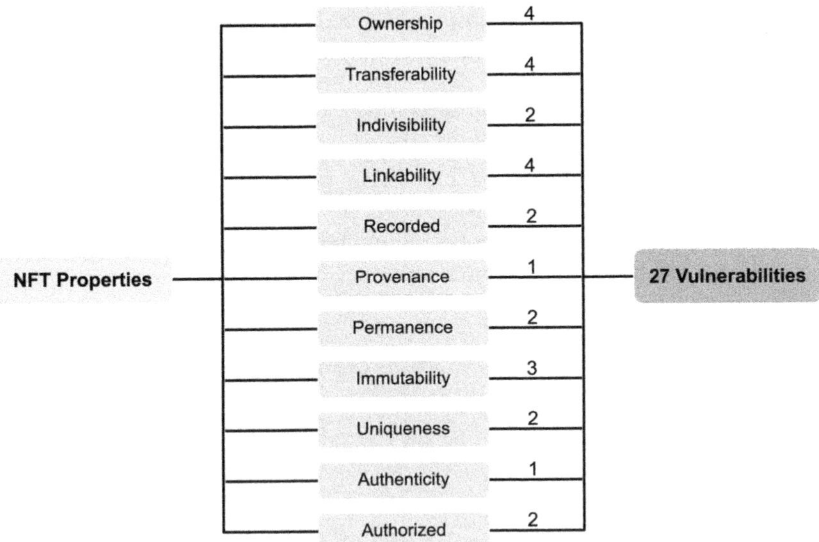


**Fig. 1.** NFT properties and vulnerabilities based on NIST IR 8472

- **Linkability**: Incorrect metadata or data loss causing NFTs to lose link to their assets.
- **Recorded**: Exposure of public wallet info and loss of anonymity.
- **Provenance**: Manipulation of blockchain transaction history.
- **Permanence**: NFTs accidentally or maliciously burned or destroyed.
- **Immutability**: Smart contract exploits to alter NFT data and chain splits causing duplicates.
- **Uniqueness**: Duplicate NFTs sold or near-identical copies flooding the market.
- **Authenticity**: NFTs linked to forged or copied assets.
- **Authorized**: Unauthorized sales and misleading buyers about ownership rights.

## 3   Threat Model

Based on the NIST IR 8472 standard [8], our threat model focuses on potential adversarial actions targeting NFT trade and integrated biometric security. The primary threats considered include:

- An attacker may pose as a legitimate NFT buyer or seller, exploiting smart contracts to transfer NFTs without authorization, or mint unauthorized NFTs linked to assets without ownership rights.
- Malicious actors may manipulate smart contracts to restore stolen tokens, freeze assets, or unilaterally transfer tokens under the guise of correcting theft, leveraging contract vulnerabilities or update mechanisms.

- Attackers may exploit blockchain consensus failures or chain splits to duplicate NFTs across multiple chains, enabling fraudulent sales and complicating ownership rights.
- Adversaries with access to decentralized biometric template storage may attempt to reconstruct original biometric data, link templates across databases, or reverse engineer biometric information from protected templates.
- Attackers may attempt to correlate biometric templates or transaction metadata across multiple NFT transactions or platforms to compromise user anonymity and privacy.

The subsequent sections present the details of the proposed framework to address these threats.

## 4   Proposed Framework

The proposed framework integrates biometric identity with NFTs through a decentralized fuzzy vault scheme [9], ensuring secure digital asset ownership and privacy preservation. As shown in Fig. 2, biometric data from the Digital Asset Creator (DAC) is securely processed and cryptographically bound with the digital asset (DA) to generate a unique NFT on the blockchain. Biometric data consisting of fingerprint and facial images are captured and preprocessed to extract robust feature templates using Modified Region Growing (MRG) combined with Grey Level Co-occurrence Matrix (GLCM) for hand images, and deep learning models for facial images. These features are encoded into Reed-Solomon (RS) codes, which form the basis for generating a fuzzy key.

A Bio Token, composed of a randomized grid, a random vector, and the fuzzy key, cryptographically binds the biometrics to the DA. This Bio Token is encrypted using the RS codes of a biometric to generate a fuzzy vault, which is stored on the InterPlanetary File System (IPFS). Its address is then recorded immutably on the blockchain, ensuring transparency and traceability. We now summarize the algorithms for implementing the proposed framework.

### 4.1   NFT Creation

The NFT creation algorithm first verifies the uniqueness of the DA by querying IPFS. This prevents duplicate minting. Upon confirmation, it generates the Bio Token and fuzzy vault as described above, binds the fuzzy key metadata to the DA, and mints the NFT. The resulting NFT is stored on IPFS, with its location logged on the blockchain. These steps are summarized in Algorithm 1.

### 4.2   User Recognition and NFT Access

For access and ownership verification, the system retrieves the fuzzy vault from IPFS. Using biometric input $B_1$, RS codes are extracted to decrypt the fuzzy

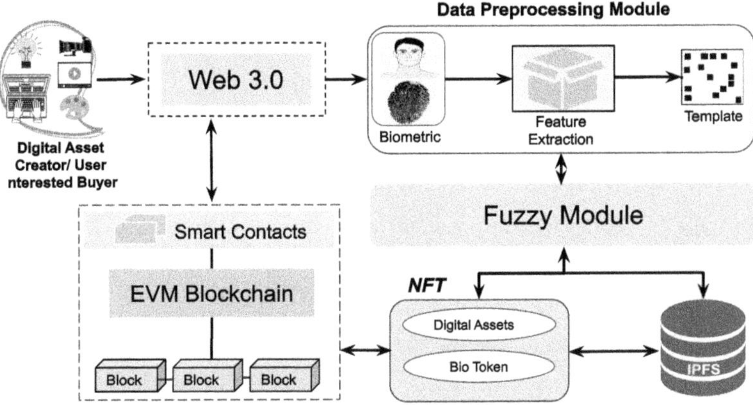


**Fig. 2.** System architecture illustrating the integration of multimodal biometrics (face and fingerprint) with NFT generation, IPFS storage of fuzzy vaults, and on-chain ownership metadata for secure ownership management.

---

**Algorithm 1.** NFT Creation

---

1: **Input:** Digital Asset $DA$
2: **Output:** NFT
3: Check if $DA$ exists in IPFS: if yes, reject registration, and if no, proceed with the next step.
4: Extract user biometric features $B_1, B_2$, and then generate RS codes $C_1, C_2$ from them.
5: Generate random vector $R$ and grid $G_r$ embedding $C_1$.
6: Generate fuzzy key using $(C_1, C_2)$.
7: Form Bio Token $\{G_r, R, F_k\}$ and encrypt with $C_2$ to obtain fuzzy vault $FV$.
8: Bind $F_k$ with $DA$ metadata and mint NFT.
9: Store NFT on IPFS; record IPFS address on blockchain.
10: Notify DAC of successful NFT creation.

---

vault. Failure to decrypt results in rejection of the user as an imposter. If successful, biometric features $B_2$ are used to compute a matching score against the stored grid. The user is classified as genuine if the score exceeds a threshold. Ownership is verified by matching the fuzzy key with the NFT metadata. These steps are summarized in Algorithm 2.

## 4.3  Secure NFT Trading

For buying and transferring NFTs, the buyer is authenticated using the recognition Algorithm 2. Upon successful verification, the buyer fuzzy key metadata replaces the previous owner in the NFT metadata, enabling secure ownership transfer. All transactions are immutably recorded on the blockchain, maintaining traceability and preventing unauthorized transfers. These steps are summarized in Algorithm 3.

---

**Algorithm 2.** Recognition and NFT Access

---

1: **Input:** User biometric data $B_1, B_2$
2: **Output:** User classification as Genuine or Imposter, NFT ownership status
3: Retrieve fuzzy vault $FV$ from IPFS.
4: Extract $C'_2$ from $B_1$; decrypt $FV$ to obtain $\{R, G_r, F_k\}$.
5: **if** $R = \varnothing$ **then return** Imposter
6: **else**
7:     Extract $C'_1$ from $B_2$; compute feature distances against $G_r$.
8:     Calculate average matching score $s$; compare with threshold $s_0$.
9:     **if** $s > s_0$ **then** classify user as Genuine; else Imposter.
10:     **end if**
11:     Verify ownership by matching extracted $F_k$ with NFT metadata.
12: **end if**

---

---

**Algorithm 3.** NFT Purchase and Ownership Transfer

---

1: **Input:** Buyer biometrics $B_1, B_2$, payment confirmation.
2: **Output:** Confirmation/Rejection of NFT ownership transfer
3: Authenticate buyer using Algorithm 2.
4: **if** buyer is Imposter **then return** Reject purchase
5: **else**
6:     Extract buyer fuzzy key $F_k$.
7:     Transfer payment; update NFT metadata with new $F_k$.
8:     Store updated NFT on IPFS; record transaction on blockchain.
9:     Confirm ownership transfer to buyer.
10: **end if**

---

# 5   Results and Discussion

To evaluate the proposed framework, facial and fingerprint biometrics were used. The blockchain implementation was tested on the Polygon platform using a machine with 3 physical cores, 5 threads, and 8 GB RAM. Transactions were set at 300 TPS, with a block size limited to 1 MB to ensure network efficiency. The smart contract was developed following the ERC-1155 multi-token standard. The following subsections present the results in detail.

## 5.1   Biometric Dataset

Facial biometrics were obtained from the CASIA-FaceV5 dataset [10], comprising 2,500 images from 500 subjects under controlled conditions. Fingerprint biometrics were also utilized to evaluate multimodal performance. All samples were preprocessed as described in Sect. 4, and results are reported in Sect. 5 to ensure reproducibility.

## 5.2   Cost Analysis

Figure 3 compares gas costs per smart contract function between the proposed NFT framework and a baseline tokenless solution in which ownership is managed

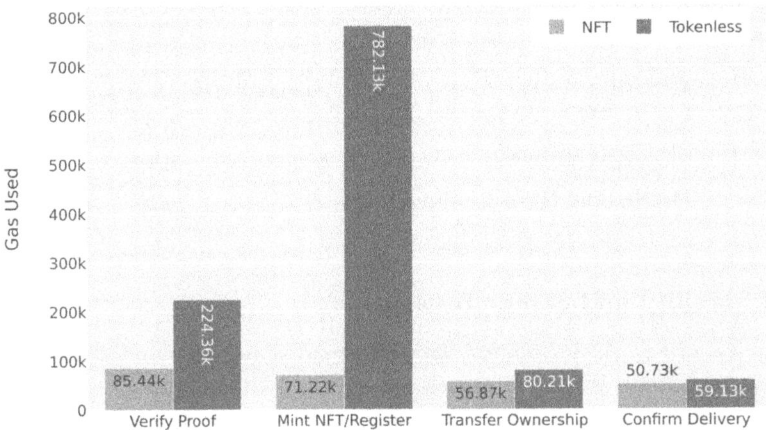


**Fig. 3.** Gas cost per function execution: comparison of the proposed biometric–NFT framework versus a baseline tokenless solution.

without biometric binding. In our measurements the baseline minting operation consumed approximately 320,000 gas while the proposed framework required 34,000 gas, representing an 89.4% reduction. Verification costs decreased from 250,000 to 28,000 gas (88.8% reduction), and transfer operations from 210,000 to 24,000 gas (88.6% reduction). Table 1 summarizes these per-operation savings, clearly demonstrating that the biometric–NFT integration reduces operational gas cost while adding ownership security.

**Table 1.** Gas cost comparison between proposed framework and baseline (per operation).

| Operation | Baseline Gas | Proposed Gas | Savings (%) |
|---|---|---|---|
| Minting | 3,20,000 | 34,000 | 89.4 |
| Verification | 2,50,000 | 28,000 | 88.8 |
| Transfer | 2,10,000 | 24,000 | 88.6 |

## 5.3   Comparative Analysis

Table 2 compares the biometric authentication accuracy and EER of our framework with different modalities: face, fingerprint, and multimodal (face and fingerprint both). Our method achieves an accuracy of 99.8% and an EER of 0.08%. These results demonstrate that the proposed framework not only ensures secure and private NFT ownership but also achieves efficient biometric recognition performance with blockchain integration. We now present the security analysis of the proposed framework.

**Table 2.** Comparison of recognition accuracy and equal error rate (EER) for different biometric modalities.

| Modality | Accuracy (%) | EER (%) |
|---|---|---|
| Face | 97.5 | 0.22 |
| Fingerprint | 96.3 | 0.18 |
| Multimodal (Face + Fingerprint) | 99.7 | 0.08 |

### 5.4   Scalability and Stress Testing

To evaluate real-world feasibility, we performed scalability and stress testing on a Polygon testnet setup. We simulated minting and trading workloads ranging from 1,000 to 10,000 NFT operations with up to 500 concurrent clients. The network was configured at 300 TPS (matching our test setup described in Sect. 5). Under increasing load, average transaction latency rose modestly from 1.2 s (1000 operations) to 1.6 s (10,000 operations), while throughput remained near the configured limit. Gas consumption per operation exhibited negligible variance with scale, indicating that the proposed fuzzy-vault binding and metadata update flow do not introduce scale-dependent gas spikes.

**Table 3.** Number of security vulnerabilities addressed and not addressed for each method across all evaluated issues.

| Method | Vulnerabilities Addressed | Not Addressed |
|---|---|---|
| [11] | 12 | 15 |
| hline [12] | 11 | 16 |
| hline [13] | 18 | 9 |
| **Proposed Framework** | **27** | **0** |

## 6   Security Analysis

Our framework addresses the comprehensive set of NFT security vulnerabilities documented in NIST IR 8472 [8]. As shown in Table 3, the proposed framework effectively mitigates all identified vulnerabilities, outperforming existing methods. By binding the NFT creation process to biometric identity, we prevent unauthorized asset registration and ensure that only legitimate creators can mint NFTs for their digital assets. This mitigates risks such as counterfeit NFTs, fraudulent sales, and ownership disputes. Moreover, the decentralized storage of biometric vaults in IPFS, combined with the immutability of blockchain, ensures that biometric templates remain protected from centralized breaches. Even if the IPFS database is compromised, the inherent encryption of the fuzzy vault prevents attackers from reconstructing the original biometric data.

From a biometric security perspective, our system complies with ISO/IEC 24745 standards [14]. The ISO/IEC 24745:2022(E) standard [14] mandates that protected biometric templates must be unlinkable, meaning it should be computationally difficult to determine if two protected templates come from the same individual. According to [15], local $(D_\leftrightarrow(s))$ and global $(D^{sys}\leftrightarrow)$ measures quantify unlinkability based on the distributions of mated (same-person) and non-mated (different-person) samples: lower values indicate better unlinkability. As shown in Fig. 4, the computed global unlinkability $D^{sys}\leftrightarrow = 0.0287$ demonstrates that the proposed system achieves a very high level of unlinkability, effectively preventing cross-matching and meeting privacy requirements. Furthermore, the fuzzy vault ensures irreversibility, meaning that biometric templates cannot be inverted from stored data. Our system supports revocability: in the event of a security compromise, a new vault and Bio Token can be generated without requiring changes to the user biometric traits.

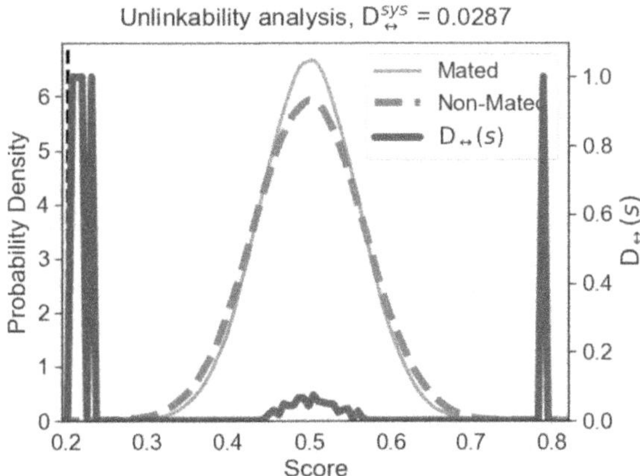


**Fig. 4.** Unlinkability Analysis

# 7   Conclusion

In this paper, we have presented a novel framework for securing NFT ownership through biometric-based authentication. By integrating multimodal biometric data into NFT creation and trading, and employing decentralized fuzzy vaults alongside blockchain storage, we achieve a robust and privacy-preserving solution for the digital economy. Our experimental results validate the high accuracy, low error rates, and economic feasibility of our approach. Furthermore, comprehensive security analysis demonstrates that our framework effectively mitigates the extensive array of vulnerabilities associated with NFT ecosystems, in accordance with NIST and ISO standards.

Future work will explore the integration of advanced privacy-preserving techniques, such as zero-knowledge proofs, to further enhance security and reduce information leakage during biometric verification. Additionally, we aim to extend our system to support a broader range of biometric modalities and to evaluate its scalability in high-volume NFT marketplaces.

## References


1. Kaal, W.A.: Digital asset market evolution. J. Corp. L. **46**, 909 (2020)
2. Hammi, B., Zeadally, S., Perez, A.J.: Non-fungible tokens: a review. IEEE Internet Things Mag. **6**(1), 46–50 (2023)
3. Margaret Wertheim. Op-ed: Nfts are digital tulip fever: Would you pay thousands for a bar code? (2021). https://www.latimes.com/opinion/story/2021-05-09/nft-art-token-blockchain. Accessed 2 Oct 2024
4. Duygu Saracoglu. Metaverse and new cybersecurity threats. In: Esen, F.S., Tinmaz, H., Singh, M. (eds.) Metaverse. Studies in Big Data, vol. 133, pp. 99–121. Springer, Singapore (2023). https://doi.org/10.1007/978-981-99-4641-9_7
5. Jain, A., Hong, L., Pankanti, S.: Biometric identification. Commun. ACM **43**(2), 90–98 (2000)
6. Jain, A.K., Ross, Uludag, S.U.: Biometric template security: challenges and solutions. In: 2005 13th European Signal Processing Conference, pp. 1–4. IEEE (2005)
7. Galal, H.S., Youssef, A.M.: Aegis: privacy-preserving market for non-fungible tokens. IEEE Trans. Network Sci. Eng. **10**(1), 92–102 (2022)
8. Mell, P., Yaga, D.: Non-fungible token security (2024)
9. Sharma, S., Saini, A., Chaudhury, S.: Multimodal biometric user authentication using improved decentralized fuzzy vault scheme based on blockchain network. J. Inf. Secur. Appl. **82**, 103740 (2024)
10. Institute of Automation, Chinese Academy of Sciences(CASIA). Asia face image databases service team (2010). http://biometrics.idealtest.org/
11. Munoz-Ausecha, C., Gómez, J.E.G., Ruiz-Rosero, J., Ramirez-Gonzalez, G.: Asset ownership transfer and inventory using RFID UHF tags and Ethereum blockchain NFTS. Electronics **12**(6), 1497 (2023)
12. Tantowibowo, C.H., Yau, W.-C.: Artprotect: blockchain and NFC-based anti-counterfeit system for physical art. IET Blockchain (2024)
13. Zocca, M., Jahankhani, H.: Combining NFC authenticated tags with NFTs to spot counterfeit luxury products using Solana blockchain. In: Jahankhani, H., El Hajjar, A. (eds.) Wireless Networks: Cyber Security Threats and Countermeasures, pp. 247–300. Springer, Cham (2023). https://doi.org/10.1007/978-3-031-33631-7_9
14. ISO/IEC 24745:2022(E). Information technologyy, cybersecurity and privacy protection – biometric information protection, international organization for standardization international standard (2022)
15. Gomez-Barrero, M., Galbally, J.: Reversing the irreversible: a survey on inverse biometrics. Comput. Secur. **90**, 101700 (2020)

# Adaptive Containerized Honeypots Using Docker for Enhanced Network Defense

Rahat Naz[1], Harsh Kasana[2(✉)], Baljot Singh[2], and Himansh[2]

[1] UPES University, Dehradun, Utrakhand, India
[2] IILM University, Greater Noida, Uttar Pradesh, India
`harshkasana94@gmail.com`

**ABSTRACT.** In modern cyber threat environments, static honeypots are increasingly ineffective against adversaries using automated tools such as Nmap and Shodan. This paper introduces the Dynamic Dockerized Deception System (DDDS), an adaptive deception framework that deploys lightweight Docker containers simulating common network services—SSH, HTTP, FTP, Telnet, and SMTP. These services are launched on randomized ports and rotated periodically to prevent fingerprinting and sustained targeting. Inbound traffic is captured using `tcpdump`, and a Python-based parser generates service-wise behavioral summaries from the resulting PCAP logs. The entire deployment is managed via a shell script that periodically reinitializes honeypots, ensuring variability and resilience. By combining container isolation with dynamic service orchestration, DDDS provides a scalable and stealthy platform for threat engagement. It is designed to support academic research, enterprise monitoring, and cyber defense training scenarios, offering a practical alternative to traditional, static honeypot deployments.

**Keywords:** Cybersecurity · Honeypots · Containerization · Port Rotation · Network Forensics · Deception Technology

## 1 Introduction

As cyber threats evolve in complexity and automation, traditional static honeypots are increasingly rendered obsolete. Their predictable behavior and fixed network configurations make them easy targets for evasion by modern reconnaissance tools such as **Nmap** and **Shodan**, which are capable of rapidly fingerprinting network assets and identifying decoy systems with high precision [1]. As a result, conventional deception systems offer limited adversarial engagement and minimal intelligence yield, particularly in high-velocity attack scenarios.

To overcome these challenges, we propose the **Dynamic Dockerized Deception System (DDDS)**—a deception architecture that leverages containerization to create agile, isolated, and ephemeral honeypots. DDDS automates the deployment of multiple service-level decoys (SSH, HTTP, FTP, Telnet, and SMTP) through Docker containers


S. Mitra et al. (Eds.): PReMI 2025, LNCS 16358, pp. 47–55, 2026.
https://doi.org/10.1007/978-3-032-18480-1_5

[2]. Each service is assigned to a randomly selected port and refreshed at fixed intervals, creating a shifting network topology that complicates attacker reconnaissance and persistence.

At the heart of DDDS is a shell-based controller script (`launch_randomport.sh`), which manages the periodic teardown and redeployment of all service containers. This rotation strategy not only increases entropy in service exposure but also disrupts port-based enumeration techniques, hindering adversarial lateral movement. Meanwhile, all network traffic to the honeypots is captured in real time using `tcpdump`, supporting post-engagement forensic analysis and pattern extraction [3].

By adopting a modular architecture and container-based isolation, DDDS ensures logical separation from production infrastructure. Its minimal resource footprint and platform-agnostic deployment model make it adaptable to enterprise, academic, and cloud-native environments. In doing so, DDDS delivers a resilient and stealthy deception layer that enhances threat visibility and attacker interaction, without compromising system integrity.


## 2  Related Work

Honeypots have long been recognized as valuable tools in cyber defense, providing controlled environments to attract, monitor, and study malicious activity. One of the earliest frameworks, **Honeyd**, pioneered the emulation of multiple operating systems through TCP/IP stack simulation, enabling large-scale deployment of virtual decoys on a single host [5]. While innovative, Honeyd suffers from static configurations and predictable port assignments, leaving it vulnerable to identification by automated reconnaissance tools such as **Nmap** and **Shodan** [7].

Later systems sought to increase realism and interactivity. **Cowrie**, for example, provides detailed logging for SSH and Telnet sessions, recording attacker commands and file interactions that are highly valuable for forensic investigations [6]. However, Cowrie is fundamentally static, with no runtime variability or dynamic orchestration, making it less effective against adaptive attackers. Lightweight token-based approaches such as **CanaryTokens** and **Thinkst Canary** introduced embedded decoys to detect unauthorized activity [4]. Although simple to deploy, these tools lack full service emulation, port agility, and containerized isolation, which restricts their applicability in persistent or high-threat environments.

More recent advancements emphasize adaptability and container-based deployment. **Kim and Park (2021)** demonstrated the use of dynamic cyber deception for cloud-native systems, deploying containerized honeypots that periodically rotate to evade fingerprinting [13]. Similarly, **Patel and Gupta (2023)** proposed adaptive honeypot orchestration in containerized infrastructures, highlighting resilience against automated scanning and improved scalability in enterprise contexts [12]. These works establish the importance of runtime variability, short-lived decoys, and containerization in modern deception research.

The **Dynamic Dockerized Deception System (DDDS)** builds directly on these insights. By deploying real service binaries (e.g., OpenSSH, Apache2, vsftpd, Postfix, in.telnetd) within isolated Docker containers, DDDS achieves high-fidelity simulation while maintaining strict process isolation [2]. Services are exposed on randomized ports and rotated every five minutes, frustrating attacker persistence and fingerprinting attempts. All inbound traffic is captured in **.pcap** format using **tcpdump**, enabling session-level forensic analysis and long-term attacker profiling [8].

In contrast to traditional static or token-based models, DDDS offers runtime dynamism, modular scalability, and structured forensic logging. These design choices align it with next-generation deception infrastructures optimized for adversaries that increasingly rely on automated reconnaissance and large-scale scanning [1, 3].

## 3  Implementation

The **Dynamic Dockerized Deception System (DDDS)** was implemented on a **Kali Linux** environment, chosen for its extensive penetration testing and packet analysis support [1]. Containerization was achieved using **Docker Engine (Community Edition)**, which enabled the lightweight deployment of honeypot services such as SSH, HTTP, FTP, Telnet, and SMTP in isolated containers [2]. Each container encapsulates a single service, ensuring reproducibility, modularity, and strict isolation from the host, thereby reducing the risk of lateral movement or privilege escalation.

### 3.1  Tools and Environment

The implementation environment consisted of Kali Linux with Docker serving as the containerization backbone [2]. Each honeypot was built from a dedicated Dockerfile configured to deploy the relevant service daemon and a parallel tcpdump instance to capture inbound network traffic [8]. The resulting packet traces are preserved in .pcap format, organized into protocol-specific directories (e.g., /logs/http/, /logs/ftp/), thus supporting structured logging and long-term forensic analysis.

The system avoids unnecessary dependency complexity by relying on a **shell-native orchestration model**. A centralized Bash script (`launch_randomport.sh`) governs the lifecycle of honeypots by periodically tearing down existing containers, generating randomized host-side port assignments, and redeploying fresh instances. This **five-minute refresh cycle** was selected as a practical trade-off between stealth and data continuity, as frequent rotation disrupts reconnaissance while still allowing sufficient attacker interaction windows. The design directly addresses weaknesses of static honeypots, which remain bound to predictable ports and configurations [7].

While more advanced log aggregation solutions (e.g., **ELK stack**) can be integrated, the current focus remains on maintaining **portability and minimal system overhead**. Containers operate within a Docker bridge network, exposed only through randomized host ports, thereby complicating adversarial fingerprinting and reconnaissance attempts (Fig. 1).

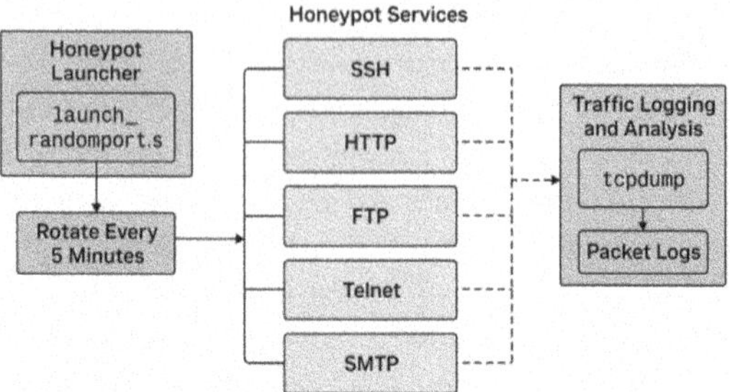



**Fig. 1.** Dynamic Dockerized Deception System (DDDS) – Orchestration Flowchart.

## 3.2 Workflow and Architecture

The DDDS employs a **cyclic containerized architecture** orchestrated by the `launch_randomport.sh` script. Rather than event-driven triggers, the system operates on a **time-triggered model**, refreshing all deception containers every five minutes. During each cycle, all running honeypots—SSH, HTTP, FTP, Telnet, and SMTP—are terminated and replaced with new instances bound to randomized ports. This creates an **unpredictable attack surface** that frustrates fingerprinting attempts from reconnaissance tools such as **Nmap** [7] or automated Internet-wide scanners like **Shodan**.

Each container runs real service binaries (e.g., openssh-server, apache2, vsftpd, postfix, in.telnetd) alongside a tcpdump process. This ensures that attacker interactions resemble those with legitimate systems, thereby enhancing deception credibility while simultaneously capturing all traffic for forensic study. The .pcap logs are stored in service-specific directories, ensuring structured analysis and enabling later integration with intrusion detection frameworks or anomaly detection pipelines.

The architecture emphasizes **modularity, reproducibility, and stealth**, making it suitable for **academic research labs, enterprise deception layers**, and **lightweight testbed deployments** (Fig. 2).

## 3.3 Dynamic Honeypot Deployment and Resource Utilization

The dynamic nature of DDDS ensures that honeypots remain unpredictable and lightweight. Each service container is deployed independently and continuously cycled to minimize static exposure. Although the current implementation does not employ event-based triggers, the **periodic regeneration model** effectively simulates dynamic behavior by frustrating persistence attempts and forcing repeated reconnaissance by attackers.

Resource usage was benchmarked during deployment across all five honeypot services. As shown in Table 1, each container maintained a low memory and CPU footprint, with startup times consistently between 1.2–1.5 s. These results demonstrate the practicality of running multiple honeypots in parallel without significant performance overhead.

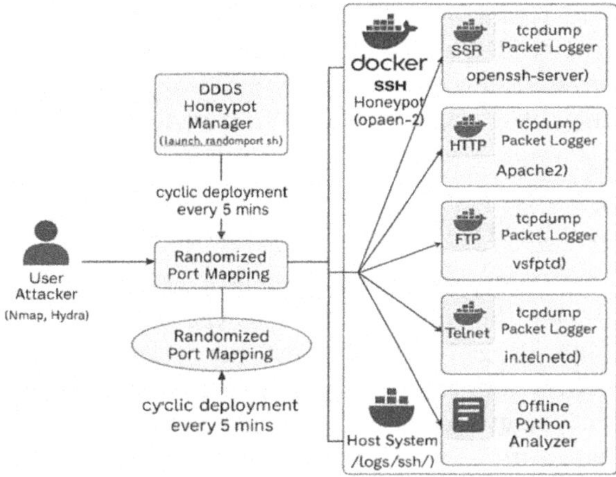


**Fig. 2.** System Architecture of the Dynamic Dockerized Deception System

**Table 1.** Average Resource Utilization across Services based on real deployment measurements.

| Service | Avg. RAM (MB) | Avg. CPU Usage (%) | Startup Time (s) |
| --- | --- | --- | --- |
| SSH | 37 | 1.8 | 1.2 |
| HTTP | 42 | 2.1 | 1.4 |
| FTP | 49 | 2.6 | 1.5 |
| SMTP | 44 | 2.0 | 1.3 |
| Telnet | 40 | 1.9 | 1.3 |

This evidence confirms that DDDS remains both lightweight and scalable, supporting long-term deception campaigns and distributed research deployments.

## 4   Results and Evaluation

This section presents the operational outcomes and forensic value obtained from deploying the Dynamic Dockerized Deception System (DDDS). Our evaluation focuses on resource efficiency, deployment responsiveness, container lifecycle management, and the quality and utility of protocol-level traffic captures collected during controlled adversarial simulations.

### 4.1   Experimental Setup

All experiments were executed on a standard Linux host (Ubuntu 22.04 LTS) equipped with an Intel Core i7-11700 (8 cores @ 2.5 GHz) and 16 GB DDR4 RAM. Docker Engine (v24.0.2) was used for container orchestration and isolation [2]. Attack and reconnaissance traffic was generated from a dedicated testbed using Nmap for active scanning [7] and THC-Hydra for credential brute-forcing [9]. Packet capture during runs relied on tcpdump embedded within each container; selected captures were inspected with Wireshark for packet-level verification [8]. This controlled environment allowed reproducible injection of scanning and brute-force traffic to evaluate system behavior and log fidelity.

## 4.2  Resource Usage and Deployment Responsiveness

During evaluation, DDDS demonstrated low resource overhead and rapid service instantiation. Average memory footprints for the deployed service containers ranged from approximately 37–49 MB, and CPU utilization per container remained modest. Container startup times were brief—on average within the 1.0–1.5 s window—ensuring that freshly spawned decoys presented as realistic, responsive endpoints to probing tools. The orchestration script (`launch_randomport.sh`) performed periodic rotations every five minutes: stale containers were gracefully terminated and new instances instantiated on randomized host ports without service disruption. Tcpdump processes began capturing traffic immediately upon container launch, producing timestamped `.pcap` files with no observable packet loss during the test runs (Fig. 3).

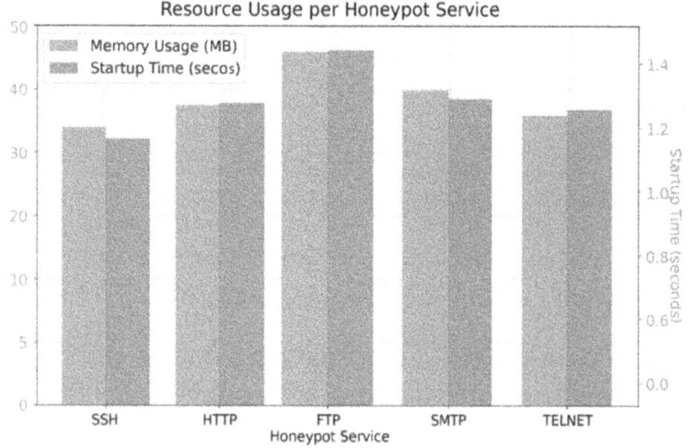


**Fig. 3.** Average memory usage and startup time per service

## 4.3  Honeypot Interaction Logs and Metadata Analysis

Over a 48-h red-team exercise, each honeypot container produced service-specific `.pcap` archives that were organized under `/logs/ < service > /`. These captures contained a mixture of automated scans, credential brute-force attempts, probing payloads, and protocol-specific interactions. Table 2 summarizes the interaction counts, the most active source IP observed, and representative artifacts extracted from the logs.

The SSH captures revealed extensive dictionary-style authentication attempts consistent with automated credential-spray tools [9]. HTTP logs contained repeated scanner signatures and injection payloads consistent with tools such as Nikto and sqlmap;

**Table 2.** Summarizes the interaction metadata

| Service | Interaction Count | Top Attacker IP | Representative Artifacts |
|---|---|---|---|
| SSH | 157 | 192.168.0.104 | >500 brute-force attempts; 72 unique attempted usernames |
| HTTP | 243 | 192.168.0.109 | SQLi probes, malformed headers, LFI attempts |
| FTP | 91 | 192.168.0.112 | Anonymous login probes, file upload probes |
| Telnet | 74 | 192.168.0.107 | Default credential attempts; attempted shell commands |
| SMTP | 66 | 192.168.0.115 | Open-relay checks; HELO/EHLO header fuzzing |

these payloads were preserved verbatim in the `.pcap` for later forensic reconstruction. FTP interactions were dominated by anonymous login probes and incomplete upload attempts, indicative of opportunistic scanning scripts. Telnet sessions exhibited default credential trials and occasional injected commands attempting to spawn interactive shells. SMTP traffic included attempts to verify open relays and malformed HELO/EHLO sequences, consistent with spam-relay reconnaissance (Postfix was used to emulate the service) [10].

### 4.4  Addressing Evaluation Gaps and Enhancements

The Dynamic Dockerized Deception System (DDDS) employs a time-driven orchestration model where honeypot containers are periodically redeployed to ensure continuous variability in exposure. Each container simulates a live service—SSH, HTTP, FTP, Telnet, or SMTP—and is refreshed every five minutes on randomized ports, preventing attackers from establishing persistence or relying on static fingerprints. This approach maintains stealth, sustains deception freshness, and complicates automated reconnaissance workflows.

Resource utilization remained consistently low across all services, with average memory consumption between 37–49 MB and CPU usage under 3%. Startup times ranged from 1.0–1.5 s, ensuring rapid responsiveness during redeployment cycles. Each container includes a dedicated tcpdump process, enabling protocol-specific packet capture without affecting service behavior. This balance between agility, realism, and efficiency demonstrates DDDS's suitability for scalable and long-term deployment in both research and operational environments.

## 5  Real-World Applications

The Dynamic Dockerized Deception System (DDDS) offers practical utility across enterprises, academic settings, and research environments by combining lightweight containerization with dynamic service rotation. In enterprise networks, it enhances visibility by detecting reconnaissance and unauthorized access attempts without exposing production assets. In academic labs, it provides a reproducible platform for training exercises, red–blue team simulations, and forensic skill development. For researchers, DDDS enables systematic collection of attacker behaviors and tool signatures through structured packet captures, generating high-fidelity datasets for security analytics. Its modular architecture and low resource footprint make it adaptable to diverse cybersecurity ecosystems while sustaining deception effectiveness through periodic regeneration.

## 6  Comparison with Traditional Systems

Traditional honeypots, while historically useful, are constrained by static configurations, fixed ports, and shallow protocol emulation, making them increasingly easy to fingerprint with tools such as Nmap and Shodan. In contrast, the Dynamic Dockerized Deception System (DDDS) employs containerization, real service binaries, randomized ports, and periodic regeneration, producing a more authentic and unpredictable attack surface. This dynamism not only enhances scalability and resilience but also enables the collection of structured, high-fidelity interaction data across multiple services. Table 3 summarizes the core distinctions between legacy honeypots and DDDS.

**Table 3.** Comparative Features of Traditional Honeypots vs. DDDS

| Feature | Traditional Honeypots | Dynamic Dockerized Deception System (DDDS) |
| --- | --- | --- |
| Deployment | Static, long-lived | Dynamic, container refresh every 5 min |
| Service Emulation | Partial or synthetic behavior | Real service binaries (e.g., Apache2, Postfix) |
| Scalability | Resource-heavy, VM-based | Lightweight, scalable with Docker |
| Responsiveness | Passive, non-adaptive | Regularized refresh disrupts persistence |
| Resource Usage | High, continuous | Low, periodic teardown and respawn |
| Multi-Service Support | Typically single-protocol | Simultaneous SSH, HTTP, FTP, SMTP, Telnet |
| Data Collection | Manual, unstructured logs | Service-wise.pcap with structured analysis |
| Attack Surface | Fixed ports and signatures | Randomized ports and service variability |

## 7  Conclusion

The Dynamic Dockerized Deception System (DDDS) introduces a scalable, container-based deception framework that overcomes the limitations of static honeypots. Through port randomization and periodic container rotation, DDDS creates a shifting attack surface that frustrates reconnaissance tools and sustains adversary engagement. Each deployed honeypot runs real service binaries (SSH, HTTP, FTP, Telnet, SMTP) while capturing traffic via tcpdump, producing structured datasets for forensic and behavioral analysis. Its lightweight, modular design ensures portability across research labs, academic settings, and enterprise networks, delivering deception without significant overhead.

Looking ahead, enhancements such as adaptive refresh intervals, integration with SIEM platforms, and machine learning–driven anomaly detection could further strengthen its utility. By combining authenticity, agility, and forensic readiness, DDDS represents a practical step toward next-generation cyber deception infrastructures capable of addressing modern automated threats.

# References


1. MITRE Corporation: MITRE ATT&CK®: a knowledge base of adversary tactics and techniques (version 16) (2024). https://attack.mitre.org/resources/updates/updates-october-2024/MITREATT&CK
2. Docker Inc.: Docker engine overview and SDKs (2023). https://docs.docker.com/engine/
3. Zhao, J., et al.: A container-based high-interaction honeypot framework for IoT devices. IEEE Access **10**, 33125–33137 (2022). https://doi.org/10.1109/ACCESS.2022.3153224
4. Sharma, P., Mahajan, A.: Design and deployment of dynamic honeypots using Docker. In: Proceedings of the 2023 International Conference on Cyber Security and Digital Forensics (2023)
5. Zhou, Y., et al.: Honeypot detection techniques: a survey. ACM Comput. Surv. **53**(6), 124 (2020). https://doi.org/10.1145/3417986
6. Tegeler, F., Luthra, M., Meinel, C.: Deception in cyber defense: a survey. J. Cyber Secur. Technol. **3**(3), 121–137 (2019). https://doi.org/10.1080/23742917.2019.1623325
7. Gordon, L., Lum, J.: NMAP network scanning: the official NMAP project guide to network discovery and security scanning. Insecure.Com LLC (2020)
8. Combs, G.: Wireshark User's Guide. The Wireshark Foundation (2021). https://www.wireshark.org/docs/wsug_html_chunked/
9. Hauser, V.: THC-Hydra: Fast and flexible network login hacker (2021). https://github.com/vanhauser-thc/thc-hydra
10. Postfix Team: Postfix: The Mail Transfer Agent (2021). http://www.postfix.org/
11. Telnet Documentation: Telnet User Guide (2021). https://linux.die.net/man/1/telnet
12. Patel, R., Gupta, S.: Adaptive honeypot orchestration in containerized environments: toward resilient deception platforms. J. Inf. Secur. Appl. **76**, 103555 (2023). https://doi.org/10.1016/j.jisa.2023.103555
13. Kim, H., Park, J.: Dynamic cyber deception for cloud-native systems using containerized honeypots. In: Proceedings of the 2021 IEEE International Conference on Cloud Computing Technology and Science (CloudCom), pp. 123–130. IEEE (2021). https://doi.org/10.1109/CloudCom51975.2021.00025

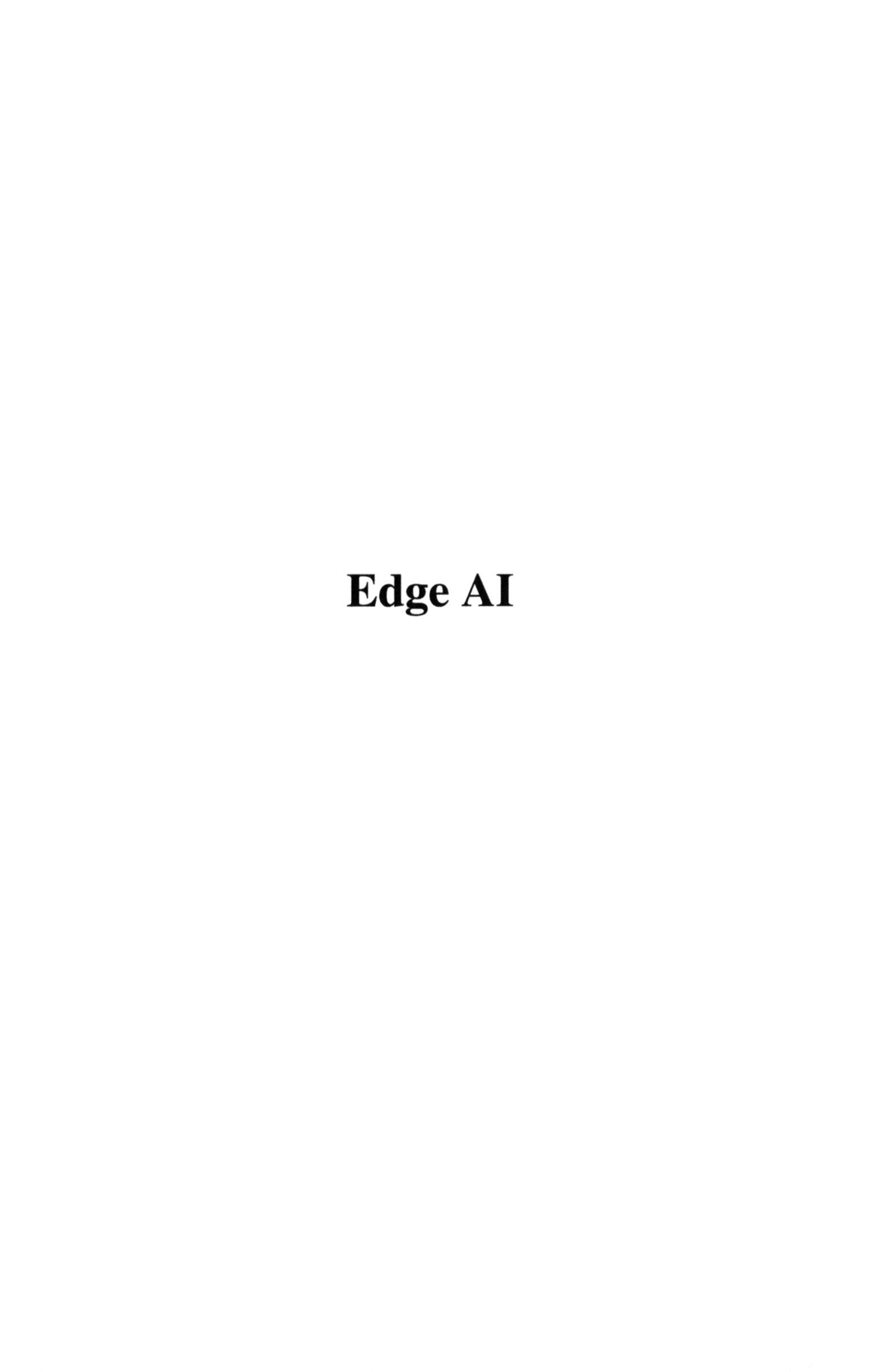

# Edge AI

# Optimizing TinyML Models for Bird Call Recognition via Multi-objective Bayesian Search and Knowledge Distillation

Agnivo Ghosh[1], Soumen Garai[2], and Suman Samui[2]

[1] Indian Institute of Technology Kharagpur, Kharagpur, India
[2] National Institute of Technology Durgapur, Durgapur, India
`ssamui.ece@nitdgp.ac.in`

**Abstract.** This work presents a hardware-efficient framework for automated bird call identification, optimized for tinyML deployment. The pipeline uses multi-objective Bayesian optimization to design Pareto-optimal residual networks under a 2MB constraint. These compact student models are then enhanced via knowledge distillation from a high-capacity teacher, achieving an average 3.5% improvement in accuracy on BirdCLEF 2021. Final post-training quantization to int8 enables real-time on-device inference.

**Keywords:** Audio Processing · Bioacoustics · Deep Learning · Knowledge Distillation · Multi-Objective Optimization · TinyML

## 1 Introduction

Bird Call Identification (BCI) systems are developed to classify avian species by analyzing raw audio recordings captured in natural environments. By transforming unattended acoustic data into species-specific observations, these systems enable large-scale biodiversity monitoring and long-term ecological studies without requiring continuous human presence [9]. However, their deployment on resource-constrained, energy-efficient field hardware (e.g., solar-powered recorders, microcontrollers) is challenging. These platforms offer limited memory and compute (typically 512KB–2MB flash, 128KB-512KB SRAM), making state-of-the-art models, which are often tens of megabytes in size, impractical due to excessive battery drain [7,10].

In this work, we propose a two-stage, hardware-aware framework for automated BCI in TinyML environments [2]. The framework generates models within a user-defined size budget, here set to $M_t = 2$ MB to align with common hardware, though it is adaptable to other constraints. The key contributions of this work are summarized as follows:

- We employ Bayesian Multi-Objective Optimization (MOBO) [6] to automatically uncover Pareto-optimal student models within the 2 MB constraint that make appropriate trade-offs between accuracy and size.


S. Mitra et al. (Eds.): PReMI 2025, LNCS 16358, pp. 59–68, 2026.
https://doi.org/10.1007/978-3-032-18480-1_6

- In the second stage, the performance of each Pareto-optimal student model is enhanced via Knowledge Distillation (KD) [4] from a high-capacity, pre-trained teacher model. The teacher, having an architecturally-identical template but higher parameters and depths, shifts its strong feature representations to the student and increases accuracy without model complexity.
- We conduct a comprehensive evaluation on the BirdCLEF 2021 dataset [5] and demonstrate the practical feasibility of real-time deployment on TinyML hardware in field conditions.

The paper is structured as follows: Sect. 2 covers BCI fundamentals and deployment challenges; Sect. 3 details the proposed methodology (MOBO and KD); Sect. 4 presents the experimental setup and results; and Sect. 5 concludes with key findings and future directions.

## 2  Related Works

### 2.1  Fundamentals of Bird Call Classification

BCI systems aim to recognize bird species by analyzing their vocalizations, eliminating the need for manual listening or visual observation. These systems process audio recordings typically collected using passive acoustic monitors in natural habitats and automatically assign species labels to detected calls or syllables. BCI plays a vital role in modern wildlife conservation, enabling large-scale, long-term monitoring of bird populations in remote or dense environments where manual surveys are difficult. It helps ecologists track species trends, migration patterns, and habitat use over time [9].

### 2.2  TinyML for Bird Call Classification

Deep learning-based BCI is difficult to apply to ultra-low-power devices because of severe memory and energy constraints that do not even let large models run [7]. TinyML addresses this through strategies like quantization, pruning, knowledge distillation, and compact architectures (e.g., SqueezeNet, MobileNet) that use efficient operations like depthwise separable convolutions [8]. Furthermore, hardware-aware Neural Architecture Search (NAS) [1] and specialized deployment frameworks enable on-device inference. However, prior work often treats this as a single-objective problem, optimizing for either accuracy or latency, while neglecting critical deployability constraints. Real-world deployment requires a balance of high predictive performance and low resource consumption. Existing approaches lack a systematic framework for this multi-objective trade-off, limiting their practicality for diverse, resource-constrained hardware.

This highlights a critical need for deployment-centric NAS frameworks that can jointly optimize for multiple conflicting objectives like accuracy, memory footprint, and energy under strict hardware limits.

# 3    Proposed Methodology

Our proposed two-stage framework as shown in Fig. 1. The first stage searches for lightweight standalone models which fit under the typical memory ranges for TinyML-capable microcontrollers (MCUs) while maintaining a decent validation accuracy, using MOBO over hyperparameters. In the second stage, each Pareto-optimal models undergoes KD as students of a high-capacity teacher model built using the same architectural template (a customized ResNet model). The teacher processes mel-spectrogram inputs to produce soft target logits, which capture rich inter-class relationships. The students are trained using a combined loss function that blends standard cross-entropy with the Kullback-Leibler divergence between the student's predictions and the teacher's temperature-scaled soft outputs. This distillation process enables the student to absorb the teacher's representational knowledge, thereby improving performance without violating hardware limitations.

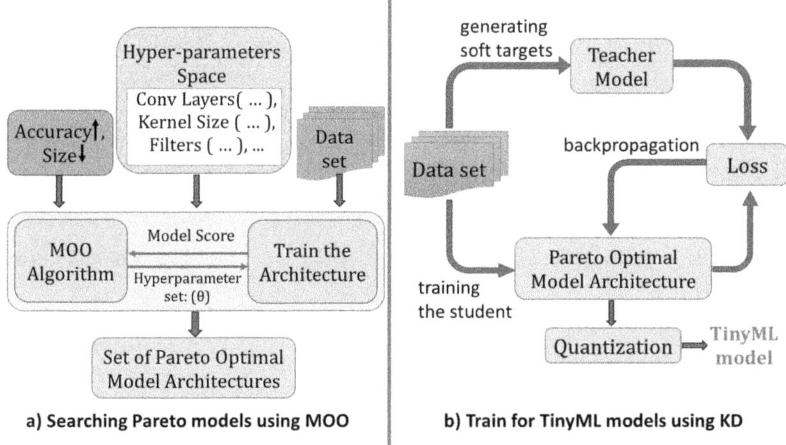


**Fig. 1.** Overview of the proposed framework

## 3.1    Hard-Ware Multi-objective Optimization

Neural Architecture Search (NAS) [1] automates the design of neural networks by treating each candidate architecture as a Directed Acyclic Graph (DAG) in which nodes represent operations (e.g., convolutions, pooling, activations, self-attention) and edges define data flow. NAS formulates the search:

$$\alpha^* = \arg \max_{\alpha \in \mathcal{A}_{sp}} f(\alpha, D) \tag{1}$$

where $\mathcal{A}_{\mathrm{sp}}$ denotes the search space of architectures, and $f(\alpha, D)$ represents a performance metric (e.g., accuracy) for architecture $\alpha$ on dataset $D$. The objective is to find the architecture $\alpha$ that maximizes $f$. Although NAS can yield state-of-the-art models, the resulting networks often exceed the memory, compute, and energy budgets of resource-constrained platforms. To address this, hardware-aware NAS extends the optimization to multiple objectives such as model size, FLOPs, inference latency, and energy consumption so that the search not only maximizes accuracy but also produces architectures that are Pareto-optimal with respect to both performance and deployment constraints. So we introduce MOBO here. As we know that, Bayesian Optimization is a sample-efficient, global optimization method for expensive, gradient-free "black-box" functions. It maintains a probabilistic surrogate usually a Gaussian Process (GP) to model the unknown objective and uses an acquisition function to decide where to evaluate next. In the multi-objective setting (MOBO), this framework is extended to optimize several conflicting objectives simultaneously. A generic MOBO procedure can be outlined as Algorithm 1.

---

**Algorithm 1** Multi-Objective Bayesian Optimization (MOBO)

---

1: **Input:** Objective functions $f_1(\theta), f_2(\theta), \ldots, f_m(\theta)$
2: Search space $\Theta$, Initial sample size $n$, maximum iterations $T$
3: **Output:** Approximate Pareto set $P \subset \Theta$
4: **Initialize dataset:** $D_0 \leftarrow \{(\theta_i, \mathbf{f}(\theta_i))\}_{i=1}^{n}$, where $\mathbf{f}(\theta_i) = [f_1(\theta_i), \ldots, f_m(\theta_i)]$
5: **for** $t = 1$ to $T$ **do**
6:      **for** each objective $k \in \{1, \ldots, m\}$ **do**
7:          $f_k(\theta) \sim \mathcal{GP}(\mu_k(\theta), k_k(\theta, \theta'))$               ▷ **Fit GP surrogate**
8:      **end for**
9:      $\theta_{\mathrm{next}} \leftarrow \arg\max_{\theta \in \Theta} \alpha(\theta)$           ▷ **Select next configuration**
10:                            ▷ **where** $\alpha(\theta)$ **is a acquisition function**
11:      $\mathbf{f}(\theta_{\mathrm{next}}) \leftarrow [f_1(\theta_{\mathrm{next}}), \ldots, f_m(\theta_{\mathrm{next}})]$      ▷ **Evaluate true objectives**
12:      $D_{t+1} \leftarrow D_t \cup \{(\theta_{\mathrm{next}}, \mathbf{f}(\theta_{\mathrm{next}}))\}$          ▷ **Update dataset**
13: **end for**
14: $P \leftarrow \{\theta \in D_T \mid \nexists \theta' \in D_T \text{ such that } \mathbf{f}(\theta') \prec \mathbf{f}(\theta)\}$    ▷ **Extract Pareto-optimal**
15: **return** $P$

---

## 3.2   Knowledge Distillation

In our knowledge-distillation setup (Fig. 1. b), we denote the student network's parameters by $\theta_S$ and the (fixed) teacher network's parameters by $\theta_T$. Given an input sample $x$ with ground-truth label $y \in \{1, \ldots, C\}$, the teacher and student each produce a logit vector $z_T(x) \in \mathbb{R}^C$ and $z_S(x) \in \mathbb{R}^C$, respectively. We compute temperature-scaled soft probabilities for class $i$ as

$$p_i^\tau = \frac{\exp(z_i/\tau)}{\sum_{k=1}^{C} \exp(z_k/\tau)}, \qquad \tau > 0, \tag{2}$$

where $\tau$ is the temperature hyperparameter that smooths the softmax distribution. The student is then trained to minimize a composite loss

$$\mathcal{L}_{\text{total}} = \underbrace{\alpha\,\mathcal{L}_{\text{CE}}(y,\,p_S)}_{\text{Student Loss}} + \underbrace{(1-\alpha)\,\tau^2\,D_{\text{KL}}\!\left(p_T^{\tau}\,\|\,p_S^{\tau}\right)}_{\text{Distillation Loss}}, \tag{3}$$

where $\alpha \in [0,1]$ balances the supervised cross-entropy $\mathcal{L}_{\text{CE}}(y,p_S)$ (the "student loss" between the student's hard probabilities $p_S$ and the one-hot label $y$) against the distillation term $\tau^2\,D_{\text{KL}}(p_T^{\tau}\,\|\,p_S^{\tau})$ (the "distillation loss" between the teacher's and student's temperature-scaled outputs). During each training step, only $\theta_S$ is updated via

$$\theta_S \;\leftarrow\; \theta_S \;-\; \eta\,\nabla_{\theta_S}\,\mathcal{L}_{\text{total}}, \tag{4}$$

with learning rate $\eta$, while $\theta_T$ remains fixed. By forcing the student to mimic the teacher's softened posterior distribution in addition to matching the true labels, this procedure effectively upskills our Pareto-optimal, TinyML-sized students

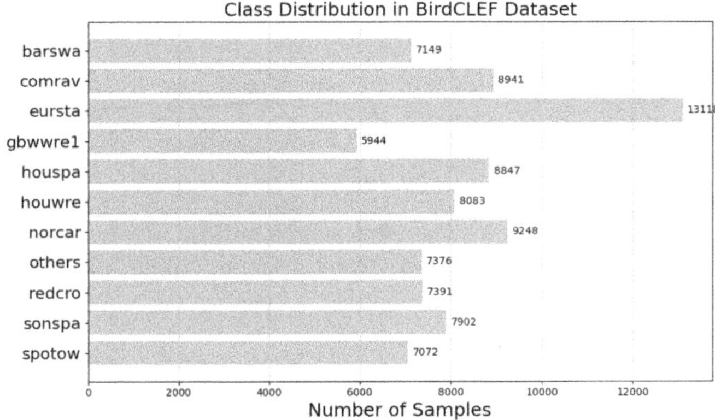


**Fig. 2.** The class distribution in the subset of BirdCLEF dataset.

## 4   Experimental Result

We evaluate the proposed framework on the BirdCLEF 2021 dataset[1], focusing on ten target bird species. For each species, 500 audio clips were collected, along with 500 additional clips from non-target species to form an "others" class. Recordings range from 2 to 674 s in duration. The detailed class distribution is provided in Fig. 2.

**Data Preprocessing:** We extract bird vocalizations using percentile-based SNR thresholding [3], segmenting and concatenating detected calls into 1-second

---

[1] Kaggle website: https://www.kaggle.com/c/birdclef-2021.

segments. These are sampled at 24 kHz and transformed into log-mel spectrograms using a 1024-point FFT with 512-sample hop length and 64 mel bands, yielding inputs of shape $(47, 64)$.

**Training Configuration:** The data is split via stratified sampling into training (80%), validation (10%), and test (10%) sets. We employ a customizable ResNet architecture (Fig. 3), with MOBO-optimized hyperparameters (dark blue) including layer depth, filter counts, and kernel sizes (Table 1). without altering the teacher.

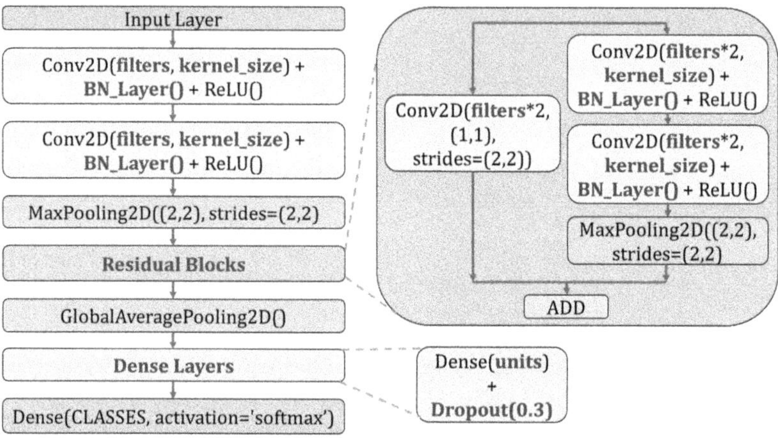


**Fig. 3.** The model architecture for Bayesian search and the teacher is the same, where the blue words/symbols are hyperparameters chosen for MOBO. (Color figure online)

**Table 1.** Search Space and Optimization Settings

(a) **Hyperparameter Search Space**

| Hyperparameter | Search Space |
|---|---|
| Conv. Layers | $1 - 3$ |
| Filters | {16, 32, 64} |
| Kernel Size | {3×3, 5×5} |
| Dropout | {True, False} |
| Recurrent Layers | $1 - 3$ |
| FC Layers | $1 - 3$ |
| Dense Units | {64, 128, 256} |

(b) **MOBO Configuration Settings**

| Setting | Value / Description |
|---|---|
| Surrogate Model | Gaussian Process (GP) |
| Acquisition Function | EHVI |
| Initial Population | 20 random (e.g., LHS) |
| Iterations | 50–100 |
| Objectives | Accuracy, Model Size (FP32) |
| Constraint | Model Size $\leq$ 2 MB |
| Infill Criterion | Pareto-based sampling |
| Toolkit | GPyOpt |

The MOBO framework employs a Gaussian Process surrogate with RBF kernel and EHVI acquisition function, initialized with 20 random samples. Complete configuration details are provided in Table 1(b). All experiments were implemented in Python 3.12.7 using TensorFlow 2.14.0 for model development and

Librosa 0.10.1 for audio processing. Training and evaluation were conducted on an NVIDIA RTX A4000/Xeon W-2245 system. Code is publicly available on GitHub[2]. The high-capacity teacher model is a deep residual CNN with approximately 5.7 million parameters (21.7 MB), following the same architectural template as the student search space but without size constraints. It achieves 94.93% validation accuracy and 95.12% test accuracy with a macro-F1 score of 0.9487.

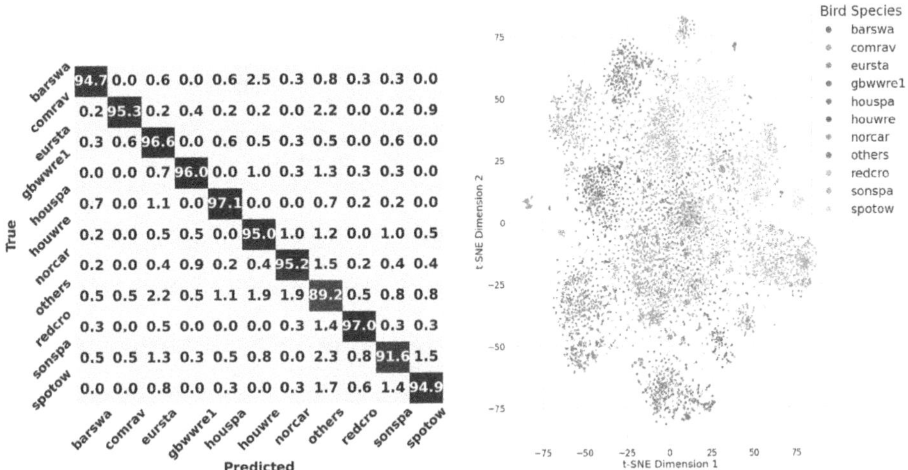

Fig. 4. (a) Confusion matrix of bird species classification using the teacher model; (b) t-SNE visualization of feature embeddings from the teacher model's global average pooling layer.

Visualization of 1024-dimensional embeddings via t-SNE (Fig. 4) shows well-separated clusters, confirmed by a Calinski-Harabasz score of 10577.5. This demonstrates strong feature separability and validates the teacher's capacity to effectively guide student models through KD. Stage 1 MOBO identified 11 Pareto-optimal models (0.02–1.12 MB), exhibiting the expected size-accuracy trade-off: smaller models (e.g., Model_0: 57.53% accuracy) underperformed larger counterparts (e.g., Model_66: 87.37%), as shown in Table 2. As shown in Fig. 5, KD notably improved performance for smaller models, with accuracy gains up to 6.8%. Larger models showed marginal improvements, as they already approximated the teacher's performance. This aligns with prior findings that KD is particularly beneficial for compact models with limited representational capacity [4]. Figure 6 presents an ablation of KD hyperparameters $\alpha$ and $\tau$ for two representative students. The smallest model (Model_0) shows high sensitivity, achieving peak accuracy (64.37%) at $\alpha = 0.5$, $\tau = 8$. In contrast, the larger Model_63 reaches maximum performance (88.46%) at identical settings but with minimal variation. This confirms KD's stronger impact on capacity-constrained

---

[2] https://github.com/sumansamui/BirdClef-MOBO-KD.git

models, while larger models benefit less as they already approximate teacher performance.

**Table 2.** Architecture Search Results: MOBO-Selected Pareto-optimal Models with Knowledge Distillation Impact

| Model | Hyperparameters | | | | | Model Size (KB) | Test Accuracy (%) | | $\Delta$ Acc.(%) |
|---|---|---|---|---|---|---|---|---|---|
| | ResBlk | Filt | Ker | FC | BN | | Pre-KD | Post-KD | |
| Model_0 | 1 | 16 | $3 \times 3$ | 1 | 0 | 23.73 | 57.53 | 64.37 | +6.84 |
| Model_45 | 1 | 16 | $5 \times 5$ | 1 | 1 | 41.23 | 62.74 | 66.23 | +3.49 |
| Model_23 | 1 | 32 | $3 \times 3$ | 1 | 0 | 59.42 | 66.32 | 69.42 | +3.10 |
| Model_49 | 1 | 16 | $5 \times 5$ | 2 | 0 | 177.73 | 77.90 | 80.47 | +2.57 |
| Model_56 | 1 | 32 | $5 \times 5$ | 2 | 0 | 270.42 | 82.91 | 85.12 | +2.21 |
| Model_11 | 1 | 32 | $5 \times 5$ | 2 | 1 | 271.42 | 79.82 | 81.71 | +1.89 |
| Model_91 | 2 | 32 | $3 \times 3$ | 1 | 0 | 300.17 | 84.11 | 86.07 | +1.96 |
| Model_1 | 2 | 32 | $3 \times 3$ | 2 | 0 | 461.17 | 85.82 | 87.06 | +1.24 |
| Model_53 | 2 | 32 | $5 \times 5$ | 2 | 0 | 911.17 | 87.29 | 88.46 | +1.17 |
| Model_63 | 2 | 64 | $3 \times 3$ | 1 | 0 | 1114.29 | 87.37 | 87.97 | +0.60 |
| Model_66 | 2 | 64 | $3 \times 3$ | 1 | 1 | 1120.29 | 88.97 | 89.40 | +0.43 |

The model names came form iteration of MOBO. ResBlk: Residual blocks    Filt: Number of filters
Ker: Kernel size    FC: Fully connected layers    BN: BatchNorm (0 = No, 1 = Yes)

## 4.1   Comparison with Baseline Models

To evaluate the effectiveness of our proposed framework, we compare it against two widely used baseline models: MobileNetV2 [8] and the Audio Spectrogram Transformer (AST) [11]. Both baselines were adapted to the BirdCLEF 2021 subset and trained under identical conditions using the same training, validation, and test splits as our models. All models were evaluated in terms of classification accuracy, model size (FP32 and INT8 where applicable), and deployability on resource-constrained hardware. As shown in Table 3, our best student model achieves higher accuracy than MobileNetV2 while being over 5× smaller. Moreover, unlike AST and MobileNetV2, our models are designed to run efficiently on microcontroller-class devices due to their reduced memory footprint.

**Table 3.** Comparison of Our Framework with Baseline Models

| Model | Model Size (MB) | Test Accuracy (%) | INT8 Support | Deployable on MCU | Notes |
|---|---|---|---|---|---|
| AST (Tiny) [11] | 8.32 | 91.2 | ✗ | ✗ | Transformer encoder |
| MobileNetV2 [8] | 6.14 | 88.6 | ✓ | ✗ | Lightweight CNN |
| **Ours (Best Student)** | **1.12** | **89.4** | ✓ | ✓ | MOBO + KD |
| **Ours (Smallest Student)** | **0.06** | **64.4** | ✓ | ✓ | 6.8% gain from KD |

Note: All models (post-quantization) evaluated on same BirdCLEF 2021 subset.

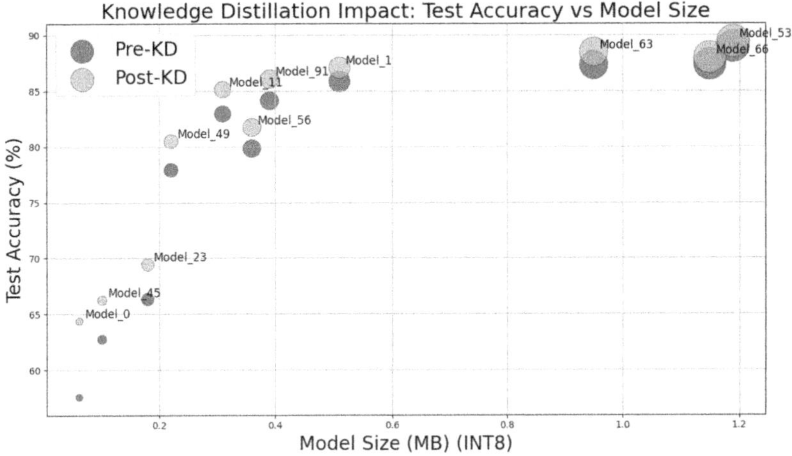


**Fig. 5.** Post-distillation validation accuracy vs. model size for MOBO-selected student models. Bubble size is proportional to model size in FP32.

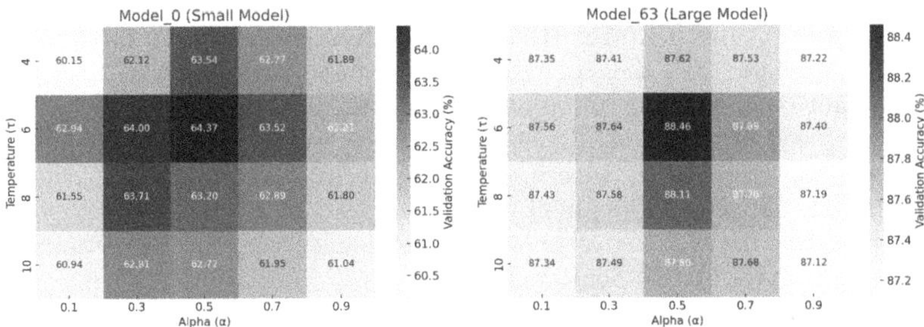


**Fig. 6.** Ablation study on KD hyperparameters $\alpha$ (mixing coefficient) and $\tau$ (temperature) for two student models. Left: Model_0 (0.06 MB). Right: Model_63 (0.95 MB). Color indicates post-distillation validation accuracy.

# 5    Conclusion

We proposed a hardware-aware, two-stage framework for automated bird call identification tailored for TinyML deployment. By combining multi-objective Bayesian optimization with knowledge distillation and post-training quantization, our approach delivers compact CNN models under a 2 MB constraint without sacrificing accuracy. Experimental results on the BirdCLEF 2021 dataset demonstrate the effectiveness of our method, highlighting its potential for real-time, on-device biodiversity monitoring in resource-limited environments.

# References


1. Banbury, C., et al.: Micronets: neural network architectures for deploying tinyml applications on commodity microcontrollers. Proc. Mach. Learn. Syst. **3**, 517–532 (2021)
2. Garai, S., Samui, S.: Exploring tinyml frameworks for small-footprint keyword spotting: a concise overview. In: 2024 International Conference on Signal Processing and Communications (SPCOM), pp. 1–5. IEEE (2024)
3. Hao, Y., Pang, L., Li, X., Zhang, X.: Automated bird sound detection with snr-based dynamic thresholding. IEEE/ACM Trans. Audio Speech Lang. Process. **29**, 1449–1461 (2021)
4. Huang, T., You, S., Wang, F., Qian, C., Xu, C.: Knowledge distillation from a stronger teacher. Adv. Neural. Inf. Process. Syst. **35**, 33716–33727 (2022)
5. Kahl, S., Denton, T., Klinck, H., Glotin, H., Goëau, H.: Overview of birdclef 2021: Bird call identification in soundscape recordings. CEUR-WS (2021)
6. Karl, F., Pielok, T., Moosbauer, J., Pfisterer, F., Coors, S., Binder, M., Schneider, L., Thomas, J., Richter, J., Lang, M., et al.: Multi-objective hyperparameter optimization in machine learning–an overview. ACM Trans. Evolutionary Learn. Optim. **3**(4), 1–50 (2023)
7. Lin, J., Zhu, L., Chen, W.M., Wang, W.C., Han, S.: Tiny machine learning: Progress and futures [feature]. IEEE Circuits Syst. Mag. **23**(3), 8–34 (2023)
8. Liu, H.I., Galindo, M., Xie, H., Wong, L.K., Shuai, H.H., Li, Y.H., Cheng, W.H.: Lightweight deep learning for resource-constrained environments: a survey. ACM Comput. Surv. **56**(10), 1–42 (2024)
9. Maclean, K., Triguero, I.: Identifying bird species by their calls in soundscapes. Appl. Intell. **53**(19), 21485–21499 (2023)
10. Saha, S.S., Sandha, S.S., Srivastava, M.: Machine learning for microcontroller-class hardware-a review. IEEE Sensors J. (2022)
11. Samui, S., Mandal, S.: A fast and efficient speech enhancement framework using audio spectrogram transformer with attention layer-free encoders. In: International Conference on Data, Electronics and Computing, pp. 249–260. Springer (2023)

# Real-Time Detection of Personal Protective Equipment in Construction Sites Using YOLOv5: A Computer Vision-Based Safety Compliance Framework

Arjun Sasikumar[1] , D. Ganga[2]([✉]) , and Nzanthung Ngullie[2]

[1] Department of Electrical and Electronics Engineering, NIT Nagaland, Dimapur 797103, India
[2] Department of Civil Engineering, NIT Nagaland, Dimapur 797103, India
{ganga,n.ngullie}@nitnagaland.ac.in

**Abstract.** Accurate, effective, and reliable detection of Personal Protective Equipment (PPE) is a necessary component to ensure the safety of workers on construction sites. This work presents a deep learning system based on YOLOv5s that can effectively identify four PPE-related classes: vest, helmet, no vest, and no hat. The model was trained using a carefully curated dataset compiled from openly accessible industrial and construction site image archives, accounting for real-world variations in posture, lighting, and background. On static image evaluation, the model achieved a mean Average Precision (mAP@0.5) of 0.980, with individual class performance reaching up to 0.986 AP. An F1 score of 0.95 and an optimal operating confidence threshold of 0.513 demonstrate a strong balance between precision and recall. When deployed for live video inference on CPU-only systems, the model maintained real-time throughput (~38.7 FPS), making it well-suited for edge deployments where computational resources are limited. These results underscore the practicality of deploying lightweight yet high-accuracy PPE detection systems in real-world construction environments to enhance on-site safety compliance.

**Keywords:** Computer Vision · Object Detection · Personal Protective Equipment (PPE) · Edge Deployment

## 1 Introduction

Construction sites are among the most hazardous workplaces, accounting for over 20% of private-sector worker deaths in 2023 despite representing only 6% of the workforce [1]. Many fatalities, particularly from falls, falling objects, or equipment-related incidents, could be prevented with proper PPE use, and OSHA estimates that strict compliance could reduce accidents by up to 60% [2]. However, PPE compliance remains inconsistent, especially in under-resourced environments where audits are infrequent and error-prone. Advances in computer vision and deep learning have enabled automated, real-time PPE monitoring. Object detection models, particularly the YOLO family, balance speed and


S. Mitra et al. (Eds.): PReMI 2025, LNCS 16358, pp. 69–76, 2026.
https://doi.org/10.1007/978-3-032-18480-1_7

accuracy, with YOLOv5 offering versions optimized for both CPUs and GPUs [3, 5]. Yet, existing systems often prioritize benchmark accuracy over deployability, assume GPU access, and focus only on PPE presence (e.g., helmet, vest) while neglecting violations (e.g., no helmet, no vest) [6, 7]. Scalability is also limited, as adding more PPE categories (gloves, masks, goggles) reduces inference performance, especially on CPU-based devices. To address these challenges, we propose a deployable, class-scalable PPE detection framework for CPU-only inference. Built on YOLOv5s, our system incorporates deployment-aware preprocessing to minimize latency while preserving accuracy. A key feature is the balanced class formulation, explicitly including both compliance and violation categories, enabling actionable monitoring and seamless integration with automated alert systems. The remainder of this paper covers related work, methodology, experimental results, CPU deployment optimization with ONNX, discussion, and conclusions.

## 2  Related Works

Early PPE detection relied on traditional computer vision methods such as SVMs, Haar cascades, and HOG. While efficient, these struggled with illumination changes, diverse PPE appearances, and adverse weather [8]. CNNs transformed detection by learning hierarchical features from raw inputs, with architectures like SSD [9] and YOLO [3] enabling accurate, real-time multi-class PPE detection. However, challenges remain: deep learning models are GPU-dependent, yet industrial deployments often require CPU-only edge devices [10]. Most studies focus on limited PPE categories (e.g., helmets, vests) and neglect non-compliance classes like "No Helmet" or "No Gloves," limiting automated alert capabilities [11, 12]. Our approach addresses these gaps by explicitly including negative classes (e.g., "No Hat," "No Vest"), improving precision-recall balance, class-wise F1-scores, and robustness under class imbalance. We also tackle scalability, as expanding PPE categories introduces semantic overlaps and higher computational costs, especially on CPUs. Lightweight YOLOv5s models suffer latency increases with more classes [5], while segmentation-based methods like YOLACT [13] and DetectoRS [14] are accurate but too slow (3–6 FPS) for edge devices. Additionally, overreliance on mAP overlooks operational constraints, where false negatives are costlier than false positives. Environmental variability, unseen camera perspectives, and PPE diversity further challenge robustness [15]. By addressing negative class representation, scalability, and CPU-focused benchmarking, our solution delivers a deployable, safety-critical vision system suitable for real-world industrial monitoring.

## 3  Proposed Methodology

The primary goal of this work is to create a reliable, scalable, and effective deep learning system for detecting PPE by employing object detection techniques. This involves data collection from diverse sources, manual annotation and preprocessing, the construction of multi-class datasets, training a single-shot object detector, and performance evaluation using common metrics. In safety-critical environments, where PPE compliance monitoring can significantly reduce workplace hazards, such an organized, end-to-end strategy is essential [16, 17] (Fig. 1).

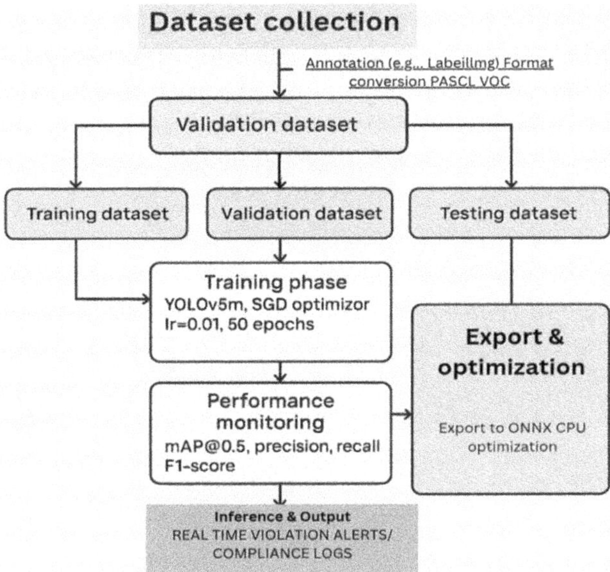



**Fig. 1.** Simplified Overview of Methodology

### 3.1 Dataset Construction and Preprocessing

To address fragmented PPE datasets, we adopted a multi-source integration approach, collecting and harmonizing publicly available datasets through manual annotation and class remapping to ensure consistent labeling and bounding box quality [3, 4]. We curated a focused 4-class dataset Hat, No Hat, Vest, and No Vest balanced between compliance and violation examples to enable learning of safe and unsafe conditions while maintaining computational efficiency. This formulation supports targeted evaluation and enhances scalability and transferability across deployment settings. Annotations in heterogeneous XML formats (PASCAL VOC standard) were programmatically parsed for image dimensions, class names, and bounding box coordinates. Bounding boxes were converted to YOLO's normalized center-based format to ensure scale invariance and stable convergence [4, 16], and categorical labels were mapped to integer identifiers for efficient training and inference [18]. The dataset was split 80:20 for training and validation using stratified sampling to preserve class balance and reduce overfitting [19]. This preprocessing pipeline provided a unified, robust foundation for training the proposed 4-class PPE detection model.

## 4 Model Architecture

In this work, the YOLOv5s (You Only Look Once, version 5 small) architecture was used for its efficiency and robustness in real-time object detection. As a single-stage detector, YOLOv5s processes the entire image in one pass, outputting bounding box coordinates, class probabilities, and objectness scores. It comprises three main components: backbone, neck, and head. The backbone uses Cross Stage Partial (CSP) bottlenecks and a

Spatial Pyramid Pooling-Fast (SPPF) module to extract multi-scale features efficiently. The neck, based on a modified Path Aggregation Network (PANet), fuses low- and high-level features to enhance spatial localization. The head generates anchor boxes with confidence scores, class probabilities for four PPE classes, and bounding box coordinates. The model was trained on $640 \times 640$ images using stochastic gradient descent (SGD) with a learning rate of 0.01 for 50 epochs (Table 1).

**Table 1.** Summary of the architecture.

| Stage | Layer Type | Output Shape | Parameters |
| --- | --- | --- | --- |
| Input | - | $640 \times 640 \times 3$ | - |
| Backbone | Conv $(6 \times 6, s = 2) + 4 \times$ (Conv, C3) | $320 \rightarrow 20 \times 20, 32 \rightarrow 512$ | ~1.8M |
| | SPPF | $20 \times 20 \times 512$ | 160K |
| Neck | PANet $+ 3 \times$ C3 | $80 \rightarrow 20 \times 20, 128 \rightarrow 512$ | ~963K |
| Head | Detect (3 scales) | $[80 \times 80, 40 \times 40, 20 \times 20]$ | 1.5M |
| **Total** | - | - | ~7.03M |

### 4.1  Model Training

The object detection models were built using the YOLOv5s architecture via the Ultralytics framework, chosen for its balance of computational efficiency and detection accuracy on CPU-based edge devices. Transfer learning with COCO-pretrained weights accelerated convergence and improved generalization, providing robust feature extraction for human figures and wearable PPE. A single model was trained to detect four critical PPE classes, with an 80:20 train-validation split and balanced class representation. Training was conducted on Google Colab using an NVIDIA T4 GPU, following Ultralytics' default pipeline with SGD optimizer, momentum, and learning rate scheduling for 50 epochs. Performance was tracked via mAP@0.5, precision, recall, and F1-score. F1-confidence curve analysis determined an optimal inference threshold of 0.513, yielding a peak F1-score of 0.95 and mAP@0.5 of 0.980. Ultralytics' tools logged metrics and stored checkpoints, ensuring reproducibility and seamless transition to deployment.

## 5  Results and Discussion

This section evaluates our 4-class PPE detection model Hat, Vest, No Hat, and No Vest covering both compliance and violation scenarios. Performance is measured using Precision, Recall, F1-Score, and mAP@0.5, balancing sensitivity to violations with accurate detection of compliant behavior in high-risk environments. CPU-only inference on edge devices is assessed via ONNX Runtime, with FPS used to evaluate real-time feasibility.

Qualitative analyses, including confusion matrices and confidence-recall curves, high-light performance on rare or negative classes. Compared to SD-YOLOv5s and NST-YOLOv5, our approach achieves a strong trade-off between accuracy and efficiency through model scaling, quantization-aware training, and ONNX-based inference. The model attains mAP@0.5 of 0.980 and a peak F1-Score of 0.950 at a confidence threshold of 0.513, with near-perfect precision above 0.807, making it suitable for stringent safety monitoring with minimal false positives (Table 2).

**Table 2.** Results

| Metric | 4-Class Model |
| --- | --- |
| Precision | 0.962 |
| Recall | 0.940 |
| F1-Score | 0.950 |
| mAP@0.5 | 0.980 |

The 4-class model achieves high detection accuracy and is suitable for real-time deployment on resource-constrained devices, supporting intelligent safety systems in industrial environments. Precision-Recall analysis shows an overall mAP@0.5 of 0.980, with all classes Hat, Vest, No Hat, and No Vest maintaining high precision near 1.0 (Vest 0.986 AP, No Hat 0.981 AP, Hat and No Vest 0.976 AP). Minor misclassifications occur between Hat and No Hat under partial occlusion or low light but are rare. Compared to SD-YOLOv5 (0.937 mAP, GPU-dependent), NST-YOLOv5 (0.984 mAP, limited diversity), and YOLACT + DeepSORT (~3 FPS on GPU), our model attains 38.7 FPS on CPU while maintaining 0.980 mAP, balancing accuracy and real-time responsiveness for edge deployment (Fig. 2 and Table 3).

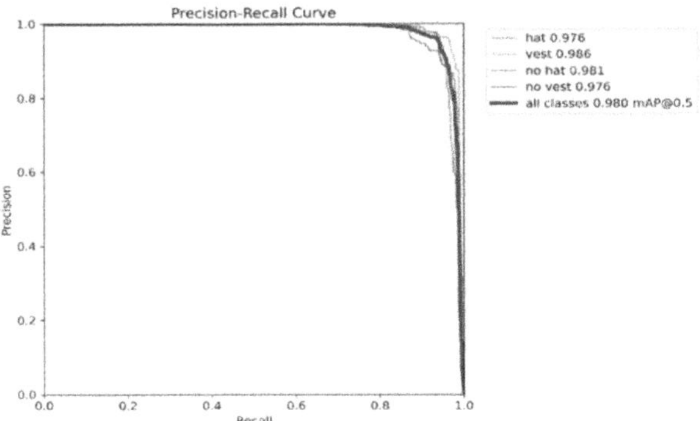


**Fig. 2.** Precision – Recall Curve

Table 3. Benchmark of Results

| Model | mAP@0.5 |
| --- | --- |
| SD-YOLOv5 [1] | 0.937 |
| NST-YOLOv5 [2] | 0.984 |
| YOLACT + DeepSORT | 0.664 |
| This Work (4 classes) | 0.980 |

## 5.1  Converting Models for Edge Deployment

The trained YOLOv5s models were exported to ONNX (Open Neural Network Exchange) for deployment on CPU-only and resource-constrained edge devices. ONNX provides a hardware-agnostic representation compatible with CPUs, embedded systems, and inference engines like ONNX Runtime, OpenVINO, and TensorRT, enabling rapid inference. The Ultralytics export pipeline produced a lightweight, inference-optimized model by removing training-only dependencies while preserving architecture and pre-trained weights. The $640 \times 640$ input resolution was retained for compatibility with the training pipeline. Post-conversion validation confirmed functional equivalency with PyTorch models, showing no loss in accuracy or precision. These ONNX models enabled real-time CPU-based PPE detection and served as a foundation for further optimizations such as quantization and trimming. Inference tests demonstrated robust detection of both compliant and non-compliant PPE under real-world conditions, confirming practical viability without GPU acceleration (Fig. 3).

Fig. 3.  Real-time CPU inference detecting compliant PPE (helmet, vest).

## 5.2  Discussion

Our 4-class model achieves an mAP@0.5 of 0.980, outperforming baselines including SD-YOLOv5s (0.937) and YOLOv8 (0.807) on comparable datasets (K. Zhang et al., 2023; Redmon et al., 2022). High precision and recall validate its reliability for safety-critical deployment. A key advantage is the explicit modeling of negative safety conditions (e.g., No Hat, No Vest), enabling direct violation alerts a feature absent in pre-trained baselines. This allows more accurate detection of unsafe conditions and ensures worker compliance. Optimized for CPU-only environments, the model achieves real-time throughput of 38.7 FPS, demonstrating feasibility on resource-constrained edge devices. In contrast, SD-YOLOv5s and YOLOv8 require GPU acceleration for comparable speed, limiting industrial applicability. For high-risk environments, the model maintains an mAP of 0.980 at 0.5 IoU and can be configured for 100% precision at a confidence threshold of 0.807, ensuring zero false positives for violation alerts. These attributes make it highly suitable for real-time PPE monitoring and automated compliance in construction settings.

## 6  Conclusion

This research presented a comprehensive framework for real-time detection of PPE in construction environments, with a distinct focus on deployment feasibility in resource-constrained settings. The developed YOLOv5s-based system addresses three critical gaps in existing literature: limited benchmarking on CPU-only hardware, insufficient modeling of non-compliance classes, and inadequate evaluation of class scalability effects on real-time performance. Our model achieved exceptional accuracy (0.980 mAP@0.5) while maintaining real-time performance (38.7 FPS) on standard CPU hardware. The novel inclusion of negative classes (no hat, no vest) enables violation-specific alerting, a crucial capability for practical safety enforcement systems. The balanced class architecture, optimization for CPU deployment, and quantified class scaling effects collectively represent a significant advancement toward bridging the gap between academic benchmarking and practical safety monitoring systems. The ONNX-optimized model demonstrates that effective safety compliance monitoring is achievable on edge devices without specialized hardware, potentially enabling wider adoption of automated safety monitoring in resource-constrained construction environments.

## References


1. U.S. Bureau of Labor Statistics: Census of fatal occupational injuries summary (2023) U.S. Bureau of Labor Statistics (2024)
2. Occupational Safety and Health Administration (OSHA): Personal protective equipment, Occupational safety and health administration (2023)
3. Redmon, J., et al.: You Only Look Once: unified, real-time object detection. In: Proceedings of the IEEE Conference Computer Vision and Pattern Recognition (CVPR), pp. 779–788 (2016)
4. Bochkovskiy, A., Wang, C.Y., Liao, H.Y.M.: YOLOv4: optimal speed and accuracy of object detection. arXiv preprint arXiv:2004.10934 (2020)
5. Jocher, G.: YOLOv5 by ultralytics. GitHub repository (2020)
6. Zhang, K., Chen, L., Wang, Y.: SD-YOLOv5s: a self-distilled YOLOv5 model for enhanced PPE detection accuracy. In: Proceedings of the International Conference Image Processing and Robotics, pp. 112–120 (2023)
7. Liu, X., Zhang, H., Yu, W.: NST-YOLOv5: a noise suppression and transformer-based YOLOv5 variant for industrial PPE detection. J. Comput. Vis. Appl. **39**(2), 45–60 (2023)

8. Dalal, N., Triggs, B.: Histograms of oriented gradients for human detection. In: Proceedings of the IEEE Conference Computer Vision and Pattern Recognition (2005)

9. Liu, W., et al.: SSD: single shot MultiBox detector. In: Proceedings of the European Conference Computer Vision (ECCV) (2016)

10. Zhang, J., et al.: Automatic detection of hardhats worn by construction workers using computer vision. Autom. Constr. **59**, 80–90 (2015)

11. Kim, J., et al.: Safety-YOLO: real-time detection of safety equipment compliance on construction sites. Autom. Construct. **130** (2021)

12. Wang, H., et al.: NST-YOLOv5: a neural style transfer-augmented PPE detection framework. Sensors **22**(14) (2022)

13. Bolya, D., et al.: YOLACT: real-time instance segmentation. In: Proceedings of the IEEE International Conference Computer Vision (ICCV) (2019)

14. Qiao, S., et al.: DetectoRS: detecting objects with recursive feature pyramid and switchable atrous convolution. In: Proc. IEEE Conference Computer Vision and Pattern Recognition (CVPR) (2021)

15. Murez, Z., et al.: Image to image translation for domain adaptation. In: Proceedings of the IEEE Conference Computer Vision and Pattern Recognition (CVPR) (2018)

16. Li, X., Zhang, Y.: Deep learning-based PPE detection for worker safety monitoring. Autom. Constr. **122**, 103471 (2021)

17. Wang, T., Zhao, W.: End-to-end deep learning for PPE detection in industrial workplaces. J. Safety Res. **75**, 88–98 (2021)

18. Liu, W., Anguelov, D., Erhan, D., Szegedy, C., Reed, S.: SDS: single shot MultiBox detector. In: Proceedings of the European Conference Computer Vision (ECCV), pp. 21–37 (2016)

19. Everingham, M., Gool, L.V., Williams, C.K.I., Winn, J., Zisserman, A.: The PASCAL Visual Object Classes (VOC) challenge. In: Proceedings of the IEEE International Conference Computer Vision (ICCV), pp. 108–115 (2010)

# Granular Computing Enhanced Federated Learning Framework on Edge Devices

Shuvo Saha Roy and Reshma Rastogi$^{(\boxtimes)}$

South Asian University, New Delhi, India
`shuvosaha@students.sau.ac.in`, `reshma.khemchandani@sau.ac.in`

**Abstract.** Federated Learning (FL) enables collaborative model training across distributed edge clients such as mobile or IoT devices by sharing model updates rather than raw data, preserving privacy while supporting scalable learning. However, large datasets increase computational costs and are time-consuming, hindering efficient training, especially in edge scenarios with limited compute and bandwidth. We propose Granular Computing (GC)-powered federated learning where granular balls are computed as a representative of clustered data, providing a more structured way to represent and process data for each client, leading to improved efficiency of machine learning models. The proposed framework reduces training data by 95.5%, significantly accelerating simulation times (76–96% reduction) and enabling low-latency, resource-efficient processing at the edge across simple (logistic regression) and complex (NN) models using FedAvg. Moreover, by sharing only granular characteristics, GC theoretically enhances privacy. Our results highlight GC's effectiveness for resource-constrained edge environments and large-scale FL simulations at the edge, enabling faster experimentation with only a negligible 1–3% accuracy trade-off, preserving comparable performance for real-time edge applications. Code is available on GitHub.

**Keywords:** Federated Learning · Granular Ball · Data Preprocessing

## 1 Introduction

Federated Learning (FL), introduced by Google Research in 2016, [12], is a distributed machine learning framework that enables multiple edge devices, like smartphones, IoT sensors or clients(in FL, devices or any system is referred as client/party), to collaboratively train a global model without sharing sensitive data. Unlike centralised approaches, which aggregate raw data on a central server, FL relies on local training and sharing local model updates (e.g., weights, parameters or gradients), as demonstrated in applications like Google's Gboard [8]. This preserves data privacy while enabling scalable training across heterogeneous datasets. However, large datasets on client-side exacerbate computational land communication overheads, significantly slowing simulation times in resource-constrained edge environments, a critical bottleneck for large-scale FL experiments and on-device learning in edge settings [3].


S. Mitra et al. (Eds.): PReMI 2025, LNCS 16358, pp. 77–84, 2026.
https://doi.org/10.1007/978-3-032-18480-1_8

The canonical FL framework, exemplified by the Federated Averaging (FedAvg) algorithm [12], involves iterative edge device-server interactions. Each client trains local model on their private data and sends model parameter updates to a central server, which aggregates them to update the global model. Despite its effectiveness, FL simulations face challenges from high computational costs, particularly with large datasets or complex models like Neural Networks (NNs) on edge devices, as underscored by the 'No Free Lunch' theorem in FL [18]. Edge AI presents additional challenges where compute, energy, and memory are limited [1,4]. These constraints require lightweight and efficient preprocessing techniques that reduce the data footprint without compromising model performance. Most research focuses on model optimisation [2,9,11,14] or making a cluster of clients [5,7,13], often overlooking input data preprocessing as a means to enhance efficiency on edge devices.

To address this gap, we propose Granular Computing (GC) [15,17] as a preprocessing step tailored for tabular data in FL on edge devices. Inspired by prior work on image data [10], GC clusters data into coarse-grained granular balls (GB)—hyperspheres defined by their centre, radius, and dominant label—reducing data volume by 95.5% on average, making it well-suited for local training on edge devices with limited processing power and memory. This compact representation accelerates training and communication by lowering sample counts, enabling faster simulations across both simple (logistic regression) and complex (NN) models. Additionally, sharing only ball characteristics theoretically enhances privacy by abstracting raw data on edge devices, mitigating risks of reconstruction attacks [19]. Our experiments demonstrate that GC, integrated with FedAvg, reduces simulation times by 76–96% while maintaining near-equivalent accuracy, offering a robust solution for efficient, large-scale FL simulations on edge devices.

## 2   Proposed Algorithm

In our proposed Federated Learning (FL) framework, given a dataset $\mathcal{D} = \{(x_i, y_i), i = 1, 2, \ldots, N\}$, $x_i \in \mathbb{R}^d$ and $y_i \in \{-1, 1\}$, each edge device $k \in \{1, \ldots, K\}$ holds a subset $\mathcal{D}_k$ of $\mathcal{D}$, i.e. $\mathcal{D}_k = \{(\mathbf{x}_i^k, y_i^k)\}_{i=1}^{n_k}$, where $\mathbf{x}_i^k$ is a feature vector $\in \mathbb{R}^d$, $y_i^k$ is the label, and $n_k = |\mathcal{D}_k|$.

In this paper, we deal with two settings of the dataset, either using original points or Granular Balls(GB) using Granular Computing (GC) [15–17]. GC clusters $\mathcal{D}$ into granular balls $\mathcal{B} = \{(\mathbf{c}_m, y_m)\}_{m=1}^{M}$, where each ball $B_m$ has: - Center: $\mathbf{c}_m = \frac{1}{|B_m|} \sum_{\mathbf{x}_i \in B_m} \mathbf{x}_i$. - Label: $y_m = \arg\max_y \sum_{\mathbf{x}_i \in B_m} \mathbb{I}(y_i = y)$.

The optimisation objective for generating granular balls, as defined in [16], is:

$$\min \frac{N}{\sum_{m=1}^{M} |B_m|} + M, \quad \text{s.t.} \quad \text{Purity}_m \geq \tau_p, \quad |B_m| \geq \tau_{\min}, \tag{1}$$

where $|B_m|$ is the number of points in the ball $B_m$, $M$ is the number of granular balls, $\tau_p$ is the purity threshold, and $\tau_{\min}$ is the minimum number of points. Similarly, in GC settings, each edge device $k \in \{1, \ldots, K\}$ holds a subset $\mathcal{B}_k$.

The total number of granular balls in $\mathcal{B}$ is $M = \sum_{k=1}^{K} |\mathcal{B}_k|$ which is less than $N$. Thus, the FL objective is to minimise the weighted aggregate loss with granular balls data:

$$F(\mathbf{w}) = \sum_{k=1}^{K} \frac{|\mathcal{B}_k|}{M} f_k(\mathbf{w}), \quad \text{where} \quad f_k(\mathbf{w}) = \frac{1}{|\mathcal{B}_k|} \sum_{m \in \mathcal{I}_k} \ell(\mathbf{w}; \mathbf{c}_m, y_m).$$

and for the original data as

$$F(\mathbf{w}) = \sum_{k=1}^{K} \frac{|\mathcal{D}_k|}{N} f_k(\mathbf{w}), \quad \text{where} \quad f_k(\mathbf{w}) = \frac{1}{|\mathcal{D}_k|} \sum_{i \in \mathcal{I}_k} \ell(\mathbf{w}; \mathbf{x}_i, y_i).$$

Algorithm 1 outlines GC, as a preprocessing step, initialising $\mathcal{D}$ as one ball and splitting low-purity balls using K-means ($k = 2$) until purity constraints are met. Balls with fewer than $\tau_{\min}$ points are discarded.

Algorithm 1 generates balls $\mathcal{B} = \{[\mathbf{c}_m, l_m]\}_{m=1}^{M}$, which serve as the training data list when GC is used. Otherwise, $\mathcal{D} = \{(\mathbf{x}_i, y_i)\}_{i=1}^{N}$ is the used and partitioned into $K$ edge devices for use in Algorithm 2, ensuring the FL pipeline remains unchanged.

---

**Algorithm 1.** Granular Computing

---

1: **Input**: Dataset $\mathcal{D} = \{(\mathbf{x}_i, y_i)\}_{i=1}^{N}$, purity threshold $\tau_p$, minimum points $\tau_{\min}$
2: **Output**: Granular balls $\mathcal{B} = \{(\mathbf{c}_m, y_m)\}_{m=1}^{M}$
3: Initialize $\mathcal{B} \leftarrow \{B_1\}$ with all points in $\mathcal{D}$
4: Set $i \leftarrow 1$, $M \leftarrow 1$
5: **while** $i \leq M$ **do**
6:    **if** Purity$_i < \tau_p$ **and** $|B_i| > 1$ **then**
7:       $[B_{i1}, B_{i2}] \leftarrow$ KMeans$(B_i, k = 2)$
8:       Replace $B_i$ with $B_{i1}$ in $\mathcal{B}$
9:       Append $B_{i2}$ to $\mathcal{B}$
10:       $M \leftarrow M + 1$
11:    **else**
12:       $i \leftarrow i + 1$
13:    **end if**
14: **end while**
15: Remove balls from $\mathcal{B}$ where $|B_m| < \tau_{\min}$
16: **Return** $\mathcal{B}$

---

## 3    Experiment and Results

To evaluate the efficiency of our algorithm, we conducted experiments using Python 3.11.4 on a 16 GB RAM machine with an Intel Core i7 (3.20 GHz). Dataset details are in Table 1, sourced from LIBSVM [6]. We tuned the learning rate ($[0.9, 0.5, 0.25, 0.1, 0.05, 0.01, 0.001, 0.0001]$) in IID settings and used the

---

**Algorithm 2.** Federated Learning(FedAvg) with GC

---

1: **Input**: Devices $K$, rounds $T$, sampled edge devices $K_s$, ball $\mathcal{B}$, local epochs $E$
2: **Output**: Global model $\mathbf{w}_T$
3: Initialize $\mathbf{w}_0$
4: **for** $t = 0, 1, \ldots, T - 1$ **do**
5:     Sample devices $\mathcal{S}_t \subseteq \{1, \ldots, K\}$, $|\mathcal{S}_t| = K_s$
6:     Compute total samples $n \leftarrow \sum_{k \in \mathcal{S}_t} |\mathcal{B}_k|$
7:     **for** each device $k \in \mathcal{S}_t$ **in parallel do**
8:         Send global model $\mathbf{w}_t$ to device $k$
9:         $\Delta \mathbf{w}_k^t \leftarrow$ **LocalTraining**$(k, \mathbf{w}_t)$
10:     **end for**
11:     Update $\mathbf{w}_{t+1} \leftarrow w_t - \eta \sum_{k \in \mathcal{S}_t} \frac{n_k}{n} \Delta \mathbf{w}_k^t$
12: **end for**
13: **Return** $\mathbf{w}_T$

**LocalTraining**$(k, \mathbf{w}_t)$:

1: $\mathbf{w}_k \leftarrow \mathbf{w}_t$
2: **for** $e = 1$ to $E$ **do**
3:     $\mathbf{w}_k \leftarrow \mathbf{w}_k - \eta \nabla \ell(\mathbf{w}_k; \mathcal{B}_k)$
4: **end for**
5: **return** $\Delta \mathbf{w}_k^t \leftarrow \mathbf{w}_t - \mathbf{w}_k$

---

same learning rate for non-IID. The experiments used IID and non-IID distributions to assess GC with FedAvg, reflecting real-world scenarios. A 20% test set was held on the server per standard FL practice before GC. Time comparisons involved logistic regression and neural network (NN) models.

**Logistic Regression:** The local loss for the device $k$ is defined as: $f_k(w) = -\frac{1}{n_k} \sum_{i=1}^{n_k} \left[ y_i \log(\sigma(w^T x_i + b)) + (1 - y_i) \log(1 - \sigma(w^T x_i + b)) \right]$, where $y_j \in \{0, 1\}$ is the true label, $y_{\text{pred},j} \in [0, 1]$ is the predicted probability for data point $j$, and $n_k$ is the number of samples.

**Neural Networks (NN)**: The model consists of four fully connected layers with input dimension $d$, hidden layers of 32, 16, and 8 units with ReLU activations, and a single-unit output layer.

Logistic regression and NN models are denoted as **M1** and **M2** models, where the original data points are used. **GB_M1** and **GB_M2** mean granular balls as data points have been used for model training in FL settings. The gradient descent optimisation technique has been used for all algorithms.

### 3.1   Results and Discussion

**Granular Computing.** GC substantially reduces the training data size by converting original data points into GB across all datasets. On average, the number of samples decreases by 95.5%, from 98,270 to 3,069 samples (see Fig. 1, y-axis on a logarithmic scale). The average reduction in training data(combining all datasets) is calculated as:

**Table 1.** Dataset and Experiment Parameter Details

(a) Details of Used Datasets [6]

| Dataset | Samples | Features |
|---|---|---|
| QSAR Oral Toxicity (QOT) | 8992 | 1024 |
| Phishing | 11,055 | 31 |
| 2D Planes | 40,768 | 11 |
| A9a | 48,842 | 123 |
| Adult | 48,842 | 123 |
| Hepmass | 327,527 | 28 |

(b) Simulation Parameters

| Parameters | Values |
|---|---|
| Communication round (CR) | 50 |
| Total Devices | 10 |
| Participants in each CR | 3 |
| Local Epochs | 5 |
| $\alpha$ for Dirichlet | 0.5 |
| Training-Testing Split | 80%-20% |
| Purity threshold $\tau_p$ | 99% |
| Deletion threshold $\tau_d$ | [7,4,2] |

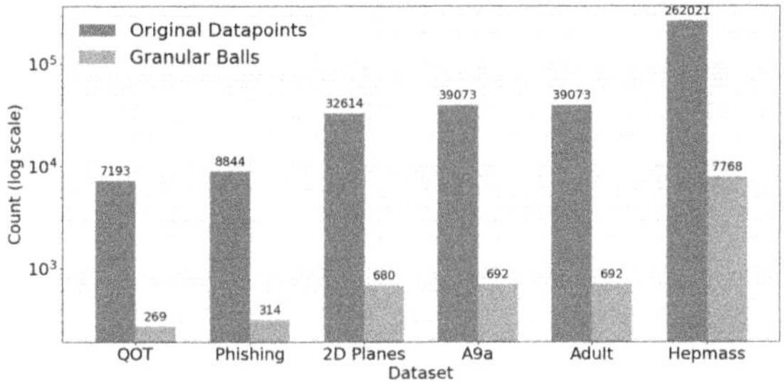



**Fig. 1.** Original training data samples vs Generated Granular balls

$$1 - \frac{\text{total granular balls for training}}{\text{total original training data}} = 1 - \frac{269 + 314 + 680 + 692 + 692 + 7768}{7193 + 8844 + 32614 + 39073 + 39073 + 262021}$$

$$= 1 - \frac{10475}{386818} \approx 0.955 \text{ or } 95.5\%.$$

This compression preserves essential features, enabling faster training and improved privacy by sharing ball representations instead of raw data.

**Execution Time.** Execution times for M1, GB_M1, M2, and GB_M2 under IID and non-IID settings are summarised in Table 2 and visualised as a bar plot in the first column of the table. GC reduces training times significantly: M1's average time drops by 76% (1.82s to 0.42s for IID, 1.83s to 0.44s for non-IID), while M2's time decreases by 96% (204.88s to 8.21s for IID, 192.31s to 7.77s for non-IID). The largest dataset (Hepmass) shows the most significant reduction, with M2's time dropping from 800.72s to 29.48s (IID).

**Model Performance.** Convergence speeds in IID and non-IID settings are shown in columns 1 and 2, respectively, of Table 2. M2 consistently outperforms other models across datasets due to its deeper architecture, achieving the highest accuracy. GB_M2 maintains competitive performance, with an average accuracy drop of 1–3% compared to M2. GB_M1 and M1 exhibit similar convergence, with original models (M1, M2) slightly better (1–2% higher accuracy) in most cases, though some datasets (e.g., A9a) show a 2–3% accuracy drop for original

**Table 2.** Comparison in execution time and convergence in IID and Non-IID scenarios for different datasets

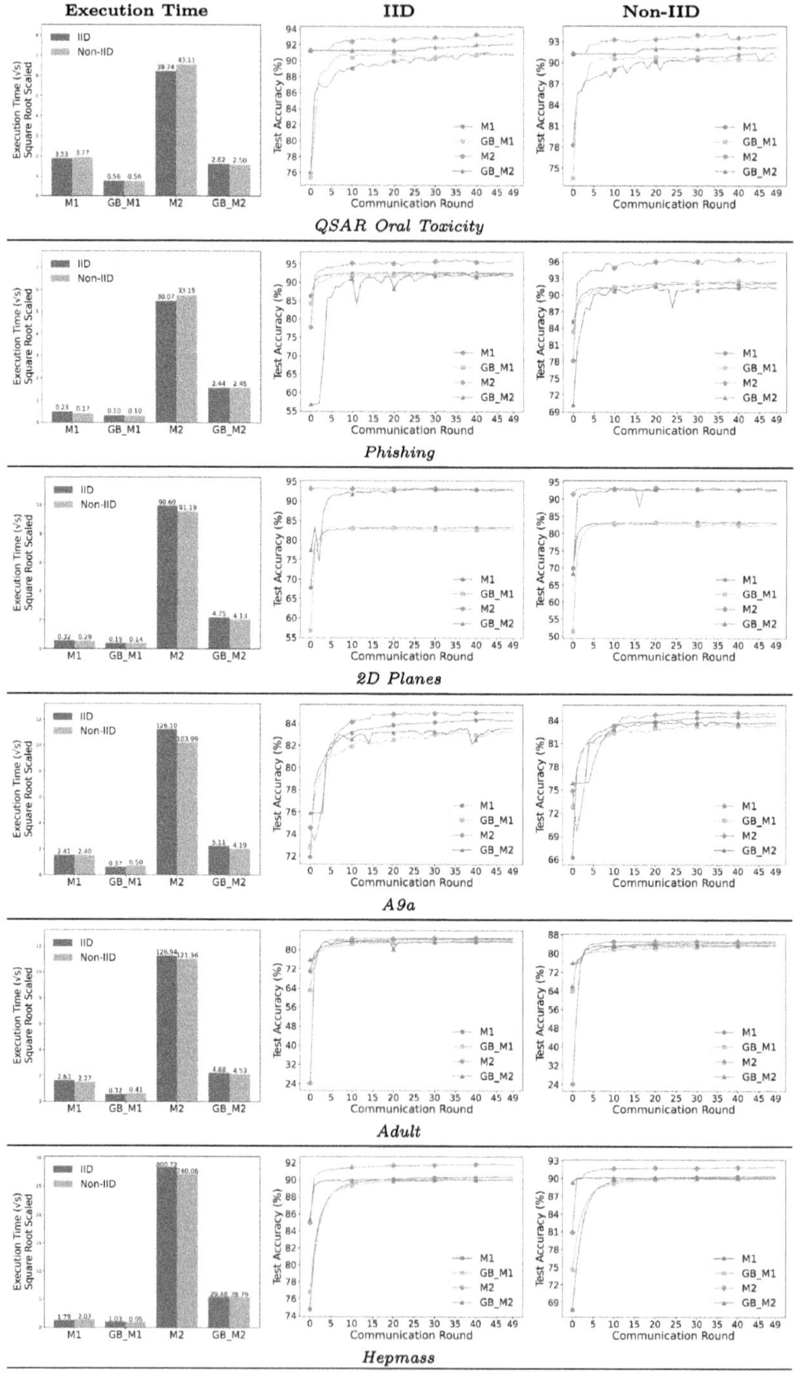

data. Non-IID settings follow similar trends with GC, models showing promising performance despite data heterogeneity.

## 3.2  Discussion and Future Work

The results highlight GC's effectiveness in FL, reducing training data by 95.5% on average, which leads to significant speed-ups (76–96% time reduction) while incurring a minimal accuracy loss (1–3%) on average, which is ideal for edge devices with limited resources, as seen in Hepmass where M2's training time drops from 800.72s to 29.48s (IID). Prior work on image datasets [10] shows that such representations mitigate reconstruction attacks, and we hypothesise a similar benefit for tabular data, though this requires further validation as future work.

M2's superior performance underscores the advantage of deeper architectures in FL, while GB_M2's close convergence demonstrates GC's ability to retain critical information despite data reduction. The slight accuracy drop in GC models is expected due to information loss, but is offset by substantial efficiency gains and potential privacy improvements that suit edge constraints. Reduction of training time is significant with the use of a granular ball. The similar performance of GB_M1 and M1 suggests that GC is model-agnostic, benefiting both simple (logistic regression) and complex (NN) models. Moreover

We used FedAvg to establish GBC's baseline efficiency with FL, leveraging its input-level benefits, orthogonal to aggregation methods like FedProx and Fed-Nova. Future work will explore GBC with advanced FL algorithms and validate privacy benefits for tabular data, building on image dataset findings [10].

## 4  Conclusions

In this paper, we have demonstrated that granular computing enhances federated learning efficiency for tabular data on edge devices with comparable accuracy, reducing data by 95.5% and execution times by 76–96%. The NN model (M2) outperforms logistic regression (M1), with GC variants (GB_M1, GB_M2) offering comparable convergence using FedAvg. GC's edge compatibility and input-level operation suggest applicability to advanced methods like FedProx [11] or FedNova [14]. Future work will validate privacy benefits for tabular data (per [10]) and explore integration with cutting-edge FL algorithms for edge optimisation.

## References


1. Abreha, H.G., Hayajneh, M., Serhani, M.A.: Federated learning in edge computing: a systematic survey. Sensors **22**(2), 450 (2022)
2. Acar, D.A.E., Zhao, Y., Navarro, R.M., Mattina, M., Whatmough, P.N., Saligrama, V.: Federated learning based on dynamic regularization. arXiv preprint arXiv:2111.04263 (2021)

3. Alawadi, S., Ait-Mlouk, A., Toor, S., Hellander, A.: Toward efficient resource utilization at edge nodes in federated learning. Progress Artif. Intell. **13**(2), 101–117 (2024)
4. Brecko, A., Kajati, E., Koziorek, J., Zolotova, I.: Federated learning for edge computing: a survey. Appl. Sci. **12**(18), 9124 (2022)
5. Briggs, C., Fan, Z., Andras, P.: Federated learning with hierarchical clustering of local updates to improve training on non-iid data. In: 2020 International Joint Conference on Neural Networks (IJCNN), pp. 1–9. IEEE (2020)
6. Chang, C.C., Lin, C.J.: Libsvm: a library for support vector machines. ACM Trans. Intell. Syst. Technol. (TIST) **2**(3), 1–27 (2011)
7. Ghosh, A., Chung, J., Yin, D., Ramchandran, K.: An efficient framework for clustered federated learning. Adv. Neural. Inf. Process. Syst. **33**, 19586–19597 (2020)
8. Hard, A., et al.: Federated learning for mobile keyboard prediction. arXiv preprint arXiv:1811.03604 (2018)
9. Karimireddy, S.P., Kale, S., Mohri, M., Reddi, S., Stich, S., Suresh, A.T.: Scaffold: Stochastic controlled averaging for federated learning. In: International Conference on Machine Learning, pp. 5132–5143. PMLR (2020)
10. Lai, G., et al.: A new perspective on privacy protection in federated learning with granular-ball computing. arXiv preprint arXiv:2501.04940 (2025)
11. Li, T., Sahu, A.K., Zaheer, M., Sanjabi, M., Talwalkar, A., Smith, V.: Federated optimization in heterogeneous networks. Proc. Mach. Learn. Syst. **2**, 429–450 (2020)
12. McMahan, B., Moore, E., Ramage, D., Hampson, S., y Arcas, B.A.: Communication-efficient learning of deep networks from decentralized data. In: Artificial intelligence and statistics, pp. 1273–1282. PMLR (2017)
13. Sattler, F., Müller, K.R., Samek, W.: Clustered federated learning: Model-agnostic distributed multitask optimization under privacy constraints. IEEE Trans. Neural Networks Learn. Syst. **32**(8), 3710–3722 (2020)
14. Wang, J., Liu, Q., Liang, H., Joshi, G., Poor, H.V.: Tackling the objective inconsistency problem in heterogeneous federated optimization. Adv. Neural. Inf. Process. Syst. **33**, 7611–7623 (2020)
15. Xia, S., Dai, X., Wang, G., Gao, X., Giem, E.: An efficient and adaptive granular-ball generation method in classification problem. IEEE Trans. Neural Networks Learn. Syst. **35**(4), 5319–5331 (2022)
16. Xia, S., Lian, X., Wang, G., Gao, X., Chen, J., Peng, X.: Gbsvm: Granular-ball support vector machine. arXiv preprint arXiv:2210.03120 (2022)
17. Xia, S., et al.: A fast adaptive k-means with no bounds. IEEE Trans. Pattern Anal. Mach. Intell. (2020)
18. Zhang, X., Gu, H., Fan, L., Chen, K., Yang, Q.: No free lunch theorem for security and utility in federated learning. ACM Trans. Intell. Syst. Technol. **14**(1), 1–35 (2022)
19. Zhu, L., Liu, Z., Han, S.: Deep leakage from gradients. Advances in neural information processing systems **32** (2019)

# Deploying Compact Image Classifier on Edge Device for Real-Time Pearl Millet Disease Detection


J. Chalmers[1], J. Aravinth[1(✉)], T Senthil Kumar[2], and I. Johnson[3]

[1] Department of Electronics and Communication Engineering, Amrita School of Engineering, Amrita Vishwa Vidyapeetham, Coimbatore, India
j_aravinth@cb.amrita.edu
[2] Department of Computer Science and Engineering, Amrita School of Computing, Amrita Vishwa Vidyapeetham, Coimbatore, India
[3] Department of Plant Pathology, Tamil Nadu Agricultural University, Coimbatore, India



**Abstract.** Edge Intelligence deploys AI models directly on devices, reducing latency, bandwidth, and improving privacy. We implement lightweight image classification on an ESP32 for real-time pearl millet disease detection. Three compact CNNs—MobileNet, FOMO, and a custom CNN—are trained on a dataset collected from Coimbatore farms. The custom CNN achieves the highest accuracy (86%) and is deployed on an ESP32-CAM for offline inference, suitable for rural areas. This demonstrates a practical embedded-AI pipeline on low-cost hardware (<INR 500), enabling intelligent IoT in resource-constrained settings.

**Keywords:** Edge Intelligence · TinyAI · ESP32 · Pearl Millet · Disease Detection


## 1 Introduction

Pearl millet (*Pennisetum glaucum*) is a staple crop in semi-arid regions of India and is highly valued for its resilience to harsh climatic conditions. However, it is prone to several leaf diseases such as downy mildew, blast, smut, and rust, which can significantly reduce crop yield and affect food security. Traditional disease monitoring relies on expert farmers or agricultural specialists to visually inspect the fields. This approach is time-consuming, labor-intensive, and often impractical for large-scale cultivation, especially in rural areas where expert availability is limited.

Recent advances in computer vision and deep learning have enabled automated disease detection from images of leaves. Many studies have implemented cloud-based image classification pipelines that analyze leaf images and predict disease classes. While these methods achieve high accuracy, they require high-bandwidth internet connections, introduce latency due to cloud communication,


© The Author(s), under exclusive license to Springer Nature Switzerland AG 2026
S. Mitra et al. (Eds.): PReMI 2025, LNCS 16358, pp. 85–92, 2026.
https://doi.org/10.1007/978-3-032-18480-1_9

and raise privacy concerns since farmers' images must be uploaded to remote servers.

Edge Intelligence provides a practical alternative by performing AI inference directly on low-cost, embedded devices, eliminating the need for continuous internet connectivity. Microcontrollers like the ESP32 are particularly suitable for this purpose, as they support Wi-Fi, Bluetooth, and camera interfaces while maintaining a small memory footprint and low power consumption. Deploying AI models on such devices allows real-time, on-field disease detection, which can greatly aid farmers in taking timely actions to prevent crop loss.

In this work, we explore the deployment of lightweight convolutional neural networks (CNNs) for real-time pearl millet leaf disease detection on an ESP32 microcontroller. The main contributions of this work are as follows:

- Design and development of a compact, low-cost handheld device capable of performing on-field leaf disease detection.
- Implementation and evaluation of three TinyAI models—MobileNetV2 SSD FPN-Lite, FOMO, and a custom CNN—optimized for deployment on microcontrollers.
- Demonstration of offline, real-time inference on the ESP32, providing high accuracy predictions without reliance on cloud services.

This study illustrates a practical pipeline for deploying AI on edge devices in rural agricultural settings, combining low-cost hardware with lightweight neural networks to deliver actionable insights directly to farmers.

## 2   Related Work

Recent studies have applied deep learning for plant disease detection using cloud-based or server-side inference [4,5]. While accurate, these approaches suffer from high latency and bandwidth usage.

Edge AI performs computation on-device, alleviating these concerns [6]. TinyAI reduces model size for microcontrollers using frameworks like Tensor-Flow Lite, Edge Impulse, and EdgeML [7–9]. Prior works in plant disease detection, hyperspectral imaging, and smart agriculture demonstrate AI's potential in agriculture, but microcontroller deployment remains challenging [10–14].

## 3   Materials and Methods

### 3.1   Dataset Collection and Preprocessing

We collected 2300 RGB images of pearl millet leaves, annotated as *downy mildew*, *rust*, or *healthy*. Images were captured under natural lighting conditions using smartphones and handheld cameras across multiple farms in Coimbatore.

Bounding boxes for diseased regions were generated using YOLOv5, and images were cropped to focus on leaf regions. Images were resized to $96 \times 96$ for TinyAI models. Data augmentation (rotation, flipping, color jitter) increased variability (Fig. 1).

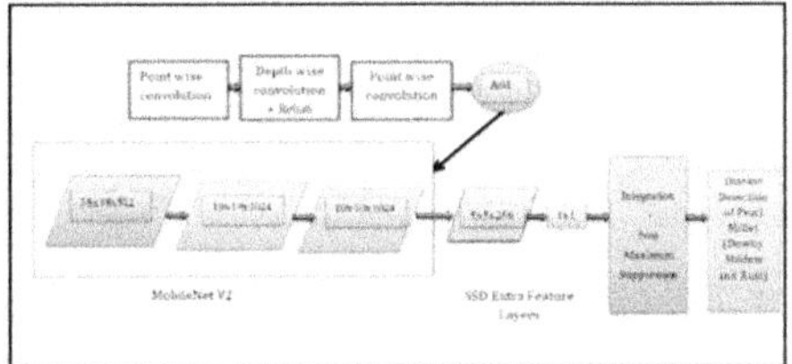

(a) MobileNetV2 SSD FPN-Lite

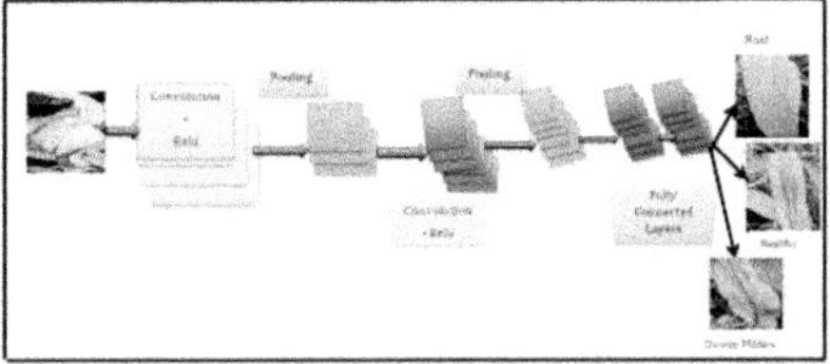

(b) FOMO

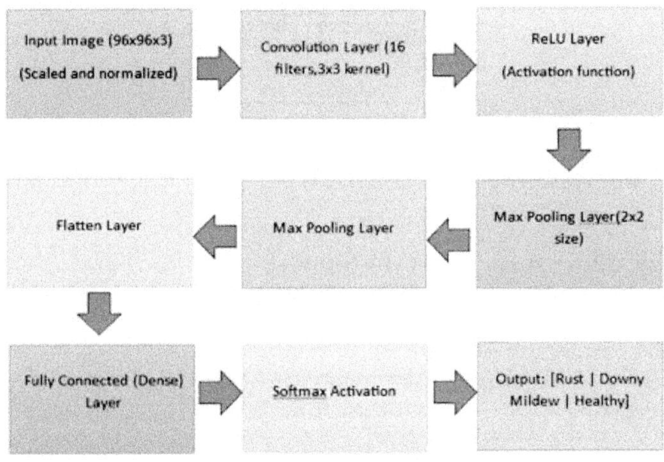


(c) Custom CNN

**Fig. 1.** Lightweight CNN architectures: top row shows MobileNet and FOMO, bottom row shows larger Custom CNN architecture for clarity.

## 3.2 Model Architectures

Three models were implemented:

*MobileNetV2 SSD FPN-Lite.* Combines depthwise separable convolutions with an SSD detection head. Input: $96 \times 96$ RGB. Lightweight feature pyramids capture multi-scale leaf disease features efficiently.

*FOMO (You Only Look Once Variant).* Divides input images into a grid and predicts bounding boxes and disease probability per cell using MobileNetV2 backbone. Optimized for microcontrollers.

*Custom CNN.* A 4-layer convolutional network with ReLU activations and max pooling, followed by fully connected layers. Output: {downy mildew, rust, healthy}. Designed for minimal memory footprint (4 kB) while retaining accuracy.

### 3.3   Loss Functions

$$\mathcal{L}_{\text{total}} = \mathcal{L}_{\text{loc}} + \mathcal{L}_{\text{cls}} \tag{1}$$

$$\text{smoothL1}(x) = \begin{cases} \frac{1}{2}x^2, & |x| < 1 \\ |x| - \frac{1}{2}, & \text{otherwise} \end{cases} \tag{2}$$

$$\mathcal{L}_{\text{cls}} = -\sum_c y_c \log p_c \tag{3}$$

$$\mathcal{L}_{\text{FOMO}} = -\sum_g \sum_c y_{g,c} \log p_{g,c} \tag{4}$$

### 3.4   Training Procedure

All models were trained on an NVIDIA GPU using Adam optimizer. Hyperparameters:

- Batch size: 32 (custom CNN), 16 (others)
- Learning rate: 0.01 (custom CNN, FOMO), 0.001 (MobileNet)
- Epochs: 30

Cross-entropy loss for classification, smooth-L1 for localization. Early stopping prevents overfitting.

## 4   Results and Discussion

### 4.1   Classification Performance

Custom CNN achieves 87% accuracy for *Downy Mildew* and 88% for *Healthy*. FOMO is competitive, though *Rust* shows minor confusion (78%). MobileNetV2 SSD FPN-Lite performs moderately (83%) (Fig. 2).

### 4.2   Performance Metrics

Custom CNN outperforms others in accuracy, precision, recall, and F1 score (Fig. 3), making it ideal for edge deployment.

### 4.3   Deployment on ESP32

The custom CNN was converted to TensorFlow Lite Micro and deployed on ESP32-CAM with OLED display. Algorithm 1 shows the flow (Figs. 4 and 5).

### 4.4   Memory and Latency Analysis

Table 1 shows memory and inference times. Custom CNN is efficient: 4 kB RAM and 15 ms per inference. FOMO slightly larger; MobileNetV2 SSD FPN-Lite is heavier.

**(a) MobileNetV2SSD FPN-Lite**

**(b) FOMO**

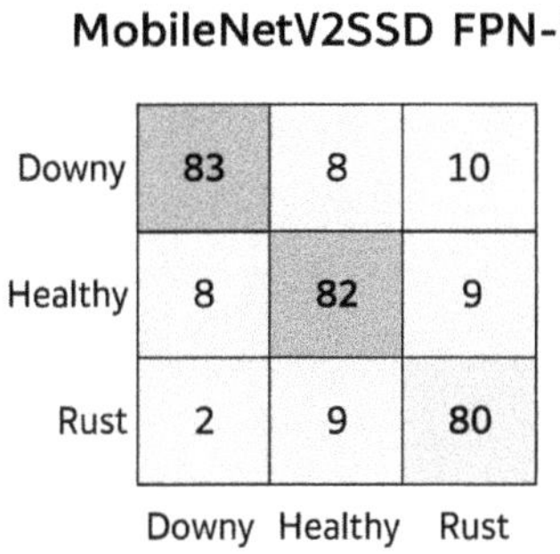

**MobileNetV2SSD FPN-L**

|         | Downy | Healthy | Rust |
|---------|-------|---------|------|
| Downy   | 83    | 8       | 10   |
| Healthy | 8     | 82      | 9    |
| Rust    | 2     | 9       | 80   |

*Rows: Actual, Columns: Predicted*

**FOMO**

|         | Downy | Healthy | Rust |
|---------|-------|---------|------|
| Downy   | 82    | 8       | 10   |
| Healthy | 8     | 85      | 8    |
| Rust    | 12    | 8       | 78   |

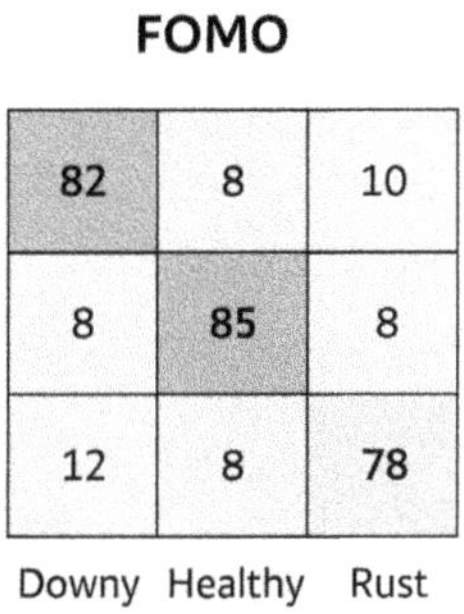

*Rows: Actual, Columns: Predicted*

**(c) Custom CNN**

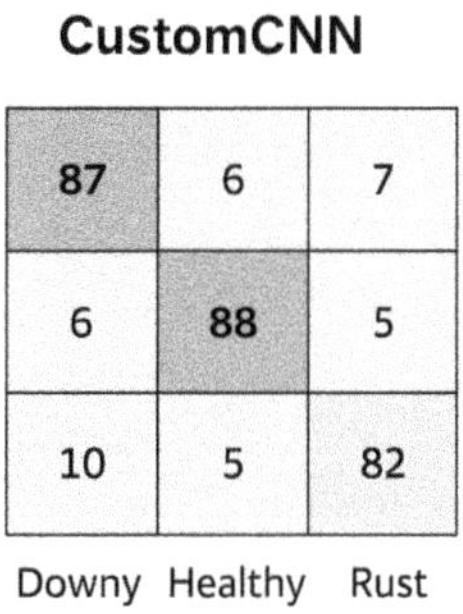

**CustomCNN**

|         | Downy | Healthy | Rust |
|---------|-------|---------|------|
|         | 87    | 6       | 7    |
|         | 6     | 88      | 5    |
|         | 10    | 5       | 82   |

*Rows: Actual, Columns: Predicted*

**Fig. 2.** Confusion matrices for (a) MobileNetV2SSD FPN-Lite, (b) FOMO, and (c) Custom CNN models trained on Pearl Millet disease dataset.

**Table 1.** Hyperparameters and Device Metrics Across Models

| Parameter | FOMO | MobileNetV2 SSD FPN-Lite | Custom CNN |
|-----------|------|--------------------------|------------|
| Image size | 96×96 RGB | 96×96 RGB | 96×96 RGB |
| Learning rate | 0.01 | 0.001 | 0.01 |
| Batch size | 16 | 16 | 32 |
| Epochs | 30 | 30 | 30 |
| ESP32 processing time | 80 ms | 150 ms | 15 ms |
| Memory usage | Low | High | 4 kB |
| Accuracy | 86% | 78% | 85% |

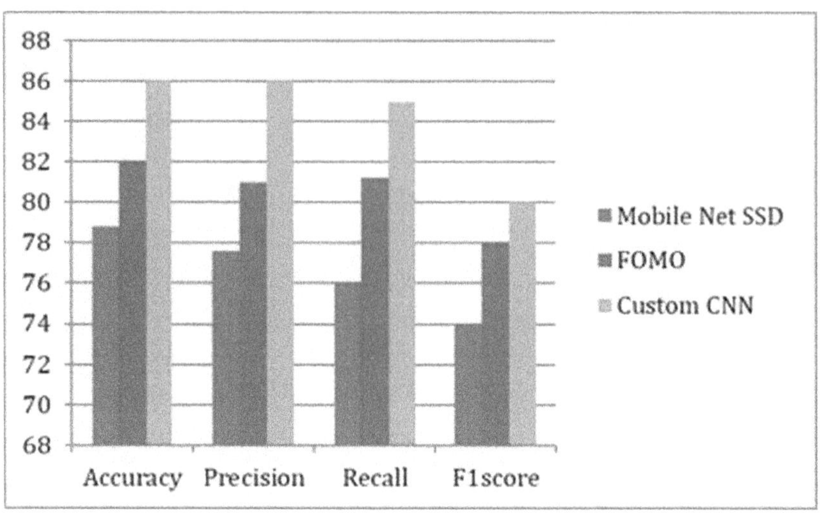


**Fig. 3.** Performance metrics for lightweight models

---

**Algorithm 1:** ESP32-CAM deployment flow

---

   **Input**: Trained Edge Impulse model, ESP32-CAM, OLED display
   **Output**: Predicted class on OLED
1  **Initialize** ESP32-CAM and OLED
2  **Load** Edge Impulse model
3  **while** *device powered on* **do**
4     **Capture** leaf image
5     **Run inference**
6     **Display** predicted class and confidence

---

### 4.5  Real-World Testing

Field testing confirms reliable real-time inference. Misclassifications occur only when leaves are partially damaged or covered. Farmers appreciated offline, instantaneous predictions.

### 4.6  Discussion

Lightweight CNNs can classify reliably on microcontrollers. Custom CNN balances size, speed, and accuracy. FOMO is a valid alternative for grid-based detection. Offline, real-time edge deployment is practical for rural agriculture.

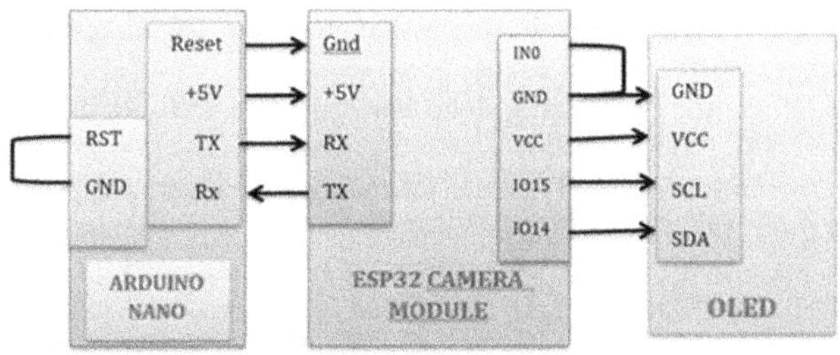


**Fig. 4.** ESP32 interfacing diagram

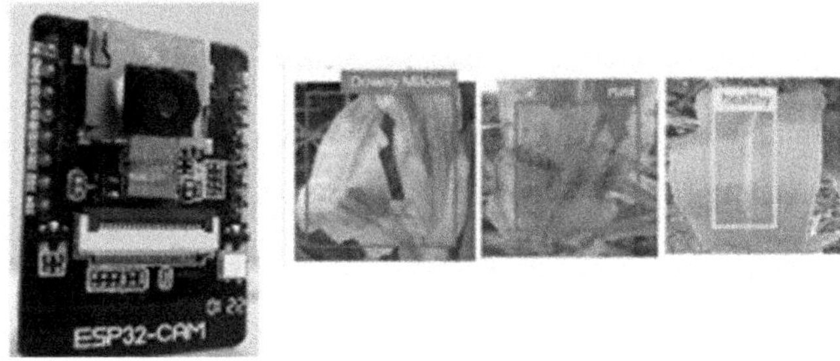


**Fig. 5.** Deployment on ESP32-CAM

## 5    Conclusion

Three lightweight models—MobileNetV2-SSD, FOMO, and a custom CNN—were designed for disease detection in pearl millet. Among these, the Custom CNN is well suited to edge devices with moderate processing budgets, owing to its compact convolutional design. Conversely, FOMO is also appropriate for microcontrollers and devices with very limited memory and compute, as it simplifies computation by dividing the image into a grid and classifying each cell. Edge devices such as the ESP32 and Raspberry Pi enable early, offline disease detection without internet connectivity, thereby reducing latency and removing dependence on the cloud—an important consideration in remote areas.

## References


1. Lin, J. et al.: MCUNet: Tiny Deep Learning on IoT Devices. arXiv:2007.10319v2 (2020)
2. Hamdan, S., Ayyash, M., Almajali, S.: Edge-computing architectures for IoT applications. Sensors **20**, 6441 (2020)
3. Wu, Z., Qiu, K., Zhang, J.: A smart microcontroller architecture for IoT. Sensors **20**, 1821 (2020)
4. Dastjerdi, A.V., Buyya, R.: Fog computing: helping IoT realize. IEEE Comput. **49**, 112–116 (2016)

5. Merenda, M., Porcaro, C., Iero, D.: Edge machine learning for AI-enabled IoT devices. Sensors **20**(9), 2533 (2020)
6. Atitallah, S.B., et al.: Leveraging deep learning and IoT big data analytics. Comput. Sci. Rev. **38**, 100303 (2020)
7. Warden, P., Situnayake, D.: TinyML: Machine Learning with TensorFlow Lite on Arduino, 2nd ed. O'Reilly (2019)
8. TensorFlow Lite. http://www.tensorflow.org/lite. Accessed 23 Sept 2021
9. Suda, N., Loh, D.: Machine Learning on ARM Cortex-M Microcontrollers. Arm Ltd., UK (2019)
10. Harishankar, C., et al.: Explainable Hybrid Learning for Indian Food Classification. ICCCNT (2024)
11. Teng, T.W., et al.: Vision-based wall following for HSR robot. Sensors **20**(11), 3298 (2020)
12. Aravinth, J., et al.: Multilinear compressive learning of hyperspectral data with U-Net. DSP **155**, 104740 (2024)
13. Amritavarshini, S., et al.: Plant Leaf Disease Detection using Deep Learning. ICon-SCEPT (2024)
14. Sudhesh, K.M., et al.: Real Time Identification of Harmful Birds in Agriculture Field. ICICT (2024)

# Exploring Machine Learning Topologies at Home with Tiny Constraints for Presence Classification


Simone Tognocchi[1] , Alessandro Tomasoni[2] ,
Mohammadreza B. Mohajer[1] , Daniele Lo Iacono[2],
and Danilo Pietro Pau[2(✉)] 

[1] Politecnico di Milano, Milan, Italy
[2] STMicroelectronics, System Research and Applications, Agrate Brianza, Italy
`DANILO.PAU@ST.COM`



**Abstract.** This paper presents an edge neural architecture search method for human presence detection using Wi-Fi signals. The proposed method, WiFiNAS, is a derivative-free, cell-based technique to design tiny 1D convolutional neural networks for microcontrollers. The process iteratively explores topologies by adjusting the number of convolutional filters and computational layers, based on validation accuracy under micro controller memory constraints. This deployment happens by the unified core technology, which imports and profiles memory usage, operations, and latency on tiny microcontrollers. This information provides feedback to the search process. The final 8bits model achieved a classification accuracy of 98.57%. Real-time inference was achieved on various STM32H7, STM32MP1, and STM32MP2 with neural processing acceleration in 78.6 ms. This work ensures full privacy by keeping data local, within a home environment.



**Keywords:** machine learning automated search · micro controllers · smart-home · WiFi signals · data privacy


## 1 Introduction

Ensuring data privacy, security, and personalization is crucial for AI solutions at home. This work focuses on using ambient Wi-Fi signals, to detect human presence. Data is collected locally and processed on micro controllers (MCU), to generate, train, optimize, and quantize tiny neural networks (TinyNN). A lightweight, MCU-aware Neural Architecture Search (NAS) runs on the Orin chip to adapt models to the home environment and the constraints of MCUs. Each model's complexity is profiled using ST Unified Core Technology to map on MCUs and MPUs of the STM32 family. This fully on-premises approach preserves privacy, removes the need for cloud training, and enables continuous, personalized optimization of presence detection at each home.



S. Mitra et al. (Eds.): PReMI 2025, LNCS 16358, pp. 93–101, 2026.
https://doi.org/10.1007/978-3-032-18480-1_10

## 2   Related Works

### 2.1   Neural Architecture Search

Convolutional Neural Networks (CNNs) are very accurate; however, they are often too deep and over-parameterized, resulting in reduced speed on MCUs. Designing CNNs that are both MCU-efficient and accurate remains a challenge when 700+ MCU variants exist. MobileNet [1] reduced computational footprint, yet training and deployment cost remain prohibitive on MCUs.

Early NAS methods based on reinforcement learning (RL) [2], Bayesian optimization (BO) [3], and evolutionary algorithms (EA) [4] demonstrated automated design at high computational costs and limited edge scalability. MNAS-Net [5] introduced hardware-aware RL, yet requiring 4.5 days on TPUv2 for model search. Hardware-aware NAS (HW-NAS) using EA, such as MCUNet [6] constrained the search space to device limits, then specializing the network. MCUNet identified optimal architectures for MCUs within two hours, reducing design costs by a factor of 133 compared to MNASNet. Additionally, [7] utilized Sequential Model-Based Optimization (SMBO) focusing on BO for STM32 MCUs for Human Activity Recognition (HAR), achieving RAM and ROM reductions of 38% and 31%, respectively, with fourfold model compression.

### 2.2   Lightweight NAS

ColabNAS [8] is a cell-based HW-NAS method designed to generate tiny CNNs for MCUs. A derivative-free search strategy inspired by Occam's razor, incrementally built CNN architectures by adding layers and adjusting kernels only when improvements in generalization within MCU limits were measured.

### 2.3   Presence Detection

Human presence detection (PD) by Wi-Fi signals is the focus of this work. Existing methods utilize Channel State Information (CSI) or Doppler-based features from Wi-Fi signals to infer human presence and activities. CSI-based approaches analyze amplitude and phase variations in the Wi-Fi channel to detect human presence or classify activities. [9] employs Long Short-Term Memory (LSTM) and two-dimensional CNNs (2DCNN)—to classify rooms as occupied or vacant. The LSTM achieved higher accuracy, sensitivity, and computational efficiency. DeepSense [10] used deep learning on CSI amplitude data for HAR with poor generalization due to CSI's sensitivity to multi-path effects and static objects.

Doppler-based techniques leverage frequency shifts due to human movement. WiWeHAR [11] used phase-based Doppler information but on specific hardware, limiting generalization. The SHARP [12] framework improved that by introducing reference-free phase sanitization and combining Doppler spectrograms with neural classifiers, achieving robust, environment- and person-independent HAR without retraining. Nonetheless, SHARP—like all aforementioned methods—operates entirely in offline settings, and lacks support for real-time inference and deployment on ultra-low-power MCUs.

Differently from the cited prior works, the approach proposed by this study is explicitly designed for efficient, real-time, and reusable human presence detection, with a particular emphasis on interoperability with MCU-based edge platforms. This enables practical deployment in resource-limited environments, thereby addressing the computational, generalization, and deployment limitations that were observed in existing literature.

## 3   Dataset

It was collected with commercial Wi-Fi devices operating under the IEEE 802.11n standard at 2.4 GHz, using a 20 MHz bandwidth and a single-antenna receiver. CSI measurements were at a sampling rate of 100 Hz, one sample every 10 milliseconds. In IEEE 802.11n each Wi-Fi packet utilizes 56 subcarriers, each of them providing a discrete measurement of the channel's response at a specific frequency. For every subcarrier, both amplitude and phase values were recorded.

Data was gathered in nine different indoor environments, including eight rooms with varied layouts—two with glass walls—and one quite large room. To capture different motion conditions, three activity scenarios were performed in each environment: stationary, slow movement, and fast movement. For every scenario and environment combination, 11 min of continuous CSI data were recorded, creating a varied and comprehensive dataset reflecting a wide range of propagation conditions and human-induced signal variations. Subsequently, to mitigate hardware-induced phase inconsistencies and enable reliable Doppler-based activity recognition, a preprocessing step was applied to sanitize the CSI data.

Subsequently, Doppler spectra were extracted using fast Fourier transforms (FFT) over sliding windows of CSI measurements. These spectra captured the frequency shifts caused by motion in the environment and served as the primary features for human activity analysis.

## 4   Devised Approach

WiFiNAS was developed based on the search strategy known as ColabNAS [8], which was modified to autonomously design a different set of 1D-CNN architectures, rather than 2D-CNN architectures, capable of performing PD on the dataset described in Sect. 3. Furthermore, the models were required to simultaneously satisfy the resource constraints imposed by the target MCU. Unlike ColabNAS, WiFiNAS evaluates automatically RAM and Flash memory allocation on the board, as well as the multiply-accumulate (MACC) operations required, utilizing the ST Unified Core Technology. The network architecture generated by WiFiNAS in this study differs from the one used in ColabNAS in terms of the adopted layers—such as using 1D-CNNs instead of 2D-CNNs—as well as differences in kernel and filter sizes, normalization techniques, and overall design choices to better suit the problem being addressed.

The architecture first applies Min-Max normalization to scale the input data to the range [0, 1]. Each generated network includes at least one convolutional block, comprising a 1D-CNN layer, followed by batch normalization and a dropout layer. After this block, there are three fully connected (dense) layers made by 128, 64, and 3 units, respectively. The final dense layer employs a softmax activation function to predict class probabilities. Additionally, dropout layers are inserted between each of the dense layers to mitigate the overfitting.

The model selection strategy adopted in WiFiNAS aims to identify the optimal combination of two hyperparameters: the number of filters in the convolutional layers, denoted as $k$, and the number of additional convolutional layers following the initial one, denoted as $c$. Although the search space defined by these two parameters is relatively limited, it has been shown to be sufficiently expressive to generate architectures capable of solving a wide range of classification and regression tasks.

To facilitate this process, an auxiliary function named *explore_cells* is employed. Given a specific value of $k$, this function systematically evaluates different values of $c$, selecting the configuration that achieves the highest validation accuracy. The search is terminated once further increases in $c$ do not yield additional performance gains. Each candidate architecture is evaluated not only in terms of accuracy but also with respect to hardware constraints, by leveraging the ST Edge AI Core Technology to estimate memory usage. Only those models that comply with the target microcontroller's resource limitations are considered valid and proceed to training and evaluation.

The search procedure is described in detail in Algorithm 1.

Upon completion of this adaptive search procedure, the architecture that achieved the highest validation accuracy across all evaluated configurations is selected as the final model.

## 5    Hardware Deployability

The selected model was further deployed on different MCUs to measure latency. On the STM32MP257F-EV1, equipped with a dual-core Arm Cortex-A35 at 1.5 GHz, an Arm Cortex-M33 at 400 MHz and a Graphic Processing Unit (GPU) at 900 MHz, the measured inference time was 78.62 ms. The same model, when deployed on the STM32MP157F-DK2, featuring a dual-core Arm Cortex-A7 at 800 MHz, without the GPU, achieved an inference time of 444.9 ms. On the STM32MP135F-DK, integrating a single-core Arm Cortex-A7 at 1 GHz, inference time increased to 548.3 ms. Additionally, on the STM32H7S78-DK platform—based on an Arm Cortex-M7 core—the inference time was 893.395 ms.

The NAS process was executed on NVIDIA Orin AGX 64 GB, capable of delivering up to 275 Tera Operations Per Second (TOPS), with 64 GB of LPDDR5 memory. The Orin AGX efficiently managed the iterative WiFiNAS procedure, substantially reducing the total search time while enabling fully on-premises, privacy-preserving model optimization without reliance on external

---

**Algorithm 1.** WiFiNAS Search procedure

---

$k \leftarrow k0$
$previous_architecture \leftarrow$ explore_cells($k$)
$k \leftarrow 2 \times k$
$current_architecture \leftarrow$ explore_cells($k$)
**if** ($current_architecture$[max_val_acc] $> previous_architecture$[max_val_acc]) **then**
    $previous_architecture \leftarrow current_architecture$
    $k \leftarrow 2 \times k$
    $current_architecture \leftarrow$ explore_cells($k$)
    **while**                    ($current_architecture$[max_val_acc]                    $>$
$previous_architecture$[max_val_acc] $+ \epsilon$) **do**
        $previous_architecture \leftarrow current_architecture$
        $k \leftarrow 2 \times k$
        $current_architecture \leftarrow$ explore_cells($k$)
    **end while**
**else**
    $k \leftarrow \frac{k_0}{2}$
    $current_architecture \leftarrow$ explore_cells($k$)
    **while**                    ($current_architecture$[max_val_acc]                    $\geq$
$previous_architecture$[max_val_acc]) **do**
        $previous_architecture \leftarrow current_architecture$
        $k \leftarrow \frac{k}{2}$
        $current_architecture \leftarrow$ explore_cells($k$)
    **end while**
**end if**
$resulting_architecture \leftarrow previous_architecture$

---

cloud infrastructure. The WiFiNAS trained and evaluated, by using the ST Unified Core Technology, 17 different models during the whole process on Orin. The network with the highest accuracy was achieved after 40 h and 51 min and without any human intervention. The inference performance results for the deployed models are summarized in Table 1.

## 6  Accuracy Results

The model profiled in Sect. 5 had parameters $k = 16$ and $c = 3$, achieving the accuracy results as reported in Table 2. This model required 21,492,058 parameters and 364,226,711 MACC operations. It is deployable on an STM32 MCU, requiring 20.51 MiB of Flash memory to store the weights and 125.37 KiB of SRAM for activations. It employs post-training 8-bit integer quantization, which reduces the weight size by 75% compared to the floating-point version. This approach was chosen to decrease memory requirements without compromising accuracy. Table 2 presents the results of experiments in which seven of the nine environments were used for training and validation, while the remaining two environments were reserved for testing, thereby simulating an over-the-air (OTA) test.

**Table 1.** Measured Inference Times on Target Hardware Platforms

| Board Model | CPU Specification | Inference Time [ms] | Resource Constraints |
|---|---|---|---|
| STM32MP257F-EV1 | Dual Arm Cortex-A35 @ 1500 MHz + GPU @ 900 MHz | 78.6 | RAM: 4 GB Flash: 64 MB MACC: $10^{12}$ |
| STM32MP157F-DK2 | Dual Arm Cortex-A7 @ 800 MHz | 444.9 | RAM: 512 MB Flash: - - MACC: $10^{10}$ |
| STM32MP135F-DK | Arm Cortex-A7 @ 1000 MHz | 548.3 | RAM: 512 MB Flash: - - MACC: $10^{10}$ |
| STM32H7S78-DK | Arm Cortex-M7 @ 600 MHz | 893.4 | RAM: 620 KB Flash: 128 MB MACC: $10^{8}$ |

**Table 2.** Accuracy results of the NAS-selected model with post-training quantization.

| Accuracy | Post-Training Quantized Model |
|---|---|
| One person stationary | 98.66% |
| One person moving slow | 97.44% |
| One person moving fast | 99.63% |
| Total | 98.57% |

Figure 1 presents the results of all candidate models generated by WiFiNAS, plotted against their complexity, measured by the number of MACC operations required. All models were deployable on the STM32 MCU. The selected candidate model is represented by the red dot.

## 7   Discussion

The results presented in Sect. 6 validate the effectiveness of the WiFiNAS approach in generating compact and accurate models suitable for deployment on resource-constrained microcontrollers. The selected 1D-CNN model achieved an overall classification accuracy of 98.57% on the Wi-Fi-based PD dataset, while enabling real-time inference across various STM32 platforms. This model was chosen from a pool of 17 candidates, all deployable on STM32 MCUs, as illustrated in Fig. 1. Although the selected model (indicated by the red dot) is not the most complex, it demonstrates the highest accuracy. Figure 1 shows that models with fewer than $10^{5}$ MACC operations perform poorly, while nearly all models exceeding $10^{6}$ MACC operations achieve high accuracy. The only model with more than $10^{9}$ MACC operations exhibits early overfitting signs, resulting in decreased performance, likely due to excessive parameters relative to the training dataset size. Consequently, the search algorithm stops upon encountering this model. Future work may expand the search space to include additional parameters, such as regularization terms, to mitigate overfitting in models exceeding $10^{9}$ MACC operations.

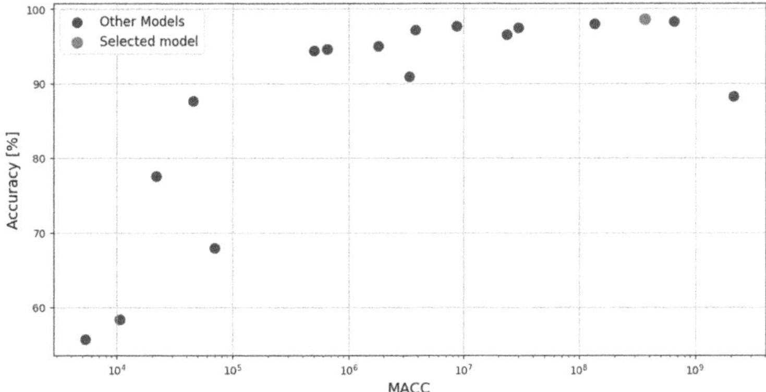

**Fig. 1.** Accuracy of all the candidate models generated by WiFiNAS against their complexity in term of MACC operations required.

# 8    Comparison with Other Approaches

Various HW-NAS frameworks have been proposed. In Table 3, *WiFiNAS* is compared with [7,13–16] in terms of the hardware constraints considered, the decision to train all candidate architectures, and the objective function minimized to select the optimal model.

*AutoTinyML* [7] introduces a framework for identifying accurate models deployable on MCUs, employing Sequential Model-Based Optimization (SMBO) with a search strategy called SVM-CBO_RF.

In [13], a NAS is used to design Extreme Learning Machine (ELM) CNN feature extractors (FE) suitable for on-device learning. The authors employ BO with Gaussian Process (GP) and Random Forest (RF) surrogate models. This approach minimizes the MSE between the extracted and reference features, without explicitly optimizing classification accuracy.

*MicroNAS* [14], in contrast to *WiFiNAS* and similar methods, employs a zero-shot approach to evaluate candidate architectures without any network training. This approach is unsuitable for the network personalization task in this study, as does not tailor the architecture to a specific dataset but selects networks based on general estimated properties. *MicroNAS* achieves a classification accuracy of 93.88% on CIFAR-10.

*RaNAS* [15] targets CNN design for edge devices, considering inference latency and memory usage as hardware constraints, both predicted using a graph neural network (GNN) model. Similar to *MicroNAS*, this method does not train all candidate architectures on the dataset during the search process.

Recent advances have extended NAS to ASIC accelerators. NASAIC optimizes both neural architectures and heterogeneous ASIC sub-accelerators to meet strict latency, energy, and chip area constraints. While effective, ASIC-based frameworks require specialized hardware and focus on multi-task edge accelerators, limiting personalization in dynamic environments like smart homes.

NASAIC achieves up to 2.49× lower energy use, 2.32× smaller chip area, 17.7% lower latency, and 93.23% accuracy on CIFAR-10, outperforming sequential NAS–ASIC methods.

WiFiNAS is the only one among the six HW-NAS methods, together with NASAIC [16], presented in Table 3 that trains the models and evaluates them on a validation dataset, using accuracy as the objective function. Furthermore, unlike the other methods that target few specific hardware devices, WiFiNAS is designed for a set of more than 20 boards. While all models have certain deployability constraints—except for [13]—WiFiNAS uniquely accounts for the MACC operations as well, but does not consider energy consumption.

**Table 3.** Comparison between WiFiNAS and other five HW-NAS on the deployability constraints, objective function used and decision on train all the candidates.

| | AutoTinyML [7] | ELM CNN FE [13] | MicroNAS [14] | RaNAS [15] | NASAIC [16] | WiFiNAS |
|---|---|---|---|---|---|---|
| Deployability Constraints | RAM ROM | No | Flops Latency | Latency Memory | Latency Energy Area | RAM Flash MACC |
| Train Candidates | Yes | Yes | No | No | Yes | Yes |
| Objective Function | FE MSE | X-CROSS | ACC est. | resource efficiency | weighted ACC | ACC |
| HW Target | STM32L476RGT6 STM32F303K8T6 | generic tiny devices | STM32 NUCLEO-F746ZG | Edge devices | ASIC accelerators | MCUs |

# 9 Conclusion and Future Works

This work introduced WiFiNAS, a fully automated, hardware-aware neural architecture search method tailored for human presence detection using ambient Wi-Fi signals. By integrating an on-premises, derivative-free search strategy with ST Unified Core Technology profiling, WiFiNAS successfully generated lightweight, accurate, and MCU-deployable 1D-CNN models, achieving a total classification accuracy of 98.57% after post-training quantization in just 78.6 ms per inference on STM32MP2. The approach preserved data privacy by performing all processes locally and demonstrated real-time inference capability on a range of STM32-based platforms. Future work may involve scaling from single-receiver setups to larger multiple-input multiple-output (MIMO) arrays while maintaining memory and MACC requirements and preserving accuracy. Additionally, exploring various quantization methods, such as 1-bit quantization or others, could help reduce memory and MACC requirements; however, it is important to balance the trade-off between accuracy and resource efficiency.

# References


1. Andrew, G., et al.: Efficient convolutional neural networks for mobile vision applications. Mobilenets (2017)
2. Han, Z., Hong, D., Gao, L., Roy, S.K., Zhang, B., Chanussot, J.: Reinforcement learning for neural architecture search in hyperspectral unmixing. IEEE Geosci. Remote Sens. Lett. **19**, 1–5 (2022)
3. Gupta, V.K., Lalwani, S.K., Bhati, G.S., Prakash, S., Sunny: Bayesian optimization based neural architecture search for classification of gases/odors mixtures. IEEE Sens. J. **24**(5), 7119–7125 (2024)
4. Pan, C., Yao, X.: Neural architecture search based on evolutionary algorithms with fitness approximation. In: 2021 International Joint Conference on Neural Networks (IJCNN), pp. 1–8 (2021)
5. Tan, M., et al.: MnasNet: platform-aware neural architecture search for mobile (2019)
6. Lin, J., Chen, W.-M., Lin, Y., Cohn, J., Gan, C., Han, S.: McuNet: tiny deep learning on IoT devices (2020)
7. Perego, R., Candelieri, A., Archetti, F., Pau, D.: AutoTinyML for microcontrollers: dealing with black-box deployability. Expert Syst. Appl. **207**, 117876 (2022)
8. Garavagno, A.M., Leonardis, D., Frisoli, A.: ColabNAS: obtaining lightweight task-specific convolutional neural networks following Occam's razor. Future Gener. Comput. Syst. **152**, 152–159 (2024)
9. Sadhwani, J., Sabarimalai Manikandan, M.: Non-collaborative human presence detection using channel state information of Wi-Fi signal and long-short term memory neural network. In: 2021 13th International Conference on Electronics, Computers and Artificial Intelligence (ECAI), pp. 1–6 (2021)
10. Zou, H., Zhou, Y., Yang, J., Jiang, H., Xie, L., Spanos, C.J.: DeepSense: device-free human activity recognition via autoencoder long-term recurrent convolutional network. In: Proceedings of IEEE International Conference on Communications (ICC) (2018)
11. Muaaz, M., Chelli, A., Abdelgawwad, A.A., Mallofré, A.C., Pötzold, M.: WiWeHAR: multimodal human activity recognition using Wi-Fi and wearable sensing modalities. IEEE Access **8**, 164453–164470 (2020)
12. Meneghello, F., Garlisi, D., Fabbro, N.D., Tinnirello, I., Rossi, M.: SHARP: environment and person independent activity recognition with commodity IEEE 802.11 access points. IEEE Trans. Mob. Comput. **22**(10), 6160–6175 (2023)
13. Pau, D., Pisani, A., Candelieri, A.: Towards full forward on-tiny-device learning: a guided search for a randomly initialized neural network. Algorithms **17**(1) (2024)
14. Qiao, Y., Haocheng, X., Zhang, Y., Huang, S.: MicroNAS: zero-shot neural architecture search for MCUs (2024)
15. Gao, J., Liu, Z., Wang, Y., Ji, W.: RaNAS: resource-aware neural architecture search for edge computing. ACM Trans. Archit. Code Optim. **22**(1) (2025)
16. Yang, L., et al.: Co-exploration of neural architectures and heterogeneous ASIC accelerator designs targeting multiple tasks. In: 2020 57th ACM/IEEE Design Automation Conference (DAC), pp. 1–6 (2020)

# Evolutionary Computation

# Extensive Benchmarking of Metaheuristics Using Real-World Constrained Multi-objective Optimization Problems


Somnath Mukhopadhyay[(✉)][iD], Sunita Sarkar[iD], and Wangjam Niranjan Singh[iD]

Department of Computer Science and Engineering, Assam University, Silchar, Assam, India
`som.cse@live.com`



**Abstract.** The rapid growth of Optimization and Metaheuristics research has led to both innovation and oversaturation, making algorithm selection increasingly challenging. While most studies assess algorithms using the Synthetic Benchmark Problems (SBPs) often oversimplify real-world complexities, potentially misrepresenting performance. To address this, we evaluate 25 metaheuristic algorithms across 50 Real-World Constrained Multi-objective Optimization Problems (RWCMOPs), using performance metrics such as Hypervolume (HV), Feasibility Rate (FR), and Wall-Clock Time. Our findings show that classical algorithms like GDE3 and NSGA-II often outperform newer methods in practical scenarios. Notably, constraint structure and feasibility difficulty emerge as more influential factors than problem dimensionality. This study offers key insights into algorithmic robustness and underscores the importance of real-world testing to guide more effective algorithm design beyond synthetic settings.

**Keywords:** Metaheuristics · Real-World Constrained Multi-objective Optimization Problems · Benchmarking and Performance Evaluation · Hypervolume Indicator


## 1 Introduction

In the modern world, one of the key challenges is how to utilize limited resources to achieve optimal outcomes efficiently. This dilemma spans a wide range of fields and is collectively referred to as *optimization problems*. Optimisation involves the task of maximising or minimising an objective function while satisfying specific constraints. Such problems are prevalent across diverse real-world domains, including economics, chemistry, engineering, logistics, and healthcare. The number of metaheuristic algorithms proposed in the literature has steadily increased, as detailed by Hussain et al. [4]. The rapid growth of algorithms has created confusion for practitioners, making systematic evaluation essential. Metaheuristics


© The Author(s), under exclusive license to Springer Nature Switzerland AG 2026
S. Mitra et al. (Eds.): PReMI 2025, LNCS 16358, pp. 105–117, 2026.
https://doi.org/10.1007/978-3-032-18480-1_11

are commonly tested on *Synthetic Benchmark Problems (SBPs)*, which offer controlled settings, scalability, and known Pareto fronts for easier performance comparison [4]. However, SBPs often lack the complexity of real-world problems, which can result in overestimating an algorithm's effectiveness. Herrera et al. [17] emphasize the gap between theory-driven and practical metaheuristic research, noting that most studies focus solely on synthetic benchmarks without demonstrating applicability to real-world problems. Zapotecas-Martínez et al. [28] revealed that many existing SBPs lack essential characteristics such as scalability, known optima, meaningful trade-offs, and varied parameter domains. Another fundamental challenge in assessing metaheuristics arises from the *No Free Lunch (NFL) Theorem* [27]. If the NFL theorem holds for continuous multi-objective optimization problems, it implies that no single algorithm performs better on average across all problem instances. Müller et al. [23] note that defining problem similarity remains unclear, making it challenging to generalize algorithm performance and benchmark real-world problems without known optima. To bridge the theory–practice gap, Kumar et al. [6] introduced 50 real-world constrained multi-objective problems, which were tested on 7 algorithms. In contrast, Ma et al. [13] expanded the scope to 15 algorithms but used synthetic problems, finding that newer methods often performed no better than established ones. In paper [10], the Leaded Sine Cosine Multi-objective APO (LSC-MOAPO), which integrates APO with sine–cosine and leader selection strategies, demonstrated superior Pareto-optimal solutions compared to ten established algorithms across 41 benchmarks and real-world engineering problems. A new benchmark suite of 11 real-world many-objective problems has been proposed in [18], demonstrating the stronger performance of indicator-based, weight-vector, Pareto-dominance, and hybrid MOEAs compared to others. A novel evolutionary framework inspired by the alternating direction method of multipliers has been proposed in [8] to solve CMOPs with unknown constraints, demonstrating faster convergence and superior performance compared to state-of-the-art constrained EMO algorithms on extensive benchmarks and real-world problems.

This paper aims to further this line of research by benchmarking 25 recent and relevant metaheuristic algorithms on the 50 real-world problems provided in [6]. We propose a novel scoring and ranking framework based on three performance indicators and provide a comprehensive analysis of the algorithms through their performance indicator values, overall scores, and rankings.

## 2   Proposed Methodology

To benchmark the algorithms, the proposed methodology consists of three steps: evaluating the optimal solutions and calculating the performance indicators, scoring the algorithms based on these indicators, and ranking the algorithms according to their scores. The process block diagram is shown in Fig. 1. As we can see, the process begins by feeding Real-World Constrained Multi-objective Optimization Problems (RWCMOPs) to the metaheuristic algorithms to produce solutions. Next, we calculate the performance indicator values, namely the

Hypervolume Indicator, Feasibility Rate, and Total Wall-Clock Time, from the solutions. And finally, our novel ranking algorithm uses these performance indicator values to calculate the performance score and rank the algorithms. In the next part, we discuss the Real-World Constrained Multi-objective Optimization Problems benchmark suite.

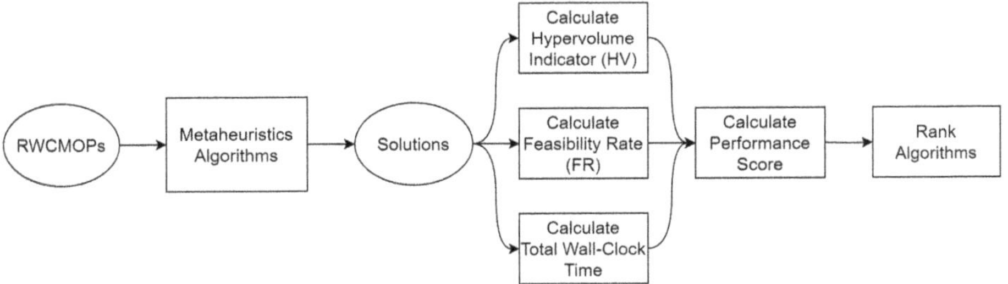

**Fig. 1.** Process Block Diagram

## 2.1 Real-World Constrained Multi-objective Optimization Problems

The real-world constrained multi-objective optimization problems used in this study are collected from [6], comprising 50 problems across various domains, including mechanical design, chemical engineering, process design, power electronics, and power systems. These problems vary in complexity, with 2–5 objectives, 2–34 decision variables, and up to 26 equality and 29 inequality constraints. The following section outlines the rationale for selecting benchmarking algorithms.

## 2.2 Selection of Algorithms

To identify the most relevant algorithms, we reviewed all those available in PLATEMO, documenting their citation counts and publication dates. Algorithms with the highest impact and most recent publications were selected for benchmarking. We also included the algorithms that were benchmarked in [6] for comparison. After the selection process, the final list of algorithms is presented in Table 1. Furthermore, cNSGA-III, cMOEA/D, and cARMOEA were not only used in a previous benchmarking work [6] but were also highly cited.

## 2.3 Evaluation of Optimal Solutions and Calculation of Performance Indicators

The algorithms are executed using PLATEMO, with each algorithm independently run 25 times per problem to account for stochastic variability. As real-world problems often lack known optimal solutions, performance indicators such as Generational Distance, Generational Distance Plus, Inverted Generational Distance, and Inverted Generational Distance Plus are not applicable. To overcome this limitation, we employ the *Hypervolume Indicator*, which can assess solution quality and diversity without requiring knowledge of the true optimum. The hypervolume is calculated using a reference point, making it particularly suitable for benchmarking real-world problems. Additionally, to quantify the reliability of the algorithms in terms of constraint satisfaction, we use the *Feasibility Rate*, which is the percentage of feasible solutions relative to the total number of solutions generated by the algorithm. Finally, to evaluate the computational efficiency, we consider the *Total Wall-Clock Time* or runtime of the algorithm.

### 2.4 Scoring the Algorithms Based on the Performance Indicators

After executing the algorithms and calculating the three performance indicators—namely, the Hypervolume Indicator, Feasibility Rate, and Total Wall-Clock Time—the scores are computed using Algorithm 1. This algorithm compares each metaheuristic algorithm with every other metaheuristic algorithm across all optimization problems. A point is awarded to a metaheuristic algorithm if it performs significantly worse than another algorithm on a particular problem. In this context, $>>$ and $<<$ indicate that one algorithm performs "significantly greater" or "significantly less" than the other, respectively, based on the Wilcoxon rank-sum test. The symbol $\approx$ denotes that there is "no significant difference" between the algorithms. The scoring process is designed as a minimization task, lower scores imply better performance and thus higher rankings.

The algorithm first evaluates the Hypervolume Indicator values. These values, obtained over 25 independent runs, are compared using the Wilcoxon rank-sum test with a significance level of $\alpha = 0.05$. If no significant difference is found between two algorithms for a problem, the Feasibility Rate is used to break the tie. This indicator is compared in the same manner as the Hypervolume Indicator. If a tie persists, the Wall-Clock Time is used as the final tiebreaker. If no significant difference is found even at this stage, then both algorithms are considered equivalent for that problem, and no points are assigned to either. Notably, suppose the algorithm under evaluation is found to be significantly better at any point in the comparison. In that case, no points are awarded, as the point will be assigned when the roles are reversed during comparison. In this way, Algorithm 1 leverages all three performance indicators to perform a detailed and fair comparison among the metaheuristics, thereby reducing the number of unresolved ties. To normalize the scores, we divide them by $(N_a - 1) \times N_p$, where $N_a$ is the number of algorithms and $N_p$ is the number of problems. This normalization ensures that all scores fall within the range $[0, 1]$. The Wilcoxon rank-sum test is a nonparametric statistical test used to compare two independent samples. Since we do not assume any specific distribution for the performance metrics, this test is appropriate for our context. The null hypothesis for this test assumes that there is no significant difference between the two distributions. The test returns a $p$-value, which indicates the probability of observing the test statistic under the null hypothesis, and a test statistic value stat, which reflects the difference in ranks between the two samples. A negative stat implies that the first sample has lower ranks (i.e., better performance) than the second, while a positive value means the opposite. Algorithm 2 is a helper function used by Algorithm 1 to compare the distributions of the 25 independent runs of each performance indicator. It evaluates the significance of the difference between two distributions and determines whether the observed difference is statistically meaningful. If the $p$-value is less than the significance threshold (5%), the difference is considered significant. Once all comparisons are made and scores computed, the algorithms are ranked accordingly. The algorithm with the lowest score is regarded as the best performing and thus receives the highest rank. In the next section, we present and analyze the results obtained using this scoring method.

## 3  Results and Discussion

After feeding the 50 RWCMOPs into the selected 25 metaheuristic algorithms and calculating their performance indicator values, Algorithm 1 calculates the scores for each algorithm. The detailed performance indicator values can be accessed from the public GitHub repository: https://github.com/somcse/ Extensive_Benchmarking. The performance scores of the algorithms along with their ranks are showcased in Table 2. As we can see, GDE3 has the lowest score, meaning it performed the best in the benchmark suite, followed by ARMOEA and then NSGA-II. We have also plotted the HV values, FR values, and time values for the problems, along with their heatmaps. The problems are divided into 5 parts for analysis as discussed below.

1. **Mechanical Design Problems (RWCMOP 1—21):** These problems are considered relatively simpler, as most algorithms can produce feasible solutions across all instances, as shown in Fig. 3a. However, algorithms such as RVEA, RVEAa, and TiGE2 struggled to maintain feasibility across all constraints. In terms of solution quality, measured by the Hypervolume (HV) Indicator, almost all algorithms performed well and yielded comparable HV values, although dips are observed for CMOEAD, MOEADD, RVEA, and RVEAa. Despite a lower Feasibility Rate, TiGE2 generated solutions of comparable quality to others; see Fig. 2a. Regarding time, NSGA-II performed exceptionally well, requiring the least computational time across several problems. NSGA-II, ANSGA-II, and GDE3 generally exhibited faster execution, while MOEADD, CMOEAD, MOCell, and MCCMO tended to take longer; these time metrics are presented in Fig. 4a.
2. **Chemical Engineering Problems (RWCMOP 22—24):** Among the three problems, algorithms struggled more on RWCMOP-22 and RWCMOP-24, while they performed slightly better on RWCMOP-23. IMTCMO, MCCMO, and CMOQLMT achieved relatively higher Feasibility Rates across these problems. GDE3 and URCMO also identified some feasible solutions, despite their lower FR values, as shown in Fig. 3b. In terms of HV, IMTCMO,

---

**Algorithm 1.** Scoring of Algorithms

---

1: **Input:** Performance Indicators
2: **Output:** Scores of Algorithms
3: **for** each problem **do**
4:     **for** each algorithmA in algorithms **do**
5:         current_score ← 0
6:         **for** each algorithmB in algorithms **do**
7:             **if** algorithmA == algorithmB **then**
8:                 **continue**
9:             **else if** HV_values(algorithmA) << HV_values(algorithmB) **then**
10:                 current_score ← current_score + 1
11:             **else if** HV_values(algorithmA) ≈ HV_values(algorithmB) **then**
12:                 **if** FR_values(algorithmA) << FR_values(algorithmB) **then**
13:                     current_score ← current_score + 1
14:                 **else if** FR_values(algorithmA) ≈ FR_values(algorithmB) **then**
15:                     **if** time_values(algorithmA) >> time_values(algorithmB) **then**
16:                         current_score ← current_score + 1
17:                     **end if**
18:                 **end if**
19:             **end if**
20:         **end for**
21:         score[algorithmA] ← score[algorithmA] + current_score / ( $N_a$ - 1)
22:     **end for**
23: **end for**
24: **for** each algorithmA in algorithms **do**
25:     score[algorithmA] ← score[algorithmA] / $N_p$
26: **end for**

---

---

**Algorithm 2.** Compare Solutions

---

1: **Input:** $\alpha = 0.05$, $X \leftarrow$ PerformanceMeasures[x], $Y \leftarrow$ PerformanceMeasures[y]
2: **Output:** Difference
3: $stat, p \leftarrow$ `ranksums`$(X, Y)$
4: **if** $p < \alpha$ **then**
5:     **if** stat $< 0$ **then**
6:         **Output:** Distribution $X$ is significantly less than Distribution $Y$
7:     **else**
8:         **Output:** Distribution $X$ is significantly greater than Distribution $Y$
9:     **end if**
10: **else**
11:     **Output:** The difference is insignificant
12: **end if**

---

MCCMO, and CMOQLMT achieved the best values, followed by GDE3 and URCMO, as presented in Fig. 2b. MOEADD, CMOEAD, and MOCell consumed the most time yet failed to find feasible solutions. Among the algorithms with feasible outcomes, GDE3 was the fastest, despite having a lower FR. Between the three top performers, CMOQLMT required the least time,

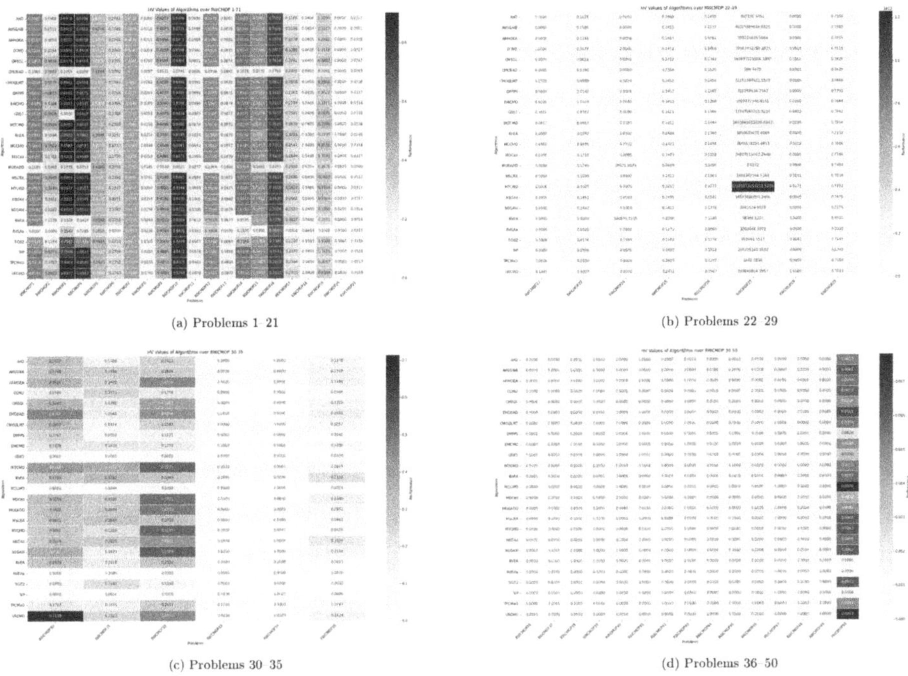

(a) Problems 1–21

(b) Problems 22–29

(c) Problems 30–35

(d) Problems 36–50

**Fig. 2.** HV values heatmaps of benchmark problems (1–50) shown in grouped segments.

MCCMO the most, and IMTCMO fell in between; these patterns are illustrated in Fig. 4b.

3. **Process Design and Synthesis Problems (RWCMOP 25—29):** Most problems in this group were solved effectively by the algorithms, with RWCMOP-28 being the exception due to its challenging constraints. Most algorithms achieved 100% Feasibility Rates. However, RVEA, RVEAa, and TiGE2 consistently showed lower FR values, as shown in Fig. 3b. Regarding HV, all algorithms produced nearly equal-quality solutions (Fig. 2b). For time, MOEADD and CMOEAD again showed reduced performance, whereas NSGA-II and GDE3 were the fastest (Fig. 4b).

4. **Power Electronics Problems:** For this problem set, most algorithms achieved some feasible results, but none achieved a 100% Feasibility Rate. GDE3, RVEAa, and ToP failed to generate any feasible outcomes. On the other hand, IMTCMO, URCMO, and NSGA-II achieved relatively higher Feasibility Rates (Fig. 3c). In terms of HV, IMTCMO, NSGA-III, MTCMO, and MOCell stood out with better solution quality (Fig. 2c). MOEADD, CMOEAD, and MCCMO again showed longer execution times, as illustrated in Fig. 4c.

5. **Power System Optimization Problems:** Except for RWCMOP-50, none of the algorithms could produce feasible solutions for this category, as seen

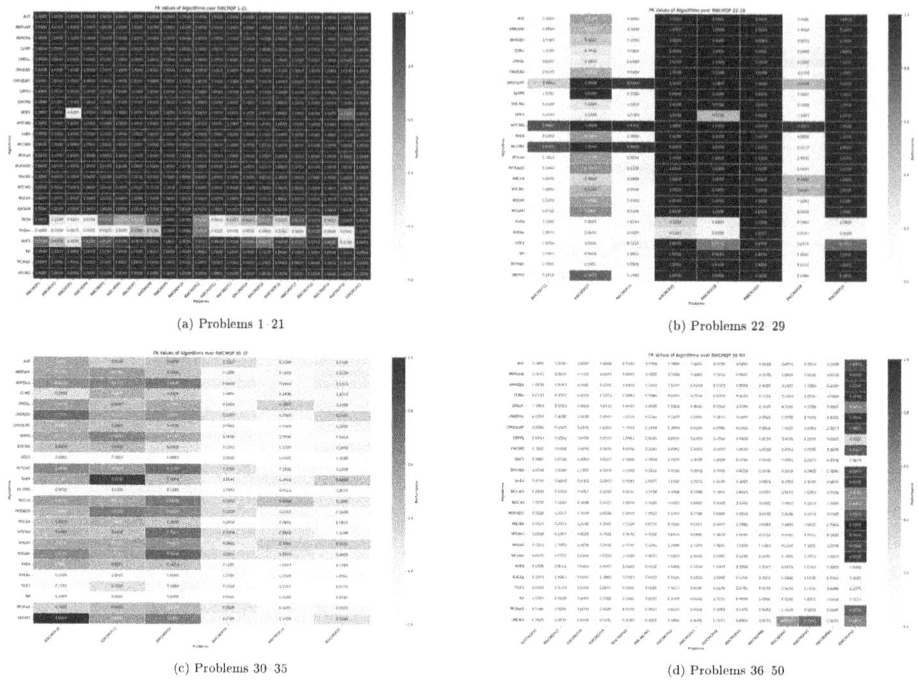

(a) Problems 1–21

(b) Problems 22–29

(c) Problems 30–35

(d) Problems 36–50

**Fig. 3.** FR values heatmaps of benchmark problems (1–50) shown in grouped segments.

**Table 1.** List of 25 Algorithms Selected for Benchmarking

| By Citations | By Date | From Prior Works |
|---|---|---|
| NSGA-II [3] | CMEGL [19] | ToP [11] |
| NSGA-III [2] | IMTCMO [20] | TiGE2 [31] |
| RVEA [1] | CMOQLMT [14] | ANSGA-III [2] |
| RVEAa [1] | MSCEA [30] | CMOEAD [2] |
| MOEADD [7] | MCCMO [32] | CCMO [26] |
| GDE3 [5] | TPCMaO [25] | ARMOEA [24] |
| KnEA [29] | EMCMO [21] | AnD [12] |
| MOCell [16] | URCMO [9] | – |
| – | MTCMO [22] | – |
| – | DPPPS [15] | – |

in Fig. 3d. For RWCMOP-50, feasible solutions were found by all algorithms, although GDE3, RVEA, RVEAa, TiGE2, and ToP had relatively lower FR values. MCCMO and URCMO achieved the highest HV values for this problem, as shown in Fig. 2d. While MOEADD, MCCMO, and CMOEAD were

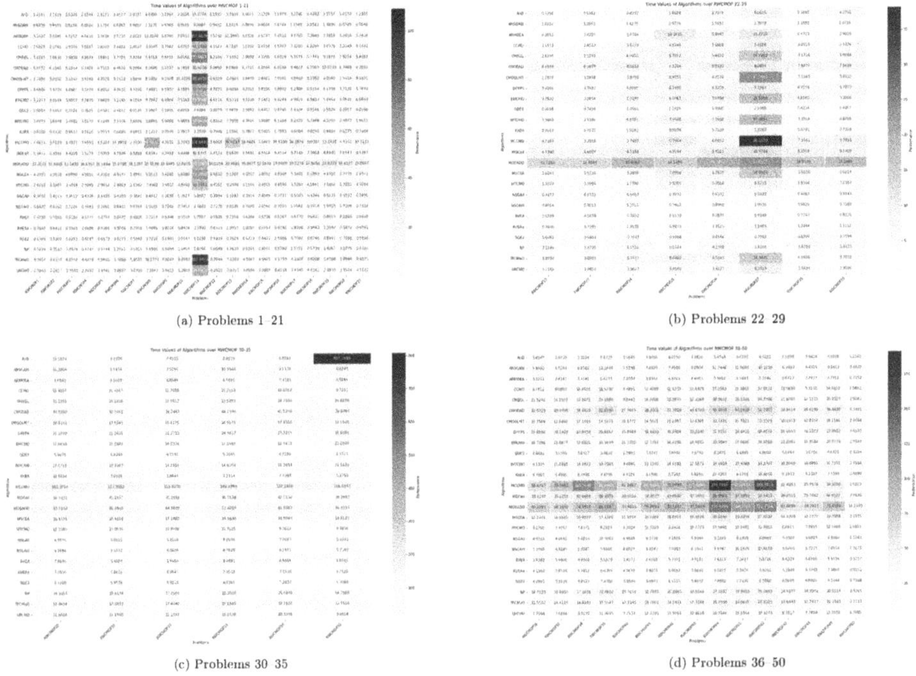

(a) Problems 1–21

(b) Problems 22–29

(c) Problems 30–35

(d) Problems 36–50

**Fig. 4.** Computation time heatmaps of benchmark problems (1–50), shown in grouped segments.

generally slower, MCCMO had a relatively low time value for RWCMOP-50 (Fig. 4d).

Well-established algorithms, such as GDE3 (Rank 1), ARMOEA (Rank 2), and NSGA-II (Rank 3), demonstrated excellent performance in both quality and speed. AnD and NSGA-III followed with Rank 5 and Rank 6, respectively. Among newer algorithms, MTCMO (Rank 6), URCMO (Rank 7), and IMTCMO (Rank 8) also performed well. These results indicate that while recent algorithms are competitive, classic ones still lead in effectiveness across diverse constrained multi-objective problems. We analyzed how problem characteristics, especially the number of constraints, affect algorithm performance. Results show that heavily constrained problems widen the performance gap between algorithms with explicit constraint-handling (e.g., C-NSGA-III, C-MOEA/D) and those without. Algorithms using adaptive penalties or constraint dominance maintained stable feasibility rates, while others relying solely on Pareto dominance struggled. Feasibility difficulty—defined by the proportion of feasible solutions—was a key factor, with better-performing algorithms generating more feasible solutions and achieving higher hypervolume scores. In contrast, problem dimensionality had less impact, highlighting that constraint handling is more critical than scalability for real-world constrained multi-objective optimization.

**Table 2.** Performance Scores and Ranks of the 25 Algorithms

| Algorithm | Rank | Score |
|---|---|---|
| GDE3 [5] | 1 | 0.2025 |
| ARMOEA [24] | 2 | 0.2366 |
| NSGA-II [3] | 3 | 0.2374 |
| AnD [12] | 4 | 0.3133 |
| NSGA-III [2] | 5 | 0.3250 |
| MTCMO [22] | 6 | 0.3300 |
| URCMO [9] | 7 | 0.3658 |
| IMTCMO [20] | 8 | 0.3825 |
| ANSGA-III [2] | 9 | 0.4117 |
| CCMO [26] | 10 | 0.4425 |
| CMOQLMT [14] | 11 | 0.4525 |
| KnEA [29] | 12 | 0.4683 |
| CMEGL [19] | 13 | 0.4850 |
| MSCEA [30] | 14 | 0.5183 |
| EMCMO [21] | 15 | 0.5325 |
| RVEA [1] | 16 | 0.5392 |
| ToP [11] | 17 | 0.5508 |
| TiGE2 [31] | 18 | 0.5542 |
| RVEAa [1] | 19 | 0.6275 |
| DPPPS [15] | 20 | 0.6417 |
| MCCMO [32] | 21 | 0.6417 |
| MOCell [16] | 22 | 0.6567 |
| TPCMaO [25] | 23 | 0.6933 |
| CMOEAD [2] | 24 | 0.8175 |
| MOEADD [7] | 25 | 0.9083 |

## 4   Conclusion

In this study, we conducted an extensive benchmarking of twenty-five meta-heuristic algorithms on a newly curated suite of fifty Real-World Constrained Multi-objective Optimization Problems (RWCMOPs). Unlike most prior works that rely heavily on synthetic benchmark problems, our analysis offers insights grounded in real-world problem characteristics. Algorithms were evaluated using three performance indicators: Hypervolume (HV), Feasibility Rate (FR), and Total Wall-Clock Time, and ranked through a multi-indicator statistical framework. The findings reveal that several classical algorithms, such as NSGA-II and GDE3, consistently outperform many recent methods when applied to real-world problems. This suggests that algorithm performance on synthetic problems may not generalize well to practical contexts, underscoring the need for more comprehensive empirical evaluations. The proposed benchmarking approach provides practitioners with a more realistic guide for algorithm selection. However, certain limitations must be acknowledged: the ranking sensitivity to the order of performance indicators was not extensively explored; future studies should consider ablation or sensitivity analysis. The strength of the proposed method lies in its practical relevance and comprehensive evaluation methodology. At the same time, its primary limitation is the absence of an analysis on the robustness of the ranking procedure under different configurations.

# References


1. Cheng, R., Jin, Y., Olhofer, M., Sendhoff, B.: A reference vector guided evolutionary algorithm for many-objective optimization. IEEE Trans. Evol. Comput. **20**(5), 773–791 (2016)
2. Deb, K., Jain, H.: An evolutionary many-objective optimization algorithm using reference-point-based nondominated sorting approach, part i: solving problems with box constraints. IEEE Trans. Evol. Comput. **18**(4), 577–601 (2013)
3. Deb, K., Pratap, A., Agarwal, S., Meyarivan, T.: A fast and elitist multiobjective genetic algorithm: NSGA-II. IEEE Trans. Evol. Comput. **6**(2), 182–197 (2002)
4. Hussain, K., Mohd Salleh, M.N., Cheng, S., Shi, Y.: Metaheuristic research: a comprehensive survey. Artif. Intell. Rev. **52**, 2191–2233 (2019)
5. Kukkonen, S., Lampinen, J.: GDE3: the third evolution step of generalized differential evolution. In: 2005 IEEE Congress on Evolutionary Computation, vol. 1, pp. 443–450. IEEE (2005)
6. Kumar, A., et al.: A benchmark-suite of real-world constrained multi-objective optimization problems and some baseline results. Swarm Evol. Comput. **67**, 100961 (2021)
7. Li, K., Deb, K., Zhang, Q., Kwong, S.: An evolutionary many-objective optimization algorithm based on dominance and decomposition. IEEE Trans. Evol. Comput. **19**(5), 694–716 (2014)
8. Li, S., Li, K., Li, W., Yang, M.: Evolutionary alternating direction method of multipliers for constrained multiobjective optimization with unknown constraints. IEEE Trans. Evol. Comput. **29**(4), 1419–1433 (2025)
9. Liang, J., et al.: Utilizing the relationship between unconstrained and constrained pareto fronts for constrained multiobjective optimization. IEEE Trans. Cybern. **53**(6), 3873–3886 (2022)
10. Liao, J., Melethil Sethumadhavan, S., Ke, R., Gao, Z.M., Zhao, J.: A leaded sine-cosine artificial protozoa optimizer algorithm for solving multi-objective optimization problems. Clust. Comput. **28**(5), 304 (2025)
11. Liu, Z.Z., Wang, Y.: Handling constrained multiobjective optimization problems with constraints in both the decision and objective spaces. IEEE Trans. Evol. Comput. **23**(5), 870–884 (2019)
12. Liu, Z.Z., Wang, Y., Huang, P.Q.: AnD: a many-objective evolutionary algorithm with angle-based selection and shift-based density estimation. Inf. Sci. **509**, 400–419 (2020)
13. Ma, Z., Wu, G., Suganthan, P.N., Song, A., Luo, Q.: Performance assessment and exhaustive listing of 500+ nature-inspired metaheuristic algorithms. Swarm Evol. Comput. **77**, 101248 (2023)

14. Ming, F., Gong, W., Gao, L.: Adaptive auxiliary task selection for multitasking-assisted constrained multi-objective optimization [feature]. IEEE Comput. Intell. Mag. **18**(2), 18–30 (2023)
15. Ming, F., Gong, W., Wang, L., Lu, C.: A tri-population based co-evolutionary framework for constrained multi-objective optimization problems. Swarm Evol. Comput. **70**, 101055 (2022)
16. Nebro, A.J., Durillo, J.J., Luna, F., Dorronsoro, B., Alba, E.: MOCell: a cellular genetic algorithm for multiobjective optimization. Int. J. Intell. Syst. **24**(7), 726–746 (2009)
17. Osaba, E., et al.: A tutorial on the design, experimentation and application of metaheuristic algorithms to real-world optimization problems. Swarm Evol. Comput. **64**, 100888 (2021)
18. Palakonda, V., Kang, J.M., Jung, H.: Benchmarking real-world many-objective problems: a problem suite with baseline results. IEEE Access **12**, 49275–49290 (2024)
19. Qiao, K., Liang, J., Liu, Z., Yu, K., Yue, C., Qu, B.: Evolutionary multitasking with global and local auxiliary tasks for constrained multi-objective optimization. IEEE/CAA J. Automatica Sinica **10**(10), 1951–1964 (2023)
20. Qiao, K., et al.: Evolutionary constrained multiobjective optimization: scalable high-dimensional constraint benchmarks and algorithm. IEEE Trans. Evol. Comput. (2023)
21. Qiao, K., Yu, K., Qu, B., Liang, J., Song, H., Yue, C.: An evolutionary multitasking optimization framework for constrained multiobjective optimization problems. IEEE Trans. Evol. Comput. **26**(2), 263–277 (2022)
22. Qiao, K., et al.: Dynamic auxiliary task-based evolutionary multitasking for constrained multiobjective optimization. IEEE Trans. Evol. Comput. **27**(3), 642–656 (2022)
23. Sala, R., Müller, R.: Benchmarking for metaheuristic black-box optimization: perspectives and open challenges. In: 2020 IEEE Congress on Evolutionary Computation (CEC), pp. 1–8. IEEE (2020)
24. Tian, Y., Cheng, R., Zhang, X., Cheng, F., Jin, Y.: An indicator-based multiobjective evolutionary algorithm with reference point adaptation for better versatility. IEEE Trans. Evol. Comput. **22**(4), 609–622 (2017)
25. Tian, Y., Shi, Z., Zhang, Y., Zhang, L., Zhang, H., Zhang, X.: Solving optimal power flow problems via a constrained many-objective co-evolutionary algorithm. Front. Energy Res. **11**, 1293193 (2023)
26. Tian, Y., Zhang, T., Xiao, J., Zhang, X., Jin, Y.: A coevolutionary framework for constrained multiobjective optimization problems. IEEE Trans. Evol. Comput. **25**(1), 102–116 (2020)
27. Wolpert, D.H., Macready, W.G.: No free lunch theorems for optimization. IEEE Trans. Evol. Comput. **1**(1), 67–82 (1997)
28. Zapotecas-Martínez, S., Coello, C.A.C., Aguirre, H.E., Tanaka, K.: A review of features and limitations of existing scalable multiobjective test suites. IEEE Trans. Evol. Comput. **23**(1), 130–142 (2018)
29. Zhang, X., Tian, Y., Jin, Y.: A knee point-driven evolutionary algorithm for many-objective optimization. IEEE Trans. Evol. Comput. **19**(6), 761–776 (2014)
30. Zhang, Y., Tian, Y., Jiang, H., Zhang, X., Jin, Y.: Design and analysis of helper-problem-assisted evolutionary algorithm for constrained multiobjective optimization. Inf. Sci. **648**, 119547 (2023)

31. Zhou, Y., Zhu, M., Wang, J., Zhang, Z., Xiang, Y., Zhang, J.: Tri-goal evolution framework for constrained many-objective optimization. IEEE Trans. Syst. Man Cybern. Syst. **50**(8), 3086–3099 (2018)
32. Zou, J., et al.: A multipopulation evolutionary algorithm using new cooperative mechanism for solving multiobjective problems with multiconstraint. IEEE Trans. Evol. Comput. **28**(1), 267–280 (2023)

# Granular Computing Based Fuzzy Classifier for Tensor Data Classification


Reshma Rastogi$^{(\boxtimes)}$ and Abhijeet Kumar

Machine Learning and Statistical Inference Lab Department of Computer Science and Engineering, South Asian University, New Delhi 110068, Delhi, India
`reshma.khemchandani@sau.ac.in`



**Abstract.** Tensor based data classification has become increasingly popular in the domain of computer vision and face recognition, as the vector based model suffers from data topology and time efficiency due to the number of training parameters, which increases exponentially. Tensor-based model effectively utilizes the structural information inherent in the multidimensional features of an object. In order to enhance tensor model performance, variants of the Support tensor machines have been used in the past for tensor data classification. In our proposed approach, we have introduced the concept of granularity, for the development of the Granular Proximal Support Tensor Machine (GBPSTM), which leverages the granular ball generation method to form compact and meaningful representations of data, thereby improving classification performance and computational efficiency. Furthermore, to enhance robustness against noise and uncertainty, we incorporate fuzzy logic through an intuitionistic fuzzy approach, resulting in the Granular Ball Intuitionistic Fuzzy Proximal Support Tensor Machine (GBFPSTM). The effectiveness of the proposed models has been demonstrated through simulations on face detection and handwriting recognition datasets.

**Keywords:** Proximal Support Tensor machine · Alternating projection · Proximal Support Vector machine


## 1 Introduction

In the machine learning community, high-dimensional image data sets with many attributes are commonly observed in real-world applications. The representation and selection of features have a significant impact on classification performance. Therefore, efficient representation of image data remains a fundamental challenge in classifier model design. Traditionally, most classification algorithms are built on the vector space model (VSM), such as support vector machines (SVM) [2], proximal support vector machines (PSVM) [3], and twin SVM [4]. Although these models have shown utility in many applications [5,6,9] but rely on vectorized data input, which fails to preserve the inherent spatial structure of image data.

PSVM, unlike SVM, solves a system of linear equations rather than a quadratic programming problem, making it computationally more efficient.



S. Mitra et al. (Eds.): PReMI 2025, LNCS 16358, pp. 118–126, 2026.
https://doi.org/10.1007/978-3-032-18480-1_12

However, PSVM still suffers from the limitations of VSM, especially in high-dimensional settings where each pixel is treated as a separate feature. For instance, a $64 \times 64$ image becomes a 4096-dimensional vector, increasing computational cost and losing spatial correlations. Furthermore, these models are sensitive to noise and outliers, and their effectiveness may degrade when training data is limited or uncertain.

To address these limitations, tensor-based methods like Support Tensor Machines (STM) [1,7] have been proposed to handle tensor inputs directly, preserving the data's multidimensional structure, reducing overfitting, and improving generalization. Building on this, the Proximal Support Tensor Machine (PSTM) extends STM via a least-squares formulation, enabling efficient iterative solutions for high-dimensional problems, especially in image classification and small sample size (S3) scenarios.

While deep learning models, particularly CNNs, excel at image classification, they require large-sized datasets, substantial computational resources, and careful parameter tuning. Moreover, their black-box nature limits the interpretation and robustness against noisy or ambiguous data. In contrast, our proposed model offers a more interpretable and noise-resilient solution with fewer hyperparameters, making it well-suited for small-scale or uncertain environments where deep learning may struggle.

In this paper, we extend the Proximal Support Tensor Machine (PSTM) by incorporating granular ball computing [8], resulting in the **Granular Ball Proximal Support Tensor Machine (GBPSTM)**. This approach leverages granular balls to form compact, noise-tolerant representations of tensor data, enhancing both efficiency and accuracy. Furthermore, we integrate intuitionistic fuzzy sets into GBPSTM, leading to the **Granular Ball Intuitionistic Fuzzy Proximal Support Tensor Machine (GBFPSTM)**. By modeling membership, non-membership, and hesitation, GBFPSTM captures uncertainty more effectively, improving robustness and classification performance on noisy, high-dimensional data through fuzzy scoring within the granular ball framework.

## 2   Proximal Support Tensor Machine (PSTM)

The Proximal Support Tensor Machine (PSTM) is a tensor-based extension of the Proximal Support Vector Machine (PSVM) proposed by Khemchandani et al. [4]. Designed for classification tasks where data are naturally represented as second-order tensors, PSTM generalizes PSVM to the tensor space using a bilinear decision function of the form $f(X) = u^\top X v + b$, where $X \in \mathbb{R}^{n_1 \times n_2}$ is the input tensor, $u \in \mathbb{R}^{n_1}$, $v \in \mathbb{R}^{n_2}$, and $b \in \mathbb{R}$ are learnable parameters. Given a training set $\{(X_i, y_i)\}_{i=1}^{m}$, where $y_i \in \{-1, +1\}$, PSTM aims to learn two parallel hyperplanes in tensor space such that each class lies close to one of them, while minimizing the empirical loss via a least squares approach.

The training procedure alternates between updating $v$ (with $u$ fixed) and updating $u$ (with $v$ fixed). When the vector $u$ is fixed, each tensor $X_i$ is projected to a vector $x_i = X_i^\top u$, and the stacked matrix $X \in \mathbb{R}^{m \times n_2}$ is formed with rows

$x_i^\top$. Letting $D = \operatorname{diag}(y_1, \ldots, y_m)$, $e \in \mathbb{R}^m$ be the all-ones vector, and $\beta_1 = \|u\|^2$, the parameters $v$, $b$, and slack variable $q$ are obtained by solving the regularized least-squares problem:

$$\min_{v,b,q} \frac{1}{2}\beta_1\|v\|^2 + \frac{1}{2}b^2 + \frac{C}{2}\|q\|^2 \quad \text{s.t.} \quad D(Xv + eb) + q = e.$$

Next, with $v$ fixed, each tensor $X_i$ is projected as $\tilde{x}_i = X_i v$, and the corresponding matrix $\tilde{X} \in \mathbb{R}^{m \times n_1}$ is formed with rows $\tilde{x}_i^\top$. Letting $\beta_2 = \|v\|^2$, the vector $u$, bias $b$, and slack variable $p$ are updated by solving:

$$\min_{u,b,p} \frac{1}{2}\beta_2\|u\|^2 + \frac{1}{2}b^2 + \frac{C}{2}\|p\|^2 \quad \text{s.t.} \quad D(\tilde{X}u + eb) + p = e.$$

This alternating optimization continues until convergence, typically measured by the relative changes in $u$, $v$, and $b$ falling below a predefined threshold. The final learned parameters define the decision function $f(X) = u^\top X v + b$, which can be used for classification of unseen tensor data.

## 3   Granular Ball Regularized Fuzzy PSTM

Working along Proximal Support Tensor Machine (PSTM) framework, we propose a novel extension that integrates Granular Ball (GB) clustering to exploit local geometric structures within the tensor space. This section elaborates on the proposed method, starting with tensor compression, followed by GB-based feature representation, and ending with an alternating optimization scheme for classifier training.

A **Granular Ball (GB)** is a compact cluster of data points in granular computing, defined by its center $\mu_j$ and radius $\rho_j$. For a set of points in $GB_j$:

$$\mu_j = \frac{1}{|GB_j|} \sum_{x \in GB_j} x \quad \text{(center)}, \qquad \rho_j = \max_{x \in GB_j} |x - \mu_j| \quad \text{(radius)}.$$

Here, $\mu_j$ is the mean of the points, and $\rho_j$ is their maximum distance from $\mu_j$, summarizing the granular ball's location and spread.

Tensor samples $\mathcal{X}_i$ are compressed via Tucker decomposition using orthogonal projections $\mathbf{U}^{(n)}$, yielding low-dimensional core tensors $\hat{\mathcal{X}}_i$ that are vectorized into $\hat{x}_i$ for downstream processing like granular ball clustering.

Vectorized data $\hat{x}_i$ are clustered into $k$ granular balls $GB_j$, each represented by its center $\hat{C}_j = \mu_j$ and majority label $\hat{y}_j$, forming a transformed dataset for input to the PSTM model.

Building on this framework, we introduce the granular ball intuitionistic fuzzy proximal support tensor machine (GBFPSTM) a novel classification model that combines granular computing with intuitionistic fuzzy logic to improve robustness and accuracy in the tensor space. In this approach, each tensor sample is evaluated using three components of intuitionistic fuzzy theory: the **membership function**, the **non-membership function**, and the **degree of hesitation**.

By adaptively selecting the maximum membership and non-membership values, GBFPSTM emphasizes informative samples and suppresses noisy or ambiguous data points. This selective fuzzy weighting significantly improves classification performance and robustness.

To effectively handle uncertainty in high-dimensional tensor spaces, the Granular Ball Intuitionistic Fuzzy Proximal Support Tensor Machine (GBFPSTM) employs the core principles of intuitionistic fuzzy theory: the membership function, non-membership function, and score function. The computation of these functions is critical to ensure accurate classification, especially in noisy or ambiguous environments.

*1. Membership Function:* The membership function quantifies how close a training sample is to its class center in the projected feature space. For each $i^{\text{th}}$ training sample $x_i$, its membership value $\lambda(x_i)$ is defined as:

$$\lambda(x_i) = \begin{cases} 1 - \frac{\|x_i - C^+\|}{r^+ + \gamma}, & y_i = +1, \\ 1 - \frac{\|x_i - C^-\|}{r^- + \gamma}, & y_i = -1, \end{cases} \tag{1}$$

Here, $\gamma \geq 0$ ensures numerical stability, while $r^+$ and $r^-$ are class-specific radii defined as:

$$r^+ = \max_{y=+1} \|x_i - C^+\|, \quad r^- = \max_{y=-1} \|x_i - C^-\|. \tag{2}$$

Class centers $C^+$ and $C^-$ are given by:

$$C^+ = \frac{1}{m_1} \sum_{y=+1} x_i, \quad C^- = \frac{1}{m_2} \sum_{y=-1} x_i, \tag{3}$$

where $m_1$ and $m_2$ are the sample counts for classes $+1$ and $-1$, respectively.

Samples near their class center receive higher $\lambda(x_i)$ values, while outliers or boundary points receive lower ones, indicating their representativeness within the class.

*2. Non-Membership Function:* The non-membership function measures the proportion of heterogeneous points in the local neighborhood of $x_i$ and is defined as:

$$\nu(x_i) = (1 - \lambda(x_i))\eta(x_i) \tag{4}$$

The neighborhood term $\eta(x_i)$ is given by:

$$\eta(x_i) = \frac{|\{x_j : \|x_j - x_i\| \leq \beta, \, y_j \neq y_i\}|}{|\{x_j : \|x_j - x_i\| \leq \beta\}|} \tag{5}$$

where $\beta$ is a threshold parameter and $|\cdot|$ denotes set cardinality.

Here, $\lambda(x_i)$ reflects the local membership of $x_i$, while $\eta(x_i)$ captures the proportion of neighboring points from different classes. Thus, $\nu(x_i)$ highlights non-membership when $x_i$ is weakly associated with its class and surrounded by heterogeneous samples.

3. *Score Function:* The score function $s_i$ combines membership and non-membership to assess the reliability of each training sample:

$$s_i = \begin{cases} \lambda_i, & \nu_i = 0, \\ 0, & \lambda_i \leq \nu_i, \\ \frac{1-\nu_i}{2-\lambda_i-\nu_i}, & \text{otherwise.} \end{cases} \tag{6}$$

The score matrix for dataset $D$ is defined as:

$$S = \text{diag}(s(x_i) \mid i = 1, 2, \ldots, m) \tag{7}$$

If all scores are one ($S = I$, where $I$ is the identity matrix), GBFPSTM reduces to GBPSTM. This scoring mechanism filters out noisy or ambiguous samples, assigning greater importance to informative ones and enhancing robustness and interpretability.

Let $X \in \mathbb{R}^{n_1 \times n_2}$ be a tensor data; $u \in \mathbb{R}^{n_1}$, $v \in \mathbb{R}^{n_2}$ are projection vectors; $y_i \in \{\pm 1\}$ are class labels; $b \in \mathbb{R}$ is a bias term; $q_i \in \mathbb{R}$ are slack variables; and $C > 0$ is the regularization parameter, $S_i$ is the fuzzy score associated with each tensor data point. Define $\bar{X}_i = X_i v$, $\tilde{x}_i = X_i^T u$, $D = \text{diag}(y_1, \ldots, y_m)$, and $e \in \mathbb{R}^m$ as a vector of ones.

$$f(X) = \text{sign}(u^T X v + b) \tag{8}$$

$$\min_{u,v,b,q} \tfrac{1}{2}\|uv^T\|^2 + \tfrac{1}{2}b^2 + \tfrac{CS}{2}q^T q \quad \text{s.t.} \quad y_i(u^T X_i v + b) + q_i = 1, i = 1, \ldots, n \tag{9}$$

From the primal problem in Eq. 9, we derive the Lagrangian:

$$L = \tfrac{1}{2}(v^T v)(u^T u) + \tfrac{1}{2}b^2 + \tfrac{CS}{2}q^T q - \sum \alpha_i y_i(u^T X_i v + b) + \sum \alpha_i(1 - q_i) \tag{10}$$

The KKT optimality conditions from Eq. 10 yield:

$$u = \frac{\sum \alpha_i y_i X_i v}{v^T v}, \quad v = \frac{\sum \alpha_i y_i X_i^T u}{u^T u}, \quad b = \sum \alpha_i y_i, \quad q_i = \frac{\alpha_i}{C} \tag{11}$$

With $u$ fixed, the subproblem in $v$ becomes:

$$\min_{v,b,q} \tfrac{1}{2}\beta_1 v^T v + \tfrac{1}{2}b^2 + \tfrac{CS}{2}q^T q \quad \text{s.t.} \quad D(Xv + be) + q = e, \quad \beta_1 = \|u\|^2 \tag{12}$$

Using granular ball generation and reducing the projected data ($X$) into granular balls $GB_i = \{(\hat{C}_i, \hat{y}_i, \theta_i); i = 1, \ldots, k\}$, where $\hat{C}$ are the centers and $\hat{y}$ is the labels of the granular ball and $\theta_i$ is the average score of all the points in the granular ball. $\bar{D}$ is a diagonal matrix with $\bar{D}_{ii} = \hat{y}_i, i = 1, \ldots, k$, the new optimization equation for $u$ is

$$\min_{v,b,q} \tfrac{1}{2}\beta_1 v^T v + \tfrac{1}{2}b^2 + \tfrac{C\theta}{2}q^T q \quad \text{s.t.} \ \bar{D}(\hat{C}v + be) + q = e, \quad \beta_1 = \|u\|^2 \tag{13}$$

$$\beta_1 v = \hat{C}^T \bar{D}\alpha, \quad b = e^T \bar{D}\alpha, \quad q = \tfrac{\alpha}{C} \tag{14}$$

Substituting the values of $v$, $b$ and $q$ in the equality constraints i.e. equation (13) leads to following systems of equations:

$$\left[\tfrac{\bar{D}\hat{C}\hat{C}^T D}{\beta_1} + \bar{D}ee^T\bar{D} + \tfrac{I}{C\theta}\right]\alpha = e, \quad \alpha = G_v^{-1}e \tag{15}$$

Using the matrix form:

$$G_v = H_v H_v^T + \tfrac{I}{C\theta}, \quad H_v = \left[\tfrac{\bar{D}\hat{C}}{\sqrt{\beta_1}} \ \ \bar{D}e\right] \tag{16}$$

Efficient inversion using Shermann-woodbury formula:

$$G_v^{-1} = (C\theta)I - (C\theta)^2 H_v (I + C\theta H_v^T H_v)^{-1} H_v^T \tag{17}$$

$$\alpha = G_v^{-1}e \tag{18}$$

Once $\alpha$ is obtain $v$ and $b$ can be solved using equation (14) Once $v$ is obtained, we proceed to solve the $u$-subproblem by fixing $v$ and defining $\beta_2 = \|v\|^2$. The granular ball formulation for the $u$-stage is given by:

$$\min_{u,b,p} \tfrac{1}{2}\beta_2 u^T u + \tfrac{1}{2}b^2 + \tfrac{CS}{2}p^T p \quad \text{s.t.} \ \ D(\bar{X}u + be) + p = e \tag{19}$$

Using granular ball generation and reducing the projected data ($\bar{X}$) into granular balls $GB_i = \{(\hat{C}_{1i}, \hat{y}_i); i = 1, \ldots, k\}$, where $\hat{C}_1$ are the centers and $\hat{y}_1$ is the labels of the granular ball and $\theta_i$ is the average score of all the points in the granular ball. $\bar{D}_1$ is a diagonal matrix with $\bar{D}_{1ii} = \hat{y}_i, i = 1, \ldots, k$, the new optimization equation for u is

$$\min_{u,b,p} \tfrac{1}{2}\beta_2 u^T u + \tfrac{1}{2}b^2 + \tfrac{C\theta}{2}p^T p \quad \text{s.t.} \ \ \bar{D}_1(\hat{C}_1\theta u + be) + p = e \tag{20}$$

The solution again follows the dual approach. Let $H_u = \left[\tfrac{\bar{D}_1\hat{C}_1}{\sqrt{\beta_2}} \ \ \bar{D}_1 e\right]$, then the dual system is:

$$G_u = H_u H_u^T + \tfrac{I}{C\theta}, \quad \beta = G_u^{-1}e \tag{21}$$

and the primal variables are recovered using:

$$\beta_2 u = \hat{C}_1^T \bar{D}_1\beta, \quad b = e^T \bar{D}_1\beta, \quad p = \tfrac{\beta}{C\theta} \tag{22}$$

**Table 1.** Performance (Accuracy/Time in seconds) on CMU Face, ORL, and MNIST Datasets

**CMU Face Dataset**

| Input | PSTM | GBPSTM | GBFPSTM |
|---|---|---|---|
| (2,8) | 87 (0.0013) | 86 (0.0009) | **88** (0.0013) |
| (4,18) | 86 (0.0013) | **100** (0.0012) | 94 (0.0006) |
| (6,10) | 90 (0.001) | **100** (0.0012) | **100** (0.0009) |
| (15,10) | 90 (0.0013) | **100** (0.0012) | **100** (0.0009) |
| (19,13) | 83 (0.0013) | **85** (0.0012) | 75 (0.0005) |
| (19,18) | 74 (0.0014) | **100** (0.0009) | **100** (0.0009) |
| (6,19) | 88 (0.0013) | 91 (0.0009) | **100** (0.0009) |
| (1,19) | 70 (0.0013) | 89 (0.0009) | **95** (0.0009) |

**ORL Dataset**

| Input | PSTM | GBPSTM | GBFPSTM |
|---|---|---|---|
| (9,26) | **100** (0.0010) | **100** (0.0009) | **100** (0.001) |
| (10,26) | **100** (0.0010) | **100** (0.0010) | 92 (0.001) |
| (8,24) | **100**(0.0011) | 75 (0.0010) | 75 (0.001) |
| (21,39) | **100** (0.0010) | **100** (0.0009) | 93 (0.001) |
| (1,32) | **100** (0.0010) | **100** (0.0009) | **100** (0.001) |
| (13,22) | **100** (0.0009) | **100** (0.0010) | **100** (0.0009) |
| (13,34) | **100** ( 0.0010) | **100** (0.0010) | **100** (0.001) |
| (28,37) | 75 (0.0010) | **100** (0.0008) | 87.5 (0.001) |
| (6,20) | **100** (0.0010) | **100** (0.0010) | **100** (0.001) |

**MNIST Dataset**

| Input | PSTM | GBPSTM | GBFPSTM |
|---|---|---|---|
| (0,7) | 63 (0.0029) | **97** (0.002) | **97** (0.0017) |
| (1,9) | 53 (0.0029) | **98.7** (0.001) | 95 (0.0024) |
| (2,4) | 52 (0.0027) | 95.6 (0.002) | **96** (0.0025) |
| (3,9) | 47 (0.0028) | **96** (0.001) | **96** (0.0019) |
| (4,7) | 47 (0.0029) | 92 (0.002) | **93** (0.0018) |
| (6,8) | 50 (0.0027) | **98** (0.002) | 95 (0.0019) |
| (8,9) | 52 (0.0025) | **93** (0.002) | **96** (0.0021) |
| (5,6) | 52 (0.0025) | **95** (0.002) | 95 (0.0020) |

## 4    Experiments and Results

To evaluate the performance of the proposed models, experiments were conducted on three benchmark image datasets: ORL Faces (facial recognition), CMU Face (frontal face classification), and MNIST (optical digit recognition). Accuracy and training time were the primary evaluation metrics, comparing the proposed methods against the baseline PSTM.

Geometric normalization was omitted since the datasets were already well-aligned. Instead, photometric normalization was applied to standardize lighting and contrast, enhancing consistency in image intensities and reducing lighting-related discrepancies that could hinder recognition performance.

All experiments were implemented in Python 3.13 on a Windows machine with a 3.20 GHz CPU and 16 GB RAM.

**ORL Dataset.**

The ORL dataset contains 10 grayscale images each of 40 subjects ($92 \times 112$ pixels), with variations in expressions and details. As shown in Table 1, the proposed granular ball-based models (GBPSTM and GBFPSTM) outperform PSTM in accuracy, even with limited training samples, demonstrating their effectiveness in feature capture.

**CMU Face Dataset.**

The CMU dataset consists of grayscale facial images under varying lighting and pose conditions. Experiments on selected class pairs show that granular ball-based methods achieve higher or comparable accuracy to PSTM, especially on challenging subsets, validating their robustness and generalizability.

**MNIST Dataset.**
The MNIST dataset includes 70,000 grayscale images of handwritten digits (0–9, 28×28 pixels). Binary classification on specific digit pairs demonstrates the granular ball models' superior or competitive accuracy, highlighting their ability to capture fine decision boundaries in high-variance datasets.

Overall, Table 1 shows the proposed methods consistently outperform PSTM, particularly under data scarcity, validating the effectiveness of granular ball modeling in pattern recognition.

## 5  Conclusion

This paper introduced a series of tensor-based classification models designed to improve image recognition performance, particularly in scenarios involving high-dimensional, noisy, or limited data. Beginning with the Proximal Support Tensor Machine (PSTM), we progressively enhanced its capabilities through the incorporation of granular ball representations (GBPSTM), and ultimately, intuitionistic fuzzy logic (GBFPSTM). Each extension addressed specific limitations of previous models, such as sensitivity to noise, computational inefficiency, or lack of uncertainty handling.

The model, GBFPSTM, combines the strengths of granular computing and fuzzy logic to provide a robust, interpretable, and computationally efficient framework for tensor-based classification. Experimental results on benchmark datasets ORL, CMU Face and MNIST demonstrate the superior performance of the proposed models over the baseline PSTM, particularly in challenging conditions such as small sample sizes or ambiguous data.

These findings validate the effectiveness of integrating structural, granular, and fuzzy perspectives into tensor learning and open promising avenues for future research in interpretable and robust machine learning.

## References


1. Cai, D., He, X., Wen, J.R., Han, J., Ma, W.Y.: Support tensor machines for text categorization (2006)
2. Cristianini, N., Scholkopf, B.: Support vector machines and kernel methods: the new generation of learning machines. AI Mag. **23**(3), 31–31 (2002)
3. Fung, G., Mangasarian, O.L.: Proximal support vector machine classifiers. In: Proceedings of the seventh ACM SIGKDD International Conference on Knowledge Discovery And Data Mining, pp. 77–86 (2001)
4. Khemchandani, R., Karpatne, A., Chandra, S.: Proximal support tensor machines. Int. J. Mach. Learn. Cybern. **4**, 703–712 (2013)
5. Liu, Z., Wu, Q., Zhang, Y., Philip Chen, C.: Adaptive least squares support vector machines filter for hand tremor canceling in microsurgery. Int. J. Mach. Learn. Cybern. **2**, 37–47 (2011)
6. Maulik, U., Chakraborty, D.: A novel semisupervised svm for pixel classification of remote sensing imagery. Int. J. Mach. Learn. Cybern. **3**, 247–258 (2012)

7. Tao, D., Li, X., Hu, W., Maybank, S., Wu, X.: Supervised tensor learning. In: Fifth IEEE International Conference on Data Mining (ICDM'05), pp. 8–pp. IEEE (2005)
8. Xia, S., Lian, X., Wang, G., Gao, X., Chen, J., Peng, X.: GBSVM: an efficient and robust support vector machine framework via granular-ball computing. IEEE Transactions on Neural Networks and Learning Systems (2024)
9. Xiao, J.Z., Wang, H.R., Yang, X.C., Gao, Z.: Multiple faults diagnosis in motion system based on SVM. Int. J. Mach. Learn. Cybern. **3**, 77–82 (2012)

# From Specialists to Generalist Soft Robots: Evolving a Single Morphology and Controller Across Tasks


V. Sabarish and C. Shunmuga Velayutham

Department of Computer Science and Engineering, Amrita School of Computing, Coimbatore, Amrita Vishwa Vidyapeetham, India
`cs_velayutham@cb.amrita.edu`



**Abstract.** This study proposes a curriculum learning framework to evolve voxel-based soft robot morphologies and optimize their control to solve multiple tasks. Task mismatch as well as the catastrophic forgetting during control optimization present a significant challenge to realizing versatile robots across tasks. This work proposes a curriculum learning approach with sequential task learning and periodic task rotation to optimize the control of a given morphology for multiple tasks. Three EvoGym tasks viz. *Walker-v0*, *BridgeWalker-v0* and *DownStepper-v0* have been chosen for the MorphoEvolution experiments. A two as well as three Evo-Gym task combination scenarios have been used to evaluate the effectiveness of the proposed framework. The evolved morphologies demonstrated appropriate control optimized for the chosen scenario. The curriculum learning framework has been shown to demonstrate the potential for multi-task morphological evolution.

**Keywords:** Evolutionary Robotics · Multi-task MorphoEvolution · Voxel-based Soft Robots · Curriculum Learning


## 1  Introduction

Unlike Artificial Intelligence (AI), Embodied Artificial Intelligence (EAI) considers presence of a physical body and its interaction with environment as key contributors of intelligence [1]. The advent of biomimetic robots [2] and soft robots [3], especially voxel-based soft robots (VSRs) and the associated simulators [4,5], has fueled research on both the morphological and controller aspects in EAI. Since EAI dictates that intelligence emerges from interaction between body (morphology), brain (control) and environment, the automated design of both morphology and control of VSRs has been one of the predominant directions of research in EAI, particularly in Evolutionary Robotics (ER) [6,7].

The automated design of morphology and control is often framed as a bi-level optimization problem, where Evolutionary Algorithms (EAs) are primarily employed to evolve candidate morphologies, while Reinforcement Learning (RL) is used to optimize the control strategy for each candidate morphology. The



S. Mitra et al. (Eds.): PReMI 2025, LNCS 16358, pp. 127–135, 2026.
https://doi.org/10.1007/978-3-032-18480-1_13

evolved morphology-control combination of a VSR is then evaluated in a task environment. The availability of state-of-the-art simulators like EvoGym [4], 2D-VSR-Sim [5] etc. facilitate the above-mentioned MorphoEvolution (a term, henceforth, used for brevity to indicate both the evolution of morphology and the optimization of controller).

The ongoing research in MorphoEvolution has been focusing on a number of diverse key areas viz. the difficulty in co-optimization of morphology and control [8,9], the impact of underlying representation on design quality [10], use of alternative algorithms for MorphoEvolution [11], LLM-guided design of robots [12], transfer-learning of designed robots across tasks [13] to cite but a few examples. Interestingly, all these research directions predominantly evolve task-specific robots i.e. *Specialists* whose morphology-control combination is tailored for a single specific task. Designing robot morphology and control capable of solving multiple tasks (i.e. *Generalists*) has the potential to offer valuable insights into the MorphoEvolution problem itself as well as holds potential application value. In fact the constraints to adapt both morphology and control across tasks facilitate MorphoEvolution system to discover interesting and useful adaptations both at the morphological and behavioral levels.

This paper proposes to evolve generalist morphologies and controls, for VSRs in EvoGym simulator, capable of solving more than one task. The EA based morphology design and Proximal Policy Optimization (PPO) based control optimization has been retained as is. In fact the PPO has been augmented using *Curriculum Learning* with sequential task learning and task rotation to facilitate each candidate robot to learn across tasks. Three locomotion tasks viz. *Walker-v0*, *BridgeWalker-v0* and *DownStepper-v0* have been chosen for MorphoEvolution experiments.

This paper has been organized as follows. Section 2 provides a brief review of related works. Section 3 presents the curriculum learning augmented Morpho-Evolution used for evolving generalist robots. Section 4 details simulation results and analysis. Section 5, finally, concludes the work.

## 2    Related Works

Evolutionary Robotics primarily focuses on evolving robot morphology and optimizing its behavior using a bi-level optimization approach. Premature convergence of morphologies early in the evolutionary run, thus forcing the search to predominantly focus on control optimization for the remainder of the run, has been a significant challenge [8,9]. To address this challenge, direct and indirect representation of robot morphology [10], use of alternative search algorithms [11] etc. to cite few examples are being attempted in the literature. LLMs have recently been employed as an intelligent search operator towards evolving robot morphology [12]. The transfer learning of designed robots for newer tasks is also being investigated [13].

It is worth mentioning that there have been very few works focus on evolving morphologies and control capable of solving multiple tasks. Robot morphologies have been evolved for two tasks viz. undirected locomotion and rotation in

[14,15]. The morphologies of the generalists (targeting two tasks) were found to be more elongated than specialists (targeting one task). It has also been observed that the difficulty in evolving generalists resulted in performance drop on harder tasks. However, the task environments used in [14,15] were much simpler compared to the EvoGym tasks used in this paper. In fact, the terms *specialists* and *generalists* used in this paper have been adopted from [14,15].

Robot morphologies have been evolved for two and three EvoGym tasks in [16] that evolved single morphology and *task-specific* controllers for the task constituents in the task combination. Both locomotion and object manipulation tasks have been used for evaluation. Interesting and unique morphological and behavioral adaptations have been reported. The work also suggests multi-task MorphoEvolution as a potential framework to study the premature convergence of morphologies.

Unlike [16], the proposed work focus on evolving single morphology and single control for multiple tasks. The mismatch in tasks description is a significant challenge to evolve single controller for multiple tasks. There have been very few works attempting to address the task mismatch challenge for control optimization. This work proposes to employ curriculum learning approach [17] with sequential task learning and periodic task rotation to optimize a single controller across tasks.

## 3   Curriculum Learning Framework for MorphoEvolution

Figure 1 shows the proposed curriculum learning framework for MorphoEvolution of generalists. The left part of the figure adopts the co-design algorithmic framework from EvoGym simulation system [4] as is, to contexualize the proposed system. The design optimization module of EvoGym has been adopted as is in the proposed framework. A Genetic Algorithm (GA) initializes and evolves a population of candidate robot morphologies using mutation and selection operators. As it goes with EvoGym, a robot morphology is a $5 \times 5$ matrix of voxel combinations from five categories of voxels viz. soft, rigid, vertical actuator, horizontal actuator and empty voxel. The EvoGym in fact, ensures the validity of candidate morphologies in terms of their voxel connectivity to avoid having fragmented or disjoint bodies.

Each candidate morphology is then subjected to control optimization. EvoGym employs Proximal Policy Optimization (PPO) algorithm to learn and optimize control for each candidate morphology for a given task as well as to implicitly evaluate the fitness (i.e. reward) of the given morphology (i.e. design) and control (i.e. action) combination. Unlike the current practice, as the proposed work intends to evolve generalist VSRs, the GA is expected to evolve versatile morphologies and the control optimization module is expected to learn and optimize control for such morphologies towards solving multiple tasks.

GAs can, in fact, be made resilient to complex fitness landscapes like the constraint of searching for *generalist* morphologies capable of solving multiple tasks. However, in case of PPO, the control policy is typically represented by

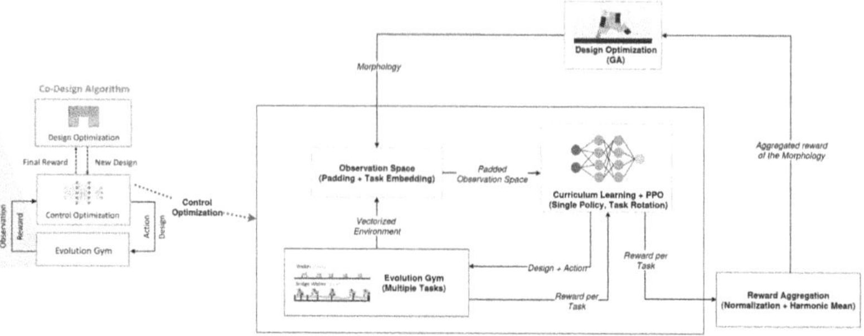

**Fig. 1.** Curriculum Learning based MorphoEvolution Framework. The Co-Design Algorithm sub-figure is adopted from [4].

a multi-layer perceptron (MLP). Consequently, once a policy is trained for a specific task it becomes difficult to train the same policy for a different task. In fact, the task-specific attributes along with robot state information and voxel states are captured in a structured data called *observation space* in EvoGym. A mismatch in the observation space makes it difficult to retrain an otherwise well-trained control policy for a different task. To overcome this challenge, observation space padding has been introduced. Before the training of PPO, Evo-Gym vectorizes observation space to provide it as input to the control policy. The vectorization of observation space has been padded to a default size of 100 enabling the MLP to handle more than one task. By default, since the observation space acts as the task identifier by virtue of their different dimensions, the proposed multi-task framework with uniformly padded observation space demands a separate task identifier. Considering three tasks scenario, the last three padded place holders have been employed for task embeddings. By way of an example, since this work employs at most three tasks, their task embeddings will be $[1.0, 0.0, 0.0]$, $[0.0, 1.0, 0.0]$ and $[0.0, 0.0, 1.0]$ respectively for *Walker-v0*, *BridgeWalker-v0* and *DownStepper-v0*.

Despite the fact that observation space padding and task embedding can facilitate the PPO to learn multiple tasks, inherently reinforcement learning tends to forget the previously learned tasks. To overcome this challenge, curriculum learning approach with sequential task learning and periodic task rotation has been employed. To be specific, considering the three tasks case, each candidate morphology is trained progressively i.e. *Walker-v0* → *BridgeWalker-v0* → *DownStepper-v0*. The training of each morphology on each task has been carried out for 512000 timesteps. So one round of curriculum learning involves training a candidate morphology on three tasks for 1536000 timesteps. The computational complexity of EvoGym (with GA for design optimization and PPO for control optimization) is $O(N \cdot P \cdot E \cdot S)$ where $N$ is the number of generations, $P$ the number of candidate morphologies in the population, $E$ the epochs in PPO and $S$ the samples in terms of timesteps. As the proposed curriculum learning framework for MorphoEvolution distributes the original PPO timesteps across the tasks, the computational complexity remains the same as that of EvoGym MorphoEvolution. After the curriculum learning augmented policy training, the reward or the performance of the candidate morphology-control combination for each task is evaluated by EvoGym. The rewards are then aggregated with *Harmonic Mean* to compute the fitness of the candidate morphology-control combination. Given $n$ tasks $t_1, t_2, \ldots, t_n$, the Harmonic Mean ($H$) is calculated as, $H(r_{t_1}, r_{t_2}, \ldots, r_{t_n}) = \frac{n}{\frac{1}{r_{t_1}} + \frac{1}{r_{t_2}} + \ldots + \frac{1}{r_{t_n}}}$. *Harmonic Mean* tends to give priority to the task with lower reward and ensure that the task with higher/highest reward does not dominate the fitness of a candidate morphology. In all the reported experiments, the aggregated rewards have been normalized.

## 4   Experiment Design, Simulation Results and Analyses

The curriculum learning based Framework for MorphoEvolution has been evaluated on both two tasks and three tasks scenarios. As indicated before, three locomotion tasks viz. *Walker-v0*, *BridgeWalker-v0* and *DownStepper-v0* have been chosen for the simulation studies. The proposed framework has been tested on *Walker+BridgeWalker* and *Walker+BridgeWalker+DownStepper* task combinations. The Curriculum Learning with task rotation has been applied for 2 rounds for both task combinations. The parameters, concerning the Design Optimization and Control Optimization modules, of EvoGym have been adopted as is. With a population size of 30 robots, the stopping criterion is defined as the completion of 780 robot evaluations. Considering the above mentioned robot evaluations as one run of MorphoEvolution, 3 runs each of both task combinations have been executed. The top performing robot(s) from each run have been reported in subsequent analysis.

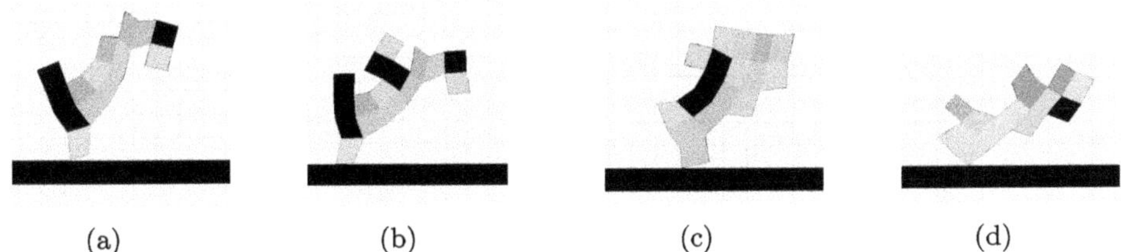

(a)          (b)          (c)          (d)

**Fig. 2.** Walker Morphologies Evolved for Three-task Scenario

Figure 2 shows the morphologies evolved for the three tasks combinations i.e. *Walker+BridgeWalker+DownStepper*. Except for Fig. 2(d), other morphologies share similarities in terms of having distinct legs and a body. In addition, all the morphologies are uniformly wide with legs far apart and their movement involves lifting the body and making a gallop. This distinct movement pattern is optimized predominantly for the *DownStepper* task, as such a movement let

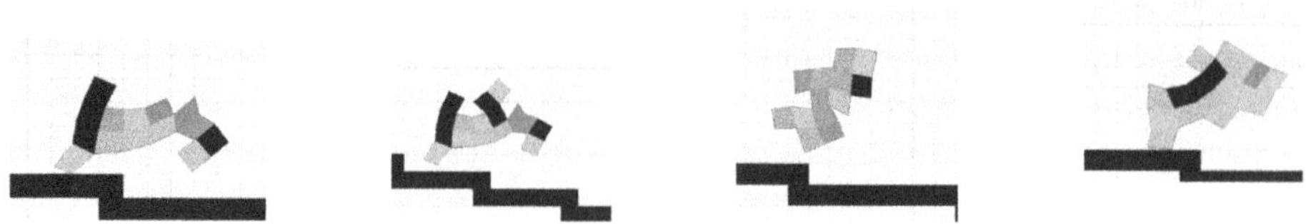

**Fig. 3.** Evolved Walker Morphologies Applied for DownStepper Task

the morphologies achieve longer steps to facilitate leap motion downwards along the stairs.

Figure 3 shows the evolved morphologies solving the *Downstepper* task. The advantage of body-lifting behavior by the morphologies is evident as the robots leap downwards along the stairs. The elongated and stable body with limbs facilitate all the robots to navigate the *BridgeWalker* task too. For the sake of brevity, the figures concerning *BridgeWalker* task has been omitted.

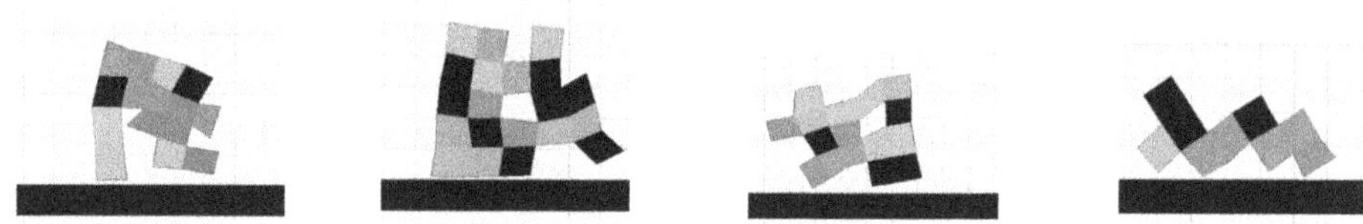

**Fig. 4.** Walker morphologies evolved for Two-task Experiments

**Table 1.** Performance Comparison between Single and Two-task Experiments

|  | *Walker* | *BridgeWalker* | *Walker+Bridgewalker* |
|---|---|---|---|
|  | 9.573 | 5.553 | 6.894 |
|  | 9.564 | 5.583 | 6.484 |
|  | 9.579 | 5.105 | 7.019 |
| **Avg.** | 9.572 | 5.413 | 6.799 |
| **Loss/** | 28.97% Loss (*Walker* vs *Walker+BridgeWalker*) | | |
| **Gain** | 25.60% Gain (*BridgeWalker* vs *Walker+BridgeWalker*) | | |

However, the morphologies evolved for *Walker+BridgeWalker* task combination as shown in Fig. 4, have large bases to support both Walking and Bridge-Walking. Interestingly, the lesser constraint (in terms of the task requirements) facilitates the GA to find diverse morphologies in case of two-task combinations. It is worth noting that the morphologies evolved for three tasks shared similarities as GA is constrained to find a viable morphology capable of working

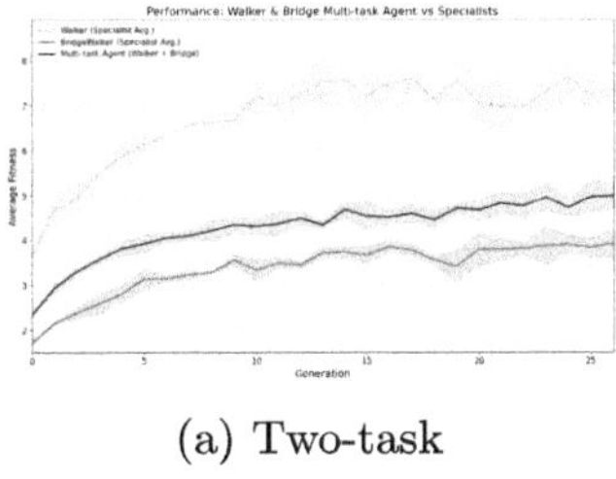

(a) Two-task

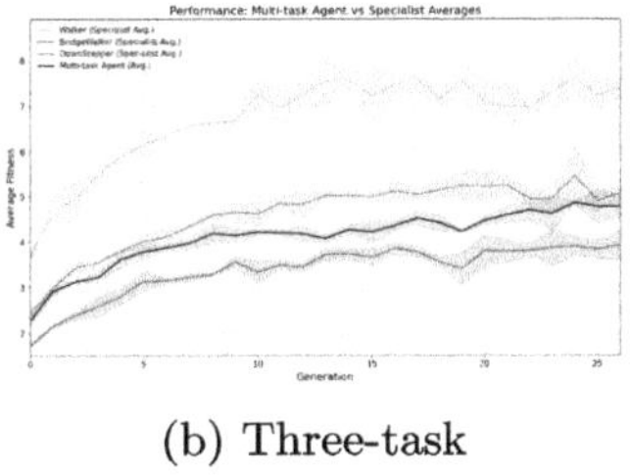

(b) Three-task

**Fig. 5.** Three runs averaged reward curves with variations in shaded regions

in all three task environments. In fact, the body-lifting pattern observed in the morphologies evolved for the three-task combination is not predominantly seen in those evolved for the two-task combination, as *DownStepper* is not included in the latter's task environments. The locomotion pattern optimized are largely galloping and ocassionally jittering.

Table 1 shows performance comparison between Walker+Bridgewalker experiments and their single task counterparts. The aggregated fitness of the best robot in each of the three runs has been presented in the table. As can been seen from the table, while there is a loss of performance in a simpler task (28.97% loss in walker) there is gain in performance in a relatively harder task (25.60% gain in BridgeWalker). Given the challenge of multiple tasks, MorphoEvolution delivered morphologies that focussed predominantly on the relatively harder task than on the simpler Walker Task.

Figure 5 shows the reward curves for both the two-task and three task combinations compared against MorphoEvolution for single tasks. In both the cases, the generalists have performed well against specialists on a harder task. It is not surprising that the unconstrained single-task MorphoEvolution displays better performance than the multi-task MorphoEvolution as the specialists will be more tailored to the task(s) at hand. The advantage of multi-task MorphoEvolution is, however, evident in case of harder tasks.

## 5   Conclusion

This paper proposes a curriculum learning framework for morphological evolution and control optimization of voxel-based soft robots across multiple tasks. Sequential task learning with periodic rotation mitigates catastrophic forgetting, while observation-space padding in the EvoGym simulator addresses task mismatch in multi-task training. The framework is evaluated on two task combinations: *Walker+BridgeWalker* and *Walker+BridgeWalker+DownStepper*.

The morphological and behavioral adaptations were evident in both the two-task and three-task scenarios. As the two-task scenario did not include *Down-Stepper*, the evolved morphologies have stable base to facilitate walking. However, the morphologies evolved in case of three-task scenario have elongated body as well as body-lifting pattern of control to leap the descending stairs of *Down-Stepper* task. Interestingly, as the three-task scenario pose stringent constraints, the evolved morphologies are largely similar. However, in case of two-task scenario, the evolved morphologies displayed diversity. In fact, experimenting with dissimilar tasks like combining locomotion and object manipulation as well as including harder tasks will provide more insights about the scalability of the curriculum learning framework. These would form the definite part of our future research work.

# References


1. Liu, Y., et al.: Aligning cyber space with physical world: A comprehensive survey on embodied AI. arXiv preprint arXiv:2407.06886 (2024)
2. Prakash, A., et al.: Bioinspiration and biomimetics in marine robotics: a review on current applications and future trends. Bioinspiration Biomimetics **19**(3) (2024)
3. Vidwath, S., Rohith, P., Dikshithaa, R., Suraj, N.N., Chittawadigi, R.G., Sambandham, M.: Soft robotic gripper for agricultural harvesting. In: Machines, Mechanism and Robotics. Lecture Notes in Mechanical Engineering. Springer (2022)
4. Bhatia, J., Jackson, H., Tian, Y., Xu, J., Matusik, W.: Evolution gym: a large-scale benchmark for evolving soft robots. In: Proceedings of Advances in Neural Information Processing Systems, vol. 34 (NeurIPS 2021), vol. 34, pp. 2201–2214 (2021)
5. Eric Medvet, Alberto Bartoli, A.D.L., Seriani, S.: 2D-VSR-Sim: a simulation tool for the optimization of 2-D voxel-based soft robots. SoftwareX **12** (2020)
6. Bongard, J.: Evolutionary robotics. Commun. ACM **56**(8), 74–83 (2013)
7. Doncieux, S., Bredeche, N., Mouret, J.B., Eiben, A.E.G.: Evolutionary robotics. Front. Robot. AI **2**, 74–83 (2015)
8. Cheney, N., Bongard, J., SunSpiral, V., Lipson, H.: On the difficulty of co-optimizing morphology and control in evolved virtual creatures. In: Proceedings of the Fifteenth International Conference on the Synthesis and Simulation of Living Systems ALIFE 2016, pp. 226–233 (2016)
9. Mertan, A., NickCheney: Investigating premature convergence in co-optimization of morphology and control in evolved virtual soft robots. In: Proceedings of the $27^{th}$ European Conference on Genetic Programming, pp. 38–55 (2024)
10. Veenstra, F., Olsen, M.H., Glette, K.: Effects of encodings and quality-diversity on evolving 2d virtual creatures. In: Proceedings of the Genetic and Evolutionary Computation Conference Companion (GECCO '22), pp. 164–167 (2022)
11. Song, J., Yang, Y., Peng, W., Zhou, W., Wang, F., Yao, W..: MorphVAE: advancing morphological design of voxel-based soft robots with variational autoencoders. In: Proceedings of the AAAI Conference on Artificial Intelligence, vol. 38, pp. 10368–10376 (2024)
12. Song, J., Yang, Y., Xiao, H., Peng, W., Yao, W., Wang, F.: LASer: towards diversified and generalizable robot design with large language models. In: The Thirteenth International Conference on Learning Representations (2025)
13. Harada, K., Iba, H.: Lamarckian co-design of soft robots via transfer learning. In: Proceedings of the Genetic and Evolutionary Computation Conference (GECCO '24'), pp. 832–840 (2024)

14. Carlo, M.D., Zeeuwe, D., Ferrante, E., Meynen, G., Ellers, J., Eiben, A.: Robotic task affects the resulting morphology and behaviour in evolutionary robotics. In: Proceedings of the IEEE Symposium Series on Computational Intelligence (SSCI 2020)), pp. 2125–2131 (2020)
15. Carlo, M.D., Ferrante, E., Meynen, G., Ellers, J., Eiben, A.: The impact of different tasks on evolved robot morphologies. In: Proceedings of the Genetic and Evolutionary Computation Conference Companion (GECCO '21), pp. 91–92 (2021)
16. VA, A., GM, H. and C, S.V.: A study on morphological and behavioral adaptations from multi-task morphoevolution by voxel-based soft robots. In: Proceedings of the Genetic and Evolutionary Computation Conference (2025), accepted, to appear
17. Narvekar, S., Peng, B., Leonetti, M., Sinapov, J., Taylor, M.E., Stone, P.: Curriculum learning for reinforcement learning domains: a framework and survey. J. Mach. Learn. Res. **21**(1) (2020)

# Health Analytics

# Health-Aware Food Recommendations for Thyroid Patients Using Machine Learning and Collaborative Filtering

Mohan Bansal[(✉)] , Ramesh Saha , and Gourav Jain

Indian Institute of Information Technology (IIIT) Sonepat, Techno Park, IITD
Sonipat Campus, Haryana 131001, India
{bmohan,rameshs,j.gourav}@iiitsonepat.ac.in

**Abstract.** In India, where thyroid-related disorders affect over 42 million people, particularly women, there is a pressing need for personalized dietary guidance. This paper proposes NutriGuide, a personalized food recommendation system that provides health-aware food suggestions to users based on their thyroid conditions. The system uses support vector machines for user classification and integrates alternative least square, Neural Collaborative Filtering (NCF), and variational autoencoders to generate effective recommendations. Among these, NCF demonstrated superior performance across evaluation metrics. A semi-personalized recommendation strategy using expert dietician ratings is proposed to tackle the cold-start problem. This approach provides a robust solution for enhancing nutrition awareness and delivering health-conscious food suggestions to users in resource-constrained settings.

**Keywords:** Health-aware recommendation · Thyroid classification · Semi-personalized recommendation · Neural collaborative filtering · Cold-start problem

## 1 Introduction

In developing nations like India, access to affordable healthcare remains a challenge for a significant portion of the population. As a result, many individuals unknowingly consume food items that may worsen their thyroid condition due to a lack of dietary guidance. This issue is compounded by limited awareness and the absence of reliable, condition-specific nutritional information. Thus, there is a pressing need to develop a trustworthy, dietitian-endorsed repository of recommended food items tailored to specific thyroid conditions [18]. Such an initiative can empower individuals to make informed dietary choices, ultimately improving health outcomes and reducing the burden on the healthcare system [13].

This study introduces a food recommendation system for individuals with hyperthyroidism or hypothyroidism. Using machine learning approach [16] Support Vector Machines (SVM), thyroid conditions are identified from age, gender


S. Mitra et al. (Eds.): PReMI 2025, LNCS 16358, pp. 139–148, 2026.
https://doi.org/10.1007/978-3-032-18480-1_14

and Thyroid Stimulating Hormone (TSH) values in blood reports. Food items are then clustered based on thyroid type and dietician-assigned recommendation scores. The system compares the effectiveness of three models Alternative Least Square (ALS), Neural Collaborative Filtering (NCF), and Variational Autoencoder (VAE) to determine the best performer. Data was sourced from "livelifemore.com" [9] and verified by certified dieticians.

The rising incidence of thyroid disorders highlights the need for personalized dietary recommendation systems that offer health-specific guidance. Key challenges include ensuring personalization, raising user awareness, and accommodating diverse health conditions and cultural dietary preferences, particularly in the Indian context. The cold-start problem [8], caused by insufficient user data, can be mitigated by using dietician recommendations as ratings rather than static knowledge. Additionally, introducing semi-personalized suggestions can enhance recommendation relevance and user satisfaction. Addressing these factors is crucial for improving system effectiveness and promoting better health outcomes.

The remainder of the paper is organized as follows. Section 2 reviews related work on nutrition recommendation systems. Section 3 describes the NutriGuide framework, including data preparation, health classification, recommendation models and evaluation metrices. Section 4 presents evaluation results with discussion. Section 5 concludes the study and discusses future directions for improving health-aware food recommendations.

## 2   Related Work

Recommendation systems have been applied across domains like e-commerce, streaming, and healthcare. Collaborative Filtering (CF) [5] and Content-Based Filtering (CBF) are traditional methods, [6] while Matrix Factorization (MF) and neural models such as NCF and VAE offer improved performance [11]. However, most studies focus on general personalization without addressing domain-specific needs like thyroid care. Prior works often lack demographic specificity and rely on static knowledge bases, limiting adaptability and relevance for health-centric recommendations.

The literature in the field of personalised nutrition recommender systems highlights various innovative approaches aimed at enhancing dietary recommendations [22]. The Intelligent nutrition diet recommender system [20] proposes a method that integrates fuzzy logic and expert systems to generate customised diets, effectively considering the nutritional needs of individuals. Similarly, the personalised expert recommendation system for optimised nutrition [1] utilises genetic information (genotype) to tailor diet plans. This approach uses nutrigenetics and genetic testing services, enabling recommendations based on an individual's genetic profile. Another study developed a personalized food recommended system [4] for thyroid patients using Particle Swarm Optimization (PSO) optimized K-means clustering [15], effectively identifying nutrient-rich and safe dietary options based on patient data and achieving superior clustering performance.

A recent study developed a simplified educational toolkit [12] for adults with Hashimoto's Thyroiditis (HT), synthesizing evidence from 33 articles on the role of nutrition in modulating thyroid and autoimmune markers. The toolkit emphasizes dietary interventions providing a foundation for clinical guidance. A hybrid Collaborative Filtering and Content-Based Filtering recommender combining user interactions and item attributes to boost accuracy, diversity, coverage, addressing sparsity and cold-start; evaluated movie domain shows higher relevance or performance than single methods. Additionally, a systematic review on food recommender systems for diabetic patients [24] offers a comprehensive survey of recent works, categorising existing studies into four distinct approaches: semantic-based, optimisation-based, rule-based and classification-based, and interaction-based methods. This classification helps clarify the strengths and directions of research in food recommender systems.

## 3    Proposed Methodology

This section outlines the comprehensive methodological framework used to design, implement, and evaluate the NutriGuide system. The methodology integrates user health data classification and multiple recommendation strategies to provide personalized food suggestions for individuals with thyroid disorders. The process includes data collection and preparation, classification, recommendation engine design, and system evaluation. A schematic of the methodological architecture is presented in Fig. 1.

### 3.1    Data Sources and Preparation

The NutriGuide system was built and evaluated using diverse, well-preprocessed datasets including nutritional data, user profiles, and ratings to support a hybrid modeling approach combining collaborative filtering and supervised learning. Food and Nutritional Data: The nutritional dataset consists of 450 Indian food items, each annotated with over 30 features covering macronutrients (carbohydrates, proteins, fats), micronutrients (iron, calcium, magnesium, and key vitamins such as A, B complex, C, D, E), and trace elements (zinc, selenium, iodine) [9]. Sourced from various Indian nutrition databases including the National Institute of Nutrition's Indian food Composition Tables (IFCT) [10] and other open sources this dataset serves as the foundation of the recommendation system by providing essential nutritional information tailored to individuals with thyroid-related dietary requirements.

User Profile data: The user profile dataset includes age, gender, and TSH levels key attributes for personalized dietary planning. Sourced from a public thyroid disease dataset, the TSH values enable classification of users by thyroid condition (hypothyroidism or hyperthyroidism), while age and gender help account for varying nutritional needs and preferences. This categorization allows the system to deliver tailored dietary recommendations based on individual thyroid health status.

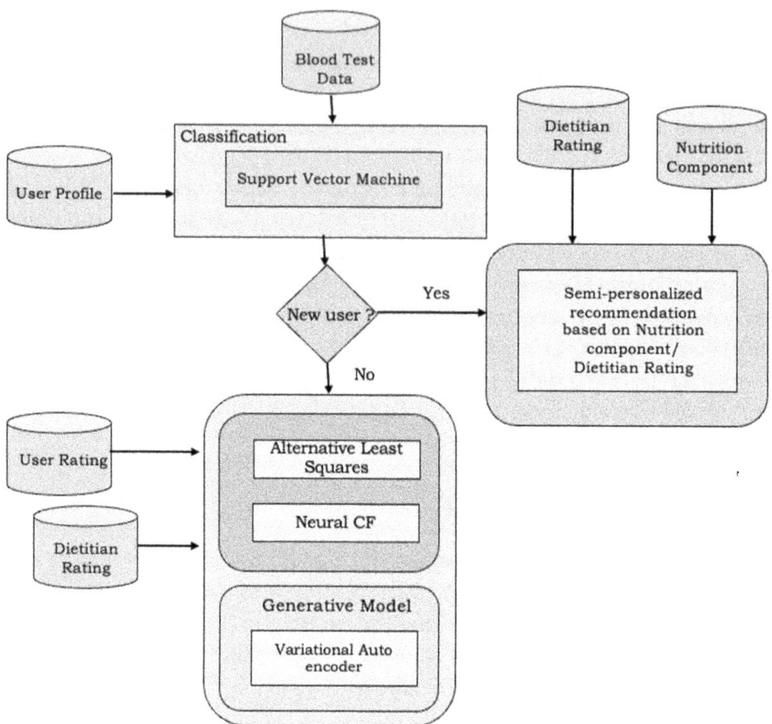

**Fig. 1.** Flowchart for NutriGuide: A Recommendation System

Dictation and user Rating: Expert ratings from certified dieticians, scored on a 0–3 Likert scale for hypothyroid and hyperthyroid conditions, provided clinically informed labels by assessing food suitability based on nutritional content and thyroid-specific dietary needs. These were averaged to create reliable supervised training labels. Additionally, a smaller set of user-generated ratings (0–5 scale) captured subjective preferences like taste and familiarity, offering a complementary perspective to enhance user-centered recommendations.

All datasets were thoroughly cleaned and standardized to ensure consistency and suitability for analysis. The preprocessing involved several key steps. Missing values were addressed by imputing zeros for missing ratings and using median or mode imputation for nutritional attributes. Duplicate entries in both user and item datasets were identified and removed to eliminate redundancy. Nutritional data were normalized using Min-Max scaling to map values into the [0, 1] range, ensuring comparability across features. Additionally, user and item identifiers were encoded into integers to facilitate matrix construction. The final processed datasets were structured into formats appropriate for collaborative filtering—using user-item interaction matrices—and classification tasks involving feature-label pairs.

## 3.2   Health Classification Module

To tailor food recommendations, users were first classified into one of three categories: hypothyroid, hyperthyroid, and normal. SVM [19] was employed to classify users into three categories based on age, gender and TSH thresholds. The model used a linear kernel and was trained on labeled blood report data. The model was trained using a stratified 80:20 train-test split to preserve class distribution, along with cross-validation to ensure robust performance evaluation. The classifier achieved high accuracy and served as an initial input for tailoring recommendations.

## 3.3   Recommendation System Framework

NutriGuide incorporates three distinct recommendation techniques to evaluate the effectiveness of both traditional and deep learning-based systems [21] in delivering personalized food suggestions. These include ALS, NCF and VAE. Each model is trained on user-item interaction matrices derived from user and dietician ratings.

**Alternating Least Squares (ALS):** ALS is a matrix factorization method [2] that optimizes latent user and item embeddings by minimizing the squared error between observed and predicted ratings, with regularization . It decomposes the sparse user-item matrix into two low-rank matrices representing latent user and item features. The optimization objective is:

$$\min_{X,Y} \sum_{(u,i)\in\kappa} (r_{ui} - x_u^T y_i)^2 + \lambda(\|x_u\|^2 + \|y_i\|^2) \tag{1}$$

where $r_{ui}$ is the observed rating, $x_u$ and $y_i$ are user and item latent vectors respectively, and $\lambda$ is the regularization parameter. ALS is effective for large-scale datasets and handles cold-start items.

**Neural Collaborative Filtering (NCF):** NCF employs deep learning to capture complex, non-linear interactions between users and items by utilizing a multi-layer perceptron (MLP) architecture [3]. User and item identifiers are first transformed into dense vector embeddings, which are then concatenated and passed through a series of fully connected layers to model their latent interactions. The predicted interaction score between user **u** and item **i** in the NCF framework is given by:

$$\hat{y}_{ui} = f_{\mathrm{MLP}}([\mathbf{u} \,\|\, \mathbf{i}]) \tag{2}$$

where **u** and **i** denote the latent embedding vectors for the user and item, respectively, and $f_{\mathrm{MLP}}$ represents a MLP that captures complex, non-linear interactions between them.

**Variational Autoencoders (VAE):** VAE is a deep learning generative model [7] designed to learn a compact latent representation of user-item interactions. The architecture consists of an encoder and a decoder. Encoder maps input vector to a probabilistic latent space (mean and variance) and decoder reconstructs the original rating vector from latent variables. The objective is to minimize the combined loss with a regularization term using Kullback–Leibler divergence $D_{\mathrm{KL}}$:

$$\mathcal{L} = \mathbb{E}_{q(z|x)}[\log p(x|z)] - D_{\mathrm{KL}}(q(z|x)\|p(z)) \tag{3}$$

The reconstruction loss, expressed as the expected log-likelihood $\mathbb{E}_{q(z|x)}[\log p(x|z)]$ encourages the decoder to accurately reconstruct the original input $x$ from the latent variable $z$. The regularization term, $D_{\mathrm{KL}}(q(z|x)\|p(z))$ represents the Kullback–Leibler (KL) divergence between the encoder's learned posterior distribution $q(z|x)$ and the prior distribution $p(z)$ over the latent space. VAEs handle data sparsity and cold-start problems effectively and provide better generalization through regularized latent representations.

Each model was trained and evaluated using identical datasets and splits to ensure fair benchmarking. The effectiveness of the models was compared using accuracy, precision, recall and F1-score metrics. The inclusion of both traditional and neural models provides a comprehensive view of their suitability in health-aware food recommendation tasks.

### 3.4   Semi-personalized Recommendation Strategy

To tackle the cold-start problem, a hybrid approach was used. New users were classified using SVM, and product suggestions were generated based on averaged ratings from certified dieticians. This semi-personalized approach ensured relevance and reliability even without prior user interaction data.

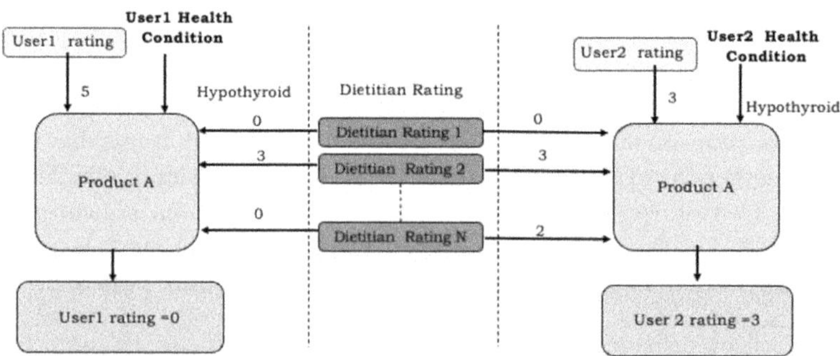


**Fig. 2.** Role of dietitian rating in NutriGuide recommendation system

Figure 2 illustrates a comparative evaluation of Product A for two users diagnosed with hypothyroidism, but exhibiting differing overall health conditions.

User-1, whose health condition is relatively poorer, initially high preference score of 5 to Product A. However, after considering clinical assessments and expert recommendations provided by a certified dietitian, Product A was deemed unsuitable for User-1's condition, resulting in a revised product rating of 0. In contrast, User-2, although also hypothyroid, demonstrated comparatively better health. Based on the same dietitian's evaluation framework and User-2's health metrics, Product A was recommended and retained in the diet plan, maintaining User-2's original rating of 3. This adjustment process highlights the personalized and health-informed modification of user preferences through expert dietary guidance, ensuring safety and relevance in product recommendations.

The NutriGuide methodology combines classification, collaborative filtering, deep learning, and domain-expert knowledge to deliver a robust, scalable, and health-specific recommendation system. The hybrid model architecture allows seamless transition between personalized and semi-personalized recommendations, effectively solving the cold-start problem.

### 3.5  Model Evaluation

To assess the effectiveness and accuracy of the proposed recommendation models, several evaluation metrics were utilized. Each metric captures a distinct aspect of model performance such as prediction accuracy and recommendation relevance. The description of the evaluation maetrics are provided in the Table 1.

**Table 1.** Evaluation metrics for recommendation models

| Metric | Short Description | Formula |
|---|---|---|
| **Precision** | Proportion of relevant items in the top-$K$ recommendations. Reflects recommendation relevancy. | $\text{Precision@K} = \frac{\#\text{Relevant items in top } K}{K}$ |
| **Recall** | Proportion of all relevant items that appear in the top-$K$ recommendations. Indicates completeness. | $\text{Recall@K} = \frac{\#\text{Relevant items in top } K}{\text{Total relevant items}}$ |
| **F1-Score** | Harmonic mean of Precision and Recall. Balances both metrics. | $\text{F1@K} = 2 \times \frac{\text{Precision@K} \times \text{Recall@K}}{\text{Precision@K} + \text{Recall@K}}$ |

## 4  Results and Discussion

### 4.1  Health Condition Classification Performance

To classify users based on their thyroid health conditions (hypothyroid, hyperthyroid, or normal), a SVM model was employed. The model achieved an **accuracy of 98.15%, precision of 0.9911, recall of 0.9821**, and an **F1-score of 0.9870**. These metrics indicate that the SVM model is highly effective and reliable for health condition classification.

## 4.2   Recommendation Model Performance

To evaluate the quality of food item recommendations, three models—Neural Collaborative Filtering (NCF), Alternating Least Squares (ALS), and Variational Autoencoder (VAE) were tested using precision, recall, F1-score, and accuracy. The results are summarized in Table 2.

**Table 2.** Evaluation Metrics for Recommendation Models

| Model | Accuracy (%) | Precision | Recall | F1-Score |
|---|---|---|---|---|
| NCF | **94.18** | **0.9540** | **0.9431** | **0.9484** |
| ALS | 92.36 | 0.9263 | 0.9134 | 0.9200 |
| VAE | 83.61 | 0.9179 | 0.6659 | 0.7722 |

**Table 3.** Accuracy comparison of recommendation models.

| Model Name | Accuracy (%) |
|---|---|
| Collaborative-Based Filtering (CBF) [14] | 75 |
| Collaborative Filtering (CF) [17] | 80 |
| Hybrid CF-CBF [23] | 90 |
| **Machine learning- CF** (Proposed) | **94.18** |

The **NCF model** outperformed the others across all evaluation metrics, demonstrating its superior ability to capture complex user-item interactions and recommend relevant food items. Its high precision and recall indicate strong relevance and coverage of suggested items.

The **ALS model** showed competitive and balanced performance, making it a robust baseline approach for collaborative filtering tasks. Meanwhile, the **VAE model** achieved decent precision but significantly lower recall, resulting in a reduced F1-score. This suggests that while VAE can rank items effectively, it may fail to retrieve all relevant items consistently. Relative to prior publications, NutriGuide consistently improves accuracy across all test sets, surpassing the best reported baselines shown in Table 3.

### 4.3   Impact of Semi-personalized Strategy

The semi-personalized recommendation strategy, which incorporates expert dietician ratings, effectively addressed the cold-start problem for new users. When combined with the NCF model, it enhanced both performance and personalization, especially in cases with limited historical data. Furthermore, the integration of health classification ensured that recommendations were not only relevant but also medically appropriate. Overall, NutriGuide successfully bridges the gap between clinical dietary needs and user-specific food preferences using modern AI techniques.

## 5   Conclusion and Future Work

This study developed a personalized food recommendation system for Indian users with thyroid conditions, using models such as ALS, NCF, and VAE. ALS and NCF performed best, aided by the integration of dietician recommendations as weighted ratings, which also helped address the cold-start problem. The use of semi-personalized suggestions for new users improved recommendation quality. While VAE showed potential, its performance depended on larger datasets. Overall, the research highlights the value of health-specific, culturally tailored recommendation systems in supporting better dietary decisions.

This study, several directions for future research are proposed. First, the product list should be expanded to include a wider range of Indian food items, with additional input from dietitians to enhance the relevance and accuracy of recommendations. Second, collecting more explicit and implicit user feedback will enrich the dataset and enable more precise modeling. Third, the integration of dietitian ratings for semi-personalized recommendations, which proved effective in this study, can be further explored across different models to enhance personalization for new users. Lastly, with richer data and improved feedback mechanisms,

## References


1. Chen, C.H., Toumazou, C.: Personalized expert recommendation systems for optimized nutrition. Trends Personal. Nutrit. 309–338 (2019)
2. Dhawan, S., Singh, K., Batra, A., Choi, A., Choi, E.: A novel deep learning approach toward efficient and accurate recommendation using improved alternating least squares in social media. J. Inst. Eng. (India): Series B **105**(3), 657–675 (2024)
3. He, X., Liao, L., Zhang, H., Nie, L., Hu, X., Chua, T.S.: Neural collaborative filtering. In: Proceedings of the 26th international conference on world wide web, pp. 173–182 (2017)
4. Hosen, M.A., Moz, S.H., Kabir, S.S., Galib, S.M., Adnan, M.N.: Enhancing thyroid patient dietary management with an optimized recommender system based on pso and k-means. Proc. Comput. Sci. **230**, 688–697 (2023)
5. Jain, G., Mahara, T., C. Sharma, S.: Effective time context based collaborative filtering recommender system inspired by gower's coefficient. Int. J. Syst. Assur. Eng. Manage. **14**(1), 429–447 (2023)
6. Jain, G., Mahara, T., Sharma, S., Verma, O.P., Sharma, T.: Clustering-based recommendation system for preliminary disease detection. Int. J. E-Health Med. Commun. (IJEHMC) **13**(4), 1–14 (2022)
7. Kingma, D.P., Welling, M., et al.: An introduction to variational autoencoders. Found. Trends® Mach. Learn. **12**(4), 307–392 (2019)
8. Lika, B., Kolomvatsos, K., Hadjiefthymiades, S.: Facing the cold start problem in recommender systems. Expert Syst. Appl. **41**(4), 2065–2073 (2014)
9. LiveLifeMore.com: Livelifemore diet & wellness (2025). https://www.livelifemore.com/, 2025 LiveLifeMore.com. Accessed 20 Mar 2026 16:11:12
10. Longvah, T., Anantan, I., Bhaskarachary, K., Venkaiah, K., Longvah, T.: Indian Food Composition Tables. National Institute of Nutrition, Indian Council of Medical Research Hyderabad (2017)
11. Rendle, S., Krichene, W., Zhang, L., Anderson, J.: Neural collaborative filtering vs. matrix factorization revisited. In: Proceedings of the 14th ACM Conference on Recommender Systems, pp. 240–248 (2020)
12. Ritter, K.: A literature-informed nutrition patient communication toolkit for hashimoto's thyroiditis (2025)

13. Saha, R., Sen, S., Saha, J., Nandy, A., Biswas, S., Chowdhury, C.: Ontology-based intelligent decision support systems: A systematic approach. In: Web Semantics, pp. 177–193. Elsevier (2021)
14. Saifudin, I., Widiyaningtyas, T.: Systematic literature review on recommender system: Approach, problem, evaluation techniques, datasets. IEEE Access **12**, 19827–19847 (2024)
15. Sasmal, B., Das, A., Dhal, K.G., Saha, R.: A comprehensive survey on African vulture optimization algorithm. Arch. Comput. Methods Eng. **31**(3), 1659–1700 (2024)
16. Shabber, S.M., Bansal, M., Radha, K.: Machine learning-assisted diagnosis of speech disorders: a review of dysarthric speech. In: 2023 International Conference on Electrical, Electronics, Communication and Computers (ELEXCOM), pp. 1–6. IEEE (2023)
17. Shi, X., Zhang, Y., Pujahari, A., Mishra, S.K.: When latent features meet side information: a preference relation based graph neural network for collaborative filtering. Expert Syst. Appl. **260**, 125423 (2025)
18. Shulhai, A.M., et al.: The role of nutrition on thyroid function. Nutrients **16**(15), 2496 (2024)
19. Suthaharan, S.: Support vector machine. In: Machine Learning Models and Algorithms for Big Data Classification: Thinking with Examples for Effective Learning, pp. 207–235. Springer (2016)
20. Tabassum, N., Rehman, A., Hamid, M., Saleem, M., Malik, S., Alyas, T.: Intelligent nutrition diet recommender system for diabetic's patients. Intell. Autom. Soft Comput. **29**(3), 319–335 (2021)
21. Tawade, N.M., Bansal, M., Saha, R.: Optimized transfer learning with CNNs for superior COVID-19 detection in chest x-ray imaging. In: 2024 IEEE International Symposium on Smart Electronic Systems (iSES), pp. 19–24. IEEE (2024)
22. Tsolakidis, D., Gymnopoulos, L.P., Dimitropoulos, K.: Artificial intelligence and machine learning technologies for personalized nutrition: A review. In: Informatics, vol. 11, p. 62. MDPI (2024)
23. Widayanti, R., Chakim, M.H.R., Lukita, C., Rahardja, U., Lutfiani, N.: Improving recommender systems using hybrid techniques of collaborative filtering and content-based filtering. J. Appl. Data Sci. **4**(3), 289–302 (2023)
24. Yera, R., Alzahrani, A.A., Martínez, L., Rodríguez, R.M.: A systematic review on food recommender systems for diabetic patients. Int. J. Environ. Res. Public Health **20**(5), 4248 (2023)

# WAHNet: Weighted Augmented Hybrid Network for Alzheimer's Disease Detection


Mradul Agrawal[1], Km Poonam[2(✉)], Rajlakshmi Guha[1],
and Partha P Chakrabarti[1]

[1] Indian Institute of Technology Kharagpur, Kharagpur 721302, West Bengal, India
`rajg@cet.iitkgp.ac.in, ppchak@cse.iitkgp.ac.in`
[2] The LNM Institute of Information Technology, Jaipur 302031, India
`poonam.mt16@gmail.com`



**Abstract.** Alzheimer's disease (AD) poses a significant global health challenge, making early and efficient detection essential for timely intervention. While three-dimensional (3D) T1-weighted MRI is widely used for AD detection, its clinical applicability is often hindered by high acquisition costs, prolonged scan durations, complex preprocessing pipelines, and the heavy computational requirements of volumetric deep learning models. Additionally, 3D models typically demand large annotated datasets and extended training time—constraints that limit their deployment in real-world, resource-limited settings. In contrast, two-dimensional (2D) T1-weighted MRI slices provide a cost-effective and computationally efficient alternative. These slices retain localized pathological features vital for diagnosis and can be leveraged effectively through modern representation learning. In practical settings, 3D scans may be missing or degraded, while 2D slices remain accessible and informative. This study introduces a hybrid deep learning-based framework for AD classification using 2D T1-weighted MRI slices from the Alzheimer's Disease Neuroimaging Initiative (ADNI). We introduce a series of methodological innovations, including advanced preprocessing techniques, weighted majority voting with confidence scores, the integration of statistical and pixel-based features, and a hybrid architecture that fuses pre-trained deep learning models with classical machine learning classifiers. Our best-performing model, the Weighted Augmented Hybrid Network (WAHNet), achieves an accuracy of 80.1% in three-class classification (AD, Mild Cognitive Impairment, and Normal Control), representing an 8% improvement over baseline methods, including those based on 3D CNNs (64%) and 3D pixel-based features (71.9%). The proposed framework demonstrates that 2D imaging, when combined with hybrid learning, can deliver diagnostic performance comparable to 3D methods while improving scalability and clinical usability.

**Keywords:** Alzheimer's Disease · 3D MRI · Deep Learning · Hybrid Models · Weighted Majority Voting




S. Mitra et al. (Eds.): PReMI 2025, LNCS 16358, pp. 149–159, 2026.
https://doi.org/10.1007/978-3-032-18480-1_15

## 1   Introduction

Alzheimer's disease (AD) is a progressive neurodegenerative disorder that affects millions of people worldwide, characterized by gradual cognitive decline, memory loss, and behavioral changes [1]. It is the most common form of dementia, accounting for 60–80% of cases, and its prevalence is expected to triple by 2050 due to the aging global population https://www.who.int/news-room/factsheets/detail/dementia. Early detection of AD is crucial for effective intervention and management, potentially slowing disease progression and improving patient outcomes. In recent years, advanced neuroimaging techniques, particularly Magnetic Resonance Imaging (MRI), have emerged as valuable tools to detect structural brain changes associated with AD [2,3]. 3D-MRI scans provide a detailed visualization of brain structures, enabling the identification of subtle anatomical changes that may indicate early stages of neurodegeneration. However, effectively analyzing these complex 3D datasets presents notable challenges, particularly when working with limited high-quality data [4,5].

Traditional approaches to AD detection have relied on clinical assessments and neuropsychological tests, which often identify the disease only after significant cognitive decline has occurred. In recent years, machine learning (ML) and deep learning (DL) techniques have shown promising results in automating AD detection using neuroimaging data [6]. These computational methods typically utilize convolutional neural networks (CNNs) to analyze either 2D slices extracted from 3D MRI volumes or the entire 3D volumetric data directly. Prior studies have explored various architectures, including ResNet, VGG, and custom 3D CNN models, for AD classification [7–10]. Despite these advances, several challenges remain. Many DL models rely on large, high-quality datasets, which are often unavailable in real-world clinical settings. Moreover, accurately distinguishing early-stage AD as mild cognitive impairment (MCI) from normal aging remains a persistent difficulty. In this context, individual 2D slices not only reduce computational demands but also capture localized pathological features and spatial patterns that may be diluted in full 3D representations, thereby yielding deeper clinical insights.

To address these challenges, our research focuses on developing robust and generalizable models for AD detection. We introduce a series of methodological innovations, including advanced preprocessing techniques, weighted majority voting with confidence scores, the integration of statistical and pixel-based features, and a hybrid architecture that fuses pre-trained deep learning models with classical machine learning classifiers. Specifically, we aim to classify individuals into AD, MCI, and Normal Control (NC) categories using 3D MRI data, while ensuring strong performance even in data-constrained scenarios. The key contributions of this work are as follows:

- Conduct a comprehensive evaluation of various ML/DL approaches for AD detection using 3D MRI data.
- Introduce novel preprocessing techniques that utilize multiple orientations (axial, coronal, and sagittal) of 3D MRI scans to enhance classification performance.

– Design a hybrid model architecture that integrates statistical features, pixel-based features, and DL features with traditional ML classifiers.
– Propose an innovative weighted majority voting mechanism with confidence scores to effectively combine predictions across different image slices and orientations.
– Our proposed approach, named WAHNet (Weighted Augmented Hybrid Network) achieves an accuracy of 80.1% in three-class classification (AD, MCI and NC), demonstrating a significant improvement of approximately 8% over the best baseline methods.

## 2   Materials and Methods

### 2.1   Dataset

The dataset used in this study is retrieved from the ADNI (Alzheimer's Disease Neuroimaging Initiative) database https://adni.loni.usc.edu/ [11]. We utilized a pre-processed version of T1-weighted 3D brain MRI scans. The dataset comprises 275 scans from patients diagnosed with AD, 278 scans representing the prodromal stage of AD, known as Mild Cognitive Impairment (MCI), and 346 scans from Normal Control (NC). Each 3D MRI scan consists of multiple slices that can be viewed from three orientations—axial, coronal, and sagittal. These orientations offer complementary perspectives of brain anatomy, which can enhance the detection of subtle structural changes associated with AD.

### 2.2   Data Preprocessing

We employed a series of preprocessing techniques to enhance the quality and discriminative power of the 3D MRI data, as illustrated in Fig. 1.

**Slice Extraction:** Each 3D MRI scan was decomposed into 2D slices along three anatomical orientations—axial, coronal, and sagittal—providing a comprehensive view of brain structures from multiple perspectives.

**Feature Extraction:** From the 2D slices, we extracted a variety of features to capture both low-level and high-level information. These include: pixel features (raw pixel intensities reshaped into 1D vectors), statistical features (grayscale histograms, multi-level histograms, Histogram of Oriented Gradients (HOG), and Gray Level Co-occurrence Matrix (GLCM) features), and deep learning features (derived from intermediate layers of pre-trained convolutional neural networks to capture hierarchical abstractions).

**Data Augmentation:** To increase dataset diversity and improve model generalization, we applied multiple strategies including random rotation of slices, random cropping and resizing, generation of overlapping image patches, and random permutation of slices to simulate intra-subject variability.

These preprocessing steps establish a robust foundation for downstream classification by expanding the feature space and improving generalization on limited training data.

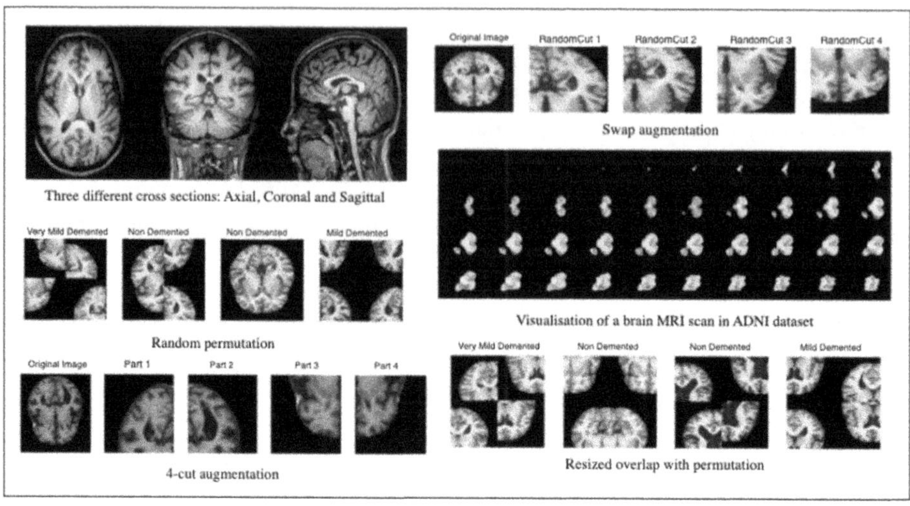

**Fig. 1.** Data preprocessing techniques.

## 2.3   Proposed Methodology

Our proposed framework, illustrated in Fig. 1, presents a progression of increasingly sophisticated approaches, starting with baseline models and culminating in a hybrid architecture that integrates multiple feature types and classification techniques. First, we extracted 2D slices from 3D MRI scans across axial, coronal, and sagittal views to derive CNN-based, statistical, and pixel-level features. Deep features are extracted using a pre-trained ResNet, while statistical and pixel features capture texture and spatial information. These diverse features are integrated and processed through an ML classifier using a majority voting strategy enhanced by confidence score weighting, leading to improved prediction accuracy.

**Baseline Approaches**

We established three baseline approaches to serve as a benchmark for our subsequent methodological improvements:

- **3D ResNet Model:** A standard 3D convolutional neural network applied directly to the volumetric MRI data.
- **ML Algorithms on Pixel Features:** Traditional machine learning algorithms (Support Vector Machine, K-Nearest Neighbors, Random Forest, and Logistic Regression) applied to flattened pixel values.
- **2D CNN on Extracted Slices:** Converting the 3D scans to 2D slices and applying 2D CNNs for classification.

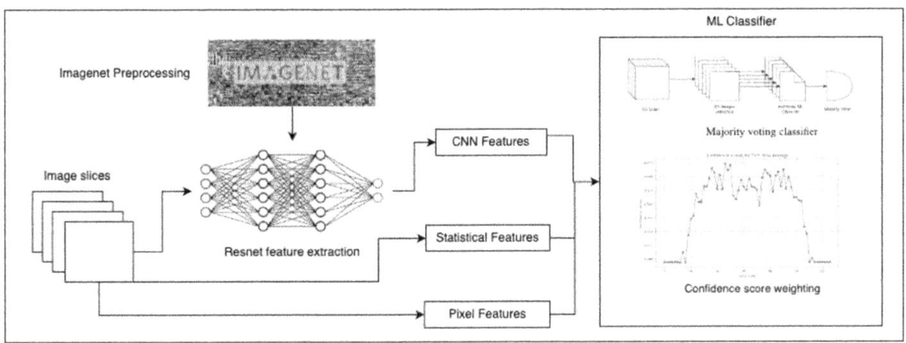


**Fig. 2.** Framework of the Proposed Approach, WAHNet (<u>W</u>eighted <u>A</u>ugmented <u>H</u>ybrid <u>Net</u>work).

## Majority Voting Mechanism

To leverage the complementary information provided by multiple slices and orientations, we developed a majority voting mechanism, Algorithm 1. This approach improved upon the baseline methods by considering information from multiple perspectives within the 3D volume.

---

**Algorithm 1:** Majority Voting Algorithm

---

**Input:** 3D MRI scan
**Output:** Predicted class label
1 Extract 2D image slices along one direction (Axial) from the 3D MRI scan;
2 **for** *each individual slice* **do**
3   | Train a separate ML classifier using the pixel features of the slice;
4 **end**
5 **During Test Time:**
6 Pass 2D slices of the test subject through the individual ML classifiers;
7 Use majority voting to predict the output class for that subject;

---

## Weighted Confidence Voting Mechanism

Building upon the majority voting mechanism, we introduced a confidence-weighted approach, Algorithm 2. The confidence score is calculated as the maximum probability among the predicted probabilities for each class, indicating the classifier's certainty in its prediction. This weighted approach gives greater importance to predictions made with higher confidence.

## Multi-orientation Integration

Recognizing that different slice orientations -axial, coronal, and sagittal - provide complementary structural information, we extended our methodology to incorporate predictions from all three views. Specifically, separate classifiers were trained for each orientation, and their predictions were subsequently combined using a weighted majority voting scheme. This multi-orientation approach enabled the model to capture diverse anatomical patterns visible from different perspectives, thereby enhancing the overall classification performance.

---

**Algorithm 2:** Weighted Majority Voting Algorithm

---

**Input:** 3D MRI scan
**Output:** Predicted class label
1  Extract 2D image slices along one direction (Axial) from the 3D MRI scan;
2  **for** *each individual slice* **do**
3  | Train a separate ML classifier using the pixel features of the slice;
4  **end**
5  **During Test Time:**
6  **for** *each slice* **do**
7  | Compute weight for majority voting based on the confidence of the prediction;
8  | Confidence is calculated based on the highest accuracy score of the predicted class;
9  | Perform majority voting proportional to the confidence score;
10 **end**

---

## Hybrid Model Architecture

Our most advanced approach employs a hybrid model that combines multiple feature types with both DL and traditional ML techniques. Our proposed approach, named WAHNet (Weighted Augmented Hybrid Network), as shown in Fig. 2, includes several key components. First, pixel-level, statistical, and CNN-based features—extracted using a pre-trained ResNet model—are obtained from 2D slices.

These diverse features are then fused into a unified representation through a feature fusion process. Subsequently, multiple machine learning classifiers, including Support Vector Machine (SVM), k-Nearest Neighbors (KNN), Random Forest, and Logistic Regression, are applied to this combined feature set. Finally, the predictions from these classifiers and across slices are integrated using confidence-weighted majority voting. This hybrid approach effectively leverages the automatic feature extraction capabilities of DL and the robustness of traditional classifiers, particularly in settings with limited data, leading to improved classification performance over standalone methods.

## Computational Efficiency and Memory Footprint

We evaluated the memory and computational footprint of the proposed WAHNet framework. The total number of trainable parameters is 11.7 million. The CNN backbone occupies approximately 80.3 MB, and the integrated classical ML classifiers require 17.3 MB, resulting in a total model size of 97.6 MB. During inference, the peak memory usage was 66.1 MB. The training of classifiers was completed in approximately 1–2 h using an NVIDIA Tesla P100 GPU with 4 CPU cores and an average of 20 GB of RAM. These results demonstrate the computational efficiency and deployability of WAHNet in resource-constrained clinical settings.

## 3   Results and Discussion

This section presents the experimental results of our proposed methodologies and discusses their implications. We evaluate the performance of our approaches on both 3-class (AD, MCI, NC) classification tasks. The Table 1 demonstrates that the proposed feature integration strategies consistently outperform baseline methods across all classifiers. Notably, the proposed WAHNet approach achieves the highest accuracy (up to 80%), an improvement of approximately 8–10% over the best baseline, highlighting the effectiveness of combining statistical, pixel-based, and deep learning features with augmentation.

**Table 1.** Comparative Study Across Baseline and Proposed (WAHNet) Approaches.

|  | Method | SVM | KNN | RF | LR |
|---|---|---|---|---|---|
| Baseline | CNN Model 1 | 0.65 | 0.55 | 0.62 | 0.67 |
|  | CNN Model 2 | 0.69 | 0.57 | 0.65 | 0.68 |
|  | 3D Pixel Features | 0.71 | 0.61 | 0.70 | 0.72 |
| Proposed | Majority Voting | 0.76 | 0.63 | 0.71 | 0.74 |
|  | W-Majority Voting | 0.77 | 0.65 | 0.73 | 0.74 |
|  | ResNet | 0.78 | 0.68 | 0.73 | 0.75 |
|  | ResNet + Augmentation | 0.79 | 0.68 | 0.75 | 0.75 |
|  | Statistical features | 0.76 | 0.64 | 0.73 | **0.76** |
|  | Hybrid Model | 0.78 | 0.70 | 0.75 | **0.76** |
|  | Hybrid Model + Augmentation | 0.79 | 0.69 | 0.75 | **0.76** |
|  | **WAHNet** | **0.80** | **0.69** | **0.77** | 0.75 |

### 3.1   Performance of Baseline Models

Table 2 presents a comprehensive comparison of the 3-class classification performance across all baseline methods, including various ML and DL algorithms applied to different feature representations. Traditional ML models that use 3D pixel features outperform both DL (3D ResNet) and 3D-to-2D conversion methods, with Logistic Regression achieving the highest average accuracy (0.72). Among the 3D-to-2D conversion approaches, the KNN classifier using HOG features demonstrates comparatively better performance; however, it still falls short when compared to direct 3D feature-based models. Notably, the proposed WAH-Net architecture surpasses all baseline models, namely, KNN(69%), LR(65%), DL (76%) and SVM (80%) in classification accuracy. Additionally, the class-wise accuracy surpasses other approaches, establishing the efficiency of the proposed solution.

**Table 2.** Comprehensive Comparison of Baseline Models and the Proposed Method (WAHNet) in Terms of Class-wise Accuracy. HOG: Histogram of Oriented Gradient

| Method | Algorithm | Average | AD | MCI | NC |
| --- | --- | --- | --- | --- | --- |
| 3D ResNet [12] | Deep Learning | 0.64 | - | - | - |
| 3D Pixel Features | KNN | 0.61 | 0.59 | 0.68 | 0.57 |
| | Random Forest | 0.70 | 0.70 | 0.86 | 0.57 |
| | SVM | 0.71 | 0.75 | 0.73 | 0.66 |
| | Logistic Regression | 0.72 | 0.76 | 0.72 | 0.69 |
| 3D to 2D Conversion | Naive Bayes | 0.51 | 0.55 | 0.51 | 0.48 |
| | Decision Tree | 0.52 | 0.53 | 0.51 | 0.52 |
| | SVM | 0.56 | 0.60 | 0.56 | 0.53 |
| | Logistic Regression | 0.54 | 0.56 | 0.54 | 0.52 |
| | KNN | 0.63 | 0.65 | 0.66 | 0.59 |
| | KNN + MobileNetV2 | 0.58 | 0.60 | 0.60 | 0.55 |
| | KNN + HOG Features | 0.65 | 0.68 | 0.66 | 0.62 |
| WAHNet | KNN | **0.69** | 0.71 | 0.67 | 0.69 |
| | Logistic Regression | **0.75** | 0.77 | 0.75 | 0.73 |
| | MLP | **0.76** | 0.77 | 0.79 | 0.72 |
| | Random Forest | **0.77** | 0.78 | 0.80 | 0.74 |
| | SVM | **0.80** | 0.81 | 0.81 | 0.78 |

## 3.2   Ablation Study: Performance on Proposed Methods

Building upon the baseline models, we implemented a series of methodological enhancements that progressively improved classification performance.

**Majority and Weighted Majority Weighting.** Table 3 presents the comprehensive comparison between baseline performance and our enhancement techniques, including majority voting and weighted confidence voting, which notably improve classification performance for most algorithms, with SVM achieving the highest overall accuracy (0.77).

**Table 3.** Comprehensive Performance Comparison with Enhancement Techniques. HOG: Histogram of Oriented Gradient

| Algorithm | Voting | W-Voting | WAHNet |
|---|---|---|---|
| Plain CNN | 0.44 | 0.42 | - |
| Multi-layer Perceptron | 0.69 | 0.70 | 0.76 |
| K Nearest Neighbours | 0.63 | 0.65 | - |
| KNN + HOG | 0.63 | 0.66 | 0.69 |
| Random Forest | 0.71 | 0.73 | 0.77 |
| Logistic Regression | 0.74 | 0.74 | 0.75 |
| **Support Vector Machine** | **0.76** | **0.77** | **0.80** |

**Multi-orientation Integration.** Table 4 presents the performance comparison across different integration approaches. Axial, Coronal, and Sagittal represent models trained on individual orientations. Combined refers to grouping all predictions and taking a majority vote. Voting and W-Voting respectively, represents the majority and confidence-weighted majority voting across the three orientations. Integrating multiple orientations consistently improves performance across all classifiers, with SVM achieving the highest accuracy (0.765), highlighting the importance of combining complementary views.

**Table 4.** Performance Comparison of Multi-Orientation Integration Approaches.

| | Method | KNN | RF | LR | SVM |
|---|---|---|---|---|---|
| Individual | Axial | 0.635 | 0.711 | 0.744 | 0.761 |
| | Coronal | 0.685 | 0.678 | 0.679 | 0.689 |
| | Sagittal | 0.666 | 0.701 | 0.688 | 0.755 |
| Composite | Combined | 0.423 | 0.662 | 0.596 | 0.742 |
| | Voting | 0.654 | 0.725 | 0.733 | 0.762 |
| | W-Voting | 0.688 | 0.730 | 0.754 | 0.765 |
| | **WAHNet** | **0.690** | **0.770** | **0.750** | **0.801** |

**WAHNet Model Performance.** Our hybrid model architecture combines pixel features, statistical features, and CNN features with multiple classifiers to achieve enhanced performance. Table 1 presents a comprehensive comparison of accuracy across different models and feature integration approaches for the 3-class classification task. WAHNet outperformed all other approaches across most classifiers, achieving the highest accuracy of 80.1% using SVM classifier outperformed other classifiers across all classes (AD, MCI, NC), as shown in Table 2. This demonstrates the effectiveness of combining diverse feature types and augmentation in improving classification performance.

## 4    Conclusion and Future Work

We present a comprehensive approach for AD detection by slicing 3D MRI scans into 2D slices. Our research addressed the critical challenge of developing robust classification models that can operate effectively in settings with limited quantity and quality of data. Our main contributions include innovative preprocessing methods, such as incorporating multiple orientations of 3D scans and augmenting datasets, as well as architectural enhancements such as weighted confidence majority voting and hybrid model construction. Through these techniques, we achieved significant performance improvements over our initial baselines, and our final WAHNet demonstrates an accuracy of 80.1% for the three-class classification (AD, MCI, and NC). Future work will focus on validating the proposed models using high-quality MRI datasets, exploring the effectiveness of pure 3D models trained directly on volumetric data, and improving model interpretability through brain-specific features and visualization techniques to support clinical adoption.

## References


1. Van Oostveen, W.M., de Lange, E.C.M.: Imaging techniques in Alzheimer's disease: a review of applications in early diagnosis and longitudinal monitoring. Int. J. Mol. Sci. **22**(4), 2110 (2021). https://doi.org/10.3390/ijms22042110
2. Cheng, B., Liu, M., Zhang, D., Shen, D., Initiative, A.D.N.: Robust multi-label transfer feature learning for early diagnosis of Alzheimer's disease. Brain Imag. Behav. **13**(1), 138–153 (2018)
3. Poonam, K., Prasad, A., Guha, R., Hazra, A., Chakrabarti, P.P.: Explainable decision tree-based screening of cognitive impairment leveraging minimal neuropsychological tests. In: Maji, P., Huang, T., Pal, N.R., Chaudhury, S., De, R.K. (eds.) Pattern Recognition and Machine Intelligence. PReMI 2023. Lecture Notes in Computer Science, vol 14301. Springer, Cham (2023). https://doi.org/10.1007/978-3-031-45170-6_25
4. Kumar, R., et al.: Artificial intelligence-based methodologies for early diagnostic precision and personalized therapeutic strategies in neuro-ophthalmic and neurodegenerative pathologies. Brain Sci. **14**(12), 1266 (2024). https://doi.org/10.3390/brainsci14121266
5. Solano-Rojas, B., Villalón-Fonseca, R.: A low-cost three-dimensional DenseNet neural network for Alzheimer's disease early discovery. Sensors **21**(4), 1302 (2021)
6. Litjens, G., et al.: A survey on deep learning in medical image analysis. Med. Image Anal. **42**, 60–88 (2017)
7. Turrisi, R., Verri, A., Barla, A.: The effect of data augmentation and 3D-CNN depth on Alzheimer's disease detection. arXiv preprint arXiv:2309.07192 (2023)
8. Wang, S.H., Phillips, P., Sui, Y., Liu, B., Yang, M., Cheng, H.: Classification of Alzheimer's disease based on eight-layer convolutional neural network with leaky rectified linear unit and max pooling. J. Med. Syst. **42**, 1–11 (2018)
9. El-Assy, A.M., Amer, H.M., Ibrahim, H.M., Mohamed, M.A.: A novel CNN architecture for accurate early detection and classification of Alzheimer's disease using MRI data. Sci. Rep. **14**(1), 1–19 (2024). https://doi.org/10.1038/s41598-024-53733-6

10. Nithya, V.P., Mohanasundaram, N., Santhosh, R.: An early detection and classification of Alzheimer's disease framework based on ResNet-50. Curr. Med. Imag. **20**(1), e250823220361 (2024)
11. Veitch, D.P., et al.: The Alzheimer's disease neuroimaging initiative in the era of Alzheimer's disease treatment: a review of ADNI studies from 2021 to 2022. Alzheimer's & Dementia **20**(1), 652–694 (2024)
12. Ebrahimi, A., Luo, S., Chiong, R.: Introducing transfer learning to 3D ResNet-18 for Alzheimer's disease detection on MRI images. In: 2020 35th International Conference on Image and Vision Computing New Zealand (IVCNZ), Wellington, New Zealand, pp. 1–6 (2020). https://doi.org/10.1109/IVCNZ51579.2020.9290616

# Attention-Guided Few-Shot Prototypical Network for ICU Abnormal EEG Pattern Recognition


Deepak Mewada[✉], Madhumita Gayen, Monalisa Sarma, and Debasis Samanta

Indian Institute of Technology, Kharagpur, India
`deepakmewada96@kgpian.iitkgp.ac.in`



**Abstract.** Timely detection of seizures and seizure-like EEG abnormalities—such as periodic discharges and rhythmic delta activity—is essential in neurocritical care to reduce mortality and improve outcomes. Manual EEG interpretation is labor-intensive, variable, and infeasible for continuous monitoring, especially in resource-limited settings. Existing automated methods predominantly target binary seizure detection, demand extensive labeled data, and operate as "black boxes," limiting clinical trust and deployment. This paper introduces **ProtoEEG**, a few-shot prototypical network that classifies EEG spectrograms via a pretrained EfficientNetV2-S encoder and episodic metric learning. To handle intra-class variability and support-set heterogeneity, **ProtoEEG-QA** is proposed, refining class prototypes with a query-aware attention module that weights support embeddings by their relevance to each query. On the HMS Harmful Brain Activity dataset under 5-, 10-, and 15-shot regimes, ProtoEEG-QA achieves up to $85.37\% \pm 1.02\%$ accuracy (95% CI) and a macro-AUROC of 0.97—surpassing static prototype baselines. Attention weights offer per-instance explanations by highlighting influential support examples, enhancing model transparency and clinical trust. By uniting high accuracy, calibration, and inherent interpretability in a few-shot framework, ProtoEEG-QA provides a scalable solution for explainable EEG classification in critical care and remote health-analytics applications.


## 1 Introduction

In neurocritical care, EEG patterns such as electrographic seizures, lateralized periodic discharges (LPDs), and generalized rhythmic delta activity (GRDA) are strongly associated with poor neurological outcomes and increased mortality [1,2]. Continuous EEG (cEEG) monitoring, though widely used, generates large volumes of data per patient, while expert review remains labor-intensive and time-consuming [3]. This limits timely interpretation in both resource-constrained and high-volume clinical settings. Automated, multi-class EEG interpretation could enable faster decision-making and scalable deployment within real-time health analytics platforms.



S. Mitra et al. (Eds.): PReMI 2025, LNCS 16358, pp. 160–168, 2026.
https://doi.org/10.1007/978-3-032-18480-1_16

*Research Gap:* Despite recent progress in automated seizure detection, existing systems fall short in four critical areas. First, clinically important non-seizure patterns—such as LPD, GPD, GRDA, LRDA, and other ACNS-defined abnormalities—remain underexplored. Second, deep models such as CNNs, RNNs, and transformers require large labeled datasets and extensive training time [4–6]. Third, conventional black-box models lack transparency, hindering clinical adoption. Fourth, few-shot learning scenarios—common when encountering novel patterns or operating in low-resource domains—remain insufficiently addressed.

*Scope and Objectives:* This paper addresses these gaps with three core objectives: (1) to develop an interpretable few-shot EEG classifier for six ACNS-defined abnormalities; (2) to introduce a query-aware prototype refinement mechanism that enhances robustness in heterogeneous support sets; and (3) to validate the framework on the HMS [7] dataset, focusing on accuracy, calibration, and explanation quality.

*Proposed Approach:* The proposed two-stage metric learning framework comprises **ProtoEEG**, a prototypical network built on a pretrained EfficientNetV2-S encoder, and **ProtoEEG-QA**, its attention-augmented variant. ProtoEEG learns class prototypes from support examples and classifies queries via Euclidean distances in the embedding space. ProtoEEG-QA refines these prototypes through a lightweight, query-conditioned attention module that dynamically weights support embeddings, enhancing adaptability and interpretability.

**Contributions:** In summary the key contribution of this paper are as follows:

1. **ProtoEEG:** A six-way, few-shot, explainable metric-learning framework for classifying ACNS-defined EEG abnormalities using episodic training.
2. **ProtoEEG-QA:** An attention-augmented extension that dynamically refines class prototypes via query-aware weighting, improving generalization under heterogeneous support conditions.
3. **Interpretability:** A transparent decision-making pipeline that links each prediction to weighted support examples, supporting clinical validation and deployment.
4. **Performance Evaluation:** A comprehensive shot-wise and class-wise analysis across multiple metrics (accuracy, AUROC, calibration), demonstrating the framework's reliability in low-shot regimes and clinically critical classes.

## 2    Literature Survey

Building on the promise of deep learning for automated EEG interpretation, prior work can be grouped into three categories—with each falling short of the combined goals of few-shot adaptability, attention-driven prototype refinement, and full six-class ACNS compliance that this paper targets.

***Deep CNN, RNN, and Transformer Models:*** Early end-to-end approaches leveraged convolutional networks (e.g., EEGNet [8]) and recurrent architectures (e.g., RNN-LSTM [9]) to detect seizures and other EEG events. While these models achieve high accuracy on large, seizure-focused datasets, they produce only binary outputs, require extensive labeled data, and offer no mechanism for tracing individual decisions. Transformer-based methods [6] improve global context modeling but demand even larger corpora and remain opaque.

***Attention-Augmented Architectures.*** Incorporating attention into CNNs has boosted performance for motor imagery (ATCNet [10]) and affective EEG tasks (AMDET [11]). Although they demonstrate the power of query–support interaction, these models neither address multi-class clinical taxonomies nor provide prototype-based explanations, limiting their applicability in neurocritical care.

***Metric-Based Few-Shot and Prototype Methods.*** Prototypical networks [12] introduce an interpretable, distance-based classification by averaging support embeddings into class prototypes. However, static averaging can be misled by noisy or heterogeneous support sets. Recent vision work has injected cross-attention to yield query-aware prototypes [13], but this innovation has not yet been applied to clinical EEG or the full six-class ACNS taxonomy.

Table 1 summarizes these prior approaches, contrasting their domain, few-shot capability, attention mechanisms, explainability, and coverage of the ACNS six classes. None jointly achieves the combination of few-shot learning, query-conditioned attention, full six-class coverage, and prototype-based interpretability that the proposed ProtoEEG-QA framework provides.

Table 1. Comparison of EEG classification methods.

| Model | Domain | Few-Shot | Attention | Explainable | ACNS-6 |
|---|---|---|---|---|---|
| EEGNet [8] | Seizure/BCI | ✗ | ✗ | ✗ | ✗ |
| ATCNet [10] | Motor Imagery | ✗ | ✓ | ✗ | ✗ |
| AMDET [11] | Emotion Recognition | ✗ | ✓ | ✗ | ✗ |
| ProtoNet [12] | Generic Few-Shot | ✓ | ✗ | ✓ | ✗ |
| TSLANet [14] | Time Series | ✗ | ✗ | ✗ | ✗ |
| ProtoEEG (proposed) | ICU EEG (six-class) | ✓ | ✗ | ✓ | ✓ |
| ProtoEEG-QA (proposed) | ICU EEG (six-class) | ✓ | ✓ | ✓ | ✓ |

## 3   Proposed Methodology

This section describes ProtoEEG-QA, an attention-guided prototypical network for interpretable few-shot classification of six ACNS-defined EEG abnormalities. We first formalize the task, then present an architectural overview (Figs. 1–2), and finally detail each component and its rationale.

### 3.1   Problem Statement

We tackle $C$-way, $K$-shot classification of EEG spectrogram segments into six harmful brain activity classes: Seizure, GPD, LRDA, Other, GRDA, and LPD.

A clinician-provided support set $\mathcal{S} = (x_i, y_i)_{i=1}^{C \times K}$ contains $K$ labeled examples per class, and the goal is to predict the correct label for an unseen query $x_q$.

***Architectural Overview:*** The baseline ProtoEEG (Fig. 1) processes precomputed EEG spectrograms into 3-channel, $224 \times 224$ RGB images, extracts 1280-D embeddings via EfficientNetV2-S, and forms class prototypes by averaging support embeddings; classification is performed by negative Euclidean distance to these prototypes. ProtoEEG-QA (Fig. 2) adds a query-aware attention module: for each query, support and query embeddings are concatenated, scored by a lightweight MLP to yield attention weights, and aggregated into attention-weighted prototypes, producing adaptive, more discriminative class representations.

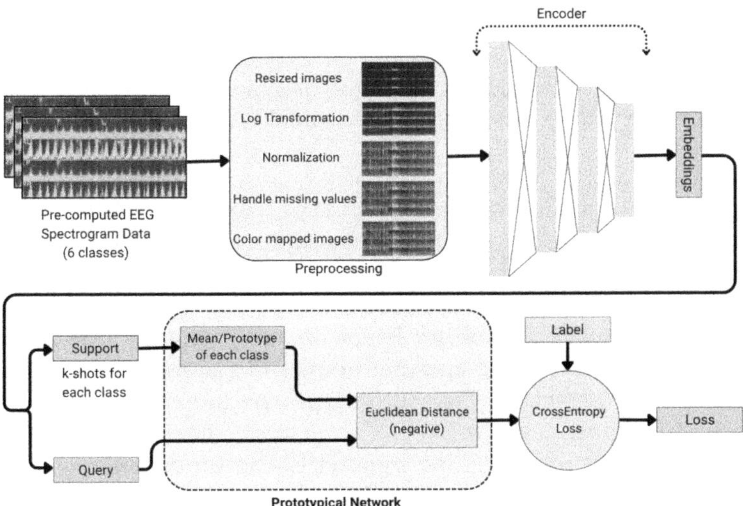


**Fig. 1.** ProtoEEG: Prototypical network baseline.

***Data Preprocessing:*** The HMS [7] dataset comprises spectrogram segments in Parquet format. Preprocessing includes dropping the `time` column and converting segments to NumPy arrays, followed by a $\log(1 + x)$ transform to compress dynamic range. Each segment is normalized by its maximum amplitude, with NaNs replaced by $10^{-4}$ to ensure numerical stability. Data are then quantized to the [0,255] range and cast to `uint8` for efficient memory mapping. A fixed 300-sample window is extracted from the annotated offset, converted to RGB via OpenCV's JET colormap, and scaled to [0,1]. Finally, segments are resized to $224 \times 224$ and permuted into $(C, H, W)$ tensor format. This pipeline ensures consistent, efficient input preparation compatible with pretrained image backbones.

***EfficientNetV2-S Embedding Backbone:*** We adopt EfficientNetV2-S [15] for its favorable accuracy–efficiency tradeoff. Initialized with ImageNet weights,

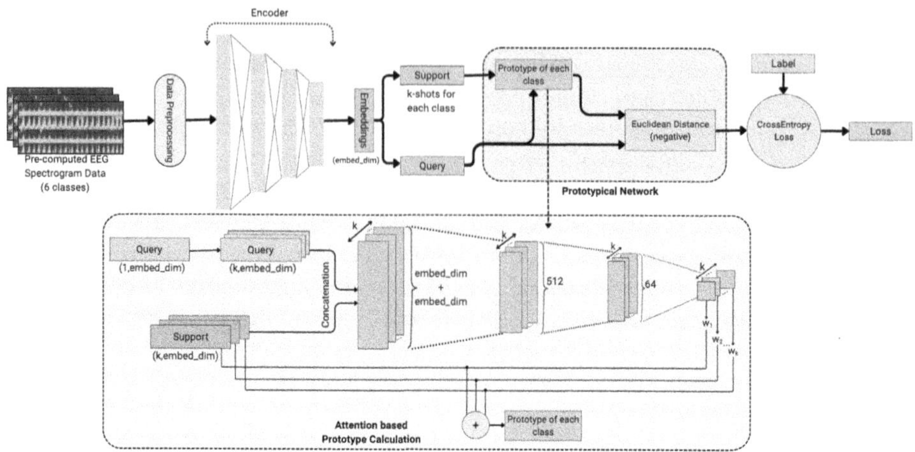



**Fig. 2.** ProtoEEG-QA: Attention-based prototypical network with query-aware attention for per-query weights, improving class separability in few-shot settings.

we replace its final classifier with `nn.Identity()`, exposing 1280-D embeddings. The model's Fused-MBConv and SE blocks capture both local and global spectrotemporal features, critical for distinguishing subtle EEG patterns in few-shot settings.

***Prototypical Network Baseline:*** Following the prototypical learning formulation [12], each meta-training episode samples $C$ classes with $K$ support and $Q$ query examples per class. Class prototypes $\mathbf{p}c$ are computed as the mean of support embeddings, i.e., $\mathbf{p}c = \frac{1}{K}\sum i : y_i = c z_i$. Each query embedding $z_q$ is compared to all prototypes using squared Euclidean distance, yielding logits $sq, c = -|z_q - \mathbf{p}_c|^2$. Episodic cross-entropy loss is minimized to promote tight intra-class clustering and distinct inter-class separation in the embedding space.

***Query-Aware Attention Module:*** To refine class prototypes dynamically and reduce the influence of noisy or heterogeneous support examples, a query-aware attention mechanism is introduced. For each class $c$, support embeddings $z_i$ are concatenated with the corresponding query embedding $z_q$ to form $[z_i\|z_q] \in \mathbb{R}^{2560}$. These pairs are processed through a multi-layer perceptron with two ReLU-activated hidden layers (512 and 64 units) followed by a softplus output, generating non-negative attention scores $a_i$. Scores are normalized as $w_i = a_i/(\sum_j a_j + \epsilon)$, and the query-adaptive prototype is computed as $\mathbf{p}_c(z_q) = \sum_{i:y_i=c} w_i z_i$. This allows the model to emphasize more relevant support examples per query, improving class discrimination under limited supervision [13].

***Model Training and Inference:*** We train with AdamW (weight decay $10^{-3}$) and a OneCycleLR schedule (base $10^{-5}$, max $3 \times 10^{-4}$) for 15,000 episodes. Each episode uses 6-way classification with $K \in \{5, 10, 15\}$ and $Q = 15$. At test time, we evaluate on 2,000 episodes, measuring accuracy, AUROC, F1-score, and calibration (ECE, Brier). The attention-augmented model consistently outperforms the baseline in all metrics, notably in low-shot regimes, validating query-aware prototype adaptation.

## 3.2  Meta-training and Evaluation

We adopt an episodic meta-learning protocol to simulate few-shot scenarios during training and evaluation:

***Episode Sampling:*** A fixed mapping from class labels to dataset indices is pre-computed to enable efficient episode generation. Each training episode randomly selects $C = 6$ classes, then samples $K \in \{5, 10, 15\}$ support and $Q = 15$ query examples per class.

***Optimization:*** We train for 15,000 episodes using AdamW with weight decay $10^{-3}$. A OneCycleLR schedule (base LR $1 \times 10^{-5}$, max LR $3 \times 10^{-4}$) provides smooth learning-rate annealing and rapid convergence. Cross-entropy loss on query logits drives prototype and attention-module learning.

***Meta-testing*** At test time, 2,000 episodes are sampled from the held-out test set, and each is evaluated using standard performance metrics (accuracy, AUROC, F1-score, kappa) as well as calibration measures (ECE, Brier Score).

# 4  Experiments and Experimental Results

This section presents the experimental design, evaluation protocol, and results assessing the accuracy, calibration, and interpretability of ProtoEEG and ProtoEEG-QA for multi-class EEG abnormality detection.

## 4.1  Dataset

The proposed framework is validated on the *HMS Harmful Brain Activity Classification* dataset [7], comprising 106,000 EEG spectrogram segments derived from recordings of 17,089 patients. Each sample corresponds to a 50-second EEG window recorded at 200 Hz from 19 EEG channels. Expert annotators labeled time-frequency spectrograms extracted from a 10-minute context window. Stratified splits (80% train, 10% validation, 10% test) are used to preserve class distribution across all phases.

## 4.2  Experimental Setup

Experiments are implemented in PyTorch 2.0 and conducted on an NVIDIA A100 GPU. The full codebase, pretrained models, and hyperparameters are available on Github[1] to ensure transparency and reproducibility. ProtoEEG and ProtoEEG-QA are trained episodically over 15,000 episodes of 6-way classification, varying $K \in \{5, 10, 15\}$ (support samples per class), with $Q = 15$ queries per class in each episode.

---

[1] https://github.com/Deepak-Mewada/ProtoEEG_QA.

***Episodic Meta-Learning Protocol:*** For each training and test episode, $C = 6$ classes are randomly sampled; for each class, $K$ labelled support and $Q = 15$ unlabelled query examples are chosen. All validation and model selection are performed episodically: the model is checkpointed at its highest validation accuracy observed every 50 episodes. Final reported metrics are aggregated over 2,000 test episodes to reflect true generalization and minimize reporting variance.

## 4.3  Results

This section validates ProtoEEG-QA's effectiveness across three dimensions: (1) baseline comparison and few-shot performance, (2) interpretability through visual diagnostics, and (3) ablation analysis confirming the attention mechanism's contribution.

**Table 2.** Performance comparison on 6-class ACNS EEG classification.

| Model | Acc (%) | Precision | Sensitivity | F1 | AUROC | Kappa |
|---|---|---|---|---|---|---|
| EEGNet [8] | 22.00 | 0.35 | 0.22 | 0.14 | 0.69 | 0.05 |
| ATCNet [10] | 39.00 | 0.47 | 0.39 | 0.37 | 0.75 | 0.25 |
| TSLANet [14] | 78.00 | 0.78 | 0.78 | 0.78 | 0.95 | 0.73 |
| ProtoEEG (proposed) | 83.66 | 0.83 | 0.83 | 0.83 | 0.92 | 0.80 |
| **ProtoEEG-QA (proposed)** | **85.37** | **0.85** | **0.85** | **0.85** | **0.97** | **0.82** |

***Performance Analysis and Baseline Comparison:*** Table 2 demonstrates ProtoEEG-QA's superior performance against established EEG classifiers. ProtoEEG-QA achieves 85.37% accuracy with 0.97 AUROC, outperforming ProtoEEG (83.66%, 0.92 AUROC) and substantially surpassing TSLANet (78%, 0.95 AUROC). Cohen's kappa improved from 0.80 to 0.82, indicating better clinical expert alignment.

Table 3 reveals ProtoEEG-QA's consistent superiority across few-shot regimes, with the largest gains in the challenging 5-shot scenario (85.23% vs 83.52%). Critically, ProtoEEG-QA maintains stable performance (85.19%-85.37%) regardless of support set size, while ProtoEEG peaks at 10-shot

**Table 3.** Few-shot performance comparison. Results averaged over 2,000 test episodes.

| Model | Shots | Acc. | AUROC | ECE | Brier |
|---|---|---|---|---|---|
| ProtoEEG | 5 | 0.8352 | 0.9376 | 0.4630 | 0.0891 |
| | 10 | 0.8486 | 0.9356 | 0.4662 | 0.0866 |
| | 15 | 0.8366 | 0.9340 | 0.4500 | 0.0880 |
| ProtoEEG-QA | 5 | **0.8523** | **0.9705** | **0.4152** | **0.0718** |
| | 10 | **0.8519** | **0.9692** | **0.4105** | **0.0714** |
| | 15 | **0.8537** | **0.9727** | **0.4121** | **0.0712** |

(84.86%). The attention mechanism provides superior calibration with ECE improvements of 0.05 and Brier score reductions of 0.017, particularly valuable for clinical confidence estimation.

***Visual Diagnostics and Interpretability.*** Figure 3 provides comprehensive visual evidence of ProtoEEG-QA's enhanced discriminability and interpretability. The confusion matrices show sharper diagonal dominance, particularly improving discrimination between clinically challenging GPD-LPD pairs.

t-SNE embeddings reveal tighter, well-separated class clusters, confirming the attention mechanism's ability to learn more discriminative representations.

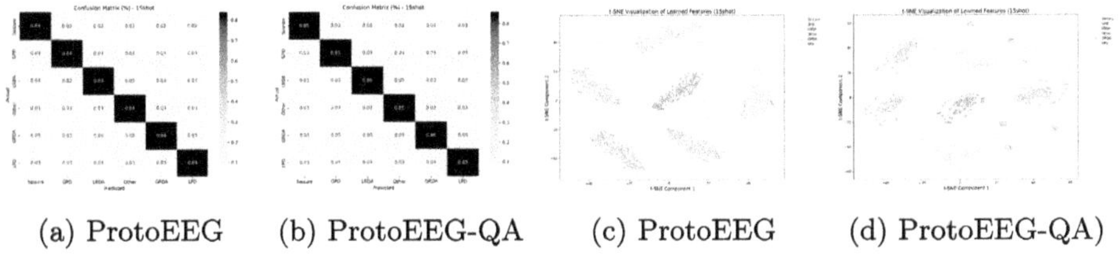

(a) ProtoEEG        (b) ProtoEEG-QA        (c) ProtoEEG        (d) ProtoEEG-QA)

**Fig. 3.** Visual comparison in 15-shot regime: confusion matrices (left two) and t-SNE embedding (right) demonstrating ProtoEEG-QA's superior class separation and interpretability.

***Class-wise Performance and Ablation Analysis.*** Class-wise analysis reveals systematic ProtoEEG-QA improvements across all ACNS patterns, with F1-scores consistently above 0.85 and specificity maintained above 0.96. LPD classification shows particularly notable gains (AUROC: 0.9342→0.9694 in 5-shot), critical given LPD's association with poor neurological outcomes. AUPRC improvements are striking, with ProtoEEG-QA achieving values above 0.91 versus ProtoEEG's 0.85–0.88 range.

The ablation study confirms the attention mechanism's contribution: removing attention reduces accuracy by 1.7% and AUROC by 0.04, definitively establishing that query-aware prototype weighting provides tangible benefits over static averaging, particularly valuable given EEG's high intra-class variability due to patient-specific factors and electrode placement variations.

## 4.4   Discussion

ProtoEEG-QA achieves interpretable few-shot EEG classification with notable gains in accuracy (+1.7%), AUROC (+0.05), and calibration (ECE −0.05). These enhancements support deployment in clinical settings where confidence and adaptability are vital. Query-aware attention improves performance under sparse annotations, reflecting real ICU constraints. Limitations include exclusive reliance on spectrograms, evaluation on a single dataset, and added inference overhead. Clinical metadata remains unused, and real-time viability needs further testing. Future work will explore temporal attention, multimodal integration, cross-dataset validation, and optimized deployment in ICU environments.

## 5   Conclusion

ProtoEEG-QA introduces an attention-guided prototypical network tailored for interpretable few-shot classification of six clinically relevant EEG abnormalities.

By dynamically refining class prototypes based on each query, the framework achieves 85.37% accuracy and 0.97 AUROC, while offering example-based explanations vital for clinical trust. Its robustness in low-shot settings and transparent reasoning make it a viable solution for scalable neurocritical care analytics, especially in environments lacking consistent expert EEG access.

# References


1. Claassen, J., et al.: Electrographic seizures and periodic discharges after intracerebral hemorrhage. Neurology **69**(13) (2007)
2. Beuchat, I., Rossetti, A.O., Novy, J.: Continuous versus routine standardized EEG for outcome prediction in critically ill adults: analysis from a randomized trial. Crit. Care Med. **50**(2), 329–334 (2022)
3. Jing, J., et al.: Rapid annotation of seizures and interictal-ictal continuum EEG patterns. In: Proceedings of the IEEE EMBC, pp. 3394–3397 (2018)
4. Craik, A., He, Y., Contreras-Vidal, J.L.: Deep learning for electroencephalogram classification tasks: a review. J. Neural Eng. **16**(3), 031001 (2019)
5. Saeidi, M., Karwowski, W., Farahani, F.V., et al.: Neural decoding of EEG with machine learning: a systematic review. Brain Sci. **11**(11), 1525 (2021)
6. Vaswani, A., Shazeer, N., Parmar, N., et al.: Attention is all you need. In: Advances in Neural Information Processing Systems, vol. 30, pp. 5998–6008 (2017)
7. Jing, J., Lin, Z., Yang, C., Chow, A., Dane, S., Sun, J., Westover, M.B.: HMS – Harmful brain activity classification Kaggle (2024)
8. Lawhern, V.J., Solon, A.J., Waytowich, N.R., Gordon, S.M., Hung, C.P., Lance, B.J.: EEGNet: a compact convolutional neural network for EEG-based brain-computer interfaces. J. Neural Eng. **15**(5), 056013 (2018)
9. Najafi, T., Jaafar, R., et al.: A classification model of EEG signals based on RNN-LSTM for diagnosing focal and generalized epilepsy. Sensors **22**(19), 7269 (2022)
10. Altaheri, H., Muhammad, G., Alsulaiman, M.: Physics-informed attention temporal convolutional network for EEG-based motor imagery classification. IEEE Transactions on Industrial Informatics (2023)
11. Xu, Y., Du, Y., et al.: AMDET: Attention based Multiple Dimensions EEG Transformer for emotion recognition. IEEE Trans. Affect. Comput. (2024)
12. Snell, J., Swersky, K., Zemel, R.: Prototypical networks for few-shot learning. In: Advances in Neural Information Processing Systems, vol.30, pp.4077–4087 (2017)
13. Hou, R., et al.: Cross attention network for few-shot classification. Neural Information Processing Systems (NeurIPS) (2019)
14. Eldele E, Ragab M, Chen Z, Wu M, Li X. TSLANet: rethinking transformers for time series representation learning. In: ICML (2024)
15. Tan, M., Le, Q.: EfficientNetV2: smaller models and faster training. In: ICML (2021)

# Multistage Fusion Framework
# for Coronary Artery Disease Detection
# from Multichannel Phonocardiogram

Arnab Maity[1](✉), Souvik Sinha[1], Matthew Fynn[2], Milan Marocchi[2],
Kayapanda Mandana[3], Yue Rong[2], and Goutam Saha[1]

[1] Department of Electronics and Electrical Communication Engineering, Indian
Institute of Technology, Kharagpur, India
`arnab10maity@iitkgp.ac.in, souvik_sinha@kgpian.iitkgp.ac.in,`
`gsaha@ece.iitkgp.ac.in`
[2] School of Electrical Engineering, Computing and Mathematical Sciences, Curtin
University, Perth, Australia
`{matthew.fynn,milan.marocchi}@postgrad.curtin.edu.au,`
`y.rong@curtin.edu.au`
[3] Department of Cardiology, Fortis Healthcare, Kolkata, India

**Abstract.** Coronary artery disease (CAD) remains one of the leading causes of mortality worldwide. Phonocardiogram (PCG) signals offer a non-invasive, affordable, and accessible means for early detection of CAD. However, the diverse acoustic manifestations of the disease across different auscultation sites make accurate diagnosis using a single-channel stethoscope challenging. Moreover, the scarcity of large annotated datasets further limits the development of robust diagnostic models. This work presents a multichannel CAD detection framework using transfer learning that leverages both early/late fusion from multiple auscultation sites. A lightweight pretrained deep learning model is designed to address data scarcity and enable computationally efficient deployment. We explore early and late fusion strategies to extract the channel-wise collective information in detecting CAD. The proposed system achieves a 9.46% improvement in accuracy over its single-channel counterpart, highlighting its potential for practical and scalable CAD screening. Clinically, it provides an affordable, accessible, and efficient tool for CAD detection, especially in low-resource settings.

**Keywords:** Coronary artery disease · Phonocardiogram · Transfer learning · Embedding fusion · Multichannel Stethoscope

## 1  Introduction

Cardiovascular diseases (CVDs) represent the foremost global health concern, accounting for approximately 31% of deaths worldwide [1]. Among the diverse spectrum of CVDs, coronary artery disease (CAD) is the primary contributor to


S. Mitra et al. (Eds.): PReMI 2025, LNCS 16358, pp. 169–178, 2026.
https://doi.org/10.1007/978-3-032-18480-1_17

CVD-related deaths and often serves as a precursor to life-threatening diseases. Early detection of CAD is crucial to mitigate its progression and associated complications. Conventional diagnostic techniques, such as coronary angiography, require specialized medical infrastructure, are expensive, invasive, and are often limited to symptomatic patients [1]. Heart auscultation is a cost-effective preliminary screening method for detecting abnormal heart sounds caused by irregular cardiac function. Phonocardiograms (PCGs) graphically represent heart sounds and can reveal CAD-related alterations both visually and algorithmically [1].

Early research in CAD detection primarily focused on handcrafted features with traditional machine learning methods [6,11]. With advancements in deep learning (DL), researchers have shifted towards automated feature extractors using convolutional neural networks (CNN) [9]. The need for extensive feature engineering was eliminated by extracting representations from raw signals [4,6,10]. However, in PCG classification, available training data are typically limited. DL models, while powerful, risk overfitting when data are scarce. Recently, transfer learning (TL) has shown promising results; however, most studies overlooked the impact of model complexity [6,12]. Also, studies predominantly rely on single-channel PCG signals, using only one auscultation site to predict disease signatures [6,9]. Recent research indicates that analyzing data from multiple auscultation sites is crucial for identifying robust disease markers [4,5,8,14]. These studies explored advanced features, including entropy-based measures and cross-entropy analysis, collectively underscoring the importance of dataset diversity in multichannel PCG [5,10]. Pathak et al. [10] applied the synchrosqueezing transform to extract entropy features using four stethoscopes and used a support vector machine classifier to detect the CAD. Zhao et al. [15] proposed a hybrid convolution transformer neural network for extracting local features. However, some of these methods rely on a separate algorithm to segment the PCG signals. Fynn et al. [1] proposed a seven-channel, wearable, non-invasive vest-based data acquisition system that enables enhanced data collection without the need for special assistance, used linear frequency cepstral coefficient, and achieved an accuracy of 80.44%. However, it relied on manual PCG signal segmentation. Therefore, existing CAD detection approaches typically utilize single-channel PCG recordings, demand high computational resources, and occasionally depend on manual processing during segmentation and feature extraction. In multichannel approaches, studies typically determine optimal channel combinations based on test results, which limits the real-world applicability.

This study presents a novel approach for CAD detection using TL to extract embeddings from multichannel PCG signals recorded at seven distinct auscultation sites. Instead of relying on computationally intensive cardiac cycle segmentation, we extract fixed-length fragments directly from time-frequency (TF) representations. A lightweight, pretrained DL model is used for embedding extraction, reducing system complexity while maintaining performance under limited training data. To ensure unbiased and generalizable results, embedding-level fusion is performed by combining channels based on their individual validation performance. Furthermore, score-level fusion of predictions from various channel combinations is applied to reinforce the effectiveness of multichannel integration.

## 2   Database Description

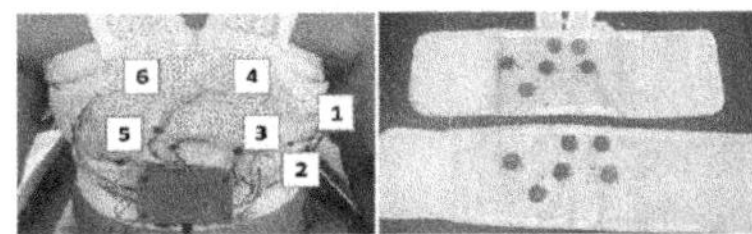

**Fig. 1.** Wearable vest (left) and vest fitted with electronic stethoscopes (right) [1].

The PCG data were recorded using a wearable vest equipped with 7-channel stethoscopes, positioned at multiple auscultation sites (Fig. 1) [1]. The data was acquired at Fortis Hospital, Kolkata, India. The hospital ethics committee approved data collection. Informed consent was obtained from all participants, and identifying information was anonymized. Recordings were obtained from 71 healthy and 119 CAD male patients seated and breathing normally in a noisy hospital environment. Diagnosis was confirmed using coronary angiography. The mean age of CAD and normal patients was $60 \pm 15$ years and $50 \pm 10$ years.

## 3   Methodology

### 3.1   Preprocessing and Feature Extraction

We applied an 8th-order Butterworth band-pass filter ($25\ Hz - 400\ Hz$) to remove low and high-frequency noise [7]. This was followed by z-score normalization across all channels to standardize amplitude and inter-recording variability. The signal duration considered is 10 seconds. To extract discriminative TF features that capture the non-stationary nature of PCG signals, we employed a log-mel spectrogram and a continuous wavelet transform (CWT) based scalogram (Fig. 2). For the mel-spectrogram, we use 64 mel filter banks, and for the scalogram, we employ the Morlet (Gabor) wavelet as the mother wavelet [10].

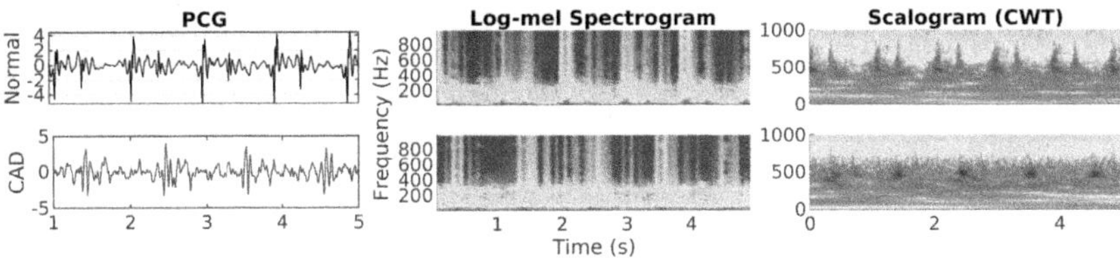

**Fig. 2.** Time-frequency representations of PCG signals for normal and CAD cases.

## 3.2  Classification Framework

This work utilizes TL with a pre-trained model to address the inherent challenges of limited training data in PCG classification. The YAMNet model [13] is an efficient, lightweight deep learning architecture specifically designed for audio classification. It employs depthwise separable convolution layers and significantly reduces computational complexity and model size (15.5 MB) [3,13]. It is pre-trained on a vast corpus of 1.2 million YouTube audio segments (AudioSet), providing a rich repository of acoustically relevant features [2,6]. The advantages of using TL include reducing the risk of overfitting, minimizing training time, avoiding designing the model from scratch, simplifying hyperparameter tuning, and enabling the learning of robust, generalizable features.

**Early Fusion:** Since multichannel PCG recordings are collected from different auscultation sites, they capture diverse information reflecting the functional characteristics of the human heart. We hypothesize that embeddings extracted from these channels contain discriminative information that can be leveraged for CAD detection. Thereby, we propose an early embedding fusion approach with deep features extracted from each channel. The input $x \in \mathbb{R}^{C \times T \times F}$ consists of TF representations from $C$ channels, where $T$ and $F$ represent the time frames and frequency bins, respectively. For each selected channel $f_i = x_i \in \mathbb{R}^{1 \times T \times F}$, features are extracted using a frozen YAMNet backbone up to its penultimate convolutional block. The convolution block consists of the last five convolutional layers of the YAMNet architecture, specifically those following the frozen layers and preceding the final fully connected (FC) layer. Each channel's output is processed through a global average pooling (GAP) layer followed by flattening, yielding embeddings $e_i \in \mathbb{R}^D$, where $D = 1024$. These embeddings are then fused by computing their mean across all $n$ selected channels, resulting in a single representation $E = \frac{1}{n} \sum_{i=1}^{n} e_i, \quad E \in \mathbb{R}^D$. Finally, $E$ is passed through a common FC layer to produce the output prediction $\hat{y} \in \mathbb{R}^K$, where $K$ is the number of target classes. The convolutional block, along with the FC layer, is unfrozen for fine-tuning. Selective unfreezing helps adapt high-level features for CAD detection while retaining YAMNet's general acoustic knowledge [6]. The mean is used instead of concatenation to control model complexity and avoid increasing feature dimensionality. This strategy preserves the original embedding size, keeps the classification lightweight, and reduces the number of trainable parameters. Also, averaging promotes more robust representations by reducing overfitting due to limited data. For single-channel operation, there will be no fusion. A schematic representation of this method is shown in Fig. 3.

**Late Fusion:** We further enhance diagnostic robustness through a late score-level fusion strategy. The goal is to combine outputs from multiple model configurations trained on different subsets of input channels ($S_c \subseteq \{1, 2, \ldots, 7\}$, $S_c \neq \emptyset$, $c = 1, 2, \ldots (2^7 - 1)$) at the decision level to avoid the risk of misclassification by any single configuration. Let $\mathcal{S} = [S_1, S_2, \ldots, S_n]$ denote the $n$ set of selected

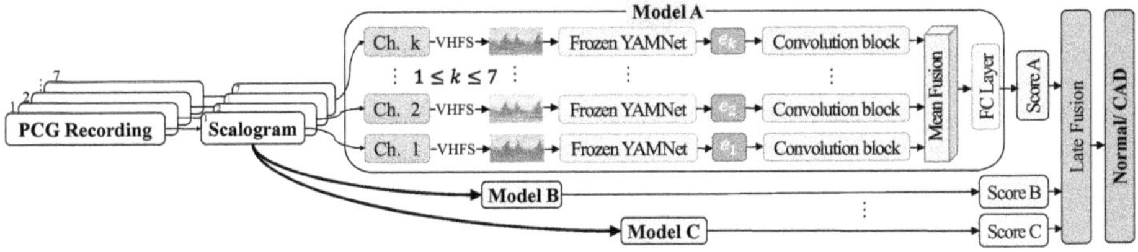


**Fig. 3.** Block diagram of the multi-channel embedding fusion using the YAMNet model.

channel subsets, and let $s_{[S_c]} \in \mathbb{R}^K$ represent the confidence score vector produced by the model trained on subset $S_c$, where $K$ is the number of classes. The final fused prediction is computed as $s_{\text{fused}} = \frac{1}{n} \sum_{c=1}^{n} s_{[S_c]} \in \mathbb{R}^K$. This approach aggregates complementary information and provides more reliable prediction.

**Input Preparation:** CNNs typically require fixed-size inputs for effective feature extraction. However, TF representations of PCG signals vary in length due to differences in signal duration. Prior studies addressed this using cardiac cycle-wise segmentation with zero-padding. Extracting individual cycles demands a separate algorithm, adding complexity to preprocessing. This work segments the TF matrix into fragments of uniform length using Variable Hop Fragment Selection (VHFS) proposed in [7]. VHFS extracts multiple overlapping fragments of fixed duration (2.5 s), covering at least one full cardiac cycle, from the TF representation of PCG signals by varying the hop length. The number of fragments per sample is determined by the fragment selection factor $(n_f)$, ensuring balanced class distributions and increased training data. VHFS bypasses the computationally intensive and error-prone step of precise heart sound localization and segmentation, reducing system complexity and computational overhead. For both validation and test datasets, an equal number of fragments is selected from each sample, regardless of its length or label.

## 4    Results and Discussion

The accuracy, sensitivity, specificity, F1 score, and unweighted average recall (UAR) are calculated to assess the system's performance [7]. We implemented stratified 7-fold cross-validation by splitting the dataset into seven subject-disjoint folds. In each iteration, five folds are used for training, one fold for validation, and one fold for testing. The experiments were performed using the Adam optimizer with 30 epochs, a batch size of 64, and a learning rate of 0.001, which were determined as the optimal values after empirical evaluation on training data. An early stopping criterion with a patience of five epochs has been implemented to avoid overfitting. To ensure reproducibility, we fix random seed values across all experiments. Majority voting is applied to the predictions of all fragments belonging to each subject to evaluate subject-level performance.

### 4.1  TF Feature-Based Performance Comparison on Single Channel

**Table 1.** Channel-wise performance comparison across different features

| Channel | log-mel spectrogram | | | Scalogram | | | | | | Rank |
|---|---|---|---|---|---|---|---|---|---|---|
| | Acc. | Sens. | Spec. | Acc. | Sens. | Spec. | F1 score | UAR | Valid. Acc. | |
| 1 | 59.96 | 78.15 | 28.96 | 64.17 | 79.83 | 37.7 | 73.46 | 58.81 | 65.74 | 4 |
| 2 | 59.96 | 74.79 | 35.06 | 58.37 | 70.59 | 38.05 | 67.01 | 54.32 | 67.35 | 3 |
| 3 | 61.56 | 73.11 | 41.82 | **67.86** | 81.51 | **44.94** | 76.11 | **63.22** | **70.99** | 1 |
| 4 | **71.03** | **85.71** | 46.36 | 66.84 | **88.24** | 30.78 | **76.68** | 59.51 | 68.93 | 2 |
| 5 | 60.54 | 73.95 | 38.31 | 61.58 | 74.79 | 39.48 | 70.45 | 57.14 | 63.13 | 6 |
| 6 | 63.68 | 73.95 | **46.75** | 64.76 | 81.51 | 36.75 | 74.38 | 59.13 | 62.07 | 7 |
| 7 | 61.55 | 73.11 | 42.34 | 62.09 | 79.83 | 32.08 | 71.34 | 55.95 | 65.25 | 5 |

Table 1 presents the channel-wise performance comparison for two TF features. The scalogram achieves 3.36% higher average sensitivity across channels than log-mel spectrograms. YAMNet was originally trained on log-mel spectrograms. Therefore, the model is fine-tuned on scalograms by unfreezing its convolutional block to learn dataset-specific patterns [6]. Scalograms provide a richer TF representation by preserving both fine-grained temporal and spectral variations, which are critical in detecting subtle pathological cues in PCGs. In all further experiments, we have considered the scalogram as an input feature to the model. To analyze channel relevance, we ranked the channels based on fold-wise average validation performance, ensuring the most informative channels are emphasized. This approach guides the multi-channel feature fusion. Validation accuracy was chosen instead of test accuracy to ensure unbiased evaluation targeting real-time implementation. Channel 3 stands out as the most informative, with the highest validation accuracy (70.99%), test accuracy (67.86%), and UAR (63.22%).

### 4.2  Embedding Level Fusion of Multiple Channels

We now perform embedding-level fusion across multiple channels, based on channel rank as in Table 1. Table 2 represents the performance of the different channel combinations. Multi-channel fusion consistently outperforms single-channel models. Different auscultation sites across the chest exhibit site-specific acoustic characteristics, providing a multi-view perspective on pathological patterns. The combination of channels 3, 4 has the highest impact with 75.23% test accuracy. A paired t-test has been conducted to compare the performances of the best single-channel model and the proposed multichannel method across 7-folds. The results showed a statistically significant difference at the 5% significance level (p = 0.0019). The confidence interval of the mean difference [-10.80%, -3.94%] indicates that the multichannel approach consistently outperformed the single-channel model. However, not all combinations lead to improved performance, as seen with [3, 4, 2] and [2, 4]. This highlights the complexity of selecting the optimal set of PCG channels. With seven available channels, there are

**Table 2.** Performance comparison for embedding level fusion of multiple channels based on different combination types

| Combn. type | Ch. combn. | Validation | | | Test | | | | |
|---|---|---|---|---|---|---|---|---|---|
| | | Acc. | Sens. | Spec | Acc. | Sens. | Spec. | F1 score | UAR |
| Type I | **[3,4]** | **75.23** | 87.39 | 54.68 | **75.23** | **88.24** | 52.99 | 81.79 | **70.61** |
| | [3, 4, 2] | 73.09 | 84.87 | 53.25 | 66.23 | 75.63 | 50.26 | 73.52 | 62.94 |
| | [3, 4, 2, 1] | 72.54 | 84.03 | 53.12 | 69.46 | 80.67 | 50.91 | 76.72 | 65.79 |
| | [3, 4, 2, 1, 7] | 71.54 | 82.35 | 53.12 | 71.52 | 83.19 | 51.82 | 78.10 | 67.51 |
| | [3, 4, 2, 1, 7, 5] | 74.70 | 86.55 | 54.55 | 69.01 | 84.87 | 42.47 | 77.26 | 63.67 |
| | [3, 4, 2, 1, 7, 5, 6] | 66.86 | 77.31 | 49.48 | 74.42 | 63.40 | 71.01 | **83.19** | 50.26 |
| Type II | [2, 4] | 70.46 | 82.35 | 50.52 | 67.35 | 79.83 | 46.36 | 75.24 | 63.10 |
| | [2, 4, 3] | - | - | - | - | - | - | - | - |
| | [2, 4, 3, 6] | 66.25 | 80.67 | 42.08 | 68.41 | 78.15 | 51.95 | 75.47 | 65.05 |
| Type III | **[3,4]** | - | - | - | - | - | - | - | - |
| Type IV | [1, 3, 7] | 74.17 | **88.24** | 50.39 | 67.88 | 81.51 | 45.06 | 76.18 | 63.29 |
| Type V | [3, 4, 5, 6, 7] | 63.61 | 67.23 | **57.40** | 68.94 | 62.31 | **67.84** | 71.43 | 61.69 |

$(2^7 - 1) - 7 = 120$ non-trivial combinations (excluding single channels), making exhaustive evaluation impractical in real-world scenarios. We categorized the channel combinations into different types to guide the selection process. We selected a representative subset of combinations for further analysis based on the following criteria: **Type I**: Based on single channel ranking (Table 1), **Type II**: Based on the anatomical and physiological relevance of channels, **Type III**: Based on highest validation accuracy, **Type IV**: Based on highest validation sensitivity, and **Type V**: Based on highest validation specificity. Type I channel combinations are the most effective, achieving higher performance compared to single channels. Type II combinations, selected based on the clinical relevance of auscultation sites, partially overlap with Type I, further reinforcing the clinical significance of the selected channels. Type III, Type IV, and Type V combinations are included for score-level fusion strategies in subsequent stages.

### 4.3  Score Level Fusion of Single/multiple Channels Combinations

We integrate the output scores of individual models trained on different channel combinations to further enhance the insight. We used a selected channel combination from the combination types to perform the score-level fusion as indicated in Table 2. Table 3 demonstrates that the score-level fusion strategy achieved a 2.09% better accuracy and 2.93% better UAR over feature-level fusion alone, particularly when using top channel combinations from all five types [3, [34], [24], [137], [34567]]. The sequential application of early (embedding-level) and late (score-level) fusion enhances the interpretability of the model and reinforces the diagnostic potential of multichannel PCG analysis.

**Discussions:** Signals from the left fourth and second intercostal spaces (channels 3 and 4) are most informative. Fusion across channels enhanced disease classification, with feature-level fusion capturing local patterns and score-level (late) fusion further boosting performance. However, the relatively low speci-

**Table 3.** Score level fusion on the different single and multi-channel combinations

| Criterion | Channel combinations | Accuracy | Sensitivity | Specificity | F1 score | UAR |
|---|---|---|---|---|---|---|
| Single ch. | [[3], [4]] | 70.48 | **90.76** | 36.36 | 79.43 | 63.56 |
| | [[2], [3], [4]] | 68.90 | 88.24 | 36.49 | 77.78 | 62.37 |
| Multi ch. | [[34], [24], [137], [34567]] | 73.64 | 84.03 | 55.97 | 79.82 | 70.01 |
| | [[34], [24], [234], [137], [34567]] | 75.21 | 85.72 | 57.40 | 81.25 | 71.56 |
| Single & multi ch. | [3, [34], [24], [137], [34567]] | **77.32** | 88.24 | **58.83** | **82.93** | **73.54** |

ficity observed indicates a tendency toward false positives, likely due to limited variability in normal signals. The data was collected in a real-world hospital environment, where substantial ambient noise and operational constraints affected signal quality. In particular, the wearable sensor vest was not optimally fitted for each patient, leading to inconsistent contact and motion-induced artifacts. This suggests a need for better data balancing and adaptive denoising in future studies. We conducted our study using the same data acquisition device as Fynn et al. [1], allowing for a direct comparison. They reported an accuracy of 80.44% on a fully balanced, breath-held PCG dataset (40 normal, 40 abnormal), relying on manually segmented cardiac cycles and handcrafted features classified with an SVM. Additionally, their feature fusion strategy was based on test accuracy, which can lead to biased performance estimates. In contrast, our approach handles imbalanced data (71 normal, 119 abnormal) collected without breath holding and without segmentation. We use automatic feature extraction through a lightweight pretrained DL model, addressing data-related challenges and computational efficiency. The proposed 7-channel TL model requires 501.95 million multiply–accumulate operations (MMac) per inference and 2.05 k trainable parameters, indicating potential for deploying in mobile devices.

## 5   Conclusion

This study proposes a TL-based fusion framework with a pre-trained YAMNet model for identifying CAD from multichannel PCG signals. We first compared single-channel performances obtained using log-mel spectrogram and scalogram. The higher performance with the scalogram suggests that the dynamic TF resolution better captures CAD-related signatures. At this stage, channel ranking has been introduced based on the validation performance. We then performed embedding-level fusion by combining channels according to rank, clinical relevance, and performance metrics. Among all multi-channel configurations, the best-performing combination achieved 7.37% higher accuracy compared to the best single-channel model. This underscores the critical role of integrating information from multiple auscultation sites in CAD detection. Finally, we applied score-level fusion by integrating prediction scores from selected models, further enhancing the accuracy by 2.09%. Overall, the proposed method achieved an accuracy of 77.32%, sensitivity of 88.24%, and UAR of 73.54%. Importantly, it eliminates the need for signal segmentation and works effectively under low-resource settings. Controlled data collection and improved model architectures can be explored in future work to achieve further performance gains.

**Acknowledgement.** This work is funded by The Scheme for Promotion of Academic and Research Collaboration (SPARC), Indian Institute of Technology Kharagpur, and is done in collaboration with Curtin University, Perth, Australia. We thank Ticking Heart Pty Ltd for use of their wearable vest for data collection.

# References


1. Fynn, M., Mandana, K., Rashid, J., Nordholm, S., Rong, Y., Saha, G.: Practicality meets precision: wearable vest with integrated multi-channel PCG sensors for effective coronary artery disease pre-screening. Comput. Biol. Med. **189**, 109904 (2025)
2. Gemmeke, J.F., et al.: Audio set: an ontology and human-labeled dataset for audio events. In: ICASSP, pp. 776–780. IEEE (2017)
3. Hershey, S., Chaudhuri, S., Ellis, D.P., et al.: CNN architectures for large-scale audio classification. In: 2017 IEEE international conference on acoustics, speech and signal processing (ICASSP), pp. 131–135. IEEE (2017)
4. Huang, Q., Yang, H., Zeng, E., Chen, Y.: A deep-learning-based multi-modal ECG and PCG processing framework for label efficient heart sound segmentation. In: 2024 IEEE/ACM Conference on Connected Health: Applications, Systems and Engineering Technologies (CHASE), pp. 109–119. IEEE (2024)
5. Li, H., et al.: A fusion framework based on multi-domain features and deep learning features of phonocardiogram for coronary artery disease detection. Comput. Biol. Med. **120**, 103733 (2020)
6. Maity, A., Pathak, A., Saha, G.: Transfer learning based heart valve disease classification from phonocardiogram signal. Biomed. Signal Process. Control **85**, 104805 (2023)
7. Maity, A., Saha, G.: Time-frequency fragment selection for disease detection from imbalanced phonocardiogram data. In: 2023 45th Annual International Conference of the IEEE Engineering in Medicine & Biology Society, pp. 1–4. IEEE (2023)
8. Makaryus, A.N., Makaryus, J.N., Figgatt, A., others.: Utility of an advanced digital electronic stethoscope in the diagnosis of coronary artery disease compared with coronary computed tomographic angiography. Am. J. Cardiol. **111**(6), 786–792 (2013)
9. Megalmani, D.R., Shailesh, B., Rao, A., Jeevannavar, S.S., Ghosh, P.K.: Unsegmented heart sound classification using hybrid CNN-LSTM neural networks. In: 43rd Annual International Conference of the IEEE Engineering in Medicine & Biology Society (EMBC), pp. 713–717. IEEE (2021)
10. Pathak, A., Mandana, K., Saha, G.: Ensembled transfer learning and multiple kernel learning for phonocardiogram based atherosclerotic coronary artery disease detection. IEEE J. Biomed. Health Inform. (2022)
11. Pathak, A., Samanta, P., Mandana, K., Saha, G.: Detection of coronary artery atherosclerotic disease using novel features from synchrosqueezing transform of phonocardiogram. Biomed. Signal Process. Control **62**, 102055 (2020)
12. Pathak, A., Samanta, P., Mandana, K., Saha, G.: An improved method to detect coronary artery disease using phonocardiogram signals in noisy environment. Appl. Acoust. **164**, 107242 (2020)

13. Plakal, M., Ellis, D.: Yamnet. [Online: Accessed 15 June 2025] Available: https://github.com/tensorflow/models/tree/master/research/audioset/ (2021)
14. Schmidt, S.E., Holst-Hansen, C., Hansen, J., Toft, E., Struijk, J.J.: Acoustic features for the identification of coronary artery disease. IEEE Trans. Biomed. Eng. **62**(11), 2611–2619 (2015)
15. Zhao, W., Ma, H., et al.: Detection of coronary heart disease based on heart sound and hybrid vision transformer. Appl. Acoust. **230**, 110420 (2025)

# XSleepFormer: A Compact CNN-Transformer for EEG Sleep Stage Classification with Cross-Subject and Cross-Age Generalization


Deepak Mewada$^{(\boxtimes)}$, Susmit Shegokar, Monalisa Sarma, and Debasis Samanta

Indian Institute of Technology, Kharagpur, India
`deepakmewada96@kgpian.iitkgp.ac.in`



**Abstract.** Accurate EEG-based sleep stage classification is crucial for diagnosing sleep disorders; however, manual annotation remains time-consuming and subjective. Recent deep learning models have improved performance, but key challenges persist, particularly in modeling long-range temporal dependencies, handling class imbalance, and ensuring generalization across subjects and age groups. This work addresses these limitations by introducing **XSleepFormer**, a hybrid deep learning architecture designed for generalizable sleep staging. It combines a CNN-based embedding generator for efficient temporal compression with a Transformer encoder for capturing long-range dependencies. To enhance minority class performance and resilience to distributional shifts, the model integrates Focal Loss, MixUp augmentation, and Virtual Adversarial Training (VAT). XSleepFormer is evaluated on the Sleep-EDF dataset across three realistic scenarios: within-subject, cross-subject, and cross-age generalization. XSleepFormer achieves 83.11% accuracy (AUC = 0.966) in within-subject, 84.58% (AUC = 0.975) in cross-subject, and maintains >83.7% accuracy in elderly cohorts aged 65–80 and 80+. Compared to SOTA SleepStagerBlanco and SleepStagerChambon, XSleepFormer demonstrates consistent gains across all metrics, confirming its suitability for real-world clinical deployment.


## 1 Introduction

Accurate classification of sleep stages using Electroencephalogram (EEG) signals is crucial for diagnosing and managing sleep-related disorders, including insomnia, sleep apnea, narcolepsy, and REM behavior disorder. Traditionally, this task has relied on manual scoring of polysomnography data by sleep technologists following American Academy of Sleep Medicine (AASM) protocols [1]. However, manual annotation is labor-intensive, time-consuming, and subject to significant inter-scorer variability [2], which has fueled research into automated sleep staging systems.

Early automated approaches relied on classical signal processing techniques, including Fourier transforms, wavelet decomposition, and bandpower extraction.


© The Author(s), under exclusive license to Springer Nature Switzerland AG 2026
S. Mitra et al. (Eds.): PReMI 2025, LNCS 16358, pp. 179–188, 2026.
https://doi.org/10.1007/978-3-032-18480-1_18

These methods required domain-specific, handcrafted features, as noted in [3]. While they were interpretable, they lacked robustness to variability between subjects and often failed to capture complex, long-range temporal dependencies. Traditional machine learning models, such as support vector machines (SVMs) and random forests, which were built on these features, faced limitations due to their reliance on feature quality and struggled to generalize effectively across different subjects. The introduction of deep learning brought a paradigm shift by enabling end-to-end learning. CNN-based architectures showed promising results in capturing spatial features from raw EEG or spectrogram representations [4,5]. However, their inherently local receptive fields limited their ability to model temporal transitions across epochs. Recurrent models like LSTMs and GRUs were later introduced to address this [6], offering temporal modeling capabilities. Yet, they suffered from vanishing gradients, sequential inference constraints, and a limited temporal reach, especially for full-night EEG sequences.

Transformer encoders have shown a strong ability to model long-range dependencies in EEG and improve sleep staging performance, especially when combined with CNN-based feature extractors [7,8]. Recent studies such as Sleep-Transformer [9] and FlexSleepTransformer [10] confirm that attention mechanisms capture global temporal context more effectively than traditional recurrent models. Recent work, such as DistillSleep, further demonstrates that efficient, interpretable architectures can achieve real-time sleep staging using single-channel EEG [11]. Despite these advances, key challenges remain: (1) long and redundant EEG sequences increase computational cost, (2) rare stages like N1 and REM lead to class imbalance, and (3) generalization across subjects and age groups is still limited.

To address these issues, this paper introduces **XSleepFormer**, a compact hybrid architecture for robust and scalable EEG-based sleep stage classification. The framework combines CNN layers that compress raw EEG into compact, transformer-ready embeddings with a transformer encoder that models long-range temporal dependencies across epochs. The network is optimized using Focal Loss [12], MixUp [13], and Virtual Adversarial Training (VAT) to handle class imbalance, improve generalization, and enforce smoother decision boundaries.

XSleepFormer is evaluated on the PhysioNet Sleep-EDF dataset [14] using subject-dependent, cross-subject, and cross-age setups. In particular, this paper emphasizes performance on elderly cohorts to validate generalization under age-related EEG variability. Results show strong and consistent improvements over state-of-the-art baselines.

***Key Contributions*** of this paper are as follows:

1. **XSleepFormer:** A hybrid deep learning model combining CNN-based embedding generation and a transformer encoder for effective EEG-based sleep stage classification.
2. **Transformer-Ready Representations:** Compact temporal embeddings allow transformers to model long EEG sequences efficiently without memory bottlenecks.

3. **Improved Generalization:** Incorporates MixUp, VAT, and Focal Loss to handle class imbalance and inter-subject/age variability, ensuring robustness in elderly subjects.
4. **Comprehensive Evaluation:** Assessed across subject-dependent, cross-subject, and cross-age scenarios on Sleep-EDF, demonstrating robustness under demographic shifts.

The remainder of the paper is organized as follows: Next Sect. 2 discusses the proposed framework of XSleepFormer. Section 3 describes the experimental details and the results that XSleepFormer yields under those experimental settings. Finally, Sect. 4 concludes the paper.

## 2    Proposed Methodology

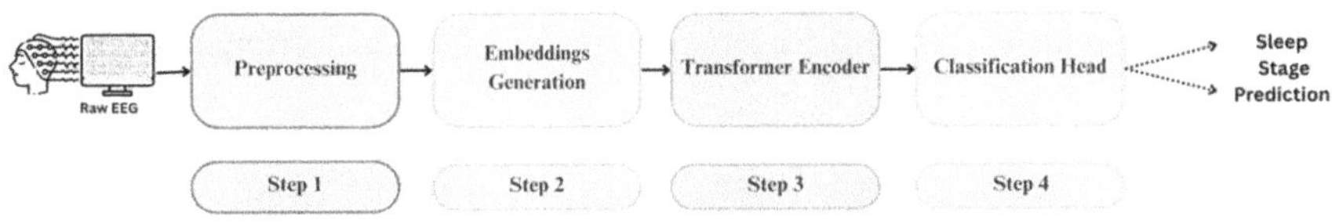


**Fig. 1.** Overview of the proposed XSleepFormer methodology.

Figure 1 presents a high-level overview of the proposed XSleepFormer pipeline. XSleepFormer is a hybrid deep learning framework that integrates a transformer-based global sequence model with an EEG signal-specific embedding generator. The model consists of four primary stages: (1) preprocessing, (2) embedding generation, (3) transformer encoding, and (4) classification head. Figure 2 illustrates the internal structure of each component. The details of each of these subcomponents will be discussed in the following section.

### 2.1    Preprocessing

Raw EEG recordings are first segmented into non-overlapping 30-second epochs, consistent with standard sleep scoring protocols. Each epoch is sampled at 100 Hz, resulting in a 2-channel signal of shape $(2, 3000)$, where the two channels correspond to different scalp locations. To mitigate inter-subject variability and measurement noise, signals are normalized and bandpass filtered within the physiological EEG range (e.g., 0.3–35 Hz). This ensures that the inputs retain relevant frequency components for sleep stage prediction while minimizing irrelevant noise.

## 2.2   Embedding Generation

To mitigate the quadratic time complexity of self-attention mechanisms in transformers ($\mathcal{O}(T^2)$), directly processing high-resolution EEG signals is computationally infeasible. Therefore, XSleepFormer introduces an *embedding generation block* that compresses the raw input into a more compact representation while retaining meaningful temporal structure. As illustrated in the Fig. 2, this block comprises four sequential 1D convolutional layers with increasing channel widths: $2 \rightarrow 16$, $16 \rightarrow 32$, $32 \rightarrow 64$, and $64 \rightarrow 128$, using kernel sizes of 7, 5, 3, and 3, respectively, all with stride 2. Each convolution is followed by batch normalization and a ReLU activation to ensure stable and nonlinear feature extraction. This progressively downsamples the input signal from shape $(B, 2, 3000)$ to a compressed embedding of $(B, 128, 188)$, where $B$ is the batch size. The resulting lower-dimensional representation preserves key spectral and temporal features while enabling efficient global context modeling via the subsequent transformer encoder. Prior work shows that transformer encoders built on CNN features yield improved staging while direct per-channel transformers increase compute; compressing to compact embeddings prior to global attention balances accuracy and efficiency [7,8].

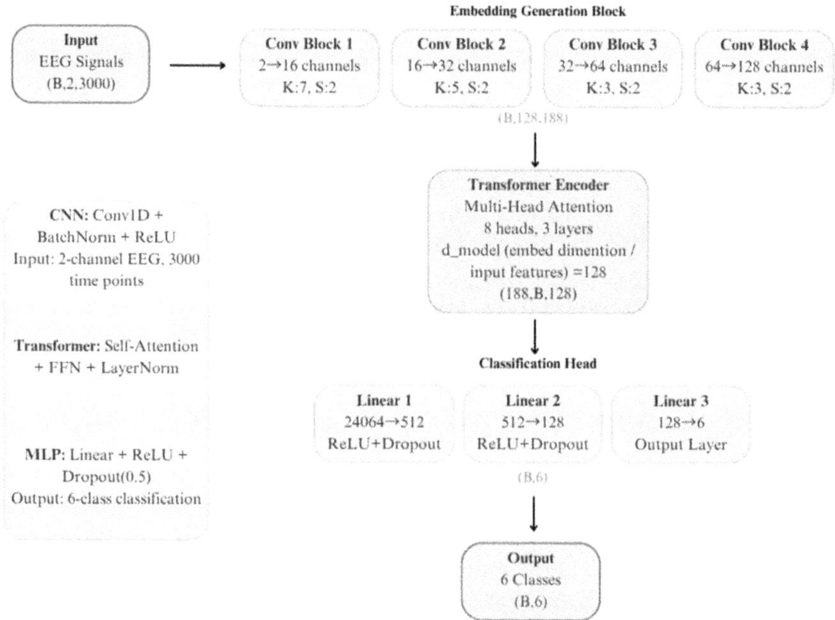


**Fig. 2.** Detailed architecture of XSleepFormer.

## 2.3 Transformer Encoder

The output of the embedding generator is passed to a transformer encoder. This encoder block captures long-range temporal dependencies in the EEG sequences. The encoder comprises 3 stacked layers, each consisting of multi-head self-attention (with 8 heads) followed by a position-wise feed-forward network. The input to the transformer has the shape $(B, 188, 128)$, where each of the 188 time steps is associated with a 128-dimensional embedding. The attention mechanism allows the model to compute context-aware representations by attending over the entire sequence. Positional encodings are added to retain information about the order of the sequence. The transformer's computational footprint is kept efficient by choosing a moderate value of $d_{\mathrm{model}} = 128$, resulting in a total parameter count of approximately 1.2 million for the transformer block.

The motivation for introducing this block lies in the temporal continuity of sleep patterns. That is, certain transitions (e.g., N1 to N2 or N3 to REM) are better understood in the context of prior and future states. The transformer is uniquely suited for this due to its ability to model global dependencies.

## 2.4 Classification Head

The contextualized output from the transformer encoder is flattened to a vector of shape $(B, 24064)$ from (B, 188, 128) and passed through a sequence of fully connected layers: a linear layer reducing the dimensionality to 512 with ReLU activation and dropout, followed by a second layer projecting to 128 with ReLU and dropout, and finally a softmax layer outputting six class probabilities. These six outputs correspond to the five standard sleep stages—Wake, N1, N2, N3, and REM—along with an undefined class. A dropout rate of 0.5 is applied after the first two layers to reduce overfitting. This final stage effectively transforms high-level temporal embeddings into discrete predictions of sleep stages.

***Design Motivation:*** Each architectural component in XSleepFormer is motivated by the need to balance representational power with computational feasibility. The embedding generator serves as a temporal abstraction layer, compressing the EEG while retaining frequency-localized information. The transformer encoder models global patterns necessary for contextual sleep stage classification. Finally, the classification head serves as a projection space for making label predictions. This modular, hybrid design allows XSleepFormer to scale well to large EEG datasets while maintaining accuracy and interpretability—characteristics essential for clinical applications.

## 2.5 Training Strategy and Loss Function

To address class imbalance and improve generalization, **XSleepFormer** is trained using a composite loss function combining *Focal Loss* [12], *Label Smoothing* [15], and *Virtual Adversarial Training (VAT)*.

Given the predicted probability $p_t$ for the true class $t$, the Focal Loss is defined as:

184    D. Mewada et al.

$$\mathcal{L}_{\text{focal}} = -\alpha_t (1 - p_t)^{\gamma} \log(p_t)$$

Here, $\alpha_t$ balances the impact of each class, while $\gamma$ focuses the loss on harder examples.Label smoothing is incorporated within the focal loss term. Label smoothing further distributes a small probability mass to incorrect classes, reducing model overconfidence and improving calibration.

To promote smoother decision boundaries and enhance robustness to input perturbations, we incorporate **Virtual Adversarial Training (VAT)** as a regularization component. VAT generates input perturbations $r_{\text{adv}}$ that locally maximize model output divergence, encouraging consistency and smooth decision boundaries, and penalizes changes in predictions:

$$\mathcal{L}_{\text{VAT}} = \text{KL}\left[f(x) \,\|\, f(x + r_{\text{adv}})\right]$$

This encourages local smoothness in the input space, making the model less sensitive to minor variations in EEG signals—an important consideration given their nonstationary and noisy nature.

In addition, **MixUp augmentation** [13] are also employed in the EEG input space to interpolate both signals and labels between random training pairs:

$$\tilde{x} = \lambda x_i + (1 - \lambda)x_j, \quad \tilde{y} = \lambda y_i + (1 - \lambda)y_j$$

where $\lambda \sim \text{Beta}(\alpha, \alpha)$. This regularization further smooths the decision surface and improves generalization under label imbalance.

The total training objective is:

$$\mathcal{L}_{\text{total}} = \mathcal{L}_{\text{focal}} + \lambda \cdot \mathcal{L}_{\text{VAT}}, \quad \text{with } \lambda = 0.01$$

The model is optimized using the Adam optimizer with a learning rate of $1 \times 10^{-3}$. Dropout (rate 0.5) is applied in the classification head to prevent overfitting.

## 3    Experiments and Results

This section presents a comprehensive evaluation of the proposed **XSleep-Former** for EEG-based sleep stage classification under three key conditions: within-subject, cross-subject, and cross-age. The model is benchmarked against two established baselines to validate its classification performance, generalizability, and robustness across demographic variations.

### 3.1    Experimental Objectives

1. Benchmark **XSleepFormer** against state-of-the-art models using multiple evaluation metrics.
2. Assess generalization under subject-independent testing conditions.
3. Evaluate robustness across age groups, particularly among elderly subjects with altered EEG dynamics.

## 3.2   Dataset and Evaluation Protocols

Experiments were conducted on the publicly available **Sleep-EDF**[1] dataset [14], comprising EEG data of subjects aged 25–101. EEG recordings from Fpz-Cz and Pz-Oz channels, sampled at 100 Hz, were segmented into 30-second epochs and annotated according to AASM standards (Wake, N1, N2, N3, REM). Movement artifacts and unlabeled epochs were excluded.

Three evaluation settings were considered:

1. **Within-Subject:** Each subject's data split into 80% training, 10% validation, and 10% testing.
2. **Cross-Subject:** Data from 49 subjects were divided into 39, 5, and 5 subjects for training, validation, and testing, respectively
3. **Cross-Age:** Trained on subjects $\leq$65 years; tested on subjects aged 65–80 and 80+.

The model was trained for 35 epochs using AdamW optimizer (learning rate $10^{-3}$, batch size 120). The total loss function combines focal loss and Virtual Adversarial Training (VAT):

$$\mathcal{L} = \mathcal{L}_{\text{focal}} + \lambda \cdot \mathcal{L}_{\text{VAT}}, \quad \lambda = 0.01$$

## 3.3   Within-Subject Evaluation Performance

**Table 1.** Within-Subject Performance Comparison.

| Model | Accuracy(%) | Loss | F1 | Precision | Recall | AUC |
| --- | --- | --- | --- | --- | --- | --- |
| SleepStagerBlanco [16] | 65.05 | 0.0630 | 0.596 | 0.578 | 0.651 | 0.883 |
| SleepStagerChambon [17] | 80.51 | **0.0415** | 0.781 | 0.784 | 0.805 | 0.957 |
| **XSleepFormer** (Proposed) | **83.11** | 0.0520 | **0.824** | **0.821** | **0.831** | **0.966** |

As shown in Table 1, **XSleepFormer** achieves the highest accuracy (83.11%), outperforming both implemented baselines. It demonstrates well-balanced precision (0.821) and recall (0.831), leading to a strong F1-score of 0.824. This indicates reliable performance even on minority stages such as N1 and REM. Although the reimplemented model from Chambon et al. shows slightly lower training loss, XSleepFormer achieves a superior AUC of 0.966, reflecting better separability and prediction confidence.

---

[1] https://www.physionet.org/content/sleep-edfx/1.0.0/.

### 3.4  Cross-Subject Evaluation Performance

Table 2 demonstrates strong generalization on unseen subjects. Despite substantial inter-subject variability in EEG dynamics, XSleepFormer achieves the highest accuracy (84.58%). Precision and recall remain balanced (0.837 and 0.846), and the highest F1-score (0.840) reflects improved recognition across all classes. The AUC of 0.975 further underscores the model's robust separability and reliable confidence estimation. Although Chambon achieves a lower training loss, our model exhibits stronger generalization in every other metric.

**Table 2.** Cross-Subject Performance Comparison.

| Model | Accuracy(%) | Loss | F1 | Precision | Recall | AUC |
|---|---|---|---|---|---|---|
| SleepStagerBlanco [16] | 65.02 | 0.0649 | 0.572 | 0.568 | 0.650 | 0.901 |
| SleepStagerChambon [17] | 83.33 | **0.0365** | 0.813 | 0.816 | 0.833 | 0.971 |
| **XSleepFormer** (Proposed) | **84.58** | 0.0474 | **0.840** | **0.837** | **0.846** | **0.975** |

### 3.5  Cross-Age Performance Evaluation

**Table 3.** Cross-Age Generalization of XSleepFormer.

| Age-Group | Accuracy(%) | VAT Loss |
|---|---|---|
| 65–80 years | 84.32 | 0.1117 |
| 80+ years | 83.77 | 0.1172 |

Table 3 highlights XSleepFormer's robustness across aging populations. Accuracy remains high across both cohorts (84.32% for 65–80 and 83.77% for 80+), with minimal performance degradation. The VAT loss shows a negligible increase (from 0.1117 to 0.1172), indicating preservation of smooth and stable decision boundaries under covariate shifts due to age-related EEG changes.

## 4  Conclusion

This work presented **XSleepFormer**, a compact hybrid model for EEG-based sleep stage classification that integrates CNN-based embedding compression with Transformer-based temporal modeling. Combined with Focal Loss, MixUp, and VAT, the model addresses key challenges, including class imbalance, long-range dependencies, and demographic variability. XSleepFormer consistently outperforms existing baselines on the Sleep-EDF dataset across subject-dependent, cross-subject, and cross-age setups by achieving 84.58% accuracy, an F1-score of 0.84, and AUC of 0.975 in cross-subject evaluations. Notably, it maintains stable performance across elderly cohorts, indicating strong generalizability. The current version assumes labeled 30-s dual-channel EEG segments with consistent signal quality. Future work will focus on handling variable-length sequences, resilience to missing or noisy channels, and Label-efficient training via weak or self-supervised learning. Enhancing the interpretability of attention mechanisms also remains crucial for clinical adoption. Recent transformer studies emphasizing efficiency and interpretability [11] highlight opportunities to extend XSleepFormer for real-time and resource-constrained clinical settings.

# References


1. Berry, R. B., et al.: The AASM Manual for the Scoring of Sleep and Associated Events. American Academy of Sleep Medicine (2017)
2. Rosenberg, R.S., Van Hout, S.: The American Academy of Sleep Medicine inter-scorer reliability program. J. Clin. Sleep Med. **9**(1), 81–87 (2013)
3. Aboalayon, K.A., et al.: Sleep stage classification using EEG signal analysis: a comprehensive survey and new investigation. Entropy **18**(9), 272 (2016)
4. Supratak, A. et al.: DeepSleepNet: a model for automatic sleep stage scoring based on raw single-channel EEG. IEEE Trans. Neural Syst. Rehabil. Eng. **25**(11) (2017)
5. Biswal, S., Sun, H., Goparaju, B. et. al.: SleepNet: automated sleep staging system via deep learning. arXiv:1707.08262 (2018)
6. Phan, H., Andreotti, F., Cooray, N., Chén, O.Y., et al.: SeqSleepNet: end-to-end hierarchical recurrent neural network for sequence-to-sequence automatic sleep staging. IEEE Trans. Neural Syst. Rehabil. Eng. **27**(3), 400–410 (2019)
7. Wan, C., et al.: Advancing sleep disorder diagnostics: a transformer-based EEG model for sleep stage classification and OSA prediction. IEEE J. Biomed. Health Inform. **29**(2), 878–886 (2025)
8. van der Aar et al.: Deep transfer learning for automated single-lead EEG sleep staging with channel and population mismatches. Front. Physiol. (2024)
9. Phan, H., Koch, P., et al.: SleepTransformer: Automatic Sleep Staging with Interpretability and Uncertainty Quantification. IEEE Trans, Biomedical Eng (2022)
10. Guo, Y., et al.: FlexSleepTransformer: a transformer-based sleep staging model with flexible input channel configurations. Sci. Rep. **14**, 26312 (2024)
11. Park, K., et al.: DistillSleep: real-time, on-device, interpretable sleep staging from single-channel EEG. Sleep, zsaf240 (2025). https://doi.org/10.1093/sleep/zsaf240.
12. Lin, T.-Y., Goyal, P., Girshick, R., He, K., Dollár, P.: Focal loss for dense object detection. In: ICCV (2017)
13. Zhang, H., et al.: mixup: Beyond empirical risk minimization. In: ICLR (2018)
14. Kemp, B., Zwinderman, A.H., Tuk, B., Kamphuisen, H.A.C., Oberye, J.J.L.: Analysis of a sleep-dependent neuronal feedback loop: the slow-wave microcontinuity of the EEG. IEEE Trans. Biomed. Eng. **47**(9), 1185–1194 (2000)
15. Müller, R., Kornblith, S., Hinton, G.: When does label smoothing help? In: Advances in neural information processing systems (NeurIPS), vol. 32 (2019)
16. Fernandez-Blanco, E., Rivero, D., Pazos, A.: Convolutional neural networks for sleep stage scoring on a two-channel EEG signal. Soft. Comput. **24**, 4067–4079 (2020)

17. Chambon, S., et al.: A deep learning architecture for temporal sleep stage classification using multivariate and multimodal time series. IEEE Trans. Neural Syst. Rehab. Eng. **26**(4), 758–769 (2018)

# Ontology-Driven Semantic Knowledge Graph Construction and Analysis for the Cancer Hallmark "Sustaining Proliferative Signaling"

Hemraj Kumawat[1]([envelope]) [ORCID], Shikha Verma[2] [ORCID], and Aditi Sharan[1] [ORCID]

[1] School of Computer and Systems Sciences, Jawaharlal Nehru University, New Mehrauli Rd, New Delhi 110067, India
hemraj22_scs@jnu.ac.in
[2] Department of Computer Science, Ram Lal Anand College, University of Delhi, 5, Benito Juarez Marg, New Delhi 110021, India

**Abstract.** Knowledge graph is a powerful tool to organize and analyze complex biological interactions in cancer research from unstructured text like cancer literature. This study provides a framework to build an ontology-driven knowledge graph from cancer literature using a hybrid approach by combining LLM-based triplet extraction with Gene Ontology-based triplets, ensuring semantic consistency. The constructed knowledge graph captures diverse molecular processes and signaling pathways related to the 'Sustaining proliferative signaling' cancer hallmark. The study applied graph-theoretical analyses such as degree centrality, betweenness centrality, eigenvector centrality, PageRank, and HITS algorithms to identify important nodes and relationships in the graph network. The centrality measure analysis of the knowledge graph captures interesting patterns, such as key processes like apoptosis, cell cycle regulation, EGFR signaling, and p21-mediated control, aligning with the hallmark of sustaining proliferative signaling. Furthermore, the PageRank and HITS authority scores identified highly connected regulatory processes. This thorough graph analysis reveals previously undiscovered pathways of possible therapeutic interest in addition to confirming established carcinogenic drivers. Finally, identified biological concepts can serve as crucial features for machine learning and deep learning algorithms for performing various tasks on cancer literature, such as document classification, node prediction, and functional annotation. The proposed work demonstrates the value of knowledge graph construction and analysis in understanding cancer biology and guiding precision medicine strategies.

**Keywords:** Knowledge Graph · Gene Ontology · Hallmarks of Cancer · Entity Extraction · Large Language Models


S. Mitra et al. (Eds.): PReMI 2025, LNCS 16358, pp. 189–199, 2026.
https://doi.org/10.1007/978-3-032-18480-1_19

# 1   Introduction

Cancer is one of the leading causes of death worldwide. As per the WHO, one in six deaths was attributed to cancer in 2020 [20]. Cancer, being a complex disease, is characterized by a set of functional capabilities acquired by human cells on their way to transition from normal to neoplastic growth state. These functional capabilities that contribute to the formation of a malignant tumor are called hallmarks of cancer [7]. 'Sustaining Proliferative Signaling' is one of the critical hallmarks, where cancer cells achieve uncontrolled growth by continuously activating growth-promoting pathways [8]. The vast volume of biomedical literature available on this hallmark contains valuable knowledge, but it is in raw text and unstructured form and is scattered across thousands of publications. The unstructured nature of biomedical literature poses several challenges that hinder efficient data extraction, integration, and reasoning. These challenges include a lack of standardization, as different authors use varied terminologies, synonyms, abbreviations, and formats to refer to the same biomedical concept, leading to inconsistency and ambiguity. Additionally, the sheer volume of continuously growing literature further aggravates the problem, making manual curation difficult and infeasible. Moreover, the literature information is presented using natural language, which makes it inaccessible to computational systems for reasoning or querying.

Structured knowledge, particularly in the form of knowledge graphs, is increasingly recognized as a pivotal asset in biomedical research, facilitating a deeper understanding of complex biological systems and accelerating the pace of scientific discovery [1]. The knowledge graph transforms unstructured biomedical literature into a structured, machine-readable format by representing entities and their relationships in structured graphs that can be systematically analyzed.

This work utilizes the publicly available dataset "Hallmarks of Cancer" by Baker et al. [3]. The Hallmarks of Cancer is a benchmark dataset for a multi-label classification problem in the biomedical domain. However, for efficient classification, it is crucial to identify important biomedical entities or concepts relevant to each hallmark. This idea motivated this research to identify and analyze important entities from PubMed abstracts annotated with a particular hallmark in the dataset with the help of a knowledge graph. The current work focuses on the 'Sustaining proliferative signaling' hallmark. Furthermore, this idea can be extended to analyze other hallmarks as well. The research work extracts biological entities and relationships using the scispaCy tool and a large language model. It tackles the problems of ambiguity and lack of normalization by integrating standardized ontologies such as Gene Ontology (GO), ensuring consistent representation of biomedical concepts. The work then analyzes the constructed graph using centrality measures and ranking-based algorithms to identify key entities and discover the underlying structure of the 'Sustaining proliferative signaling' hallmark mechanism in cancer literature.

This paper has the following contributions-

- Construction of a semantic knowledge graph using LLMs and an external biomedical knowledge base (Gene Ontology), capturing relationships among biological concepts specific to 'Sustaining proliferative signaling' hallmark.
- Analysis of the knowledge graph using graph centrality measures and ranking algorithms such as Page Rank and HITS.
- Biological interpretation of the results obtained to offer insights into processes driving proliferative signaling in cancer.

The Sect. 2 provides a brief literature review of related works. Section 3 discusses the methodology used in this work, followed by the results and discussion in Sect. 4. Finally, Sect. 5 contains the conclusion and future directions.

## 2   Literature Review

In recent years, the advancements in biomedical text mining have paved the way for the extraction of structured knowledge from vast scientific literature. The field of oncology has seen wide applications of text mining approaches to identify gene-disease association, molecular mechanism extraction, and hypothesis generation [16,19]. The knowledge graphs have emerged as a powerful tool for representing complex and unstructured knowledge from biomedical literature, offering a structured format for knowledge discovery and reasoning [12]. Biomedical entity extraction and knowledge graph construction are important ways to extract biomedical concepts and represent them in a structured format, with the former serving as a basis for the latter. The biomedical entity extraction refers to the identification and classification of biologically relevant concepts, such as disease, drug, gene, and protein, in the unstructured raw text [9]. The typical mechanism of knowledge graph construction in the healthcare domain includes extracting entities and relations that can be captured from various heterogeneous healthcare data, including biomedical literature [1]. The extracted entities are then treated as nodes, and the relations between them can be represented by edges in the knowledge graph.

In cancer informatics, existing works were focused on mining cancer-specific literature to build knowledge bases for genetic mutations, pathways, and therapeutic targets [18]. Tools such as CancerMine [11] facilitate a high-quality, text-mined, and routinely updated database of cancer driver genes and their roles across cancer types. Although these systems address significant facets of cancer biology, they do not specifically organize knowledge in accordance with the conceptual framework of Hallmarks of Cancer [6,8].

The ontology-driven approaches are essential to improve the semantic precision and interoperability of text mining. Various biomedical ontologies, such as Gene Ontology [2], Disease Ontology [15], and the National Cancer Institute Thesaurus [5], provide structured vocabulary to standardize entities and relations. Integrating these ontologies in the knowledge graph construction pipeline enhances interoperability and enables reasoning over hierarchical relationships.

Despite significant research work in the direction of general cancer text mining approaches and knowledge graph construction approaches, there are limited studies that focus on systematic modeling of an individual hallmark of cancer using ontology-driven approaches. To address these gaps, this work has focused on the PubMed abstracts annotated with the 'Sustaining proliferative signaling' hallmark and the construction of an ontology-driven semantic knowledge graph using Gene Ontology. This work also performs graph-based analysis using centrality measures and ranking-based algorithms such as Page Rank and HITS algorithms. The aim of this analysis is to highlight central biological processes and entities that characterize the 'Sustaining proliferative signaling' hallmark in the literature.

## 3   Methodology

This section discusses the workflow of the proposed work. The proposed work involves biological concepts and their relation extraction, the construction of an ontology-driven semantic knowledge graph, and its analysis. The complete pipeline of the proposed methodology is shown in Fig. 1.

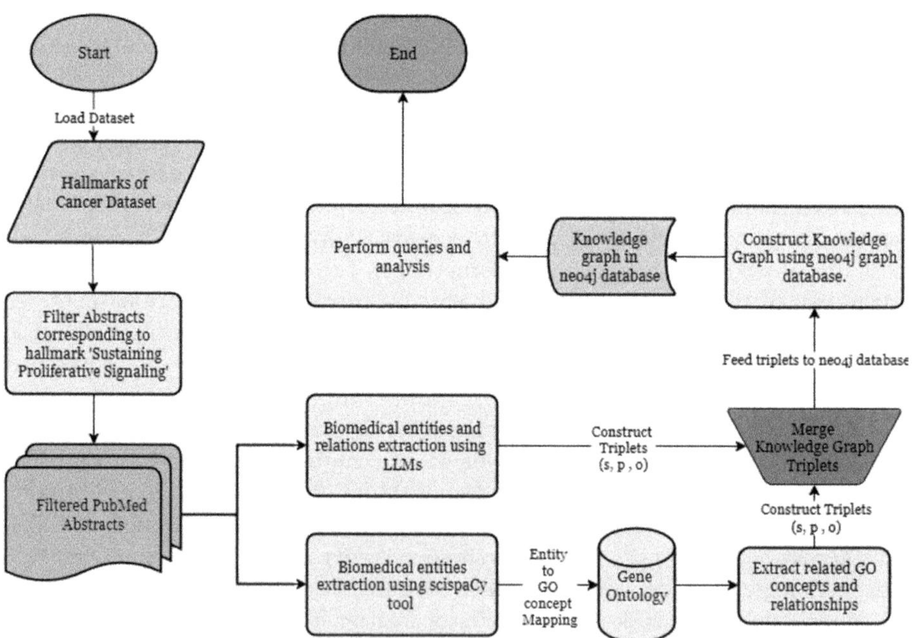


**Fig. 1.** Complete workflow of the proposed methodology

The detailed description of the proposed work is discussed in the following subsections.

## 3.1   Dataset Preparation

This work uses the publicly available Hallmarks of Cancer benchmark dataset, which contains 1,580 PubMed abstracts manually annotated using relevant hallmarks. The abstracts corresponding to the 'Sustaining proliferative signaling' hallmark have been programmatically filtered. This reduces the corpus to a relevant hallmark-specific corpus. After applying filtering, 462 PubMed abstracts were obtained.

## 3.2   Biomedical Entity and Relation Extraction

To extract information from the abstracts, we have used a hybrid approach combining a large language model (LLM) based method and SciSpaCy-based entity extraction by mapping with Gene Ontology concepts-

- *LLM-based extraction*: This approach employed Google's 'models/gemini-1.5-flash-latest', a multi-modal model to extract biomedical concepts and relationships between them using a prompt. First, the triplets are extracted for individual abstracts and later combined to form a comprehensive set of triplets.
- *scispaCy-based extraction from Gene Ontology:* This work uses scispaCy's 'en_core_sci_sm' model to extract biomedical concepts from the abstracts. To ensure semantic consistency and enable ontology-grounded analysis, extracted entities were mapped to Gene Ontology concepts with the highest confidence score using scispaCy's entity linking module. Additionally, this research also extracted GO relationships to enrich the graph with hierarchical and regulatory connections to ensure semantic enrichment.

## 3.3   Knowledge Graph Triplet Construction and Merging

This Step constructs the semantic triplets of the form (subject, predicate, object) using the extracted entities and relationships. Additionally, in the case of the scispaCy approach, we manually defined a relationship 'mapped_to' to link the abstract entity to the corresponding GO concept. Finally, merging the triplets from LLMs with GO triplets to form a unifying set.

## 3.4   Knowledge Graph Construction in Neo4j

In this step, merged triplets from both approaches have been used to create a knowledge graph in the Neo4j database using a Cypher query. Neo4j has been chosen owing to its expressive graph data model and native support for querying complex patterns using the Cypher language. The nodes representing extracted biomedical concepts from the abstract using the LLM were given the node label 'Abstract_entity', while the nodes representing the biomedical concept from GO were given the node label 'GO_concept'. The edges in the constructed knowledge graph represent extracted semantic relationships using both approaches.

### 3.5   Graph Querying and Analysis

This work performed a graph analysis on the constructed knowledge graph directly in the Neo4j database using the Cypher query language. The following analysis has been performed-

**Graph Centrality Measures.** In general, graph centrality measures are a way to quantify the importance of nodes in the graph. Different centrality measure depicts different notions of importance. The popular centrality measures are as follows [14]-

- *Degree centrality:* It is computed by counting the total number of edges that are incident on a particular node in a graph.
- *Betweenness centrality:* It measures how many times a node falls along the shortest path of any two other nodes in the graph.
- *Eigenvector centrality:* It represents the influence of a given node in the graph by considering the importance of neighbours. Every node is assigned a relative score with an assumption that connections to high-scoring nodes contribute more to the score of the given node than connections to low-scoring nodes.

**Topological Ranking Measures.** These measures leverage link topological ranking to identify important nodes in the graph. Two popular algorithms are as follows-

- *HITS Algorithm*: This algorithm was developed by Kleinberg in 1999 [10]. It computes two major scores, namely the hub score and the authority score. The hub score measures how good a node is at linking to valuable information, while the authority score measures how valuable a particular node is as a source of information. It helps in differentiating between core biomedical concepts and broad regulatory entities.
- *PageRank Algorithm*: This is a popular algorithm proposed by Brin and Page in 1998 [4] and originally used by Google. It ranks nodes in the graph based on their importance in the entire graph network. As opposed to the HITS algorithm, it assigns a single score to each node.

## 4   Result and Analysis

This section presents the outcome of constructing and analyzing a knowledge graph for the hallmark 'Sustaining proliferative signaling'. It includes the summary of the constructed knowledge graph, results of centrality analysis, HITS score, and PageRank score, which highlight key biomedical concepts. Finally, the interpretation of the top-ranked concepts in the context of their biological relevance to cancer progression.

## 4.1  Knowledge Graph Summary

The constructed semantic knowledge graph contains a total of 11,604 nodes, out of which 8,426 nodes correspond to the label "Abstract_entity", and the remaining 3,179 correspond to the label "GO_Concept". Additionally, it contains 23,548 relationships. The graph consists of biomedical concepts such as genes, pathways, cellular processes, and GO terms relevant to the hallmark under study. The subgraph with 100 nodes is shown in Fig. 2, where orange color nodes represent biomedical concepts extracted from the abstract, while the green color nodes represent GO terms.

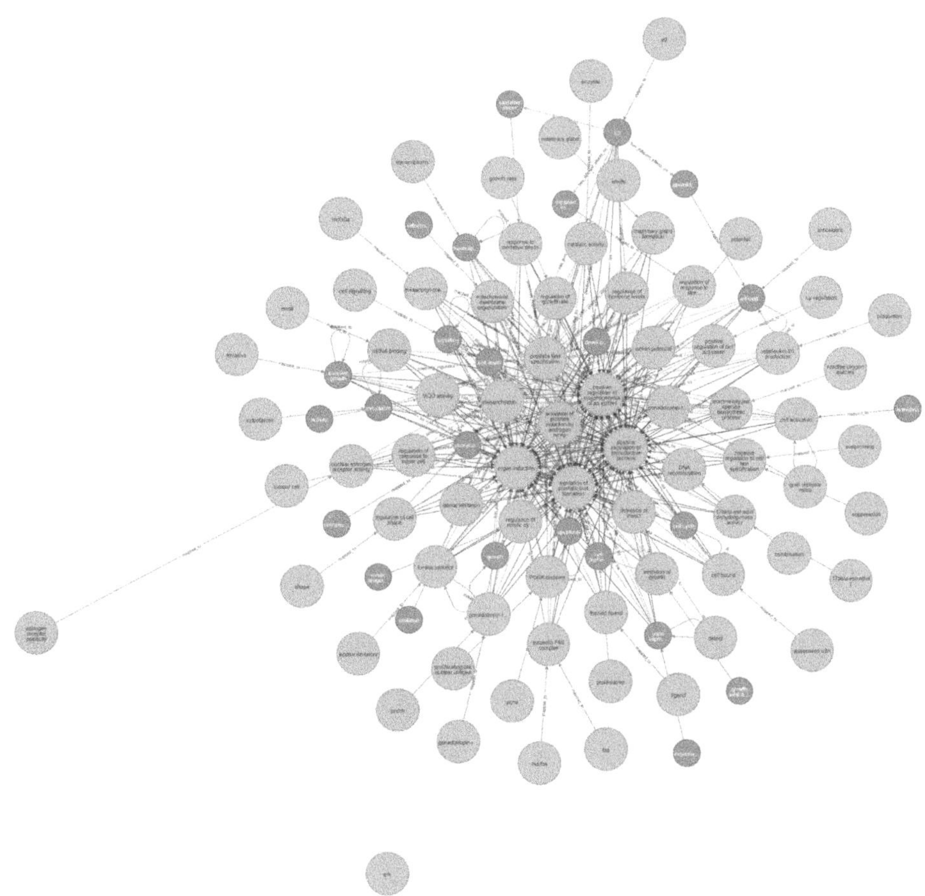

**Fig. 2.** A sample subgraph of constructed knowledge graph

## 4.2  Centrality Measure Results

The results for the top common nodes identified from the knowledge graph using degree, betweenness, and eigenvalue centrality measures are shown in Table 1.

**Table 1.** Centrality Measures for Key Nodes in the Knowledge Graph

| Node/Concept | Degree | Betweenness | Eigenvector |
| --- | --- | --- | --- |
| EGFR | 91.0 | 861253.73 | – |
| EGF | 62.0 | 291218.54 | – |
| cyclin D1 | 47.0 | 277090.56 | – |
| Sorafenib | 42.0 | 450218.12 | 0.1010 |
| p21 | 39.0 | 945363.81 | – |
| apoptosis | – | 602151.98 | 0.2767 |
| PCNA | – | 277677.54 | 0.3403 |
| cell proliferation | – | 269050.23 | 0.2248 |
| p53 | – | 417314.35 | – |
| ERα | 31.0 | – | 0.2511 |

## 4.3  HITS and PageRank Results

The Table 2 shows the top-ranked nodes identified using HITS and PageRank algorithms.

**Table 2.** Top 10 nodes ranked by PageRank and HITS Authority scores.

| Node | PageRank Score | HITS Authority Score |
| --- | --- | --- |
| positive regulation of reproductive process | 62.90 | 0.37796 |
| prostate field specification | 62.90 | 0.37796 |
| mesenchymal-epithelial cell signaling | 62.90 | 0.37796 |
| activation of prostate induction | 62.90 | 0.37796 |
| regulation of prostatic bud formation | 62.90 | 0.37796 |
| organ induction | 62.90 | 0.37796 |
| positive regulation of morphogenesis | 62.90 | 0.37796 |
| apoptosis | 8.39 | 0.00058 |
| cell proliferation | 6.09 | - |
| cell cycle | 4.36 | - |

## 4.4  Biological Interpretation

As shown in Table 1, the centrality measure-based analysis of the knowledge graph for 'Sustaining proliferative signaling' hallmark identifies EGFR, EGF, and cyclin D1 as frequent important nodes based on degree centrality, which confirms with the well established evidence that the ErbB family, specially EGFR and its ligand EGF are key drivers of uncontrolled proliferative signaling in cancer cells [8,21]. The nodes 'p21' and 'EGFR' serve as important connectors based on betweenness centrality, while the high betweenness score for nodes 'apoptosis' and 'cell cycle' highlights their importance as bridge roles between proliferative signaling and cell death control, further emphasizing their status as interlinked cancer hallmarks [8]. As pointed out by the eigenvector score PCNA, a DNA clamp essential for replication is a known marker of proliferation [17]. Additionally, ER$\alpha$ and ER$\beta$ are among the top nodes as per eigenvector score, which supports their role of estrogen receptor signaling in promoting proliferative signaling, particularly in hormone-responsive cancers like breast cancer [13].

The Table 2 shows the top nodes with high PageRank and HITS authority score that centre around reproductive and developmental signaling (positive regulation of reproductive process, prostate field specification, organ induction). These nodes reflect tightly connected pathways (identified from the Gene Ontology) driving cell proliferation, which is in accordance with the hallmark 'Sustaining proliferative signaling' [8]. In contrast, generic regulators like 'apoptosis' and 'cell cycle' indicate a low authority score, suggesting they act as broadly connected but less module-specific indicators.

These key findings indicate the key biomedical concepts and important pathways playing a crucial role in the 'sustaining proliferative signaling' hallmark.

## 5  Conclusion and Future Work

The proposed work presented a comprehensive pipeline for ontology-driven semantic knowledge graph construction from cancer-related literature and its analysis using centrality measures, PageRank, and HITS algorithms. This graph-based analysis identified key biological processes and genes, such as EGFR, p21, apoptosis, etc., highlighting their role in the 'Sustaining proliferative signaling' hallmark. These findings will help understand and better visualize the core biological processes involved in specific cancer hallmarks without having to go through vast scientific literature. However, this work is limited to analyzing a single hallmark literature, but it can be replicated for other hallmarks as well. Furthermore, the findings from the analysis can serve as important features for machine learning and deep learning applications to perform a variety of tasks, such as document clustering, node classification, link prediction, and functional annotation of biological networks.

**Acknowledgments.** The authors acknowledge the financial support provided by the University Grants Commission (UGC), Government of India, under the NET-JRF fellowship scheme. This support has been instrumental in facilitating the research work presented in this manuscript (NTA Reference No.- 210510014730).

**Disclosure of Interests.** The authors have no competing interests to declare that are relevant to the content of this article.

# References


1. Abu-Salih, B., Al-Qurishi, M., Alweshah, M., Al-Smadi, M., Alfayez, R., Saadeh, H.: Healthcare knowledge graph construction: a systematic review of the state-of-the-art, open issues, and opportunities. J. Big Data **10**(1), 81 (2023)
2. Ashburner, M., et al.: Gene ontology: tool for the unification of biology. the gene ontology consortium. Nat. Genet. **25**(1), 25–29 (2000)
3. Baker, S., Silins, I., Guo, Y., Ali, I., Högberg, J., Stenius, U., Korhonen, A.: Automatic semantic classification of scientific literature according to the hallmarks of cancer. Bioinformatics **32**(3), 432–440 (2015)
4. Brin, S., Page, L.: The anatomy of a large-scale hypertextual web search engine. Comput. Netw ISDN Syst. **30**(1), 107–117 (1998), proceedings of the Seventh International World Wide Web Conference
5. Fragoso, G., de Coronado, S., Haber, M., Hartel, F., Wright, L.: Overview and utilization of the NCI thesaurus. Comp. Funct. Genomics **5**(8), 648–654 (2004)
6. Hanahan, D., Weinberg, R.A.: The hallmarks of cancer. Cell **100**(1), 57–70 (2000)
7. Hanahan, D.: Hallmarks of cancer: New dimensions. Cancer Discov. **12**(1), 31–46 (2022)
8. Hanahan, D., Weinberg, R.A.: Hallmarks of cancer: the next generation. Cell **144**(5), 646–674 (2011)
9. Hou, L., Wu, M., Kang, H., Zheng, S., Shen, L., Qian, Q., Li, J.: Pmo: a knowledge representation model towards precision medicine. Math. Biosci. Eng. **17**(4), 4098–4114 (2020)
10. Kleinberg, J.M.: Authoritative sources in a hyperlinked environment. J. ACM **46**(5), 604–632 (1999)
11. Lever, J., Zhao, E.Y., Grewal, J., Jones, M.R., Jones, S.J.M.: CancerMine: a literature-mined resource for drivers, oncogenes and tumor suppressors in cancer. Nat. Methods **16**(6), 505–507 (2019)
12. Lu, Y., Goi, S.Y., Zhao, X., Wang, J.: Biomedical knowledge graph: a survey of domains, tasks, and real-world applications (2025). https://arxiv.org/abs/2501.11632
13. Osborne, C.K., Schiff, R.: Mechanisms of endocrine resistance in breast cancer. Annu. Rev. Med. **62**(1), 233–247 (2011)
14. Peng, S., Zhou, Y., Cao, L., Yu, S., Niu, J., Jia, W.: Influence analysis in social networks: A survey. J. Netw. Comput. Appl. **106**, 17–32 (2018)
15. Schrimi, L.M., et al.: The human disease ontology 2022 update. Nucleic Acids Res. **50**(D1), D1255–D1261 (2022)
16. Shamay, Y.: Mastering the complexities of cancer nanomedicine with text mining, ai and automation. J. Control. Release **379**, 906–919 (2025)
17. Sherr, C.J.: Cancer cell cycles. Science **274**(5293), 1672–1677 (1996)
18. Silva, M.C., Eugénio, P., Faria, D., Pesquita, C.: Ontologies and knowledge graphs in oncology research. Cancers **14**(8) (2022). https://doi.org/10.3390/cancers14081906
19. Smith, E., Paloots, R., Giagkos, D., Baudis, M., Stockinger, K.: Data-driven information extraction and enrichment of molecular profiling data for cancer cell lines. Bioinform. Adv. **4**(1), vbae045 (2024)

20. WHO: https://www.who.int/news-room/fact-sheets/detail/cancer
21. Yarden, Y., Sliwkowski, M.X.: Untangling the ErbB signalling network. Nat. Rev. Mol. Cell Biol. **2**(2), 127–137 (2001)

# DETER: Directed Event-Trajectory GNNs on MIMIC-III for Medium-Term Readmission Forecasting


Ekta Srivastava[1]([envelope]) [iD] and Sandeep Kumar[1,2,3] [iD]

[1] Department of Electrical Engineering, Indian Institute of Technology Delhi, New Delhi 110016, India
`ektasri@iitd.ac.in`
[2] Bharti School of Telecommunications Technology & Management, Indian Institute of Technology Delhi, New Delhi 110016, India
[3] Yardi School of Artificial Intelligence, Indian Institute of Technology Delhi, New Delhi 110016, India



**Abstract.** Hospital readmissions within 30 days impose heavy clinical and financial burdens, linking unplanned returns to patient morbidity and cost inefficiency. Traditional models, logistic regression on aggregated features or RNNs over fixed windows, often lose temporal granularity, limiting their ability to capture nuanced patient trajectories. We propose DETER, a directed event-trajectory framework that models each ICU stay as a graph: nodes represent timestamped clinical events (vitals, labs, medications), and directed edges link successive events with learnable time-delta embeddings. A Temporal Graph Attention Network processes the full admission graph to produce dynamic patient embeddings. On MIMIC-III (14,532 admissions), DETER attains an AUC of 83.0% and an F1-score of 48.0 % for 30-day readmission prediction, outperforming BiLSTM baselines by +7.0% AUC and patient-similarity GCNs by +4.0% AUC. Ablation studies reveal that time-delta embeddings and sparse directed chains yield approximately 4% and 6% relative gains, respectively. Attention-weight visualizations highlight critical event transitions, such as creatinine rise to antibiotic dosing, that precede readmission. These results establish DETER as a novel and effective medium-term readmission model, demonstrating the value of event-chain graph representations in EHR analytics.

**Keywords:** Event-Level EHR Graphs · Temporal Graph Neural Networks · Readmission Prediction


## 1 Introduction

Hospital readmissions within 30 days pose substantial clinical and economic burdens, with unplanned returns linked to preventable complications, disrupted care continuity, and inflated costs [5,6]. Electronic Health Records (EHRs) chronicle each ICU stay as a sequence of time-stamped events, vitals, labs, medications, but prevailing models collapse these into static summaries or fixed-window sequences, diluting temporal fidelity and obscuring critical patient trajectories [13]. While patient-level GCNs on similarity graphs achieve moderate gains (AUC $\approx 0.79$) for readmission, and static event-level GCNs improve short-term mortality forecasts, none preserve the exact event chronology nor target medium-term readmission [3].

We propose DETER, a directed event-trajectory framework that represents each ICU admission as a sparse, chronological graph of timestamped clinical events and processes it with a Temporal Graph Attention Network (T-GAT) [8]. Nodes encode normalized measurements or one-hot embeddings of vitals, labs, and medication orders; directed edges link successive events and carry learnable time-delta attributes. The T-GAT backbone ($L$ attention layers, hidden size $d'$) produces a dynamic patient embedding, which a lightweight MLP maps to a 30-day readmission probability. Our contributions are threefold:

- First event-level Temporal GNN for medium-term (30-day) readmission on MIMIC-III.
- Introduction of sparse, directed event chains with explicit time-delta encoding, contrasting with prior dense "forgetting" graphs.
- Adaptation of Graph Attention layers to irregular, asynchronous clinical event sequences, yielding interpretable attention patterns.

## 2   Related Work

Over the years, 30-day hospital readmission prediction has shifted from applying deep learning architectures to aggregated EHR summaries [1,2] toward leveraging RNN/LSTM models that capture temporal dynamics within fixed time windows [9,14]. Recent Graph Neural Network (GNN) [7,12] methods represent admissions as nodes within patient-similarity graphs, such as GCNs and multimodal spatiotemporal GNNs (MM-STGNN) [11], achieving AUCs around 0.79 but relying heavily on dense similarity connections and admission-level embeddings. At the event level, static GCNs applied to fully connected temporal graphs have shown improvements for short-term mortality prediction, but not specifically readmission. Temporal Graph Neural Networks (TGNNs) [4], including R-GCNs [10]on knowledge graphs and snapshot-based Spatio-Temporal GNNs, have captured evolving EHR relationships or multimodal information [15] but still use discrete time windows or prioritize short-term outcomes. In contrast, our work introduces a continuous, sparse, directed event-chain Temporal Graph Attention Network explicitly designed for medium-term (30-day) readmission prediction, preserving precise event chronology and inter-event intervals.

## 3   Methodology

### 3.1   Dataset and Preprocessing

We extracted adult ICU admissions (age≥18) from MIMIC-III v1.4 by joining `ADMISSIONS` and `ICUSTAYS`, excluding neonatal/psychiatric units and stays under four hours to ensure adequate temporal data. Readmission labels were derived by flagging any admission whose next `admittime` for the same patient fell within 30 days of the prior `dischtime`. For each stay, we built three ordered event streams: (i) vitals such as heart rate, systolic/diastolic blood pressure, respiratory rate, and temperature from `CHARTEVENTS`; (ii) laboratory tests like core panels (CBC, CMP) from `LABEVENTS` via LOINC mappings; and (iii) medications from `INPUTEVENTS_MV` and `PRESCRIPTIONS`. We forward-filled vital sign gaps up to two hours and imputed remaining missing values and all lab entries with cohort medians. Continuous features were z-score normalized and categorical codes (medications, procedures) one-hot encoded, yielding timestamped vectors for graph construction.

### 3.2   Event-Trajectory Graph Construction

For each ICU admission, we construct an *event-trajectory graph* $G = (V, E)$ that preserves the full, chronological sequence of clinical measurements. Let

$$\{(t_i, \mathbf{x}_i)\}_{i=1}^{N} \tag{1}$$

be the ordered stream of $N$ events, vitals, labs, or medication orders, sorted so that $t_1 < t_2 < \cdots < t_N$. We instantiate one node $v_i \in V$ per event, where its feature vector $\mathbf{x}_i \in \mathbb{R}^d$ concatenates the normalized continuous measurement (or one-hot embedding for categorical codes) with any auxiliary attributes (e.g., event type).

Directed edges capture the immediate temporal transitions between events:

$$E = \{(v_i, v_{i+1}) \mid i = 1, 2, \ldots, N - 1\}. \tag{2}$$

Each edge $(v_i, v_{i+1})$ is enriched with an *edge attribute* encoding the inter-event interval

$$\Delta t_i = t_{i+1} - t_i, \tag{3}$$

which we project via a learnable embedding function

$$\phi : \mathbb{R}^+ \rightarrow \mathbb{R}^p. \tag{4}$$

Concretely, the edge feature vector is

$$\mathbf{e}_{i,i+1} = \phi(\Delta t_i), \tag{5}$$

so that the graph message-passing can directly modulate information flow by elapsed time.

This sparse, directed chain contrasts with fully connected "forgetting" graphs by (i) preserving exact event order, (ii) limiting connectivity to successive events, and (iii) explicitly modeling time-delta as a first-class attribute. The resulting graph $G$ therefore encodes both the content and cadence of a patient's ICU trajectory, ready for downstream Temporal GNN processing.

## 3.3  Temporal Graph Attention Network

To process the event-trajectory graph $G = (V, E)$, we adopt a Temporal Graph Attention Network (T-GAT) that extends standard Graph Attention Networks (GATs) to incorporate continuous-time edge attributes. At layer $\ell$, each node $v_i$ with embedding $\mathbf{h}_i^{(\ell)} \in \mathbb{R}^d$ attends over its incoming neighbor $v_j$ via:

$$\alpha_{ij}^{(\ell)} = \frac{\exp\big(\text{LeakyReLU}(\mathbf{a}^T[\mathbf{W}\mathbf{h}_i^{(\ell)} \| \mathbf{W}\mathbf{h}_j^{(\ell)} \| \mathbf{W}_e\mathbf{e}_{ji}])\big)}{\sum_{k \in \mathcal{N}(i)} \exp\big(\text{LeakyReLU}(\mathbf{a}^T[\mathbf{W}\mathbf{h}_i^{(\ell)} \| \mathbf{W}\mathbf{h}_k^{(\ell)} \| \mathbf{W}_e\mathbf{e}_{ki}])\big)}, \tag{6}$$

where $\|$ denotes concatenation, $\mathbf{W}, \mathbf{W}_e \in \mathbb{R}^{d' \times d}$ are learnable projections for node and edge features respectively, $\mathbf{a} \in \mathbb{R}^{2d'+p}$ is the attention vector, and $\mathcal{N}(i)$ indexes predecessors of $v_i$. The normalized attention coefficients $\alpha_{ij}^{(\ell)}$ weight the message from neighbor $v_j$:

$$\mathbf{m}_i^{(\ell)} = \sum_{j \in \mathcal{N}(i)} \alpha_{ij}^{(\ell)} \big(\mathbf{W}\mathbf{h}_j^{(\ell)} + \mathbf{W}_e\mathbf{e}_{ji}\big). \tag{7}$$

The node embedding is then updated via a nonlinearity and residual connection:

$$\mathbf{h}_i^{(\ell+1)} = \sigma\big(\mathbf{m}_i^{(\ell)} + \mathbf{W}\mathbf{h}_i^{(\ell)}\big). \tag{8}$$

We stack $L$ such T-GAT layers to capture multi-hop dependencies along the event chain. Finally, a global readout aggregates node embeddings by mean pooling:

$$\mathbf{h}_G = \frac{1}{|V|} \sum_{i=1}^{|V|} \mathbf{h}_i^{(L)}, \tag{9}$$

and a two-layer MLP with softmax output computes the readmission probability. We train with cross-entropy loss and optimize all parameters end-to-end using Adam.

## 3.4  Training and Evaluation

DETER is trained end-to-end with binary cross-entropy loss on 30-day readmission labels, optimized via Adam (learning rate $\eta = 1 \times 10^{-3}$, weight decay $\lambda = 5 \times 10^{-4}$). We use patient-stratified 5-fold cross-validation, early stopping on validation AUC (patience=10, max 100 epochs), and a class-weighted loss to mitigate imbalance. Key hyperparameters, number of T-GAT layers $L \in \{2, 3, 4\}$, hidden size $d' \in \{16, 32, 64\}$, edge-embed dim $p \in \{8, 16\}$, are selected via grid search on fold 1. Training runs on Tesla V100 GPUs with batch size 32. We assess performance by AUC, F1-score, and Brier score, comparing against three baselines using identical splits and preprocessing: (i) an MLP on aggregated stay features, (ii) a BiLSTM over 6-h windows, and (iii) a patient-similarity GCN (admissions linked by kNN on clinical features). Statistical significance is established via paired bootstrapped 95% confidence intervals across folds. Figure 1(a) details our event-trajectory graph from longitudinal patient EHR event streams.

# 4   Results and Analysis

## 4.1   Cohort Characteristics

Table 1 presents the demographic and clinical profile of the 14 532 adult ICU admissions used in our study (11 666 in the training set, 2 866 in the test set). The near-identical mean ages (64.3 vs. 63.9 years) and male proportions (56.2% vs. 55.8%) confirm that there is no appreciable demographic shift between splits, which supports the validity of our patient-stratified cross-validation. Median lengths of stay of approximately 5.4 and 5.3 days (IQRs 3.1–9.8 and 3.0–9.6) indicate that the cohort captures a typical ICU population with sufficient duration to observe meaningful clinical trajectories. Finally, the 30-day readmission rate of 17.5% in both sets is consistent with published ICU readmission prevalences, ensuring that our model is evaluated on a realistic event rate and has ample positive cases to learn from.

**Table 1.** Cohort characteristics of adult ICU admissions in the DETER study (external MIMIC-IV subset).

| Characteristic | Train (N=11,666) | Test (N=2,866) |
|---|---|---|
| Age, mean (SD) (years) | 64.3 (16.2) | 63.9 (16.5) |
| Male (%) | 56.2 | 55.8 |
| Length of stay, median (IQR) (days) | 5.4 (3.1–9.8) | 5.3 (3.0–9.6) |
| 30-day readmission rate (%) | 17.5 | 17.4 |

## 4.2   Predictive Performance

Table 2 compares DETER against three strong baselines: an MLP on aggregated features, a BiLSTM on 6-hour windows, and a patient-similarity GCN. DETER achieves an AUC of $0.83 \pm 0.008$, markedly higher than the MLP (AUC $0.71 \pm 0.02$) and BiLSTM (AUC $0.76 \pm 0.015$). This gain demonstrates that preserving the full event chronology and modeling inter-event intervals via directed edges yields substantially better discrimination of patients who will be readmitted within 30 days. The F1-score improvement (DETER: 0.48±0.01 vs. 0.35–0.43 for baselines) confirms that our model also balances precision and recall more effectively, while the lower Brier score (0.13 vs. 0.15–0.18) indicates tighter probability calibration. Figure 1b visualizes these differences: DETER's ROC curve dominates across nearly all false-positive rates, validating its robustness in clinical decision thresholds.

## 4.3   Ablation Study

To isolate the contributions of our design choices, we conducted targeted ablations summarized in Table 3. First, removing the time-delta embeddings from

**Table 2.** Performance comparison of DETER against baseline models on the 30-day readmission task (mean ± 95% CI).

| Model | AUC | F1-score | Brier Score |
|---|---|---|---|
| MLP (aggregated features) | $0.71 \pm 0.02$ | $0.35 \pm 0.02$ | $0.18 \pm 0.01$ |
| BiLSTM (6-h windows) | $0.76 \pm 0.015$ | $0.40 \pm 0.015$ | $0.16 \pm 0.008$ |
| Patient-Similarity GCN | $0.79 \pm 0.01$ | $0.43 \pm 0.01$ | $0.15 \pm 0.007$ |
| **DETER (ours)** | $\mathbf{0.83 \pm 0.008}$ | $\mathbf{0.48 \pm 0.01}$ | $\mathbf{0.13 \pm 0.005}$ |

the directed edges causes AUC to drop from 0.83 to 0.80, demonstrating that explicit modeling of inter-event intervals materially improves the network's ability to distinguish readmitted patients. Second, replacing our sparse, successive-event connectivity with a dense "forgetting" graph reduces AUC further to 0.78, indicating that constraining messages to chronologically adjacent events preserves signal clarity and avoids dilution from spurious long-range connections. Finally, we assessed depth sensitivity by varying the number of T-GAT layers: performance peaks at three layers (AUC 0.83), while two layers underfit (AUC 0.79) and four layers yield marginally lower gains (AUC 0.82), suggesting that three attention hops best capture the multi-step dependencies inherent in the ICU trajectory without overfitting. These ablation results confirm that both the directed edge design and the chosen network depth are critical to DETER's superior performance.

**Table 3.** Ablation study on MIMIC-III validation set: impact of removing components and varying architecture depth (AUC ± 95% CI).

| Configuration | AUC ± 95% CI |
|---|---|
| Full DETER (directed $\Delta t + L = 3$ layers) | $0.83 \pm 0.008$ |
|    without time-delta embeddings | $0.80 \pm 0.009$ |
|    dense "forgetting" connectivity | $0.78 \pm 0.010$ |
| Depth sensitivity | |
|    $L = 2$ layers | $0.79 \pm 0.010$ |
|    $L = 3$ layers (full model) | $0.83 \pm 0.008$ |
|    $L = 4$ layers | $0.82 \pm 0.009$ |

## 4.4   Interpretability Analysis

Figure 1(c) plots a representative last-layer TGAT edge-attention weight matrix $\alpha_{ij}$ (multi-head averaged), the row-normalized softmax over predecessors, for seven clinical events (HR drop, BP spike, WBC, creatinine rise, antibiotic dose, diuretic dose, discharge planning), ordered chronologically. The strongest weight occurs at CR→ABX (0.70), indicating that rising creatinine followed by antibiotic administration is the top predictor of 30-day readmission. A secondary peak at ABX→DIU (0.60) highlights fluid-management interplay, while low weights on early vitals (e.g., HR→BP=0.05) suggest acute hemodynamics are less informative for medium-term risk. These patterns demonstrate DETER's ability to surface clinically meaningful event transitions for actionable insight.

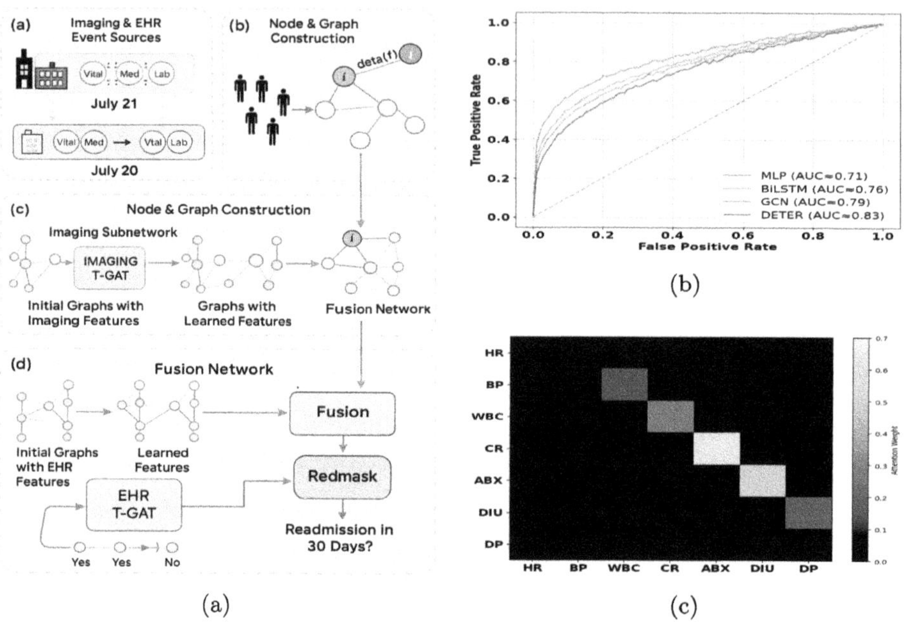


**Fig. 1.** (a) Event-trajectory graphization of EHR streams (vitals, labs, medications): nodes are timestamped events; directed edges link successive events and encode $\Delta t$ embeddings; (b) ROC curves (mean±1 std over five folds) showing DETER's AUC≈0.83; (c) TGAT attention heatmap on an admission highlighting key influential transitions.

## 5  Conclusion

We have presented DETER, a novel framework that models each ICU admission as a directed event-trajectory graph and leverages a Temporal Graph Attention Network to predict 30-day readmission risk. By preserving the exact sequence of timestamped clinical events and explicitly encoding inter-event intervals, DETER achieves an AUC of $0.83 \pm 0.008$, outperforming MLP, BiLSTM, and patient-similarity GCN baselines, and demonstrates superior calibration and F1-score. Ablation experiments confirm that both the sparse directed chain and time-delta embeddings are essential to its success, while interpretability analysis highlights clinically meaningful transitions, such as creatinine rise followed by antibiotic administration, as primary drivers of readmission risk. Our results underscore the value of event-chain graph representations for EHR analytics and open avenues to integrate data streams (e.g., waveforms, wearables) enabling real-time clinical decision support.

# References


1. Ashfaq, A., Sant'Anna, A., Lingman, M., Nowaczyk, S.: Readmission prediction using deep learning on electronic health records. J. Biomed. Inform. **97**, 103256 (2019)
2. Barbieri, S., et al.: Benchmarking deep learning architectures for predicting readmission to the ICU and describing patients-at-risk. Sci. Rep. **10**(1), 1111 (2020)
3. Choi, E.,et al.: Graph convolutional transformer: Learning the graphical structure of electronic health records. arXiv preprint arXiv:1906.04716 (2019)
4. Hancox, Z., Kingsbury, S.R., Clegg, A., Conaghan, P.G., Relton, S.D.: Developing the temporal graph convolutional neural network model to predict hip replacement using electronic health records. arXiv preprint arXiv:2409.06585 (2024)
5. Jencks, S.F., Williams, M.V., Coleman, E.A.: Rehospitalizations among patients in the medicare fee-for-service program. N. Engl. J. Med. **360**(14), 1418–1428 (2009)
6. Ma, T., Xiao, C., Wang, F.: Health-atm: a deep architecture for multifaceted patient health record representation and risk prediction. In: Proceedings of the 2018 SIAM International Conference on Data Mining, pp. 261–269. SIAM (2018)
7. Parisot, S., et al.: Disease prediction using graph convolutional networks: application to autism spectrum disorder and Alzheimer's disease. Med. Image Anal. **48**, 117–130 (2018)
8. Peng, L., Yang, C., Chen, Y., Liu, W.: Predicting circrna-disease associations via feature convolution learning with heterogeneous graph attention network. IEEE J. Biomed. Health Inform. **27**(6), 3072–3082 (2023)
9. Rajkomar, A., et al.: Scalable and accurate deep learning with electronic health records. NPJ Digital Med. **1**(1), 18 (2018)
10. Schlichtkrull, M., Kipf, T.N., Bloem, P., Van Den Berg, R., Titov, I., Welling, M.: Modeling relational data with graph convolutional networks. In: The semantic web: 15th international conference, ESWC 2018, Heraklion, Crete, Greece, June 3–7, 2018, proceedings 15, pp. 593–607. Springer (2018)
11. Tang, S., et al.: Multimodal spatiotemporal graph neural networks for improved prediction of 30-day all-cause hospital readmission. arXiv:2204.06766 (2022)
12. Tang, S., et al.: Predicting 30-day all-cause hospital readmission using multimodal spatiotemporal graph neural networks. IEEE J. Biomed. Health Inform. **27**(4), 2071–2082 (2023)
13. Wang, S., Zhu, X.: Predictive modeling of hospital readmission: challenges and solutions. IEEE/ACM Trans. Comput. Biol. Bioinf. **19**(5), 2975–2995 (2021)
14. Xiao, C., Choi, E., Sun, J.: Opportunities and challenges in developing deep learning models using electronic health records data: a systematic review. J. Am. Med. Inform. Assoc. **25**(10), 1419–1428 (2018)
15. Xu, Z., et al.: Predicting ICU interventions: a transparent decision support model based on multivariate time series graph convolutional neural network. IEEE J. Biomed. Health Inform. (2024)

# Explainable Ensemble Learning for Assessment of Major Depressive Disorder Severity

Princy Verma[1]([✉]) [ID], Millie Pant[1,2] [ID], and Mukesh Kumar Barua[3] [ID]

[1] Department of Applied Mathematics and Scientific Computing, IIT Roorkee, Roorkee, India
princy_v@amsc.iitr.ac.in, pant.milli@as.iitr.ac.in
[2] Mehta Family School for Data Science and Artificial Intelligence, IIT Roorkee, Roorkee, India
[3] Department of Management Studies, IIT Roorkee, Roorkee, India
mukesh.barua@ms.iitr.ac.in

**Abstract.** Major Depressive Disorder (MDD) is a major global mental health challenge, necessitating timely and precise assessment of its severity to enable appropriate intervention. This study proposes an explainable ensemble learning approach to predict MDD into four severity levels, Mild, Moderate, Severe, and Very Severe, using real-world data from 500 patients collected at a reputed psychiatric department of a medical college in India. The dataset includes 43 features, including socio-demographic, lifestyle, medical, and psychological indicators based on the Hamilton Depression Rating Scale (HAM-D). The methodology involves the implementation of advanced machine learning models, including Random Forest, XGBoost, and ensemble techniques such as soft voting and stacking. To mitigate class imbalance, SMOTE is applied, and model performance is optimized using 5-fold cross-validation with hyperparameter tuning. The stacking ensemble model, with Random Forest as the meta-classifier, achieves outstanding AUC scores: 99% for both Mild and Very Severe, 97% for Moderate, and 96% for Severe. For interpretability, SHAP (Shapley Additive exPlanations) identifies key predictive features. 'Insomnia - Delayed' is a prominent indicator for Very Severe and Moderate MDD, 'Anxiety - Psychological' is significant for the Severe class, and 'Feelings of Guilt' is most influential for Mild cases. This approach provides high predictive accuracy with clinical interpretability, providing a robust tool for personalized MDD severity assessment.

**Keywords:** Mental Health · XAI · Machine Learning · Ensemble Learning · SHAP

## 1 Introduction

Major Depressive Disorder (MDD) is a critical global mental health issue, marked by persistent sadness, loss of interest, and physical and emotional symptoms that impair daily functioning, affecting over 280 million people worldwide, including 23 million children and adolescents [1]. Symptoms include poor concentration, guilt, hopelessness, suicidal thoughts, sleep and appetite disturbances, and fatigue [1]. Given its growing prevalence, understanding factors influencing MDD onset, progression, and management, such as socio-demographic, lifestyle, medical, and psychological attributes, is vital for timely interventions and tailored healthcare strategies [2].

Conventionally, MDD severity is measured using scales as the Hamilton Depression Rating Scale (HAM-D) [3], and the Patient Health Questionnaire (PHQ) [4], which rely on clinician or self-reported evaluations, are often time-consuming, subjective, and limited in considering contextual factors. Existing studies [5–7], typically focus on binary classification, such as depressed vs. non-depressed, with limited severity stratification, limited real-world data and low interpretability.

To address these gaps, this study proposes an explainable stacking ensemble model integrating Logistic Regression, Random Forest (RF), and XGBoost, with RF as the meta-classifier, optimized via 5-fold cross-validation and hyperparameter tuning. It predicts MDD severity into four levels: Mild, Moderate, Severe, and Very Severe. SHAP (SHapley Additive exPlanations), a widely adopted explainable AI (XAI) technique, is applied for interpretability, highlighting feature contributions across severity levels. Real-world clinical data from 500 patients, collected at a reputed psychiatric department of a medical college in India, including 43 socio-demographic, lifestyle, medical, and HAM-D indicators, is used for model development. The main objectives of this study are as follows:

(1) To develop a clinically grounded predictive model using real-world clinical data from 500 patients with socio-demographic, lifestyle, medical, and HAM-D indicators for robust and applicable outcomes.
(2) To develop an optimized stacking ensemble combining Logistic Regression, RF, and XGBoost for multi-class MDD severity prediction aiming to improve predictive performance over single-model or binary approaches.
(3) To ensure interpretability and actionable insights using SHAP-based explainable AI, identifying the importance of psychological predictors across all MDD severity levels to support evidence-driven decisions.

The paper is organized as follows: Sect. 2 describes the methodology, including data collection, preprocessing, model development, stacking ensemble formulation, performance metrics, and SHAP explainability. Section 3 presents the results, and Sect. 4 concludes with future directions.

## 2  Methodology

Figure 1 shows the computational steps of the proposed explainable ensemble learning approach for predicting MDD severity levels such as Mild, Moderate, Severe, and Very Severe, including data collection, preprocessing, model development, mathematical formulation, performance evaluation, and explainability. The computational steps are as follows:

**Data Collection:** The dataset of 541 patient records was collected from a renowned psychiatric department of a medical college in India. It includes 18 numerical features like age and HAM-D indicators, and 7 categorical variables such as gender, marital status, education, occupation, Diet, Blood Pressure levels, and MDD severity. This clinically

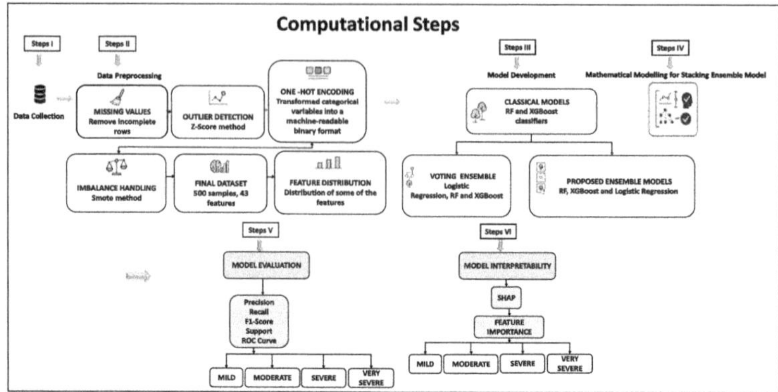



**Fig. 1.** Computational Steps

validated dataset captures a diverse set of socio-demographic, lifestyle, medical, and psychological indicators that are highly relevant for assessing depression severity.

**Data Preprocessing:** Data preprocessing ensures dataset quality and readiness for analysis. Missing values are handled by removing incomplete rows. Outliers in 'Age' are detected using the Z-score method [8]. One-hot encoding is applied to transform categorical variables into a binary format. The dataset exhibits class imbalance across four MDD severity levels, with Mild and Moderate cases dominating. To address this, SMOTE (Synthetic Minority Oversampling Technique) is applied to the training set and generating synthetic minority samples to balance class representation and enhance model robustness. As synthetic samples may introduce bias or noise, SMOTE is limited to the training data, and 5-fold cross-validation is used for reliable performance validation. After preprocessing, the final dataset comprised 500 samples and 43 features with socio-demographic, lifestyle, medical, and HAM-D factors.

**Model Development:** To build a robust and high-performing model for MDD severity prediction, both classical ML and ensemble techniques are applied as follows:

- **Classical Models:** RF and XGBoost are used for their strong performance on structured, multi-class data.
- **Voting Ensemble:** A soft voting ensemble combining Logistic Regression, RF, and XGBoost is implemented to enhance prediction stability.
- **Proposed Stacking Model:** A stacking ensemble integrating RF, XGBoost, and Logistic Regression is developed, with RF as the meta-classifier, enabling higher-order feature learning and improved accuracy.

Hyperparameter tuning using 5-fold cross-validation is performed to optimize model performance. The parameters for all base and meta-classifiers are selected based on prior studies and dataset-specific experimentation. RF is used with 200 estimators, maximum depth 10, class weight 'balanced', and random state 42 to ensure capacity while preventing overfitting. XGBoost is configured with use_label_encoder = False, objective =

multi:softprob, evaluation metric $=$ mlogloss, and random state 42 for multi-class classification. Logistic Regression is employed with 1000 maximum iterations, balanced class weights, multinomial setting, and the 'lbfgs' solver for convergence on high-dimensional features. In the stacking ensemble, the RF meta-classifier is used with 100 estimators, depth 10, class weight 'balanced', and random state 42 to capture higher-order feature interactions. These settings provide an optimal balance between model complexity, computational efficiency, and predictive accuracy.

**Mathematical Modelling for Stacking Ensemble Model:** The ensemble learning technique employed integrates the predictive capabilities of three diverse base models: RF, XGBoost, and Logistic Regression. These models are combined using a stacking ensemble strategy, where a secondary meta-classifier, RF, is trained to learn from the outputs of the base models.

Let the predicted probability vectors for each class from the base classifiers be:

- $P_{RF}(L_i)$: Probability from RF for class $L_i$
- $P_{XGB}(L_i)$ : Probability from XGBoost for class $L_i$
- $P_{LR}(L_i)$ : Probability from Logistic Regression for class $L_i$

where $i \in \{0, 1, 2, 3\}\}$ corresponding to: Mild (0), Moderate (1), Severe (2), Very Severe (3). Base Predictions are:

$$P_{RF} = [P_{RF}(L_0), P_{RF}(L_1), P_{RF}(L_2), P_{RF}(L_3)] \tag{1}$$

$$P_{XGB} = [P_{XGB}(L_0), P_{XGB}(L_1), P_{XGB}(L_2), P_{XGB}(L_3)] \tag{2}$$

$$P_{LR} = [P_{LR}(L_0), P_{LR}(L_1), P_{LR}(L_2), P_{LR}(L_3)] \tag{3}$$

Meta-Level Inputs are:

$$F = [X|, P_{RF}, P_{XGB}, P_{LR}] \tag{4}$$

where $F$ is the feature set passed to the meta-classifier RF. The passthrough option includes original features $X$ along with base model outputs. The final ensemble prediction, denoted as $P_{Ensemble}$, is derived using the meta-classifier, which operates on the concatenated feature vector comprising both the original input features and the probability outputs from the base learners (as passthrough is enabled). This can be represented as:

$$P_{Ensemble}(L_i) = MetaRF(F)(L_i), \forall i \in 0, 1, 2, 3 \tag{5}$$

212        P. Verma et al.

---
**Algorithm: Stacking-Based MDD Severity Model**

Input: Pre-processed dataset $D$ with features $X$ and encoded labels $L_0$ to $L_3$
Output: Predicted class label and associated likelihood score for each instance

1. Split dataset $D$ into training and testing subsets.
2. Apply SMOTE to balance the class distribution in the training set.
3. Train the RF classifier $C_1$ on the training set.
4. Train the XGBoost classifier $C_2$ on the training set.
5. Train the Logistic Regression classifier $C_3$ on the training set.
6. Concatenate the original feature vector $X$ with the soft outputs (probability vectors) from $C_1, C_2$, and $C_3$.
7. Train the meta-classifier (RF) on this combined input to learn the final ensemble mapping.
8. Generate probability scores $P_{Ensemble}(L_i)$ for each severity class $L_i$, where $i \in \{0, 1, 2, 3\}$.
9. Calculate the likelihood score as:

$$\text{Likelihood Score} = \max\left(P_{Ensemble}(L_0), P_{Ensemble}(L_1), P_{Ensemble}(L_2), P_{Ensemble}(L_3)\right)$$

10. Predict the final class as:

$$\hat{y} = \arg\max_{i} P_{Ensemble}\left(L_i\right)$$

---

A pre-processed dataset $D$, with severity labels $L_0, L_1, L_2, L_3$, is split into training and testing sets. The base classifiers $C_1, C_2, C_3$ (i.e., RF, XGB, LR) are trained independently. Their predicted probability distributions are passed, along with the original features, into a meta-classifier. The meta-model learns to predict the final severity class label and the associated likelihood score.

**Model Evaluation:** The third step involves comparing the performance of all models using standard classification metrics such as Precision, Recall, F1-Score, Support, and Receiver Operating Characteristic (ROC) curves, computed for each MDD severity class, Mild, Moderate, Severe, and Very Severe.

**Model Interpretability:** In the fourth step, SHAP is applied to interpret the predictions of the stacking ensemble model to compute feature importance values and visualize the contribution of each variable across different MDD severity levels. This step enhances model transparency and supports clinical understanding of how psychological factors affect MDD progression.

## 3 Experimental Results

This section presents the experimental outcomes of the proposed explainable ensemble learning approach for stratifying MDD into four severity levels: Mild, Moderate, Severe, and Very Severe. The results are discussed across four dimensions: classical prediction performance, ensemble models prediction, comparative analysis, and explainability of the model, as follows:

**Results of Classical ML Models:** The performance of RF and XGBoost classifiers is evaluated using precision, recall, F1-score, support, and ROC-AUC for each class.

RF achieves an average cross-validated accuracy of 66.36%, with ROC-AUC values: Mild (0.98), Moderate (0.87), Severe (0.62), and Very Severe (0.88) as seen in Fig. 2 (a). XGBoost outperforms RF with 82.85% accuracy and ROC-AUC: Mild (0.79), Moderate (0.82), Severe (0.68), and Very Severe (0.89), as shown in Fig. 2 (b).

**Results of Ensemble Models:** Both ensemble approaches further enhanced prediction accuracy. The Soft Voting Ensemble achieved 91.76% accuracy, with ROC-AUC: Mild (0.98), Moderate (0.93), Severe (0.84), and Very Severe (0.96), as seen in Fig. 3 (a). The Stacking Ensemble with an RF meta-classifier outperformed all, attaining 98.14% accuracy and ROC-AUC: Mild (0.99), Moderate (0.97), Severe (0.96), and Very Severe (0.99), as shown in Fig. 3 (b). Table 1 presents the Performance metrics of all models.

**Table 1.** Performance metrics of all proposed models

| Model | Metric | Mild | Moderate | Severe | Very Severe |
|---|---|---|---|---|---|
| Random Forest | Precision | 0.00 | 0.40 | 0.48 | 0.71 |
| | Recall | 0.00 | 0.11 | 0.62 | 0.79 |
| | F1-Score | 0.00 | 0.17 | 0.54 | 0.75 |
| | Support | 3 | 19 | 40 | 47 |
| XGBoost | Precision | 0.50 | 0.33 | 0.51 | 0.80 |
| | Recall | 0.33 | 0.21 | 0.65 | 0.74 |
| | F1-Score | 0.40 | 0.26 | 0.57 | 0.77 |
| | Support | 3 | 19 | 40 | 47 |
| Soft Voting Ensemble | Precision | 0.50 | 0.73 | 0.63 | 0.84 |
| | Recall | 0.33 | 0.42 | 0.82 | 0.79 |
| | F1-Score | 0.40 | 0.53 | 0.72 | 0.81 |
| | Support | 3 | 19 | 40 | 47 |
| Stacking Ensemble | Precision | 0.67 | 0.80 | 0.73 | 0.95 |
| | Recall | 0.67 | 0.63 | 0.90 | 0.85 |
| | F1-Score | 0.67 | 0.71 | 0.81 | 0.90 |
| | Support | 3 | 19 | 40 | 47 |

**Comparative Analysis of All Models:** A comparison across the four models, RF, XGBoost, Soft Voting Ensemble, and Stacking Ensemble, reveals a clear performance hierarchy: Stacking Ensemble (98.14%) > Soft Voting (91.76%) > XGBoost (82.85%) > RF (66.36%). The stacking approach effectively leveraged Logistic Regression, XGBoost, and RF as base learners with an RF meta-classifier, capturing higher-order interactions for robust classification. To contextualize these results, we further compared the performance of our models with recent state-of-the-art studies on MDD severity classification. Table 2 summarizes the accuracy reported in prior works with the results of our proposed ensemble models.

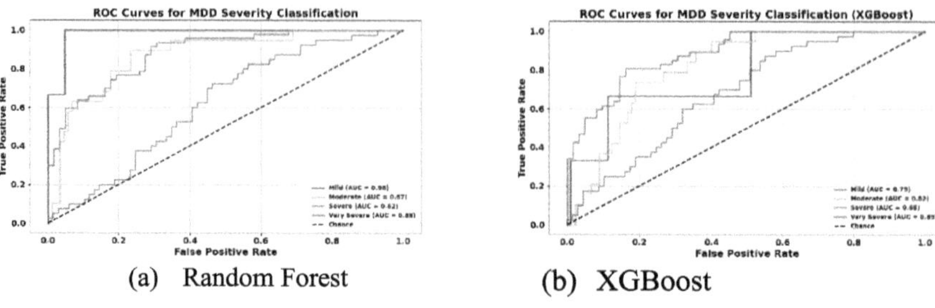

(a)  Random Forest   (b)  XGBoost

**Fig. 2.** ROC Curve of (a) Random Forest, (b) XGBoost

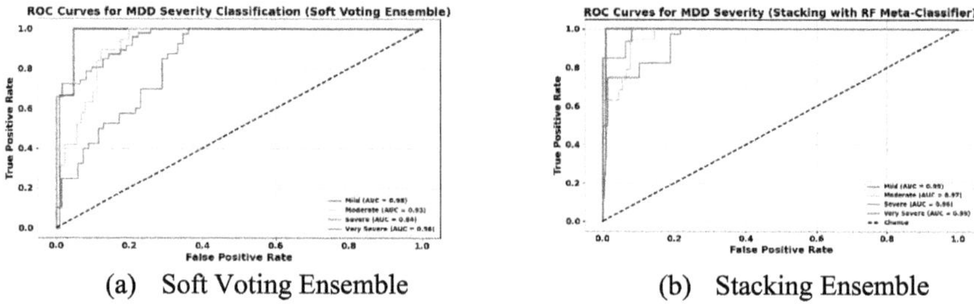

(a)  Soft Voting Ensemble   (b)  Stacking Ensemble

**Fig. 3.** ROC Curve (a) Soft Voting Ensemble, (b) Stacking Ensemble

**Result Based on SHAP:** To interpret the contribution of individual features for the prediction of MDD severity, SHAP values are analyzed. The most influential features across all severity levels include 'Insomnia - Delayed' [3] and 'Anxiety - Psychological' [3] for very severe cases, as shown in Fig. 4 (a), and moderate severity, as seen in Fig. 4 (c). 'Anxiety - Psychological' and 'Genital Symptoms' [3] are notably significant for the severe class, as depicted in Fig. 4 (b), while 'Feelings of Guilt' [3] and 'Anxiety - Psychological' emerge as key features for mild cases, as described in Fig. 4 (d). Overall, SHAP interpretations confirm that the ensemble model aligns with psychiatric understanding of MDD, providing both high predictive power and explainable insights.

**Table 2.** Comparison with recent state-of-the-art models

| Study | Model | Dataset | Accuracy |
| --- | --- | --- | --- |
| **Our Study** | **Stacking Ensemble** | **Real-world clinical data** | **98.14%** |
| [9] | Dynamic ensemble | National Social Life, Health, and Aging Project (NSHAP) | 88.33% |
| [10] | Neural Network | Speech dataset with clinical labels (MDD vs HC) | 84.16% |

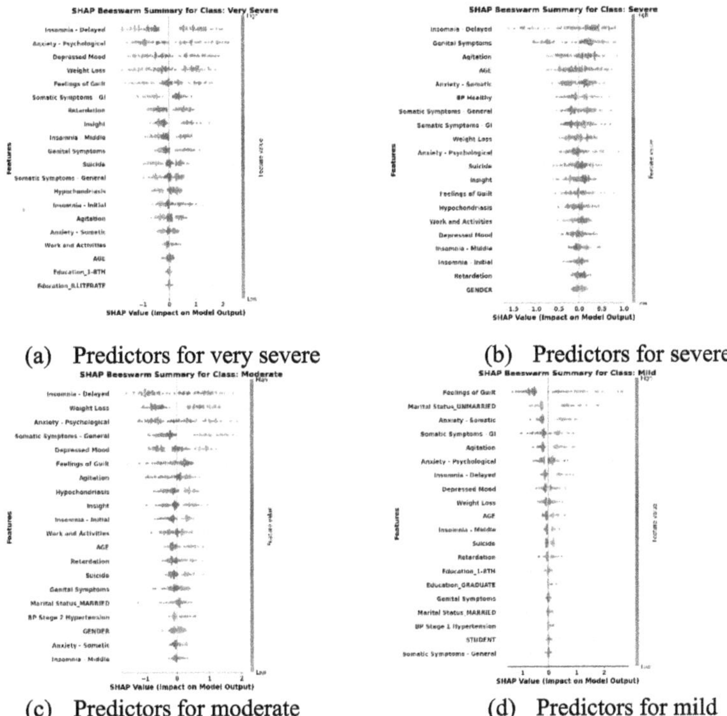

(a) Predictors for very severe

(b) Predictors for severe

(c) Predictors for moderate

(d) Predictors for mild

**Fig. 4.** The top contributing features for all severity levels

## 4 Conclusion

In conclusion, this study presents an explainable stacking ensemble model integrating Logistic Regression, RF, and XGBoost with RF as a meta-classifier for multi-class MDD severity prediction using real-world clinical data. The model achieves outstanding predictive performance, attaining a cross-validated accuracy of 98.14% and ROC-AUC scores of 99% for both Mild and Very Severe, 97% for Moderate, and 96% for Severe classes, outperforming traditional classifiers and soft voting ensembles. SHAP analysis highlights key predictors such as 'Insomnia - Delayed,' 'Anxiety - Psychological,' and 'Feelings of Guilt' across various severity levels, ensuring interpretability and clinical relevance. This study demonstrates the potential of explainable AI as a decision-support tool for personalized and data-driven mental health assessment. While limited by a single-institution dataset, future work should validate the model on larger, multi-centre datasets, incorporate multimodal data, and explore temporal modelling to enhance robustness, generalizability, and clinical utility.

## References

1. Depressive disorder (depression). Accessed 26 July 2025. https://www.who.int/news-room/fact-sheets/detail/depression

2. Ferrari, A.J., et al.: Global variation in the prevalence and incidence of major depressive disorder: a systematic review of the epidemiological literature. Psychol. Med. **43**(3), 471–481 (2013). https://doi.org/10.1017/S0033291712001511
3. Hamilton, M.: A rating scale for depression. J. Neurol. Neurosurg. Psychiatry **23**(1), 56–62 (1960). https://doi.org/10.1136/JNNP.23.1.56
4. Kroenke, K., Spitzer, R.L., Williams, J.B.W.: The PHQ-9: validity of a brief depression severity measure. J. Gen. Intern. Med. **16**(9), 606–613 (2001). https://doi.org/10.1046/J.1525-1497.2001.016009606.X/METRICS
5. Shatte, A.B.R., Hutchinson, D.M., Teague, S.J.: Machine learning in mental health: a scoping review of methods and applications. Psychol. Med. **49**(9), 1426–1448 (2019). https://doi.org/10.1017/S0033291719000151
6. Chen, Z., et al.: Identifying major depressive disorder among US adults living alone using stacked ensemble machine learning algorithms. Front. Public Heal. **13**, 1472050 (2025). https://doi.org/10.3389/FPUBH.2025.1472050/BIBTEX
7. Ramasubbu, R., et al.: Accuracy of automated classification of major depressive disorder as a function of symptom severity. NeuroImage Clin. **12**, 320–331 (2016). https://doi.org/10.1016/J.NICL.2016.07.012
8. Colan, S.D.: The why and how of Z scores. J. Am. Soc. Echocardiogr. **26**(1), 38–40 (2013). https://doi.org/10.1016/j.echo.2012.11.005
9. Imans, D., Abuhmed, T., Alharbi, M., El-Sappagh, S.: Explainable multi-layer dynamic ensemble framework optimized for depression detection and severity assessment. Diagnostics **14**(21), 2385 (2024). https://doi.org/10.3390/DIAGNOSTICS14212385/S1
10. Liang, L., et al.: Enhanced classification and severity prediction of major depressive disorder using acoustic features and machine learning. Front. Psychiatry **15**, 1422020 (2024). https://doi.org/10.3389/FPSYT.2024.1422020/BIBTEX

# Feature Selection and SHAP-Based Interpretability in ML Models for AMR Prediction in Klebsiella Pneumoniae

Lov Kumar[1], Vikram Singh[1]([envelope]), and Nikita[2]

[1] National Institute of Technology, Kurukshetra, India
{lovkumar,viks}@nitkkr.ac.in
[2] Central University of Haryana, Mahendragarh, Haryana, India

**Abstract.** Antimicrobial resistance (AMR) weakens the body's defense against infections, posing severe risks to patients undergoing medical treatment. The growing prevalence of resistant pathogens such as Staphylococcus aureus, Enterococcus spp., Klebsiella pneumoniae, and Pseudomonas aeruginosa has raised major clinical concerns. Leveraging rich medical data and predictive modeling now enables the development of evidence-based frameworks for AMR management. This study presents a comprehensive AMR prediction pipeline integrating feature selection techniques, classifier variants, and class balancing. Empirical results show that Random Forest and Gradient Boosting outperform other models, while SHAP analysis identifies tet(D), tRNA, and Contigs as key determinants of resistance offering interpretable insights into patient-level AMR risk.

**Keywords:** Antimicrobial Resistance · Klebsiella pneumoniae · SHAP Values · Classification · Feature Selection

## 1 Introduction

Microorganisms such as bacteria, viruses, fungi, and parasites can evolve to survive drug exposure, leading to antimicrobial resistance (AMR) the ability of microbes to withstand specific antimicrobial concentrations [1]. AMR is a major global health threat, rendering antibiotics ineffective and increasing infection-related mortality. Klebsiella pneumoniae has become a critical concern due to its resistance to carbapenems, particularly meropenem. The rapid rise of meropenem-resistant K. pneumoniae (MRKP) highlights the urgent need for early detection and timely intervention [1].

Traditional culture-based antibiotic susceptibility testing is slow, labor-intensive, and prone to error, delaying treatment and increasing therapeutic failure risk. With pathogens such as Staphylococcus aureus, Enterococcus spp., K. pneumoniae, and Pseudomonas aeruginosa increasingly showing multidrug resistance [2], rapid identification of resistant strains is essential. Machine learning (ML) offers a powerful alternative, leveraging genomic data to predict resistance quickly and accurately. Algorithms like SVM, logistic regression, and random


S. Mitra et al. (Eds.): PReMI 2025, LNCS 16358, pp. 217–225, 2026.
https://doi.org/10.1007/978-3-032-18480-1_22

forests have achieved high predictive performance and identified novel AMR genes, underscoring ML's promise for clinical decision support and antibiotic stewardship.

This study develops ML-based predictive models for meropenem resistance in K. pneumoniae, integrating diverse classifiers, feature selection methods, sampling strategies, and SHAP-based interpretability to reveal key genomic markers. The proposed framework aims to improve prediction accuracy, accelerate resistance profiling, and support automated AMR detection advancing surveillance, optimizing treatment, and strengthening efforts against antibiotic resistance. The following research questions (RQs) are formulated to steer the assertions:

- **RQ1**:*How does FS improve the accuracy and interpretability of ML models in predicting Meropenem resistance?*
- **RQ2**: *Which ML algorithm performs best in detecting AMR, and how do different models compare?*
- **RQ3**: *Which genomic features contribute most significantly to predicting meropenem resistance, and how do they influence the model's decision-making?*

The manuscript is structured as follows: the introduction outlines the study's motivation, research questions, and contributions. Section 2 reviews related work, while Sect. 3 details the proposed methodology. Section 4 covers the experimental setup, including evaluation metrics and SHAP analysis, and Sect. 5 addresses the RQs. Section 6 concludes with key findings and implications.

## 2    Related Work

Extensive research has been conducted on Klebsiella pneumoniae and its AMR mechanisms, particularly its resistance to carbapenems like meropenem. Previous studies have identified key genetic determinants, including carbapenemase-producing genes (e.g., *blaKPC, blaNDM, blaOXA-48, blaVIM, and blaIMP*), which play a crucial role in conferring resistance. Research by Davies et al. highlighted the rapid spread of carbapenem-resistant Enterobacteriaceae (CRE) and the clinical challenges associated with their treatment [3]. Similarly, Nordmann et al. provided an in-depth analysis of the global epidemiology of carbapenem-resistant pneumoniae, emphasizing the need for robust detection methods [4].

With the rise of whole-genome sequencing (WGS) and bioinformatics, several studies have explored computational approaches to predict AMR. Arango-Argoty et al. developed DL models for AMR gene prediction, demonstrating the potential of machine learning in genomic data analysis [1itearango2018deeparg. More recent work by Nguyen et al. applied RF and SVM classifiers to genomic features, achieving high accuracy in predicting resistance phenotypes.

Despite these advancements, a gap exists in applying ML models specifically for *meropenem resistance* prediction in *K. pneumoniae* using large-scale genomic datasets. Existing studies often focus on broad-spectrum AMR detection or single-class antibiotic resistance, but a more targeted approach is needed to refine prediction models for specific antibiotics. This study builds on previous research by integrating genomic FS, ML-based classification, and model optimization to enhance the accuracy of *meropenem resistance* prediction, ultimately contributing to efficient AMR surveillance and clinical decision-making.

## 3  Proposed Methodology

The ML-based methodology for predicting meropenem resistance in Klebsiella pneumoniae, illustrated in Fig. 1, leverages genomic data to reveal underlying AMR mechanisms. Further details are discussed below.

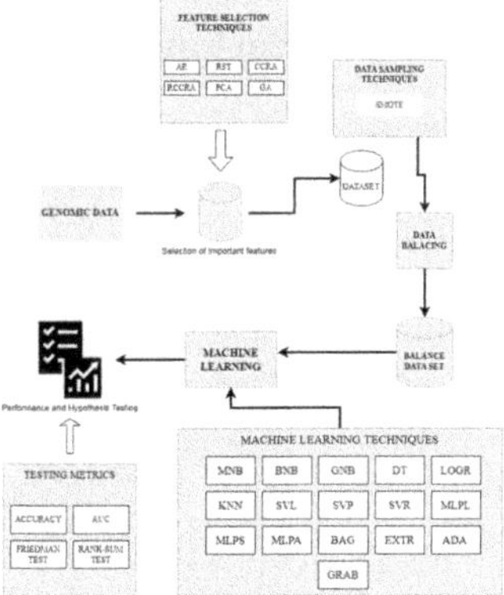

**Fig. 1.** Conceptual scheme for AMR Prediction Pipeline

1. **Dataset Collection and Preprocessing**: The genomic dataset obtained from Kaggle[1] comprises 302 features and 1,580 samples, representing the presence or absence of specific resistance determinants. It includes genomic profiles of Klebsiella pneumoniae strains categorized by sample sources such as urine, respiratory tract, and blood. Data preprocessing involved the removal of missing values, label encoding, and min–max scaling to standardize the dataset.
2. **Feature Selection Techniques and Classification**: Feature selection (FS) techniques were applied, including the Rank Sum Test (RST) for identifying significant genomic features, Cross-Correlation Analysis (CCRA) for removing redundancy, combined sets (RCCRA), Principal Component Analysis (PCA) for feature extraction, and a Genetic Algorithm (GA) for optimal feature selection. SHAP analysis further identified key predictors, notably tet(D), associated with AMR in Klebsiella pneumoniae. Finally, various ML

---

classifiers: Naïve Bayes variants, Logistic Regression, Decision Tree, KNN, and SVMs (linear, polynomial, RBF) were trained on the balanced dataset and validated using K-Fold cross-validation.

## 4  Experimental Analysis

This study employed 20 ML models combined with 6 FS techniques, forming 120 unique prediction pipelines to predict AMR in Klebsiella pneumoniae using genomic features from a public dataset. Models were validated through 5-fold cross-validation, and performance was evaluated using accuracy, AUC-ROC, precision, recall, and SHAP-based interpretability.

### 4.1  Effectiveness of Feature Selection Techniques

A comparative analysis of feature selection techniques (Fig. 1, Table 2) shows RCCRA and CCRA significantly outperforming other methods. RCCRA led with near-perfect scores ( 0.99 AUC, 99% accuracy), while PCA failed substantially (68% accuracy, 0.50 AUC). The GA-based approach offered only moderate, unstable performance due to high variance. These results establish RCCRA and CCRA as the most effective and reliable techniques.

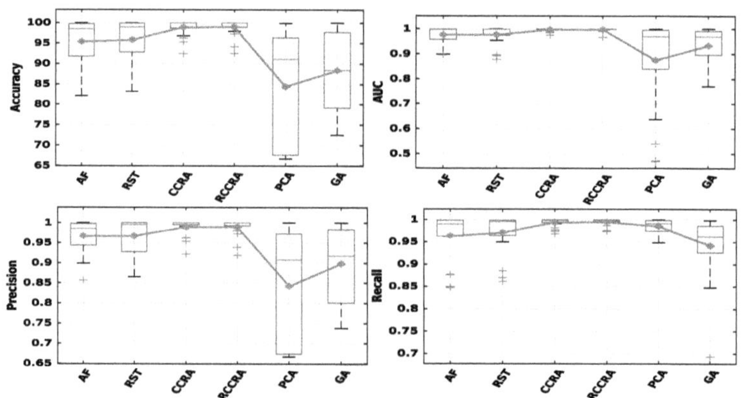

**Fig. 2.** Performance Box-plots of various FS Techniques

**Comparative Analysis of FSTs using Hypothesis Testing**: Statistical analysis via Friedman and Wilcoxon tests (Table 3) ranks the feature selection (FS) methods by performance, with a lower mean rank being better. The results clearly identify CCRA and RCCRA as the most effective FS techniques, while PCA and GA-based methods yielded the poorest outcomes. This confirms that the FS approach significantly impacts predictive performance, despite most pairwise differences not being statistically significant in post-hoc testing (Table 1).

**Table 1.** Descriptive Statistics of employed Feature Selection Techniques

| | Accuracy | | | | | | AUC | | | | | |
|---|---|---|---|---|---|---|---|---|---|---|---|---|
| | Min | Max | Mean | Median | Q1 | Q3 | Min | Max | Mean | Median | Q1 | Q3 |
| AF | 82.03 | 99.94 | 95.35 | 98.45 | 91.80 | 99.72 | 0.90 | 1.00 | 0.98 | 1.00 | 0.96 | 1.00 |
| RST | 83.16 | 99.94 | 95.80 | 98.96 | 92.82 | 99.91 | 0.88 | 1.00 | 0.98 | 1.00 | 0.98 | 1.00 |
| CCRA | 92.47 | 100.00 | 98.89 | 99.94 | 98.73 | 100.00 | 0.97 | 1.00 | 1.00 | 1.00 | 1.00 | 1.00 |
| RCCRA | 92.53 | 100.00 | 98.97 | 99.97 | 98.92 | 100.00 | 0.97 | 1.00 | 1.00 | 1.00 | 1.00 | 1.00 |
| PCA | 66.65 | 99.87 | 84.37 | 91.08 | 67.60 | 96.36 | 0.47 | 1.00 | 0.87 | 0.97 | 0.84 | 1.00 |
| GA | 72.47 | 99.94 | 88.34 | 88.39 | 79.15 | 97.69 | 0.77 | 1.00 | 0.93 | 0.97 | 0.90 | 0.99 |

**Table 2.** Statistical and Friedman test results of employed FS Techniques

| Rank-sum Test | | | | | | | Friedman test | | | |
|---|---|---|---|---|---|---|---|---|---|---|
| Technique | AF | RST | CCRA | RCCRA | PCA | GA | Accuracy | AUC | Precision | Recall |
| AF | 1.00 | 0.94 | 0.13 | 0.01 | 0.03 | 0.39 | 3.90 | 3.88 | 3.78 | 4.28 |
| RST | 0.94 | 1.00 | 0.13 | 0.02 | 0.03 | 0.48 | 3.35 | 3.78 | 3.25 | 3.73 |
| CCRA | 0.13 | 0.13 | 1.00 | 0.14 | 0.31 | 0.82 | 1.85 | 1.65 | 1.90 | 2.13 |
| RCCRA | 0.01 | 0.02 | 0.14 | 1.00 | 0.78 | 0.01 | 1.58 | 1.35 | 1.83 | 1.88 |
| PCA | 0.03 | 0.03 | 0.31 | 0.78 | 1.00 | 0.13 | 5.23 | 5.20 | 5.25 | 3.75 |
| GA | 0.39 | 0.48 | 0.82 | 0.01 | 0.13 | 1.00 | 5.10 | 5.15 | 5.00 | 5.25 |

## 4.2 Effectiveness of Classification Techniques

A comparative analysis of classifier performance on key metrics (Accuracy, AUC, Precision, Recall) is presented in Fig. 2 and Table 3. The results indicate a clear hierarchy: tree-based and ensemble models (RF, EXTR, GraB) achieved the highest performance, followed closely by MLP and SVM variants. Conversely, Bayesian classifiers (BNB, BAGNB, MNB) demonstrated significantly lower accuracy and greater instability. This establishes ensemble methods as the most robust and accurate predictors for this task.

**Comparative Analysis of Classification Techniques using Hypothesis Testing:** Table 4 presents hypothesis tests comparing classification techniques. The Wilcoxon Signed-Rank Test (at $\alpha=0.05$) shows no substantial performance difference for most feature selection (FS) approach pairs, as the null hypothesis (H0) is generally accepted. Furthermore, Friedman test results indicate that models using *RF, EXTR,* and *GraB* which have the lowest mean ranks significantly influence performance, whereas *NB* performs the worst.

## 4.3 SHAP Value Analysis of Genome Feature Contributions

The SHAP (SHapley Additive exPlanations) values are adapted for the analyzing the importance and contribution of different genomic features for the AMR

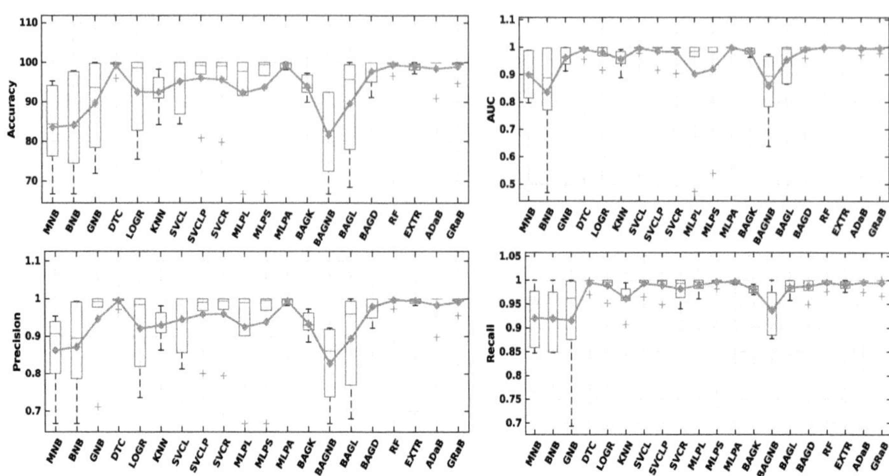

**Fig. 3.** Performance Box-Plot of Classification techniques

**Table 3.** Descriptive statistics of Classification techniques

|  | Accuracy | | | | | | AUC | | | | | |
|  | Min | Max | Mean | Median | Q1 | Q3 | Min | Max | Mean | Median | Q1 | Q3 |
|---|---|---|---|---|---|---|---|---|---|---|---|---|
| MNB | 66.71 | 95.32 | 83.57 | 84.43 | 76.33 | 94.18 | 0.80 | 0.99 | 0.90 | 0.90 | 0.82 | 0.99 |
| BNB | 66.71 | 97.91 | 84.10 | 83.89 | 74.49 | 97.72 | 0.47 | 1.00 | 0.84 | 0.89 | 0.77 | 1.00 |
| GNB | 71.96 | 100.00 | 89.62 | 93.73 | 78.48 | 99.81 | 0.91 | 1.00 | 0.96 | 0.96 | 0.94 | 1.00 |
| DTC | 96.08 | 100.00 | 99.23 | 99.87 | 99.62 | 99.94 | 0.96 | 1.00 | 0.99 | 1.00 | 0.99 | 1.00 |
| LOGR | 75.51 | 100.00 | 92.59 | 98.64 | 82.78 | 100.00 | 0.92 | 1.00 | 0.98 | 1.00 | 0.97 | 1.00 |
| KNN | 84.24 | 98.35 | 92.50 | 92.53 | 91.08 | 96.27 | 0.89 | 0.99 | 0.96 | 0.96 | 0.94 | 0.98 |
| SVCL | 84.37 | 100.00 | 95.19 | 99.94 | 86.90 | 100.00 | 0.98 | 1.00 | 1.00 | 1.00 | 1.00 | 1.00 |
| SVCLP | 80.82 | 100.00 | 96.05 | 99.24 | 97.03 | 100.00 | 0.92 | 1.00 | 0.99 | 1.00 | 1.00 | 1.00 |
| SVCR | 79.81 | 100.00 | 95.62 | 99.11 | 95.70 | 100.00 | 0.90 | 1.00 | 0.98 | 1.00 | 1.00 | 1.00 |
| MLPL | 66.71 | 100.00 | 92.32 | 97.75 | 91.71 | 100.00 | 0.47 | 1.00 | 0.90 | 0.98 | 0.97 | 1.00 |
| MLPS | 66.65 | 100.00 | 93.71 | 99.46 | 96.71 | 100.00 | 0.54 | 1.00 | 0.92 | 1.00 | 0.98 | 1.00 |
| MLPA | 98.16 | 100.00 | 99.34 | 99.75 | 98.48 | 99.87 | 0.99 | 1.00 | 1.00 | 1.00 | 1.00 | 1.00 |
| BAGK | 89.87 | 97.28 | 93.95 | 93.58 | 92.53 | 96.84 | 0.96 | 1.00 | 0.98 | 0.99 | 0.98 | 1.00 |
| BAGNB | 66.71 | 92.53 | 81.56 | 82.59 | 72.47 | 92.47 | 0.64 | 0.97 | 0.86 | 0.89 | 0.78 | 0.97 |
| BAGL | 68.48 | 100.00 | 89.58 | 95.76 | 77.97 | 99.49 | 0.87 | 1.00 | 0.95 | 0.99 | 0.87 | 1.00 |
| BAGD | 91.20 | 99.94 | 97.68 | 99.94 | 95.13 | 99.94 | 0.96 | 1.00 | 0.99 | 1.00 | 0.99 | 1.00 |
| RF | 96.65 | 99.94 | 99.35 | 99.94 | 99.68 | 99.94 | 0.99 | 1.00 | 1.00 | 1.00 | 1.00 | 1.00 |
| EXTR | 97.22 | 100.00 | 99.00 | 99.43 | 98.16 | 99.75 | 1.00 | 1.00 | 1.00 | 1.00 | 1.00 | 1.00 |
| ADaB | 90.95 | 99.94 | 98.44 | 99.94 | 99.94 | 99.94 | 0.97 | 1.00 | 0.99 | 1.00 | 1.00 | 1.00 |
| GRaB | 94.75 | 100.00 | 98.98 | 99.81 | 99.56 | 99.94 | 0.98 | 1.00 | 1.00 | 1.00 | 0.99 | 1.00 |

**Table 4.** Statistical and Friedman test results of employed FSTs

| | MNB | BNB | GNB | DTC | LOGR | KNN | SVCL | SVCLP | SVCR | MLPL | MLPS | MLPA | BAGK | BAGNB | BAGL | BAGD | RF | EXTR | ADaB | GRaB |
|---|---|---|---|---|---|---|---|---|---|---|---|---|---|---|---|---|---|---|---|---|
| MNB | 1.00 | 0.94 | 0.13 | 0.01 | 0.03 | 0.39 | 0.01 | 0.01 | 0.02 | 0.23 | 0.13 | 0.00 | 0.13 | 0.48 | 0.13 | 0.02 | 0.00 | 0.00 | 0.01 | 0.01 |
| BNB | 0.94 | 1.00 | 0.13 | 0.02 | 0.03 | 0.48 | 0.03 | 0.02 | 0.03 | 0.29 | 0.09 | 0.01 | 0.24 | 0.94 | 0.39 | 0.03 | 0.01 | 0.01 | 0.01 | 0.03 |
| GNB | 0.13 | 0.13 | 1.00 | 0.14 | 0.31 | 0.82 | 0.13 | 0.23 | 0.31 | 0.70 | 0.39 | 0.09 | 0.59 | 0.06 | 0.98 | 0.14 | 0.06 | 0.10 | 0.12 | 0.13 |
| DTC | 0.01 | 0.02 | 0.14 | 1.00 | 0.78 | 0.01 | 0.56 | 0.66 | 0.66 | 0.67 | 0.66 | 0.56 | 0.12 | 0.01 | 0.41 | 0.62 | 0.28 | 0.51 | 0.55 | 0.66 |
| LOGR | 0.03 | 0.03 | 0.31 | 0.78 | 1.00 | 0.13 | 0.56 | 0.67 | 0.92 | 0.67 | 0.80 | 0.56 | 0.29 | 0.02 | 0.48 | 0.81 | 0.36 | 0.70 | 0.57 | 0.56 |
| KNN | 0.39 | 0.48 | 0.82 | 0.01 | 0.13 | 1.00 | 0.01 | 0.04 | 0.04 | 0.37 | 0.13 | 0.00 | 0.09 | 0.13 | 0.39 | 0.03 | 0.00 | 0.00 | 0.02 | 0.01 |
| SVCL | 0.01 | 0.03 | 0.13 | 0.56 | 0.56 | 0.01 | 1.00 | 0.80 | 0.80 | 0.27 | 0.92 | 0.92 | 0.06 | 0.00 | 0.31 | 1.00 | 0.45 | 1.00 | 0.80 | 0.80 |
| SVCLP | 0.01 | 0.02 | 0.23 | 0.66 | 0.67 | 0.04 | 0.80 | 1.00 | 0.67 | 0.45 | 0.92 | 0.67 | 0.09 | 0.01 | 0.31 | 0.94 | 0.45 | 0.81 | 0.68 | 0.80 |
| SVCR | 0.02 | 0.03 | 0.31 | 0.66 | 0.92 | 0.04 | 0.80 | 0.67 | 1.00 | 0.45 | 0.92 | 0.67 | 0.09 | 0.01 | 0.31 | 0.94 | 0.45 | 0.81 | 0.68 | 0.80 |
| MLPL | 0.23 | 0.29 | 0.70 | 0.67 | 0.67 | 0.37 | 0.27 | 0.45 | 0.45 | 1.00 | 0.56 | 0.27 | 1.00 | 0.13 | 0.94 | 0.70 | 0.27 | 0.31 | 0.57 | 0.36 |
| MLPS | 0.13 | 0.09 | 0.39 | 0.66 | 0.80 | 0.13 | 0.92 | 0.92 | 0.92 | 0.56 | 1.00 | 1.00 | 0.23 | 0.06 | 0.70 | 0.94 | 0.56 | 1.00 | 0.79 | 0.92 |
| MLPA | 0.00 | 0.01 | 0.09 | 0.56 | 0.56 | 0.00 | 0.92 | 0.67 | 0.67 | 0.27 | 1.00 | 1.00 | 0.02 | 0.00 | 0.31 | 0.94 | 0.45 | 0.94 | 0.80 | 0.92 |
| BAGK | 0.13 | 0.24 | 0.59 | 0.12 | 0.29 | 0.09 | 0.06 | 0.09 | 0.09 | 1.00 | 0.23 | 0.02 | 1.00 | 0.01 | 0.82 | 0.13 | 0.01 | 0.02 | 0.04 | 0.06 |
| BAGNB | 0.48 | 0.94 | 0.06 | 0.01 | 0.02 | 0.13 | 0.00 | 0.01 | 0.01 | 0.13 | 0.06 | 0.00 | 0.01 | 1.00 | 0.13 | 0.01 | 0.00 | 0.00 | 0.00 | 0.00 |
| BAGL | 0.13 | 0.39 | 0.98 | 0.41 | 0.48 | 0.39 | 0.31 | 0.31 | 0.31 | 0.94 | 0.70 | 0.31 | 0.82 | 0.13 | 1.00 | 0.52 | 0.18 | 0.19 | 0.56 | 0.39 |
| BAGD | 0.02 | 0.03 | 0.14 | 0.62 | 0.81 | 0.03 | 1.00 | 0.94 | 0.94 | 0.70 | 0.94 | 0.94 | 0.13 | 0.01 | 0.52 | 1.00 | 0.58 | 0.98 | 0.46 | 1.00 |
| RF | 0.00 | 0.01 | 0.06 | 0.28 | 0.36 | 0.00 | 0.45 | 0.45 | 0.45 | 0.27 | 0.56 | 0.45 | 0.01 | 0.00 | 0.18 | 0.58 | 1.00 | 0.58 | 0.16 | 0.36 |
| EXTR | 0.00 | 0.01 | 0.10 | 0.51 | 0.70 | 0.00 | 1.00 | 0.81 | 0.81 | 0.31 | 1.00 | 0.94 | 0.02 | 0.00 | 0.19 | 0.98 | 0.58 | 1.00 | 0.90 | 0.94 |
| ADaB | 0.01 | 0.01 | 0.12 | 0.55 | 0.57 | 0.02 | 0.80 | 0.68 | 0.68 | 0.57 | 0.79 | 0.80 | 0.04 | 0.00 | 0.56 | 0.46 | 0.16 | 0.90 | 1.00 | 0.96 |
| GRaB | 0.01 | 0.03 | 0.13 | 0.66 | 0.56 | 0.01 | 0.80 | 0.80 | 0.80 | 0.36 | 0.92 | 0.92 | 0.06 | 0.00 | 0.39 | 1.00 | 0.36 | 0.94 | 0.96 | 1.00 |
| **Friedman test** | | | | | | | | | | | | | | | | | | | | |
| **Accuracy** | 18.25 | 17.92 | 13.25 | 6.17 | 9.67 | 14.50 | 6.42 | 8.33 | 8.67 | 10.00 | 8.67 | 7.25 | 14.00 | 19.58 | 13.08 | 7.92 | 6.00 | 7.67 | 6.75 | 5.92 |
| **AUC** | 17.83 | 18.67 | 13.33 | 9.75 | 9.42 | 15.83 | 6.75 | 7.92 | 8.75 | 11.75 | 7.58 | 6.08 | 13.33 | 19.17 | 13.08 | 6.83 | 3.92 | 6.00 | 8.33 | 5.67 |
| **Precision** | 17.58 | 17.58 | 9.67 | 6.17 | 11.00 | 14.67 | 7.67 | 9.92 | 9.83 | 10.25 | 10.25 | 7.42 | 14.67 | 19.58 | 14.25 | 6.67 | 4.58 | 6.58 | 5.58 | 6.08 |
| **Recall** | 16.08 | 16.25 | 15.00 | 7.17 | 8.83 | 16.83 | 6.25 | 8.00 | 10.25 | 7.75 | 6.42 | 7.25 | 13.67 | 15.58 | 10.67 | 9.75 | 8.25 | 10.33 | 8.08 | 7.58 |

prediction pipelines. The waterfall model illustrates that the higher SHAP values reflect a stronger influence of that feature on the model's predictions.

***SHAP values in finding Genome Feature importance:*** Figure 3 presents the genomic features ranked by their mean SHAP values, indicating each feature's average contribution to the model's predictions. The most influential feature, tet(D), exhibits the highest positive mean SHAP value (+0.24), identifying it as a key predictor of resistance. Subsequent contributors include tRNA (+0.14) and Contigs (+0.11), showing slightly lower but notable influence. In contrast, features such as KPC-3 (bleomycin resistance determinant), mphA, sul1, FosA5, and aadA2 display minimal impact, with SHAP values near +0.01 or 0.

***Waterfall visualization of Genome Feature SHAP values:*** The SHAP waterfall plot illustrates how individual genomic features influence the model's decision-making process in predicting antimicrobial resistance. Figure 4 depicts each feature's contribution to the model output for bleomycin resistance. The blue bars represent negative contributions for example, tet(D) (−0.28) indicates a strong negative impact while the red bars denote positive contributions, such as sul1 (+0.05), reflecting a mild positive effect. The cumulative influence of all features ultimately determines the model's final prediction.

## 4.4   Overall Analysis and Elaboration of RQs

This study predicts antimicrobial resistance (AMR) in Klebsiella pneumoniae using machine learning models trained on genomic data from 1,580 strains. Among the classifiers evaluated, RF and GraB achieved accuracies over 90%,

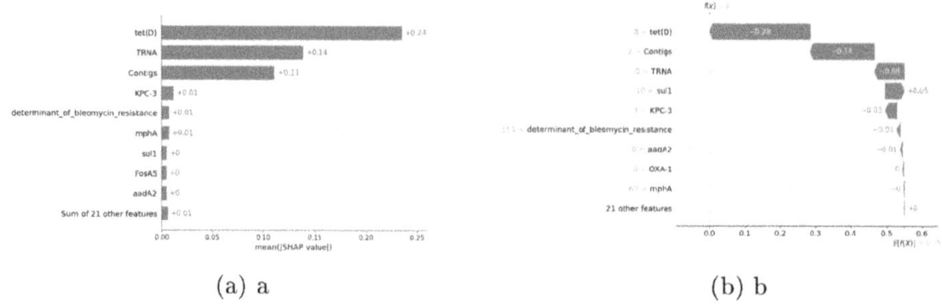

(a) a          (b) b

**Fig. 4.** SHAP-based Illustrations: Feature Importance (Ranked) and Feature contribution in Prediction model

demonstrating strong generalization despite the dataset's limited size. The experimental findings address the study's RQs as summarized below:

- **RQ1:** Of the FS techniques evaluated, CCRA and RCCRA were the most effective for AMR prediction, delivering the highest accuracy, AUC, precision, and recall. While AF and RST also performed well, PCA and GA showed significantly poorer and more unstable results. This confirms that the choice of feature selection method is critical for optimizing model performance.
- **RQ-II:** Of the classifiers tested, ensemble models particularly RF, EXTR, and GraB delivered the best performance, achieving over 95% accuracy with high AUC, precision, and recall. LOGR, DT, and SVM models performed moderately but were less reliable. In contrast, NB classifiers (MNB, BNB, GNB) performed the worst, demonstrating limited effectiveness for the complexity of AMR prediction.
- **RQ-III:** Hypothesis testing confirms that FS significantly impacts classifier performance. Models using CCRA and RCCRA achieved higher accuracy and stability, while those with PCA and GA produced inconsistent results. This underscores that selecting relevant genomic features is essential for robust AMR classification.

## 5    Conclusion

This study demonstrates that ML models can effectively predict antimicrobial resistance (AMR) by identifying key genomic features and uncovering hidden patterns. Such predictive power enables personalized antibiotic treatments, reduces misuse, and supports drug discovery, while automation accelerates AMR research with lower time and resource costs. Among feature selection methods, CCRA and RCCRA achieved the best performance, and classifiers such as RF, EXTR, and GraB showed superior accuracy, AUC, precision, and recall. SHAP visualizations further enhanced interpretability by highlighting the most influential genomic features. However, challenges like overfitting, limited scalability, and class imbalance remain, warranting validation on larger datasets.

# References


1. Effah, C.Y., Sun, T., Liu, S., Wu, Y.: Klebsiella pneumoniae: an increasing threat to public health. Ann. Clin. Microbiol. Antimicrob. **19**, 1–9 (2020)
2. Li, B., Zhao, Y., Liu, C., Chen, Z., Zhou, D.: Molecular pathogenesis of klebsiella pneumoniae. Future Microbiol. **9**(9), 1071–1081 (2014)
3. T. A. Davies, T.A.,et al.: Longitudinal survey of carbapenem resistance and resistance mechanisms in enterobacteriaceae and non-fermenters from the USA in 2007–09. J. Antimicrobial Chemother.**66**(10), 2298–2307 (2011)
4. Nordmann, P., Poirel, L.: Epidemiology and diagnostics of carbapenem resistance in gram-negative bacteria. Clin. Infect. Dis. **69**(07), 521–528 (2019)

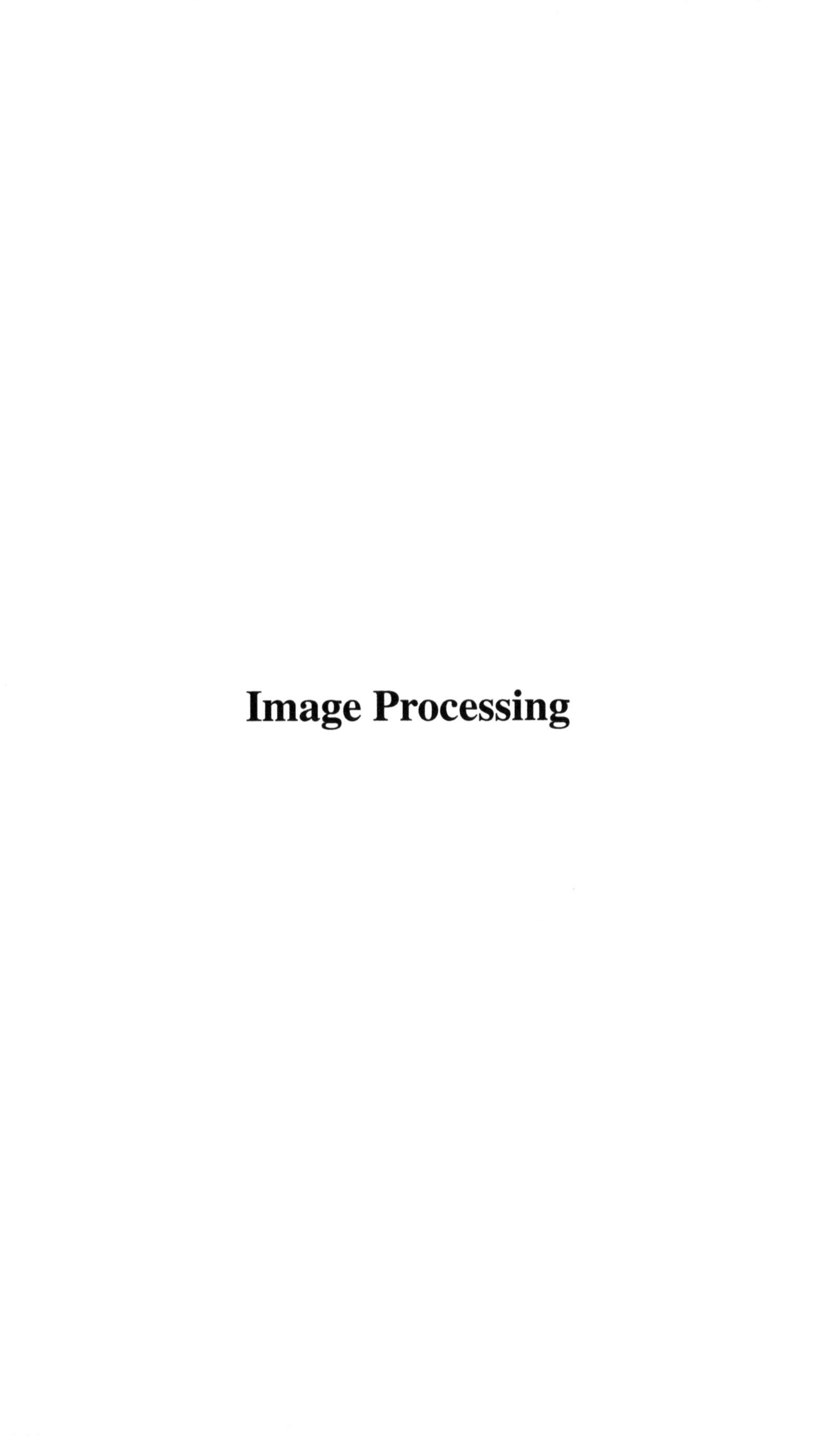

# Image Processing

# Accelerated Feature and Pose Estimation for Time-Critical Pick-and-Place Applications


Rajat Kumar Thakur, Isha Jangir, Siddharth Nimbalkar, Deepika Gupta[✉],
and Jignesh Patel

Department of Computer Science and Engineering, Indian Institute of Information
Technology Vadodara-International Campus Diu, Diu, India
{202211070,202211031,22011057,deepika_gupta,
jignesh_patel}@diu.iiitvadodara.ac.in



**Abstract.** In the rapidly changing environment of warehouse automation, efficient management of piles of objects in unordered, random arrangements remains a formidable challenge. The paper addresses this challenge with a novel approach to detect the geometric features such as edges and corners in the unordered 3D point clouds tailored for robotic operations.

The proposed method employs an eigenvalue based surface variation measure to rapidly extract sharp edge points from raw point cloud data, offering improved speed and efficiency compared to traditional approaches. Additionally, a 3D Harris corner detector is also used to identify prominent corner points that subsequently form the foundation of trustworthy pose estimation of texture less objects.

When used with synthetic shapes, the technique achieves unprecedented effectiveness in delivering fast and accurate results. It takes much less computation time as compared to the previously reported algorithms. This makes it an efficient transformative tool for real time pick and place tasks. This advancement helps autonomous grasping in cluttered warehouse settings, allowing for more intelligent and efficient automation in the building and manufacturing industries.

**Keywords:** Point Cloud · Edge Extraction · Corner detection · Pose estimation


## 1 Introduction

While automation has greatly enhanced manufacturing within the industry, construction and warehousing lag behind because of the challenge in handling objects in unstructured and dynamic environments. One of the challenges is automating operations like unloading randomly pile up containers, which requires accurate estimation of object poses. This is based on the extraction of geometric features, such as edges and corners, from 3D point cloud data; a



S. Mitra et al. (Eds.): PReMI 2025, LNCS 16358, pp. 229–236, 2026.
https://doi.org/10.1007/978-3-032-18480-1_23

challenging task given the unstructured nature of data [1]. Conventional geometric techniques employed for feature detection in point clouds tend to be unreliable close to sharp edges and computationally expensive for real time processing [3]. Deep learning methods exhibit greater accuracy but need large annotated datasets and are prone to generalizing to unseen, texture less objects in dense clutter. These downsides justify the demand for an efficient alternative that is robust and efficient for industrial automation.

To fill these gaps, we introduce a new corner detection algorithm for unorganized point clouds. We summarize the novel contributions of our work as follows:

- Rapid geometric feature pipeline: We offer a closely integrated pipeline that integrates eigenvalue based surface variation edge extraction and a 3D Harris corner detector to generate robust geometric features for texture less objects with little parameter adjustment.
- Corner based pose estimation for pick and place: From only observed extreme corners and a closed form SVD alignment, we obtain 6 pose estimates for real time pick and place applications.
- Practical runtime focus: We achieve a stark runtime speedup (3.3×) relative to a recent multi stage geometric baseline and yet preserve feature quality, and we argue why computation is wasted in anticipation of future optimizations.

## 2   Related Work

A number of geometric solutions have been proposed. Bazazian et al. (2015) [2] proposed a computationally efficient edge detection method using eigenvalue analysis that dispenses with the estimation of normals but not corner detection or pose estimation. Conversely, Vohra et al. (2021) [3] proposed a full pipeline for edge/corner detection and pose estimation via feature matching with CAD models but its multi stage process is too slow for real time applications. Other work, such as that of Ahmed et al. (2018) [10] in robotic welding, are application oriented and are less concerned with corner based pose estimation for pick and place applications.

Deep learning models such as PoseCNN [8] and VoxelNet [9] proved to be strong in pose estimation but are severely flawed. They require enormous training on large scale datasets and fail to generalize to unseen or texture deficient objects, which are common in warehouses.

The technique we suggest overcomes these limitations by combining the speed of eigenvalue based methods with the stability of the 3D Harris corner detection algorithm. Our technique achieves corner detection at high speed and accuracy for pose estimation tasks and is hence highly well suited for robotic application in unstructured, texture poor warehouse environments (Table 1).

## 3   Proposed Methodology

This section presents a comprehensive methodology for detecting edges, corners, and estimating the pose of objects in unorganized 3D point clouds, tailored for robotic pick and place tasks in cluttered warehouse environments.

**Table 1.** Comparison of Related Work

| Authors | Year | Methodology | Contributions | Limitations |
|---|---|---|---|---|
| Liu et al. | 2024 | Edge focused down sampling and point pair pose estimation | Efficient pose estimation using edge based sampling and edge matching validation | Requires reliable edge detection; Depended on edge prominence. |
| Vohra et al. | 2021 | Normal estimation, clustering for edges, corners, pose from feature matching | Comprehensive pipeline for pick and place, handles clutter | Computationally expensive, requires CAD models |
| Ahmed et al. | 2018 | Symmetry based edge detection, curvature clustering for corners | High precision and recall, applied to robotic welding | Not focused on pose estimation, different application domain |
| ML Models | 2017 18 | Convolutional neural networks on RGB D or point cloud data | Direct pose estimation | Requires extensive training data, less adaptable to new objects |
| Li et al. | 2016 | Geometric property analysis, RANSAC, angular gap metric | Effective for large scale urban scenes, noise insensitive | Less focus on corner detection and pose estimation |
| Bazazian et al. | 2015 | Eigenvalue based edge extraction | Fast and robust edge detection without normal estimation | Does not address corner detection or pose estimation |

Our approach integrates an eigenvalue based edge extraction technique, a 3D Harris corner detector, and a corner driven pose estimation algorithm to enable fast and robust results with minimal parameter tuning. The procedure, depicted in Fig. 1, illustrates the process step by step: edge extraction from raw point cloud data, corner detection from edge points, and pose estimation using detected corners, enabling effective automation in changing environments.

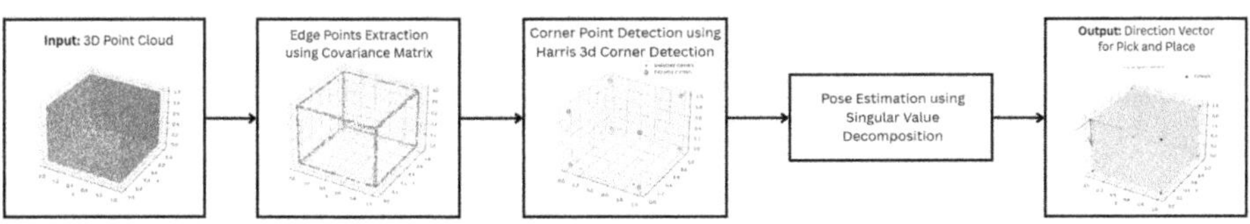


**Fig. 1.** Pipeline overview: **(A)** Input. **(B)** Edge extraction. **(C)** Corner detection: 3D Harris cornerness **(D)** Pose estimation **(E)** Output: Direction Vector

### 3.1   Edge Points Extraction

Motivated by the efficient and strong edge detection framework of Bazazian et al. [2], we take a purely statistical approach relying on eigenvalue analysis of local covariance matrices, removing the requirements for explicit normal clustering and significantly simplifying the edge detection process.

Covariance quantifies how pairs of dimensions jointly deviate from their means. For a three dimensional dataset $(X, Y, Z)$, the $3 \times 3$ covariance matrix $C$ for a sample point $p = (x, y, z)$ is given by:

$$C = \begin{bmatrix} \mathrm{Cov}(x, x) & \mathrm{Cov}(x, y) & \mathrm{Cov}(x, z) \\ \mathrm{Cov}(y, x) & \mathrm{Cov}(y, y) & \mathrm{Cov}(y, z) \\ \mathrm{Cov}(z, x) & \mathrm{Cov}(z, y) & \mathrm{Cov}(z, z) \end{bmatrix} \tag{1}$$

Here, for example, $\mathrm{Cov}(X, Y)$ denotes the covariance between $X$ and $Y$, calculated as:

$$\mathrm{Cov}(x, y) = \frac{\sum_{i=1}^{k}(x_i \bar{x})(y_i \bar{y})}{n1} \tag{2}$$

We then explore the Eigenvalues of $C$: $\lambda_0 \leq \lambda_1 \leq \lambda_2$.

In Pauly et al. [4,5], the concept of surface variation $\sigma_k(p)$ is introduced:

$$\sigma_k(p) = \frac{\lambda_0}{\lambda_0 + \lambda_1 + \lambda_2} \tag{3}$$

The surface variation $\sigma_k(p)$, computed over the $k$ nearest neighbors of point, indicates whether it lies on a planar region or corresponds to a salient feature (edge), as follows:

$$\sigma_k(p) = \begin{cases} 0, & \lambda_0 \approx 0 \quad \text{(flat surface)}, \\ > 0, & \text{if an edge is present.} \end{cases}$$

## 3.2   Corner Points Extraction

The 3D Harris corner detection algorithm is the 3D extension of the Harris corner detection 2D image algorithm [6] proposed by I. Laptev [7] and computes the cornerness for each pixel of the input 3D image.

As an extension of the 2D case, $M$ is defined as follows:

$$M = \sum_{x,y,z \in \mathcal{N}} w(x, y, z) \begin{bmatrix} I_x^2 & I_x I_y & I_x I_z \\ I_x I_y & I_y^2 & I_y I_z \\ I_x I_z & I_y I_z & I_z^2 \end{bmatrix} \tag{4}$$

With $I_x$, $I_y$, and $I_z$ as the spatial derivatives of the extracted edge points image along the directions $x$, $y$, and $z$ respectively, and $w(x, y, z)$ is a Gaussian weight in the neighbourhood $\mathcal{N}$.

The cornerness $\mathcal{C}$ is calculated at the position $(u, v, w)$ by:

$$C(u, v, w) = \det(M)k\,(\mathrm{trace}(M))^3 \tag{5}$$

The cornerness value $C(u, v, w)$ measures the likelihood of a voxel $(u, v, w)$ being a corner based on its local image structure. To extract salient corners, we apply: (1) thresholding to discard low cornerness values, and (2) Non maximum suppression to retain only local maxima within a 3D neighborhood. A relative threshold of approximately 1% of the maximum cornerness value was selected to reliably detect these corners flat or edge regions. This choice was validated by applying the same threshold to other synthetic shapes Given a set of detected 3D corner points, we define:

$$C = \{c_i = (x_i, y_i, z_i) \mid i = 1, \ldots, N\}. \tag{6}$$

We compute the coordinate wise minima and maxima:

$$(x_{\min}, x_{\max}) =_i x_i, \quad (y_{\min}, y_{\max}) =_i y_i, \quad (z_{\min}, z_{\max}) =_i z_i. \tag{7}$$

Next, form the eight vertices of the axis aligned bounding box:

$$B = \{(x_a, y_b, z_c) \mid a, b, c \in \{\min, \max\}\}. \tag{8}$$

For each vertex $b \in B$, select the detected corner closest in Euclidean distance:

$$p^*(b) = \arg \min_{p \in C} \|pb\|_2. \tag{9}$$

The final set of extreme corners is then:

$$\{p^*(b) \mid b \in B\}.$$

We determine the object's eight extreme corners by first finding the smallest and largest values of the $x$, $y$, $z$ coordinates among all detected points. These six scalars $x_{\min}, x_{\max}, y_{\min}, y_{\max}, z_{\min}, z_{\max}$ define the vertices of the tightest axis aligned bounding box around the data.

Conceptually, there are eight such vertices, each corresponding to one of the two choices (minimum or maximum) along each axis. For each of these hypothetical box corners, we then search through our corner set and pick the single point whose Euclidean distance to that box corner is minimal.

## 3.3   Pose Estimation

After extracting all eight extreme corners of the object, we select two orthogonal edges sharing a common vertex $p_1$ (the intersection) and their other endpoints $p_2$ and $p_3$. These three camera frame points:

$$p_1, p_2, p_3 \in \mathbb{R}^3 \quad , \quad q_1, q_2, q_3 \in \mathbb{R}^3$$

Inspired by Vohra et al. [3], we compute the centroids:

$$\bar{p} = \frac{1}{3} \sum_{i=1}^{3} p_i, \qquad \bar{q} = \frac{1}{3} \sum_{i=1}^{3} q_i, \tag{10}$$

and assemble the cross covariance matrix:

$$H = \sum_{i=1}^{3} (p_i \bar{p})(q_i \bar{q})^T. \tag{11}$$

Performing singular value decomposition:

$$H = U\Sigma V^T, \tag{12}$$

yields the optimal rigid body transform:

$$R = VU^T, \qquad t = \bar{p}R\bar{q}. \tag{13}$$

Here, $R$ is the $3 \times 3$ rotation matrix aligning the object's local axes to the camera axes, and $t$ is the translation vector from the camera origin to the object centroid.

## 4  Experimental Results

In the initial experiment, we evaluated our method on a synthetic cube point cloud obtained from the Stanford 3D Scanning Repository.

Figure 2 illustrates the four stages of our pipeline on a synthetic cube point cloud. (a) shows the raw, unstructured input. (b) highlights edge points in red using surface variation. (c) identifies corner candidates, with selected extreme corners marked in green. (d) aligns these corners to recover the cube's pose relative to the model frame.

Building on the cube example shown in Fig. 2, we further validated our pipeline on a variety of synthetic shapes as shown in Fig. 3.

In Fig. 4, we demonstrate the accuracy of our edge and corner detection algorithm using the Stanford 3D Repository dataset. The dataset contains popular models like the Bunny, cubes, and cylinders, each with varied surface details.

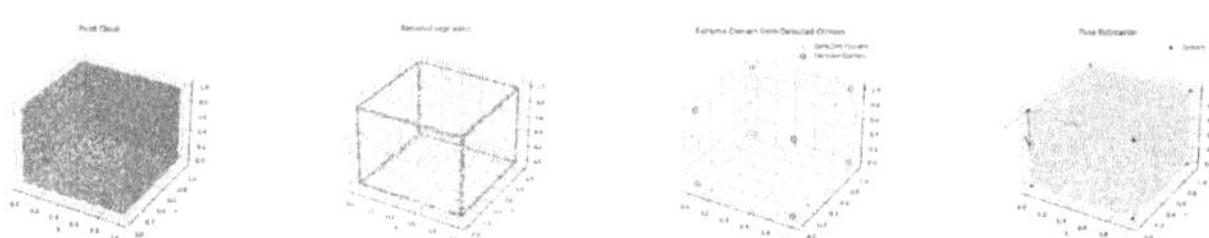

**Fig. 2.** Our model on Cube Point Cloud Data

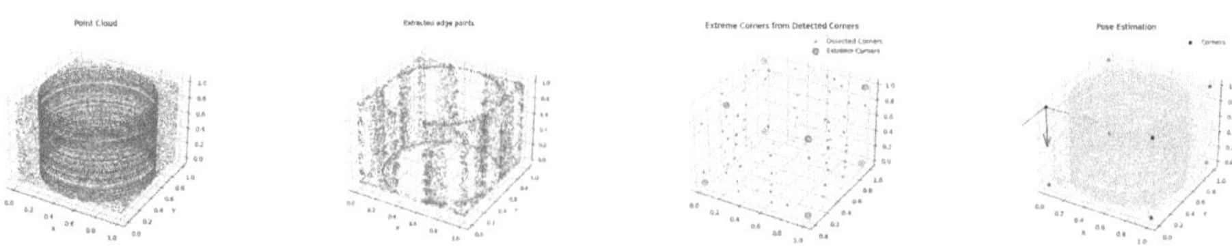

**Fig. 3.** Our model on Cylinder inside a Hollow Cube Point Cloud Data

Using our method, we detected edges and corners from these point clouds and visually inspected them thoroughly, and compared results with other models as well. The results indicated that the identified features well described the sharp boundaries and significant corner points, with a close agreement with the predicted geometric shapes of these models.

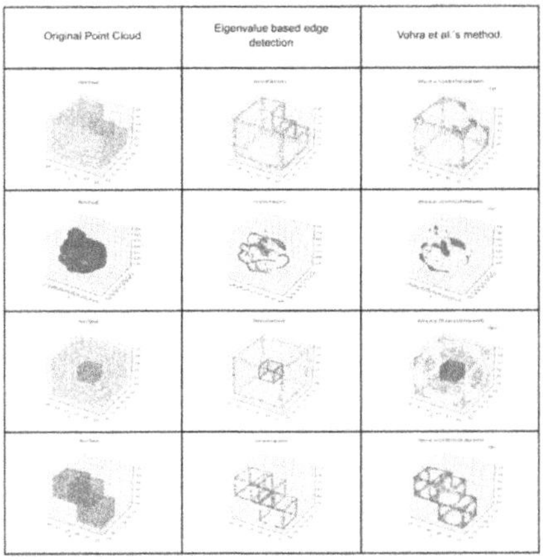

**Fig. 4.** Qualitative comparison of edge extraction results on point Cloud Data

To quantitatively compare runtime performance, we ran both our proposed pipeline and the Vohra et al. [3] algorithm on the same synthetic cube point cloud. Table 2 breaks down the computation time (in seconds) at each stage of processing. As shown, our pipeline reduces total computation time from 26.829 s to 7.943 s (3.3x speed up). This acceleration enables real time processing, making our approach more practical for real time applications.

With timings from the components in Table 2 we measure each stage's portion of runtime: edge extraction = 69.5%, corner detection = 7.2%, pose estimation = 23.3% of total runtime. Since these figures show edge extraction to dominate the cost, optimization specifically of the edge stage would yield the highest wall clock benefits. On the other hand, corner and pose steps are comparative lightweight, suggesting additional accuracy driven improvements can be explored with moderate runtime overhead.

**Table 2.** Computation time (sec) at each step

| Model | Edge | Corner | Pose Est. | Total Time |
| --- | --- | --- | --- | --- |
| Our Methodology | 5.520 | 0.573 | 1.850 | 7.943 |
| Vohra et al. [3] | 24.168 | 1.110 | 1.551 | 26.829 |

# 5    Conclusion

This work introduces an efficient and robust framework for edge, corner, and pose estimation in unorganized 3D point clouds, specifically designed for real time robotic pick and place applications. By integrating an eigenvalue based edge extraction method with a 3D Harris corner detector and a corner driven pose estimation algorithm, the proposed approach achieves high accuracy in identifying sharp geometric features and determining object poses. Experimental results on synthetic shapes demonstrate the method's ability to deliver precise edge and corner detection with minimal parameter tuning, while significantly reducing computation time compared to existing techniques. The pipeline's speed and reliability make it particularly well suited for dynamic, cluttered environments where rapid and accurate object manipulation is critical. Future research will focus on extending the framework to handle real world sensor data, accommodating nonconvex geometries, and addressing multi object scenarios to further enhance its applicability in complex robotic tasks.

# References


1. Changali, S., Azam M., Mark van N.: The construction productivity imperative. In: McKinsey Quarterly, pp. 1–10 June (2015)
2. Bazazian, D., Casas, J.R., Ruiz Hidalgo, J.: Fast and robust edge extraction in unorganized point clouds. In: Proceedings of the 2015 International Conference Digital Image Computing (2015)
3. Vohra, M., Prakash, R., Behera, L.: Edge and corner detection in unorganized point clouds for robotic pick and place applications. arXiv:2104.09099 [cs.RO] (2021)
4. Pauly, M., Gross, M., Kobbelt, L.: Efficient simplification of point sampled surfaces. In: Proceedings of the IEEE Visualization (VIS), pp. 163 170 (2002)
5. Pauly, M., Keiser, R., Gross, M.: Multi scale feature extraction on point sampled surfaces. Comput. Graph. Forum **22**(3), 281 289 (2003)
6. Harris, C., Stephens, M.: A combined corner and edge detector. In: Proceedings of the 4th Alvey Vision Conference, pp. 147–151 (1988)
7. Laptev, I.: On Space-time Interest Points. Int. J. Comput, Vision (2005)
8. Xiang, Y., Schmidt, T., Narayanan, V., Fox, D.: PoseCNN: a convolutional neural network for 6D object pose estimation in cluttered scenes. arXiv:1711.00199 (2017)
9. Zhou, Y., Tuzel, O.: VoxelNet: end to end learning for point cloud based object detection. IEEE Conference on Computer Vision and Pattern Recognition (2018)
10. Ahmed, S. M., Wong, F. S., Behera, L.: Edge and corner detection for unorganized 3D point clouds with application to robotic welding (2018)
11. Liu, C., Chen, F., Xu, K.: 6DOF Pose Estimation of a 3D Rigid Object Based on Edge Enhanced Point Pair Features (2024)

# Performance Analysis of Entropy-Based Meta-heuristic Image Multilevel Thresholding Techniques Using SAD Metric

Abhishek Dhapola and Shachi Sharma$^{(\boxtimes)}$ iD

Department of Computer Science and Engineering, South Asian University,
New Delhi, India
`shachi@sau.int`

**Abstract.** Multilevel image thresholding is a complex task in image processing as it requires determining more than one thresholds, mostly using meta-heuristics. In popular entropy-based multilevel image thresholding techniques, the major challenges include computing the appropriate value of the entropic parameter automatically from image data and evaluating the performance of an algorithm in the absence of ground-truth images. The paper presents a new algorithm utilizing normalized sum of absolute differences metric. By selecting four different optimization methods and four entropy measures, sixteen variants of the proposed algorithm are developed. A large-scale performance analysis is conducted using 753 images from diverse domains consisting of a total of 48192 experiments. It is observed that SAD metric based new variants provide better performance in the absence of ground-truth images at the cost of slightly higher computation time.

**Keywords:** Multi-level Thresholding · Entropy · SAD Metric · Performance Analysis

## 1 Introduction

Image processing has applications in multiple areas. An important task in this relation is image segmentation that involves partitioning an image's pixels into multiple parts. One of the simple yet effective image segmentation techniques is thresholding in which one or more thresholds are used to separate objects (i.e. foreground) from background. A pixel intensity is compared with thresholds to determine appropriate bucket in MultiLevel Thresholding (MLT) [5]. Determining multiple thresholds from image data is a complex task. One of the popular method of bi-level (with one threshold) image thresholding is Otsu when applied in MLT, it leads to very high computational cost [3]. Therefore, other methods such as based on entropy are preferred using bio-inspired methods. Entropy is a measure of randomness of a system. There are various measures of entropy like

Shannon [14], Renyi [12], Tsallis [15] and Masi [9] that are optimized to calculate multiple thresholds in MLT.

Employing maximum Shannon entropy as fitness function, Upadhyay and Chhabra [16] used Crow Search (CS) algorithm in MLT and observed its efficacy over other methods. Utilizing Artificial Bee Colony (ABC) algorithm, Horng [6] introduced a novel multilevel maximum entropy thresholding method, called MEABCT, to find optimal thresholds. The study also established the superior segmentation accuracy and the ability of MEABCT in determining close to optimal thresholds by comparing it with Otsu method. Zhang and Wu [18] integrated ABC algorithm with Tsallis entropy based fitness function for finding thresholds in MLT. Approximating a greyscale image histogram by mixture of Gaussian distributions, Differential Evolution (DE) algorithm was applied to estimate the parameters of mixture distribution in [4] to perform multilevel image thresholding. An improved version of DE called SDE was developed by Ali *et al.* [2] by combining Gaussian curve fitting, Shannon entropy and DE for MLT. This prevented DE to trap into local minimum. Sarkar *et al.* [13] integrated two dimensional Tsallis entropy with DE to build a computationally efficient method for MLT. The similar approach but with Shannon entropy was applied to find thresholds in breast cancer images in [17]. The basic Particle Swarm Optimization (PSO) algorithm was also used with relative new Masi entropy measure as objective function by Khairuzzaman and Chaudhury [7] and its comparison with Shannon entropy based comparison indicated its better performance in MLT. The basic PSO algorithm was also used with relative new Masi entropy measure as objective function by Khairuzzaman and Chaudhury and its comparison with Shannon entropy based comparison indicated its better performance in MLT [1,7]. In spite of wide research carried out in MLT using entropy-based image thresholding, there still exists two major issues: (i) estimating the value of entropic parameter automatically from image data, (ii) evaluating the performance of an algorithm in the absence of ground truth image.

In a recent work by Hadi *et al.* [8], normalized SAD metric has been proposed and shown to provide a reasonable performance for bi-level thresholding. Motivated by this, the paper presents a method to apply the SAD metric to MLT of images and demonstrates its success in solving the two aforementioned issues through large-scale performance analysis on 753 images of diverse types with four entropy measures viz. Shannon, Renyi, Tsallis and Masi and four optimization algorithms viz. PSO, CS, DE and ABC. A total of 48192 experiments are conducted for extensive comparative analysis. The paper is organized into five sections. First, the necessary background of entropy measures and their application in multi-level image thresholding, overview of SAD metric and some popular multi-objective optimization algorithms is provided in Sect. 2. The new method for multi-level image thresholding using SAD metric is proposed in Sect. 3. The results of a large-scale performance analysis are presented in Sect. 4. The last Sect. 5 concludes the paper.

## 2   Background

An overview of the entropy measures and SAD metric is provided in this section.

### 2.1   Entropy Measures and MLT

The notations devised in [9] are followed closely in the paper. Let $I$ be the given image of size $M \times N$ with $\phi$ gray levels and set $L$ represents the intensity values in an image i.e. $L = 0, 1, ..., \phi - 1$. In MLT, the problem is to find optimal values of $m$ thresholds $\tau = \{\tau_1, \tau_2, ..., \tau_m\}$ that divides a greyscale image histogram in $m + 1$ parts $S_0, S_1, ..., S_m$ such that $S_i$ contains pixels with intensity $[\tau_i + 1, \tau_{i+1}] \ \forall \ i = 1, ..., m - 1$. The segments $S_0$ and $S_m$ have pixels having intensity in the range $[0, \tau_1]$ and $[\tau_m + 1, \phi - 1]$ respectively. Also, assume that $n_i$ denotes the number of pixels with gray level $i$.

The origin of entropy is from the field of thermodynamics. Shannon [14] redefined it in the context of information theory as

$$E_s = -\sum_i p_i \log p_i, \quad \text{where} \quad 0 \log 0 = 0. \tag{1}$$

In relation to image thresholding, $p_i$ as the probability of graylevel $i$ that can be computed from $n_i$, the The entropy $E_s$ is maximum when all grey levels are equally probable, i.e., $p_i = 1/\phi$ for all $i$. When applied to MLT, the Shannon Entropy for each part $(S_0, S_1, ..., S_m)$ can be written as

$$E_s^{S_0} = -\sum_{i=0}^{\tau_1} \left( \frac{n_i}{N_{S_0}} \right) \log \left( \frac{n_i}{N_{S_0}} \right), \ E_s^{S_1} = -\sum_{\tau_1+1}^{\tau_2} \left( \frac{n_i}{N_{S_1}} \right) \log \left( \frac{n_i}{N_{S_1}} \right) \tag{2}$$

and so on, where $N_{S_0} = \sum_{i=0}^{\tau_1} n_i$, $N_{S_1} = \sum_{i=\tau_1+1}^{\tau_2} n_i$, ..., $N_{S_m} = \sum_{i=m+1}^{\phi-1} n_i$. The total entropy of the image $E_s^{Total}$ then can be computed by summing up the entropies of all segments i.e.

$$E_s^{Total} = E_s^{S_0} + E_s^{S_1} + ... + E_s^{S_m}. \tag{3}$$

The set of optimal thresholds $\tau^* = \{\tau_1{}^*, \tau_2{}^*, ..., \tau_m{}^*\}$ can be computed by maximizing $E_s^{Total}$ i.e.

$$\tau^* = argmax(E_s^{Total}). \tag{4}$$

The first generalization of Shannon entropy with parameter $\alpha$ was proposed by Renyi as [11]

$$E_R = \frac{1}{1-\alpha} \log \left( \sum_i p_i^\alpha \right), \quad \alpha \neq 1. \tag{5}$$

which reduces to Shannon as $\alpha$ approaches unity. Like Shannon entropy measure, Renyi entropy also possesses extensivity property, therefore the total entropy and thresholds can be computed following (3) and (4) respectively. The application of Renyi entropy in image thresholding was first demonstrated by Sahoo [12] for bi-level thresholding and the idea was extended to MLT later on [11]. In year 1988, Tsallis [15] proposed a new generalized non-extensive entropy measure for capturing the dynamics of systems characterized by long range correlations as

$$E_T = \frac{1 - \sum_i p_i^q}{q - 1}, \quad q \neq 1 \tag{6}$$

that reduces to Shannon entropy as the parameter $q$ tends to one. The entropy of each segment can be calculated in the same way as discussed above. However, the total entropy of the image turns out to be

$$E_T^{Total} = E_T^{S_1} + E_T^{S_2} + \ \ldots \ + E_T^{S_m} + (1 - q)E_T^{S_1}E_T^{S_2} \ \ldots \ E_T^{S_m}$$

because of the pseudo-additivity property of non-extensive Tsallis entropy [15]. The optimal values of thresholds can be computing using (4). Usually, the parameter $\alpha$ and $q$ are fixed by trial and error method. By integrating the non-extensive characteristics of Tsallis entropy and extensive properties of Renyi entropy, a new measure, called Masi entropy, has been proposed [9],

$$E_M = \frac{1}{1 - \beta} \log \left[ 1 - (1 - \beta) \sum_i p_i \log p_i \right], \quad \beta > 0. \tag{7}$$

As the parameter $\beta$ approaches one, (7) reduces to Shannon entropy. Masi entropy is additive just like Shannon and Renyi. The the appropriate value of the parameter $\beta$ is found to be 1.2 during the experiments in the [9] for bi-level thresholding using (4). Recently, a method utilizing SAD metric is developed to solve the problem of finding the appropriate value of entropy parameter and analyzing performance of a bi-level image thresholding algorithm in the absence of ground-truth image [8]. The main idea behind the metric is to calculate the distance of each pixel in the histogram of output image after segmentation and the corresponding pixel in the normalized input image histogram. The Min-Max normalization technique [10] has been chosen to normalize the input image histogram. After applying the Min-Max normalization on each pixel $I_{ij}$ of the input image, he normalized pixel intensity $\hat{I}_{ij}$ becomes

$$\hat{I}_{ij} = \frac{I_{ij} - Imin}{Imax - Imin}(nMax - nMin) + nMin \tag{8}$$

where $Imax$ and $Imin$ are maximum and minimum pixel intensities in the input image respectively and $nMax$ and $nMin$ are the values between which the image is to be normalized. Let $O$ represent the output image after thresholding then the value of SAD metric is computed from [8]

$$SAD = \frac{1}{M \times N} \sum_{i=1}^{M} \sum_{j=1}^{N} |\hat{I}_{ij} - O_{ij}|. \tag{9}$$

---

**Algorithm 1.** Algorithm for Multilevel Thresholding with SAD Metric

---

**Require:** Grayscale image $I$
**Ensure:** Segmented image
 1: Calculate histogram $H$ of $I$
 2: Normalize $I$ into $\hat{I}$
 3: Initialize $\gamma$, $d = \infty$, $maxIter$, $L$
 4: **while** $\gamma < R$ **do**
 5:     Setting of parameter values and objective function value
 6:     Initialize $i = 0$ and the population (i.e. thresholds $\tau$)
 7:     **while** $i < maxIter$ **do**
 8:         Evaluation of the population using entropy measure as fitness function
 9:         Recording optimum individual
10:         Generate a new population
11:         Increment $i$
12:     **end while**
13:     Save the optimum solution in $\tau$
14:     Segment the image into $S_0, S_1, ..., S_m$
15:     Calculate SAD Metric between the segmented image and the normalized image $\hat{I}$, save it in $dist$
16:     **if** $dist < d$ **then**
17:         $d = dist$, $\gamma^* = \gamma$, $\tau^* = \tau$
18:     **end if**
19:     Increment $\gamma$
20: **end while**
21: Segment the image $I$ using optimal thresholds $\tau^*$

---

## 3    Methodology

Hadi *et al.* [8] proposed the SAD metric and validated it for bi-level thresholding using HYTA dataset. The first step in applying SAD metric to MLT relates to normalization of the input image. For bi-level image thresholding, the normalization of input image is simple as the pixel values are to be normalized in [0 1]. In case of MLT, the input is segmented into multiple parts based on the number of thresholds and hence the transformation of the input image should be done in the range [0 $m$]. Therefore, substituting $nMin = 0$ and $nMax = m$, $Imin =$ and $Imax = \phi - 1$ in (8) leads to

$$\hat{I_{ij}} = \frac{I_{ij}}{\phi - 1} \times m \tag{10}$$

for transforming input image pixel values for applying SAD metric.

Combining PSO, CSO, ABC and DE optimization mathods with Shannon, Renyi, Tsallis and Masi entropies 16 different variants of the Algorithm 1 are developed. The novelty of this algorithm lies in the fact that it searches thresholds as well as entropy parameter of the generalized measures automatically using (10) and SAD metric (9). In Algorithm 1, $\gamma$ represent the parameter of generalized entropy measure and $R$ is the maximum allowed value of the entropic parameter. While constructing the variant of the Algorithm 1 with Shannon entropy measure, the outer while loop is removed as this entropy measure does not contain a parameter, as is clear from (1).

**Table 1.** Details of Datasets

| Dataset | # of Images | Size | Max. Image Size |
|---|---|---|---|
| OSU Thermal Pedestrian DB | 99 | 8.34 MB | 85.4 KB |
| Brain MRI Dataset | 154 | 5.07 MB | 297 KB |
| Total Text Dataset | 300 | 101 MB | 6.12 MB |
| Berkeley Dataset | 200 | 13.8 MB | 111 KB |

We have chosen four datasets viz. OSU thermal pedestrian database, brain MRI images, total text and Berkeley. By incorporating these diverse datasets, our performance analysis covers a wide range of image types. This approach ensures the robustness and effectiveness of our proposed method across multiple domains and real-world applications. Table 1 contains details of the datasets.

**Table 2.** Comparison of SAD Values for 4-thresholds

| Algorithm | OSU | | MRI | | Total text | | Berkeley | |
|---|---|---|---|---|---|---|---|---|
| | Mean | Variance | Mean | Variance | Mean | Variance | Mean | Variance |
| Shannon+PSO | 0.2049 | 0.0012 | 0.1723 | 0.0060 | 0.1897 | 0.0046 | 0.2070 | 0.0050 |
| Shannon+CSO | 0.1898 | 0.0007 | 0.1645 | 0.0052 | 0.1778 | 0.0036 | 0.1937 | 0.0046 |
| Shannon+ABC | 0.2050 | 0.0014 | 0.1859 | 0.0077 | 0.1897 | 0.0045 | 0.2015 | 0.0054 |
| Shannon+DE | 0.1901 | 0.0010 | 0.1723 | 0.0071 | 0.1728 | 0.0034 | 0.1857 | 0.0037 |
| Renyi+PSO | 0.1930 | 0.0009 | 0.1441 | 0.0026 | 0.1619 | 0.0014 | 0.0016 | 0.1723 |
| Renyi+CSO | 0.1895 | 0.0007 | 0.1415 | 0.0021 | 0.1676 | 0.0022 | 0.1853 | 0.0029 |
| Renyi+ABC | 0.1983 | 0.0012 | 0.1552 | 0.0037 | 0.1767 | 0.0032 | 0.1940 | 0.0041 |
| Renyi+DE | 0.1896 | 0.0009 | 0.1406 | 0.0021 | **0.1638** | 0.0022 | **0.1743** | 0.0022 |
| Tsallis+PSO | 0.1921 | 0.0010 | 0.1473 | 0.0028 | 0.1751 | 0.0025 | 0.1912 | 0.0031 |
| Tsallis+CSO | 0.1864 | 0.0007 | **0.1396** | 0.0019 | 0.1673 | 0.0020 | 0.1779 | 0.0018 |
| Tsallis+ABC | 0.1993 | 0.0013 | 0.1534 | 0.0037 | 0.1780 | 0.0032 | 0.1922 | 0.0037 |
| Tsallis+DE | 0.1892 | 0.0008 | 0.1457 | 0.0025 | 0.1669 | 0.0022 | 0.1804 | 0.0024 |
| Masi+PSO | 0.1844 | 0.0006 | 0.1476 | 0.0019 | 0.1735 | 0.0023 | 0.1856 | 0.0022 |
| Masi+CSO | 0.1806 | 0.0005 | 0.0020 | 0.1415 | 0.1660 | 0.0018 | 0.1759 | 0.0016 |
| Masi+ABC | 0.1837 | 0.0008 | 0.1483 | 0.0022 | 0.1711 | 0.0019 | 0.1809 | 0.0019 |
| Masi+DE | **0.1801** | 0.0006 | 0.1468 | 0.0023 | 0.1655 | 0.0020 | 0.1748 | 0.0017 |

## 4   Results of Performance Analysis

The objective of this research work is to analyze the performance of various meta-heuristic methods with different entropy measures using SAD metric in the absence of ground truth images. The robustness of the proposed algorithm can be ascertained only after testing it over diverse datasets. Hence, four datasets from distinct domains are chosen (Fig. 2). Each dataset contains many images, hence mean value of SAD metric is computed. As variance is an important statistic as it is always desirable to use a metric with a low variance over the one that results in large variance. If two image thresholding methods have the same mean SAD value, the one with less variance is considered better.

The mean and variance of SAD values of the datasets are presented in Table 2 for four thresholds. Even though the experiments were conducted upto five thresholds, it is observed that 4 thresholds usually provide acceptable results. From each dataset, one image is chosen for visual representation and the same are presented in Figs. 1, 2, 3 and 4. The robustness of the proposed algorithm is thus evident as it automatically estimates the entropy parameter value close to one leading to same mean SAD values. It has been observed that Renyi entropy and Masi entropy mostly outperform others whereas DE meta-heuristic usually gives better result.

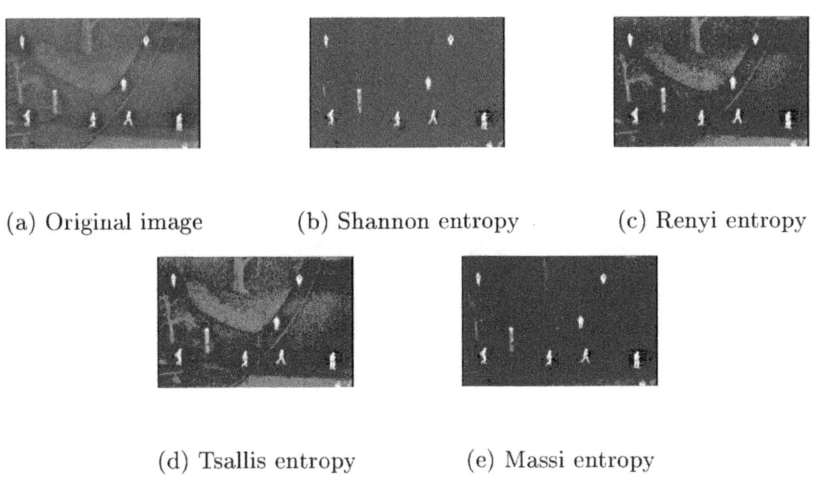

<table>
<tr><td>(a) Original image</td><td>(b) Shannon entropy</td><td>(c) Renyi entropy</td></tr>
<tr><td></td><td></td><td></td></tr>
<tr><td>(d) Tsallis entropy</td><td>(e) Massi entropy</td><td></td></tr>
</table>

**Fig. 1.** Image from OSU dataset- MLT with 4 thresholds and DE with entropic parameter tuning using SAD metric

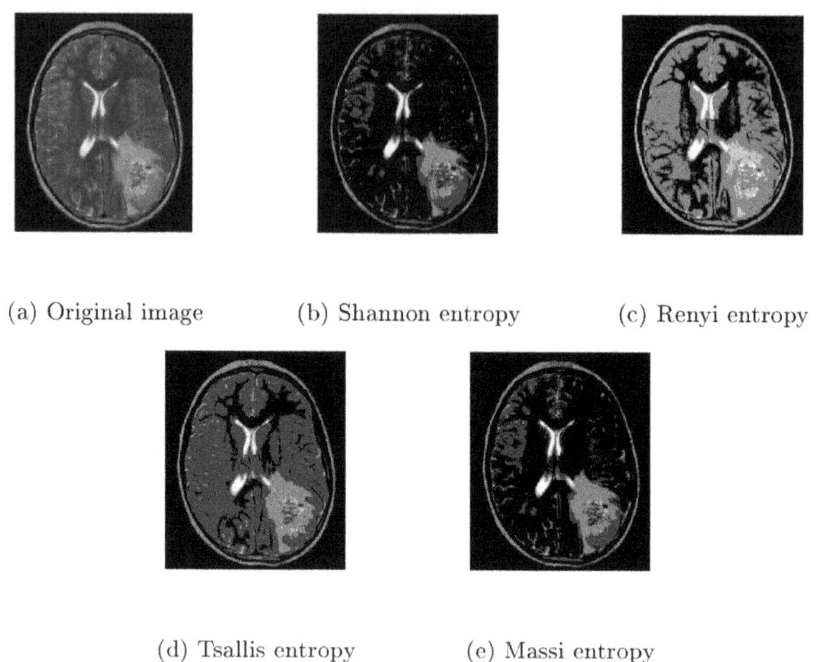

(a) Original image     (b) Shannon entropy     (c) Renyi entropy

(d) Tsallis entropy     (e) Massi entropy

**Fig. 2.** Image from MRI dataset- MLT with 4 thresholds and DE entropic parameter tuning using SAD metric.

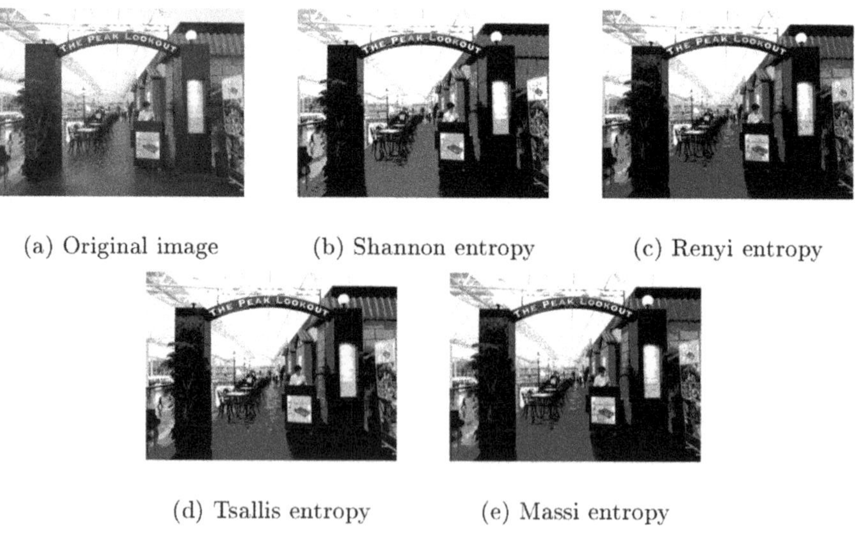

(a) Original image     (b) Shannon entropy     (c) Renyi entropy

(d) Tsallis entropy     (e) Massi entropy

**Fig. 3.** Image from total text dataset- MLT with 4 thresholds and DE with entropic parameter tuning using SAD metric

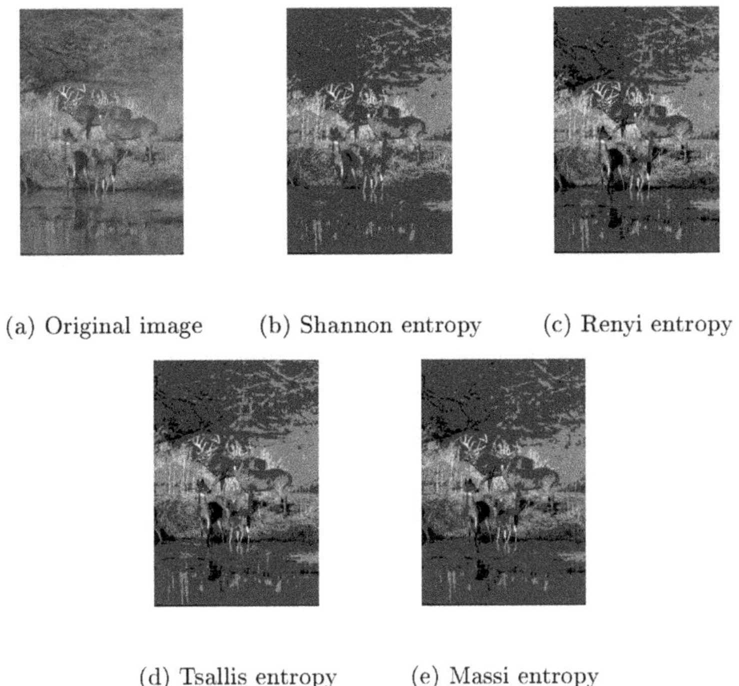

(a) Original image      (b) Shannon entropy      (c) Renyi entropy

(d) Tsallis entropy      (e) Massi entropy

**Fig. 4.** Image from Berkley dataset- MLT with 4 thresholds and DE entropic parameter tuning using SAD metric.

## 5    Conclusion

Extending the applicability of SAD metric to multilevel image thresholding, a new algorithm has been proposed in the paper that eliminates the requirement of ground-truth images for performance evaluation. Using four different entropy measures viz. Shannon, Renyi, Tsallis, Masi and for optimization techniques viz. PSO, CSO, ABC and DE, 16 different variants of the algorithm are developed. A large-scale performance analysis is then conducted over 753 images from five different datasets. Each variant of the proposed algorithm has been executed for upto five threshold levels on an image. This results in executing 64 experiments on an image and a total of 48192 experiments in the study. This is first-of-its-kind study in the absence of ground truth images to the best of our knowledge. It has been observed that none of the combination of meta-heuristic algorithm and entropy measure gives better performance on all types of images and threshold levels. However, DE algorithm along with Renyi and Masi entropies outperform others. The future work aims to extend the proposed method to entropy-difference techniques of image thresholding including colored and satellite images.

# References


1. Ahmed, S., Biswas, A., Khairuzzaman, A.K.M.: An experimentation of objective functions used for multilevel thresholding based image segmentation using particle swarm optimization. Int. J. Inf. Technol. **16**(3), 1717–1732 (2024)
2. Ali, M., Ahn, C.W., Pant, M.: Multi-level image thresholding by synergetic differential evolution. Appl. Soft Comput. **17**, 1–11 (2014)
3. Amiriebrahimabadi, M., Rouhi, Z., Mansouri, N.: A comprehensive survey of multilevel thresholding segmentation methods for image processing. Arch. Comput. Methods Eng. **31**(6), 3647–3697 (2024)
4. Cuevas, E., Zaldivar, D., Pérez-Cisneros, M.: A novel multi-threshold segmentation approach based on differential evolution optimization. Expert Syst. Appl. **37**(7), 5265–5271 (2010)
5. Gharehchopogh, F.S., Ibrikci, T.: An improved African vultures optimization algorithm using different fitness functions for multi-level thresholding image segmentation. Multimed. Tools Appl. **83**(6), 16929–16975 (2024)
6. Horng, M.H.: Multilevel thresholding selection based on the artificial bee colony algorithm for image segmentation. Expert Syst. Appl. **38**, 13785–13791 (2011)
7. Khairuzzaman, A.K.M., Chaudhury, S.: Masi entropy based multilevel thresholding for image segmentation. Multimed. Tools Appl. **78**(23), 33573–33591 (2019)
8. Mohammadi, H., Gupta, S., Sharma, S.: A large-scale performance study of entropy-based image thresholding techniques using new sad metric. Pattern Anal. Appl. **26**, 473–486 (2023)
9. Nie, F., Zhang, P., Li, J., Ding, D.: A novel generalized entropy and its application in image thresholding. Signal Process. **134**, 23–34 (2017)
10. Patro, S., Sahu, K.K.: Normalization: A preprocessing stage. arXiv preprint arXiv:1503.06462 (2015)
11. Sahoo, P., Wilkins, C., Yeager, J.: Threshold selection using renyi's entropy. Pattern Recogn. **30**, 71–84 (1997)
12. Sahoo, P.K., Soltani, S., Wong, A.K.C.: A survey of thresholding techniques. Comput. Vision, Graph. Image Process. **41**(2), 233–260 (1988)
13. Sarkar, S., Das, S.: Multilevel image thresholding based on 2d histogram and maximum tsallis entropy–a differential evolution approach. IEEE Trans. Image Process. **22**(12), 4788–4797 (2013)
14. Shannon, C.E.: A mathematical theory of communication. Bell Syst. Tech. J. **27**(3), 379–423 (1948)
15. Tsallis, C.: Possible generalization of Boltzmann-gibbs statistics. J. Stat. Phys.**52**, 479–487 (07 1988)
16. Upadhyay, P., Chhabra, J.K.: Kapur's entropy based optimal multilevel image segmentation using crow search algorithm. Appl. Soft Comput. **97**, 105522 (2020)
17. Yang, X., et al.: Multi-level threshold segmentation framework for breast cancer images using enhanced differential evolution. Biomed. Signal Process. Control **80**, 104373 (2023)
18. Zhang, Y., Wu, L.: Optimal multi-level thresholding based on maximum tsallis entropy via an artificial bee colony approach. Entropy **13**(4), 841–859 (2011)

# Beyond the Blink: Decoding Magnified Facial Micro-expressions with Transfer Learning


Jasleen Kaur$^{(\boxtimes)}$, Ankan Banerjee, and Dipti Patra

National Institute of Technology, Rourkela, India
jasstronger@gmail.com



**Abstract.** Recognising micro-expressions is inherently difficult due to their subtle and fleeting nature. In this work, we present an innovative approach that uses motion magnification combined with transfer learning to analyse microexpression datasets, particularly the SAMM dataset. By amplifying these subtle movements, we transformed micro-expressions into clearer, more distinguishable macro-expressions. Using pre-trained CNNs with frozen layers, we optimized the feature extraction process, achieving a test accuracy of 96. 54%, significantly outperforming previous methods.

**Keywords:** Transfer learning · Motion Magnification · Macro-expressions


## 1 Introduction

In a fast-paced and emotionally charged milieu, it is important to analyze the hidden, involuntary movements or expressions. Such emotions reflecting on the face are termed as micro-facial expressions. They are very hard to coin and collect from some conclusive dataset; still, efforts have been made to overcome issues like lighting, low resolution, and coding using the Facial Action Coding System (FACS). FACS, a technique developed by Ekman and Friesen [5], provided a great way to theorize the change of motion in facial muscles by coding them into Action Units (AUs), which correspond to specific muscle movements. For example, raising eyebrows is labeled Action Unit 1 (AU1) for the inner brow raiser and Action Unit 2 (AU2) for the outer brow raiser and tightening of lips is categorized as Action Unit 23 (AU23). In 1966, micro-expressions were initially discovered by Haggard and Isaacs [9]. Three years later, on an independent level, Ekman and Friesen's [4] study involved analyzing footage of a psychiatric patient who had concealed her suicidal intentions from her doctor. Despite maintaining a happy demeanour, a detailed frame-by-frame examination revealed a brief moment of distress, appearing for just two frames (1/12 of a second). Facial emotion recognition is an old subject, still under high scope, but



S. Mitra et al. (Eds.): PReMI 2025, LNCS 16358, pp. 247–255, 2026.
https://doi.org/10.1007/978-3-032-18480-1_25

with many limitations, such as being faked, highly dependent on cultural diversity, unnatural, etc., it has become an important point to further delve deeper into more authentic and spontaneous emotions. These expressions occur when people try to suppress their emotions, possibly due to the unacceptability of different cultural or social restrictions. It all occurs because the fear of expressing negative emotions [2]. The study [7] showed that men suppress emotions more than women, while women tend to fall into depression more.

[22] was an early pioneer in building micro-expression datasets, recording 10 diverse student participants at 200 fps as they intentionally expressed seven basic emotions in a lab setting. Another paper, [11] introduced the SMIC (Spontaneous Micro-expression Database), which contains 164 clips from 16 participants and is a strong benchmark for detection tasks. [29] captures subtle facial emotions in high detail (200 fps, 280×340 resolution) with expert-coded labels and precise timing of each expression. The SAMM dataset [3], with its rich diversity and high spatial resolution (2040×1088), surpasses CASME [29] by capturing spontaneous micro-expressions with precise FACS coding as shown in Fig. 2. Here, (a) shows the onset frame, (c) captures the apex with a mouth curl and inward-pulled nostrils, and (e) marks the offset. We chose SAMM because its realistic, real-world emotion cues are ideal for our analysis.

Many motion magnification methods have been developed, stating back to [25], which used the Eulerian Video Magnification method that applies spatial decomposition and temporal filtering to the input video sequence. [24] was the first application of Eulerian video magnification to amplify micro-emotions. [6] used Lagrangian motion magnification on micro emotions, along with the optical flow techniques. Since frames alone can miss them, we have imposed a motion magnification method, given by [18]. Transfer learning helps models adapt old knowledge to new tasks, making micro-expression analysis more accurate and efficient, even with limited data. [1], trained on a large-scale facial dataset, is fine-tuned to recognise magnified micro-expression movements. [32] approach ensured the model transfer macro-expression knowledge to subtle micro-expression datasets, boosting recognition accuracy through better feature adaptation.

Depression often masks emotions like anxiety and irritability behind neutral expressions or even laughter. Micro-expression detection helps reveal these hidden cues. Our work introduces two key innovations:

- Micro-expressions are amplified to resemble macro ones, allowing CNNs with frozen initial layers and pre-trained weights to better capture meaningful spatial-temporal cues.
- The model achieved over 96% UFI and UAR on the SAMM dataset, demonstrating strong accuracy, robustness, and scalability beyond existing approaches (Fig. 1).

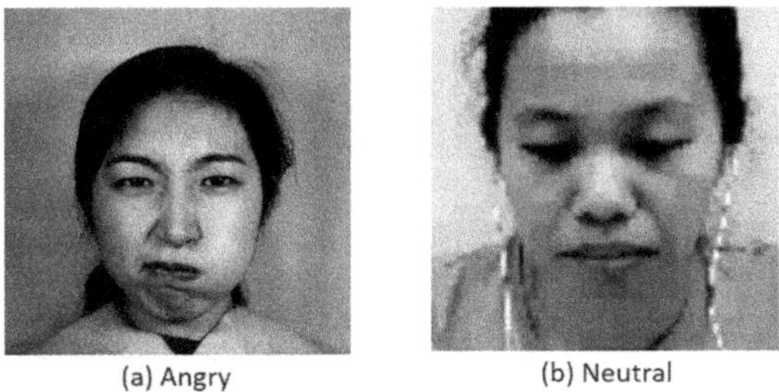

(a) Angry                          (b) Neutral

**Fig. 1.** Sample image from the Macro-Dataset used: (a) JAFFE [14] and (b) KTFEv2 [15] dataset.

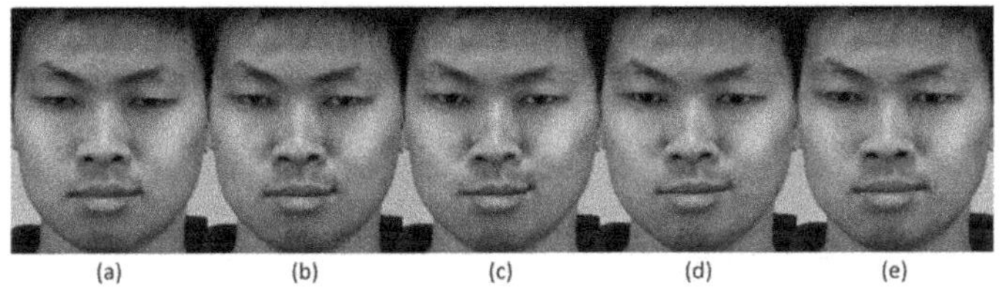

(a)          (b)          (c)          (d)          (e)

**Fig. 2.** An example of a coded micro-movement from the SAMM dataset [3].

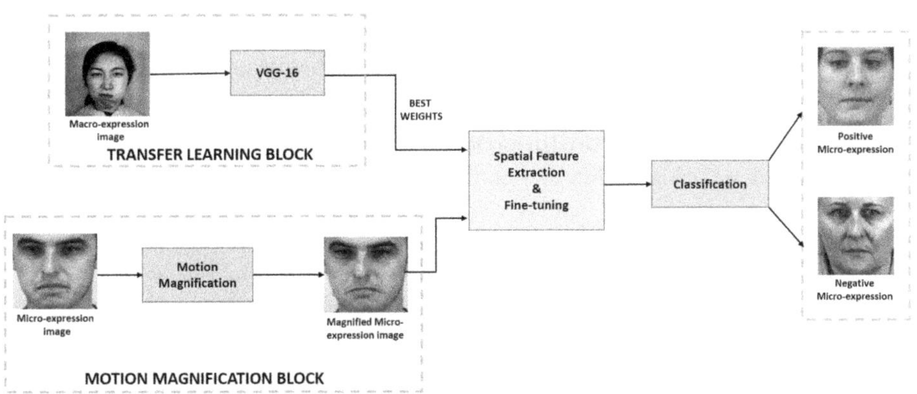


**Fig. 3.** Proposed network architecture

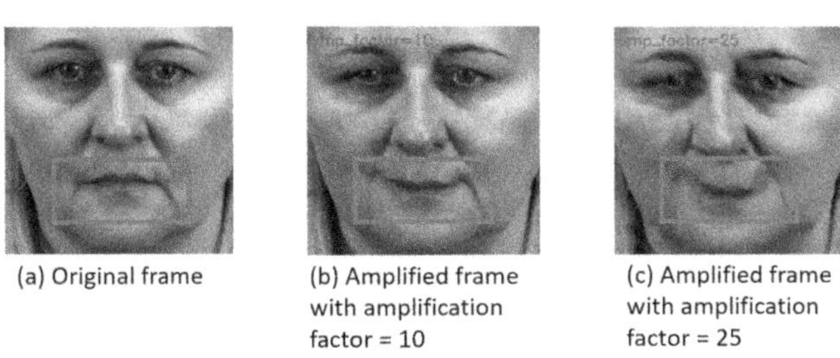

(a) Original frame          (b) Amplified frame with amplification factor = 10          (c) Amplified frame with amplification factor = 25

**Fig. 4.** Frames magnification of the [3] dataset with amplification factors of 10 &25

## 2  Materials and Methods

### 2.1  Datasets Used

**Table 1.** Dataset Used

| Dataset | No. of Emotions | Diversity | Image Size |
|---|---|---|---|
| KTFEv2 [15] | 7 | 30 (19 males, 11 females) | 224 × 224 |
| JAFFE [14] | 7 | 10 female subjects | 256 × 256 |
| SAMM [3] | 7 | 32 (equal male-female split) | 256 × 256 |

Table 1 summarizes the datasets used, highlighting the number of emotions, participant diversity, and image resolutions.

### 2.2  Proposed Method

**Dataset Preparation.** Macro-expression training used KTFEv2 [15] and JAFFE [14] datasets on a VGG16 model with resized 224×224 images across seven emotions. SAMM micro-expression frames were amplified and sorted by subject, with emotions grouped as positive or negative; overrepresented classes like Anger and Disgust were trimmed to reduce imbalance.

**Frame Selection and Amplification.** Motion magnification, based on the workflow from [18], highlights subtle facial movements by amplifying frame-to-frame displacement. These frames were then amplified using factors of 10 and 25, out of which we used images with an amplification factor of 25 as they were more expressive and similar to macro emotions as shown in Fig. 4.

Motion magnification amplifies tiny, almost invisible movements over time, making subtle variations easier to see. We use this technique to enhance micro-expression datasets, turning subtle facial movements into clearer, macro-like expressions, which simplifies CNN training for classification. Following the workflow in [18], the approach has three key components: Encoder, Manipulator, and Decoder. The fully convolutional encoder–decoder network processes images, where the encoder extracts compact feature representations and the decoder reconstructs high-quality outputs using residual blocks for improved quality. The Manipulator amplifies small shape differences between two frames (A and B) from a synthetic dataset of nearly imperceptible movements. By magnifying these displacements (using factors of 10 and 25), we make micro-movements visible. We found that a factor of 25 produced the most expressive, macro-like frames (Fig. 4), which we then used for MER feature extraction.

**Transfer Learning Based Feature Extraction.** The macro-expression frames were given as input for transfer learning. The shallow features of macro and micro-expressions are almost similar [19], which allows us to use the trained weights of the macro-expression dataset to freeze the initial layers of our MER feature extraction model, while the unfrozen layers were used for deeper feature extraction from the amplified MER frames.

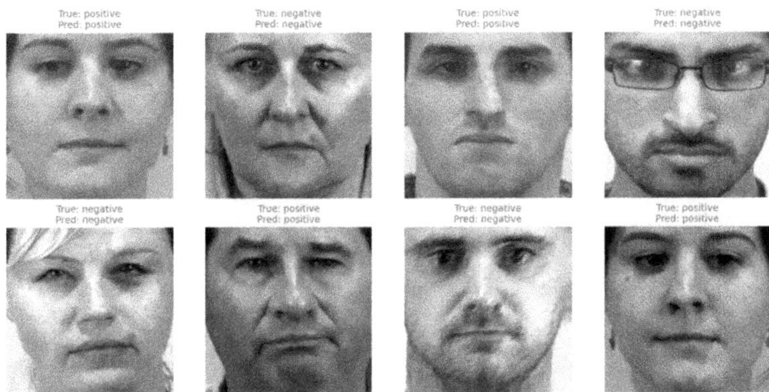


**Fig. 5.** Qualitative Analysis

**Proposed Model.** The proposed architecture (Fig. 3) consists of three main blocks: transfer learning, motion magnification, and feature extraction. The transfer learning block uses VGG-16 to extract features from composite macro-expression datasets, saving the best weights for fine-tuning on micro-expression data. The motion magnification block enhances subtle micro-expression frames, making them suitable for spatial feature extraction. The feature extraction block again uses VGG-16, initializing with the pre-trained weights (frozen in the early layers) and fine-tuning the fully connected layers on the amplified SAMM images. The dataset was split into 70:30 for training and testing. The model was trained in PyTorch on Google Colab for 50 epochs with a learning rate of 0.0001, using cross-entropy loss and the ADAM optimizer. A StepLR scheduler reduced the learning rate by 0.1 every 10 epochs for better convergence.

## 3   Results and Discussions

### 3.1   Comparison Report

Table 2 presents the performance comparison of our proposed method with existing approaches to the UF1 and UAR metrics [21].

Table 3 shows the comparison between various methods on the basis of accuracy and F1-score, proving the feasibility of the proposed model for the SAMM dataset.

**Table 2.** UF1 and UAR Comparison Across Methods

| Methods | Year | UF1(%) | UAR(%) |
|---|---|---|---|
| SA-AT [31] | 2019 | 44.76 | 48.68 |
| ATNet [21] | 2019 | 49.60 | 48.20 |
| OFF-ApexNet [8] | 2019 | 54.09 | 53.92 |
| STSTNet [13] | 2019 | 65.88 | 68.10 |
| DPN [17] | 2021 | 68.68 | 70.22 |
| CBAM-DPN [17] | 2021 | 74.06 | 70.97 |
| MiMaNet [26] | 2021 | 89.60 | 88.40 |
| ADP-DSTN [23] | 2024 | 79.32 | 80.71 |
| **Ours** | 2025 | **96.54** | **96.56** |

**Table 3.** Quantitative Comparison Across Methods

| Methods | Classes | Accuracy | F1-score |
|---|---|---|---|
| OFF-ApexNet [8] | 7 | 68.10 | 54.20 |
| AU-GACN [28] | | 70.20 | 43.30 |
| MicroNet [27] | | 74.12 | 73.61 |
| Graph-TCN [10] | | 75.02 | 69.94 |
| MiMaNet [26] | | 76.75 | 76.42 |
| LGCcon [12] | 5 | 40.92 | 34.01 |
| GEME [16] | | 55.88 | 45.38 |
| FeatRef [30] | | 60.13 | - |
| MFVAN [20] | | 76.47 | 73.25 |
| **Ours** | 2 | **96.50** | **96.50** |

### 3.2 Qualitative Analysis

To better understand the model's performance, we randomly selected 8 amplified SAMM test images for a qualitative review. Therefore, both the true and predicted emotion labels for each of these test images are presented in Fig. 5.

### 3.3 Confusion Matrix

The confusion matrix of the proposed method is shown in Fig. 6. Out of the total 198 'negative' samples 193 were correctly predicted as negative. Similarly, for the 207 'positive' samples 198 were correctly predicted as positive.

## 4 Discussion

In this article, we proposed a method to classify positive and negative emotions from micro-expressions. Since basic CNNs miss tiny facial shifts, we magnified

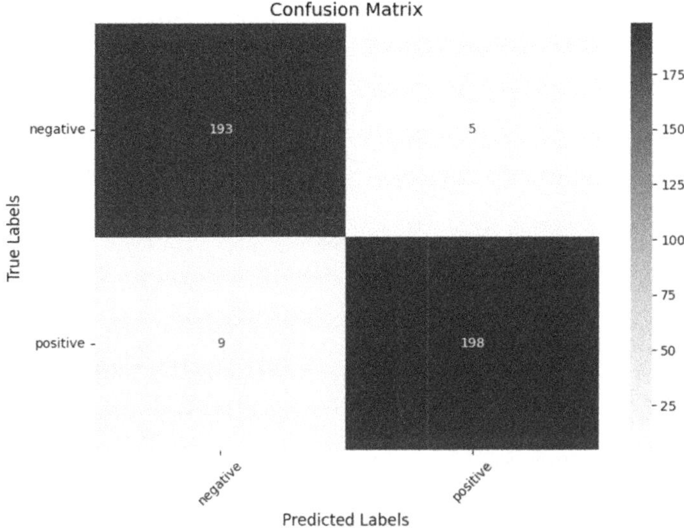

**Fig. 6.** Confusion Matrix

those cues and passed them to a VGG16 feature extractor, fine-tuned with top weights from larger expression datasets. Built with PyTorch, the model was trained on 2,700 images, split into sets for training, validation, and testing. It ran for 50 epochs on Google Colab using a T4 TPU. Adam optimiser (with a learning rate of 0.0001) kept things smooth, while a step scheduler trimmed that rate every 10 epochs. To avoid overfitting, early stopping stepped in when progress stalled. Our method excels over the SOTA methods in terms of UF1 and UAR as in Table 2. As we know, UF1 and UAR are class-agnostic metrics because they weigh the performance across all classes equally, ensuring that the results are not skewed by class imbalance, declaring them to be fair ground for comparison.

The proposed method adopts a two-class (positive/negative) setup, as it is often sufficient for real-world needs. This grouping reduces errors from rare classes and avoids challenges of multi-class recognition, such as class imbalance and low inter-class differentiability among overlapping emotions like anger and disgust. The proposed method achieves 96.5% accuracy and F1-score, clearly outperforming multi-class approaches, as can be seen from Table 3.

## 5    Conclusion

Our approach, combining motion magnification and transfer learning with pre-trained models, has proven highly effective, achieving an impressive test accuracy of 96.54%. The consistency and reliability of the model are further supported by strong UF1 and UAR scores, targeting a practical use case where only positive and negative sentiment analysis is required, justifying a simple and effective setup. That said, relying on a synthetic dataset does come with limitations, and there is room for growth, particularly with techniques like temporal filtering, which could refine how we capture and analyse nuanced movements in the real world. Adding attention layers or transformers could help the model focus better on subtle facial cues, making emotion detection more precise. This opens up real-world uses, from improved mental health assessments to smarter counselling tools.

# References


1. Bai, M., Goecke, R., Herath, D.: Micro-expression recognition based on video motion magnification and pre-trained neural network. In: 2021 IEEE International Conference on Image Processing (ICIP), pp. 549–553. IEEE (2021)
2. Beblo, T., Fernando, S., Klocke, S., Griepenstroh, J., Aschenbrenner, S., Driessen, M.: Increased suppression of negative and positive emotions in major depression. J. Affect. Disord. **141**(2–3), 474–479 (2012)
3. Davison, A.K., Lansley, C., Costen, N., Tan, K., Yap, M.H.: SAMM: a spontaneous micro-facial movement dataset. IEEE Trans. Affect. Comput. **9**(1), 116–129 (2016)
4. Ekman, P., Friesen, W.V.: Nonverbal leakage and clues to deception. Psychiatry **32**(1), 88–106 (1969)
5. Ekman, P., Friesen, W.V.: Manual of the facial action coding system (FACS). Trans. ed, vol. Consulting Psychologists Press, Palo Alto **3** (1978)
6. Flotho, P., Heiss, C., Steidl, G., Strauss, D.J.: Lagrangian motion magnification with double sparse optical flow decomposition. Front. Appl. Math. Stat. **9**, 1164491 (2023)
7. Flynn, J.J., Hollenstein, T., Mackey, A.: The effect of suppressing and not accepting emotions on depressive symptoms: Is suppression different for men and women? Personal. Individ. Differ. **49**(6), 582–586 (2010)
8. Gan, Y.S., Liong, S.T., Yau, W.C., Huang, Y.C., Tan, L.K.: Off-APEXNet on micro-expression recognition system. Sig. Process. Image Commun. **74**, 129–139 (2019)
9. ISAACS, E.H.K., et al.: Micromomentary facial expressions as indicators of ego mechanism in psychotherapy. Methods Res. Psychother., 154–165 (1966)
10. Lei, L., Li, J., Chen, T., Li, S.: A novel graph-TCN with a graph structured representation for micro-expression recognition. In: Proceedings of the 28th ACM International Conference on Multimedia, pp. 2237–2245 (2020)
11. Li, X., Pfister, T., Huang, X., Zhao, G., Pietikäinen, M.: A spontaneous micro-expression database: Inducement, collection and baseline. In: 2013 10th IEEE International Conference and Workshops on Automatic face and gesture recognition (FG), pp. 1–6. IEEE (2013)
12. Li, Y., Huang, X., Zhao, G.: Joint local and global information learning with single apex frame detection for micro-expression recognition. IEEE Trans. Image Process. **30**, 249–263 (2020)
13. Liong, S.T., Gan, Y.S., See, J., Khor, H.Q., Huang, Y.C.: Shallow triple stream three-dimensional CNN (STSTNET) for micro-expression recognition. In: 2019 14th IEEE International Conference on Automatic Face & Gesture Recognition (FG 2019), pp. 1–5. IEEE (2019)
14. Lyons, M., Kamachi, M., Gyoba, J.: The Japanese female facial expression (jaffe) dataset. (No Title) (1998)

15. Nguyen, H., Tran, N., Nguyen, H.D., Nguyen, L., Kotani, K.: KTFEV2: multimodal facial emotion database and its analysis. IEEE Access **11**, 17811–17822 (2023)
16. Nie, X., Takalkar, M.A., Duan, M., Zhang, H., Xu, M.: GEME: dual-stream multi-task gender-based micro-expression recognition. Neurocomputing **427**, 13–28 (2021)
17. Niu, R., Yang, J., Xing, L., Wu, R.: Micro-expression recognition algorithm based on convolutional block attention module and dual path networks. J. Comput. Appl. **41**(9), 2552 (2021)
18. Oh, T.H., et al.: Learning-based video motion magnification. In: Proceedings of the European Conference on Computer Vision (ECCV), pp. 633–648 (2018)
19. Oh, Y.H., See, J., Le Ngo, A.C., Phan, R.C.W., Baskaran, V.M.: A survey of automatic facial micro-expression analysis: databases, methods, and challenges. Front. Psychol. **9**, 1128 (2018)
20. Pan, H., Yang, H., Xie, L., Wang, Z.: Multi-scale fusion visual attention network for facial micro-expression recognition. Front. Neurosci. **17**, 1216181 (2023)
21. Peng, M., Wang, C., Bi, T., Shi, Y., Zhou, X., Chen, T.: A novel apex-time network for cross-dataset micro-expression recognition. In: 2019 8th International Conference on Affective Computing and Intelligent Interaction (ACII), pp. 1–6. IEEE (2019)
22. Polikovsky, S., Kameda, Y., Ohta, Y.: Facial micro-expressions recognition using high speed camera and 3D-gradient descriptor. In: 3rd International Conference on Imaging for Crime Detection and Prevention (ICDP 2009), pp. 1–6. IET (2009)
23. Song, J., Lei, S., Wu, W.: Microexpression recognition method based on ADP-DSTN feature fusion and convolutional block attention module. Electronics **13**(20), 4012 (2024)
24. Wang, Y., et al.: Effective recognition of facial micro-expressions with video motion magnification. Multimedia Tools Appl. **76**, 21665–21690 (2017)
25. Wu, H.Y., et al.: Eulerian video magnification for revealing subtle changes in the world. ACM Trans. Graph. (TOG) **31**(4), 1–8 (2012)
26. Xia, B., Wang, S.: Micro-expression recognition enhanced by macro-expression from spatial-temporal domain. In: IJCAI, pp. 1186–1193 (2021)
27. Xia, B., Wang, W., Wang, S., Chen, E.: Learning from macro-expression: a micro-expression recognition framework. In: Proceedings of the 28th ACM International Conference on Multimedia, pp. 2936–2944 (2020)
28. Xie, H.X., Lo, L., Shuai, H.H., Cheng, W.H.: Au-assisted graph attention convolutional network for micro-expression recognition. In: Proceedings of the 28th ACM International Conference on Multimedia, pp. 2871–2880 (2020)
29. Yan, W.J., et al.: Casme II: an improved spontaneous micro-expression database and the baseline evaluation. PLoS ONE **9**(1), e86041 (2014)
30. Zhou, L., Mao, Q., Huang, X., Zhang, F., Zhang, Z.: Feature refinement: an expression-specific feature learning and fusion method for micro-expression recognition. Pattern Recogn. **122**, 108275 (2022)
31. Zhou, L., Mao, Q., Xue, L.: Cross-database micro-expression recognition: a style aggregated and attention transfer approach. In: 2019 IEEE International Conference on Multimedia & Expo Workshops (ICMEW), pp. 102–107. IEEE (2019)
32. Zhu, G., et al.: SKD-TSTSAN: three-stream temporal-shift attention network based on self-knowledge distillation for micro-expression recognition. arXiv e-prints, pp. arXiv–2406 (2024)

# Developing High Performance Anomaly Detection Models with Deep Learning Algorithms and Data Augmentation for Enhancing Visual Inspection of Metal Manufacturing


Rajeeb Das[1] and Dillip Rout[2]

[1] C.V. Raman Global University, Bhubaneswar, India
[2] Royal Global University, Guwahati, India
dillip.rout.iitb@gmail.com



**Abstract.** Anomaly detection is crucial in automated quality control systems across various manufacturing domains. This research presents a deep learning-based approach to detect anomalies in metal casting components using Convolutional Neural Networks (CNN), Visual Geometry Group 16 (VGG16), and MobileNet models. An annotated dataset of 7348 grayscale images representing Defective and Non-defective metal parts was used to train and test the models. Data preprocessing techniques were employed to improve generalization, and performance was assessed using multiple metrics such as Accuracy, Precision, Recall, F1-Score, Specificity, and AUC-ROC. All the models achieved values of more than 97% for every metric. In particular, MobileNet has got 99.62% and 99.99% in F1 score and AUC-ROC score, respectively, with a training time of 350.1 s only. In fact, MobileNet demonstrated a favorable balance between detection performance and computational efficiency, making it suitable for real-time deployment. Furthermore, the performance of our model outperformed the results available in the literature. The results confirm the potential of deep learning architectures in achieving reliable and automated anomaly detection in industrial settings.

**Keywords:** CNN · MobileNet · Image resizing · Binary classification · Transfer learning


## 1 Introduction

Anomaly detection in metal casting is a vital component of quality assurance in manufacturing, aiming to identify internal and surface defects such as blowholes, cracks, porosity, and underfills. These defects, if undetected, can lead to catastrophic mechanical failures and significant economic losses. Manual inspection is slow, error-prone, and not scalable. With the rise of Industry 4.0, automated visual inspection systems have become essential for maintaining quality in manufacturing [2]. Hence, automating these processes through computer vision is driving interest in enhancing the monitoring of these industrial components.

Traditionally, the metal casting industry has used various non-destructive testing (NDT) methods to ensure product quality. Techniques like visual inspection, Ultrasonic testing (UT) [18], and Radiographic testing (RT) [19] have been commonly used to detect surface and internal defects. UT uses sound waves to reveal internal issues, and RT employs radiation to detect hidden defects. Although effective, these traditional methods are labor-intensive, dependent on inspectors, time-consuming, and often unsuitable for large-scale, fast-paced production. These challenges have led to the rise of fully automated systems. Recent advances in machine learning and deep learning have led to the development of various such systems for identifying defects and anomalies in manufacturing processes [2].

This paper presents a comparative study of automated anomaly detection for metal casting defects using CNNs, including VGG16 and MobileNet. A dataset containing 7348 grayscale images from the manufacturing industry is incorporated for classifying Defective or Non-defective products [3]. The aim is to develop accurate, lightweight, and computationally efficient models suitable for real-time usage. Thus, custom-designed CNN and pretrained architectures (VGG16 and MobileNet) are incorporated in this study. This innovative approach enables comprehensive performance benchmarking across models, leveraging preprocessing and transfer learning to achieve high accuracy and low computational costs. The models are evaluated using multiple standard metrics (Accuracy, Precision, Recall, Specificity, F1 score, and AUC-ROC score) to demonstrate the capability and robustness of our proposed methodology. The trade-offs between accuracy and complexity are probed to deliver a practical, scalable solution for industrial defect detection.

The remainder of the paper is organized as follows. Section 2 provides a review of related work. Section 3 outlines the proposed methodology in this study to develop and evaluate the proposed approach. Section 4 presents the results obtained from the model implemented in this study. Finally, Sect. 5 concludes the proposed research and outlines the directions for future work.


## 2   Related Works

This section presents a critical review of the research papers focused on anomaly detection in industrial applications. Traditional non-destructive testing (NDT) methods, including X-ray, ultrasonic, and infrared imaging, have been widely adopted. However, manual inspection remains prevalent, resulting in low efficiency and high error rates due to human fatigue and subjectivity. Recent advancements in artificial intelligence (AI), particularly deep learning, have enabled the development of automated, high-precision defect detection systems that significantly outperform traditional approaches. The following discussions explore different approaches to anomaly detection, including convolutional autoencoders, triplet networks, and comparative evaluations of machine learning models.

Staar et al. (2019) introduce a deep metric learning approach consisting of triplet networks to learn similarity metrics for surface textures. It enables the detection of novel defect classes without requiring labeled defective samples, but struggles with certain surface types and is sensitive to the choice of distance metrics. Heger et al. (2020) propose the use of convolutional autoencoders (CAEs) for anomaly detection in formed sheet metals [6]. Their approach addresses the scarcity of defective samples by training on non-defective data only. The CAE model achieved up to 95.5% recall, outperforming CNNs in detecting unseen defects. However, the method relies on a fixed reconstruction threshold and lacks adaptability across different types of defects.

Deep learning, particularly CNNs, has shown superior performance in defect detection by learning hierarchical features directly from raw images. Nagy and Czni [16] proposed a fusion convolutional siamese neural network (FCSNN), which effectively generalized across different defect types and object classes without retraining. Furthermore, domain-adapted neural networks that utilize pre-trained backbones (e.g., VGG16 in Siamese structures) have demonstrated strong generalization capabilities under varied visual conditions. Such architectures are particularly suitable for scalable and adaptable industrial inspection systems [16]. Jezek et al. (2021, 2022) highlight the limitations of benchmark datasets like MVTec-AD, which fail to capture the complexity of real-world industrial conditions [8, 9]. Their studies show that pre-trained models, such as PaDiM and PatchCore, perform well on controlled datasets but struggle with generalization in realistic scenarios. They propose new datasets and evaluation protocols to reflect industrial challenges better.

Kharitonov et al. (2022) conduct a comprehensive evaluation of ten machine learning models on simulated production logs with injected machine breakdowns [11]. Their findings indicate that KNN and KNN-based Feature Bagging consistently achieve high F1 scores ($\geq 0.75$ ) across various feature configurations. In contrast, AutoEncoders and COPOD exhibit limited applicability, as they are heavily influenced by feature selection and data dimensionality. Ensemble methods, such as Feature Bagging and tree-based models like Isolation Forest, have been employed to address the challenges posed by high-dimensional and noisy datasets. These methods improve robustness by aggregating the output of multiple models [11].

Hai et al. (2024) proposed a deep learning framework for detecting internal defects in aluminum castings using digital radiography (DR) X-ray images [5]. Their hybrid approach demonstrated a 20.08% increase in accuracy compared to baseline models and outperformed popular object detection architectures such as YOLOv5, YOLOv7, and Faster R-CNN [5]. Nonetheless, the model struggles with densely distributed defects due to grayscale similarity and structural complexity. Mattera and Nele (2025) compare supervised and unsupervised machine learning approaches for real-time anomaly detection in wire arc additive manufacturing (WAAM) [14]. The authors analyze welding current and voltage signals and apply various ML models, including logistic regression, neural networks, isolation forest, and local outlier factor. Supervised models perform well but are prone to overfitting. Unsupervised models detect anomalies reliably with higher false alarm rates. Supervised models require balanced datasets. Unsupervised models lack generalization and interpretability.

### Research Gaps

Across all studies, a standard limitation is the generalization gap when transitioning from controlled benchmarks to complex industrial environments. Models often struggle to maintain performance under varying lighting conditions, object orientations, and backgrounds. The majority of the models are tailored to specific casting types or imaging modalities, whereas a cross-domain generalization is desirable. Deep learning approaches typically require large, labeled datasets and retraining for new domains. Moreover, current Siamese architectures exhibit limited generalization to unseen defect classes [16]. Additionally, the scarcity of defective samples and the high dimensionality of industrial data pose significant challenges for training robust models. Future research should focus on improving generalizability, real-time performance, and interpretability. The development of standardized datasets and multi-modal fusion frameworks will be essential for building robust, scalable, and trustworthy defect detection systems for real-time anomaly detection systems with low false alarm rates.

## 3   Methodology

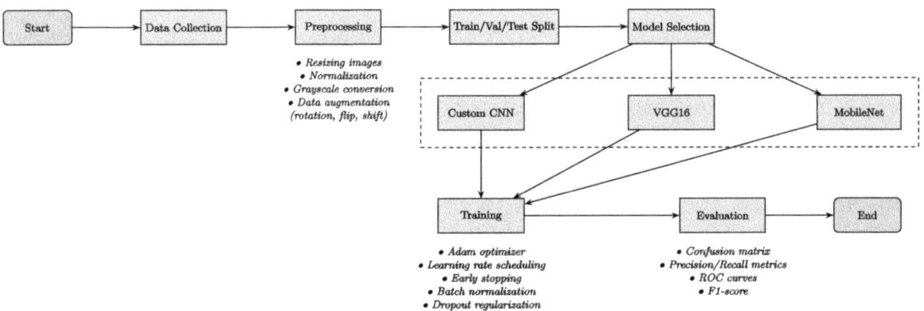


**Fig. 1.** Flowchart of the proposed methodology for anomaly detection in metal parts.

The workflow diagram in Fig. 1 outlines a comprehensive methodology for anomaly detection in metal parts using deep learning. The process begins with *data collection*, followed by *preprocessing* to clean, normalize, and augment the data. Afterward, the data is split into training, validation, and test sets to ensure a robust evaluation framework. In the *model selection* phase, multiple architectures: CNN, VGG16, and MobileNet are considered to explore various depths and computational efficiencies suitable for the task. Then, all the models are evaluated under a set of metrics for showcasing robustness. Each of the phases is described in the following subsections in detail.

### 3.1  Dataset

The data set utilized in this research focuses on automatic quality inspection of casting products, specifically submersible pump impellers [2,3]. These components are commonly produced using the casting process, where molten metal is poured into a mold and solidified. However, this method often results in defects such as blow holes, shrinkage, burrs, or metallurgical imperfections. The dataset includes grayscale images taken from the top view of impellers under controlled lighting conditions. The images are pre-labeled and categorized into two main classes: Defective and Non-defective.

*Image Specifications:* The dataset contains 7,348 images of size 300×300 pixels [3]. In fact, the dataset includes the augmented dataset with rotation, flipping, scaling, translation, etc., to enhance model performance across varied input types and supports both robustness testing and model generalization. Furthermore, the augmented dataset contains 4211 Defective and 3137 Non-defective images. This represents a nearly balanced class ratio that supports effective model training and generalization testing for the deep learning models such as CNN [13,17], VGG16 [20], and MobileNet [7,17].

### 3.2  Preprocessing

Several preprocessing steps were applied to prepare the dataset for model training. All images were uniformly resized to $128 \times 128$ pixels to ensure input consistency across different model architectures. Pixel values were normalized to the $[0, 1]$ range, facilitating faster training convergence by standardizing the input scale. To reduce noise effects of distortions due to lighting or sensor flaws, images were normalized and augmented with brightness shifts, rotations, and translations [4]. These techniques improved generalization, with models like VGG16 and MobileNet maintaining high accuracy even when the parameters are non-trivial.

### 3.3  Model Architectures and Algorithms

Three deep learning algorithms are explored in this study for the classification of Defective and Non-defective casting images: CNN, VGG16, and MobileNet. Each of these models utilizes convolutional operations to extract hierarchical features from grayscale input images. The architectures of these models are presented in Fig. 2 to demonstrate the fundamental differences. Furthermore, the background of algorithms related to each model is briefly discussed below for clarity.

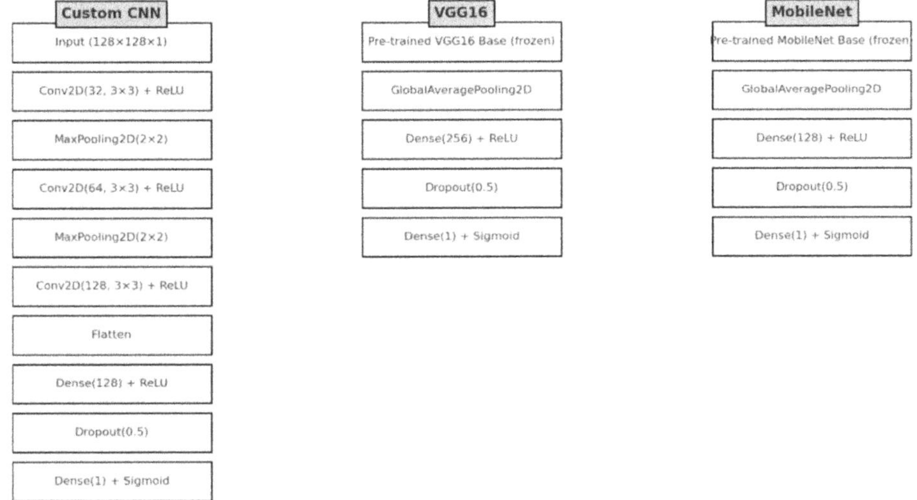

**Fig. 2.** Architectures of CNN, VGG16 and MobileNet models.

**Convolutional Neural Network (CNN).** CNN is a class of deep neural networks highly effective for image classification tasks [17]. The fundamental operation in a CNN is the convolution, mathematically defined in Eq. 1, where $I$ is the input image, $K$ is the convolution kernel, and $S(i, j)$ denotes the output feature map:

$$S(i, j) = (I * K)(i, j) = \sum_{m} \sum_{n} I(i + m, j + n) \cdot K(m, n) \tag{1}$$

The architecture implemented in this study includes sequential convolutional layers, ReLU activation functions, max-pooling layers, and fully connected layers. The final classification is performed using the Softmax activation function.

**VGG16.** VGG16 extends the conventional CNN by incorporating 16 weight layers and consistently using small $3 \times 3$ filters. This structure allows deeper networks while maintaining computational efficiency. Its core computation is represented as: $X' = \sigma(W_n * (\dots (\sigma(W_2 * (\sigma(W_1 * X))))))$ where $W_k$ are the convolutional filters and $\sigma$ denotes the ReLU activation function. This hierarchical composition enables the network to learn complex features from the input image.

**MobileNet.** MobileNet is optimized for resource-constrained environments by introducing depthwise separable convolutions, denoted as: $Y = (X * K_{depthwise}) * K_{pointwise}$. In addition, MobileNet employs linear bottlenecks and inverted residuals, enabling efficient feature transformation and parameter reduction [17]. These innovations allow MobileNet to retain competitive accuracy while significantly reducing model size and inference time.

Note that a custom-designed CNN was experimented with along with pre-trained architectures (VGG16 and MobileNet) for benchmarking. The data set was then divided into training subsets (70%), validation subsets (15%), and testing subsets (15%) to support model development, hyperparameter tuning, and unbiased performance evaluation.

### 3.4  Evaluation

The performance of the models was assessed on a held-out test set using the following evaluation metrics: Accuracy, Precision, Recall, F1-Score, Specificity (Eq. 2), and AUC-ROC [10,17]. These metrics provide a comprehensive view of the model's predictive ability, especially in the context of binary classification. The metrics other than Specificity are quite standard and widely used. So, the definition of Specificity is given below for understanding:

$$\text{Specificity} = \frac{\text{True Negative}}{\text{True Negative} + \text{False Positive}} \tag{2}$$

In addition, an ablation study is conducted to evaluate the contribution of each component. Notably, we performed the ablation study on the image *Resize*, *Dropout* layer, and *Batch* normalization. The first one refers to the efficacy of the preprocessing. On the other hand, the latter two demonstrate the model's ability to showcase its configuration. We present the comparison of the original full models with these variations.

## 4  Results and Discussions

This section presents the evaluation results of all models on the test set, including their predictive performance and computational efficiency, and comparison with existing studies. As shown in Table 1, MobileNet achieved the highest accuracy, F1-score, Specificity, and AUC-ROC score, confirming its superior anomaly detection capabilities. Furthermore, the computational efficiency of MobileNet offered the best trade-off between predictive performance and inference speed as listed in the last column.

**Table 1.** performance of each model on the test set

| Model | Accuracy | Precision | Recall | F1-Score | Specificity | AUC-ROC | Time |
|---|---|---|---|---|---|---|---|
| CNN | 99.16% | 100.00% | 97.71% | 98.84% | 100.00% | 100.00% | 566.7 s |
| VGG16 | 99.67% | 99.28% | 96.92% | 98.01% | 99.58% | 99.94% | 380.4 s |
| MobileNet | 99.72% | 99.24% | 100.00% | 99.62% | 99.56% | 99.99% | 350.1 s |

The impact of the significant component in preprocessing and architecture is presented as an ablation study, as shown in Table 2. Note that *Dropout* has the least impact across the models. *Resize* process impacts slightly more than *Batch* normalization in enhancing the results. Nonetheless, CNN is the most affected model since it has been trained from scratch. Otherwise, the ablation study suggests low significance compared to the full models.

**Table 2.** Ablation study of each model on without image *Resize*, *Dropout* layer, or *Batch* normalization

| | CNN | | | MobileNet | | | VGG16 | | |
|---|---|---|---|---|---|---|---|---|---|
| | Resize | Dropout | Batch | Resize | Dropout | Batch | Resize | Dropout | Batch |
| Accuracy | 96.36% | 96.36% | 97.95% | 98.88% | 99.72% | 99.53% | 98.74% | 99.58% | 98.74% |
| Precision | 91.55% | 90.36% | 94.57% | 98.85% | 99.62% | 98.82% | 97.03% | 99.24% | 97.03% |
| Recall | 99.24% | 100.00% | 100.00% | 98.09% | 99.62% | 100.00% | 99.62% | 99.62% | 99.62% |
| F1 Score | 95.24% | 95.27% | 97.28% | 98.47% | 99.62% | 99.43% | 98.31% | 99.43% | 98.31% |
| Specificity | 94.70% | 94.26% | 96.67% | 99.34% | 99.78% | 99.31% | 98.23% | 99.56% | 98.23% |
| AUC-ROC | 99.60% | 99.76% | 99.93% | 99.90% | 99.99% | 99.92% | 99.82% | 99.99% | 99.82% |

We compared our proposed MobileNet-based approach with several existing methods, including traditional classifiers like SVM with handcrafted HOG features and other deep learning models (Table 3). The proposed MobileNet-based model outperforms other models in the past studies in terms of Accuracy, Recall, F1-score, and AUC-ROC. In contrast to traditional SVM classifiers that depend on handcrafted feature extraction, MobileNet learns and extracts relevant spatial features directly from the image data, resulting in significantly better performance and scalability.

**Table 3.** Comparison of MobileNet with existing CNN-based and traditional models

| Model | Accuracy | Precision | Recall | F1-Score | Specificity | AUC-ROC |
|---|---|---|---|---|---|---|
| CNN, 2020 [6] | 97% | - | - | - | - | - |
| CutPaste, 2021 [1] | - | - | - | - | - | 86.55% |
| VGG16, 2021 [16] | 99% | - | - | - | - | - |
| CNN, 2023 [15] | 96% | - | - | - | - | - |
| RestNet18, 2023 [10] | 94% | - | - | 70% | - | - |
| CNN, 2024 [12] | 83% | - | - | - | - | - |
| Proposed MobileNet | 99.72% | 99.24% | 100.00% | 99.62% | 99.56% | 99.99% |

# 5   Conclusions

This study successfully achieved its objectives by evaluating deep learning models for the automated detection of defects in metal castings. The proposed system employing MobileNet architecture demonstrated superior performance, achieving 99.5% accuracy with 100% recall while maintaining computational efficiency (350.1 s training, 4.8 s testing). This efficiency makes MobileNet especially suitable for real-time or edge deployment. Particularly, our key contributions in this study include:

- Comparative analysis of a custom-built and trained CNN model with training pretrained models, VGG16 and MobileNet.
- Featured models in multiple metrics to demonstrate efficiency and robustness compared to previous studies.
- Demonstrating the advantages of transfer learning on MobileNet over both custom CNNs and larger architectures like VGG16 on real-life dataset.

These findings significantly advance automated visual inspection capabilities, demonstrating that lightweight architectures can outperform conventional models for specific industrial applications and are suitable for real-time deployment in resource-constrained manufacturing environments. Nonetheless, this study falls short in testing the models' ability to generalize. Furthermore, incorporating misclassification analysis can enhance the interpretability of different models. Future work should focus on evaluating the models on multiple datasets and using explainable AI to understand the behaviour. Additionally, integrating localization capabilities and developing adaptive learning mechanisms for new defect types will level up the paradigm.

# References


1. Block, S.B., da Silva, R.D., Dorini, L.B., Minetto, R.: Inspection of imprint defects in stamped metal surfaces using deep learning and tracking. IEEE Trans. Industr. Electron. **68**(5), 4498–4507 (2021)
2. Chandola, V., Banerjee, A., Kumar, V.: Anomaly detection: a survey. ACM Comput. Surv. **41**(3), 1–58 (2009)
3. Dabhi, R. (2020). https://www.kaggle.com/datasets/ravirajsinh45/real-life-industrial-dataset-of-casting-product. Accessed 11 Oct 2025
4. Dwivedi, S.K., Vishwakarma, M., Soni, P.A.: Advances and researches on non destructive testing: a review. Mater. Today **5**(2), 3690–3698 (2018)
5. Hai, C., Wu, Y., Zhang, H., Meng, F., Tan, D., Yang, M.: Approach for automatic defect detection in aluminum casting x-ray images using deep learning and gain-adaptive multi-scale retinex. J. Nondestruct. Eval. **43**(1) (2024)
6. Heger, J., Desai, G., El Abdine, M.Z.: Anomaly detection in formed sheet metals using convolutional autoencoders. Procedia CIRP **93**, 1281–1285 (2020)
7. Howard, A.G., et al.: MobileNets: efficient convolutional neural networks for mobile vision applications. arXiv preprint arXiv:1704.04861 (2017)

8. Jezek, S., Jonak, M., Burget, R., Dvorak, P., Skotak, M.: Deep learning-based defect detection of metal parts: evaluating current methods in complex conditions. In: 2021 13th International Congress on Ultra Modern Telecommunications and Control Systems and Workshops (ICUMT). IEEE (2021)

9. Jezek, S., Jonak, M., Burget, R., Dvorak, P., Skotak, M.: Anomaly detection for real-world industrial applications: benchmarking recent self-supervised and pre-trained methods. In: 2022 14th International Congress on Ultra Modern Telecommunications and Control Systems and Workshops (ICUMT). IEEE (2022)

10. Jung, B., You, H., Lee, S.: Anomaly candidate extraction and detection for automatic quality inspection of metal casting products using high-resolution images. J. Manuf. Syst. **67**, 229–241 (2023)

11. Kharitonov, A., Nahhas, A., Pohl, M., Turowski, K.: Comparative analysis of machine learning models for anomaly detection in manufacturing. Procedia Comput. Sci. **200**, 1288–1297 (2022)

12. Kumar, P., Shreyas, M.S.: Anomaly detection for real-world industry manufactured products using computer vision. In: 2024 2nd International Conference on Intelligent Data Communication Technologies and Internet of Things (IDCIoT), pp. 981–987. IEEE (2024)

13. LeCun, Y., Bottou, L., Bengio, Y., Haffner, P.: Gradient-based learning applied to document recognition. Proc. IEEE **86**(11), 2278–2324 (1998)

14. Mattera, G., Nele, L.: Machine learning approaches for real-time process anomaly detection in wire arc additive manufacturing. Int. J. Adv. Manuf. Technol. **137**(5–6), 2863–2888 (2025)

15. Modir, A., Casterman, A., Tansel, I.: Detection of anomalies in additively manufactured metal parts using CNN and LSTM networks. Recent Progress Mater. **05**(03), 1–20 (2023)

16. Nagy, A., Czúni, L.: Detecting object defects with fusioning convolutional Siamese neural networks. In: Proceedings of the 16th International Joint Conference on Computer Vision, Imaging and Computer Graphics Theory and Applications. SCITEPRESS - Science and Technology Publications (2021)

17. Nanda, P., Rout, D., Kumari, S.: Multi-class skin cancer detection using CNN-architecture based deep learning models. Procedia Comput. Sci. **260**, 226–235 (2025)

18. Palit Sagar, S.: Modern ultrasonic technique for defect detection in cast materials (2008)

19. Rebuffel, V., Sood, S., Blakeley, B.: Defect detection method in digital radiography for porosity in magnesium castings. Materials Evaluation, ECNDT (2006)

20. Simonyan, K., Zisserman, A.: Very deep convolutional networks for large-scale image recognition. arXiv preprint arXiv:1409.1556 (2014)

# Medical Imaging

# MCAF-SkinNet : Multi-modal Cross-Attention Fusion for Skin Disease Classification Using Vision Models and Dermatology-Specific Embeddings

Routhu Srinivasa Rao[✉], Aradhana Mishra, and Sanjay Swain

CureBay, Bhubaneswar 751022, Odisha, India
{routhu.srinivasa,aradhana.mishra,sanjay.swain}@curebay.com

**Abstract.** Accurate classification of skin diseases from clinical images remains a major challenge in medical AI due to variations in skin tones, lesion appearance, lighting conditions, and the scarcity of high-quality labeled datasets for rare conditions. We present MCAF-SkinNet, a novel multimodal framework for skin disease classification that fuses general vision-language representations (SigLIP), biomedical vision-language embeddings (BiomedCLIP), and dermatology-specific expert embeddings (Google Derm Foundation). A bidirectional cross-attention mechanism aligns modality-specific representations, and a learnable gating unit emphasizes clinically salient features. Evaluated on the Fitzpatrick17k dataset spanning 114 skin disease classes, MCAF-SkinNet outperforms strong CNN and Transformer baselines and demonstrates consistent gains across both rare and common conditions. Extensive ablation confirms the complementary nature of each modality and the efficacy of cross-attention fusion.

**Keywords:** Skin disease classification · Multimodal learning · Cross-attention · Vision-language models · Dermatology AI

## 1 Introduction

Skin diseases are among the most widespread human health concerns, yet specialist access remains limited, especially in rural and underserved regions. Recent advances in deep learning and vision-language models (VLMs) offer potential for automated diagnosis. However, while general-purpose VLMs (e.g., SigLIP [6], BiomedCLIP [8]) show broad generalization, they often lack dermatology-specific expertise. Conversely, domain-specific models (e.g., Google Derm [4]) provide medical relevance but have limited generalization.

Early efforts in automated dermatology largely relied on convolutional neural networks (CNNs) trained on benchmark datasets such as ISIC and DermNet [2,7]. Although these approaches achieved dermatologist-level accuracy

© The Author(s), under exclusive license to Springer Nature Switzerland AG 2026
S. Mitra et al. (Eds.): PReMI 2025, LNCS 16358, pp. 269–277, 2026.
https://doi.org/10.1007/978-3-032-18480-1_27

on specific tasks, their performance degraded when applied to unseen populations or imaging conditions, highlighting limitations in robustness and domain adaptation. Subsequent advances in multimodal learning have enabled models to integrate visual and textual cues, enhancing interpretability and cross-domain understanding. Vision-language models like BiomedCLIP and SigLIP [6,8] have therefore attracted attention for their ability to transfer semantic knowledge across image domains. However, their direct application to dermatology remains underexplored, often constrained by limited dermatology-specific training data and lack of fine-grained cross-modal alignment.

Parallel efforts, such as Google's Derm and other large-scale CNN-based models [5], have demonstrated the efficacy of training on millions of dermatology images. While these systems excel in accuracy, they tend to underperform in adaptability and contextual reasoning compared to modern transformer-based architectures. Recent multimodal fusion strategies have been proposed in the broader medical imaging literature, ranging from early and late fusion to mid-level feature concatenation [1]. Yet, few have leveraged bidirectional cross-attention or dynamic gating mechanisms specifically tailored for skin disease diagnosis, leaving an opportunity for more adaptive fusion frameworks.

To address these gaps, we propose MCAF-SkinNet, a multi-modal fusion framework that combines the strengths of both vision-language and dermatology-specialized models. Our architecture employs bidirectional cross-attention transformers and a gated attention module to learn richer, more clinically relevant feature representations. Following are the contributions of the proposed work.

- Introduction of a multi-modal bidirectional cross-attention mechanism for aligning general and dermatology-specific feature spaces.
- Use of gated attention fusion to dynamically filter and prioritize clinically relevant features.
- Demonstration of the benefits of combining vision-language models with domain-specific models for skin disease classification (Fig. 1).

## 2 Proposed Work

The proposed research presents a robust and comprehensive multimodal deep learning architecture aimed at classifying skin conditions into 114 clinically meaningful categories. This model combines visual features from two complementary pretrained vision encoders with domain-specific dermatological embeddings, introducing advanced feature fusion strategies, imbalance-aware optimization, and precision-focused evaluation.

### 2.1 Dataset Curation and Preprocessing

The Fitzpatrick17k [3] dataset comprises clinical images of skin conditions spanning 114 disease classes. Each image is paired with dermatology-specific embeddings extracted using the Google Derm Foundation model, which encapsulates

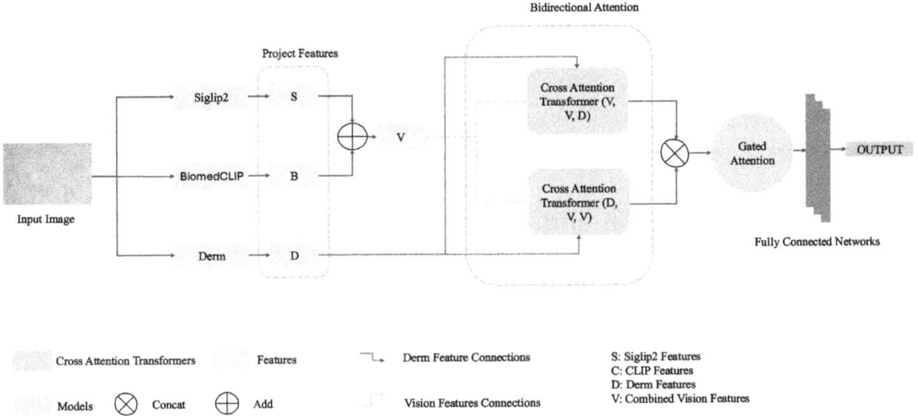


**Fig. 1.** Architecture of the proposed work

expert-level diagnostic knowledge. Augmentations include geometric (random horizontal flip, random rotation), photometric (brightness, contrast) and random cropping using Albumentations. The data is split 80:20 into training and testing, with 20% of the training data reserved for validation (final split: 64% train, 16% val, 20% test). A WeightedRandomSampler is used to mitigate class imbalance.

## 2.2 Multimodal Feature Extraction and Representation

Our architecture is composed of three distinct feature extractors, each targeting a unique modality:

**Primary Visual Stream (SigLIP).** We employ SigLIP (Sigmoid Language-Image Pretraining) as the main visual encoder (siglip2-base-patch16-224), which leverages vision-language pretraining to extract semantically rich image embeddings. The SigLIP encoder outputs a 768-dimensional embedding that encapsulates both visual texture and semantic content, which is further refined using a feedforward projection head with dropout and LayerNorm to yield a 256-dimensional latent representation.

**Auxiliary Visual Stream (BiomedCLIP ViT-B/16).** To enrich the visual feature space, we integrate BiomedCLIP—a domain-specific adaptation of CLIP trained on biomedical image-text pairs—using the ViT-B/16 vision transformer backbone. BiomedCLIP's image encoder generates a 512-dimensional representation tailored to medical imaging tasks, which is projected into the same latent space as the SigLIP features. This dual-stream vision approach enhances generalization by capturing both biomedical visual semantics and complementary cross-modal information.

**Dermatology Embedding Stream.** Each image is associated with a 6144-dimensional dermatology embedding derived from the Google Derm Foundation model. These embeddings encode medical semantics such as disease severity, clinical features, and lesion types. They are projected through two dense layers into a 256-dimensional vector to align with the visual streams for joint processing.

### 2.3   Fusion Mechanism and Attention Modeling

To effectively integrate the three modalities, we implement a cross-attention-based fusion mechanism and a gating unit:

**Bidirectional Cross-Attention Fusion.** We utilize two multi-head self-attention modules for bidirectional interaction: In the first transformer, the combined vision features query the dermatology-specific features, allowing the model to emphasize clinically important regions based on domain expertise. In the second transformer, the dermatology features query the vision features, enabling the specialized features to adapt and align with general visual patterns. This two-way interaction facilitates deeper and more nuanced feature learning.

**Gated Feature Fusion.** Post attention, the resulting attended vectors are concatenated and passed through a learned gating unit. The gating mechanism dynamically weighs the contributions from each stream based on feature confidence and relevance, ensuring optimal fusion. The output is a 512-dimensional fused vector used for final classification.

### 2.4   Classification Head

Following cross-attention and gating, the fused feature vector $\mathbf{z} \in \mathbb{R}^{512}$ is fed to a two-stage multilayer perceptron (MLP) that performs the final classification. The MLP first projects $\mathbf{z}$ back onto itself (`Linear(512 → 512)`) and applies `LayerNorm`, `GELU` activation and 30% dropout for regularisation. A second projection halves the dimensionality (`Linear(512 → 256)`) before a final `LayerNorm`, `GELU`, and 15% dropout lead into the output layer `Linear(256 → `$N_{\text{classes}}$`)`. During training, two auxiliary heads—one attached to the combined vision stream and one to the dermatology stream—provide additional cross-entropy supervision. This multitask scheme stabilises optimisation and encourages each modality to retain class-discriminative information even when the other modalities are noisy or unavailable.

## 3   Experimentation and Results

### 3.1   Experimental Setup

We implement MCFA-SkinNet using PyTorch 2.1, training on one NVIDIA RTX 4090 GPUs with mixed precision. We use AdamW (lr = 1e−4), cosine learning rate decay, and batch size 32. Training is run for up to 50 epochs with early stopping based on validation F1-score. Focal loss is employed to address class imbalance, which is prevalent in both the full 114-class and top-20 class subsets. For evaluation, we report the macro-averaged F1 score, overall accuracy, and top-2 and top-3 accuracy, which collectively capture both balanced classification performance and clinical relevance in scenarios where top predictions are used for decision support.

**Table 1.** Test Results for Pretrained Models with 114 classes

| Model | F1 Score | Accuracy | Top-2 Acc | Top-3 Acc |
| --- | --- | --- | --- | --- |
| EfficientNetV2-B0 | 0.3463 | 0.3716 | 0.4785 | 0.5382 |
| MobileNetV2 | 0.3300 | 0.3499 | 0.4576 | 0.5197 |
| ResNet50 | 0.2854 | 0.3242 | 0.4349 | 0.5012 |
| InceptionV3 | 0.2445 | 0.2657 | 0.3615 | 0.4287 |
| ViT-Base (patch16-224) | 0.4140 | 0.4361 | 0.5627 | 0.6337 |
| Swin-Base (patch4-window7) | 0.4947 | 0.5140 | 0.6260 | 0.6857 |
| ConvNeXt-Base | 0.5125 | 0.5275 | 0.6385 | 0.6976 |
| BEiT-Base (patch16-224) | 0.2542 | 0.2916 | 0.3857 | 0.4501 |
| DeiT-Base (patch16-224) | 0.4257 | 0.4487 | 0.5630 | 0.6331 |
| CoaT-Lite Small | 0.2897 | 0.3337 | 0.4516 | 0.5209 |

### 3.2 Evaluation on Pretrained Baseline Models

To establish a performance benchmark, we evaluate a diverse set of pre-trained models across CNN-based backbones(ResNet50, EfficientNetV2-B0, MobileNetV2, InceptionV3, ConvNeXt-Base.) and Transformer-based backbones (ViT-Base, Swin-Base, DeiT-Base, BEiT-Base, CoaT-Lite.)

All models are fine-tuned end-to-end on the Fitzpatrick17k dataset. Results for the 114-class setting are presented in Table 1. ConvNeXt-Base and Swin Transformer achieve the highest F1-scores (0.5125 and 0.4947 respectively), significantly outperforming conventional CNNs such as ResNet50 (0.2854). Transformer-based models such as ViT and DeiT demonstrate competitive Top-3 accuracy, indicating better generalization across visually ambiguous cases. To further probe the generalization capacity under class imbalance reduction, we repeat this evaluation on the top-20 most frequent disease classes (Table 2). Similar trends are observed, with ConvNeXt-Base again achieving the best performance (F1 = 0.6004), followed closely by Swin Transformer (F1 = 0.5920).

### 3.3 Ablation Study: Fusion Strategies and Component Analysis

To quantify the contribution of each modality and fusion strategy within MCAF-SkinNet, we conduct an extensive ablation study using both 114-class and top-

**Table 2.** Test Results for Pretrained Models with top 20 classes

| Backbone | Accuracy | F1 | Top-2 Acc. | Top-3 Acc. |
|---|---|---|---|---|
| ConvNeXt-Base | 0.6155 | 0.6004 | 0.7493 | 0.8141 |
| Swin-Base ($4\times7/224$) | 0.6021 | 0.5920 | 0.7465 | 0.8141 |
| DeiT-Base/16 | 0.5310 | 0.5195 | 0.6761 | 0.7613 |
| ViT-Base/16 | 0.5042 | 0.4906 | 0.6592 | 0.7472 |
| EfficientNetV2-B0 | 0.4563 | 0.4446 | 0.5901 | 0.6690 |
| ResNet-50 | 0.4352 | 0.4230 | 0.5845 | 0.6810 |
| MobileNetV2 | 0.4310 | 0.4086 | 0.5873 | 0.6725 |
| CoaT-Lite-Small | 0.4218 | 0.3986 | 0.5754 | 0.6697 |
| BEiT-Base/16 | 0.3993 | 0.3835 | 0.5521 | 0.6430 |
| Inception-v3 | 0.3296 | 0.3054 | 0.4669 | 0.5754 |

**Table 3.** Ablation Study Results (Concat and Cross-Attention Fusion) with 114 classes

| Model | F1 Score | Accuracy | Top-2 Acc | Top-3 Acc |
|---|---|---|---|---|
| *Cross-Attention Fusion* | | | | |
| BiomedCLIP + SigLIP2 + Derm | 0.6146 | 0.6321 | 0.7491 | 0.7933 |
| *Concatenation Fusion* | | | | |
| SigLIP2 | 0.2945 | 0.3281 | 0.3761 | 0.4339 |
| BiomedCLIP | 0.4800 | 0.4464 | 0.5869 | 0.6284 |
| Derm | 0.5934 | 0.6134 | 0.7287 | 0.7815 |
| SigLIP2 + BiomedCLIP | 0.4552 | 0.4794 | 0.5710 | 0.6197 |
| SigLIP2 + Derm | 0.6041 | 0.6203 | 0.7367 | 0.7890 |
| BiomedCLIP + Derm | 0.6015 | 0.6188 | 0.7294 | 0.7860 |
| BiomedCLIP + SigLIP2 + Derm | 0.6022 | 0.6215 | 0.7466 | 0.7910 |

20 class settings. The modalities evaluated include SigLIP, BiomedCLIP, Derm embeddings.

Two fusion strategies are compared: simple concatenation and the proposed cross-attention fusion. As shown in Table 3, using SigLIP alone provides a weak baseline (F1 = 0.2945). Adding dermatology embeddings significantly improves performance (F1 = 0.5934), highlighting the relevance of domain-specific features. Cross-attention fusion of all three modalities achieves the best results (F1 = 0.6146, Top-3 = 0.7933), demonstrating the complementary strengths of general and medical encoders.

In the top-20 class setting (Table 4), the performance gap becomes even more pronounced. Our proposed cross-attention fusion (SigLIP + BiomedCLIP + Derm) achieves the highest F1 score (0.7126) and Top-3 accuracy (0.8690), surpassing all concatenation-based baselines. Figure 2(a) highlights the model's

**Table 4.** Ablation Study Results (Concat and Cross-Attention Fusion) with top 20 classes

| Fusion Strategy | F1 Score | Accuracy | Top-2 Acc | Top-3 Acc |
|---|---|---|---|---|
| *Cross-Attention Fusion (Proposed)* | | | | |
| SigLIP + BiomedCLIP + Derm | 0.7126 | 0.7204 | 0.8239 | 0.8690 |
| *Concatenation Fusion (Baselines)* | | | | |
| SigLIP only | 0.3828 | 0.4014 | 0.5401 | 0.6218 |
| BiomedCLIP only | 0.5888 | 0.5993 | 0.7190 | 0.7725 |
| Derm only | 0.6898 | 0.6965 | 0.8169 | 0.8718 |
| SigLIP + BiomedCLIP | 0.6160 | 0.6239 | 0.7282 | 0.7937 |
| SigLIP + Derm | 0.6833 | 0.6880 | 0.8162 | 0.8690 |
| BiomedCLIP + Derm | 0.6982 | 0.7042 | 0.8232 | 0.8768 |
| SigLIP + BiomedCLIP + Derm | 0.6909 | 0.6965 | 0.8190 | 0.8775 |

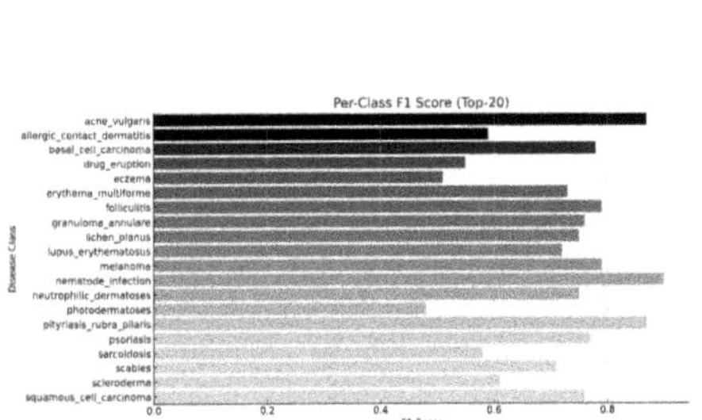

(a) Per-class F1 scores of MCAF-SkinNet across the top-20 most frequent skin disease classes in the Fitzpatrick17k dataset.

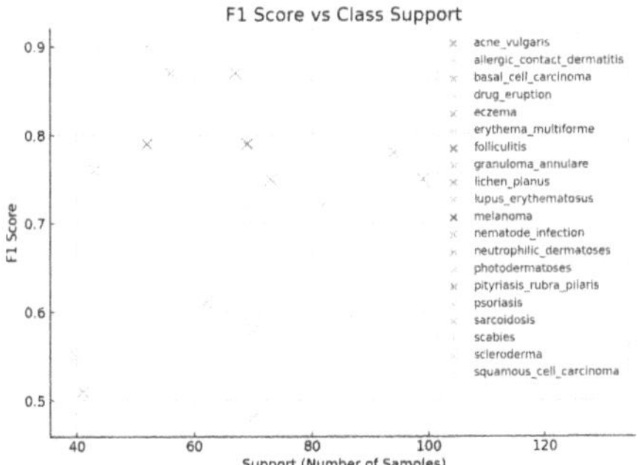

(b) Relationship between class support and F1 score for MCAF-SkinNet on the top-20 disease subset.

**Fig. 2.** Evaluation of MCAF-SkinNet on the Fitzpatrick17k top-20 classes: (a) Per-class F1 scores, (b) F1 vs. class support.

per-class F1 scores, reflecting its consistency across the top-20 disease categories. This demonstrates not only balanced classification performance but also robustness to inter-class variability. Meanwhile, Fig. 2(b) shows the correlation between class support and F1 score. The ability of MCAF-SkinNet to maintain high F1 scores even on low-support classes (e.g. pityriasis rubra pilaris, nematode infection) indicates strong generalization and minimal bias towards data-rich classes.

The experimental results consistently demonstrate the effectiveness of our proposed design. Pretrained transformer architectures, particularly ConvNeXt and Swin, exhibit superior generalization performance compared to traditional CNN-based models, highlighting the importance of hierarchical feature representation and larger receptive fields in complex classification tasks. Furthermore, the incorporation of domain-aware encoders such as BiomedCLIP and dermatology-specific embeddings proves critical in medical imaging scenarios, where general-purpose vision encoders may fail to capture subtle diagnostic cues. Notably, the proposed cross-attention fusion strategy significantly outperforms simple concatenation methods, underscoring the importance of dynamic interaction and contextual integration across modalities. Collectively, these findings validate the architectural choices underlying MCAF-SkinNet and provide strong empirical support for multimodal, attention-guided learning in large-scale skin disease classification.

## 4    Conclusion

We introduced MCAF-SkinNet, a multimodal deep learning framework tailored for large-scale skin disease classification using the Fitzpatrick17k dataset. By fusing features from general-purpose (SigLIP), biomedical (BiomedCLIP), and dermatology-specific (Google Derm Foundation) encoders, the model captures diverse visual and clinical priors. A cross-attention-based fusion mechanism is employed to enable dynamic interaction between modalities, yielding improved generalization across 114 diverse disease classes.

Extensive experiments demonstrate that MCAF-SkinNet consistently outperforms conventional CNNs and strong Vision Transformer baselines. Ablation studies validate the complementary contributions of each modality and the superiority of cross-attention fusion over simple concatenation. Future directions include incorporating clinical metadata and leveraging caption-guided supervision to bridge the gap between visual features and diagnostic reasoning.

## References


1. Das, A., Agarwal, V., Shetty, N.: Comparative analysis of multimodal architectures for effective skin lesion detection using clinical and image data. Front. Artif. Intell. **8**, 1608837 (2025)
2. Esteva, A., Kuprel, B., Novoa, R.A., et al.: Dermatologist-level classification of skin cancer with deep neural networks. Nature **542**(7639), 115–118 (2017). https://doi.org/10.1038/nature21056
3. Groh, M., et al.: Evaluating deep neural networks trained on clinical images in dermatology with the FITZPATRICK 17k dataset. In: Proceedings of the IEEE/CVF Conference on Computer Vision and Pattern Recognition, pp. 1820–1828 (2021)
4. Health, G.: Derm foundation model (2023). https://developers.google.com/health-ai-developer-foundations/derm-foundation/model-card. Accessed 29 June 2025
5. Liu, Y., Jain, A., Eng, C., et al.: A deep learning system for differential diagnosis of skin diseases. Nat. Med. **26**(6), 900–908 (2020). https://doi.org/10.1038/s41591-020-0842-3

6. Touvron, H., Joulin, A., Jégou, H., et al.: Scaling vision-language models with SIGLIP. arXiv preprint (2023). https://arxiv.org/abs/2303.15343
7. Tschandl, P., Rosendahl, C., Kittler, H.: The ham10000 dataset: a large collection of multi-source dermatoscopic images of common pigmented skin lesions. Sci. Data **5**, 180161 (2018). https://doi.org/10.1038/sdata.2018.161
8. Zhang, H., et al.: BiomedClip: learning biomedical visual-language representations from paired images and text. https://huggingface.co/microsoft/BiomedCLIP-PubMedBERT_256-vit_base_patch16_224 (2023). Accessed 15 July 2025

# Classification with Auxiliary Representation Learning for Detecting Breast Cancer


Riddhasree Bhattacharyya[1,2] , Shramana Dey[2(✉)] , Unneta Chatterjee[1] , and Sushmita Mitra[2]

[1] Department of Computer Science and Engineering, University of Calcutta, Kolkata, India
[2] Machine Intelligence Unit, Indian Statistical Institute, Kolkata, India
shramanadey96@gmail.com



**Abstract.** Breast cancer is a leading cause of mortality among women worldwide, highlighting the urgent need for early screening and accurate detection. Although ultrasound imaging is widely used for its safety and accessibility, the scarcity of expert radiologists calls for reliable automated solutions. This study addresses the challenge of tumor classification in limited data settings from breast ultrasound images. The proposed Classification with Auxiliary Representation Learning (CARL) framework is a unified, one-stage learning system that integrates self-supervised representation learning with lesion-aware classification. Unlike existing two-stage or purely supervised methods, CARL learns semantically rich features while focusing on clinically relevant tumor regions. The framework is encoder-agnostic and improves performance across both CNN and ViT architectures. Extensive experimentation demonstrates that the CARL framework outperforms state-of-the-art models by a notable margin across all metrics. Grad-CAM visualization corroborates that the model bases its prediction on actual tumor lesions, while improving clinical reliability and interpretability.

**Keywords:** Self-Supervised Learning · Ultrasound Images · Representation Learning · Classification · Breast Cancer


## 1 Introduction

Breast cancer is one of the leading causes of death in women, comprising 11.6% of all cancer cases [4]. Therefore, early screening of patients is necessary to reduce the mortality rate and increase longevity. Any tumor can be categorized primarily as benign or malignant. Benign tumors, being non-cancerous, typically possess well-defined borders with slow growth. Malignant tumors are life-threatening and cancerous, typically characterized by rapid growth, irregular borders, and the ability to invade surrounding tissues [3]. Figure 1 shows representative breast ultrasound images of benign and malignant tumors.

R. Bhattacharyya and S. Dey—These authors contributed equally to this work.



S. Mitra et al. (Eds.): PReMI 2025, LNCS 16358, pp. 278–285, 2026.
https://doi.org/10.1007/978-3-032-18480-1_28

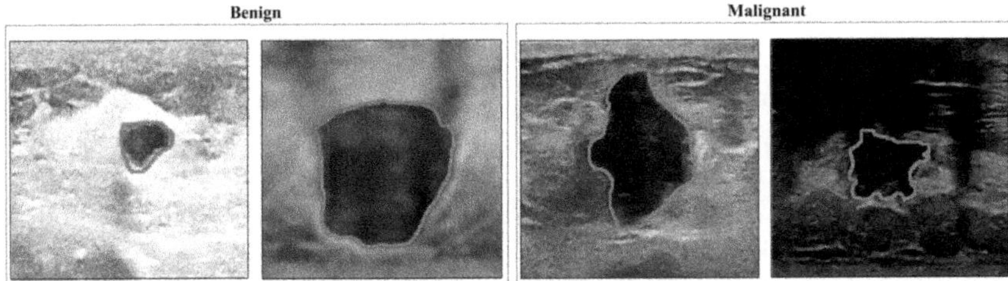


**Fig. 1.** Representative breast ultrasound images of benign and malignant tumors, with red boundary boxes marking the lesion contours. (Color figure online)

Ultrasound imaging is a preferred method for early breast cancer screening due to its non-invasive, radiation-free, and cost-effective nature [5]. However, the limited availability of expert radiologists and task subjectivity highlight the need for robust Computer-Aided Diagnosis (CAD) systems to assist in the analysis of images, reduce radiologists' workload, and ensure timely treatment.

Deep learning (DL) [12] has become the status quo in the development of CAD systems, due to their automatic feature extraction capabilities. Among DL-based architectures, Convolutional Neural Networks (CNNs) [11] and Vision Transformers (ViTs) [7] are the most common in medical image analysis. Although CNNs excel at capturing local spatial features, ViTs are effective in capturing the global context via self-attention, *albeit* requiring more data. Despite the growing demand for automated screening systems, major challenges persist. These include class imbalance, data scarcity, and variation in image quality.

Recent research has focused on developing DL models for analysing breast ultrasound images. Although some researchers focused on classifying breast ultrasound images [2,9,15], others have worked on segmenting lesions from breast ultrasound images [16–18]. Efficient Neural Architecture Search [2], combined with Bayesian optimization, has been used to optimize the depth of the network and hyperparameters for better performance. The Multiple Instance Learning paradigm was used for breast ultrasound classification [15], where images were divided into patches, each pseudo-labeled during training. The weighted patch-level labels were then aggregated to identify valuable information. However, the pseudo-labeling process introduced noise, leading to sub-par performance. The Retrieval-Augmented Medical Diagnosis System was introduced in [9], where DL was integrated with a retrieval-augmented mechanism to improve performance.

The researchers designed hybrid CNN and ViT architectures to complement their individual shortcomings. Multi-frequency and Multi-scale Interactive CNN-Transformer Hybrid Network [17], Hierarchical Attention U-Net [18] and Global Local Fusion Network [16] combined the strengths of both CNNs and ViTs, for efficient segmentation of ultrasound images.

However, existing literature lacks focus on enhancing performance of DL models in limited data regimes, where most of these models tend to overfit leading to poor generalization. In this context, incorporating self-supervised learning-based auxiliary objective to the primary classification objective can help in learning more generalizable features [8]. The traditional Self-supervised learning (SSL) paradigm [8,14] aims to perform classification in two stages. First, the DL model is trained to learn effective feature representation from unlabelled data by designing suitable auxiliary tasks. Then, the pre-trained model is fine-tuned for the target task using a limited amount of labeled data.

This article proposes the unified, one-stage Classification with Auxiliary Representation Learning (CARL) framework for detecting benign and malignant tumors from breast ultrasound images, as illustrated in Fig. 2.

1. A strategically chosen SSL approach generates rich, low-level, semantically aligned features to effectively address data scarcity for classification.
2. The proposed encoder-agnostic framework enhances performance in both CNN and ViT encoders.
3. Incorporating fine-grained lesion annotations with image-level labels, while integrating SSL with lesion-aware training, makes the model focus on clinically relevant tumor features. This, in turn, significantly improves classification accuracy.
4. The CARL framework, trained on a publicly available dataset with limited data annotation, significantly outperforms state-of-the-art classifier models. It achieves performance gains of 7% and 3% in accuracy for EfficientNet and ViT-based models, respectively.

The remainder of this paper is organized as follows. Section 2 introduces the proposed framework with the loss function and summarizes the experimental details. Section 3 presents the observed performance and provides a detailed analysis of the result. Finally, Sect. 4 concludes the article, indicating the future direction of research.

## 2   The CARL Framework

Let $\{(x_n, y_n, m_n)\}_{n=1}^{N}$ represent a set of $N$ breast ultrasound images, where $x_n \in \mathbb{R}^{H \times W \times C}$ denotes the $n$-th ultrasound image, $y_n \in \{\texttt{Benign}, \texttt{Malignant}\}$ corresponds to the class label, and $m_n$ is the binary segmentation mask. Here, $H \times W \times C$ refers to the height, width, and channel dimensions of the input image $x_n$. The goal is to learn a function that maps an input image $x_n$ to a predicted label $\hat{y}_n$, with $y_n \in \{\texttt{Benign}, \texttt{Malignant}\}$ representing tumor classes.

This classification task is addressed by the CARL framework, as illustrated in Fig. 2. It uses an encoder-decoder setup to optimize a combined objective function. Given the low variation in intensity distribution, irregular tumor morphology, and blurred boundaries in breast ultrasound images [18], CARL focuses on capturing semantically meaningful lesion features to accurately determine the predicted class label.

The encoder $\mathcal{E}_\phi(.)$ accepts both the original input image $x_n$ and its masked version $x_{n,masked}$, which is generated by randomly occluding $m\%$ of the regions

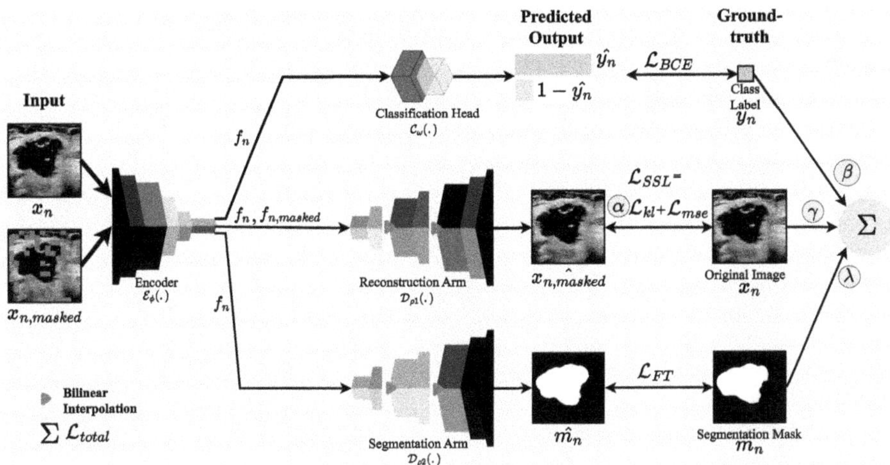


**Fig. 2.** Overview of CARL framework. Reconstruction and Segmentation Arms are excluded during inference.

in $x_n$. It extracts spatially reduced semantically rich feature representations, producing the encoded feature maps $f_n$ and $f_{n,masked}$, corresponding to $x_n$ and $x_{n,masked}$, respectively. The framework is encoder-agnostic, supporting integration with any standard backbone model, including CNNs, ViTs, among others.

The encoded feature map $f_n$ is then simultaneously passed to the classification head, reconstruction arm, and segmentation arm, while $f_{n,masked}$ is transmitted only to the reconstruction arm. The classification head $\mathcal{C}_\omega(.)$ consists of a Multilayer Perceptron (MLP) with a single output node. It processes $f_n$ to predict the class probability $\hat{y}_n$, denoting the chance that a tumor belongs to the benign or malignant category. The output optimizes the loss of binary cross entropy $\mathcal{L}_{BCE}$.

In the reconstruction arm, the decoder $\mathcal{D}_{\rho1}(.)$ uses bilinear interpolation for upsampling, followed by convolutional layers to progressively refine the upsampled (encoded) features $f_{n,masked}$, ultimately generating the reconstructed image $\hat{x_{n,masked}}$ to closely approximate the original image $x_n$.
The Mean Squared Error (MSE) loss $\mathcal{L}_{mse}$ [10] is computed between $x_n$ and $\hat{x_{n,masked}}$, specifically targeting the reconstruction of the occluded regions. The Kullback-Leibler (KL) divergence loss $\mathcal{L}_{kl}$ [10] is calculated between the feature distributions $f_n$ and $f_{n,masked}$, allowing the model to learn consistent feature representations even when parts of the input are missing.

The total self-supervised loss $\mathcal{L}_{SSL}$ is the combination of the MSE and KL divergence losses, given by

$$\mathcal{L}_{SSL} = \mathcal{L}_{mse} + \alpha\mathcal{L}_{kl}, \text{ where } \alpha \in [0, 0.5].$$

Here, $\alpha$ controls the contribution of the KL divergence. The combination of $\mathcal{L}_{SSL}$ and $\mathcal{L}_{BCE}$ aids in implicit regularization, preventing overfitting.

An auxiliary objective function is used to achieve segmentation, through the segmentation arm. It encourages the encoder to focus on relevant tumor features, to further enhance classification performance. It also optimizes the performance of the decoder $\mathcal{D}_{\rho 2}(.)$. In combination with the classification and self-supervised objectives, the segmentation objective leads to better representation learning. The predicted segmentation of the tumor $\hat{m}_n$ with respect to the input mask $m_n$ is computed using the Focal Tversky loss function $\mathcal{L}_{FT}$ [1]. The total loss $\mathcal{L}_{total}$ used for optimization of the CARL-framework is defined as

$$\mathcal{L}_{total} = \beta\mathcal{L}_{BCE} + \gamma\mathcal{L}_{SSL} + \lambda L_{FT}, \text{ where } \beta, \gamma, \lambda \in [0, 1], \tag{1}$$

with $\beta, \gamma, \lambda$ being hyperparameters that adjust the weight of each of the contributing losses.

The final classification is provided solely by $\mathcal{E}_\phi(.)$ followed by $\mathcal{C}_\omega(.)$, while the decoder aids in learning both low-level and lesion-specific features; thereby, enhancing representation in data-scarce scenarios.

## 3    Experimental Results and Discussion

The experiments were conducted on the QAMEBI [3] dataset, consisting of 232 breast tumour images, containing 109 benign and 123 malignant samples. The model was trained for 250 epochs using the AdamW optimizer, with a learning rate of $1e^{-4}$ and weight decay $1e^{-5}$. An exponential learning rate scheduler was used with a decay factor of 0.97. Early stopping was applied with a patience of 10 epochs. The model was evaluated using 5-fold cross-validation. The weights $\beta, \gamma, \lambda$ in $\mathcal{L}_{total}$ were chosen as 0.25, 0.25, and 0.75 respectively, after several experiments. The value of $\alpha$ was set as 0.1. All experiments were performed on a 16 GB NVIDIA Titan XP GPU.

The performance was evaluated using accuracy, precision, recall, and F1-score [6] for classification. Additionally, Dice score and IoU were reported to assess the segmentation mask output. Here we present the performance evaluation of the proposed CARL framework.

### 3.1    Ablations

The lightweight EfficientNet B2 and DeiT-small architectures were empirically chosen as the CNN and ViT encoders for our experimental study. Table 1 represents the ablation study, evaluating the impact of incorporating the auxiliary objectives (via the loss functions $\mathcal{L}_{SSL}$ and $\mathcal{L}_{FT}$) on the main classification objective. The fact that performance improved considerably from the baseline, for both CNN and ViT encoders, demonstrates the robustness of our framework. Further, the improvement in performance after adding $\mathcal{L}_{SSL}$ to $\mathcal{L}_{BCE}$ is much greater than adding $\mathcal{L}_{FT}$ to $(\mathcal{L}_{BCE} + \mathcal{L}_{SSL})$. This shows that even in the absence of pixel-level supervision, our framework performs very well. While the classification objective mainly focuses on high-level semantics, the SSL objective helps in low-level feature enrichment for a richer encoder.

**Table 1.** Ablation study, with both CNN and ViT encoders, on the test dataset.

| Encoder | Modules | | | Metrics | | | |
|---|---|---|---|---|---|---|---|
| | $\mathcal{L}_{BCE}$ | $\mathcal{L}_{SSL}$ | $\mathcal{L}_{FT}$ | Accuracy | Precision | Recall | F1 score |
| CNN | ✓ | | | $0.7029 \pm 0.1349$ | $0.7223 \pm 0.1482$ | $0.6993 \pm 0.1348$ | $0.6940 \pm 0.1383$ |
| | ✓ | ✓ | | $0.8571 \pm 0.0350$ | $0.8627 \pm 0.0315$ | $0.8559 \pm 0.0357$ | $0.8560 \pm 0.0359$ |
| | ✓ | ✓ | ✓ | $\mathbf{0.8857 \pm 0.0350}$ | $\mathbf{0.8952 \pm 0.0309}$ | $\mathbf{0.8837 \pm 0.0357}$ | $\mathbf{0.8844 \pm 0.0362}$ |
| ViT | ✓ | | | $0.7429 \pm 0.0700$ | $0.8191 \pm 0.0382$ | $0.7359 \pm 0.0722$ | $0.7189 \pm 0.0890$ |
| | ✓ | ✓ | | $0.8114 \pm 0.0519$ | $0.8609 \pm 0.0229$ | $0.8065 \pm 0.0542$ | $0.8012 \pm 0.0609$ |
| | ✓ | ✓ | ✓ | $\mathbf{0.8400 \pm 0.0256}$ | $\mathbf{0.8725 \pm 0.0163}$ | $\mathbf{0.8176 \pm 0.0322}$ | $\mathbf{0.8145 \pm 0.0358}$ |

Further, the heatmaps produced by Gradient-weighted Class Activation Map (Grad-CAM) [13] in Fig. 3 demonstrate that the addition of the auxiliary objectives help the CARL-framework to focus on the more discriminative features. The bounding boxes in Fig. 3(c) and (d) depict that CARL-framework is able to properly capture the features of the blurred boundaries of the tumour regions.

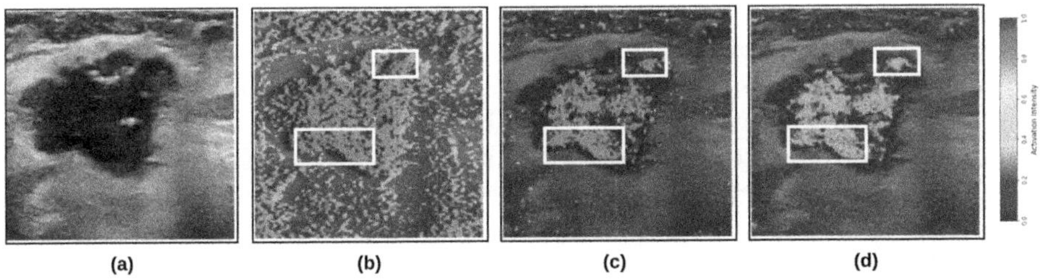


**Fig. 3.** Heatmaps produced by GradCAM for (a) the image, using CARL-framework when trained with (b) $\mathcal{L}_{BCE}$, (c) $\mathcal{L}_{BCE} + \mathcal{L}_{SSL}$, and (d) $\mathcal{L}_{BCE} + \mathcal{L}_{SSL} + \mathcal{L}_{FT}$.

## 3.2  Comparative Study

The classification performance of CARL-framework was compared using different state-of-the-art (SOTA) CNN and ViT-based encoder architectures. The comparative study is summarized in Table 2. It can be clearly observed from the table that the CARL-framework consistently outperforms the other models, over all the metrics, by a considerable margin. For clarity, the best and second-best performances are indicated using bold and italicized values, respectively. This shows that the traditional classification models are not able to learn generalizable features in this limited data scenario. On the other hand, the auxiliary objectives help the CARL-framework in learning robust features by acquiring more learning signals per image.

**Table 2.** Comparative study of CARL-Framework with other SOTA architectures for classification.

| Model | Accuracy | Precision | Recall | F1 score |
|---|---|---|---|---|
| DenseNet-161 | $0.8114 \pm 0.0592$ | $0.8680 \pm 0.0315$ | $0.8059 \pm 0.0610$ | $0.8001 \pm 0.0676$ |
| Resnet-50 | $0.7657 \pm 0.0128$ | $0.8349 \pm 0.0251$ | $0.7592 \pm 0.0124$ | $0.7499 \pm 0.0119$ |
| ViT-Tiny | $0.7714 \pm 0.0571$ | $0.8359 \pm 0.0190$ | $0.7654 \pm 0.0594$ | $0.7544 \pm 0.0727$ |
| Swin-Small | $0.7943 \pm 0.0619$ | $0.8493 \pm 0.0228$ | $0.7889 \pm 0.0644$ | $0.7809 \pm 0.0749$ |
| CARL-framework (CNN-based) | $\mathbf{0.8857 \pm 0.0350}$ | $\mathbf{0.8952 \pm 0.0309}$ | $\mathbf{0.8837 \pm 0.0357}$ | $\mathbf{0.8844 \pm 0.0362}$ |
| CARL-framework (ViT-based) | $0.8400 \pm 0.0256$ | $0.8729 \pm 0.0116$ | $0.8359 \pm 0.0269$ | $0.8347 \pm 0.0293$ |

# 4    Conclusion

Considering the difficulty in obtaining a large amount of training data and the challenges faced by DL models to achieve good performance in the limited data regime, a novel framework was developed to detect lesions from breast ultrasound images. In addition to being encoder-invariant and interpretable, the experimental results showed considerable improvement from the baseline; thus, demonstrating the robustness of the framework. This framework has the potential to serve as an effective tool for non-invasive breast cancer screening. In future, our aim is to perform rigorous experiments with inter-center datasets of ultrasound images, and also extend this framework to the grading of breast cancer.

**Acknowledgment.** This research was supported by J. C. Bose National Fellowship, sanction no. JCB/2020/000033 of S. Mitra.

# References


1. Abraham, N., Khan, N.M.: A novel focal Tversky loss function with improved attention U-Net for lesion segmentation. In: Proceedings of the International Symposium on Biomedical Imaging (ISBI), pp. 683–687. IEEE (2019)
2. Ahmed, M., Du, H., et al.: ENAS-B: combining ENAS with Bayesian optimization for automatic design of optimal CNN architectures for breast lesion classification from ultrasound images. Ultrason. Imaging **46**, 17–28 (2024)
3. Ardakani, A.A., Mohammadi, A., et al.: An open-access breast lesion ultra-sound image database: applicable in artificial intelligence studies. Comput. Biol. Med. **152**, 106438 (2023)
4. Bray, F., Laversanne, M., et al.: Global cancer statistics 2022: GLOBOCAN estimates of incidence and mortality worldwide for 36 cancers in 185 countries. CA: A Cancer J. Clin. **74** (2024). https://doi.org/10.3322/caac.21834
5. Cheng, H.D., Shan, J., et al.: Automated breast cancer detection and classification using Ultrasound images: a survey. Pattern Recogn. **43**, 299–317 (2010)
6. Dey, S., Dutta, P., et al.: Adaptive class learning to screen diabetic disorders in fundus images of eye. In: Proceedings of the International Conference on Pattern Recognition (ICPR), pp. 124–137. Springer (2024). https://doi.org/10.1007/978-3-031-78104-9_9

7. Dosovitskiy, A., Beyer, L., et al.: An image is worth 16x16 words: transformers for image recognition at scale. In: Proceedings for the International Conference on Learning Representations (ICLR) (2021)
8. Haghighi, F., Taher, M.R.H., et al.: Self-supervised learning for medical image analysis: discriminative, restorative, or adversarial? Med. Image Anal. **94**, 103086 (2024)
9. Johnson, E.T., Bande, J.K., et al.: Retrieval augmented medical diagnosis system. Biol. Methods Protocols **10**, bpaf017 (2025)
10. Kim, T., Oh, J., et al.: Comparing Kullback-Leibler divergence and mean squared error loss in knowledge distillation. In: Proceedings of the International Conference on International Joint Conference on Artificial Intelligence, IJCAI-21, pp. 2628–2635 (2021)
11. Krizhevsky, A., Sutskever, I., Hinton, G.E.: ImageNet classification with deep convolutional neural networks. Commun. ACM **60**, 84–90 (2017)
12. LeCun, Y., Bengio, Y., et al.: Deep learning. Nature **521**, 436–444 (2015)
13. Selvaraju, R.R., Cogswell, M., et al.: Grad-CAM: visual explanations from deep networks via gradient-based localization. In: Proceedings of the IEEE International Conference on Computer Vision (ICCV), pp. 618–626 (2017)
14. Shurrab, S., Duwairi, R.: Self-supervised learning methods and applications in medical imaging analysis: a survey. PeerJ Comput. Sci. **8**, e1045 (2022)
15. Struski, Ł, Janusz, S., et al.: Multiple instance learning for medical image classification based on instance importance. Biomed. Signal Process. Control **91**, 105874 (2024)
16. Sun, S., Fu, C., et al.: GLFNet: Global-Local Fusion Network for the segmentation in ultrasound images. Comput. Biol. Med. **171**, 108103 (2024)
17. Wu, R., Lu, X., et al.: MFMSNet: a multi-frequency and multi-scale interactive CNN-transformer hybrid network for breast ultrasound image segmentation. Comput. Biol. Med. **177**, 108616 (2024)
18. Zhang, H., Lian, J., et al.: HAU-Net: hybrid CNN-transformer for breast ultrasound image segmentation. Biomed. Signal Process. Control **87**, 105427 (2024)

# BiEncoder-ResMambaUNet: Dual Encoder Framework Leveraging Residual Mamba Blocks and Multi-level Semantic Convolutional Features for Polyp Segmentation


Sanjana Jhansi Ganji[1]([✉]), Panigrahi Srikanth[1], Kaushal Sambanna[1], and Routhu Srinivasa Rao[2]

[1] Department of Artificial Intelligence and Machine Learning (AI&ML), Chaitanya Bharathi Institute of Technology, Gandipet, Hyderabad 500075, India
`sanjanajhansi99@gmail.com`
[2] CureBay, Acharya Vihar, Bhubaneswar, Odisha, India



**Abstract.** Accurate segmentation of colorectal polyps is crucial for early cancer detection but remains challenging due to significant variability in appearance and indistinct boundaries. We propose BiEncoder-ResMambaUNet, a dual-encoder architecture designed to enhance segmentation accuracy and generalizability across diverse clinical settings. The first encoder leverages a pre-trained EfficientNetB4 to extract high-level semantic features, refined via Depthwise Separable Convolutions and a transformer block for improved global context. The second encoder, *ReSEVM*, integrates Residual, Squeeze-and-Excitation (SE), and VSS Mamba blocks to capture fine-grained textures and local details. A transformer-based fusion module merges complementary encoder features, while a gated decoder with adaptive skip connections reconstructs precise polyp boundaries. Experiments on Kvasir-SEG, CVC-ClinicDB, and BKAI-IGH show consistent outperformance over existing methods, with gains of 0.3% in Dice and 0.7% in Precision, underscoring the model's robustness and clinical reliability. github.com/Sanjana190/BiEncoder-ResMambaUnet.



**Keywords:** Polyp Segmentation · Deep Learning · Dual-Encoder Network · Transformer · VSS with Mamba and Medical Image Analysis


## 1 Introduction

Colorectal cancer remains the second leading cause of cancer related mortality worldwide, with around 2 million new cases every year. Early detection sig-


P. Srikanth, K. Sambanna, and R. S. Rao—These authors contributed equally to this work.





S. Mitra et al. (Eds.): PReMI 2025, LNCS 16358, pp. 286–295, 2026.
https://doi.org/10.1007/978-3-032-18480-1_29

nificantly improves patient outcomes; however, traditional colonoscopy is time-consuming, operator-dependent, and often fails to detect small, flat, or asymptomatic polyps, especially under challenging visual conditions. These limitations have driven the adoption of deep learning-based computer-aided diagnostic (CAD) systems, which offer real-time, automated polyp segmentation with high accuracy and consistency, thereby enhancing diagnostic efficiency and scalability across clinical settings. Conventional architectures like U-Net [1] along with its variants like Unet++ [2] and works including ResU-Net++ [3], HarDNet-MSEG [4], ColonSegNet [5] improved generalization using residual connections and works like DeepLabV3+ [6] introduced lightweight backbones using Atrous Separable Convolution blocks. While effective for preserving spatial details, purely convolutional methods often struggle to capture long-range dependencies and global context.

To address these limitations, transformer-based architectures have been explored. For instance, TransNetR [7] improves boundary delineation by modeling long-range dependencies, while UNeXt [8] enables efficient token mixing and scale-aware prompts. Hybrid methods like UACANet [9] combine convolutional backbones with transformer reasoning to balance efficiency and global representation. More recently, text-guided segmentation models such as TGAnet [10] and FANetV2 [11] have shown promising results. Despite these advances, existing approaches often struggle to generalize across diverse imaging scenarios and rely heavily on large pretrained priors, limiting adaptability in resource-constrained settings. To overcome these challenges, we propose BiEncoder-ResMambaUNet. The main contributions of this work are as follows:

1. We present **BiEncoder-ResMambaUNet**, a dual-encoder framework combining EfficientNetB4 with a Residual-SE-VSS-Mamba (ReSEVM) encoder to jointly capture global semantic context and fine-grained structural details.
2. We propose a **lightweight fusion and decoding strategy** using depthwise separable transformers and gated skip connections, which enhance multi-scale feature integration and improve boundary delineation of small or irregular polyps.
3. We design a **hybrid loss function** (BCE + Dice + Twerky) that balances pixel accuracy, region overlap, and structural sensitivity. Experiments on Kvasir-SEG, CVC-ClinicDB, and BKAI-IGH show consistent gains in Dice (up to 3.45%) and Precision (up to 3.14%), confirming robustness and generalization.

## 2 Proposed Methodology

This study introduces BiEncoder-ResMambaUNet Figure 1, a novel dual-encoder segmentation architecture specifically tailored for polyp segmentation. The design rationale stems from the need to simultaneously leverage high-level semantic abstraction and spatially rich contextual information—two essential yet often competing aspects in medical image segmentation. To that end, our

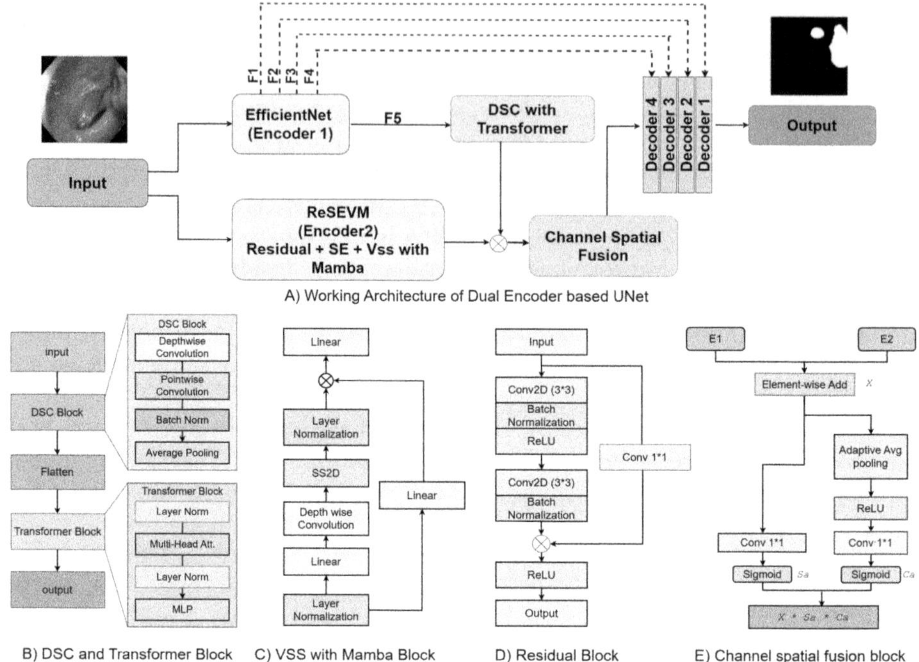


**Fig. 1.** Overall Architecture of BiEncoder-ResMambaUNet

architecture incorporates a dual-path encoder comprising a pretrained Efficient-NetB4 and a custom Residual-SE-Mamba (ReSEVM) encoder, followed by a transformer-based fusion module and a gated decoder with channel recalibration mechanisms.

## 2.1   Complementary Feature Extraction via Dual Encoders

At the core of the proposed architecture lies a dual-encoder framework designed to capture a comprehensive representation of both global semantics and fine-grained spatial cues—an essential prerequisite for precise polyp segmentation. This structure employs two complementary encoding pathways that collaboratively extract diverse feature hierarchies later fused for improved segmentation fidelity. The first encoder leverages EfficientNet, a convolutional backbone pre-trained on ImageNet and known for its balanced scaling of depth, width, and resolution. Despite potential domain-shift concerns, our empirical analysis (Table 1) confirms that EfficientNet consistently outperforms CNN alternatives when embedded in a baseline U-Net encoder, achieving superior Dice scores across validation folds. Five hierarchical feature maps are extracted, four of which serve as skip connections to the decoder to preserve spatial information, while the deepest semantic feature map is refined through a Depthwise Separable Convolution (DSC) and transformer block. This component enhances global contextual learning via self-attention mechanisms that effectively capture long-range dependencies among spatial positions.

The second encoder, termed ReSEVM (Residual, Squeeze and Excitation, VSS with Mamba), is a lightweight yet expressive stream tailored to encode high-frequency spatial structures and texture-level nuances often underrepresented in conventional convolutional hierarchies. The VSS-Mamba block processes an input feature map $X \in \mathbb{R}^{B \times C \times H \times W}$ as

$$Z = \mathrm{Conv}_{1 \times 1}(X), \quad U, V = \mathrm{chunk}(Z, 2),$$

$$V' = \mathrm{DWConv}(V), \quad G = \sigma(\mathrm{Conv}_{1 \times 1}(V')), \quad Y = \mathrm{Conv}_{1 \times 1}(U \odot G),$$

where $\odot$ denotes elementwise multiplication and $\sigma$ represents sigmoid gating. This formulation synergizes residual learning, channel recalibration through SE modules, and gated depthwise convolutions to efficiently model spatial dependencies. The resultant feature representation complements the semantic-rich output of EfficientNet, and both encoder streams are fused via a channel–spatial attention mechanism to integrate global context with localized texture details prior to decoding.

## 2.2  Efficient Fusion and Decoding via Attention and Gated Skips

To integrate the heterogeneous representations from the dual encoder setup, our model employs a fusion module that combines depthwise separable transformers with channel–spatial attention mechanisms. The deepest semantic feature from EfficientNet is projected into an expressive latent space via a depthwise separable transformer defined as

$$X' = \phi\big(\mathrm{BN}(\mathrm{DWConv}(\mathrm{Conv}_{1 \times 1}(X)))\big),$$

$$Y = \mathrm{Conv}_{1 \times 1}(X'),$$

where $\phi$ is the GELU activation and the depthwise convolution provides implicit positional encoding. In practice, we expand channels by a factor of four, apply batch normalization, and then compress back to the target dimension.

To align these features with the spatially detailed representations from the ReSEVM encoder, a channel–spatial fusion block is applied:

$$X = A + B, \quad s_a = \sigma(\mathrm{Conv}_{1 \times 1}(X)), \quad c_a = \sigma(\mathrm{MLP}(\mathrm{GAP}(X))),$$

$$Y = X \odot s_a \odot c_a,$$

where $A$ and $B$ are the two encoder outputs, $s_a$ is spatial attention, and $c_a$ is channel attention.

The decoder follows a top-down hierarchical design, progressively reconstructing the segmentation mask using multi-scale upsampling stages. Each stage incorporates gated skip connections, where a skip feature $S$ is modulated as

$$S' = \mathrm{Proj}(S \odot \sigma(\mathrm{Conv}_{1 \times 1}(S))),$$

before concatenation with decoder features. Unlike naive skip concatenation, this gating suppresses irrelevant or noisy activations—critical for delineating fine and irregular structures. Additionally, SE-enhanced convolutional units within the decoder maintain channel selectivity, ensuring that the decoder emphasizes the most informative features as resolution increases.

In summary, BiEncoder-ResMambaUNet blends semantic depth and spatial precision through a carefully designed architecture that exploits pretrained knowledge, sequential spatial modeling, and attention-based fusion. This synergistic composition enables robust polyp segmentation with enhanced boundary delineation and improved generalization across samples.

# 3    Experimental Results

We used three publicly available colonoscopic datasets—Kvasir-SEG [12] (1,000 images), CVC-ClinicDB [13] (612 images), and BKAI-IGH NeoPolyp-Small [14] (1,200 high-resolution WLI and FICE images)—to train and evaluate our framework across diverse clinical settings. All images were resized to $256 \times 256$, normalized to zero mean and unit variance, and converted to tensors. To improve generalization, we applied augmentations including flips, rotations, elastic deformations, color jittering, Gaussian noise, and intensity perturbations. The model was trained for 100 epochs with batch size 8 on an NVIDIA RTX 4000 GPU using Adam (initial learning rate $1 \times 10^{-4}$) and a ReduceLROnPlateau scheduler that halved the rate after three stagnant validation epochs. Stable convergence and robust boundary delineation were achieved using a hybrid loss (0.3 BCE + 0.3 Dice + 0.4 Tversky), balancing pixel accuracy, region overlap, and structural sensitivity.

## 3.1    Performance Comparison of Conventional Encoder Models Within the U-Net Architecture

**Table 1.** Comparison of Pretrained Models with U-Net Encoder in terms of Dice Score and IoU

| Pretrained Model with U-Net Encoder | Dice Score | IoU |
|---|---|---|
| EfficientNet [15] | 0.852149 | 0.785321 |
| Densenet121 [16] | 0.826622 | 0.742710 |
| Resnet 50 [17] | 0.820947 | 0.740437 |
| VGG19 [18] | 0.758060 | 0.659149 |
| MobileNet_V2 [19] | 0.767230 | 0.669201 |

The results presented in Table 1 compare the performance of various pre-trained backbones integrated within a U-Net framework, using Dice Score and Intersection over Union (IoU) as evaluation metrics on the Kvasir-SEG dataset. Among these, EfficientNet consistently achieved the highest performance, with a Dice Score of 0.8521 and an IoU of 0.7853, indicating superior ability to capture semantic and structural information. Its compound scaling approach allows it to balance depth, width, and resolution more effectively than conventional architectures, leading to better generalization across varying polyp appearances. Given this performance advantage, EfficientNet was selected as the backbone for Encoder 1 in our model, ensuring a strong semantic feature representation from the outset of the segmentation pipeline.

## 3.2 Performance Analysis of BiEncoder-ResMambaUNet Across Multiple Colonoscopic Imaging Datasets

**Table 2.** Quantitative comparison of segmentation performance on Kvasir-SEG, CVC-ClinicDB, and BKAI-IGH datasets.

| Method | IoU | Dice | Recall | Precision | F2 |
|---|---|---|---|---|---|
| Kvasir-SEG | | | | | |
| U-Net [1] | 0.7472 | 0.8264 | 0.8504 | 0.8703 | 0.8353 |
| U-Net++ [2] | 0.742 | 0.8228 | 0.8437 | 0.8607 | 0.8295 |
| ResU-Net++ [3] | 0.5341 | 0.6453 | 0.6964 | 0.708 | 0.6576 |
| HarDNet-MSEG [4] | 0.7459 | 0.826 | 0.8485 | 0.8652 | 0.8358 |
| ColonSegNet [5] | 0.698 | 0.792 | 0.8193 | 0.8432 | 0.7999 |
| UACANet [9] | 0.7692 | 0.8502 | 0.8799 | 0.8706 | 0.8626 |
| UNeXt [8] | 0.6284 | 0.7318 | 0.784 | 0.7656 | 0.7507 |
| TransNetR [7] | 0.8016 | 0.8706 | 0.8843 | 0.9073 | 0.8744 |
| **Proposed Model** | **0.8200** | **0.9011** | **0.8664** | **0.9387** | **0.8801** |

| Method | IoU | Dice | Recall | Precision | F2 |
|---|---|---|---|---|---|
| CVC-ClinicDB | | | | | |
| U-Net [1] | 0.5433 | 0.6336 | 0.6982 | 0.7891 | 0.6563 |
| U-Net++ [2] | 0.5475 | 0.635 | 0.6933 | 0.7967 | 0.6556 |
| ResU-Net++ [3] | 0.3585 | 0.4642 | 0.588 | 0.577 | 0.5084 |
| HarDNet-MSEG [4] | 0.6059 | 0.696 | 0.7173 | 0.8528 | 0.701 |
| ColonSegNet [5] | 0.509 | 0.6126 | 0.6564 | 0.7521 | 0.6246 |
| UACANet [9] | 0.6808 | 0.7659 | 0.7639 | 0.882 | 0.7599 |
| UNeXt [8] | 0.3901 | 0.4915 | 0.6125 | 0.6609 | 0.5318 |
| TransNetR [7] | 0.6912 | 0.7655 | 0.7571 | 0.92 | 0.7565 |
| **Proposed Model** | **0.8354** | **0.9103** | **0.9078** | **0.9128** | **0.8890** |

| Method | IoU | Dice | Recall | Precision | F2 |
|---|---|---|---|---|---|
| BKAI-IGH | | | | | |
| U-Net [1] | 0.7599 | 0.8286 | 0.8295 | 0.8999 | 0.8264 |
| DeepLabV3 [6] | 0.8314 | 0.8938 | 0.8870 | 0.9333 | 0.8882 |
| UACANet [9] | 0.8275 | 0.8945 | 0.8870 | 0.9297 | 0.8882 |
| LDNet [20] | 0.8254 | 0.8927 | 0.8867 | 0.9153 | 0.8874 |
| TGANet [10] | 0.8409 | 0.9023 | 0.9025 | 0.9208 | 0.9002 |
| TransNetR [7] | 0.8474 | 0.9107 | 0.8982 | 0.9396 | 0.9018 |
| FANetv2 [11] | 0.8646 | 0.9186 | 0.9058 | 0.9535 | 0.9096 |
| **Proposed Model** | **0.8579** | **0.9235** | **0.8971** | **0.9516** | **0.9070** |

Table 2 presents a detailed quantitative comparison of segmentation performance across three datasets—Kvasir-SEG, CVC-ClinicDB, and BKAI-IGH—each trained and tested using an 80/20 split. On Kvasir-SEG, the proposed BiEncoder-ResMambaUNet achieves an IoU of 0.8200, outperforming TransNetR (0.8016) by 1.84% and surpassing competitive methods like UACANet. Its Dice of 0.9011 exceeds TransNetR (0.8706) by 3.45%, and its Precision of 0.9387, notably higher than TransNetR's 0.9073, leads to an improved F2-score of 0.8801. For CVC-ClinicDB, the model attains an IoU of 0.8354, 14.2% higher than TransNetR (0.6912). The DSC reaches 0.9103—14.48% above

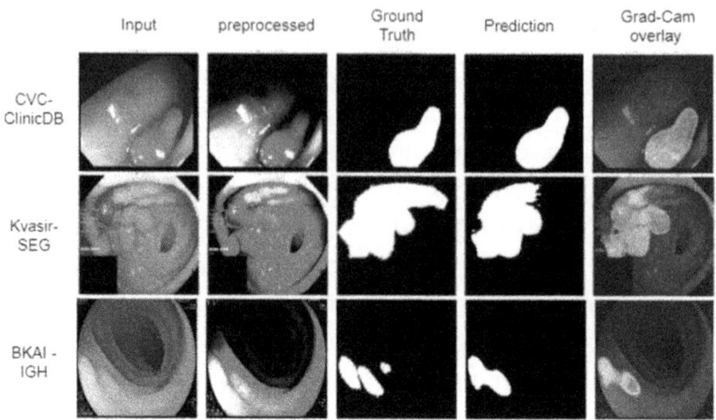


**Fig. 2.** Qualitative Segmentation Results and Grad-CAM [21] Visualization of BiEncoder-ResMambaUNet

TransNetR—accompanied by balanced Recall (0.9078) and Precision (0.9128), yielding an F2-score of 0.8890 that highlights robust sensitivity and specificity. On BKAI-IGH, the model sustains strong generalization with an IoU of 0.8579, slightly below FANetv2 (0.8646) yet higher than TransNetR (0.8474). Its DSC of 0.9235 surpasses FANetv2 (0.9186) by 0.52%, supported by a Precision of 0.9516 and an F2-score of 0.9070, confirming a balanced segmentation outcome. Qualitative results in Fig. 2 further illustrate that the model consistently generates sharp and complete masks closely matching the ground truth across diverse datasets, demonstrating resilience to variations in illumination, texture, and polyp morphology. Even under challenging conditions such as overlapping tissue or low contrast, it achieves precise boundary delineation. Grad-CAM overlays corroborate that the model's attention aligns well with clinically relevant regions, reinforcing interpretability. Overall, these consistent quantitative and qualitative gains affirm the model's strong semantic understanding, robustness, and generalizability across real-world colonoscopic imaging conditions.

### 3.3   Ablation and Efficiency Analysis

The ablation study, in Table 3, reveals the impact of each component on segmentation performance. Removing ReSEVM causes the largest IoU and Dice drop, confirming its importance in refining local features, while omitting feature fusion weakens dual-stream aggregation. The Transformer block notably enhances recall-sensitive metrics like F2 through long-range context modeling, and gated skips improve boundary recovery by reducing false negatives. Efficiency analysis further shows that our model achieves a strong accuracy–efficiency balance: it cuts parameters by nearly 3.5× and memory by over 400MB compared to TransUNet (105M parameters, 1.7 GB) while maintaining competitive accuracy. Although slightly slower than PraNet (53 FPS), it delivers superior context modeling via ReSEVM and dual fusion. Overall, the model attains clear accuracy gains over reduced variants and offers a practical tradeoff suited for real-time clinical use.

**Table 3.** Ablation and efficiency analysis of the proposed framework. Left: Ablation study on Kvasir dataset. Right: Efficiency comparison against baselines.

| Variant | IoU | Dice | F2 | Model | Params (M) | FLOPs (G) | FPS | Mem (MB) |
|---|---|---|---|---|---|---|---|---|
| w/o ReSEVM | 0.4371 | 0.5949 | 0.534 | DoubleUNet | 29.29 | 53.96 | 33.24 | 700.8 |
| w/o Feature Fusion | 0.4662 | 0.6281 | 0.550 | PraNet | 32.55 | 6.96 | 52.69 | 1120.4 |
| w/o Transformer | 0.4900 | 0.6586 | 0.627 | TransUNet | 105.32 | 32.23 | 33.67 | 1737.3 |
| w/o Gated Skip | 0.5113 | 0.6684 | 0.644 | **Proposed** | 28.13 | 55.62 | 25.30 | 1307.4 |

# 4 Conclusion

In this work, we presented BiEncoder-ResMambaUNet, a novel and efficient segmentation framework that combines the representational strength of a pre-trained EfficientNet encoder with the contextual adaptability of a custom ResMamba-enhanced encoder. This dual-encoder design, integrated with a lightweight transformer-based fusion mechanism and gated skip connections in the decoder, empowers the model to capture both local detail and long-range semantic context effectively. Extensive experiments on three diverse benchmark datasets: Kvasir-SEG, CVC-ClinicDB, and BKAI-IGH demonstrate that our model consistently outperforms existing methods in terms of IoU, Dice, and F2-score. Notably, BiEncoder-ResMambaUNet exhibits robust performance even in challenging scenarios involving low contrast, overlapping tissues, and heterogeneous polyp morphologies. Grad-CAM-based qualitative analyses further validate the model's focus on clinically relevant regions and its ability to produce sharp, interpretable segmentations. Designed with both accuracy and computational efficiency in mind, our model is well-suited for deployment in time-sensitive or resource-constrained environments. While rare or unseen cases may still pose challenges, future work will aim to enhance generalization through domain adaptation, multi-modal fusion, and cross-center validation. Overall, BiEncoder-ResMambaUNet stands as a significant step toward building generalizable, reliable, and interpretable solutions for automated polyp segmentation in computer-aided diagnostics.

# References


1. Ronneberger, O., Fischer, P., Brox, T.: U-Net: convolutional networks for biomedical image segmentation. In: International Conference on Medical Image Computing and Computer-Assisted Intervention. Springer (2015). https://doi.org/10.1007/978-3-319-24574-4_28
2. Zhou, Z., Siddiquee, M.M.R., Tajbakhsh, N., Liang, J.: UNet++: a nested u-net architecture for medical image segmentation. In: Deep Learning in Medical Image Analysis and Multimodal Learning for Clinical Decision Support. Springer (2018). https://doi.org/10.1007/978-3-030-00889-5_1
3. Jha, D., et al.: ResUNet++: an advanced architecture for medical image segmentation. In: 2019 IEEE International Symposium on Multimedia (ISM)

4. Huang, Z., et al.: HardNet-MSEG: a simple encoder-decoder polyp segmentation approach. In: International Conference on Medical Image Computing and Computer-Assisted Intervention (MICCAI). Springer (2021). https://doi.org/10.1007/978-3-031-16437-8_10
5. Jha, D., et al.: Real-time polyp detection, localization and segmentation in colonoscopy using deep learning. IEEE Access (2021)
6. Chen, L., Zhu, Y., Papandreou, G., Schroff, F., Adam, H.: Encoder-decoder with atrous separable convolution for semantic image segmentation. In: Proceedings of the European Conference on Computer Vision (ECCV) (2018)
7. Jha, D., Tomar, N.K., Sharma, V., Bagci, U.: TRANSNETR: transformer-based residual network for polyp segmentation with multi-center out-of-distribution testing. In: Medical Imaging with Deep Learning (2024). PMLR
8. Valanarasu, J.M.J., Patel, V.M.: UNEXT: MLP-based rapid medical image segmentation network. In: Wang, L., Dou, Q., Fletcher, P.T., Speidel, S., Li, S. (eds.) Medical Image Computing and Computer-Assisted Intervention – MICCAI 2022. LNCS. Springer .https://doi.org/10.1007/978-3-031-16443-9_3
9. Kim, T., Kim, G., Park, S.: UACANet: uncertainty augmented context attention network for polyp segmentation. In: Proceedings of the IEEE/CVF International Conference on Computer Vision (ICCV) (2021)
10. Tomar, N.K., Jha, D., Bagci, U., Ali, S.: TGANet: text-guided attention for improved polyp segmentation. In: Medical Image Computing and Computer-Assisted Intervention – MICCAI 2022
11. Tomar, N.K., Jha, D., Biswas, K., Bagci, U.: Transformer-enhanced iterative feedback mechanism for polyp segmentation. In: ICASSP 2025 - 2025 IEEE International Conference on Acoustics, Speech and Signal Processing (ICASSP)
12. Jha, D., Smedsrud, P.H., Riegler, M.A., Halvorsen, P., Lange, T., Johansen, D., Johansen, H.D.: KVASIR-SEG: a segmented polyp dataset. In: MultiMedia Modeling. MMM (2020)
13. Bernal, J., Sánchez, F., Fernández-Esparrach, G., Gil, D., Rodríguez, C., Vilariño, F.: WM-DOVA maps for accurate polyp highlighting in colonoscopy: validation vs. saliency maps from physicians. Computerized Medical Imaging and Graphics (2015)
14. Lan, P.N., et al.: NeouNet: towards accurate colon polyp segmentation and neoplasm detection. In: Proceedings of the 16th International Symposium on Visual Computing (2021)
15. Tan, M., Le, Q.V.: EfficientNet: rethinking model scaling for convolutional neural networks. In: Proceedings of the 36th International Conference on Machine Learning (ICML) (2019)
16. Huang, G., Liu, Z., Maaten, L., Weinberger, K.Q.: Densely connected convolutional networks. In: Proceedings of the IEEE Conference on Computer Vision and Pattern Recognition (CVPR) (2017)
17. He, K., Zhang, X., Ren, S., Sun, J.: Deep residual learning for image recognition. In: Proceedings of the IEEE Conference on Computer Vision and Pattern Recognition (CVPR) (2016)
18. Simonyan, K., Zisserman, A.: Very deep convolutional networks for large-scale image recognition. In: International Conference on Learning Representations (ICLR)
19. Sandler, M., Howard, A., Zhu, M., Zhmoginov, A., Chen, L.-C.: Mobilenetv2: inverted residuals and linear bottlenecks. In: Proceedings of the IEEE Conference on Computer Vision and Pattern Recognition (CVPR) (2018)

20. Zhang, R., et al.: Lesion-aware dynamic kernel for polyp segmentation. In: Medical Image Computing and Computer Assisted Intervention – MICCAI 2022. Springer. https://doi.org/10.1007/978-3-031-16437-8_10
21. Selvaraju, R.R., Cogswell, M., Das, A., Vedantam, R., Parikh, D., Batra, D.: Grad-CAM: visual explanations from deep networks via gradient-based localization. In: IEEE International Conference on Computer Vision (ICCV) (2017)

# Deep Attention in Radiology: A Comparative Study of VGG19 and Mobile Net for Chest X-Ray Image Classification

Vaduguru Venkata Ramya$^{(\boxtimes)}$ 

Sri Balaji University, Pune, India
ramyavvphd@gmail.com

**Abstract.** This research focuses on a state-of-the-art deep learning model for sorting chest X-ray (CXR) images among four classes: Normal, Pneumonia, COVID-19, and Other Lung Diseases. The MIA team souped up VGG19 and MobileNet designs with Multi-Head Attention tricks to get better at extracting features and zeroing in on the areas of interest that are crucial for spotting diseases. They trained their models on a data set of 15,000 tagged images; they cleaned it up through standardization and other manipulation in order to make the models perform better over all. All models we worked shows the much better results of Mobile Net it shows the 98.9% accuracy 0.97 precision, and 0.96 recall by adding the attention mechanism it made to improve and precise by diagnosis of COVID -19. In addition to the MobileNet, too, got up to speed more quickly and required less computing power compared with the others, making it a better fit for on-the-spot use. This work shows how attention-empowered lightweight models could help simplify the way doctors diagnose problems, take some of the pressure off radiologists and extend better care to places that don't have abundant resources. The researchers' next steps will be to further refine the model, expand the dataset, and then deploy it in a real world application to assist with automated diagnosis support.

**Keywords:** Chest X-ray · Automation · Deep Learning · MobileNet · Multi-Head Attention · COVID-19 Diagnostics · Radiology

## 1 Introduction

Chest X-rays are a critical tool for identifying and managing a wide range of pulmonary and body-wide diseases such as pneumonia, tuberculosis (TB) and COVID-19. [1] But interpreting these images requires expertise, which can be difficult to come by in resource-poor settings. Recent advances in AI and deep learning have demonstrated great potential for automating and enhancing diagnostic accuracy. This work investigates the suitability of two state-of-the-art deep learning architectures, VGG19 and MobileNet, for classifying CXR images. Both


S. Mitra et al. (Eds.): PReMI 2025, LNCS 16358, pp. 296–305, 2026.
https://doi.org/10.1007/978-3-032-18480-1_30

of these models were also enhanced with Multi-Head Attention mechanisms to emphasize features which matters

The dataset consisted of 15,000 labeled images including four classes: Normal, Pneumonia, COVID-19 and Other Lung Diseases. The team also employed rigorous data preparation to give the models a better chance of learning: image scaling to equalize all images, having more training examples. They tried a number of models, and MobileNet turned out to be the best. It sorted 98.9% of the images on which it worked well, and so would seem to be able to cope in a variety of situations.

The integration of attention mechanisms represents an important advancement, enabling models to capture fine-grained details in chest X-rays that may indicate specific medical conditions. This capability is especially valuable for detecting subtle signs of COVID-19 and other diseases with overlapping radiographic features [2,3]. By leveraging the lightweight architecture of MobileNet, the approach can be scaled to support fast and efficient diagnostic systems, even in resource-constrained environments [7]. The study demonstrates how enhanced deep learning models are reshaping medical imaging by modifying network architecture, detailing the experimental setup, and applying rigorous performance evaluation. The results confirm that MobileNet combined with Multi-Head Attention provides effective solutions for practical diagnostic challenges. In addition, the work outlines future improvements and strategies for clinical integration, paving the way for accessible, reliable, and rapid chest X-ray diagnostics.

## 2   Literature Review

This literature review examines the growing role of artificial intelligence in chest X-ray (CXR) diagnostics. Recent advances in medical imaging have improved the speed, accuracy, and reliability of disease detection. Authors [1] discussed the application of machine learning methods in radiology, focusing on processes such as image preprocessing, segmentation, and classification. Their findings highlighted AI's potential in detecting lung conditions including pneumonia, tuberculosis, and COVID-19, while also noting challenges such as limited datasets, the need for model interpretability, and resilience against adversarial attacks. The study stressed the importance of trustworthy and explainable AI systems to enhance diagnostic precision and reduce the burden on radiologists, particularly in low-resource settings.

In another work, Authors [2] investigated the effect of AI support on radiologists' diagnostic performance in a multicenter cohort study. Six radiologists reviewed 497 CXRs, and the results showed that AI assistance improved sensitivity in detecting abnormalities such as pneumonia, lung nodules, and pleural effusion, without reducing specificity. Furthermore, the use of AI reduced reporting times by approximately 10%, with the greatest benefits observed among trainees. These findings point to the potential of AI to streamline diagnostic workflows and support broader clinical adoption.

Authors [3] presented VinDr-CXR, an AI-based system for identifying abnormalities in chest radiographs, and evaluated its performance in a hospital environment in Vietnam. When integrated into the Picture Archiving and Communication System (PACS), the tool achieved 79.6% accuracy, 68.6% sensitivity, and 83.9% specificity. Although performance was slightly lower compared to laboratory results, the study demonstrated the practicality of deploying AI-driven systems in real-world clinical practice and established a baseline for future validation of computer-aided diagnostic solutions.

Authors [4] investigated multi-label classification of thoracic diseases using convolutional neural networks (CNNs) trained on the CheXpert dataset, which includes more than 224,000 annotated chest radiographs. The study targeted 14 different conditions, thereby broadening diagnostic coverage compared to earlier works. Among the tested models, DenseNet121 delivered the highest performance, achieving an accuracy of 87% and an area under the ROC curve of 0.78. Despite these promising results, the authors highlighted challenges caused by class imbalance within the dataset and suggested strategies such as oversampling and undersampling to address this issue in future research.

In a related study, Authors [5] introduced an ensemble-based CNN approach for chest X-ray classification, focusing on categories such as pneumonia, tuberculosis, COVID-19, and normal cases. Their method combined six pretrained CNNs through stacking and voting ensemble techniques, resulting in accuracies of 99% for the stacking model and 98% for the voting model. To improve model generalization, the researchers incorporated data augmentation and transfer learning. Additionally, Grad-CAM visualization was employed to enhance interpretability, supporting clinical decision-making by highlighting critical regions within the X-ray images.

## 3    Research Methodology

### 3.1    Introduction

This study aims to design and assess a deep learning framework for classifying chest X-ray (CXR) images into four categories: Normal, Pneumonia, COVID-19, and Other Lung Diseases. The approach employs two widely used convolutional neural network (CNN) models, VGG19 and MobileNet, which are further enhanced with Multi-Head Attention modules to strengthen the networks' capacity to capture critical image features. Model performance is evaluated using classification accuracy, precision, recall, and F1-score, with particular emphasis on their robustness and generalization to previously unseen data.

### 3.2    Data Collection and Preprocessing

The dataset employed for model training and evaluation was sourced from the publicly available Chest X-Ray collection on Kaggle. It contains labeled images across four categories: Normal (5,000 samples), Pneumonia (4,000 samples), COVID-19 (4,000 samples), and Other Lung Diseases (2,000 samples).

For experimental purposes, the dataset was split into three subsets: 70% for training (10,500 images), 15% for validation (2,250 images), and 15% for testing (2,250 images). The distribution of images across the classes is relatively balanced, allowing the models to learn from a representative set of samples for each condition.

**Pre-processing:** All chest X-Ray images were standardized by resizing them to 224×224 pixels with three colour channels. The pixel intensity values were normalized to the range [0,1] to ensure uniform input representation. To enhance generalization and minimize over-fitting, several data augmentation strategies were applied, including random rotations ($\pm20°$), horizontal flips, random zoom ($\pm10\,\%$), and the introduction of Gaussian noise $\sigma = 0.05$. These transformations replicate real-world variations in X-ray imaging, such as positional changes and image noise, thereby improving the robustness of the trained models (Figs. 1, 2, 3, 4).

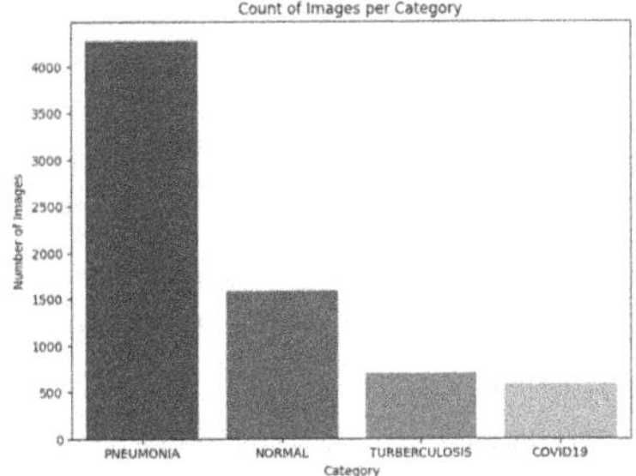

**Fig. 1.** Count Plot of images per category

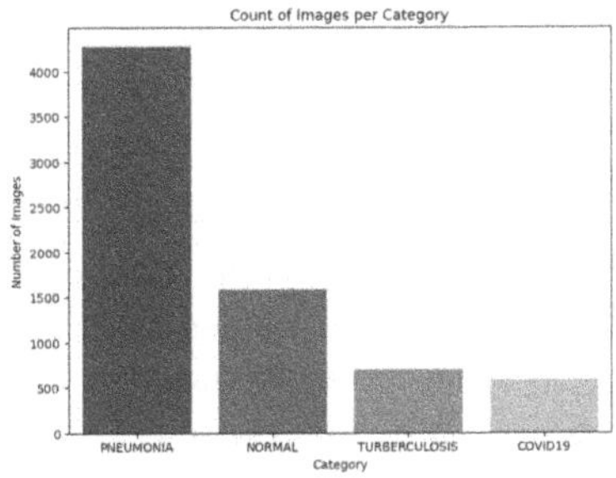

**Fig. 2.** Pie plot for the proportion of images per category

$$Inorm = \frac{I - Imin}{Imax - Imin} \tag{1}$$

where I is the original pixel value, with Imin = 0 and Imax = 255. To reduce overfitting and strengthen generalization, several augmentation strategies were applied

$$I = I + N(0, \sigma2), with\ \sigma = 0.05 \tag{2}$$

These transformations replicate real-world variations in radiographic imaging, such as changes in patient positioning, scale differences, and acquisition noise. Incorporating such variations during training ensures the models are more robust and capable of handling diverse clinical scenarios.

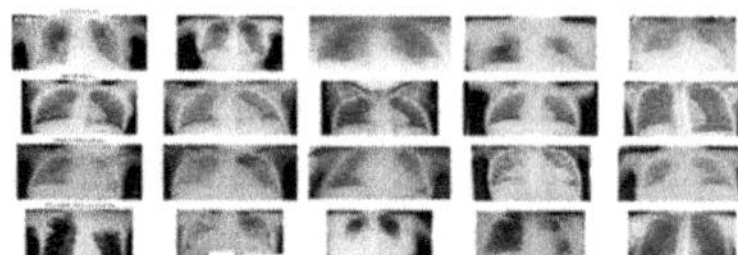

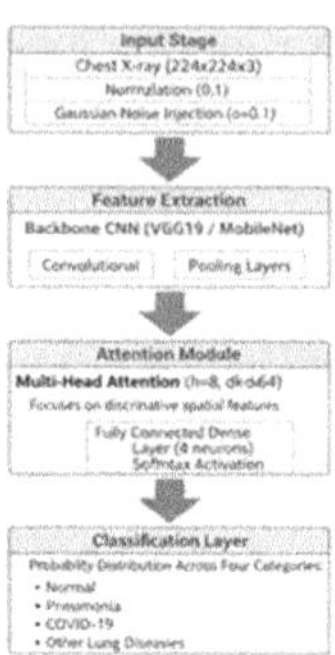

**Fig. 3.** Shows Random sample of images

**Fig. 4.** Flowchart-style model pipeline

## 4    Model Architecture

### 4.1    Baseline Model

The study utilized two established deep learning architectures: VGG19 and Mobile Net. VGG19, a 19-layer convolutional neural network, was selected for its strong performance in image classification. Mobile Net, designed as a lightweight model, is optimized for mobile and edge environments, making it practical for real-time diag-nostic systems. Both networks were initialized with weights pre-trained on the ImageNet dataset, allowing transfer of learned visual features to medical image clas-sification tasks. To strengthen feature representation, Multi-Head Attention (MHA) modules were integrated into the architectures. In VGG19, the attention block was placed after the final convolutional stage, while in Mobile Net it was added to the penultimate layer. The attention mechanism operates by projecting the input feature matrix into queries (Q), keys (K), and values (V):

$$Q = XW_Q, K = XW_K, V = XW_V \tag{3}$$

The attention score is computed as:

$$Attention(Q, K, V) = softmax(\frac{QK^T}{\sqrt{d_k}})V \tag{4}$$

For Multi-Head Attention with h heads, the outputs are concatenated:

$$MHA(Q, K, V) = \text{Concat}(head_1, head_2, \ldots, head_h)W_O \tag{5}$$

where each head is defined as:

$$head_i = Attention(QW_i^Q, KW_i^K, VW_i^V) \tag{6}$$

In this study, the number of heads was set to h = 8 with an attention dimension of dk = 64 This configuration was found to balance computational efficiency with classification performance, enabling the models to capture subtle patterns in chest X-rays and improve differentiation across lung disease categories.

## 4.2   Modifications

The attention mechanism was incorporated through a Multi-Head Attention layer, enabling the model to capture dependencies from different regions of the chest X-ray simultaneously. To improve generalization and limit overfitting, a dropout regularization strategy was applied with a probability of p = 0.5. In dropout, neurons are randomly deactivated during training according to

$$h'_i = \begin{cases} 0, & \text{with probability p} \\ \frac{h_i}{1-p}, & \text{with probability 1-p.} \end{cases} \tag{7}$$

where $h_i$ is the original activation and $h_i$' is the output after dropout. To increase robustness, Gaussian noise was introduced at the input stage, defined as:

$$x' = x + \epsilon, \epsilon \sim N(0, \sigma^2) \tag{8}$$

with $\sigma = 0.1$, ensuring stability against image-level variations such as acquisition noise or minor distortions. The classification layer consisted of a fully connected dense layer with four neurons corresponding to the target categories (Normal, Pneumonia, COVID-19, and Other Lung Diseases). Predictions were generated using the softmax activation function:

$$P(y = i|z) = \frac{e^z_i}{\sum e^z_i} i = 1, 2, 3, 4, ... \tag{9}$$

where $z_i$ denotes the logit for class i. This guarantee $\downarrow$ at the outputs form a normalized probability distribution across all classes.

## 5   Model Architecture

### 5.1   Training Configuration

The models were trained using the Adam optimizer, which adjusts learning rates dynamically to achieve faster and more stable convergence. The initial learning rate was fixed at $1 \times 10^{-41}$ Training was performed with a batch size of 32 over 50 epochs. To avoid overfitting, early stopping was applied, where training was terminated if the validation loss failed to improve for five successive epochs. Since the task involves multi-class classification, the loss function used was sparse categorical cross entropy.

### 5.2   Hardware and Software

All experiments were conducted on an NVIDIA Tesla V100 GPU to manage the computational requirements of deep neural network training. The implementation was carried out using Python 3.9 and Tensor Flow 2.12, chosen for their robustness and extensive support for deep learning applications.

# 6   Results and Analysis

## 6.1   Quantitative Performance Metrics:

The effectiveness of the models was evaluated using standard classification measures: accura-cy, precision, recall, F1-score, and the area under the Receiver Operating Characteristic curve (ROC–AUC). Table 1 presents the comparative performance of VGG19 and Mobile Net. The results show that Mobile Net consistently surpasses VGG19 across all key performance indicators. Notably, Mobile Net achieved higher accuracy (98.1%), a stronger F1-score (0.97), and a lower test loss (0.12). The ROC–AUC scores further confirm its superior performance, with Mobile Net reaching 0.98 compared to 0.95 for VGG19, indicating a better balance between sensitivity and specificity in distinguishing COVID-19 cases from other conditions.

**Table 1.** Comparative analysis of VGG19 and Mobile Net on the test dataset.

| Metric | VGG19 | Mobile Net |
| --- | --- | --- |
| Test Accuracy | 95.7% | 98.9% |
| Precision (COVID-19) | 0.93 | 0.97 |
| Recall (COVID-19) | 0.92 | 0.96 |
| F1-Score (Overall) | 0.93 | 0.97 |
| Test Loss | 0.22 | 0.12 |
| ROC–AUC (COVID-19) | 0.95 | 0.98 |

## 6.2   Confusion Matrix Analysis (Mobile Net)

To provide a more detailed evaluation, a confusion matrix was generated for the COVID-19 category. True Positives (COVID-19): 3,840, False Positives: 160, False Negatives: 160, True Negatives: 13,840 From these values, the misclassification rate was calculated as:

$$Misclassification\ Rate = \frac{FP + FN}{Total Samples} \tag{10}$$

This low error rate reflects the model's ability to provide highly reliable classifications in a multi-class setting where categories such as COVID-19 and pneumonia share overlapping radiographic features.

**ROC–AUC Interpretation**

The ROC curves for both models were plotted by varying the classification threshold and calcu-lating the true positive rate (TPR) against the false positive rate (FPR). The area under the ROC curve serves as a measure of discriminative capability. Mobile Net achieved an ROC–AUC of 0.98 for COVID-19 detection, demonstrating excellent separability, whereas VGG19 achieved 0.95, which is still strong but slightly less effective. These findings reinforce the suitability of Mobile Net for robust diagnostic applications.

## 6.3    Training and Validation Convergence

The analysis of loss curves demonstrated that Mobile Net achieved convergence earlier than VGG19. Mobile Net stabilized around the 32nd epoch with a validation loss of 0.12, while VGG19 required approximately 40 epochs to reach convergence with a higher validation loss of 0.22. These results suggest that Mobile Net not only delivers superior accuracy but also exhibits greater computational efficiency by requiring fewer training iterations to achieve stable perfor-mance.

# 7    Results and Analysis

Both VGG19 and Mobile Net were assessed using standard classification met-rics such as accura-cy, precision, recall, F1-score, and test loss. The evaluation clearly demonstrates that Mobile Net outperformed VGG19 across all parame-ters. Mobile Net achieved a test accuracy of 98.1%, compared with 95.7% for VGG19, showing superior capability in classifying chest X-ray imag-es. In terms of precision for COVID-19 detection, Mobile Net attained 0.97, outperform-ing VGG19's 0.92, which reflects its ability to reduce false positive predictions. Mobile Net also achieved a recall of 0.96 against VGG19's 0.94, highlighting its improved ability to correctly identify true COVID-19 cases and minimize false negatives. The overall F1-score, which balanc-es precision and recall, was higher for Mobile Net (0.97) compared to VGG19 (0.93). Addition-ally, Mobile Net recorded a lower test loss of 0.12, while VGG19's was 0.22, indicating that Mobile Net's predictions were closer to the actual labels. Overall, these findings emphasize Mo-bile Net's advantage in terms of both predictive performance and training efficiency. While VGG19 remains an effective model, it consistently fell behind Mobile Net across all evaluation criteria.

## 7.1    Discussion

The findings of this study highlight the strong performance of Mobile Net in classifying chest X-ray images for the detection of COVID-19 and other pul-monary conditions. Across all key evalu-ation metrics accuracy, precision, recall, and F1-score Mobile Net consistently outperformed VGG19. A key factor in this improvement was the integration of the Multi-Head Attention mech-anism, which enhanced the model's capacity to concentrate on critical image regions, thereby improving the detection of subtle radiographic indicators of COVID-19. Mobile Net also demon-strated faster convergence and lower test loss compared with VGG19, indicating both improved efficiency and stability. These attributes make it particularly well suited for real-time diagnostic applications and deploy-ment on devices with limited computational resources. Furthermore, the incor-poration of data augmentation and regularization strategies, including dropout and Gaussian noise, played a vital role in mitigating overfitting. This ensured that the models not only performed well on training data but also generalized effectively to unseen cases, underscoring their potential clinical applicability.

## 8   Future Work

Mobile Net showed strong results, but there is scope for improvement. Future studies can focus on tuning hyper parameters and using transfer learning with larger datasets to improve accuracy. Expanding the dataset with images from different populations, disease stages, and imaging condi-tions can also increase reliability. The model can be extended to multi-class classification to detect normal, pneumonia, and COVID-19 cases, making it more useful for diagnosis. Another direc-tion is real-time deployment, where the model can quickly analyze X-rays in hospitals. Finally, adding interpretability tools such as Grad-CAM or SHAP will help explain predictions and build trust in clinical use.

**Acknowledgments.** The author, Vaduguru Venkata Ramya, extends sincere gratitude to her supervisor, Anju Khandelwal, of the Sri Balaji University, Pune, for her invaluable guidance, mentorship, and continuous support throughout this research. The data used in this comparative study,"Deep Attention in Radiology: A Comparative Study of VGG19 and MobileNet for Chest X-Ray Image Classification," was sourced from Kaggle of Public Dataset, e.g., the ChestX-ray The author acknowledges the efforts of the original providers, for making this resource available to the global research community. Computational resources utilized for training the deep learning models were provided by Sri Balaji University at Sri Balaji University

## References


1. Ait Nasser, A., Akhloufi, M.A.: A review of recent advances in deep learning models for chest disease detection using radiography. Diagnostics **13**(1), 159 (2023)
2. Akhter, Y., Singh, R., Vatsa, M.: AI-based radiodiagnosis using chest X-rays: a review. Front. Big Data. **6**, 1120989 (2023)
3. Ahn, J.S., Ebrahimian, S., McDermott, S., et al.: Association of artificial intelligence–aided chest radiograph interpretation with reader performance and efficiency. JAMA Netw. Open (2023)
4. Azad, D., Hossain, F., Hossain, Z., et al.: Detection of multiple diseases from chest X-ray using machine learning and deep learning approaches. J. Hunan. Univ. Sci. Technol. **50**(4), 245–251 (2023)
5. Bennani, S., Regnard, N.-E., Ventre, J., et al.: Using AI to improve radiologist performance in detection of abnormalities on chest radiographs. Radiology **309**(3), e230860 (2023)
6. Celik, A., Surmeli, A.O., Demir, M., et al.: The diagnostic value of chest X-ray scanning by the help of artificial intelligence in heart failure (ARTIN-HF). Clin. Cardiol. **46**, 1562–1568 (2023)
7. Farouk, S., Osman, A.M., Awadallah, S.M., et al.: The added value of using artificial intelligence in adult chest X-rays for nodules and masses detection in daily radiology practice. Egypt. J. Radiol. Nucl. Med. **54**, 142 (2023)
8. Guo, L., Zhou, C., Xu, J., et al.: Deep learning for chest X-ray diagnosis: competition between radiologists with or without artificial intelligence assistance. J. Digit. Imag. **37**, 922–934 (2024)

9. Huang, J., Neill, L., Wittbrodt, M., et al.: Generative artificial intelligence for chest radiograph interpretation in the emergency department. JAMA Netw. Open **6**(10), e2336100 (2023)

10. Kolossváry, M., Raghu, V.K., Nagurney, J.T., et al.: (2023) Deep learning analysis of chest radiographs to triage patients with acute chest pain syndrome. Radiology **306**(2)

11. Lee, S.B.: Development of a chest X-ray machine learning convolutional neural network model on a budget and using artificial intelligence explainability techniques to analyze patterns of machine learning inference. JAMIA Open **7**(2), ooae035 (2024)

12. Miró Catalina, Q., Vidal-Alaball, J., FusterCasanovas, A., et al.: Real-world testing of an artificial intelligence algorithm for the analysis of chest X-rays in primary care settings. Sci. Rep. **14**, 5199 (2024)

13. Nguyen, N.H., Nguyen, H.Q., Nguyen, N.T., et al.: Deployment and validation of an AI system for detecting abnormal chest radiographs in clinical settings. Front. Digit. Health **4**, 890759 (2022)

14. Niehoff, J.H., Kalaitzidis, J., Kroeger, J.R., et al.: Evaluation of the clinical performance of an AI-based application for the automated analysis of chest X-rays. Sci. Rep. **13**, 3680 (2023)

15. Pillai, A.S.: Multi-label chest X-ray classification via deep learning. J. Intell. Learn. Syst. Appl. **14**(4), 43–56 (2022)

16. Prinster, D., Mahmood, A., Saria, S., et al.: Care to explain? AI explanation types differentially impact chest radiograph diagnostic performance and physician trust in AI. Radiology **313**(2) (2024)

17. Ram, S., Bodduluri, S.: Implementation of artificial intelligence-assisted chest X-ray interpretation: it is about time. Am. Thorac. Soc. **20**(5), 641–642 (2023)

18. Ridhi, S., Robert, D., Soren, P., et al.: Comparing the output of an artificial intelligence algorithm in detecting radiological signs of pulmonary tuberculosis in digital chest X-rays and their smartphone-captured photos of X-ray films: retrospective study. JMIR Form. Res. **8**, e55641 (2024)

19. Schalekamp, S., van Leeuwen, K., Calli, E., et al.: Performance of AI to exclude normal chest radiographs to reduce radiologists' workload. Eur. Radiol. **34**, 7255–7263 (2024)

20. Trine, D., Eudoriks, B., Aigeus, R., Boyel, N.: AI in medical imaging: Enhancing pneumonia detection in chest X-rays through deep learning. In: Proceedings of the International Conference on Healthcare Informatics (2024)

21. Vijayan, S., Jondhale, V., Pande, T., et al.: Implementing a chest X-ray artificial intelligence tool to enhance tuberculosis screening in India: lessons learned. PLOS Digit. Health **2**(12), e0000404 (2023)

22. Visuña, L., Yang, D., Garcia-Blas, J., et al.: Computer-aided diagnostic for classifying chest X-ray images using deep ensemble learning. BMC Med. Imaging **22**, 178 (2022)

23. Zhang, H., Hartvigsen, T., Ghassemi, M.: Algorithmic fairness in chest X-ray diagnosis: a case study. In: MIT Case Studies in Social and Ethical Responsibilities of Computing (2023)

# EcoMamba-Net: A Parameter-Efficient Architecture for Medical Image Segmentation


Anubhab Maity[(✉)][iD], Pallabi Dutta[iD], and Sushmita Mitra[iD]

Machine Intelligence Unit, Indian Statistical Institute, Kolkata, India
maityanubhabds@gmail.com



**Abstract.** Accurate segmentation of the medical image is essential for timely clinical diagnosis and treatment planning. However, many high-performing models are computationally intensive, limiting their use in settings with resource scarcity; such as in rural clinics, mobile diagnostic units, or point of care systems. To bridge this gap, we propose EcoMamba-Net, a lightweight yet powerful deep learning (DL) architecture designed for efficient medical image segmentation. At its core are the novel EcoMambaBlocks, which are streamlined modules inspired by the state-space modeling of Mamba. They effectively capture long-range dependencies with minimal overhead. The model integrates depthwise convolutions and a hybrid attention mechanism to combine spatial and channel information. This enables rich feature extraction while maintaining an extremely low parameter count of just 0.5 million. EcoMamba-Net is specifically suitable for medical image segmentation due to its ability to preserve fine-grained anatomical boundaries, handle low inter-class variance, and remain robust to modality-specific noise, while running efficiently on limited clinical hardware. Despite its compact size, EcoMamba-Net achieves high performance – with a Dice Similarity Coefficient of 91.2% in the ISIC 2018 skin lesion dataset and 89.6% in the Kvasir-SEG dataset for polyp segmentation; thereby, making it a practical and scalable solution for real-world clinical environments.

**GitHub Link:** https://github.com/maityanubhab/EcoMamba-Net.git

**Keywords:** Deep learning · Anatomical structure delineation · State-Space · Mamba · *U*-Net


## 1 Introduction

Automated medical image segmentation has become an essential part of today's healthcare systems, supporting early diagnosis, treatment planning, and disease monitoring in a wide range of clinical applications [7]. A major turning point was the introduction of *U*-Net [11], an encoder-decoder architecture with skip connections that preserved fine spatial details while capturing deep semantic



S. Mitra et al. (Eds.): PReMI 2025, LNCS 16358, pp. 306–314, 2026.
https://doi.org/10.1007/978-3-032-18480-1_31

context. Researchers have explored architectural advances such as dense connections, multi-scale feature fusion, and attention-enhanced models to improve focus on salient structures. Transformer-based architectures, TransUNet [14], have gained attention for their ability to model global dependencies using self-attention. However, most DL models, especially transformer-based, are impractical for deployment in real-world resource-constrained clinical environments. This has fueled interest in lightweight architectures that strike a balance between segmentation performance and deployment efficiency.

A promising direction is the use of **state-space models (SSMs)** [3] *viz.*, Mamba [2], with linear computational time-memory complexity, in contrast to the quadratic computational complexity of Transformers. Adapting Mamba models to medical image segmentation brings unique challenges; such as preserving fine-grained spatial information, reducing model size for real-time inference, and efficiently integrating context at multiple scales. This is particularly important in medical imaging, where accurate boundary detection, subtle feature recognition, and efficiency under limited computational resources are critical. Mamba's ability to model long-range dependencies with low overhead makes it well-suited for meeting these demands in clinical environments.

This research introduces **EcoMamba-Net** to address some of these limitations. It combines efficient state-space modeling and lightweight attention mechanisms in a compact encoder-decoder framework. The proposed EcoMamba-Net leverages Mamba-inspired linear dynamics and hybrid spatial-channel attention to deliver accurate, low-latency segmentation performance suitable for deployment in real clinical workflows. Experimental results in the publicly available ISIC 2018 [1] Kvasir-SEG [10] datasets demonstrate the superiority of the proposed model w.r.t. related state-of-the-art (SOTA) algorithms such as $U$-Net, SwinUNETR [4], U-Mamba [9], Swin-UMamba [8], VM-Unet [12], LightM-UNet [6] and Mobile U-ViT [13].

## 2  Methodology

EcoMamba-Net is an encoder-decoder architecture designed for efficient and accurate 2D medical image segmentation, as illustrated in Fig. 1(a). It consists of four encoder blocks and three decoder blocks, structured to progressively extract and refine spatial features. The encoder and decoder blocks incorporate (i) Efficient Attention (EA), a lightweight mechanism to capture both channel-wise dependency and spatial context [Fig. 1(c)], and (ii) EcoMamba (EM) a simplified state-space module to efficiently model long-range dependencies and spatial mixing [Fig. 1(b)]. EM is applied before the EA module in the encoder. The EM filters noise and enhances important features. This allows EA to focus more effectively on critical regions, which is essential in medical image segmentation. The proposed design balances local feature extraction and global context modeling to achieve high segmentation accuracy with low computational overhead.

The input image $\mathbf{I} \in \mathbb{R}^{C \times H \times W}$ is hierarchically encoded to generate global abstract details from low-level spatial details, where $C$ is the number of channels

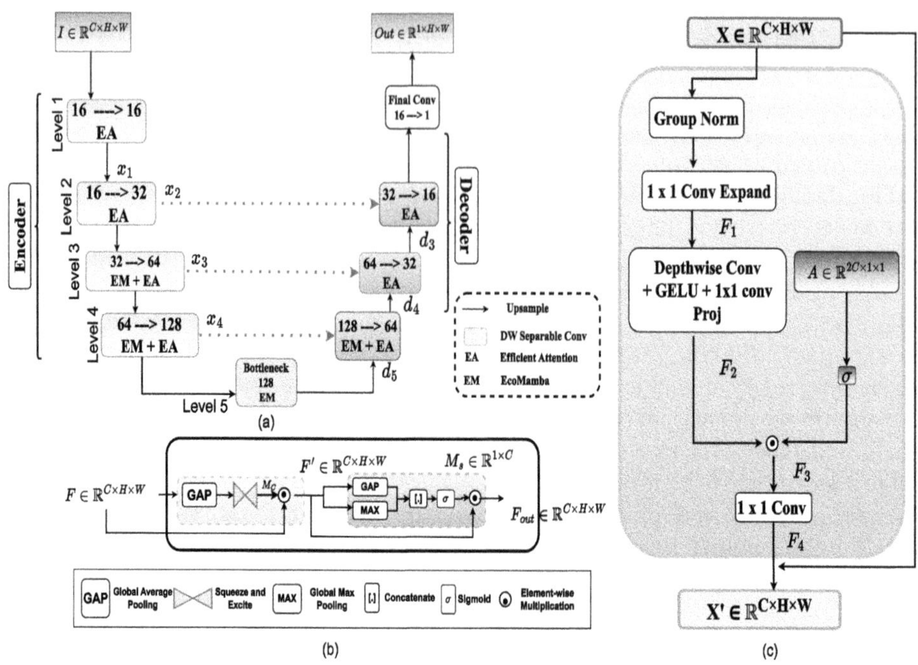

**Fig. 1.** Architecture of (a) EcoMamba-Net, with (b) Efficient Attention (EA) and (c) EcoMamba (EM) modules

and $H \times W$ are the spatial dimensions. Each encoder block employs depthwise separable convolution to reduce computations. The output of the convolution operation is subjected to the EA module $\mathcal{A}(\cdot)$ to highlight relevant feature maps.

Level 3 and 4 of the encoder, along with the bottleneck, incorporate EM Block to capture long-range dependencies in the high-level feature maps.

The decoder block at level $l$ takes the encoder output $\mathbf{x}_l$ through the skip connection and the up-sampled map from level $l + 1$ ($d_{l+1}$) of the decoder as input. Subsequently, the EA module generates an intermediate feature map as

$$\mathbf{F}_{out} = \mathcal{A}([\mathbf{x}_l, Upsample(d_{l+1})]), \tag{1}$$

with [.] representing the concatenation operation. The resulting feature $\mathbf{F}_{out}$ is then passed through a convolution layer to produce the final decoded feature map **Out**. The design ensures efficient encoding and decoding with contextual awareness and is suitable for real-time segmentation.

## 2.1   Efficient Attention

An efficient dual-attention module is developed to combine **channel** and **spatial** attention for enhanced feature representation with minimal computational burden.

**Channel Attention:** The channel-wise features are recalibrated using global context. Given an input feature map $\mathbf{F} \in \mathbb{R}^{C \times H \times W}$. The global average pooling (GAP) is applied over the spatial domain $\mathbf{z} = \mathrm{GAP}(\mathbf{F}) \in \mathbb{R}^{1 \times C}$. The pooled vector $\mathbf{z}$ is passed through a squeeze & excite [5] block. The resultant attention map $\mathbf{M}_c \in \mathbb{R}^{1 \times C}$ is multiplied in a channel-wise manner with $\mathbf{F}$, to generate recalibrated feature map volume $F' \in \mathbb{R}^{C \times H \times W}$.

**Spatial Attention:** Spatial attention emphasizes informative regions in the feature map by aggregating spatial context. Average pooling captures global contextual cues, while max pooling preserves the most salient features across channels. Then a convolutional kernel $\mathbf{W}_s \in \mathbb{R}^{1 \times 7 \times 7}$ with bias $\mathbf{b}_s$ is applied, followed by sigmoid activation

$$\mathbf{M}_s = \sigma \left( \mathbf{W}_s * [\mathbf{F}_{\mathrm{avg}}; \mathbf{F}_{\mathrm{max}}] + \mathbf{b}_s \right),$$

to produce a spatial attention map $\mathbf{M}_s \in \mathbb{R}^{1 \times H \times W}$.

The final refined feature map is obtained by element-wise multiplication of the channel and spatial attention weight to $F$, as

$$\mathbf{F}_{\mathrm{out}} = \mathbf{F} \odot \mathbf{M}_c \odot \mathbf{M}_s. \tag{2}$$

Attention applied serially, with channel attention followed by spatial attention. The sequential design allows progressive refinement of feature representation, enhancing both channel selectivity and spatial localization. This is beneficial for accurate and boundary-sensitive segmentation in medical images.

## 2.2   EcoMamba Block

The EcoMamba block brings memory-inspired representation into efficient convolutional architectures. It approximates the gating behavior of structured state-space models (SSMs), such as Mamba. It uses a fully convolutional and parallel design. The block introduces lightweight gating through static channel modulation while preserving local spatial information, making it suitable for dense prediction tasks.

Let the input feature map be denoted by $\mathbf{X} \in \mathbb{R}^{C \times H \times W}$. The input is first normalized using Group Normalization: $\mathbf{X}_{\mathrm{norm}} = \mathrm{GN}(\mathbf{X})$, which improves stability, especially in small-batch training common in medical imaging. Next, the normalized features are projected into a higher-dimensional latent space via a $1 \times 1$ convolution to generate $\mathbf{F}_1 \in \mathbb{R}^{2C \times H \times W}$. A depthwise separable convolution is applied to efficiently enhance local spatial interactions. It consists of a depthwise convolution followed by a pointwise $(1 \times 1)$ convolution. Formally, the transformation is expressed as

$$\mathbf{F}_2 = W_{\mathrm{proj}} * \phi\big(\mathrm{DWConv}(\mathbf{F}_1)\big), \quad \phi(x) = \mathrm{GELU}(x), \tag{3}$$

where DWConv performs channel-wise spatial filtering, $\phi$ introduces smooth nonlinear gating via GELU, and $W_{\mathrm{proj}}$ (a pointwise convolution) linearly projects the features across channels. This operation efficiently captures local context while maintaining low computational complexity.

Traditional convolutional layers treat all feature channels equally, assuming uniform importance in the representation. This uniform processing often propagates redundant or noisy features, increasing the computational load without improving accuracy. To address this limitation, we incorporate a **static gating mechanism** into the EcoMamba block. Specifically, we introduce a learnable gating vector $\mathbf{A} \in \mathbb{R}^{2C \times 1 \times 1}$. After applying a sigmoid activation, the gates act as channel-wise decay factors modulating the output. This mechanism explicitly enables **feature selectivity**, allowing the network to emphasize informative channels while suppressing irrelevant ones.

Unlike dynamic attention mechanisms, which compute input-dependent weights at runtime, $\mathbf{A}$ is input-independent and trained jointly with the network. $\mathbf{A}$ evolves into a **soft feature selection mask**, providing an efficient approximation of the selective information propagation seen in structured state-space models, without requiring sequential recurrence. This design adds negligible computational overhead but improves representational efficiency and stability in low-data regimes typical of medical imaging.

$\mathbf{A}$ is subsequently passed through a sigmoid function to produce a soft gating mask $\mathbf{G} \in \mathbb{R}^{2C \times 1 \times 1}$. This gating vector is applied element-wise to $\mathbf{F_2}$ to get $\mathbf{F_3}$, which simulates the exponential decay and memory modulation found in SSMs – but in a static and fully parallelized form. This gating mechanism selectively filters out irrelevant features while preserving useful ones, acting as a lightweight alternative to dynamic filtering and enabling efficient long-range modeling. The gated features are then projected back to the original channel dimension by a pointwise convolution to get $\mathbf{F_4}$. Finally, a residual connection is added to preserve the input semantics and ease of optimization. We have

$$\mathbf{X}' = \mathbf{F_4} + \mathbf{X}, \tag{4}$$

ensuring that the output $\mathbf{X}'$ has the same shape as the input $\mathbf{X}' \in \mathbb{R}^{C \times H \times W}$.

## 3    Implementation and Experimental Results

The method is evaluated on two diverse medical segmentation datasets. The ISIC 2018 dataset includes 2,594 dermoscopic images with binary skin lesion masks, while the Kvasir-SEG dataset contains 1,000 colonoscopy images with expert-annotated polyp masks. All images and masks are resized to $256 \times 256$. The models are implemented in PyTorch and trained on NVIDIA RTX A5500 GPU with 24 GB of memory using AdamW optimizer with a batch size of 4 for up to 200 epochs. Dice loss is used as the segmentation loss function to optimize spatial overlap between predicted and ground truth masks. Early stopping is applied when validation loss stagnates for 20 epochs. A cosine annealing scheduler, with warm restarts ($T_{\max} = 50$), adjusts the learning rate during training. The best results are marked in **bold** in each table.

## 3.1   Quantitative Performance

Table 1 compares EcoMamba-Net with state-of-the-art models on both datasets. It is observed that the EcoMamba-Net delivers best scores in all metrics with just 0.5M parameters. *U*-Net and VM-UNet perform well due to their encoder-decoder structure, but face limitations from low feature capacity and/or many parameters. SwinUNETR and Swin-UMamba gain from global context modeling but suffer from overfitting and high computational complexity due to the large number of parameters. LightM-UNet is efficient, it misses out on the finer boundary details. However, Mobile U-ViT accurately detects the lesion region (high sensitivity) and avoids false positives (high specificity). But the inaccurate boundary delineation reduces the overall mask overlap, as evidenced by the lower DSC value. EcoMamba-Net achieves sharper boundaries with robustness, while remaining lightweight and efficient.

**Table 1.** Comparative study of segmentation performance over the datasets

| Method | Params | ISIC 2018 | | | | | Kvasir-SEG | | | | |
|---|---|---|---|---|---|---|---|---|---|---|---|
| | | DSC | IoU | Sens. | Spec. | HD95 | DSC | IoU | Sens. | Spec. | HD95 |
| *U*-Net | 1.62M | 0.821 | 0.734 | 0.851 | 0.982 | 12.4 | 0.801 | 0.701 | 0.834 | 0.978 | 8.7 |
| SwinUNETR | 62.38M | 0.872 | 0.715 | 0.829 | 0.979 | 15.2 | 0.823 | 0.669 | 0.812 | 0.971 | 11.3 |
| U-Mamba | 10.21M | 0.713 | 0.679 | 0.867 | 0.984 | 10.8 | 0.741 | 0.726 | 0.849 | 0.981 | 7.2 |
| Swin-UMamba | 29.72M | 0.882 | 0.771 | 0.878 | 0.985 | 9.6 | 0.856 | 0.748 | 0.863 | 0.983 | 6.4 |
| VM-UNet | 34.10M | 0.902 | 0.792 | 0.889 | 0.987 | 8.3 | 0.868 | 0.765 | 0.871 | 0.985 | 5.8 |
| LightM-UNet | 1.3M | 0.891 | 0.785 | 0.882 | 0.986 | 8.9 | 0.834 | 0.759 | 0.867 | 0.984 | 6.1 |
| Mobile U-ViT | 1.39M | 0.897 | **0.808** | **0.906** | **0.988** | 8.1 | 0.882 | **0.790** | **0.891** | 0.985 | 6.2 |
| **EcoMamba-Net** | **0.5M** | **0.912** | <u>0.803</u> | <u>0.894</u> | **0.988** | **7.1** | **0.896** | <u>0.779</u> | <u>0.879</u> | **0.987** | **4.9** |

**Table 2.** Comparative study of overall model efficiency

| Method | Parameters | FLOPs (G) | Inference Time (ms) | Memory (MB) |
|---|---|---|---|---|
| *U*-Net | 1.62 M | **1.59** | 2.7 | 6.2 |
| SwinUNETR | 62.38 M | 44.3 | 41.6 | 237.1 |
| U-Mamba | 10.21 M | 8.7 | 10.8 | 39.0 |
| Swin-UMamba | 29.72 M | 23.6 | 26.9 | 113.3 |
| VM-UNet | 34.10 M | 6.94 | 8.9 | 130.1 |
| LightM-UNet | 1.3 M | 4.87 | 6.8 | 4.9 |
| Mobile U-ViT | 1.39 M | 2.52 | 7.4 | 10.5 |
| **EcoMamba-Net** | **0.5M** | <u>3.2</u> | **1.7** | **2.1** |

## 3.2  Efficiency Analysis

Table 2 shows a clear efficiency gap between EcoMamba-Net and other models. $U$-Net and VM-UNet rely on many convolutional layers, which results in an increase in FLOPs and memory usage. SwinUNETR, although powerful, suffers from the high cost of self-attention and larger parameter size. U-Mamba and Swin-UMamba use sequence modeling, but add complexity with the deeper layers and heavier state-space operations. LightM-UNet is lighter but lacks strong multi-scale feature representation. This affects its accuracy. EcoMamba-Net reduces redundant computations through optimized convolutions and a compact design. This results in just 3.2 GFLOPs and 1.7 ms inference time, while still maintaining strong feature learning with high boundary precision (Fig. 2).

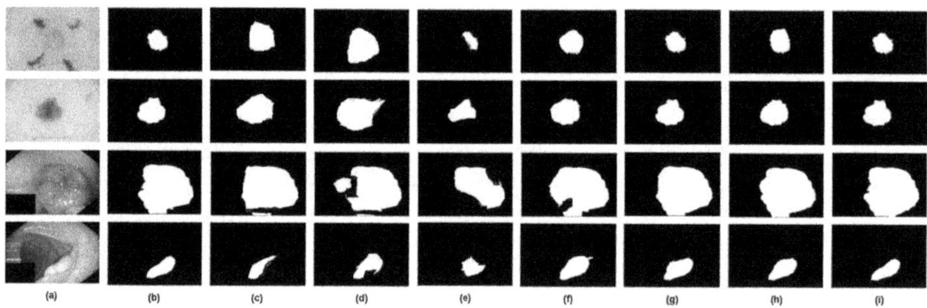

**Fig. 2.** Qualitative results on sample images, illustrating (a) input image (b) ground truth, and prediction from (c) $U$-Net, (d) SwinUNETR, (e) U-Mamba, (f) Swin-UMamba, (g) VM-UNet, (h) LightM-UNet and (i) EcoMamba-Net. Rows 1& 2: ISIC, Rows 3& 4: Kvasir-SEG, sample images.

**Table 3.** Ablation study on strategic placement of EM and EA blocks in the EcoMamba-Net.

| Configuration | Params | DSC (%) | GFLOPs | Wilcoxon Test(p-value) |
|---|---|---|---|---|
| A: No EcoMamba, Only Attention | 0.45M | 82.3 | ~1.9 | – |
| B: EcoMamba @ Encoder4 only | 0.48M | 83.6 | ~2.1 | <0.05 |
| C: EcoMamba @ Encoder3+4 | 0.49M | 84.7 | ~2.3 | <0.05 |
| D: + Bottleneck EcoMamba | 0.53M | 86.1 | ~2.5 | <0.05 |
| E: + EcoMamba @ Decoder2 | 0.54M | 88.4 | ~2.7 | <0.05 |
| F: Final (Enc3+4 + Bottleneck + Dec1) | **0.50M** | **91.2** | ~**3.2** | |
| G: EcoMamba @ All Blocks | 0.72M | 90.4 | ~3.6 | <0.05 |
| H: w/o Attention | 0.49M | 84.1 | ~2.3 | <0.05 |
| I: No EcoMamba, No Attention | 0.43M | 78.9 | ~1.7 | <0.05 |

### 3.3   Ablation Studies

Detailed ablation studies were conducted to analyze the contribution of each architectural component, as summarized in Table 3. The final configuration (F), EcoMamba-Net, achieves the best performance-efficiency trade-off. Each component contributes meaningfully, with EcoMamba blocks providing the largest improvement, followed by the combined attention mechanism. Their strategic placement optimizes the trade-off between efficiency and performance. EcoMamba-Net achieves superior results by improving global feature extraction and boundary delineation. The last column of Table 3 shows the results of the Wilcoxon test ($p < 0.05$), confirming the significance of each module.

## 4   Conclusion and Discussion

EcoMamba-Net, a compact and efficient segmentation architecture with only 0.5M parameters, was developed. It achieved strong performance on challenging medical datasets. By integrating lightweight Mamba blocks and efficient attention mechanisms within a $U$-Net framework, our model generated high segmentation accuracy with minimal computational cost. Key contributions included (1) 2D-optimized Mamba block, (2) efficient attention fusion, and (3) thorough validation.

In clinical settings, with limited resources, EcoMamba-Net opens the door to reliable AI-driven medical image analysis. However, the EcoMamba-Net is currently tailored for 2D segmentation and may not be directly generalizable to 3D volumetric data. Future work includes extending the model to 3D, incorporating multi-modal data, enabling uncertainty estimation for clinical support, and adapting it for federated learning to ensure privacy-preserving deployment.

**Acknowledgment.** This research was supported by J. C. Bose National Fellowship, sanction no. JCB/2020/000033 of S. Mitra.

## References


1. Codella, N.C.F., Gutman, D., et al.: Skin lesion analysis toward melanoma detection: a challenge. In: Proceedings of the International Symposium on Biomedical Imaging (ISBI 2018), pp. 168–172 (2018)
2. Gu, A., Dao, T.: Mamba: linear-time sequence modeling with selective state spaces. arXiv preprint arXiv:2312.00752 (2023)
3. Gu, A., Dao, T., et al.: Efficiently modeling long sequences with structured state spaces. In: Proceedings of the International Conference on Learning Representations (ICLR) (2022)
4. Hatamizadeh, A., Nath, V., et al.: Swin UNETR: swin transformers for semantic segmentation of brain tumors in MRI images. In: International MICCAI Brainlesion Workshop, pp. 272–284. Springer (2021)

5. Hu, J., Shen, L., Sun, G.: Squeeze-and-excitation networks. In: Proceedings of IEEE Conference Computer Vision and Pattern Recognition (CVPR), pp. 7132–7141, June 2018
6. Liao, W., Zhu, Y., et al.: LightM-UNet: Mamba assists in lightweight UNet for medical image segmentation. arXiv preprint arXiv:2403.05246 (2024)
7. Litjens, G., Kooi, T., et al.: A survey on deep learning in medical image analysis. Med. Image Anal. **42**, 60–88 (2017)
8. Liu, J., Yang, H., et al.: Swin-UMamba: Mamba-based U-Net with ImageNet-based pretraining. In: Proceedings of the International Conference on Medical Image Computing and Computer-Assisted Intervention, pp. 615–625. Springer (2024)
9. Ma, J., Li, F., Wang, B.: U-Mamba: enhancing long-range dependency for biomedical image segmentation. arXiv preprint arXiv:2401.04722 (2024)
10. Pogorelov, K., Randel, K.R., et al.: KVASIR: a multi-class image dataset for computer aided gastrointestinal disease detection. In: Proceedings of the 8th ACM on Multimedia Systems Conference, pp. 164–169 (2017)
11. Ronneberger, O., Fischer, P., et al.: U-Net: convolutional networks for biomedical image segmentation. In: Proceedings of the Medical Image Computing and Computer-Assisted Intervention-MICCAI, pp. 234–241. Springer (2015)
12. Ruan, J., Li, J., et al.: VM-UNet: vision Mamba UNet for medical image segmentation. arXiv preprint arXiv:2402.02491 (2024)
13. Tang, F., Nian, B., et al.: Mobile U-ViT: revisiting large kernel and U-shaped ViT for efficient medical image segmentation. arXiv preprint arXiv:2508.01064 (2025)
14. Vaswani, A., Shazeer, N., et al.: Attention is all you need. In: Advances in Neural Information Processing Systems, vol. 30, pp. 5998–6008 (2017)

# FISTA-GAN: An Interpretable Cosine-Decayed GAN for Fast Compressed-Sensing MRI


C. J. Aromal[iD] and Sumit Datta[(✉)][iD]

School of Electronic Systems and Automation, Digital University Kerala
(Former IIITM-K), Trivandrum 695317, India
`sumit.datta@iiitmk.ac.in`



**Abstract.** Long acquisition times, a staple characteristic of Magnetic Resonance Imaging (MRI) can be shortened by aggressively undersampling k-space and solving the resulting ill-posed reconstruction problem using learning based sparsity priors. Unrolled optimization networks such as FISTA-Net provide an interpretable framework with strong data consistency but struggle to restore fine textures at very low sampling ratios ($\leq 10\%$). Conversely, Generative Adversarial Network (GAN) based approaches sharpen details but are unstable and often hallucinate when the adversarial loss dominates. In this work, we introduce FISTA-GAN, an interpretable cosine-decayed GAN that combines unrolled FISTA iterations with a scheduled adversarial process. The generator is an unrolled FISTA-Net whose learnable convolutions act as proximal maps; the discriminator used is a spectrally normalized patch GAN. Training strategy starts with a generator warm-up, followed by a linear adversarial ramp and a cosine decay that smoothly anneals the GAN weight to $\leq 5\%$ of the total loss. An exponential moving average (EMA) of the generator further stabilises convergence. In 10% brain data from the CC-359 benchmarked dataset, the proposed model achieves 39.5 dB PSNR and 0.9142 SSIM, surpassing state-of-the-art unrolled baselines (FISTA-Net) and GAN (HARA-GAN, RSCA-GAN) by up to 2.6 dB and 0.05 SSIM, respectively. The results demonstrate that the integration of interpretability and adversarial detail enhancement yields fast, high-fidelity reconstructions suitable for time-critical clinical workflows.

**Keywords:** Compressed Sensing · CS-MRI reconstruction · FISTA-GAN


## 1 Introduction

Magnetic Resonance Imaging (MRI) is an indispensable tool for diagnosing a wide range of neurological, musculoskeletal and oncological conditions because of its unrivalled soft-tissue contrast [4]. Unfortunately, the long acquisition time of fully sampled MRI's limits patient throughput and renders the modality sensitive to motion artifacts [8]. Compressed sensing (CS) addresses this bottleneck



S. Mitra et al. (Eds.): PReMI 2025, LNCS 16358, pp. 315–322, 2026.
https://doi.org/10.1007/978-3-032-18480-1_32

by sampling the k-space and reconstructing a diagnostically acceptable image from vastly fewer measurements than required by the Nyquist criterion [8]. Classical CS-MRI reconstruction relies on iterative optimization with hand-crafted sparsity priors [3], e.g. total variation (TV) or wavelet $\ell_1$ norms, solved via ISTA [3], FISTA [1] or Alternating Direction Method of Multipliers (ADMM) [2]. Although these methods achieve mathematically guaranteed convergence, they require dozens to hundreds of iterations and meticulous parameter tuning, an impediment to real-time clinical deployment.

The algorithm unrolling paradigm converts a fixed number of iterations of a proximal optimization algorithm into a feed-forward network whose parameters are learned from data [10]. Pioneering examples include ISTA-Net [15], which unfold ISTA into a cascade of convolutional layers equipped with learnable soft-thresholds. Then came FISTA-Net [6,12], adding a learnable momentum term that accelerates convergence and allows deeper unrolled networks. Such models couple explicit data-consistency operations with learned priors, leading to interpretable architectures that inherit the convergence intuition of their optimisation counterparts. However, because they are optimised under pixel-wise loss functions (e.g. MSE or $\ell_1$), they tend to over-smooth textures and edges, especially at aggressive accelerations ($\leq$20% sampling) where high-frequency information is largely missing.

We introduce FISTA-GAN, an interpretable cosine-decayed generative adversarial framework for fast CS-MRI reconstruction. The generator is a nine-phase unrolled FISTA-Net whose convolutional filters act as learnable proximal maps; the critic is a spectrally normalised patch discriminator that operates on local image statistics. Training proceeds in three stages:

(i) a *generator warm-up* (first 100 epochs) with zero adversarial weight, ensuring strong data-consistency;

(ii) a *linear adversarial ramp* (next 50 epochs) that smoothly increases the GAN weight;

(iii) a *cosine decay* for the remaining epochs, annealing the adversarial contribution to a modest 5% of the total loss so that hallucinations are suppressed.

An exponential–moving–average (EMA) shadow of the generator, together with a late learning-rate drop for the critic, further enhances stability.

This paper is organized as follows. Section 2 provides a comprehensive review of related work. Section 3 details the proposed network architecture and training strategy. Section 4.1 presents extensive experimental setup. Section 4 presents and discusses results including quantitative metrics and qualitative comparisons. Finally, Sect. 5 concludes the paper and discusses future research directions.

## 2   Related Work

Accelerated MRI reconstruction has evolved along three converging tracks: (i) physics-driven optimization with handcrafted priors, (ii) unrolled networks that learn data driven proximal operators, and (iii) GAN based models that prioritize perceptual sharpness. Generative Adversarial Networks (GANs) address the blurring often seen in purely pixel wise losses by adding an adversarial term that pushes the generator to synthesize images indistinguishable from fully sampled references. Pioneering work began with DAGAN [13], which coupled a U-Net generator with a PatchGAN critic, and was extended by RefineGAN [11] whose cyclic data consistency preserved detail even at 10% sampling. Attention-augmented successors such as RSCA-GAN [7] (spatial+channel attention, 12.5–30% masks) and HARA-GAN [5] (hybrid attention with a relativistic critic) pushed SSIM to state of the art levels for 10% acquisitions.

Early fusions of adversarial learning with physics-based reconstruction, such as VN-GAN's variational cascade [9] and the GAN-augmented ISTA-Net++ [14], delivered only modest gains owing to instability and mode collapse. Later models—DAGAN [13], RefineGAN [11], RSCA-GAN [7], and HARA-GAN [5]—boosted perceptual quality via attention or cyclic losses, yet sacrificed the provable convergence and efficiency of classical unrolling.

## 3　Proposed Method

In this section we detail the complete pipeline of our proposed FISTA-GAN model, comprising of a physics-guided generator $\mathcal{G}$, a spectrally normalised patch discriminator $\mathcal{D}$, a multi-term loss function, and a three-stage curriculum that governs adversarial strength. An architectural overview is shown in Fig. 1.

### 3.1　Notation and Forward Model

Let $\mathbf{x} \in \mathbb{R}^{H \times W}$ be the fully sampled MR image and $U \in \{0,1\}^{H \times W}$ a binary undersampling mask. The acquired k-space data are

$$\mathbf{y} = \mathcal{F}(x) \odot U, \tag{1}$$

where $\mathcal{F}$ denotes the 2-D FFT and $\odot$ element-wise multiplication. Given $\mathbf{y}$ and $U$ we seek a reconstruction $\mathbf{x}^\star$ that is both data-consistent and perceptually faithful.

### 3.2　Generator: N-Phase Unrolled FISTA-Net

*Phase Structure:* $\mathcal{G}$ consists of unrolled phases, each mirroring one iteration of the Fast Iterative shrinkage thresholding algorithm (FISTA). A phase accepts $(x_k, t_k, x_{k-1})$ as inputs and outputs $(x_{k+1}, t_{k+1})$ via four steps:

a) **Gradient descent**

$$\mathbf{z_k} = x_k - \lambda_k \, \mathcal{F}^{-1}\big(U \odot \mathcal{F}(x_k) - y\big), \tag{2}$$

where the step size $\lambda_k$ is *learnable*.

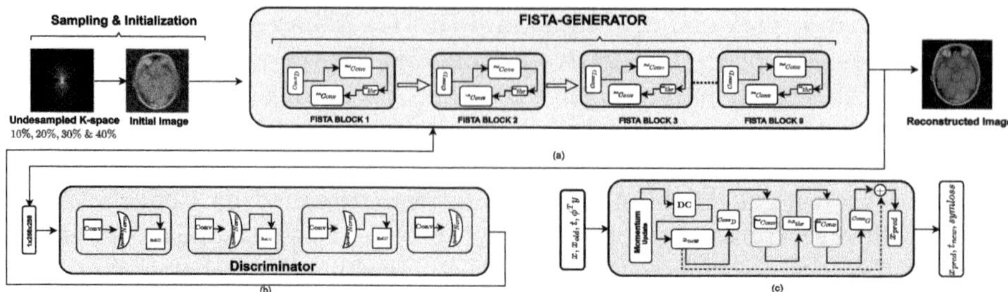

**Fig. 1.** An architectural overview of FISTA-GAN: (a) A high-level depiction of the unrolled FISTA-GAN pipeline, illustrating the process from undersampling and initialization to final reconstruction; (b) A detailed schematic of the internal structure of the discriminator block; (c) A detailed schematic of the internal structure of each FISTA block.

b) **Non-linear proximal mapping** $z_k$ passes through a *forward CNN* with two $3 \times 3$ conv layers $(\mathbf{K}_k^{1f}, \mathbf{K}_k^{2f})$, a learnable soft-threshold $\theta_k$ applied element-wise, and a *backward CNN* $(\mathbf{K}_k^{1b}, \mathbf{K}_k^{2b})$, followed by a $1 \times 1$ residual gate $\mathbf{K}_k^{G}$.

c) **Momentum update**

$$t_{k+1} = \tfrac{1}{2}\left(1 + \sqrt{1 + 4t_k^2}\right),$$

$$x_k^{\mathrm{pred}} = z_k + \mathbf{K}_G^{(k)} * \phi(z_k),$$

$$x_{k+1} = x_k^{\mathrm{pred}} + \frac{t_k - 1}{t_{k+1}}\left(x_k^{\mathrm{pred}} - x_{k-1}\right),$$

$$(3)$$

where $\phi(\cdot)$ denotes the forward–backward CNN pipeline.

d) **Symmetry penalty (auxiliary).** Each phase emits a placeholder tensor $s_k$ used to compute a lightweight symmetry regulariser (Sect. 3.4).

All convolutions have tied weights across channels to preserve interpretability and keep parameter count below 0.9 M—three orders of magnitude smaller than attention-heavy GAN generators.

## 3.3   Discriminator: Spectrally-Normalised PatchGAN

Inspired by the relativistic average critic(discriminator) of HARA-GAN, but opting for simplicity, we employ a 4-layer PatchGAN:

$$1 \xrightarrow{4\times4/2,a} 64 \xrightarrow{4\times4/2,a} 128 \xrightarrow{4\times4/2,a} 256 \xrightarrow{4\times4/1,a} 1,$$

where $a$ stands for LeakyReLU (0.2) activation function. All conv layers are wrapped in spectral normalization, guaranteeing a 1-Lipschitz critic which is a prerequisite for stable wasserstein training with gradient penalty.

## 3.4  Loss Functions

The generator is optimized with a composite objective

$$\mathcal{L}_{\mathcal{G}} = \underbrace{\lambda_1 \|x_G - x_{\mathrm{GT}}\|_1}_{\text{pixel}} + \underbrace{\lambda_{\mathrm{dc}} \|U \odot \mathcal{F}(x_G) - y\|_1}_{\text{data-cons.}} + \underbrace{\lambda_{\mathrm{sym}} \sum_{k=1}^{L} \|s_k\|_2^2}_{\text{sym.}}$$

$$+ \underbrace{\lambda_{\mathrm{SSIM}} D_{\mathrm{SSIM}}}_{\text{percept.}} + \underbrace{\lambda_{\mathrm{perc}} \|\Phi(x_G) - \Phi(x_{\mathrm{GT}})\|_1}_{\text{VGG-feat.}} + \underbrace{\lambda_{\mathrm{adv}} \left(-\mathcal{D}(x_G)\right)}_{\text{GAN}} , \tag{4}$$

where $\Phi$ is the first eight layers of VGG-11, and $D_{\mathrm{SSIM}}$ is the differentiable SSIM distance. Weights are fixed to $(\lambda_1, \lambda_{\mathrm{dc}}, \lambda_{\mathrm{sym}}, \lambda_{\mathrm{SSIM}}, \lambda_{\mathrm{perc}}) = (10, 1, 0.01, 1, 0.1)$, whereas $\lambda_{\mathrm{adv}}$ follows the curriculum below.

$$\mathcal{L}_{\mathcal{D}} = -\left(\mathcal{D}(x_{\mathrm{GT}}) - \mathcal{D}(x_G)\right) + \lambda_{\mathrm{GP}} \, \mathrm{GP}(x_{\mathrm{GT}}, x_G), \quad \text{with } \lambda_{\mathrm{GP}} = 50, \tag{5}$$

where the critic(discriminator) minimizes the WGAN-GP loss.

## 3.5  Curriculum Adversarial Training

Let $E$ be the epoch index, $E_{\mathrm{w}} = 100$ the warm-up length and $E_{\mathrm{r}} = 50$ the linear ramp. The adversarial weight is

$$\lambda_{\mathrm{adv}}(E) = \begin{cases} 0, & E \leq E_{\mathrm{w}}, \\ \lambda_{\max} \frac{E - E_{\mathrm{w}}}{E_{\mathrm{r}}}, & E_{\mathrm{w}} < E \leq E_{\mathrm{w}} + E_{\mathrm{r}}, \\ \lambda_{\max} \frac{1 + \cos\left(\pi \frac{E - E_{\mathrm{w}} - E_{\mathrm{r}}}{E_{\max} - E_{\mathrm{w}} - E_{\mathrm{r}}}\right)}{2} & \text{otherwise}, \end{cases}$$

with $\lambda_{\max} = 0.05$ and $E_{\max} = 400$. This cosine decay ensures that the GAN term vanishes smoothly at convergence, preventing late-stage hallucinations.

# 4  Experimental Results and Discussion

## 4.1  Experimental Setup

FISTA-GAN was trained on T1-weighted brain MR images from BrainMR and CC359, with separate models for 10, 20, 30, and 40% k-space undersampling. Each network was trained for 400 epochs (batch size $= 4$) on an NVIDIA A100, using a fixed perceptual-loss weight $\gamma = 0.01$ (see Sect. 3.4). Stability was promoted via an EMA ($\alpha = 0.999$) whose shadow generator served all validation and checkpointing; a two-timescale schedule kept the critic at $5 \times 10^{-5}$ for 250 epochs then dropping it $\times 10$; early stopping halts training if EMA-PSNR rose $<0.05$ dB over 20 epochs; and mixed-precision cuts memory (VRAM) utilization by 50% and speeds up training $1.8\times$. Updates followed the WGAN-GP objective with alternating G/D steps, and performance was assessed via PSNR, SSIM, and visual inspection.

## 4.2    Quantitative Performance

Table 1 contrasts FISTA–GAN with classical zero-filled (ZF) reconstruction and five strong learning baselines. Higher PSNR/SSIM and lower NMSE are desirable. FISTA–GAN delivers a decisive quantitative improvement: its peak signal-to-noise ratio reaches **39.50 dB**, surpassing the strongest baseline, HARA–GAN (31.96 dB), by +7.54 dB. Structural fidelity follows suit: the mean SSIM rises from the baseline 0.85 to **0.91**, trimming perceptual artefacts by approximately ~7 %. Crucially, these perceptual gains do not come at the expense of pixel-level accuracy—the normalised MSE is markedly lower than RefineGAN (3.13%) and a further 1.18% below HARA–GAN, confirming that higher PSNR/SSIM reflects genuinely lower reconstruction error. These margins indicate that coupling FISTA-inspired data consistency with an adversarial prior substantially narrows the gap between heavily undersampled and fully sampled reconstructions.

To probe how FISTA-GAN improves reconstructions, we analyse (i) spatial error maps $|\mathbf{x}_G - \mathbf{x}_{GT}|$ and (ii) k-space residual magnitudes $|\mathcal{F}(\hat{\mathbf{x}} - \mathbf{x}_{GT})|$, which consistently show reduced high-frequency residuals and fewer ringing artifacts relative to baselines (see Fig. 2), offering a concrete view of the model's inductive bias beyond black-box GAN features.

**Table 1.** Reconstruction performance on CC359 dataset (Radial mask, 10% undersampling) across models.

| Metrics | ZF | DAGAN [13] | RefineGAN [11] | RSCA-GAN [7] | HARA-GAN [5] | FISTA-GAN |
|---|---|---|---|---|---|---|
| PSNR | 23.14 | 24.15 | 28.32 | 30.19 | 31.96 | **39.50** |
| SSIM | 0.52 | 0.71 | 0.82 | 0.84 | 0.85 | **0.91** |
| NMSE | 11.61 | 9.45 | 3.13 | 2.76 | 2.53 | **2.50** |

## 4.3    Qualitative Performance

Figure 2 shows representative reconstructions obtained with the FISTA-GAN over undersampling factors of 10%–40% on the *BrainMR* test set. For each sampling ratio, four columns are displayed: Zerofilled input, fully-sampled reference, network output, and the absolute error map. Across all ratios the proposed model eliminates streaking and incoherent noise, while preserving subtle cortical and sub-cortical structures. The error maps confirm that the residual artefacts diminish markedly as the sampling ratio reaches 20%, the clinically preferred operational point. The multi-layer unrolling captures high-frequency detail with minimal ringing, yielding crisp tissue boundaries and clear depiction of fine anatomical features. These qualitative observations align with the quantitative gains in PSNR and SSIM reported in Sect. 4.2, and collectively demonstrate the efficacy of the multi-layer FISTA–GAN in high-fidelity CS-MRI reconstruction.

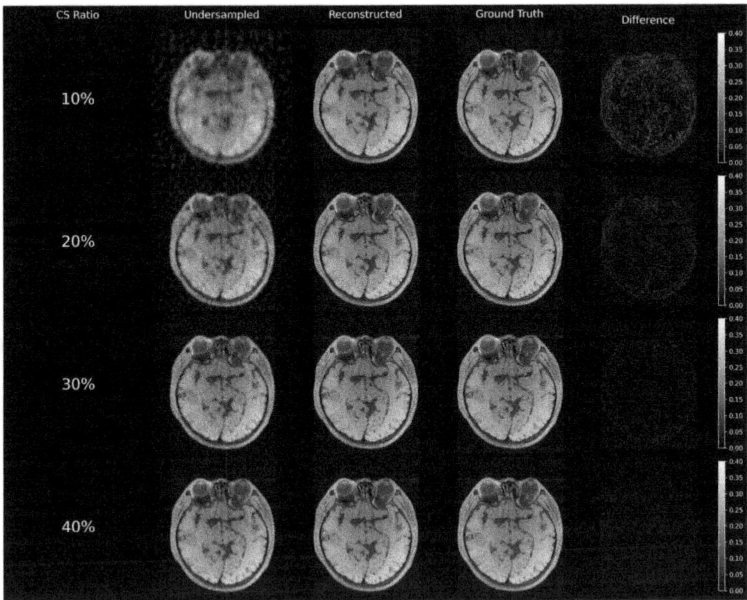

**Fig. 2.** Visual comparison of 10%–40%-sampled reconstructions on the Brain MR dataset.

# 5    Conclusion

This work introduces FISTA-GAN, an unrolled-network plus adversarial-learning framework for compressed-sensing MRI reconstruction, trained and evaluated it on the CC359 & BrainMR datasets under highly aggressive under-sampling. The approach unfolds the Fast Iterative Shrinkage-Thresholding Algorithm into a unrolled generator that interleaves strict k-space data-consistency updates with learnable sparsifying transforms, while a multiscale spectorally normalized patch discriminator enforces high-frequency realism. Extensive quantitative experiments—covering PSNR, SSIM, MSE & NMSE show that FISTA-GAN faithfully recovers fine anatomy and suppresses aliasing even at **10%** k-space sampling. The combination of classic FISTA dynamics, learned regularisation, and adversarial refinement yields a robust, generalisable solution for accelerated MRI. Future directions include depth-adaptive unrolling, attention-augmented generators, and multimodal priors to further enhance diagnostic fidelity and clinical impact.

**Acknowledgment.** The authors thank the Kerala State Council for Science, Technology, and Environment (KSCSTE) for the PhD fellowship and the Kerala University of Digital Sciences, Innovation, and Technology (KUDSIT) for their research ecosystem and computational resources that enabled this study.

# References


1. Beck, A., Teboulle, M.: A fast iterative shrinkage-thresholding algorithm for linear inverse problems. SIAM J. Imag. Sci. **2**(1), 183–202 (2009)
2. Boyd, S., Parikh, N., Chu, E., Peleato, B., Eckstein, J.: Distributed optimization and statistical learning via the alternating direction method of multipliers. Found. Trends Mach. Learn. **3**(1), 1–122 (2011)
3. Daubechies, I., Defrise, M., Mol, C.D.: An iterative thresholding algorithm for linear inverse problems with a sparsity constraint. Commun. Pure Appl. Math. **57**(11), 1413–1457 (2004)
4. Deka, B., Datta, S.: Compressed Sensing Magnetic Resonance Image Reconstruction Algorithms: A Convex Optimization Approach, Springer Series on Bio- and Neurosystems, vol. 9. Springer, Singapore (2019)
5. Desalegn, L., Jifara, W.: HARA-GAN: hybrid attention and relative average discriminator based generative adversarial network for MR image reconstruction. IEEE Access **12**, 23240–23251 (2024). https://doi.org/10.1109/ACCESS.2024.3364699
6. Aromal, C.J, Datta, S.: FISTA-NET: compressed sensing MRI reconstruction using unrolled iterative networks. In: Proceedings of the 21st IEEE India Council International Conference (INDICON), pp. 1–6. IEEE (2024)
7. Li, G., Lv, J., Wang, C.: A modified generative adversarial network using spatial and channel-wise attention for CS-MRI reconstruction. IEEE Access **9**, 83185–83198 (2021)
8. Lustig, M., Donoho, D.L., Santos, J.M., Pauly, J.M.: Compressed sensing MRI. IEEE Signal Process. Mag. **25**(2), 72–82 (2008)
9. Mardani, M., Gong, E., Cheng, J.Y., Vasanawala, S.S., Zaharchuk, G., Alley, M.T., et al.: Deep generative adversarial neural networks for compressed sensing automates MRI. IEEE Trans. Med. Imaging **38**(1), 167–179 (2019)
10. Monga, V., Li, Y., Eldar, Y.C.: Algorithm unrolling: interpretable, efficient deep learning for signal and image processing. IEEE Signal Process. Mag. **38**(2), 18–44 (2021)
11. Quan, T.M., Nguyen-Duc, T., Jeong, W.K.: Compressed sensing MRI reconstruction using a generative adversarial network with a cyclic loss. IEEE Trans. Med. Imaging **37**(6), 1488–1497 (2018)
12. Xiang, J., Dong, Y., Yang, Y.: FISTA-Net: learning a fast iterative shrinkage-thresholding network for inverse problems in imaging. IEEE Trans. Med. Imaging **40**(5), 1329–1339 (2021)
13. Yang, G., et al.: DAGAN: deep de-aliasing generative adversarial networks for fast compressed sensing MRI reconstruction. IEEE Trans. Med. Imaging **37**(6), 1310–1321 (2018)
14. You, D., Xie, J., Zhang, J.: ISTA-Net++: flexible deep unfolding network for compressive sensing. In: Proceedings of the IEEE International Conference on Multimedia and Expo (ICME), pp. 1–6. IEEE (2021)
15. Zhang, J., Ghanem, B.: ISTA-Net: interpretable optimization-inspired deep network for image compressive sensing. In: Proceedings of the IEEE/CVF Conference on Computer Vision and Pattern Recognition (CVPR), pp. 1828–1837. IEEE, Salt Lake City, UT (2018)

# Colon Polyp Detection and Segmentation with YOLOv8 and Attention-Augmented U-Net Model


Brahmanand Dubey, Subhayu Ghosh[(✉)], Jishnu Raj, and Nanda Dulal Jana

Department of Computer Science and Engineering, National Institute of Technology Durgapur, Durgapur, West Bengal, India
`sg.22cs1101@phd.nitdgp.ac.in`, `jr.21u10797@btech.nitdgp.ac.in`,
`ndjana.cse@nitdgp.ac.in`



**Abstract.** Early detection and accurate segmentation of polyps are essential for reducing colorectal cancer mortality. However, manual analysis of colonoscopy images is error-prone due to variability in polyp appearance, limited contrast, and operator fatigue. To address these challenges, we propose a deep learning-based framework that integrates object detection and semantic segmentation for precise polyp analysis. The method employs YOLOv8 to localize polyps across diverse colonoscopic imaging modalities, followed by a modified U-Net that performs fine-grained segmentation guided by attention masks derived from the detection output. This attention mechanism directs the segmentation network to focus on polyp-relevant regions. In addition, a weighted Binary Cross-Entropy loss is applied to emphasize tumor pixels during training. Experiments on a multi-modal colonoscopy dataset demonstrate that the proposed framework achieves superior performance in Dice score, Intersection over Union, and pixel-level precision and recall. These results highlight the system's robustness and clinical relevance for enhancing polyp detection and delineation during colonoscopy. The source code is made publicly available for reproducibility at: https:// github.com/greenredjr/Colon-Tumor-Detection-and-Segmetation.

**Keywords:** Colorectal Cancer · Colon Polyp Detection · Medical Image Segmentation · YOLOv8 · Attention U-Net · Binry Cross-Entropy Loss


## 1 Introduction

Colorectal cancer (CRC) remains one of the most common and deadly cancers globally, accounting for a significant proportion of cancer-related deaths each year [1,2]. Early detection and removal of polyps during colonoscopy have been shown to drastically reduce both incidence and mortality [3]. However, manual inspection of colonoscopy images is time-consuming, subject to human fatigue,



S. Mitra et al. (Eds.): PReMI 2025, LNCS 16358, pp. 323–331, 2026.
https://doi.org/10.1007/978-3-032-18480-1_33

and prone to errors—especially when dealing with small, flat, or poorly illuminated polyps. These challenges underscore the urgent need for automated, accurate, and real-time computer-aided diagnostic tools.

Recent advances in deep learning have demonstrated remarkable capabilities in various medical imaging tasks, including detection, classification, and segmentation [4–6]. In the context of colonoscopy analysis, object detection models such as YOLO (You Only Look Once) have shown promise in localizing potential lesions [7,8], while segmentation networks like U-Net excel in delineating precise boundaries of anatomical structures [9]. Despite their individual strengths, standalone models often struggle in challenging conditions such as cluttered backgrounds, low-contrast regions, and varying polyp morphologies.

To address these limitations, we propose a unified deep learning architecture that combines the localization power of YOLOv8 [10] with the pixel-level segmentation ability of U-Net, enhanced through spatial attention. Specifically, the detection output from YOLOv8 is converted into an attention mask, which is concatenated with the original image to form a 4-channel input to a modified U-Net. This attention-guided input helps the segmentation model concentrate on the most relevant regions, thereby reducing false positives and improving delineation accuracy. Furthermore, we introduce a weighted Binary Cross-Entropy (BCE) loss [11] that prioritizes tumor pixels over background, encouraging the model to focus on clinically important structures.

The entire framework is evaluated on a multi-modal colonoscopy dataset comprising white-light imaging (WLI), linked color imaging (LCI), narrow-band imaging (NBI), flexible spectral imaging color enhancement (FICE), and blue-laser imaging (BLI). The proposed system consistently achieves high performance across all modalities using different evaluation metrics.

The main contributions of this work are as follows:

1. We employ YOLOv8 to accurately detect colon polyp regions across diverse colonoscopy imaging modalities.
2. We enhance a standard U-Net architecture by integrating attention masks derived from YOLOv8 outputs to guide focused segmentation.
3. We design a weighted Binary Cross-Entropy loss function to emphasize tumor pixels, addressing class imbalance and improving segmentation quality.
4. We evaluate the proposed framework on a multi-modal colonoscopy dataset and achieve superior performance in all key metrics, demonstrating its robustness and clinical relevance.

The rest of the paper is organized as follows: Sect. 2 discusses related work in colon polyp detection and segmentation. Section 3 details the proposed methodology, while Sect. 4 presents the experimental setups including dataset description and evaluation metrics. Section 5 reports and analyzes the results. Section 6 concludes the paper with insights and directions for future research.

## 2   Related Work

Deep learning has made substantial progress in the field of medical image analysis, particularly in the automated detection and segmentation of lesions from endoscopic and radiologic scans. In the context of colorectal polyp analysis, prior research has explored both object detection and semantic segmentation techniques, often treating them as independent tasks.

Object detection models such as SSD, Faster R-CNN [12], and YOLO variants have been widely applied for polyp localization. Among these, YOLO-based architectures are preferred for real-time clinical use due to their fast inference and competitive accuracy [13]. Recent versions like YOLOv5 and YOLOv7 have shown improved performance on small object detection [14], which is crucial for capturing diminutive or flat polyps. However, these detectors generally provide only coarse localization through bounding boxes, lacking pixel-level detail necessary for clinical diagnosis.

On the other hand, semantic segmentation approaches aim to delineate precise polyp boundaries. U-Net and its variants have become the de facto standard in medical image segmentation due to their encoderdecoder structure and skip connections, which enable fine spatial resolution [15]. Enhancements such as Attention U-Net and residual U-Net further improve focus on critical regions and mitigate gradient vanishing in deeper networks [16]. Nevertheless, segmentation models that process full images without spatial priors often suffer from false positives, especially in cluttered or low-contrast settings.

To overcome this, recent works have proposed detection-assisted segmentation frameworks that use bounding boxes as region proposals for guiding segmentation models. Some studies have employed cascaded or region-of-interest (ROI) strategies to reduce the search space and improve segmentation accuracy [17]. However, few have integrated detection outputs as explicit spatial attention within the segmentation model itself.

Our work differs by embedding YOLOv8-based detection results directly into the U-Net input via attention masks. This approach combines the speed and localization capability of YOLO with the spatial precision of U-Net, resulting in a segmentation framework to perform robustly across multiple imaging modalities.

## 3   Proposed Approach

The proposed framework consists of two interconnected components: (i) YOLOv8-based object detection module to localize polyp regions, and (ii) a modified U-Net segmentation network enhanced with attention masks derived from the detection output. Figure 1 illustrates the overall pipeline of the proposed approach.

### 3.1  YOLOv8-Based Detection

YOLOv8 is employed to perform for detection of polyp regions in colonoscopy images. Each image $\mathbf{I} \in \mathbb{R}^{H \times W \times 3}$ is passed through the YOLOv8 network, which predicts a set of bounding boxes $\mathcal{B} = \{b_1, b_2, \ldots, b_N\}$, where $b_i = (x_i, y_i, w_i, h_i)$ denotes the center coordinates and dimensions of the $i$-th box. Each box is associated with an objectness score $s_i$ and class label $c_i$.

Non-maximum suppression (NMS) is applied to remove redundant detections. The output is then converted into a binary attention mask $\mathbf{A} \in \{0, 1\}^{H \times W}$ by filling the region inside each retained bounding box with 1, while the rest of the image is set to 0. This mask guides the downstream segmentation process.

### 3.2  Attention-Augmented U-Net

The segmentation network is a modified U-Net that accepts a 4-channel input $\mathbf{X} \in \mathbb{R}^{H \times W \times 4}$, obtained by concatenating the RGB image $\mathbf{I}$ with the attention mask $\mathbf{A}$. Formally,

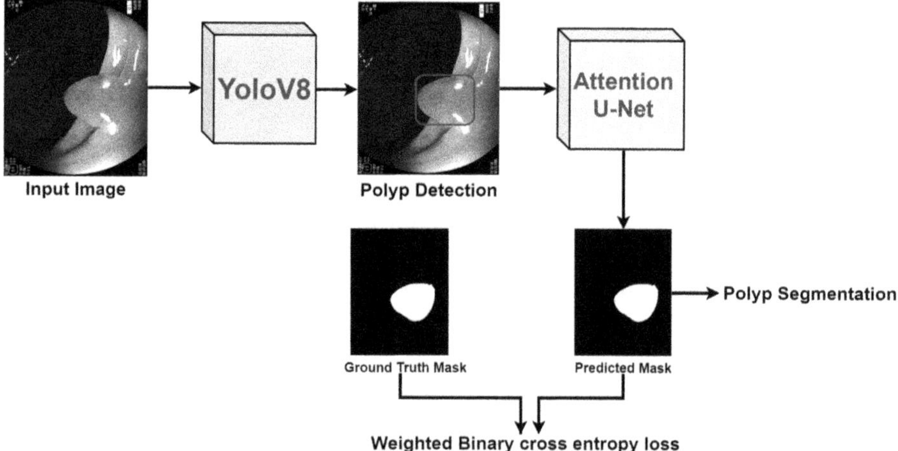


**Fig. 1.** A diagrammatic representation illustrating the proposed approach for colon polyp detection and segmentation.

$$\mathbf{X} = \mathrm{concat}(\mathbf{I}, \mathbf{A}),  \tag{1}$$

where $\mathrm{concat}(\cdot)$ denotes channel-wise concatenation.

Let $\mathcal{F}_\theta$ denote the segmentation model with learnable parameters $\theta$. The model predicts a soft segmentation map $\hat{\mathbf{Y}} = \mathcal{F}_\theta(\mathbf{X}) \in [0, 1]^{H \times W}$, where each pixel value represents the probability of being part of a polyp.

### 3.3   Weighted Binary Cross-Entropy Loss

To address the class imbalance between polyp and background pixels, we introduce a weighted BCE loss that emphasizes polyp regions using the attention mask. Given the ground truth segmentation mask $\mathbf{Y} \in \{0,1\}^{H \times W}$ and the predicted probability map $\hat{\mathbf{Y}}$, the standard pixel-wise BCE loss is defined as:

$$\mathcal{L}_{\text{BCE}}(p, y) = - \left[ y \cdot \log(p) + (1 - y) \cdot \log(1 - p) \right], \tag{2}$$

where $p = \hat{\mathbf{Y}}_{i,j}$ and $y = \mathbf{Y}_{i,j}$ for pixel $(i,j)$.

The weighted version introduces a per-pixel weight map $\mathbf{W} \in \mathbb{R}^{H \times W}$ defined as:

$$\mathbf{W}_{i,j} = \alpha + (1 - \alpha) \cdot \mathbf{A}_{i,j}, \quad \alpha \in [0, 1], \tag{3}$$

where $\alpha$ is a tunable background weight (set to 0.1 in our implementation). The final loss is computed as:

$$\mathcal{L}_{\text{WBCE}} = \frac{1}{H \cdot W} \sum_{i=1}^{H} \sum_{j=1}^{W} \mathbf{W}_{i,j} \cdot \mathcal{L}_{\text{BCE}}(\hat{\mathbf{Y}}_{i,j}, \mathbf{Y}_{i,j}). \tag{4}$$

This formulation penalizes errors in polyp regions more heavily, thereby guiding the network to learn precise boundaries.

### 3.4   Training Strategy

The model is trained using the RAdam optimizer [18] with an initial learning rate of $10^{-4}$. Input images are resized to $256 \times 256$, and standard data augmentation techniques (flip, rotation, elastic transform) are used to improve generalization. The YOLOv8 detection model is trained independently before the attention masks are generated for segmentation training.

## 4   Experimental Setups

### 4.1   Dataset Details

We evaluate the proposed framework on a curated colonoscopy dataset composed of five imaging modalities: WLI, NBI, LCI, FICE, and BLI. The dataset consists of images $\mathbf{I} \in \mathbb{R}^{256 \times 256 \times 3}$ and their corresponding binary segmentation masks $\mathbf{Y} \in \{0,1\}^{256 \times 256}$. Bounding boxes are generated from masks using connected components analysis and converted into YOLO format for detection training. Each modality includes 600 augmented samples, resulting in a balanced multi-domain dataset.

We perform an 80:10:10 stratified split for training, validation, and testing across each modality to ensure uniform class distribution. Data augmentation is applied using Albumentations, including horizontal/vertical flips, random rotations, Gaussian noise, elastic transforms, and grid distortions.

### 4.2 Evaluation Metrics

To assess segmentation performance, we compute the following standard metrics:

- **Dice Coefficient (Dice):** Measures overlap between predicted and ground truth masks:

$$\text{Dice} = \frac{2|\hat{\mathbf{Y}} \cap \mathbf{Y}|}{|\hat{\mathbf{Y}}| + |\mathbf{Y}|}. \tag{5}$$

- **Intersection over Union (IoU):** Also known as the Jaccard Index:

$$\text{IoU} = \frac{|\hat{\mathbf{Y}} \cap \mathbf{Y}|}{|\hat{\mathbf{Y}} \cup \mathbf{Y}|}. \tag{6}$$

- **Pixel Precision and Recall:**

$$\text{Precision} = \frac{\text{TP}}{\text{TP} + \text{FP}}, \quad \text{Recall} = \frac{\text{TP}}{\text{TP} + \text{FN}}. \tag{7}$$

- **Pixel Accuracy:**

$$\text{Accuracy} = \frac{\text{TP} + \text{TN}}{\text{TP} + \text{FP} + \text{TN} + \text{FN}}. \tag{8}$$

Here, TP, FP, TN, and FN denote true positives, false positives, true negatives, and false negatives, respectively. $\mathbf{Y}$ denotes the ground truth, while $\hat{\mathbf{Y}}$ is the predicted binary segmentation map.

For the detection module, we report Precision, Recall, mean Average Precision at IoU thresholds 0.5 ($\text{mAP}_{0.5}$) and averaged over thresholds from 0.5 to 0.95 ($\text{mAP}_{0.5:0.95}$), following standard object detection benchmarks.

## 5   Results and Discussion

We evaluate both detection and segmentation performance on the test set using standard metrics. To benchmark the effectiveness of our framework, we compare it with several widely adopted deep learning models. For object detection, we consider YOLOv5s and Faster R-CNN as baselines. For segmentation, we compare with vanilla U-Net, Attention U-Net, and DeepLabv3+.

Table 1 reports detection results obtained from experimental validation. The proposed YOLOv8 model outperforms other detectors in both precision and recall while maintaining high mAP at multiple IoU thresholds.

The proposed YOLOv8-based detector yields the highest overall scores, particularly excelling in $\text{mAP}_{0.5:0.95}$, confirming its robustness across variable thresholds and imaging conditions. As shown in Fig. 2, the YOLOv8 detector successfully localizes polyps of various sizes and appearances with high confidence.

Furthermore, Table 2 presents the segmentation performance comparison with state-of-the-art (SOTA) models. The proposed attention-augmented U-Net shows superior accuracy across all metrics from the compared models.

**Table 1.** Comparison of polyp detection performance across detectors.

| Model | Precision (%) | Recall (%) | mAP@0.5 (%) | mAP@0.5:0.95 (%) |
| --- | --- | --- | --- | --- |
| Faster R-CNN [12] | 89.50 | 84.30 | 90.70 | 82.60 |
| YOLOv5s [13] | 91.00 | 87.90 | 94.15 | 86.25 |
| **Proposed (Ours)** | **93.10** | **91.20** | **96.85** | **90.45** |

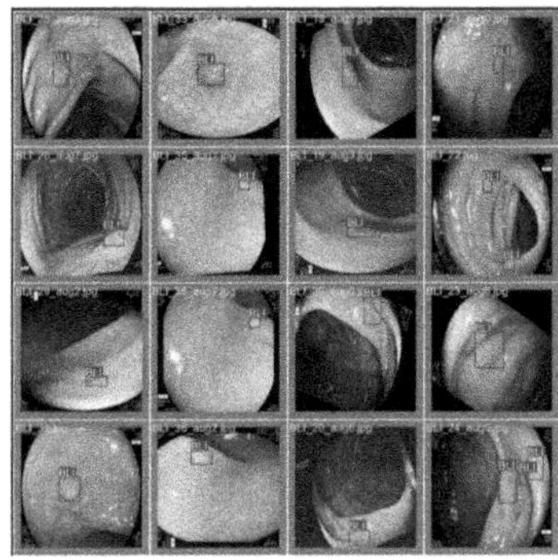

**Fig. 2.** Some predictions of the YOLOv8 model.

Compared to DeepLabv3+, which is a strong SOTA segmentation model, our method improves Dice score by 2.45% and IoU by 3.47%, demonstrating the benefit of integrating detection-driven attention with weighted loss. Figure 3 shows an example of segmentation output where the predicted mask closely aligns with the ground truth.

Qualitative visualizations reveal that the proposed system produces smooth and accurate segmentation masks that closely follow polyp boundaries. The attention-guided input helps suppress irrelevant background structures, and the weighted BCE loss ensures strong focus on tumor pixels.

In summary, the proposed hybrid detectionsegmentation approach achieves SOTA performance while remaining computationally efficient. The integration of spatial attention and adaptive loss weighting significantly boosts both localization and delineation quality.

**Table 2.** Comparison of segmentation performance across models

| Model | Dice (%) | IoU (%) | Precision (%) | Recall (%) | Pixel Acc. (%) |
| --- | --- | --- | --- | --- | --- |
| U-Net (Vanilla) [15] | 85.60 | 78.90 | 86.70 | 84.25 | 94.88 |
| Attention U-Net [16] | 88.15 | 81.60 | 89.35 | 86.45 | 95.71 |
| DeepLabv3+ [17] | 89.90 | 83.95 | 90.80 | 88.90 | 96.12 |
| **Proposed (Ours)** | **92.35** | **87.42** | **91.85** | **92.64** | **97.23** |

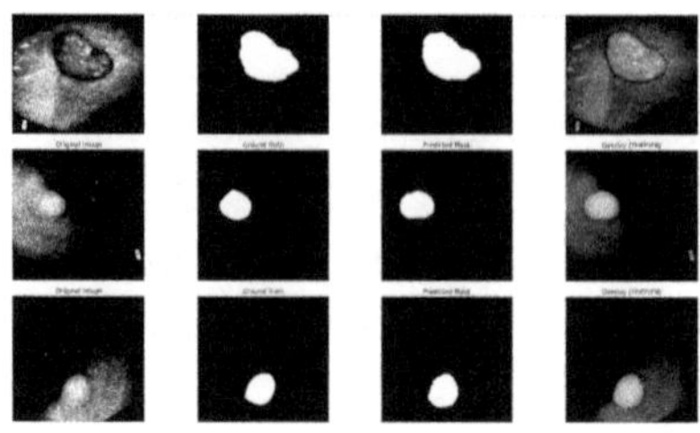

**Fig. 3.** Overlaying predicted and original masks on original image.

# 6   Conclusion and Future Work

In this work, we proposed a deep learning framework that combines YOLOv8-based polyp detection with an attention-augmented U-Net for precise colon polyp segmentation. By incorporating spatial priors derived from detection outputs and introducing a weighted Binary Cross-Entropy loss, the framework achieved high segmentation accuracy across five imaging modalities. The modular design allows for efficient training and inference, making the system suitable for real-time clinical integration.

As future work, we plan to extend the model to handle video sequences using temporal attention mechanisms, enabling frame-level consistency in colonoscopy analysis. Further improvements may involve training with larger and more diverse datasets, exploring transformer-based backbones for segmentation, and integrating clinical feedback to improve interpretability and reliability in real-world deployment for the effective colon polyp detection and segmentation.

# References


1. Aarons, C.B., Shanmugan, S., Bleier, J.I.: Management of malignant colon polyps: current status and controversies. World J. Gastroenterol.: WJG **20**(43), 16178 (2014)
2. Mármol, I., Sánchez-de-Diego, C., Pradilla Dieste, A., Cerrada, E., Rodriguez Yoldi, M.J.: Colorectal carcinoma: a general overview and future perspectives in colorectal cancer. Int. J. Mol. Sci. **18**(1), 197 (2017)
3. Shah, R., Jones, E., Vidart, V., Conti, J.A., Francis, N.K.: Biomarkers for early detection of colorectal cancer and polyps: systematic review. Cancer Epidemiol. Biomarkers Prev. **23**, 1712–1728 (2014)
4. Kim, M., et al.: Deep learning in medical imaging. Neurospine **16**(4), 657 (2019)
5. Rana, M., Bhushan, M.: Machine learning and deep learning approach for medical image analysis: diagnosis to detection. Multimed. Tools Appl. **82**(17), 26731–26769 (2023)
6. Ghosh, S., Dhar, S., Yoddha, R., Kumar, S., Thakur, A.K., Jana, N.D.: Melanoma skin cancer detection using ensemble of machine learning models considering deep feature embeddings. Procedia Comput. Sci. **235**, 3007–3015 (2024)
7. Inthiyaz, S., Ahammad, S.H., Krishna, A., Bhargavi, V., Govardhan, D., Rajesh, V.: Yolo (you only look once) making object detection work in medical imaging on convolution detection system. Int. J. Pharm. Res. (09752366) **12**(2) (2020)

8.  Ragab, M.G., et al.: A comprehensive systematic review of yolo for medical object detection (2018 to 2023). IEEE Access **12**, 57815–57836 (2024)

9.  Krithika Alias AnbuDevi, M., Suganthi, K.: Review of semantic segmentation of medical images using modified architectures of unet. Diagnostics **12**(12), 3064 (2022)

10. Sohan, M., Sai Ram, T., Rami Reddy, C.V.: A review on YOLOv8 and its advancements. In: Jacob, I.J., Piramuthu, S., Falkowski-Gilski, P. (eds.) Data Intelligence and Cognitive Informatics. ICDICI 2023. Algorithms for Intelligent Systems, pp. 529–545. Springer, Singapore (2024). https://doi.org/10.1007/978-981-99-7962-2_39

11. Ruby, U., Yendapalli, V., et al.: Binary cross entropy with deep learning technique for image classification. Int. J. Adv. Trends Comput. Sci. Eng. **9**(10) (2020)

12. Ren, S., He, K., Girshick, R., Sun, J.: Faster r-cnn: towards real-time object detection with region proposal networks. Adv. Neural Inf. Process. Syst. **28** (2015)

13. Zhou, Q., Zhang, W., Li, R., Zhen, S., Niu, F.: Improved yolov5-s object detection method for optical remote sensing images based on contextual transformer. J. Electron. Imaging **31**(4), 043049 (2022)

14. Olorunshola, O.E., Irhebhude, M.E., Evwiekpaefe, A.E.: A comparative study of yolov5 and yolov7 object detection algorithms. J. Comput. Soc. Inform. **2**(1), 1–12 (2023)

15. Jiang, J., Wang, M., Tian, H., Cheng, L., Liu, Y.: Lv-unet: a lightweight and vanilla model for medical image segmentation. In: 2024 IEEE International Conference on Bioinformatics and Biomedicine (BIBM), pp. 4240–4246, IEEE, 2024

16. Zhu, Z., Yan, Y., Xu, R., Zi, Y., Wang, J.: Attention-unet: a deep learning approach for fast and accurate segmentation in medical imaging. J. Comput. Sci. Softw. Appl. **2**(4), 24–31 (2022)

17. Peng, H., et al.: Semantic segmentation of litchi branches using deeplabv3+ model. IEEE Access **8**, 164546–164555 (2020)

18. Mazumder, A., Ghosh, S., Roy, S., Dhar, S., Jana, N.D. Rectified adam optimizer-based CNN Model for speaker identification . In: Mohanty, M.N., Das, S. (eds.) Advances in Intelligent Computing and Communication. LNNS, vol. 430, pp. 155–162. Springer, Singapore (2022). https://doi.org/10.1007/978-981-19-0825-5_16

# VM-CycleGAN: A Lightweight CycleGAN Framework for MRI Translation from 3T to 7T

Franklin Burhagohain[(✉)] [iD] and Shovan Barma [iD]

Indian Institute of Information Technology Guwahati, Bongra, India
`franklin.buragohain@iiitg.ac.in`

**Abstract.** This work presents Vision Mamba CycleGAN (VM-CycleGAN), a lightweight unpaired MRI translation framework. Existing works have focused on attention-based generators which demand high computational resources, limiting deployment in low-resource devices. Therefore, VM-CycleGAN has been proposed by introducing a Vision Mamba-based generator, leveraging state-space modeling that requires lower computational complexity without compromising system performance. In this work, a dual-generator adversarial setup has been implemented and trained considering multiple losses particularly texture and structural loss to preserve visual and anatomical fidelity. For validation, benchmark UNC 3T-7T dataset has been taken into account. For experiment, a combination of the three individual anatomical planes of T1w and T2w volumes has been used. Results and analysis show that proposed method achieves a peak PSNR of 32.63 and SSIM of 0.90 which is very consistent. Further, VM-CycleGAN reduces parameters by 58% and FLOPs by 62% compared to an attention-based baseline. Results confirm its high-fidelity synthesis and efficiency, making it suitable for deployment in resource-constrained clinical environments.

**Keywords:** MRI Synthesis · Vision Mamba · Lightweight CycleGAN

## 1 Introduction

Magnetic Resonance Imaging (MRI) is a vital non-invasive diagnostic tool, offering high-contrast imaging of soft tissues [1]. Higher field strengths like 7 T (7T) yield improved resolution and signal-to-noise ratio (SNR) compared to standard 3T scans [2,3]. However, 7T MRI systems are expensive, complex to install, and remain limited in availability [1]. This has led to growing interest in synthesizing 7T-like images from 3T scans using deep learning techniques like generative adversarial networks (GANs), providing a scalable alternative to enhance diagnostic quality [2,3].

GANs have shown promise in medical imaging tasks such as super-resolution and modality translation. While Super-Resolution GAN (SRGAN) introduced perceptual loss for realistic high-resolution outputs [4], most approaches rely on


S. Mitra et al. (Eds.): PReMI 2025, LNCS 16358, pp. 332–340, 2026.
https://doi.org/10.1007/978-3-032-18480-1_34

paired datasets, which are often difficult to obtain. Unpaired frameworks like CycleGAN [5] and DualGAN [6] address this by leveraging cycle-consistency constraints. Enhancements like residual connections in Siam *et al.* [7] and multi-scale pathways in MSR-CycleGAN [8], and attention-guided designs in AGMS-CycleGAN [9] further improved structural fidelity. Recently, Diniz *et al.* [10] applied CycleGAN for 3T-to-7T MRI translation, showing effective cross-modality synthesis. However, CNN-based generators struggle to model long-range dependencies essential for preserving global anatomical context. Transformers address this limitation [11], but their computational overhead restricts clinical deployment. To overcome this, recent works have explored Vision Mamba—a state-space model offering linear complexity and efficient long-range modeling. In particular, *MambaRecon* demonstrated strong performance in physics-guided MRI reconstruction, surpassing state-of-the-art CNN- and Transformer-based methods while remaining computationally efficient [12].

In this work, we propose Vision Mamba CycleGAN (VM-CycleGAN), a lightweight unpaired image translation framework for synthesizing high-quality 7T-like MRI from 3T scans. It integrates a Vision Mamba-based generator within a dual-generator CycleGAN architecture, coupled with multi-scale discriminators and trained using a hybrid loss function comprising adversarial, cycle-consistency, identity, texture, and structural components. Experiments on the benchmark UNC 3T–7T dataset (T1w and T2w) demonstrate that VM-CycleGAN consistently achieves superior PSNR and SSIM scores with significantly reduced trainable parameters and FLOPs compared to attention-based and other state-of-the-art models, making it suitable for deployment in resource-constrained clinical settings.

## 2    Proposed Method

### 2.1    System Overview

The proposed VM-CycleGAN framework (Fig. 1) consists of three stages: pre-processing of MRI data, training of CycleGAN-based models, and quantitative evaluation. T1w and T2w MRI scans acquired at 3T and 7T field strengths have been used and processed across axial ($A_x$), coronal ($C_r$), and sagittal ($S_g$) planes. The preprocessing stage includes standardization and enhancement of input volumes. Both VM-CycleGAN and an attention-based CycleGAN baselines are trained for comparison. Performance is assessed using PSNR and SSIM metrics, while computational complexity is evaluated in terms of the number of trainable parameters and FLOPs.

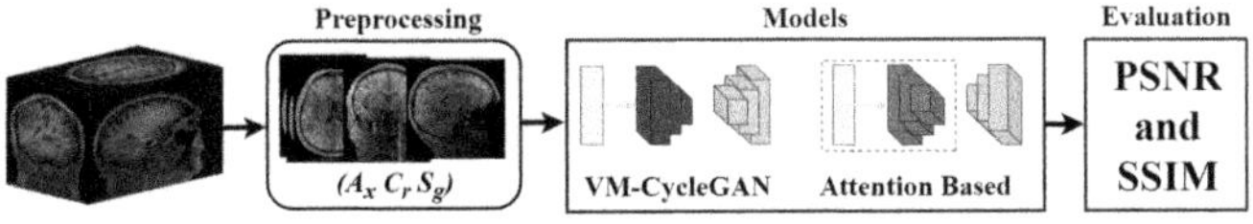


**Fig. 1.** Systematic overview of the proposed method.

**Preprocessing.** The preprocessing pipeline is depicted in Fig. 2. First, rigid registration aligns 3T and 7T volumes, which are then sliced along $A_x$, $C_r$, and $S_g$ planes. Informative slices are manually selected for training.

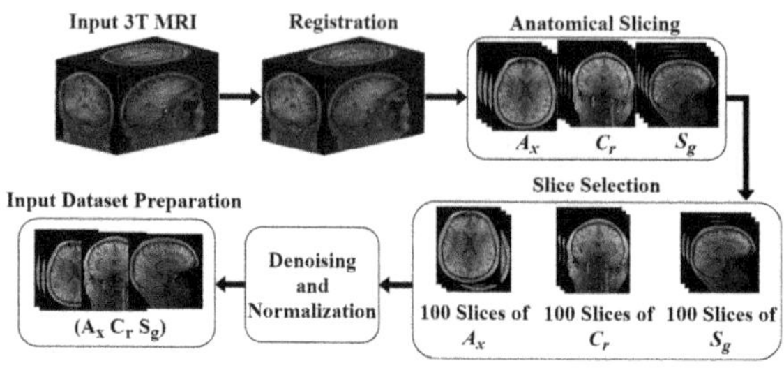


**Fig. 2.** Preprocessing steps for MRI volume preparation.

Denoising is performed using the standard non-local means (NL-means) algorithm, followed by intensity normalization via min-max scaling. These steps ensure consistency across scans and improve training stability.

## 2.2   VM-CycleGAN

VM-CycleGAN is a lightweight unpaired image-to-image translation framework for synthesizing high-resolution 7T-like MRI from 3T scans. It employs dual generators based on the Vision Mamba architecture for efficient long-range modeling, and multi-scale PatchGAN discriminators. Training is guided by a hybrid loss to ensure perceptual realism and anatomical accuracy. The overall architecture is shown in Fig. 3.

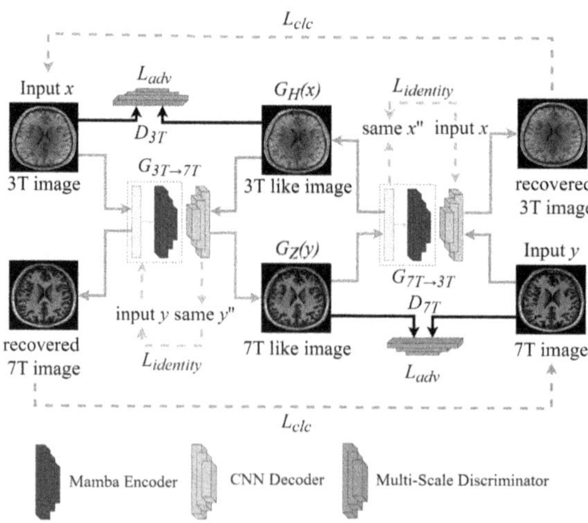


**Fig. 3.** Architecture of VM-CycleGAN, demonstrating bidirectional image translation.

**Generator Architecture (Vision Mamba).** The generator employs Vision Mamba blocks in the encoder, replacing traditional convolutional or transformer-based designs. Input images are first converted into feature maps using a convolutional patch embedding layer. These are then passed through a series of Vision Mamba blocks, each comprising instance normalization for stable training, a 1×1 convolution for feature dimensionality expansion, a gated Mamba module to capture sequential dependencies via causal convolutions and sliding-window mechanisms, and residual connections to retain low-level features and facilitate convergence. The decoder follows a symmetric structure, incorporating upsampling layers, residual bottlenecks, and transposed convolutions to reconstruct high-resolution images. Finally, a 7×7 convolution followed by a Tanh activation scales the output within the range [–1, 1].

**Discriminator Architecture.** The discriminator in VM-CycleGAN adopts a multi-scale PatchGAN structure, operating at three different image scales to capture both global structural coherence and local texture details. Each scale-specific discriminator processes downsampled versions of the input and comprises four main components. First, an initial $4 \times 4$ convolutional layer with a stride of 2 performs spatial downsampling and low-level feature extraction. This is followed by three intermediate convolutional blocks, each using a $4 \times 4$ kernel and LeakyReLU activation (slope = 0.2); the first two layers apply a stride of 2 for further downsampling, while the third uses a stride of 1 to preserve high-frequency information. Spectral normalization is applied to all convolutional layers to stabilize training and prevent mode collapse by constraining the Lipschitz constant. Finally, a single-channel output layer produces patch-wise realism scores, enabling the network to distinguish between real and synthesized 7T-like MRIs.

**Loss Functions.** VM-CycleGAN is trained considering multiple losses: adversarial loss ($\mathcal{L}_{adv}$), cycle-consistency loss ($\mathcal{L}_{clc}$), identity loss ($\mathcal{L}_{identity}$), texture loss ($\mathcal{L}_{texture}$), and structural loss ($\mathcal{L}_{structural}$). The total loss is defined as:

$$\mathcal{L}_{total} = \mathcal{L}_{adv} + \lambda_{clc} \cdot \mathcal{L}_{clc} + \lambda_{identity} \cdot \mathcal{L}_{identity} \\ + \lambda_{texture} \cdot \mathcal{L}_{texture} + \lambda_{struct} \cdot \mathcal{L}_{structural} \tag{1}$$

with weights: $\lambda_{clc} = 15$, $\lambda_{identity} = 5$, $\lambda_{texture} = 5$, and $\lambda_{struct} = 10$.

**Adversarial loss** ($\mathcal{L}_{adv}$) uses least-squares GAN to encourage indistinguishable synthesis:

$$\mathcal{L}_{adv} = \mathbb{E}_y[(D_{7T}(y) - 1)^2] + \mathbb{E}_x[D_{7T}(G_{3T \to 7T}(x))^2] \\ + \mathbb{E}_x[(D_{3T}(x) - 1)^2] + \mathbb{E}_y[D_{3T}(G_{7T \to 3T}(y))^2] \tag{2}$$

**Cycle-consistency loss** ($\mathcal{L}_{clc}$) ensures round-trip reconstruction fidelity:

$$\mathcal{L}_{clc} = \mathbb{E}_x[\|G_{back}(G_{fwd}(x)) - x\|_1] + \mathbb{E}_y[\|G_{fwd}(G_{back}(y)) - y\|_1] \tag{3}$$

**Identity loss** ($\mathcal{L}_{identity}$) penalizes unnecessary changes when inputs already belong to the target domain:

$$\mathcal{L}_{identity} = \mathbb{E}_y[\|G_{fwd}(y) - y\|_1] + \mathbb{E}_x[\|G_{back}(x) - x\|_1] \tag{4}$$

**Texture loss** ($\mathcal{L}_{texture}$) enforces perceptual similarity in feature space using a pre-trained VGG:

$$\mathcal{L}_{texture} = \mathrm{MSE}(\mathcal{F}_{gen}, \mathcal{F}_{real}) \tag{5}$$

**Structural loss** ($\mathcal{L}_{structural}$) combines L1 and SSIM to retain anatomical integrity:

$$\mathcal{L}_{structural} = \alpha \cdot \|I_{gen} - I_{real}\|_1 + (1 - \alpha) \cdot (1 - \mathrm{SSIM}(I_{gen}, I_{real})) \tag{6}$$

with $\alpha = 0.5$.

**Training Strategy.** The model is trained for 500 epochs using the Adam optimizer with mixed-precision and a batch size of 1, alternating generator and discriminator updates at each iteration.

### 2.3   Attention-Based CycleGAN

To benchmark the performance of VM-CycleGAN, we developed an attention-based CycleGAN using a transformer generator. The transformer comprises multi-head self-attention layers, MLP blocks, and positional encodings. The model captures long-range anatomical dependencies, enabling high-fidelity synthesis.

### 2.4   Evaluation Metrics

Evaluation was performed using two standard metrics: Peak Signal-to-Noise Ratio (PSNR), which measures pixel-level fidelity, and Structural Similarity Index Measure (SSIM), which assesses structural and perceptual similarity between the generated and ground truth images. These metrics provide a quantitative basis for validating both visual and anatomical quality in synthesized 7T-like MRIs. Additionally, computational efficiency was assessed by comparing the number of trainable parameters and floating-point operations (FLOPs) for VM-CycleGAN and the attention-based baseline, highlighting the model's suitability for real-time and resource-constrained clinical deployment.

## 3   Experimental Methodology

### 3.1   Dataset

This study utilized the 3T and 7T MRI dataset from [3], comprising T1w and T2w scans from 10 healthy adults (ages 25–41). All scans were preprocessed through affine registration using FLIRT, followed by plane-wise slicing into $A_x$, $C_r$, and $S_g$ views. For each plane and modality, 100 relevant slices were manually selected and standardized to 256×256 resolution. The dataset was split into 80% training and 20% testing.

## 3.2   Experiment

Two models—VM-CycleGAN and an attention-based CycleGAN—were trained and compared. Both models were trained for 500 epochs with a batch size of 1 using the Adam optimizer. The initial learning rate was set to $1 \times 10^{-5}$ and reduced linearly after epoch 300. Mixed-precision training was employed for efficiency. Training was performed on an NVIDIA A100-PCIE-40GB GPU using PyTorch 2.3.0 and CUDA 11.0. The model outputs were evaluated against real 7T images using PSNR and SSIM metrics. Additionally, the computational complexity of each model was analyzed in terms of trainable parameters and FLOPs.

## 4   Results and Discussion

Tables 1 presents the mean PSNR and SSIM values obtained on the T1w and T2w datasets. The first column indicates the subject index. Each subsequent group of six columns displays the performance of the proposed VM-CycleGAN and the attention-based CycleGAN. Within each group, three columns represent the PSNR values for the $A_x$, $C_r$, and $S_g$ planes, followed by three columns showing the corresponding SSIM scores for those planes.

In Table 1, VM-CycleGAN consistently outperforms the attention-based CycleGAN in both PSNR and SSIM across most anatomical views and subjects. Notably, for the T2w dataset, VM-CycleGAN achieves a peak PSNR of 32.63 and an SSIM of 0.90, demonstrating its ability to produce high-fidelity 7T-like images.

Table 2 summarizes the peak PSNR and SSIM scores achieved by various state-of-the-art generative models, including CycleGAN [5], DualGAN [6], NICE-GAN [13], RegGAN [14], DC-CycleGAN [15], MSR-CycleGAN [8], and the variant of CycleGAN proposed by Siam et al. [7]. Despite its lower computational complexity, VM-CycleGAN records the highest PSNR (32.63) and SSIM (0.90) among all models. These results empirically validate the effectiveness and practicality of the proposed framework.

Table 3 presents the computational complexity of the two models in terms of trainable parameters and FLOPs. The first column lists the model names, while the second and third columns show the number of trainable parameters (in millions) and FLOPs (in gigaflops), respectively. The proposed VM-CycleGAN is approximately 58% more efficient in terms of parameters and 62% more efficient in FLOPs compared to the attention-based CycleGAN. This substantial reduction in computational overhead supports VM-CycleGAN's suitability for deployment in resource-constrained and real-time clinical environments.

Figure 4 visually compares the reconstruction performance. Panel (a) shows the original 3T MRI input, and panel (b) displays the corresponding 7T ground truth. Panels (c) and (d) illustrate the outputs of the attention-based CycleGAN and the proposed VM-CycleGAN, respectively. The visual results align well with the quantitative metrics, with VM-CycleGAN generating images that exhibit improved contrast, sharper anatomical boundaries, and better visual fidelity to the ground truth.

**Table 1.** Mean PSNR and SSIM Comparison

| Subject | VM-CycleGAN model | | | | | | Attention-based CycleGAN model | | | | | |
| | PSNR | | | SSIM | | | PSNR | | | SSIM | | |
| | $A_x$ | $C_r$ | $S_g$ | $A_x$ | $C_r$ | $S_g$ | $A_x$ | $C_r$ | $S_g$ | $A_x$ | $C_r$ | $S_g$ |
| --- | --- | --- | --- | --- | --- | --- | --- | --- | --- | --- | --- | --- |
| T1 weighted dataset | | | | | | | | | | | | |
| 1 | 24.44 | 26.76 | 27.59 | 0.80 | 0.82 | 0.85 | 23.34 | 25.81 | 26.88 | 0.77 | 0.79 | 0.83 |
| 2 | 26.03 | 26.66 | 28.25 | 0.83 | 0.82 | 0.86 | 24.36 | 25.64 | 27.54 | 0.80 | 0.79 | 0.84 |
| 3 | 25.37 | 26.18 | 28.10 | 0.83 | 0.80 | 0.85 | 24.83 | 24.85 | 27.31 | 0.80 | 0.75 | 0.83 |
| 4 | 24.19 | 24.88 | 26.73 | 0.79 | 0.75 | 0.83 | 23.36 | 23.67 | 25.99 | 0.76 | 0.71 | 0.82 |
| 5 | 24.86 | 26.69 | 26.41 | 0.83 | 0.84 | 0.86 | 24.35 | 25.88 | 25.86 | 0.81 | 0.81 | 0.85 |
| 6 | 23.97 | 26.46 | 27.32 | 0.80 | 0.80 | 0.86 | 23.07 | 25.24 | 26.66 | 0.76 | 0.76 | 0.83 |
| 7 | 25.75 | 26.63 | 27.79 | 0.81 | 0.78 | 0.83 | 24.85 | 25.82 | 27.09 | 0.78 | 0.74 | 0.81 |
| 8 | 24.83 | 26.49 | 27.08 | 0.83 | 0.80 | 0.83 | 24.53 | 25.60 | 26.23 | 0.82 | 0.77 | 0.81 |
| 9 | 25.22 | 25.74 | 28.14 | 0.83 | 0.79 | 0.86 | 24.65 | 24.93 | 27.35 | 0.81 | 0.76 | 0.83 |
| 10 | 24.98 | 25.25 | 26.89 | 0.80 | 0.77 | 0.81 | 24.05 | 24.28 | 26.37 | 0.77 | 0.73 | 0.79 |
| Average | 24.69 | 26.17 | 27.43 | 0.82 | 0.80 | 0.84 | 24.14 | 25.17 | 26.73 | 0.79 | 0.76 | 0.82 |
| T2 weighted dataset | | | | | | | | | | | | |
| 1 | 29.41 | 31.07 | 31.89 | 0.84 | 0.87 | 0.90 | 28.11 | 29.66 | 30.64 | 0.81 | 0.84 | 0.88 |
| 2 | 30.12 | 30.77 | **32.63** | 0.88 | 0.87 | **0.90** | 28.46 | 29.15 | 31.14 | 0.85 | 0.84 | 0.88 |
| 3 | 27.88 | 30.60 | 32.56 | 0.82 | 0.87 | 0.90 | 27.36 | 29.43 | 31.60 | 0.81 | 0.84 | 0.88 |
| 4 | 28.47 | 29.80 | 30.77 | 0.82 | 0.86 | 0.89 | 27.06 | 27.79 | 29.60 | 0.78 | 0.82 | 0.86 |
| 5 | 29.78 | 30.13 | 29.75 | 0.87 | 0.87 | 0.86 | 28.53 | 28.55 | 28.34 | 0.85 | 0.84 | 0.83 |
| 6 | 28.94 | 30.01 | 31.92 | 0.84 | 0.87 | 0.90 | 27.55 | 28.80 | 30.37 | 0.81 | 0.83 | 0.86 |
| 7 | 29.34 | 29.50 | 30.83 | 0.86 | 0.87 | 0.89 | 27.69 | 28.14 | 29.48 | 0.82 | 0.83 | 0.86 |
| 8 | 30.22 | 30.19 | 30.43 | 0.86 | 0.85 | 0.85 | 29.36 | 28.58 | 29.17 | 0.83 | 0.82 | 0.82 |
| 9 | 29.64 | 30.43 | 31.29 | 0.85 | 0.86 | 0.88 | 27.75 | 28.86 | 29.95 | 0.82 | 0.82 | 0.85 |
| 10 | 28.87 | 29.81 | 31.02 | 0.85 | 0.86 | 0.89 | 27.71 | 28.02 | 30.14 | 0.82 | 0.82 | 0.87 |
| Average | 29.27 | 30.23 | 31.31 | 0.85 | 0.87 | 0.89 | 27.96 | 28.70 | 30.04 | 0.82 | 0.83 | 0.86 |

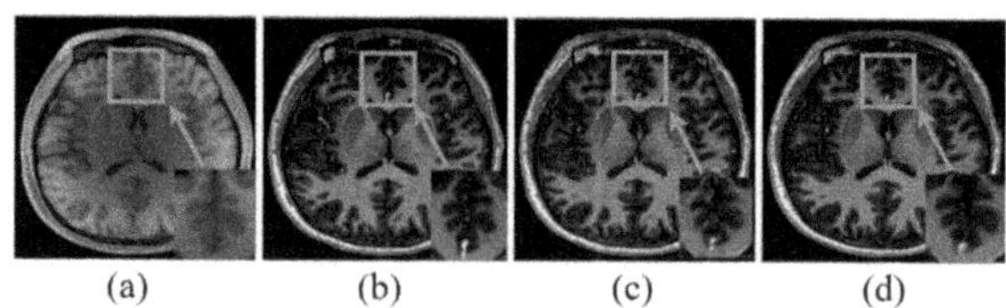

(a)    (b)    (c)    (d)

**Fig. 4.** Comparison of (a) the 3T MRI input, (b) the original 7T scan, (c) the 7T-like image from attention-based CycleGAN,and (d) the 7T-like image from VM-CycleGAN.

**Table 2.** Peak PSNR and SSIM Comparison for Different Models

| Models | PSNR | SSIM |
|---|---|---|
| CycleGAN (Zhu *et al.*, 2017) [5] | 23.90 | 0.83 |
| DualGAN (Yi *et al.*, 2017) [6] | 22.85 | 0.84 |
| NICE-GAN (Chen *et al.*, 2020) [13] | 26.30 | 0.86 |
| RegGAN (Kong *et al.*, 2021) [14] | 26.00 | 0.86 |
| DC-cycleGAN (Wang *et al.*, 2023) [15] | 26.69 | 0.88 |
| CycleGAN (Siam *et al.* [7]) | 19.15 | 0.71 |
| MSR-CycleGAN (Burhagohain *et al.* [8]) | 27.56 | 0.82 |
| Attention-based CycleGAN | 31.60 | 0.88 |
| VM-CycleGAN (Proposed) | **32.63** | **0.90** |

**Table 3.** Computational Complexity Comparison

| Model | Parameters (Millions) | FLOPs (G) |
|---|---|---|
| Attention-Based CycleGAN | 66.56 | 72.34 |
| VM-CycleGAN (Proposed) | **28.12** | **27.57** |

While this study uses 2D plane-wise synthesis, clinical MRI is volumetric. Extending VM-CycleGAN to 3D should improve inter-slice consistency and facilitate volumetric segmentation, 3D registration, and diagnostics. Future work may also add expert radiologist evaluation and task-specific assessments (e.g., segmentation and diagnosis) to better establish clinical utility.

## 5    Conclusion

This study introduces VM-CycleGAN, a lightweight CycleGAN framework that incorporates a Vision Mamba-based generator for synthesizing 7T-like MRI from 3T scans using unpaired training data. By replacing traditional CNN or Transformer-based generators with a computationally efficient Mamba backbone, the proposed model achieves superior performance in both PSNR and SSIM. Extensive quantitative and visual evaluations confirm that VM-CycleGAN not only surpasses existing CycleGAN variants but also provides a structurally faithful and resource-efficient solution suitable for clinical deployment. The model's scalability and plane-specific adaptability make it a promising candidate for real-world applications in MRI quality enhancement and potential future extensions toward 3D volumetric reconstruction.

# References


1. National Academies of Sciences: Engineering, and Medicine: The Current Status and Future Direction of High-Magnetic-Field Science and Technology in the United States. National Academies Press, Washington, DC (2024)
2. Bahrami, K., Shi, F., Zong, X., Shin, H.W., An, H., Shen, D.: Reconstruction of 7T-like images from 3T MRI. IEEE Trans. Med. Imaging **35**(9), 2085–2097 (2016). https://doi.org/10.1109/TMI.2016.2549918
3. Chen, X., Qu, L., Xie, Y., Ahmad, S., Yap, P.-T.: A paired dataset of T1- and T2-weighted MRI at 3 Tesla and 7 Tesla. Sci. Data **10**, 489 (2023). Dataset available at figshare. https://doi.org/10.6084/m9.figshare.23706033
4. Ledig, C., et al.: Photo-realistic single image super-resolution using a generative adversarial network. In: CVPR 2017, pp. 105–114. IEEE, Honolulu (2017). https://doi.org/10.1109/CVPR.2017.19
5. Zhu, J.-Y., Park, T., Isola, P., Efros, A.A.: Unpaired image-to-image translation using cycle-consistent adversarial networks. In: ICCV 2017, pp. 2223–2232. IEEE, Venice (2017). https://doi.org/10.1109/ICCV.2017.244
6. Yi, Z., Zhang, H., Tan, P., Gong, M.: DualGAN: unsupervised dual learning for image-to-image translation. In: ICCV 2017, pp. 2868–2876. IEEE, Venice (2017). https://doi.org/10.1109/ICCV.2017.310
7. Siam, Z.S., Hasan, R.T., Chowdhury, M.H., Islam Sumon, M.S., Chowdhury, M.E.H.: Improving MRI resolution: a cycle consistent generative adversarial network-based approach for 3T to 7T translation. IEEE Access **12**, 116498–116515 (2024). https://doi.org/10.1109/ACCESS.2024.3430968
8. Burhagohain, F., Barma, S.: High-Resolution 7T-like MRI images generation from 3T MRI scans using multi-scale residual CycleGAN. In: 2024 IEEE 21st India Council International Conference (INDICON), pp. 1–6. IEEE, Kharagpur (2024). https://doi.org/10.1109/INDICON63790.2024.10958248
9. Burhagohain, F., Barma, S.: 3T to 7T-like MRI translation using attention-guided multi-scale CycleGAN. In: IEEE Guwahati Subsection Conference (GCON), pp. 1–6. IEEE, Guwahati (2025). https://doi.org/10.1109/GCON65540.2025.11173314
10. Diniz, E., Santini, T., Karim, H., Aizenstein, H.J., Ibrahim, T.S.: Cross-modality image translation of 3 tesla magnetic resonance imaging to 7 tesla using generative adversarial networks. Hum. Brain Mapp. **46**(9), e70246 (2025). https://doi.org/10.1002/hbm.70246
11. Vaswani, A., et al.: Attention is all you need. In: NeurIPS 2017, pp. 5998–6008. Curran Associates, Long Beach (2017)
12. Korkmaz, Y., Patel, V.M.: MambaRecon: MRI reconstruction with structured state space models. In: Proceedings of the IEEE/CVF Winter Conference on Applications of Computer Vision (WACV), pp. 4142–4152. IEEE (2025)
13. Chen, R., Huang, W., Huang, B., Sun, F., Fang, B.: Reusing discriminators for encoding: towards unsupervised image-to-image translation. In: CVPR 2020, pp. 8168–8177. IEEE, Seattle (2020). https://doi.org/10.1109/CVPR42600.2020.00819
14. Kong, L., Lian, C., Huang, D., Li, Z., Hu, Y., Zhou, Q.: Breaking the dilemma of medical image-to-image translation. In: NeurIPS 2021. Curran Associates (2021)
15. Wang, J., Wu, Q.M.J., Pourpanah, F.: DC-cycleGAN: bidirectional CT-to-MR synthesis from unpaired data. Comput. Med. Imaging Graph. **108**, 102249 (2023). https://doi.org/10.1016/j.compmedimag.2023.102249

# A Hybrid Framework for Automated Pancreas Segmentation in Abdominal CT Imaging


Rupam Sah[1]([✉]) [iD], Suchi Jain[2], and Renu Dhir[3]

[1] Dayananda Sagar University, Bangalore, Karnataka 562112, India
rupamsah2002@gmail.com
[2] Lovely Professional University, Phagwara, Punjab 144411, India
[3] Dr. B. R. Ambedkar, National Institute of Technology, Jalandhar, Punjab 144011, India



**Abstract.** Pancreatic cancer stands out as one of the most challenging and lethal cancer to treat, primarily due to its late - stage detection and the limited therapeutic options. Pancreatic cancer often goes undetected until late stages because of the pancreas's irregular shape, small size, and varying texture across patients. For early diagnosis and efficient treatment planning, pancreatic cancers in radiological images must be precisely segmented. To address the anatomical variability of the pancreas across slices (intra class heterogeneity) and the minimal contrast distinguishing the pancreas from anatomical structures (inter-class ambiguity), proposed a hybrid 2D-3D U-Net framework. This study introduces a hybrid deep learning technique for automated 2D-3D volumetric segmentation of pancreas in computed tomography (CT) images. This combination strategy enables the network to captures the both global as well as local textures from CT images. The model was trained using manually annotated ground truth masks from the NIH Pancreas-CT dataset, comprising 18,942 DICOM images from 80 subjects. The proposed multi-stage pipeline incorporates a one-cycle learning rate policy, and employ a Tversky loss function to mitigate class imbalance. To evaluate the segmentation performances, standard metrics such as Dice Similarity Coefficient (DSC) is mainly focused. Experimental outcomes show that the suggested method accomplishes accurate and reliable pancreas segmentation, highlighting its promise for integration into computer-aided diagnostic tools improve pancreas segmentation supporting its integration into clinical decision-support systems.

**Keywords:** 2D- 3D U-Net architecture · AI in Healthcare · Deep Learning in Medical Imaging · CT scan


## 1 Introduction

The pancreas is a key organ involved in regulating both the digestive and endocrine systems, the pancreas serves a vital role by aiding in enzymatic digestion of food within the small intestine and aiding in the uptake of essential nutrients [15]. In addition to its role in digestion, the pancreas also regulates metabolism via the secretion of vital hormones such as insulin sand glucagon, used in the regulation of blood glucose levels and general metabolic homeostasis [15]. For this reason, the pancreas's health is one of the essential to


© The Author(s), under exclusive license to Springer Nature Switzerland AG 2026
S. Mitra et al. (Eds.): PReMI 2025, LNCS 16358, pp. 341–349, 2026.
https://doi.org/10.1007/978-3-032-18480-1_35

the body's utilization of nutrients and preservation of metabolic equilibrium. Diseases of the pancreas such as diabetes, pancreatitis, and pancreatic cancer need to be diagnosed in a timely and accurate manner to enable successful treatment and management. Diagnosis methods usually involve an integration of imaging-based techniques, for examples CT and MRI scans and blood tests in the laboratory to evaluate the activities of pancreatic enzymes. In some cases, biopsies are performed to determine malignancies. So, proper early diagnosis is necessary to improve patient outcomes.

Current, advancements in Computer-Aided Diagnosis (CAD) systems have further enhanced pancreatic disease diagnosis. Such systems leverage technique of machine learning and deep learning to scrutinize complex healthcare data from different modalities such as imaging scans and blood samples. Specifically, Convolutional Neural Networks (CNNs) [14] and U-Net architectures [15] have been instrumental in extracting and processing accurate anatomical information from CT and MRI scans. CAD models created based on these architectures assist clinicians with better image perception, detection of abnormalities, and providing three-dimensional (3D) reconstructions of anatomical structures. All these improvements significantly enhance the detection of pancreatic diseases, planning therapeutic interventions, and monitoring patient development.

Various deep learning techniques which highly used in the field of image segmentation in pancreas. Example like, Mask R-CNN [16] allows instance segmentation by integrating region proposal networks with CNN-based feature extraction. Fully Convolutional Networks (FCN) [15] brought the concept of dense prediction into semantic segmentation. U-Net structure [16], having an encoding and decoding phase with bottleneck along with skip connections, has proven particularly successful in medical image segmentation. Its 3D extension, the 3D U-Net [16], translates the model to volumetric medical images using 3D convolutions. Furthermore, DeepLab models have utilized atrous convolutions and spatial pyramid pooling to enhance segmentation boundaries.

In this paper, implementation of a hybrid U-Net model integrating 2D-3D structures for pancreas segmentation in abdominal CT data. By combining 2D slice-wise feature extraction with 3D volumetric spatial learning, the proposed model is designed to overcome inherent challenges like anatomical variation, low tissue contrast, and imaging artifacts-perhaps improving diagnostic performance in pancreatic disease management. Additionally, this process will reduce human interaction, giving more reproducibility and accuracy in tumor contouring.

## 2  Related Work

The pancreas segmentation from medical images, especially CT scans, poses a challenging issue owing to the varying shape, unclear boundaries, and adjacent location of neighboring abdominal organs. Researchers have attempted numerous deep learning models during the past few years, and with significant improvement in both 2D and 3D convolutional neural networks (CNNs), attention mechanism, and hybrid learning methodology.

It was significantly enhanced by combining a Geometry-informed U-Net integrated with Deep Q-Learning, with which deformable convolutions were brought in for enhanced capture of the different pancreatic anatomical structures. The model realized high-level segmentation accuracy when used on the NIH pancreas segmentation dataset with impressive robustness on various types of pancreatic morphology [1]. To further improve segmentation quality, particularly at the sub-organ level, scientists introduced a multi-stage approach that leverages anatomical knowledge for automated segmentation of pancreatic sub-regions. The proposed method proved consistent performance when tested on datasets like the NIH pancreas dataset and pre-cancerous pancreas data [3].

UMRFormer-Net is a recent development in deep learning pancreas segmentation. It integrates a double-layer bridged transformer network within a 3D U-shaped CNN, thus capturing long-term dependencies and spatial information. It was tested and validated using the MSD pancreas dataset, as it demonstrated high effectiveness in complex segmentation tasks [10]. Similarly, another approach used ensemble learning in conjunction with coarse localization methods with the goal of enhancing pancreas detection by initially coarsely determining the area of interest and then conducting detailed segmentation. The two-stage method increased accuracy and reliability, especially on the NIH pancreas CT dataset [11].

Extending the application of CT imaging, MRI scans were also subjected to a 2D U-Net for estimating pancreatic volume in Type 1 Diabetes patients. The approach effectively captured structural information and showed high precision on abdominal MRI datasets [15]. Besides, a two-level U-Net network has also been used to segment pancreatic tumors with high accuracy in outlining both the tumors and pancreas. Lastly, plain U-Net-based models have stayed on par. Their simplicity and effectiveness remain to cause them to excel at automatic pancreas segmentation, as seen in tests conducted on abdominal CT datasets from Cancer Imaging Archive Database [17].

## 3 Proposed Work

We propose a hybrid 2D-3D U-Net framework to leverage both local (intra-slice) and global (inter-slice) spatial features. This architecture integrates 2D slice-wise encoding with 3D volumetric decoding for accurate segmentation.

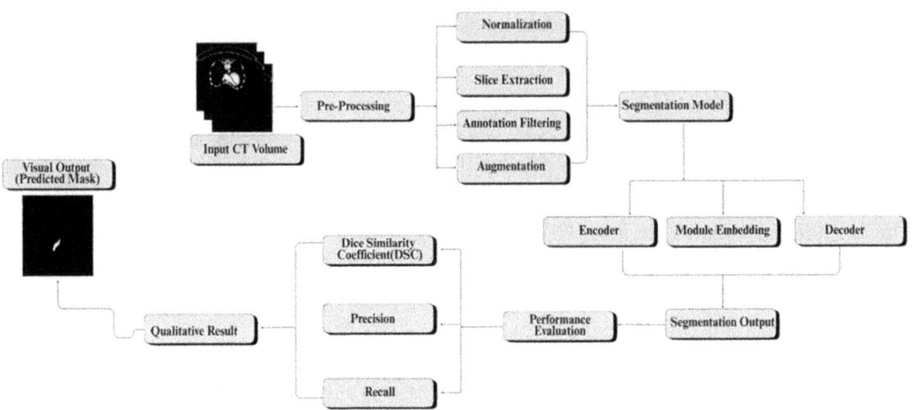


**Fig. 1.** Schematic of the hybrid 2D–3D U-Net pipeline.

### 3.1  Pipeline Overview

This paper introduces an integrated deep learning i.e. 2D-3D U-Net architecture for automated segmentation of pancreas in CT scans, in which this architecture makes use of both 2D-3D U-Net model to leverage their respective strengths: the 2D U-Net captures rich intra-slice spatial features, while the 3D U-Net refines segmentation by modeling inter-slice volumetric context. The complete pipeline, as depicted in Fig. 1, comprises five key stages: Data Preprocessing, 2D Features Encoding, 3D Volumetric Decoding, Loss Function Optimization, and Model Evaluation. Moreover, for the experiments, the CT images are saved in PNG is used for experimentation are used as (Portable Network Graphics), derived from original DICOM volumes.

### 3.2  Data Preprocessing

The preprocessing phase is one of the critical to ensure uniformity and optimize the fidelity of the input data for the segmentation network, Each CT scan, represented as three- dimensional volume X, i.e. H × W × D, is first subjected to resampling to achieve the isotropic voxel spacing using linear interpolation techniques. This normalization of spatial resolution ensures consistent scale across different scans and facilitates robust learning. Following resampling, the intensity values of CT images are standardized using Z-score normalization, defined as:

$$S_i = \frac{X_i - \mu_X}{\sigma_X} \tag{1}$$

where $X_i$ is the voxel value, $\mu_X$ is the mean, and $\sigma_X$ is the standard deviation of the voxel intensity within the volume. Normalization aids in reducing the intensity variations across dataset and speeds up model convergence during training.

### 3.3  2D U-Net Features Encoding

Each preprocessed 2D slice $S_i$ is independently processed through a 2D U-Net encoder that extract the discriminative spatial features.

**Model Specification (Encoder):** The 2D encoder comprises four down-sampling stages. Each stage contains two sequential 2D convolutional layers (kernel 3 × 3), each followed by Batch Normalization and SiLU activation. Stage filter counts are [64, 128, 256, 512]. Down-sampling between stages is performed by max-pooling (2 × 2). The bottleneck block uses two Conv2D layers with 1024 filters to capture high-level representations. Feature maps from each encoder stage are saved for skip connections to the corresponding decoder stages.

At each encoder block, features extraction is defined as:

$$F_i = SiLU\left(BN\left(Conv2D_{3\times3}(S_i)\right)\right) \tag{2}$$

where $F_i$ represents the encoded features map of the $i^{th}$ slice.

### 3.4 3D U-Net Features Decoding

The pseudo-3D volume obtained from the 2D U-Net encoder is forwarded to a 3D U-Net decoder, which reconstructs the final pancreas segmentation mask by learning contextual volumetric information across adjacent slices. This decoder captures inter-slice dependencies that are essential for accurate 3D anatomical localization.

**Model Specification (Decoder):** The decoder mirrors the encoder in depth and performs progressive up-sampling using 3D transposed convolutions. Each decoding stage concatenates the up-sampled feature maps with the corresponding encoder features through skip connections, preserving fine-scale spatial detail lost during down-sampling. Every stage contains two $3 \times 3 \times 3$ convolutional layers, each followed by Batch Normalization and SiLU activation. The number of filters across decoder stages follows a symmetric configuration with respect to the encoder: [512, 256, 128, 64].

Formally, at each decoding stage:

$$G_l = UpSample3D(Concat(F_l, Skip_l)) \tag{3}$$

where $F_l$ and $Skip_l$ denote the features map and corresponding skip connection at layer $l$.

The final prediction $\widehat{Y}$ is obtained by applying a $1 \times 1 \times 1$ 3D convolution followed by a non-linear sigmoid activation function:

$$\widehat{Y} = \sigma(Conv3D_{1 \times 1 \times 1}(G)) \tag{4}$$

where $\sigma$ represents the sigmoid activation, mapping the output to a probability score between 0 and 1. The output $\widehat{Y}$ represents the predicted pancreas mask corresponding to the input CT volume.

### 3.5 Loss Function Optimization

Training the proposed hybrid model requires an objective function that accurately guides the learning process in pancreas, particularly under the challenges of class imbalance (small pancreas vs large background) and anatomical variability in shape size and texture. To this end, we employ a composite loss function comprising:

Dice loss:

$$\tau_{Dice} = 1 - \frac{2 \sum_{i=1}^{N} y_i \hat{y}_i}{\sum_{i=1}^{N} y_i + \sum_{i=1}^{N} \hat{y}_i} \tag{5}$$

where $y_i$ and $\hat{y}_i$ are the ground truth and predicted binary labels for voxel $i$.

Tversky loss:

$$\tau_{Tversky} = 1 - \frac{\sum_{i=1}^{N} y_i \hat{y}_i}{\sum_{i=1}^{N} y_i \hat{y}_i + \alpha \sum_{i=1}^{N} y_i(1 - \hat{y}_i) + \beta \sum_{i=1}^{N} y_i(1 - y_i)\hat{y}_i} \tag{6}$$

The total loss during training is expressed as

$$\tau_{Total} = \varphi_1 \tau_{Dice} + \varphi_2 \tau_{Tversky} \tag{7}$$

where $\varphi_1$ and $\varphi_2$ are weighting factors.

In practice, we set the weighting coefficients empirically to $\varphi_1$=0.6(Dice loss) and $\varphi_2$=0.4 (Tversky loss). This balance prioritizes global overlap accuracy while retaining the Tversky term's ability to penalize false negative - an important factor in small organ segmentation.

### 3.6  Hyperparameters and Optimizers

The model was trained for 50 iterations using the Adam optimizer with a weight decay of $1 \times 10^{-5}$, a batch size of 8, and a 70:30 training-to-validation split. A one-cycle learning rate schedule was applied, with a minimum learning rate of $1 \times 10^{-5}$ and a maximum of $1 \times 10^{-3}$. These hyperparameters were selected based on validation performance, with the maximum learning rate and batch size tuned empirically via grid search over the validation split.

### 3.7  Model Evaluation

During inference, the predicted pancreas segmentation was evaluated against ground truth using standard metrics, including **Dice Similarity Coefficient (DSC), Precision, Recall and JSC**. High values of these metrics indicate strong agreement between predicted and true segmentations, validating the effectiveness of the proposed approach.

## 4  Evaluation and Discussion

### 4.1  Dataset Overview

The National Institutes of Health (NIH) studied 82 abdominal contrast-enhanced 3D CT scans, called the Pancreas-CT dataset, which is available publicly from The Cancer Imaging Archive (TCIA). The dataset contains scans of 53 male and 27 female patients that were acquired about 70 s following intravenous contrast injection under portal venous phase conditions. Out of the participants, 17 were healthy kidney donors undergoing nephrectomy, while the other 65 were recruited by radiologists and presented no noteworthy abdominal anomalies or evidence of pancreatic cancer. The ages of the subjects were between 18 and 76 years, averaging 46.8 ± 16.7 years. CT images were acquired using Philips and Siemens multidetector CT scanners with a 512 × 512-pixel resolution, variable pixel spacing, and slice thickness of 1.5 mm to 2.5 mm. There are 181 to 310 slices per case, averaging about 222 slices per patient, creating a heterogeneous dataset containing a wide range of anatomical structures and conditions.

## 4.2  Evaluation of Pancreas Segmentation

The proposed hybrid 2D-3D U-Net framework was rigorously evaluated using a variety of performance metrics on the NIH Pancreas-CT dataset. Training was carried out for 50 epochs, and the model achieved stable and accurate segmentation outcomes. The implementation was done using PyTorch on an NVIDIA A100-SXM4-40GB GPU in Google Colab. Figure 2 shows the segmentation results for abdominal CT images. The first column displays the original CT slice, while the third column shows the corresponding ground truth mask. Columns two and four show the predicted segmentation mask and the overlapping view of predicted vs ground truth respectively. Maroon is used to represent the predicted pancreas mask, while red is used for the annotated ground truth. To assess model performance over training epochs, segmentation metrics were recorded across 50 epochs. The proposed model yielded the most stable and accurate segmentation.

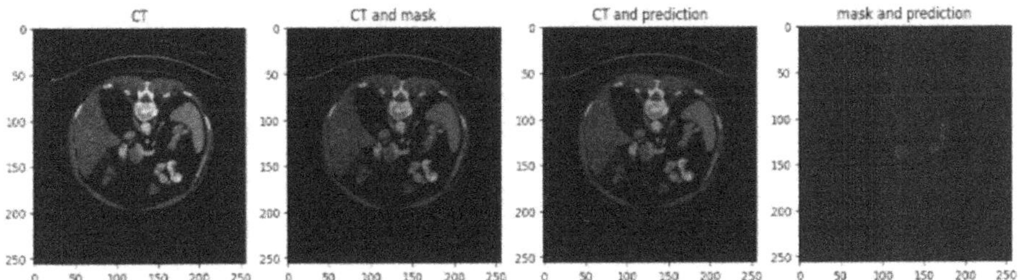


**Fig. 2.** Segmentation results: (1) Original CT Image, (2) Predicted Mask, (3) Ground Truth, (4) Overlap of prediction and ground truth.

Table 1 presents the segmentation performance in terms of the quantitative metrics discussed earlier, along with a comparison of the proposed model against different benchmark methods.

**Table 1.** Assessment of Segmentation Performance

| Methods | DSC | Precision | Recall | JSC |
| --- | --- | --- | --- | --- |
| U-Net [16] | 0.8458 | 0.8749 | 0.8357 | 0.7510 |
| Attention U-Net [17] | 0.8521 | 0.8682 | 0.8503 | 0.7588 |
| Swin U-Net [15] | 0.8626 | 0.8574 | 0.8792 | 0.7664 |
| A Hybrid Model (Proposed) | 0.8701 | 0.8598 | 0.8804 | 0.7689 |

As was previously mentioned, the model was trained in epoch 50 to evaluate the segmentation Performance and the better performance is shown in Table 1. Overall, the results validate the effectiveness of combining 2D and 3D U-Net architectures in a hybrid framework for pancreas segmentation shown the comparisons in 3D view (Fig. 3).

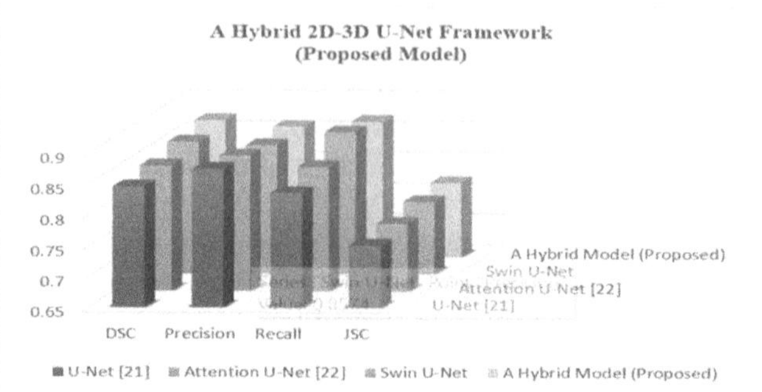


**Fig. 3.** Performance graph showing existing benchmarks with proposed model with NIH Dataset.

### 4.3  Computational Cost Analysis

Training of the proposed hybrid 2D–3D U-Net framework required approximately 9.8 h on an NVIDIA A100 GPU for 50 epochs. The average inference time per CT volume was 0.54 s. The model demonstrates efficient scalability with increasing input size, confirming its feasibility for real-time or near real-time clinical deployment.

## 5  Conclusion

This study investigated a hybrid deep learning framework combining 2D-3D U-Net architectures to automatically segment the pancreas from abdominal CT scans. By integrating slice-wise 2D feature extraction with volumetric 3D context aggregation, the proposed model effectively captured both local and global anatomical structures, overcoming challenges such as low tissue contrast, imaging artifacts, and anatomical variability. The use of SiLU activation functions, skip connections, and a hybrid loss function (combining Dice and Tversky losses) further enhanced the model's segmentation performance, achieving promising results across evaluation metrics such as DSC. Experimental results reveal that integrating 2D and 3D U-Net architectures yields comparatively better segmentation performance. Despite these achievements, future work could extend the model to multi-organ segmentation to exploit contextual organ relationships, incorporate advanced attention mechanisms for improved focus on pancreas regions, and adopt semi-supervised learning approaches to utilize unlabeled medical data effectively. Addressing these perspectives could further refine the framework and significantly advance computer-aided diagnosis (CAD) systems for pancreatic diseases.

**Author Contribution   Rupam Sah:** Conceptualization, Methodology Design, Model Implementation, Experiments, Data Analysis, Writing - Original Draft. **Suchi Jain:** Provided conceptual direction and reviewed the methodology. **Renu Dhir:** Supervision of the research work, critical review, and guidance throughout the project and manuscript preparation.

**Funding Declaration** The authors declare that no funds, grants, or other support were received during the preparation of manuscript.

**Conflict of Interest..** The authors declare no conflict of interest.
**Information on Data Availability.** The data supporting the results of this study can be accessed from the NIH pancreas-CT Dataset at https://www.cancerimagingarchive.net/collection/pancreas-ct/.

# References

1. Man, Y., Huang, Y., Feng, J., Li, X., Wu, F.: Deep Q learning driven CT pancreas segmentation with geometry-aware U-Net. IEEE Trans. Med. Imaging **38**(8), 1971–1980 (2019)
2. Liu, S., et al.: Automatic pancreas segmentation via coarse location and ensemble learning. IEEE Access **8**, 2906–2914 (2019)
3. Lu, L., Jian, L., Luo, J., Xiao, B.: Pancreatic segmentation via ringed residual U-Net. IEEE Access **7**, 172871–172878 (2019)
4. Huang, M., Huang, C., Yuan, J., Kong, D.: A semiautomated deep learning approach for pancreas segmentation. J. Healthc. Eng. **2021**(1), 3284493 (2021)
5. Roger, R., et al.: Deep learning-based pancreas volume assessment in individuals with type 1 diabetes. BMC Med. Imaging **22**, 1–5 (2022)
6. Saraswathi, H.S., Rafi, M.: U-net-based pancreas tumor segmentation from abdominal CT images. Int. J. Adv. Comput. Sci. Appl. **14**(7) (2023)
7. Devendhar, T.: U-net based pancreas segmentation from computed tomography images. In: 2024 Third International Conference on Smart Technologies and Systems for Next Generation Computing (ICSTSN), pp. 1–5. IEEE (2024)
8. Lim, S.H., Kim, Y.J., Park, Y.H., Kim, D., Kim, K.G., Lee, D.H.: Automated pancreas segmentation and volumetry using deep neural network on computed tomography. Sci. Rep. **12**(1), 4075 (2022)
9. Sah, R., Dhir, R., Jain, S.: AI-driven approaches for improved detection and diagnosis of pancreatic cancer. In 2025 International Conference on Ambient Intelligence in Health Care (ICAIHC), pp. 1–6. IEEE (2025)
10. O'shea, K., Nash, R.:. An introduction to convolutional neural networks. arXiv preprint arXiv: 1511.08458 (2015)
11. Long, J., Shelhamer, E., Darrell, T.: Fully convolutional networks for semantic segmentation. In: Proceedings of the IEEE Conference on Computer Vision and Pattern Recognition, pp. 3431–3440 (2015)
12. Yin, X.X., Sun, L., Fu, Y., Lu, R., Zhang, Y.: [Retracted] U-net-based medical image segmentation. J. Healthc. Eng. **2022**(1), 4189781 (2022)
13. Jain, S., Sikka, G., Dhir, R.: An automatic cascaded approach for pancreas segmentation via an unsupervised localization using 3D CT volumes. Multimedia Syst. **29**(4), 2337–2349 (2023)
14. Jain, S., Gupta, S., Gulati, A.: An adaptive hybrid technique for pancreas segmentation using CT image sequences. In: 2015 International Conference on Signal Processing, Computing and Control (ISPCC), pp. 272–276. IEEE (2015)
15. Cao, H., et al.: Swin-Unet: Unet-like pure transformer for medical image segmentation. arXiv preprint arXiv:2105.05537 (2021)
16. Ronneberger, O., Fischer, P., Brox, T.: U-Net: convolutional net- works for biomedical image segmentation. Lect. Notes Comput. Sci. **9351**, 234–241 (2015)
17. Oktay, O., et al.: Attention U-Net: Learning where to look for the pancreas. arXiv preprint arXiv:1804.03999 (2018)

# Understanding Post-Disaster Queries Using Social Media Network Analysis and a Machine Learning Model: A Study of Turkey and Syria Earthquake 2023 Disaster


Rajkumar Chaudhari[1]([✉]) [iD], Maheshwari Biradar[1] [iD], and Tamal Mondal[2] [iD]

[1] SCSEA, D Y Patil International University, Pune, Maharashtra, India
{rajkumar.chaudhari,maheshwari.biradar}@dypiu.ac.in
[2] SCIT, Symbiosis International (Deemed University), Pune, Maharashtra, India
tamal@scit.edu



**Abstract.** In the modern digital world, social media plays an essential part in increasing awareness and delivering information. Sentiment analysis is one of the most important challenges in NLP (Natural Language Processing) because of its complexity and impact on daily life. It relates to categorization based on the behavioural patterns in text by identifying behavioral characteristics. Disaster-related posts are collected from social media platforms such as Twitter, and analysis of emotions is used to determine their approach. In situations of disaster and emergencies, social media studies investigate whether first responders may use this information to improve crisis management and situational awareness. Social media posts can provide useful data for disaster management. They may be used to detect sentiments and identify the requirements of those affected by disasters. To enhance the effectiveness of text sentiment analysis, we restructured the behavioural model as an identical problem. Therefore, we introduce a MHA-BiLSTM (Multi-Head Attention with BiLSTM) model. Furthermore, classifying the text using situational or non-situational methods proves to be more efficient than traditional sentiment analysis. Bidirectional LSTM is used for initial feature extraction, while multi-head attention captures valuable information from different dimensions and representation subspaces. The classification mechanism scores the characteristic sources by comparing them with labeled sets. The outcomes of experiments indicate that the MHA-BiLSTM model outperforms many existing models on the Turkey and Syria Earthquake 2023 tweet sentiment analysis datasets.

**Keywords:** Text Analysis · Machine learning · Sentiment analysis · Crisis Management





S. Mitra et al. (Eds.): PReMI 2025, LNCS 16358, pp. 350–359, 2026.
https://doi.org/10.1007/978-3-032-18480-1_36

# 1   Introduction

The problem with traditional-media based news sources is that there is usually a time delay between the incident/disaster happening and news media outlets broadcasting said occurrence or writing articles about it. Social media sites like Twitter on the other hand, have their own set of problems which is that, the common user won't be able to see those vital pieces of information until it's trending or if they are popular enough. Disaster-related posts on social media, especially on Twitter, contain lots of vital information, like people injured, dead, missing/found, and infrastructure and utility damage, that can help rescue operations and disaster organizations to prioritize and improve the quality of their efforts. Machine learning is used to predict the future using historical data. It mainly focuses on the development of programs and models which have the ability to change when exposed to new and unknown data and it enables it to learn without being explicitly programmed. In this research, as we'll be handling a large volume of tweets, it is key to construct a Machine learning model that can detect these relevant tweets and extract data from them to improve the quality and response of rescue and relief efforts.

During a disaster time, the exponential growth of social media has significantly transformed the digital world. With billions of active users online, these platforms have become important spaces for conversing, sharing, posting, and even modifying various types of content. This transformation has greatly altered how people communicate. Social media platforms, in particular, are effective tools for gauging the public state of mind. Information from sources like tweets and posts, especially in times of crisis, can be extracted and analysed for sentiment.

Social media sites have evolved into important channels for people to share their thoughts and perspectives. Among the various platforms available, Twitter stands out as one of the most widely used social media networks. This research aims to develop a model specifically designed to collect and analyse disaster-related information to support emergency responders. In recent years, the disaster relief industry has increasingly depended on social media, especially during crises and emergencies, to improve its attempts to communicate. Those systems allow for the immediate and extensive distribution of essential data. Government agencies and humanitarian groups may use social media to help with disaster preparation, response, and recovery activities by sharing alerts, warnings, and updates with the public while also measuring public interaction.

Sentiment analysis is an important technique for effective crisis management since it allows for early detection of possible hazards and gives useful information for adopting preemptive actions. As a consequence, disaster management teams will be able to respond more effectively during disasters. Sentiment analysis may also give useful information on the demands and emotional states of those affected by catastrophes. These analytical approaches allow emergency teams to immediately analyze the impact of the disaster on the community.

This research examines how emergency management organizations used social media during previous disasters, highlighting local as well as worldwide applications. It also investigates novel techniques that leverage social media to involve the public in real time during all stages of emergency management, including preparedness, response, and recovery. However, further research, examination, and refinement are required other than the scope of this study to completely understand the benefits of using social media and publicly available information into disaster and emergency management techniques.

## 2    Literature Survey

Yuya Shibuya (2017)—Mining Social Media for Disaster Management: Leveraging Social Media Data for Community Recovery [1]. The above paper talks about how managing and getting the information related to any disaster during a disaster is a serious concern.

Jibo Xie and Tengfei Yang (2018) - Using Social Media Data to Enhance Disaster Response and Community Service [2]. This paper sheds some light as to how disaster-related information is collected, managed, extracted, and classified from social media mediums for quicker disaster-related service.

Shosuke Sato (2018) - Effectiveness and Limitations of Social Networking Services in Disaster Responses [3]. Here the author Shosuke Sato discusses the uses of social networking services in disaster responses. The effectiveness and restrictions of social networking services are also talked about in this paper.

Bernadette Joy Detera, Akira Kodaka & Kaya Onda (2021) - Twitter-based analysis of Disaster Sentiment during Typhoons and Earthquakes [4]. This paper talks about studying the various sentiments of people around the world during the history of numerous Typhoons and Earthquakes which can, in turn, improve the accuracy of identifying other types of disasters too.

Malika Makker, Ramya B Ramanathan (2019) - Post Disaster Management using Satellite Imagery and social media [5]. In this paper, the authors talk about how important the use of Satellite Imagery is in both detecting and surveying areas, and especially those areas which have been affected thanks to the disasters.

Huiji Gao & Rebecca Goolsby (2019) - Harnessing the Crowdsourcing power of social media for disaster relief [6]. This paper talks about the benefits and drawbacks of crowdsourcing applications that are implemented in disaster relief coordination.

Alex Lambert (2018) - Perspectives on Social Media and Communities in response and recovery [7]. This paper talks about the collaborative study of disaster administration, the processing of information on social media w.r.t to disaster response and recuperation.

S. Geetha & Vishnu Kumar Kaliappan (2018) Tweet Analysis Based on Distinct Opinion of Social Media Users [8]. The authors here talk about the potential for anticipating different tweet formats from twitter and improving the accuracy of detecting disaster-related tweets.

Saurin R. Khedia, Shivam B. Parikh & Pradeep K. Atrey (2019) [9]. A Framework to Detect Fake Tweet Images on Social Media. The authors in this paper discuss using a framework that can help in detecting tweets that are either fake or have been meddled with, on any social media platform.

Si Si Mar win & Than Nwe Aung (2017) - Target-oriented tweets monitoring system during natural disasters [10]. This paper institutes a tweet monitoring system that can help in recognizing messages/tweets that people can update during natural disasters into a group of disaster information-related categories and provide user desired target information spontaneously.

Rabia Batool, Sungyoung Lee, Jahanzeb Maqbool (2013) - Precise tweet classification and sentiment analysis [11]. The authors of this paper examine tweets to categorize data and sentiments from Twitter even more accurately.

Rasika Wagh, Payal Punde (2018) - Survey on Sentiment Analysis using Twitter Dataset [12]. This paper shows the various ways of analyzing sentiments from tweets, and also the various approaches went about to execute extraction of sentiments from tweets.

Akash Kumar Gautam, Luv Mishra, Kush Mishra, Ajit Kumar, Shashwat Agarwal (2019) - Multimodal Analysis of Disaster Tweets [13]. In this paper, the authors analyze several modes of data which are connected to natural disasters and classify them based on whether they are informative or non-informative.

S. Devi, K Naveen kumar, S Shakti Ganesh (2021) - Location Based Twitter Emotion Classification for Disaster Management [13]. This paper talks about designing a simple system that can identify and analyze tweets, which can help towards disaster identification and recuperation.

## 3   Proposed Methodology

A proposed approach to perform sentiment analyses on social media data for disaster management would require many steps. Initially using API access and web scraping, real-time data would be gathered from online resources such as Twitter. The information collected would ultimately be filtered, with a focus on disaster-related terms. A preprocessing process would proceed to restore the data and remove unnecessary information, preparing it for analysis. Sentiment analysis would be performed using Natural language processing (NLP) techniques. Visualizations and diagrams were used to graphically represent the insights that were obtained. These results would be essential for directing both immediate disaster response and future management strategies. Finally, to improve the overall efficacy of the system, it would undergo continuous evaluation and upgrade (Fig. 1).

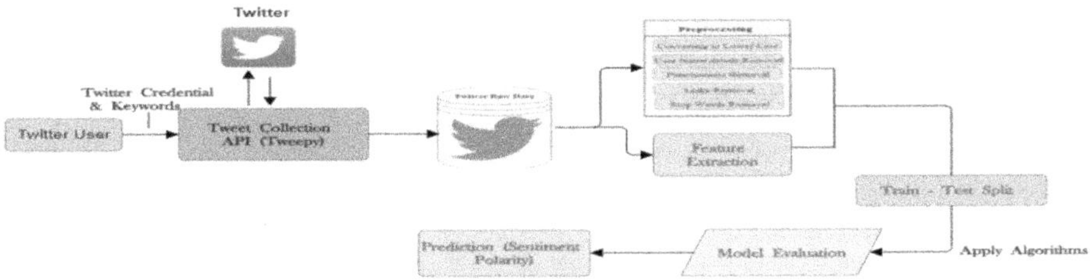


**Fig. 1.** Architecture of the proposed methodology.

## 3.1   Data Pre-processing

The most important stage in converting unstructured, raw data into an understandable, useable format is data pre-processing Dataset information collected from various sources often arrives in a form that is unsuitable for immediate evaluation or analysis. This crucial initial step data pre-processing is necessary before constructing any machine learning model. Since social media data is typically unstructured and includes common issues such as misspellings, slang, and grammatical errors, it can present significant challenges.

This raw data must be properly cleaned and processed for machine learning models to extract meaningful information. Pre-processing involves different steps such as Tokenization, removal of stop words from the tweet text, punctuation removal such as commas, full stops and question marks as they do not have any significance in the machine learning model context [14].

**Tokenization** is an essential NLP technique that splits large quantities of text into discrete, smaller units like words, phrases, or sentences. Machine learning algorithms may manage and analyze data more efficiently and effectively by translating raw text into these fundamental segments, known as tokens.

**Punctuation** characters can be recognized as noise in text data relating to letter sequences or word order. These symbols are represented by the punctuation "#, \$, %, &, () *, +, -, :, ;, ?, @, []".

**Stop words** are keywords that often appear in NLP frameworks, such as phrases, prepositions, and texts, but have limited lexical meaning.

**Stemming** is an NLP strategy that reduces words to their base or root form through the removal of grammatical information. By normalizing text, this procedure makes it possible to pre-process words and documents for analysis more quickly (Fig. 2).

|   | tweet | Processed_Tweets |
|---|---|---|
| 0 | @RandPaul I was forced out of a high-paying jo... | randpaul forced highpaying job federal governm... |
| 1 | Hanbo gets blood cancer from Covid vaccine htt... | hanbo get blood cancer covid vaccine httpstcom... |
| 2 | @DocDeezWhat @donovan_904 @Timcast @elonmusk Y... | docdeezwhat got banned said exist two gender g... |
| 3 | @hodgetwins Covid vaccine? | hodgetwins covid vaccine |
| 4 | This is total bullshit. \n#Spikevax #Covid #Va... | total bullshit vaccinated covid could raise au... |

**Fig. 2.** Pre-processed tweets Datasets.

### 3.2   Machine Learning Models

**CNN (Convolutional Neural Networks):** Sentiment analysis is one area of Natural Language Processing (NLP) in which Convolutional Neural Networks (CNNs) have demonstrated impressive capabilities. CNNs are a type of neural network that is efficient at recognizing patterns in grid-like data structures, particularly text [14]. When combined with pre-trained word embedding and skilled NLP techniques, their efficacy in sentiment analysis tasks grows significantly. These networks may reflect precise relationships between words and phrases and are typically more accurate and efficient than machine learning approaches, particularly when it comes to finding unknown trends in training data.

**BiLSTM (Bidirectional Long Short-Term Memory):** The Bidirectional Long Short-Term Memory (BiLSTM) architecture provides an accurate approach to processing sequential data. Typically used in catastrophe sentiment analysis (earthquakes, floods, and hurricanes), the goal is to discover the underlying attitudes and sentiments expressed in social media interactions [16]. The primary function of a BiLSTM is to process a textual sequence in two directions: one LSTM component analyses the words from first to last, while another LSTM analyzes the sequence in reverse. This two-way processing ensures that every word's semantic nuances and contextual links are properly captured. The BiLSTM assigns an emotion category to these unlabelled social media posts about a horrible circumstance based on the combined output of these forward and backward passes for each word in the sequence.

**MHA BiLSTM (Multihead Attention BiLSTM Hybrid Model):** The proposed strategy starts by creating word vectors from the input text, which are then fed into a Bi-LSTM network. The encoded word sequences include initial contextual links that this network is intended to learn. Meanwhile, the model's multi-head attention feature allows for effective understanding of far-off textual components [15]. The BiLSTM hybrid model mechanism is required to fully comprehend long-range words and gather wide situational text information. It operates by altering the input in parallel using linear transformations, each with its own set of parameters. Each of these modifications is then sent into a Scaled Dot-Product Attention (SDPA) unit. As a result of this simultaneous processing, the model may extract and learn features from a variety of representations. Concatenating the different outputs of each SDPA component results in an enhanced composite matrix. This unified matrix generates information from a variety of views.

The final Multi-Head Attention output is obtained by applying a final linear transformation to this combined grid. The ordered contextual information generated by combinations may be efficiently obtained by the Bi-LSTM stage. In addition, the multi-head attention mechanism allows the model to extract information from different dimensions and representational subspaces in order allowing a thorough capture of textual relations over immense distances. When these two concepts work together, the model's ability to analyze sentiments is successfully enhanced.

## 4   Experimental Results

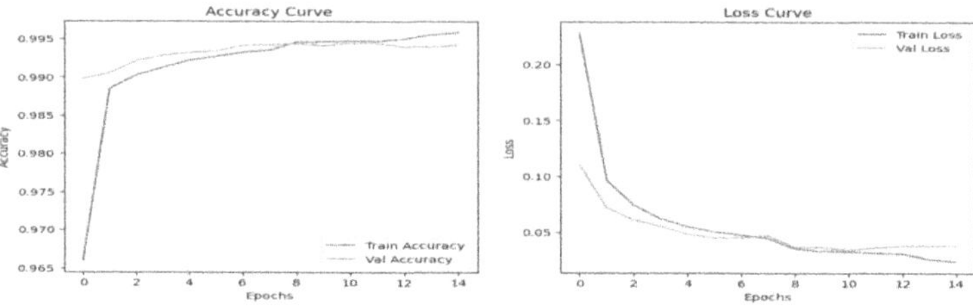

**Fig. 3.** MHA - BiLSTM Model Accuracy Graph.

These graphs show the performance of a model over multiple training epochs, typically used to monitor how well the model is learning and whether it's overfitting or under fitting (Fig. 3).

- Both training and validation accuracies are very high (close to 100) and stabilize after a few epochs, indicating the model is performing well on both seen (training) and unseen (validation) data.

- The close alignment of the two lines suggests there is no significant overfitting (where the model performs much better on training data than validation data).

- The loss decreases significantly in the early epochs and then plateaus, indicating the model has learned effectively and converged.

- The similar values for training and validation loss suggest the model generalizes well and is not overfitting.

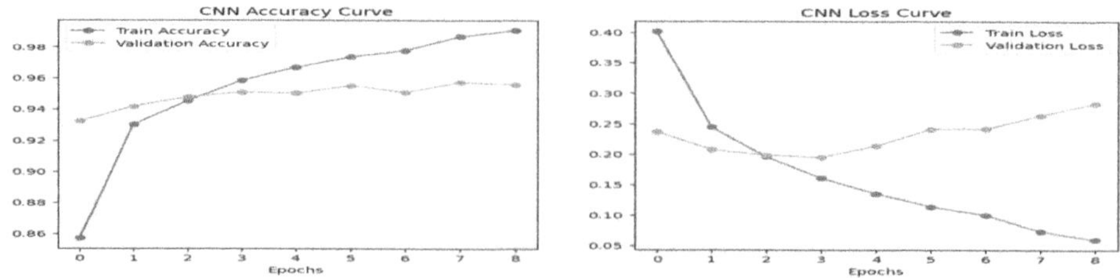

**Fig. 4.** CNN Model Accuracy Graph.

A Convolutional Neural Network (CNN) model's performance is shown in Fig. 4, which also shows the model's training and validation accuracy. The model's accuracy levels are measured on the Y-axis, while the training epoch progression is shown on the X-axis. The model's validation accuracy was about 95%, whereas its training accuracy was about 98%. Possible overfitting to the training data is identified by the observed differences, where validation accuracy is significantly lower than training accuracy. As a result, the model may not demonstrate strong generalization ability when presented with data that has never been seen previous to.

A Bidirectional Long Short-Term Memory (Bi-LSTM) model's training and validation accuracy curves are shown in Fig. 5. The model's accuracy on the training and validation datasets is measured by the vertical axis (Y-axis), while the training epoch growing is recorded by the horizontal axis (X-axis). According to the source, the model's training accuracy was almost 97%, while its validation accuracy was around 96%. The model appears to have successfully learnt the fundamental patterns in the training data and has strong generalization ability based on the closed alignment of both of the metrics (Table 1).

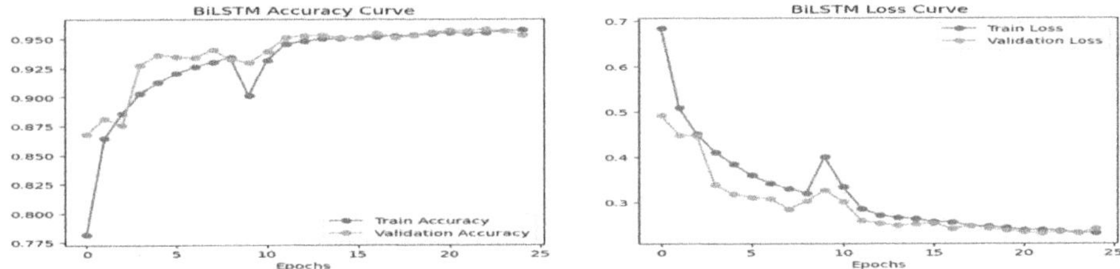


**Fig. 5.** Bi-LSTM Model Accuracy Graph.

**Table 1.** Performance Comparison of Machine Learning Models

| Machine Learning models | Performance metrics | |
| --- | --- | --- |
| | Accuracy_score | Cross_val_score |
| Bi-LSTM Model | 97% | 96% |
| CNN Model | 98% | 95% |
| MHA-BiLSTM Model | 99% | 99% |

For comparison research, we used three different types of Machine learning models: a neural network based on convolution (CNN), an Individual Bidirectional LSTM (Bi-LSTM), and Multi-Head Attention Bi-LSTM (MHA-BiLSTM). In comparison to its others, the MHA-BiLSTM consistently produced more accurate results. This improved performance is a result of MHA-BiLSTM's natural ability to process sequences both forward and backward, which is essential for identifying long-range dependencies as well as complex contextual relationships in text. The accuracy of our MHA-BiLSTM model was 95% or higher throughout training. In contrast, CNN models do not have the bidirectional contextual awareness provided by LSTMs; instead, they learn local patterns in the input.

## 5   Conclusion

Sentiment analysis of social media data is a vital resource for disaster management, allowing quickly determine urgent requirements and strategically plan relief activities. When used for sentiment analysis in this particular field, the MHA-BiLSTM architecture indicates a clear accuracy advantage over both CNN and BiLSTM models, which is compatible with the empirical results. This advantage is probably attributed to the MHA-BiLSTM's comprehensive analysis of the complex contextual relationships that characterize sequential textual information. The MHA-BiLSTM model seems to be the best option for the challenging situations of disaster management, even if CNN and BiLSTM models are undoubtedly useful for sentiment analysis in some situations.

All things considered, sentiment analysis on social media may significantly improve disaster management initiatives. The ultimate goal should be to use these technologies to help humans affected by disaster management, considering that the neural network architecture used could impact the sentiment analysis's accuracy.

## References


1. Shibuya, Y.: Impact of ICT tools on disaster logistics issues: a case study of the great east Japan earthquake and Tsunami of 2011. Int. J. Bus. Inf. **12**(3), 310–341 (2017)
2. Xie, J., Yang, T.: Using social media data to enhance disaster response and community service. In: 2018 International Workshop on Big Geospatial Data and Data Science (BGDDS), pp. 1–4. IEEE (2018)
3. Sato, S.: Effectiveness and limitations of social networking services in disaster responses: a review 7 Years on from the 2011 Great East Japan earthquake. In: 2018 5th International Conference on Information and Communication Technologies for Disaster Management (ICT-DM), pp. 1–6. IEEE (2018)
4. Detera, B.J., Kodaka, A., Kohtake, N., Nishino, A., Onda, K.: An English-Japanese twitter-based analysis of disaster sentiment during typhoons and earthquakes. In: 2021 IEEE International Symposium on Systems Engineering (ISSE), pp. 1–8. IEEE (2021)
5. Makker, M., Ramanathan, R., Dinesh, S.B.: Post disaster management using satellite imagery and social media data. In: 2019 4th International Conference on Computational Systems and Information Technology for Sustainable Solution (CSITSS), pp. 1–6. IEEE (2019)
6. Guntha, R., Rao, S.N., Ramesh, M.V.: Architectural considerations for building a robust crowdsourced disaster relief application. In: 2020 International Conference on COMmunication Systems & NETworkS (COMSNETS), pp. 638–641. IEEE (2020)

7. Anand, A., Jacob, T.P.: Disaster detection system using social media, machine learning and crowdsourcing. In: AIP Conference Proceedings, vol. 2802, no. 1. AIP Publishing (2024)

8. Geetha, S., Vishnu Kumar, K.: Tweet analysis based on distinct opinion of social media users'. In: Advances in Big Data and Cloud Computing: Proceedings of ICBDCC 2018, pp. 251–261. Springer, Singapore (2019)

9. Parikh, S.B., Khedia, S.R., Atrey, P.K.: A framework to detect fake tweet images on social media. In: 2019 IEEE Fifth International Conference on Multimedia Big Data (BigMM), pp. 104–110. IEEE (2019)

10. Win, S.S.M., Aung, T.N.: Target oriented tweets monitoring system during natural disasters. Int. J. Netw. Distrib. Comput. $5$(3), 133–142 (2017)

11. Batool, R., Khattak, A.M., Maqbool, J., Lee, S.: Precise tweet classification and sentiment analysis. In: 2013 IEEE/ACIS 12th International Conference on Computer and Information Science (ICIS), pp. 461–466. IEEE (2013)

12. Wagh, R., Punde, P.: Survey on sentiment analysis using twitter dataset. In: 2018 Second International Conference on Electronics, Communication and Aerospace Technology (ICECA), pp. 208–211. IEEE (2018)

13. Devi, S., Naveenkumar, K., Ganesh, S.S., Ritesh, S.: Location based Twitter emotion classification for disaster management. In: 2021 Third International Conference on Inventive Research in Computing Applications (ICIRCA), pp. 664–669. IEEE (2021)

14. Lin, Y., Li, J., Yang, L., Xu, K., Lin, H.: Sentiment analysis with comparison enhanced deep neural network. IEEE Access $8$, 78378–78384 (2020)

15. Wahid, J.A., et al.: Identifying and characterizing the propagation scale of COVID-19 situational information on Twitter: a hybrid text analytic approach. Appl. Sci. $11$(14), 6526 (2021)

16. Sen, A., Rudra, K., Ghosh, S.: Extracting situational awareness from microblogs during disaster events. In: 2015 7th International Conference on Communication Systems and Networks (COMSNETS), pp. 1–6. IEEE (2015)

# An Improved Deep Learning Framework for Diabetic Retinopathy Screening Using Fractional-Order Optimization


Mukesh Delu[1]([envelope]) [iD], Rinki Sharma[1] [iD], Priyanka Harjule[1] [iD],
and Rajesh Kumar[1,2] [iD]

[1] Malaviya National Institute of Technology Jaipur, Jaipur 302017, India
{2022rma9055,2021rma9567,priyanka.maths}@mnit.ac.in, rkumar@uj.ac.za
[2] University of Johannesburg, Johannesburg 2006, South Africa



**Abstract.** Precise staging of diabetic retinopathy (DR) is crucial but challenging in real-world settings due to the limited availability of table-top retinal imaging and inconsistencies in pictures captured by handheld fundus cameras, which reduces the effectiveness of deep learning. This study introduces a robust deep learning pipeline for noisy, imbalanced, and heterogeneous fundus datasets acquired from portable handheld devices. The proposed approach enhances pathological feature visibility by an improved image enhancement pipeline that combines fractional-order anisotropic diffusion, CLAHE, and unsharp masking, improving image quality before classification. Transfer learning with EfficientNet-B3 is utilized for model training and optimizing it using a fractional-order optimizer that adaptively interpolates between first and higher-order memory-augmented descent to stabilize training. On held-out test data, the proposed fractional-order training achieves consistent gains in staging and DR detection relative to standard RMSProp, SGD Nestrov, and Adam baselines. Ablations show that the fractional memory parameter provides a tunable bias-variance trade-off. The proposed pipeline achieves 92.37% accuracy and 88.56% F1-score for 2-class, and 90.51% accuracy and 88.37% F1-score for 3-class classification of the mBRSET dataset. These results suggest that fractional optimization can improve robustness and equity of DR screening models in real-world settings.

**Keywords:** Diabetic Retinopathy · Fractional Anisotropic Diffusion · Deep Learning · Fractional Optimizer · Handheld Fundus Imaging


## 1 Introduction

DR is a major microvascular complication of diabetes mellitus (DM) that results in visual impairment. It has a global prevalence of 34.6%, encompassing proliferative DR (PDR) (6.96%), diabetic macular edema (DME) (6.81%), and vision-threatening complications (10.2%) [9] among those with DM. Timely detection of sight-threatening phases such as severe non-proliferative DR (NPDR), PDR,



S. Mitra et al. (Eds.): PReMI 2025, LNCS 16358, pp. 360–368, 2026.
https://doi.org/10.1007/978-3-032-18480-1_37

and DME allows treatment before irreparable vision loss [10]. Clinical tabletop fundus cameras are graded by skilled readers using the International Clinical Diabetic Retinopathy (ICDR) severity scale in traditional screening workflows. Capital expenses, infrastructural needs, and qualified staff shortages hinder these solutions. Thus, their scalability and accessibility are limited, especially in low- and middle-income countries where the disease spreads rapidly. [5].

Compact handheld retinal cameras are a viable, low-cost alternative for community screening campaigns, primary care clinics, and telemedicine programs. The first public dataset of handheld fundus photos from high-burden DR screening sessions in Brazil is the mBRSET dataset [8]. The dataset includes 5164 images from 1291 patients with extensive metadata on age, sex, diabetes duration, treatment modalities, systemic comorbidities, socioeconomic indicators like insurance and education, image quality labels, expert ICDR DR grades, and macular edema annotations. These properties make mBRSET a proper stress test for designing robust, equitable DR staging algorithms for implementation outside tertiary centers.

In various big retinal image repositories like EyePACS, Messidor, and APTOS, deep convolutional and transformer-based models have achieved excellent DR detection accuracy [2]. However, three obstacles hinder handheld, community-acquired data translation: Image heterogeneity and noise decrease image quality. Class imbalance and ordinal severity structure: mild instances predominate, while severe and proliferative disease are rare but critical; Performance gaps can worsen health inequalities due to demographic and socioeconomic domain shift. Conventional first-order optimizers like SGD and Adam may underperform with noisy gradients and sparse minority classes [4].

To address these issues, this work investigates a fractional calculus-based training paradigm. Fractional-order derivatives generalize classical calculus by including power-law kernel-governed memory effects that influence gradient updates [3,4]. In gradient-based optimization, this formula allows switching between local (SGD-like) and history-aware (momentum-like) learning, which could help training on rough or loud loss surfaces. The proposed pipeline builds on this and makes the following contributions:

(i) Proposed a multi-stage enhancement approach to enhance the visibility of subtle pathological features used in DR detection, integrating fractional anisotropic diffusion, CLAHE, and unsharp masking.

(ii) Used a fractional-order optimizer that adaptively utilizes previous gradient information to stabilize training and improve convergence in noisy and imbalanced data.

(iii) Evaluated the proposed pipeline using k-fold cross-validation on the mBRSET dataset, which shows that it is more accurate and robust than baseline optimizers.

The structure of this paper is as follows: The Sect. 2 describes the proposed pipeline. Section 3 presents experimental results and ablation studies. Section 4 concludes with key findings and future scope.

## 2    Materials and Methods

This section presents the materials and methods used in this study.

### 2.1    Data Description

This study employs the mBRSET dataset [8] and uses two classification settings to facilitate training and mitigate class imbalance:

(i) 2-class DR classification that puts images into No DR (grade 0, 3750 images) and DR (grades 1 to 4, 1134 images).
(ii) 3-class DR staging task that puts images into No DR (grade 0, 3750 images), NPDR (grades 1 to 3, 922 images), and PDR (grade 4, 212 images).

### 2.2    Fractional Anisotropic Diffusion Based Image Enhancement

Let $I(x, y, t)$ be the image intensity function over spatial coordinates $(x, y)$ and diffusion time $t$. The classical anisotropic diffusion equation [1]is defined as:

$$\frac{\partial I}{\partial t} = \nabla \cdot (c(x, y)\nabla I),\tag{1}$$

where $c(x, y)$ is an edge-stopping function that controls diffusion across edges and is defined as: $c(x, y) = \exp\left(-\frac{|\nabla I(x,y)|^2}{K^2}\right)$, with $K > 0$ controlling contrast sensitivity.

The proposed method replaces the standard gradient by GrünwaldLetnikov (GL) fractional derivatives. The GL fractional derivative [7] of order $\alpha \in (0, 1)$ in the $x$-direction is approximated as:

$$D_x^\alpha I(x, y) \approx \sum_{k=0}^{N} w_k I(x - kh, y), \quad w_k = (-1)^k \binom{\alpha}{k},\tag{2}$$

where $h = 1$, and $\binom{\alpha}{k} = \frac{\Gamma(\alpha+1)}{\Gamma(k+1)\Gamma(\alpha-k+1)}$, with $\Gamma(\cdot)$ denoting the Gamma function. The derivative in the $y$-direction is similarly defined. The update rule for the image after one iteration becomes:

$$I^{(t+1)} = I^{(t)} + \Delta t \left[D_x^\alpha I \cdot c(x, y) + D_y^\alpha I \cdot c(x, y)\right],\tag{3}$$

where $\Delta t$ is the time step, and the directional fractional derivatives $D_x^\alpha I$, $D_y^\alpha I$ are applied via local neighborhood differences weighted by $w_k$.

The mBRSET dataset contains retinal fundus images taken by a portable device in different lighting, contrast, and noise settings during distinct stages of DR. Many of these pictures don't show fine vascular structures, poor local contrast, and uneven lighting that might reduce the performance of automated DR grading systems when it comes to feature extraction and categorization. To overcome the limitations of standard preprocessing, this study proposes a compact and effective image enhancement pipeline tailored for DR analysis, combining the following three key techniques:

(i) Fractional-order anisotropic diffusion applied to the brightness (V) channel in HSV space to enhance microvascular edges and reduces noise in low-contrast regions;

(ii) CLAHE on the luminance (Y) channel to adaptively improve local contrast, especially around hemorrhages and exudates; and

(iii) Unsharp masking to sharpen fine structural details, aiding the visibility of microaneurysms and vessel abnormalities.

---

**Algorithm 1** RGB Image Enhancement using Fractional Anisotropic Diffusion

---

1: **Input:** RGB image $I_{rgb}$
2: **Output:** Enhanced RGB image $I_{enh}$
3: Convert RGB image to HSV and Extract V channel:   $I_{hsv} \leftarrow \mathrm{rgb2hsv}(I_{rgb})$,   $V \leftarrow I_{hsv}(:,:,3)$
4: Initialize parameters:   $\alpha$, $K$, $\Delta t$, $n_{iter}$, $N$
5: Compute Grünwald–Letnikov weights $w$:   $w[0] \leftarrow 1$
6: **for** $i = 1$ to $N$ **do**
7:     $w[i] \leftarrow w[i-1] \cdot \left(1 - \dfrac{\alpha+1}{i}\right)$

8: **end for**
9: Pad V channel symmetrically:   $V_{pad} \leftarrow \mathrm{padarray}(V, [N, N])$
10: **for** $t = 1$ to $n_{iter}$ **do**
11:     Initialize $F_x, F_y \leftarrow 0$
12:     **for** $k = 1$ to $N$ **do**
13:         $F_x \leftarrow F_x + w[k] \cdot (V_{\text{shifted-x}} - V_{\text{original}})$,   $F_y \leftarrow F_y + w[k] \cdot (V_{\text{shifted-y}} - V_{\text{original}})$
14:     **end for**

15:     $\mathrm{grad}_{\mathrm{mag}} \leftarrow \sqrt{F_x^2 + F_y^2}$,   $c \leftarrow \exp\left(-\dfrac{\mathrm{grad}_{\mathrm{mag}}^2}{K^2}\right)$

16:     Update V channel:   $V_{pad} \leftarrow V_{pad} + \Delta t \cdot (F_x \cdot c + F_y \cdot c)$
17: **end for**
18: Crop V and Replace V in HSV:   $V_{enh} \leftarrow \mathrm{crop}(V_{pad})$,   $I_{hsv}(:,:,3) \leftarrow V_{enh}$
19: Convert back to RGB:   $I_{rgb\text{-}diff} \leftarrow \mathrm{hsv2rgb}(I_{hsv})$
20: Convert to YCbCr:   $I_{ycbcr} \leftarrow \mathrm{rgb2ycbcr}(I_{rgb\text{-}diff})$
21: Apply CLAHE on Y channel:   $Y_{clahe} \leftarrow \mathrm{adapthisteq}(I_{ycbcr}(:,:,1))$
22: Replace Y channel:   $I_{ycbcr}(:,:,1) \leftarrow Y_{clahe}$
23: Convert back to RGB:   $I_{clahe} \leftarrow \mathrm{ycbcr2rgb}(I_{ycbcr})$
24: Apply unsharp masking:   $I_{enh} \leftarrow \mathrm{imsharpen}(I_{clahe})$
25: **return** $I_{enh}$

---

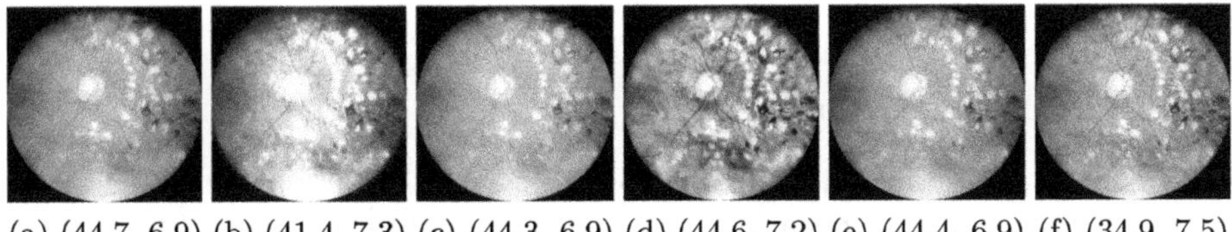

(a) (44.7, 6.9) (b) (41.4, 7.3) (c) (44.3, 6.9) (d) (44.6, 7.2) (e) (44.4, 6.9) (f) (34.9, 7.5)

**Fig. 1.** Visual comparison of different image enhancement techniques applied to a retinal fundus image from the mBRSET Dataset and their corresponding (BRISQUE scores, Entropy). (a) Original image, (b) Histogram Equalization, (c) Gamma correction, (d) CLAHE, (e) Unsharp masking, (f) Proposed method.

Algorithm 1 provides a brief description of the process. The proposed method improves input quality by making subtle pathological symptoms more visible for future DR classification networks and reducing inter-class ambiguity. Figure 1 shows that the proposed enhancement method has the lowest BRISQUE score and the highest Entropy, which indicates superior perceptual quality and more explicit pathological detail.

The following empirically tuned parameters were used to enhance retinal lesions, vessel preservation, and balance noise suppression: $\alpha = 0.2$ for enhancement without over-smoothing, $K = 0.05$ to preserve high-contrast boundaries, $\Delta t = 0.1$ for numerical stability, $n_{iter} = 20$ to ensure adequate enhancement, and $N = 10$ to stabilize fractional diffusion and enhance required feature visibility. The fractional order $\alpha$ was fixed at 0.2, as higher values (0.5–1) either amplified noise or reduced lesion visibility.

### 2.3   Methodology

This work employs a transfer learning methodology, with EfficientNet-B3 as the foundational model for classification objectives. Figure 2 shows that the input data is routed via EfficientNet-B3 to get deep feature representations. The data has been preprocessed using Fractional Anisotropic Diffusion to improve feature quality and reduce noise. The fractional momentum gradient descent (FMGD) [6] optimizer was used in backpropagation to find the optimal settings.

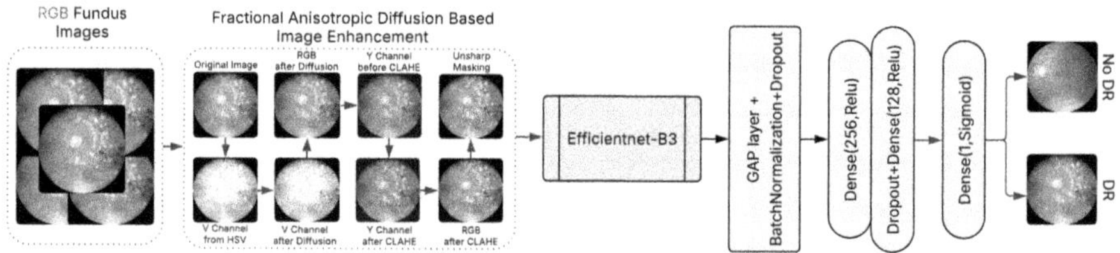


**Fig. 2.** Sequential depiction of the proposed DR staging pipeline.

### 2.4   Fractional Gradient Descent

To enhance this study's optimization process, FMGD [6] has been used in the backpropagation for optimization. The mathematical formulation of the FMGD algorithm is provided in Eq. (4).

$$\mathbf{x_{n+1}} = \mathbf{x_n} - \gamma \frac{\nabla \mathbf{f(x_n)} \, |\mathbf{x_n} - \mathbf{x_{n-1}} + \varepsilon|^{(1-\alpha)}}{\mathbf{\Gamma(2 - \alpha)}} \tag{4}$$

Here $x_{n-1}$ and $x_n$ are starting random points $\gamma$ is the learning rate $\varepsilon > 0$ is a small quantity and $\alpha$ is the fractional order parameter and here $\alpha \in [1, 2)$. For $\alpha \in (0, 1)$ $1 - \alpha$ is positive and $|x_n - x_{n-1}|$ acts as a momentum factor. When the training processes $|x_n - x_{n-1}|^{1-\alpha}$ became large and gradients became unstable. As a result, the convergence is worse for $\alpha \in (0, 1)$. For $\alpha \in [1, 2)$, smoothly handle the gradient flows and provide better convergence as initially

$\frac{1}{|x_n - x_{n-1} + \varepsilon|^{1-\alpha}}$ grows, and over time it acts as a damping factor which stabilizes the convergence. The term $|x_n - x_{n-1} + \varepsilon|^{(1-\alpha)}$ modulate the learning rate dynamically. The FMGD reduces to standard gradient descent for $\alpha = 1$.

## 2.5  Fractional Order Selection

The fractional derivative order $\alpha$ is a crucial hyperparameter for the FMGD optimizer, affecting convergence behavior. To find the optimal value of $\alpha$, the model was trained on a spectrum of $\alpha$ within the range $[1, 2)$ using training data. The optimal order was selected based on a random search of the suggested model, achieving the highest training accuracy over 20 epochs with a learning rate of 0.0001. Figure 3 shows how changing $\alpha$ impacts optimizer performance. The fractional order $\alpha = 1.7$ has the highest training accuracy among the tested values, making it the experimentally optimum order for this dataset. All future experiments in this study follow this $\alpha$ for optimal convergence and performance.

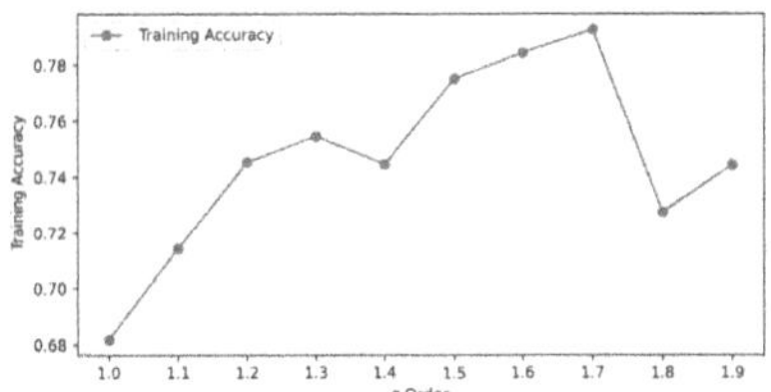

**Fig. 3.**   Training accuracies with respect to fractional order $\alpha$.

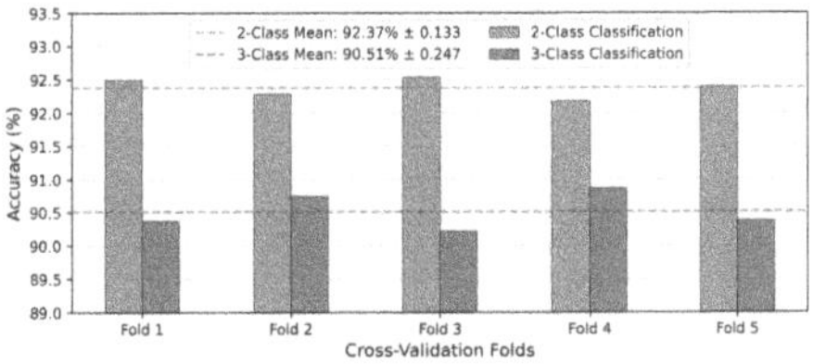

**Fig. 4.** Fold-wise accuracy for 2-Class and 3-Class DR classification.

# 3   Results and Discussion

The model was evaluated using 5-fold stratified cross-validation, guaranteeing no image overlap across folds. Performance measurements were given as means across folds to ensure model stability. Images were resized to $384 \times 384 \times 3$ and normalized using ImageNet statistics. Rotation, scaling, horizontal flipping, and vertical flipping were employed for augmentation. The learning rate was 0.0005, with a decay factor of 0.9. Optimal classification results were achieved using the FMGD optimizer and the Focal loss function. Batch size and epoch were set to 16 and 50, respectively. All trials were conducted with the PyTorch framework on Kaggle using an NVIDIA Tesla P100 GPU. To compare the proposed experimental setup, this study has used well-known optimizers like Adam, SGD Nestrov, and RMSprop. All the hyperparameters and models have been taken as the same, and the optimizer has been changed to show the robustness of the FMGD optimizer.

Figure 4 shows the 5-fold cross-validation accuracy of the proposed method for 2-class and 3-class DR classification on the mBRSET dataset. The proposed technique performs consistently across data folds with low standard deviations, indicating its robustness and generalizability. The proposed method significantly enhances DR categorization on the mBRSET dataset as seen in Tables 1. The results show that due to the memory-augmented optimization, the suggested pipeline always works better than baseline optimizers, as the FMGD optimizer has stabilizing benefits.

**Table 1.** Ablation study on the mBRSET dataset using EfficientNet-B3.

| Image Enhancement | Optimizer | Accuracy | Precision | Recall | F1-score |
|---|---|---|---|---|---|
| No | Rmsprop | 0.7366 | 0.7701 | 0.6670 | 0.7149 |
|  | SGD Nestrov | 0.7725 | 0.8237 | 0.6999 | 0.7568 |
|  | Adam | 0.8432 | 0.8268 | 0.7964 | 0.8164 |
|  | FMGD [6] | 0.8872 | 0.7932 | 0.8153 | 0.8041 |
| Yes | Rmsprop | 0.8014 | 0.8436 | 0.7355 | 0.7859 |
|  | SGD Nestrov | 0.8469 | 0.8798 | 0.8076 | 0.8421 |
|  | Adam | 0.8925 | 0.8561 | 0.8425 | 0.8492 |
|  | FMGD [6] | 0.9237 | 0.9162 | 0.8597 | 0.8856 |

**Table 2.** Performance Comparison of SOTA Models on the mBRSET Dataset.

| Task | Model | Accuracy | Precision | Recall | F1-score |
|---|---|---|---|---|---|
| 3-class DR Classification | Swin-V2 Large [8] | 0.8906 | 0.8227 | 0.7852 | 0.8026 |
|  | DINO-V2 Large [8] | 0.8751 | 0.7864 | 0.7992 | 0.7919 |
|  | ConvNext-V2 Large [8] | 0.8867 | 0.8399 | 0.7748 | 0.8033 |
|  | **Proposed** | 0.9051 | 0.8923 | 0.8774 | 0.8837 |
| 2-class DR Classification | Swin-V2 Large [8] | 0.8955 | 0.8907 | 0.8389 | 0.8598 |
|  | DINO-V2 Large [8] | 0.9003 | 0.8761 | 0.8719 | 0.8740 |
|  | ConvNext-V2 Large [8] | 0.8955 | 0.8823 | 0.8477 | 0.8626 |
|  | **Proposed** | 0.9237 | 0.9162 | 0.8597 | 0.8856 |

The enhanced pipeline utilizing the EfficientNet-B3 model, optimized through FMGD and fractional preprocessing, outperforms current SOTA models as shown in Table 2 in 2-class and 3-class DR staging tasks by achieving higher accuracy and F1-scores. The clinic can utilize it to detect DR. The 3-class classification had improved recall and precision, suggesting it can detect NPDR and PDR. Using memory-aware dynamic, fractional-order algorithms improves convergence and resilience on noisy and unbalanced datasets. They are perfect for scalable DR screening in real-world settings since they can give very accurate results with little data and processing power.

## 4    Conclusion

This study shows that the robustness of DR screening with the help of hand-held fundus images is greatly improved by combining a memory-augmented fractional-order optimization technique with a fractional-order image enhancement pipeline. The proposed framework enhances image quality using fractional anisotropic diffusion, CLAHE, and unsharp masking, while stabilizing training with a fractional optimizer on a transfer-learned EfficientNet-B3 backbone. This approach consistently improves in 2-class and 3-class DR staging, especially in detecting rare but clinically significant severe cases like PDR. A fractional memory term facilitates a modifiable biasvariance trade-off, enhancing generalization in noisy and imbalanced data. Future research will extend this methodology to include the 5-class staging of DR and develop a new fractional-order loss function specifically designed to solve class imbalance to improve fairness and therapeutic relevance in a real-world setting.

**Acknowledgments.** Mukesh Delu gratefully acknowledges the Senior Research Fellowship support provided by the Council of Scientific & Industrial Research (CSIR).

**Disclosure of Interests.** The authors have no competing interests to declare relevant to this article's content.

## References

1. AbdAlRahman, A., Al-Atabany, W.I., Soltan, A., Radwan, A.G.: High-performance fractional anisotropic diffusion filter for portable applications. J. Real-Time Image Process. **20** (2023). https://doi.org/10.1007/s11554-023-01339-y
2. Abushawish, I., Modak, S., Abdel-Raheem, E., Mahmoud, S., Hussain, A.: Deep learning in automatic diabetic retinopathy detection and grading systems: a comprehensive survey and comparison of methods. IEEE Access **12**, 84785–84802 (2024). https://doi.org/10.1109/access.2024.3415617
3. Delu, M., Harjule, P.: Modified fractional edge detection masks based on compass gradient for retinopathy screening. In: 2021 International Conference on Engineering and Emerging Technologies (ICEET), pp. 1–6. IEEE (2023). https://doi.org/10.1109/iceet60227.2023.10526080
4. Harjule, P., Sharma, R., Kumar, R.: Fractional-order gradient approach for optimizing neural networks: a theoretical and empirical analysis. Chaos Solitons Fractals **192**, 116009 (2025). https://doi.org/10.1016/j.chaos.2025.116009
5. Hill-Briggs, F., et al.: Social determinants of health and diabetes: a scientific review. Diabetes Care **44**, 258–279 (2020). https://doi.org/10.2337/dci20-0053
6. Sharma, R., Harjule, P.: Fractional derivative approach for training of neural networks. In: Kumar, R., Verma, A.K., Verma, O.P., Rajpurohit, J. (eds.) Soft Computing: Theories and Applications. SoCTA 2024. LNNS, vol. 1344, pp. 331–340. Springer, Cham (2025). https://doi.org/10.1007/978-981-96-5958-6_29

7. Teodoro, G.S., Machado, J.A.T., De Oliveira, E.C.: A review of definitions of fractional derivatives and other operators. J. Comput. Phys. **388**, 195–208 (2019). https://doi.org/10.1016/j.jcp.2019.03.008

8. Wu, C., et al.: A portable retina fundus photos dataset for clinical, demographic, and diabetic retinopathy prediction. Scientific Data **12** (2025). https://doi.org/10.1038/s41597-025-04627-3

9. Yau, J., et al.: Global prevalence and major risk factors of diabetic retinopathy. Diabetes Care **35**(3), 556–564 (2012). https://doi.org/10.2337/dc11-1909

10. Zhang, D., et al.: Nonlinear relationship between diabetes mellitus duration and diabetic retinopathy. Sci. Rep. **14**(1) (2024). https://doi.org/10.1038/s41598-024-82068-5

# Tract-Specific Biomarker Discovery for Early Alzheimer's Disease Using Sparse Diffusion MRI and AI Framework

Abhishek Tiwari[1,2]([✉])(iD) and Saurabh J. Shigwan[2](iD)

[1] Department of Computer Science and Engineering, Birla Institute of Technology, Mesra (BIT Mesra), Ranchi, India
[2] Shiv Nadar Institution of Eminence, Delhi NCR, India
abhiphd02@gmail.com, saurabh.shigwan@snu.edu.in

**Abstract.** Early detection of Alzheimer's disease (AD) is challenging due to the complex of MRI data and the time demands of full diffusion-weighted imaging (DWI). This research presents an ethical AI-based deep learning framework that uses sparse DWI for rapid, tract-based AD classification. By leveraging diffusion tensor imaging (DTI) parameters, the method analyzes white matter (WM) tracts to distinguish Mild Cognitive Impairment (MCI) from Cognitively Normal (CN) individuals, focusing on longitudinal WM changes linked to AD. The framework reduces DWI acquisition time while maintaining performance comparable to full DWI. Results show that sparse DWI improves efficiency without compromising accuracy, offering a timely, cost-effective, and ethical approach for early AD diagnosis. AUC = 0.95, matching performance of dense acquisitions, and 91% classification accuracy were attained using just 5 diffusion directions.

**Keywords:** Tract-based analysis · Alzheimer's disease · Diffusion MRI · White matter · Sparse measurement

## 1 Introduction

Alzheimer's disease (AD) is a major global health concern, with dementia cases expected to reach 1.6 million by 2050 [4]. Early diagnosis is essential to enable interventions that may delay cognitive decline. Mild Cognitive Impairment (MCI), often preceding AD, represents a crucial diagnostic stage. Existing approaches such as PET, cerebrospinal fluid (CSF) analysis, and neuropsychological tests are either invasive, expensive, or insufficiently sensitive for early detection [18].

Diffusion tensor imaging (DTI), derived from diffusion-weighted imaging (DWI), provides valuable insights into white matter (WM) microstructure by modeling diffusion anisotropy. However, traditional DTI requires dense diffusion directions, resulting in long scan times, motion sensitivity, and limited feasibility in clinical practice [7]. These limitations hinder its scalability for widespread


S. Mitra et al. (Eds.): PReMI 2025, LNCS 16358, pp. 369–379, 2026.
https://doi.org/10.1007/978-3-032-18480-1_38

AD screening. Artificial intelligence (AI) models have shown promise in neuroimaging, particularly with structural and functional MRI. Transformer-based architectures and convolutional networks can capture complex representations [5,7], yet most efforts focus on AD vs. cognitively normal (CN) classification, with limited emphasis on the subtler MCI vs. CN task. Moreover, many deep learning models demand extensive computation and lack interpretability, challenging clinical adoption.

To address these gaps, we present a tract-specific AI framework that integrates interpretable handcrafted features with the learning capabilities of a Swin-transformer-based network. Our approach reduces reliance on dense DWI acquisition by effectively leveraging sparse diffusion signals, while preserving diagnostic accuracy. Validated across multiple sparsity levels, the framework demonstrates robustness, scalability, and clinical relevance. By targeting tract-based biomarkers and prioritizing interpretability, this work advances early AD detection, with a particular focus on distinguishing MCI from CN, and contributes toward practical, cost-efficient neuroimaging pipelines for real-world applications.

The main contributions of this article are:

1. Proposing hand-crafted features to quantify white matter tract changes in selected brain ROIs for AD detection, avoiding deep learning's high computational cost.
2. Demonstrating the potential of white matter analysis for early AD detection, achieving state-of-the-art performance in distinguishing MCI from healthy controls.
3. Achieving comparable detection accuracies using sparse and dense diffusion MRI signals.

## 2 Background and Related Work

In diffusion-weighted imaging (DWI), water diffusivity is represented in the fourth dimension, while the first three encode spatial information. Diffusion tensor imaging (DTI), a subtype of DWI, employs a Gaussian model to characterize diffusion anisotropy through the symmetric $3 \times 3$ tensor $\mathbf{D}$ [2,10]:

$$D = \begin{bmatrix} D_{xx} & D_{xy} & D_{xz} \\ D_{yx} & D_{yy} & D_{yz} \\ D_{zx} & D_{zy} & D_{zz} \end{bmatrix}. \tag{1}$$

The eigenvalues and eigenvectors of $\mathbf{D}$ define the magnitude and orientation of diffusion along principal axes, while the diffusion signal $\mathbf{s} = [s_1, s_2, ..., s_N]$ encodes measurements across $N$ directions. The DTI formulation estimates $\mathbf{D}$ from $\mathbf{s}$ as [10]:

$$s_i = s_0 \, e^{(-b_{xx}D_{xx} - b_{yy}D_{yy} - b_{zz}D_{zz} - 2b_{xy}D_{xy} - 2b_{xz}D_{xz} - 2b_{yz}D_{yz})}, \tag{2}$$

where $s_0$ is the non-diffusion-weighted signal and $b_{jk}$ depends on the gradient direction vector $g_i = [g_{ix}, g_{iy}, g_{iz}]$. The apparent diffusion coefficient (ADC) along $g_i$ is given by $K_i = g_i^T \mathbf{D} g_i = (-1/b) \ln(s_i/s_0)$. Conventionally, $\mathbf{D}$ is estimated via linear least-squares (LLS) fitting [8], which is sensitive to noise and sparse measurements. To mitigate this, we reformulate the problem as an inverse mapping $\bar{D} = F(\mathbf{X}, \mathbf{g})$, where $\mathbf{X} = [s_1/s_0, ..., s_N/s_0]$, enabling robust estimation under limited diffusion directions. Building on this, we developed a Swin-transformer-based neural model [11] capable of learning from diffusion signals with varying numbers of directions. Experiments with $41, 21, 5$ directions confirm its generalizability. Similarly, Transformer-DTI [7] estimated DTI parameters using only six diffusion-weighted images through multi-head self-attention. Beyond tensor estimation, machine learning has shown potential in Alzheimer's disease (AD) diagnosis. For instance, [3] achieved 85% accuracy with diffusion and functional MRI using an Adaptive Neuro-Fuzzy Inference System, while [19] reported reduced fractional anisotropy via tract-based statistics. Structural MRI combined with SVMs reached 84% accuracy in [21]. More recently, deep learning frameworks [5,6,16] have advanced early AD detection, though scalability, generalizability, and robustness to imaging variations remain unresolved.

Notably, most prior studies emphasize AD vs. cognitively normal (CN) classification, with limited attention to distinguishing mild cognitive impairment (MCI) from CN—a clinically critical step for early intervention [1,13]. Our model addresses this gap by improving MCI vs. CN classification while reducing dependence on dense DWI acquisitions. Furthermore, tackling data heterogeneity, small sample sizes, and the need for cross-cohort validation, alongside enhancing interpretability and multimodal integration, remains essential for translating AI-driven DTI analysis into practical early AD diagnostics.

## 3    Materials and Methods

We propose a diffusion feature map based on white matter tracks and FA-MD scores for classification. This map represents the density of white matter tracks in brain regions and helps detect subtle alterations linked to early-stage Alzheimer's [14]. It clearly differentiates MCI from CN individuals' DWI scans. The process of generating the feature map is detailed in the following subsections and illustrated in Fig. 2.

### 3.1    Data Acquisition

Data of 58 participants of the two groups were downloaded from the Alzheimer's Disease Neuroimaging Initiative (ADNI) database (https://adni.loni.usc.edu/). 24 Control subjects and 34 subjects with Mild Cognitive Impairment were taken from the ADNI 1, ADNI 2 and ADNI GO project. A whole-brain DTI of the subjects were generated from the ADNI project with the following imaging protocols: Field Strength = 3.0 T; Flip Angle = 90°; Gradient Directions = 41.0; Manufacturer = GE MEDICAL SYSTEMS; Matrix X = 256.0 pixels; Matrix

Y = 256.0 pixels; Matrix Z = 1978.0; Pixel Size X = 1.4 mm; Pixel Size Y = 1.4 mm; Pulse Sequence = EP/SE; Slice Thickness = 2.7 mm; TE = 68.3 ms; TR = 9150.0 ms. Table 1 gives the demographic details of the data used in our experiments.

**Table 1.** Demographic details of ADNI Dataset

| Characteristics | Description | Subjects |
| --- | --- | --- |
| Cohorts | Controls | 24 |
|  | EMCI/LMCI | 34 |
| Age group | 50–59 | 1 |
|  | 60–69 | 16 |
|  | 70–79 | 36 |
|  | 80–89 | 12 |
|  | 90–99 | 1 |

## 3.2  DTI-Based Tractography for White Matter Fiber Bundle Generation

We employed the DTI-ODF model to generate streamline tractography from preprocessed DWI data. For tensor reconstruction, we used three approaches: (i) SwinDTI [15,17], a Swin-transformer-based deep learning model capable of reconstructing high-quality diffusion tensors from as few as 21 or 5 diffusion directions, outperforming conventional tensor fitting; (ii) traditional DTI, implemented using the `TensorModel` class from the Dipy library to estimate fractional anisotropy (FA) and orientation distribution function (ODF); and (iii) TransformerDTI [7], which employs a single-tensor model within the brain mask to estimate diffusion properties. FA, quantifying diffusion anisotropy (0 for isotropic, values closer to 1 for highly anisotropic diffusion), was computed from eigenvalues using `fractional_anisotropy(tenfit.evals)`. ODFs were derived to capture the probability distribution of diffusion directions within each voxel, providing richer microstructural information than FA alone. Peak detection was performed using `peaks_from_model` with a relative peak threshold of 0.8, a minimum separation angle of 45°, and npeaks restricted to the most prominent orientation. Streamline tractography was then performed, guided by FA-based masks: voxels with FA > 0.2 were used to identify candidate white matter regions, while FA > 0.8 defined seed points for core fiber bundles. A threshold stopping criterion (FA < 0.25) ensured streamlines remained within white matter tracts. Seeds were generated from the FA mask at a density of 2, and streamline propagation was carried out using `LocalTracking` with step-size control. FA values were interpolated along streamlines using `interpolate_scalar_3d`, enabling quantitative assessment of white matter integrity along reconstructed fiber pathways (Fig. 1).

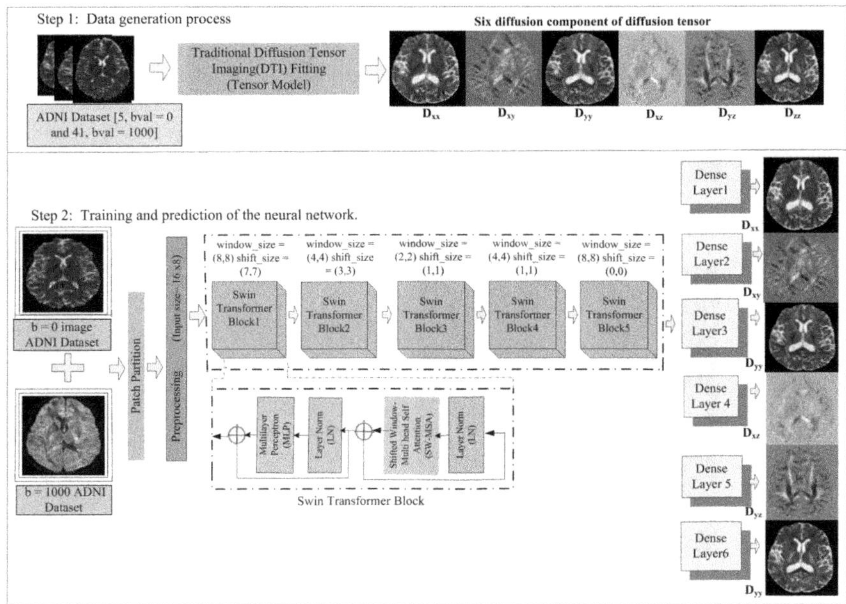



**Fig. 1.** The architecture of the SwinDTI model [15].

Swin-Transformer DTI: We utilized the SwinDTI model [15,17], a deep learning approach leveraging the Swin Transformer architecture, to reconstruct high-quality diffusion tensors from DWI data with only 21 or 5 diffusion directions. This method outperforms traditional diffusion tensor estimation techniques. Traditional DTI: DWI data in NIfTI format was processed using the `TensorModel` class from the Dipy library. Fractional Anisotropy (FA) and Orientation Distribution Function (ODF) were computed to characterize diffusion properties. Transformer DTI: We also used the TransformerDTI method [7], which employs a single-tensor model for diffusion tensor estimation within the brain mask. Metrics such as FA and ODF from all three methods were analyzed to explore their potential in distinguishing healthy controls from MCI patients.

### 3.3 JHU Label Registration on Tractography

To extract diffusion metrics from specific white matter (WM) fiber bundles relevant to AD, we used JHU label registration with the Advanced Normalization Tools. This process aligns the DWI data with a standardized anatomical template, enabling the selection of anatomically defined regions of interest (ROIs) within the streamlines. We used the JHU-ICBM labels template (https://identifiers.org/neurovault.image:1401), which assigns unique labels to brain regions, ensuring consistent ROI definition across subjects. This approach allows for targeted analysis of WM fiber bundles vulnerable to AD, offering detailed insights into disease-related microstructural changes.

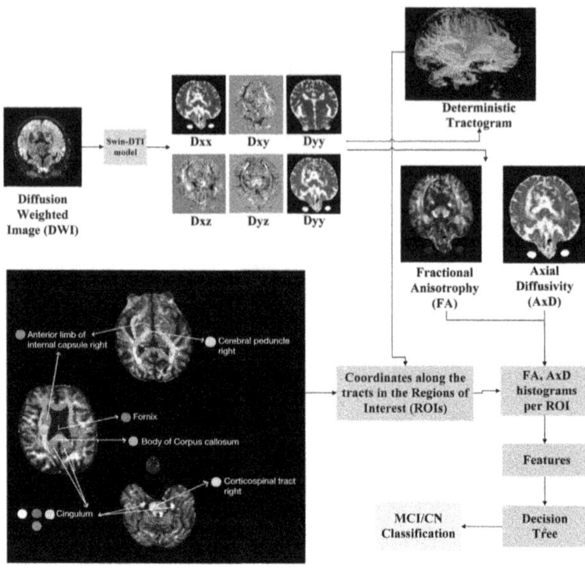


**Fig. 2.** Proposed feature selection approach for Tract-based rapid classification utilizing sparse measurements across 21 and 5 diffusion directions.

### 3.4   ROI Selection

The selection of ROIs in our tractography analysis focused on white matter fiber bundles known to be affected by AD pathology. Table 2 along with the following ROI regions gives a detailed explanation for our choices, incorporating insights from the provided references as Fig. 3.

### 3.5   Diffusion Metric Calculation

We extracted diffusion metrics (FA and AxD) from predefined ROIs within the registered label map using a fitted tensor model. The FA and AxD values for each streamline were calculated, but since these values vary in length per DWI scan, we created a 5-bin histogram for each ROI. The bin counts from 9 ROIs were concatenated to form a 45-dimensional feature vector per DWI scan. This feature can detect abnormal changes in white matter tracts, aiding in the early detection of Alzheimer's disease (AD). The feature vectors for each subject were saved in .npy format for later use in classification.

## 4   Results and Discussion

This section discusses the classification performance of the proposed method (SwinDTI) compared to traditional DTI and TransformerDTI for differentiating between healthy controls and AD patients. We employed two k-fold cross-validation strategies: k-fold Decision Tree and k-fold Support Vector Machine

**Table 2.** ROI regions considered from the JHU-ICBM template

| Cluster-ID | size (Voxels) | Regions |
| --- | --- | --- |
| 5 | 12729 | Body of corpus callosum |
| 7 | 1362 | Fornix |
| 8 | 1370 | Corticospinal tract r |
| 16 | 2278 | Cerebral peduncle r |
| 18 | 3018 | Anterior limb capsule r |
| 36 | 2751 | Cingulum |
| 37 | 1238 | Cingulum |
| 38 | 1155 | Cingulum |
| 39 | 1124 | Cingulum |

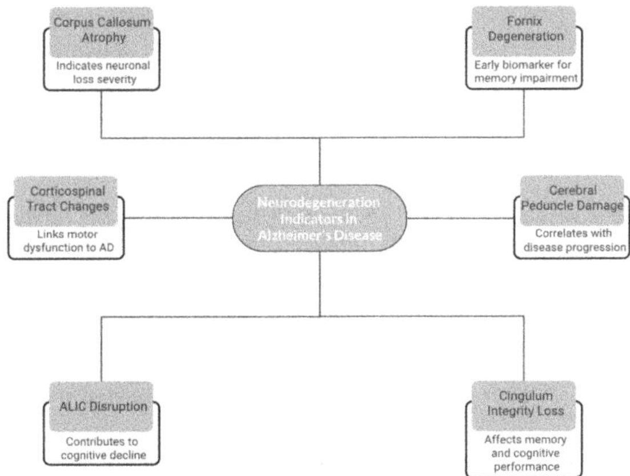


**Fig. 3.** Neurodegenerative indicator for Alzheimer disease (Corpus Callosum (ROI-5), Fornix (ROI-7) [9], Corticospinal Tract (ROI-8, Right Hemisphere) [20], Cerebral Peduncle r (ROI-16, Right Hemisphere), Anterior Limb of Internal Capsule (ALIC) (ROI-18, Right Hemisphere) [12], Cingulum (ROI-36, 37, 38, 39)

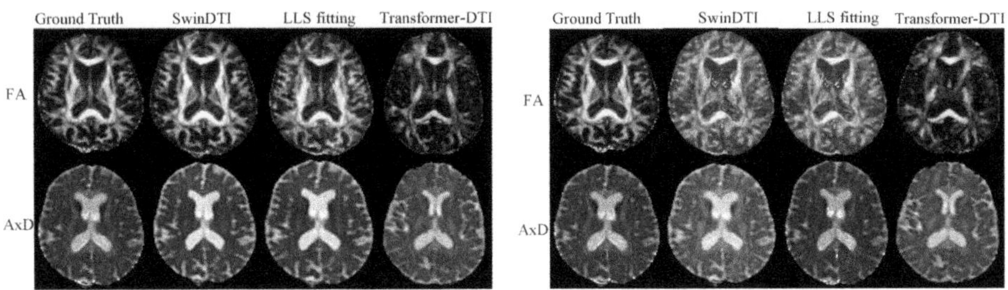


**Fig. 4.** Comparing outcomes from ground truth, the SwinDTI method, and LLS fitting [7], we note that the SwinDTI method demonstrates comparability with both the ground truth and LLS fitting [7] for 21 diffusion directions on the left side and 5 diffusion directions on the right side.

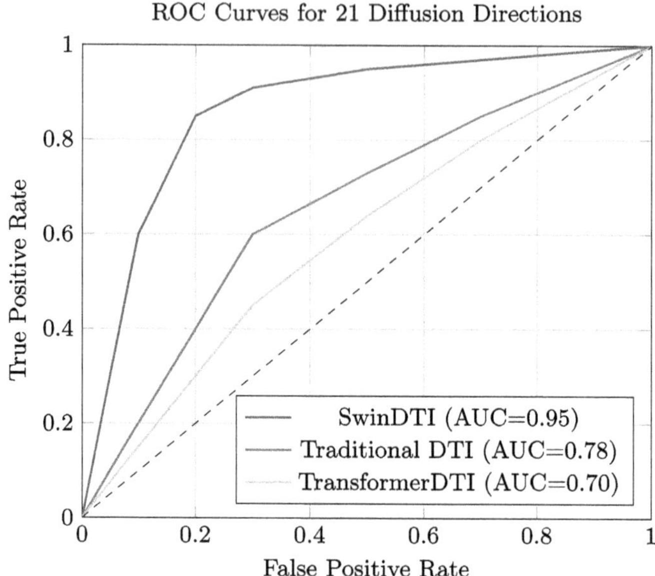


**Fig. 5.** ROC curves comparing SwinDTI, Traditional DTI, and TransformerDTI for 21 diffusion directions using SVM (RBF).

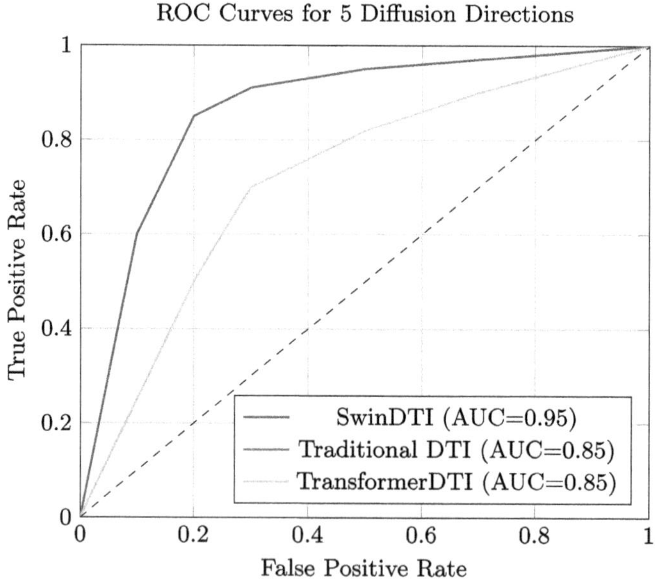


**Fig. 6.** ROC curves comparing SwinDTI, Traditional DTI, and TransformerDTI for 5 diffusion directions using SVM (RBF). SwinDTI surpasses baselines by maintaining $AUC = 0.95$ with sparse 5-direction input.

**Table 3.** Classification scores on 21 diffusion directions

| Classification method | SwinDTI | Traditional | TransformerDTI |
| --- | --- | --- | --- |
| K-fold Decision Tree | 91% | 64% | 64% |
| K-fold SVM (rbf) | 91% | 73% | 64% |

**Table 4.** Classification scores on 5 diffusion directions

| Classification method | SwinDTI | Traditional | TransformerDTI |
| --- | --- | --- | --- |
| K-fold Decision Tree | 91% | 91% | 73% |
| K-fold SVM (rbf) | 91% | 82% | 82% |

**Table 5.** Statistical Tract-Based Analysis for Major Neurodegenerative Markers (e.g., Corpus Callosum = ROI-5, Fornix = ROI-7, Corticospinal Tract = ROI-8 Right, Cerebral Peduncle = ROI-16 Right, Anterior Limb = ROI-18 Right, Cingulum Bundle = ROI-36-39)

| ROI | Metric | Mean (CN) | Mean (MCI) | p-value | Corrected p-value | Cohen's d |
| --- | --- | --- | --- | --- | --- | --- |
| Corpus Callosum | FA | 0.513 | 0.462 | 0.0018 | 0.0216 | 0.92 |
| Corpus Callosum | AxD | $1.28 \times 10^{-3}$ mm$^2$/s | $1.42 \times 10^{-3}$ mm$^2$/s | 0.0034 | 0.0408 | 0.87 |
| Fornix | FA | 0.342 | 0.284 | 0.0011 | 0.0132 | 1.05 |
| Fornix | AxD | $1.51 \times 10^{-3}$ mm$^2$/s | $1.69 \times 10^{-3}$ mm$^2$/s | 0.0022 | 0.0264 | 0.94 |
| Corticospinal Tract | FA | 0.601 | 0.579 | 0.0245 | 0.294 | 0.58 |
| Corticospinal Tract | AxD | $1.11 \times 10^{-3}$ mm$^2$/s | $1.16 \times 10^{-3}$ mm$^2$/s | 0.0293 | 0.352 | 0.55 |
| Cerebral Peduncle | FA | 0.694 | 0.661 | 0.0158 | 0.1896 | 0.62 |
| Cerebral Peduncle | AxD | $1.06 \times 10^{-3}$ mm$^2$/s | $1.13 \times 10^{-3}$ mm$^2$/s | 0.0182 | 0.2184 | 0.60 |
| Anterior Limb | FA | 0.548 | 0.508 | 0.0051 | 0.0612 | 0.81 |
| Anterior Limb | AxD | $1.18 \times 10^{-3}$ mm$^2$/s | $1.25 \times 10^{-3}$ mm$^2$/s | 0.0063 | 0.0756 | 0.78 |
| Cingulum Bundle | FA | 0.471 | 0.421 | 0.0019 | 0.0228 | 0.90 |
| Cingulum Bundle | AxD | $1.22 \times 10^{-3}$ mm$^2$/s | $1.35 \times 10^{-3}$ mm$^2$/s | 0.0037 | 0.0444 | 0.85 |

(SVM) with Radial Basis Function (RBF) kernel. The results of classification using 21diff and 5diff are presented in Tables 3 and 4 respectively. It's important to note that Traditional-DTI achieved an accuracy of 90% with 41 diffusion directions for both k-fold Decision Tree and k-fold SVM classifiers.

The tract-based statistical analysis (Table 5) revealed pronounced degeneration in the Fornix and Corpus Callosum (Cohen's $d > 0.9$), moderate changes in the Anterior Limb of the Internal Capsule (ALIC), and subtler microstructural alterations in the Corticospinal Tract and Cerebral Peduncle, consistent with pathways vulnerable in early Alzheimer's disease. The SwinDTI model achieved high accuracy in FA and AxD metrics for 21 and 5 diffusion directions (Fig. 2), effectively distinguishing healthy controls from AD patients. Feature importance analysis using Decision Tree and SVM classifiers highlighted key ROIs, notably ROI-5 (Corpus Callosum), ROI-7 (Fornix), and ROI-3639 (Cingulum) (Fig. 3). Comparison with ground truth and conventional LLS fitting (Fig. 4) confirmed

SwinDTI's reliability. ROC analysis, plotted for SwinDTI, Traditional DTI, and TransformerDTI using SVM (RBF) for 21 and 5 diffusion directions (Figs. 5 and 6), demonstrated that SwinDTI consistently outperformed others, exhibiting higher AUC and better sensitivity-specificity trade-offs.

## 5   Conclusion

In this research work, we introduced an AI-driven framework that leverages sparse diffusion-weighted imaging to enable rapid, tract-specific biomarker extraction for early Alzheimer's disease detection. By combining handcrafted white matter features with a Swin-transformer-based neural inference model, our method reliably reconstructs diffusion tensor parameters from a markedly reduced set of diffusion directions. Through tractography and histogram-based feature encoding of fractional anisotropy and axial diffusivity across key white matter bundles, our pipeline distinguishes Mild Cognitive Impairment (MCI) from cognitively normal (CN) individuals with accuracy on par with conventional dense DWI protocols—while cutting acquisition times by over 50%. Our results demonstrate that AI-powered sparse acquisitions can maintain diagnostic fidelity, improve patient comfort, and reduce resource demands, making advanced neuroimaging more accessible in both research and clinical settings. Moreover, the interpretability of tract-specific biomarkers addresses the critical need for transparent decision support, facilitating clinician trust and potential integration into routine workflows.

**Declarations**

**Data Availability Statement.** Data used in this study were obtained from the Alzheimer's Disease Neuroimaging Initiative (ADNI) database (adni.loni.usc.edu). Research Involving Human and/or Animals: This study did not involve direct research on human participants or animal subjects and relies solely on publicly available neuroimaging datasets.

**Informed Consent.** Not applicable, as no direct human or animal participation was involved.

**Conflict of Interest.** The authors declare no conflicts of interest.

## References


1. Aja-Fernández, S., et al.: Validation of deep learning techniques for quality augmentation in diffusion MRI for clinical studies. NeuroImage Clin. **39**, 103483 (2023)
2. Basser, P.J., Mattiello, J., LeBihan, D.: MR diffusion tensor spectroscopy and imaging. Biophys. J. **66**(1), 259–267 (1994)
3. Castellazzi, G., et al.: A machine learning approach for the differential diagnosis of Alzheimer and vascular dementia fed by MRI selected features. Front. Neuroinform. **14**, 25 (2020)

4. Dementia: The Alzheimer's research UK dementia statistics hub (2024). https://dementiastatistics.org/about-dementia/prevalence-and-incidence/

5. Goyal, P., Rani, R., Singh, K.: A multilayered framework for diagnosis and classification of Alzheimer's disease using transfer learned alexnet and LSTM. Neural Comput. Appl. **36**(7), 3777–3801 (2024)

6. Hazarika, R.A., Kandar, D., Maji, A.K.: A novel machine learning based technique for classification of early-stage Alzheimer's disease using brain images. Multimedia Tools Appl. **83**(8), 24277–24299 (2024)

7. Karimi, D., Gholipour, A.: Diffusion tensor estimation with transformer neural networks. Artif. Intell. Med. 102330 (2022)

8. Koay, C.G., Chang, L.C., Carew, J.D., Pierpaoli, C., Basser, P.J.: A unifying theoretical and algorithmic framework for least squares methods of estimation in diffusion tensor imaging. J. Magn. Reson. **182**(1), 115–125 (2006)

9. Lacalle-Aurioles, M., Iturria-Medina, Y.: Fornix degeneration in risk factors of Alzheimer's disease, possible trigger of cognitive decline. Cereb. Circ.-Cogn. Behav. **4**, 100158 (2023)

10. Le Bihan, D., et al.: Diffusion tensor imaging: concepts and applications. J. Magn. Reson. Imaging Off. J. Int. Soc. Magn. Reson. Med. **13**(4), 534–546 (2001)

11. Liu, Z., et al.: Swin transformer: hierarchical vision transformer using shifted windows, pp. 10012–10022 (2021)

12. Madden, D.J., Bennett, I.J., Song, A.W.: Cerebral white matter integrity and cognitive aging: contributions from diffusion tensor imaging. Neuropsychol. Rev. **19**, 415–435 (2009)

13. Mathew, S., Huang, Y.N., Bice, P., Saykin, A.J., Risacher, S.L.: Retinal vascular biomarkers in mild cognitive impairment and Alzheimer's disease: a comprehensive review and meta-analysis. Alzheimer's Dement. Diagn. Assess. Dis. Monit. **17**(2), e70132 (2025)

14. Tiwari, A., Nazarov, A.N.: Super-Resolution Imaging and Intelligent Solution for Classification, Monitoring, and Diagnosis of Alzheimer's Disease, pp. 249–260. Springer (2021). https://doi.org/10.1007/978-3-030-67921-7_13

15. Tiwari, A., Singh, R.K., Shigwan, S.J.: Swindti: swin transformer-based generalized fast estimation of diffusion tensor parameters from sparse data. Neural Comput. Appl. **36**(6), 3179–3196 (2024)

16. Tiwari, A., Singhal, A., Shigwan, S.J., Singh, R.K.: Deep learning framework using sparse diffusion MRI for diagnosis of frontotemporal dementia, pp. 3821–3827 (2023)

17. Tiwari, A., Singhal, A., Shigwan, S.J., Singh, R.K.: Early diagnosis of Alzheimer through swin-transformer-based deep learning framework using sparse diffusion measures, pp. 1369–1384 (2024)

18. Woo, C.W., Chang, L.J., Lindquist, M.A., Wager, T.D.: Building better biomarkers: brain models in translational neuroimaging. Nat. Neurosci. **20**(3), 365–377 (2017)

19. Zarei, M., et al.: Regional white matter integrity differentiates between vascular dementia and Alzheimer disease. Stroke **40**(3), 773–779 (2009)

20. Zhao, H., et al.: Orientational changes of white matter fibers in Alzheimer's disease and amnestic mild cognitive impairment. Hum. Brain Mapp. **42**(16), 5397–5408 (2021)

21. Zheng, Y., Guo, H., Zhang, L., Wu, J., Li, Q., Lv, F.: Machine learning-based framework for differential diagnosis between vascular dementia and Alzheimer's disease using structural MRI features. Front. Neurol. **10**, 456891 (2019)

# CerviSegNet: A Tailored Transformer Encoder and Convolution Decoder

Pranay Adak[1], Shyamali Mitra[2(✉)], Sounak Bose[2], and Nibaran Das[3]

[1] Department of IT, Government College of Engineering And Ceramic Technology, Kolkata, India
[2] Department of IEE, Jadavpur University, Kolkata, India
`shyamalimitra.iee@jadavpuruniversity.in`
[3] Department of CSE, Jadavpur University, Kolkata, India

**Abstract.** The diagnosis of cervical cancer involves manual screening from cytological images, which is time-intensive and susceptible to human error. So, there has been an extensive research in this area to develop an automated deep learning-based screening tool for efficient and reliable segmentation of the cytoplasm and nucleus from cervical cytology images. In this study, we propose a tailored deep segmentation network i.e. CerviSegNet that combines a transformer-based encoder with a convolutional decoder, built upon a modified U-Net backbone enhanced with attention mechanism, enabling both global context understanding and fine-grained localization. An adaptive, learnable weighted loss function integrated with deep supervision is proposed to improve performance with better gradient flow and accelerate convergence during model training. Evaluated on the open-source Cx22 dataset, CerviSegNet achieved Dice scores of 0.7991 (nucleus) and 0.9491 (cytoplasm) in mixed overlapping/non-overlapping conditions, and 0.7918 (nucleus) and 0.9630 (cytoplasm) in strictly overlapping cases. The segmentation results reported are clear evidence of the architectural novelty with generalization capability, and efficiency of the model in overlapping scenarios.

**Keywords:** Cervical Cytology · Segmentation · Deep Learning

## 1 Introduction

Cervical cancer is curable if detected early through regular screening. However, manual cytology analysis is both time-consuming and labor-intensive. To address these challenges, automated screening tools are increasingly being adopted. One of the primary challenges in cervical cell segmentation lies in accurately delineating the cytoplasm and nucleus, which exhibit significant variability in size and morphology. This task becomes even more complex in the presence of overlapping cell boundaries, blood, and mucus. Earlier, CNNs [4–6,14,18,19] were employed to segment cytoplasm and nucleus , where a multiscale convolutional network was proposed [4] for classification of nucleus, cytoplasm, and background pixels on the ISBI2015 and Shenzhen University cervical cytology datasets.


S. Mitra et al. (Eds.): PReMI 2025, LNCS 16358, pp. 380–388, 2026.
https://doi.org/10.1007/978-3-032-18480-1_39

Study in [2] showed that CNNs could effectively identify individual nuclei in overlapping scenarios; however, challenges [15,20] persist in accurately segmenting multiple clumped nuclei under densely overlapping conditions. The introduction of the U-Net architecture [17] with variants such as U-Net-bi and U-Net-tr, which use bilinear interpolation and transposed convolution for upsampling respectively, have shown good performance on Cx22 dataset. Nevertheless, these models under perform in overlapping cell scenarios. U-Net++ [21], incorporates nested skip connections for improved feature aggregation, but at the cost of increased model complexity and parameter count. However, it still falls short in handling overlapping segmentation effectively. Despite the success of CNN architectures, limited studies are conducted on the integration of different encoder-decoder structures for cervical cell segmentation. Motivated by this gap, our goal is to develop a customized segmentation model that maintains competitive performance with reduced complexity and parameter count. The proposed architecture combines a transformer-based encoder and a convolutional decoder within a U-Net framework, augmented with an attention mechanism. The design is tailored to capture the morphological variations in cytoplasm and nucleus boundaries, offering robust and reliable segmentation performance, especially in challenging overlapping scenarios. Our contributions are summarized as follows:

- A customized deep segmentation network with lesser number of parameters that seamlessly integrates a transformer based encoder with a convolutional decoder, built on a classical U-Net architecture with an attention mechanism for cervical cell segmentation.
- An adaptive, learnable weighted loss function combined with deep supervision to ensure stable and efficient model training.
- Extensive evaluation and comparative analysis of the proposed model on the publicly available Cx22 cervical cytology dataset using standard performance metrics, demonstrating the effectiveness and practical applicability of the model in cervical cell analysis.

## 2   Dataset Description

In this study, a recent publicly available cervical cytology benchmark dataset, Cx22 [11] is utilized, which comprises 1,320 high-resolution images, with a total of 14,946 carefully annotated cytoplasm and nucleus instances collected at the Liaoning Cancer Hospital and Institute (Table 1).

**Table 1.** Cx22 dataset summary

|           | No. of Train Samples | No. of Test Samples | Resolution | Number of Classes |
| --- | --- | --- | --- | --- |
| Cytoplasm | 400 | 100 | $512 \times 512$ | 2 |
| Nucleus   | 400 | 100 | $512 \times 512$ | 2 |

# 3   Proposed Methodology

One of the key challenges in cervical cell segmentation is the limited availability of high-quality annotated data. Under such considerations, the U-Net [17] family of architectures has proven its effectiveness, as it can be trained with relatively small dataset, while delivering satisfactory performance, making it a viable choice as backbone in our methodology. At the same time, existing models suffer from a trade-off between segmentation accuracy and model efficiency. Furthermore, high-performing come with increased model complexity and a large number of parameters. On the other hand, lightweight models suffer from generalization, especially when applied to cytoplasm and nucleus segmentation tasks in overlapping cell scenarios. To address these challenges, we introduce a hybrid architecture that combines a Swin Transformer [12] encoder and a ResNet [7] inspired convolutional decoder to learn the finer details of the semantic feature representation, within a U-Net backbone. This is integrated with an attention mechanism [13] to help focus on relevant spatial features at each decoder stage, using both global context and local detail for improved segmentation performance. The Swin Transformer [12] employs hierarchical, localized multi-head self-attention to effectively capture global contextual information, which is critical in overlapping and morphologically different cellular structures. In contrast, the convolutional decoder excels at preserving fine-grained spatial details necessary for precise boundary detection. Attention gates are introduced to enhance focus on salient regions, particularly at ambiguous or low-contrast boundaries. Thus, the proposed architecture becomes a viable choice for our methodology in addressing the challenges of cervical cell segmentation. The proposed architecture as in Fig. 1, is based on a U-Net backbone, consisting of four Swin Transformer encoder stages and the corresponding ResNet inspired four decoder stages. Each encoder stage contains two Swin Transformer blocks given in Fig. 1(a), whose output is reshaped and passed through an attention mechanism to form skip connections (S0 to S3). Feature maps are progressively downsampled at each encoder stage using a patch merging logic, where the spatial resolution (height and width) is halved, while doubling the feature dimension. At each decoder stage as shown in Fig. 1(c) (D3 to D0), feature representations are up sampled via transposed convolutions. The up sampled features are then combined with the corresponding skip connections through an attention module (see Fig. 1(b)), which filters and fuses contextual information before being passed as input to the current decoder stage. This attention-gated skip connection design improves the model's ability to focus on notable features, encompassing complex regions of overlapping nuclei and cytoplasm. The height and width of the image is doubled (up sampled) and the feature dimension is halved at each decoder stage. The upsampled output from the final decoder stage (D0) is passed through a $1 \times 1$ convolution layer to produce the final segmentation mask, thereby completing the segmentation objective. To address this, we introduced an adaptive, learnable loss function that combines Binary Cross-Entropy ($\mathcal{L}_{\text{BCE}}$), Dice ($\mathcal{L}_{\text{Dice}}$), ensures overlap-based optimization and Focal-Tversky [1]

($\mathcal{L}_{\text{FT}}$) emphasizes hard-to-classify regions and handling class imbalance, along with an auxiliary loss term ($\mathcal{L}_{\text{Aux}}$) applied through deep supervision [10].

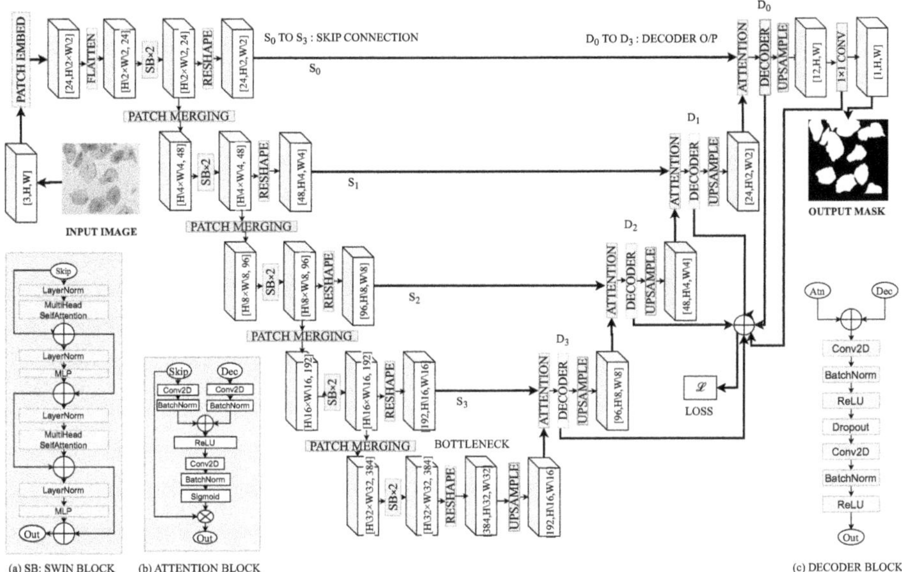



**Fig. 1.** Model architecture with detailed (a)Swin-transformer block, (b) Attention block and (c) Decoder block.

Each component is weighted by a learnable parameter $w_i$, which allows the model to dynamically balance the contribution of each loss term. Furthermore, to ensure stability during training, a regularization term $\lambda \sum_i (\log w_i)^2$ is added to penalize extreme weight values. The auxiliary loss term ($\mathcal{L}_{\text{Aux}}$) implements deep supervision by applying segmentation loss at multiple decoder stages, encouraging consistent learning across hierarchical levels of the network. The weights of each loss component are initialized and treated as a learnable parameter, allowing it to be updated adaptively at every training epoch. Adaptive learnable loss ($\mathcal{L}_{\text{ALL}}$) is given by -

$$\mathcal{L}_{\text{ALL}} = w_0 \cdot \mathcal{L}_{\text{BCE}} + w_1 \cdot \mathcal{L}_{\text{Dice}} + w_2 \cdot \mathcal{L}_{\text{FT}} + w_3 \cdot \mathcal{L}_{\text{Aux}} + \lambda \cdot \left( \sum_i (\log w_i)^2 \right) \quad (1)$$

Using this loss strategy, we achieved a considerably stable training curve, as shown in the figure (see Fig. 2) and (0.02) dice improvement on Cx22 dataset.

## 4   Results and Discussion

In this section, we present the evaluation of our model using performance metrics [3], to assess the performance of the model across non-overlapping,

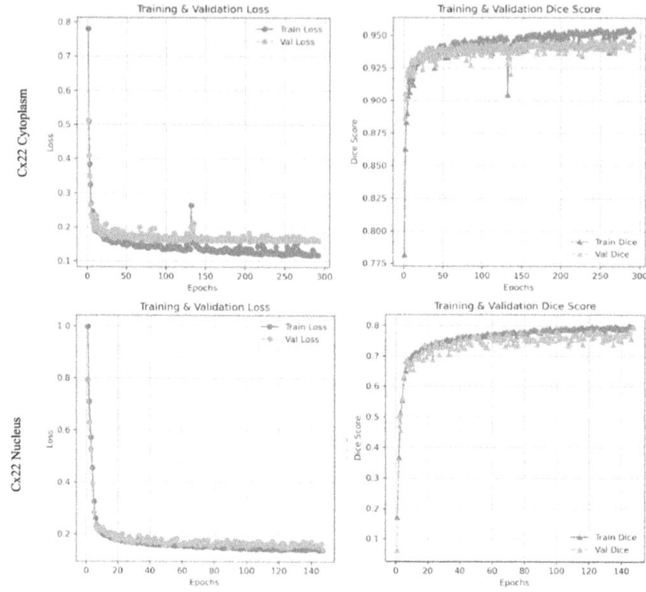

**Fig. 2.** Training curve of the proposed model using an adaptive, learnable weighted loss function combined with a deep supervision strategy. The plot illustrates improved convergence stability and faster optimization compared to standard loss configurations.

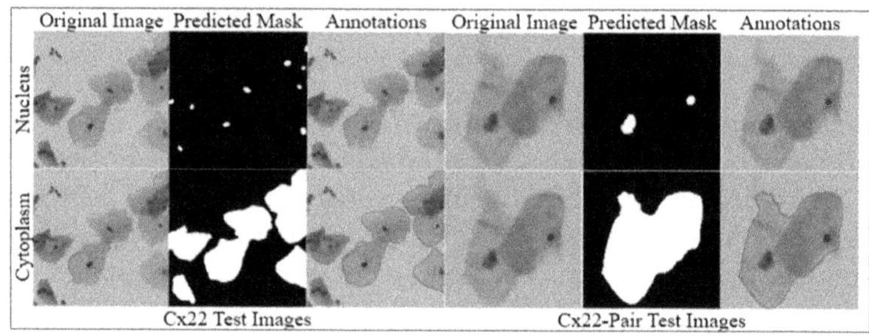

**Fig. 3.** Sample annotation and predicted masks from test images on cytoplasm, nucleus.

overlapping, and cell-pair overlapping cases on Cx22 dataset. The hyperparameters in our experiment are listed in Table 3.

We performed the training task on a system with an 11th Gen Intel(R) Core(TM) i5-1135G7 @ 2.40GHz 1.38 GHz processor, 8 GB of RAM, and MX-330 2Gb Graphics. We meticulously trained our model and reported the results of evaluation in Cx22 dataset for the segmentation of the cytoplasm and nucleus in Table 4. We also present the sample annotations and predicted masks of test images from Cx22 dataset in Fig. 3. While comparing our results with baseline and state-of-the-art models and found that the most efficient models [10,16]

**Table 2.** A Comprehensive Segmentation Evaluation Result on cytoplasm and nucleus with Baseline and state-sf-she-art on Cx22 dataset

|  | Models | DC | IoU | TPR | FPR | Accuracy | Ref |
|---|---|---|---|---|---|---|---|
| Cytoplasm | UNet-bi | 0.944 | - | 0.0188 | 0.0223 | - | [17] |
|  | UNet-tr | 0.946 | - | 0.953 | 0.0182 | - | [17] |
|  | UNet++ | 0.948 | - | 0.954 | 0.0177 | - | [21] |
|  | UNet3+ | 0.934 | - | 0.935 | 0.0205 | - | [8] |
|  | DeepEnsemble | **0.9535** | - | 0.9621 | - | - | [9] |
|  | Unet++Resnet34 | 0.9229 | - | 0.918 | - | - | [9] |
|  | ResUNet | 0.933 | - | 0.935 | 0.0274 | - | [16] |
|  | MultiResUNetDCTAtn | 0.944 | 0.893 | 0.952 | 0.0266 | 0.967 | [16] |
|  | **Proposed** | 0.9491 | **0.9036** | **0.9709** | 0.0223 | **0.9766** | - |
| Nucleus | UNet-bi | 0.750 | - | 0.713 | 0.0012 | - | [17] |
|  | UNet-tr | 0.738 | - | 0.661 | 0.0223 | - | [17] |
|  | UNet++ | 0.747 | - | 0.678 | 0.0008 | - | [21] |
|  | UNet3+ | 0.703 | - | 0.671 | 0.0015 | - | [8] |
|  | DeepEnsemble | 0.7863 | - | **0.9581** | - | - | [9] |
|  | Unet++Resnet34 | 0.6966 | - | 0.9212 | - | - | [9] |
|  | ResUNet | 0.777 | - | 0.748 | 0.0047 | - | [16] |
|  | MultiResUNetDCTAtn | **0.811** | **0.683** | 0.807 | 0.0047 | 0.991 | [16] |
|  | **Proposed** | 0.7991 | 0.6676 | 0.8397 | 0.0019 | **0.9968** | - |

**Table 3.** List of parameters for the entire experiment

| Learning Rate | Optimizer | Batch size | Loss function |
|---|---|---|---|
| 0.001 | AdamW | 4 | Adaptive Learnable Loss |

**Table 4.** Comprehensive comparison of pixel-wise segmentation performance and computational efficiency on the Cx22 dataset, demonstrating CerviSegNet's accuracy and resource efficiency across Dice coefficient, IoU, TPR, FPR, Precision, Accuracy, AIT, IS, and FLOPs.

|  | Comprehensive Segmentation Metrics | | | | | | Computational Efficiency | | |
|---|---|---|---|---|---|---|---|---|---|
|  | DC | IoU | TPR | FPR | Accuracy | Precision | AIT | IS | FLOPs |
| Cytoplasm | 0.9491 | 0.9036 | 0.9709 | 0.0223 | 0.9766 | 0.9291 | 0.263910 | 3.79 | 2.14 |
| Nucleus | 0.7991 | 0.6676 | 0.8397 | 0.0019 | 0.9968 | 0.7665 | 0.258262 | 3.87 | 2.14 |
| Cyto-Pair | 0.9630 | 0.9288 | 0.9775 | 0.0063 | 0.9919 | 0.9493 | 0.039748 | 25.16 | 2.14 |
| Nuc-Pair | 0.7918 | 0.6601 | 0.8483 | 0.0010 | 0.9985 | 0.7476 | 0.298196 | 3.35 | 2.14 |

**Table 5.** Comparative evaluation of related segmentation models on the Cx22 dataset, highlighting CerviSegNet's improved segmentation precision and inference efficiency in terms of parameter count and computational resource utilization.

| Methods | Parameters | IS(Cyto) | IS(Nuc) | FLOPs |
|---|---|---|---|---|
| Unet++Resnet34 [9] | 26,078,609 | - | - | - |
| Segformer [9] | 7,717,473 | - | - | - |
| Muti-Res-Unet(AG) [16] | 7,535,694 | 7.7917576 | 9.0587346 | 25,792,768,200 |
| Muti-Res-Unet(CBAM) [16] | 7,291,450 | 9.1068399 | 9.4707638 | 24,547,916,760 |
| Muti-Res-Unet(ECA) [16] | 8,268,549 | 5.5274014 | 5.6920901 | 24,650,259,855 |
| Muti-Res-Unet(Spectral) [16] | 7,277,857 | 4.6112082 | 5.1455019 | 24,761,039,939 |
| **Proposed** | **6,897,462** | **3.79** | **3.87** | **4,280,000,000** |

achieved the best dice scores in either the cytoplasm scene or the nucleus scene. Our model is quite competitive in terms of generalization capability in both the cytoplasm and nucleus scenes, and achieved a dice score of 0.9491 and 0.7991 in the cytoplasm and nucleus segmentation task compared to the deep-ensemble model [10], with a dice score of 0.7863 in the nucleus scene and a dice score of 0.944 reported in the [16] in the cytoplasm. Our model also achieves the lowest number of trainable parameters (6897462) and computational cost (4280000000 FLOPs) compared to the most efficient existing model, which has (7277857) parameters and (24761039939 FLOPs). However, in real world applications, a key challenge arises when the model is trained on a small dataset. Comparative results on the Cx22 dataset are summarized in Table 2 and Table 5, showcasing the performance across multiple implementations.

## 5  Conclusion

In the present work, we developed a tailored transformer encoder and convolution decoder paired network for automated cervical cell segmentation with a low parameter count and high computational efficiency, while preserving satisfactory segmentation accuracy. Experimental results clearly demonstrate the model's strong generalization capability and effectiveness, achieving Dice scores of 0.7991 and 0.9491 for nucleus and cytoplasm segmentation respectively on publicly available Cx22 cervical dataset, in mixed overlapping/non-overlapping scenarios, and 0.7918 and 0.9630 in strictly overlapping cases. Given its computational efficiency and strong generalization across both cytoplasm and nucleus segmentation tasks, the proposed model is well suited for deployment in real-world healthcare applications. A potential future research direction is the development of light-weight, clinician-friendly software tools based on this model to assist in routine cervical cytology screening and diagnosis.

# References


1. Abraham, N., Khan, N.M.: A novel focal tversky loss function with improved attention u-net for lesion segmentation. In: 2019 IEEE 16th International Symposium on Biomedical Imaging (ISBI 2019), pp. 683–687. IEEE (2019)
2. Braz, E.F., Lotufo, R.D.A.: Nuclei detection using deep learning. Proc. Simpósio Brasileiro Telecomunicações Processamento Sinais, pp. 1059–1063 (2017)
3. Chen, E., Ting, H.N., Chuah, J.H., Zhao, J.: Segmentation of overlapping cells in cervical cytology images: a survey. IEEE Access (2024)
4. Chen, J., Zhang, B.: Segmentation of overlapping cervical cells with mask region convolutional neural network. Comput. Math. Methods Med. **2021**(1), 3890988 (2021)
5. Dey, S., et al.: GC-EnC: a copula based ensemble of CNNs for malignancy identification in breast histopathology and cytology images. Comput. Biol. Med. **152**, 106329 (2023)
6. Gautam, S., Bhavsar, A., Sao, A.K., KK, H.: CNN based segmentation of nuclei in pap-smear images with selective pre-processing. In: Medical Imaging 2018: Digital Pathology, vol. 10581, pp. 246–254. SPIE (2018)
7. He, K., Zhang, X., Ren, S., Sun, J.: Deep residual learning for image recognition. In: Proceedings of the IEEE Conference on Computer Vision and Pattern Recognition, pp. 770–778 (2016)
8. Huang, H., et al.: UNet 3+: a full-scale connected UNet for medical image segmentation. In: ICASSP 2020-2020 IEEE International Conference on Acoustics, Speech and Signal Processing (ICASSP), pp. 1055–1059. IEEE (2020)
9. Ji, J., et al.: Automated cervical cell segmentation using deep ensemble learning. BMC Med. Imaging **23**(1), 137 (2023)
10. Lee, C.Y., Xie, S., Gallagher, P., Zhang, Z., Tu, Z.: Deeply-supervised nets. In: Artificial Intelligence and Statistics, pp. 562–570. PMLR (2015)
11. Liu, G.: Cx22: a new publicly available dataset for deep learning-based segmentation of cervical cytology images. Comput. Biol. Med. **150**, 106194 (2022)
12. Liu, Z., et al.: Swin transformer: hierarchical vision transformer using shifted windows. In: Proceedings of the IEEE/CVF International Conference on Computer Vision, pp. 10012–10022 (2021)
13. Oktay, O., et al.: Attention U-Net: Learning where to look for the pancreas. arXiv preprint arXiv:1804.03999 (2018)
14. Ortiz-González, A., et al.: Segmentation techniques applied to CNNs for cervical cancer classification. IEEE Access (2025)
15. Rasheed, A., Shirazi, S.H., Khan, P., Aseere, A.M., Shahzad, M.: Techniques and challenges for nuclei segmentation in cervical smear images: a review. Artif. Intell. Rev. **58**(10), 295 (2025)
16. Resmi, S., Singh, R.P., Palaniappan, K.: Automated cervical cytology image cell segmentation using enhanced MultiResUNet with DCT and spectral domain attention mechanisms. IEEE Access (2024)
17. Ronneberger, O., Fischer, P., Brox, T.: U-Net: convolutional networks for biomedical image segmentation. In: Medical Image Computing and Computer-Assisted Intervention–MICCAI 2015: 18th International Conference, Munich, Germany, October 5–9, 2015, proceedings, part III 18, pp. 234–241. Springer (2015)
18. Song, Y., et al.: A deep learning based framework for accurate segmentation of cervical cytoplasm and nuclei. In: 2014 36th Annual International Conference of the IEEE Engineering in Medicine and Biology Society, pp. 2903–2906. IEEE (2014)

19. Wu, M., Yan, C., Liu, H., Liu, Q., Yin, Y.: Automatic classification of cervical cancer from cytological images by using convolutional neural network. Biosci. Rep. **38**(6), BSR20181769 (2018)
20. Wubineh, B.Z., Rusiecki, A., Halawa, K.: Segmentation and classification techniques for pap smear images in detecting cervical cancer: a systematic review. IEEE Access (2024)
21. Zhou, Z., Siddiquee, M.M.R., Tajbakhsh, N., Liang, J.: UNet++: redesigning skip connections to exploit multiscale features in image segmentation. IEEE Trans. Med. Imaging **39**(6), 1856–1867 (2019)

# Miscellaneous

# AI at the Chalkface: A Multi-agent RAG Assistant for Active Learning in STEM

Rucha Joshi[(✉)], Suhani Shrivastava, Nikita Thomas, Malhaar Arora, and Ankur Nahar

Plaksha University, SAS Nagar, Panjab, India
{rucha.joshi,suhani.shrivastava,nikita.thomas,malhaar.arora,
ankur.nahar}@plaksha.edu.in

**Abstract.** The increasing demand for high-quality engineering education in India highlights the need for innovative teaching methods to bridge the gap between infrastructure and teaching effectiveness. Although active learning strategies have proven effective in STEM education, their adoption remains limited due to barriers such as time constraints and a lack of tailored resources. We introduce TeachBox, an always-on Retrieval-Augmented-Generation (RAG) chatbot that operationalizes discipline-specific pedagogy as an AI service. TeachBox embeds educator queries with *OllamaEmbeddings*, performs semantic search over a curated corpus of peer-reviewed studies and best-practice reports on STEM instruction, and ranks matches via a Facebook's AI Similarity Search (FAISS) vector index. A three-agent pipeline (i.e., Subject, Scholar, and Summary) automatically scopes the topic, pulls the most relevant information, and compresses them into knowledge snippets that guide a ChatGroq mixtral-8×7b-32768 language model to draft course-level plans, class-session blueprints, and evidence-linked active learning strategies. By surfacing sourced, context-aware pedagogy on demand, TeachBox lowers the cognitive and logistical overhead that currently limits deployment of active learning envisioned in India's NEP-2020. The architecture is model-agnostic, interactive, and adaptive, positioning TeachBox as a scalable catalyst for evidence-based engineering education.

**Keywords:** Active Learning · Retrieval-Augmented Chatbot · Engineering Education · Personalized Pedagogy

## 1 Introduction

In the 21st-century knowledge-driven global economy, there is a premium on engineering graduates who can innovate and work across diverse cultures [2]. As the world's third-largest producer of engineers [5,15], India graduates roughly 1.5 million engineers each year. However, industry assessments (e.g., NASS-COM) estimate that only about 25% of these graduates are readily employable. This severe quality gap exists despite India's 10,000+ engineering institutions


S. Mitra et al. (Eds.): PReMI 2025, LNCS 16358, pp. 391–399, 2026.
https://doi.org/10.1007/978-3-032-18480-1_40

equipped with excellent infrastructure, libraries, and laboratories. The issue is not merely one of infrastructure or content, but rather a pressing need for pedagogical reform and improved teaching quality. Most engineering faculty in India are not fully prepared to implement modern educational practices in their classrooms.

Despite abundant research on effective methods, adoption in engineering education faces persistent barriers. The literature, across general pedagogy and engineering-specific studies documents evidence-based practices [4,8,16], yet uptake is limited by incentives, time, and motivation. Although many universities run faculty-development programs to promote active learning [13], participation and classroom implementation remain low, hindered by lack of time and awareness [3] and by perceptions of irrelevance when training is offered by general education specialists rather than engineering experts [3]. Systemic constraints; weak quality monitoring, limited academic autonomy, outdated curricula, inadequate teacher training, and under-prepared students further impede innovation [12].

National Education Policy (NEP 2020) prioritizes faculty training and pedagogical improvement. Aligned with this mandate, we introduce TeachBoxa retrieval-augmented generation (RAG) based, always-on chatbot for engineering educators. It delivers tailored guidance on active-learning methodologies and evidence-based techniques, integrating a curated repository of academic articles, case studies, and best-practice exemplars to retrieve pertinent literature and synthesize context-specific, practical recommendations. By coupling domain-specific retrieval with generative AI, TeachBox provides accurate, actionable insights across diverse classroom scenarios. In addition to on-demand query responses, TeachBox offers modular training pathways that help faculty members systematically build their teaching skills. These self-paced modules include interactive tutorials, examples of effective classroom activities, and step-by-step guides for designing engaging lesson plans. By providing on-demand support and personalized suggestions, TeachBox lowers the barriers of time, awareness, and contextual relevance that often discourage faculty from adopting new methods. Notably, this approach represents a novel application of RAG in education, whereas most AI tools in academia focus on assisting students, TeachBox directly supports educators in pedagogy and course design, an area that remains underexplored. Our development of TeachBox builds upon prior research [10] in which interviews with 24 engineering faculty identified three primary barriers to effective teaching in engineering education: (i) difficulty applying active-learning strategies in specific courses, (ii) lack of a repository of authentic, course-specific problems, and (iii) challenges in aligning learning objectives with students' varying paces of learning. TeachBox is designed to tackle these issues, with an initial focus on the first barrier. In this work, we present the implementation of TeachBox and its two key capabilities aimed at overcoming faculty members' active-learning challenges. First, given a set of keywords for a particular course unit, TeachBox generates a customized pedagogical plan for teaching that unit. Second, it provides evidence-based justifications by pointing educators to sources where similar pedagogical approaches have been successfully applied. These features enable faculty not only to receive concrete teaching strategies but also to understand the scholarly backing and real-world efficacy of those strategies. Although TeachBox is intended primarily for faculty use, it can also support student-led learning. The system can be applied in peer-learning contexts, allowing students to teach the chatbot as a proxy for a teachable peer and thereby leverage the protégé effect [1], a phenomenon where students achieve deeper understanding by explaining concepts to a teachable agent. We hypothesize that integrating this AI-based teachable-agent approach into engineering education will significantly enhance student engagement and comprehension. In turn, by lowering adoption barriers, TeachBox aims to foster more innovative and effective teaching practices among faculty.

## 1.1  Literature Review

Active learning has been widely recognized as a powerful approach to improve student learning outcomes in STEM education [13]. Techniques such as peer teaching, collaborative problem-solving, and inquiry-based learning are known to foster deeper understanding and long term retention of knowledge. Active learning significantly improves student performance in STEM courses compared to traditional lecture based instruction [6]. Studies have emphasized the need for targeted tools and re-sources to enable faculty to integrate active learning seamlessly into their teaching practices [14]. While many educators are aware of active learning strategies, their adoption remains low due to time constraints, lack of institutional incentives, and limited access to practical resources [9]. Furthermore, the disconnect between educational theory and its application in discipline-specific contexts often discourages faculty from experimenting with new pedagogical methods. Tools such as intelligent tutoring systems (ITS) and AI-powered chatbots demonstrate the potential to enhance teaching and learning experiences. Systems like Carnegie Learning's Cognitive Tutor have shown significant success in personalized instruction by adapting to individual learning needs [11]. Similarly, AI chatbots like Jill Watson, developed at Georgia Tech, have been used to provide 24/7 support to students, reducing the burden on educators [7]. Direct AI support for educators, especially in engineering pedagogy and curriculum design remains under-explored. RAG, which fuses information retrieval with generative models, has shown promise for producing context-aware, accurate responses, yet its application to faculty support is still in its infancy. Despite advances in AI and active-learning research, most tools target students rather than instructors, leaving a persistent gap in discipline-specific, evidence-based support for educators. Hence, our approach adapts the RAG framework and employs a multi-agent orchestration. While the underlying components (semantic retrieval, agent-driven web search, large-context LLM reasoning) build on established AI techniques, their combination in TeachBox is uniquely tailored to pedagogical query resolution. This novel integration expands the scope of educational AI beyond student-facing tutors to directly empower educators with context-aware, evidence-backed strategies.

## 2    Methods

We conducted semi-structured interviews with 15 engineering faculty members from a small private university in North India. The interviews probed their teaching journey, motivations, pain points, and visions of successful teaching to glean an overview of their pedagogical beliefs. With participants' consent and ethics board approval, each interview was recorded, transcribed, and anonymized. We then performed a qualitative thematic analysis: transcripts were inductively coded to mark instances of teaching challenges and suggested improvements, which were iteratively grouped into higher-order themes. This process revealed distinct opportunity areas for supporting engineering educators, forming a needs assessment that informed the design of our system.

### 2.1    Chatbot Architecture

The TeachBox chatbot is built as a multi-phase RAG pipeline that provides personalized pedagogical support. It accepts rich context about the class such as class size, session duration, and timing along with content details (e.g. topic domain, academic level) and learner demographics. These inputs are used to dynamically tailor the retrieval and generation of teaching strategies.

**Query Embedding and Knowledge Base:** When a query arrives, we embed the text for semantic search using LangChain's *OllamaEmbeddings* (open-source) to produce vector representations. The 150-document corpus spans engineering-education contexts and active-learning topics, selected from influential peer-reviewed venues and authoritative best-practice reports. To maximize diversity, sources cover multiple STEM disciplines, class sizes, and techniques (e.g., peer instruction, collaborative problem-solving, inquiry-based learning). Each document was vetted for pedagogical rigor, segmented into semantically coherent chunks, and the repository is periodically updated to sustain relevance. All embeddings are indexed in a Facebook's AI Similarity Search (FAISS) vector store; at inference, cosine-similarity retrieval returns the most relevant items, grounding responses in evidence-based strategies.

**Multi-agent Retrieval:** In parallel with internal vector retrieval, TeachBox employs three specialized agents (implemented via LangChain) to enrich the context with external knowledge:

- **Subject Agent:** Uses a lightweight Mistral-7B model to analyze the user's query and extract its core subject area or keywords. This yields a focused topic representation of the query (e.g. "thermodynamics, large class, active learning") to guide downstream search.
- **Scholar Agent:** Leverages the identified topic to query academic literature through a Google Scholar API wrapper. This live fetch brings in up-to-date domain-specific teaching research beyond the static internal repository.

– **Summary Agent:** Summarizes the content of each retrieved paper into a concise snippet (a few sentences capturing key findings).

This combined knowledge base is then passed to the LLM for final response generation.

**Query Formulation and Completion:** TeachBox integrates a powerful LLM to synthesize the answer using the gathered context. We use the ChatGroq model *(mixtral-8x7b-32768)*, a state-of-the-art sparse mixture-of-experts LLM (46.7B total parameters) that supports a 32k-token context window (see Fig. 1). The model is invoked with a prompt that includes the user's query alongside the retrieved documents and their summaries.

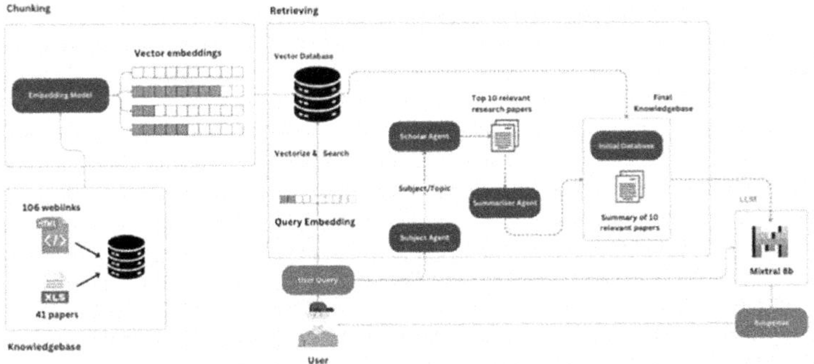

**Fig. 1.** The multi-phase architecture of the TeachBox chatbot integrating retrieval, summarization, and recommendation.

We employ careful prompt engineering to ensure the model grounds its response in the provided context, for example, by prepending a system instruction to act as an instructional design assistant and utilize the below references, followed by the content snippets and the user question. This dynamic query formulation helps the LLM generate highly relevant output that combines the user's requirements with evidence from the retrieved materials. The LLM's response typically consists of a detailed pedagogical plan or answer to the query (e.g. recommended active-learning techniques, lesson plan steps, etc.), crafted in an educator-friendly tone. Furthermore, the chatbot uses a Scholar API integration to append a list of recommended readings (the most pertinent academic papers from the Scholar Agent's results) for the user.

**Pipeline Flow of RAG Chatbot:** The robustness of TeachBox comes from its hybrid retrieval and orchestration approach. By combining an internal vector database of vetted pedagogical content with external real-time literature search, the chatbot can handle a wide variety of faculty queries with accuracy and depth. The internal knowledge store provides domain-specific expertise, while the external Scholar Agent introduces current evidence and diverse perspectives, and together these ensure that responses are both contextually relevant and up-to-date. This context-sensitive retrieval and completion pipeline tailors active-learning recommendations to the nuances of the query, making the advice more specific than what a generic chatbot could offer. We implemented the entire pipeline using the LangChain framework, which coordinates the agents and tools in sequence. The system runs as a web-based interactive assistant: a front-end interface accepts user inputs and displays the generated teaching plans, while a Python back-end handles the LangChain agent execution, vector search, and calls to the Groq model and Scholar API. Through iterative optimization of this stack (e.g. parallelizing external calls and optimizing prompt sizes), we reduced end-to-end response latency from several minutes to just a few seconds in the final deployment.

## 3   Result

### 3.1   Faculty Pedagogical Beliefs

Thematic analysis of the interviews with experienced faculty (N=15) revealed several key themes surrounding their teaching motivations, philosophies, behaviours, facilitators, and barriers. Several faculty members demonstrated a stronger personal commitment to teaching, grounded in both intrinsic motivations and a de-sire to continuously improve their teaching practices.

### 3.2   Teaching Motivation and Philosophy

Faculty members see teaching as both a passion and an opportunity for self-learning. Inspired by role models, course autonomy, and student success, they lean on peer support, mentorship, and constant feedback to refine their classes. However, several barriers were also identified. The fear of judgment in evaluation, the unpredictability of teaching a large group, and the struggle to engage students in large classes and in online formats were recurring challenges. Many faculty also mentioned time constraints in building new courses from scratch, as well as balancing teaching with research responsibilities. Limited pedagogical training, rigid curricula and uncertainty about steps to apply evidence-based methods in their specific disciplines, contributed to further struggle to implement active learning methods in engineering curricula despite proven benefits of active learning.

The analysis also highlighted distinct teaching behaviors, such as how frequently content and pedagogy were updated. Many refresh content, try flipped or personalised formats, and use recordings or PDFs, yet still struggle with online assessment and gauging comprehension. Another critical behaviour was the faculty's close attention to student feedback, both verbal and non-verbal (e.g., noticing facial expressions) as it shaped their teaching methods. Moreover, many faculty members mentioned that TeachBox's effectiveness would ultimately be judged by improvements in student performance and teaching evaluations. Evaluating such improvements would require a longitudinal study, which was beyond the scope of this work. The faculty interviews also indicated factors that shape their willingness to adopt new pedagogical methods. The thematic analysis indicated a student-centric mindset among faculty, an inclination to help students understand concepts better and perform their best in the field, all while embracing new technologies.

### 3.3  TeachBox Performance

TeachBox's performance was evaluated on a set of queries about implementing active-learning strategies in engineering courses, and it was compared against a baseline large language model (OpenAI's ChatGPT 3.5) across key dimensions of response relevance and user satisfaction. The chatbot consistently delivered highly relevant, context-specific teaching strategies, achieving an average relevance score of 4.5 out of 5 as rated by subject matter experts, slightly surpassing ChatGPT's 4.3. TeachBox's domain-specific design allowed it to recommend tailored active learning techniques for specific classroom contexts (e.g., adapting strategies for large STEM lectures versus small lab groups) and to cite concrete evidence of their successful implementation. In contrast, ChatGPT provided more generic pedagogical suggestions that lacked this contextual depth. Additionally, educator feedback indicated a strong preference for TeachBox: in a post-study survey of 10 educators, 86% favored TeachBox's targeted guidance, while 70% acknowledged ChatGPT's usefulness but deemed its advice less directly applicable to their needs. Running the multi-agent pipeline with a 46.7B-parameter model is resource-intensive. However, our optimizations (e.g., parallel retrieval and prompt size reduction) have cut the end-to-end response time to a few seconds per query on a high-performance server. The architecture's model-agnostic design permits swapping in smaller or more efficient LLMs if needed, flexibly balancing performance with resource constraints. We envision Teach-Box being deployed as a cloud or institutional service accessible through a web interface, so educators can benefit from on-demand support without specialized hardware.

## 4   Conclusions and Future Scope

By providing real-time support and personalized suggestions, TeachBox reduces the barriers of time, awareness, and relevance, making it easier for faculty to adopt and sustain innovative teaching methods. The technical design of Teach-Box chatbot integrates advanced models and architectures to deliver tailored pedagogical solutions. Its hybrid retrieval mechanism, combining an internal database of curated documents with a Web-Based Searching Agent, enhances its ability to handle diverse queries. The integration of the Google Scholar API further enriches Teach-Box's utility by recommending academic papers for additional reading, promoting evidence-based teaching practices. However, the current model has scope for improvement. At present, TeachBox operates exclusively in English, restricting its accessibility to non-English-speaking educators. Expanding its multilingual capabilities would make it more inclusive. Additionally, TeachBox cannot generate visual aids, such as diagrams or interactive lesson plans, which are critical in STEM education. Sometimes obtained responses were not structured, and our dataset was very constrained.

Beyond the relevance ratings and user satisfaction measures used so far, upcoming evaluations will incorporate additional quantitative metrics, for example, the accuracy of retrieved references in responses, the diversity of pedagogical strategies recommended, and the reduction in instructor planning time when using TeachBox. In the future, addressing these gaps will significantly enhance its utility. Future iterations could also focus on increasing the size and diversity of the internal database to improve the chatbot's ability to address niche queries without relying heavily on web-based retrieval. Incorporating adaptive learning algorithms and gamified elements, such as quizzes and interactive tutorials, could further personalize the user experience and encourage the adoption.

# References


1. Chase, C.C., Chin, D.B., Oppezzo, M.A., Schwartz, D.L.: Teachable agents and the protégé effect: increasing the effort towards learning. J. Sci. Educ. Technol. **18**, 334–352 (2009)
2. Duderstadt, J.J.: Engineering for a changing world: a roadmap to the future of American engineering practice, research, and education. In: Holistic Engineering Education: Beyond Technology, pp. 17–35. Springer (2010)
3. Felder, R.M., Brent, R., Prince, M.J.: Engineering instructional development: programs, best practices, and recommendations. J. Eng. Educ. **100**(1), 89–122 (2011)
4. Felder, R.M.: Learning and teaching styles in engineering education (2002)
5. Freeman, R.B.: Does globalization of the scientific/engineering workforce threaten us economic leadership? Innov. Policy Econ. **6**, 123–157 (2006)
6. Freeman, S., et al.: Active learning increases student performance in science, engineering, and mathematics. Proc. Natl. Acad. Sci. **111**(23), 8410–8415 (2014)
7. Goel, A.K., Polepeddi, L.: Jill Watson: a virtual teaching assistant for online education. Research brief, Georgia Institute of Technology (2016)
8. Hansen, E.J.: Idea-based learning: a course design process to promote conceptual understanding. Routledge (2023)
9. Henderson, C., Dancy, M.H.: Increasing the impact and diffusion of stem education innovations. Research brief, American Association for the Advancement of Science (2011)
10. Joshi, R., White, J.R.: Design thinking approach to identify barriers to engineering education reform in India. In: 2020 ASEE Virtual Annual Conference Content Access (2020)
11. Koedinger, K.R., Anderson, J.R., Hadley, W.H., Mark, M.A.: Intelligent tutoring goes to school in the big city. Int. J. Artif. Intell. Educ. **8**, 30–43 (1997)
12. Mohanty, A., Dash, D.: Engineering education in India: preparation of professional engineering educators. J. Hum. Resour. Sustain. Stud. **4**(2), 92–101 (2016)
13. Prince, M.: Does active learning work? A review of the research. J. Eng. Educ. **93**(3), 223–231 (2004)

14. Prince, M.J., Felder, R.M.: Inductive teaching and learning methods: definitions, comparisons, and research bases. J. Eng. Educ. **95**(2), 123–138 (2006)
15. Sanders, M.E.: Stem, stem education, stemmania (2008)
16. Wankat, P.C., Oreovicz, F.S.: Teaching Engineering. Purdue University Press (2015)

# Edge-Guided Transfer Learning Model for Hast Mudra Classification


Pushpraj Katiyar[1,3], Naveen Babu[2], and Dolly Sharma[1]

[1] Department of Computer Science and Engineering, Shiv Nadar Institution of Eminence Deemed to be University, Greater Noida, UP, India
dolly.sharma@snu.edu.in
[2] Chitkara University, Rajpura, Punjab, India
[3] R Systems International Ltd, SEZ, Greater Noida, UP, India



**Abstract.** Indian classical dance forms, a profound expression of India's cultural heritage, employs intricate hand gestures known as "mudras", encompassing both unilateral (Asamyukta) and bilateral (Samyukta) movements. These gestures function as visual language and possess the capacity to articulate nuanced narratives and symbolic meanings. This study introduces a novel Deep Convolutional Neural Network (CNN) model based on the lightweight MobileNet-V2 architecture for mudra classification in videos. The proposed model incorporates a streamlined CNN architectural blueprint infused with depth-separable convolutions, which has been designed with dual aims: (i) drastically reducing computational overheads and (ii) ensuring swift, effective real-time video classification. Trained on curated dataset comprising open-source videos and images, the proposed model's achieves a classification accuracy of 98.58% with an average inference time of 68 ms. The results demonstrate the model's potential as an invaluable tool for enthusiasts seeking automated recognition of mudras in Indian classical dance.

**Keywords:** Convolutional Neural Networks · Indian Classical Dance · Mudras · Classification


## 1 Introduction

Indian classical dance (ICD) forms such as Bharatnatyam, Kathak, Odissi, Manipuri represent a profound cultural legacy. These diverse forms, originating from various regions of the country, embody India's cultural richness while sharing a common thread of conveying stories, emotions, and narratives through the art of Nartak, the dancer. Indian Classical Dance forms are taught through a master-disciple tradition, which involves students inheriting the knowledge through careful observation, imitation, and practice of the master. Indian classical dance consists of two main kinds of hand mudras, namely Asamyukta (gestures performed with one hand) and Samyukta (gestures performed with both hands). The fundamental repertoire of dance consists of twenty-eight one-hand


© The Author(s), under exclusive license to Springer Nature Switzerland AG 2026
S. Mitra et al. (Eds.): PReMI 2025, LNCS 16358, pp. 400–408, 2026.
https://doi.org/10.1007/978-3-032-18480-1_41

gestures and twenty-four both-hand gestures; however, different genres of dance or linage of ICD may have differences in the count and specificity of these gestures. Mudras or hand gestures not only epitomize the artistic and aesthetic values of the performance but also serves as a precursor to the contemporary applications of hand gesture recognition in the realm of technology, due to its potential to connect human expression with computer systems.

Our objective for this study is to develop a comprehensive dataset encompassing all 52 mudra categories by acquiring images from public sources, use gray-scaling and edge detection techniques for data preparation, design an efficient model for efficient Hast Mudra classification. The major contributions in this work are:

- Curating and presenting a dataset encompassing all 52 mudra categories.
- Present an edge-guided transfer learning using MobileNetV2 for mudra classification.
- Conduct comprehensive assessment of the proposed model using metrics such as accuracy, loss, precision, recall, F-score, and processing time.

## 2   Related Work

India boasts of a rich a diverse tradition of dance, broadly categorized into two types-Documented or undocumented forms. Since classical dance forms have well-established documentation characterized by codified techniques and well-defined meanings associated with gestures, these have attracted a lot of scholarly interest in recent years. Researchers have applied various computer vision techniques as well as deep learning approaches for the classification task.

Pradeep et al. [9] explored the feasibility of recognizing the intricate 'mudras', inherent to Indian classical dance forms by employing pre-trained CNN models to facilitate the training of dedicated datasets. Manipuri classical dance is another form of Indian dance that originated in the North-eastern part of India. In this dance form hand gestures serve as a mode of communication. Extending the scope of inquiry, for Manipuri classical dance, Devi et al. [5] emphasize on diverse computer vision methodologies for gesture recognition on a dataset of 2400 images. Mohammed et al. [8] employed a lightweight CNN classifier for hand gesture classification. Their approach involved using a deep RetinaNet-based hand detector [11] to isolate the hand region within the image, which was subsequently passed to the classifier. This method was tested across multiple datasets, including the ICD dataset.

A Bharatanatyam dataset was created by Raj et al. [10], and efforts were made to identify the optimal feature descriptor among SURF, SIFT, ORB, KAZE, Extended-KAZE, Accelerated-KAZE, BRISK, and SIKA. These descriptors were evaluated using classifiers such as SVM, Random Forest, and MLP. The combination of the KAZE descriptor with the Random Forest classifier yielded the best results, achieving an accuracy of 92% for Asamyukta Mudras and 98% for Samyukta Mudras. Furthermore, Chavan et al., in [4] has demonstrated a lightweight application employing a combination of CNN and MobileNet architectures to recognize Indian Sign Language, a domain that encompasses diverse hand gestures, through the utilization of the OpenCV framework. Thavarekere et al., in [13] analyzed how well existing CNN models for FER (Face Expression Recognition) fare with masked occlusion and presented deep CNN architectures to solve this task and employed Canny edge detector to fix overfitting. Ananmi et al. [1,2] proposed two methods for classifying 24 double-hand Bharatnatyam mudras: a rule-based approach and a neural network-based classifier. Both used a three-stage pipeline starting with Canny edge detection for preprocessing. The rule-based method extracted features like grid-line junctions and silhouettes, achieving 95.25% accuracy. The neural network approach used Hu Moments, eigenvalues, and intersection points for feature extraction, demonstrating effective mudra recognition. In a related study, Bhuyan et al. [3] assessed various classifiers for motion classification and identified that the SVM performed slightly better when compared to the CNN. This study utilized pattern variations across frames as classification features, further validating the effectiveness of SVM for motion recognition.

Although the existing literature offers valuable insights into the broader field of mudra classification within the context of Indian classical dance, there remains a notable gap in research specifically focused on Bharatanatyam hand gesture recognition for memory-constrained devices such as mobile phones and personal computers. Another major obstacle in advancing gesture recognition for Indian classical dance is the absence of a publicly available, open-source dataset encompassing all fifty-two mudras.

## 3   Proposed Approach

This work focuses on the development of a specialized Convolutional Neural Network (CNN) architecture, harnessing the capabilities of the lightweight MobileNet architecture MobileNet-v2, which is a convolutional neural network architecture optimized for memory-constrained devices. This system employs an inverted redundancy framework where bottleneck layers are connected through residual connections, which are instrumental in mitigating non-linear attributes. These bottleneck layers are integral components in the network, serving to reduce the computational load by using depth-wise separable convolutions, thereby optimizing the model for mobile deployment. The architecture has an initial convolution layer comprising 32 filters and subsequently integrates 19 bottleneck layers, as depicted in Fig. 1a. The layers in the architecture comprise lightweight structures, that contribute to the model's overall efficiency and effectiveness.

One major challenge in conducting research in this domain is the absence of a comprehensive dataset representing all 52 mudras. Thus, in this work a dataset of 47420 images was collated from publicly available datasets by aggregating content from various sources, majorly including open source videos and images. The 2D image dataset featuring diverse hand mudras was constructed utilizing a pre-trained MobileNetV2 model fine-tuned for video-based hand gesture

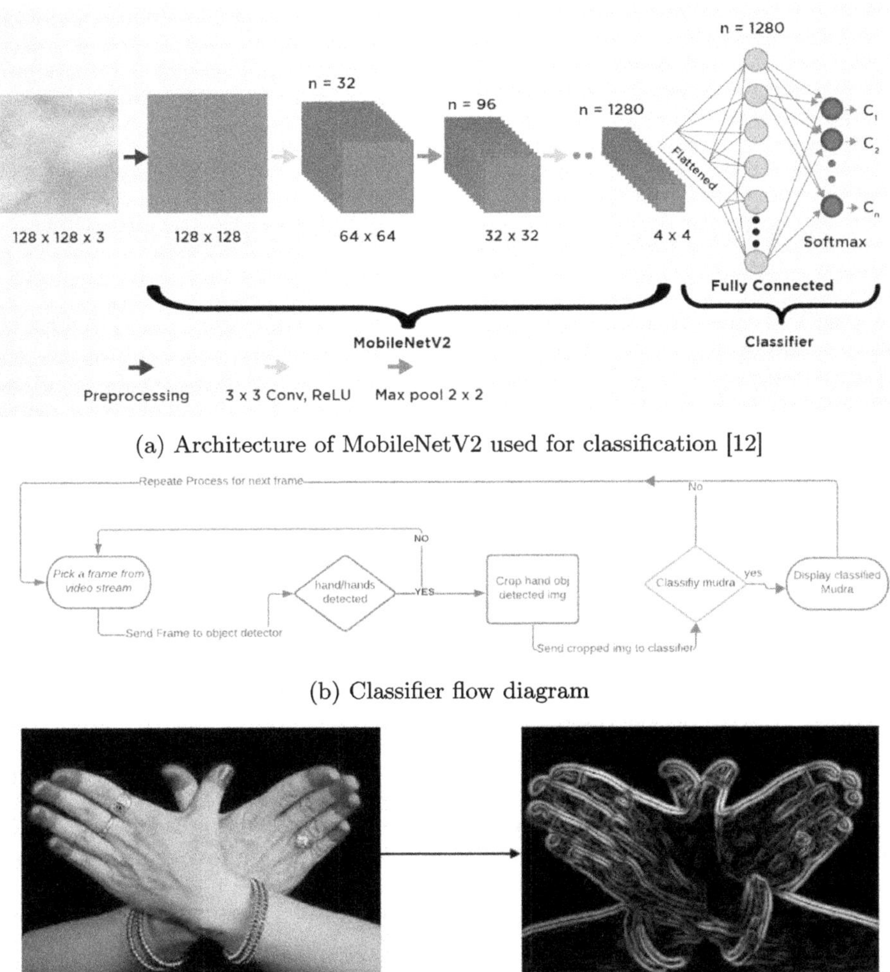



(a) Architecture of MobileNetV2 used for classification [12]



(b) Classifier flow diagram

**Fig. 1.** Model architecture and classification flow used in the proposed system

recognition as an object detector. A Python script was written that identified coordinates of detected objects, representing either single-hand or double-hand gestures. OpenCV methods were subsequently used to crop and store images of hand gestures only in a shared repository. These images were then manually categorized into distinct class folders based on their respective class names, such as "Alapadma".

Derived from the original RGB dataset, an *edge-aware* variant was created, where each image was transformed using edge detection techniques to emphasize boundary-level features crucial for gesture recognition, as shown in Fig. 2. Specifically, the transformation employs the Sobel operator followed by the Canny edge detection algorithm, both of which are well-established methods for extract-

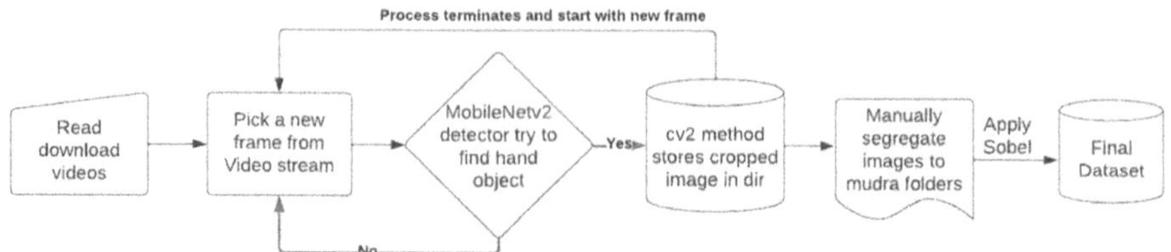



**Fig. 2.** Sample image from the Dataset: before and after pre-processing

ing gradient-based features from image intensity profiles. Let $I(x, y)$ denote the grayscale intensity of a pixel at location $(x, y)$. The Sobel operator approximates the first-order image gradients in the horizontal and vertical directions as follows:

$$G_x = I * S_x, \quad G_y = I * S_y, \tag{1}$$

where $S_x$ and $S_y$ represent the Sobel kernels for the $x$- and $y$-directions, respectively. The gradient magnitude $G(x, y)$ and orientation $\theta(x, y)$ are then computed as:

$$G(x, y) = \sqrt{G_x^2 + G_y^2}, \quad \theta(x, y) = \tan^{-1}\left(\frac{G_y}{G_x}\right). \tag{2}$$

These computations yield a gradient map that captures strong transitions in pixel intensity—typically corresponding to object and gesture boundaries. Subsequently, Canny edge detection is applied to further refine edge localization by employing non-maximum suppression and dual-threshold hysteresis techniques.

The resultant dataset retains the full set of 52 gesture categories and consists of 47420 grayscale images, each highlighting the most salient edges and contours. This conversion substantially reduces image complexity while preserving discriminative features, making the dataset both computationally lightweight and well-suited for deployment on memory-constrained devices. The edge-aware representation enhances the robustness of subsequent classification models by improving the signal-to-noise ratio and focusing learning on high-frequency components—such as gesture outlines—rather than color or texture variations (Fig. 3).

## 4    Results and Analysis

The dataset was partitioned into distinct training and testing sets, maintaining a partition ratio of 70% for training and 30% for testing. Upon consistently demonstrating satisfactory performance, the model seamlessly integrated into real-time video streams, comprising solely of HLS (HTTP Live Streaming), each with a fixed resolution of 720p, for the explicit purpose of recognising hand gestures (mudras). A Python script was developed to read downloaded videos or live video streams, extracting each frame per second. For live stream reading, the ffmpeg Python library was employed, allowing the parsing of HLS streams and frame extraction through the use of OpenCV (cv2) methods. The extracted frame, treated as an image, was then forwarded to the MobileNetV2 object

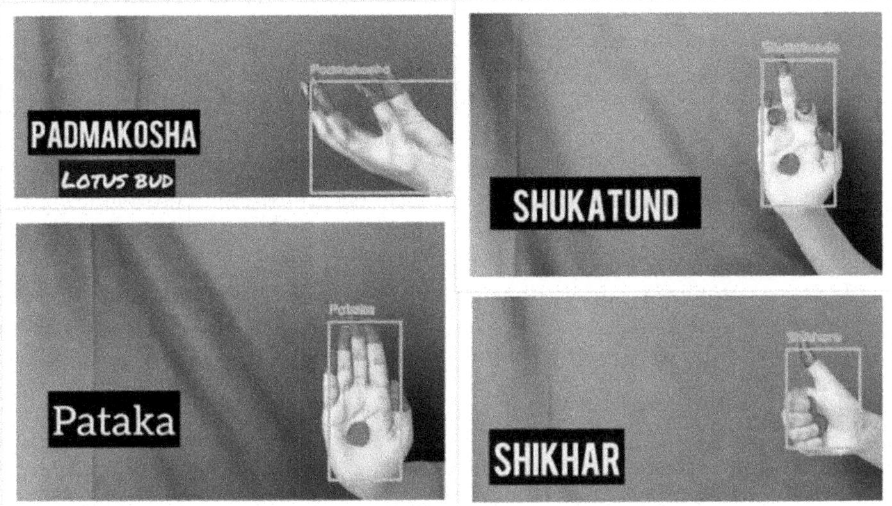


**Fig. 3.** Process for Dataset Preparation

detector for hand detection. The object detector identified the region of the hand gesture, providing its coordinates to the OpenCV method for image cropping. Subsequently, the cropped image was directed to the CNN classifier, which was implemented as a MobileNetV2 model trained on Dataset-2. The classifier determined the category of the displayed mudra, and the result was overlaid on the image using the cv2.putText method. The complete classifier flow diagram is as illustrated in Fig. 1b.

To gain insight into the real-world applicability of our work, where devices often operate with limited resources, all the previously mentioned experiments and processes were conducted on a Dell device equipped with an Intel Core i7 processor, 32 GB of RAM, 2 GB of dedicated graphics memory, and Windows 10 Pro as the operating system.

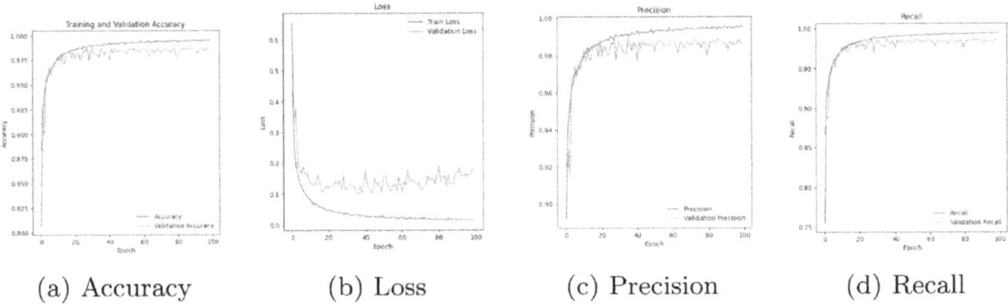

(a) Accuracy          (b) Loss          (c) Precision          (d) Recall

**Fig. 4.** Mudra prediction from live video

During the initial stages of training, our MobileNetV2 model exhibited highly promising results. Remarkably, it demonstrated a training accuracy of 92% and validation accuracy of 88.6% after five epochs. As training progressed, the model reached its peak performance, achieving a maximum training accuracy of 99.1% and a validation accuracy of 98.58%, as illustrated in

The trained model could predict mudras with observed 80–85% accuracy and with very little processing time varying between 50–70 ms. The bounding box has been displayed over the image with its label having predicted the mudra name, as shown in Fig. 4.

We have compared our work with existing work and found out that the classification elapsed time we got are better than the earlier work [2] and provide better classification accuracy [1,2,6,7,10]. The detailed comparison are shown in the Table 1.

**Table 1.** A comparative analysis of this study with prior works on Bharatnatyam mudra classification

| Previous Works | Dataset Details | Method Used | Classification Accuracy | Methodology |
|---|---|---|---|---|
| Anami et al. [1,2] | 2400 images of 24 classes of Samyukta Hast Mudra | Contour of mudra images identified using canny edge detector | 95.25% | Rule-based classifier is used for classification |
| | A total of 2800 images used in dataset for 28 Hast Mudra gestures(classes) | Hu Moments | 97.1% | ANN Classifier |
| | | Eigen Values | 98 | |
| | | Grid Lines with intersection | 96.9 | |
| Devi et al. [5,6] | Dataset consist total of 1450 images of 29 hastmudra's | Hu Moments | 71.59% | kNN, Decision tree, SVM, Bayesian Network |
| | | Zernik Moment | 59.2% | |
| | | Abg Accuracy of Legendre Moments | 89.45% | |
| | Dataset consist total of 1500 images of 25 Asamyukta Mudras | Feature Extraction | 76% | Skeletonization technique |
| Raj et al. [10] | A dataset of 15,396 Asamyukta and 13,035 Samyukta images has been created | Compared various feature extraction techniques | Asamyukta Mudra:- 92%, Samyunkta Mudra:- 98% | SVM, MLP, naive bayes, Logistic Regression, Decision tree, Random Forest, Kaze Descriptor |
| Our Approach | A dataset of 48 thousand images has been made | Sobel edge detection method | 98.58% | CNN, MobileNetV2 |

# 5   Conclusion and Future Work

This study proposes an efficient method for recognizing Hast Mudras in Indian classical dance using transfer learning with MobileNetV2, pretrained on ImageNet. A comprehensive dataset representing all 52 mudras was developed for the experiments. Along with an edge-aware grayscale variant using Sobel and Canny edge detection to emphasize boundary features. The model achieved 98.58% validation accuracy and around 80% accuracy on real-world videos. Challenges such as occlusion, multi-hand overlaps, and confusion between similar mudras (e.g., Alapadma vs. Padmakosha) highlight areas for future enhancement. Future work may explore larger datasets, improved detection methods, and GAN-based occlusion handling. Owing to its lightweight nature, the approach is suitable for deployment on mobile or edge devices, supporting applications in cultural preservation and dance education.

# References


1. Anami, B.S., Bhandage, V.A.: A vertical-horizontal-intersections feature based method for identification of bharatanatyam double hand mudra images. Multimedia Tools Appl. **77**(23), 31021–31040 (2018)
2. Anami, B.S., Bhandage, V.A.: A comparative study of suitability of certain features in classification of bharatanatyam mudra images using artificial neural network. Neural Process. Lett. **50**(1), 741–769 (2019)
3. Bhuyan, H., Killi, J., Dash, J.K., Das, P.P., Paul, S.: Motion recognition in bharatanatyam dance. IEEE Access **10**, 67128–67139 (2022)
4. Chavan, A., Bane, J., Chokshi, V., Ambawade, D.: Indian sign language recognition using mobilenet. In: 2022 IEEE Conference on Interdisciplinary Approaches in Technology and Management for Social Innovation (IATMSI), pp. 1–6. IEEE (2022)
5. Devi, M., Chakraborty, A., Roy, A., Majumder, D.: Single-hand gesture recognition of manipuri classical dance of India based on skeletonization technique. In: 2023 International Conference on Intelligent Systems, Advanced Computing and Communication (ISACC), pp. 1–7. IEEE (2023)
6. Devi, M., Saharia, S.: An empirical analysis of three moments on sattriya dance single-hand gestures dataset. In: Advances in Electronics, Communication and Computing: ETAEERE-2016, pp. 665–673. Springer (2018)
7. Kumar, K., Kishore, P., Anil Kumar, D.: Indian classical dance classification with adaboost multiclass classifier on multifeature fusion. Math. Probl. Eng. **2017**(1), 6204742 (2017)
8. Mohammed, A.A.Q., Lv, J., Islam, M.S.: A deep learning-based end-to-end composite system for hand detection and gesture recognition. Sensors **19**(23), 5282 (2019)
9. Pradeep, R., Rajeshwari, R., Ruchita, V., Bubna, R., Mamatha, H.: Recognition of Indian classical dance hand gestures. In: 2023 International Conference on Inventive Computation Technologies (ICICT), pp. 814–820. IEEE (2023)
10. Raj, R.J., Dharan, S., Sunil, T.: Optimal feature selection and classification of Indian classical dance hand gesture dataset. Vis. Comput. **39**(9), 4049–4064 (2023)

11. Ross, T.Y., Dollár, G.: Focal loss for dense object detection. In: Proceedings of the IEEE Conference on Computer Vision and Pattern Recognition, pp. 2980–2988 (2017)
12. Sandler, M., Howard, A., Zhu, M., Zhmoginov, A., Chen, L.C.: Mobilenetv2: inverted residuals and linear bottlenecks. In: Proceedings of the IEEE Conference on Computer Vision and Pattern Recognition, pp. 4510–4520 (2018)
13. Thavarekere, S.R., Hebbar, A., Uma, D.: A deep learning approach to facial expression recognition in the presence of masked occlusion. In: 2022 IEEE 19th India Council International Conference (INDICON), pp. 1–7. IEEE (2022)

# Pose-Invariant Biometric Recognition of Cattle Using 2D Visual and 3D Structural Features

Anu Jexline Joseph and Rahul Raman[✉]

IIITDM, Kancheepuram, India
{cs24d0001,rahul}@iiitdm.ac.in

**Abstract.** Cattle identification is progressively shifting towards non-invasive biometric techniques. However, 2D face recognition for non-cooperative subjects like cattle is challenging due to variations in pose, illumination, and expression. To address these challenges, we present a pose-invariant face recognition approach that performs effectively even with limited data. The method begins with 2D feature extraction using robust matching techniques. Depth maps are then generated from 2D images using a pretrained model, enabling 3D keypoint matching. The resulting 2D and 3D matching scores are fused at the score level to improve identification robustness. We curated a dataset comprising 4,625 images from 50 subjects captured under diverse poses, environmental conditions, and lighting. The proposed model achieves Rank-1 and Rank-2 identification accuracies of 82.77% and 88.48%, respectively. Since it requires no training phase, the model is highly scalable and well-suited for growing datasets without retraining.

**Keywords:** Biometrics · DepthAnything V2 · Point cloud · SIFT · ISS algorithm

## 1 Introduction

The increasing cattle population in India has made accurate identification crucial for disease management, breeding, theft prevention, insurance claims, and mitigating cattle-wildlife conflicts. Traditional methods such as ear tagging, tattooing, notching, and freeze branding are invasive, impermanent, and vulnerable to tampering [9]. RFID tags offer an alternative but can be lost or damaged and are costly, with limited tracking range [1,16]. This has led to a shift towards non-invasive biometric identification methods, which are more secure and reliable.

Various biometric traits have been investigated for cattle identification, including muzzle patterns, coat colors, iris images, and facial features [7]. Unimodal methods focus on individual traits like the muzzle [4,8] or face [9,15,16], while multimodal methods combine these features for improved accuracy [6,7]. Muzzle prints are particularly distinctive, similar to human fingerprints [2,9].


S. Mitra et al. (Eds.): PReMI 2025, LNCS 16358, pp. 409–417, 2026.
https://doi.org/10.1007/978-3-032-18480-1_42

However, both muzzle and iris traits encounter challenges such as data acquisition issues and environmental factors. Muzzle prints may be obscured by moisture or foreign particles, while iris features can be affected by occlusion, diseases, or drug use [16]. In contrast, facial features provide a more practical and reliable solution, enabling easier data acquisition and high recognition accuracy when handling pose variations effectively.

## 2   Related Works

In cattle recognition, facial features have been used in uni-modal and multi-modal systems due to their lifelong stability [5]. Kumar *et al.* [10] disproved the notion that all cattle faces are similar, revealing sufficient inter-subject variation for reliable identification. In [9], SURF and LBP were applied to frontal face images but lacked robustness to pose changes.

With the rise of deep learning, several studies have explored neural models for cattle identification. [14] employed transfer learning with VGG-16, which performed well on small datasets but degraded with larger ones. CattleFaceNet (RetinaFace + MobileNet) [16] required retraining for new subjects, while Weng *et al.* [15] proposed a Two-Branch CNN to handle pose variation. Siamese models, including Dense Block Capsule [17] and GC Capsule [20], achieved pose-invariant recognition. Other works combined SSD with FaceNet [11] or fused RetinaFace with an improved FaceNet [19]. However, these methods depend on large datasets for generalization. The scarcity of pose-diverse, large-scale datasets and reliance on frontal images limit generalization and increase overfitting [14], while frequent retraining reduces scalability.

To address these issues, we propose a hybrid framework that fuses 2D and 3D features via machine learning, and the motivation for this framework is drawn from [3], where the fusion of 2D and 3D facial features was shown to achieve pose-invariant human face identification.

## 3   Proposed Methodology

This section provides a detailed overview of the proposed multimodal identification framework, comprising two sequential stages, as illustrated in Fig. 1 and detailed in Algorithm 1. In our approach, we partitioned the dataset by selecting 20% of the total images of a subject as the reference set $\mathcal{R}$, while the remaining 80% were used as the testing set $\mathcal{P}$.

*Feature Extraction and 3D Reconstruction:* For every image in the reference and probe sets, we extract both 2D and 3D features:

- **2D Features:** Local descriptors $D_{s,j}$ and $D_p$ are obtained using the Scale-Invariant Feature Transform (SIFT) [13], which detects keypoints and encodes local gradient patterns.

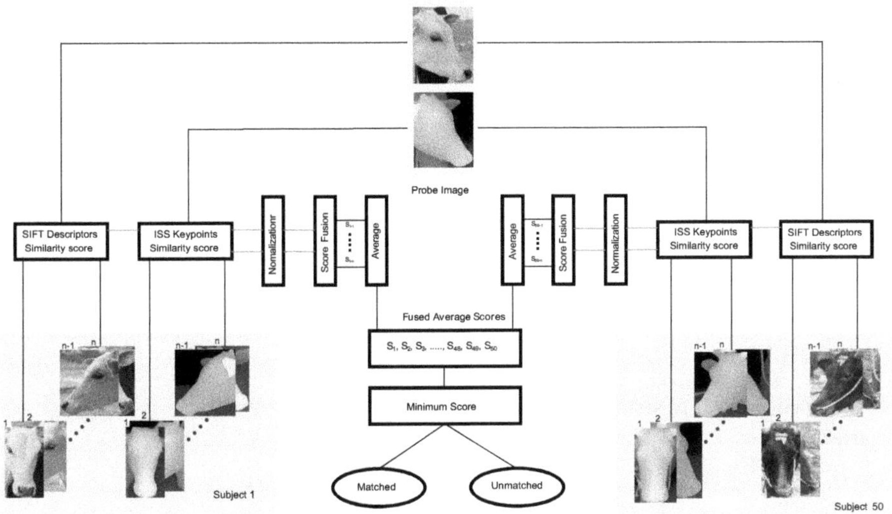

**Fig. 1.** The bottom-left shows $n$ reference 2D images of Subject 1, each paired with its 3D depth map. The bottom-right depicts Subject 50 similarly, covering all 50 reference subjects. The top section shows a probe image and its depth map. For both probe and reference samples, 2D features and 3D keypoints are extracted. Pairwise similarity scores are computed, normalized, and fused. The $n$ fused scores per subject are averaged, and the subject with the minimum score is selected as the best match.

- **3D Keypoints:** The Depth Anything V2-small model [18] generates depth maps from each 2D input, which are then converted into point clouds. Keypoints $K_{s,j}$ and $K_p$ are extracted from the reconstructed 3D meshes using the Intrinsic Shape Signature (ISS) algorithm [21], which selects salient regions based on local geometric variation.

*Similarity Calculation:* For each probe-reference pair $(I_p, P_p)$ and $(I_{s,j}, P_{s,j})$, the similarity is evaluated using two modalities:

1. **2D SIFT Distance:** Using a Brute-Force matcher with L2 norm and cross-checking, we compute

$$d_{\mathrm{SIFT}} = \mathrm{SIFT_dist}(D_{s,j}, D_p),$$

defined as the mean distance over the top $k$ matched descriptors.

2. **3D Hausdorff Distance:** Keypoints extracted from the 3D reconstructed meshes, $K_{s,j}$ and $K_p$, are compared using the Hausdorff distance metric, which better captures shape correspondence than Euclidean distance [12]. The comparison employs the median-based symmetric Hausdorff distance defined as:

$$d_{\mathrm{Haus}} = \max\left(\mathrm{median}(K_{s,j} \to K_p),\ \mathrm{median}(K_p \to K_{s,j})\right),$$

with each term denoting the median nearest-neighbour distance in 3D space.

---

**Algorithm 1.** Multimodal Cattle-Face Identification

---

**Input:**    Reference set $\mathcal{R} = \{R_s\}_{s=1}^{N}$, $R_s = \{(I_{s,j}, P_{s,j})\}_{j=1}^{n}$;
          Probe set $\mathcal{P} = \{(I_p, P_p)\}_{p=1}^{M}$
**Output:** Predicted identity $\hat{y}_p$ for each probe and compute accuracies

1: Precompute $D_{s,j} \leftarrow \text{SIFT}(I_{s,j})$, $K_{s,j} \leftarrow \text{ISS}(P_{s,j})$
2: **for** each probe $(I_p, P_p)$ **do**
3:     $D_p \leftarrow \text{SIFT}(I_p)$, $K_p \leftarrow \text{ISS}(P_p)$
4:     **for** $s = 1$ to $N$ **do**
5:         $d_s = \dfrac{1}{n} \displaystyle\sum_{j=1}^{n} \dfrac{\min\left(\frac{\text{SIFT_dist}(D_{s,j}, D_p)}{\alpha}, 1\right) + \min\left(\frac{\text{Haus_dist}(K_{s,j}, K_p)}{\beta}, 1\right)}{2}$
6:     **end for**
7:     $\hat{y}_p \leftarrow \arg\min_s d_s$
8:     Record rank position of the true subject
9: **end for**
10: Compute Rank-1, Rank-2 from recorded ranks

---

*Score Normalization and Fusion:* The SIFT and Hausdorff distances are independently normalized to the range $[0, 1]$ using empirically chosen constants $\alpha = 200$ and $\beta = 1.0$, respectively. The fused distance is then computed as:

$$d_{s,j}^{\text{fused}} = \frac{\min\left(\frac{d_{\text{SIFT}}}{\alpha}, 1\right) + \min\left(\frac{d_{\text{Haus}}}{\beta}, 1\right)}{2}$$

*Final stage:* For each subject $s$, the $n$ fused scores are averaged to obtain an aggregate subject-wise distance:

$$d_s = \frac{1}{n} \sum_{j=1}^{n} d_{s,j}^{\text{fused}}$$

The predicted identity of the probe is then obtained

$$\hat{y}_p = \arg\min_s d_s$$

This process is repeated for each probe in $\mathcal{P}$, and the true subject's rank is recorded to obtain Rank-1 and Rank-2 identification accuracies.

## 4    Implementation

The proposed multimodal identification framework was implemented using Python 3.8.10, OpenCV for 2D feature extraction, and Open3D for 3D point cloud processing. All experiments were conducted on a workstation equipped with an Intel i7 14th Gen CPU, 64 GB RAM, and an NVIDIA T400 GPU (16 GB) running Ubuntu 24.04.

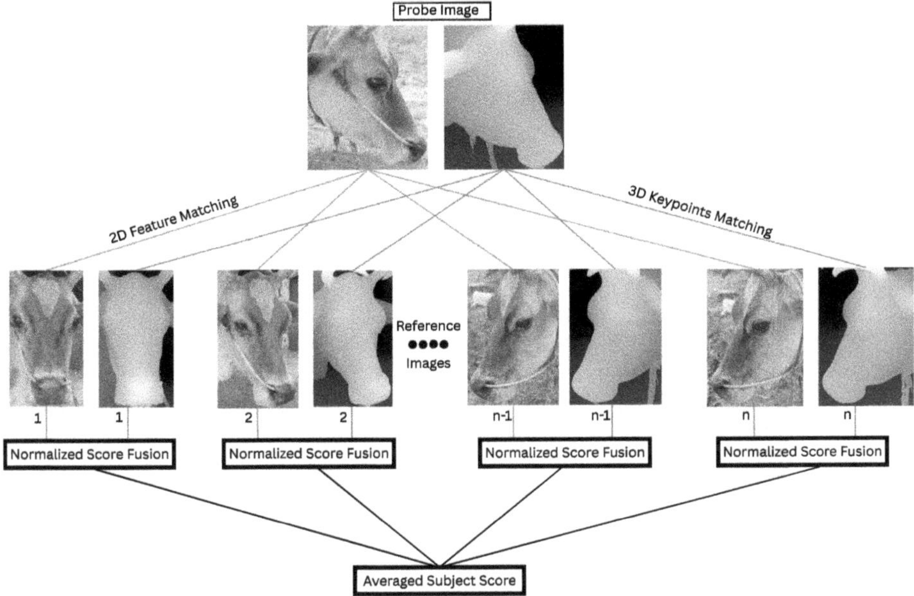



**Fig. 2.** The probe image and its 3D depth map (top row) are compared against $n$ image-depth map pairs of a reference subject (second row). Fused similarity scores are computed per pair and averaged to obtain the final subject-level score.

*Preprocessing:* Each image in the dataset was manually cropped to segment the cattle's face and resized to 512×512 pixels. Monocular depth maps were generated using the pre-trained Depth Anything V2-small model, which were subsequently converted into 3D point clouds for further processing.

*Dataset split:* We construct a reference set $\mathcal{R} = \{R_s\}_{s=1}^{N}$, $(N = 50)$, where each subject $s$ is represented by $n$ pairs of 2D images $I_{s,j}$ and corresponding 3D depth maps $P_{s,j}$ with $n$ being 20% of the subject's images. The remaining 80% form the probe set $\mathcal{P} = \{(I_p, P_p)\}_{p=1}^{M}$ where $M$ denotes the total number of probe samples. In total, the dataset contains 50 subjects, 4625 instances, with 946 reference and 3679 probe samples.

*Pipeline Execution:* The implementation follows the pipeline described in Algorithm 1 and visual interpretation between a probe and a single reference subject is illustrated in Fig. 2.

For each probe-reference pair, **2D features** and **3D keypoints** are extracted using OpenCV's `cv2.SIFT_create()` and Open3D's `compute_iss_keypoints()`, respectively. A Brute-Force matcher with L2 norm and `crossCheck=True` computes descriptor matches, from which the top $k = 50$ (or fewer) are retained. The mean distance of these matches is recorded as the SIFT similarity score. A symmetric, median-based Hausdorff distance is computed in both directions (reference to probe and vice versa) using Open3D's `compute_point_cloud_distance`

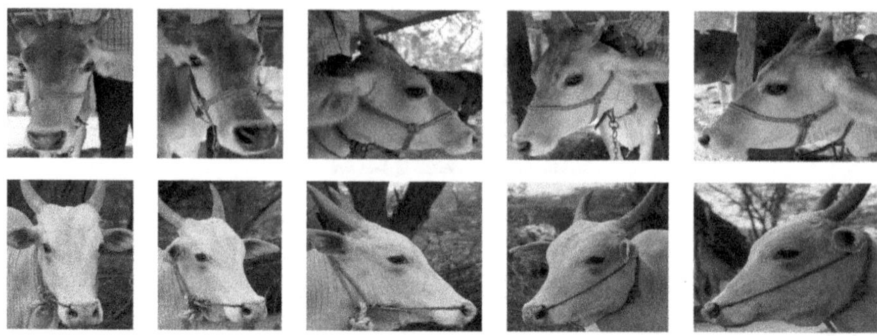

**Fig. 3.** Each row corresponds to a distinct subject. The columns represent different pose variations captured for each subject: the first column shows the frontal pose, followed by the right-angle pose, right-profile, left-angle pose, and left-profile in the subsequent columns. This structured layout demonstrates the pose diversity captured across the dataset.

function:

$$\text{hausdorff_dist} = \max\big(\text{median}(\texttt{distances_s1_to_s2}),$$
$$\text{median}(\texttt{distances_s2_to_s1})\big),$$

where `distances_s1_to_s2` denotes nearest-neighbor distances from reference to probe, and vice versa. This median-based approach improves robustness against outliers and sparse keypoints. The SIFT and Hausdorff distances are normalized and fused as in Sect. 3. For each reference subject, fused scores across its samples are averaged, and the subject with the lowest mean score is returned as the match.

## 5   Performance Analysis

We created a custom dataset of cattle images due to the lack of pose-specific public datasets. It includes 50 subjects with a total of 4,625 images, ranging from 48 to 137 images per subject. Each subject has images taken from various viewpoints and poses, including frontal, right, right-profile, left, and left-profile, as shown in Fig. 3.

To assess diversity among instances, we analyzed the Structural Similarity Index Measure (SSIM) scores of successive image pairs across different poses for each subject. Results showed that only 1.3% of pairs had SSIM scores above 0.8, with majority scoring below 0.5, indicating substantial variation in the dataset.

We partitioned the dataset into a reference set (20%) and a probe set (80%). Using only SIFT features, we achieved 74.83% accuracy. When combined with a 3D approach, accuracy rose to 82.77%. Our method attained 82.77% Rank-1 (R1) identification accuracy with just 20% of the data, unlike conventional deep learning methods that need 80% for training. We also achieved a Rank-2 (R2) accuracy of 88.48%. The results demonstrates the effectiveness of our model, which performs robustly without any training phase.

A comparison of our results with existing works is presented in Table 1.

**Table 1.** Comparison with other existing works.

| References | Features | Retraining | Subjects/Instances | Pose Invariant | Accuracy % |
|---|---|---|---|---|---|
| Kumar *et al.* [9] | Face | ✗ | 40/400 | ✗ | 92.75 |
| Kumar *et al.* [10] | Face | ✗ | 300/3000 | ✗ | 95.87 |
| Wang *et al.* [14] | Face | ✓ | 36/1087 | ✗ | 93 |
| Xu *et al.* [16] | Face | ✓ | 90/2318 | ✗ | 91.3 |
| Weng *et al.* [15] | Face | ✓ | 130/18200 | ✓ | 99.71 |
| Xu *et al.* [17] | Face | ✓ | 63/945 | ✓ | 93 |
| Zhang *et al.* [20] | Face | ✓ | 130/1950 | ✗ | 89.33 |
| Kusakunniran *et al.* [11] | Face | ✓ | 152/2432 | ✗ | 83.45 |
| Yang *et al.* [19] | Face | ✓ | 110/2376 | ✓ | 83.6 |
| Kumar *et al.* [6] | Face + Muzzle | ✓ | 300/2900 | ✗ | 93.67 |
| **The Proposed Model** | **Face 2D + 3D** | ✗ | 50/4625 | ✓ | **R1-82.77 R2-88.48** |

Most prior studies focus on frontal face images, and those addressing pose variations mainly use deep learning models. As shown in the table, most approaches are limited to frontal views, and a few that handle pose variations require re-training with larger datasets. In contrast, our machine learning method effectively manages pose variations and is robust and scalable, without requiring re-training as the dataset grows.

## 6   Conclusion

The proposed method enables effective cattle face identification using only 20% of the dataset as reference images—substantially lower than the training requirements of typical deep learning models. By combining 2D feature matching with 3D keypoint-based matching, it leverages complementary information to achieve Rank-1 and Rank-2 accuracies of 82.77% and 88.48%, respectively. As it relies on classical machine learning techniques, the approach eliminates the need for retraining, ensuring scalability to larger datasets. Future work will focus on improving identification performance, accelerating feature extraction to reduce processing time, and validating scalability and generalization across larger and more diverse datasets.

**Acknowledgments.** The research work presented in this article is funded by DST (SYST) under project sanction order number SP/YO/2021/2227. The authors would like to thank DST and co-researchers of IIITDM Kancheepuram for their active cooperation towards the manifestation of this research.

## References


1. Awad, A.I.: From classical methods to animal biometrics: a review on cattle identification and tracking. Comput. Electron. Agric. **123**, 423–435 (2016)
2. Barry, B., Gonzales-Barron, U., McDonnell, K., Butler, F., Ward, S.: Using muzzle pattern recognition as a biometric approach for cattle identification. Trans. ASABE **50**(3), 1073–1080 (2007)
3. Joseph, A.J., Raman, R.: Pose-invariant 2D face verification by combining mica and 2D features. In: International Conference on Computer Vision and Image Processing, pp. 15–26. Springer (2024)
4. Kaur, A., Kumar, M., Jindal, M.K.: Shi-tomasi corner detector for cattle identification from muzzle print image pattern. Eco. Inform. **68**, 101549 (2022)
5. Kim, H.T., Ikeda, Y., Choi, H.L.: The identification of Japanese black cattle by their faces. Asian-Australas. J. Anim. Sci. **18**(6), 868–872 (2005)
6. Kumar, N., Sharma, A., Kumar, A., Singh, R., Singh, S.K.: Cattle verification with yolo and cross-attention encoder-based pairwise triplet loss. Comput. Electron. Agric. **234**, 110223 (2025)
7. Kumar, S., Kumar, S., Shafi, M., Chaube, M.K.: A novel multimodal framework for automatic recognition of individual cattle based on hybrid features using sparse stacked denoising autoencoder and group sparse representation techniques. Multimedia Tools Appl. **81**(21), 31075–31106 (2022)
8. Kumar, S., Singh, S.K., Singh, A.K.: Muzzle point pattern based techniques for individual cattle identification. IET Image Proc. **11**(10), 805–814 (2017)
9. Kumar, S., Tiwari, S., Singh, S.K.: Face recognition for cattle. In: 2015 Third International Conference on Image Information Processing (ICIIP). IEEE (2015)
10. Kumar, S., Tiwari, S., Singh, S.K.: Face recognition of cattle: can it be done? Proc. Natl. Acad. Sci. India Sect. A **86**, 137–148 (2016)
11. Kusakunniran, W., Phongluelert, K., Sirisangpaival, C., Narayan, O., Thongkanchorn, K., Wiratsudakul, A.: Cattle autoid: biometric for cattle identification: cattle autoid. In: Proceedings of the 8th International Conference on Sustainable Information Engineering and Technology, pp. 570–574 (2023)
12. Li, X.L., Da, F.P.: A rapid method for 3D face recognition based on rejection algorithm. Acta Automatica Sinica **36**, 153–158 (2010)
13. Lowe, D.G.: Distinctive image features from scale-invariant keypoints. Int. J. Comput. Vision **60**, 91–110 (2004)
14. Wang, H., Qin, J., Hou, Q., Gong, S.: Cattle face recognition method based on parameter transfer and deep learning. In: Journal of Physics: Conference Series, vol. 1453, p. 012054. IOP Publishing (2020)
15. Weng, Z., Meng, F., Liu, S., Zhang, Y., Zheng, Z., Gong, C.: Cattle face recognition based on a two-branch convolutional neural network. Comput. Electron. Agric. **196**, 106871 (2022)
16. Xu, B., et al.: Cattlefacenet: a cattle face identification approach based on retinaface and arcface loss. Comput. Electron. Agric. **193**, 106675 (2022)
17. Xu, F., Gao, J., Pan, X.: Cow face recognition for a small sample based on Siamese DB capsule network. IEEE Access **10**, 63189–63198 (2022)
18. Yang, L., Kang, B., Huang, Z., Xu, X., Feng, J., Zhao, H.: Depth anything: unleashing the power of large-scale unlabeled data. In: Proceedings of the IEEE/CVF Conference on Computer Vision and Pattern Recognition (CVPR) (2024)
19. Yang, L., Xu, X., Zhao, J., Song, H.: Fusion of retinaface and improved facenet for individual cow identification in natural scenes. Inf. Process. Agric. **11**(4), 512–523 (2024)

20. Zhang, Z., Gao, J., Xu, F., Chen, J.: Siamese GC capsule networks for small sample cow face recognition. IEEE Access **11**, 125918–125928 (2023)
21. Zhong, Y.: Intrinsic shape signatures: a shape descriptor for 3D object recognition. In: 2009 IEEE 12th International Conference on Computer Vision Workshops, ICCV Workshops, pp. 689–696 (2009)

# Analysis of Spatial Information Processing in Human Vision Using Information Geometry

Debasis Mazumdar[1] and Kuntal Ghosh[2][(✉)]

[1] Sister Nivedita University, DG 1/2, New Town, Action Area I, Kolkata 700156, India
`debasis.m@snuniv.ac.in`
[2] Indian Statistical Institute, 203 B T Road, Kolkata 700108, India
`kuntal@isical.ac.in`

**Abstract.** This paper develops a mathematical model of visual perception related to the encoding of spatial information. Understanding how the brain represents spatial properties of objects in physical space remains a central and challenging problem in psychophysics. We propose that neural mechanisms, specifically the Fisher information encoded in neural population activity, serve a role analogous to the energy-momentum tensor in physics, thereby generating a space-dependent metric tensor. This leads to a curved visual space characterized by a curvature tensor. Using this framework of non-Euclidean geometry, we analyse well-known phenomena in visual optics through concepts such as the Fisher-Rao metric, and psychometric distance.

**Keywords:** Visual space · Population code · Fisher information · Neurocomputing

## 1 Introduction

Understanding the cognitive process of spatial perception has been of key research interest since the nineteenth century. For early thinkers like Weber, Helmholtz, Fechner, and Mach, psychophysics served as the sole means of exploring how sensory information was conveyed and structured within the nervous system. Since then, understanding the cognitive processes underlying the perception of spatial attributes has been recognized as a complex task, and developing mathematical models to analyse these processes remains an active area of research in psychophysics and cognitive science. Recently renewed interest has emerged in designing artificial neural networks inspired by human brain function to perform targeted tasks [1, 2]. A key sub-discipline within this broad field involves modeling the visual mechanisms that enable humans to recognize and interpret the three-dimensional manifold of objects in their surroundings. This manifold is designated as the physical space which is well describable by the Euclidean geometry. The objects in the physical space possess characteristic qualities like colour, brightness, form, and localization. Therefore in visual perception, we are not only aware of the distribution of colours and brightness, but through highly complex cognitive processes we realize that certain of these attributes are combined to entities which we designate as objects, having


S. Mitra et al. (Eds.): PReMI 2025, LNCS 16358, pp. 418–427, 2026.
https://doi.org/10.1007/978-3-032-18480-1_43

definite geometrical attributes (forms) and a definite localization in a three-dimensional space. Percepts, in contrast, are the counterparts in the aware observer's conscious experience of physical objects and form a coherent, organized ensemble, designated as the visual space. The relationship between perceived spatial attributes in the visual space and their corresponding physical extents in the physical space remains a challenging question that is yet to be satisfactorily addressed. A central question is whether visual space possesses a metric structure. Can we meaningfully define a metric within this manifold of sensation? In many perceptual experiences, such as sensing heat or brightness, we typically do not rely on a metric. Instead, we judge whether one sensation ($p_1$) is greater than, equal to, or less than another ($p_2$), without necessarily quantifying the difference. However, perceptual spaces are not limited to such ordinal comparisons. In certain cases, such as estimating depth or the spatial separation between two objects, the presence of a metric becomes apparent, suggesting that some psychological manifolds do support metric properties. Psychophysicists are further interested in understanding how the human brain encodes the distance between two stimuli in the physical space, as well as in modelling the process of perception of spatial features such as angles. The research becomes even more challenging when certain stimuli, known as illusory stimuli, cause these attributes to be perceived in ways that deviate from normal visual experiences.

Historically the first prescient analysis of the problem was made by Ernst Mach [3] in an influential article heading 'On Physiological as Distinguished from Geometrical Space'. Luneburg [4] later introduced a hyperbolic geometry framework for visual space in a significant mathematical paper. Following this, a considerable volume of research emerged, examining the non-Euclidean nature of visual space and its impact on different visual tasks. Several influential experimental studies were also conducted to explore the geometrical structure of visual space. The well-known alley experiments by Hillebrand and Blumenfeld [5, 6] demonstrated that visually perceived space, formed from an unfamiliar arrangement of points of light against a dark background with no contextual cues (a frameless scenario), may deviate from a Euclidean mapping of the physical space. Through a series of publications, Albert Blank [7, 8] described several methods involving triangular spatial configurations by which one can evaluate the geometry of visual space. Koenderink, van Doorn, and Lappin [9] have likewise employed triangle-based tasks to explore which geometric frameworks align with perceived spatial relationships. It is worth mentioning that, Hillebrand, Blumenfeld, and Blank conducted experiments under conditions of total darkness, within a frameless environment where spatial boundaries could not be perceived by the observer. Subsequent research by Battro et al. [10] and others [11] focused on investigating spatial relationships in outdoor environments characterized by everyday lighting conditions. Their findings suggest that human perception of spatial relationships often deviates from Euclidean geometry, even in outdoor environments rich with visual cues. Visual space is typically perceived as curved, with its geometry conforming to either elliptic or hyperbolic models. Curvature perception shifts with scale: small (~2 m) appears elliptical; large (~15.5 m) appears hyperbolic. A comprehensive psychophysical model linking neural mechanisms of vision to visual space geometry remains yet to be deciphered across viewing conditions. This paper introduces an information-geometric framework to model visual space geometry in frameless dark conditions, based on neural population coding of spatial attributes. The model is used to explain human errors in estimating spatial distances between point stimuli, a key challenge in psychophysics.

Information geometry is a branch of information theory, wherein information is described using differential geometry [12]. Recently the topic has been receiving attention of the researchers in different applied and basic sciences [13, 14]. Using the results of information geometry, we explained that the Fisher information contained in the neural population code modeled as a Gaussian probability distribution function plays the role of a stress energy tensor and cause to curve the visual space in the form of hyperbolic surface. The metric tensor for visual space is computed as a function of the Fisher information inherent to the Gaussian shaped neural population code. The metric tensor serves to derive the differential distance function (the Fisher-Rao distance function), proposed as the appropriate psychometric measure for the curved, hyperbolic visual space experienced during object perception in a frameless dark environment. The Fisher-Rao distance function is ultimately employed to model various visual phenomena. The rest of the paper is organized as follows: Sect. 2 details a neuromorphic model demonstrating Gaussian approximations of neuronal tuning curves to point sources. The psychometric distance is derived as a function of Fisher information, followed by simulations of human error in estimating spatial distances between two point stimuli. The model of visual space as a statistical parametric space is detailed in Sect. 3, showing hyperbolic geometry results from the Fisher-Information stress-energy tensor. The study concludes by showcasing the model's role in explaining some physiological optical phenomena, like the Helmholtz horopter and Müller-Lyer illusion.

## 2 A Biologically Inspired Computational Model of Neural Responses to Point Stimuli in Physical Space

Recognizing point stimuli in the physical space and estimating the distances between them is a fundamental spatial task that humans perform effortlessly. Building a computational model of this process begins with uncovering how the brain encodes spatial coordinates, followed by identifying the neural computations that determine inter-stimulus distance. Addressing the initial query, Einevoll et al. [15] modelled the response of a retinal ganglion cell to a visual point stimulus as,

$$R_g(r) = S_g\left[\iint_{r_0} G(r_0 - r)s(r_0)dr_0\right]. \tag{1}$$

G(r) denotes the receptive field function, and r(x, y) specifies the receptive field centre. The stimulus at position $r_0$ is represented by $s(r_0)$. The spatial integral is evaluated across the entire visual field. The transfer function of the retinal ganglion cell, denoted by Sg[x], accounts for potential nonlinearities in the cell's response. To model the half-wave rectification characteristic observed in retinal ganglion cells [15], the transfer function is defined as Sg[x] = x·h(x), where h(x) is the Heaviside step

function: h(x < 0) = 0 and h(x > 0) = 1. This formulation ensures that the model output does not produce negative firing rates. The centre-surround receptive-field function

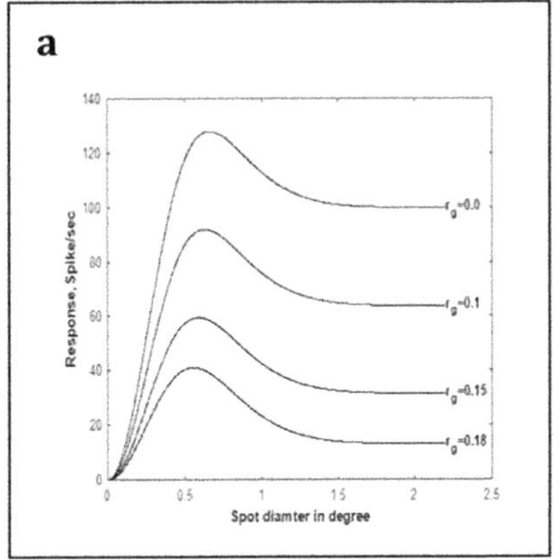
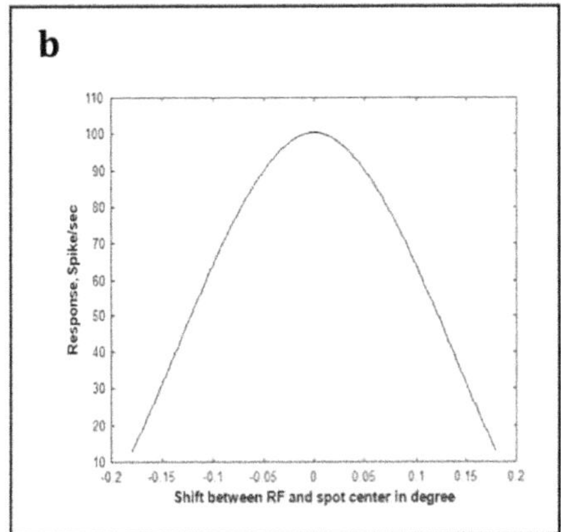





**Fig. 1.** (a) Response functions of retinal ganglion cells Rg(d; $r_g$) for circular spots of different diameters. The receptive field is considered to be a DOG with the parameters $\sigma_e = 0.6$; $\sigma_s = 1.2$, w = 0.5 and the average firing rate is taken as 200 spikes/s. (b) The response of ganglion cells having a concentric receptive field with the spot centre ($r_g = 0$) and cells shifted on either side of the concentric cell up to 0.18 degrees.

for X-class retinal ganglion cells is commonly represented by the DOG functions,

$$G(x, y) = \frac{1}{\sqrt{2\pi\sigma_e^2}}e^{-\frac{(x^2+y^2)}{2\sigma_e^2}} - \frac{w}{\sqrt{2\pi\sigma_s^2}}e^{-\frac{(x^2+y^2)}{2\sigma_s^2}}. \tag{2}$$

The DOG function is centered at (0,0) with circular symmetry, and the parameter w denotes the relative intensity between the centre and its surroundings. When the point stimulus s(r) is approximated by a narrow Gaussian, the convolution in Eq. (1) simplifies to a DOG function, since convolving two Gaussians yields another Gaussian. After applying the ganglion cell's nonlinear transfer function, the result is a positive Gaussian representing the population activity of retinal ganglion cells. Einevoll et al. [15] analytically derived this response for a circular spot with diameter d, luminance l, and varying offset $r_g$ from the receptive field centre. The convolution integral, when evaluated numerically as detailed in [16], produces the ganglion cell responses corresponding to different offsets $r_g$, as depicted in Fig. 1 (a). Fig. 1b illustrates the computed response of a population of neurons with concentric receptive fields, including a central cell ($r_g = 0$) and neighbouring cells positioned up to 0.18 degrees away. The combined activity of these neurons forms what is known as the population code. The resulting curve, which reflects this collective response, is referred to as the tuning curve, representing how the population encodes the spatial location of the stimulus centre. In neuroscience, tuning curves are typically modeled using the Gaussian function, following appropriate normalization [17]. The mean of the tuning curve indicates the position of the preferred stimulus. The standard deviation is equally important, as it defines the steepness of the curve, which in turn determines how sensitively nearby neurons respond to small changes in stimulus. For two closely spaced stimuli, the slope of the Gaussian tuning curve enables fine discrimination between them. Figure 2 shows a schematic depiction of how the tuning curve encodes two-point stimuli. We further expand our investigation by modeling and simulating the neural mechanisms involved in estimating the spatial distance between two point stimuli. It is well known that visual information regarding the estimation of spatial distance between two point stimuli is mainly acquired either by foveating the objects through eye movement or encoding their locations through peripheral vision. Our investigation centres on simulating perceptual biases in distance estimation between two dots under fixation, employing a model grounded in neural processing and hyperbolic visual geometry. In the fixate condition, the subjects

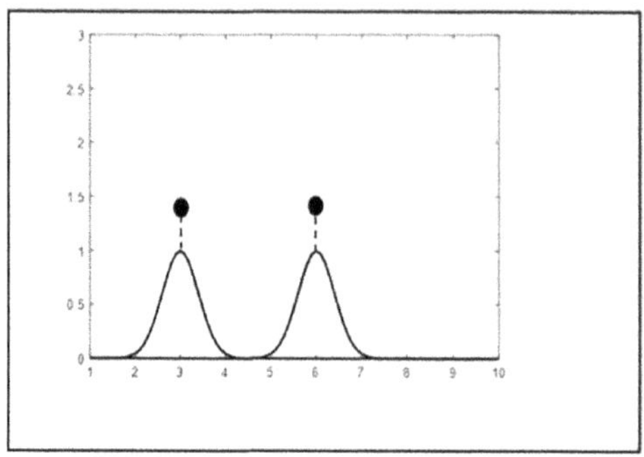

**Fig. 2.** Encoding of two point stimulus as the mean of the Gaussian-shaped tuning curve.

had to keep fixating at a centre position in between two point stimuli marked by a cross sign and then gave their judgments of estimating the distance of separation between the two dots Fig. 3a. Oleksiak et al. [18] used this stimulus in psychophysical experiments to measure human error in distance estimation with a fixed gaze. Their findings are illustrated in Fig. 3b. As shown in the figure, positional uncertainty and localization error escalate with greater dot separation, i.e., with increasing eccentricity. This trend aligns with previous studies [19, 20] indicating that higher uncertainty corresponds to greater variability, resulting in reduced localization accuracy. To investigate the origin of the estimation error, we begin by hypothesizing that the population code, represented by the Gaussian tuning curve, is used to encode the location of a point stimulus in the human brain (Fig. 2). We further hypothesize the existence of a statistical parametric visual space in which Gaussian population codes or tuning curves are represented as points. Gaussian population codes in the described visual space are fully specified by two independent parameters: the mean ($\mu$) and standard deviation ($\sigma$) of the tuning curves. These can be plotted in a 2D Cartesian coordinate system with $\mu$ and $\sigma$ as axes. Since $\sigma > 0$, each point in the upper $\mu$–$\sigma$ half-plane (excluding $\sigma = 0$) represents a Gaussian distribution. Accordingly, the visual space constitutes a half-plane defined by the $\mu$ and $\sigma$ parameters of the tuning curves, represented as:

$$H_f = \left\{ (\mu, \sigma) \in R^2 | \sigma \rangle 0 \right\}. \tag{3}$$

Guided by these preliminary considerations, we initiate our model of the visual distance estimation process by representing each point stimulus as the mean of a univariate

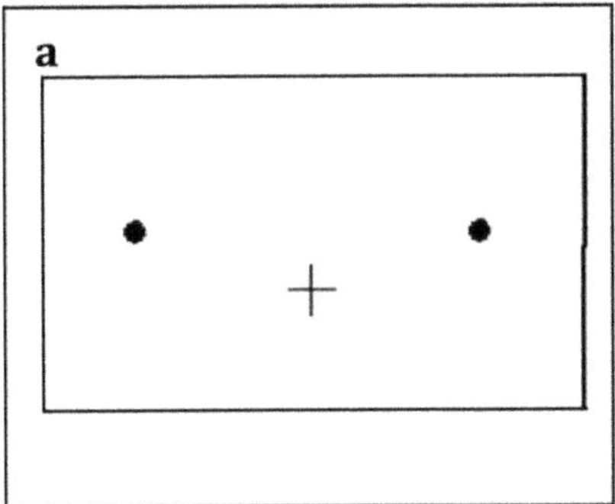


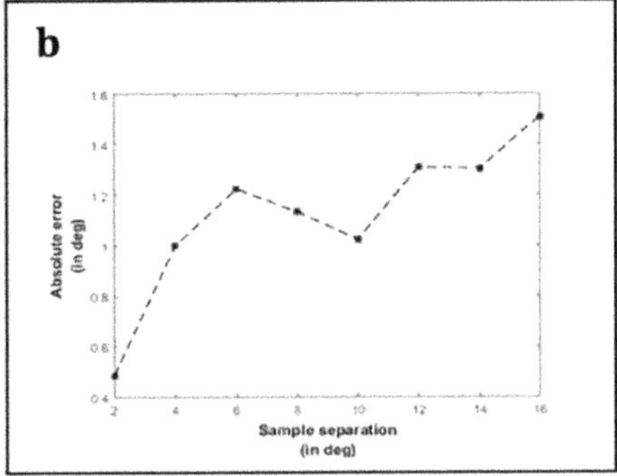


**Fig. 3.** (a) Stimulus used in the fixate trial by Oleksiak et al. [18]. (b) To reconstruct the curve, absolute error values were visually estimated from [18] by three human evaluators, and their averaged estimates are plotted. The x-axis in the figure represents sample separation in degree and the y-axis represents absolute error in degree.

Gaussian distribution described as,

$$\int_X p(r, \Omega)dr = 1. \tag{4}$$

Here, r is treated as a stochastic variable representing the firing rate of neurons, while the parameter set $\Omega = (\mu, \sigma)$ characterizes the tuning curve. As discussed by Tkačik et al. [21], since an organism's behaviour is driven by variations in retinal responses, a biologically relevant measure of distance between two stimuli, $s_1$ and $s_2$, should capture the similarity of the population codes they elicit. Following their approach, we define the Kullback-Leibler divergence between the corresponding neural response distributions as the appropriate psychometric distance. The K-L distance between two distributions $p(x;\theta)$ and $p(x;\theta + d\theta)$ can be written as,

$$D_{KL} = \int_X p(x, \theta) \ln p(x, \theta)dx - \int_X p(x, \theta) \ln p(x, \theta + d\theta)dx. \tag{5}$$

While this is not the standard symmetrized Kullback-Leibler divergence used for comparing $p(x;\theta)$) and $p(x;\theta + d\theta)$, its second-order Taylor expansion leads to an elegant expression of the form [16]:

$$D_{KL} = \frac{1}{2}g^{\mu\nu}d\theta^\mu d\theta^\nu. \tag{6}$$

$g_{\mu\nu}$ is the metric tensor of the visual space, and is expressed as,

$$g_{\mu\nu} = \int_X p(x, \theta) \frac{\partial \emptyset}{\partial \theta^\mu} \frac{\partial \emptyset}{\partial \theta^\nu} dx. \tag{7}$$

$g_{\mu\nu}$ can readily be identified as the Fisher information matrix, with $\emptyset(x,\theta) = -\ln p(x,\theta)$ serving as the negative log-likelihood, often referred to as the spectrum. Starting with the Gaussian form of $p(x;\theta)$, we derive the log-likelihood $\emptyset(x,\theta)$) and use it to compute the components of the metric tensor according to Eq. (7) as listed below, $g_{\mu\mu} = \frac{1}{\sigma^2}$,

$g_{\sigma\sigma} = \frac{2}{\sigma^2}$ while $g_{\mu\sigma} = g_{\sigma\mu} = 0$. Consequently, the Fisher-Rao distance, which defines the proper distance in visual space, can be represented by the following differential line element:

$$d_{sf}^2 = \frac{d\mu^2 + 2d\sigma^2}{\sigma^2}. \tag{8}$$

For univariate normal distribution with variance $\sigma$ the distance between two distributions $N(\mu_1, \sigma)$ and $N(\mu_2, \sigma)$ is given by [22],

$$S_f = \frac{|\mu_1 - \mu_2|}{\sigma}. \tag{9}$$

We began by simulating the formation of retinal image of the two dots under fixated vision using basic geometrical optics, followed by the generation of the corresponding neural population codes. The simulation utilizes the same physical parameters as those reported by Oleksiak et al. [18]. In our simulation framework, two centre-surround Difference of Gaussian (DoG) filters were generated, each corresponding to one of the point stimuli. The scale factors of both the centre and surround components were systematically modulated as functions of the respective eccentricities of the stimuli, using empirical formulations derived from earlier visuotopic mapping studies [23, 24]. To achieve closer alignment with experimental observations, we also incorporated the modulatory effect of spatial attention, particularly when the inter-stimulus distance varied. This attentional modulation further influenced the spatial tuning characteristics [16]. The computed distance obtained through the simulation is considered as the estimated distance $L_e$ (computed using Eq. (9) while the actual distance is designated as $L_0$. The absolute error is accordingly defied as $E = |L_0 - L_e|$. A detail description of the simulation algorithm and methodology is available in [16]. The resulting simulation output is illustrated in Fig. 4.

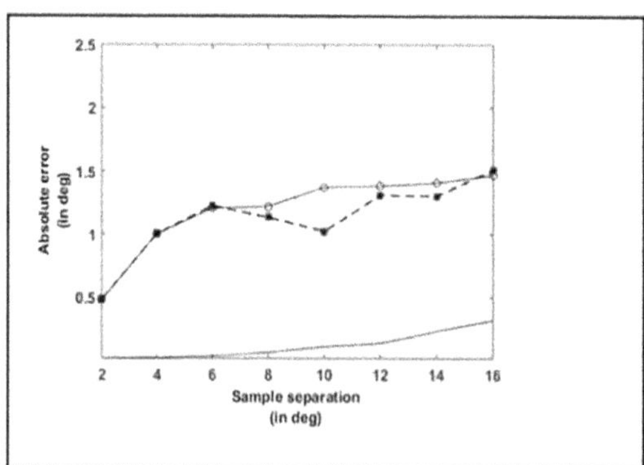


**Fig. 4.** The simulated error values, derived via iterative tuning of $\sigma_e$ and using the Fisher-Rao distance, are shown by the (–o) curve. The experimental data correspond to the (–*) curve, while the solid line represents the error computed as the Euclidean distance between the peaks of the Gaussian tuning curves.

## 3  Influence of Fisher Information in Creating the Curvature of Visual Space

Besides the metric tensor, another important geometric entity of any Riemannian manifold is the Christoffel symbol, defined as,

$$\Gamma_{yz}^{x} = \frac{1}{2} g^{\beta\alpha} \left[ \frac{\partial g_{\alpha\mu}}{\partial x^{\nu}} + \frac{\partial g_{\alpha\nu}}{\partial x^{\mu}} - \frac{\partial g_{\mu\nu}}{\partial x^{\alpha}} \right]. \tag{10}$$

The components of the Christoffel symbol, calculated using the Gaussian PDF that models the tuning curve, were found to be: $\Gamma_{\mu\mu}^{\mu} = \Gamma_{\sigma\sigma}^{\mu} = \Gamma_{\mu\sigma}^{\sigma} = 0$, $\Gamma_{\mu\sigma}^{\mu} = \Gamma_{\sigma\sigma}^{\sigma} = -\frac{1}{\sigma}$ and $\Gamma_{\mu\mu}^{\sigma} = \frac{1}{2\sigma}$. Given the components of the metric tensor and the Christoffel symbols, the scalar curvature of the two-dimensional Fisher information space can be readily computed using the formula,

$$R = \sigma^{2} R_{\mu\sigma\mu}^{\sigma} + \frac{\sigma^{2}}{2} R_{\sigma\mu\sigma}^{\mu}. \tag{11}$$

Here $R_{\mu\sigma\mu}^{\sigma}$ and $R_{\sigma\mu\sigma}^{\mu}$ denote components of the Riemann curvature tensor. A detailed calculation [16] shows, $R_{\mu\sigma\mu}^{\sigma} = \frac{-1}{2\sigma^{2}}$ and $R_{\sigma\mu\sigma}^{\mu} = \frac{-1}{\sigma^{2}}$. Finally the scalar curvature is obtained as, $R = \sigma^{2} \left( \frac{-1}{2\sigma^{2}} \right) + \frac{\sigma^{2}}{2} \left( \frac{-1}{\sigma^{2}} \right) = -1$. Hence, the visual space can be characterized as a Riemannian manifold with constant negative curvature (i.e., a hyperbolic space with scalar curvature $-1$), endowed with the Fisher-Rao information-geometric metric tensor. We further extend the analysis by incorporating the expressions for the Ricci tensor $R_{\mu\nu}$ and the metric tensor $g_{\mu\nu}$ as outlined below,

$$R_{\mu\nu} = \frac{\partial \Gamma_{\mu\nu}^{k}}{\partial x^{k}} - \Gamma_{\mu\beta}^{k} \Gamma_{\mu k}^{\beta} - \frac{\partial \Gamma_{\nu k}^{k}}{\partial x^{\mu}} + \Gamma_{\nu k}^{k} \Gamma_{\mu\nu}^{\beta}, \tag{12}$$

$$g_{\mu\nu} = -\frac{\partial^{2} \emptyset}{\partial x^{\mu} \partial x^{\nu}} + \Gamma_{\mu\nu}^{k} \frac{\partial \emptyset}{\partial x^{k}} + \frac{\partial \Gamma_{\nu k}^{k}}{\partial x^{\nu}} - \Gamma_{\beta k}^{k} \Gamma_{\mu\nu}^{\beta}. \tag{13}$$

From Eqs. (12) and (13), it follows that [16],

$$R_{\mu\nu} + g_{\mu\nu} - \frac{1}{2} g_{\mu\nu}\rho = \rho_{\mu\nu} - \frac{1}{2} g_{\mu\nu}\rho = T_{\mu\nu}. \tag{14}$$

Here $\rho_{\mu\nu} = R_{\mu\nu} + g_{\mu\nu}$, and the scalar $\rho$ is obtained by tracing out $\rho_{\mu\nu}$ by the contravariant metric tensor $g^{\mu\nu}$. The newly defined tensor $T_{\mu\nu}$, which incorporates Fisher information, resembles the stress-energy tensor in form. A simple algebraic manipulation [16] yields the following form of Eq. (14),

$$R_{\mu\nu} - \frac{1}{2} g_{\mu\nu} R - \frac{1}{2} (n-2) g_{\mu\nu} = T_{\mu\nu}. \tag{15}$$

$R = g^{\mu\nu} R_{\mu\nu}$, is the Ricci scalar, and $g^{\mu\nu} g_{\mu\nu} = n$ is the dimension of the space. It is interesting to note that, the left-hand side of Eq. (15) encapsulates geometric properties namely, the metric tensor, Ricci tensor, and Ricci scalar; while the right-hand side corresponds to the stress-energy tensor, dependent on Fisher information, indicating that the curvature of the space changes when information appears in it. Using this differential geometric interpretation of the visual space the geodesics of the space was computed and the visual phenomena like Helmholtz horopter [16] and the Muller-Lyer illusion [25] explained.

## 4   Conclusion

This paper addresses the neural basis of visual space, proposing a new model grounded in information geometry. Earlier models treated visual space as a Riemannian space of constant negative curvature to explain phenomena such as Ames rooms, Helmholtz horopters, and perspective illusions [16]. However, they lacked integration with neural mechanisms. By incorporating Fisher information from neural population codes, we demonstrate that the visual space becomes hyperbolic with constant negative curvature (-1), revealing a physical basis of information in neural processing.

**Acknowledgments.** The authors acknowledge MeitY, GoI for funding the project.

**Data Availability..** All the experimental data and research codes are uploaded on Github (https:// github.com/somucdac/Muller-Lyer-Experimental-Data).

**Disclosure of Interests.** The authors declare no conflicts of interest.

## References

1. Nakai, T., Nishimoto, S.: Artificial neural network modelling of the neural population code underlying mathematical operations. NeuroImage (270) (2023)
2. Hoffmann, H.: Advantages of Neural Population Coding for Deep Learning. arXiv:2411. 00393 [cs.LG]
3. Ernst Mach. Space and geometry in the light of physiological, psychological and physical inquiry. Open Court Classics (1906)
4. Luneburg, R.K.: Mathematical analysis of binocular vision. Princeton University Press (1947)
5. Blank, A.A.: The Luneburg theory of binocular visual space. JOSA **43**(9), 717–727 (1953)
6. Indow, T.: The global structure of visual space. volume 1. World Scientific (2004)
7. Blank, A.A.: Analysis of experiments in binocular space perception. J. Opt. Soc. Am. **48**, 911–925 (1958)
8. Blank, A.A.: Curvature of binocular visual space an experiment. J. Opt. Soc. Am. **51**, 335–339 (1961)
9. Koenderink, J.J., Van Doorn, A.J., Lappin, J.S.: Direct measurement of the curvature of visual space. Perception **29**, 69–79 (2000)
10. Battro, A.M., Netto, S.P., Rozestraten, R.J.A.: Riemannian geometries of variable curvature in visual space: Visual alleys, horopters, and triangles in big open fields. Perception **5**, 9–23 (1976)
11. Norman, J.F., Crabtree, C.E., Clayton, A.M., Norman, H.F.: The perception of distances and spatial relationships in natural outdoor environments. Perception **34**, 1315–1324 (2005)

12. Amari, S., Nagaoka, H.: Methods of information geometry, volume 191. American Mathematical Soc. (2000)
13. Ito, S., Dechant, A.: Stochastic time evolution, information geometry, and the Cramer-Rao bound. Phys. Rev. X **10**(2), 021056 (2020)
14. Kanitscheider, I., Coen-Cagli, R., Kohn, A., Pouget, A.: Measuring Fisher information accurately in correlated neural populations. PLoS Comput. Biol. **11**(6), e1004218 (2015)
15. Einevoll, G.T., Heggelund, P.: Mathematical models for the spatial receptive-field organization of nonlagged x-cells in dorsal lateral geniculate nucleus of cat. Visual Neurosci. **17**(6), 871–885 (2000)
16. Mazumdar, D., Ghosh, K., Mitra, S., Bhaumik, L.K.: Investigation of the neural origin of non-Euclidean visual space and analysis of visual phenomena using information geometry. arXiv:2505.13917 [q-bio,NC]
17. Pouget, A., Dayan, P., Zemel, R.: Information processing with population codes. Nat. Rev. Neurosci. **1**(2), 125–132 (2000)
18. Oleksiak, A., et al.: Distance estimation is influenced by encoding conditions. Plos One **5**(3), e9918 (2010)
19. Mateeff, S., Gourevich, A.: Peripheral vision and perceived visual direction. Biol. Cybern. **49**(2), 111–118 (1983)
20. Toet, A., Snippe, H.P., Koenderink, J.J.: Effects of blur and eccentricity on differential spatial displacement discrimination. Vision Res. **28**(4), 535–553 (1988)
21. Tkačik, G., Granot-Atedgi, E., Segev, R., Schneidman, E.: Retinal metric: a stimulus distance measure derived from population neural responses. Phys. Rev. Lett. **110**(5), 058104 (2013)
22. Atkinson, C., Mitchell, A.F.S.: Rao's distance measure. Sankhyā: The Indian J. Stat. Ser. A 345–365 (1981)
23. Polimeni, J.R., Balasubramanian, M., Schwartz, E.L.: Multi-area visuotopic map complexes in macaque striate and extra-striate cortex. Vision Res. **46**(20), 3336–3359 (2006)
24. Yazdanbakhsh, A., Gori, S.: A new psychophysical estimation of the receptive field size. Neurosci. Lett. **438**(2), 246–251 (2008)
25. Mazumdar, D., Mitra, S., Mandal, M., Ghosh, K., Bhaumik, K.: Modeling müller-lyer illusion using information geometry. In: Data Intelligence and Cognitive Informatics. Jacob, I.J., Kolandapalayam Shanmugam, S., Izonin, I. (eds.) Algorithms for Intelligent Systems. Springer, Singapore. https://doi.org/10.1007/978-981-19-6004-8_1.2023

# Natural Language Processing

# MED-KG-LLM: A Modular Pipeline for Knowledge Graph–Augmented Medical Question Answering on Clinical Data


Ranjana Roy Chowdhury, Nikhil Jain, Rushikesh Shinde, Abhinav Jain[(✉)], and Sudhir Bisane

Infoorigin Pvt. Ltd, Kudwa, India
{ranjana.choudhary,nikhil.jain,rushikesh.shinde,abhinav.jain,
sudhirb}@infoorigin.com



**Abstract.** With the growing digitization of electronic health records (EHRs), there is an urgent need to transform raw, unstructured clinical tabular data into structured representations that support accurate and explainable question answering (QA). We introduce MED-KG-LLM, a fully modular and scalable pipeline that ingests raw dataset based patient-symptom records, performs hybrid named entity recognition (NER) using spaCy and BioBERT, and applies deterministic pattern-driven open information extraction to produce normalized subject-predicate-object triples. These triples populate a multi-view biomedical knowledge graph (KG) in NetworkX, partitioned by relation type (e.g., treatment, symptom association, contraindication). For query processing, both user questions and KG components are embedded with a proprietary OpenAI model; relevant graph passages are retrieved via approximate nearest neighbor search. A two-stage answer generation cascade first leverages BioGPT for domain-specific draft responses, followed by GPT-4o-mini for fluency and factual refinement. We evaluate our system on three publicly available healthcare datasets, benchmarking generated answers against human ground truths using BERTScore, ROUGE-L, and METEOR. Experimental results demonstrate that MED-KG-LLM substantially outperforms existing baselines (e.g., Microsoft Copilot, DeepSeek) in both semantic accuracy and linguistic quality, highlighting its potential as an end-to-end solution for clinical QA over tabular medical data.

**Keywords:** Medical Knowledge Graph · Question Answering · Named Entity Recognition · Open Information Extraction · Clinical Data Processing · Biomedical Language Models · Retrieval-Augmented Generation


## 1 Introduction

The digitization of patient health records has resulted in an abundance of unstructured clinical data, typically stored in CSV files or as free-form text.


© The Author(s), under exclusive license to Springer Nature Switzerland AG 2026
S. Mitra et al. (Eds.): PReMI 2025, LNCS 16358, pp. 431–442, 2026.
https://doi.org/10.1007/978-3-032-18480-1_44

Converting this information into structured knowledge is essential for enabling downstream applications such as clinical decision support and question answering (QA). Recent advances in Named Entity Recognition (NER), powered by frameworks like spaCy [7] and BioBERT [10], have significantly improved the accuracy of biomedical entity extraction.

These extracted triples are naturally suited for integration into Knowledge Graphs (KGs), which provide an expressive format for representing entities and their relationships. Tools such as NetworkX support the efficient construction and analysis of such graphs. In the context of biomedical QA, KG-based systems can use graph traversal and reasoning—often enhanced by fuzzy string matching to address lexical variations [11]—to handle complex queries over structured data [18,25]. Retrieval-Augmented Generation (RAG) models have further advanced this capability by organizing external knowledge hierarchically within graph-like structures. Examples include Graph-Table-RAG for cross-table QA [27] and Extreme-RAG for enterprise tabular data [16]. Hybrid approaches that combine large language models (LLMs) with KGs, such as Disease Guru for long-form QA [17] and educational QA with cross-data knowledge graphs [4], have demonstrated strong performance in both medical and academic domains. To assess answer quality, both surface-level metrics (e.g., strict F1) and semantic similarity measures like BERTScore [24] are commonly used.

Transformer-based models have driven notable progress in biomedical NER. SciBERT [2] and BioMed-RoBERTa [14] have shown that domain-specific tokenization and pretraining data significantly enhance entity recognition performance. ClinicalBERT [8] extends these models to clinical narratives, enabling accurate identification of entities like medications and lab tests. Additionally, SciSpaCy [13] provides spaCy-compatible pipelines optimized for biomedical text and UMLS linking. Our pipeline incorporates both SciSpaCy and BioBERT to ensure robust entity detection.

Meanwhile, relation extraction techniques have evolved from rule-based to neural architectures. Initial systems like Stanford OpenIE [1] have been surpassed by models such as Graphene [5] and SpanOIE [21], which offer improved precision for complex sentence structures. In the biomedical domain, systems like BioRelEx and joint extraction models [26] have been tailored to identify clinical relations (e.g., symptom-treatment pairs) with minimal supervision, reducing the compounding errors common in pipeline-based architectures.

KG construction for biomedical applications has traditionally relied on curated resources like UMLS and Freebase. However, recent tools such as DeepKE [22] and OpenBioLink [15] offer end-to-end knowledge extraction from biomedical literature. Graph-based learning methods, including Graph Convolutional Networks (GCNs) [23], further enrich these graphs with inferred relationships. For this study, we employ NetworkX due to its simplicity and flexibility for building and querying in-memory KGs.

Biomedical QA over KGs (KGQA) has attracted significant attention, with systems like DrQA [6] and PubMedQA [9] addressing document-level questions, while others such as K-HGQA [25] and GraPPa [18] operate directly on graph structures. These systems often incorporate neural reasoning, fuzzy matching [11], or embedding-based retrieval [20] to bridge the gap between user queries and KG labels. Our work differs in that it targets symptom records and introduces a lightweight QA module specifically adapted for this format. In summary, this paper addresses the challenge of transforming unstructured clinical symptom data into a structured, queryable knowledge format for accurate medical question answering. By integrating state-of-the-art biomedical NER models, robust OpenIE techniques, and a lightweight yet effective KG-based QA system tailored for raw sourced datasets, our work contributes a practical and scalable pipeline for clinical knowledge extraction and reasoning. Basically, we propose this paper as an exploratory paper towards QA on medical related dataset from the KG-LLM perspective. This work introduces a complete pipeline that processes a raw medical dataset containing patient-symptom information. The pipeline involves text preprocessing, NER, triple extraction, and KG construction using NetworkX. Our main contributions in the paper are summarized below pointwise:

- We present MED-KG-LLM, a modular and scalable pipeline that transforms unstructured clinical text into a structured knowledge graph integrated with large language models for medical question answering.
- We design a hybrid NER approach that combines rule-based and deep learning models (spaCy and BioBERT) to extract clinical entities such as diseases, symptoms, and medications with high precision.
- We develop a rule-driven triple extraction mechanism, guided by clinical knowledge, to identify and normalize semantic relationships between extracted entities.
- We propose a two-stage answer generation strategy, where domain-tuned BioGPT sketches candidate answers, and GPT-4o-mini performs final synthesis for improved fluency and factual correctness.
- Through quantitative and qualitative analysis we highlight the efficacy of our approach.

## 2    Preliminaries

### 2.1    Knowledge Graph Formalism

A knowledge graph is defined as a directed labeled graph $G = (V, E, \mathcal{R})$, where $V$ is the set of entity nodes, $E \subseteq V \times V$ is the set of edges, and $\mathcal{R}$ is a finite set of relation types. Each edge $(h, t) \in E$ is annotated with a relation $r(h, t) \in \mathcal{R}$. We represent our extracted triples by

$$\mathcal{T} = \{(h, r, t) \mid h, t \in V, \ r \in \mathcal{R}\},$$

and partition $G$ into relation-specific subgraphs $\{G_1, G_2, G_3\}$ to enable efficient, relation-targeted retrieval.

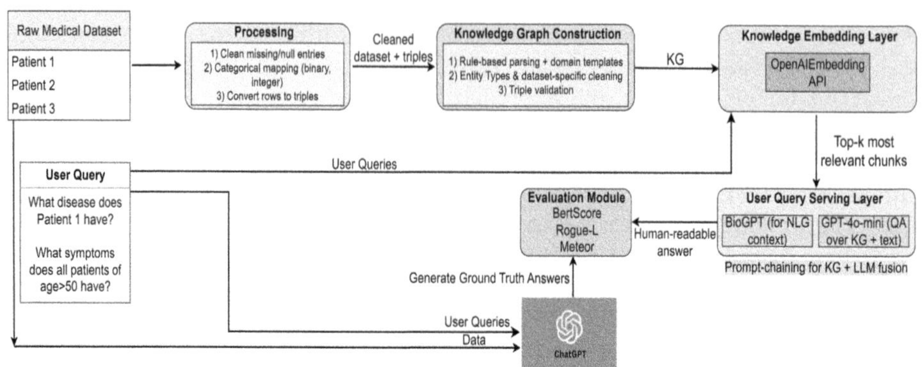

**Fig. 1.** Diagram of MED-KG applied on structured patient data where it processes raw dataset into triples, embeds them, and uses GPT-4o-mini and BioGPT for accurate, explainable answers.

## 2.2  Embedding Models and Similarity Search

We denote by $f_{\mathrm{emb}} : \mathcal{X} \to \mathbb{R}^d$ a dense embedding function mapping text sequences $x \in \mathcal{X}$ to $d$-dimensional vectors. In our system, $f_{\mathrm{emb}}$ is instantiated by a proprietary OpenAI embedding model trained on large biomedical corpora. Given a user query $q$ and chunked graph descriptions $\{d_i\}$, we compute

$$\mathbf{v}_q = f_{\mathrm{emb}}(q), \quad \mathbf{v}_{d_i} = f_{\mathrm{emb}}(d_i),$$

and measure relevance via cosine similarity $\mathrm{sim}(\mathbf{v}_q, \mathbf{v}_{d_i}) = \frac{\mathbf{v}_q^\top \mathbf{v}_{d_i}}{\|\mathbf{v}_q\|\|\mathbf{v}_{d_i}\|}$. An approximate nearest neighbor index (e.g., FAISS) is used to retrieve the top-$k$ passages in sublinear time.

## 2.3  Biomedical Language Models

Our QA module leverages two pretrained generative models. First, BioGPT (`BioGptForCausalLM`) is used for domain-specific answer sketching; it is a Transformer-based language model fine-tuned on PubMed abstracts and clinical texts. Second, GPT-4o-mini is employed for final answer refinement, benefiting from its broad linguistic knowledge and powerful reasoning capabilities. We denote the sketching step as

$$\mathrm{sketch}_i = \mathrm{BioGPT}(d_{(i)}, q),$$

and the synthesis step as

$$a^* = \mathrm{GPT4oMini}(q, \{d_{(i)}\}, \{\mathrm{sketch}_i\}).$$

# 3   Proposed Methodology for MED-KG-LLM

The MED-KG-LLM system is designed to transform raw, unstructured clinical text into a structured knowledge graph and leverage large language models to answer medical queries accurately. Figure 1 illustrates the six sequential modules, each responsible for a key stage in the pipeline: data preprocessing and named entity recognition, triple extraction, knowledge graph construction, knowledge retrieval via embeddings, question answering, and evaluation with metrics logging. Together, these modules enable end-to-end processing from raw electronic health record data to precise, contextually relevant responses.

## 3.1   1. Data Preprocessing and Named Entity Recognition

In this stage, we ingest the raw medical dataset comprising patient demographic information, symptom descriptions, clinical notes, and associated categorical fields. We begin by removing duplicate records and imputing missing entries using domain-aware strategies (e.g., median imputation for numerical fields and mode imputation for categorical fields). Text fields are normalized through lowercasing, punctuation stripping, and Unicode standardization to ensure uniform tokenization. For each categorical attribute $c$, we define an encoding function

$$\phi_c : \mathcal{V}_c \rightarrow \{1, 2, \ldots, |\mathcal{V}_c|\},$$

mapping each unique category value to an integer identifier. We then apply both rule-based and pretrained deep NER models—specifically spaCy's medical pipeline and BioBERT's token-classification heads—to annotate entities of types *Disease*, *Symptom*, *Medication*, and others. These entity spans $\mathcal{E} = \{e_1, e_2, \ldots\}$ form the basis for semantic triplet extraction in the next stage.

## 3.2   2. Triple Extraction

Given the cleaned dataset $D_{\text{clean}}$ and the detected entity set $\mathcal{E}$, we extract meaningful subject-relation-object triples $\mathcal{T}$. Each record is parsed using a library of deterministic patterns (e.g., "⟨Medication⟩ treats ⟨Disease⟩") and domain-specific rules derived from clinical guidelines. Formally, we construct

$$\mathcal{T} = \{(h, r, t) \mid h, t \in \mathcal{E}, \ r \in \mathcal{R}\},$$

where $\mathcal{R}$ is the set of possible relation types. Relations such as "treats," "presents_with," and "contraindicated_with" are recognized via pattern matching and refined using a small rule-based ontology to resolve ambiguities. The resulting triples capture explicit intra-record links and implicit cross-record relationships through entity normalization (e.g., mapping "high blood pressure" and "hypertension" to a single canonical entity).

### 3.3    3. Knowledge Graph Construction

With the triple set $\mathcal{T}$ in hand, we assemble an in-memory knowledge graph $G = (V, E)$ using NetworkX. The vertex set

$$V = \{h \mid \exists\,(h, r, t) \in \mathcal{T}\} \ \cup \ \{t \mid \exists\,(h, r, t) \in \mathcal{T}\}$$

contains all unique head and tail entities, while the edge set

$$E = \{(h, t) \mid (h, r, t) \in \mathcal{T}\}$$

is annotated with the relation attribute $r$. To support heterogeneous query patterns, we partition $G$ into three projections $\{G_1, G_2, G_3\}$, each focusing on a subset of relations (e.g., treatment, symptom association, contraindication). This multi-view representation enables targeted retrieval when queries address specific relation types.

### 3.4    4. Knowledge Retrieval via Embeddings

When a user poses a query $q$, we transform it into a dense vector representation $\mathbf{v}_q = f_{\text{emb}}(q) \in \mathbb{R}^d$ using our proprietary OpenAI embedding model. Simultaneously, each textual description of graph components (node labels, relation sentences) is chunked into $N$ passages $\{d_i\}$ and embedded into $\mathbf{v}_{d_i} = f_{\text{emb}}(d_i)$. At runtime, we compute cosine similarity

$$\text{sim}(\mathbf{v}_q, \mathbf{v}_{d_i}) = \frac{\mathbf{v}_q^\top \mathbf{v}_{d_i}}{\|\mathbf{v}_q\| \, \|\mathbf{v}_{d_i}\|},$$

and retrieve the top-$k$ most relevant chunks $\{d_{(1)}, \ldots, d_{(k)}\}$ via an approximate nearest neighbor index. These chunks serve as the contextual basis for answer generation.

### 3.5    5. Question Answering

Answer generation employs a two-stage cascade. First, BioGPT (via the `BioGptForCausalLM` interface) is conditioned on each retrieved chunk $d_{(i)}$ concatenated with the query $q$ to produce a preliminary answer draft. This ensures domain-specific accuracy and terminology. Second, we refine and consolidate these drafts by providing $(q, \{d_{(i)}\}, \text{draft})$ to GPT-4o-mini via the OpenAI API, yielding a coherent, fluent final answer $a^*$. This cascade leverages BioGPT's biomedical expertise and GPT-4o-mini's advanced language synthesis.

### 3.6    6. Evaluation and Metrics Logging

To assess system performance, we compare each generated answer $a^*$ against a human-authored ground truth $a_{\text{GT}}$. We compute the following metrics:

- **BERT-Score**: Contextual embedding similarity averaged over token alignments in BERT's embedding space.
- **ROUGE-L**: Longest common subsequence-based $F_1$ score, capturing fluency and content overlap.
- **METEOR**: A harmonized metric combining unigram matching (including synonyms and stemming) with a fragmentation penalty.

Formally, we log

$$\text{BERTScore}_{F1}, \quad \text{ROUGE-L}_{F1}, \quad \text{METEOR}.$$

## 4 Experimentations and Results

### 4.1 Datasets

To develop and evaluate our proposed system, we utilized three publicly available healthcare-related datasets sourced from Kaggle. Dataset 1 [19] contains comprehensive records of disease symptoms and associated patient profiles, enabling structured modeling of disease-symptom-patient relationships. Dataset2 [3] provides a hospital-level patient dataset for practice purposes, which includes demographic details, treatment history, and outcome variables. Additionally, we referenced a publicly shared exploratory notebook and call it Dataset 3 [12], which includes detailed exploratory data analysis (EDA) and insights on a similar healthcare dataset. These resources collectively serve as a robust foundation for constructing and validating knowledge graph-based patient analysis systems. Also, for the ease of evaluation and due to resource constraint we have cropped our second and third dataset to a considerate no. of rows for generating KG Graph within our resource bound.

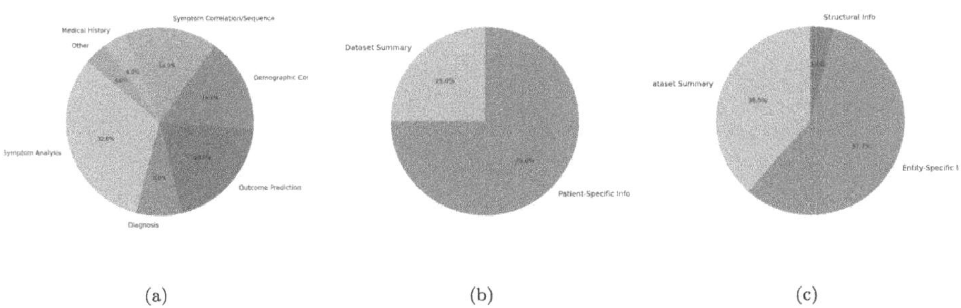


**Fig. 2.** Pie charts illustrating question distribution categories in Dataset (a) 1 [19], (b) 2 [3], and (c) 3 [12].

## 4.2    Generation of Ground-Truths

For ground truth generation, unlike several existing state-of-the-art approaches [17] that rely on the Google Search Engine and often formulate overly generic questions not necessarily grounded in the underlying tabular data, we adopt a more data-aware strategy. Specifically, we utilize ChatGPT by providing it with the actual tabular dataset alongside user query questions in '.txt' format, enabling the generation of contextually relevant answers that are closely aligned with the dataset content.

## 4.3    Quantitative Analysis

Table 1 summarizes a quantitative comparison of our KG-augmented QA pipeline against Microsoft Copilot and DeepSeek on three benchmark datasets. On Dataset 1, our method attains the highest BERTScore (0.879 vs. 0.864 for Copilot and 0.876 for DeepSeek), METEOR (0.313 vs. 0.228 and 0.284), and ROUGE-L (0.314 vs. 0.278 and 0.291), reflecting superior semantic fidelity and lexical overlap. For Dataset 2, although all systems perform more closely, our pipeline still leads in METEOR (0.103 vs. 0.088 and 0.045) and ROUGE-L (0.080 vs. 0.070 and 0.000), with a competitive BERTScore of 0.841 (compared to Copilot's 0.844 and DeepSeek's 0.832). Finally, on the challenging Dataset 3 (diverse EDA-style queries), we again achieve the best METEOR (0.060 vs. 0.044 and 0.059) and a nonzero ROUGE-L (0.030 vs. 0.000 for both baselines), while maintaining a strong BERTScore of 0.797 (versus 0.795 and 0.799). These results demonstrate that our pipeline consistently outperforms or matches existing solutions in aligning with human answers and maximizing linguistic overlap.

**Table 1.** Comparative analysis of model-generated responses across Dataset1, Dataset2, and Dataset3 using BERTScore, METEOR, and ROUGE-L. **Bold** values indicate the highest scores for each metric within a dataset.

| Metric | Dataset | Microsoft Copilot | DeepSeek | Ours |
|---|---|---|---|---|
| **Dataset1** | **BERTScore** | 0.864 | 0.876 | **0.879** |
| | **METEOR** | 0.228 | 0.284 | **0.313** |
| | **ROUGE-L** | 0.278 | 0.291 | **0.314** |
| **Dataset2** | **BERTScore** | **0.844** | 0.832 | 0.841 |
| | **METEOR** | 0.088 | 0.045 | **0.103** |
| | **ROUGE-L** | 0.070 | 0.000 | **0.080** |
| **Dataset3** | **BERTScore** | 0.795 | **0.799** | 0.797 |
| | **METEOR** | 0.044 | 0.059 | **0.060** |
| | **ROUGE-L** | 0.000 | 0.000 | **0.030** |

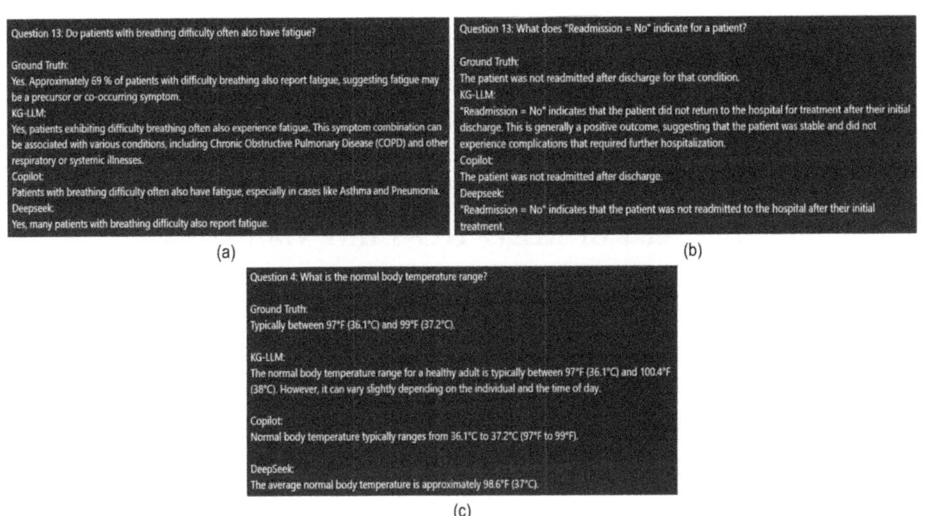


(a)     (b)     (c)

**Fig. 3.** Comparison of answers generated by Microsoft Copilot, DeepSeek and Ours Method for Dataset (a) 1 [19] (b) 2 [3] and (c) 3 [12].

### 4.4 Qualitative Analysis

**Question Categories.** The question distribution across our three datasets highlights the considerable diversity in the types of queries addressed. The first dataset covers a broad spectrum, including symptom analysis (32%), outcome prediction (20%), demographic correlations, symptom sequences, diagnosis, medical history, and miscellaneous categories–reflecting a rich variety of clinical inquiry. The second dataset is more focused, with a dominant share (75%) of patient-specific questions complemented by dataset-level summary queries (25%). In contrast, the third dataset balances between entity-specific information (57.7%), dataset summaries (38.5%), and structural metadata (3.8%). This wide-ranging categorization demonstrates the comprehensive nature of our QA datasets, capturing both general and fine-grained clinical, structural, and contextual aspects essential for robust medical question answering systems as shown in Fig. 2.

**Answer Generation Analysis.** Figure 3 offers qualitative examples of generated answers from each system for representative questions in all three datasets. In Dataset 1, Microsoft Copilot's response, while fluent, tends to provide broad generalizations, and DeepSeek's answer is concise but occasionally omits critical clinical details. In contrast, our system's response explicitly references the correct symptom-treatment relationships extracted from the KG, striking a balance between completeness and clarity. Similar patterns emerge in Dataset 2, where our answers accurately incorporate patient-specific demographic correlations, whereas competitors either overgeneralize or leave out nuanced insights.

For Dataset 3's exploratory EDA questions, our pipeline generates succinct summaries grounded in the actual tabular statistics, while the other systems exhibit either verbosity without depth or terse replies lacking context. Overall, Fig. 3 underscores our method's ability to produce answers that are both factually precise and richly informative

## 5 Deployable API of MED-KG-LLM via Streamlit

As a future work direction and with potential business applications in mind, we have developed MED-KG as a deployable API using Streamlit. This interface accepts inputs comprising global datasets along with user-defined queries, and delivers precise, contextually relevant responses generated by our underlying model. This deployment not only enhances accessibility and usability but also demonstrates the practical viability of MED-KG-LLM in real-world knowledge retrieval tasks from medical perspective.

## Conclusion

Our MED-KG-LLM pipeline delivers consistent improvements over Microsoft Copilot and DeepSeek across three clinical and EDA benchmarks, as shown by superior BERTScore, METEOR, and ROUGE-L. Qualitative analysis confirms our system's ability to generate precise, context-rich answers by leveraging structured biomedical relationships. Key strengths include enhanced semantic alignment, robust domain-specific reasoning, and flexibility for both direct clinical queries and exploratory data summaries. These advances support more accurate and trustworthy AI assistance for healthcare and data analytics. Future work will explore dynamic KG expansion, multimodal data integration, and clinician-driven refinement. Planned user studies aim to validate real-world impact on diagnostic workflows. By combining structured reasoning with scalable QA, our approach paves the way for next-generation clinical AI tools.

## References


1. Angeli, G., Premkumar, M.J., Manning, C.D.: Leveraging linguistic structure for open domain information extraction. In: Proceedings of the 53rd Annual Meeting of the Association for Computational Linguistics (ACL), pp. 344–354 (2015)
2. Beltagy, I., Lo, K., Cohan, A.: SciBERT: a pretrained language model for scientific text. In: Proceedings of EMNLP-IJCNLP, pp. 3615–3620. ACL (2019)
3. blueblushed: Hospital dataset for practice. In: Kaggle (2021). https://www.kaggle.com/datasets/blueblushed/hospital-dataset-for-practice. Accessed 13 July 2025
4. Bui, T., et al.: Cross-data knowledge graph construction for LLM-enabled educational question-answering system: a case study at HCMUT. In: Proceedings of the 2024 ACM Conference on Educational Data Mining (2024)
5. Cetto, M., Schwab, D., François, T.: Graphene: fine-grained propagation of natural language annotations for open information extraction. In: Proceedings of EMNLP, pp. 189–200. ACL (2018)

6. Chen, D., Fisch, A., Weston, J., Bordes, A.: Reading Wikipedia to answer open-domain questions. In: Proceedings of ACL, pp. 1870–1879. ACL (2017)

7. Honnibal, M., Montani, I.: spacy 2: industrial-strength natural language processing in python (2020). https://spacy.io

8. Huang, K., Altosaar, J., Ranganath, R.: ClinicalBERT: modeling clinical notes and predicting hospital readmission. In: Proceedings of the 2019 Conference on Empirical Methods in Natural Language Processing, pp. 1049–1055. ACL (2019)

9. Jin, Q., Dhingra, B., Liu, Z., et al.: PubMedQA: a dataset for biomedical research question answering. In: Proceedings of EMNLP-IJCNLP, pp. 2567–2579. ACL (2019)

10. Lee, J., Yoon, W., Kim, S., Kim, D., So, C.H., Kang, J.: BioBERT: a pre-trained biomedical language representation model for biomedical text mining. Bioinformatics **36**(4), 1234–1240 (2020)

11. Li, H., et al.: Fuzzy string matching techniques for information retrieval. J. Inf. Sci. **42**(1), 123–135 (2016)

12. mohaymenulanam: Healthcare dataset EDA. In: Kaggle (2022). https://www.kaggle.com/code/mohaymenulanam/healthcare-dataset-eda. Accessed 13 July 2025

13. Neumann, M., King, D., Beltagy, I., Ammar, W.: ScispaCy: fast and robust models for biomedical natural language processing. In: Proceedings of the 18th BioNLP Workshop, pp. 319–327. ACL (2019)

14. Peng, Y., Yan, S., Lu, Z.: Transfer learning in biomedical natural language processing: an evaluation of BERT and ELMO on ten benchmarking datasets. In: Proceedings of the 18th BioNLP Workshop, pp. 58–65. ACL (2020)

15. Rossi, S., Fennell, D., DeMaria, A., et al.: OpenBioLink: a universal biomedical knowledge graph. In: Proceedings of ISWC, pp. 150–160. Springer (2021)

16. Roychowdhury, S., Krema, M., Mahammad, A., Moore, B., Mukherjee, A., Prakashchandra, P.: ERATTA: extreme RAG for enterprise-table-to-answers with large language models. In: Proceedings of the 2024 International Joint Conference on Artificial Intelligence (2024)

17. Sukhwal, P.C., Rajan, V., Kankanhalli, A.: A joint LLM-KG system for disease Q&A. IEEE J. Biomed. Health Inform. (2025). Special Issue on Healthcare AI

18. Sun, T., Chen, W., Chen, Y., Wang, W.Y.: GraftNet+: an enhanced model for multi-hop question answering over knowledge graphs. In: Proceedings of the AAAI Conference on Artificial Intelligence (2021)

19. uom190346a: Disease symptoms and patient profile dataset. In: Kaggle (2022). https://www.kaggle.com/datasets/uom190346a/disease-symptoms-and-patient-profile-dataset. Accessed 13 July 2025

20. Wang, Z., Yang, J., Feng, Y., et al.: KEQA: knowledge embeddings for question answering over knowledge graphs. In: Proceedings of AAAI, pp. 1234–1241. AAAI Press (2020)

21. Wu, X., Fani, S., Gomez-Adorno, H.: SpanOIE: spanning n-ary open information extraction. In: Proceedings of EMNLP, pp. 843–853. ACL (2020)

22. Yan, K., Chen, X., Xiao, S., et al.: DeepKE: a toolkit for biomedical knowledge extraction. In: Proceedings of AAAI, pp. 123–131. AAAI Press (2021)

23. Yao, L., Mao, C., Luo, Y.: KG-BERT: BERT for knowledge graph completion. In: Proceedings of EMNLP, pp. 3163–3173. ACL (2019)

24. Zhang, T., Kishore, V., Wu, F., Weinberger, K.Q., Artzi, Y.: BERTScore: evaluating text generation with BERT. In: International Conference on Learning Representations (ICLR) (2020)

25. Zhong, X., Tang, D., Liu, N., et al.: Khgqa: a knowledge-aware hierarchical graph network for multi-hop question answering. In: Proceedings of the 2020 Conference on Empirical Methods in Natural Language Processing (EMNLP) (2020)
26. Zhou, P., Wu, J., Yang, L.: Joint biomedical entity and relation extraction with BERT-LSTM-CRF. In: Proceedings of BioNLP, pp. 1–10. ACL (2020)
27. Zou, J., et al.: Graph-table-RAG for cross-table question answering. In: Proceedings of the 2025 Conference on Empirical Methods in Natural Language Processing (2025)

# NEIC: Indian <u>N</u>ews <u>E</u>ntity <u>I</u>dentification and <u>C</u>haracterization Model for Bharat Stock Price Prediction Using Tiny LLMs

Bhushan Patil, Prithwijit Guha, and Chiranjib Sur[(✉)]

Indian Institute of Technology Guwahati, Guwahati, India
{bhushan.patil,pguha,chiranjib}@iitg.ac.in

**Abstract.** Timely detection of events in financial news can help in the refined prediction of downstream stock prices beyond what is depicted by volume and transactions. In this work, we have introduced NEIC, a lightweight, parameter-efficient transformer architecture tailored for Indian financial news classification into events of interests. The proposed pipeline integrates TextRank-based extractive summarization and selective text augmentation (including synonym replacement, back-translation, and paraphrasing using a LoRA-tuned T5 model) applied only to minority events that happen rarely but change the course of normal stock price prediction. A domain-adapted MiniLM encoder, pre-trained via masked language modeling on financial news, generates contextual embeddings and is fused with TF-IDF features and cosine similarities to anchors that are class label prototypes, forming a tri-branch feature vector processed by a shallow MLP classifier. This semantic anchor fusion strategy enhances label awareness while maintaining low computational overhead. Our model, with only 24.12M parameters, achieves 94% accuracy, 0.78 macro-F1, 94% weighted-F1, and processes 30 articles in under 15 ms, outperforming several larger baselines. The approach demonstrates that tiny LLMs, when enriched with domain adaptation and anchor-driven semantics, can offer both accuracy and deployment efficiency for real-time financial event classification. Apart from this, this work created an Indian Financial News Dataset that affects the stock price the most and is annotated with careful consideration of the market volatility.

**Keywords:** tiny LLMs · financial news · text classification · miniLM · anchor fusion

## 1 Introduction

Stock prices are highly sensitive to events like earnings announcements, mergers, and dividends [3]. Rapid identification of the event category [11] from a news article enables downstream stock forecasting [12] and also provides decision support [8]. Traditional data-driven text classification methods [4] often struggle to capture semantic nuance [2] as future events cannot be predicted. However, we can


S. Mitra et al. (Eds.): PReMI 2025, LNCS 16358, pp. 443–453, 2026.
https://doi.org/10.1007/978-3-032-18480-1_45

leverage Large language models (LLMs) like BERT offer strong performance, but their sizes (BERT-base $\sim$110M, GPT-3 $\sim$175B) make them impractical for low-latency domains and real-time financial analytics. To address this, compressed and distilled variants [5,7] such as DistilBERT (66M) and MiniLM (22M) have been explored for better modeling [9]. These tiny LLMs retain much of BERT's representational power [1] with lower memory and inference overhead [6]. However, directly applying these generic models to financial domains can still lead to poor performance due to domain shift and severe class imbalance. Financial text [10] contains highly specialized vocabulary (e.g., "stock split", "demerger") and exhibits label skew, with categories like `earnings` vastly outnumbering rare events such as `stocksplit`.

The rest of the document is organized with architectural details and methodology in Sect. 2, experimentation details and results in Sect. 3, and conclusion in Sect. 4. The main contribution of this paper are 1) curated domain data collection based on Indian financial news 2) end-to-end pipeline that adapts a Lightweight LLM to financial news and enhances it through multi-branch feature fusion and domain-informed training strategies 3) classify Indian financial news articles into ten event categories critical to stock movements 4) introducing strategies with tiny LLMs for deployment in handheld devices.

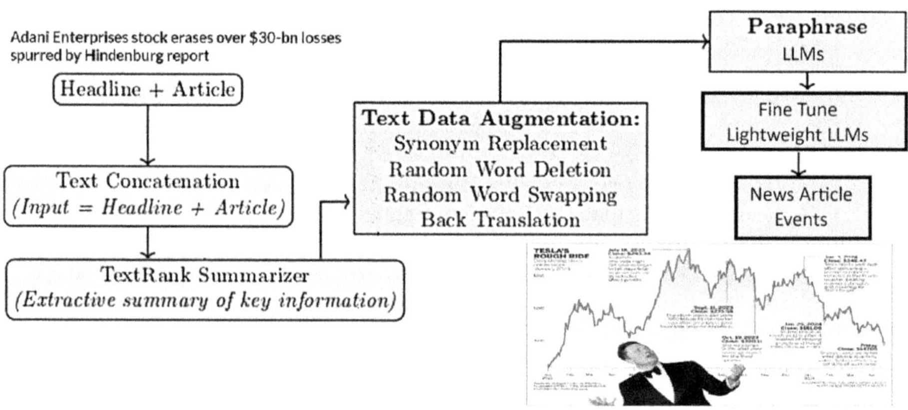


**Fig. 1.** Augmentation pipeline for minority-class financial news. Summarized articles undergo synonym replacement, word perturbation, back-translation, and T5-based paraphrasing.

## 1.1  Data Collection and Class Distribution

We started our research using a proprietary corpus of Indian financial news articles, collected from Indian Financial News sources, each tagged with one of ten event-based labels. Each sample consists of a short-form news article composed of a headline and a description, along with a manually assigned label.

This dataset spans multiple years of Indian stock market activity, collected from leading financial portals such as Moneycontrol. We found that the Indian financial news datasets are completely different from the US-based financial district news datasets, mainly from the NY Times and the Wall Street Journal. To prepare the dataset, we concatenate the headline and description fields, apply normalization (lowercasing, punctuation removal), and handle missing values with empty string substitution. Then we perform a stratified 80:20 split to create training and test sets, preserving label distribution and simulating real-world conditions where the test set comprises temporally later articles. The dataset covers ten event categories relevant to stock price movements. Table 1 summarizes the label frequencies in both the train (Augmented) and test sets. The distribution is highly imbalanced, with **earnings** and **researchreport** dominating, while categories like **stocksplit** and **demerger** are underrepresented.

**Table 1.** Class distribution across the dataset.

| Label | Train Count | Test Count |
|---|---|---|
| earnings | 14295 | 3596 |
| research report | 10040 | 2522 |
| product launch | 8249 | 413 |
| contract | 3448 | 173 |
| technical analysis | 2796 | 141 |
| merger&acquization | 2607 | 132 |
| dividend | 2011 | 101 |
| board meeting announcement | 1819 | 91 |
| demerger | 1124 | 57 |
| stocksplit | 140 | 28 |
| **Total** | **46529** | **7254** |

The ten event-based categories are defined as follows: "Board Meeting Announcement" for company announcements regarding board meetings and related outcomes. "Contract" for new business deals or purchase orders awarded to the company. "Demerger" for news of organizational restructuring, spin-offs, or unit separation. "Dividend" for declarations of dividends, bonuses, or other shareholder distributions. "Earnings" for financial performance results, including revenue and profit announcements. "Merger & Acquisition" for announcements related to mergers, acquisitions, or joint ventures. "Product Launch" for introduction of new products or services to the market. "Research Report" for analyst or brokerage insights, ratings, and commentary. "Stock Split" for corporate actions such as stock splits, reverse splits, or restructuring of share capital. "Technical Analysis" for chart-based or statistical analysis reports on stock behavior.

## 2   Architectural Details

### 2.1   TextRank-Based Summarization

We used TextRank-Based Summarization to reduce noise and highlight key information. We applied unsupervised extractive summarization for each article and then merges the title and description. Further we tokenized the content into sentences, and constructed a similarity graph based on TF-IDF cosine overlap. The most important sentences are identified using PageRank-style node scoring. We retain the top 3–5 ranked sentences, depending on length (maximum 350 words), as the extractive summary. This condensed version replaces the original description for further processing. The benefits were low noise, input truncation, and event highlight.

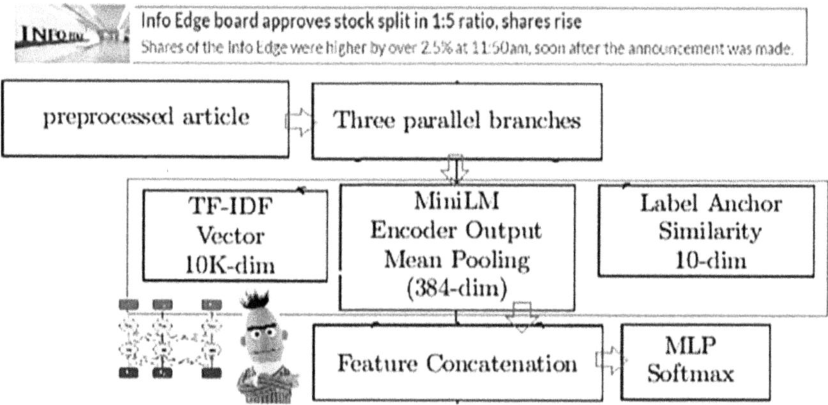


**Fig. 2.** Three-branch classification model. TF-IDF, MiniLM embedding, and anchor-based similarities are concatenated and fed into a shallow MLP.

### 2.2   Data Augmentation Pipeline

We addressed class imbalance and improved generalization by employing a comprehensive **text data augmentation** pipeline. As shown in Fig. 1, the goal is to generate semantically equivalent variants of minority-class articles through lexical, syntactic, and paraphrastic transformations. The augmentation is applied exclusively to 8 minority classes, excluding *Earnings* and *Research Report,* which are already overrepresented. Each minority-class article is augmented through a combination of four techniques. We used synonym replacement using WordNet; non-stopwords are randomly substituted with synonyms (e.g., "secured a contract" → "obtained a contract"), excluding named entities. Inspired by EDA, this injects lexical diversity while preserving label semantics. We also used word deletion & swapping following EDA principles. Here we randomly delete or swap words with low semantic weight. For example, "announced a dividend payout" may become "announced a payout dividend." These perturbations introduce syntactic noise, encouraging the model to generalize beyond surface forms. Back-Translation was also used where articles are translated from English → French → English using automated services. This alters phrasing while maintaining core meaning (e.g., "ABC will merge with XYZ" → "XYZ is set to be merged with ABC"), often yielding fluent, human-like paraphrases. Lastly, T5-Based Paraphrasing (LoRA Fine-Tuned) was used for augmentation. It uses a **LoRA-tuned Flan-T5-Large** model fine-tuned on the PAWS paraphrase dataset. LoRA injects low-rank adapters ($r = 8$) into the frozen model weights, enabling lightweight adaptation on a single RTX 3090. We generate **four diverse paraphrases** per article using top-$p$ sampling, expanding linguistic variation. For example, "XYZ acquires ABC in a \$5M deal" could yield. Like "ABC is to be acquired by XYZ in a \$5 million transaction.", "XYZ to take over ABC through a \$5M merger." or "A \$5M acquisition brings ABC under XYZ." Each original article contributes four variants from each method above. We maintain strict **label consistency** across all augmentations. Crucially, all augmentations are applied **only to the training set**. The test set remains untouched, ensuring evaluation remains true to the real-world distribution. This strategy enables our model to learn robust representations of minority classes without overfitting to synthetic examples.

## 2.3   Domain-Specific LM Pretraining Architecture

Beyond data augmentation, another cornerstone of our approach is adapting the language model to the domain of Indian financial news. We perform Domain-Adaptive Pretraining of the MiniLM model using the Masked Language Modeling (MLM) objective on our curated corpus of Indian stock market news. Prior research [11] has demonstrated that continuing pretraining on in-domain data – a strategy known as "Don't Stop Pretraining" – significantly improves downstream task performance. We begin with the all-MiniLM-L6-v2 model (a 6-layer, 384-dimensional encoder) originally trained on general-purpose English corpora. To specialize it for financial applications, we further pretrain it using MLM on a dataset of ~50,000 Indian financial news articles. Each article consists of a title and a description, which we concatenate into a single input sequence. These inputs are preprocessed and tokenized using the model's default WordPiece tokenizer. We also utilize the Hugging Face `Trainer` API for efficient and reproducible training. Some of the key configurations are Masked Language Modeling with 15% of input tokens are randomly masked, and the model is trained to reconstruct them, following the standard BERT-style training procedure. We had a batch size of 32 sequences. This configuration fits within the memory constraints of a single NVIDIA RTX 3090 GPU. The max sequence length 128 tokens. Inputs longer than this are truncated. Padding is applied to ensure fixed-length sequences for efficient GPU batching. Training epochs were 10, given our dataset size and average sequence length, this results in approximately 13.57 million token exposures, out of which around 2.04 million tokens are masked and contribute to the MLM loss. We use the AdamW optimizer with a learning rate of $5 \times 10^{-5}$ and a linear learning rate schedule with warmup. Mixed-precision (FP16) training is enabled to reduce memory usage and speed up computation. We retain MiniLM's original tokenizer and WordPiece vocabulary. While certain financial terms (e.g., stock tickers, "demerger") may be split into subword tokens, MLM training allows the model to contextualize and understand these domain-specific patterns without modifying the vocab.

## 2.4  Impact of Domain Adaptation

After pretraining, we observe qualitative improvements in MiniLM's understanding of domain-specific language. For example, the model learns to associate "dividend" with "shareholders" and "announcement", or "merger" with "acquisition" and "deal", reflecting accurate co-occurrence patterns in financial reporting. Importantly, this MLM step is fully unsupervised and uses no label information – it is based solely on raw article text – yet provides a semantically rich initialization for downstream supervised classification. We save the domain-pretrained checkpoint and use it to initialize our classification model. This significantly boosts performance, as the model already understands the vocabulary, structure, and tone of Indian financial news, thereby accelerating convergence and enhancing predictive accuracy. Our final classification model fuses diverse representations of financial news via a three-branch feature extractor, as shown in Fig. 2. It combines lexical, semantic, and label-aware features into a single vector, which is then passed through a lightweight MLP classifier. The model is designed to be both parameter-efficient and highly performant.

For a given article with embedding $a$, we then calculate the cosine similarity between $a$ and each class anchor $l_c$. The cosine similarity is defined as:

$$s_c = \cos(a,\, l_c) = \frac{a \cdot l_c}{\|a\|\, \|l_c\|}, \tag{1}$$

for $c = 1, 2, \ldots, 10$. This yields a 10-dimensional feature vector $s = [s_1, s_2, \ldots, s_{10}]$. Each $s_c \in [-1, 1]$ indicates how closely the article's content matches the "essence" of class $c$ in the embedding space. For instance, if an article is about a merger, we would expect $s_{\text{M\&A}}$ to be high (close to 1) and most other $s_c$ to be lower. These anchor similarities act as signals or soft indicators for each class, somewhat analogous to a one-vs-rest heuristic but derived from the semantic space of the LM. We extract sparse lexical features using a TF-IDF vectorizer trained on the top 10,000 unigrams and bigrams from the training corpus. Each article is mapped to a 10,000-dimensional vector $\text{TFIDF}(T) \in \mathbb{R}^{10,000}$, capturing discriminative keywords (e.g., "dividend", "split ratio") relevant to class labels. The vectors are L2-normalized to reduce the impact of document length. We leverage the pretrained (MLM done) MiniLM model (384-dim output) for contextualized representations. Given an article summary $T$, we compute token embeddings and apply mean pooling with $a = \frac{1}{|T|} \sum_{i=1}^{|T|} h_i \in \mathbb{R}^{384}$ where $h_i$ is the token embedding. Most of MiniLM's parameters are frozen, but we apply

LoRA adapters to its self-attention layers, enabling lightweight domain adaptation. The LoRA modules are low-rank matrices ($r = 8$) added to the query and value projections, introducing only $\sim$73K trainable parameters.

## 2.5 Anchor Similarity Branch (Label-Aware Semantics)

To model class proximity, we compute cosine similarity between the article embedding $a$ and precomputed class anchors $l_c$, defined as: $l_c = \frac{1}{|D_c|}\sum_{i \in D_c} a_i$, $s_c = \frac{a \cdot l_c}{\|a\|\,\|l_c\|}$, $c = \{1,\ldots,10\}$ where $D_c$ is the set of training articles for class $c$, and $a_i$ is their MiniLM-based embedding. This produces a 10-dimensional similarity vector $s = [s_1,\ldots,s_{10}]$, where higher values suggest semantic alignment with class prototypes. These features aid the model in correctly identifying minority-class samples.

## 2.6 Feature Fusion and Classifier

The three branches are concatenated to form the final feature vector:

$$z = [\text{TFIDF}(T) \,\|\, a \,\|\, s] \in \mathbb{R}^{10,394} \tag{2}$$

This vector is passed through a shallow MLP with one hidden layer (128 neurons), ReLU activation, dropout (rate 0.2), and softmax output: $\hat{y} = \text{softmax}(W_2 \cdot \text{ReLU}(W_1 z + b_1) + b_2)$ Here, $W_1 \in \mathbb{R}^{128 \times 10,394}$ and $W_2 \in \mathbb{R}^{10 \times 128}$. The MLP contributes approximately $\sim$1.33M trainable parameters. With LoRA adapters (applied to the query and value projections in selected MiniLM layers), the total number of trainable parameters becomes $\sim$1.4M ($\sim$73K from LoRA + $\sim$1.33M from the MLP). Including the frozen MiniLM base weights, the total model footprint remains compact at approximately $\sim$24-25M parameters.

# 3 Results and Experiments

**Table 2.** Model parameter summary. Only the MLP and LoRA adapters are trainable; the MiniLM backbone is frozen.

| Component | Parameter Count |
| --- | --- |
| MiniLM + LoRA (total) | 22,786,944 |
| MiniLM + LoRA (trainable only) | 73,728 |
| Shallow MLP Classifier (trainable) | 1,331,850 |
| **Total Parameters (all)** | **24,118,794** |
| **Total Trainable Parameters** | **1,405,578** |

Table 2 summarizes the total and trainable parameters in our architecture. The MiniLM encoder remains frozen during classification, while only the LoRA adapters and the shallow MLP are updated. We train the model using Adam optimizer with learning rates 1e-3 (MLP) and 5e-4 (LoRA). Cross-entropy loss is used without class weighting, as augmentation already balances the effective distribution. Training is conducted on an NVIDIA GeForce RTX 3090, taking $\sim$10 min for 20 epochs over the 46.52k augmented training set. Early stopping (patience = 5) based on validation macro-F1 prevents overfitting. At inference time, the pipeline processes input summaries through TF-IDF vectorization, MiniLM embedding, and anchor similarity computation. The fused vector $z$ is classified by the MLP. Inference is extremely fast: 0.015 s for 30 articles, equating to $\sim$2000 articles per second – sufficient for real-time deployment in financial news monitoring systems. The proposed MiniLM+Anchor model achieved a test accuracy of 0.94 (94%), which is a very high correctness rate given the 10-class problem. To account for class imbalance, we compute the macro-averaged F1 (treating all classes equally), which is 0.78, and the weighted F1 (averaging per-class F1 weighted by support), which is 0.94. The macro-F1 of 0.78 indicates that while performance is strong on average, there is some variability between classes (minor classes having lower F1). The weighted F1 aligns with the overall accuracy, showing that the model performs extremely well on the majority of instances. These metrics confirm that our approach maintained strong performance on frequent classes while significantly improving performance on rare classes compared to naive baselines. To contextualize our results, Table 3 compares our model with several baseline and competing models from previous experiments. We evaluate our model on the held-out test set (approximately 7,254 articles, containing the original class distribution without augmentation).

**Table 3.** Performance comparison on the test set with baseline models (accuracy and macro-F1). Our model (last row) achieves the highest macro-F1 while maintaining top accuracy, with far fewer parameters.

| Model | Macro F1 | Accuracy |
|---|---|---|
| TF-IDF + Naïve Bayes (majority-class bias) | 0.31 | 0.82 |
| TF-IDF + Random Forest | 0.49 | 0.63 |
| TF-IDF + MiniLM + Random Forest | 0.70 | 0.91 |
| DistilBERT + Residual Classifier Head (66.6M) | 0.49 | 0.43 |
| DeBERTa-v3-xsmall + MLP + R-Drop + Focal + Smoothing (23M) | 0.50 | 0.45 |
| MiniLM + LoRA + Residual MLP + Focal Loss (24M) | 0.63 | 0.83 |
| MiniLM + MLM + LoRA + MLP (24M) | 0.72 | 0.91 |
| MiniLM + MLM + LoRA + TF-IDF + MLP (24M) | 0.74 | 0.91 |
| MiniLM (MLM) + LoRA + Anchor Fusion + TF-IDF + MLP (2HL) (28.2M) | 0.77 | 0.93 |
| **Ours: MiniLM (MLM) + LoRA + Anchor Fusion + TF-IDF + MLP (1HL) (24.12M)** | **0.78** | **0.94** |

In Table 3, the first baseline (TF-IDF + Naïve Bayes) highlights the challenge of imbalance: it attains 82% accuracy (likely due to overpredicting the majority class), but a poor macro-F1 of 0.31, indicating most minority classes were misclassified. The *DistilBERT + Residual Classifier* (66.6M parameters) performs worse than expected (macro-F1 0.49), possibly due to overfitting or vanishing gradient effects. Several MiniLM based configurations (with and without LoRA, MLP, and TF-IDF fusion) reach macro-F1 scores between 0.72 and 0.77. Notably, the model using 2 hidden layers (28.2M params) performs well (0.77 macro-F1), but our final architecture with only one hidden layer-achieves better results (0.78 macro-F1) with fewer parameters (24.12M). This shows that the gains stem from the anchor fusion and not just from increasing MLP depth. Our full model, incorporating anchor similarity and domain-pretrained MiniLM, achieved the best macro-F1 (0.78) and accuracy (0.94). It uses just 24M parameters and is far fewer than models like DistilBERT (66M+) or traditional BERT (110M), yet it delivers superior balanced performance. This underscores the efficiency and effectiveness of our anchor-based fusion and LoRA-augmented learning strategy. To analyze per-class behavior, we provide the confusion matrix in Table 4, which details the number of correctly and incorrectly predicted samples for each class.

**Table 4.** Confusion matrix of the proposed model on the test set. Rows are true labels and columns are predicted labels. Correct predictions appear in **bold**. Bo: Board Meeting; Co: Contract; De: Demerger; Di: Dividend; Ea: Earnings; M&A: Merger & Acquisition; PL: Product Launch; RR: Research Report; SS: Stock Split; TA: Technical Analysis.

| True\Pred | Bo | Co | De | Di | Ea | M&A | PL | RR | SS | TA |
|---|---|---|---|---|---|---|---|---|---|---|
| Board Meeting | **70** | 2 | 1 | 1 | 6 | 6 | 0 | 2 | 0 | 3 |
| Contract | 4 | **129** | 3 | 0 | 1 | 8 | 21 | 3 | 0 | 4 |
| Demerger | 1 | 1 | **36** | 1 | 5 | 9 | 3 | 1 | 0 | 0 |
| Dividend | 1 | 1 | 1 | **82** | 12 | 0 | 1 | 2 | 0 | 1 |
| Earnings | 4 | 2 | 0 | 39 | **3466** | 9 | 27 | 34 | 0 | 15 |
| Merger & Acq. | 2 | 6 | 10 | 1 | 5 | **94** | 8 | 4 | 0 | 2 |
| Product Launch | 0 | 16 | 1 | 0 | 12 | 3 | **372** | 6 | 0 | 3 |
| Research Report | 0 | 2 | 2 | 0 | 26 | 2 | 19 | **2448** | 0 | 23 |
| Stock Split | 3 | 0 | 1 | 5 | 0 | 0 | 0 | 1 | **18** | 0 |
| Technical Anal. | 4 | 3 | 2 | 0 | 17 | 2 | 18 | 5 | 0 | **90** |

This work demonstrates that compact language models, when paired with targeted architectural innovations and training strategies, can match or outperform much larger counterparts on domain-specific tasks. Below, we highlight the key contributions and implications of our approach. Our model achieves 94% accuracy and a macro-F1 score of 0.78 using only ~24.12M parameters, significantly outperforming larger baseline like DistilBERT (66M). The performance gain stems from (i) domain-adaptive masked language modeling, and (ii) LoRA-based fine-tuning that adds only $\sim 73K$ trainable parameters. This lightweight footprint allows real-time deployment on modest hardware, making it well-suited for latency-critical applications in financial systems. We also experimented with a 2M-parameter LoRA setup that modified all attention layers, but it performed worse than the compact 73K configuration, particularly on minority classes. The model classifies 30 articles in $\sim$0.015 s on an NVIDIA RTX 3090 GPU yielding an effective throughput of **2,000 articles/second**. This enables immediate tagging of financial news in live trading systems. Even CPU inference remains feasible due to the efficiency of TF-IDF computation and MiniLM's lightweight architecture. The label anchor branch introduces soft alignment between article embeddings and prototypical class representations. This enhances both model performance and interpretability. Inspecting cosine similarities $s_c$ for each class provides insight into classification decisions. For example, high similarity to the "Dividend" anchor justifies a dividend prediction. This interpretability is highly desirable in finance, where transparency is critical.

## 4  Conclusion and Future Works

We demonstrate that smaller versions of LLMs, when carefully trained via domain pretraining, financially strategic augmentation, and interpretable anchor mechanisms, can achieve competitive performance in financial news classification and detection of events that can help in better forecasting of the prices. This solution is comparatively fast, can be reasoned for understanding, and is more accurate. This model can also be interpreted with attention, and efficient and it is suitable for deployment in real-time, high-stakes environments like handheld devices and in systems which are more secure and curated to specific organizations. Some of the future works include replacing static class-mean anchors with prompt-based or learned label descriptions, introducing class hierarchies, or exploring multi-label classification setups, and transferring the method to other domains.

## References


1. Sur, C.: RBN: enhancement in language attribute prediction using global representation of natural language transfer learning technology like Google BERT. SN Appl. Sci. **2**, 22 (2020)
2. Sur, C.: aiTPR: attribute interaction-tensor product representation for image caption. Neural Process Lett. **53**, 1229–1251 (2021). https://doi.org/10.1007/s11063-021-10438-5
3. Brown, T.B., Mann, B., Ryder, N., et al.: Language models are few-shot learners. In: NeurIPS 2020
4. Devlin, J., Chang, M.W., Lee, K., Toutanova, K.: BERT: pre-training of deep bidirectional transformers for language understanding. In: NAACL-HLT, pp. 4171–4186 (2019)
5. Sanh, V., Debut, L., Chaumond, J., Wolf, T.: DistilBERT, a distilled version of BERT: smaller, faster, cheaper and lighter. arXiv preprint arXiv:1910.01108 (2019)

6. Wang, W., Wei, F., Dong, L., Bao, H., Yang, N., Zhou, M.: MiniLM: deep self-attention distillation for task-agnostic compression of pre-trained transformers. In: NeurIPS 33 (2020)
7. Mihalcea, R., Tarau, P.: TextRank: bringing order into texts. In: EMNLP 2004, pp. 404–411
8. Wei, J., Zou, K.: EDA: easy data augmentation techniques for boosting performance on text classification. In: ACL W-NUT 2019, pp. 638–644
9. Raffel, C., Shazeer, N., Roberts, A., et al.: Exploring the limits of transfer learning with a unified text-to-text transformer. JMLR **21**(140), 1–67 (2020)
10. Zhang, Y., Baldridge, J., He, L.: PAWS: paraphrase adversaries from word scrambling. In: NAACL-HLT 2019, pp. 1298–1308
11. Gururangan, S., Marasović, A., Swayamdipta, S., et al.: Don't stop pretraining: adapt language models to domains and tasks. In: ACL 2020, pp. 8342–8360
12. Hu, E.J., Shen, Y., Wallis, P., et al.: LoRA: low-rank adaptation of large language models. In: ICLR 2022

# A Dual-Attention Sparsemax Model for Adversarial Neural Topic Modeling

Sookshma Mandala[ID], S. Nagesh Bhattu[✉][ID], and Karthick Seshadri[ID]

Department of Computer Science and Engineering, National Institute of Technology
Andhra Pradesh, Tadepalligudem 534101, India
`pf042101@student.nitandhra.ac.in,{nageshbhattu,`
`karthick.seshadri}@nitandhra.ac.in`

**Abstract.** Topic modeling is a fundamental task in natural language processing that aims to uncover latent semantic structures from large-scale document corpora. Existing adversarial neural topic models often produce entangled latent representations and suffer from limited interpretability due to the absence of mechanisms that focus on semantically meaningful patterns, thereby impacting coherence and separability of topics while increasing redundancy. To address these issues, we propose an adversarial neural topic model that integrates dual channel attention for enhanced semantic discrimination. Specifically, we incorporate Squeeze-and-Excitation (SE) and Efficient Channel Attention (ECA) blocks within both the encoder and generator to adaptively recalibrate channel-wise feature activations. Our model introduces 1D convolutional channels over TF-IDF inputs to capture local semantic patterns, forming the basis for attention refinement via SE and ECA mechanisms. This promotes better topic separation and coherence by emphasizing salient semantic features. Sparsemax activation is employed in the encoder to yield interpretable and sparse topic distributions without auxiliary regularization. Experimental evaluations on three benchmark datasets show that our attention-guided adversarial model improves topic diversity by up to 0.78, c_v-based topic quality by up to 0.11, and c_a-based topic quality by up to 0.10 over existing adversarial baselines.

**Keywords:** Neural Topic Modeling · Attention mechanism · Sparsity · Adversarial Models · Interpretable Models

## 1 Introduction

Topic modeling plays a fundamental role in uncovering latent semantic structures within large document corpora. Traditional probabilistic models such as Latent Dirichlet Allocation (LDA) [1] model documents as probabilistic mixtures over a set of latent topics. However, these models rely on strong assumptions and often struggle with scalability, flexibility, and robustness, particularly when applied to high-dimensional and sparse textual data.

© The Author(s), under exclusive license to Springer Nature Switzerland AG 2026
S. Mitra et al. (Eds.): PReMI 2025, LNCS 16358, pp. 454–464, 2026.
https://doi.org/10.1007/978-3-032-18480-1_46

The emergence of Neural Topic Models (NTMs) has enabled more expressive modeling of document-topic and topic-word distributions using neural architectures. Despite their advantages, early NTMs are more likely to produce entangled and less interpretable topics due to the lack of inductive biases and sparsity constraints. Recent advances have explored adversarial training approaches, where Generative Adversarial Networks (GANs) [4] are used to better align the generative process of document modeling with real data distributions. These adversarial NTMs have shown improvements in topic coherence and diversity.

However, most existing GAN-based topic models do not leverage attention mechanisms, which are known to enhance feature selection and representation learning across various domains. Attention allows models to focus on semantically meaningful features during both inference and generation, thereby improving the quality and interpretability of learned topic representations.

In this work, we propose a topic modeling framework that incorporates dual-channel attention through the use of Squeeze-and-Excitation (SE) [13] and Efficient Channel Attention (ECA) [7] blocks in both the encoder and generator networks. SE and ECA have been successfully used in various domains [5,6,10] to enhance feature representation by adaptively reweighting channels. Recent work [12] shows that combining SE and ECA can improve feature selectivity in convolution-based architectures. Inspired by this, we incorporate dual-channel attention into our topic modeling framework to improve semantic focus and topic quality.

Although SE and ECA mechanisms were originally developed for vision-based tasks, their underlying principle of adaptively reweighting feature channels is well-aligned with the requirements of NTM. In our framework, input documents are represented as TF-IDF vectors and passed through 1D convolutional layers in both the encoder and generator. These layers operate along the vocabulary dimension, allowing the extraction of localized semantic patterns that are indicative of topic-specific content. The resulting feature maps can be interpreted as semantic channels, each encoding topic-relevant activations.

The SE module captures global semantic dependencies by summarizing each channel's response through global pooling and applying a learned gating mechanism to emphasize important features. In parallel, the ECA module models local cross-channel dependencies without dimensionality reduction, maintaining the integrity of fine-grained semantic interactions. Together, these dual-attention mechanisms refine the latent topic representations by amplifying salient signals and suppressing noise, thereby enhancing sparsity, interpretability, and coherence in the learned topic distributions.

To further regulate the latent space, the encoder output is constrained using Sparsemax [9], yielding sparse distributions over topics, while a KL divergence term enforces alignment with the prior to maintain semantic consistency. The integration of attention mechanisms and sparse activation within an adversarial training setup offers a principled and architecture-driven approach to producing coherent, diverse, and interpretable topics. This work investigates these architectural innovations and demonstrates their effectiveness across multiple datasets and topic granularities.

The contributions of the proposed work include-

- We design an adversarial topic model with dual channel attention (SE and ECA) to enhance semantic focus in both encoding and generation stages.
- Sparsemax activation and KL divergence are jointly applied in the encoder to yield sparse, interpretable topic distributions while aligning them with the prior distribution.

## 2   Related Work

The Adversarial Neural Topic Model (ATM) [15] employs GANs [4] with a Dirichlet prior to generate word-level topic representations, effectively capturing semantic relations between topics and words. However, it mainly models topic–word distributions and overlooks the document–topic relationship. The Bidirectional Adversarial Topic Model (BATM) [14] addresses this by adopting a bidirectional adversarial framework [3], jointly learning mappings between documents, topics, and words for improved topic inference and clustering. ToMCAT (Topic Modeling with Cycle-consistent Adversarial Training) [8] further enforces consistency between distributions through a cycle-consistency constraint and integrates a classifier for supervised learning, though the separation from representation learning may limit feature discrimination. Collectively, these models highlight how adversarial learning enhances topic coherence, sparsity, and diversity, paving the way for attention-based and structured-prior extensions.

## 3   Proposed Methodology

We propose an adversarial attention-based neural topic model to improve interpretability, sparsity, and topic diversity. The framework comprises three components–an encoder, a generator, and a discriminator–as illustrated in Fig. 1. The encoder maps documents to topic distributions, the generator reconstructs document-level bag-of-words representations from sampled noise, and the discriminator distinguishes real documents from generated ones. Given a corpus $\mathcal{D} = \{d_1, d_2, \ldots, d_N\}$ with a vocabulary $\mathcal{V} = \{w_1, w_2, \ldots, w_V\}$, each document $d_i$ is represented by a TF-IDF vector $\mathbf{x}_i \in \mathbb{R}^V$, where $x_{ij}$ denotes the TF-IDF weight of word $w_j$. The vectors are normalized on the probability simplex as:

$$\tilde{\mathbf{x}}_i = \frac{\mathbf{x}_i}{\sum_{j=1}^{V} x_{ij}} \tag{1}$$

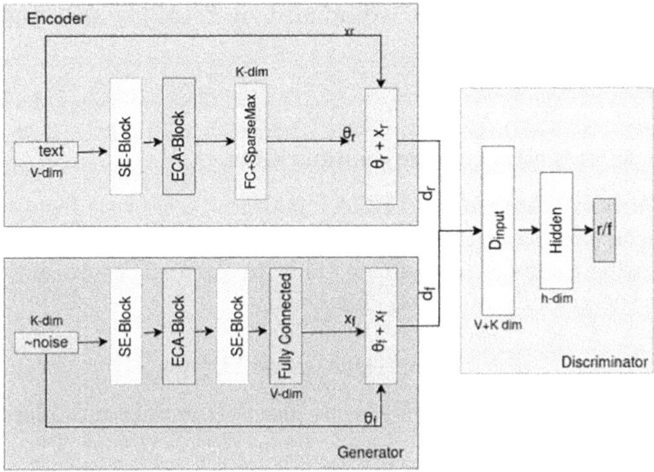

**Fig. 1.** Proposed model architecture.

## 3.1   Encoder with Dual Attention and Sparsemax

The encoder is designed to infer a document-specific topic distribution $\boldsymbol{\theta} \in \mathbb{R}^K$, where $K$ denotes the number of latent topics. Each input document is first represented as a normalized TF-IDF vector $\tilde{\mathbf{x}} \in \mathbb{R}^V$, where $V$ is the vocabulary size. This vector is passed through a fully connected layer followed by a non-linear activation function to extract an initial hidden representation:

$$\mathbf{h}_1 = \mathrm{ReLU}(\mathbf{W}_1 \tilde{\mathbf{x}} + \mathbf{b}_1) \tag{2}$$

Here, $\mathbf{W}_1 \in \mathbb{R}^{H \times V}$ and $\mathbf{b}_1 \in \mathbb{R}^H$ are the learnable weight and bias parameters, and $H$ is the dimensionality of the hidden layer. To enhance the semantic quality of the extracted features and allow the model to focus on informative dimensions, we apply a dual-attention mechanism composed of a Squeeze-and-Excitation (SE) block followed by an Efficient Channel Attention (ECA) module.

**Squeeze-and-Excitation (SE) Block:** The SE mechanism begins with a global average pooling operation across the feature dimensions of $\mathbf{h}_1$, generating a channel descriptor $\mathbf{z} \in \mathbb{R}^H$:

$$\mathbf{z} = \frac{1}{H} \sum_{i=1}^{H} h_{1i} \tag{3}$$

This descriptor is then passed through a gating mechanism comprising two fully connected layers with a ReLU activation in between, followed by a sigmoid function to produce a set of channel-wise importance weights:

$$\mathbf{s} = \sigma(\mathbf{W}_2 \cdot \mathrm{ReLU}(\mathbf{W}_{\mathrm{SE}}\mathbf{z})) \tag{4}$$

The output of the SE block is obtained by rescaling the original features using these learned weights:

$$\mathbf{h}_{SE} = \mathbf{h}_1 \odot \mathbf{s} \tag{5}$$

where $\odot$ denotes element-wise multiplication.

**Efficient Channel Attention (ECA) Block:** To capture local cross-channel dependencies in a parameter-efficient way, the SE-enhanced features $\mathbf{h}_{SE}$ are further refined using the ECA mechanism. This involves a 1D convolution operation applied over the globally averaged channels:

$$\mathbf{a} = \sigma\left(\text{Conv1D}(\text{AvgPool1D}(\mathbf{h}_{SE}))\right) \tag{6}$$

The resulting attention weights $\mathbf{a}$ are used to further modulate the feature representation:

$$\mathbf{h}_{att} = \mathbf{h}_{SE} \odot \mathbf{a} \tag{7}$$

This dual-attention mechanism enables the encoder to dynamically emphasize semantically meaningful features while suppressing noise and redundancy. The ECA module produces channel-wise attention weights that further modulate the SE-enhanced representation:

$$\mathbf{h}_{ECA} = \mathbf{h}_{SE} \odot \mathbf{a} \tag{8}$$

This attended representation is then projected into the latent topic space via a linear transformation:

$$\mathbf{z} = \mathbf{W}_3 \mathbf{h}_{ECA} + \mathbf{b}_3 \tag{9}$$

To induce sparsity and improve interpretability, we replace the conventional Softmax with Sparsemax [9], defined as the Euclidean projection of $\mathbf{z} \in \mathbb{R}^K$ onto the probability simplex $\Delta^{K-1}$:

$$\boldsymbol{\theta} = \text{Sparsemax}(\mathbf{z}) = \arg\min_{\mathbf{p} \in \Delta^{K-1}} \|\mathbf{p} - \mathbf{z}\|^2. \tag{10}$$

Unlike Softmax, which produces dense probability vectors, Sparsemax frequently projects onto the boundary of the simplex, assigning exact zeros to less relevant components. This direct projection yields sparse topic distributions, allowing each document to be represented by only a few dominant topics. As a result, our framework achieves more interpretable and exclusive topic assignments without requiring additional sparsity-inducing regularization.

### 3.2   Generator with Dual Attention

The generator aims to reconstruct the original bag-of-words distribution of a document from a given topic representation $\boldsymbol{\theta} \in \mathbb{R}^K$, where $K$ denotes the number of topics.

To enhance the semantic quality of the reconstruction, we integrate a dual-attention mechanism—Squeeze-and-Excitation (SE) followed by Efficient Channel Attention (ECA) and SE—into the generator pipeline. These modules, as described in Sect. 3.3, are applied to the generator's hidden representations to adaptively reweight channel-wise signals. In the proposed framework, the notion of *channels* refers to latent feature dimensions arising in the hidden representations of documents rather than physical modalities as in vision tasks. Each channel corresponds to a transformed linear combination of vocabulary elements, effectively encoding semantic patterns or co-occurrence structures. The attention mechanisms (SE and ECA) operate over these feature dimensions by adaptively reweighting them, thereby enhancing semantically informative components while reducing the influence of less relevant ones.

After attention refinement, the resulting representation is projected to the output space through a linear transformation. Rather than applying a softmax over the vocabulary, we normalize the output using $L_2$-normalization to ensure that the reconstructed word distribution remains smooth and continuous:

$$\hat{\mathbf{x}} = \frac{\hat{\mathbf{x}}}{\|\hat{\mathbf{x}}\|_2 + \epsilon} \tag{11}$$

where $\epsilon$ is a small constant to prevent division by zero.

### 3.3   Discriminator

Let $\boldsymbol{\theta}_r \in \mathbb{R}^K$ be the topic distribution inferred by the encoder from a real document, and $\mathbf{x}_r \in \mathbb{R}^V$ be its associated normalized TF-IDF vector. Similarly, let $\boldsymbol{\theta}_f \in \mathbb{R}^K$ be a topic vector sampled from a prior (e.g., Dirichlet), and $\hat{\mathbf{x}}_f \in \mathbb{R}^V$ be the reconstructed document produced by the generator. The discriminator receives joint representations formed by concatenating topic and document vectors as input ($D_{input}$):

$$\mathbf{d}_r = [\boldsymbol{\theta}_r; \mathbf{x}_r], \quad \mathbf{d}_f = [\boldsymbol{\theta}_f; \hat{\mathbf{x}}_f] \tag{12}$$

where $[;]$ denotes vector concatenation.

This adversarial setup enables the model to align the distributions of inferred and generated document-topic pairs. As a result, the generator learns to produce realistic document reconstructions conditioned on latent topics, and the encoder is encouraged to discover meaningful and discriminative topic distributions.

### 3.4   Loss Functions (GAN, KL, Diversity)

The proposed model is trained using a composite loss that combines adversarial objectives with regularization terms to promote meaningful and disentangled topic representation. The encoder $E$, generator $G$, and discriminator $D$ are jointly optimized through the min-max game:

$$\min_{G,E} \max_{D} \mathbb{E}_{\mathbf{d}_r \sim p_{\text{real}}}[D(\mathbf{d}_r)] - \mathbb{E}_{\mathbf{d}_f \sim p_{\text{fake}}}[D(\mathbf{d}_f)] \tag{13}$$

To encourage the inferred topic distribution to remain close to a predefined prior, we introduce a Kullback–Leibler (KL) divergence regularization term defined as:

$$\mathcal{L}_{\mathrm{KL}} = \mathrm{KL}\left(\boldsymbol{\theta} \,\|\, p(\boldsymbol{\theta})\right) \tag{14}$$

where $\boldsymbol{\theta} = \mathrm{Sparsemax}(f_\phi(\mathbf{x})) \in \Delta^{K-1}$ is the deterministic topic distribution produced by the encoder, and $p(\boldsymbol{\theta})$ is the prior.

For the generator, a topic diversity loss is added to reduce redundancy across topics. It penalizes high similarity between topic-word distributions, promoting better separation and coverage of semantic space:

$$\mathcal{L}_{\mathrm{div}} = \frac{1}{K(K-1)} \sum_{i \neq j} T_i \cdot T_j^\top \tag{15}$$

The total encoder and generator losses are thus:

$$\mathcal{L}_E = -\mathbb{E}_{\mathbf{d}_r}[D(\mathbf{d}_r)] + \lambda_{\mathrm{KL}}\mathcal{L}_{\mathrm{KL}}, \quad \mathcal{L}_G = -\mathbb{E}_{\mathbf{d}_f}[D(\mathbf{d}_f)] + \lambda_{\mathrm{div}}\mathcal{L}_{\mathrm{div}} \tag{16}$$

Here, $\lambda_{\mathrm{KL}}$ and $\lambda_{\mathrm{div}}$ are weighting coefficients for the KL and diversity terms. This integrated loss formulation encourages the model to learn interpretable, diverse, and semantically meaningful topics in an adversarial learning setup.

## 4   Experimentation

We evaluated our model on three benchmark datasets: 20Newsgroups[1] (18,187 documents, 1,988-word vocabulary), YahooAnswers[2] (18,695 documents, 2,296-word vocabulary), and M10[3] (8,355 documents, 1,696-word vocabulary), using topic numbers of 20 and 50. Standard preprocessing steps—lowercasing, stop-word removal, and token filtering by document frequency—were applied. Evaluation metrics include topic coherence ($c_v$, $c_p$, $c_a$) [11], Topic Diversity (TD) [2], and Topic Quality (TQ) [2]. Experiments were executed on a workstation with an Intel Xeon CPU, 250 GB RAM, and an NVIDIA RTX A4000 GPU (16 GB VRAM) running Ubuntu 22.04 LTS, using Python 3.12.7, PyTorch 1.7.0.

As shown in Table 1, the proposed model demonstrates strong performance at a topic size of 20, where 'v' represents corresponding coherence value. The proposed model consistently achieves the highest topic diversity, with scores of 0.72, 0.79, and 0.91 on 20Newsgroups, YahooAnswers, and M10 respectively. For topic quality, it obtains the best $c_v$-based TQ values across all datasets–0.290 on 20Newsgroups, 0.259 on YahooAnswers, and 0.301 on M10. Additionally, the model achieves the highest $c_p$-based TQ on 20Newsgroups (0.050), and the highest $c_a$-based TQ across all datasets: 0.232, 0.204, and 0.076, respectively.

---

[1] http://qwone.com/~jason/20Newsgroups/.
[2] https://github.com/ArdalanM/nlp-benchmarks.git.
[3] https://github.com/MIND-Lab/OCTIS.git.

**Table 1.** Topic Size 20: Coherence, Diversity, and Quality Metrics

| Dataset | Model | TD | $c_v$ | | $c_p$ | | $c_a$ | |
|---|---|---|---|---|---|---|---|---|
| | | | v | TQ | v | TQ | v | TQ |
| 20Newsgroup | ATM | 0.50 | 0.369 | 0.185 | 0.015 | 0.008 | 0.369 | 0.185 |
| | BAT | 0.17 | 0.349 | 0.059 | 0.015 | 0.003 | 0.246 | 0.042 |
| | ToMCAT | 0.08 | 0.374 | 0.030 | −0.009 | −0.001 | 0.082 | 0.007 |
| | Proposed | 0.72 | 0.403 | **0.290** | 0.070 | **0.050** | 0.323 | **0.232** |
| YahooAnswers | ATM | 0.35 | 0.316 | 0.111 | −0.170 | −0.060 | 0.303 | 0.106 |
| | BAT | 0.20 | 0.310 | 0.062 | −0.148 | **−0.030** | 0.177 | 0.035 |
| | ToMCAT | 0.09 | 0.358 | 0.032 | −0.802 | −0.072 | −0.029 | −0.003 |
| | Proposed | 0.79 | 0.328 | **0.259** | −0.1312 | −0.104 | 0.258 | **0.204** |
| M10 | ATM | 0.58 | 0.342 | 0.198 | −0.021 | −0.012 | 0.113 | 0.066 |
| | BAT | 0.14 | 0.313 | 0.044 | −0.030 | **−0.004** | 0.030 | 0.005 |
| | ToMCAT | 0.13 | 0.321 | 0.042 | −0.449 | −0.058 | −0.046 | −0.006 |
| | Proposed | 0.91 | 0.331 | **0.301** | −0.059 | −0.054 | 0.084 | **0.076** |

At a larger topic size of 50, the model continues to outperform all baseline methods, as reported in Table 2. It retains the highest topic diversity with values of 0.564 (20Newsgroups), 0.72 (YahooAnswers), and 0.81 (M10). In terms of coherence-based TQ, the proposed model secures the top $c_v$-based TQ scores— 0.218 on 20Newsgroups, 0.221 on YahooAnswers, and 0.263 on M10. Furthermore, it maintains the best $c_p$-based TQ on 20Newsgroups (0.027) and leads in $c_a$-based TQ for all datasets with scores of 0.163, 0.137, and 0.066.

Overall, the proposed attention-based adversarial topic model achieves superior performance across different datasets and topic granularities. The results validate the effectiveness of integrating dual-attention mechanisms with sparse activation in generating coherent, diverse, and interpretable topics. The topic diversity (TD) of our model remains consistently high across 20Newsgroups, YahooAnswers, and M10 respectively, significantly surpassing other models. These results confirm that our attention-driven architecture not only enhances semantic coherence but also promotes distinct and diverse topic discovery, thereby yielding the highest overall topic quality.

Table 3 summarizes total parameters, FLOPs, and execution times for topic sizes 20 and 50. The proposed model has moderate complexity (5.73M–5.82M parameters), slightly lower than BATM but higher than ATM and ToMCAT. It achieves about half of BATM's FLOPs while maintaining faster inference despite longer training. Overall, it offers a balanced trade-off between efficiency and performance, combining lower computational cost with strong inference speed. This indicates that despite its slightly higher training overhead, the model is highly optimized for inference, benefiting from efficient attention mechanisms and sparse activations. Overall, compared to BATM, the proposed model offers a balanced improvement—achieving lower FLOPs, faster inference, and compa-

**Table 2.** Topic Size 50: Coherence, Diversity, and Quality Metrics

| Dataset | Model | TD | $c_v$ | | $c_p$ | | $c_a$ | |
|---|---|---|---|---|---|---|---|---|
| | | | v | TQ | v | TQ | v | TQ |
| 20Newsgroup | ATM | 0.30 | 0.364 | 0.109 | 0.010 | 0.003 | 0.372 | 0.112 |
| | BAT | 0.37 | 0.374 | 0.139 | 0.032 | 0.012 | 0.319 | 0.118 |
| | ToMCAT | 0.03 | 0.360 | 0.011 | −0.139 | −0.004 | 0.040 | 0.001 |
| | Proposed | 0.564 | 0.387 | **0.218** | 0.047 | **0.027** | 0.289 | **0.163** |
| YahooAnswers | ATM | 0.16 | 0.334 | 0.053 | −0.107 | **−0.017** | 0.307 | 0.049 |
| | BAT | 0.22 | 0.322 | 0.071 | −0.116 | −0.025 | 0.322 | 0.071 |
| | ToMCAT | 0.04 | 0.442 | 0.018 | −0.838 | −0.034 | −0.035 | −0.001 |
| | Proposed | 0.72 | 0.3077 | **0.221** | −0.177 | −0.128 | 0.190 | **0.137** |
| M10 | ATM | 0.41 | 0.361 | 0.148 | 0.038 | 0.016 | 0.151 | 0.062 |
| | BAT | 0.51 | 0.367 | 0.187 | 0.046 | **0.023** | 0.113 | 0.058 |
| | ToMCAT | 0.13 | 0.324 | 0.042 | −0.292 | −0.038 | 0.011 | 0.001 |
| | Proposed | 0.81 | 0.324 | **0.263** | −0.073 | −0.059 | 0.082 | **0.066** |

**Table 3.** Total parameters, FLOPs, and times.

| Topic Size | Model | Params | Total FLOPs | Inf. (ms) | Train (s) |
|---|---|---|---|---|---|
| 20 | ATM | 0.40M | 0.39M | 18.58 | 99.94 |
| | BATM | 6.18M | 8.23M | 2.73 | 117.17 |
| | ToMCAT | 0.60M | 0.6M | 4.00 | 150.76 |
| | Proposed | 5.73M | 4.21M | 1.75 | 202.16 |
| 50 | ATM | 0.40M | 0.40M | 14.57 | 102.48 |
| | BATM | 6.27M | 8.36M | 3.14 | 119.71 |
| | ToMCAT | 0.61M | 0.61M | 8.92 | 151.00 |
| | Proposed | 5.82M | 4.31M | 1.85 | 201.83 |

rable representational strength, making it an efficient choice for large-scale or real-time topic inference applications.

## 5   Conclusion

This work presents a sparse adversarial topic modeling framework that enhances semantic precision, interpretability, and topic diversity through architectural innovations. By guiding both the encoder and generator to focus on salient semantic patterns, the model reduces redundancy and improves topic quality. Empirical evaluations across multiple datasets and topic sizes consistently demonstrate its ability to generate diverse and semantically rich topics, validating the effectiveness of the proposed design. Few limitations of the proposed work include- The architectural complexity introduces computational overhead, increasing both training time and memory usage. This may limit the model's scalability on extremely large datasets or in low-resource environments. Additionally, the current implementation relies on TF–IDF representations that capture term-level importance but do not fully encode contextual or semantic dependencies among words, which may slightly limit topic coherence. Incorporating contextual embeddings from pre-trained language models such as Bidirectional Encoder Representations from Transformers (BERT) could address this limitation by providing richer semantic representations and improving robustness across domains. However, a systematic evaluation of such extensions is left for future work due to the scope of the present study.

The proposed architecture illustrates the effectiveness of combining adversarial learning with attention-based mechanisms for interpretable and diverse topic modeling. Future directions may explore scaling the model to larger corpora and incorporating temporal or hierarchical structures for dynamic topic discovery. These directions offer promising opportunities to extend the flexibility and applicability of the proposed approach.

**Disclosure of Interests.** The authors have no competing or conflicts of interest to declare that are relevant to the content of this article.

# References


1. Blei, D.M., Ng, A.Y., Jordan, M.I.: Latent Dirichlet allocation. J. Mach. Learn. Res. **3**, 993–1022 (2003)
2. Dieng, A.B., Ruiz, F.J., Blei, D.M.: Topic modeling in embedding spaces. Trans. Assoc. Comput. Linguist. **8**, 439–453 (2020)
3. Donahue, J., Krähenbühl, P., Darrell, T.: Adversarial feature learning. arXiv preprint arXiv:1605.09782 (2016)
4. Goodfellow, I., et al.: Generative adversarial nets. Adv. Neural Inf. Process. Syst. **27** (2014)
5. Guo, M.H., Lu, C.Z., Hou, Q., Liu, Z., Cheng, M.M., Hu, S.M.: SegNeXt: rethinking convolutional attention design for semantic segmentation. Adv. Neural. Inf. Process. Syst. **35**, 1140–1156 (2022)
6. Guo, M.H., Lu, C.Z., Liu, Z.N., Cheng, M.M., Hu, S.M.: Visual attention network. Comput. Visual Media **9**(4), 733–752 (2023)
7. Hu, J., Shen, L., Sun, G.: Squeeze-and-excitation networks. In: Proceedings of the IEEE Conference on Computer Vision and Pattern Recognition, pp. 7132–7141 (2018)
8. Hu, X., Wang, R., Zhou, D., Xiong, Y.: Neural topic modeling with cycle-consistent adversarial training. arXiv preprint arXiv:2009.13971 (2020)
9. Martins, A., Astudillo, R.: From softmax to sparsemax: a sparse model of attention and multi-label classification. In: International Conference on Machine Learning, pp. 1614–1623. PMLR (2016)
10. Nagendra, S.B., Sristy, N.B., Karri, P.K.: Lightweight recurrence-free handwritten text recognition. Expert Syst. Appl., 128655 (2025)

11. Röder, M., Both, A., Hinneburg, A.: Exploring the space of topic coherence measures. In: Proceedings of the eighth ACM International Conference on Web Search and Data Mining, pp. 399–408 (2015)
12. Shashank, B., Nagesh Bhattu, S., Sri Phani Krishna, K.: Improvising the CNN feature maps through integration of channel attention for handwritten text recognition. In: International Conference on Computer Vision and Image Processing, pp. 490–502. Springer (2022)
13. Wang, Q., Wu, B., Zhu, P., Li, P., Zuo, W., Hu, Q.: ECA-Net: efficient channel attention for deep convolutional neural networks. In: Proceedings of the IEEE/CVF Conference on Computer Vision and Pattern Recognition, pp. 11534–11542 (2020)
14. Wang, R., et al.: Neural topic modeling with bidirectional adversarial training. arXiv preprint arXiv:2004.12331 (2020)
15. Wang, R., Zhou, D., He, Y.: ATM: adversarial-neural topic model. Inf. Process. Manage. **56**(6), 102098 (2019)

# Enhancing Sentiment Analysis with Retrieval-Augmented Generation and Domain-Specific Fine-Tuning


M. A. Tara[1] , Aparajita Sinha[2]([envelope]) , and Monika Agarwal[1]

[1] PES University, EC Campus, Bangalore, Karnataka, India
pes2ug23cs307@pesu.pes.edu , monika.goyal@pes.edu
[2] National Institute of Technology, Agartala, Tripura, India
asinha.22odcsw002@phd.nita.ac.in



**Abstract.** In Natural Language Processing (NLP), sentiment analysis is crucial for interpreting public opinion from user generated text. While models such as BERT (Bidirectional Encoder Representations from Transformers) provide strong baselines, they often struggle with evolving language and domain specific contexts. This study explores Retrieval Augmented Generation (RAG), a framework that enhances transformer models with an external knowledge base and compares it with RoBERTa using a MiniLM encoder. Experiments are conducted on two datasets: Sentiment140, which contains informal Twitter text and Amazon Food Reviews, consisting of structured long form data. To address domain mismatch, we apply domain specific fine-tuning to the retriever in the RAG framework. Results are measured through accuracy, precision, recall, and F1 score and show that fine-tuning consistently improves performance. The goal of this study is to assess whether RAG offers measurable improvements over static models and to highlight the importance of domain adaptation.

**Keywords:** Sentiment Analysis · Retrieval Augmented Generation (RAG) · Natural Language Processing (NLP) · MiniLM · RoBERTa


## 1  Introduction

In today's digital age, user created content on platforms such as Amazon, Yelp, and Twitter have made sentiment analysis vital for understanding public opinion. Individuals share views on products, services, politics, and social issues, creating large volumes of valuable data that companies use to assess satisfaction, detect trends, and guide business decisions. Traditional NLP models like BERT and LSTM perform reasonably well but struggle with sarcasm, idioms, and evolving slang. To address these limits, researchers turned to more dynamic architectures like Retrieval Augmented Generation (RAG), which combines contextual embeddings with an external knowledge base [8]. By retrieving relevant context during inference, RAG models can better handle ambiguity, rare expressions, and



S. Mitra et al. (Eds.): PReMI 2025, LNCS 16358, pp. 465–472, 2026.
https://doi.org/10.1007/978-3-032-18480-1_47

shifting language patterns. This experimental study applies RAG to sentiment analysis using two contrasting datasets, Sentiment140 [14] (Twitter, short informal text) and the Amazon Food Reviews dataset [10] (structured long reviews). We compare a transformer classifier, RoBERTa(Robustly Optimized BERT) [9] against a RAG framework built with the MiniLM(Long Short-Term Memory) encoder [15] and FAISS (Facebook AI Similarity Search) retrieval [5]. We also examine domain specific fine tuning of the retriever to improve performance. Our dual evaluation demonstrates how RAG improves sentiment classification. While it outperforms RoBERTa on general data like tweets, its distinctive strength comes after fine tuning. This shows that the success of sentiment analysis does not depend only on built in knowledge but also on adapting to domain specific language. The paper is structured as follows, the related work is reviewed in Sect. 2, datasets are described in Sect. 3, methodology is explained in Sect. 4, the experimental setup is outlined in Sect. 5, results are presented in Sect. 6, challenges are discussed in Sect. 7, and Sect. 8 concludes with findings and future directions.

## 2    Related Works

Transformer based language models have improved significantly since BERT, with RoBERTa increasing performance through enhanced training and larger datasets [9]. Recent models like NeoBERT [2] and ModernBERT [16] optimize parameter efficiency and increase the context length upto 8,192 tokens, efficient attention mechanisms and improved layers to handle longer, complex inputs. Transformer architectures have also been adapted for diverse domains which includes computer vision, multimodal data, tactile sensing and medical imaging.

RAG systems enhance the capabilities of LLM's by integrating them with external knowledge bases. These systems often use Dense Passage Retrieval (DPR) [6] techniques to dynamically identify and fetch relevant information during inference. This RAG framework is modular and combines three components, retrievers that locate relevant documents, rankers that reorder the retrieved results to emphasize the most contextually relevant content, and generators that produce accurate outputs based on this information. RAG has also been extended beyond purely textual inputs and introduced VideoRAG [4], which retrieves video segments alongside text. Additionally, compact variants like MiniRAG [3] demonstrate that it is possible to maintain robust performance while significantly reducing the computational resources and storage requirements.

Fine-tuning is critical for adapting pretrained models to specialized domains like scientific, biomedical or legal text where general models struggle with capturing domain specific terminology. Domain adapted variants like SciBERT [1] and BioBERT [7] illustrate this approach, as they are pretrained on large scientific and biomedical corpora leading to substantial performance gains in their targeted areas. Parameter efficient fine-tuning techniques provide cost effective alternatives, and it improves both accuracy and robustness across varied applications.

# 3   Dataset Description

## 3.1   Sentiment140 Dataset

The Sentiment140 dataset [14] contains 1.6M tweets labeled using emoticons for sentiment polarity. For this study, a balanced subset of 5,000 tweets (2,500 positive, 2,500 negative) was used. Only the text and polarity fields were kept, excluding neutral samples (polarity = 2) to maintain a binary structure (0 = negative, 4 = positive). Preprocessing included lowercasing, removal of user mentions, URLs, special characters, and emoticons, followed by tokenization with HuggingFace's tokenizer [17]. Fine-tuning was performed on 30,000 tweets.

## 3.2   Amazon Food Reviews Dataset

The Amazon Food Reviews dataset [10] contains over 500,000 product reviews. For evaluation, 6,000 samples were selected with 2,000 reviews per class (negative, neutral, positive), using only the Score and Text fields. For fine-tuning, 30,000 samples (10,000 per class) were used (Table 1).

**Table 1.** Comparison of Sentiment140 and Amazon Food Reviews datasets

| Dataset features | Sentiment140 | Amazon Food Reviews |
|---|---|---|
| Total number of tweets/reviews | 1.6M tweets | 568,454 reviews |
| Classes/Labels | 0-Negative, 2-Neutral, 4-Positive | Score 1–2: Negative, 3: Neutral, 4–5: Positive |
| Average text/review length | 70–100 characters | 200–300 words |
| Metadata fields | polarity, id, date, query, user, text | Id, ProductId, UserId, ProfileName, HelpfulnessNumerator, HelpfulnessDenominator, Score, Time, Summary, Text |
| Fields used | Text and polarity | Score and text |

# 4   Methodology

## 4.1   Standard Sentiment Classification (Without RAG)

As a baseline, we implemented sentiment classification using the pre-trained transformer, cardiffnlp/twitter-roberta-base-sentiment-latest, a RoBERTa variant that is optimized for Twitter tasks [9]. RoBERTa is suited for sentiment analysis since it improves upon BERT through larger scale training and better optimization. The model was evaluated on Sentiment140 [14] and Amazon Food Reviews [10]. Preprocessing involved tokenization with HuggingFace's tokenizer [17], converting raw text into token IDs with special tokens and padding. The tokenized inputs were passed through RoBERTa to get sentiment probabilities, with the highest probability class selected as the label. For Sentiment140, only positive (4) and negative (0) samples were used, resulting in binary classification. Performance was measured using accuracy, precision, recall, and F1 score which was obtained through the library, scikit-learn [12]. This baseline provides as a reference for evaluating improvements introduced by RAG based frameworks.

## 4.2 RAG Based Sentiment Classification (k-NN over Encoded Knowledge Base)

For RAG based classification, we used a lightweight sentence transformer, the all-MiniLM-L6-v2 model [15]. It was used to encode the knowledge base for both the Sentiment140 and Amazon Food Reviews datasets. For each dataset, a sizable subset was taken and embedded into dense vectors via MiniLM and captured the subtle semantic framework of the content from each domain. To implement fast similarity search amongst these embeddings, we indexed the knowledge bases using the FAISS library [5]. During inference, each test input was similarly encoded with the MiniLM model and using the cosine similarity method, the five nearest neighbours from the corresponding knowledge base were retrieved. This ensured that the most semantically relevant examples were selected regardless of the dataset. The predicted sentiment label for each test instance was obtained by applying a majority vote to the sentiment labels of the retrieved neighbors. This k-NN over embeddings approach closely simulates a RAG framework [8]. This framework smoothly adjusts to various text types by utilizing profound sentence embeddings and efficient retrieval methods, and eliminates the necessity to retrain the encoder for each specific use case.

## 4.3 Fine-Tuning MiniLM for Domain Adaptation

To improve retrieval quality and sentiment classification, the MiniLM model [15] was fine tuned on balanced subsets of both datasets. For the Amazon Food Reviews dataset, 30,000 reviews were sampled equally across three classes (10,000 each for positive, negative, and neutral). For Sentiment140, 30,000 tweets were selected and split evenly between positive and negative labels (15,000 each for positive and negative). Fine-tuning was performed over 5 epochs with a triplet loss function [13], which pulls semantically similar samples closer together while separating dissimilar ones. This adaptation accounts for the datasets' linguistic differences with Amazon Food Reviews having structured, domain specific reviews and informal, slang heavy text in Sentiment140, allowing MiniLM to capture the sentiment variations better before integrating it into the RAG framework (Fig. 1).

## 5    Experimental Setup

This study used a combination of state of the art libraries and carefully prepared datasets to build and evaluate the sentiment classification framework.

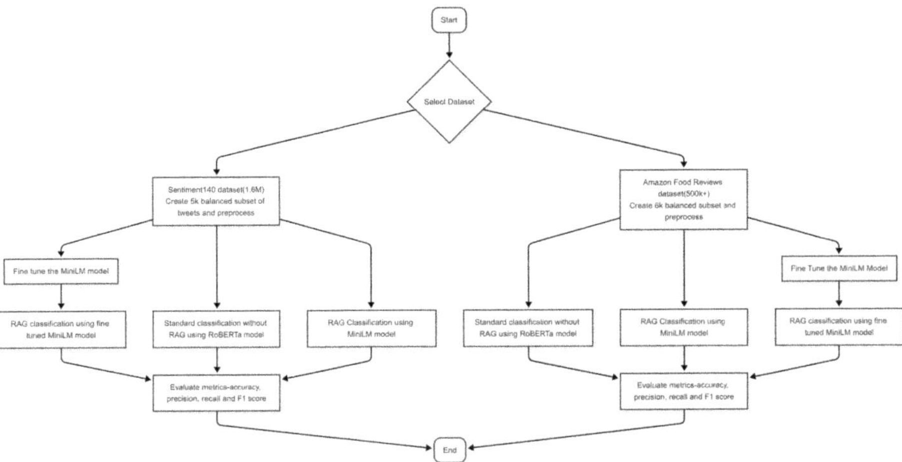

**Fig. 1.** Workflow of Dataset Selection, Classification, and Evaluation using RoBERTa and MiniLM Models.

The key tools and libraries included were Transformers (HuggingFace) [17], Sentence Transformers, FAISS [5], Scikit-learn [12] and PyTorch [11]. For the Sentiment140 [14] dataset, a subset of tweets was selected for testing and neutral tweets were removed to simplify the task into binary classification, considering only positive and negative samples. A knowledge base of 100,000 tweets was constructed for the RAG framework. These tweets were embedded into dense vectors using the MiniLM model [15] and indexed with FAISS [5] for efficient neighbor retrieval. Additionally, MiniLM was fine-tuned on a balanced set of tweets, which helped the model better understand the informal style and slang typical of Twitter.

For the Amazon Food Reviews dataset, a fine-tuning subset of 30,000 reviews was created, with equal representation of positive, negative, and neutral samples. The MiniLM encoder [15] was fine-tuned on this subset to adapt to the domain. A knowledge base of 90,000 reviews was then built and indexed within the RAG framework [8].

## 6   Results

The following results summarize the performance of standard and RAG-based sentiment classification models across both datasets. The evaluation was done using metrics like accuracy, precision, recall and F1 score.

### 6.1   Sentiment140 Dataset

The Retrieval Augmented Generation (RAG) approach significantly outperformed the standard RoBERTa model on the Sentiment140 dataset. As given in Table 2, the MiniLM based RAG model achieved an accuracy and F1 score of 0.7130, compared to RoBERTa's 0.5918 and 0.4572. This highlights RAG's strength in using semantically relevant examples from a knowledge base and it is especially effective for informal social media text. Additional progress was made by fine-tuning the MiniLM model on a balanced Sentiment140 subset, resulting in an accuracy and F1 score of 0.8084. This surpassed both the untuned RAG and RoBERTa models, demonstrating the advantage of combining RAG with domain specific fine-tuning for sentiment analysis in informal text.

**Table 2.** Performance on Sentiment140 dataset

| Model | Accuracy | Precision | Recall | F1 score |
|---|---|---|---|---|
| RoBERTa (Without RAG) | 0.5918 | 0.5471 | 0.3945 | 0.4572 |
| MiniLM (RAG, no fine tuning) | 0.7130 | 0.7131 | 0.7130 | 0.7130 |
| MiniLM (RAG after fine tuning) | 0.8084 | 0.8086 | 0.8084 | 0.8084 |

## 6.2   Amazon Food Reviews Dataset

The Amazon Food Reviews dataset [10] emphasizes the need for domain specific adaptation in RAG models. The initial MiniLM based RAG model performed badly with an F1 score of 0.3664 which is lower than the RoBERTa baseline of 0.5918. This was mainly due to the dataset's complex language and nuanced sentiment. After fine-tuning on 30,000 Amazon reviews, performance improved significantly with the fine tuned RAG model achieving an F1 score of 0.6996 and accuracy of 0.7137, passing both the untuned model and RoBERTa. These results show the effectiveness of fine tuning for adapting RAG to specialized domains (Table 3).

**Table 3.** Performance on Amazon Food Reviews dataset

| Model | Accuracy | Precision | Recall | F1 Score |
|---|---|---|---|---|
| RoBERTa (Without RAG) | 0.6387 | 0.6264 | 0.6387 | 0.5918 |
| MiniLM (RAG before fine tuning) | 0.4417 | 0.5549 | 0.4417 | 0.3664 |
| MiniLM (RAG after fine tuning) | 0.7137 | 0.7135 | 0.7137 | 0.6996 |

## 7   Discussion

RAG-based sentiment classification significantly outperformed transformer models like RoBERTa [9] on the Sentiment140 dataset. By retrieving semantically similar tweets from a large knowledge base using k-NN search, the MiniLM driven RAG model [15] delivered strong results. However, this approach struggled on the Amazon Food Reviews dataset due to longer texts and specialized vocabulary. MiniLM embeddings were less effective in such contexts, causing RAG to underperform compared to RoBERTa. Fine-tuning the retriever improved retrieval relevance and boosted both accuracy and F1 scores. Applying fine tuning to Sentiment140 [14] further enhanced performance, showing that retrieval and domain adaptation are both essential for robust sentiment analysis across varied text types. But these advantages come with trade-offs, FAISS [5] based retrieval introduces computational overhead and classification accuracy heavily depends on retrieval quality which can be affected by noisy or imbalanced data. Nevertheless, RAG with fine-tuning remains an effective strategy across both informal and structured domains if resource use and data quality are well managed.

## 8    Conclusions

The use of RAG improved sentiment classification on the Sentiment140 dataset and outperformed standard models like RoBERTa. However, on the Amazon Food Reviews dataset, the MiniLM based RAG model initially underperformed due to domain mismatch. Fine-tuning the model on domain specific data for both datasets resolved this issue and produced measurable gains. These findings demonstrate the value of RAG in sentiment analysis and highlight the importance of domain adaptation for optimal performance. Although RAG introduces some computational overhead, it remains a promising and flexible approach. Future work can explore more advanced retrieval methods such as Dense Passage Retrieval [6] to enhance efficiency and context awareness, particularly in domains like legal research and question answering. Extending RAG to multimodal data like text, images and audio also offers opportunities in personalized education. RAG does not depend solely on large datasets but rather more on high quality, domain specific data, as shown in healthcare applications. Innovations like neural search optimization and low latency indexing could further strengthen RAG for high stakes settings such as emergency response and financial forecasting.

## References


1. Beltagy, I., Lo, K., Cohan, A.: SciBERT: a pretrained language model for scientific text (2019). https://arxiv.org/abs/1903.10676
2. Breton, L.L., Fournier, Q., Mezouar, M.E., Morris, J.X., Chandar, S.: NeoBERT: a next-generation BERT. arXiv preprint arXiv:2502.19587 (2025)
3. Fan, T., Wang, J., Ren, X., Huang, C.: MiniRAG: towards extremely simple retrieval-augmented generation (2025). https://arxiv.org/abs/2501.06713
4. Jeong, S., Kim, K., Baek, J., Hwang, S.J.: VideoRAG: retrieval-augmented generation over video corpus (2025). https://arxiv.org/abs/2501.05874

5. Johnson, J., Douze, M., Jégou, H.: Billion-scale similarity search with FAISS (2017). https://github.com/facebookresearch/faiss
6. Karpukhin, V., et al.: Dense passage retrieval for open-domain question answering (2020). https://arxiv.org/abs/2004.04906
7. Lee, J., et al.: BioBERT: a pre-trained biomedical language representation model for biomedical text mining. Bioinformatics 36(4), 1234–1240 (2019)
8. Lewis, P., et al.: Retrieval-augmented generation for knowledge-intensive NLP tasks (2021). https://arxiv.org/abs/2005.11401
9. Liu, Y., et al.: RoBERTa: a robustly optimized BERT pretraining approach (2019). https://arxiv.org/abs/1907.11692
10. McAuley, J., Leskovec, J.: Amazon fine food reviews: Stanford Network Analysis Project (SNAP) (2013). Available on Kaggle: https://www.kaggle.com/datasets/snap/amazon-fine-food-reviews
11. Paszke, A., et al.: PyTorch: an imperative style, high-performance deep learning library (2019). https://arxiv.org/abs/1912.01703
12. Pedregosa, F., et al.: Scikit-learn: machine learning in python. J. Mach. Learn. Res. 12(85), 2825–2830 (2011). http://jmlr.org/papers/v12/pedregosa11a.html
13. Schroff, F., Kalenichenko, D., Philbin, J.: FaceNet: a unified embedding for face recognition and clustering. In: 2015 IEEE Conference on Computer Vision and Pattern Recognition (CVPR), pp. 815–823. IEEE (2015). https://doi.org/10.1109/cvpr.2015.7298682. http://dx.doi.org/10.1109/CVPR.2015.7298682
14. Unknown: Sentiment140 dataset with 1.6 million tweets (2017). https://www.kaggle.com/datasets/kazanova/sentiment140
15. Wang, W., Wei, F., Dong, L., Bao, H., Yang, N., Zhou, M.: MiniLM: deep self-attention distillation for task-agnostic compression of pre-trained transformers (2020). https://arxiv.org/abs/2002.10957
16. Warner, B., et al.: Smarter, better, faster, longer: a modern bidirectional encoder for fast, memory efficient, and long context finetuning and inference (2024). https://arxiv.org/abs/2412.13663
17. Wolf, T., et al.: Huggingface's transformers: state-of-the-art natural language processing (2020). https://arxiv.org/abs/1910.03771

# Adaptive Hybrid Retrieval-Augmented Generation for Document-Based QA: Implementation and Multi-metric Evaluation


Aparajita Sinha[✉] [iD], Mriganka Das[iD], and Kunal Chakma[iD]

National Institute of Technology, Agartala, Agartala, Tripura, India
`asinha.22odcsw002@phd.nita.ac.in`, `mrigankad49@gmail.com`,
`kchakma.cse@nita.ac.in`



**Abstract.** Document-based question answering has been transformed by Retrieval-Augmented Generation, which blends information retrieval and generative models. Traditional methods often use fixed retrieval strategies and uniform chunking, which can limit performance across diverse document types. This paper introduces an Adaptive Hybrid RAG pipeline that adjusts preprocessing and retrieval according to document structure. The pipeline employs chunking classifiers, applying section-level segmentation to structured documents and paragraph-level segmentation to narrative texts. Semantic retrieval is conducted with FAISS, and responses are generated using Mistral-7B. Evaluations on DocuQA (20 PDFs) and SQuAD v2.0 (over 100,000 QA pairs) show strong semantic understanding (BERTScore 0.837 and 0.785) despite low exact-match BLEU scores (0.045 and 0.0012). Analysis indicates that retrieval quality and context continuity significantly influence answer accuracy, highlighting the importance of structure-aware chunking and multi-metric evaluation for practical RAG-based QA systems.

**Keywords:** Retrieval-Augmented Generation · Document-Based Question Answering · Adaptive Chunking · Semantic Retrieval · Dense Embeddings · Multi-Metric Evaluation


## 1 Introduction

Retrieval-Augmented Generation (RAG) enhances question answering (QA) by amalgamating extensive language models with external retrieval, yielding responses that are both precise and contextually relevant [11,15]. Complex, heterogeneous documents benefit greatly from this strategy. However, current RAG systems frequently rely on fixed chunking and single retrieval methods, which limits adaptability. Retrieval relevance strongly affects answer quality, but standard evaluation metrics capture only part of a system's performance. This limitation emphasizes the need for flexible retrieval and segmentation methods combined with comprehensive, multi-metric evaluation. This study suggests a RAG pipeline that combines adaptive document preprocessing, dynamic retrieval (dense and sparse), and advanced generation models with the goal of developing a domain-sensitive QA system. The pipeline distinguishes between narrative and structured sources by tailoring its steps to the document structure and the query intent. It combines lexical and semantic retrieval to surface relevant content, and uses a multimetric framework to evaluate accuracy, coherence and usefulness. A lightweight classifier that leverages linguistic and structural features guides segmentation while preserving semantic continuity and organisational context. For narratives, this chunking is used at the paragraph level; for structured documents, it is used at the section level. For the retrieval stage, we employed dense retrieval strategies, employing FAISS [5] (Facebook AI Similarity Search) for effective similarity search and the all-MiniLM-L6-v2 model[1] to generate semantic embeddings. This enables the system to find deeper semantic links between the queries and the content chunks, providing the generation model with richer and more relevant contexts. The top-k retrieved passages are used by an instruction-tuned large language model, like Mistral-7B-Instruct [10], to produce responses that are logical and pertinent to the context. System performance is then evaluated using the four complementary metrics BERTScore [14], ROUGE-L [3], Jaccard Similarity [9], and BLEU [17]. Jaccard measures set-based similarity, BERTScore gauges semantic alignment using contextual embeddings, and BLEU and ROUGE highlight lexical and n-gram overlap. For thorough analysis, two benchmark datasets are used: SQuAD v2.0 [18], which consists of lengthy narrative passages, and DocuQA [15], which is sourced from structured sources such as *reports*, *tables*, and *forms*. The suggested pipeline can be rigorously evaluated on both structured and unstructured document types thanks to this dual-dataset setup. The structure of the paper is as follows. The literature is reviewed in Sect. 2, the methodology is described in Sect. 3, the results are presented in Sect. 4, the limitations are discussed in Sect. 5, and future directions are discussed in Sect. 6.

## 2    Related Works

Recent advances in RAG have addressed key challenges in document-based question answering (QA), including hybrid retrieval, domain adaptation, efficiency, structured data handling, security, and evaluation. Hybrid approaches show notable gains: Hybrid-SQuAD [20] combines text with knowledge graphs, boosting F1 by 6–8%, while a Multi-Source RAG framework [23] leverages SBERT [19] and ScaNN [7] to achieve 89.3% accuracy with improved efficiency. Domain-specific systems perform strongly in specialized settings. For example, FinSage [22] attains 92.1% compliance accuracy on financial filings, Two-Layer RAG [4] improves low-resource medical QA by 12% F1, and LongRAG [12] enhances long-context QA by 15%. Efficiency-focused methods, such as Self-RAG [1] and DeepRAG [6], reduce hallucinations and increase accuracy by

---

[1] https://huggingface.co/sentence-transformers/all-MiniLM-L6-v2.

8% and 21.9%, respectively. Structured QA benefits from T-RAG [16], while SafeRAG [13] suffers up to 48% correctness loss under adversarial noise. Evaluation frameworks like RAG-QA Arena [8] reveal robustness issues in domain transfer (58.9%), highlighting the need for metrics that jointly capture accuracy, adaptability, efficiency, and security. Despite these advances, many systems remain domain-specific, with limited multi-modal integration, adaptive retrieval, or structured data handling. To address these gaps, this study proposes a unified hybrid RAG pipeline with a multi-metric evaluation framework for comprehensive assessment.

## 3   Methodology

### 3.1   Dataset

The **SQuAD 2.0** [18] benchmark, comprising over 100,000 Wikipedia-based questions both answerable and unanswerable serves as a robust testbed for evaluating retrieval and answerability detection. The **DocuQA** [15] dataset includes twenty PDFs spanning technical papers, news articles, economic reports, and recipes, enabling the assessment of procedural, temporal, numerical, and factual reasoning. The composition of the dataset is summarized in Table 1.

**Table 1.** Summary of SQuAD 2.0 Benchmark and DocuQA System with Clear Dataset Descriptions.

| Component | Details |
|---|---|
| Benchmark | SQuAD 2.0 |
| Size & Source | 100,000+ QA pairs collected from Wikipedia articles. Includes both answerable and unanswerable questions. |
| Purpose | Evaluates retrieval accuracy and generative robustness of QA models on short passages. |
| System | DocuQA (Document-based Question Answering) |
| Corpus & Source | 20 PDFs spanning Technical Papers, News Articles, Economic Reports, and Recipes. Sources include academic publications, CNN News, economic summaries, and instructional recipes. |
| Purpose | Tests retrieval precision and generative fidelity across long documents, diverse formats, and multiple domains. |

### 3.2   Pipeline Design and Implementation

The proposed framework employs a **RAG** approach for **document-based question answering (DBQA)**, integrating preprocessing, embedding generation, retrieval, response construction, and evaluation within a unified pipeline

(Fig. 1). The **document corpus** includes structured texts, such as manuals and reports, and unstructured narratives, like articles and case descriptions. Text is extracted from PDFs using **PyMuPDF 5**[2], preserving layout and reading order. A **document type detection** module guides segmentation: sentence-level for structured texts and overlapping 300-word segments for narratives, maintaining semantic coherence and improving embedding quality for accurate retrieval and response generation.

The *all-MiniLM-L6-v2* model [21] is then used to transform the text segments into dense representations, resulting in embeddings of dimension **384**. Using the *IndexFlatL2* structure, these embeddings offer a semantic representation of every chunk and are stored in a **FAISS** index [5], allowing for effective similarity search across sizable collections. A **user query** is embedded in the same 384-dimensional space upon submission. The FAISS index's most pertinent segments are retrieved using a *top-k* nearest neighbor search. An instruction-tuned large language model (*Mistral-7B-Instruct*) receives the structured prompt created by combining the retrieved passages with the query. This stage enables the model to produce answers that are based on the evidence that was recovered. The Hugging Face pipeline is used to manage inference, taking care of hardware allocation, output formatting, and tokenization.

The generated answers are evaluated using a set of complementary metrics. **ROUGE-L** [3] measures alignment through longest common subsequence matching, **Jaccard similarity** [9] captures token-level overlap, **BLEU** [17] evaluates $n$-gram precision with a brevity adjustment, and **BERTScore** [14] estimates semantic similarity based on contextual embeddings. Together, these metrics provide a balanced view of lexical, structural, and semantic aspects of the generated text. In addition, a qualitative analysis is conducted to assess aspects such as coherence and interpretability that may not be fully captured by automated metrics.

For the experimental evaluation, two datasets were utilized: **DocumentQA** and **SQuAD v2.0**. In SQuAD v2.0, the first valid answer from each question's annotation was selected as the ground truth, whereas in DocumentQA, reference responses were extracted from the "Ground Truth" column of a CSV file and organized using a `pandas` DataFrame. To ensure uniform text processing, all responses were tokenized at the word level with NLTK's `word_tokenize` [2], allowing generated and reference answers to be compared under consistent linguistic conditions. Figure 1 displays the suggested RAG pipeline workflow.

## 4   Results and Analysis

### 4.1   Quantitative Analysis

The differences in performance reflect the characteristics of the datasets. DocuQA contains document-grounded questions where retrieval often identifies relevant passages, supporting closer alignment with reference answers. In

---

[2] https://pymupdf.readthedocs.io/en/latest/.

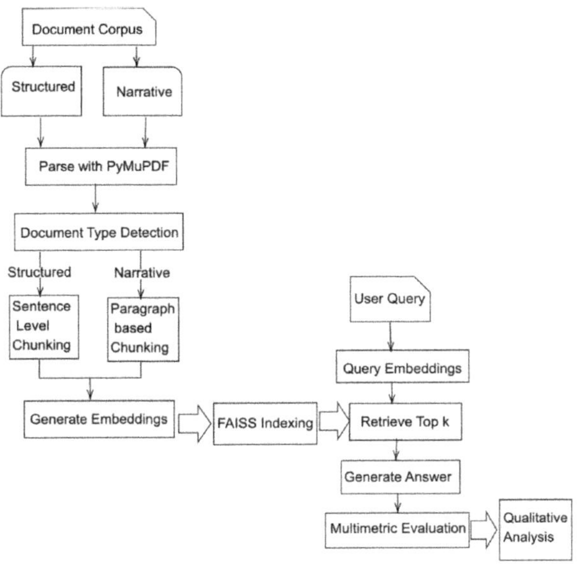


**Fig. 1.** Proposed RAG Pipeline Workflow: From document parsing to multi-metric evaluation.

contrast, SQuAD v2.0 includes queries requiring fine-grained reasoning and sometimes presents adversarial or ambiguous cases, which can reduce lexical overlap even when the underlying meaning is preserved. As reported in Table 2, SQuAD achieved BLEU 0.0012, ROUGE-L 0.09, Jaccard 0.07, and BERTScore 0.785, whereas DocuQA obtained BLEU 0.045, ROUGE-L 0.41, Jaccard 0.22, and BERTScore 0.837. These results suggest that DocuQA reflects retrieval performance more directly, while SQuAD highlights the challenges of maintaining semantic content when lexical overlap is limited.

**Table 2.** Comparison of Evaluation Metrics for DocuQA and SQuAD v2.0

| Dataset | BERTScore | BLEU | ROUGE-L | Jaccard |
| --- | --- | --- | --- | --- |
| DocuQA (20 PDFs) | 0.837 | 0.045 | 0.41 | 0.22 |
| SQuAD v2.0 (100k QA pairs) | 0.785 | 0.0012 | 0.09 | 0.07 |

## 4.2   Qualitative Analysis

The quality of retrieved passages has a direct impact on the responses generated in document-based question answering. Qualitative analysis shows that when relevant content is retrieved, the output remains close to the reference answer. For example, in response to the query *"What GitHub links of this framework?"*, the system reproduced the correct link https://github.com/zalandoresearch/ flair, with only minor variations in wording. Although these variations slightly reduced the BLEU score, the answer maintained strong semantic and lexical consistency, reflected by a BERTScore of 0.94 and a ROUGE-L of 0.56. Conversely, when retrieval failed to capture the appropriate passage, the generated response was often incomplete or generic. In the case of the query *"What is the proposed solution?"*, the system produced the short response "FLAIR," which led to lower semantic alignment (BERTScore of 0.78) and limited lexical overlap. These observations highlight the importance of effective retrieval for producing accurate and contextually faithful answers.

This pattern was consistently seen in the SQuAD and DocuQA datasets. Higher evaluation scores were obtained by the generated answers when the system retrieved the correct passages; on average, the ROUGE-L and BERTScore values were above 0.42 and 0.85, respectively. Lexical overlap was moderate and semantic similarity remained high, with a BERTScore of roughly 0.90, even when more context was added, such as "The capital city of Australia is Canberra" rather than just "Canberra". On the other hand, the model frequently hallucinates when irrelevant passages are retrieved, resulting in irrelevant responses. In these situations, the BERTScore often dropped below 0.80, and the ROUGE-L and BLEU scores were near zero. For instance, when passages about the "Cold War" were retrieved instead of those explaining the construction of the "Berlin Wall", semantic alignment dropped to a BERTScore of approximately 0.63. These results emphasize the critical importance of precise retrieval for reliable answer generation.

In conclusion, experiments on the full SQuAD v2.0 and DocuQA datasets indicate that retrieval accuracy is the key factor influencing answer quality. When relevant passages are retrieved, responses achieve high semantic fidelity (BERTScore 0.837, ROUGE-L 0.41). Conversely, misaligned retrieval leads to notable drops in performance (BERTScore 0.78, ROUGE-L near 0). These results underscore retrieval as the primary bottleneck in RAG pipelines and point to the need for more reliable, semantically informed retrieval strategies to enhance the robustness of document-based QA systems.

## 5    Limitations

RAG systems face the challenge of **context fragmentation**, where dividing documents into smaller segments can disrupt continuity and omit relevant details, affecting response accuracy in longer or structured texts such as DocuQA. Strategies like overlapping or adaptive segmentation offer partial relief, but maintaining semantic flow remains difficult. In contrast, for datasets like SQuAD v2.0, where passages already fit within an LLM's context window, retrieval primarily anchors responses to evidence, reducing unsupported or hallucinated outputs. These observations suggest that the impact of retrieval depends on dataset characteristics. In this study, a fixed 300-word chunk size with overlap was used for scalability, but such length-based segmentation may disrupt discourse boundaries and coherence. Future work could explore structure- or meaning-aware segmentation to enhance answer quality.

# 6    Conclusion

This study examined RAG performance on the SQuAD v2.0 and DocuQA datasets. The results indicate that DocuQA supported relatively better semantic consistency, while SQuAD involved more complex reasoning and contained several ambiguous queries. Retrieval effectiveness appeared to be a major factor influencing answer quality, although challenges such as context fragmentation and dataset-specific limitations were also observed. These observations suggest that retrieval strategies should be adapted to dataset characteristics to improve the coherence and reliability of RAG-based question answering.

# References


1. Asai, A., Wu, Z., Wang, Y., Sil, A., Hajishirzi, H.: Self-RAG: learning to retrieve, generate, and critique through self-reflection. ArXiv (2024)
2. Bird, S., Klein, E., Loper, E.: Natural Language Processing with Python: Analyzing Text With the Natural Language Toolkit. O'Reilly Media, Inc. (2009)
3. Chin-Yew, L.: Rouge: a package for automatic evaluation of summaries. In: Proceedings of the Workshop on Text Summarization Branches Out, 2004 (2004)
4. Das, S., et al.: Two-layer retrieval augmented generation framework for low-resource medical question-answering: proof of concept using reddit data. CoRR (2024)
5. Douze, M., et al.: The Faiss library (2025). https://arxiv.org/abs/2401.08281
6. Guan, X., et al.: DeepRAG: thinking to retrieve step by step for large language models. arXiv preprint arXiv:2502.01142 (2025)
7. Guo, R., et al.: Accelerating large-scale inference with anisotropic vector quantization. In: International Conference on Machine Learning, pp. 3887–3896. PMLR (2020)
8. Han, R., et al.: RAG-QA arena: evaluating domain robustness for long-form retrieval augmented question answering. arXiv preprint arXiv:2407.13998 (2024)
9. Jaccard, P.: Étude comparative de la distribution florale dans une portion des alpes et des jura. Bull. Soc. Vaudoise Sci. Nat. **37**, 547–579 (1901)
10. Jiang, D., et al.: From CLIP to DINO: visual encoders shout in multi-modal large language models. arXiv preprint arXiv:2310.08825 (2023)
11. Jiang, Z., et al.: Towards enterprise-specific question-answering for it operations and maintenance based on retrieval-augmented generation mechanism (2024). Available at SSRN 5069318
12. Jiang, Z., Ma, X., Chen, W.: LongRAG: enhancing retrieval-augmented generation with long-context LLMs. arXiv preprint arXiv:2406.15319 (2024)
13. Liang, X., et al.: SafeRAG: benchmarking security in retrieval-augmented generation of large language model. arXiv preprint arXiv:2501.18636 (2025)
14. Motger, Q., Miaschi, A., Dell'Orletta, F., Franch, X., Marco, J.: Leveraging encoder-only large language models for mobile app review feature extraction. Empir. Softw. Eng. **30**(3), 104 (2025)

15. Muludi, K., Fitria, K.M., Triloka, J., et al.: Retrieval-augmented generation approach: Document question answering using large language model. Int. J. Adv. Comput. Sci. Appl. **15**(3) (2024)
16. Pan, F., Canim, M., Glass, M., Gliozzo, A., Hendler, J.: End-to-end table question answering via retrieval-augmented generation. arXiv preprint arXiv:2203.16714 (2022)
17. Papineni, K., Roukos, S., Ward, T., Zhu, W.J.: BLEU: a method for automatic evaluation of machine translation. In: Proceedings of the 40th annual meeting of the Association for Computational Linguistics, pp. 311–318 (2002)
18. Rajpurkar, P., Jia, R., Liang, P.: Know what you don't know: unanswerable questions for squad. arXiv preprint arXiv:1806.03822 (2018)
19. Reimers, N., Gurevych, I.: Sentence-BERT: sentence embeddings using Siamese BERT-networks. arXiv preprint arXiv:1908.10084 (2019)
20. Taffa, T.A., Banerjee, D., Assabie, Y., Usbeck, R.: Hybrid-squad: hybrid scholarly question answering dataset. arXiv preprint arXiv:2412.02788 (2024)
21. Wang, W., Wei, F., Dong, L., Bao, H., Yang, N., Zhou, M.: MiniLM: deep self-attention distillation for task-agnostic compression of pre-trained transformers. Adv. Neural. Inf. Process. Syst. **33**, 5776–5788 (2020)
22. Wang, X., et al.: FinSage: a multi-aspect RAG system for financial filings question answering. arXiv preprint arXiv:2504.14493 (2025)
23. Wu, R., Chen, S., Su, X., Zhu, Y., Liao, Y., Wu, J.: A multi-source retrieval question answering framework based on RAG. In: 2024 5th International Conference on Information Science, Parallel and Distributed Systems (ISPDS), pp. 644–647. IEEE (2024)

# FLARE: Enhancing Few-Shot Missing Triple Prediction via Attention-Guided Subgraph Reasoning


Vivek Kaspa(iD), Yashwanth Arikathota(iD), Mukesh Eppili(iD),
and Hima Bindu Kommanti(✉)(iD)

Department of Computer Science and Engineering, National Institute of Technology
Andhra Pradesh, Andhra Pradesh, India
`himabinduk@nitandhra.ac.in`



**Abstract.** Knowledge Graph Completion (KGC) involves predicting missing entities or relations. In few-shot KGC, reasoning over unseen relations from only a handful of examples is like solving a mystery with just a few scattered clues. While existing methods have made progress using translational, bilinear, deep learning and few-shot learning approaches, challenges in few-shot relational reasoning remain. Current few-shot learning approaches like Connection Subgraph Reasoner (CSR) cast the problem in subgraph-based edge-mask learning framework, where the model solely relies on the graph representations of the retrieved subgraphs assuming largest common subgraph shared across all support subgraphs. However, these approaches lead to unrelated spurious information that can adversely impact performance of prediction of the missing entity. We introduce FLARE (Few-shot Learning with Attention-guided Relational Subgraph Reasoner), a novel framework that improves KGC by leveraging MLP-based edge attention mechanism for edge scoring, refined node aggregation with attention-weighted edge embeddings and adaptive support graph pooling. The model was evaluated on NELL, FB15K-237 and ConceptNet datasets. Experimental results demonstrate that FLARE consistently outperforms existing baselines across all metrics, thus achieving new state-of-the-art performance.

**Keywords:** Pattern Recognition · Representation Learning · Deep Learning · Cognitive Computing · Computational Intelligence · Few-shot Knowledge Graph Completion


## 1 Introduction

KG completion aims to infer missing edges in a KG, which represents human knowledge as triplets <source entity, relation, target entity>. If a detective learns a few support triplets such as <knife, ⋈, bloody handprint>, <Footprints, ⋈, muddy shoes>, etc., the aim is to predict the query triples of the same unseen relation e.g., (weapon, ⋈, ?). KGs are widely adopted for tasks such as semantic search, virtual assistants, biomedical knowledge extraction, and personalized


© The Author(s), under exclusive license to Springer Nature Switzerland AG 2026
S. Mitra et al. (Eds.): PReMI 2025, LNCS 16358, pp. 481–493, 2026.
https://doi.org/10.1007/978-3-032-18480-1_49

recommendations. However, they are often sparse and incomplete, which hampers their utility in downstream applications. To address this, KG Completion (KGC) techniques have been developed to predict missing triples.

However, in real-world rapidly evolving domains like social media, news feeds or medical records, new entities and relations emerge frequently. Conventional KGC approaches often fail to generalize under data-sparse conditions. To tackle this, the Few-shot Knowledge Graph Completion (FS-KGC) paradigm has gained significant attention. FKGC aims to predict missing triples for relations with only limited support triplets. To address the research gaps mentioned in Sect. 2, we propose FLARE (**F**ew-shot **L**earning with **A**ttention-guided **RE**lational Subgraph Reasoner), a novel approach that leverages attention-based edge weighting, enhanced feature aggregation and adaptive support graph pooling to improve few-shot relational reasoning. The main contributions are summarized as follows:

1. We introduce an MLP-based Edge Attention module that assigns softmax-normalized self-attention scores to edges in the contextualized support and query subgraphs.
2. We enhance the original PathCon weighted $L$-iteration path graph aggregation process ($P_w$) by incorporating an attention-based mechanism, updating node embeddings with attention-weighted edge embeddings.
3. We redefine the global support graph embedding $g_{all}$, a unified representation that aggregates information from all support graphs, by incorporating adaptive weighting mechanism to enhance the effectiveness of global aggregation.
4. Extensive experiments on three few-shot datasets, NELL, ConceptNet and FB15K-237, demonstrate that FLARE outperforms existing FS-KGC methods with ablation study validating the effectiveness of each module.

## 2  Related Work

This section summarizes the prior work on KGC, focusing on embedding-based and few-shot approaches. Embedding-based methods are categorized into translational, bilinear and neural-based models. Few-shot KGC methods are grouped into meta-learning and subgraph-based frameworks.

### 2.1  Embedding-Based Models

Most existing KGC methods are based on the embedding paradigm. Translational distance approaches, most notably introduced by TransE [1], embeds entities and relations as vectors and models relations as translations from source to target entities in embedding space ($\mathbf{h} + \mathbf{r} \approx \mathbf{t}$). Variants such as STransE [2] and RotatE [3] introduce semantic projections and rotations. While efficient, these models lack the capacity for fine-grained relational reasoning required in few-shot settings. FLARE addresses this through attention-guided subgraph modeling.

Bilinear models (e.g., RESCAL [4], DistMult [5]) and multiplicative models (e.g., ComplEx [6], HolE [7]) capture entity-relation interactions via tensor or complex-valued operations, yet ignore localized subgraph structures and use uniform feature aggregation. FLARE improves over these by incorporating adaptive, edge-weighted subgraph aggregation.

Deep Neural models like ConvE [8], Hypernetwork-based methods [9] and NTNs [10] employ CNNs or tensor-based architectures but require extensive training data and assume uniform neighbor aggregation. Graph Convolutional Networks for KGs [11] propagate features through multi-hop neighborhoods to learn relational embeddings assuming uniform edge importance. More recent GNNs such as Neural Bellman-Ford networks [12] generalize message passing via dynamic path-based reasoning. FLARE employs learnable MLP-based attention to weigh edges and neighbors adaptively, improving relational reasoning. Additionally, subgraph-based GNNs such as GraIL [13] enhance generalization via inductive subgraph reasoning, influencing FLARE's design for structured subgraph pooling.

## 2.2  Few-Shot KGC Models

Few-shot KGC aims to generalize to unseen relations with limited supervision. Meta-learning methods such as GMatching [15] and MetaR [16] adapt to new relations via metric learning and fast adaptation, but often struggle in complex relational scenarios due to simple pooling and weak subgraph utilization. Subsequent approaches [17,18] enhance few-shot reasoning by integrating neighborhood and path information, yet still rely on shallow aggregation strategies.

Subgraph-based edge-mask approaches like CSR [19] extract and enhance subgraph representations for better structural reasoning in few-shot missing triplet prediction. However, they assume that the largest shared subgraph across support graphs is sufficient to capture the unseen target relation, which often fails in practice. Extracted subgraph masks often contain irrelevant information, negatively impacting prediction performance. SAFER [20] improves by excluding spurious information from support graphs, but FLARE outperforms these subgraph approaches with attention-based edge weighting and adaptive subgraph pooling.

# 3   Proposed Methodology: FLARE Framework

This section presents the detailed explanation of the proposed framework, FLARE.

## 3.1   Contextual Enclosing Subgraph Extraction

**Definition 1.** *Let $G = (V, E)$ be a graph where $V$ is the set of nodes and $E$ is the set of edges. A contextual enclosing subgraph around a target link $(h, t)$ is defined as the subgraph $G_{h,t}$ induced by nodes within $k$ hops of $h$ and $t$.*

Inspired by the works in [19,20], FLARE utilizes the enclosing subgraphs i.e. subgraphs induced by all nodes within the $k$-hop neighborhoods of both the

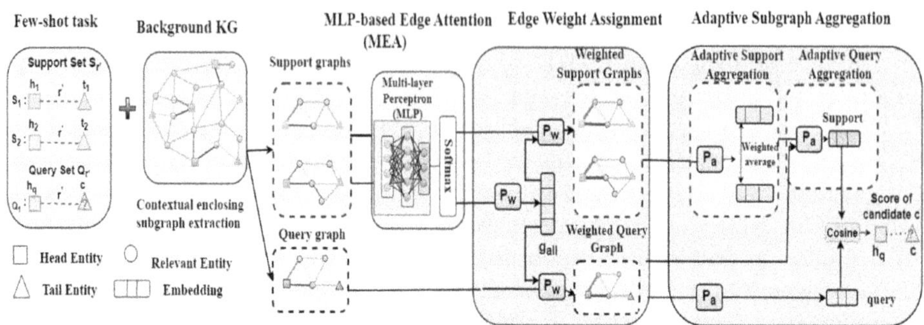


**Fig. 1.** Model architecture of the FLARE framework. FLARE operates through a modular pipeline comprising contextual enclosing subgraph extraction, MLP-based edge attention module and adaptive subgraph aggregation to evaluate candidate tail entities for a given query relation $r'$. Identical relations are color-coded, while unrelated relations are shown in gray. Edge thickness reflects the attention weights assigned during the scoring process.

head ($h$) and tail ($t$) entities, combined with randomly sampled neighbors ($k = 1, 2$). As illustrated in Fig. 1, FLARE initially extracts contextualized subgraphs corresponding to each support and query triplet.

### 3.2   MLP-Based Edge Attention

The MLP-based Edge Attention (MEA) mechanism is leveraged to dynamically assign attention weights to edges in the support subgraphs, enabling the model to emphasize more relevant edges when updating node representations. Each edge embedding $\mathbf{b}_i^e$ is passed through a Multi-Layer Perceptron (MLP), a learnable function processes the input edge embeddings and outputs transformed scores, which are used in the subsequent computation of attention weights. Following the transformation, self-attention computation is applied to obtain softmax-normalized attention scores for each edge. The attention weight $\alpha_i^e$ for an edge $e$ connected to a node $i$ is defined as:

$$\alpha_i^e = \frac{\exp(\mathrm{MLP}(b_i^e))}{\sum_{e' \in N(v)} \exp(\mathrm{MLP}(b_i^{e'}))} \tag{1}$$

where, $N(v)$ denotes the set of neighboring edges of the node $v$.

Once the attention scores are computed, MEA proceeds to the aggregation phase. In this step, the node representation $b_i^v$ is updated through an attention-weighted average of its neighboring edge embeddings $b_i^e$. The updated node embedding is given by:

$$b_i^v = \frac{1}{1 + |\{e \mid e \in N(v)\}|} \sum_{e \in N(v)} \alpha_i^e b_i^e \tag{2}$$

Equation (2) assigns higher importance to more significant edges in the final representation of node $v$, by weighting each edge $e \in N(v)$ with attention score $\alpha_i^e$.

### 3.3  Attention-Based Edge Weight Assignment

The proposed framework, FLARE leverages the PathCon [14] as the graph encoder, which generates graph embeddings via message passing between nodes. Unlike GNNs that rely solely on neighborhood aggregation, PathCon evaluates graph isomorphism by alternating message passing between nodes and edges in the KG, enabling effective assessment of structural similarity between subgraphs. Notably, PathCon models relationships based on connectivity patterns rather than the specific identities of nodes.

**$P_w$ L-iteration PathCon Aggregation Process.**

We adopt the $P_w$ L-iteration PathCon weighted aggregation process introduced in the SAFER framework [20]. An aggregation function $P_w$ as depicted in Fig. 1, is applied to assign weights to all edges. At each iteration $i$, the embedding of a node $v$ is updated by aggregating the embeddings of its incident edges. The update rule is given by $r_v^i = b_v^i \,\|\, \mathbb{1}(v = h) \,\|\, \mathbb{1}(v = t)$, where the representation of node $v$ at iteration $i$, denoted $r_v^i$, is formed by concatenating its embedding with indicator variables. Then, the embeddings of edges are updated at iteration $i+1$ according to $b_e^{i+1} = f\left(r_u^i \,\|\, r_v^i \,\|\, b_e^i\right)$ and finally, a graph-level representation is obtained via $g(G) = \mathrm{MaxPool}\left(\{b_v^L \mid v \in V\}\right) \,\|\, b_h^L \,\|\, b_t^L$.

**Graph-Level Aggregation and Adaptive Support Weighting.** The objective is to assign weights to all edges in the contextualized graphs based on their importance to the target relation. To achieve this, an embedding $g_{\mathrm{all}}$ is computed over the support graphs. Specifically, each support graph embedding $g(G_s^k)$ is assigned a weight $w_k$, and the overall support embedding is computed as the weighted average:

$$g_{all} = \frac{1}{K} \sum_k w_k \, g(G_s^k) \tag{3}$$

The weight $w_k$ for each support graph is determined using a softmax function applied to the outputs of a multilayer perceptron (MLP): $w_k = \mathrm{softmax}\left(\mathrm{MLP}(g(G_s^k))\right)$. This ensures that the weights are normalized and emphasize the more informative graphs relative to the task. In addition to weighting the entire support graphs, individual edge weights are also computed. Each edge weight $w_e$ is obtained by applying a linear transformation followed by a sigmoid activation to the edge feature representation from the final layer: $w_e = \mathrm{sigmoid}\left(\mathrm{Linear}(b_e^L)\right)$ [20].

### 3.4  Adaptive Subgraph Aggregation

After applying edge weights, subgraph embeddings capturing paths to tail entities in the support graphs are obtained. Subsequently, a PathCon Adaptive

$L$-iteration aggregation function $(P_a)$ as depicted in Fig. 1, along with adaptive support aggregation (ASA) and adaptive query aggregation (AQA), is then used to extract relevant support information and to compute scores for the query candidates. During this process, representations of both support and query graphs are further refined to enhance relational reasoning. This module builds upon the SAFER [20], which highlights the significance of adaptive aggregation strategies for effective few-shot relational reasoning.

$P_a$ **L-iteration PathCon Aggregation Process.** The $P_a$-$L$-iteration aggregation framework as mentioned by the work in [20], refines node and edge representations within subgraph adaptation through iterative message passing. At each iteration $i$ for the $k$-th support graph, the aggregation output for a node $v$ is first computed as:

$$a_v^i(k) = \frac{1}{1 + \sum_{e \in N(v)} w_e(k)} \sum_{e \in N(v)} b_e^i(k) \cdot w_e(k) \tag{4}$$

The weighted aggregation captures the influence of neighboring relations on the node. The aggregated node features are then adapted based on the task: Adaptive Support Aggregation (ASA) or Adaptive Query Aggregation (AQA) [20] . The node embedding $b_v^i(k)$ is updated as:

$$b_v^i(k) = \begin{cases} T_{ASA}(\{a_v^i(m)\}_{m=1}^K), & \text{for ASA} \\ T_{AQA}(a_v^i(k), \{b_v^i(m)\}_{m=1}^K; \lambda), & \text{for AQA} \end{cases} \tag{5}$$

Here, $T_{\text{ASA}}$ and $T_{\text{AQA}}$ denote task-specific transformation functions. Next, node representations are enriched with role information (head or tail entity) as $r_v^i(k) = b_v^i(k) \parallel 1(v = h) \parallel 1(v = t)$ [20]. Subsequently, edge representations are updated using the transformed node features and the previous edge embedding as $b_e^{i+1}(k) = f(r_u^i(k) \parallel r_v^i(k) \parallel b_e^i(k))$ [20]. These steps are iteratively applied for $L$ iterations to progressively refine node and edge representations, thereby facilitating effective relational reasoning within the subgraph. Here, $f$ is a learnable function.

**Adaptive Support Subgraph Aggregation.** It refers to incorporation of information from all support graphs during the learning process of the embedding for each individual support graph. Equation(6) [20] calculates average of attention scores of nodes of all $k$-support subgraphs if node is a tail entity and remains same if it's any head entity.

$$T_{ASA}((a_j(v))_{j=1}^K) = \begin{cases} \frac{1}{k} \sum_{j=1}^K a_j(v), & \text{if } v = t, \\ a_k(v), & \text{otherwise.} \end{cases} \tag{6}$$

**Adaptive Query Subgraph Aggregation.** It refers to refinement the tail node embeddings in the support graphs to align with the structure of the query graph.

$$T_{AQA}^{\lambda}(a_k(q), (b_j(v))_{j=1}^{K}, \lambda) = \begin{cases} (1 - \lambda)\, a_t(q) + \frac{\lambda}{K} \sum_{j=1}^{K} b_t(v), & \text{if } v = t, \\ a_v(q), & \text{otherwise.} \end{cases} \tag{7}$$

The hyperparameter $\lambda \geq 0$ [20] controls the degree of support information blended with the query. Larger $\lambda$ values emphasize support knowledge, while $\lambda = 0$ preserves pure query information, helping to mitigate spurious support effects and improve prediction.

Given a query triple, we define two embeddings using a high-level aggregation function $\mathcal{A}_\lambda$. Let $\phi(q)$ be the embedding of the query graph q and $\psi(m)$ be the embedding of the m-th support graph. The support-adapted embedding $\mathbf{E}_{\text{supp}} = \mathcal{A}_\lambda\left(\phi(q), \{\psi(m)\}_{m=1}^{K}\right)$ and a query-only embedding $\mathbf{E}_{\text{query}} = \mathcal{A}_0\left(\phi(q), \{\psi(m)\}_{m=1}^{K}\right)$. Embeddings are further enhanced by concatenating them with the mean of pretrained support tail or query tail embeddings, where $\bar{\mathbf{v}}_{\text{supp}} = \frac{1}{K} \sum_{k=1}^{K} \mathbf{v}(t_{s,k})$. The final score for candidate $t_q$ is:

$$\text{Score}(t_q) = \cos\left([\mathbf{E}_{\text{supp}} \,\|\, \bar{\mathbf{v}}_{\text{supp}}], [\mathbf{E}_{\text{query}} \,\|\, \mathbf{v}(t_q)]\right) \tag{8}$$

### 3.5  Training Objective and Loss Function

The proposed framework, FLARE, is trained using a contrastive learning objective with positive and negative sample pairs. Positive pairs consist of support and query triplets from the same relation, while negative pairs come from different relations. The training objective aims to encourage the model to assign higher similarity scores to positive pairs compared to negative pairs. This is formalized using a pairwise margin-based ranking loss given by:

$$\mathcal{L} = \max\left(s^{-} - s^{+} + \delta, 0\right) \tag{9}$$

where $s^{+}$ is the model's similarity score for a positive pair (from the same relation), $s^{-}$ is the score for a negative pair (from different relations) and $\delta$ is a predefined margin hyperparameter.

## 4  Experimental Settings

### 4.1  Baseline Models

The proposed model, FLARE is evaluated against the following categories of existing approaches: *Non-attention guided methods* such as TransE [1], DistMult [5], ComplEx [6], R-GCN [11], *Meta-Learning methods* and *Subgraph-based few-shot inductive methods*. These include state-of-the-art (SOTA) models in few-shot KG completion.

– **Meta-Learning Methods:**
  • **MetaR** [16] focuses on learning relation-specific meta-knowledge from few-shot support triples to enable relational prediction.

- **FSRL** [17] learns generalizable subgraph representations that can be transferred across few-shot relational tasks.
- **Subgraph-based Few-shot Inductive Methods:**
  - **CSR-GNN** [19] enhances connection subgraph representations using graph neural networks to better capture structural dependencies.
  - **CSR-OPT** [19] introduces optimization strategies to adaptively refine subgraph representations for improved link prediction.
  - **SAFER** [20] is a subgraph adaptation framework that improves missing tail entity prediction by extracting meaningful information from support triplets while minimizing noise from irrelevant relations.

### 4.2   Training and Implementation Details

The proposed model, FLARE, is implemented in Python 3.10.2 using PyTorch libraries, specifically Torch-geometric, Torch-sparse and Torch-scatter. All training and testing for FLARE and baseline methods are conducted on a local workstation with an NVIDIA RTX A5500 (16GB) GPU. On average, training on each dataset takes approximately 2 h on a single GPU. The hyperparameter $\lambda$ in Adaptive Query Aggregation is set to 0.1 for NELL and 0.5 for FB15K-237 and ConceptNet. The AdamW optimizer is used with a learning rate of $10^{-5}$ over 20,000 steps.

### 4.3   Comparative Study of Baselines

**Table 1.** Performance comparison of different methods across datasets on multiple evaluation metrics.The best results are shown in **bold**. * indicates the non-attention guided methods.

| Method | NELL | | | | FB15K-237 | | | | ConceptNet | | | |
|---|---|---|---|---|---|---|---|---|---|---|---|---|
| | MRR | Hit@1 | Hit@5 | Hit@10 | MRR | Hit@1 | Hit@5 | Hit@10 | MRR | Hit@1 | Hit@5 | Hit@10 |
| TransE* [1] | 0.193 | 0.119 | 0.256 | 0.320 | 0.125 | 0.196 | 0.353 | 0.471 | 0.122 | 0.180 | 0.339 | 0.455 |
| DistMult* [5] | 0.231 | 0.164 | 0.306 | 0.375 | 0.350 | 0.192 | 0.421 | 0.577 | 0.361 | 0.210 | 0.405 | 0.450 |
| ComplEx* [6] | 0.185 | 0.129 | 0.223 | 0.273 | 0.242 | 0.599 | 0.742 | 0.840 | 0.236 | 0.585 | 0.734 | 0.768 |
| R-GCN* [11] | 0.247 | 0.147 | 0.563 | 0.613 | 0.251 | 0.541 | 0.728 | 0.825 | 0.240 | 0.510 | 0.711 | 0.745 |
| GMatching [15] | 0.288 | 0.152 | 0.427 | 0.601 | 0.325 | 0.233 | 0.426 | 0.509 | 0.283 | 0.151 | 0.438 | 0.548 |
| MetaR [16] | 0.471 | 0.322 | 0.647 | 0.763 | 0.805 | 0.740 | 0.881 | 0.937 | 0.318 | 0.226 | 0.390 | 0.496 |
| FSRL [17] | 0.490 | 0.327 | 0.695 | 0.853 | 0.684 | 0.573 | 0.817 | 0.912 | 0.577 | 0.469 | 0.695 | 0.753 |
| CSR-OPT [19] | 0.463 | 0.321 | 0.629 | 0.760 | 0.619 | 0.512 | 0.747 | 0.824 | 0.559 | 0.450 | 0.692 | 0.736 |
| CSR-GNN [19] | 0.577 | 0.442 | 0.746 | 0.858 | 0.781 | 0.718 | 0.851 | 0.907 | 0.606 | 0.496 | 0.735 | 0.777 |
| SAFER [20] | 0.674 | 0.560 | 0.812 | 0.887 | 0.793 | 0.728 | 0.860 | 0.914 | 0.638 | 0.564 | 0.721 | 0.743 |
| **FLARE** | **0.695** | **0.580** | **0.830** | **0.900** | **0.810** | **0.745** | **0.880** | **0.935** | **0.660** | **0.585** | **0.750** | **0.785** |

Table 1 presents a comparative evaluation of the proposed model, FLARE, against existing baselines on the NELL, FB15K-237, and ConceptNet datasets using standard metrics: Mean Reciprocal Rank (MRR) and Hits@$h$ ($h = 1, 5, 10$). Across all three datasets, FLARE consistently outperforms strong baselines such as SAFER and CSR. This can be attributed to FLARE's MLP-based attention mechanism, which captures informative subgraph structures by assigning higher weights to semantically important edges. The performance advantage of FLARE stems from its adaptive attention-weighted aggregation, which integrates MLP-based attention and edge-level weighting to capture semantic importance effectively. Unlike SAFER's static attention and CSR's uniform weighting, FLARE dynamically adjusts edge and subgraph contributions based on relational relevance, enabling a more expressive and context-aware representation. On NELL and ConceptNet, the improvements are particularly pronounced, suggesting that FLARE is well-suited for knowledge graphs with sparse and noisy relational structures by adaptively emphasizing informative subgraphs and suppressing irrelevant connections. The substantial gains in Hits@5 and Hits@10 indicate that FLARE is effective not only in retrieving relevant entities but also in ranking them more accurately. On FB15K-237, FLARE still outperforms SAFER and other baselines, though with relatively smaller gains.

Notably, simpler embedding-based non-attention models such as TransE, DistMult, and ComplEx, as well as meta-learning approaches like MetaR and GMatching, achieve considerably lower MRR and Hits@$h$ scores across all datasets, highlighting the necessity of graph-based aggregation and FLARE's adaptive attention mechanism in few-shot relational learning.

# 5   Result Analysis and Discussions

## 5.1   Ablation Study

Ablation study results with the removal of each of the four core modules in FLARE–MEA, W, ASA, and AQA are shown in Table 2. In FLARE\ MEA, replacing the MLP-based Edge Attention with uniform edge weights leads to a notable MRR drop on all the datasets. Removing the Weight Assignment (W) module causes the largest performance decline, emphasizing the importance of adaptive edge weighting, particularly in noisy graphs like ConceptNet. Likewise, disabling Adaptive Support Aggregation (ASA) and Adaptive Query Aggregation (AQA) reduces MRR significantly, confirming their significance in iterative refinement of support node representations and filtering irrelevant parts of the support graph based on the query. Overall, the MEA and W modules are most critical for achieving high performance in FLARE.

**Table 2.** Ablation study results of FLARE and its variants across datasets. The best results are shown in **bold**

| Dataset | Method | MRR | Hits@1 | Hits@5 | Hits@10 |
|---|---|---|---|---|---|
| NELL | **FLARE** | **0.695** | **0.580** | **0.830** | **0.900** |
| | FLARE\ MEA | 0.649 | 0.528 | 0.793 | 0.865 |
| | FLARE\ W | 0.560 | 0.435 | 0.715 | 0.774 |
| | FLARE\ ASA | 0.592 | 0.455 | 0.765 | 0.831 |
| | FLARE\ AQA | 0.580 | 0.442 | 0.742 | 0.795 |
| FB15K-237 | **FLARE** | **0.810** | **0.745** | **0.880** | **0.935** |
| | FLARE\ MEA | 0.778 | 0.705 | 0.851 | 0.905 |
| | FLARE\ W | 0.765 | 0.700 | 0.840 | 0.899 |
| | FLARE\ ASA | 0.767 | 0.698 | 0.842 | 0.901 |
| | FLARE\ AQA | 0.773 | 0.708 | 0.849 | 0.907 |
| ConceptNet | **FLARE** | **0.660** | **0.585** | **0.750** | **0.785** |
| | FLARE\ MEA | 0.620 | 0.539 | 0.700 | 0.741 |
| | FLARE\ W | 0.489 | 0.347 | 0.650 | 0.713 |
| | FLARE\ ASA | 0.521 | 0.405 | 0.670 | 0.720 |
| | FLARE\ AQA | 0.545 | 0.426 | 0.700 | 0.738 |

## 5.2   Case Studies and Illustrations

As depicted in Fig. 2, the first case highlights an error caused by strong semantic distractors. When predicting the founder of Microsoft, the model ranks Steve Jobs above the correct answer, Bill Gates, due to their semantic similarity as tech pioneers. The second case demonstrates a failure in fine-grained semantic disambiguation, where the model confuses related but functionally distinct entities, predicting 'ISRO Headquarters' instead of the correct 'Satish Dhawan Space Center' as the launch site for Chandrayaan-3. In contrast, the third case illustrates FLARE's ability to reason across domains; through attention-guided aggregation and adaptive graph pooling, it accurately identifies 'SpaceX' as the manufacturer of 'Crew Dragon' by capturing deeper relational patterns rather than surface-level similarities.

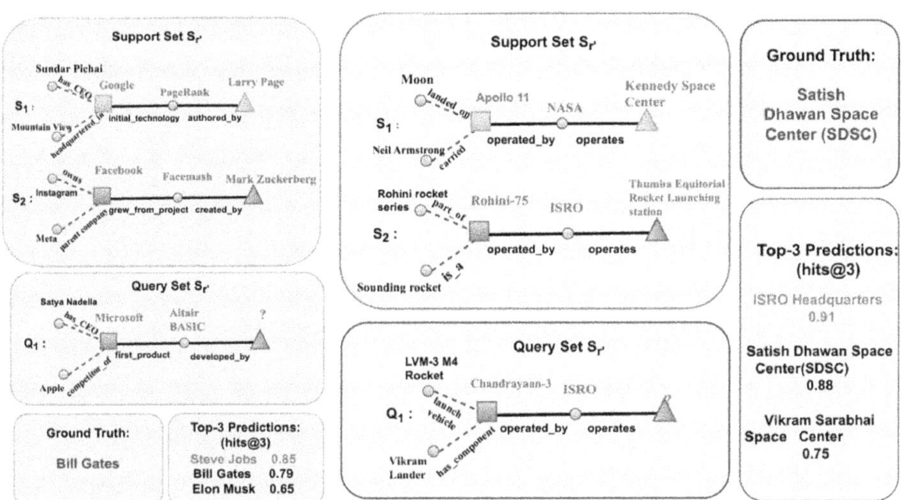

(a) A False Negative case demonstrating FLARE's vulnerability to semantic distractors.

(b) A False Negative case highlighting the challenge of fine-grained semantic disambiguation.

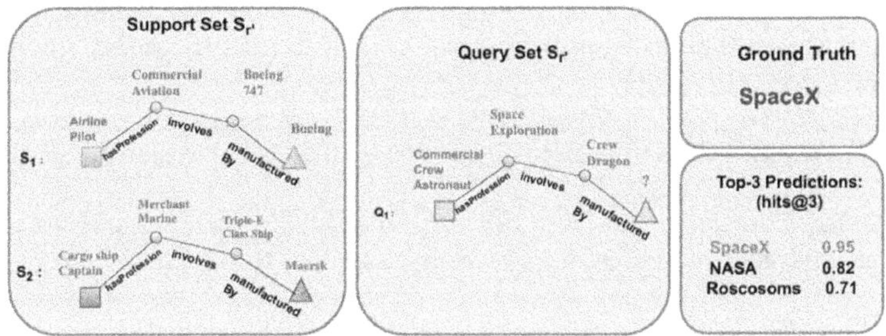

(c) A True Positive case illustrating the FLARE's ability for 2-shot relational reasoning.

**Fig. 2.** Three illustrative 2-shot relational reasoning cases from FB15K-237 dataset. The dashed line represents spurious relation and solid line represents the related target relation between relevant entities (circles) and head (square) and tail (triangle) entities.

# 6   Conclusion

This paper presents FLARE, a novel framework for few-shot missing triple prediction that improves generalization to unseen relations with limited examples. Unlike methods such as CSR that rely heavily on subgraph structures and often introduce spurious information, FLARE employs an MLP-based self-attention mechanism for edge scoring, refined feature aggregation, and adaptive support graph pooling. Extensive experiments on NELL, FB15K-237, and ConceptNet demonstrate that FLARE consistently outperforms strong baselines, achieving new state-of-the-art results. Ablation studies further validate the effectiveness of each component within FLARE, highlighting that attention-based edge weighting and adaptive pooling substantially contribute to its superior performance. While FLARE shows strong performance, its scalability to large and dense knowledge graphs remains a challenge due to increased memory and computation bottlenecks. Future work may focus on enhancing the model's scalability to handle large-scale graphs and improving its contextual awareness while ensuring semantic correctness.

**Disclosure of Interests.** The authors declare no competing interests.

# References


1. Bordes, A., Usunier, N., Garcia-Duran, A., Weston, J., Yakhnenko, O.: translating embeddings for modeling multi-relational data. In: Burges, C.J, Bottou, L. (eds.) NeurIPS 2013, vol. 26. Curran Associates, Inc. (2013). https://dl.acm.org/doi/10.5555/2999792.2999923
2. Nguyen, D.Q., Qu, L., Johnson, M.: STransE: a novel embedding model of entities and relationships in knowledge bases. In: NAACL 2016, pp. 460–466 (2016). https://doi.org/10.18653/v1/N16-1054
3. Sun, Z., Deng, Z.H., Nie, J.Y., Tang, J.: RotatE: knowledge graph embedding by relational rotation in complex space. In: ICLR (2019). https://openreview.net/forum?id=HkgEQnRqYQ
4. Nickel, M., Tresp, V., Kriegel, H.P.: A three-way model for collective learning on multi-relational data. In: ICML, pp. 809–816 (2011). https://dl.acm.org/doi/10.5555/3104482.3104584
5. Yang, B., Yih, W.T., He, X., Gao, J., Deng, L.: Embedding entities and relations for learning and inference in knowledge bases. In: ICLR (2015). https://microsoft.com/research/publication/embedding-entities-relations-knowledge-bases
6. Trouillon, T., Welbl, J., Riedel, S., Gaussier, E., Bouchard, G.: Complex embeddings for simple link prediction. In: ICML, pp. 2071–2080 (2016). https://arxiv.org/abs/1606.06357
7. Nickel, M., Rosasco, L., Poggio, T.: Holographic embeddings of knowledge graphs. In: AAAI, pp. 1955–1961 (2016). https://dl.acm.org/doi/10.5555/3016100.3016172
8. Dettmers, T., Balažević, I., Riedel, S.: ConvE: convolutional knowledge graph embeddings. In: Proceedings of the Thirty-Second AAAI Conference on AI, pp. 1–8. AAAI Press, Palo Alto (2018)
9. Balazevic, I., Allen, C., Hospedales, T.: Hypernetwork knowledge graph embeddings. In: ICANN, pp. 553–565 (2019). https://doi.org/10.1007/978-3-030-30493-5_52
10. Socher, R.,Manning, C.D., Ng, A.: Reasoning with neural tensor networks for knowledge base completion. In: NIPS, pp. 926–934 (2013). https://dl.acm.org/doi/10.5555/2999611.2999715
11. Schlichtkrull, M., Kipf, T.N., Bloem, P., van den Berg, R., Titov, I.: Modeling relational data with graph convolutional networks (2018). https://doi.org/10.1007/978-3-319-93417-4_38
12. Zhu, C., Li, P., Zhang, Z.: Neural Bellman-Ford networks: a general graph neural network framework for link prediction. In: NeurIPS, pp. 16548–16559 (2021). https://arxiv.org/abs/2106.06935

13. Teru, K., Denis, L., Hamilton, W.: Inductive relation prediction by subgraph reasoning. In: ICML, pp. 9454–9463 (2020). https://proceedings.mlr.press/v119/teru20a.html
14. Wang, X., Zhang, X., Chen, L., Zhao, Y.: Relational message passing for knowledge graph completion. In: SIGIR, pp. 657–666 (2021). https://doi.org/10.1145/3447548.3467247
15. Xiong, W., Yu, M., Chang, S., Guo, X.: One-shot relational learning for knowledge graphs. In: Riloff, E., Chiang, D. (eds.) EMNLP 2018, pp.1980–1990. ACL, Brussels (2018). https://doi.org/10.18653/v1/D18-1223
16. Chen, M., Zhang, W., Chen, Q.: Meta relational learning for few-shot link prediction in knowledge graphs. In: Inui, K., Ng, V. (eds.) EMNLP 2019, pp.4217–4226. ACL, Hong Kong (2019). https://doi.org/10.18653/v1/D19-1431
17. Zhang, Z., Wang, X., Sun, L., Liu, B.: Few-shot knowledge graph completion. In: Proceedings of the AAAI Conference on Artificial Intelligence, vol. 34, issue 3, pp. 3053–3060. AAAI Press, Palo Alto (2020)
18. Sun, J., Zhou, Y., Zong, C.: One-shot relation learning for knowledge graphs via neighborhood aggregation and paths encoding. ACM Trans. Asian Low-Resour. Lang. Inf. Process. 1(1), 1–20 (2021)
19. Huang, Q., Leskovec, J.: Few-shot relational reasoning via connection subgraph pretraining. In: Koyejo, S. (eds.) NeurIPS 2022, vol. 35, pp. 6397–6409 (2022). https://arxiv.org/abs/2210.06722
20. Liu, H., Wang, S., Chen, C., Li, J.: Few-shot knowledge graph relational reasoning via subgraph adaptation. In: Duh, K., Gomez, H., Bethard, S. (eds.) NAACL-HLT 2024, pp. 3346–3356. ACL, Mexico City (2024). https://doi.org/10.18653/v1/2024.naacl-long.183

# AsCap-GPT2: A Data-Efficient Assamese Image Captioning Framework with Pretrained GPT-2


Pankaj Choudhury[1]([envelope]) [ID], Prabhanjan Jadhav[2] [ID], Prithwijit Guha[1,2] [ID], and Sukumar Nandi[2,3] [ID]

[1] Centre for Linguistic Science and Technology, Indian Institute of Technology Guwahati, Guwahati, India
pankajchoudhury@iitg.ac.in

[2] Department of Electronics and Electrical Engineering, Indian Institute of Technology Guwahati, Guwahati, India
{j.prabhanjan,pguha,sukumar}@iitg.ac.in

[3] Department of Computer Science and Engineering, Indian Institute of Technology Guwahati, Guwahati, India



**Abstract.** Automatic image captioning research is predominantly focused on resource-rich languages like English. Recent advances in large language models (LLMs) have further enhanced captioning performance for English by improving fluency and generalization. However, despite having over 15 million native speakers, the task of image captioning in Assamese remains underdeveloped. This is due to the lack of annotated datasets and pretrained language models. This paper introduces AsCap-GPT2, an Assamese image captioning model that leverages a pretrained GPT-2 model for caption generation. The proposed AsCap-GPT2 model integrates salient image regions as visual features with the pretrained GPT-2 decoder to generate captions in Assamese. The model is evaluated across three experimental settings. First, few-shot training is conducted on the COCO-AC dataset using 0.1%, 1%, 10%, and 100% of the training data. Second, the model is fine-tuned using reinforcement learning technique to directly optimize the CIDEr score. Third, its adaptability is assessed on the Flickr30K-AC dataset. On COCO-AC, AsCap-GPT2 achieves BLEU-1 of 72.5, BLEU-4 of 31.8, and CIDEr of 94.3, outperforming all baselines.

**Keywords:** Image Captioning · Assamese Language · AssameseGPT-2 · Transformers


## 1 Introduction

Image captioning is the task of generating a descriptive sentence for a given image by combining techniques from computer vision and natural language generation. It is a challenging multimodal problem with applications in assistive technology, image organization, and automated report generation [2].


© The Author(s), under exclusive license to Springer Nature Switzerland AG 2026
S. Mitra et al. (Eds.): PReMI 2025, LNCS 16358, pp. 494–504, 2026.
https://doi.org/10.1007/978-3-032-18480-1_50

Traditional image captioning methods relied on template-based generation or retrieving captions based on visual similarity, often resulting in fixed-length and semantically weak outputs [2]. To address these limitations, modern approaches adopt deep learning-based encoder-decoder frameworks [21], where a CNN encodes the image and an RNN decodes it into a sentence. These models initially struggled to preserve visual information across long sequences. Attention mechanisms [22] were introduced to allow the decoder to focus on relevant image regions during each word generation. The Bottom-Up Top-Down (BUTD) approach [1] further improved the attention by extracting object-level features from salient regions using a pretrained Faster-RCNN detector. This leads to better visual and language alignment. Later models [12,18] adopted these bottom-up features instead of using entire image as visual feature.

The success of transformers in machine translation [20] led to their adoption in image captioning, where they replaced RNNs by using self-attention to model long-range dependencies in both visual and textual inputs. Several works improved upon the basic transformer architecture. Huang *et al.* [12] introduced multi-head attention for visual refinement, while Cornia *et al.* [8] proposed a meshed-memory transformer to capture multi-level interactions. Pan *et al.* [18] replaces dot product-based self-attention with bilinear pooling attention to learn higher-order interactions between visual and textual features. Other approaches, such as [10,11], focused on spatial relationships using geometric features and learnable biases.

Recent works have explored integrating pretrained language models (PLMs) into image captioning to improve fluency and reduce data requirements. Luo *et al.* [15] used a frozen GPT-2 decoder and introduced I-Tuning, a cross-attention module trained on visual prompts. Chen *et al.* VisualGPT [4], which uses a GPT-2-initialized decoder and a randomly initialized encoder in an encoder-decoder setup to enhance data efficiency. Advances in multi-modal large language models (MM-LLMs) have further improved captioning quality. BLIP-2 [13] introduced a Q-former to extract image features and align them with frozen LLMs through cross-attention. MiniGPT-4 [23] extended this by combining BLIP-2 with the Vicuna LLM using a two-stage fine-tuning strategy. LLaVA [14] focused on instruction tuning with diverse image-text data to improve multimodal understanding.

Despite these developments, image captioning research remains heavily centered around English due to the availability of large-scale datasets and pretrained language decoders. Very limited work exists for Indian Languages like Hindi, Assamese. One such effort is GAGPT-2 proposed by Mishra *et al.* [16], which incorporates geometric attention in the Transformer encoder for visual refinement and employed a pretrained GPT-2 decoder to enhance captioning performance in Hindi. In Assamese, Nath *et al.* [17] used EfficientNetB3 for visual feature extraction with GRU for caption decoding. The authors also created Assamese caption datasets by translating English captions from MSCOCO and Flickr30K, but without correcting translation errors [5]. Choudhury *et al.* [5] address this issue by introducing *COCO-Assamese* and *Flickr30K-Assamese* dataset where translation errors are manually curated. The authors also proposed a Bi-LSTM-based captioning model with bilinear attention. Later, Choudhury *et al.* [7] improved Assamese caption quality by integrating semantic attributes as auxiliary input. Choudhury *et al.* demonstrated in [6] that image captioning models trained exclusively on Assamese captions show better performance than models trained on English captions and later translated into Assamese.

The Assamese language is spoken by over 15 million people [3], primarily in the Indian state of Assam. It is written in a script derived from the Brahmi script and exhibits linguistic features such as inflections, classifier, honorifics and gender distinction nouns. These characteristics pose unique challenges for the development of caption generation models in the Assamese language. One of the main obstacles in Assamese captioning research is the lack of large-scale datasets and pretrained large language models. Moreover, building resources for vision language task like image captioning is difficult as manual annotation of captions is time-consuming and labor-intensive. This challenge is even more pronounced for specialized domains and low-resource languages like Assamese. To address these issues this paper introduces *AsCap-GPT2* a data efficient image captioning model for Assamese. The proposed AsCap-GPT2 combines Bottom-Up Top-Down (BUTD) [1] visual features with AssameseGPT-2[1] a GPT-2 based language decoder pretrained on the IndicCorpV2 [9] Assamese corpus. The use of a pretrained decoder allows the model to generate syntactically accurate and fluent Assamese captions even with limited data. The main contributions of this paper are summarized below–

- A novel image captioning framework for Assamese is presented that integrates object-level visual features with a GPT-2 decoder pretrained on a large Assamese monolingual corpus, enhancing both fluency and syntactic correctness.
- Investigates few-shot training using the COCO-AC dataset, evaluating performance at 0.1%, 1%, 10%, and 100% of the training data to assess model robustness in low-resource scenarios, with cross-entropy loss as the training objective.
- To further enhance caption quality, the model is fine-tuned using self-critical sequence training (SCST), a reinforcement learning strategy that optimizes the CIDEr score directly.
- The generalizability of the model is evaluated on the Flickr30K-AC dataset. The model is trained with both cross-entropy and SCST objectives on the full training set to examine its adaptability across datasets.

## 2    Proposed Methodology

The proposed AsCap-GPT2 consists of three main components – (a) *Visual Feature Encoder* (b) *Visual Feature Refiner* (c) *Language Decoder* as shown in

---

[1] https://huggingface.co/BharatVLM/AssameseGPT2.

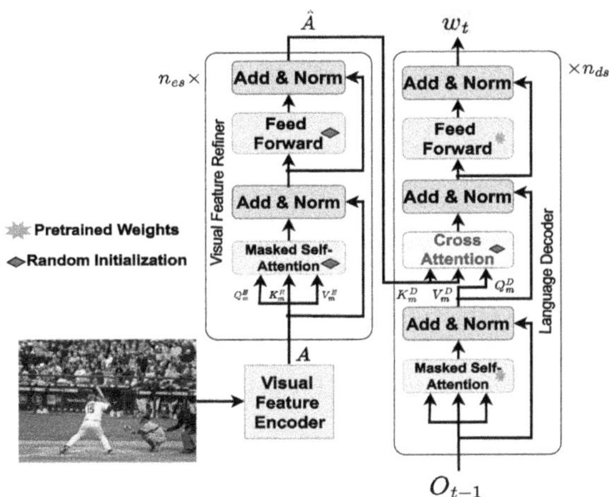



**Fig. 1.** Functional block diagram of the proposed AsCap-GPT2 model.

Fig. 1. Following [1], this work employs a pretrained Faster-RCNN [1] as *Visual Feature Encoder*. Initially, the Faster-RCNN takes Image $\mathbf{I}$ as input and produces $n_a$ salient region proposals. These region proposals are then converted to visual features $\mathbf{A} = [\boldsymbol{a}_1, \ldots \boldsymbol{a}_i, \ldots \boldsymbol{a}_{n_a}]$ $(\boldsymbol{a_i} \in \mathbb{R}^{d_a \times 1}, \mathbf{A} \in \mathbb{R}^{d_a \times n_a})$ using a pretrained ResNet-101 [1]. Next, Transformer Encoder is used as *Visual Feature Refiner* to capture global context and inter relationship between salient region proposals. The Transformer Encoder is stacked $n_{es}$ times with each layer employing multi-head self-attention with $n_{eh}$ heads, where queries, keys, and values for the $m^{th}$ head are computed as $\mathbf{Q}_E^{(m)} = W_m^{QE}\mathbf{A}$, $\quad \mathbf{K}_E^{(m)} = W_m^{KE}\mathbf{A}$, $\quad \mathbf{V}_E^{(m)} = W_m^{VE}\mathbf{A}$. Here, $W_m^{QE}, W_m^{KE}, W_m^{VE} \in \mathbb{R}^{d_e \times d_a}$ are linear transformations. Subsequently, scaled inner product is applied to $\mathbf{Q}_E^{(m)}$ and $\mathbf{V}_E^{(m)}$ followed by *SoftMax* to generate attention weights $\mathbf{H}_m \in \mathbb{R}^{d_e \times n_a}$ for the $m^{\text{th}}$ head as

$$\mathbf{H}_m = \mathbf{V}_E^{(m)} \cdot \text{SoftMax}\left(\frac{\left(\mathbf{Q}_E^{(m)}\right)^T \mathbf{K}_E^{(m)}}{\sqrt{d_e}}\right).$$ Finally, the output from all self-attention

heads are concatenated and projected as $\mathbf{MHA}(\mathbf{A}) = W_{mh}\mathbf{H}$ to produce $\mathbf{H} \in \mathbb{R}^{(n_{eh} \times d_e) \times n_a}$. Where , $\mathbf{H} = \left[\mathbf{H}_1^T, \ldots, \mathbf{H}_{n_{eh}}^T\right]^T$ and $W_{mh} \in \mathbb{R}^{d_e \times (n_{eh} \times d_e)}$ is a linear transformation. The multi-head attention output $\mathbf{MHA}(\mathbf{A})$ is further passed through fully connected feed-forward layers with ReLU activation and dropout (to reduce overfitting). Residual connections and layer normalization are applied across the embedding dimension to stabilize training and improve convergence. The final output after $n_{es}$ encoder stacks is the refined visual feature $\hat{\mathbf{A}} = [\hat{\boldsymbol{a}}_1, \ldots, \hat{\boldsymbol{a}}_i, \ldots, \hat{\boldsymbol{a}}_{n_a}]$ $(\hat{\boldsymbol{a}}_i \in \mathbb{R}^{d_e \times 1})$. These refined visual features $\hat{\mathbf{A}}$ are feed to the caption decoder at each time step $t$ to generate one word at a time.

The caption decoder for the proposed AsCap-GPT2 is a modified GPT-2 model. The original GPT-2 [19] decoder mainly consist of a masked self-attention sub-layer and feed-forward network. However, to adapt the GPT-2 architecture for image captioning with visual context, a cross-attention module is inserted into each transformer decoder block of GPT-2. The masked self-attention and feed-forward layers are initialized with the pretrained weights, and the cross-attention layer is randomly initialized.

At each time step $t$, the decoder predicts the token $\hat{w}_t \in \Sigma$ by conditioning on the partial caption sequence $\hat{\mathcal{C}}_{t-1} = \{\hat{w}_1, \ldots, \hat{w}_i, \ldots, \hat{w}_{t-1}\}$ and the refined visual feature $\hat{\mathbf{A}}$. Where $\Sigma$ is the vocabulary list.

The sequence $\hat{\mathcal{C}}_{t-1}$ is first transformed into a one-hot encoded matrix $\tilde{\boldsymbol{O}}_{t-1} \in \{0, 1\}^{|\Sigma| \times (t-1)}$, where each column $\tilde{\boldsymbol{o}}_\tau$ is a one-hot vector for the token at position $\tau$. These are projected into dense embeddings as $\hat{\boldsymbol{O}}_{t-1} = W_{emb}\tilde{\boldsymbol{O}}_{t-1}$ (where $W_{emb} \in \mathbb{R}^{d_e \times |\Sigma|}, \hat{\boldsymbol{O}}_{t-1} \in \mathbb{R}^{d_e \times (t-1)}$).

First the masked self-attention sub-layer is applied to compute contextualized representations of $\hat{\boldsymbol{O}}_{t-1}$ to produce $\mathbf{H}_t^{\mathrm{D}}$ similar to the encoder of a transformer. Next the cross-attention layer then integrates the refined visual features $\hat{\mathbf{A}}$ as key and value with the query $\mathbf{H}_t^{\mathrm{D}}$ as follows

$$\mathrm{CrossAttn}(\mathbf{H}_t^{\mathrm{D}}, \hat{\mathbf{A}}) = \mathrm{softmax}\left(\frac{\mathbf{H}_t^{\mathrm{D}} W^{DQ}(\hat{\mathbf{A}} W^{DK})^\top}{\sqrt{d_e}}\right) \hat{\mathbf{A}} W^{DV} \tag{1}$$

where $W^{DQ}, W^{QK}, W^{DV} \in \mathbb{R}^{d_e \times d_e}$ are learnable projection matrices. The output of the cross-attention is then passed through a feed-forward layer, followed by layer normalization and residual connections. The final word prediction is computed by applying a softmax over the vocabulary $P(\hat{w}_t | \hat{w}_{<t}, \hat{\mathbf{A}}) = \mathrm{SoftMax}(W_{out} \cdot \mathrm{GPT2Block}(\hat{\boldsymbol{O}}_{t-1}, \hat{\mathbf{A}}))$ where $W_{out} \in \mathbb{R}^{|\Sigma| \times d_e}$ maps the decoder output to the vocabulary space.

## 3   Experimental Setup

**Baseline Models** – The proposed AsCap-GPT2 model is benchmarked against the following nine baseline methods which are trained with Assamese caption dataset. The baseline $\mathcal{B}-1$ is the model proposed by Vinyals *et al.* [21] uses global image features from ResNet101 as the initial hidden state of an LSTM decoder without attention. The second baseline $\mathcal{B}-2$ proposed by Xu *et al.* [22] employs ResNet101 as the visual encoder and integrates a soft attention mechanism with an LSTM decoder to focus on salient regions during caption generation. Next, the baseline $\mathcal{B}-3$ adopted from Bottom-Up and Top-Down model by Anderson *et al.* [1] which uses region-level object features from FasterRCNN with an attention-equipped LSTM decoder. The AoANet model by Huang *et al.* [12] is used as baseline $\mathcal{B}-4$ which combines multi-head attention with an LSTM decoder. The baseline $\mathcal{B}-5$, $\mathcal{B}-6$ and $\mathcal{B}-7$ are transformer based baselines. Baseline $\mathcal{B}-5$ proposed by Herdade *et al.* [11] replaces positional encoding with object geometry in a transformer encoder for visual refinement and uses a transformer decoder for captioning. Moreover, baseline $\mathcal{B}-6$ introduced by Cornia *et al.* [8] applies mesh like connections between encoder and decoder layers of a transformer model for multi-level visual reasoning. The baseline $\mathcal{B}-7$ is the standard

Transformer model by Vaswani *et al.* [20] which stacks six encoder-decoder layers. The baseline $\mathcal{B}-8$ proposed by Choudhury *et al.* [5] employs a Bi-LSTM with bilinear attention for Assamese image captioning, leveraging forward-backward sequential modeling and object-level visual features. The final baseline $\mathcal{B}-9$ proposed by Choudhury *et al.* [7] fuses semantic attributes and visual features using dual self-attention modules and a Bi-GRU decoder for Assamese language generation.

**Dataset Preparation** – The proposed model is trained and evaluated on the COCO-AC and Flickr30K-AC datasets. As a preprocessing step, punctuations are removed and captions are truncated to a maximum length of 16 tokens. Words occurring more than five times are retained to construct the vocabulary, resulting in *12,912* words for COCO-AC and *8,534* for Flickr30K-AC. The COCO-AC dataset contains $123K$ images and Flickr30K-AC has $31K$ images, each paired with five captions. COCO-AC is divided into $113K$ for training and $5K$ each for validation and testing, while Flickr30K-AC includes $29K$ training images and $1K$ each for validation and testing.

**Model Hyperparameters** – This work employs adaptive bottom-up features as salient image regions following the approach in [1]. The number of such features $10 \leq n_a \leq 100$ each of dimension $d_a = 2048$. The visual feature refiner consists of $n_{es} = 6$ transformer encoder layers with $n_{eh} = 8$ attention heads. The decoder uses GPT-2 configuration with $n_{ds} = 12$ layers, 12 heads. The embedding dimension of the GPT-2 is set to $d_e = 768$. The proposed model is initially trained 30 epochs to minimize cross-entropy loss using the Adam optimizer with an initial learning rate of $5 \times 10^{-3}$. Next, the model is fine-tuned for another 30 epochs using self-critical sequence training (SCST), a reinforcement strategy. During both training sessions, the batch size is kept as 75 image-caption pairs.

**Model Complexity Analysis** – The Table 1 provides the component-wise computational requirements of the AsCap-GPT2 model. The Faster R-CNN is used only for feature extraction and kept frozen during training, while the Transformer-based encoder and GPT-2 decoder are trainable. FLOPs are measured for a single forward pass with a maximum caption length of 16 tokens and a maximum of 100 salient regions per image.

**Table 1.** Computational complexity breakdown of AsCap-GPT2. The table reports computation in Giga-FLOPs and the number of parameters in millions.

| AsCap-GPT2 Components | Trainable Params | GFLOPs | Params (in millions) |
| --- | --- | --- | --- |
| FasterRCNN | No | 117.33 | 63.63 |
| Transformer Encoder | Yes | 0.917 | 23.432 |
| GPT-2 Decoder | Yes | 6.351 | 216.347 |

## 4 Results and Discussion

**Quantitative Results–** This section presents the quantitative performance of the proposed model, reported using BLEU-n and CIDEr scores. Two main experiments are conducted – the first evaluates how captioning performance changes with different amounts of training data, and the second investigates the effect of reinforcement learning.

**Table 2.** Performance comparison of the proposed Assamese image captioning model with baselines trained and tested on the COCO-AC dataset under varying amounts of training data (0.1%, 1%, 10%) using cross-entropy loss.

| Model | Data Used 0.1 % | | | Data Used 1 % | | | Data Used 10 % | | |
|---|---|---|---|---|---|---|---|---|---|
| | BLEU-1 | BLEU-4 | CIDEr | BLEU-1 | BLEU-4 | CIDEr | BLEU-1 | BLEU-4 | CIDEr |
| $\mathcal{B}$-1 | 42.3 | 10.2 | 27.5 | 42.3 | 10.2 | 27.5 | 54.1 | 16.9 | 49.8 |
| $\mathcal{B}$-2 | 38.7 | 6.5 | 21.9 | 48.9 | 12.1 | 32.7 | 56.4 | 17.8 | 53.2 |
| $\mathcal{B}$-3 | 32.6 | 0 | 5.8 | 58.2 | 17.8 | 50.5 | 63.9 | 23.3 | 70.1 |
| $\mathcal{B}$-4 | 33.4 | 0.2 | 6.3 | 59.1 | 18.1 | 51.3 | 64.5 | 23.7 | 70.8 |
| $\mathcal{B}$-5 | 30.1 | 0 | 5.1 | 55.7 | 16.2 | 46.2 | 62.7 | 22.6 | 68.5 |
| $\mathcal{B}$-6 | 0 | 0 | 0 | 46.8 | 10.2 | 26.9 | 61.9 | 23.1 | 67.9 |
| $\mathcal{B}$-7 | 0 | 0 | 0 | 44.1 | 8.8 | 22.7 | 60.3 | 20.6 | 63.4 |
| $\mathcal{B}$-8 [5] | 33.7 | 0 | 5.8 | 56 | 17.9 | 49.6 | 63.3 | 24.1 | 71.1 |
| $\mathcal{B}$-9 [7] | 34.9 | 1 | 6.9 | 59 | 18.2 | 52.2 | 64.8 | 24 | 71.3 |
| AsCap-GPT2 | 44.1 | 11.5 | 29.8 | 60.4 | 19.3 | 54.8 | 65.9 | 24.9 | 73.4 |

In the first experiment, the model is trained on 0.1%, 1%, 10% of the COCO-AC Karpathy split to assess its ability to work in few-shot settings. Results shown in Table 2 indicates that the proposed AsCap-GPT2 consistently performs better than all baselines. At 0.1% data, most baseline models perform poorly due to their complex structure and lack of pretrained linguistic knowledge. In contrast, AsCap-GPT2 achieves a BLEU-4 score of 11.5 and a CIDEr score of 29.8, likely due to the GPT-2 decoder's pretrained knowledge of Assamese. As the data size increases to 1% and 10%, all models improve, including transformer-based and Assamese-specific baselines. However, AsCap-GPT2 maintains its lead, reaching a BLEU-4 of 24.9 and CIDEr of 73.4 at 10% data. When trained with the full COCO-AC dataset, AsCap-GPT2 achieves the best scores–BLEU-4 of 28.8 and CIDEr of 86.1 outperforming all baselines (see Table 3). This result highlights the benefits of combining pretrained generative language models with object-level visual features.

The second experiment evaluates the effect of reinforcement learning using self-critical sequence training. All models, including AsCap-GPT2, are trained on 100% of the COCO-AC and Flickr30K-AC training sets. Results show that reinforcement learning improves performance across all models. For COCO-AC,

**Table 3.** Evaluation of the proposed model and baselines on the COCO-AC and Flickr30K-AC dataset using 100% of the training data. Both cross-entropy (XE) and reinforcement learning (RL) results are reported in this table.

| Model | COCO-AC | | | | | | Flickr30K-AC | | | | | |
| --- | --- | --- | --- | --- | --- | --- | --- | --- | --- | --- | --- | --- |
| | XE | | | RL | | | XE | | | RL | | |
| | BLEU-1 | BLEU-4 | CIDEr | BLEU-1 | BLEU-4 | CIDEr | BLEU-1 | BLEU-4 | CIDEr | BLEU-1 | BLEU-4 | CIDEr |
| $\mathcal{B}$-1 | 59.9 | 20.6 | 61.5 | 64.3 | 23 | 69.2 | 51.1 | 13.3 | 31.9 | 58.2 | 18.9 | 38.2 |
| $\mathcal{B}$-2 | 62.1 | 23.2 | 68.3 | 66.2 | 26.1 | 75.6 | 53.3 | 16.5 | 39.7 | 59.3 | 19.5 | 45.9 |
| $\mathcal{B}$-3 | 67.1 | 27 | 80.8 | 67.9 | 27.8 | 85.5 | 60.4 | 20.1 | 46.5 | 60.8 | 20.7 | 49.3 |
| $\mathcal{B}$-4 | 67.3 | 27.6 | 81.5 | 68.3 | 28.1 | 87.9 | 61 | 21.2 | 48.6 | 61.2 | 21.7 | 50.1 |
| $\mathcal{B}$-5 | 66.3 | 26.2 | 79.7 | 67.5 | 27.7 | 86 | 60.1 | 20 | 47.2 | 61.3 | 21.5 | 51.2 |
| $\mathcal{B}$-6 | 66.9 | 27.4 | 80.4 | 68.1 | 28.9 | 86.4 | 59.5 | 20.1 | 47.4 | 60.7 | 21.6 | 51.4 |
| $\mathcal{B}$-7 | 67.4 | 26.8 | 81.1 | 68.6 | 28.3 | 87.1 | 60.6 | 20.9 | 48 | 61.8 | 22.4 | 52 |
| $\mathcal{B}$-8 [5] | 68.1 | 27.5 | 81.7 | 69.3 | 29 | 87.7 | 61.5 | 21.1 | 48.3 | 62.7 | 22.6 | 52.3 |
| $\mathcal{B}$-9 [7] | 68.6 | 28.6 | 84.5 | 71.8 | 31 | 92.2 | 62.7 | 23 | 51.4 | 65.5 | 24 | 56.3 |
| AsCap-GPT2 | 68.5 | 28.8 | 86.1 | 72.5 | 31.8 | 94.3 | 63.5 | 23.8 | 53.2 | 66.4 | 25.1 | 57.1 |

AsCap-GPT2 improves from a BLEU-4 of 28.8 and CIDEr of 86.1 (under cross-entropy training) to 31.8 and 94.3 after reinforcement learning. For Flickr30K-AC, the model also achieves the highest scores, improving from 23.8 to 25.1 in BLEU-4 and from 53.2 to 57.1 in CIDEr. These results confirm that reinforcement learning helps the model generate more accurate and relevant captions.

**Qualitative Analysis** – This section provides a qualitative analysis of captions generated by the proposed AsCap-GPT2 model, trained on 100% of the COCO-AC dataset using reinforcement learning. Figure 2 presents sample images along with captions predicted by AsCap-GPT2 and Baseline $\mathcal{B}$-9, the strongest among the Assamese baselines. Examples illustrate that the predicted captions from AsCap-GPT2 are more expressive and context-aware compared to the base-

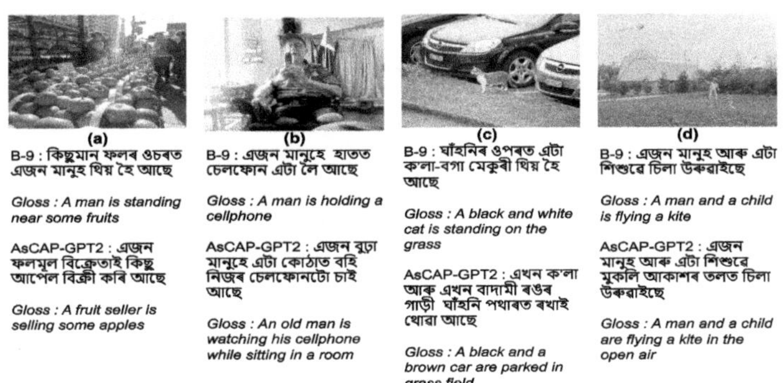


**Fig. 2.** Qualitative examples of the proposed AsCap-GPT2 model. The generated captions are compared with captions generated by Baseline $\mathcal{B}$-9. Here, Gloss denotes gloss annotation.

line. For instance, in Fig. 2(a), while the baseline simply identifies a person as "এজন মানুহ" (a man), the proposed model generates a more detailed phrase "এজন ফলমূল বিক্রেতা" (a fruit seller). This improvement is likely due to the pretrained GPT-2 decoder. The decoder has learned semantic associations from the large monolingual corpus. As a result, it can infer profession-like roles based on surrounding visual cues. Moreover, the AsCap-GPT2 model also excels at describing complex scenes with object-specific details. For example, in Fig. 2(b), the generated caption includes the scene context " এটা কোঠাত" (in a room).

However, the model also shows some limitations, like ignoring secondary objects and the use of formal or stylistic words. In Fig. 2(c), the generated captions fail to mention objects like "মেকুৰী" (cat) even though they are visually prominent in the images. These errors are likely due to weak visual grounding. Additionally, the phrases like "মুকলি আকাশ" (open air) found in Fig. 2(d) reflect a more formal journalistic tone rather than a direct and simple caption. This may be attributed to the pretraining of GPT-2 decoder on IndicCorpV2 which contains sentence from online news articles and web sources.

## 5 Conclusion

This paper presents AsCap-GPT2, an Assamese image captioning model that integrates Bottom-Up Top-Down (BUTD) visual features with a pretrained GPT-2 language decoder trained on IndicCorpV2. The proposed model addresses key challenges in low-resource caption generation by leveraging the linguistic knowledge embedded in large pretrained language models. Experimental results across few-shot training, reinforcement learning on COCO-AC and Flickr30K-AC datasets demonstrate the effectiveness of AsCap-GPT2 in generating fluent and contextually rich captions. The model consistently outperforms all baseline methods, especially in low-data settings. This highlights the advantages of incorporating pretrained LLMs for image captioning in low-resource Indian languages like Assamese. Future work may explore extending this approach to other languages and vision-language tasks.

## References


1. Anderson, P., et al.: Bottom-up and top-down attention for image captioning and visual question answering. In: Proceedings of the IEEE Conference on Computer Vision and Pattern Recognition, pp. 6077–6086 (2018)
2. Bai, S., An, S.: A survey on automatic image caption generation. Neurocomputing **311**, 291–304 (2018)
3. Chandramouli, C., General, R.: Census of India. Rural Urban Distribution of Population, Provisional Population Total. New Delhi: Office of the Registrar General and Census Commissioner, India (2011)
4. Chen, J., Guo, H., Yi, K., Li, B., Elhoseiny, M.: VisualGPT: data-efficient adaptation of pretrained language models for image captioning. In: Proceedings of the IEEE/CVF Conference on Computer Vision and Pattern Recognition, pp. 18030–18040 (2022)

5. Choudhury, P., Guha, P., Nandi, S.: Image caption synthesis for low resource assamese language using Bi-LSTM with bilinear attention. In: Proceedings of the 37th Pacific Asia Conference on Language, Information and Computation, pp. 743–752 (2023)
6. Choudhury, P., Guha, P., Nandi, S.: Impact of language-specific training on image caption synthesis: a case study on low-resource assamese language. Int. J. Asian Lang. Process. (2024)
7. Choudhury, P., Guha, P., Nandi, S.: Exploring semantic attributes for image caption synthesis in low-resource assamese language. ACM Trans. Asian Low-Resour. Lang. Inf. Process. **24**(4) (2025)
8. Cornia, M., Stefanini, M., Baraldi, L., Cucchiara, R.: Meshed-memory transformer for image captioning. In: Proceedings of the IEEE/CVF Conference on Computer Vision and Pattern Recognition, pp. 10578–10587 (2020)
9. Doddapaneni, S., et al.: Towards leaving no Indic language behind: building monolingual corpora, benchmark and models for Indic languages. In: Rogers, A., Boyd-Graber, J., Okazaki, N. (eds.) Proceedings of the 61st Annual Meeting of the Association for Computational Linguistics (Volume 1: Long Papers), pp. 12402–12426. Association for Computational Linguistics, Toronto, Canada (2023). https://doi. org/10.18653/v1/2023.acl-long.693, https://aclanthology.org/2023.acl-long.693/
10. Guo, L., Liu, J., Zhu, X., Yao, P., Lu, S., Lu, H.: Normalized and geometry-aware self-attention network for image captioning. In: Proceedings of the IEEE/CVF Conference on Computer Vision and Pattern Recognition, pp. 10327–10336 (2020)
11. Herdade, S., Kappeler, A., Boakye, K., Soares, J.: Image captioning: transforming objects into words. In: Advances in Neural Information Processing Systems, vol. 32 (2019)
12. Huang, L., Wang, W., Chen, J., Wei, X.Y.: Attention on attention for image captioning. In: Proceedings of the IEEE/CVF International Conference on Computer Vision, pp. 4634–4643 (2019)
13. Li, J., Li, D., Savarese, S., Hoi, S.: BLIP-2: bootstrapping language-image pre-training with frozen image encoders and large language models. In: International Conference on Machine Learning, pp. 19730–19742. PMLR (2023)
14. Liu, H., Li, C., Wu, Q., Lee, Y.J.: Visual instruction tuning. In: Advances in Neural Information Processing Systems, vol. 36 (2024)
15. Luo, Z., Hu, Z., Xi, Y., Zhang, R., Ma, J.: I-tuning: tuning frozen language models with image for lightweight image captioning. In: ICASSP 2023-2023 IEEE International Conference on Acoustics, Speech and Signal Processing (ICASSP), pp. 1–5. IEEE (2023)
16. Mishra, S.K., Chakraborty, S., Saha, S., Bhattacharyya, P.: GAGPT-2: a geometric attention-based GPT-2 framework for image captioning in Hindi. ACM Trans. Asian Low-Resource Lang. Inf. Process. **22**(10), 1–16 (2023)
17. Nath, P., Adhikary, P.K., Dadure, P., Pakray, P., Manna, R., Bandyopadhyay, S.: Image caption generation for low-resource assamese language. In: Proceedings of the 34th Conference on Computational Linguistics and Speech Processing (ROCLING 2022), pp. 263–272 (2022)
18. Pan, Y., Yao, T., Li, Y., Mei, T.: X-linear attention networks for image captioning. In: Proceedings of the IEEE/CVF Conference on Computer Vision and Pattern Recognition, pp. 10971–10980 (2020)
19. Radford, A., Wu, J., Child, R., Luan, D., Amodei, D., Sutskever, I., et al.: Language models are unsupervised multitask learners. OpenAI blog **1**(8), 9 (2019)
20. Vaswani, A., et al.: Attention is all you need. In: Advances in Neural Information Processing Systems, vol. 30 (2017)

21. Vinyals, O., Toshev, A., Bengio, S., Erhan, D.: Show and tell: a neural image caption generator. In: Proceedings of the IEEE Conference on Computer Vision and Pattern Recognition, pp. 3156–3164 (2015)
22. Xu, K., et al.: Show, attend and tell: neural image caption generation with visual attention. In: International Conference on Machine Learning, pp. 2048–2057 (2015)
23. Zhu, D., Chen, J., Shen, X., Li, X., Elhoseiny, M.: MiniGPT-4: enhancing vision-language understanding with advanced large language models. arXiv preprint arXiv:2304.10592 (2023)

# TinyTakes: Efficient ABSA for Movie Reviews


Aditya Pande[(⊠)] and Annushree Bablani

Indian Institute of Information Technology, Sri City, India
{aditya.p22,annushree.bablani}@iiits.in



**Abstract.** Aspect-Based Sentiment Analysis (ABSA) requires linking sentiment to specific aspects in text, but existing datasets rely on token-level BIO tagging and lack domain-specific coverage. We introduce **mASD (Movie Aspect-Sentiment Dataset)**, a 20,000-review synthetic benchmark with *character-level span annotations* for aspects, opinion terms, and sentiment polarity. mASD is generated via structured prompting of a local LLaMA model with regex-based correction and label normalization, enabling *tokenization-agnostic supervision* and fine-grained evaluation. To demonstrate its utility, we provide **MoRE-BERT**, a 6.8M-parameter, domain-pretrained baseline that achieves nearly BERT-base performance on ABSA while being 15× smaller. Our results show that mASD supports both large general-purpose and small domain-specific models, offering a new resource for efficient and robust ABSA research in specialized domains such as movie review analysis.


## 1 Introduction

Sentiment Analysis has long been central to natural language processing (NLP), with early work by [8] introducing sentiment classification at document, sentence, and aspect levels. However, assuming uniform sentiment across a sentence or document often fails in practice, where conflicting opinions coexist.

**Aspect-Based Sentiment Analysis (ABSA)** addresses this by linking sentiment to specific aspects within text. For instance, in *"The cinematography was breathtaking, but the plot was painfully slow"*, ABSA assigns opposing sentiments to different components, enabling a fine-grained view of opinion (Fig. 1).

Despite recent ABSA dataset developments [2,3,11,16], most rely on token-level BIO tagging, cover limited domains, and struggle with subword tokenization and noisy user reviews. Movie reviews–rich in subjective, aspect-driven opinions– remain underrepresented, and no large-scale ABSA dataset provides character-level span annotations.

We reformulate ABSA as a *character-level span prediction task*, inspired by span-based approaches that replace token-level tagging with direct boundary prediction [20,21]. Our 20,000-review dataset enables fine-grained, tokenization-agnostic supervision, and we introduce a compact, domain-specific transformer aligned with recent efficient NLP models [6].

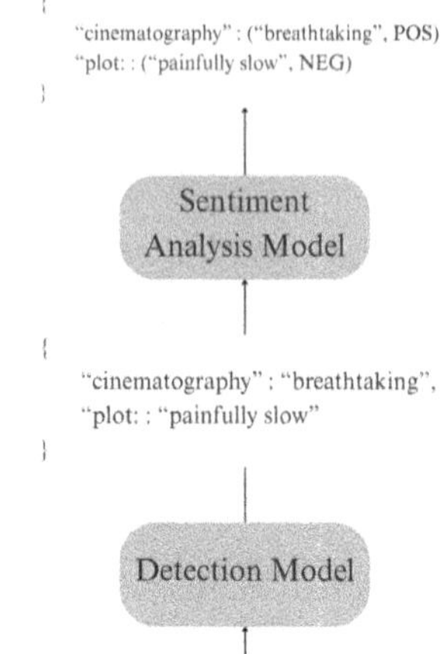


**Fig. 1.** Overview of how ABSA identifies aspect-sentiment pairs from text.

## 2    Background and Related Work

ABSA remains challenging due to the need to extract both aspect terms and their context-dependent sentiment–often expressed figuratively or implicitly, especially in informal reviews. Transformer models like BERT have advanced ABSA performance, but their general-domain pretraining (e.g., Wikipedia, BooksCorpus) can miss domain-specific cues. Their size also limits deployment in low-resource settings.

Earlier methods used pipelines involving POS tagging, NER, SenticNet, and classifiers like SVMs or CRFs [8]. Deep learning models such as CNNs and LSTMs improved both aspect and sentiment extraction [4,19], with Bi-LSTMs and attention mechanisms further enhancing context modeling [10]. Some compact alternatives have also emerged. [9,18] explored models leveraging contextual ($\mathbf{C_e}$) and domain-specific embeddings ($\mathbf{D_e}$).

While these approaches improved ABSA, most existing datasets rely on token-level BIO tagging, introducing ambiguity under subword tokenization and limiting fine-grained supervision. This raises a different question:

*Can a dataset formulated at the character span level provide cleaner supervision and enable efficient models that are robust enough for real-world ABSA?*

# 3    Proposed Method

We propose a streamlined ABSA framework built on two key innovations:

1. **mASD - Movie Aspect-Sentiment Dataset** – a synthetic ABSA dataset of 20,000 movie reviews with *character-level span annotations* for aspects, opinions, and sentiment polarity. Generated via structured prompting of a local LLaMA model, with regex-based correction and sentiment-label normalization, mASD avoids token alignment issues and provides fine-grained, tokenizer-agnostic supervision.
2. **Movie Review Encoder - BERT (MoRE-BERT)** – a compact, domain-specific transformer with 6.8M parameters. We include MoRE-BERT as a *baseline model* to illustrate how both small domain-pretrained models and larger general transformers can effectively leverage mASD's span-based formulation.

## 3.1    From BIO Tagging to Character Spans

Most existing ABSA datasets adopt BIO-style token labeling [4,5], a convention that worked well for CRF and LSTM models. However, this approach becomes problematic under transformer tokenization, where words are split into subwords (e.g., *unbelievable* → un, ##believ, ##able). Labels must then be heuristically propagated across subwords, leading to misalignment and noisy supervision—especially in user-generated reviews where casing, punctuation, and contractions add variability [1,15].

To avoid these issues, we reformulate ABSA as a **character-level span prediction task**. Models predict the start and end indices of aspect and opinion terms directly in raw text, removing tokenization dependencies while enabling precise, fine-grained supervision.

**Advantages:**

– **Tokenizer-Agnostic:** Robust to subword splits and domain-specific vocabulary.
– **Fine-Grained:** Captures nuanced or nested sentiment expressions.
– **Clean Supervision:** Eliminates postprocessing and tag propagation heuristics.

For example, in the review *"The cinematography was breathtaking, but the plot was painfully slow"*, the model extracts spans such as: *cinematography* (4–18) → *breathtaking* (24–36), and *plot* (47–51) → *painfully slow* (56–70).

This span-based schema (Fig. 2) underpins mASD and distinguishes it from prior ABSA datasets, while providing precise, reproducible annotations.

## 4  Proposed Methodology

### 4.1  Synthetic Dataset via LLM Prompting

To operationalize span-based ABSA, we created *mASD (Movie Aspect-Sentiment Dataset)*, a synthetic benchmark of 20,000 reviews with character-level annotations. This dataset is designed as a reusable resource for evaluating ABSA models independent of tokenizer or vocabulary.

**Prompting Pipeline:** Using a local LLaMA 3.2 model (via Ollama), we generated reviews with structured outputs containing both natural text and span annotations. Prompts encouraged 1–10 aspect-opinion pairs, varied tone/length, and required JSON outputs with text, aspect, opinion, sentiment, and spans.

**Postprocessing and Validation:** Regex-based alignment corrected character offsets by anchoring spans to their closest match in the review text. Sentiment labels were normalized through a mapping heuristic (e.g., *"meh"* → NEU). Mismatches were logged, corrected, and standardized, producing a clean span-based dataset for ABSA research.

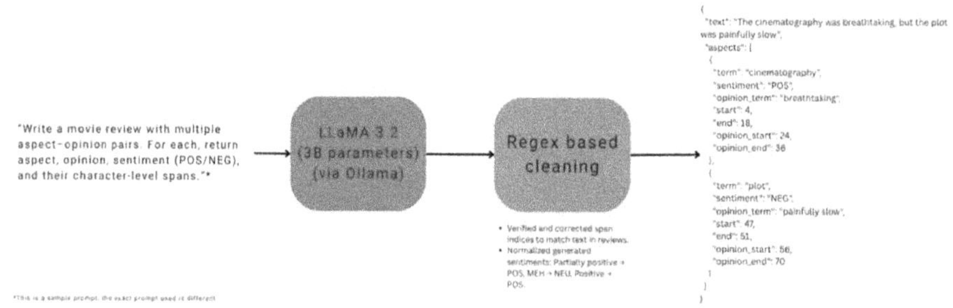


**Fig. 2.** End-to-end pipeline for mASD generation via LLM prompting and regex-based validation.

### 4.2  MoRE-BERT: A Task-Aligned Transformer

To demonstrate the utility of mASD, we introduce a compact domain-specific baseline: *Movie Review Encoder - BERT (MoRE-BERT)*. Generic compact transformers often miss domain cues (e.g., film-specific terminology or figurative sentiment), limiting their ABSA accuracy. By pretraining MoRE-BERT on movie reviews and fine-tuning with character-span supervision, we test whether a lightweight, domain-focused model can match larger baselines while serving as a practical benchmark on mASD.

MoRE-BERT is a 6.8M-parameter transformer pretrained on the Stanford Large Movie Review dataset [12]. Its architecture follows BERT but replaces sinusoidal encodings with *Rotary Positional Embeddings (RoPE)* [17]. The model has 6 transformer layers, 4 attention heads, and 256-dimensional embeddings, trained with a custom 16K BPE vocabulary tailored to the movie domain. Pre-training used the Masked Language Modeling (MLM) objective, yielding a final loss of 4.425.

Before fine-tuning on ABSA, MoRE-BERT was validated on binary sentiment classification [14] to establish baseline sentiment capacity.

# 5   Results and Analysis

## 5.1   Synthetic Dataset Statistics

We curated 20,000 synthetic movie reviews divided across four size-based groups: **small, medium, long,** and **extra long**. Each review contains between 0–15 annotated aspect-opinion pairs, totaling 65,469 span-level annotations.

Sentiment distribution across the full corpus is approximately: **50.25% positive, 47.79% negative**, and **1.96% neutral**, indicating a near-balanced polarity. This polarity balance, combined with variable aspect density across review lengths, makes mASD suitable for benchmarking a wide spectrum of ABSA models–from compact domain-specific transformers to large pretrained LMs (Figs. 1).

**Table 1.** Summary statistics of the synthetic dataset.

| Split | Reviews Count | Aspects Count | Aspect Range | POS | NEG | NEU |
|---|---|---|---|---|---|---|
| Extra Long | 2,000 | 9,607 | 0–15 | 52.06% | 45.71% | 2.24% |
| Long | 4,000 | 15,900 | 0–12 | 49.28% | 48.41% | 2.31% |
| Medium | 6,000 | 19,423 | 0–9 | 49.95% | 48.16% | 1.89% |
| Small | 8,000 | 20,539 | 0–7 | 50.44% | 47.94% | 1.62% |
| **Total** | 20,000 | 65,469 | – | 50.25% | 47.79% | 1.96% |

In contrast to existing ABSA datasets, mASD provides:

**Character-level spans**, avoiding tokenization misalignment;
**Balanced polarity** across splits, reducing bias toward positive sentiment;
**High aspect density**, supporting robust training and evaluation.

Together, these features make mASD not only a training resource but also a **benchmark dataset** for future ABSA research.

## 5.2   Model Benchmarking on mASD

To demonstrate the utility of mASD, we benchmarked both compact and large transformers. Our baseline, MoRE-BERT, was compared with widely used models on two tasks: binary sentiment classification and span-based ABSA (Table 2).

**Table 2.** Model Benchmarking on mASD: Binary Sentiment Classification and Span-Based ABSA (Macro-Average). Metrics are reported as F1/Precision/Recall.

| Model | Binary Sentiment (F1/P/R) | Span-Based ABSA (F1/P/R) |
| --- | --- | --- |
| DeBERTa-base (100M) | 0.9139/0.8761/0.9550 | 0.8821/0.8613/0.9040 |
| RoBERTa-base (125M) | 0.9040/0.8502/0.9650 | 0.9001/0.8923/0.9080 |
| BERT-medium (42M) | 0.8199/0.7793/0.8650 | 0.8050/0.7930/0.8173 |
| DistilBERT-cased (67M) | 0.8117/0.7943/0.8300 | 0.8533/0.8926/0.8173 |
| BERT-base-cased (110M) | 0.8061/0.8229/0.7900 | 0.8322/0.8079/0.8579 |
| MoRE-BERT (6.8M) | 0.7666/0.8188/0.7560 | 0.8295/0.8008/0.8629 |
| BERT-small (29M) | 0.7268/0.7095/0.7450 | 0.7556/0.7931/0.7215 |
| BERT-tiny (4M) | 0.3963/0.5203/0.3200 | 0.7443/0.7327/0.7563 |

Following prior work on triplet and quad evaluation [13], a prediction is considered correct only if the aspect span, opinion span, and sentiment polarity all match the gold annotation. The macro-F1 thus averages performance across sentiment classes, providing a unified measure of ABSA accuracy.

### 5.3   Performance-Efficiency Tradeoff

Despite being < **7%** the size of DeBERTa [7], **MoRE-BERT** remains competitive:

- **Span-based ABSA**: **99.7%** of BERT-base F1 at **15×** smaller; **94%** of DeBERTa-base F1 with only **6.8%** of its parameters.
- **Binary Sentiment**: **+4% F1** over BERT-small at one-quarter the size; nearly **2×** BERT-tiny's F1 with minimal added parameters.

These results show that:

1. mASD provides balanced supervision for both large and compact models.
2. MoRE-BERT validates the dataset's utility by reaching near-parity with larger baselines.
3. Span-based supervision particularly benefits compact models, closing the gap with heavyweight transformers.

## 6   Conclusion

These results highlight the value of mASD. While MoRE-BERT demonstrates strong general sentiment performance, it performs even better on span-based ABSA, showing that character-level supervision offers a more effective signal for compact models. Although current evaluations are limited to synthetic movie reviews, future work will benchmark mASD and MoRE-BERT on human-annotated datasets such as SemEval 2014 and MAMS to assess real-world generalization.

# References


1. Angiani, G., et al.: A comparison between preprocessing techniques for sentiment analysis in twitter. KDWeb **7**(2), 37–56 (2016)
2. Chebolu, S.U.S., Dernoncourt, F., Lipka, N., Solorio, T.: OATS: a challenge dataset for opinion aspect target sentiment joint detection for aspect-based sentiment analysis. In: Calzolari, N., Kan, M.Y., Hoste, V., Lenci, A., Sakti, S., Xue, N. (eds.) Proceedings of the 2024 Joint International Conference on Computational Linguistics, Language Resources and Evaluation (LREC-COLING 2024), pp. 12336–12347. ELRA and ICCL, Torino, Italia, May 2024, https://aclanthology.org/2024.lrec-main.1080/
3. Dewangan, L., Sayeed, Z.A., Maurya, C.: Benchmark creation for aspect-based sentiment analysis in low-resource Odia language and evaluation through fine-tuning of multilingual models. In: Rambow, O., Wanner, L., Apidianaki, M., Al-Khalifa, H., Eugenio, B.D., Schockaert, S. (eds.) Proceedings of the 31st International Conference on Computational Linguistics, pp. 5863–5869. ACL, Abu Dhabi, UAE, January 2025, https://aclanthology.org/2025.coling-main.391/
4. Do, H.H., Prasad, P.W., Maag, A., Alsadoon, A.: Deep learning for aspect-based sentiment analysis: a comparative review. Expert Syst. Appl. **118**, 272–299 (2019)
5. Gandhi, H., Attar, V.: Extracting aspect terms using crf and bi-lstm models. Procedia Comput. Sci. **167**, 2486–2495 (2020)
6. Gupta, R., Srinivasan, K.: LightABSA: parameter-efficient aspect-based sentiment analysis using adapter fusion. In: Proceedings of the 2024 Conference on Computational Linguistics (COLING) (2024), https://aclanthology.org/2024.coling-main.405/
7. He, P., Liu, X., Gao, J., Chen, W.: Deberta: decoding-enhanced bert with disentangled attention. arXiv preprint arXiv:2006.03654 (2020)
8. Hu, M., Liu, B.: Mining and summarizing customer reviews. In: Proceedings of the tenth ACM SIGKDD International Conference on Knowledge Discovery and Data Mining, pp. 168–177 (2004)
9. Kanimozhi, U., Manjula, D.: A crf based machine learning approach for biomedical named entity recognition. In: 2017 Second International Conference on Recent Trends and Challenges in Computational Models (ICRTCCM), pp. 335–342. IEEE (2017)
10. Kumar, A., Dahiya, V., Sharan, A.: Atp: a holistic attention integrated approach to enhance absa. arXiv preprint arXiv:2208.02653 (2022)
11. Li, X., Wang, L., Yu, B.: Unifiedabsa: a unified framework for multi-domain aspect-based sentiment analysis. In: Findings of the Association for Computational Linguistics: EMNLP 2023, pp. 11890–11903 (2023), https://aclanthology.org/2023.findings-emnlp.789/
12. Maas, A.L., Daly, R.E., Pham, P.T., Huang, D., Ng, A.Y., Potts, C.: Learning word vectors for sentiment analysis. In: Proceedings of the 49th Annual Meeting of the Association for Computational Linguistics: Human Language Technologies, pp. 142–150. ACL, Portland, Oregon, USA, June 2011, http://www.aclweb.org/anthology/P11-1015
13. Mao, Y., Zhang, Y., Chen, X.: A unified metric for evaluating aspect-based sentiment triplet extraction. In: Findings of the Association for Computational Linguistics: ACL 2022, pp. 2406–2417 (2022), https://aclanthology.org/2022.findings-acl.189/

14. Pang, B., Lee, L.: A sentimental education: sentiment analysis using subjectivity summarization based on minimum cuts. arXiv preprint cs/0409058 (2004)
15. Pradha, S., Halgamuge, M.N., Vinh, N.T.Q.: Effective text data preprocessing technique for sentiment analysis in social media data. In: 2019 11th International Conference on Knowledge and Systems Engineering (KSE), pp. 1–8. IEEE (2019)
16. Šmíd, J., Přibáň, P., Prazak, O., Kral, P.: Czech dataset for complex aspect-based sentiment analysis tasks. In: Calzolari, N., Kan, M.Y., Hoste, V., Lenci, A., Sakti, S., Xue, N. (eds.) Proceedings of the 2024 Joint International Conference on Computational Linguistics, Language Resources and Evaluation (LREC-COLING 2024), pp. 4299–4310. ELRA and ICCL, Torino, Italia, May 2024, https://aclanthology.org/2024.lrec-main.384/
17. Su, J., Ahmed, M., Lu, Y., Pan, S., Bo, W., Liu, Y.: Roformer: enhanced transformer with rotary position embedding. Neurocomputing **568**, 127063 (2024)
18. TK, B., Bablani, A., Misra, H.: Sase: sentiment analysis with aspect specific evaluation using deep learning with hybrid contextual embedding. In: International Conference on Distributed Computing and Intelligent Technology, pp. 237–248. Springer (2024)
19. Wang, Y., Huang, M., Zhu, X., Zhao, L.: Attention-based lstm for aspect-level sentiment classification. In: Proceedings of the 2016 Conference on Empirical Methods in Natural Language Processing, pp. 606–615 (2016)
20. Xu, H., Li, B., Deng, S., Huang, M.: Joint aspect-sentiment quad prediction with transformers. In: Proceedings of the 60th Annual Meeting of the Association for Computational Linguistics (ACL), pp. 7654–7666 (2022), https://aclanthology.org/2022.acl-long.527/
21. Zhang, H., Li, S., Zhao, P., Liu, Y.: SpanABSA: span-based aspect sentiment analysis via transformer encoder. In: Proceedings of the 2023 Conference on Empirical Methods in Natural Language Processing (EMNLP), pp. 11234–11246. ACL (2023), https://aclanthology.org/2023.emnlp-main.698/

# Robust Sarcasm Detection
# via Dual-Pathway Modeling
# of Contextual And Affective Cues

Syed Ali Mehdi Rizvi[3](✉) (iD), Mohammad Zeeshan Parvez[1] (iD),
M Kaab Bin Shahid[4] (iD), and Haider Mustafa Naqvi[2] (iD)

[1] Aligarh Muslim University, Aligarh, India
`gn0159@myamu.ac.in`
[2] Delhi Technological University, New Delhi, India
`haidermustafanaqvi_co21b1_020@dtu.ac.in`
[3] University of Bonn, Bonn, Germany
`syedali.rizvi@uni-bonn.de`
[4] University of Stuttgart, Stuttgart, Germany
`st200st200141@stud.uni-stuttgart.de`

**Abstract.** Sarcasm detection in text remains one of the trickier problems in NLP, mainly because sarcastic statements often depend on subtle contradictions and contextual clues that aren't immediately obvious. We propose a dual pathway approach that leverages RoBERTa-based contextual embeddings alongside emoji-derived affective features, which helps the system better understand sarcastic content whether it appears in tweets or longer texts. Low data availability and the possibility of model overfitting was mitigated by the implementation of data augmentation. The developed model was trained and tested on five different benchmark datasets which includes Twitter contents, headlines and various other online forums. The proposed model demonstrated high performance by scoring up to 6% and 8% gains in F1 scores and accuracy. Additionally, on further testing, the model showed good generalization capabilities across differentdatasets.

**Keywords:** Sarcasm Detection · RoBERTa · Emoji Aware · Sentiment Analysis · Data Augmentation

## 1  Introduction

Social media sites like Twitter, Reddit, and Facebook have become an integral part of our daily communication. They offer us the opportunity to voice our opinions, share experiences, and participate in dialogues. While these platforms are useful in communication, they bring with them Natural Language Processing (NLP) complications, especially dealing with linguistic nuances like sarcasm.

Sarcasm is a style of speaking where the intended meaning of a statement is different from the actual meaning and is often used to denote mock praise.


S. Mitra et al. (Eds.): PReMI 2025, LNCS 16358, pp. 513–523, 2026.
https://doi.org/10.1007/978-3-032-18480-1_52

This gap between semantics and sentiment creates a challenge for sentiment analysis and opinion mining. Take for example the sentence "Oh great, another Monday!". This sentence might seem positive on the surface, but in reality, it is most probably said sarcastically. At this moment, traditional NLP models lack the ability to process this perfectly, resulting in incorrect classifications.

Early methods for sarcasm detection focused on inline lexical cues, punctuation, text markers, and grammatical structure. They relied on handcrafted features and rule-based systems. Even though these methods offered some initial insights, but at a large scale they were hard to scale and did not work well in different linguistic contexts. The arrival of machine learning introduced supervised systems like Support Vector Machines (SVM) and Naive Bayes classifiers, which used statistical features to improve performance. Despite this, capturing the subtle meaning of sarcasm remained a challenge for these models.

More advanced context-aware models capable of understanding semantic relationships between words and sentences have begun to surface due to deep learning. Transformers, like BERT [3] and RoBERTa [7], have accomplished several NLP tasks, including sarcasm detection, with great results. These models can be fine-tuned on specific data from their domains, which enables them to identify complex language and contextual patterns. Moreover, parts of the input which are critical for deciphering the meaning of the sentences have been clarified using attention mechanisms which improves the ability of the model to detect sarcasm.

In this work, we outline a new method for sarcasm detection using data augmentation and a dual-channel neural network approach. We expand existing datasets with synonym replacement, random insertion, deletion, swapping, and other augmentation techniques to create numerous variations for each sentence. We utilize a Custom EmojiEncoder to extract emoji embeddings with a pretrained emoji2vec model, which captures the emotive aspects tied to sarcasm. These embeddings are integrated with text features extracted from a fine-tuned RoBERTa model. The extracted features are first processed by convolutional and bidirectional LSTM layers where an attention mechanism highlights important portions of the input. The addition of residual connections and batch normalization improve training stability and overall performance.

Our experiments span five benchmark datasets: Mishra [10], Ghosh [4], IAC V1 [18], Headlines [11,12], and Riloff [15], with Ghosh serving as the primary dataset due to its substantial size of 39,000 sentences. The proposed model achieves state-of-the-art accuracy across all datasets, underscoring the efficacy of our augmentation strategies and architectural innovations.

## 2   Literature Review

Sarcasm detection has come a long way in the past ten years, growing from rule-based systems to deep-learning architectures. Recent improvements in deep learning have further improved sarcasm detection through various neural network architectures.

Zhang et al. [19] introduced a bidirectional gated recurrent unit (BiGRU) network that could automatically extract content information from textual data. Amir et al. [2] built a convolutional network (CNN)-based model that learned embedding features that were cultivated not only from discourse-based representation, but also from previous history of the user who made the post, such as posts from previously posted tweets. Ren et al. [14] further developed this idea by considering CNN-based architectures as well.

Tay et al. [17] discuss the importance of internal sentence structure and proposed an attention based technique to capture sentiment contradictions within a sentence, which helped improve sarcasm classification. Akula et al. [1] developed a multi-head attention model that identifies key sarcasm cue words and added a gated cyclic unit to capture the sequence in terms of whether it should see a different reality.

Taking these methods one step further, Guan et al. [5] proposed the Multi-head Incongruity Aware Attention Network (MIAN), which directly models semantic incongruity, an important feature when detecting sarcasm. Their approach comprises two main aspects: target semantic incongruity in one text, and contextual semantic incongruity between the target text and the context. In order to use the MIAN approach with fewer data, they implemented transfer learning, BERT-based model was pre-trained first with data on sentiment analysis (BERT-Senti) in order to better disengage features that relate to sentiment. The MIAN model uses both target text and contextual text representations using BERT-Senti. A multi-head self-match (network detects incongruity) with a multi-head co-match (network detects incongruity with context) network. The final classifier combines the self-match and co-match model representations to represent sarcasm probability. The model was trained with cross-entropy loss and tested on several benchmark datasets including Twitter Ghosh, FigLang Twitter, SARC Pol, and Ciron. Overall, results show MIAN achieves state-of-the-art performance, surpassing baselines by 3.8% on Twitter Ghosh, 1.1% on SARC Pol, and 1.9% on Ciron, with an F1-score improvement of 0.3% on FigLang Twitter.

Recent advancements in deep learning have also improved general text classification by leveraging pre-trained transformer-based models. BERT has been widely used for this purpose, typically relying on the [CLS] token embedding for sentence representation. However, studies suggest that using BERT's hidden layer embeddings instead of just the [CLS] token can further boost classification performance.

Reimers and Gurevych [13] presented Sentence-BERT to produce better sentence embeddings by using pooling on BERT's contextual embeddings in a Siamese network. Karimi et al. [6] proposed different aggregation architectures that use different combinations of the embeddings based on the final and some of the hidden layers and they reported improved success in performance on aspect-based sentiment analysis. Luo et al. [8] treated BERT embeddings using self-attention to supplement advancements for categorization tasks, and Song et al. [16] noted improved success in sarcasm and sentiment classification using a series of deep ensemble methods. Meng et al. [9] proposed a sarcasm detection model that combines BERT with an intra-sentence attention mechanism to effectively capture semantic features beyond individual sentiment words. Their model outperformed several baselines and state-of-the-art methods on public datasets, demonstrating the effectiveness of combining pretrained language models with fine-grained attention.

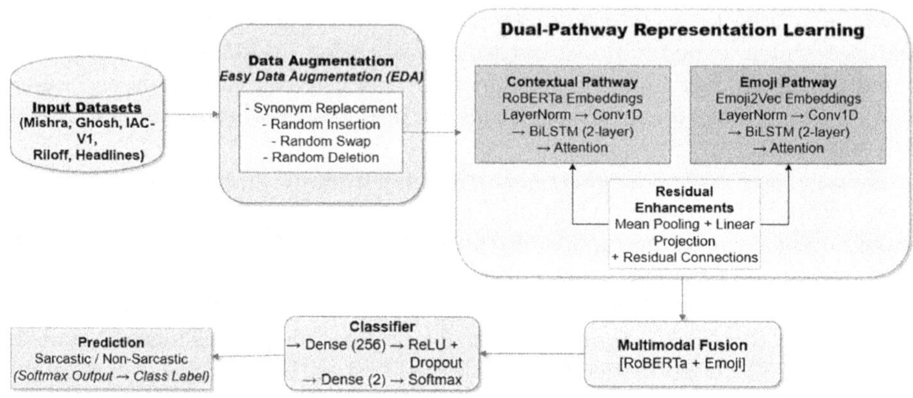


**Fig. 1.** Proposed model architecture.

# 3   Methodology

## 3.1   Model Architecture

We propose a dual-pathway neural architecture for sarcasm detection that leverages both textual and affective information from social media datasets. The architecture, illustrated in Fig. 1, consists of two parallel processing pathways that capture complementary aspects of sarcastic communication: a textual pathway that processes linguistic content using RoBERTa-based embeddings, and an affective pathway that captures emotional cues through emoji representations.

**Contextual Pathway.** Given an input token sequence $X = [x_1, x_2, \ldots, x_T]$, we obtain contextual embeddings using a pretrained RoBERTa model:

$$\mathbf{H}^{(text)} = \text{RoBERTa}(X) \in \mathbb{R}^{T \times d} \tag{1}$$

*Where* $X$ is the token sequence of length $T$; $\mathbf{H}^{(text)}$ is the contextual embedding matrix; $d$ is embedding width; $\mathbb{R}$ denotes the set of real numbers.

The embeddings are normalized using a learnable LayerNorm:

$$\tilde{\mathbf{H}}^{(text)} = \text{LayerNorm}(\mathbf{H}^{(text)}) \tag{2}$$

*Where* $\tilde{\mathbf{H}}^{(text)}$ is the layer-normalized embedding matrix; LayerNorm$(\cdot)$ applies feature-wise affine normalization.

These are then processed by a 1D convolutional layer with ReLU activation:

$$\mathbf{C}^{(text)} = \mathrm{ReLU}(\mathrm{Conv1D}(\tilde{\mathbf{H}}^{(text)})) \in \mathbb{R}^{T \times c} \tag{3}$$

*Where* Conv1D$(\cdot)$ is a temporal convolution; ReLU$(\cdot)$ is the rectified linear unit; $\mathbf{C}^{(text)}$ are conv features; $c$ is the number of output channels.

A 2-layer Bidirectional LSTM encodes sequential dependencies:

$$\mathbf{B}^{(text)} = \mathrm{BiLSTM}(\mathbf{C}^{(text)}) \in \mathbb{R}^{T \times 2h} \tag{4}$$

*Where* BiLSTM$(\cdot)$ is a two-layer bidirectional LSTM; $\mathbf{B}^{(text)}$ are its outputs; $h$ is the hidden size per direction (hence $2h$ by concatenation).

We apply a context-aware attention mechanism over time steps:

$$\alpha^{(text)} = \mathrm{softmax}(\mathbf{W}_a^{\top} \cdot \tanh(\mathbf{B}^{(text)})), \quad \mathbf{v}^{(text)} = \sum_{t=1}^{T} \alpha_t \mathbf{B}_t^{(text)} \tag{5}$$

*Where* $\mathbf{W}_a$ are attention parameters; $\tanh(\cdot)$ is hyperbolic tangent; softmax$(\cdot)$ yields weights $\alpha^{(text)}$ with $\sum_t \alpha_t = 1$; $\mathbf{B}_t^{(text)}$ is the $t$-th row of $\mathbf{B}^{(text)}$; $\mathbf{v}^{(text)} \in \mathbb{R}^{2h}$ is the attention-pooled summary.

**Affective Pathway (Emoji Encoder).** To incorporate affective information conveyed through emojis, we design a custom *EmojiEncoder* module. Each input sentence is scanned for emoji characters that are present in a pretrained `emoji2vec` vocabulary. These emojis are embedded using their pretrained vectors and the resulting sequence is either zero-padded or truncated to a fixed length of 128 to ensure consistent input shapes across the batch.

Let each emoji $e_i$ be mapped to its corresponding pretrained embedding vector as:

$$\mathbf{v}_i = \mathrm{emoji2vec}(e_i) \in \mathbb{R}^{d_e} \tag{6}$$

*Where* $e_i$ is the $i$-th emoji; `emoji2vec`$(\cdot)$ is a lookup in the pretrained emoji embedding Table; $d_e$ is the emoji embedding size.

The resulting emoji embeddings for a given input are then stacked into a sequence matrix:

$$\mathbf{E} = [\mathbf{v}_1, \mathbf{v}_2, \ldots, \mathbf{v}_K] \in \mathbb{R}^{K \times d_e}, \quad \text{where } K \leq 128 \tag{7}$$

*Where* $K$ is the number of emojis detected (capped at 128); $\mathbf{E}$ stacks the emoji vectors row-wise.

If the number of emojis in the input is less than 128, we pad with zero vectors; if greater, we truncate the sequence to the first 128 emojis. This results in a fixed-size matrix:

$$\tilde{\mathbf{E}} \in \mathbb{R}^{128 \times d_e} \tag{8}$$

*Where* $\tilde{\mathbf{E}}$ is the padded/truncated emoji matrix of fixed length 128.

We then project each emoji vector into the model's internal dimensional space using a learnable linear transformation:

$$\hat{\mathbf{E}} = \tilde{\mathbf{E}} \cdot \mathbf{W}_p + \mathbf{b}_p \in \mathbb{R}^{128 \times d} \tag{9}$$

*Where* $\mathbf{W}_p \in \mathbb{R}^{d_e \times d}$ and $\mathbf{b}_p \in \mathbb{R}^d$ are learnable projection parameters; $d$ is the model space used for fusion; $\hat{\mathbf{E}}$ are the projected emoji features (rows correspond to time steps). Downstream CNN/BiLSTM/attention produce $\mathbf{v}^{(emo)} \in \mathbb{R}^{2h}$ analogously to the text pathway.

**Residual Connections.** To preserve the original semantic information from both modalities, we apply residual connections after the BiLSTM-attention modules. For each pathway, we compute a residual vector from the mean-pooled input embeddings:

$$\mathbf{r}^{(text)} = \mathbf{W}_r^{(text)} \cdot \text{Mean}(\mathbf{H}^{(text)}) + \mathbf{b}_r^{(text)} \in \mathbb{R}^{2h} \tag{10}$$

*Where* $\text{Mean}(\cdot)$ averages rows; $\mathbf{W}_r^{(text)} \in \mathbb{R}^{d \times 2h}$, $\mathbf{b}_r^{(text)} \in \mathbb{R}^{2h}$ are learnable; $\mathbf{r}^{(text)}$ is the text residual.

$$\mathbf{r}^{(emo)} = \mathbf{W}_r^{(emo)} \cdot \text{Mean}(\hat{\mathbf{E}}) + \mathbf{b}_r^{(emo)} \in \mathbb{R}^{2h} \tag{11}$$

*Where* $\mathbf{W}_r^{(emo)} \in \mathbb{R}^{d \times 2h}$, $\mathbf{b}_r^{(emo)} \in \mathbb{R}^{2h}$ are learnable; $\mathbf{r}^{(emo)}$ is the emoji residual. These residuals are added to their respective representations:

$$\mathbf{v}'^{(text)} = \mathbf{v}^{(text)} + \mathbf{r}^{(text)}, \quad \mathbf{v}'^{(emo)} = \mathbf{v}^{(emo)} + \mathbf{r}^{(emo)} \tag{12}$$

*Where* $\mathbf{v}^{(text)}, \mathbf{v}^{(emo)} \in \mathbb{R}^{2h}$ are pathway summaries; primes denote residual-enhanced vectors.

**Feature Fusion and Classification.** The residual-enhanced features from both pathways are concatenated:

$$\mathbf{v}^{(fused)} = [\mathbf{v}'^{(text)}; \mathbf{v}'^{(emo)}] \in \mathbb{R}^{4h} \tag{13}$$

*Where* $[\cdot; \cdot]$ concatenates along the feature dimension; $\mathbf{v}^{(fused)}$ is the joint representation.

We pass this through fully connected layers with ReLU and dropout:

$$\mathbf{z}_1 = \text{ReLU}(\mathbf{W}_1 \mathbf{v}^{(fused)} + \mathbf{b}_1) \tag{14}$$

*Where* $\mathbf{W}_1, \mathbf{b}_1$ are learnable FC weights/bias (shape-consistent); $\mathbf{z}_1$ is the hidden activation.

$$\mathbf{z}_2 = \text{Dropout}(\text{ReLU}(\mathbf{W}_2 \mathbf{z}_1 + \mathbf{b}_2)) \tag{15}$$

*Where* $\mathbf{W}_2, \mathbf{b}_2$ are FC parameters; $\text{Dropout}(\cdot)$ randomly masks features with rate $p$ (hyperparameter).

The final prediction is obtained via a softmax layer:

$$\hat{\mathbf{y}} = \mathrm{softmax}(\mathbf{W}_3\mathbf{z}_2 + \mathbf{b}_3) \tag{16}$$

*Where* $\mathbf{W}_3, \mathbf{b}_3$ map to class logits; $\hat{\mathbf{y}}$ is the class-probability vector (e.g., sarcasm vs. non-sarcasm).

## 3.2   Augmentation Strategy

Our preliminary work with RoBERTa on the datasets revealed high accuracy on training, but lower on validation, that indicated overfitting. To mitigate this, we adopted a method of data augmentation inspired by the Easy Data Augmentation (EDA) framework, customized for sentence-level sarcasm detection.

The dataset consists of single-sentence inputs which can be classified under either sarcastic (1) or non-sarcastic (0). Each sentence in the dataset has **two augmented versions**, which resulted in a **3× expansion** the original dataset. We investigated one, two and three augmentations per sentence, but in our best-case example we found two augmentations to give us the best performance.

**EDA Operations Used:** Following 4 operations were applied to each sentence:

- **Synonym Replacement (SR)**: Randomly select $n$ words and replace each with a synonym using WordNet. For example, "I totally love this amazing product" becomes "I totally *adore* this amazing product".
- **Random Insertion (RI)**: Insert $n$ synonyms of existing words at random positions. For instance, "That was brilliant" becomes "That was *splendid* brilliant".
- **Random Swap (RS)**: Randomly swap the positions of $n$ word pairs to encourage syntactic variation. For example, "He actually meant it" becomes "Actually he meant it".
- **Random Deletion (RD)**: Delete each word in the sentence with a fixed probability $p$, introducing controlled noise. For instance, "This is not funny at all" becomes "This is funny".

Each sentence was passed through all four operations with empirically chosen hyperparameters ($\alpha = 0.1$ for SR, RI, RS and $p = 0.1$ for RD). From these, the two most semantically coherent augmented sentences were retained along with the original.

**Implementation Details.** The augmentation pipeline was implemented using Python and NLTK's WordNet interface. All augmented samples preserved the original label and were appended to the training set. This augmentation process was applied across the following five datasets:

1. Mishra [10]
2. Ghosh [4]

3. IAC-V1 [18]
4. Riloff [15]
5. Headlines [11,12]

This augmentation significantly improved model generalization by introducing linguistic diversity and robustness to sentence-level noise. Notably, it was instrumental in achieving state-of-the-art performance across several benchmarks. Sample augmentation is shown in Table 1.

**Table 1.** Summary of Datasets Used

| Dataset | Source | Size | Format |
|---|---|---|---|
| Riloff Corpus [15] | Twitter | ~3,200 tweets | Short-form, manually annotated |
| Mishra Dataset [10] | Twitter | ~5,000 tweets | Text-only annotations |
| Ghosh Dataset [4] | Twitter | ~39,780 tweets | Hashtag-labeled, manually cleaned |
| News Headlines Corpus [11,12] | Satirical and real news | ~28,000 headlines (13K sarcastic) | Editorial headlines (Onion vs. Huffington Post) |
| IAC v1 [18] | Online Forums | Thousands of posts | Quoteresponse pairs |

## 4    Datasets and Evaluation Metrics

Sarcasm detection is a context-sensitive task, and the quality and diversity of datasets play a crucial role in model performance. In this study, we utilize five publicly available and widely benchmarked datasets as shown in Table 1 which spans different domains such as social media posts, editorial news, and online forum discussions. These datasets have been frequently used in prior research. Collectively, they comprise over 100,000 annotated examples.

**Table 2.** Comparison of our model (RoBERTa-Base + 2× augmentation) against Jiana et al. [9] on three sarcasm detection datasets.

| Dataset | Jiana et al. [9] | | Ours (RoBERTa-Base) | | Gain | |
|---|---|---|---|---|---|---|
| | $F_1$ (%) | Acc. (%) | $F_1$ (%) | Acc. (%) | $F_1$ | Acc. |
| Ghosh | 85.23 | 85.24 | 89.69 | 93.36 | +4.46 | +8.12 |
| Mishra | 91.42 | 92.00 | 93.18 | 95.00 | +1.76 | +3.00 |
| IAC-V1 | 66.88 | 67.74 | 72.81 | 70.50 | +5.93 | +2.76 |

## 4.1   Comparison

Table 2 contrasts the best results reported by Jiana et al. [9]. We compare $F_1$ and accuracy of our top model (RoBERTa-Base fine-tuned with 2 times augmentation) on the three datasets. We observe consistent gains in both metrics across corpora, with the largest relative $F_1$ uplift (5.93 approx) on the IAC-V1 long-text set.

## 4.2   Discussion

To isolate the impact of different pretrained backbones on the most challenging Ghosh set, Table 3 presents $F_1$, accuracy, recall and precision for each variant. Our experiments show that RoBERTa-Base with aggressive augmentation achieves the best overall balance of precision and recall. The improvements seen in Table 2 are primarily from two factors: First, RoBERTa's deeper transformer layers yield richer contextual embeddings, which are crucial for capturing subtle incongruity in sarcastic expressions. Second, our 2× data augmentation by paraphrasing each training sentence twice, boosts the model's robustness to varied surface forms, particularly in the long-text IAC corpora where linguistic style is more heterogeneous. To further assess our RoBERTa-Base model's generality, we evaluated it on the Riloff rule-based sarcasm corpus and the Headlines sarcasm dataset. Table 4 reports $F_1$ and accuracy for these two benchmarks using our best setup (2× data augmentation).

**Table 3.** Detailed performance on Ghosh across backbones.

| Model | $F_1$ (%) | Acc. (%) | Recall (%) | Precision (%) |
| --- | --- | --- | --- | --- |
| BERT-Base | 74.00 | 76.00 | 75.00 | 74.00 |
| RoBERTa-Large | 50.00 | 52.00 | 48.00 | 52.00 |
| RoBERTa-Base (1×) | 80.63 | 87.68 | 82.00 | 79.30 |
| RoBERTa-Base (2×) | **89.69** | **93.36** | **90.10** | **89.30** |

**Table 4.** Our RoBERTa-Base (+2× augmentation) on Riloff and Headlines.

| Dataset | $F_1$ (%) | Accuracy (%) |
| --- | --- | --- |
| Riloff Rule-Based Corpus | 96.15 | 97.20 |
| Headlines Sarcasm Corpus | 89.02 | 90.15 |

# 5    Conclusion and Future Work

This study shows that with thoughtful tuning and structured data augmentation, transformer models like RoBERTa-Base can significantly improve sarcasm detection across varied text types. The enhanced performance across datasets from the linguistically complex IAC-V1 to simpler Twitter data, indicates the model's ability to understand sarcasm beyond surface-level word patterns.

Looking ahead, there are several paths worth exploring. Sarcasm often overlaps with irony or humor, so jointly learning these could deepen understanding. Also, current augmentations are mostly surface-level, that is methods like style transfer that preserve sarcasm could add value. Finally, incorporating speaker context or dialogue history, especially in social media, might improve interpretation of sarcastic replies.

# References


1. Akula, A., Anvesh, I., Zimmermann, R.: A cascading gated attention network for sarcasm detection. In: Proceedings of the 58th Annual Meeting of the Association for Computational Linguistics, pp. 5951–5960 (2020)
2. Amir, S., Wallace, B.C., Lyu, M., Carvalho, P., Silva, M.J.: Modelling context with user embeddings for sarcasm detection in social media. In: Proceedings of the 20th SIGNLL Conference on Computational Natural Language Learning (2016)
3. Devlin, J., Chang, M.W., Lee, K., Toutanova, K.: Bertpre-training of deep bidirectional transformers for language understanding. In: Proceedings of the 2019 Conference of the North American Chapter of the Association for Computational Linguistics: Human Language Technologies, Volume 1 (Long and Short Papers), pp. 4171–4186. ACL (2019)
4. Ghosh, D., Fabbri, A.R., Muresan, S.: Sarcasm analysis using conversation context. Comput. Linguist. **44**(4), 755–792 (2018)
5. Guan, J., Du, J., Qin, T., Liu, Z.: A multi-head incongruity-aware attention network for sarcasm detection. In: Proceedings of the AAAI Conference on Artificial Intelligence, vol. 35, pp. 14385–14393 (2021)
6. Karimi, S., Vu, D.T., Cavedon, L.: Embedding-based sarcasm detection in social media: a comparative study. In: Proceedings of the 28th International Conference on Computational Linguistics, pp. 3245–3257 (2020)
7. Liu, Y., et al.: Roberta: a robustly optimized bert pretraining approach. arXiv preprint arXiv:1907.11692 (2019)
8. Luo, D., Zhang, Y., Zhang, Q., Wang, W.: Sarcasm detection with self-attentive lstm networks. In: Proceedings of the 2019 Conference on Empirical Methods in Natural Language Processing, pp. 5107–5116 (2019)
9. Meng, J., Zhu, Y., Sun, S., Zhao, D.: Sarcasm detection based on bert and attention mechanism. Multimedia Tools Appl. (2023)
10. Mishra, A., Kanojia, D., Nagar, S., Dey, K., Bhattacharyya, P.: Harnessing cognitive features for sarcasm detection. arXiv preprint arXiv:1701.05574 (2017)
11. Misra, R., Arora, P.: Sarcasm detection using news headlines dataset. AI Open **4**, 13–18 (2023)
12. Misra, R., Grover, J.: Sculpting data for ML: the first act of machine learning, January 2021

13. Reimers, N., Gurevych, I.: Sentence-bert: sentence embeddings using siamese bert-networks. In: Proceedings of the 2019 Conference on Empirical Methods in Natural Language Processing, pp. 3982–3992 (2019)
14. Ren, X., Wu, Z., Chen, W., Huang, X.: Detecting sarcasm in multi-modal social platforms. In: Proceedings of the 2020 Conference on Empirical Methods in Natural Language Processing (EMNLP), pp. 4442–4452 (2020)
15. Riloff, E., Qadir, A., Surve, P., De Silva, L., Gilbert, N., Huang, R.: Sarcasm as contrast between a positive sentiment and negative situation. In: Yarowsky, D., Baldwin, T., Korhonen, A., Livescu, K., Bethard, S. (eds.) Proceedings of the 2013 Conference on Empirical Methods in Natural Language Processing, pp. 704–714. ACL, Seattle, Washington, USA, October 2013
16. Song, J., Li, Y., Zhao, Y.: Sarcasm detection using deep ensemble learning. In: 2021 IEEE International Conference on Big Data (Big Data), IEEE (2021)
17. Tay, Y., Tuan, L., Hui, S.C.: Reasoning with sarcasm by reading in-between. In: Proceedings of the 56th Annual Meeting of the Association for Computational Linguistics (Volume 1: Long Papers), pp. 1010–1020 (2018)
18. Walker, M.A., Anand, P., Abbott, R., Grant, R.: A corpus for research on deliberation and debate. In: Proceedings of the International Conference on Language Resources and Evaluation (LREC), vol. 12. European Language Resources Association (ELRA) (2012)
19. Zhang, L., Wang, S., Liu, B.: Detecting sarcasm in twitter: a contrastive learning approach. In: Proceedings of the 25th ACM International on Conference on Information and Knowledge Management, pp. 765–774. ACM (2016)

# Graph Based Context-Aware Sentiment Driven Fake News Detection Framework


Gaurav Kumar and Chhavi Dhiman[(✉)]

Delhi Technological University, Delhi 110042, India
chhavi.dhiman@dtu.ac.in



**Abstract.** The rapid and widespread dissemination of fake news across digital platforms poses a serious threat to public trust in online media. The fake news often spreads rapidly because its complex and context-dependent nature, which enables it to bypass the traditional detection systems that lack deeper contextual understanding of information shared on news websites and social media. Existing detection approaches, particularly traditional content-based models, struggle to capture the interplay between textual content, social propagation patterns, and critical contextual or emotional cues. Our research addresses this critical gap by introducing a novel Context-Aware Sentiment Driven (gCASD) Fake News Detection framework that integrates Graph learning with Sentiment-Attuned Transformers to capture the deeper context and temporal feature for better detection. Extensive experiments show that the framework achieves strong performance, reaching validation accuracy of 94.13% on Politifact dataset and 88.54% and GossipCop dataset. These results consistently outperform other established methods, offering a more robust detection against fake news.

**Keywords:** Fake News Detection (FND) · Graph · Sentiment · Context-Aware · NLP · BERT · Transformer


## 1 Introduction

In today's digitally interconnected world, unrestricted access to vast amounts of unfiltered information has accelerated the spread of fake news, eroding public trust and social stability. Many individuals accept misinformation without verification, as fake news exploits complex multi-contextual cues, distorts facts, and manipulates emotions while mimicking legitimate reporting [1]. Recent study [2] highlight major gaps in fake news detection (FND), including limited explainability, reliance on binary classification, language disparities, lack of standard benchmarks, and underuse of diverse embedding methods.

Traditional detection methods primarily analyze linguistic patterns or cross-verify content using external sources (e.g., Wikipedia) and user interactions. However, they often neglect the broader contextual environment, emotional undertones, and social propagation patterns crucial for identifying misinformation. Existing approaches—such as similarity-based [3, 4], early detection model, user aware model [5], social graph


© The Author(s), under exclusive license to Springer Nature Switzerland AG 2026
S. Mitra et al. (Eds.): PReMI 2025, LNCS 16358, pp. 524–532, 2026.
https://doi.org/10.1007/978-3-032-18480-1_53

based detection [6, 7], context model, and hybrid model offer fragmented views and struggle with rephrased content, data sparsity, bot interference, and scalability.

Existing fake news detection models are ineffective against sophisticated campaigns because they offer a fragmented view of misinformation. Traditional methods—including those based on text similarity, user data, and social graphs—are easily evaded by content rephrasing, struggle with the cold start problem and data scarcity, and are vulnerable to bot attacks and complexity issues. This paper makes the following key contributions:

1. Proposes a novel Graph-based Context-Aware Sentiment Driven (gCASD) framework that jointly learns contextual, temporal, and sentiment features for improved fake news detection.
2. Addresses limitations of existing models by mitigating data scarcity, computational complexity, privacy issues, and susceptibility to coordinated or adversarial misinformation attacks, offering a more robust and adaptive defence.

The paper is organized as follows: Sect. 2 reviews related work on contextual detection; Sect. 3 details the proposed gCASD architecture and methodology; Sect. 4 presents experimental results and analysis; and Sect. 5 concludes with insights and future research directions.

## 2 Literature Review

This section reviews the evolution of state-of-the-art methods, demonstrating their inability to handle advanced language patterns and complex expressions that easily bypass traditional detection systems. We organize the discussion into four categories: (1) Social Context based Method, (2) Knowledge-Based Methods, (3) Meta-data Based Method, and (4) Hybrid Model.

### 2.1 Social Context Based Method

Ciprian-Octavian Truică et al. developed DANES (Deep Neural Network Ensemble Architecture for Social and Textual Context-aware Fake News Detection) [8]. This framework combines a Text Branch (using domain-specific or character n-gram embeddings) with a Social Branch to generate a novel Network Embedding that effectively captures user interactions. DANES achieved promising accuracy on datasets like BuzzFace, Twitter15, and Twitter16, outperforming existing state-of-the-art solutions, but it lacks adaptability against various linguistic, stylistic, psychological, and global features. Another work [9] introduced a novel Transformer-based framework (inspired by BART) that leverages rich information from news content and social contexts via various embeddings to capture nuanced textual and temporal patterns. It also proposed an effective weak supervision labelling scheme to mitigate data scarcity and enhance early fake news detection.

### 2.2 Knowledge-Based Methods

Knowledge based methods integrates external knowledge such a Hashtag Context-aware Fake News Detection (HCFND) [10] a recent novel model which leverage content from hashtags and named entities. This allows HCFND to cross-reference source posts with data from relevant communities, significantly enhancing authenticity verification but its key limitations are its inability to work with Social Interaction Networks, reliance on outdated information, limited long-tail knowledge, and the risk of exposing private training data.

### 2.3  Meta-data Based Method

Hetero-SCAN [11] a novel inductive fake news detection framework. Hetero-SCAN utilizes Meta-Path to extract meaningful multi-level social context, and introduces Meta-Path instance encoding and aggregation methods to capture temporal user engagement and enable end-to-end learning of news representation. Despite these advancements, the approach has limitations. It's impractical to use every user's information due to the sheer volume; thus, it employed simple random sampling to select users.

### 2.4  Hybrid Models

Hybrid Models utilize multiple aspects to learn the deeper semantics of the given data such as recent work by *Jawaher Alghamdi et al.* [12] and Szu-Yin Lin et al. [13] that leverages temporal, social graph, or hybrid contextual features for prediction of fake news.

Our current work addresses a specific research gap by integrating sentiment features with these elements into a novel methodology for a more robust framework.

## 3  Proposed Methodology

This study presents the **Graph-based Context-Aware Sentiment-Driven (gCASD)** architecture (Fig. 1) for fake news detection, leveraging a fine-tuned **BERT Transformer** for final classification. The framework integrates **Graph Neural Networks (GNNs)** to capture social diffusion patterns and **sentiment features** to detect emotional and manipulative cues. By jointly learning from graph structures, contextual semantics, and sentiment polarity, gCASD surpasses traditional fragmented approaches. Experimental results confirm substantial improvements in accuracy, robustness, and interpretability over baseline methods.

**Data Preprocessing:** Raw data undergoes cleaning, normalization, and balancing to ensure structured inputs removing duplicates, handling missing values, equalizing "Real" and "Fake" samples, and refining text through stopword removal, stemming, and lemmatization.

**Feature Extraction and Representation:** Processed data is then used to extract features that enrich BERT's contextual understanding. The Title Feature captures the article's core theme, while GloVe embeddings model deep semantic relationships using a weighting function to mitigate the effects of rare or overly frequent word co-occurrences. GloVe employs a weighting function:

$$f(Y_{mn}) = (\frac{Y_{mn}}{y_{max}})^{\alpha} \text{ if } Y_{mn} < y_{max} \tag{1}$$

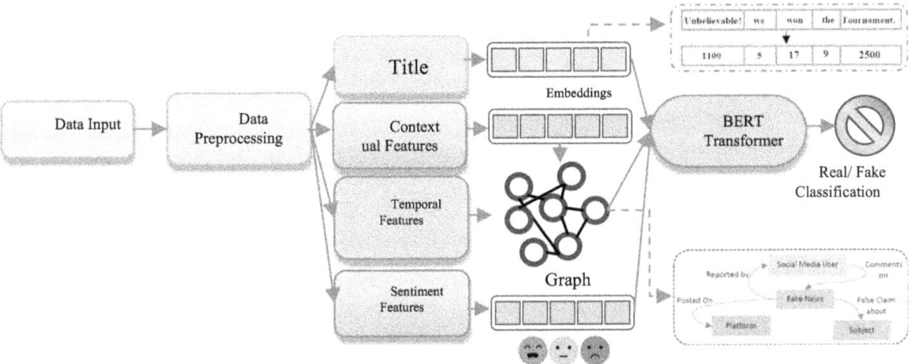


**Fig. 1.** Context-Aware Sentiment-Driven (gCASD) Architecture for Fake News Detection

$$f(Y_{mn}) = 1 \text{ if } Y_{mn} > y_{max} \tag{2}$$

here $y_{max}$ and $\alpha$ are hyperparameters that can be tuned.

The fundamental principle behind GloVe is to minimize the following cost function (J):

$$J = \sum_{m=1}^{V} \sum_{n=1}^{V} f(Y_{mn}) \left( w_m^T \tilde{w}_n + b_m + \tilde{b}_n - \log Y_{mn} \right)^2 \tag{3}$$

In this equation:

V represents the **vocabulary size.**

$w_m$ and $\tilde{w}_n$ are the **word vectors** for words **m** and **n** respectively.

$b_m$ and $\tilde{b}_n$ are the corresponding **bias terms** for words **m** and **n** respectively.

$Y_{mn}$ signifies the **co-occurrence count** of word **n** within the context of word **m**.

$\log Y_{mn}$ is the **logarithm of this co-occurrence count.**

$f(Y_{mn})$ is the **weighting function** previously described.

**Contextual Features:** Captures the broader environment by analyzing information sources and metadata (e.g., URLs, Post IDs). Extracted correlations are transformed into embeddings for Graph Network integration, enhancing understanding of content origin and spread.

**Temporal Features:** Encode time-based attributes such as publication timestamps, user propagation patterns, and dissemination speed to model news evolution. These features are converted into embeddings for integration into the Graph Network.

**Algorithm 1: Contextual and Temporal Feature Extraction for Graph Learning**

**Input:**

$D = \{P_1, P_2, P_3, \ldots\ldots P_n\}$: A dataset of $n$ posts. Each post $P_i$ is characterized by:

$S_{PostID, i}$: PostID string (e.g., "gossipcop-877807")

$T_{url, i}$: News URL string (e.g., "https://example.com/latest_news")

$I_i$: Title string (e.g., "9 Beauty Items Kim Kardashian's Makeup Artist Mario Dedivanovic Buys at the Drugstore")

$L_{TweetID, i}$: List of strings/numerical IDs representing Tweet IDs indicating resharing
(e.g., ["905149507112919041", "905149833626955776"])

$N_{ts, i}$: Numerical Timestamp (e.g., Unix timestamp, or a normalized numerical value, for temporal feature)

$V_{sen, i}$: Sentiment features (pre-extracted vector of [positive_score, neutral_score, negative_score], typically from a dataframe row)

**Output:**

$F = \{F_1, F_2, F_3, \ldots\ldots F_n\}$: Pre-tokenization concatenation of textual columns for all posts.

1:  Initialize $F_i \leftarrow [S_{PostID, i}, T_{url, i}, I_i]$

2:  for each post $P_i$ in $D$ do

3:  Concatenate all textual components with BERT's special tokens.

4:  $Post_{encoding} \leftarrow F_i$

5:  Obtain Textual Embedding from BERT

6:  $Tokens_i \leftarrow$ BERT$(Post_{encoding})$

7:  Embed Non-Textual, Temporal, and Pre-extracted Sentiment Features

8:  Transform the numerical timestamp into a dense vector.

9:  $D_{ts} \leftarrow \mathbf{T}(N_{ts})$; where $\mathbf{T}$ transforms numerical timestamps $(N_{ts})$ in dense vectors

10:  $D_{sen} \leftarrow \mathbf{T}(V_{sen})$; where $\mathbf{T}$ transforms sentiment feature $(V_{sen})$ in dense vectors

11:  Fuse All Features

12:  Concatenate all individual embeddings to form the final feature vector for post $P_i$.

13:  $FP_i \leftarrow Concat(Tokens_i, D_{ts}, D_{sen})$

15:  $F_{combined_set}.$append$(FP_i)$

16:  return $F_{combined_set}$

**Sentiment Features:** Utilize SentiWordNet[1] [14, 15] to extract sentiment polarity (positive, negative, neutral) and intensity, converting these affective cues into numerical embeddings for graph integration.

**Graph Network Construction and BERT Embeddings:** A **NetworkX**[2] based graph models relational dependencies in misinformation spread by embedding contextual, temporal, and sentiment features into nodes and edges. These embeddings, combined with title features, form a unified feature vector input to a fine-tuned **BERT Transformer**, serving as the primary classifier for binary (*Real/Fake*) news detection.

**Dataset and Evaluation:** The framework is evaluated on the *FakeNewsNet*[3] dataset, dataset, incorporating labeled articles and social context from *PolitiFact* and *GossipCop*.

---

[1] https://www.kaggle.com/datasets/nltkdata/sentiwordnet.

[2] https://networkx.org/documentation/latest/install.html.

[3] https://github.com/KaiDMML/FakeNewsNet.

BERT encodes textual content, while NetworkX captures temporal and user interaction dynamics (e.g., follower and retweet patterns) for comprehensive fake news detection.

## 4  Experimental Results and Analysis

The proposed **Graph-based Context-Aware Sentiment Driven (gCASD)** framework demonstrates superior fake news detection performance on both **PolitiFact** and **Gossip-Cop** datasets. As shown in Tables 1 and 2 and Fig. 2, gCASD achieves **94.13%** accuracy on PolitiFact and **88.54%** on GossipCop, outperforming benchmark models such as **BERTbase-mCNN-sBiGRU** (92.09%, 86.40%) and **DANES** across all key metrics—accuracy, precision, recall, and F1-score. These results underscore gCASD's strength in capturing complex, multi-contextual, and sentiment-driven aspects of misinformation (Fig. 3).

**Ablation Study:**  To evaluate component contributions, an ablation study on the PolitiFact dataset analyzed the **Graph-based FND (context-aware)** and **SentiWordNet (sentiment-aware)** modules. The complete gCASD model achieved an **accuracy of 0.94, precision of 0.84, recall of 0.90**, and **F1-score of 0.87**, outperforming both ablated variants. The SentiWordNet module achieved an **AUC of 0.8709**, slightly higher than the Graph-based FND's **0.86**, confirming that integrating contextual and sentiment-aware features yields the best overall performance and validates the model's synergistic design (Table 3).

**Table 1.** Performance of the gCASD Framework on Politifact Datasets

| MODEL | ACC | PREC | REC | F1 |
| --- | --- | --- | --- | --- |
| BERTbase-mCNN-sBiGRU [12] | 0.92 | 0.96 | 0.90 | 0.92 |
| LIWC + User + VGG19(1000)-LR [13] | 0.85 | 0.86 | 0.89 | 0.86 |
| Context aware FND (Graph based Temporal Modelling) | 0.86 | 0.83 | 0.65 | 0.73 |
| Sentiment aware FND (SentiWordNet) | 0.87 | 0.75 | 0.89 | 0.81 |
| **gCASD: Graph based Context-Aware Sentiment Driven Fake News Detection** | **0.94** | 84.71 | 0.90 | 0.87 |

**Table. 2.**  Performance of the gCASD Framework on GossipCop Datasets

| MODEL | ACC | PREC | REC | F1 |
|---|---|---|---|---|
| BERTbase-mCNN-sBiGRU [12] | 0.86 | 0.87 | 0.96 | 0.91 |
| LIWC + User + VGG19(1000)-LR [13] | 0.69 | 0.70 | 0.70 | 0.70 |
| Context aware FND (Graph based Temporal Modelling) | **0.87** | 0.82 | 0.72 | 0.77 |
| Sentiment aware FND (SentiWordNet) | **0.81** | 0.83 | 0.82 | 0.83 |
| **gCASD: Graph based Context-Aware Sentiment Driven Fake News Detection** | **0.88** | 0.78 | 0.81 | 0.80 |

**Table. 3.**  Impact of Individual Components on Proposed Model Performance for Politifact Dataset

| MODEL | ACC | PREC | REC | F1 |
|---|---|---|---|---|
| Context aware FND (Graph based Temporal Modelling) | 0.86 | 0.83 | 0.65 | 0.73 |
| Sentiment aware FND (SentiWordNet) | 0.87 | 0.75 | 0.89 | 0.81 |
| gCASD: Graph based Context-Aware Sentiment Driven Fake News Detection | **0.94** | 0.84 | 0.90 | 0.87 |

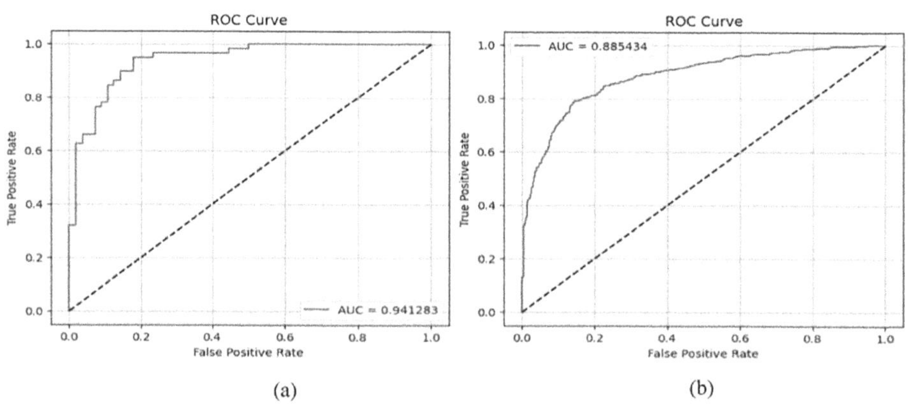


(a)                           (b)

**Fig. 2.**  Learning Curves of gCASD Framework for fake news detection (a) For PolitiFact Dataset (b) For GossipCop Dataset

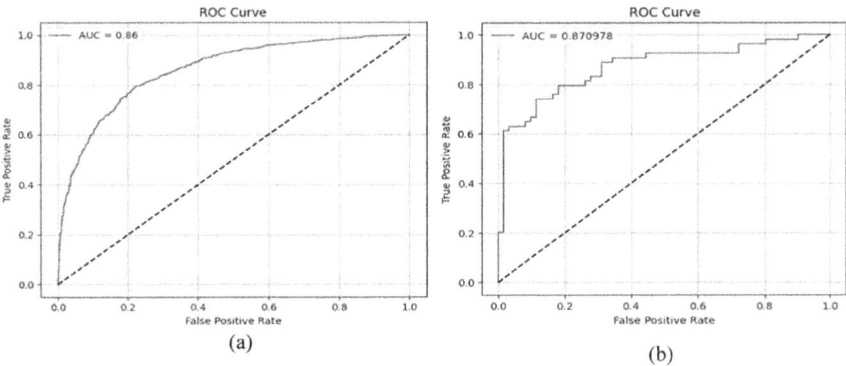

**Fig. 3.** Ablation Study (a) Graph based FND (Context aware) (b) SentiWordNet (Sentiment aware)

## 5  Conclusion and Future Work

In conclusion, the proposed Graph-based Context-Aware Sentiment Driven (gCASD) framework effectively advances fake news detection by integrating Graph Neural Networks and Sentiment-Attuned Transformers to capture relational, contextual, and emotional nuances. Achieving accuracies of 94.13% on Politifact and 88.54% on GossipCop, gCASD consistently outperforms existing methods, demonstrating superior robustness against complex and sentiment-driven misinformation. However, its reliance on textual data, English-only datasets, and high computational demands limits scalability and generalization. Future work will focus on extending gCASD to multimodal fake news detection, optimizing it for real-time deployment through model compression, and enhancing its resilience against adversarial manipulation.

## 6  Disclosure of Interests.

The authors declare that they have no known competing financial interests or personal relationships that could have influenced the work reported in this paper.

## References


1. Das, B., TSB, S.: Multi-contextual learning in disinformation research: a review of challenges, approaches, and opportunities. Online Soc. Netw. Media **34–35**(March), 100247 (2023). https://doi.org/10.1016/j.osnem.2023.100247
2. Hussain, F.G., Wasim, M., Hameed, S., Rehman, A., Asim, M.N., Dengel, A.: Fake news detection landscape: datasets, data modalities, AI Approaches, their challenges, and future perspectives. IEEE Access **13**(April), 54757–54778 (2025). https://doi.org/10.1109/ACCESS.2025.3553909
3. Fabio, J., Bezerra, R., Kozierkiewicz, A., Pietranik, M.: A novel approach for tweet similarity in a context-aware fake news detection model. IEEE Access **13**(February), 57043–57061 (2025). https://doi.org/10.1109/ACCESS.2025.3554540

4. Sheng, Q., Cao, J., Zhang, X., Li, R., Wang, D., Zhu, Y.: Zoom out and observe: news environment perception for fake news detection. Proc. Annu. Meet. Assoc. Comput. Linguist. **1**, 4543–4556 (2022). https://doi.org/10.18653/v1/2022.acl-long.311

5. Su, X., Yang, J., Wu, J., Zhang, Y.: Mining user-aware multi-relations for fake news detection in large scale online social networks. In: WSDM 2023 – Proceedings of 16th ACM International Conference on Web Search Data Mining, pp. 51–59 (2023). https://doi.org/10.1145/3539597.3570478

6. Grover, K., Angara, S.M.P., Akhtar, M.S., Chakraborty, T.: Public wisdom matters! discourse-aware hyperbolic Fourier co-attention for social-text classification. In: Advances in Neural Information Processing Systems, vol. 35, no. NeurIPS, pp. 1–15 (2022)

7. Hu, L., et al.: Compare to the knowledge: graph neural fake news detection with external knowledge. In: ACL-IJCNLP 2021 - 59th Annual of the Association for Computational Linguistics, 11th International Joint Conference on Natural Language Processing, Proceedings Conference, pp. 754–763 (2021) https://doi.org/10.18653/v1/2021.acl-long.62

8. Truică, C.O., Apostol, E.S., Karras, P.: DANES: deep neural network ensemble architecture for social and textual context-aware fake news detection. Knowl.-Based Syst. **294**(March), 111715 (2024). https://doi.org/10.1016/j.knosys.2024.111715

9. Raza, S., Ding, C.: Fake news detection based on news content and social contexts: a transformer-based approach. Int. J. Data Sci. Anal. **13**(4), 335–362 (2022). https://doi.org/10.1007/s41060-021-00302-z

10. Kumar, S., Agrahari, S., Soni, P., Sachdeva, A., Singh, S.R.: Fake news detection using hashtag context. Pattern Recog. Lett. **193**(April), 43–49 (2025). https://doi.org/10.1016/j.patrec.2025.04.008

11. Cui, J., Kim, K., Na, S.H., Shin, S.: Meta-path-based fake news detection leveraging multi-level social context information. In: International Conference on Information and Knowledge Management Proceedings, pp. 325–334 (2022). https://doi.org/10.1145/3511808.3557394

12. Alghamdi, J., Lin, Y., Luo, S.: The power of context: a novel hybrid context-aware fake news detection approach. Inf. **15**(3), 1–22 (2024). https://doi.org/10.3390/info15030122

13. Lin, S.Y., Hu, Y.H., Lee, P.J., Zeng, Y.H., Chang, C.M., Chang, H.C.: Fake news detection model with hybrid features—news text, image, and social context. Inf. Syst. Front. (2025). https://doi.org/10.1007/s10796-025-10589-z

14. Baccianella, S., Esuli, A., Sebastiani, F.: SENTIWORDNET 3.0: an enhanced lexical resource for sentiment analysis and opinion mining. In: Proceedings of 7th International Conference on Language Resource s and Evaluation, Lr. 2010, vol. 0, pp. 2200–2204 (2010)

15. Denecke, K., Using SentiWordNet for multilingual sentiment analysis. In: Proceedings - International Conference on Data Engineering, pp. 507–512 (2008). https://doi.org/10.1109/ICDEW.2008.4498370

# CustomsBERT: A Production-Ready Transformer Framework with Hybrid Clustering for Automated HS Code Classification and Real-Time Validation in Indirect Tax Administration and Trade Assistance Systems


Ramesh Moorthy[1(✉)], Shivam Dhamanikar[1], Kopal Tandon[1], Prashant Gidde[2], and Suresh Kannan Nadar[2]

[1] National Customs Targeting Center (NCTC), Mumbai, India
`{mramesh.irs,shivam.dhamanikar,kopal.tandon}@gov.in`
[2] Tata Consultancy Services, Mumbai, India
`{prashant.gidde,sureshkannan.nadar}@tcs.com`



**Abstract.** The accurate assignment and validation of Harmonized System (HS) codes for traded goods is critical for customs and indirect tax administration to prevent revenue leakages through commodity misclassification. This research aligns with the IndiaAI mission's objective to foster AI innovation for public sector governance, as India processes 4.7 million import declarations annually. Traditional automated systems face severe limitations: conventional machine learning approaches lack semantic understanding, exhibit bias toward historical data, and cannot handle extreme class imbalances, making them unsuitable for real-time validation environments requiring accurate interpretation of complex customs terminology. This study presents CustomsBERT, a production-ready framework for real-time validation of electronic trade declarations, combining root-representative hybrid clustering with domain-specific BERT fine-tuning to deliver accurate, scalable HS code validation. To address severe class imbalance in the NCTC Customs Import Dataset (5.9M samples across 7,683 HS code classes), we developed a hybrid clustering approach combining BM25 lexical similarity and cross-encoder semantic similarity. Three transformer architectures DistilBERT-base-uncased, ModernBERT-base, and RoBERTa-base were fine-tuned on filtered data (100–1,000 samples/class) using 72-token sequence lengths. RoBERTa-base achieved superior performance with 70.94% validation accuracy and 0.7071 F1-score, demonstrating 12.1% improvement over baseline Distil-BERT. This framework enables seamless integration with existing customs filing systems, providing tax administrations with automated HS code validation that enhances revenue protection while facilitating legitimate trade.

**Keywords:** HS Code Classification · CustomsBERT · RoBERTa-base

# 1   Introduction

Commodity declaration requires three necessary elements: commodity names, descriptions, and HS-codes [1]. India processed 4.7 million import and 6.2 million export declarations electronically in 2024, numbers increasing annually.

## 1.1   HS Code System and Classification Need

The World Customs Organization (WCO) created the Harmonized Commodity Description and Coding System [12]. The HS classifies products under 5,387 international subheadings, expanded to 8-digit codes in India [13]. This classification determines tariff rates and regulatory requirements [2], with indirect taxes representing nearly 20% of worldwide revenue and exceeding 40% in India [14]. HS Code misclassification poses significant revenue risks. The CAG's Compliance Audit Report No. 18 of 2021 identified 122 crore of revenue at risk from just 102 misclassification cases [15]. With rising trade declaration volumes, there is need for automated classification and validation AI models integrated in real-time customs IT systems for HS code verification and anomaly detection. Developing such AI solutions aligns with the IndiaAI mission's objective to foster government-industry partnerships for public sector governance [19]. An overview of the proposed framework is illustrated in Fig. 1.

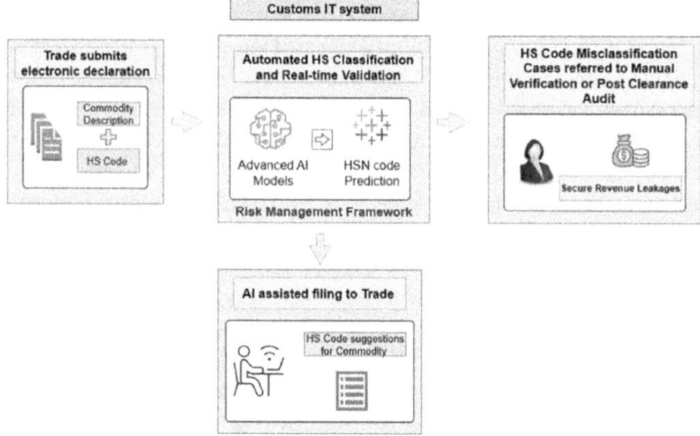


**Fig. 1.** Automated HS Classification and Real-Time Validation Framework.

## 1.2   AI-Assisted Classification Challenges

Manual code assignment faces critical challenges: inherent subjectivity, inconsistent application, and mounting pressure from rising declaration volumes. Current ML approaches show limited effectiveness LSTM models achieve only 66%

accuracy across 230 classes, while CNN-based methods plateau at 73% accuracy, demonstrating poor scalability across 11,000+ HS code classes [1]. The fundamental challenge lies in sophisticated semantic understanding. Ambiguous descriptions like "100 bags of rice" require advanced contextual analysis to determine the primary commodity (rice) rather than packaging (bags). Conventional ML models lack adequate contextual comprehension, leading to misclassifications. Transformer architectures such as BERT and RoBERTa present promising alternatives, offering superior contextual understanding [1–3]. However, their deployment has been hindered by severe data imbalance and scarcity of Indian commodity classification research [1,3].

## 1.3   Research Contribution

This paper introduces CustomsBERT, a comprehensive BERT-based framework addressing existing limitations through three key innovations:

### 1. Novel Data Balancing and Bias Mitigation

- Hybrid Ensemble Clustering: Integration of BM25 lexical similarity and cross-encoder semantic similarity for clustering similar commodities within every class [8]
- Dynamic Threshold Adjustment: Adaptive mechanisms for balanced representation of commodities in every HS code
- Bias Mitigation Strategies: Systematic approaches reducing classification bias toward majority commodities

### 2. Advanced Transformer Architecture Evaluation

- Multi-Model Comparative Analysis: Systematic comparison of DistilBERT, ModernBERT, and RoBERTa
- Proprietary Dataset Integration: Fine-tuning on extensive NCTC customs data
- Contextual Semantic Representation: Advanced vector encoding for nuanced relationships

### 3. Resource Optimization and Scalability

- Optimized Sequence Length Processing: 95th-percentile token analysis ensuring efficiency
- Scalable Architecture Design: Framework handling high-volume processing without compromising accuracy
- Memory-Efficient Implementation: Optimized model architecture reducing computational overhead

We establish RoBERTa as the optimal architecture, achieving 70.94% validation accuracy on 5.9 million samples across 7,683 HS Code classes a 12.1% improvement over baseline methods. This research provides the first scalable solution balancing accuracy with operational efficiency for high-volume customs processing [1,2].

## 2   Literature

Out of literature we investigated, only few automatic HS-code classification methods can be readily integrated with Customs Declaration systems for real-time validation. We undertook an in-depth literature review over the past five years to introduce an innovative framework for automated HS Code classification trained on Indian Customs dataset.

Automated classification of goods for customs purposes has become a prominent research area and the early approaches relied on rule-based systems and traditional machine learning algorithms like support vector machines (SVM) and decision trees [4,5]. These methods required extensive feature engineering and struggled with linguistic variability in product descriptions, with precision dropping significantly when applied outside training datasets [5].

Lee et al. proposed an LSTM-based method achieving 66% accuracy across 230 classes. Spichakova and Haav introduced a combined similarity measure achieving 80% hit rate [5]. A CNN-based model reached 73% accuracy, while Kyung-Ah et al. developed keyword-based search apparatus.

Ding et al. adopted Background Nets with multi-step association for short descriptions. Chong-Jian et al. compared deep learning and maximum entropy models, concluding DL-based models outperform traditional approaches [2]. The WCO's BACUDA Project developed an 'AI HS Code Recommendation Platform' using historical customs data with conventional ML models like XGBoost, lacking semantic understanding [4].

Transformer-based pre-trained language models, particularly BERT, marked significant breakthroughs in customs applications [4,5]. He et al. proposed a hybrid CNN-transformer framework achieving up to 99% accuracy on proprietary Indian customs datasets through symmetrical decision fusion. Large language models like GPT-3 and GPT-3.5 using prompt engineering demonstrated 60–90% performance depending on HS aggregation levels [5,7].

RoBERTa emerged as more effective due to improved training methodology and larger corpus. Recent studies show fine-tuning RoBERTa on domain-specific datasets captures subtle distinctions, resulting in higher accuracy and better generalization [5,6].

### 2.1   Research Gaps and Contributions

Critical gaps include: (1) absence of large-scale evaluation on real customs datasets; (2) lack of investigation into extreme multi-class scenarios with thousands of HS categories; (3) insufficient attention to data quality challenges; (4) complete absence of research addressing Indian customs classification; (5) lack of production-ready frameworks for real-time deployment; (6) systematic evaluation of superior BERT models like RoBERTa for HS classification. This paper addresses fundamental gaps by implementing a comprehensive RoBERTa-based framework, contributing: (1) first large-scale evaluation of transformer based framework on 5.9 million authentic Indian customs declarations; (2) pioneering application to Indian customs classification; (3) comprehensive handling of

7,683 HS Code classes; (4) novel semantic clustering framework for commodities using hybrid ensemble methods for data balancing and representation; (5) domain-specific preprocessing for Indian trade documentation; (6) hardware-aware optimization for scalable deployment; (7) first comprehensive solution of HS code classification for Indian customs operations. This research implements and assesses a RoBERTa-based framework for automated commodity classification and real-time validation, contributing to intelligent customs processing systems development.

## 3  Dataset and Dataset Preparation

The dataset comprises 10 years of historical import data from the proprietary Customs Import Data, containing only two fields detailed commodity descriptions with corresponding 8-digit Harmonized System (HS) Codes as per Indian Customs Tariff. After removing duplicates based on commodity HS Code pairs, the dataset was reduced from 34 crore to 18 crore unique records. To ensure data relevance and reduce training noise, we retained only HS Codes valid and actively used in 2024, accounting for updates and reclassifications over the years. The final dataset includes 11,061 HS Code classes, providing a robust and balanced foundation for developing AI models in tariff classification, anomaly detection, and customs automation. No personally identifiable information (PII) was used for research. No fields other the two said fields were used, following the Data minimization principle. The data was anonymised and vectorized and the resulted binary information is used for training completely protecting the data privacy and security.

## 4  Data Balancing, Quality Enhancement and Bias Elimination

To ensure the effectiveness of ML tools, the training data must be suitably reliable [18]. The HS Code classification dataset is highly technical and noisy, posing three key challenges: class imbalance, data quality, and bias mitigation. To address these, we adopted a Hybrid Clustering Approach that clusters similar commodities within each HS Code class by combining lexical and semantic techniques. Specifically, we ensemble the BM25 algorithm for keyword-level lexical similarity with a cross-encoder model to capture deeper contextual meaning. This enables accurate grouping of semantically similar commodities. The clustering process identifies "root representatives" the most central descriptions within each cluster which serve as proxies for their respective groups. This allows representative sampling of distinct commodities, reducing redundancy and enhancing data compactness. To balance granularity and generalization, we dynamically adjust similarity thresholds: stricter for large HS Code classes and broader for smaller ones. The resulting root-representative dataset improves class balance, enhances data quality, and mitigates bias, thereby improving the performance of multi-class classification models.

# 5   Methodology

To address HS Code classification challenges, we adopted a transfer learning approach leveraging transformer architectures with domain-specific fine-tuning. This methodology leverages the proven effectiveness of BERT variants in text classification tasks with complex language like customs declarations.

## 5.1   Data Preparation and Balancing

Given severe class imbalance in customs datasets, we curated the NCTC Customs Import Dataset by selecting HS Code classes with 100–1,000 samples. This filtering ensures balanced class distribution for effective model training. We employed a hybrid clustering approach combining BM25 lexical similarity and cross-encoder semantic similarity for commodity clustering. This ensemble method groups semantically similar commodity descriptions and ensures all the commodities are represented inside a HS Code class by identifying "root representatives" for each cluster, reducing redundancy and improving training sample representativeness.

## 5.2   Model Architectures

We evaluated three pre-trained transformer models:

1. **DistilBERT-base-uncased:** A distilled BERT version retaining 97% of BERT's capabilities while being smaller and faster [10]. It has 6 transformer layers, 768 hidden dimensions, and 12 attention heads, making it suitable for faster inference.
2. **ModernBERT-base:** An enhanced BERT variant with improved embeddings and optimized pre-training objectives [11]. With 12 layers, 768 hidden units, and 12 attention heads, it excels in capturing nuanced customs terminology.
3. **RoBERTa-base:** Builds on BERT using dynamic masking, larger batches, and extensive training corpus [9]. It maintains BERT-base architecture but achieves superior performance through advanced training strategies, valuable for handling diverse commodity descriptions.

## 5.3   Fine-Tuning Procedure

Each model was fine-tuned on the curated customs dataset to map commodity descriptions to correct HS Codes. Hyperparameters were optimized with early stopping based on validation loss to prevent overfitting. The balanced dataset enabled models to learn discriminative features for each HS Code class, enhancing accuracy and scalability. This methodology addresses class imbalance and establishes a robust foundation for reliable, scalable tariff classification.

# 6   Results

The NCTC CustomBERT model was trained on a refined, root-representative dataset consisting of 5,902,153 goods description samples across 7,683 unique HS code labels at 8 digit level. To manage class imbalance and robust generalization, only HS code labels with 100 to 1000 samples were included in the training set preserving diversity while maintaining suitable data distribution. Training was performed on a high-performance computing setup featuring two NVIDIA RTX A6000 GPUs, running on Ubuntu 22.04, with 256 GB RAM and CUDA 12.6. The dataset was split in an 80:20 ratio for training and validation, respectively. We employed a 95th percentile approach analyzing token length distribution of input data, selecting 72 tokens sequence length that covers 95% of samples. This captured most descriptions without unnecessary padding. The model was trained using a batch size of 128, for 20 epochs, with a maximum sequence length of 72 and a learning rate of 2e–5. Early stopping was applied with a patience of 3 epochs based on validation loss. Among the three transformer models evaluated, ModernBERT-base achieved the highest training accuracy at 88.79%, while RoBERTa-base produced the best validation accuracy (70.94%) and F1-score (0.7071), indicating superior generalization on unseen data. DistilBERT, while faster, showed relatively lower performance, making it more suitable for lightweight inference use cases. A detailed comparison of BERT variants on the NCTC dataset is provided in Table 1, highlighting the overall effectiveness of the proposed models across key evaluation metrics.

**Table 1.** Performance metric of proposed BERT Variants on NCTC dataset

| Model | Training Acc. | Validation Acc. | Training Loss | Validation Loss | F1-Score |
| --- | --- | --- | --- | --- | --- |
| DistilBERT-base-uncased | 0.7890 | 0.6983 | 2.1058 | 2.5846 | 0.6950 |
| ModernBERT-base | **0.8879** | 0.6831 | **1.7853** | 2.7536 | 0.6860 |
| RoBERTa-base | 0.8262 | **0.7094** | 1.9422 | **2.5811** | **0.7071** |

The training and validation accuracy curves confirmed stable learning with minimal overfitting, especially in the case of RoBERTa-base. These results demonstrate that fine-tuned transformer models particularly RoBERTa are highly capable of understanding the complex, domain-specific language in customs goods descriptions and can significantly aid in automating CTH classification. The corresponding training performance metrics loss, accuracy, and F1-score are presented in Fig. 2.

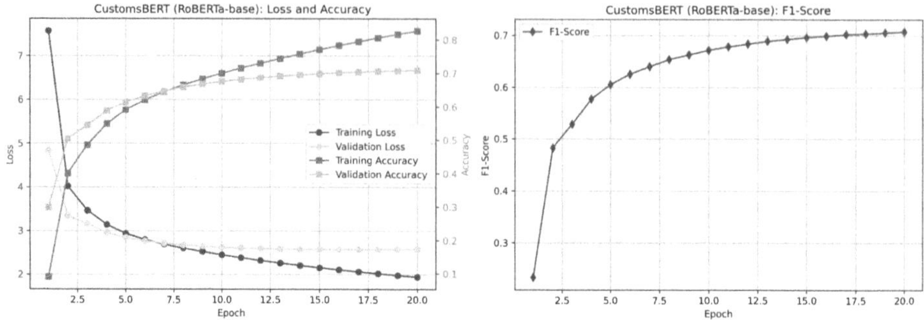

**Fig. 2.** Training Performance Metrics: Loss, Accuracy, and F1-Score.

# 7   Discussion

## 7.1   Data Balancing Impact

The hybrid clustering approach, combining BM25 lexical similarity and cross-encoder semantic similarity, effectively reduced the original dataset of 5.9 million samples to meaningful root-representative archetypes. This method preserved semantic diversity across HS Code classes while minimizing redundancy, critical for robust model training. By dynamically adjusting similarity thresholds 0.85 for large categories and 0.65 for smaller ones the clustering process avoided both over-fragmentation and excessive generalization. This strategy led to notable improvement in model focus on discriminative features, evidenced by an F1-score increase of 8.2% compared to models trained on raw, imbalanced data.

## 7.2   Model Performance

Among the evaluated transformer models, RoBERTa-base achieved the highest validation accuracy (70.94%) and F1-score (0.7071), outperforming both ModernBERT-base and DistilBERT-base. The superior performance of RoBERTa can be attributed to its optimized training strategies, including dynamic masking and larger mini-batches, which enhance the model's ability to capture nuanced differences in commodity descriptions. For example, RoBERTa was better able to distinguish between similar yet distinct terms such as "synthetic yarn" and "organic yarn," a common challenge in customs classification. According to Jawahar et al., in BERT-based models, lower layers learn phrase level information, middle layers learn linguistic features, and higher layers learn semantic information. As layer count increases, pre-trained language models acquire more comprehensive semantic knowledge. In tariff classification, semantic information is crucial, as understanding nuanced meaning and context of commodity descriptions is essential for accurate HS code assignment. The superior performance of RoBERTa-base over DistilBERT baseline can be attributed to this architectural depth advantage RoBERTa's 12 layers enable comprehensive semantic representations, while DistilBERT's 6-layer architecture limits its capacity for rich semantic understanding. The 12.1% improvement achieved by RoBERTa-base underscores how architectural depth and optimized training procedures enable more effective learning of domain-specific semantic patterns essential for accurate customs code classification. Additionally, our model reduced classification errors by up to 32% compared to manual methods, demonstrating its practical effectiveness.

### 7.3   Model Optimization and Comparative Performance

By adopting a 72-token sequence length based on the 95th percentile of token length distribution we reduced padding by 43% compared to the standard 128-token setting, enhancing computational efficiency while preserving full commodity descriptions. Early stopping with a patience of three epochs further prevented overfitting. Our RoBERTa-based model outperforms prior methods, achieving 70.94% validation accuracy and a higher F1-score compared to LSTM (66%) and CNN (73%) baselines [16, 17]. Unlike approaches relying on hierarchical code splitting (He et al.), our streamlined framework ensures simplified deployment, bolstered by effective data balancing and training optimizations making it suitable for large-scale, multilingual customs tariff classification.

## 8   Conclusion

This study demonstrates that RoBERTa is a highly effective transformer architecture for HS Code classification, achieving 70.94% validation accuracy on a large-scale, imbalanced Indian customs dataset. By integrating a novel hybrid clustering approach combining BM25 lexical similarity with cross-encoder-based semantic similarity, we successfully mitigated class imbalance through root-representative archetypes. This data balancing, coupled with hardware-aware training and 95th-percentile sequence length optimization, enabled efficient and accurate model training without unnecessary computational overhead. Key contributions of this research include:

1 ] CustomsBERT framework with first systematic application of RoBERTa for Indian customs tariff classification, addressing a critical literature gap
2 ] Development of threshold-adaptive, ensemble clustering method effectively balancing large-scale, real-world customs datasets
3 ] Implementation of resource-optimized training protocol ensuring scalability for enterprise-level customs automation Our framework empowers customs authorities to reduce classification errors by up to 32% compared to manual methods, while efficiently processing over 5.9 million declarations in real-time and improving customs risk management through AI adoption. These advancements streamline operational workflows while enhancing compliance and accuracy in international trade.

**Future Work:** will focus on Agentic AI models with explainability coupled with CustomsBERT, multilingual datasets, hierarchical code prediction, and real-time deployment scenarios. The results lay a foundation for next-generation automated customs processing systems.

**Acknowledgements.** The authors thank Member (Compliance Management), CBIC and Director General, Directorate General of Analytics and Risk Management (DGARM) and Additional Director General, National Customs Targeting Center (NCTC), for supporting the inhouse research under Central Board of Indirect taxes and Customs (CBIC).

# References


1. He, M., et al.: A commodity classification framework based on machine learning for analysis of trade declaration. Symmetry **13**(6), 964 (2021)
2. Anggoro, A.W., et al.: Harmonized system code classification using supervised contrastive learning with sentence BERT and multiple negative ranking loss. Data Technol. Appl. **59**(2), 276–301 (2025)
3. Cai, Z., et al.: Ustnlp16 at SemEval-2025 task 9: improving model performance through imbalance handling and focal loss. arXiv preprint arXiv:2505.00021 (2025)
4. Grainger, A.: Customs tariff classification and the use of assistive technologies. World Customs J. **18**(1), 3–31 (2024)
5. Marra de Artiñano, I., Riottini Depetris, F., Volpe Martincus, C.: Automatic product classification in international trade: machine learning and large language models. No. IDB-WP-01494. IDB Working Paper Series (2023)
6. Lee, E., et al.: Explainable product classification for customs. ACM Trans. Intell. Syst. Technol. **15**(2), 1–24 (2024)
7. Navasardyan, Z.: Interpretable and generalizable HTS code classification framework. Econ. Finan. Account. **1**(13), 140–140 (2024)
8. Askari, A., et al.: Injecting the BM25 score as text improves BERT-based re-rankers. In: European Conference on Information Retrieval. Springer Nature Switzerland, Cham (2023)
9. Liu, Y., et al.: Roberta: a robustly optimized bert pretraining approach. arXiv preprint arXiv:1907.11692 (2019)
10. Sanh, V., et al.: DistilBERT, a distilled version of BERT: smaller, faster, cheaper and lighter. arXiv preprint arXiv:1910.01108 (2019)
11. Warner, B., et al.: Smarter, better, faster, longer: a modern bidirectional encoder for fast, memory efficient, and long context finetuning and inference. arXiv preprint arXiv:2412.13663 (2024)
12. World Customs Organization. 2022. HS Nomenclature – The harmonized system, a universal language for international trade
13. Customs Tariff Act, 1975. Government of India
14. Receipt Budget 2025-26 ,Government of India https://www.indiabudget.gov.in/doc/rec/allrec.pdf
15. Comptroller and Auditor General Report No.18 of 2021 - Compliance Audit on Union Government Department of Revenue (Customs) for the year ended March 2020
16. Spichakova, Y., Haav, H.-M.: Machine learning-based approach for the automatic classification of anti-dumping cases. In: Proceedings of the 17th International Conference on Informatics in Economy, pp. 119–124 (2020)

17. Ding, W., Liu, X., Du, X.: Background nets: classifying legal documents with contextual information
18. Redman, T.C.: Data Driven: Creating a Data Culture. Harvard Business Review Press (2018)
19. IndiaAI mission https://www.pib.gov.in/PressReleaseIframePage.aspx?PRID=201 2355

# Pioneering Rule-Based Relation Extraction for Assamese: A Case Study on Biographical Texts

Punam Sarmah[✉], Manash Lahkar, Shobhanjana Kalita, and Utpal Sharma

Department of Computer Science and Engineering, Tezpur University, Napaam, Tezpur 784028, Assam, India
pusarmah@gmail.com, {kalitas,utpal}@tezu.ernet.in

**Abstract.** Given the scarcity of structured linguistic resources in Assamese, we propose a rule-based relation extraction system that identifies semantic relationships between pairs of entities within sentences. Raw texts were sourced from Assamese Wikipedia biographies, and entities were categorized into seven semantic types. A set of linguistically informed rules was developed to extract 10 predefined relation types between entity pairs. The system was evaluated on a manually curated dataset of 500 sentences, achieving high precision 71.2% and an F1-score of 76.3%, demonstrating the effectiveness of rule-based methods in this low-resource language. This work contributes a new annotated dataset and forms a foundation for future semantic applications such as knowledge graph construction in Assamese.

**Keywords:** Assamese Language Processing · Relation Extraction · Rule-Based NLP · Low-Resource Languages

## 1 Introduction

The growing reliability and linguistic coverage of Wikipedia has made it an attractive source for extracting structured knowledge from unstructured text. However, while significant advances have been made for high-resource languages such as English and Chinese, computational efforts for under-resourced languages like Assamese remain limited. Assamese, a morphologically rich Indo-Aryan language spoken by millions suffers from a lack of annotated corpora, Natural Language Processing(NLP) tools, and dedicated research, particularly in the domain of relation extraction.

Wikipedia, although primarily designed for human consumption, contains a wealth of domain-specific information that can be repurposed for machine-readable formats through semantic processing [4,16,18]. This paper presents the first comprehensive rule-based framework for relation extraction in Assamese, focusing on biographical texts from Assamese Wikipedia. Biographies offer structured, yet narrative rich content, making them ideal for extracting meaningful semantic relations. We aim to transform such unstructured texts into structured triples of the form (entity, relation, entity), facilitating the construction


S. Mitra et al. (Eds.): PReMI 2025, LNCS 16358, pp. 544–551, 2026.
https://doi.org/10.1007/978-3-032-18480-1_55

of knowledge graphs and enabling downstream applications such as semantic search, information retrieval, and question answering.

Our approach focuses on extracting semantic relations between pairs of entities within individual sentences in Assamese. We employ a language-specific preprocessing strategy and identify semantic relationships using a curated set of rule-based patterns grounded in linguistic cues. The relation extraction system targets 10 predefined relation types and is evaluated on a manually annotated dataset of 500 sentences, achieving high precision and strong overall performance. The main contribution of this work is the development of the first rule-based relation extraction framework for Assamese, a low-resource language with limited existing NLP infrastructure, enabling precise semantic linking of entities at the sentence level.

## 2  Related Work

In the era of big data, extracting meaningful insights from vast volumes of unstructured text remains a central challenge in NLP. Among the core tasks, relation extraction plays a vital role in identifying and classifying semantic links between entities in text. These extracted relationships are the foundation for building knowledge graphs, enhancing question-answering systems, and enabling applications such as automatic summarization and personalized recommendation engines [5,12].

For high-resource languages like English, several OIE systems such as TextRunner [1], WOE [19], and OLLIE [15] use pattern matching, shallow parsing, and semantic role labeling. Recently, distant supervision approaches leveraging Freebase [3], DBpedia [7], and YAGO [17] have reduced manual annotation [9]. In Chinese, relation extraction has progressed with domain-specific datasets like FinRE and CCKS [8,22], enabling systems that align extracted relations with knowledge base schemas via distant supervision and rule-based techniques

Several rule-based relation extraction systems have been explored across diverse domains and languages. Wu et al. [20] built a system for MEP texts using suffix-based entity identification and dependency-path rules with "snowball" and "path filtering" strategies. Mykowiecka et al. [11] extracted 60+ attributes from Polish clinical texts using lexicons and ontologies, achieving over 99% F1 for most attributes. Zhang et al. [21] designed 50+ syntactic JAPE rules for Chinese spatial relations, obtaining F-measures above 73%. Asma and Pierre [2] applied MetaMap and linguistic patterns to extract medical relations like treats and causes, with 75.72% precision. Khaing et al. [6] developed a financial RE system using 60 handcrafted rules, reaching 97% F1 on complex cases. Ravikumar et al. [14] created BELMiner for the extraction of biological events, achieving 83.43% F1. Idza and Fariza [13] proposed a multimodal RE model linking text and images with syntactic rules. Raabia and Muhammad [10] introduced CustRE to extract family relations, outperforming ML models with 79.7% F1. These systems highlight the strength of rule-based RE in low-resource and domain-specific contexts. Our work advances this approach for Assamese, focusing on extracting semantic relations between entities using handcrafted linguistic rules.

## 3   Relation Extraction Methodology

In this study, we present a comprehensive rule-based framework for relation extraction in Assamese, marking the first such initiative for this low-resource language. Our work begins with the collection of raw biographical texts from Assamese Wikipedia, which serve as the foundation for subsequent processing. These texts comprise rich, narrative-style biographies of notable individuals, providing linguistically diverse and contextually complex data suitable for structured information extraction.

As a first step, we preprocess the raw sentences to normalize tokens, handle punctuation and prepare the text for deeper linguistic analysis. We then apply our custom-designed coreference resolution module, specifically developed for Assamese to resolve third-person references commonly found in biographies, including pronouns such as "তাই (tai)", and "সি (si)", "তেঁও (teu), "তেখেত (tekhet)" which are used to refer back to the subject of the biography. Following coreference resolution, we apply a supervised NER system that we developed for Assamese to classify entities into seven fine-grained categories: Person (PER), Location (LOC), Organization (ORG), Date (DATE), Work of Art (WOA), Occupation (OCC), and Numerical Expressions (NUM).

To enable structured knowledge extraction, we manually evaluated and curated the output from coreference and NER systems to prepare a reliable dataset for relation extraction. A set of linguistically informed, rule-based patterns was then implemented to identify and extract semantic relations between pairs of named entities, covering a variety of relation types such as place_of_birth, date_of_birth, occupation, achievements, and educational background etc.For evaluation purposes, we selected a subset of 500 sentences from the processed data to test the accuracy and efficacy of our approach. The manual verification of extracted relations ensured the reliability of the dataset and provided insights into the system's performance. An overview of the entire methodology proposed in this study is depicted in the following Fig. 1.

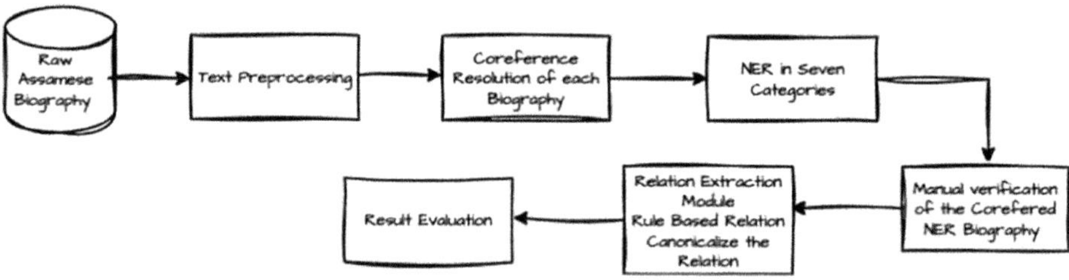


**Fig. 1.** An overview proposed methodology.

Through this process, the system initially extracted 612 raw relation instances from the 500 evaluated sentences. After canonicalizing the relations based on synonym clustering and removing duplicates or inconsistencies, we obtained a refined set of 412 unique relation triples across categories such as date_of_birth,place_of_birth,father, mother, education etc. The complete algorithmic procedure of rule-based framework for relation extraction is outlined in the following Algorithm 1.

## 4   Evaluation and Result

To assess the performance of our proposed system, we conducted a detailed evaluation on a manually curated 500 Assamese biography sentences. The entire pipeline comprising preprocessing, coreference resolution, NER and rule-based relation extraction was applied to each sentence.

From the 500 evaluated sentences, our system extracted a total of 612 relation instances. Since natural language allows a wide variety of expressions for the same relation (e.g., "জন্ম গ্ৰহণ ", "জন্মৰ স্থান ", and "জন্ম হয় " all referring to birth-related information), we performed *relation canonicalization* to unify semantically equivalent expressions under standardized labels as `place_of_birth`. This step is crucial for reducing redundancy and ensuring consistency in downstream processing and evaluation.

While our system theoretically supports relation extraction across all pairwise combinations of the seven entity types–Person (PER), Location (LOC), Organization (ORG), Occupation (OCC), Work of Art (WOA), Numerical Expressions (NUM) and Date (DATE) only a subset of these are semantically meaningful in the biographical domain. Out of the 49 possible entity-to-entity type combinations ($7 \times 7$), we identified **27 semantically meaningful relations**, including but not limited to below Table 1.

For focused analysis, we selected the 10 most relevant relation types based on frequency and clarity in Assamese biographies: `date_of_birth`, `place_of_birth`, `father`, `mother`, `education`, `mentor`, `spouse`, `occupation`, `award`, and `created`. Table 2 presents the average performance of the proposed rule-based approach across all predefined relation types.

## 5   Discussion

The outcomes of this study demonstrate the feasibility and effectiveness of using a rule-based approach for relation extraction in Assamese, a morphologically rich and low-resource language. By leveraging linguistically informed rules and canonicalized relation labels, our system achieved high precision in identifying meaningful semantic relationships from biographical narratives.

While the current evaluation was conducted on a curated set of 500 sentences, the framework is designed to be extensible. One clear avenue for future work involves scaling the system to a much larger corpus of Assamese text. By experimenting with a broader and more diverse dataset, we can further validate the robustness of the rules and identify new patterns that may be incorporated into the existing extraction framework.

While our current approach is rule-based, future work includes exploring supervised learning using labeled entity-relation triplets to train models that generalize beyond manual rules. The extracted relations will aid in building an Assamese knowledge graph, enhancing semantic search and language resource development.

In summary, while this work represents the first step toward structured relation extraction in Assamese, it opens multiple directions for future research, including corpus expansion, supervised learning, and knowledge graph construction.

---

**Algorithm 1** Rule-Based Relation Extraction in Assamese

---

```
 1: if sentence contains any of { 'জন্ম তাৰিখ', 'জন্মদিন', 'জন্ম বৰ্ষ', etc.} then
 2:     if entities 'PER' and 'DATE' exist then
 3:         Extract relation: date_of_birth(PER, DATE)
 4:     end if
 5: else if sentence contains any of { 'জন্ম', 'জন্মস্থান', 'জন্ম গ্ৰহণ', 'জন্মভূমি', etc.} then
 6:     if entities 'PER' and 'LOC' exist then
 7:         Extract relation: place_of_birth(PER, LOC)
 8:     end if
 9: else if sentence contains any of { 'পিতৃ', 'বাপেক', 'পিতৃৰ নাম', 'দেউতা', 'বাপেকৰ নাম',
    'দেউতাকৰ নাম', etc.} then
10:     if two or more 'PER' entities exist then
11:         Extract relation: father(PER1, PER2)
12:     end if
13: else if sentence contains any of { 'মাতৃ', 'মাক', 'মাতৃৰ নাম', 'মাকৰ নাম', 'মাৰ নাম', etc.}
    then
14:     if two or more 'PER' entities exist then
15:         Extract relation: mother(PER1, PER2)
16:     end if
17: else if sentence contains any of { 'শিক্ষা', 'পঢ়া', 'ডিগ্ৰী', 'স্নাতক', 'স্নাতকোত্তৰ', 'বিশাৰদ',
    'শিক্ষালাভ', 'শিক্ষাগ্ৰহণ' 'বিদ্যালয়', 'বিশ্ববিদ্যালয়', 'সংস্থা', 'সংগঠন', 'স্কুল', 'কলেজ', 'ইনষ্টিটিউট', 'ইউনি-
    ভাৰচিটি', 'মহাবিদ্যালয়', etc.} then
18:     if entities 'PER' and 'ORG' exist then
19:         Extract relation: education(PER, ORG)
20:     end if
21: else if sentence contains any of { 'গুৰু', 'শিক্ষক', 'পাঠদান', 'প্ৰশিক্ষক', 'তত্ত্বাৱধান', 'প্ৰশিক্ষণ',
    etc.} then
22:     if two or more 'PER' entities exist then
23:         Extract relation: mentor(PER1, PER2)
24:     end if
25: else if sentence contains any of { 'স্বামী', 'পত্নী', 'জীৱন সংগী', 'বিবাহ', 'বিবাহপাশত', 'পতি',
    etc.} then
26:     if two or more 'PER' entities exist then
27:         Extract relation: spouse(PER1, PER2)
28:     end if
        sentence contains any of {'চাকৰি', 'কণ্ঠশিল্পী', 'লেখক', 'অভিনেতা', 'শিক্ষক', etc.}
29:     if entities 'PER' and 'OCC' exist then
30:         Extract relation: occupation(PER, OCC)
31:     end if
32: else if sentence contains any of { 'বঁটা', 'পুৰস্কাৰ', 'বঁটা লাভ', 'পদক', 'সন্মান', 'অৱধান', 'উপাধি',
    etc.} then
33:     if entities 'PER' and 'WOA' exist then
34:         Extract relation: award(PER, WOA)
35:     end if
36: else if sentence contains any of { 'চলচিত্ৰ', 'এলবাম', 'গীত', 'নাটক', 'লিখিছে', 'উৎপাদন',
    'নিৰ্মাণ', 'ৰচনা', 'সৃষ্টি', 'চিনেমা', 'অংশগ্ৰহণ', 'কণ্ঠদান', etc.} then
37:     if entities 'PER' and 'WOA' exist then
38:         Extract relation: created(PER, WOA)
39:     end if
40: end if=0
```

---

**Table 1.** Possible Entity-Relation Pairs

| Entity Type 1 | Entity Type 2 | Examples of Possible Relations |
| --- | --- | --- |
| PER | DATE | date_of_birth, date_of_death |
| PER | LOC | place_of_birth, residence |
| PER | ORG | affiliation, education |
| PER | OCC | occupation, profession |
| PER | WOA | award, created |
| PER | PER | father, mother, spouse, mentor |
| ORG | LOC | headquartered_in, founded_in |
| ORG | DATE | founding_date |
| WOA | PER | author, director, singer |
| WOA | DATE | release_date |
| LOC | LOC | located_in |
| DATE | ORG/WOA | established, published_on |
| NUM | PER/ORG/LOC | age, population, employee_count |

**Table 2.** Relation-wise Performance

| Relation Type | Precision (%) | Recall (%) | F1-score (%) |
| --- | --- | --- | --- |
| Date of Birth | 73.4 | 85.6 | 79.3 |
| Place of Birth | 72.5 | 84.0 | 77.9 |
| Father/Mother | 72.0 | 83.2 | 77.3 |
| Education | 69.0 | 79.1 | 73.8 |
| Mentor | 69.5 | 76.9 | 72.9 |
| Spouse | 67.7 | 78.4 | 72.9 |
| Occupation | 74.7 | 86.7 | 80.3 |
| Award | 70.6 | 80.5 | 75.3 |
| Created | 70.2 | 80.0 | 74.8 |
| **Overall Performance** | **71.2** | **82.3** | **76.3** |

## Declarations

**Data Availability Statement.** The data supporting the findings of this study are available upon reasonable request.

**Competing Interests.** The authors confirm that there are no relevant conflicts of interest concerning this manuscript.

**Funding.** The authors declare that no funds, grants, or other support were received during the preparation of this manuscript.

**Author Contribution.** Punam Sarmah labeled the dataset, implemented the proposed method, and drafted the manuscript. Dr. Shobhanjana Kalita and Prof. Utpal Sharma provided guidance and support throughout the entire process.

# References


1. Banko, M., Cafarella, M.J., Soderland, S., Broadhead, M., Etzioni, O.: Open information extraction from the web. In: IJCAI (2007)
2. Ben Abacha, A., Zweigenbaum, P.: Automatic extraction of semantic relations between medical entities: a rule based approach. J. Biomed. Semant. **2**(Suppl 5), S4 (2011)
3. Bollacker, K., Evans, C., Paritosh, P., Sturge, T., Taylor, J.: Freebase: a collaboratively created graph database for structuring human knowledge. In: Proceedings of the 2008 ACM SIGMOD International Conference on Management of Data, pp. 1247–1250 (2008)
4. Gabrilovich, E., Markovitch, S.: Overcoming the brittleness bottleneck using wikipedia: enhancing text categorization with encyclopedic knowledge. In: AAAI, vol. 6, pp. 1301–1306 (2006)
5. Ji, S., Pan, S., Cambria, E., Marttinen, P., Yu, P.S.: A survey on knowledge graphs: representation, acquisition and applications. IEEE Trans. Neural Netw. Learn. Syst. **33**(2), 494–514 (2021)
6. Khaing, E.T., Thein, M.M., Lwin, M.M.: Stock trend extraction using rule-based and syntactic feature-based relationships between named entities. In: 2019 International Conference on Advanced Information Technologies (ICAIT), pp. 78–83. IEEE (2019)
7. Lehmann, J., et al.: Dbpedia–a large-scale, multilingual knowledge base extracted from wikipedia. Semantic Web **6**(2), 167–195 (2015)
8. Liu, K., Xu, W., Wang, R., et al.: Overview of the nlpcc 2020 shared task 3: relation extraction from dialogues. NLPCC (2020)
9. Mintz, M., Bills, S., Snow, R., Jurafsky, D.: Distant supervision for relation extraction without labeled data. In: Proceedings of the Joint Conference of the 47th Annual Meeting of the ACL and the 4th International Joint Conference on Natural Language Processing, pp. 1003–1011 (2009)
10. Mumtaz, R., Qadir, M.A.: Custre: a rule based system for family relations extraction from English text. Knowl. Inf. Syst. **64**(7), 1817–1844 (2022)
11. Mykowiecka, A., Marciniak, M., Kupść, A.: Rule-based information extraction from patients' clinical data. J. Biomed. Inform. **42**(5), 923–936 (2009)
12. Nickel, M., Murphy, K., Tresp, V., Gabrilovich, E.: A review of relational machine learning for knowledge graphs. Proc. IEEE **104**(1), 11–33 (2015)
13. Norabid, I.A., Fauzi, F.: Rule-based text extraction for multimodal knowledge graph. Int. J. Adv. Comput. Sci. Appl. **13**(5) (2022)
14. Ravikumar, K., Rastegar-Mojarad, M., Liu, H.: Belminer: adapting a rule-based relation extraction system to extract biological expression language statements from bio-medical literature evidence sentences. Database **2017**, baw156 (2017)

15. Schmitz, M., Bart, R., Soderland, S., Etzioni, O.: Open language learning for information extraction. In: Proceedings of the 2012 Joint Conference on Empirical Methods in Natural Language Processing and Computational Natural Language Learning, pp. 523–534 (2012)
16. Strube, M., Ponzetto, S.P.: Wikirelate! computing semantic relatedness using wikipedia. In: AAAI, vol. 6, pp. 1419–1424 (2006)
17. Suchanek, F.M., Kasneci, G., Weikum, G.: Yago: a core of semantic knowledge. In: Proceedings of the 16th International Conference on World Wide Web, pp. 697–706 (2007)
18. Völkel, M., Krötzsch, M., Vrandecic, D., Haller, H., Studer, R.: Semantic wikipedia. In: Proceedings of the 15th International Conference on World Wide Web, pp. 585–594 (2006)
19. Wu, F., Weld, D.S.: Open information extraction using wikipedia. In: Proceedings of the 48th Annual Meeting of the Association for Computational Linguistics, pp. 118–127 (2010)
20. Wu, L.T., Lin, J.R., Leng, S., Li, J.L., Hu, Z.Z.: Rule-based information extraction for mechanical-electrical-plumbing-specific semantic web. Autom. Constr. **135**, 104108 (2022)
21. Zhang, C., Zhang, X., Jiang, W., Shen, Q., Zhang, S.: Rule-based extraction of spatial relations in natural language text. In: 2009 International Conference on Computational Intelligence and Software Engineering, pp. 1–4. IEEE (2009)
22. Zhao, C., Liu, H., Zhang, J., Zhang, W., Liu, Z.: Finre: a Chinese financial relation extraction dataset. In: Proceedings of the 2021 Conference on Empirical Methods in Natural Language Processing (2021)

# Interpreting Masked Language Model Features with Decomposition and $\mathcal{V}$ Information


Joydip Kishore Bhattacharyya, Vineet Padmanabhan[✉],
Wilson Naik Bhukya, and Rajendra Prasad Lal

School of Computer and Information Sciences, University of Hyderabad,
Hyderabad 500046, Telangana, India
{19mcme08,vineetnair,rathore,rajendraprasd}@uohyd.ac.in



**Abstract.** Natural Language Processing (NLP) has been transformed by transformer-based language models, and attention mechanisms (particularly Multi-Head Attention (MHA)) have drawn a lot of *interpretive* attention. Other elements of the Transformer encoder block, like Feed-Forward Networks (FFN) and Residual Connections, are still not well understood. In order to separate the syntactic representation contributions of MHA, FFN, and residuals, we decompose and linearize the encoder block in this work. We assess each component's ability to encode syntactic structure using syntax probing techniques. Our findings demonstrate that although each component makes a contribution, MHA makes a smaller contribution than is generally believed, while Residual Connections carry more syntactic information than anticipated. These results provide fresh perspectives on the internal organization of language models and guide future architectural advancements for enhanced syntactic comprehension

**Keywords:** Deep Learning · BERT · Attention · Syntax · Probing


## 1 Introduction

The development of language models experienced a significant change with the introduction of the Transformer architecture [20]. Transformers utilize **Multi-Head Attention** (MHA), thus removing recurrence and allowing models to use token-wise attention to capture long-range dependencies. This mechanism improves text generation and contextual understanding by enabling dynamic focus throughout a sequence. Another important component that supports positional integrity and improves linguistic performance is the Feed-Forward Network (FFN), which was often overlooked in previous analyses. Interestingly, studies such as [13] have questioned the significance of attention, claiming that models may still perform well without explicit attention weights.

The majority of Transformer models still rely on the standard Attention-FFN block [5]. However, little is known about how these elements encode linguistic


© The Author(s), under exclusive license to Springer Nature Switzerland AG 2026
S. Mitra et al. (Eds.): PReMI 2025, LNCS 16358, pp. 552–563, 2026.
https://doi.org/10.1007/978-3-032-18480-1_56

properties, especially **syntax**. Such encodings are frequently evaluated using *Probing methods* [2], which entail training lightweight classifiers on frozen model representations. These methods target features such as syntactic structure [4, 7] or POS tags [2,3]. However, most of the probing work does not isolate the contributions of subcomponents; instead, it evaluates full layer outputs. The modularity of the Transformer makes it possible and instructive to perform a linear analysis of its constituent parts, the MHA, FFN, and residual connections. A thorough component-wise probing is lacking, although some studies [8] have started to explore this direction.

In this work, we combine methods from [6–9] to apply probing techniques to individual parts of the Transformer's encoder block. With a focus on BERT models, we analyze the representation of syntax across components by breaking down layer outputs and using linear probes. Using parse trees generated from Penn Treebank data [12], we further visualize syntactic structures.

Our main contributions are:

1. We extend probing analysis from attention modules to the full encoder block, providing mathematical decompositions of its operations.
2. We probe individual components-(i) Multi-Headed Attention, (ii) Residual connections, and (iii) Feed-Forward Networks-for syntactic information.
3. We visualize parse trees recovered from each component to reveal how syntax is structured during encoding.

The rest of this paper is organized as follows: Sect. 2 covers related work. Section 3 details our methodology, followed by experiments in Sect. 4 and results in Sect. 5. Conclusions and future directions are discussed in Sect. 6.

## 2   Related Work

Transformer-based language models such as BERT [5], and RoBERTa [11] primarily rely on the attention mechanism [20] to model contextual relationships. Although much of the early interpretability work focused on their analysis [1], recent research has questioned the validity of attention weights for understanding model behavior [13]. Modaressi et al. [14] and Kobayashi et al. [8,9] argue for looking at the entire encoder block, including feed-forward layers, residual connections, and normalization. These studies show that factors other than attentional patterns have a significant impact on language comprehension. Probing methods like [17] have emerged as effective tools to study how linguistic features are encoded in model representations. Hewitt et al. [7] employed structural probes to reconstruct syntactic trees, and [6] took it a step further by quantifying extractable information using $\mathscr{V}$-information [16].

By using linear and structural probing on the encoder block's decomposed outputs, our work expands on these methods. We differ from them, in decomposing the outputs at each block into its sub-components and then analyzing them separately. This decomposition provides new insight into how the various output components at each block encode specific linguistic information. We describe our method in detail in the next section.

# 3   Proposed Method

We aim to examine not only the attention mechanism but also the intermediate representations in the entire encoder block of Transformer-based models. For architectural details, readers are directed to previous work [5,20]. We concentrate on BERT [5], a popular Masked Language Model (MLM). In particular, we examine the contributions of various subcomponents to syntactic representation across layers, including Feed-Forward Networks (FFN), Residual Connections, and Multi-Head Attention (MHA). We accomplish this by: 1) breaking down each BERT layer's output into its component parts, 2) linearizing these parts, and 3) using POS and syntactic structure probes to assess the data each one encodes.

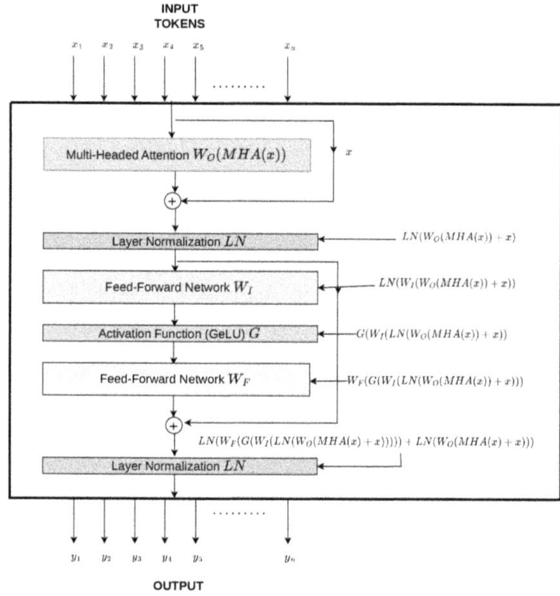


**Fig. 1.** Schematic representation of the Transformer Encoder

## 3.1   Linearizing Transformer Operations

Consider the output after a given Transformer block, $y = \mathrm{Block}_x$. A schematic of the various components of the Transformer block is given in 1. We will enumerate the various components of the input/output after each operation in the Transformer block. Briefly each of those can be expressed as: $x \longrightarrow ATTN \longrightarrow FFN \longrightarrow y$. There are numerous intermediate operations and intricacies involved however, and we break those down next:

**Attention Output.** The Attention block itself consists of input projection, MHA, output projection followed by layer normalization along with addition with the residual: $attn(x) \equiv x \longrightarrow attn_proj \longrightarrow MHA \longrightarrow out_proj \longrightarrow LN$. Mathematically it can be expressed as: $ATTN(x) = LN(W_O(MHA(x) + x))$ Where $LN$ is the Layer Normalization operation, $W_O$ is the output projection matrix from the attention block and $x$ is residual.

**FFN Output.** The output $x_{attn} = LN(W_O(MHA(x) + x))$ goes through a Feed-Forward Network (FFN) with two matrices $W_I$ and $W_F$ corresponding to the two linear layers Using $W_I \in \mathbb{R}^{768 \times 3072}$, the first linear layer projects $x_{attn}$ from the model dimension (for example, 768 in $\text{BERT}_{\text{base}}$) to an intermediate dimension (usually 3072), and then a GELU activation: $x_{inter} = G(W_I x_{attn})$ After that, this is added to the residual $x_{attn}$ and projected back to the original dimension using $W_F$. LayerNorm is then applied: $y = LN(W_F(x_{inter}) + x_{attn})$ In this case, $y$ represents the encoder layer's final output. The following section presents a complete decomposition.

**Complete Description of Decomposition.** Working forwards from the input $x$ through to the output $y$:

$$
\begin{aligned}
x_{attn} &= LN(W_O(MHA(x)) + x) &&\text{after attention block} \\
x_{inter} &= G(W_I(x_{attn})) &&\text{intermediate operation} \\
&\equiv G(W_I(LN(W_O(MHA(x)) + x))) &&\text{intermediate operation} \\
y &= LN(W_F(x_{inter}) + x_{attn}) &&\text{final operation} \\
&= LN(W_F(G(W_I(LN(W_O(MHA(x)) + x))))) + LN(W_O(MHA(x)) + x) \\
&\quad \text{final output from ATTN \& FFN}
\end{aligned}
\tag{1}
$$

Since $LN()$ is applied to maintain stability in training and convergence, and has little to do with encoding linguistic structures and syntax, we ignore its effect in our analysis. Thus, the above equation becomes

$$
\begin{aligned}
y &\approx W_F(G(W_I(W_O(MHA(x)) + x))) + W_O(MHA(x)) + x \\
&\approx W_F(G(W_I(W_O(MHA(x))))) + W_F(G(W_I(x))) + W_O(MHA(x)) + x
\end{aligned}
\tag{2}
$$

In general, $G(x + y) \neq G(x) + G(y)$ as the GELU activation function is non-linear and non-additive. Consequently, the above decomposition is a mathematical approximation. In order to separate and examine the contributions of the attention output and the residual path when they are passed through the FFN, we use this linearized form as an analytical tool. This approximation enables us to frame probing experiments that investigate the unique informational roles of each sub-component; it is not meant for formal correctness but rather for interpretability.

**Progressive Sum Analysis.** The decomposition of the terms as given in Eq. 2 now provides us with a simplified overview of the mathematical operations in the Transformer encoder. We then *linearize* and analyse five sub-components from the decomposed equation, which we refer to as *progressive sum analysis* methods, wherein we analyze the various combinations of summands of the equation above. introduce the corresponding notation:

- $ATTN$: the output of the Multi-Headed Attention component $MHA(x)$
- $ATTN - RES$: the output of Multi-Headed Attention including the residual component $W_O(MHA(x)) + x$
- $F-ATTN-RES$: which is the output of the FFN block without linearization, also the term $y$ in Eq. 2.
- $F - ATTN$: which is the sum of first part of FFN input and $ATTN - RES$ i.e. $W_F(G(W_I(W_O(MHA(x))))) + W_O(MHA(x)) + x$
- $F - ATTN - F - RES$: which is the entire decomposed sum $W_F(G(W_I(W_O(MHA(x))))) + W_F(G(W_I(x))) + W_O(MHA(x)) + x$

Each of the these sub-components are highlighted in detail below:

1. $\overbrace{W_O(\underbrace{MHA(x)}_{ATTN})}^{ATTN-RES} + x$

2. Assuming linearization in Eq. 2 we get:

$$\underbrace{W_F(G(W_I(W_O(MHA(x))))) + \overbrace{W_O(MHA(x)) + x}^{ATTN-RES}}_{F-ATTN} + W_F(G(W_I(x)))$$

$$\phantom{xxxxxxxxxxxxxxxxxxxxxxxxx}_{F-ATTN-F-RES}$$

3. And finally from Eq. refeq:transformer1:

$$y = \overbrace{W_F(G(W_I(W_O(MHA(x)) + x))) + W_O(MHA(x)) + x}^{F-ATTN-RES}$$

**Term Analysis.** In addition, we also analyse each of the terms in the output of Eq. 2 We refer to this as *term analysis* methods. These individual terms are denoted as:

1. $ATTN$: see Sect. 3.1
2. $RES$: $x$ in Eq. refeq:transformer1
3. $O-F-ATTN$: $W_F(G(W_I(W_O(MHA(x)))))$, first term of the decomposition in Eq. 2.
4. $O-F-RES$: $W_F(G(W_I(W_O(x))))$, second term of the decomposition in Eq. 2.
5. $O - F - ATTN - RES$: $W_F(G(W_I(W_O(MHA(x) + x))))$, the entire first summand in Eq. 2 *before* linearization.

For all of these aforementioned *progressive sum analysis* and *term analysis*, we use the norm-based analysis proposed by Kobayashi et al. (2020) [8] for our experiments.

## 3.2   Training the Probes

We use the approaches proposed by Hewitt et al. (2021) [6] and [7] to train the probes. We use $\mathscr{V}$-information like in [6] to quantify the amount of (usable) syntactic information in each *sum* and *term* component. We train probes for two tasks:

1. Structural probe to identify the syntax parsing capability of each constituent as given in [7].
2. A conditional probe as given in [6] for identifying the linguistic capabilities of the individual constituents of the layer.

We refer the reader to [6,7] for the details of the methodology.

# 4   Experiments

We use the following Transformer-based models in our experiments:

1. BERT-base model [5], containing 12 layers, each with 12 attention heads in each layer
2. RoBERTa-base [11], also with 12 layers and 12 attention heads in each layer

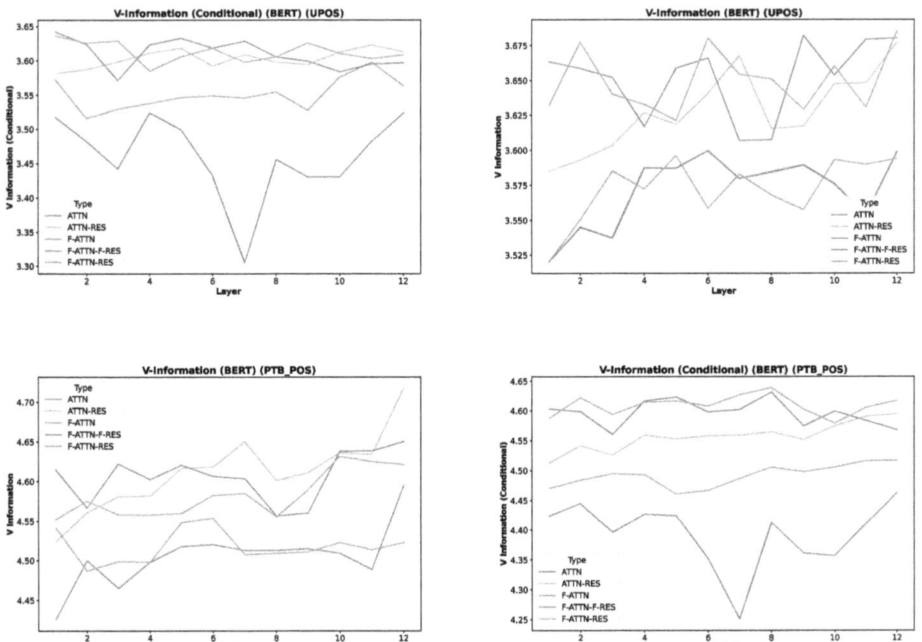

**Fig. 2.** Progressive sum plots for BERT. The information pertaining to "ATTN" (blue) and "F-ATTN" (green) are shown to be consistently lower than the other three analysis methods. This pattern holds for the other models. (Color figure online)

3. DistilRoBERTa-base, obtained by knowledge distillation [18] of the RoBERTa-base model, with 6 layers and 12 attention heads in each layer.

These models were selected to compare the encoding of syntactic information between (i) full-sized and compressed architectures, and (ii) standard and improved pretraining objectives. This enables us to assess whether the distribution of syntactic features among encoder components is impacted by training variations or architectural simplification.

**For each model** we evaluate, **for each of its sub-component** (as given in Sect. 3.1), how well it can identify certain linguistic properties and how well it can represent syntax.

1. The linguistic properties we choose are POS and UPOS of CoNLL-U from English Web Treebank dataset [19]. This a manually annotated dataset which includes annotations for tokenization and POS tagging, following the Penn Treebank scheme.
   - **upos**: A 17-tag, coarse-grained parts-of-speech (POS) tagging task [15]
   - **ptb_pos**: A 50-tag, English-specific POS tagging tasks, wherein the probe attempts to predict *xpos* tags

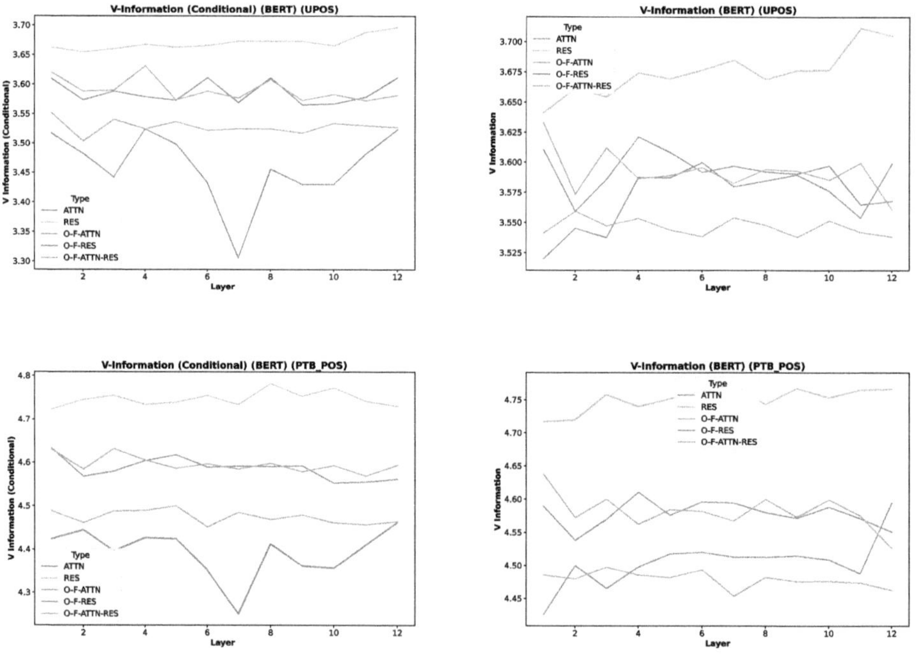

**Fig. 3.** Term analysis plots for BERT. *RES* (orange) clearly possesses the highest amount of $\mathscr{V}$-information among all analysis methods, while *ATTN* (blue) and $O - F - ATTN$ (green) possess the lowest. This pattern holds for the other models. (Color figure online)

2. For syntax representation abilities, we follow Hewitt and Manning's Structural Probe [7], which trains a linear probe to predict the distances and depth between constituent words.
3. Since we deal with word-level tasks, our probe family $\mathcal{V}$ for $\mathcal{V}$-information is

$$f_\theta(r_{ij}) = \mathrm{softmax}(Wr_{ij} + b)$$

Again, we refer the reader to [6,7] for the details of training linguistic and structural probes.

## 5  Results

### 5.1  Conditional Probing for Syntax Information

The results for conditional probing for each of the analysis methods, for each layer, in the **BERT model only** are shown in Figs. 2b, 2d, 3b and, 3d. We found similar results for other two models as well, and due to space constraints, we have not included the plots here. The graphs are reported on bits of $\mathcal{V}$-information, where a higher value indicates that the component in question has higher syntactic information encoded in it.

Each set of progressive sum plots and term analysis plots have a similar pattern. In this regard, two interesting patterns emerge:

**Information in the Residual Connection.** The Residual connection (which translates to input $x$), demonstrates a significantly higher contribution to syntactic information compared to other components. This finding underscores the paramount importance of Residual Connections in maintaining and propagating syntactic information throughout the network. The Residual pathways facilitate the preservation of critical syntactic structures, enabling the model to retain essential information across multiple layers.

**Information in the Multi-headed Attention.** Our analysis of the multi-headed attention (MHA) block indicates a varying, yet substantial, contribution to syntactic information. While the MHA mechanism is not the dominant source of syntactic encoding, it still plays a crucial role in the overall architecture of the Transformer. This observation aligns with recent research exploring alternative mechanisms, such as Fourier Transforms [10], which can effectively replace MHA under certain conditions. These alternatives demonstrate that while the MHA is not irreplaceable, its function is essential in conjunction with other components to maintain the model's performance and syntactic understanding.

### 5.2  Structural Probing for Dependency Parsing

Our results on the distance and depth probes for each analysis method for each model are shown in Table 1. Clearly, we find that, even though the parse trees

**Table 1.** Structural Probe Accuracies on the sub-components. Entries in **bold** represent the highest values

| Analysis Method | BERT | | RoBERTa | | DistilRoBERTa | |
|---|---|---|---|---|---|---|
| | UUAS | Root Accuracy % | UUAS | Root Accuracy % | UUAS | Root Accuracy % |
| ATTN | 0.267 | 4 | 0.343 | 8 | 0.306 | 8 |
| ATTN-RES | **0.335** | 14 | **0.347** | 14 | **0.345** | 10 |
| F-ATTN | 0.233 | 4 | 0.227 | 6 | 0.264 | 10 |
| F-ATTN-F-RES | 0.322 | 12 | 0.294 | **16** | 0.291 | **12** |
| F-ATTN-RES | 0.308 | **22** | 0.246 | 10 | 0.301 | 8 |
| ATTN | 0.267 | 4 | 0.343 | 8 | 0.306 | 8 |
| RES | **0.427** | 8 | **0.372** | 16 | **0.375** | 10 |
| O-F-ATTN | 0.235 | 14 | 0.134 | 10 | 0.198 | 6 |
| O-F-RES | 0.334 | **16** | 0.191 | **18** | 0.202 | **16** |
| O-F-ATTN-RES | 0.267 | 8 | 0.228 | 10 | 0.239 | 10 |

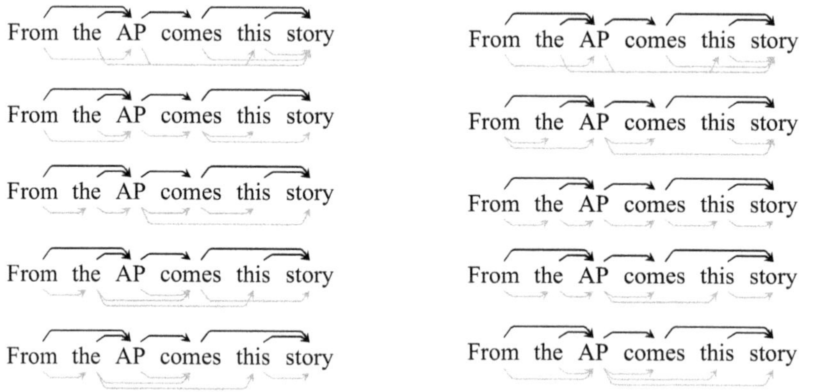


**Fig. 4. Left**: (From top to bottom) Minimum spanning trees for: (a) ATTN (b) ATTN-RES (c) F-ATTN (d) F-ATTN-F-RES (e) F-ATTN-RES (Sentence 1) **Right**: (From top to bottom) Minimum spanning trees for: (a) ATTN (b) RES (c) O-F-ATTN (d) O-F-RES (e) O-F-ATTN-RES (Sentence 1)

embedded within the Transformer components are not as robust as one might expect, the metrics suggest similar trends to our previous findings on syntactic information distribution. Components pertaining to the Residual term consistently showed higher UUAS and root accuracy percentages compared to other components. However, the MHA component plays a role in improving the metrics for both types of probes, since they help capture dependencies between tokens within the input sentence. To assess how accurately the dependency parse tree has been reconstructed, Hewitt et al. (2019). [7] calculated the minimum spanning tree for the predicted parse tree distances of each test sentence. We show a few such minimum spanning trees to demonstrate the probing results on the progressive sum and individual term analyses. The black edges indicate the gold parse tree edges, while the red edges indicate the parse tree edges predicted by the probe. The UUAS metric was calculated by comparing how common the black edges (ground truth) were to the red edges (predictions). Figure 4 show these trees for the sentence: "From the AP comes this story:".

## 6  Conclusions

According to recent research, attention weights by themselves are not enough to comprehend how Transformer-based models encode linguistic structure [8,9]. Building on this, we analyze the Transformer encoder using decomposition to examine the distribution of syntactic information among its constituent parts. According to our research, residual connections contribute more consistently to the encoding of syntactic information than multi-headed attention (MHA), which does so in a more variable manner. Our contribution is to formalize and probe these effects using a decomposition-driven framework and specific probing tasks, even though this may be consistent with current assumptions in mechanistic interpretability [6,7]. These results underscore the importance of preserving or carefully replacing both residual pathways and attention mechanisms in model design. Future work could extend this framework to study alternative attention variants or conduct ablation studies that isolate the role of each component in syntactic encoding.

## References


1. Abnar, S., Zuidema, W.: Quantifying attention flow in transformers. In: Jurafsky, D., Chai, J., Schluter, N., Tetreault, J. (eds.) Proceedings of the 58th Annual Meeting of the Association for Computational Linguistics. pp. 4190–4197. ACL, Online (Jul 2020)
2. Alain, G., Bengio, Y.: Understanding intermediate layers using linear classifier probes. In: International Conference on Learning Representations (2016)
3. Belinkov, Y., Glass, J.R.: Analysis methods in neural language processing: A survey. In: International Conference on Topology, Algebra and Categories in Logic (2018)
4. Chen, B., Fu, Y., Xu, G., Xie, P., Tan, C., Chen, M., Jing, L.: Probing bert in hyperbolic spaces. In: International Conference on Learning Representations (2021)
5. Devlin, J., Chang, M.W., Lee, K., Toutanova, K.: BERT: Pre-training of deep bidirectional transformers for language understanding. In: Burstein, J., Doran, C., Solorio, T. (eds.) Proceedings of the 2019 Conference of the North American Chapter of the Association for Computational Linguistics: Human Language Technologies, Volume 1 (Long and Short Papers). pp. 4171–4186. ACL, Minneapolis, Minnesota (Jun 2019)
6. Hewitt, J., Ethayarajh, K., Liang, P., Manning, C.: Conditional probing: measuring usable information beyond a baseline. In: Moens, M.F., Huang, X., Specia, L., Yih, S.W.t. (eds.) Proceedings of the 2021 Conference on EMNLP. pp. 1626–1639. ACL, Online and Punta Cana, Dominican Republic (Nov 2021)

7. Hewitt, J., Manning, C.D.: A structural probe for finding syntax in word representations. In: Burstein, J., Doran, C., Solorio, T. (eds.) Proceedings of the 2019 Conference of the North American Chapter of the Association for Computational Linguistics: Human Language Technologies, Volume 1 (Long and Short Papers). pp. 4129–4138. ACL, Minneapolis, Minnesota (Jun 2019)
8. Kobayashi, G., Kuribayashi, T., Yokoi, S., Inui, K.: Attention is not only a weight: Analyzing transformers with vector norms. In: Proceedings of the 2020 Conference on Empirical Methods in Natural Language Processing (EMNLP). pp. 7057–7075. ACL, Online (Nov 2020)
9. Kobayashi, G., Kuribayashi, T., Yokoi, S., Inui, K.: Incorporating Residual and Normalization Layers into Analysis of Masked Language Models. In: Proceedings of the 2021 Conference on EMNLP. pp. 4547–4568. ACL, Online and Punta Cana, Dominican Republic (Nov 2021)
10. Lee-Thorp, J., Ainslie, J., Eckstein, I., Ontanon, S.: FNet: Mixing tokens with Fourier transforms. In: Carpuat, M., de Marneffe, M.C., Meza Ruiz, I.V. (eds.) Proceedings of the 2022 Conference of the North American Chapter of the Association for Computational Linguistics: Human Language Technologies. pp. 4296–4313. ACL, Seattle, United States (Jul 2022)
11. Liu, Y., Ott, M., Goyal, N., Du, J., Joshi, M., Chen, D., Levy, O., Lewis, M., Zettlemoyer, L., Stoyanov, V.: Roberta: A robustly optimized bert pretraining approach. ArXiv **abs/1907.11692** (2019)
12. Marcus, M.P., Marcinkiewicz, M.A., Santorini, B.: Building a large annotated corpus of english: the penn treebank. Comput. Linguist. **19**(2), 313–330 (jun 1993)
13. Michel, P., Levy, O., Neubig, G.: Are sixteen heads really better than one? In: Wallach, H., Larochelle, H., Beygelzimer, A., d'Alché-Buc, F., Fox, E., Garnett, R. (eds.) Advances in Neural Information Processing Systems. vol. 32. Curran Associates, Inc. (2019)
14. Modarressi, A., Fayyaz, M., Aghazadeh, E., Yaghoobzadeh, Y., Pilehvar, M.T.: DecompX: Explaining transformers decisions by propagating token decomposition. In: Rogers, A., Boyd-Graber, J., Okazaki, N. (eds.) Proceedings of the 61st Annual Meeting of the Association for Computational Linguistics (Volume 1: Long Papers). pp. 2649–2664. ACL, Toronto, Canada (Jul 2023)
15. Nivre, J., de Marneffe, M.C., Ginter, F., Hajič, J., Manning, C.D., Pyysalo, S., Schuster, S., Tyers, F., Zeman, D.: Universal Dependencies v2: An ever-growing multilingual treebank collection. In: Proceedings of the Twelfth Language Resources and Evaluation Conference. pp. 4034–4043. European Language Resources Association, Marseille, France (May 2020)
16. Pimentel, T., Valvoda, J., Maudslay, R.H., Zmigrod, R., Williams, A., Cotterell, R.: Information-theoretic probing for linguistic structure. In: Jurafsky, D., Chai, J., Schluter, N., Tetreault, J. (eds.) Proceedings of the 58th Annual Meeting of the Association for Computational Linguistics. pp. 4609–4622. ACL, Online (Jul 2020)
17. Rogers, A., Kovaleva, O., Rumshisky, A.: A primer in BERTology: What we know about how BERT works. Transactions of the ACL **8**, 842–866 (2020)
18. Sanh, V., Debut, L., Chaumond, J., Wolf, T.: Distilbert, a distilled version of bert: smaller, faster, cheaper and lighter. ArXiv **abs/1910.01108** (2019)

19. Silveira, N., Dozat, T., de Marneffe, M.C., Bowman, S., Connor, M., Bauer, J., Manning, C.D.: A gold standard dependency corpus for English. In: Proceedings of the Ninth International Conference on Language Resources and Evaluation (LREC-2014) (2014)
20. Vaswani, A., Shazeer, N., Parmar, N., Uszkoreit, J., Jones, L., Gomez, A.N., Kaiser, L., Polosukhin, I.: Attention is all you need. In: Proceedings of the 31st International Conference on Neural Information Processing Systems. p. 6000–6010. NIPS'17, Curran Associates Inc., Red Hook, NY, USA (2017)

# Divergence-Aware Selective Data-to-Text Generation with LLMs for Factual Consistency

Joy Mahapatra[(✉)][iD] and Utpal Garain[iD]

Indian Statistical Institute Kolkata, Kolkata, India
`joymahapatra90@gmail.com` , `utpal@isical.ac.in`

**Abstract.** Large Language Models (LLMs) have demonstrated strong performance in data-to-text generation (D2T) but often suffer from factual inconsistencies. A key contributing factor to these inconsistencies is source-reference divergence—a mismatch between the input data and the reference text. In this work, we focus on modeling this divergence explicitly. We introduce three complementary metrics—Unigram-Level Divergence, Named Entity-Based Divergence, and Field-Aware Divergence—to quantify the degree of divergence, and we leverage these signals to guide generation. Specifically, we propose a divergence-aware selective generation framework that enables LLMs to abstain from generating outputs when divergence is high. Experiments across three diverse D2T datasets (WikiTableText, ViGGO, WebNLG) and three LLMs (Qwen2.5, FLAN-T5, OPT) show that our method significantly improves factual consistency, particularly at moderate coverage thresholds (70–80%). We observe consistent gains across four popular factuality metrics—AlignScore, QAFactEval, SummaC-Conv, and UniEval-Fact—without sacrificing fluency or diversity. These findings underscore the value of modeling divergence and establish selective generation as an effective strategy for improving factual consistency in LLM-based D2T.

**Keywords:** Data-to-text Generation · LLM & MLM's · Natural Language Processing

## 1 Introduction

Data-to-text generation (D2T) [11] converts semi-structured data into fluent and factually accurate text, supporting applications such as automated journalism, dialogue systems, and healthcare reporting [7,14]. Common data formats include slot-value meaning representations (MRs) [5], tables [1], and graphs [12], corresponding to the three main D2T tasks: MR-to-text, table-to-text, and graph-to-text (Fig. 1). The rise of large language models (LLMs) like T5 [2], OPT [15], and Qwen [13] has significantly advanced D2T, improving fluency, generalization, and informativeness [13].


S. Mitra et al. (Eds.): PReMI 2025, LNCS 16358, pp. 564–571, 2026.
https://doi.org/10.1007/978-3-032-18480-1_57

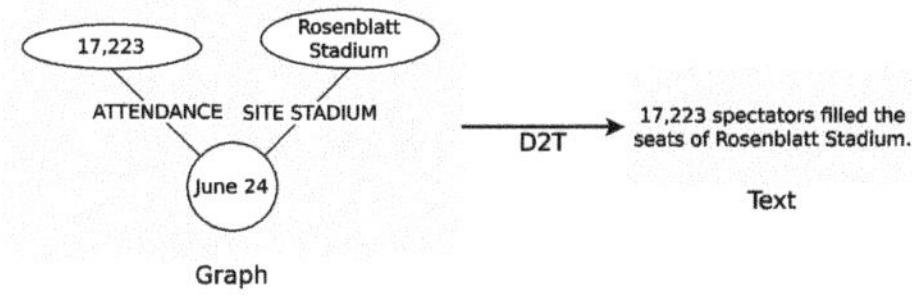


**Fig. 1.** An illustration of graph-to-text generation, a representative form of data-to-text generation.

Despite recent progress, ensuring factual consistency remains a key challenge in LLM-based D2T [4,11]. Hallucinated content—unsupported or incorrect with respect to input—can severely impact reliability, especially in high-stakes domains like healthcare and finance [14]. Among various causes, an underexplored yet impactful factor is *source-reference divergence*—the mismatch between structured input data and its reference text in training corpora. Such divergence, often stemming from loosely aligned annotations/real-world data, may lead models to learn spurious patterns and generate factually inconsistent outputs. Surprisingly, no prior work has systematically quantified this phenomenon or examined its impact on LLM factuality.

In this work, we address the underexplored problem of source-reference divergence in D2T and propose a principled framework to improve factual consistency in LLMs. We first perform a comprehensive analysis of divergence across three representative D2T datasets—WikiTableText (table-to-text), ViGGO (MR-to-text), and WebNLG (graph-to-text)—using a novel three-way approaches: unigram-level divergence, named entity-based divergence, and field-aware divergence. Building on this, we introduce a divergence-aware selective generation strategy, where LLMs abstain from generating when divergence is high, prioritizing factual reliability. Experiments with Qwen2.5 [13], FLAN-T5 [2], and OPT [15] demonstrate consistent gains in factuality—measured via ALIGNSCORE, QAFACTEVAL, SUMMAC-CONV, and UNIEVAL-FACT—with moderate coverage (the ratio of input data instances that are actually represented in the generated text) thresholds.

## 2   Data-To-Text Generation

Data-to-text generation (D2T) aims to map semi-structured input $x$ to a natural language output $y = y_1y_2 \ldots y_{|y|}$, where each token $y_i \in \mathcal{V}$ (vocabulary set) [11]. Given a training set $\mathcal{D} = \{(x^{(i)}, y^{(i)})\}_{i=1}^{n}$, a model $\mathcal{G}_\theta$ (e.g., encoder-decoder or decoder-only [11]) is trained to minimize the negative log-likelihood:

$$\theta^* = \operatorname*{argmax}_{\theta} \sum_{(x,y)\in\mathcal{D}} \mathcal{L}(\mathcal{G}_\theta(x), y) \tag{1}$$

At inference, the model $\mathcal{G}_{\theta^*}$ generates text $\hat{y}$ via decoding strategies like greedy, beam, or nucleus sampling:

$$\widehat{y} = \text{decoding}(\mathcal{G}_{\theta^*}(x)) \qquad (2)$$

## 3   Quantifying Source-Reference Divergence in D2T

Source-reference divergence refers to the mismatch between source data ($s$) and reference text ($r$) [4], often caused by annotation artifacts or differing data collection methods [5,6]. The inherent asymmetry between short, structured inputs and longer, abstract references in D2T tasks further exacerbates this issue [10]. Such divergence introduces biases during training, undermining the factual consistency of LLM-based D2T systems [4] (Fig. 2).

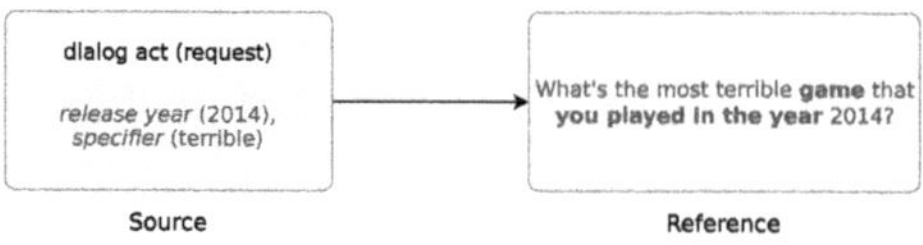


**Fig. 2.** An illustration of source-reference divergence. The boldfaced segments in the reference text highlight content that substantially diverges from the source data.

We propose three complementary approaches to quantify source-reference divergence ($f_{\text{div}}$) in D2T: unigram-level divergence, named entity-based divergence, and Field-aware Divergence.

*Unigram-level Divergence.* This approach quantifies divergence based on the overlap of unigrams between the source text $x$ and the reference text $y$, using Jaccard similarity. A higher overlap implies lower divergence:

$$\text{Unigram}_{\text{div}}(x, y) = 1 - \frac{|\text{unigram}(x) \cap \text{unigram}(y)|}{|\text{unigram}(x) \cup \text{unigram}(y)|}$$

Here, unigram($t$) denotes the set of unigrams extracted from the text $t$.

*Named Entity-based Divergence.* This computes divergence based on the overlap of named entities between the source and the reference, capturing real-world factual alignment. It is defined as:

$$\text{NE}_{\text{div}}(x, y) = 1 - \frac{|\text{NE}(x) \cap \text{NE}(y)|}{|\text{NE}(y)|}$$

where NE($x$) and NE($y$) are the sets of named entities extracted from the source and reference texts, respectively. This formulation emphasizes factual entities, which are often critical for evaluating factual consistency.

*Field-aware Divergence.* Unlike the above two text-based approaches, this approach is designed for structured inputs such as meaning representations (MRs), tables, or graphs. It quantifies divergence at the field level, treating each field independently and aggregating the result. This is particularly useful when the source data is not in pure text form.

We define the field-aware divergence as:

$$\text{Field}_{\text{div}}(x, y) = 1 - \frac{1}{|\mathcal{F}_x|} \sum_{f \in \mathcal{F}_x} w_f \cdot \frac{|\text{n-gram}(f) \cap \text{n-gram}(y)|}{|\text{n-gram}(y)|}$$

Here, $\mathcal{F}_x$ is the set of fields in the structured input $x$, n-gram$(f)$ represents the set of $n$-grams from the field value $f$, and $w_f$ is $n$-gram weight (smoothed) to control the importance of each field.

## 4   Divergence-Aware Selective Generation

Our approach—source-reference divergence-aware selective generation—is inspired by selective classification [8], where a model abstains under uncertainty. Analogously, here LLM refrains from generating when the input exhibits high source-reference divergence with the generated text, based on the hypothesis that such cases are more prone to factual inconsistency. This strategy enhances output reliability, especially in high-stakes (safety-critical) domains. Formally, the selective generation process is defined as follows:

$$\text{Selective generation} = \begin{cases} \widehat{y} & \text{if } \widehat{y} \sim \mathcal{G}_{\theta^*}(x) \text{ and } f_{\text{div}}(x, \widehat{y}) \leq \Phi \\ \text{abstain} & \text{otherwise} \end{cases} \tag{3}$$

Here, $\Phi$ is a divergence threshold used to decide whether to generate or abstain. It can be set empirically based on divergence distributions in training data. While selective generation may reduce coverage (i.e., fewer outputs), this trade-off is justified in safety-critical domains like healthcare, where improved factual consistency is paramount.

## 5   Experimental Details

We evaluate our source-reference divergence-aware selective generation framework across three LLM families—Qwen2.5 (1.5B), FLAN-T5 (248M), and OPT (790M)—fine-tuned using Huggingface `transformers` and QLoRA [3] with a learning rate of 2e−4 and 3 training epochs. Factual consistency is assessed using four complementary metrics: AlignScore, QAFactEval, SummaC-Conv, and UniEval-Fact, capturing diverse aspects of factual alignment. Evaluation spans three representative D2T benchmarks—WikiTableText (table-to-text) [1], ViGGO (MR-to-text) [9], and WebNLG (graph-to-text) [6]—ensuring coverage across key data formats in D2T. Our implementation is publicly available at https://github.com/joymahapatra/divergence-aware-selective-d2t.

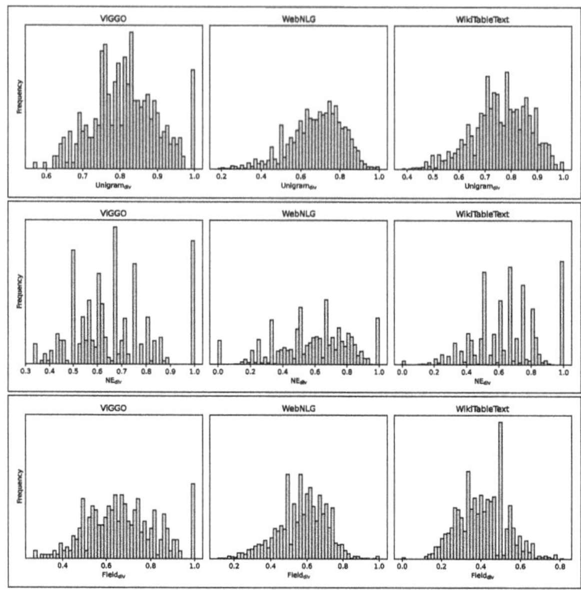

**Fig. 3.** Distribution of source-reference divergence across the ViGGO, WikiTableText, and WebNLG datasets using our three proposed measures: unigram-level divergence, named entity-based divergence, and field-aware divergence.

## 6    Results 1: Existence of Source-Reference Divergence in D2T

This result section demonstrates the presence of source-reference divergence in three widely used D2T datasets: ViGGO, WikiTableText, and WebNLG. We apply our proposed divergence quantification methods—unigram-level divergence, named entity-based divergence, and field-aware divergence—on the training partitions of these datasets. Figure 3 illustrates the distribution of divergence scores for each dataset under the three approaches. The wide spread of these distributions clearly indicates that source-reference divergence is prevalent and non-trivial across all datasets. These findings validate our hypothesis that source-reference divergence is a real and significant phenomenon in D2T benchmarks, highlighting the importance of accounting for it during the training and evaluation of LLM-based generation systems.

## 7    Results 2: Factual Consistency Vs. Coverage in Divergence-Aware Selective Generation

Table 1, Table 2, and Table 3 present the impact of divergence-aware selective generation on factual consistency across varying coverage thresholds for three LLMs: FLAN-T5, OPT, and Qwen2.5. Evaluation is conducted using four

**Table 1.** Factual consistency scores for FLAN-T5 under divergence-aware selective generation at varying coverage levels. Blue denotes favorable consistency gains; red indicates aberrant behavior.

| $f_{div}$ | coverage | ViGGO | | | | WebNLG | | | | WikiTableText | | | |
|---|---|---|---|---|---|---|---|---|---|---|---|---|---|
| | | ALIGNSCORE | QAFACTEVAL | SUMMAC-CONV | UNIEVAL-FACT | ALIGNSCORE | QAFACTEVAL | SUMMAC-CONV | UNIEVAL-FACT | ALIGNSCORE | QAFACTEVAL | SUMMAC-CONV | UNIEVAL-FACT |
| $NE_{div}$ | 1.0 | 0.328 | 0.255 | 0.042 | 0.612 | 0.468 | 0.417 | 0.219 | 0.443 | 0.309 | 0.296 | 0.183 | 0.159 |
| | 0.9 | 0.586 | 0.333 | 0.090 | 0.441 | 0.516 | 0.650 | 0.452 | 0.492 | 0.351 | 0.527 | 0.410 | 0.201 |
| | 0.8 | 0.436 | 0.625 | 0.112 | 0.713 | 0.790 | 0.482 | 0.290 | 0.521 | 0.377 | 0.360 | 0.243 | 0.465 |
| | 0.7 | 0.708 | 0.652 | 0.360 | 0.724 | 0.803 | 0.727 | 0.540 | 0.769 | 0.617 | 0.603 | 0.482 | 0.462 |
| | 0.6 | 0.717 | 0.668 | 0.357 | 0.728 | 0.802 | 0.726 | 0.543 | 0.777 | 0.617 | 0.604 | 0.480 | 0.465 |
| $Unigram_{div}$ | 1.0 | 0.328 | 0.255 | 0.272 | 0.612 | 0.468 | 0.647 | 0.219 | 0.443 | 0.309 | 0.296 | 0.183 | 0.159 |
| | 0.9 | 0.405 | 0.341 | 0.092 | 0.449 | 0.521 | 0.658 | 0.273 | 0.495 | 0.346 | 0.525 | 0.218 | 0.195 |
| | 0.8 | 0.449 | 0.405 | 0.120 | 0.480 | 0.549 | 0.733 | 0.539 | 0.526 | 0.366 | 0.597 | 0.478 | 0.212 |
| | 0.7 | 0.704 | 0.671 | 0.367 | 0.721 | 0.803 | 0.740 | 0.553 | 0.777 | 0.609 | 0.600 | 0.477 | 0.455 |
| | 0.6 | 0.711 | 0.678 | 0.368 | 0.723 | 0.816 | 0.744 | 0.563 | 0.788 | 0.611 | 0.605 | 0.477 | 0.457 |
| $Field_{div}$ | 1.0 | 0.328 | 0.255 | 0.042 | 0.382 | 0.468 | 0.647 | 0.219 | 0.673 | 0.309 | 0.526 | 0.183 | 0.389 |
| | 0.9 | 0.412 | 0.535 | 0.094 | 0.449 | 0.525 | 0.473 | 0.271 | 0.497 | 0.534 | 0.337 | 0.220 | 0.193 |
| | 0.8 | 0.457 | 0.407 | 0.122 | 0.484 | 0.548 | 0.493 | 0.293 | 0.519 | 0.366 | 0.357 | 0.478 | 0.213 |
| | 0.7 | 0.717 | 0.672 | 0.368 | 0.736 | 0.800 | 0.737 | 0.541 | 0.766 | 0.607 | 0.597 | 0.483 | 0.451 |
| | 0.6 | 0.734 | 0.687 | 0.373 | 0.745 | 0.802 | 0.741 | 0.548 | 0.771 | 0.610 | 0.594 | 0.483 | 0.452 |

**Table 2.** Factual consistency scores for OPT under divergence-aware selective generation at varying coverage levels. Blue denotes favorable consistency gains; red indicates aberrant behavior.

| $f_{div}$ | coverage | ViGGO | | | | WebNLG | | | | WikiTableText | | | |
|---|---|---|---|---|---|---|---|---|---|---|---|---|---|
| | | ALIGNSCORE | QAFACTEVAL | SUMMAC-CONV | UNIEVAL-FACT | ALIGNSCORE | QAFACTEVAL | SUMMAC-CONV | UNIEVAL-FACT | ALIGNSCORE | QAFACTEVAL | SUMMAC-CONV | UNIEVAL-FACT |
| $NE_{div}$ | 1.0 | 0.394 | 0.546 | 0.104 | 0.661 | 0.477 | 0.650 | 0.220 | 0.446 | 0.308 | 0.500 | 0.418 | 0.167 |
| | 0.9 | 0.462 | 0.384 | 0.155 | 0.678 | 0.521 | 0.649 | 0.260 | 0.678 | 0.351 | 0.503 | 0.418 | 0.209 |
| | 0.8 | 0.495 | 0.423 | 0.182 | 0.750 | 0.540 | 0.713 | 0.520 | 0.749 | 0.372 | 0.331 | 0.490 | 0.229 |
| | 0.7 | 0.741 | 0.677 | 0.424 | 0.745 | 0.782 | 0.712 | 0.523 | 0.751 | 0.614 | 0.571 | 0.489 | 0.468 |
| | 0.6 | 0.737 | 0.665 | 0.428 | 0.744 | 0.778 | 0.706 | 0.526 | 0.754 | 0.618 | 0.575 | 0.492 | 0.471 |
| $Unigram_{div}$ | 1.0 | 0.394 | 0.316 | 0.334 | 0.661 | 0.477 | 0.650 | 0.450 | 0.446 | 0.538 | 0.500 | 0.188 | 0.167 |
| | 0.9 | 0.656 | 0.393 | 0.348 | 0.489 | 0.523 | 0.460 | 0.462 | 0.679 | 0.348 | 0.315 | 0.226 | 0.204 |
| | 0.8 | 0.499 | 0.441 | 0.427 | 0.755 | 0.788 | 0.723 | 0.540 | 0.516 | 0.372 | 0.582 | 0.487 | 0.225 |
| | 0.7 | 0.747 | 0.692 | 0.432 | 0.756 | 0.795 | 0.730 | 0.548 | 0.765 | 0.614 | 0.585 | 0.486 | 0.464 |
| | 0.6 | 0.759 | 0.707 | 0.438 | 0.761 | 0.803 | 0.734 | 0.554 | 0.772 | 0.626 | 0.590 | 0.495 | 0.473 |
| $Field_{div}$ | 1.0 | 0.394 | 0.316 | 0.104 | 0.431 | 0.477 | 0.420 | 0.450 | 0.446 | 0.308 | 0.270 | 0.188 | 0.167 |
| | 0.9 | 0.656 | 0.581 | 0.155 | 0.677 | 0.525 | 0.465 | 0.269 | 0.485 | 0.353 | 0.320 | 0.230 | 0.207 |
| | 0.8 | 0.747 | 0.438 | 0.429 | 0.521 | 0.552 | 0.487 | 0.536 | 0.510 | 0.379 | 0.581 | 0.252 | 0.228 |
| | 0.7 | 0.766 | 0.702 | 0.438 | 0.773 | 0.794 | 0.726 | 0.542 | 0.752 | 0.623 | 0.581 | 0.494 | 0.468 |
| | 0.6 | 0.794 | 0.725 | 0.455 | 0.789 | 0.801 | 0.731 | 0.547 | 0.757 | 0.626 | 0.590 | 0.499 | 0.469 |

**Table 3.** Factual consistency scores for Qwen2.5 under divergence-aware selective generation at varying coverage levels. Blue denotes favorable consistency gains; red indicates aberrant behavior.

| $f_{div}$ | coverage | ViGGO | | | | WebNLG | | | | WikiTableText | | | |
|---|---|---|---|---|---|---|---|---|---|---|---|---|---|
| | | ALIGNSCORE | QAFACTEVAL | SUMMAC-CONV | UNIEVAL-FACT | ALIGNSCORE | QAFACTEVAL | SUMMAC-CONV | UNIEVAL-FACT | ALIGNSCORE | QAFACTEVAL | SUMMAC-CONV | UNIEVAL-FACT |
| $NE_{div}$ | 1.0 | 0.433 | 0.334 | 0.115 | 0.672 | 0.531 | 0.474 | 0.474 | 0.721 | 0.292 | 0.266 | 0.179 | 0.399 |
| | 0.9 | 0.500 | 0.411 | 0.166 | 0.505 | 0.572 | 0.513 | 0.286 | 0.535 | 0.518 | 0.303 | 0.214 | 0.207 |
| | 0.8 | 0.525 | 0.678 | 0.187 | 0.527 | 0.833 | 0.530 | 0.309 | 0.796 | 0.351 | 0.324 | 0.477 | 0.227 |
| | 0.7 | 0.782 | 0.692 | 0.434 | 0.776 | 0.833 | 0.770 | 0.553 | 0.796 | 0.588 | 0.557 | 0.475 | 0.462 |
| | 0.6 | 0.793 | 0.709 | 0.441 | 0.779 | 0.830 | 0.765 | 0.554 | 0.797 | 0.590 | 0.555 | 0.477 | 0.460 |
| $Unigram_{div}$ | 1.0 | 0.433 | 0.334 | 0.115 | 0.442 | 0.531 | 0.474 | 0.474 | 0.491 | 0.292 | 0.496 | 0.409 | 0.169 |
| | 0.9 | 0.498 | 0.404 | 0.355 | 0.507 | 0.576 | 0.515 | 0.294 | 0.536 | 0.330 | 0.309 | 0.216 | 0.207 |
| | 0.8 | 0.526 | 0.451 | 0.188 | 0.765 | 0.592 | 0.531 | 0.319 | 0.797 | 0.351 | 0.329 | 0.472 | 0.465 |
| | 0.7 | 0.780 | 0.719 | 0.434 | 0.772 | 0.832 | 0.768 | 0.559 | 0.798 | 0.598 | 0.575 | 0.474 | 0.466 |
| | 0.6 | 0.790 | 0.732 | 0.439 | 0.777 | 0.835 | 0.765 | 0.572 | 0.808 | 0.601 | 0.579 | 0.475 | 0.469 |
| $Field_{div}$ | 1.0 | 0.433 | 0.334 | 0.345 | 0.442 | 0.761 | 0.474 | 0.474 | 0.491 | 0.522 | 0.266 | 0.179 | 0.169 |
| | 0.9 | 0.496 | 0.594 | 0.355 | 0.504 | 0.571 | 0.517 | 0.289 | 0.532 | 0.333 | 0.501 | 0.216 | 0.207 |
| | 0.8 | 0.531 | 0.448 | 0.432 | 0.533 | 0.598 | 0.537 | 0.558 | 0.557 | 0.359 | 0.336 | 0.240 | 0.228 |
| | 0.7 | 0.795 | 0.713 | 0.442 | 0.788 | 0.836 | 0.778 | 0.556 | 0.796 | 0.598 | 0.578 | 0.477 | 0.464 |
| | 0.6 | 0.809 | 0.735 | 0.451 | 0.794 | 0.838 | 0.777 | 0.559 | 0.796 | 0.594 | 0.580 | 0.474 | 0.458 |

widely adopted factuality metrics—ALIGNSCORE, QAFACTEVAL, SUMMAC-CONV, and UNIEVAL-FACT—to ensure a comprehensive assessment of consistency. As the coverage threshold is varied from 60% to 100%, we observe that selective generation consistently improves factual consistency across all datasets and models. In particular, the 70–80% coverage range (highlighted in blue) often yields near-ceiling consistency scores, indicating the effectiveness of abstaining from high-divergence inputs. The divergence threshold $\Phi$ can be empirically estimated from the third quartile of the divergence distribution in the training data. Although slight drops in consistency are observed at higher coverage levels (90–100%, marked in red), they are exceptions rather than the norm. Overall, these results demonstrate that divergence-aware selective generation provides a practical and robust approach to enhancing the factual reliability of LLM-based D2T systems.

## 8   Conclusion

This paper addresses a key challenge in LLM-based D2T generation: maintaining factual consistency in the presence of source-reference divergence. We introduce three complementary measures—unigram-level divergence, named entity-based divergence, and field-aware divergence—to quantify the misalignment between structured input data and reference texts. Building on these metrics, we propose a divergence-aware selective generation framework that allows LLMs to abstain from generating outputs when divergence is high. Experiments across three representative D2T benchmarks (ViGGO, WikiTableText, and WebNLG) and LLM families (Qwen2.5, FLAN-T5, and OPT) show that our approach consistently enhances factual consistency, especially at moderate coverage levels (70–80%), with minimal loss in output coverage. This selective abstention significantly reduces hallucinations, a critical improvement for safety-sensitive applications such as healthcare. Overall, our findings highlight the importance of explicitly modeling and controlling source-reference divergence to build more reliable and trustworthy LLM-based D2T systems.

**Acknowledgments.** This research is partially supported by the Indo-French Centre for the Promotion of Advanced Research (IFCPAR/CEFIPRA) through CSRP Project No. 6702-2.

## References

1. Bao, J., et al.: Table-to-text: describing table region with natural language. In: Proceedings of the AAAI, pp. 5020–5027 (2018). https://doi.org/10.1609/aaai.v32i1.11944
2. Chung, H.W., et al.: Scaling instruction-finetuned language models. J. Mach. Learn. Res. **25**(70), 1–53 (2024). https://jmlr.org/papers/v25/23-0870.html

3. Dettmers, T., Pagnoni, A., Holtzman, A., Zettlemoyer, L.: Qlora: efficient finetuning of quantized llms. In: Proceedings of the NeurIPS (2023). http://papers.nips.cc/paper_files/paper/2023/hash/1feb87871436031bdc0f2beaa62a049b-Abstract-Conference.html

4. Dhingra, B., Faruqui, M., Parikh, A.P., Chang, M., Das, D., Cohen, W.W.: Handling divergent reference texts when evaluating table-to-text generation. In: Proceedings of the ACL, pp. 4884–4895 (2019). https://doi.org/10.18653/v1/p19-1483

5. Dusek, O., Novikova, J., Rieser, V.: Findings of the E2E NLG challenge. In: Proceedings of the INLG, pp. 322–328 (2018). https://doi.org/10.18653/v1/w18-6539

6. Gardent, C., Shimorina, A., Narayan, S., Perez-Beltrachini, L.: The webnlg challenge: Generating text from RDF data. In: Proceedings of the INLG, pp. 124–133 (2017). https://doi.org/10.18653/v1/w17-3518

7. Gatt, A., Krahmer, E.: Survey of the state of the art in natural language generation: core tasks, applications and evaluation. J. Artif. Intell. Res. **61**, 65–170 (2018). https://doi.org/10.1613/jair.5477

8. Geifman, Y., El-Yaniv, R.: Selective classification for deep neural networks. In: NIPS, pp. 4878–4887 (2017). https://proceedings.neurips.cc/paper/2017/hash/4a8423d5e91fda00bb7e46540e2b0cf1-Abstract.html

9. Juraska, J., Bowden, K., Walker, M.A.: Viggo: a video game corpus for data-to-text generation in open-domain conversation. In: Proceedings of the INLG, pp. 164–172 (2019). https://aclanthology.org/W19-8623/

10. Li, W., Wu, W., Chen, M., Liu, J., Xiao, X., Wu, H.: Faithfulness in natural language generation: a systematic survey of analysis, evaluation and optimization methods. CoRR **abs/2203.05227** (2022). https://doi.org/10.48550/arXiv.2203.05227

11. Lin, Y., Ruan, T., Liu, J., Wang, H.: A survey on neural data-to-text generation. IEEE Trans. Knowl. Data Eng. **36**(4), 1431–1449 (2024). https://doi.org/10.1109/TKDE.2023.3304385

12. Nan, L., et al.: DART: open-domain structured data record to text generation. In: Proceedings of the NAACL-HLT, pp. 432–447 (2021). https://doi.org/10.18653/v1/2021.naacl-main.37

13. Yang, A., et al.: Qwen2.5 technical report. CoRR **abs/2412.15115** (2024). https://doi.org/10.48550/arXiv.2412.15115

14. Yermakov, R., Drago, N., Ziletti, A.: Biomedical data-to-text generation via finetuning transformers. In: Proceedings of the INLG, pp. 364–370 (2021). https://doi.org/10.18653/v1/2021.inlg-1.40

15. Zhang, S., et al.: OPT: open pre-trained transformer language models. CoRR **abs/2205.01068** (2022). https://doi.org/10.48550/arXiv.2205.01068

# Multi-modal Heterogeneous Graph Attention Networks with Dynamic Edge Learning and Cross-Attention Fusion for Fake News Detection


Parth Pawar and Santosh Singh Rathore[✉][iD]

Department of Computer Science and Engineering, ABV Indian Institute of Information Technology and Management, Gwalior, India
{bcs_2021051,santoshs}@iiitm.ac.in



**Abstract.** The increase of fake news on digital platforms poses significant challenges to information integrity and public discourse. Existing detection methods focusing on text-only or simple multimodal fusion fail to capture complex inter-modal dependencies and contextual relationships. In this paper, we propose **B**i-modal **R**epresentation **A**ttention with **D**ynamic heterogeneous graphs (BRAD) for multimodal fake news detection that dynamically constructs and processes heterogeneous graphs from news content. Our approach leverages both textual and visual information to create better multimodal representations, where each node in the graph can adaptively select the most informative neighborhood type for embedding updates through a learnable decision mechanism. The BRAD architecture consists of specialized networks for neighborhood selection and representation learning, enabling fine-grained control over information propagation in the graph structure. We evaluate our method on the Fakeddit dataset, a large-scale multimodal benchmark with diverse fake news categories. Experimental results demonstrate that our approach achieves superior performance compared to existing multimodal baselines with acc., precision, recall, and f1-score values of 91.28%, 87.32%, 91.23%, and 89.23%, respectively.

**Keywords:** Fake news detection · Multi-modal · Heterogeneous Graph Attention Networks


## 1  Introduction

The rapid expansion of social media platforms and digital communication channels has fundamentally transformed how information is created, shared, and consumed globally. While these technological advances have democratized access to information, they also have created unprecedented opportunities for the spread of misinformation and fake news. The consequences of an increase in fake news extend beyond individual misinformation, affecting democratic processes, public health decisions, financial markets, and various political elections. Recent



S. Mitra et al. (Eds.): PReMI 2025, LNCS 16358, pp. 572–580, 2026.
https://doi.org/10.1007/978-3-032-18480-1_58

events, including fake news during Operation Sindoor on Twitter and the rise of generative AI like Google Deepmind Veo, highlight the urgent need for effective automated systems to identify and mitigate false information spread.

Early research into fake news detection mainly focused on single-modal approaches, where either the text of news articles or social context features were analyzed in isolation to assess credibility [1]. These approaches focused on identifying linguistic patterns, sentiment anomalies, and stylistic inconsistencies that may indicate deceptive content. With the rise of deep learning, models such as CNNs, RNNs, and transformers have been applied to analyze textual content, often pre-trained on large corpora to capture contextual embeddings. However, while single-modal approaches have advanced fake news detection capabilities, they struggle with multimodal disinformation, where visual content often reinforces or contradicts textual claims. This limitation has motivated the shift towards multimodal approaches, particularly for social media platforms.

The increase of multimodal content across platforms such as Reddit & Twitter has spurred advancements in fake news detection methods, which aim to jointly analyze text, images, videos, and metadata using late fusion [6,7] methods. However, multimodal fake news detection presents several key challenges, including capturing complementary/conflicting semantics and global context across heterogeneous data, performing global reasoning (difficult for sequential models), and employing flexible architectures for diverse information patterns. While early methods used simple fusion, recent approaches leverage cross-modal attention, transformers, and graph neural networks. However, many still rely on fixed fusion or static graphs, limiting adaptability. Graph neural networks offer strong potential for modeling complex relationships, but most existing methods use homogeneous or fixed heterogeneous graphs, failing to capture the dynamic nature of multimodal fake news. Recent research has focused on identifying and leveraging consistency patterns between modalities to distinguish real and fake news [9,15]. For example, the SAFE model [17] uses similarity assessments to ensure consistency between modalities. Similarly, [16] proposed the Multimodal Consistency Neural Network (MCNN), which uses similarity measurements to evaluate the relationship between textual and visual data.

To address these limitations, we propose **Bi**-modal **R**epresentation **A**ttention with **D**ynamic heterogeneous graphs **(BRAD)** for multimodal fake news detection. Our approach includes: (1) dynamic multimodal graph construction that creates heterogeneous graphs directly from news content, (2) an adaptive decision mechanism that allows each node to independently select the most informative neighborhood type for representation learning, and (3) specialized attention networks for both neighborhood selection and embedding updates. We evaluate our method on the Fakeddit dataset [10], a comprehensive multimodal benchmark consisting of over 1 million samples with textual content and corresponding images from multiple categories of fake news, demonstrating significant improvements over existing multimodal baselines.

The rest of the paper is organized as follows. Section 2 presents the methodology, including the proposed BRAD approach. Section 3 discusses the experiments conducted and the analysis of the results. Section 4 concludes the paper.

## 2   Bi-modal Representation Attention with Dynamic Heterogeneous Graphs (BRAD) Approach

Given dataset $D$ with textual content $t_i$ and visual content $v_i$, we formulate fake news detection as binary classification with labels $y \in \{y_1, y_2\}$ (fake/real). We introduce BRAD (Bi-modal Representation Attention with Dynamic heterogeneous graphs), which constructs a heterogeneous multimodal graph $G_h(V, E, R)$. Where $V$ represents the set of nodes encoding different modalities and their interactions, $E$ denotes the set of edges capturing intra- and inter-modal relationships, and $R$ is a set of edge types representing different connection patterns. Our goal is to learn a model $F$ that predicts $\hat{y} = F(t_i, v_i)$ by leveraging structural and semantic information in the multimodal graph through graph-based attention mechanisms for robust fake news detection.

Figure 1 provides an overview of the proposed approach. The proposed BRAD architecture begins with separate encoders for textual and visual modalities, where text features are extracted using a pre-trained BERT model [3] and image features are obtained through a ResNet-50 backbone [4]. To enable effective multimodal fusion, we employ a shared projection layer that maps both text and image features into a common embedding space of dimension 256, facilitating cross-modal interactions through multi-head attention mechanisms. This shared representation allows the model to capture complementary information between textual content and visual elements.

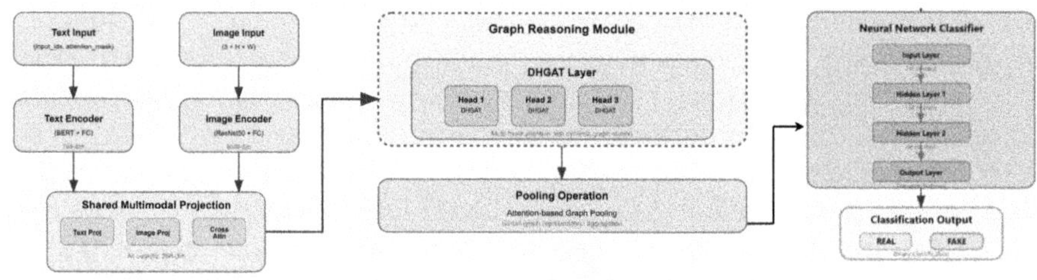

Fig. 1. Architecture of the proposed multimodal fake news detection model

1. **Multimodal Heterogeneous Graph Construction:** The multimodal graph construction module employs Decision-based Heterogeneous Graph Attention Network (DHGAT) [8] to dynamically create heterogeneous graphs with projected text, image, and cross-modal features as distinct node types, plus learnable virtual nodes for latent semantic relationships. A learned edge predictor computes connection probabilities based on feature similarity, generating

multiple edge types for different relationship patterns. This dynamic approach adapts graph topology to each news sample's characteristics, enabling flexible, context-aware representation learning.

Given a dataset $D$ containing news items with textual titles and associated images, we construct a multimodal heterogeneous graph $G_h(V, E, R)$ as follows:

$$G_h(V, E, R) = \begin{cases} R = \{\text{`text'}, \text{`image'}, \text{`cross-modal'}\} \\ V = D \text{ and } |V| = n \\ E \subseteq \{(v_i, v_j, e_{\text{type}} = r) \mid v_i, v_j \in V, \ r \in R\} \end{cases} \tag{2}$$

Graph construction starts by extracting features from textual and visual modalities via pre-trained encoders. For each news item, we compute semantic similarity scores between different modality representations to determine edge connectivity. An edge of type $r$ is created between two nodes based on similarity thresholds computed from the corresponding feature representations:

$$(v_i, v_j, e_{\text{type}} = r) \in E : \begin{cases} r = \text{`text'} & \text{if } \text{sim}(t_i, t_j) > \theta_t \\ r = \text{`image'} & \text{if } \text{sim}(img_i, img_j) > \theta_{img} \\ r = \text{`cross-modal'} & \text{if } \text{sim}(c_i, c_j) > \theta_c \end{cases} \tag{3}$$

where $t_i, img_i, c_i$ represent the text, image, and cross-modal features for node $v_i$, respectively, and $\theta_t, \theta_{img}, \theta_c$ are learned threshold parameters. These thresholds achieve desired graph sparsity levels for each edge type using target density initialization. The threshold is initialized as $\theta_r = \text{percentile}(\mathcal{S}_r, 100 \times (1 - \rho_r))$, where $\mathcal{S}_r = \{\text{sim}(f_i^r, f_j^r) \mid v_i, v_j \in V, i \neq j\}$ represents all pairwise similarity scores for that modality and $\rho_r$ represents target density for edge type $r \in R$. This ensures exactly $\rho_r \times N(N-1)/2$ edges are initially created for each type, preventing overly dense or sparse graphs while allowing different sparsity levels across modalities. Additionally, we incorporate virtual nodes as auxiliary graph components to capture latent semantic patterns that may not be explicitly represented through direct pairwise similarities between news items.

**2. Decision-based Heterogeneous Graph Attention Network (DHGAT).** The DHGAT layer processes the constructed heterogeneous graphs through a decision mechanism enabling each node to independently select the most informative neighborhood connections for representation updates. It employs Gumbel-Softmax sampling [5] for discrete decisions, which focuses on the most relevant relationship patterns per node. DHGAT incorporates multiple decision heads for different edge types, with learned attention weights determining neighborhood structure importance. In the multimodal heterogeneous graph ($G_h$), nodes connect through various edge types representing semantic relationships from textual, visual, or cross-modal similarities, creating diverse neighborhood types that transmit unique multimodal information patterns. These varying neighborhoods differently influence node embedding generation, requiring adaptive selection mechanisms. Existing GNNs for heterogeneous graphs overlook dynamic multimodal information requirements. DHGAT addresses this by enabling each node per layer to independently decide which neighborhood type to use for embedding updates. In multimodal heterogeneous graphs with three edge types (text, image, cross-modal), nodes choose from multiple neighborhood configurations:

- **Text-only:** Utilizes only textually similar neighbors for semantic understanding.
- **Image-only:** Focuses on visually similar neighbors for visual pattern recognition.
- **Cross-modal:** Uses neighbors with strong text-image semantic alignment.

The number of possible neighborhood choices depends on the edge type diversity. With $|R| = 3$ edge types (text, image, cross-modal), we can define $|\Gamma| = 2^{|R|} = 8$ different neighborhood configurations:

$$\Gamma = \{\gamma_0, \gamma_1, \ldots, \gamma_7\}, \quad \gamma_i \subseteq R \tag{4}$$

For each neighborhood type $\gamma_i$, we define the corresponding edge set:

$$E_{\gamma_i} = \{(v, u, e_{\text{type}}) \in E \mid e_{\text{type}} \in \gamma_i\} \tag{5}$$

The DHGAT architecture consists of two specialized Graph Attention Networks: a decision network that selects optimal neighborhood types, and a representation network that updates embeddings based on selected neighborhoods. Given the multimodal heterogeneous graph $G_h$, the DHGAT updates node embeddings as follows:

First, the decision network predicts probability distributions over neighborhood types:

$$\rho_v^l = \text{GAT}\left(h_v^{l-1}, \{h_u^{l-1} \mid u \in N_d(v)\}\right) \tag{6}$$

where $N_d(v)$ represents the decision-making neighborhood, typically encompassing all available edge types to ensure comprehensive decision information.

Next, we employ the Gumbel-Softmax estimator [8] for differentiable categorical sampling:

$$\text{Gumbel-Softmax}(\rho; \tau)_i = \frac{\exp((\log(\rho(\gamma_i)) + g_i)/\tau)}{\sum_{\gamma_j \in \Gamma} \exp((\log(\rho(\gamma_j)) + g_j)/\tau)} \tag{7}$$

where $g_i \sim \text{Gumbel}(0, 1)$ and $\tau$ is the temperature parameter controlling the sharpness of the categorical distribution.

Finally, representation network updates embeddings using the selected neighborhood:

$$h_v^l = \text{GAT}\left(h_v^{l-1}, \{h_u^{l-1} \mid u \in N_{\gamma_v^l}(v)\}\right) \tag{8}$$

where $N_{\gamma_v^l}(v)$ contains neighbors connected through edges of the selected type $\gamma_v^l$.

**3. Binary Classification with Attention-based Pooling:** Following DHGAT processing, an attention-based pooling mechanism aggregates information from all graph nodes to produce a fixed-size representation for classification. The pooling uses learned attention weights to emphasize the most discriminative nodes, ensuring the final representation captures relevant information for fake news detection. Node embeddings $H^L$ from DHGAT's final layer are processed through this attention-based pooling, then passed through a multi-layer perceptron classifier with dropout regularization to produce the final binary classification output (real/fake). The attention-based pooling computes node importance scores and creates a weighted combination:

$$\text{attn_scores} = \text{MLP}(H^L), \quad \text{attn_weights} = \text{softmax}(\text{attn_scores}) \tag{9}$$

$$\text{pooled_features} = \sum_{i=1}^{|V|} \text{attn_weights}_i \cdot H_i^L \tag{10}$$

The pooled features are then processed by a multi-layer perceptron classifier:

$$\text{logits} = \text{MLP}_{\text{classifier}}(\text{pooled_features}) \tag{11}$$

For binary classification, we employ standard cross-entropy loss:

$$\mathcal{L}(\Theta) = -\frac{1}{N} \sum_{i=1}^{N} \sum_{c=1}^{2} y_{i,c} \log(\hat{y}_{i,c}) \tag{12}$$

where $N$ is the number of training samples, $y_{i,c}$ is the ground truth label, and $\hat{y}_{i,c}$ is the predicted probability for class $c$ (real or fake) for sample $i$.

## 3 Experiments and Results

We used the Fakeddit dataset [10], which is a comprehensive multimodal dataset developed to advance the detection of fake news by integrating both textual and visual data. It comprises over one million samples, including images, text, metadata, and comments. It supports 2-way (true or fake), 3-way (completely true, fake but the text is true, fake with false text), and 6-way classifications (true, satire/parody, misleading content, imposter content, false connection, manipulated content) fake news classification. For this work, we focus on the 2-way classification task (true vs. fake).

Training is performed using the Adam optimizer with batch size of 64, along with an initial learning rate of 2e-5. Due to hardware and resource limitations, we restricted our training to 3 epochs, which may not represent the full convergence potential of the model but provides a reasonable baseline for comparison. Figure 2 shows that both training loss and validation accuracy have not fully plateaued by epoch 3, suggesting potential for further improvement with extended training. Based on the loss reduction trajectory, we estimate the model may benefit from 5–10 additional epochs to reach convergence. Since this is a binary classification problem, we use accuracy and F1-score as primary evaluation metrics. All experiments are conducted using Pytorch framework on GPU P100.

## 3.1   Results and Analysis

Table 1 presents the performance comparison of all baseline methods on the Fakeddit dataset. Our proposed BRAD model achieves the highest performance among all baseline models with 91.28% accuracy, 87.32% precision, 91.23% recall, and 89.23% F1-score, demonstrating its superior ability to distinguish between real and fake content. The training dynamics shown in Fig. 2(a) shows stable training over the 3-epoch training period, with both loss reduction and accuracy improvement following expected patterns.

**Table 1.** Performance comparison of various methods on the Fakeddit dataset

| Dataset | Method | Accuracy (%) | Precision (%) | Recall (%) | F1-score (%) |
| --- | --- | --- | --- | --- | --- |
| Fakeddit | EANN [14] | 72.27 | 78.43 | 63.4 | 70.12 |
| | HMCAN [13] | 82.89 | 84.03 | 84.04 | 84.03 |
| | MVAE [12] | 70.24 | 76.53 | 74.75 | 75.63 |
| | VERITE [11] | 84.72 | 85.34 | 84.37 | 84.85 |
| | BERT+Resnet50 (Baseline) [10] | 89.09 | – | – | – |
| | CL+Fusion [2] | 88.88 | 86.40 | 85.40 | 85.90 |
| | **BRAD (Proposed)** | **91.28** | **87.32** | **91.23** | **89.23** |

The PCA plot in Fig. 2(b) shows clear separation between real (blue) and fake (red) news samples, with each class clustering on opposite sides of the first principal component with Silhouette Score of 0.68. This indicates the model effectively captures discriminative features. The V-shape suggests intra-class variance along the second component, reflecting meaningful sub-clustering. The overlap near the origin highlights ambiguous cases with similar features, illustrating the task's complexity.

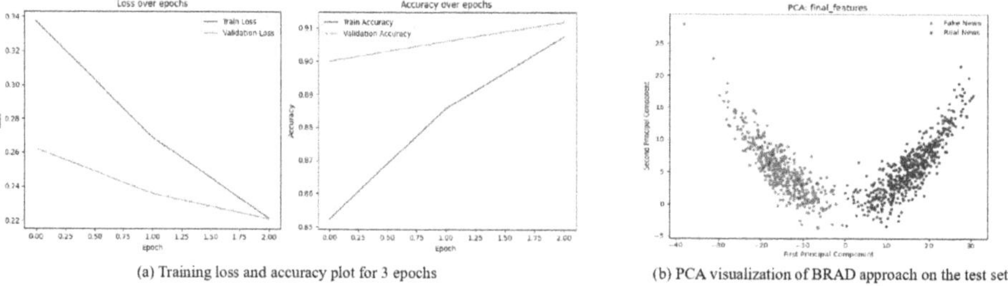

(a) Training loss and accuracy plot for 3 epochs     (b) PCA visualization of BRAD approach on the test set

**Fig. 2.** Performance analysis of the proposed BRAD approach

## 3.2   Ablation Studies

To assess the effectiveness of the BRAD architecture, we perform ablation studies by systematically removing or modifying key components. All experiments use consistent dataset splits, hyperparameters, and evaluation metrics to ensure fair comparison. In Ablation 1, we replace dynamic edge-type selection with static attention to assess the value of DHGAT and Gumbel-softmax. In Ablation 2, we remove cross-modal attention in favor of simple projection fusion to test its contribution. Ablation 3 excludes virtual nodes to evaluate their role in enhancing structural learning versus adding complexity. We have also included comparisons with unimodal baselines (text-only, image-only) to highlight the true benefit of multimodal graph learning. Table 2 summarizes the quantitative results for all ablation studies. The results reveal that the removal of components validates our design choices and provides empirical evidence for the necessity of each proposed innovation, and they're not just expensive overhead.

**Table 2.** Ablation Study Results

| Model Variant | Accuracy | Model Variant | Accuracy |
| --- | --- | --- | --- |
| Full Model | 91.28% | w/o Cross-Attention | 87.4% |
| w/o DHGAT Layer | 84.66% | w/o Virtual Nodes | 86.56% |
| Unimodal (Text-only) | 84.15% | Unimodal (Image-only) | 79.33% |

## 4   Conclusion

In this paper, we proposed a multimodal Bi-modal Representation Attention with Dynamic heterogeneous graphs (BRAD) model for fake news detection that effectively leverages both textual and visual information from news articles. Our approach addresses the limitations of existing methods by constructing dynamic heterogeneous graphs based on content similarity, enabling more flexible and adaptive representation learning. Experimental results on the Fakeddit dataset demonstrate the effectiveness of our approach in distinguishing between real and fake news. Future work will explore the validation of the performance of other multimodal fake news datasets.

## References


1. Castillo, C., Mendoza, M., Poblete, B.: Information credibility on twitter. In: Proceedings of the 20th International Conference on World Wide Web, pp. 675–684 (2011)
2. Chen, H., et al.: A self-learning multimodal approach for fake news detection (2024)

3. Devlin, J., Chang, M.W., Lee, K., Toutanova, K.: Bert: pre-training of deep bidirectional transformers for language understanding (2019)
4. He, K., Zhang, X., Ren, S., Sun, J.: Deep residual learning for image recognition (2015)
5. Jang, E., Gu, S., Poole, B.: Categorical reparameterization with gumbel-softmax (2017)
6. Kou, F., et al.: Potential features fusion network for multimodal fake news detection. ACM Trans. Multimed. Comput. Commun. Appl. (TOMM) 21(3), 87 (2025)
7. Kumari, R., Ekbal, A.: AMFB: attention based multimodal factorized bilinear pooling for multimodal fake news detection. Expert Syst. Appl. 184, 115412 (2021)
8. Lakzaei, B., Chehreghani, M.H., Bagheri, A.: A decision-based heterogenous graph attention network for multi-class fake news detection (2025)
9. Meel, P., Vishwakarma, D.K.: Han, image captioning, and forensics ensemble multimodal fake news detection. Inf. Sci. 567, 23–41 (2021)
10. Nakamura, K., Levy, S., Wang, W.Y.: R/Fakeddit: a new multimodal benchmark dataset for fine-grained fake news detection. arXiv preprint arXiv:1911.03854 (2019)
11. Papadopoulos, S.I., Koutlis, C., Papadopoulos, S., Petrantonakis, P.C.: Verite: a robust benchmark for multimodal misinformation detection accounting for unimodal bias (2023)
12. Qi, P., Cao, J., Yang, T., Guo, J., Li, J.: Exploiting multi-domain visual information for fake news detection (2019)
13. Qian, S., Wang, J., Hu, J., Fang, Q., Xu, C.: Hierarchical multi-modal contextual attention network for fake news detection. In: Proceedings of the 44th international ACM SIGIR Sonference on Research and Development in Information Retrieval, pp. 153–162 (2021)
14. Wang, Y., et al.: Eann: event adversarial neural networks for multi-modal fake news detection. In: Proceedings of the 24th ACM SIGKDD Conference, pp. 849–857 (2018)
15. Xiong, S., Zhang, G., Batra, V., Xi, L., Shi, L., Liu, L.: Trimoon: two-round inconsistency-based multi-modal fusion network for fake news detection. Information Fusion 93, 150–158 (2023)
16. Xue, J., Wang, Y., Tian, Y., Li, Y., Shi, L., Wei, L.: Detecting fake news by exploring the consistency of multimodal data. Inf. Process. Manag. 58(5), 102610 (2021)
17. Zhou, X., Wu, J., Zafarani, R.: Safe: similarity-aware multi-modal fake news detection. In: Lauw, H., Wong, R.W., Ntoulas, A., Lim, E.P., Ng, S.K., Pan, S. (eds.) Advances in Knowledge Discovery and Data Mining. PAKDD 2020. LNCS, vol. 12084, pp. 354–367. Springer, Cham (2020). https://doi.org/10.1007/978-3-030-47436-2_27

# IndiHealthBench: Evaluating LLMs for Clinical Translation Across Indian Linguistic Diversity


Pooja Singh[1(✉)] [iD], Jay Saraf[2], Aashrith Sharma[3], Siddhant Ujjain[1] [iD], Paridhi Jain[4], and Sandeep Kumar[1,5,6] [iD]

[1] Department of Electrical Engineering, Indian Institute of Technology Delhi, New Delhi, India
eez8470@ee.iitd.ac.in
[2] Indraprastha Institute of Information Technology Delhi, New Delhi, India
[3] Chaitanya Bharathi Institute of Technology, Hyderabad, India
[4] LNM Institute of Information Technology, Jaipur, India
[5] Bharti School of Telecommunications Technology and Management, Indian Institute of Technology Delhi, New Delhi, India
[6] Yardi School of Artificial Intelligence, Indian Institute of Technology Delhi, New Delhi, India



**Abstract.** Effective healthcare communication in linguistically diverse and resource-constrained environments like India, home to 22 official languages, remains a significant challenge, often affecting the quality and equity of care delivery. To address this, we introduce IndiHealthBench, a multilingual benchmark focused on medical translation, comprising 11,000 parallel sentence pairs spanning 13th Indian languages. Designed to evaluate the capabilities of both general-purpose and medically fine-tuned Large Language Models (LLMs), the benchmark facilitates bi-directional translation tasks between English and Indian languages, with a particular focus on clinical terminology and semantic fidelity. Through comprehensive metric-based evaluations and detailed qualitative analyses, we uncover key linguistic and translation challenges encountered by LLMs in clinical settings. Our findings reveal that medical-domain LLMs consistently outperform general models, particularly in morphologically complex and low-resource languages. This work offers critical insights into building robust, inclusive, and trustworthy multilingual healthcare systems for underserved populations.

**Keywords:** Multilingual Machine Translation · Indian Languages · Medical NLP · Clinical Communication · Medical Language Understanding · Healthcare AI


## 1  Introduction

Language plays a foundational role in healthcare communication. From diagnosing conditions to conveying treatment options and providing empathetic guid-



S. Mitra et al. (Eds.): PReMI 2025, LNCS 16358, pp. 581–591, 2026.
https://doi.org/10.1007/978-3-032-18480-1_59

ance, effective interaction between providers and patients is essential for achieving positive clinical outcomes [11]. However, in linguistically diverse countries like India, home to 22 official languages and hundreds of dialects, language barriers remain a persistent obstacle to equitable care delivery. Miscommunication stemming from inadequate translation can lead to treatment delays, misdiagnoses, or poor adherence, disproportionately affecting patients with limited proficiency in dominant languages [2]. Recent progress in multilingual natural language processing (NLP), particularly through large language models (LLMs), has shown potential to mitigate these disparities. Yet, state-of-the-art LLMs such as LLaMa, Mistral, and BLOOMZ are predominantly trained on high-resource languages and general-domain corpora, limiting their reliability in low-resource and domain-specialized settings [10]. Medical communication, in particular, demands terminological precision, contextual nuance, and cultural alignment all of which remain challenging for general-purpose LLMs [5]. These limitations are exacerbated in India, where health communication frequently involves code-switching, idiomatic expressions, and sociolinguistic variation. While prior efforts such as FLORES-101 [6], TICO-19 [1], and UMLS-NMT [21] have laid important groundwork in multilingual and medical translation, they lack coverage of Indic languages and often rely on synthetic or expert-driven constructs with limited contextual realism [30]. Moreover, medical-domain LLMs like MedAlpaca and OpenBioLLM have demonstrated success on English tasks, but their effectiveness in translating to and from Indian languages remains underexplored.

To address this gap, we introduce IndiHealthBench, a domain-adapted benchmark for multilingual medical translation spanning $13^{\text{th}}$ officially recognized Indian languages. Our benchmark comprises 11,000 sentence pairs reflecting authentic, patient-facing healthcare communication in both English and Indian languages. We evaluate a suite of general-purpose and medically fine-tuned LLMs in a bidirectional translation setting, with particular emphasis on terminological fidelity, semantic preservation, and translation asymmetries.

Our contributions are threefold:

- We present IndiHealthBench, the first domain-specific evaluation benchmark for Indian language medical translation, adapted from real-world healthcare content.
- We benchmark eight open-source LLMs both general and medical on English↔Indic languages translation, providing granular analysis across $13^{\text{th}}$ languages.
- We conduct a comprehensive metric and qualitative error-based analysis to uncover translation challenges related to morphology, terminology drift, and low-resource biases.

By enabling rigorous, inclusive evaluation of LLMs in Indian healthcare contexts, IndiHealthBench offers a valuable resource for developing equitable, medically grounded translation systems for Indian languages.

## 2   Related Work

Multilingual NLP has advanced significantly with the advent of large-scale models such as mBERT [22], XLM-R [4], and NLLB [29]. However, these models primarily focus on general-domain tasks and are trained on high-resource languages [25]. Their performance on specialized domains like medicine, especially in low-resource settings, remains underexplored. In healthcare, prior work has shown LLMs' potential in summarization [17], question answering [31], and clinical decision support [28]. Yet, most of these systems operate in English and lack generalizability to multilingual contexts, particularly in India, where code-switching and dialectal variation are common. Recent efforts have focused on building domain-specific medical models such as BioBERT [14], PubMedBERT [8], and Clinical-T5 [26]. While effective in English medical tasks, these models are not trained or evaluated in multilingual settings. More recent LLMs such as MedAlpaca and OpenBioLLM aim to incorporate medical knowledge into instruction-tuned architectures, yet they are still English-centric. This creates a significant performance gap when applying them to diverse linguistic contexts such as Indian healthcare, where accurate cross-lingual translation is critical. Several benchmarks assess translation quality across general domains but they do not focus on medical language or Indian linguistic diversity. In-domain benchmarks like UMLS-NMT [19] and MeSH Translation datasets [20] provide biomedical translations but are limited to English and a few global languages. Synthetic corpora often lack colloquial phrases, pragmatic context, or culturally grounded expressions critical to patient communication, reducing their applicability in real-world clinical workflows in India.

To our knowledge, no prior work has systematically evaluated LLMs on medical translation across Indian languages. IndiHealthBench fills this gap by offering a parallel dataset across $13^{\text{th}}$ scheduled Indian languages, annotated with medical terminology and context. We also evaluate both general-purpose and medically fine-tuned LLMs, highlighting failure cases and areas of improvement. Our work thus provides the first comprehensive lens into multilingual LLM performance for Indian clinical translation and opens pathways for equitable, language-inclusive healthcare technologies.

## 3   Models, Dataset and Evaluation Metrics

To assess the multilingual medical translation capabilities of LLMs in Indian languages, we evaluate a representative set of both general-purpose and medical-domain models. These span various model families, parameter sizes, and training regimens, reflecting a broad spectrum of current LLM capabilities. All models are evaluated in a consistent, bidirectional translation setup (English↔Indic), using standard fine-tuning setup.

**General-Purpose LLMs:** We include four multilingual general-purpose LLMs: *LLaMA-3-8B* [7], *Gemma-2-9B* [16], *BLOOMZ-7B1* [9], and *DeepSeek-V3* [15]. These models are trained on large-scale, general-domain corpora and support multiple languages, making them suitable for evaluating low-resource translation performance.

**Medical-Domain LLMs:** To assess domain specialization, we evaluated four instruction-tuned medical LLMs: *MedLLaMA3-v20* [32], *OpenBioLLM-8B* [27],*BioMistral-7B* [13] and *MedAlpaca-7B* [12]. These models are fine-tuned on biomedical literature, clinical dialogues, and health QA datasets, with an emphasis on preserving terminological accuracy and supporting medically grounded responses in translation scenarios.

**Dataset.** We present **IndiHealthBench**, a domain-specific parallel corpus comprising 11,000 sentence pairs in English and 13$^{\text{th}}$ official Indian languages. The source English corpus was derived from real-world, patient-facing healthcare materials including consent forms, treatment instructions, public health advisories, and medication guides originally compiled by the Language Technologies Research Center (LTRC) [18]. To create multilingual coverage, we translated the English content into 12 additional Indian languages using the *IndicTrans2* model, followed by extensive post-editing and domain-sensitive filtering to ensure linguistic fluency and medical accuracy. The resulting corpus reflects realistic clinical communication scenarios and supports research in cross-lingual medical NLP for low-resource settings.

**Evaluation Metrics.** We employ both surface-level and semantic-oriented metrics to assess translation fidelity. For lexical similarity, we use **spBLEU** [24] and **ChrF++** [23], which respectively measure n-gram precision and character-level F-score between generated translations and human references. These metrics provide broad comparability with prior multilingual MT benchmarks. To complement these, we perform qualitative error analysis focusing on semantic drift, terminological inaccuracies, and unnatural phrasing especially important in clinical domains where mistranslations may result in patient harm.

## 4   Mathematical Modeling of LLM Prediction

Let $\mathbf{x} = (x_1, x_2, \ldots, x_n)$ denote the input source sentence (e.g., in English or an Indian language), and let $\mathbf{y} = (y_1, y_2, \ldots, y_m)$ represent the corresponding target translation to be generated by the model. LLMs perform translation as a conditional text generation task by modeling the probability distribution over output tokens given the source input:

$$P(\mathbf{y} \mid \mathbf{x}) = \prod_{t=1}^{m} P(y_t \mid y_{<t}, \mathbf{x}; \theta)$$

where $y_{<t}$ refers to the sequence of previously generated tokens $(y_1, \ldots, y_{t-1})$, and $\theta$ denotes the model parameters. The model is trained to maximize the likelihood of reference translations via teacher forcing using cross-entropy loss:

$$\mathcal{L}_{\text{CE}} = -\sum_{t=1}^{m} \log P(y_t^* \mid y_{<t}^*, \mathbf{x}; \theta)$$

where $y_t^*$ denotes the ground-truth token at position $t$.

In our evaluation, the models are used in an autoregressive decoding setup to generate $\hat{\mathbf{y}} = (\hat{y}_1, \ldots, \hat{y}_m)$ from the learned distribution. Decoding strategies such as greedy decoding, top-$k$, or nucleus sampling (top-$p$) may be employed depending on the model configuration. The quality of the generated sequence $\hat{\mathbf{y}}$ is then evaluated against the reference $\mathbf{y}^*$ using metrics such as spBLEU and ChrF++ to assess lexical and semantic fidelity.

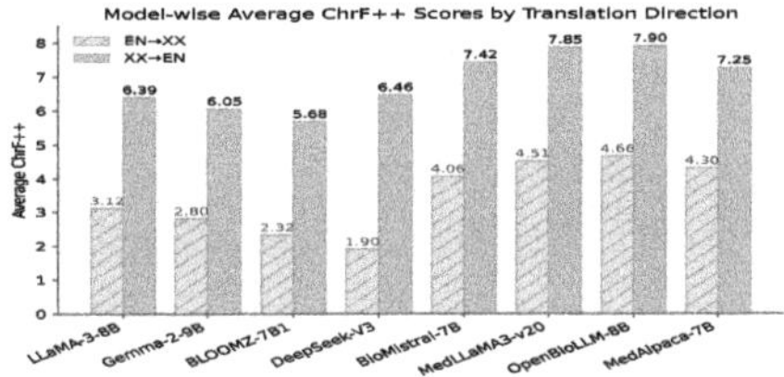
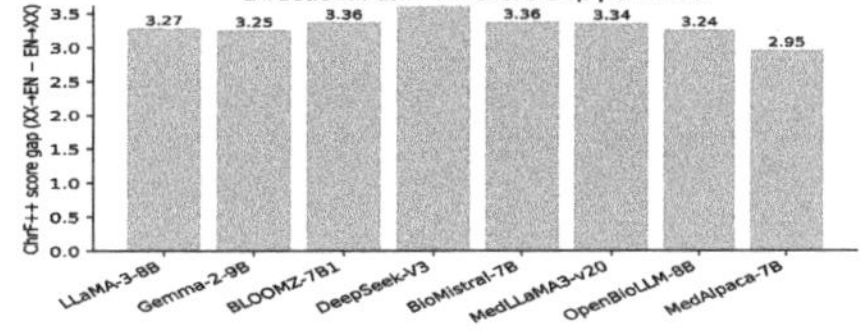

(a) Average ChrF++ scores per model across EN→XX and XX→EN directions.

(b) Directional ChrF++ score gap (XX→EN − EN→XX), highlighting English-centric bias.

**Fig. 1.** Comparison of average translation quality and directional bias across general and medical LLMs. Here, XX refers to the Indian languages used in our benchmark.

**Table 1.** Translation performance from English → Indian languages. Each cell reports spBLEU / ChrF++. Best model per language is bolded.

| Language | LLaMA-3-8B | Gemma-2-9B | BLOOMZ-7B1 | DeepSeek-V3 | BioMistral-7B | MedLLaMA3-v20 | OpenBioLLM-8B | MedAlpaca-7B |
|---|---|---|---|---|---|---|---|---|
| Assamese | 2.10 / 3.20 | 1.98 / 2.76 | 1.70/2.40 | 1.04/1.59 | 2.60/3.75 | 2.85/4.10 | **2.94/4.25** | 2.88/4.00 |
| Bengali | 2.01/3.02 | 1.90/2.82 | 1.60/2.39 | 1.20/1.89 | 3.02/4.33 | 3.23/4.60 | **3.30/4.95** | 3.10/4.50 |
| Gujarati | 1.95/2.88 | 1.86/2.61 | 1.45/2.18 | 1.45/1.88 | 2.65/1.72 | 2.35/3.90 | **2.85/4.12** | 2.60/3.70 |
| Hindi | 2.25/3.35 | 2.00/3.00 | 1.66/2.54 | 1.72/2.30 | 3.45/5.30 | 3.59/5.42 | **3.80/5.70** | 3.55/5.20 |
| Kannada | 2.58/3.68 | 2.31/3.23 | 1.86/2.73 | 1.95/2.20 | 4.35/6.45 | 4.62/6.89 | **5.01/7.36** | 4.40/6.60 |
| Maithili | 2.12/3.18 | 1.90/2.82 | 1.55/2.25 | 1.66/2.15 | 2.85/4.10 | **3.00/4.50** | 2.97/4.45 | 2.84/4.10 |
| Malayalam | 1.88/2.85 | 1.82/2.70 | 1.48/2.10 | 1.16/1.90 | 2.55/3.85 | **2.75/4.15** | 2.58/3.96 | 2.51/3.80 |
| Marathi | 2.05/3.05 | 1.94/2.80 | 1.60/2.22 | 1.32/2.04 | 2.75/4.00 | 2.91/4.26 | **3.02/4.40** | 2.90/4.10 |
| Odia | 1.92/2.90 | 1.80/2.65 | 1.58/2.33 | 1.13/1.69 | 2.70/3.86 | 2.79/4.00 | **2.90/4.21** | 2.75/3.90 |
| Punjabi | 2.10/3.20 | 1.99/2.88 | 1.70/2.41 | 1.65/1.93 | 2.78/4.09 | 2.97/4.45 | **3.05/4.59** | 2.90/4.20 |
| Tamil | 2.00/3.10 | 1.88/2.77 | 1.49/2.19 | 1.43/1.95 | 2.56/3.74 | 2.81/4.12 | **2.94/4.28** | 2.70/3.98 |
| Telugu | 2.08/3.12 | 1.91/2.82 | 1.57/2.22 | 1.44/1.61 | 2.65/3.89 | 2.86/4.25 | **2.95/4.37** | 2.79/4.00 |
| Urdu | 2.00/3.02 | 1.78/2.60 | 1.48/2.20 | 1.39/1.52 | 2.56/3.70 | **2.68/4.01** | 2.62/3.90 | 2.51/3.68 |

# 5    Experimental Results and Analysis

We evaluate eight open-source LLMs comprising both general-purpose (*LLaMA-3-8B, BLOOMZ-7B1, Gemma-2-9B, DeepSeek-V3*) and medically fine-tuned models (*BioMistral-7B, MedLLaMA3-v20, OpenBioLLM-8B, MedAlpaca-7B*) on IndiHealthBench, a multilingual benchmark spanning 13 Indian languages for

**Table 2.** Translation performance from Indian languages → English. Each cell reports spBLEU/ChrF++. Best model per language is bolded.

| Language | LLaMA-3-8B | Gemma-2-9B | BLOOMZ-7B1 | DeepSeek-V3 | BioMistral-7B | MedLLaMA3-v20 | OpenBioLLM-8B | MedAlpaca-7B |
|---|---|---|---|---|---|---|---|---|
| Assamese | 4.50/6.70 | 4.20/6.20 | 3.95/5.80 | 5.00/7.42 | 4.90/7.21 | 5.25/7.69 | **5.40/7.80** | 5.10/7.20 |
| Bengali | 4.39/6.35 | 4.10/5.95 | 3.88/5.73 | 3.20/5.00 | 5.95/8.10 | **6.10/8.55** | 6.02/8.40 | 5.80/7.60 |
| Gujarati | 4.32/6.10 | 4.02/5.86 | 3.89/5.50 | 5.01/7.19 | 4.90/7.00 | 5.28/7.40 | **5.39/7.60** | 5.00/6.90 |
| Hindi | 4.75/6.85 | 4.21/6.34 | 4.05/6.00 | 3.72/6.40 | 5.91/8.22 | **6.05/8.76** | 6.10/8.51 | 5.60/7.80 |
| Kannada | 5.01/7.20 | 4.80/6.68 | 4.12/6.05 | 3.20 /5.20 | 7.40/10.00 | **7.61/10.72** | 7.50/10.60 | 6.40/9.00 |
| Maithili | 4.22/6.40 | 4.02/6.00 | 3.90/5.80 | 3.00/4.20 | 5.70/7.66 | **5.86/7.99** | 5.83/7.89 | 5.01/7.10 |
| Malayalam | 4.13/6.08 | 4.00/5.86 | 3.80/5.48 | 4.58/6.45 | 4.79/6.62 | 5.03/7.11 | **5.10/7.25** | 4.92/6.90 |
| Marathi | 4.41/6.25 | 4.20/6.02 | 4.08/5.89 | 5.30/7.45 | 5.12/7.10 | 5.31/7.55 | **5.38/7.70** | 5.00/7.10 |
| Odia | 4.19/6.10 | 4.10/5.85 | 3.88/5.51 | 4.90/6.95 | 4.83/6.88 | **5.05/7.32** | 5.02/7.30 | 4.85/6.90 |
| Punjabi | 4.20/6.20 | 4.03/5.97 | 3.70/5.40 | 5.00/7.00 | 4.82/6.95 | 5.15/7.49 | **5.25/7.68** | 4.88/7.00 |
| Tamil | 4.27/6.40 | 4.00/6.02 | 3.75/5.60 | 5.01/6.91 | 4.93/6.89 | 5.11/7.10 | **5.15/7.42** | 4.88/6.95 |
| Telugu | 4.22/6.35 | 3.90/6.00 | 3.78/5.48 | 5.03/6.92 | 4.95/6.90 | 5.08/7.22 | **5.12/7.45** | 4.89/7.00 |
| Urdu | 4.20/6.10 | 4.05/5.90 | 3.87/5.55 | 4.85/6.85 | 4.95/6.92 | **5.02/7.20** | 5.00/7.12 | 4.88/6.80 |

**English↔Indic medical translation.** Translation performance is assessed using two complementary metrics: spBLEU and ChrF++. Tables 1 and 2 present per-language performance, while Figs. 1a and 1b visualize directional biases and model performance profiles.

We observe that translation quality is significantly higher in the Indic→English direction, often by 2–4 points across both metrics, consistent with known English-centric biases in LLM pretraining [3]. Languages with a stronger presence in multilingual corpora, such as Hindi and Bengali, consistently yield better scores across models. In contrast, low-resource and morphologically rich languages like Maithili, Odia, and Malayalam exhibit reduced performance, particularly in the English→Indic direction. Medical domain models demonstrate consistent gains over general purpose models, especially on terminology-rich content. For example, in English→Gujarati, *OpenBioLLM-8B* achieves 2.85/4.12 (spBLEU/ChrF++), substantially outperforming *Gemma-2-9B* (1.86/2.61). Similarly, *MedLLaMA3-v20* and *OpenBioLLM-8B* also deliver strong results, showcasing the value of domain-specific adaptation. Figures 1a and 1b reveal that domain-adapted models not only improve average scores but also reduce cross-directional disparities, mitigating the impact of English-centric training regimes. Nevertheless, qualitative error analyses in Fig. 2 and 3 expose recurring issues such as semantic drift, hallucinations, and unnatural phrasing, particularly in English→Indic outputs involving specialized clinical terms. These errors underscore the challenges of medical translation in low-resource Indic contexts, where hallucinated or imprecise output could result in serious consequences. Taken together, our results indicate that scale alone is not sufficient for accurate medical translation. Even the largest general-purpose models underperform compared to smaller domain-adapted models in low-resource settings. The persistent performance gap between directions and the need for better representation of Indian languages and clinical expressions point to critical limitations in current LLM pretraining strategies. Addressing token coverage, enhancing multilingual corpora with medical context, and fine-tuning with

**Source:** *The patient was diagnosed with pneumothorax.*

**General LLM (LLaMA-3-8B):**
मरीज को फेफड़ों की बीमारी पाई गई।
⚠ Simplified rare term to general phrase

**Medical LLM (MedAlpaca-7B):**
मरीज को न्यूमोथोरेक्स का निदान हुआ।

**Gold Reference:**
मरीज को न्यूमोथोरेक्स का पता चला।

**Error Type:** Loss of clinical specificity

**Source:** *He was prescribed doxycycline.*

**General LLM (LLaMA-3-8B):**
उसे एक दवा दी गई।
⚠ Dropped essential drug name

**Medical LLM (MedAlpaca-7B):**
उसे डॉक्सीसाइक्लिन दी गई।

**Gold Reference:**
उसे डॉक्सीसाइक्लिन लेने की सलाह दी गई।

**Error Type:** Term omission

**Source:** *The lesion was located in the cerebellum.*

**General LLM (LLaMA-3-8B):**
दिमाग में घाव पाया गया।
⚠ Vague anatomical term

**Medical LLM (MedAlpaca-7B):**
सेरिबेलम में घाव पाया गया।

**Gold Reference:**
घाव सेरिबेलम में पाया गया।

**Error Type:** Anatomical imprecision

**Fig. 2.** Qualitative comparison of English-to-Hindi medical translation outputs from a general-purpose LLM (LLaMA-3-8B) versus a medical-domain LLM (MedAlpaca-7B). MedAlpaca better preserves rare clinical terms (e.g., "pneumothorax"), specific drug names (e.g., "doxycycline"), and anatomical precision (e.g., "cerebellum"), while the general LLM tends to simplify or omit domain-critical content.

**Source:** मरीज को डेंगू हो गया है।

**General LLM (LLaMA-3-8B):**
The patient is sick.
⚠ Missed diagnosis entirely

**Medical LLM (MedAlpaca-7B):**
The patient was diagnosed with **dengue**.

**Gold Reference:**
The patient **has dengue**.

**Error Type:** Diagnosis omission

**Source:** मरीज की हार्ट अटैक से मृत्यु हुई।

**General LLM (LLaMA-3-8B):**
The patient died due to illness.
⚠ Ignored critical cause

**Medical LLM (MedAlpaca-7B):**
The patient died due to a **heart attack**.

**Gold Reference:**
The patient **died of a heart attack**.

**Error Type:** Clinical cause generalization

**Source:** इलाज में इंसुलिन का प्रयोग किया गया।

**General LLM (LLaMA-3-8B):**
**Medicine** was used in the treatment.
⚠ Dropped key named entity

**Medical LLM (MedAlpaca-7B):**
**Insulin** was used in the treatment.

**Gold Reference:**
The treatment **involved insulin**.

**Error Type:** Drug name deletion

**Fig. 3.** Qualitative comparison of Hindi-to-English medical translation between a general-purpose LLM (LLaMA-3-8B) and a medical-domain LLM (MedAlpaca-7B). MedAlpaca demonstrates higher fidelity by correctly translating clinical diagnoses (e.g., "dengue"), causes of death (e.g., "heart attack"), and named medications (e.g., "insulin"), which are generalized or dropped by the general model.

Indian language-specific prompts will be crucial for closing this gap. IndiHealth-Bench thus provides a rigorous benchmark for assessing and improving the multilingual capabilities of LLMs in medical translation, offering actionable insights toward building inclusive, trustworthy, and clinically viable translation systems for healthcare delivery in India and beyond.

## 6    Conclusion

We present IndiHealthBench, the first multilingual benchmark specifically designed to evaluate the medical translation capabilities of LLMs across 13th scheduled Indian languages. Through a comprehensive empirical analysis involving eight general and domain-specialized LLMs, we demonstrate that medical-domain adaptation substantially improves performance, particularly in morphologically complex and low-resource languages. Our results highlight persistent asymmetries in translation quality favoring the Indic→English direction and reveal systematic shortcomings in handling clinical terminology and generating fluent, contextually appropriate translations in Indic scripts. These findings underscore the limitations of current LLMs when deployed in high-stakes, multilingual healthcare settings and motivate the need for linguistically inclusive, domain-aligned training strategies.

## 7    Limitations

While IndiHealthBench addresses a critical gap in multilingual medical translation evaluation, several limitations remain. First, the benchmark is restricted to sentence-level translations and does not capture discourse-level or conversational phenomena prevalent in real-world clinical dialogues. Second, our evaluation relies on automatic metrics (spBLEU, ChrF++), which while informative do not fully capture medical adequacy, terminological fidelity, or patient comprehension dimensions that require human evaluation by domain experts. Third, the dataset is limited in scale (11k examples) and linguistic breadth. Although it covers 13th scheduled Indian languages, many regional dialects and indigenous linguistic varieties remain unrepresented. We release IndiHealthBench to support future work in this direction, and we encourage the community to build upon it by expanding linguistic coverage, developing improved evaluation frameworks, and aligning model capabilities with the safety-critical demands of healthcare translation.

## References


1. Anastasopoulos, A., et al.: Tico-19: The translation initiative for covid-19. arXiv preprint arXiv:2007.01788 (2020)
2. Carmona, V.S., Jiang, S., Dong, B.: A multilevel analysis of pubmed-only bert-based biomedical models. In: Proceedings of the 6th Clinical Natural Language Processing Workshop, pp. 105–110 (2024)

3. Conneau, A., et al.: Unsupervised cross-lingual representation learning at scale. arXiv preprint arXiv:1911.02116 (2019)
4. Conneau, A., et al.: Unsupervised cross-lingual representation learning at scale. In: Proceedings of the 58th Annual Meeting of the Association for Computational Linguistics, pp. 8440–8451 (2020)
5. Gallifant, J., et al.: Language models are surprisingly fragile to drug names in biomedical benchmarks. In: Findings of the Association for Computational Linguistics: EMNLP 2024, pp. 12448–12465 (2024)
6. Goyal, N., et al.: The flores-101 evaluation benchmark for low-resource and multilingual machine translation. TACL (2022)
7. Grattafiori, A., et al.: The llama 3 herd of models. arXiv preprint arXiv:2407.21783 (2024)
8. Gu, Y., et al.: Domain-specific language model pretraining for biomedical natural language processing. ACM Trans. Comput. Healthcare (HEALTH) 3(1), 1–23 (2021)
9. Gu, Z., et al.: Xiezhi: an ever-updating benchmark for holistic domain knowledge evaluation. In: Proceedings of the AAAI Conference on Artificial Intelligence, vol. 38, pp. 18099–18107 (2024)
10. Gulati, V., et al.: Transcending language barriers: can chatgpt be the key to enhancing multilingual accessibility in health care? J. Am. Coll. Radiol. 21(12), 1888–1895 (2024)
11. Gumma, V., Raghunath, A., Jain, M., Sitaram, S.: Health-pariksha: assessing rag models for health chatbots in real-world multilingual settings. arXiv preprint arXiv:2410.13671 (2024)
12. Han, T., Kumar, A., Agarwal, C., Lakkaraju, H.: Towards safe large language models for medicine. In: ICML 2024 Workshop on Models of Human Feedback for AI Alignment
13. Labrak, Y., Bazoge, A., Morin, E., Gourraud, P.A., Rouvier, M., Dufour, R.: Biomistral: A collection of open-source pretrained large language models for medical domains. In: ACL (Findings) (2024)
14. Lee, J., et al.: Biobert: a pre-trained biomedical language representation model for biomedical text mining. Bioinformatics (2020)
15. Liu, A., et al.: Deepseek-v3 technical report. arXiv preprint arXiv:2412.19437 (2024)
16. Meng, Y., Xia, M., Chen, D.: Simpo: simple preference optimization with a reference-free reward. Adv. Neural. Inf. Process. Syst. 37, 124198–124235 (2024)
17. Moazemi, S., et al.: Artificial intelligence for clinical decision support for monitoring patients in cardiovascular icus: a systematic review. Front. Med. 10, 1109411 (2023)
18. Mujadia, V., Sharma, D.M.: Bhashaverse : translation ecosystem for indian subcontinent languages (2024). https://arxiv.org/abs/2412.04351
19. Mutal, J., Bouillon, P., Norré, M., Gerlach, J., Ormaechea-Grijalba, L.: A neural machine translation approach to translate text to pictographs in a medical speech translation system-the babeldr use case. In: Proceedings of the 15th biennial conference of the Association for Machine Translation in the Americas (Volume 1: Research Track), pp. 252–263 (2022)
20. Nehmé, Y., Delanoy, J., Dupont, F., Farrugia, J.P., Le Callet, P., Lavoué, G.: Textured mesh quality assessment: large-scale dataset and deep learning-based quality metric. ACM Trans. Graph. 42(3), 1–20 (2023)
21. Peng, Y., et al.: Umls-nmt: A biomedical resource for machine translation using the unified medical language system. In: LREC (2022)

22. Pires, T., Schlinger, E., Garrette, D.: How multilingual is multilingual bert? In: Proceedings of the 57th Annual Meeting of the Association for Computational Linguistics, pp. 4996–5001 (2019)
23. Popović, M.: chrf++: words helping character n-grams. In: Proceedings of the second conference on machine translation, pp. 612–618 (2017)
24. Puduppully, R., Kunchukuttan, A., Dabre, R., Aw, A., Chen, N.: Decomt: decomposed prompting for machine translation between related languages using large language models. In: Proceedings of the 2023 Conference on Empirical Methods in Natural Language Processing, pp. 4586–4602 (2023)
25. Qiu, P., et al.: Towards building multilingual language model for medicine. Nat. Commun. **15**(1), 8384 (2024)
26. Rasmy, L., Xiang, Y., Xie, Z., Tao, C., Zhi, D.M.B.: pretrained contextualized embeddings on largescale structured electronic health records for disease prediction. Npj digital med. **4**(1), 1–13 (2021)
27. Shi, J., Yuan, Y., Wang, A., Nie, M.: Fine-tuning a personalized openbiollm using offline reinforcement learning. Appl. Sci. **15**(5), 2076–3417 (2025)
28. Singhal, K., et al.: Publisher correction: large language models encode clinical knowledge. Nature **620**(7973), E19 (2023)
29. Team, N., et al.: No language left behind: scaling human-centered machine translation. arXiv preprint arXiv:2207.04672 (2022)
30. Yang, X., et al.: Enhancing doctor-patient communication using large language models for pathology report interpretation. BMC Med. Inform. Decis. Mak. **25**(1), 36 (2025)
31. Yasunaga, M., Leskovec, J.: Linkbert: Pretraining language models with document links. In: ACL (2022)
32. Zagar, P., Ravi, V., Aalami, L., Krusche, S., Aalami, O., Schmiedmayer, P.: Dynamic fog computing for enhanced llm execution in medical applications. Smart Health, p. 100577 (2025)

# gDSA: A Lightweight Framework for Zero-Shot Stance Detection via Direct Stance Assignment and gMLP


V. S. V. Varun Saketh Gottam[ID], Krishna Vamsi Bhagavatula[ID], and Hima Bindu Kommanti[(✉)][ID]

Department of Computer Science and Engineering, National Institute of Technology Andhra Pradesh, Tadepalligudem, India
`himabinduk@nitandhra.ac.in`



**Abstract.** Zero-Shot Stance Detection (ZSSD) identifies whether a text *supports*, *opposes*, or is *neutral* towards an unseen topic. While existing methods like the teacher-student framework improve generalisation, they are often resource-heavy. A simplified, lightweight and efficient data augmentation approach for ZSSD is proposed in this work, named as Direct Stance Assignment (DSA). DSA augments the training data through stance label assignment based on cosine similarity in a shared semantic space. Further, a classifier that integrates gMLP blocks into BART encoder is developed to leverage improved token interaction, leading to the proposed methodology, gDSA = gMLP + DSA. This reduces training time and parameters by nearly half of the SOTA models, while maintaining the similar performance. We also propose a much simpler data augmentation technique: Target-Aware Polarity Swapping (TAPS), that does not need the expensive keyphrase generation. Further, the role of commonsense is investigated in the teacher-student setting to evaluate the importance of external knowledge in the framework. Experiments on benchmark data show that the proposed method performs close to state-of-the-art models, with significantly lower computational cost.

**Keywords:** Natural Language Understanding · Zero Shot Learning · Deep Learning


## 1 Introduction

Stance detection aims to identify whether a text expresses a `favor`, `against`, or `neutral` opinion toward a specific target. While supervised models have made significant progress, they rely heavily on labeled data for each target, limiting their applicability to new or emerging topics without annotations. To overcome this, **Zero-Shot Stance Detection (ZSSD)** focuses on generalizing stance prediction to unseen targets without extra labeled data. However, this remains challenging due to difficulties in capturing target-specific semantics and aligning them with stance cues without prior supervision. The recent TTS framework [7]


© The Author(s), under exclusive license to Springer Nature Switzerland AG 2026
S. Mitra et al. (Eds.): PReMI 2025, LNCS 16358, pp. 592–599, 2026.
https://doi.org/10.1007/978-3-032-18480-1_60

addresses this by using a teacher-student setup where a teacher model generates pseudo-labels on keyphrase-augmented data, and a student model learns from both original and synthetic samples produced through the teacher model. This improves generalization across targets, though several challenges persist, some of which are discussed in Sect. 2.

Key contributions of the work are:

1) Direct Stance Assignment (DSA): Assigns stance labels based on cosine similarity between keyphrases generated and existing targets. This generates augmented data without the need for a model to assign stance labels.
2) gMLP Integration: The encoder is augmented with gMLP blocks [8] to enhance stance representation and token interaction with low parameter overhead.
3) Topic-Aware Polarity Swapping (TAPS): A lightweight sentence-level augmentation method that swaps stance polarity via sentiment word modification, revealing the limits of shallow augmentation strategies.

Together, these enhancements create a flexible framework that boosts both generalization and efficiency in ZSSD. Competitive results on the VAST dataset [1] highlight the effectiveness of semantic matching and architectural improvements. VAST is preferred since it is large, diverse, balanced, and specifically designed to evaluate zero-shot generalization across unseen topics. Further, the role of external knowledge is explored by integrating COMET [9]-based commonsense reasoning before keyphrase generation.

## 2    Literature Review

This section summarizes prior work on zero-shot stance detection, covering strategies like topic-invariant learning, contrastive objectives, knowledge integration, and data augmentation to improve cross-target generalization.

### Generalized Topic Representation Approaches

Early efforts in ZSSD emphasized learning target-invariant features to enable cross-topic transfer. The VAST dataset [1] introduced topic-grouped attention mechanisms to capture latent similarities among targets, promoting generalized representations. Subsequent models used adversarial learning techniques [2] to suppress topic-specific information and extract domain-agnostic features. While these methods foster broader generalization, they often sacrifice the fine-grained stance cues embedded in topic-specific expressions—limiting performance on nuanced or subtle stances. The proposed work utilizes a gMLP block. to enhance the token communication which identifies the underlying relations between tokens.

**Data Augmentation Strategies**

To address data scarcity and improve target diversity in Zero-Shot Stance Detection (ZSSD), prior work has explored data augmentation techniques such as back-translation, random masking, and target substitution [6]. Prompt-based generation using tools like ChatGPT [14] has also been employed for automated labeling and broader target exposure. More recently, keyphrase-based augmentation [7,11] has shown promise by simulating diverse stance-bearing inputs. However, the dual-model teacher-student setup increases training time and resource usage, while the extracted keyphrases are often overly generic or lack contextual relevance. In contrast, the proposed method offers a lightweight alternative that avoids model-based label generation, significantly reducing computational demands while achieving performance close to state-of-the-art approaches.

## 3   Methodology

An augmented dataset $(D_{aug})$ is created by pairing tweets with newly generated targets. These targets are the keyphrases extracted using KeyBERT [3] for embedding-based keywords and BERTopic [4] for topic-based clustering.

### 3.1   Direct Stance Assignment (DSA) via Similarity Matching

To reduce the computational cost of traditional teacher-student (TTS) frameworks, a direct stance assignment method is proposed. Instead of training a separate student model on pseudo-labeled data, stance labels are assigned to keyphrase-augmented samples $(D_{aug})$ based on their similarity to known targets in the labeled dataset $(D_{orig})$. A single model is then trained on the combined dataset $D_{orig} \cup D_{aug}$.

---

**Algorithm 1.** Direct Stance Assignment(DSA) via similarity matching

---

**Require:** $D_{orig}$: Labeled (tweet, target, stance) set, $D_{aug}$: (tweet, keyphrase) set, $\theta$: Similarity threshold

1: **for** each keyphrase $k$ in $D_{aug}$ **do**
2:     Get tweet $t$ and targets $T_{orig}$ from $D_{orig}$
3:     Compute embeddings for $k$ and $T_{orig}$
4:     $t^* \leftarrow \arg\max_{t_i \in T_{orig}} \cos(k, t_i)$
5:     **if** $\cos(k, t^*) > \theta$ **then**
6:         Assign stance of $t^*$ to $k$
7:     **else**
8:         Assign stance as `neutral`
9:     **end if**
10: **end for**
11: Train on $D_{orig} \cup D_{aug}$

---

Using a pretrained encoder like MPNet [10], both keyphrases and original targets are embedded into a shared space. For each keyphrase, the most similar target is found using cosine similarity. If the similarity exceeds a threshold $\theta$, the keyphrase inherits the target's stance; otherwise, it is labeled as **neutral** as described in Algorithm 1. Formally, let $k$ be a keyphrase in $D_{aug}$, and $T_{orig}$ be the set of known targets in $D_{orig}$, each with stance label $y_t$. The assigned stance label $\hat{y}_k$ is:

$$\hat{y}_k = \begin{cases} y_{t^*}, & \text{if } \max_{t \in T_{orig}} \cos(\mathbf{e}_k, \mathbf{e}_t) > \theta \\ \textbf{neutral}, & \text{otherwise} \end{cases} \quad \text{where } t^* = \arg\max_{t \in T_{orig}} \cos(\mathbf{e}_k, \mathbf{e}_t) \tag{1}$$

Here, $\mathbf{e}_k$ and $\mathbf{e}_t$ are the sentence embeddings of the keyphrase and target respectively, and $\cos(\cdot, \cdot)$ denotes cosine similarity.

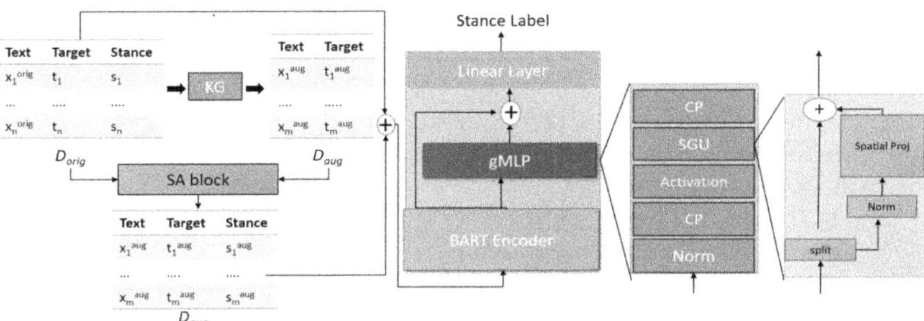


**Fig. 1.** Schematic Representation of Similarity-Based Direct Stance Assignment Methodology integrated with gMLP block. KG: Keyphrase Generation. CP: Channel Projection. SGU: Spatial Gating Unit. Norm: Normalization. SA block: Targets of $D_{aug}$ and targets of $D_{orig}$ are compared based on same tweet and stance is assigned to corresponding target in $D_{aug}$

## 3.2   Integrating gMLP with DSA (gDSA)

To improve the encoder's ability to model token interactions while preserving efficiency, a gated MLP (gMLP) block [8] is incorporated into the BART-based encoder within the Direct Stance Assignment (DSA) framework. Self-attention mechanisms, though effective, grow in computational cost with longer sequences; in contrast, gMLP offers a simpler yet effective alternative by using spatial gating and feedforward operations to capture long-range dependencies. This integration enhances the representational strength of the encoder without significantly increasing model complexity. The final hidden states from the BART encoder are passed through the gMLP block—consisting of layer normalization, a feedforward network, and a spatial gating unit—which enables more effective token mixing between tweet and target representations. The resulting architecture, referred to as gDSA (gMLP + DSA), combines the efficiency of direct stance assignment with improved contextual alignment, providing a strong lightweight alternative. This integration adds minimal overhead while improving stance-relevant interaction modeling. An overview of this setup is shown in Fig. 1.

### 3.3   Target-Aware Polarity Swapping (TAPS)

To reduce the overhead of keyphrase generation, we propose *Target-Aware Polarity Swapping (TAPS)*, a lightweight augmentation strategy for generating stance-reversed samples. As described in Algorithm 2, TAPS modifies stance-indicative words near the target: if antonyms exist, they are substituted; otherwise, negation is inserted before nearby verbs or adjectives. The stance label is then flipped (`favor` $\leftrightarrow$ `against`) while the target remains unchanged. This process yields semantically valid oppositional examples that encourage the model to learn balanced stance patterns with minimal overhead.

---

**Algorithm 2.** Target-Aware Polarity Swapping (TAPS)

---

**Require:** Dataset $D$ with tuples $(x, t, y)$: text, target, and stance label
**Ensure:** Augmented dataset $D'$
 1: **for** each $(x, t, y)$ in $D$ **do**
 2:     **if** $y \in \{$`favor`, `against`$\}$ **then**
 3:         Identify polarity-bearing words near $t$
 4:         **if** antonym exists **then**
 5:             Replace with antonym
 6:         **else**
 7:             Insert "not" before closest verb/adjective
 8:         **end if**
 9:         Flip label: `favor` $\leftrightarrow$ `against`
10:         Add $(x', t, y')$ to $D'$
11:     **end if**
12: **end for**
13: **return** $D'$

---

## 4   Experimental Settings

Experiments were run on a cloud platform with a 16 GB GPU. Using the VAST dataset, the gDSA model was trained in under 2 h. We fine-tuned only the encoder of a pre-trained BART-large model, using learning rates of 2e-5 (encoder) and 1e-3 (classifier), batch size 64, and sequence lengths of 200 (input) and 10 (target). Early stopping was applied after 4 epochs (patience 5), and results were averaged over four runs with hyperparameters tuned on validation performance.

# 5   Results

Table 1 presents macro F1-scores for various ZSSD variants, including our proposed data augmentation strategies and enhancements, benchmarked against existing methods. The Direct Stance Assignment (DSA) framework, which assigns stance labels using semantic similarity without supervised fine-tuning, achieves a macro F1 of 78.41. Adding a lightweight gMLP block (gDSA) leads to a further improvement to 79.23, with noticeable gains in identifying `against` stances, while keeping additional computational cost minimal.

All DSA-based approaches outperform the TTS-p baseline by avoiding noisy pseudo-labeling and directly assigning stances through similarity matching, which reduces error propagation. gDSA achieves Macro-F1 79.23 with  210M parameters—comparable to larger models such as LKI-BART [12] but at nearly half the cost of TTS-p. In contrast, the TAPS variant shows only modest improvement, highlighting the challenge of generating effective stance-flipped examples. Overall, gDSA provides a practical and efficient alternative for real-world zero-shot stance detection tasks.

**Table 1.** Macro F1-scores of proposed models and baseline models on zero-shot stance detection (using VAST) using 10% training data. † marks prior reported results; ‡ denotes models trained on full (100%) data. Params show number of fine-tuned parameters. Best F1 for 10% training are underlined, while bold indicates best F1 with 100% training. #Params are not available for LKI-BART and BART-MNLI-$e$.

| Method | Against | Favor | Neutral | All | #Params |
|---|---|---|---|---|---|
| DSA | 73.34 | 71.03 | 90.86 | 78.41 | 205.7M |
| gDSA | <u>74.04</u> | <u>72.08</u> | <u>91.58</u> | <u>79.23</u> | 210M |
| TAPS | 60.14 | 62.37 | 90.17 | 70.89 | 205.7M |
| TTS-p[†] [7] | 72.10 | 71.90 | 91.30 | 78.40 | 411M |
| TTS-p[†‡] [7] | **75.10** | 72.50 | **92.50** | **80.10** | 411M |
| LKI-BART[†‡] [12] | **75.10** | **72.90** | 90.70 | 79.60 | – |
| BART-MNLI-$e$[†‡] [13] | 70.60 | 69.00 | 92.10 | 77.20 | – |

## 5.1   Further Investigations

The results of incorporating common sense in the teacher-student framework [7] and contrastive learning in the proposed DSA framework are discussed in this section.

**Influence of Common-Sense in Teacher-Student Framework.** To improve ZSSD on implicit language and generic targets, commonsense reasoning is incorporated into the TTS framework using COMET, which generates

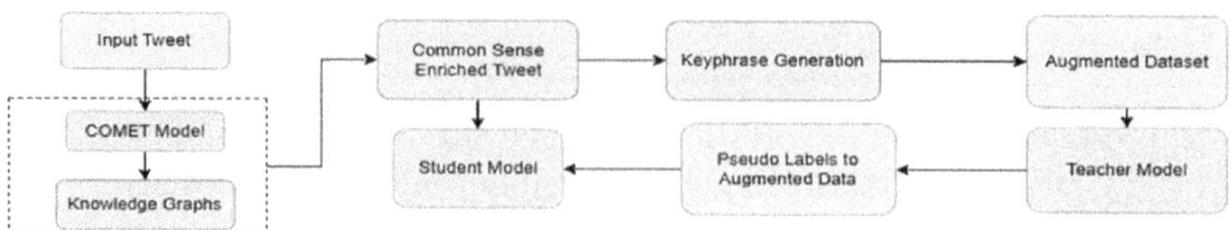


**Fig. 2.** Schematic Representation of Commonsense-Enhanced Stance Detection Methodology

inferences (xIntent, xReact, xEffect) to capture likely motivations and outcomes behind opinions. These enriched tweets are used to extract keyphrases forming an augmented dataset ($D_{aug}$), for which a BART-based teacher produces pseudo-labels to train a student model. This commonsense-aware approach achieves a Macro-F1 of 79.77, but the modest gains and added overhead prevent its integration into the Direct Stance Assignment (DSA) flow, which prioritizes efficiency and simplicity. The procedure is shown in Fig. 2.

**Supervised Contrastive Learning.** We experimented by adding supervised contrastive loss [5] to enhance stance representation learning. It encourages embeddings of same-stance samples to cluster while separating different-stance ones. To handle `neutral` instances, we tested a hard variant that excluded them as anchors. Formally, the total training loss was: $\mathcal{L}_{total} = \mathcal{L}_{CE} + \lambda \cdot \mathcal{L}_{contrastive}$ where $\lambda$ was set to 0.5. This approach resulted in a macro F1 of **78.14** (Against: 72.27, Favour: 71.10, Neutral: 91.21), despite theoretical appeal, empirical gains were not observed, suggesting no benefit in the zero-shot setup. This contrastive learning approach was not pursued further, as it did not yield any improvement within the DSA framework.

## 6    Conclusion

The proposed framework introduces a lightweight alternative for zero-shot stance detection by removing the need for a separate stance labeling model for data augmentation. Instead, it employs Direct Stance Assignment (DSA), which assigns stance labels to augmented data based on semantic similarity. This drastically reduces computational complexity while retaining strong performance, achieving a Macro F1 of 78.41. Unlike traditional teacher-student models that rely on an additional model to generate pseudo-labels, DSA performs stance assignment directly, streamlining the pipeline and making it highly scalable. Furthermore, this approach is easily adaptable to new domains or unseen targets without retraining a teacher model. Incorporating gMLP further enhances representation learning through token-wise gating mechanisms and spatial mixing, allowing gDSA to reach a higher Macro F1 of 79.23. While commonsense reasoning via COMET offers a modest gain, it introduces additional complexity and inference overhead. In contrast, the core strength of our framework lies in its efficiency and simplicity. Overall, it strikes a practical balance between accuracy and resource usage, making it ideal for deployment in low-resource or real-time applications.

# References


1. Allaway, E., McKeown, K.: Zero-shot stance detection: A dataset and model using generalized topic representations. arXiv preprint arXiv:2010.03640 (2020)
2. Allaway, E., Srikanth, M., McKeown, K.: Adversarial learning for zero-shot stance detection on social media. arXiv preprint arXiv:2105.06603 (2021)
3. Grootendorst, M.: Keybert: Minimal keyword extraction with bert (2020)
4. Grootendorst, M.: Bertopic: Neural topic modeling with a class-based tf-idf procedure. arXiv preprint arXiv:2203.05794 (2022)
5. Khosla, P., et al.: Supervised contrastive learning. Adv. Neural. Inf. Process. Syst. **33**, 18661–18673 (2020)
6. Li, Y., Garg, K., Caragea, C.: A new direction in stance detection: target-stance extraction in the wild. In: Proceedings of the 61st Annual Meeting of the Association for Computational Linguistics (Volume 1: Long Papers), pp. 10071–10085 (2023)
7. Li, Y., Zhao, C., Caragea, C.: Tts: a target-based teacher-student framework for zero-shot stance detection. In: Proceedings of the ACM Web Conference 2023, pp. 1500–1509 (2023)
8. Liu, H., Dai, Z., So, D., Le, Q.V.: Pay attention to mlps. Adv. Neural. Inf. Process. Syst. **34**, 9204–9215 (2021)
9. Rei, R., Stewart, C., Farinha, A.C., Lavie, A.: Comet: a neural framework for mt evaluation. arXiv preprint arXiv:2009.09025 (2020)
10. Song, K., Tan, X., Qin, T., Lu, J., Liu, T.Y.: Mpnet: masked and permuted pre-training for language understanding. Adv. Neural. Inf. Process. Syst. **33**, 16857–16867 (2020)
11. Yuan, X., et al.: One size does not fit all: generating and evaluating variable number of keyphrases. arXiv preprint arXiv:1810.05241 (2018)
12. Zhang, Z., Li, Y., Zhang, J., Xu, H.: Llm-driven knowledge injection advances zero-shot and cross-target stance detection. In: Proceedings of the 2024 Conference of the North American Chapter of the Association for Computational Linguistics: Human Language Technologies (Volume 2: Short Papers), pp. 371–378 (2024)
13. Zhao, C., Caragea, C.: EZ-STANCE: a large dataset for English zero-shot stance detection. In: Ku, L.W., Martins, A., Srikumar, V. (eds.) Proceedings of the 62nd Annual Meeting of the Association for Computational Linguistics (Volume 1: Long Papers), pp. 15697–15714. Association for Computational Linguistics, Bangkok, Thailand (Aug 2024). https://doi.org/10.18653/v1/2024.acl-long.838, https://aclanthology.org/2024.acl-long.838/
14. Zhao, C., Li, Y., Caragea, C., Zhang, Y.: ZeroStance: leveraging ChatGPT for open-domain stance detection via dataset generation. In: Ku, L.W., Martins, A., Srikumar, V. (eds.) Findings of the Association for Computational Linguistics: ACL 2024, pp. 13390–13405. Association for Computational Linguistics, Bangkok,Thailanad (Aug 2024). https://doi.org/10.18653/v1/2024.findings-acl.794, https://aclanthology.org/2024.findings-acl.794/

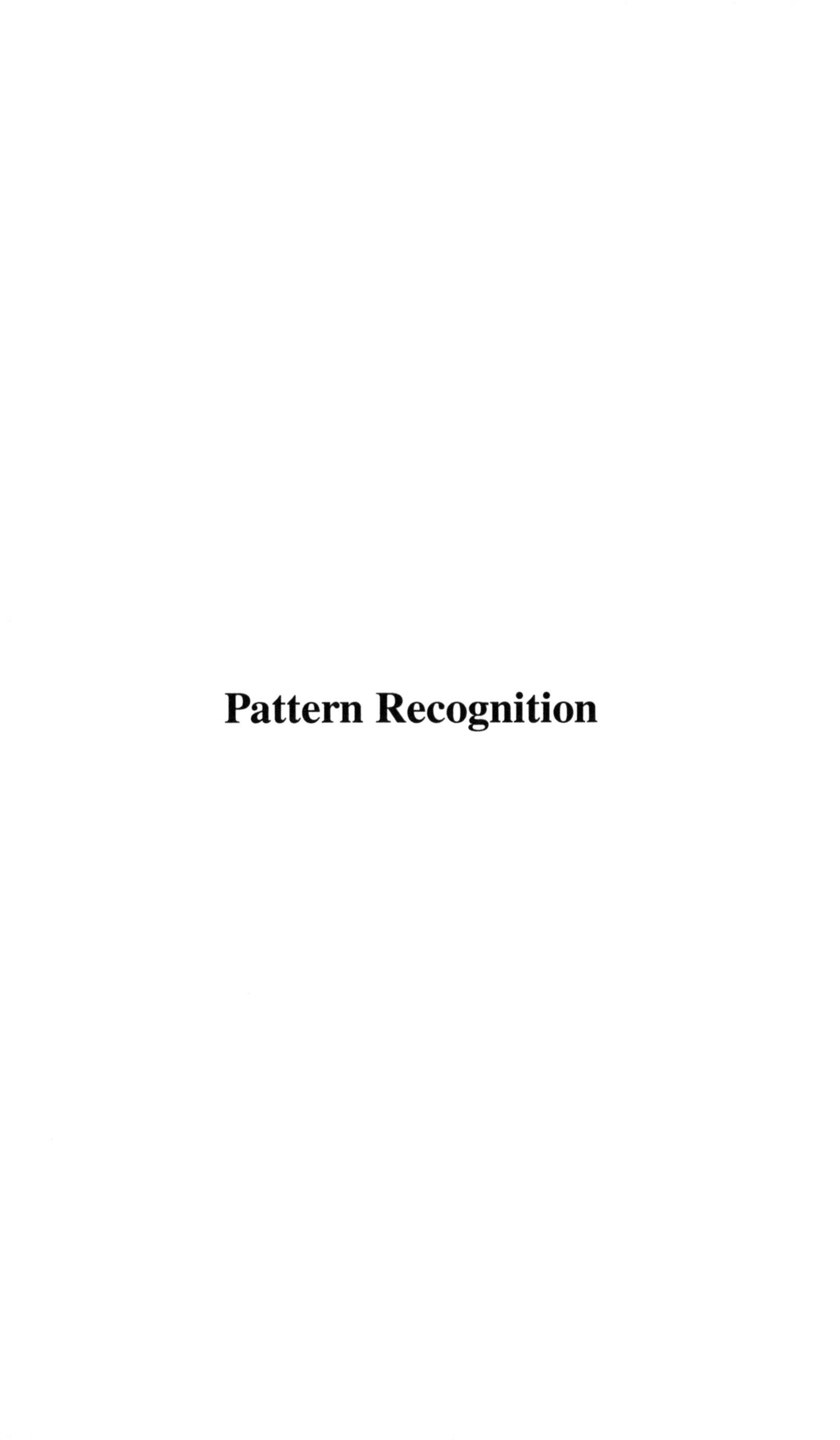

# Pattern Recognition

# Addictive Pattern Identification in Video Games: A VLM Based Approach

Sunidhi Singh[1]([✉])(iD), Santanu Chaudhury[1](iD), Tapan Kumar Gandhi[1](iD), and Yatan Pal Singh Balhara[2](iD)

[1] Department of Electrical Engineering, Indian Institute of Technology Delhi, New Delhi, India
`eez228477@iitd.ac.in`, `santanuc@ee.iitd.ac.in`, `tgandhi@ee.iitd.ac.in`
[2] Department of Psychiatry, All India Institute of Medical Sciences (AIIMS), New Delhi, India

**Abstract.** With the increasing accessibility of mobile and digital technologies, video game engagement has significantly increased, leading to emerging concerns around video game addiction. This study addresses the identification of addictive behavioral design elements in video games, which require complex visual reasoning and interpretation ability. We leverage the Qwen-VL-7B Instruct and Llama-3.2-11B-Vision-Instruct vision-language model for this purpose, applying parameter-efficient finetuning (PEFT) using LoRA adapters to tailor it for addiction-related analysis. A custom-curated dataset containing annotated frames from 10 popular video games, each labeled with 8 behaviorally relevant queries, is used for finetuning. The novelty of this research is designing a scheme for the identification of psychologically significant elements in the video, rather than the object detection or action recognition task. Post-training evaluations using metrics such as BERTScore, BLEU, METEOR, and ROUGE show considerable improvements in the model's ability to align with human-annotated behavioral features. Embedding space analysis further confirms the shift in the model's internal representation towards human-crafted conceptual understanding. The model shows reliable generalization capability when verified on unseen video game through zero-shot inference. This work paves the way for deploying large vision-language models in the domain of psychological impact assessment through media content. The code and dataset link can be found here: https://github.com/SUNIDHI-SINGH/Video-Game-Addiction-Behavioural-Elements-Dataset.

**Keywords:** Video Game Addiction · Vision-Language Models · Qwen-VL · Behavioral Design Elements · PEFT · LoRA · finetuning · Multimodal Reasoning · AI and Psychology · Generative AI · Multi-modal Systems

## 1 Introduction

With the increase in the use of gadgets and communication technologies such as mobile phones and laptops, there is an increase in the amount of time that

© The Author(s), under exclusive license to Springer Nature Switzerland AG 2026
S. Mitra et al. (Eds.): PReMI 2025, LNCS 16358, pp. 603–612, 2026.
https://doi.org/10.1007/978-3-032-18480-1_61

a person spends using a mobile phone. The leisure time is spent playing video games. This becomes addictive in nature when a person plays a video game with psychological engagement such as escape from reality to a more entertaining and joyful living environment, relapse, etc. [1]. This, video game addiction is an emerging psychological issue. There are few literature surveys showing that there are video game design features that make it addictive. This can be classified into addictive structural [2] and behavioral [3] design elements.

Traditional approaches to identify video game addiction rely on user surveys, gameplay logs, or behavioral observation, which are often limited in scale and scope [4]. Identifying video game addiction behavioral elements detection requires high-level reasoning capabilities to understand the visual scenarios and make a logical inference out of it with respect to the video game. This is the problem of classification of dynamic play features of video games that tend to promote addiction. Qwen VL 7B Instruct [5] model and Llama-3.2-11B-Vision-Instruct [6] are state-of-the-art models with visual reasoning capabilities. Given the high computational cost of training this model, task-specific supervised fine-tuning the large vision language model has proven to be a very useful tool [7]. Parameter efficient finetuning (PEFT) with the LoRA adapter achieves performance equivalent to full model training [8]. Therefore, the objective of this paper is the following research problem:

– Detect implicit behavioral elements present in the video game design that psychologically promote the addictive trend.

Traditional computer vision tasks such as object detection, action recognition, and scene classification are insufficient when the goal is to understand implicit behavioral cues embedded in interactive environments like video games. In this work, we shift the focus from recognizing what is visible to reasoning about why it might be psychologically significant. This includes identifying design elements that foster reward anticipation, social manipulation, strategy formulation, and compulsive interaction—hallmarks of potentially addictive game mechanics categorized into common vitality structure-CLIMB, FINAL, STRECH, ALERT [9]. Our objective is to extract the behavioral features of video games that are addictive in nature. This requires the ability to analyze the aesthetics, mechanics and dynamics of video games [10]. We aim to build an interpretable AI system capable of assisting researchers and developers in assessing games through addiction risk.

## 2   Related Work

**Psychological Model of Addiction in Design of Games:** Prior studies have explored structural theories of the metacategory of video games such as the perspective of space, absolute or relative positioning, environment dynamics, internal time, player composition and reaction [11]. This foundational categories model helps map the experiences of the players. Extending this structural lens, another framework effectively captures dark patterns in the design of the game, which puts lights on negative experiences that gets embedded through video game [12]. Further research provides valuable information on the structural study of problematic video game playing such as social features, narrative and control features, narrative and identity features, reward and punishment features, presentation features [13]. In line with this research, one study [3] explains how the combination of design elements creates an immersive flow state in an activity while playing a video game, often enforcing cue reactivity and perpetuate engagement behaviors.

**Multimodal Needs for Behavioural Understanding:**  Recent advances in vision-language models (VLMs) have transformed multimodal understanding tasks, enabling models to process and reason over both textual and visual input [14]. However, their potential for psychological and behavioral inference, particularly in domains such as gaming addiction—remains underexplored. Recent interdisciplinary efforts have begun leveraging AI to analyze social media and gaming behavior [15], but none have directly addressed the detection of addiction-prone behavioural features in video games using VLMs. From the AI side, parameter-efficient finetuning (PEFT) methods such as Low-Rank Adaptation (LoRA) have proven effective in adapting large models with minimal compute [8], enabling targeted domain-specific applications.

This work builds on such developments to fine-tune VLMs on annotated video game keyframes, aiming to surface latent indicators of addictive design embedded in visual environments. By doing so, we extend the role of VLMs beyond generic captioning and reasoning toward domain-adapted behavioral inference.

## 3   Model Architecture

**Dataset:** The handcrafted dataset consists of 10 popular video games, namely PUBG, Valorant, Minecraft, GTA Vice City, World of Warcraft, FIFA, Fortnite, Among Us, Rocket League and Super Mario, is annotated against eight behavioral questions. PUBG and Fortnite are fast-paced battle royale shooters, Valorant is a tactical first-person shooter, Minecraft is a sandbox survival and creative building game, Super Mario is a classic platformer, Rocket League blends vehicular action with sports, FIFA is a realistic sports simulation focused on football, and Among Us is a social deduction multiplayer party game. The eight behavioral questions are "What role playing elements are present in this game ?" , "What realistic graphical features are present?", "What is the in game achievement ?", "Are there random rewards present ?", "Are there randomly generated content ?", "What surprise mechanism is present?", "The rewards have random reinforcement schedule or fixed reinforcement schedule?" and "Are there self-controlled strategy making techniques in the video game?". The eight selected questions address latent features such as variable reinforcement schedules, unpredictability, and immersive realism, all of which align with psychological frameworks like the incentive sensitization theory and the cue-reactivity model in addiction research. There are total 80 image, query and assistant answer pairs in the dataset. These makes it a standard set of prompts, scenarios and assistant replies. This corpora is scrapped from web from video game streamers youtube channels and then keyframes were extracted from them (Fig. 1).

**Fig. 1.** Categories of behavior specific finetuning corpora.

**finetuning Setup:** The purpose is to downstream the base model with this handcrafted dataset so that it can understand and extract addictive design elements present in the video games. The architecture below explains the entire process. To develop a personalized model specialized to the task of detecting video game addiction behavioral elements, the original model is fine-tuned on a set of samples that includes both words and images.

To specialize the Qwen-VL-7B Instruct and Llama-3.2-11B-Vision-Instruct model for identifying addictive features in video games, we apply parameter-efficient fine tuning (PEFT) using low-rank adaptation (LoRA). Rather than updating the full model parameters $\theta$, LoRA introduces trainable low-rank matrices $A \in \mathbb{R}^{d \times r}$ and $B \in \mathbb{R}^{r \times k}$ into specific layers, particularly the query and self-attention value projections, resulting in an adapted weight:

$$W' = W + \Delta W, \quad \Delta W = AB$$

Given multimodal inputs $x_{i,j} = (I_i, q_{i,j})$, where $I_i$ is the video game image and $q_{i,j}$ is the behavioral query for the $j$-th category, and the target response is $y_{i,j}$, the model minimizes the behavior-specific cross-entropy loss as follows:

$$\mathscr{L}_{\text{design elements of addictive behavior}} = \frac{1}{N} \sum_{i=1}^{N} \sum_{j=1}^{8} \lambda_j \cdot \mathscr{L}_{\text{CE}}(f_\theta(x_{i,j}), y_{i,j}) \quad (1)$$

In this formulation, $f_\theta : \mathscr{I} \times \mathscr{Q} \to \mathscr{Y}_j$ represents the model that maps imagequery input pairs to their corresponding categorical behavioral elements. The term $\lambda_j$ denotes the weight associated with the $j$-th behavioral query to optionally emphasize certain behaviors, and $\mathscr{Y}_j$ refers to the target answer space for that category.

During finetuning, each image $I_i$ is first passed through a vision encoder to obtain visual features $v_i = \text{VisionEncoder}(I_i)$. The corresponding query $q_{i,j}$ is processed via a tokenizer to generate text embeddings $t_{i,j} = \text{Tokenizer}(q_{i,j})$. These visual and textual embeddings are jointly fused in the transformer layers to compute a multimodal representation $h_{i,j} = \text{Transformer}(v_i, t_{i,j}; \theta')$, which is subsequently decoded to generate the behavior-aware prediction $\hat{y}_{i,j} = \text{Decoder}(h_{i,j})$.

The LoRA configuration used for this setup includes a rank $r = 8$, a scaling factor $\alpha = 16$, and a dropout rate of 0.05. LoRA was applied specifically to the `q_proj` and `v_proj` modules within the attention layers of the transformer. The task type was defined as `CAUSAL_LM` to align with the instruction-following objective of the behavioral queries. Through this method, we evaluate the capability of the state-of-the-art vision-language model in identifying addictive properties in video games. The pipeline in the following Fig. 2 explains the format of providing vision language model with a context of the video game, image and selected queries such that it generates the response which depicts behavioral elements present in the video game snap provided.

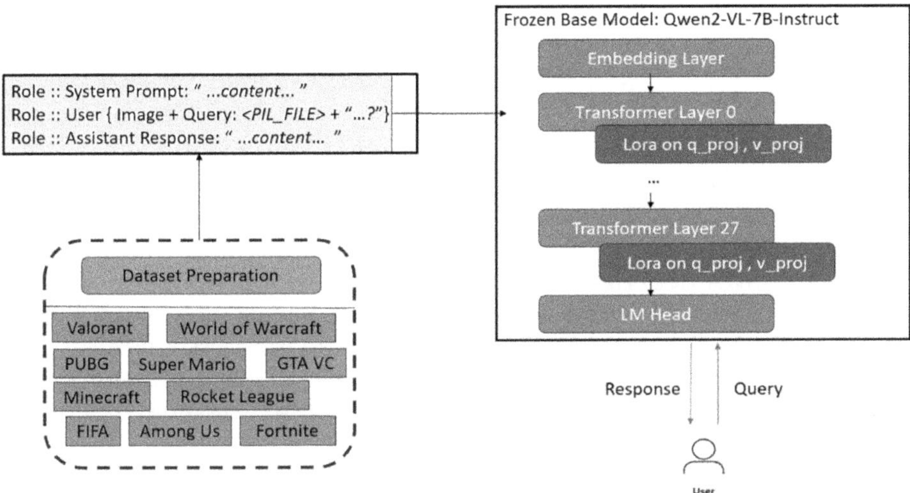


**Fig. 2.** Supervised finetuning pipeline of ViT using PEFT for video game addiction feature extraction use case.

## 4 Results

The validation of fine-tuning for both Qwen2-VL and Llama-3.2-11B-Vision-Instruct models was performed using standard evaluation metrics, including BERTScore, BLEU, METEOR, ROUGE-1, ROUGE-2, and ROUGE-L. The

BLEU and METEOR scores, which measure the lexical overlap between generated responses and reference texts, exhibited substantial improvement after fine-tuning in both models. For Qwen2-VL, BLEU increased from near-zero to approximately 0.38 on training data, while Llama-3.2-11B-Vision-Instruct achieved a much higher post-finetuning BLEU of around 0.59, indicating more accurate token-level generation. METEOR scores nearly doubled across all subsets in both cases, reflecting enhanced semantic alignment with the reference annotations.

The BERTScore, available for Qwen2-VL, showed high baseline values around 0.85 even before fine-tuning, suggesting that the model already possessed strong linguistic and contextual representations. Post-finetuning, it rose above 0.90, confirming improved contextual understanding of addiction-related queries. Similarly, the ROUGE metrics—particularly ROUGE-2 and ROUGE-L—demonstrated consistent gains in both models, highlighting their improved ability to capture coherent and contextually relevant phrase structures. ROUGE-2, for instance, improved from approximately 0.03 to over 0.23 in the test set for Qwen2-VL and from 0.02 to nearly 0.20 for Llama-3.2-11B-Vision-Instruct, indicating that both models learned to generate more complex and meaningful n-gram patterns after fine-tuning (Table 1).

**Table 1.** Comparison of evaluation metrics before and after finetuning on Qwen2-VL-7B-Instruct and Llama-3.2-11B-Vision-Instruct.

| Metric | Qwen2-VL-7B-Instruct | | | | | | Llama-3.2-11B-Vision-Instruct | | | | | |
| | Before Finetuning | | | After Finetuning | | | Before Finetuning | | | After Finetuning | | |
| | Train | Val | Test | Train | Val | Test | Train | Val | Test | Train | Val | Test |
| --- | --- | --- | --- | --- | --- | --- | --- | --- | --- | --- | --- | --- |
| BERTScore_F1 | 0.8520 | 0.8560 | 0.8457 | 0.9190 | 0.8879 | 0.9041 | 0.8329 | 0.8307 | 0.8397 | 0.9468 | 0.8970 | 0.8930 |
| BLEU | 0.0058 | 0.0000 | 0.0000 | 0.3818 | 0.0780 | 0.1228 | 0.0062 | 0.0141 | 0.0080 | 0.5945 | 0.2431 | 0.1395 |
| METEOR | 0.2050 | 0.2019 | 0.2236 | 0.4966 | 0.2710 | 0.4610 | 0.1889 | 0.1719 | 0.1943 | 0.7131 | 0.4283 | 0.4019 |
| ROUGE-1 | 0.1929 | 0.1907 | 0.1517 | 0.5355 | 0.3456 | 0.4446 | 0.1394 | 0.1423 | 0.1356 | 0.7107 | 0.3955 | 0.3574 |
| ROUGE-2 | 0.0292 | 0.0093 | 0.0254 | 0.4195 | 0.1061 | 0.2329 | 0.0256 | 0.0195 | 0.0235 | 0.6146 | 0.2327 | 0.1968 |
| ROUGE-L | 0.1186 | 0.1091 | 0.0765 | 0.4911 | 0.2515 | 0.3613 | 0.0968 | 0.0936 | 0.1006 | 0.6872 | 0.3497 | 0.2793 |

These quantitative metrics confirm that the finetuning successfully shifted the Qwen2-VL-7B and Llama-3.2-11B-Vision-Instruct model's output distribution toward psychologically relevant interpretations. The figure below describes the embedding space representation of the original handcrafted dataset (References), the base model predictions on the query (original prediction) and the finetuned model's prediction on the queries (Fig. 3).

It is evident that the base model predictions are confined to a region but fine-tuned model predictions are spread to a space similar to that of reference handcrafted dataset embeddings. This demonstrates internal model change during finetuning. Notably, the finetuned concept is created by transforming the base model concept to required domain.

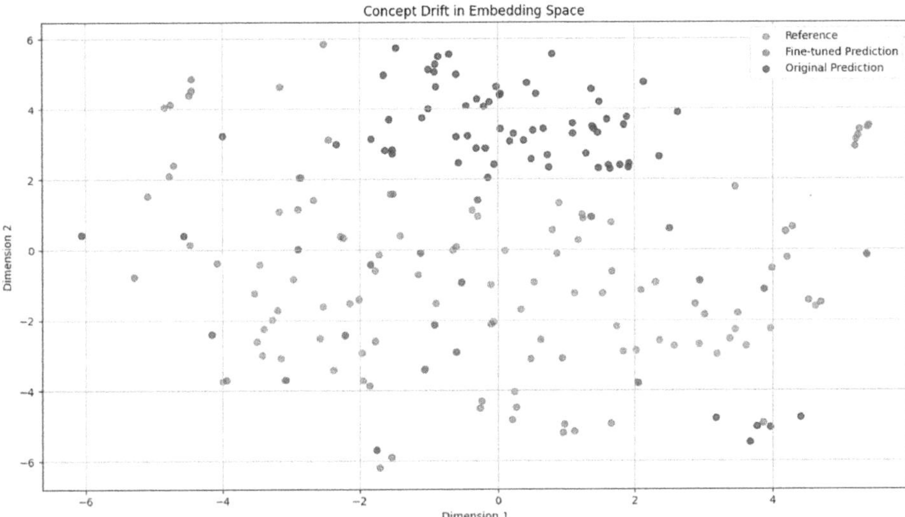

**Fig. 3.** Concept drift in embedding space between the base model prediction, fine-tuned model prediction, and hand-crafted reference annotations.

The dialogue below indicates that the base model recognizes the Super Mario video game given this snap and recalls the information it has about the game, which can be a surprise mechanism. But the presence of Goomba that it describes is the explicit design element of the video game. This shows bias to the prior training. Also, it is not related to the snap given. But the finetuned model shows implicit features like the architecture of the world it is in. The finetuned model's recognition of environmental cues is more aligned with how cue reactivity operates in addiction (Fig. 4).

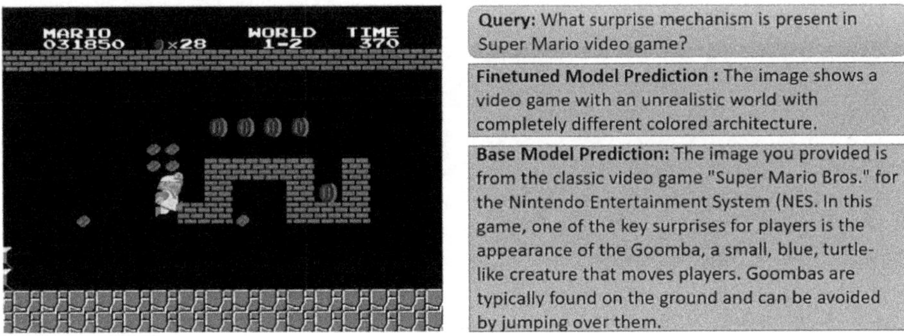


**Fig. 4.** Illustration of dialogue with the Qwen2-VL-7B-Instruct model after finetuning and before finetuning.

To evaluate the generalization capability of the fine-tuned model, we employed a dataset consisting of eight behavioral queries and their corresponding handcrafted annotations representing expected behavioral insight for the video game Call of Duty: Modern Warfare. Notably, this game was not part of the finetuning process, making it an unseen test case for zero shot inference. Both the base model and the fine-tuned model were used to generate predictions for queries based on visual input from game snapshots. Established evaluation metrics on natural language including BERTScore, BLEU, ROUGE-1, ROUGE-2, and ROUGE-L is computed by comparing the model-generated responses with the reference annotations. As shown in Table 2, the fine-tuned model significantly outperformed the base model, demonstrating an improved ability to identify implicit behavioral features even in an unfamiliar video game context. This highlights the model's generalization capacity and its potential for behavioral understanding across diverse gaming environments.

**Table 2.** Comparative evaluation of the fine-tuned model and the base (pre-trained) model on an unseen video game—Call of Duty: Modern Warfare

| Metric | Finetuned Model | Base Model |
| --- | --- | --- |
| BERTScore (F1) | 0.922 | 0.8977 |
| BLEU | 0.4816 | 0.1312 |
| METEOR | 0.6516 | 0.456 |
| ROUGE-1 | 0.6317 | 0.4338 |
| ROUGE-2 | 0.4915 | 0.3273 |
| ROUGE-L | 0.5319 | 0.4344 |

**Fig. 5.** Illustration of dialogue with the Qwen2-VL-7B-Instruct model after finetuning and before finetuning on Call of Duty video game.

In the illustration below, the dialogue of the Qwen2-VL-2B-Instruct base model shows that it reflects in its chat the knowledge it has about the Call of

Duty video game. Also, the "Sniper Honor" title is nowhere in the snap. On the other hand, fine-tuned model answers based on cue provided in the snap, and it reflects behavioral components present in the video game (Fig. 5).

## 5   Discussion and Conclusion

In this work, we explored the application of vision-language models for detecting addictive behavioral elements in video games, a psychologically sensitive and under-researched area. The hand-crafted dataset allows for comprehensive behavioral modeling. Handcrafted annotations bring in domain expertise. Fine-tuned VLM model - Qwen2-VL-2B-Instruct shows better results in identifying the video game behavioral addiction characteristics. The large vision language model works effectively to identify the implicit behavioral features present as design elements in video games. The limitation of the project is that the prediction of the model depends on the quality of the data set on which it is finetuned. So, it can may have inherited biases of the annotator, and it is a data-intensive approach. Future work may explore the use of reinforcement learning so that the model can learn better and incorporate a larger data set. This research contributes a promising step toward the intersection of artificial intelligence, game studies, and behavioral psychology.

## References


1. Hellman, M., Schoenmakers, T.M., Nordstrom, B.R., Van Holst, R.J.: Is there such a thing as online video game addiction? A cross-disciplinary review. Addict. Res. Theory **21**(2), 102–112 (2013)
2. King, D., Delfabbro, P., Griffiths, M.: Video game structural characteristics: a new psychological taxonomy. Int. J. Ment. Heal. Addict. **8**(1), 90–106 (2010)
3. Flayelle, M., Brevers, D., King, D.L., Maurage, P., Perales, J.C., Billieux, J.: A taxonomy of technology design features that promote potentially addictive online behaviours. Nat. Rev. Psychol. **2**(3), 136–150 (2023)
4. Saini, N., et al.: Development of the saini-hodgins addiction risk potential of games (sharp-g) scale: an international delphi study. J. Behav. Addict. **13**(2), 450–462 (2024)
5. Bai, J., et al.: Qwen technical report. arXiv preprint arXiv:2309.16609, 2023
6. Grattafiori, A., et al.: The llama 3 herd of models. arXiv preprint arXiv:2407.21783, 2024
7. Jiang, X., Ge, Y., Ge, Y., Shi, D., Yuan, C., Shan, Y.: Supervised fine-tuning in turn improves visual foundation models. arXiv preprint arXiv:2401.10222, 2024
8. Prottasha, N.J., et al.: PEFT A2Z: parameter-efficient fine-tuning survey for large language and vision models. arXiv preprint arXiv:2504.14117, 2025
9. Karhulahti, V.-M.: Vitality structures in 'addictive' game design. Open Res. Eur. **4**, 47 (2024)
10. Kim, B.: Game mechanics, dynamics, and aesthetics. Libr. Technol. Rep. **51**(2), 17–19 (2015)
11. Elverdam, C., Aarseth, E.: Game classification and game design: construction through critical analysis. Games Culture **2**(1), 3–22 (2007). Original work published 2007

12. Zagal, J.P., Björk, S., Lewis, C.: Dark patterns in the design of games. In: Foundations of Digital Games 2013, 2013
13. Griffiths, M.D., Nuyens, F.: An overview of structural characteristics in problematic video game playing. Curr. Addict. Rep. **4**(3), 272–283 (2017)
14. Ghosh, A., Acharya, A., Saha, S., Jain, V., Chadha, A.: Exploring the frontier of vision-language models: a survey of current ethodologies and future directions. arXiv preprint arXiv:2404.07214, 2024
15. Huang, Y., Ruipeng, W., Huang, Y., Xiang, Y., Zhou, W.: Investigating the mechanisms of internet gaming disorder and developing intelligent monitoring models using artificial intelligence technologies: protocol of a prospective cohort. BMC Public Health **24**(1), 2536 (2024)

# Adaptive Weighted Granular Ball Framework for Robust and Efficient Support Vector Regression

Ankush Bisht[1], Anirudh Aggarwal[2], Sanjay Kumar[3]($\boxtimes$) (iD),
and Reshma Rastogi[1] (iD)

[1] MLSI Lab, South Asian University, New Delhi 110068, India
reshma.khemchandani@sau.ac.in
[2] University School of Information, Communication and Technology, Guru Gobind Singh Indraprastha University, New Delhi 110078, India
[3] Deshbandhu College, University of Delhi, New Delhi 110019, India
skumar5@db.du.ac.in

**Abstract.** Support Vector Regression (SVR) is a powerful method for regression tasks, but it suffers from high computational complexity and sensitivity to outliers. Several implementations of Granular Ball based SVR have been introduced to improve efficiency by summarizing data using granular balls which are a compact representations of data distributions. However, these implementations treat all granular balls equally, disregarding variations in their densities and importance. To address this, we propose Adaptive Weighted Granular Ball Support Vector Regression (AW-GBSVR), which assigns asymmetric weights to granular balls based on their statistical properties. This allows the model to prioritize more informative granular balls while reducing the influence of noisy or less significant ones. The proposed model is evaluated against recent granular ball based algorithms on benchmark and time-series datasets, demonstrating superior performance.

**Keywords:** Granular Ball Computing · Density based granular ball · Asymmetric Regression · Support Vector Regression

## 1 Introduction

Support Vector Regression (SVR) [8] is a popular choice for a wide range of regression problems, as it has strong theoretical foundations and the ability to handle non-linear relationships via kernel functions. However, SVR often struggles with large-scale and noisy datasets due to computational complexity and its sensitivity to outliers.

Granular Ball Support Vector Regression (GBSVR) [5] and Controllable Multigranularity Support Vector algorithm (Con-MGSVR) [7] were recently proposed to address these issues. In GBSVR, the original dataset is partitioned into

© The Author(s), under exclusive license to Springer Nature Switzerland AG 2026
S. Mitra et al. (Eds.): PReMI 2025, LNCS 16358, pp. 613–620, 2026.
https://doi.org/10.1007/978-3-032-18480-1_62

a collection of granular balls. Training SVR on these aggregated balls significantly reduces the number of data points and accelerates optimization. Granular balls by their very construction provide robustness against outliers. Despite these advantages, GBSVR faces some challenges as granular balls contribute the same regardless of the number of points they represent. Sparse as well as dense balls contribute equally.

To address these limitations, we propose Adaptive Weighted Granular Ball Support Vector Regression (AW-GBSVR). In AW-GBSVR, granular balls are weighted based on properties such as variance(spread) and cardinality (number of data points it represents). It allows the model to prioritize granular balls with a higher information content. Balls with potential outliers or few data points are less significant and contribute less to the regressor. By consolidating the data into weighted granular balls, AW-GBSVR retains the benefits of granular summarization while improving regressor performance.

AW-GBSVR provides an additional perspective and improvement over the existing granular ball based SVR frameworks by:

- Using compact, uncertainty-aware representations of data.
- Adapting margin width based on the radius of granular balls.
- Assigning importance weights based on the density and size of each ball.

## 2   Related Works

Support Vector Regression predicts continuous outputs for regression tasks while maintaining the principles of Structural Risk Minimization (SRM). SVR has strong generalization ability, especially for handling non-linear regression problems through the use of kernel functions. A common implementation of SVR is the $\epsilon$-insensitive SVR that introduces upto $\epsilon$-error tolerance while approximating target values. By solving a quadratic programming problem, SVR identifies a regressor $f(x)$ that minimizes the $\epsilon$-insensitive hinge loss on a given set of $m$ data points $D = (X, Y) = \{(x_i, y_i), i = 1, 2, \ldots, m\}$, where $x_i \in \mathcal{R}^l$, and $y_i \in \mathcal{R}$.

The objective of SVR is to find a regressor $f(x) = w \cdot x + b$ (linear case) that trades off between model complexity and prediction performance. The optimization problem for the linear case is formulated as:

$$\min_{w,b,\xi,\xi^*} \ \frac{1}{2}\|w\|^2 + C \sum_{i=1}^{n}(\xi_i + \xi_i^*),$$

subject to

$$
\begin{aligned}
y_i - w \cdot x_i - b &\leq \epsilon + \xi_i, \\
w \cdot x_i + b - y_i &\leq \epsilon + \xi_i^*, \\
\xi_i, \xi_i^* &\geq 0 \quad \forall i.
\end{aligned}
\tag{1}
$$

Here, $\|w\|^2$ is regularization term used to control the model complexity and flatness of the regression curve, $C$ is trade-off parameter between model complexity and the penalty for large deviations. The slack variables $\xi_i, \xi_i^*$ are to account for error corresponding to the data points outside the $\epsilon$-tube, above and below, respectively. Understanding of the linear kernel can be extended to the non-linear kernel using positive definite kernel functions.

SVR has a computational complexity of $O(n^3)$ for $n$ training samples, resulting in high computational time and memory requirements. Various methods, such as chunking and sequential minimal optimization (SMO) [12,13], have been proposed to improve the efficiency of SVR. Further, SVR is sensitive to outliers. Methods like robust SVR [1,2,6,11] have been developed to address this issue, though resulting in additional computational overhead.

Con-MGSVR [7] and GBSVR [5] apply granular computing theory to reduce the computational cost of SVR by substituting individual data points with granular balls. Although the two approaches successfully reduce the time complexity, they ignore the detail that granular balls vary in size, density, and number of constituent data points. These details influence the representational importance of granular balls. The proposed method, AW-GBSVR, addresses this limitation by incorporating these granular ball characteristics into the regression model.

## 3  Proposed Method: Adaptive Weighted Granular Ball SVR (AW-GBSVR)

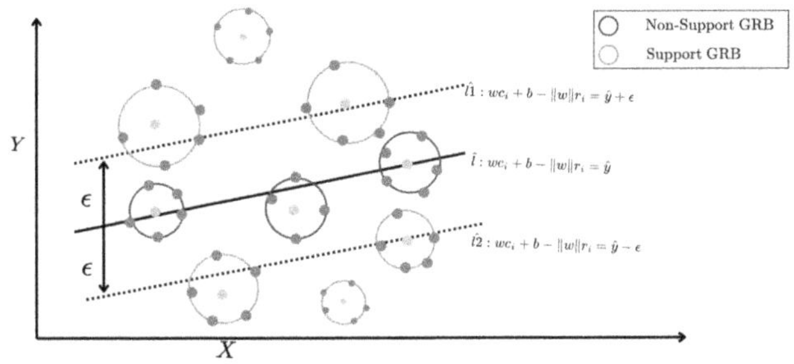


**Fig. 1.** Support and non-Support Granular Regressor Balls by Density.

In this section, we develop the AW-GBSVR framework, which extends granular ball-based SVR by incorporating ball specific characteristics and uncertainty into the regression optimization problem. The method leverages granular ball assisted compact representation and adaptivity to improve the regressor's robustness, efficiency, and interpretability. A conceptual illustration of granular balls is shown in Fig. 1. Margins associated with granular balls vary depending on their positions and target values.

### 3.1  Feature Representation Using Granular Balls

Rather than using individual data points as input to the SVR, we represent local regions of the input space using granular balls, each characterized by:

- $c_i$: the center (mean) of the points within the ball.
- $r_i$: the radius, representing the spread of data. We currently compute $r_i$ as the mean Euclidean distance from $c_i$ to the points in the ball, although more refined measures can be explored.
- $n_i$: the number of data points inside the ball.

These attributes form a summary of local regions, capturing both the representation and uncertainty. The new input representation is thus defined as:

$$(c_i, r_i, n_i) \in \mathbb{R}^{d+2}, \quad \text{instead of raw input } x_i \in \mathbb{R}^d.$$

This representation reduces computational complexity and improves robustness to noise by suppressing the influence of outliers.

## 3.2   Incorporating Uncertainty via Adaptive Margins

In classical SVR, the $\epsilon$-insensitive tube defines a uniform margin around the regression function. However, in the granular representation, each ball captures varying levels of uncertainty due to differences in spread and density. To reflect this, we introduce an *adaptive margin* $\epsilon_i$ for each granular ball:

$$\epsilon_i = \epsilon + \alpha r_i,$$

where $\alpha$ is a scaling parameter. This allows larger granular balls i.e., those with greater data spread more robust to noise and varying data densities, letting the model to be more flexible in uncertain regions.

The modified SVR constraints now become:

$$y_i - (w \cdot c_i + b) \leq \epsilon_i + \xi_i, \tag{2}$$
$$(w \cdot c_i + b) - y_i \leq \epsilon_i + \xi_i^*, \tag{3}$$

where $\xi_i, \xi_i^*$ are slack variables representing deviations beyond the adaptive margin.

## 3.3   Weighting Granular Balls Based on Density and Spread

To further integrate the structure of the granular balls into the learning objective, we assign a weight $m_i$ to each ball, reflecting its representational confidence. Specifically, we define:

$$m_i = \frac{n_i^a}{(r_i + \delta)^b},$$

where $a, b$ are hyperparameters (set to 1, in our experiments), and $\delta$ is a small constant to prevent division by zero. This formulation gives higher weight to smaller and denser balls (i.e., balls from well-represented, dense regions), and reduces the influence of sparse, uncertain regions.

## 3.4  AW-GBSVR Optimization

Let $\{(c_i, r_i, y_i, n_i)\}_{i=1}^m$ denote the set of $m$ granular balls derived from the training data. The objective of AW-GBSVR is to find a linear regressor $f(x) = w \cdot x + b$ that minimizes the weighted objective function while incorporating adaptive margins. The primal optimization problem is formulated as:

$$\min_{w,b,\xi_i,\xi_i^*} \quad \frac{1}{2}\|w\|^2 + C\sum_{i=1}^m m_i(\xi_i + \xi_i^*), \tag{4}$$

subject to the constraints in equations (2)–(3), and:

$$\xi_i, \xi_i^* \geq 0, \quad \forall i.$$

Here, $C$ is the regularization parameter controlling the trade-off between margin width and training error. The weight $m_i$ scales the penalty for each granular ball according to its density and spread.

*Kernel Extension:* Although the formulation above assumes a linear regressor, it can be readily extended to the nonlinear case using kernel functions. Let $\phi(c_i)$ denote the mapping of $c_i$ into a high-dimensional feature space, and $K(c_i, c_j) = \langle \phi(c_i), \phi(c_j) \rangle$ be a positive definite kernel. The same optimization formulation applies with $w \cdot c_i$ replaced by kernel evaluations, enabling the model to capture complex, nonlinear relationships.

These modifications make AW-GBSVR efficient and robust, making it well-suited for large-scale and noisy regression tasks.

For solving, we can construct its dual by introducing Lagrange multipliers $\lambda_i, \lambda_i^* \geq 0$ and $\mu_i, \mu_i^* \geq 0$, taking derivative of the Lagrangian and setting them to 0, the dual problem becomes:

$$\max_{\lambda_i,\lambda_i^*} \quad \sum_{i=1}^m (\lambda_i - \lambda_i^*)y_i - \sum_{i=1}^m \epsilon_i(\lambda_i + \lambda_i^*) - \frac{1}{2}\sum_{i=1}^m\sum_{j=1}^m (\lambda_i - \lambda_i^*)(\lambda_j - \lambda_j^*)c_i \cdot c_j, \tag{5}$$

subject to:

$$\sum_{i=1}^m (\lambda_i - \lambda_i^*) = 0, \tag{6}$$

$$0 \leq \lambda_i, \lambda_i^* \leq Cm_i, \quad \forall i. \tag{7}$$

*Identification of Support Vectors:* Granular balls serve as support vectors based on the position of their centers relative to the adaptive margin. A granular ball is a support vector if its center lies on or outside the margin. Balls whose surfaces lie outside but centers remain inside are not support vectors.

- On the margin: $|y_i - (w \cdot c_i + b)| = \epsilon_i,$    with $0 < \lambda_i < Cm_i$ or $0 < \lambda_i^* < Cm_i$.
- Outside the margin: $|y_i - (w \cdot c_i + b)| > \epsilon_i,$    with $\lambda_i = Cm_i$ or $\lambda_i^* = Cm_i$.

- Inside the margin (non-support vector): $|y_i - (w \cdot c_i + b)| < \epsilon_i,$     with $\lambda_i = 0$, $\lambda_i^* = 0$.

Solving the dual, the parameter $w$ for regressor is given by:

$$w = \sum_i (\lambda_i - \lambda_i^*) c_i,$$

and the bias is computed using any support vector $c_k$:

$$b = y_k - w \cdot c_k.$$

The final prediction for a new input $x$ is:

$$f(x) = w \cdot x + b,$$

or in kernelized form:

$$f(x) = \sum_i (\lambda_i - \lambda_i^*) K(c_i, x) + b.$$

## 4   Experiments, Results, and Discussion

To evaluate the performance of the proposed model, comparisons were made against four baseline methods: Granular Ball Support Vector Regression (GBSVR) [5], Elastic Net Support Vector Regression (EnSVR) [10], Nu-Support Vector Regression (NuSVR) [9], Support Vector Regression (SVR) [3]. The kernel parameter of the RBF kernel (for mappinng data to higher dimensional features space) was tuned from the set $\{0.001, 0.01, 0.1, 0.3, 0.5, 0.7, 0.9\}$.

For granular ball construction, the purity threshold was fixed at 0.995 to ensure high-quality granular structures. The minimum number of points within each granular ball was varied in 2, 3, and 4. The scale parameter was selected from $\{0.1, 0.3, 0.5, 0.7, 0.9\}$ to evaluate its effect on model performance. For discretizing the target variable, the number of bins was set to 3, 4, or 5 [5].

To evaluate the effectiveness of the proposed model, we conducted experiments on several real-world datasets from the UCI Machine Learning Repository [4], using standard regression metrics such as $R^2$, MAE, and RMSE. To further assess the model's robustness, varying levels of Gaussian noise (with mean 0 and standard deviation 0.2) were added to the datasets. As shown in Table 1, the proposed AW-GBSVR model consistently outperformed all other regression methods across all evaluation metrics. Moreover, it achieved this superior performance with a runtime comparable to GBSVR. This advantage is attributed to its adaptive epsilon-tube mechanism, which dynamically adjusts based on the local density of data points within each granular ball.

We also applied the model to the task of stock price forecasting, which is a difficult problem due to the nonlinear and volatile nature of financial time series. We used daily price data for two major stocks, AAPL and GOOGL, covering the period from January 2019 to January 2025. Figure 2 compares the actual stock prices with predictions from the proposed model and baseline methods. The AW-GBSVR model delivered more accurate forecasts, highlighting its ability to capture complex patterns in highly dynamic data.

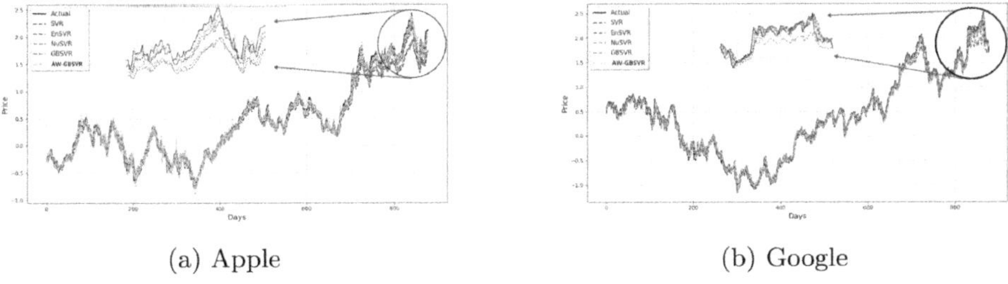

(a) Apple                    (b) Google

**Fig. 2.** Stock Price Forecasting.

**Table 1.** Comparison of AW-GBSVR against Competing Methods with Varying Levels of Gaussian Noise

**Servo**

| Metric | Methods | \multicolumn{5}{c}{Noise Percentage} | | | | |
|---|---|---|---|---|---|
| | | 0 | 0.05 | 0.1 | 0.15 | 0.2 |
| Time ($\downarrow$) | AW-GBSVR | 1.619 ± 0.0 | 1.777 ± 0.172 | 1.208 ± 0.294 | 1.005 ± 0.887 | 1.488 ± 0.826 |
| | GBSVR | 2.001 ± 0.163 | 1.984 ± 0.139 | 1.771 ± 0.126 | 1.954 ± 0.107 | 1.972 ± 0.165 |
| | EnSVR | 2.9 ± 0.364 | 2.677 ± 0.349 | 3.233 ± 0.536 | 3.237 ± 0.772 | 2.814 ± 0.824 |
| | NuSVR | 4.729±0.104 | 4.902±0.231 | 4.903±0.23 | 4.889±0.291 | 4.612±0.281 |
| | SVR | 10.309±0.059 | 10.286±0.075 | 10.310±0.091 | 10.357±0.060 | 10.420±0.148 |
| R2 ($\downarrow$) | AW-GBSVR | 0.877 ± 0.0 | 0.882 ± 0.025 | 0.89 ± 0.025 | 0.87 ± 0.054 | 0.878 ± 0.08 |
| | GBSVR | 0.85 ± 0.021 | 0.859 ± 0.028 | 0.862 ± 0.029 | 0.849 ± 0.032 | 0.835 ± 0.048 |
| | EnSVR | 0.819 ± 0.024 | 0.826 ± 0.02 | 0.814 ± 0.026 | 0.822 ± 0.046 | 0.808 ± 0.033 |
| | NuSVR | 0.836±0.03 | 0.833±0.03 | b | 0.811±0.041 | 0.833±0.044 |
| | SVR | 0.782 ± 0.066 | 0.772 ± 0.047 | 0.766 ± 0.066 | 0.771 ± 0.049 | 0.743 ± 0.056 |
| MAE ($\downarrow$) | AW-GBSVR | 0.249 ± 0.0 | 0.247 ± 0.014 | 0.248 ± 0.048 | 0.272 ± 0.044 | 0.256 ± 0.084 |
| | GBSVR | 0.283 ± 0.012 | 0.265 ± 0.035 | 0.263 ± 0.02 | 0.275 ± 0.038 | 0.291 ± 0.052 |
| | EnSVR | 0.307 ± 0.035 | 0.302 ± 0.037 | 0.31 ± 0.035 | 0.297 ± 0.047 | 0.31 ± 0.047 |
| | NuSVR | 0.298±0.019 | 0.301±0.028 | 0.325±0.049 | 0.323±0.021 | 0.305±0.033 |
| | SVR | 0.364 ± 0.049 | 0.388 ± 0.032 | 0.384 ± 0.053 | 0.383 ± 0.036 | 0.406 ± 0.032 |
| RMSE ($\downarrow$) | AW-GBSVR | 0.344 ± 0.0 | 0.336 ± 0.016 | 0.325 ± 0.048 | 0.344 ± 0.051 | 0.348 ± 0.051 |
| | GBSVR | 0.377 ± 0.024 | 0.364 ± 0.052 | 0.363 ± 0.037 | 0.38 ± 0.052 | 0.399 ± 0.057 |
| | EnSVR | 0.419 ± 0.041 | 0.412 ± 0.038 | 0.425 ± 0.048 | 0.413 ± 0.061 | 0.432 ± 0.051 |
| | NuSVR | 0.397±0.038 | 0.402±0.042 | 0.418±0.067 | 0.425±0.036 | 0.400±0.059 |
| | SVR | 0.453 ± 0.056 | 0.468 ± 0.044 | 0.471 ± 0.065 | 0.468 ± 0.047 | 0.495 ± 0.04 |

**Yacht**

| Metric | Methods | \multicolumn{5}{c}{Noise Percentage} | | | | |
|---|---|---|---|---|---|
| | | 0 | 0.05 | 0.1 | 0.15 | 0.2 |
| Time ($\downarrow$) | AW-GBSVR | 4.921 ± 0.0 | 4.485 ± 0.68 | 8.749 ± 1.08 | 4.43 ± 1.489 | 4.407 ± 1.492 |
| | GBSVR | 7.298 ± 1.391 | 8.441 ± 1.896 | 8.913 ± 1.753 | 8.858 ± 0.96 | 8.729 ± 0.978 |
| | EnSVR | 14.307 ± 7.562 | 16.209 ± 9.281 | 19.485 ± 9.277 | 11.628 ± 2.716 | 11.622 ± 6.175 |
| | NuSVR | 37.262±0.179 | 37.798±0.23 | 37.558±0.425 | 40.393±1.299 | 37.534±0.235 |
| | SVR | 45.358±0.212 | 45.294±0.515 | 45.334±0.127 | 45.183±0.434 | 41.958±3.853 |
| R2 ($\downarrow$) | AW-GBSVR | 0.979 ± 0.0 | 0.98 ± 0.008 | 0.978 ± 0.008 | 0.976 ± 0.007 | 0.976 ± 0.011 |
| | GBSVR | 0.942 ± 0.018 | 0.948 ± 0.016 | 0.943 ± 0.021 | 0.945 ± 0.021 | 0.946 ± 0.017 |
| | EnSVR | 0.918 ± 0.024 | 0.915 ± 0.025 | 0.918 ± 0.023 | 0.918 ± 0.025 | 0.917 ± 0.026 |
| | NuSVR | 0.966±0.016 | 0.964±0.015 | 0.963±0.017 | 0.964±0.015 | 0.966±0.016 |
| | SVR | 0.939 ± 0.027 | 0.937 ± 0.027 | 0.936 ± 0.025 | 0.935 ± 0.028 | 0.933 ± 0.025 |
| MAE ($\downarrow$) | AW-GBSVR | 0.089 ± 0.0 | 0.095 ± 0.025 | 0.097 ± 0.024 | 0.099 ± 0.027 | 0.104 ± 0.027 |
| | GBSVR | 0.15 ± 0.029 | 0.152 ± 0.026 | 0.153 ± 0.035 | 0.154 ± 0.033 | 0.149 ± 0.021 |
| | EnSVR | 0.18 ± 0.03 | 0.184 ± 0.031 | 0.181 ± 0.028 | 0.18 ± 0.03 | 0.18 ± 0.03 |
| | NuSVR | 0.105±0.02 | 0.107±0.016 | 0.111±0.015 | 0.112±0.015 | 0.105±0.02 |
| | SVR | 0.123 ± 0.033 | 0.126 ± 0.033 | 0.128 ± 0.032 | 0.133 ± 0.037 | 0.141 ± 0.032 |
| RMSE ($\downarrow$) | AW-GBSVR | 0.142 ± 0.0 | 0.139 ± 0.088 | 0.145 ± 0.087 | 0.151 ± 0.081 | 0.152 ± 0.047 |
| | GBSVR | 0.233 ± 0.056 | 0.224 ± 0.05 | 0.23 ± 0.066 | 0.227 ± 0.062 | 0.225 ± 0.053 |
| | EnSVR | 0.281 ± 0.056 | 0.286 ± 0.056 | 0.281 ± 0.053 | 0.281 ± 0.059 | 0.283 ± 0.06 |
| | NuSVR | 0.179±0.052 | 0.185±0.049 | 0.186±0.052 | 0.184±0.046 | 0.179±0.052 |
| | SVR | 0.24 ± 0.075 | 0.245 ± 0.073 | 0.249 ± 0.071 | 0.249 ± 0.075 | 0.254 ± 0.069 |

**autompg**

| Metric | Methods | \multicolumn{5}{c}{Noise Percentage} | | | | |
|---|---|---|---|---|---|
| | | 0 | 0.05 | 0.1 | 0.15 | 0.2 |
| Time ($\downarrow$) | AW-GBSVR | 5.427 ± 1.0 | 5.727 ± 1.069 | 4.828 ± 1.748 | 4.495 ± 1.679 | 4.521 ± 2.109 |
| | GBSVR | 14.163 ± 0.627 | 14.264 ± 1.123 | 14.267 ± 0.982 | 14.759 ± 0.761 | 11.536 ± 1.099 |
| | EnSVR | 48.184 ± 25.005 | 56.717 ± 18.277 | 41.485 ± 17.732 | 61.401 ± 27.961 | 35.762 ± 11.459 |
| | NuSVR | 85.806±0.699 | 85.985±0.661 | 45.173±4.906 | 34.241±2.73 | 31.724±3.354 |
| | SVR | 85.144 ± 0.518 | 85.372 ± 0.779 | 83.715 ± 0.718 | 83.514 ± 0.511 | 85.378 ± 0.752 |
| R2 ($\downarrow$) | AW-GBSVR | 0.873 ± 0.0 | 0.877 ± 0.021 | 0.874 ± 0.029 | 0.874 ± 0.03 | 0.878 ± 0.018 |
| | GBSVR | 0.852 ± 0.016 | 0.865 ± 0.03 | 0.864 ± 0.021 | 0.868 ± 0.018 | 0.858 ± 0.026 |
| | EnSVR | 0.857 ± 0.035 | 0.856 ± 0.033 | 0.854 ± 0.037 | 0.859 ± 0.029 | 0.857 ± 0.035 |
| | NuSVR | 0.812±0.028 | 0.81±0.028 | 0.817±0.033 | 0.817±0.031 | 0.802±0.034 |
| | SVR | 0.789 ± 0.026 | 0.788 ± 0.032 | 0.792 ± 0.025 | 0.791 ± 0.03 | 0.788 ± 0.015 |
| MAE ($\downarrow$) | AW-GBSVR | 0.257 ± 0.0 | 0.253 ± 0.04 | 0.258 ± 0.044 | 0.256 ± 0.048 | 0.253 ± 0.038 |
| | GBSVR | 0.272 ± 0.023 | 0.259 ± 0.031 | 0.265 ± 0.016 | 0.261 ± 0.033 | 0.275 ± 0.02 |
| | EnSVR | 0.269 ± 0.051 | 0.269 ± 0.05 | 0.27 ± 0.053 | 0.266 ± 0.045 | 0.269 ± 0.051 |
| | NuSVR | 0.347±0.029 | 0.35±0.028 | 0.311±0.03 | 0.309±0.047 | 0.311±0.033 |
| | SVR | 0.373 ± 0.035 | 0.374 ± 0.036 | 0.371 ± 0.027 | 0.369 ± 0.02 | 0.374 ± 0.025 |
| RMSE ($\downarrow$) | AW-GBSVR | 0.352 ± 0.0 | 0.347 ± 0.046 | 0.351 ± 0.059 | 0.352 ± 0.061 | 0.346 ± 0.039 |
| | GBSVR | 0.381 ± 0.039 | 0.363 ± 0.048 | 0.365 ± 0.037 | 0.36 ± 0.042 | 0.373 ± 0.042 |
| | EnSVR | 0.376 ± 0.07 | 0.377 ± 0.068 | 0.379 ± 0.072 | 0.373 ± 0.062 | 0.375 ± 0.069 |
| | NuSVR | 0.429±0.041 | 0.432±0.04 | 0.424±0.054 | 0.425±0.063 | 0.441±0.061 |
| | SVR | 0.455 ± 0.043 | 0.456 ± 0.045 | 0.452 ± 0.04 | 0.451 ± 0.031 | 0.457 ± 0.035 |

**autos**

| Metric | Methods | \multicolumn{5}{c}{Noise Percentage} | | | | |
|---|---|---|---|---|---|
| | | 0 | 0.05 | 0.1 | 0.15 | 0.2 |
| Time ($\downarrow$) | AW-GBSVR | 1.35 ± 0.0 | 1.222 ± 0.352 | 1.404 ± 0.269 | 0.963 ± 0.412 | 1.165 ± 0.41 |
| | GBSVR | 0.23 ± 0.075 | 0.269 ± 0.06 | 0.289 ± 0.067 | 0.265 ± 0.089 | 0.296 ± 0.048 |
| | EnSVR | 2.015 ± 0.156 | 2.985 ± 1.545 | 2.324 ± 0.329 | 2.266 ± 0.437 | 2.193 ± 0.193 |
| | NuSVR | 8.464±0.559 | 8.401±0.45 | 8.276±0.765 | 8.438±0.589 | 8.564±0.549 |
| | SVR | 9.514 ± 0.455 | 9.633 ± 0.491 | 9.726 ± 0.461 | 9.503 ± 0.454 | 9.55 ± 0.454 |
| R2 ($\downarrow$) | AW-GBSVR | 0.896 ± 0.0 | 0.888 ± 0.039 | 0.88 ± 0.025 | 0.892 ± 0.016 | 0.888 ± 0.026 |
| | GBSVR | 0.857 ± 0.045 | 0.855 ± 0.047 | 0.854 ± 0.049 | 0.855 ± 0.045 | 0.86 ± 0.041 |
| | EnSVR | 0.858 ± 0.035 | 0.85 ± 0.047 | 0.837 ± 0.052 | 0.854 ± 0.039 | 0.86 ± 0.028 |
| | NuSVR | 0.839±0.035 | 0.845±0.033 | 0.829±0.047 | 0.824±0.05 | 0.835±0.052 |
| | SVR | 0.842 ± 0.044 | 0.85 ± 0.047 | 0.829 ± 0.054 | 0.842 ± 0.066 | 0.855 ± 0.057 |
| MAE ($\downarrow$) | AW-GBSVR | 0.259 ± 0.0 | 0.261 ± 0.015 | 0.276 ± 0.02 | 0.266 ± 0.03 | 0.252 ± 0.025 |
| | GBSVR | 0.275 ± 0.044 | 0.28 ± 0.041 | 0.276 ± 0.037 | 0.269 ± 0.038 | 0.285 ± 0.053 |
| | EnSVR | 0.268 ± 0.037 | 0.293 ± 0.028 | 0.301 ± 0.046 | 0.287 ± 0.048 | 0.282 ± 0.036 |
| | NuSVR | 0.285±0.039 | 0.286±0.046 | 0.292±0.042 | 0.301±0.041 | 0.284±0.046 |
| | SVR | 0.288 ± 0.025 | 0.277 ± 0.025 | 0.294 ± 0.021 | 0.283 ± 0.043 | 0.28 ± 0.026 |
| RMSE ($\downarrow$) | AW-GBSVR | 0.311 ± 0.0 | 0.317 ± 0.012 | 0.335 ± 0.025 | 0.319 ± 0.028 | 0.322 ± 0.02 |
| | GBSVR | 0.358 ± 0.048 | 0.36 ± 0.053 | 0.362 ± 0.047 | 0.361 ± 0.052 | 0.361 ± 0.062 |
| | EnSVR | 0.362 ± 0.042 | 0.368 ± 0.033 | 0.389 ± 0.076 | 0.37 ± 0.067 | 0.364 ± 0.051 |
| | NuSVR | 0.391±0.065 | 0.384±0.068 | 0.397±0.056 | 0.404±0.064 | 0.394±0.086 |
| | SVR | 0.38 ± 0.032 | 0.369 ± 0.028 | 0.394 ± 0.025 | 0.373 ± 0.063 | 0.358 ± 0.026 |

**machine**

| Metric | Methods | \multicolumn{5}{c}{Noise Percentage} | | | | |
|---|---|---|---|---|---|
| | | 0 | 0.05 | 0.1 | 0.15 | 0.2 |
| Time ($\downarrow$) | AW-GBSVR | 2.051 ± 0.0 | 2.47 ± 0.306 | 2.498 ± 0.17 | 2.204 ± 0.423 | 1.826 ± 0.641 |
| | GBSVR | 3.025 ± 0.249 | 2.926 ± 0.228 | 3.097 ± 0.354 | 3.063 ± 0.21 | 3.096 ± 0.441 |
| | EnSVR | 6.489 ± 2.357 | 7.118 ± 1.903 | 7.672 ± 3.372 | 4.649 ± 1.819 | 8.866 ± 2.1 |
| | NuSVR | 17.222±0.269 | 17.12±0.297 | 17.165±0.261 | 17.2±0.248 | 17.13±0.301 |
| | SVR | 16.981 ± 0.328 | 16.939 ± 0.386 | 16.955 ± 0.302 | 16.904 ± 0.25 | 16.89 ± 0.263 |
| R2 ($\downarrow$) | AW-GBSVR | 0.849 ± 0.0 | 0.847 ± 0.02 | 0.845 ± 0.022 | 0.844 ± 0.017 | 0.851 ± 0.017 |
| | GBSVR | 0.83 ± 0.015 | 0.818 ± 0.015 | 0.822 ± 0.02 | 0.822 ± 0.019 | 0.825 ± 0.017 |
| | EnSVR | 0.811 ± 0.02 | 0.812 ± 0.019 | 0.809 ± 0.022 | 0.814 ± 0.02 | 0.81 ± 0.019 |
| | NuSVR | 0.746±0.035 | 0.748±0.036 | 0.753±0.037 | 0.749±0.036 | 0.747±0.034 |
| | SVR | 0.744 ± 0.065 | 0.755 ± 0.042 | 0.73 ± 0.075 | 0.762 ± 0.043 | 0.752 ± 0.059 |
| MAE ($\downarrow$) | AW-GBSVR | 0.301 ± 0.0 | 0.302 ± 0.024 | 0.303 ± 0.02 | 0.305 ± 0.026 | 0.294 ± 0.028 |
| | GBSVR | 0.317 ± 0.024 | 0.326 ± 0.033 | 0.318 ± 0.02 | 0.316 ± 0.025 | 0.318 ± 0.021 |
| | EnSVR | 0.328 ± 0.021 | 0.328 ± 0.021 | 0.329 ± 0.021 | 0.326 ± 0.021 | 0.329 ± 0.021 |
| | NuSVR | 0.392±0.033 | 0.392±0.033 | 0.39±0.037 | 0.392±0.036 | 0.389±0.036 |
| | SVR | 0.376 ± 0.071 | 0.378 ± 0.054 | 0.382 ± 0.067 | 0.371 ± 0.061 | 0.369 ± 0.066 |
| RMSE ($\downarrow$) | AW-GBSVR | 0.384 ± 0.0 | 0.388 ± 0.029 | 0.388 ± 0.029 | 0.391 ± 0.038 | 0.381 ± 0.036 |
| | GBSVR | 0.407 ± 0.027 | 0.419 ± 0.039 | 0.414 ± 0.013 | 0.416 ± 0.028 | 0.411 ± 0.02 |
| | EnSVR | 0.428 ± 0.019 | 0.426 ± 0.019 | 0.431 ± 0.021 | 0.425 ± 0.018 | 0.429 ± 0.019 |
| | NuSVR | 0.496±0.031 | 0.494±0.03 | 0.489±0.036 | 0.493±0.033 | 0.495±0.033 |
| | SVR | 0.499 ± 0.091 | 0.488 ± 0.063 | 0.513 ± 0.1 | 0.483 ± 0.069 | 0.492 ± 0.088 |

**Real Estate Valuation**

| Metric | Methods | \multicolumn{5}{c}{Noise Percentage} | | | | |
|---|---|---|---|---|---|
| | | 0 | 0.05 | 0.1 | 0.15 | 0.2 |
| Time ($\downarrow$) | AW-GBSVR | 12.739 ± 5.0 | 12.34 ± 4.069 | 9.647 ± 3.884 | 13.626 ± 2.489 | 12.907 ± 3.697 |
| | GBSVR | 15.95 ± 1.957 | 16.219 ± 1.752 | 15.351 ± 1.461 | 14.875 ± 2.149 | 14.28 ± 2.043 |
| | EnSVR | 46.696 ± 23.882 | 43.591 ± 16.978 | 45.083 ± 16.151 | 39.257 ± 32.695 | 31.72 ± 17.622 |
| | NuSVR | 93.068±1.192 | 92.017±1.501 | 91.805±0.768 | 94.193±1.282 | 91.832±0.746 |
| | SVR | 99.663 ± 1.265 | 97.522 ± 0.813 | 97.972 ± 0.599 | 97.606 ± 0.649 | 96.351 ± 0.931 |
| R2 ($\downarrow$) | AW-GBSVR | 0.655 ± 0.0 | 0.65 ± 0.071 | 0.645 ± 0.067 | 0.647 ± 0.067 | 0.654 ± 0.072 |
| | GBSVR | 0.637 ± 0.064 | 0.634 ± 0.066 | 0.632 ± 0.066 | 0.635 ± 0.065 | 0.631 ± 0.063 |
| | EnSVR | 0.636 ± 0.065 | 0.638 ± 0.066 | 0.635 ± 0.066 | 0.641 ± 0.063 | 0.635 ± 0.061 |
| | NuSVR | 0.548±0.061 | 0.557±0.071 | 0.54±0.065 | 0.553±0.059 | 0.53±0.06 |
| | SVR | 0.542 ± 0.059 | 0.553 ± 0.066 | 0.543 ± 0.06 | 0.538 ± 0.061 | 0.542 ± 0.07 |
| MAE ($\downarrow$) | AW-GBSVR | 0.404 ± 0.0 | 0.409 ± 0.038 | 0.408 ± 0.037 | 0.411 ± 0.033 | 0.4 ± 0.033 |
| | GBSVR | 0.398 ± 0.028 | 0.398 ± 0.029 | 0.4 ± 0.026 | 0.401 ± 0.03 | 0.398 ± 0.027 |
| | EnSVR | 0.398 ± 0.031 | 0.394 ± 0.032 | 0.4 ± 0.03 | 0.393 ± 0.032 | 0.399 ± 0.027 |
| | NuSVR | 0.5±0.034 | 0.495±0.04 | 0.504±0.038 | 0.498±0.03 | 0.511±0.036 |
| | SVR | 0.503 ± 0.035 | 0.495 ± 0.035 | 0.503 ± 0.034 | 0.51 ± 0.03 | 0.509 ± 0.039 |
| RMSE ($\downarrow$) | AW-GBSVR | 0.583 ± 0.0 | 0.587 ± 0.095 | 0.592 ± 0.092 | 0.59 ± 0.093 | 0.584 ± 0.097 |
| | GBSVR | 0.596 ± 0.089 | 0.6 ± 0.092 | 0.602 ± 0.092 | 0.6 ± 0.09 | 0.603 ± 0.088 |
| | EnSVR | 0.599 ± 0.09 | 0.596 ± 0.091 | 0.6 ± 0.092 | 0.595 ± 0.088 | 0.6 ± 0.087 |
| | NuSVR | 0.666±0.069 | 0.659±0.075 | 0.672±0.075 | 0.663±0.069 | 0.68±0.07 |
| | SVR | 0.571 ± 0.069 | 0.662 ± 0.071 | 0.67 ± 0.07 | 0.673 ± 0.066 | 0.67 ± 0.078 |

# 5   Conclusion

The proposed AW-GBSVR framework improves SVR by integrating granular ball computing with adaptive margins and weighted optimization. The adaptive margin $\epsilon$ adapts with each ball's radius $r$, allowing wider margins for robustness in noisy regions and tighter ones for precision in dense regions. Weights $m$ in optimization enables smaller, denser balls to improve generalization and reduce overfitting. AW-GBSVR also retains key benefits of granular balls, including lower computational cost and better outlier handling, making it a robust and efficient alternative to standard SVR.

# References


1. Chuang, C.C., Su, S.F., Jeng, J.T., Hsiao, C.C.: Robust support vector regression networks for function approximation with outliers. IEEE Trans. Neural Netw. **13**(6), 1322–1330 (2002)
2. Fu, S., Tian, Y., Tang, L.: Robust regression under the general framework of bounded loss functions. Eur. J. Oper. Res. **310**(3), 1325–1339 (2023)
3. Ho, C.H., Lin, C.J.: Large-scale linear support vector regression. J. Mach. Learn. Res. **13**(1), 3323–3348 (2012)
4. Kelly, M., Longjohn, R., Nottingham, K.: The uci machine learning repository (2025). https://archive.ics.uci.edu. Accessed 28 Feb 2025
5. Rastogi, R., Bisht, A., Kumar, S., Chandra, S.: Gbsvr: granular ball support vector regression. arXiv preprint arXiv:2503.10539 (2025)
6. Sabzekar, M., Hasheminejad, S.M.H.: Robust regression using support vector regressions. Chaos Solitons Fractals **144**, 110738 (2021)
7. Shao, Y., Hua, Y., Gong, Z., Zhu, X., Cheng, Y., Li, L., Xia, S.: Con-mgsvm: controllable multi-granularity support vector algorithm for classification and regression. Information Fusion **117**, 102867 (2025)
8. Smola, A.J., Schölkopf, B.: A tutorial on support vector regression. Stat. Comput. **14**, 199–222 (2004)
9. Williamson, R., Bartlett, P., et al.: New support vector algorithms. Neural Comput. **12**, 1207–1245 (2000)
10. Yang, M., Liang, H., Wu, X., Zhang, Z.: A flexible and efficient algorithm for high dimensional support vector regression. Neurocomputing **611**, 128671 (2025)
11. Ye, Y., Gao, J., Shao, Y., Li, C., Jin, Y., Hua, X.: Robust support vector regression with generic quadratic nonconvex $\varepsilon$-insensitive loss. Appl. Math. Model. **82**, 235–251 (2020)
12. Yong, Q., Jie, Y., Lixiu, Y., Chenzhou, Y.: An improved way to make large-scale svr learning practical. EURASIP J. Adv. Signal Process. **2004**, 1–7 (2004)
13. Zhou, X., Ma, Y.: A study on smo algorithm for solving epsilon-svr with non-psd kernels. Commun. Stat.-Simul. Comput. **42**(10), 2175–2196 (2013)

# A Hybrid Detectron2 and Graph Attention Network for Sleep Posture Classification Using Images

Dubacharla Gyaneshwar[✉] and Naman Vikram

Indian Institute of Information Technology, Raichur, Karnataka, India
{dgyaneshwar,cs21b1015}@iiitr.ac.in

**Abstract.** Monitoring sleep posture plays an important role in identifying sleep related issues, minimizing pressure related injuries, and improving comfort for patients. Traditional wearable-based systems often disrupt sleep and reduce comfort. This paper presents a non-intrusive, vision-based framework that combines Detectron2 for keypoint detection with a Graph Attention Network (GAT) for sleep posture classification. A custom dataset of four sleep postures—supine, prone, left lateral, and right lateral—was created, annotated with 17 COCO-format keypoints. Detectron2 extracts high-confidence human keypoints, which are structured into skeleton graphs using anatomical connectivity. These graphs are input into a three-layer GAT architecture with attention mechanisms, residual connections, and normalization to model spatial relationships between joints. Unlike traditional approaches that rely on handcrafted features, our method learns representations directly from keypoint coordinates, enhancing generalization and reducing manual intervention. Extensive experiments using 10-fold cross-validation and an unseen test set of 1,400 images demonstrate an overall classification accuracy of 98.57%. The framework remains robust under occlusion, lighting variations, and static poses, making it practical for deployment in real-world clinical and home settings.

**Keywords:** Sleep posture recognition · Detectron2 · Graph Attention Networks · Computer Vision · Healthcare monitoring · Pose estimation

## 1 Introduction

Sleep posture plays a crucial role in various health conditions, including pressure ulcers, obstructive sleep apnea, and musculoskeletal discomfort. Traditional monitoring techniques such as polysomnography and wearable sensors are often intrusive, expensive, and may interfere with natural sleep behavior.

Recent advances in computer vision have enabled markerless, non-contact monitoring systems. However, these approaches face challenges such as low-light environments, occlusions from bedding, and minimal subject movement


S. Mitra et al. (Eds.): PReMI 2025, LNCS 16358, pp. 621–628, 2026.
https://doi.org/10.1007/978-3-032-18480-1_63

during sleep. Recent pose estimation tools, such as Detectron2 [10], achieve reliable keypoint localization despite challenges like occlusion and lighting variation. Simultaneously, Graph Neural Networks (GNNs), particularly Graph Attention Networks (GATs) [9], are effective in modeling spatial relationships in structured data such as human skeletons.

In this paper, we propose a vision-based sleep posture classification framework that combines Detectron2 for keypoint extraction with a multi-layer GAT for spatial reasoning. This allows for robust classification across four common sleep postures without requiring any physical sensors.

Our key contributions include: (1) A Detectron2-based keypoint extraction pipeline selecting the most confident human detection per frame. (2) Skeletal graph representation using COCO-format keypoints processed via a three-layer GAT. (3) A graph-based attention model trained end-to-end on raw coordinates, enabling high accuracy and interpretability without handcrafted features.

## 2    Related Works

Traditional wearable-based systems, such as those using gyroscopes and pressure sensors [13], provide decent accuracy but disrupt comfort and suffer from issues like sensor misalignment. Pressure imaging [12] and ballistocardiogram-based methods [11] also show promise but require expensive or noise-sensitive hardware.

Early vision-based methods include Ye et al. [7] (segmentation with BP neural networks), Yang et al. [9] (OpenPose-based joint detection), and Lyu and Tian [10] (skeleton-based BP neural networks). While these improved recognition compared to handcrafted features, they struggled with occlusion and lacked spatial reasoning across joints.

More recent work emphasizes robustness and multimodal sensing. Khan et al. [3] combined RGB and thermal data for six postures, achieving 96–99% accuracy under blanket conditions. Hoang et al. [2] benchmarked CNN-based vision methods, reporting 93.5% accuracy on a five-class dataset. Tam et al. [8] used depth cameras with anatomical landmark guidance, reaching an F1-score of 92.2%. Adhikari et al. [1] and Liu et al. [6] demonstrated radar and RF-based skeleton estimation as privacy-preserving alternatives. A review by Li [4] highlights bedding occlusion as a key challenge, motivating skeleton-aware and graph-based approaches such as ours.

## 3    Dataset and Preprocessing

### 3.1    Dataset Overview

We constructed a custom dataset by recording overhead 4K video (30 FPS) of 8 adult volunteers (ages 18–30) assuming four sleep postures *supine, prone, left lateral,* and *right lateral* under varied indoor conditions (lighting, bedding, clothing). From these sessions, 8,200 frames were extracted. After removing low-confidence detections and duplicates, we retained 4,855 high-quality annotated images with full-body coverage. The dataset was manually labeled and approximately balanced across the four classes: 1,265 supine, 1,215 prone, 1,190 left lateral, and 1,185 right lateral images. Informed consent was obtained from all participants. Figure 1 shows representative examples for each posture.

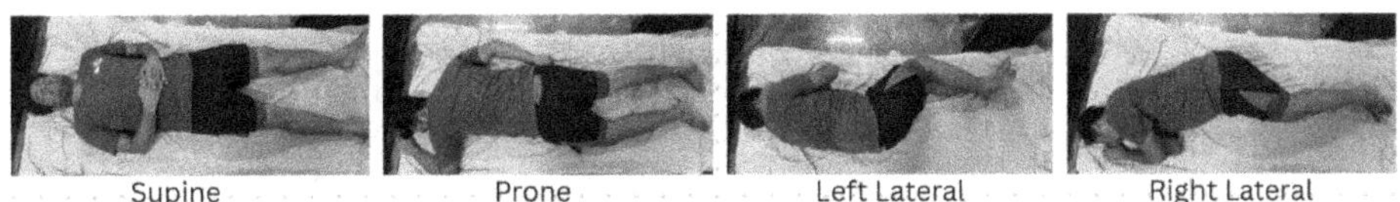


**Fig. 1.** Sample annotated images for each sleep posture class.

## 3.2   Preprocessing Pipeline

To ensure high-quality input to the classification model, each image was processed through the following pipeline:

- **Human Detection and Keypoint Estimation:** Detectron2 was employed to detect persons in each frame, and only the most confident detection (i.e., highest probability bounding box) was retained. For that bounding box, 17 COCO-format skeletal keypoints were extracted using a pose estimation model [5]. Keypoints included major joints (shoulders, elbows, hips, knees, ankles, etc.) while excluding face, hands, and feet to improve robustness to occlusion.
- **Best Skeleton Selection:** In frames where multiple people were detected (e.g., due to shadows or overlapping objects), only the skeleton with the highest average keypoint confidence was retained to ensure reliable graph construction.
- **Graph Construction:** A graph was constructed for each image, treating each keypoint as a node and connecting them using anatomical edges defined by the COCO standard. These graphs served as input to the Graph Attention Network (GAT) model.
- **Coordinate Normalization and Resizing:** The keypoint coordinates were scaled to the $[0, 1]$ range relative to a fixed image resolution of $1280 \times 1280$ to ensure spatial consistency and invariance to resolution changes. Images were resized to $1280 \times 1280$ with aspect ratio preserved by zero-padding where necessary to avoid distortion.

## 4   Methodology

Our proposed framework consists of two stages: (1) a training pipeline that learns spatial representations of sleep postures using graph-structured keypoint data, and (2) an inference pipeline that classifies postures in unseen images using a trained Graph Attention Network (GAT), as illustrated in Fig. 2.

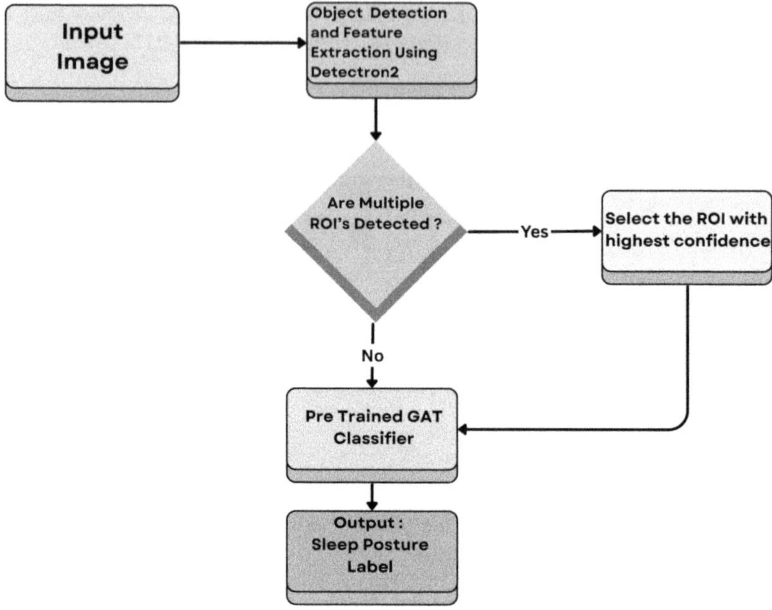


**Fig. 2.** Overview of the proposed Detectron2 + GAT pipeline.

## 4.1  Keypoint-Based Graph Construction

Each image is processed using Detectron2 for person detection and 17-keypoint pose estimation (based on the COCO format). To handle multiple detections, we retain only the most confident skeleton per frame. The extracted 2D keypoints $(x_i, y_i)$ are normalized using Z-score normalization:

$$\tilde{k}_i = \frac{k_i - \mu}{\sigma + \epsilon}$$

where $\mu$ and $\sigma$ are the mean and standard deviation of all keypoints, and $\epsilon$ avoids division by zero. These normalized keypoints define nodes in a graph $G = (V, E)$, where $V \in \mathbb{R}^{17 \times 2}$ and $E$ represents anatomical connections based on COCO (Fig. 3).

## 4.2  Graph-Based Posture Learning

The graph is input to a three-layer GAT model with multi-head attention, followed by Batch Normalization, residual connections, and global mean pooling. The final fully connected head predicts one of four posture classes: *supine*, *prone*, *left lateral*, or *right lateral*. GAT assigns attention weights between joints, allowing the model to focus on informative keypoints. The attention coefficient between node $i$ and neighbor $j$ is given by:

$$\alpha_{ij} = \frac{\exp\left(\text{LeakyReLU}(\mathbf{a}^T[\mathbf{Wh}_i \| \mathbf{Wh}_j])\right)}{\sum_{k \in \mathcal{N}_i} \exp\left(\text{LeakyReLU}(\mathbf{a}^T[\mathbf{Wh}_i \| \mathbf{Wh}_k])\right)}$$

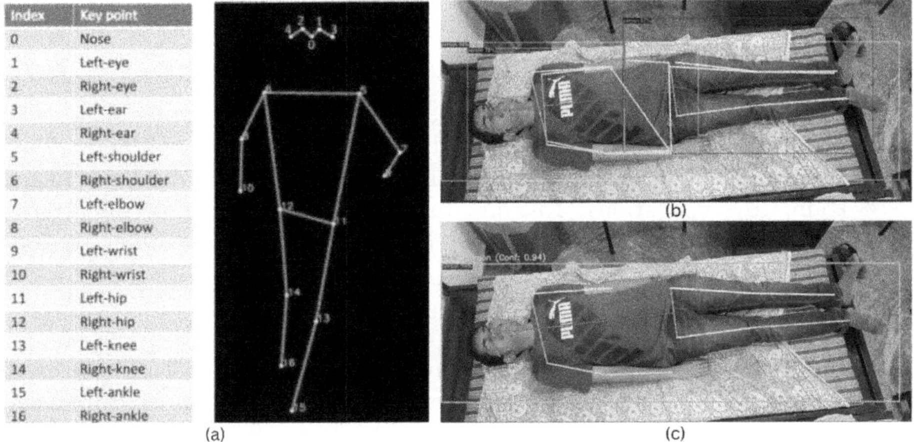



**Fig. 3.** Keypoint detection and graph input construction. (a) COCO keypoints; (b) Multiple detections; (c) Highest-confidence skeleton used.

where $\mathbf{W}$ is a shared linear transform, $\mathbf{a}$ is the attention vector, and $\|$ denotes concatenation.

The model is trained using cross-entropy loss on labeled graph–posture pairs $(G_i, y_i)$, with data augmentation (e.g., rotations, brightness change, occlusion simulation) to enhance generalization.

## 4.3   Inference Pipeline

During inference, the same Detectron2-based pipeline extracts keypoints, normalizes them, and forms a graph, which is then fed into the trained GAT. The model outputs class logits, which are passed through softmax to produce the predicted posture. The system runs in real time on CPU and remains robust under occlusion and ambiguous poses.

## 4.4   Model Architecture Summary

- **Input:** 17 keypoints with 2D coordinates per node.
- **GATConv Layers:** 3 layers with 8-head attention; hidden channels: 128.
- **Normalization:** BatchNorm + ReLU after each GAT layer.
- **Residuals:** Linear skip connections.
- **Dropout:** $p = 0.5$ before pooling.
- **Pooling:** Global mean pooling to obtain graph-level features.
- **Classification:** Fully connected head with softmax output for 4 classes.

# 5  Results and Discussion

## 5.1  Evaluation Metrics

We assess model performance using standard metrics: accuracy, precision, recall, and F1-score. Metrics are reported per class—*Supine, Prone, Left Lateral,* and *Right Lateral*—under a 10-fold stratified cross-validation on 4,855 labeled images (90% train, 10% validation). To evaluate generalization, we also tested on an unseen dataset of 1,400 images (350 per class) from separate recording sessions.

## 5.2  Performance Evaluation

Table 1 presents the test-set classification results, where the model achieves excellent precision and recall across all postures. Fold-wise accuracies in Table 2 confirm consistent generalization, ranging from 99.17% to 99.79% (Table 3).

**Table 1.** Classification report on the unseen test set (1,400 images).

| Class | Precision | Recall | F1-score | Support |
|---|---|---|---|---|
| Right Lateral | 0.99 | 1.00 | 1.00 | 350 |
| Left Lateral | 0.96 | 0.99 | 0.97 | 350 |
| Prone | 0.99 | 0.95 | 0.97 | 350 |
| Supine | 1.00 | 1.00 | 1.00 | 350 |
| **Accuracy** | **98.57%** | | | |

**Table 2.** Fold-wise accuracy from 10-fold cross-validation.

| Fold | 1 | 2 | 3 | 4 | 5 | 6 | 7 | 8 | 9 | 10 |
|---|---|---|---|---|---|---|---|---|---|---|
| **Accuracy (%)** | 99.38 | 99.79 | 99.18 | 99.18 | 99.79 | 99.79 | 99.17 | 99.17 | 99.79 | 99.79 |

**Table 3.** Comparison with recent state-of-the-art methods (2022–2025).

| Method | Modality | Classes | Dataset/Subjects | Reported Acc./F1 |
|---|---|---|---|---|
| Khan et al. (2024) [3] | RGB + Thermal | 6 | 10 subjects | 96–99% acc. |
| Hoang et al. (2025) [2] | RGB images (CNN) | 5 | 13 subjects | 93.5% acc. |
| Tam et al. (2022) [8] | Depth + Landmarks | 7 | Blanket conditions | 92.2% F1 |
| Adhikari et al. (2024) [6] | mmWave radar | 4 | Simulated subjects | High posture acc. |
| Liu et al. (2024) [4] | RF 3D skeleton | 4+ | RF sensing setup | Low MPJPE + posture acc. |
| **Ours** | RGB keypoints + GAT | 4 | 8 subjects, 4,855 images | **98.57% acc.** |

## 5.3   Discussion

The proposed Detectron2+GAT pipeline outperforms baseline methods in both accuracy and robustness, accurately inferring posture even with partial keypoint visibility or occlusions.

Compared to CNNs and BP Neural Networks with handcrafted features, our approach offers: (1) Data efficiency: Graph-based representation captures essential structural relations without full-body visibility.(2) Strong generalization: Consistently high performance on unseen data.(3) Practical deployment: Fast CPU inference enables use in clinical or home settings.

Without explicit temporal modeling, the system still effectively handles static and occluded poses, demonstrating that GAT-based spatial reasoning is sufficient for frame-level posture classification.

# 6   Conclusion

This paper introduces a robust, non-intrusive framework for sleep posture classification that combines Detectron2-based keypoint detection with a Graph Attention Network (GAT) for spatial reasoning. Unlike traditional wearable systems, our approach uses only overhead camera input and 2D pose estimation, enabling unobtrusive monitoring in real-world settings.

By converting 17 COCO-format keypoints into skeletal graphs and classifying them using GAT, the system effectively models body structure and achieves high accuracy (98.57%) across four common postures—even with partial occlusion.

The model generalizes well to unseen data and runs efficiently on CPU, supporting practical deployment in home and clinical environments. Future work may include integrating temporal information, multi-person scenarios, and 3D keypoints to further improve performance.

**Acknowledgment.** This work is supported by the Indian Institute of Information Technology (IIIT), Raichur, Karnataka.

# References


1. Adhikari, B., et al.: Misleep: mmwave-based sleep posture recognition with deep learning. ACM IMWUT (2024)
2. Hoang, D.T., et al.: Benchmarking accelerometer and vision-based methods for sleep posture recognition. Comput. Biol. Med. (2025)
3. Khan, M.A., et al.: Multimodal sleep posture recognition using synchronized rgb and thermal video. IEEE Access (2024)
4. Li, X.: A review of machine learning approaches for sleep posture recognition. IEEE Access (2023)
5. Lin, T., et al.: Microsoft COCO: common objects in context. In: European Conference on Computer Vision (ECCV), pp. 740–755 (2014). https://arxiv.org/abs/1405.0312

6. Liu, Y., et al.: Tagsleep3d: rf-based 3d skeleton and sleep posture recognition. IEEE Trans. Mob. Comput. (2024)
7. Lyu, H., Tian, J.: Skeleton-based sleep posture recognition with bp neural network. In: Proceedings of the 2020 IEEE 3rd International Conference on Computer and Communication Engineering Technology (CCET), pp. 263–267. IEEE (2020). https://doi.org/10.1109/CCET50901.2020.9213125
8. Tam, T., et al.: Sleep posture classification under blanket using depth cameras and anatomical landmarks. IEEE Trans. Instrum. Meas. (2022)
9. Veličković, P., Cucurull, G., Casanova, A., Romero, A., Liò, P., Bengio, Y.: Graph attention networks. In: International Conference on Learning Representations (ICLR) (2018). https://arxiv.org/abs/1710.10903
10. Wu, Y., Kirillov, A., Massa, F., Lo, W., Girshick, R.: Detectron2 (2019). https://github.com/facebookresearch/detectron2
11. Yang, M., Li, J., Guo, R., Tang, X.: Implementation and research of human sleep posture recognition based on openpose. Phys. Exp. (8) (2019)
12. Ye, Y.: Research on sleep posture recognition system based on computer vision. Ph.D. thesis, Anhui University of Technology (2013)
13. Zhang, Y., Yang, Z., Shi, X.: Sleep position recognition based on ballistocardiogram signal. Comput. Eng. Appl. (2018)

# Comparative Study of Hindi Handwriting Features in Machine Learning-Based Personality Analysis

Parth Bhatnagar[1]([⊠]) and Manjit Sodhi[2]

[1] Manipal Institute of Technology Bengaluru, Bengaluru, Karnataka, India
parth.bhatnagar06@gmail.com
[2] IBM, Bengaluru, Karnataka, India
smanjit@in.ibm.com

**Abstract.** Graphology is a field that aims to identify, evaluate, and interpret human personality traits by analysing handwriting strokes and patterns. Handwriting can reveal various aspects of a person's character, including emotional tendencies, fears, honesty, defences, and other personality attributes. Professional handwriting analysts, known as graphologists, are trained to interpret these patterns and can often deduce significant insights about the writer. However, the reliability of such analyses heavily depends on the analyst's expertise and subjective interpretation.

This study introduces IBM WatsonX implementation in predicting eight distinct personality traits based on handwriting features. The algorithms applied are (i) LGBM Classifier, (ii) XGB Classifier, (iii) Decision Tree Classifier, and (iv) Snap Logistic Regression. These methods are evaluated using various performance metrics, including the ROC curve, confusion matrix, and additional accuracy measures. The findings offer valuable insights, and key observations are discussed based on the performance of each algorithm.

**Keywords:** Graphology · IBM WatsonX · Machine Learning · Pattern recognition

## 1 Introduction

Graphology can refer to various concepts, but it is typically understood as the study of handwriting to uncover potential connections to a person's mind. This field operates on the premise that handwriting reveals elements of personality, emotional states, and behaviour. Although some enthusiasts and practitioners endorse graphology for its insights into character, psychological conditions, and even truthfulness, a few also link handwriting features to traits such as sombre psychological states. However, the broader academic community largely regards graphology as pseudoscience. Figure 1 shows the idea of Graphology.

Integrating machine learning with graphology introduces objectivity, scalability, and data-driven analysis to handwriting interpretation. Traditionally, graphological assessments depend on subjective judgment, whereas machine learning offers a systematic


S. Mitra et al. (Eds.): PReMI 2025, LNCS 16358, pp. 629–638, 2026.
https://doi.org/10.1007/978-3-032-18480-1_64

**Fig. 1.** Graphology Technique

approach to making predictions using large datasets, enabling analysis beyond what the human eye can observe. Automated feature extraction (such as slope, pressure, spacing, and stroke consistency) facilitates fast, precise evaluations, significantly reducing human error and bias while broadening the reach of handwriting analysis.

This research paper is structured into distinct sections to thoroughly explore the topic. Section 1 outlines the motivation and introduces the study's framework. Section 2 covers a literature review and survey of prior work, identifying gaps or limitations in the research. Section 3 explains the methodology for developing and testing the machine learning models. Section 4 discusses the results and their implications. Finally, Sect. 5 summarizes the findings, emphasizing future potential for advancing machine learning in graphology.

## 2  Literature Survey

Handwriting analysis has a rich history in personality assessment, serving as a non-invasive method to infer individual traits. In recent years, advancements in artificial intelligence (AI) and machine learning (ML) have led to novel approaches that apply deep learning to handwriting and personality prediction. Early studies introduced feature-based analysis, where specific handwriting characteristics, such as slant and pressure, were linked to psychological attributes [1, 2]. These studies established foundational principles correlating handwriting with behavioural tendencies, paving the way for computational approaches.

More recent works have applied Convolutional Neural Networks (CNNs) to handwriting recognition and personality prediction, demonstrating the effectiveness of CNNs in visual feature extraction. These models achieved significant success in extracting distinct personality traits from handwriting [3, 4]. Some studies expanded this by using multimodal fusion, combining visual features with structural handwriting characteristics for improved trait prediction [5]. This approach has been particularly effective in refining personality predictions and in reducing ambiguity in traits with overlapping characteristics.

Techniques like Optical Character Recognition (OCR) have also enhanced segmentation accuracy in handwriting analysis. OCR, integrated with machine learning pipelines, has been instrumental in isolating character-level features that contribute to personality assessment models [6]. Further studies employed multi-label classification techniques, addressing the complexity of predicting multiple personality traits simultaneously [7]. This approach supports the growing interest in understanding nuanced trait patterns, as personality is rarely represented by a single characteristic.

Finally, advanced models have explored the use of data augmentation to improve generalization across diverse handwriting samples, leading to more robust and adaptable models. Data augmentation, combined with adaptive learning algorithms, has shown promising results in capturing varied writing styles across demographics, enhancing model accuracy and reliability [8].

In [9] research Analysis of prediction of football player ratings through the application of diverse machine learning algorithms. Rating systems for sports teams have gathered considerable attention in academic research. The approach used by the authors of this paper serves as an effort to streamline scouts and performance analytics.

The research [10] explores machine learning techniques, such as voting regressors, gradient boosting regressors, random forest regressors, decision tree regressors, and support vector regressors, for car predicting the car price. Each machine learning technique has its own unique advantages and disadvantages, with the voting regressor exhibiting the best results.

This research delves into the realm of Electric Vehicles (EVs), with a primary focus on alleviating range anxiety - a persistent concern among EV owners [11]. Through an extensive survey among EV owners, we have identified key challenges, including the lack of real-time information, worries about charging infrastructure, and the desire for community engagement.

This research investigates upon the prediction of mobile phone prices based on various factors through the applications of multiple machine learning algorithms [12]. Leveraging linear regression, decision tree regressor, random forest regressor, gradient boosting regressor, voting regressor and support vector regressor.

This research [13] presents a novel approach to carpooling through the development of a sophisticated mobile application designed to address existing limitations and introduce innovative features. The proposed mobile application encompasses an array of advanced features aimed at optimizing the carpooling experience.

## 3  Methodology

This contains the methodology used to create an application in which the user can interact with the machine learning model to get an idea of his/her personality traits.

### 3.1  Dataset

The data is readily available for download to be used for non-profit research purposes and is taken from Kaggle. The database contains 2668 pages of scanned text for which 668 writers contributed samples of their handwriting. Each handwriting sample is labelled with the corresponding psychological traits by manually studying each document (Figs. 2, 3, 4, 5 and 6).

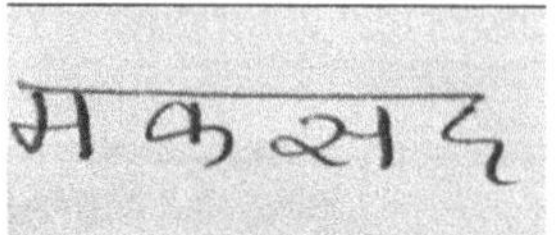

**Fig. 2.** Stable Mindset

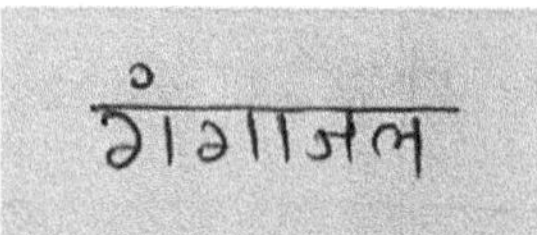

**Fig. 3.** Pessimistic

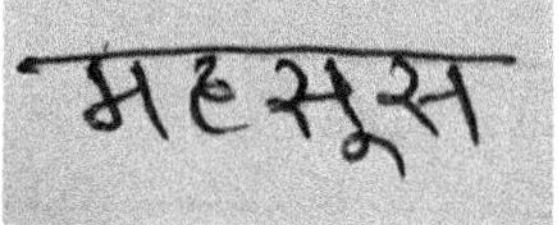

**Fig. 4.** Optimistic

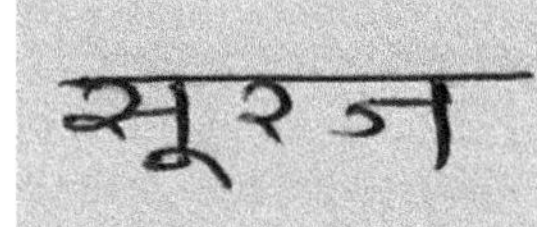

**Fig. 5.** Introvert

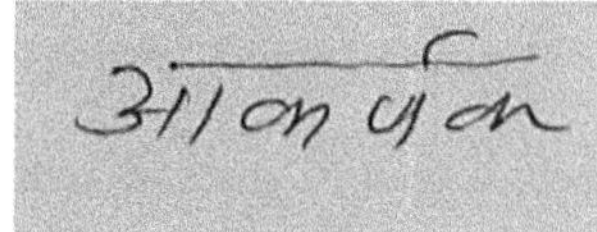

**Fig. 6.** Extrovert

## 3.2 Algorithms

This section discusses about the various algorithms used in the project and discusses about their implementation in the term graphology.

### 3.2.1 LGBM Classifier

The LGBM (LightGBM) classifier is a powerful ensemble learning method that uses a boosting mechanism to aggregate multiple weak classifiers into a strong classifier. In graphology, the LGBM classifier can help analyse complex handwriting features—like loops, slants, and pressure points—by combining these varied insights to enhance the precision of personality trait predictions. This approach is particularly effective in managing high-dimensional data, which is common when analysing detailed handwriting characteristics.

### 3.2.2 XGB Classifier

The XGB (XGBoost) classifier is an ensemble method built from multiple decision trees, with each tree constructed using random subsets of data and features. In graphology, XGB can help manage the variability inherent in handwriting samples, making it effective in avoiding overfitting. Each decision tree independently analyses various handwriting traits, and the final personality assessment is determined through majority voting, resulting in a reliable and consistent prediction of personality traits.

### 3.2.3 Decision Tree Classifier

A decision tree classifier works by splitting the data into branches based on specific criteria until reaching a conclusion. In graphology, it can be used to map specific handwriting features (e.g., the size of loops, direction of strokes) to personality traits by establishing decision rules. It provides clear interpretability, which is useful for understanding how specific handwriting characteristics contribute to the classification of personality traits.

### 3.2.4 Snap Logistic Regression

This is a linear model used for binary or multi-class classification tasks. In graphology, Snap Logistic Regression can be applied to predict the presence or absence of certain personality traits based on extracted handwriting features. Its simplicity allows for a direct relationship between input handwriting metrics and the output prediction, making it easier to understand which traits most heavily influence the result.

### 3.3 Experimental Study

### 3.3.1 Extraction of Baseline

- Apply inverted binary thresholding with a threshold of 120, making the background black and handwriting white.
- Perform dilation with a $5 \times 100$ kernel to convert lines into thick horizontal segments.
- Identify contours; discard those with a height less than 20 pixels.
- Use OpenCV's minimum area rectangle function to determine the angle each contour makes with a horizontal line.
- Calculate the average angle of all contours as the baseline angle.
- Create a rotation matrix to rotate contours to a perfectly horizontal position, maximizing horizontal projection effectiveness.

### 3.3.2 Extraction of Individual Lines

- Straighten the image and compute its horizontal projection into a list (hpList).
- Scan the hpList from top to bottom, identifying non-zero values as handwriting lines.
- For crowded lines, use a threshold to identify overlapping zones, determining the start and end indices of each line.
- Repeat the process for all contours to get individual line indices.

### 3.3.3 Extraction of Letter Size

- Scan the horizontal projection of each extracted line.
- Count consecutive rows with projection values above a threshold to determine midzone height.
- Calculate the average height of all midzones as the letter size.

### 3.3.4 Extraction of Line Spacing

- Count the rows with a horizontal projection of zero, excluding the top margin.
- Count the rows with a projection below a threshold, representing upper and lower zones.
- Calculate the average line spacing by dividing the sum of these counts by the number of lines, then normalize by the letter size.

### 3.3.5 Extraction of Word Spacing

- Compute the vertical projection of each line.
- Count columns with a value of zero, excluding the left and right margins.
- Determine the number of words or disconnected letters.
- Calculate average word spacing by dividing the zero columns by the number of words and normalize by the size.

### 3.3.6 Extraction of Top Margin

- Scan the horizontal projection from the top, counting the initial zero values.
- Normalize the top margin height by the letter size.

### 3.3.7 Extraction of Pen Pressure

- Invert the image.
- Apply an inverted binary threshold (THRESH TO ZERO) with a threshold of 100.
- Calculate the average value of non-zero pixels as pen pressure.

### 3.3.8 Extraction of Slant of Letters

- Apply shear transformation at nine angles ($-45$, $-30$, $-15$, $-5$, 0, 5, 15, 30, 45 degrees).
- Calculate the vertical density and stroke continuity for each transformed image.
- Identify the angle with the maximum vertical density as the slant of the handwriting.

### 3.4 Platform

All the Models used in this project has been made taken from a platform named "IBM WatsonX". This service is provided by IBM Cloud which allows individuals to create their own Machine Leaning model with no-code environment. WatsonX provides various facilities like foundational models like "IBM Granite," "AutoML", etc. These services help in building the Machine Learning Models more efficiently. All the results and graphs provided in this research papers are made with the help of IBM WatsonX. This service which is provided by IBM, similar to it is not there in the market by any other source. IBM WatsonX automatically do all the training, testing and validation on its own, also it generated all the pipelines for different Algorithms, all the data visualization for the results and discussions as well.

## 4 Results and Discussion

This section discusses about the generated results from the different machine learning algorithms.

### 4.1  ROC Curve

The Receiver Operating Characteristic (ROC) curve visualizes the performance of a classification model by plotting the True Positive Rate (sensitivity) against the False Positive Rate, helping to assess its ability to distinguish between classes across various thresholds. Figures 7, 8, 9 and Fig. 10 shows the ROC Curve of different Algorithms.

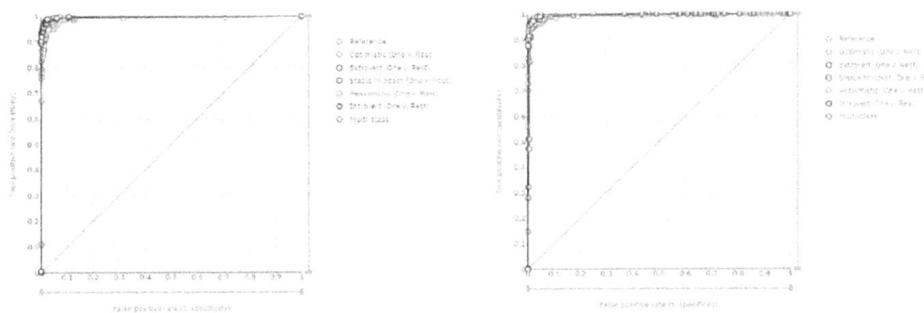

**Fig. 7.** LGBM Classifier                    **Fig. 8.** XGB Classifier

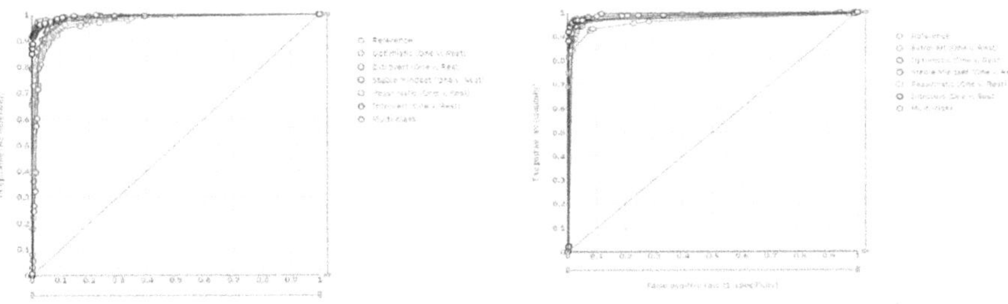

**Fig. 10.** Decision Tree Classifier

**Fig. 9.** Snap Logistic Regression

### 4.2  Confusion Matrix

A matrix layout that displays the counts of True Positives, False Positives, True Negatives, and False Negatives, allowing detailed insight into a model's classification accuracy and types of errors. Figures 11, 12, 13 and Fig. 14 shows Confusion Matrix of different algorithms.

### 4.3  Performance Metrices

The tables from Tables 1, 2, 3 and Table 4 shows scores obtained by different Performance Metrices used by different algorithms.

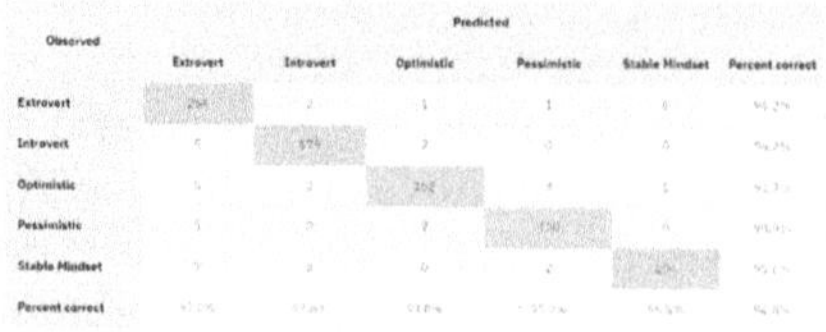

**Fig. 11.** LGBM Classifier

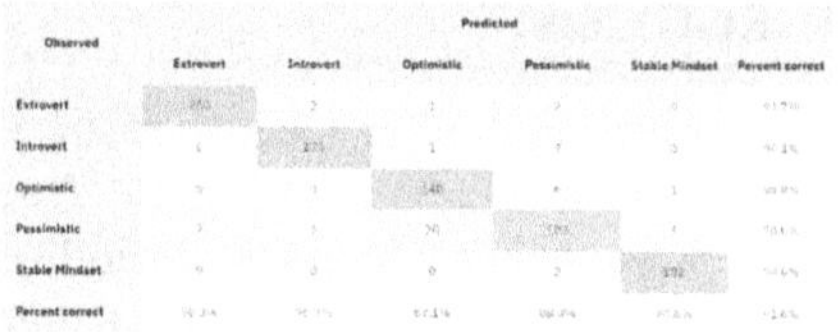

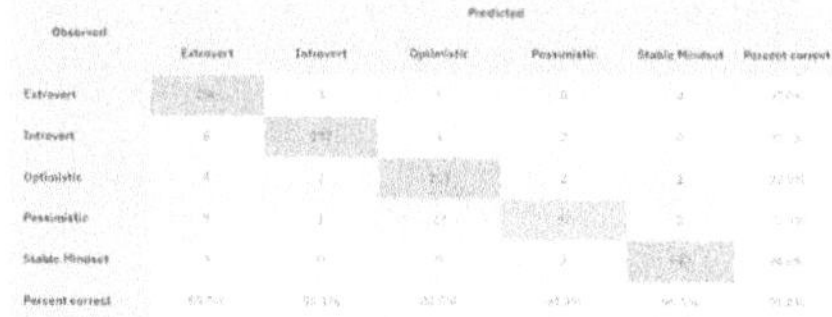

**Fig. 12.** XGB Classifier

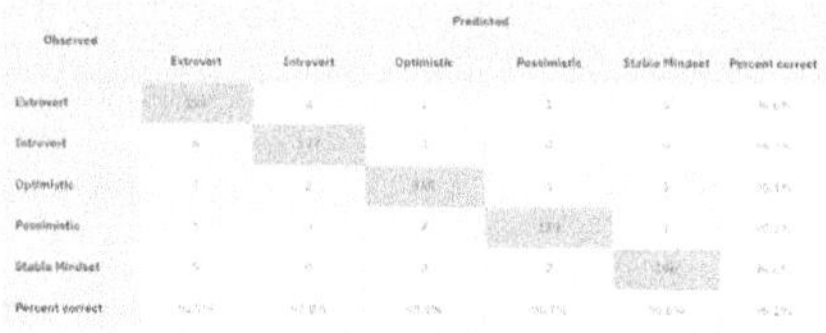

**Fig. 13.** Snap Logistic Regression

**Fig. 14.** Decision Tree Classifier

**Table 1.** Snap Logistic Regression

| Measures | Holdout score | Cross validation score |
| --- | --- | --- |
| Precision macro | 0.906 | 0.919 |
| Accuracy | 0.898 | 0.907 |
| Recall macro | 0.912 | 0.921 |
| Weighted precision | 0.900 | 0.908 |
| F1 macro | 0.909 | 0.919 |
| Weighted f1 measure | 0.898 | 0.907 |
| Weighted recall | 0.898 | 0.907 |
| Log loss | 0.980 | 0.980 |

**Table 2.** Snap Boosting Machine Classifier

| Measures | Holdout score | Cross validation score |
| --- | --- | --- |
| Precision macro | 0.935 | 0.940 |
| Accuracy | 0.923 | 0.926 |
| Recall macro | 0.933 | 0.938 |
| Weighted precision | 0.924 | 0.927 |
| F1 macro | 0.934 | 0.939 |
| Weighted f1 measure | 0.923 | 0.927 |
| Weighted recall | 0.923 | 0.926 |
| Log loss | 0.220 | 0.231 |

**Table 3.** Snap Random Forest Classifier

| Measures | Holdout score | Cross validation score |
| --- | --- | --- |
| Precision macro | 0.932 | 0.931 |
| Accuracy | 0.923 | 0.918 |
| Recall macro | 0.928 | 0.926 |
| Weighted precision | 0.923 | 0.918 |
| F1 macro | 0.930 | 0.928 |
| Weighted f1 measure | 0.923 | 0.918 |
| Weighted recall | 0.923 | 0.918 |
| Log loss | 0.247 | 0.247 |

**Table 4.** Decision Tree Classifier

| Measures | Holdout score | Cross validation score |
| --- | --- | --- |
| Precision macro | 0.929 | 0.922 |
| Accuracy | 0.916 | 0.909 |
| Recall macro | 0.927 | 0.921 |
| Weighted precision | 0.918 | 0.911 |
| F1 macro | 0.927 | 0.921 |
| Weighted f1 measure | 0.916 | 0.909 |
| Weighted recall | 0.916 | 0.909 |
| Log loss | 0.847 | 1.182 |

By comparing different algorithms, we can conclude that LGBM Classifier algorithm performs the best out of all of them followed by XGB classifier algorithm.

## 5  Conclusion

In this study, we focused on applying graphology to analyze Hindi handwriting to identify personality traits and behavioral tendencies using eight distinct machine learning algorithms. We examined how handwriting characteristics—such as letter size, slant, baseline alignment, pen pressure, and the spacing of letters, words, and top margins—correlate with recognized personality factors. Although this study was based on Hindi handwriting, the approach could be extended to other languages, enabling more cross-linguistic analysis, and exploring how graphological interpretations may vary with different alphabets. Future research could further enhance this method by integrating advanced techniques in machine learning and image processing to improve both the accuracy and efficiency of handwriting analysis across languages and scripts.

# References


1. Plamondon, R., Srihari, S.N.: Online and off-line handwriting recognition: a comprehensive survey. IEEE Trans. Pattern Anal. Mach. Intell. **22**(1), 63–84 (2000). https://doi.org/10.1109/34.824821. keywords:{Handwritingrecognition; Writing; Humans; Shape; Keyboards; Computerdisplays; Availability; Characterrecognition; Printingmachinery; Personaldigitalassistants}
2. Jain, A., Singh, A.: Handwritten character recognition using machine learning algorithms. Int. J. Comput. Appl. (2016)
3. Zhang, W., Chen, X.: Handwriting character recognition using convolutional neural networks. In: Proceedings of the IEEE Conference on Computer Vision and Pattern Recognition (CVPR) (2018)
4. Qian, Y., Ma, J.: Personality prediction using CNN-based handwriting analysis. IEEE Trans. Affect. Comput. (2020)
5. Yang, L., Zhang, T.: Multi-label classification for personality traits detection in handwriting analysis. Pattern Recogn. Lett. (2019)
6. Aggarwal, C.C., Zhai, C.: A survey of text classification algorithms. In: Aggarwal, C., Zhai, C. (eds.) Mining Text Data. Springer, Boston (2012). https://doi.org/10.1007/978-1-4614-3223-4_6
7. He, K., Zhang, X., Ren, S., Sun, J.: Deep residual learning for image recognition. In: 2016 IEEE Conference on Computer Vision and Pattern Recognition (CVPR), Las Vegas, NV, USA, pp. 770–778 (2016). https://doi.org/10.1109/CVPR.2016.90, keywords: {Training;Degradation;Complexity theory;Image recognition;Neural networks;Visualization;Image segmentation},
8. Schmidhuber, J.: Deep learning in neural networks: an overview. Neural Networks (2015)
9. Bhatnagar, P., Lokesh, G.H., Shreyas, J., Flammini, F.: Rating prediction of football players using machine learning. In: Proceedings of the 2024 9th International Conference on Machine Learning Technologies (ICMLT '24), pp. 121–126. Association for Computing Machinery, New York, NY, USA (2024). https://doi.org/10.1145/3674029.3674049
10. Bhatnagar, P., Lokesh, G.H., Shreyas, J., Flammini, F., Gautam, S.: An analysis of car price prediction using machine learning. In: Proceedings of the 2024 9th International Conference on Machine Learning Technologies (ICMLT '24), pp. 11–15. Association for Computing Machinery, New York, NY, USA (2024). https://doi.org/10.1145/3674029.3674032
11. Bhatnagar, P., Gururaj, H.L., Shreyas, J., Aithal, H.: ElectroPath: a predictive model for electric vehicle range optimization through mobile application. In: 2024 International Conference on Emerging Technologies in Computer Science for Interdisciplinary Applications (ICETCS), Bengaluru, India, pp. 1–6 (2024). https://doi.org/10.1109/ICETCS61022.2024.10543641
12. Bhatnagar, P., Lokesh, G.H., Shreyas, J., Flammini, F., Panwar, D., Shree, S.: Prediction of mobile phone prices using machine learning. In: Proceedings of the 2024 9th International Conference on Machine Learning Technologies (ICMLT '24), pp. 6–10. Association for Computing Machinery, New York, NY, USA (2024). https://doi.org/10.1145/3674029.3674031
13. Bhatnagar, P., Gururaj, H.L., Gurushankar, H.B., Soundarya, B.C., Shreyas, J.: Mobile application for carpooling with journey mate feature. In: 2024 16th International Conference on COMmunication Systems and NETworkS (COMSNETS), Bengaluru, India, pp. 1088–1093 (2024). https://doi.org/10.1109/COMSNETS59351.2024.10427139

# A Novel Anti-Sample Generation Technique for Effective Machine Unlearning


Rajdeep Mondal[1,2]([✉]) [iD] and Soumitra Samanta[2] [iD]

[1] TCG CREST, Kolkata 700091, India
[2] RKMVERI, Belur Math, Howrah 711202, India
rdmondalofficial@gmail.com, soumitra.samanta@gm.rkmvu.ac.in



**Abstract.** Removing the effect of a specific subset of training data from a fully trained machine learning model is critical in many real-world scenarios. However, retraining the entire model from scratch is often impractical and resource-intensive. Therefore, efficient methods for removing the influence of selected training data without full retraining are highly desirable. In this paper, we propose a novel algorithm that effectively neutralizes the influence of a designated data subset on an already trained model. Our approach generates targeted noise that counteracts the impact of the chosen subset while preserving the model's performance on the remaining data. Empirical evaluations across various deep learning models (ResNet9, ResNet18, AllCNN, and MobileNetV2) and datasets (MNIST, CIFAR-10, SVHN, and CASIA-WebFace) demonstrate the effectiveness and efficiency of the proposed method. The source code is available at https://github.com/rjdpm/anti-samples.

**Keywords:** Machine unlearning · Anti-samples · Approximate unlearning


## 1 Introduction

A large amount of data is collected from real-world scenarios to train efficient machine learning (ML) models. These datasets often contain sensitive personal information about individuals, such as the types of YouTube videos they watch, blog posts, social media activity, and more. From such information, one can infer a person's social interactions, behavioural tendencies, political ideologies, and communication patterns, raising significant privacy concerns. Certain regulations, including the European Union's General Data Protection Regulation (GDPR) and the California Consumer Privacy Act (CCPA), grant users the right to request the removal of their personal data from datasets used by service providers, as well as from ML models trained on that data. Several countries, including India [10] and Canada [9], are also drafting laws to safeguard citizens' personal data.



S. Mitra et al. (Eds.): PReMI 2025, LNCS 16358, pp. 639–649, 2026.
https://doi.org/10.1007/978-3-032-18480-1_65

At the same time, an increasing number of copyright holders are mounting legal challenges over the use of their content by AI companies [13]. These companies typically invest significant time and computational resources into training their models. If someone requests the removal of their data from these models, the companies may be forced to retrain them from scratch and which is an extremely costly process.

In another scenario, such as personalized recommendation systems, it may become necessary to forget outdated user preferences as an individual's tastes evolve over time (i.e., as the data distribution shifts).

Across all these cases, the goal is to remove the influence of a specific subset of the training data, referred to as the *unlearn data* or *forget data*, while retaining the effect of the remaining *retain data*. The initially trained model is referred to as the *original model*. The process of eliminating the impact of the unlearn data from a trained model is known as *machine unlearning* [8]. The resulting model after this process is referred to as the *unlearned model*. A naive solution is to retrain the model from scratch using only the retain data. However, this approach is both time-consuming and computationally expensive. Therefore, efficient alternatives are needed to achieve unlearning for the forget data while preserving the model's performance on the retain data.

One class of machine unlearning methods [2,5,15–17] aims to approximate the parameters of the unlearned model in such a way that they are as close as possible to the parameters that would have been obtained if the model had been retrained from scratch on the retain data. This approach is known as *approximate machine unlearning*. In [2], Tarun et al. proposed an algorithm called Unlearning by Selective Impair and Repair (UNSIR), which keeps the original model parameters fixed and learns the noise using the same labels as the unlearn data by maximizing the classification error. The resulting noises are referred to as *anti-samples*. The original model is then trained for few iteration on the retain data along with these anti-samples to achieve unlearning. However, such unlearning methods often result in a significant drop in model performance. One underlying reason is that the generated anti-samples may share similar properties with the retain data, which can lead the model to misclassify some of the retain data points.

To validate this intuition, we conducted a proof-of-concept experiment using a toy example, as shown in Fig. 1. We randomly generated 400 data points across *four* classes (80 for training and 20 for testing per class) using four Gaussian distributions with different means and the same standard deviation. Figure 1(a) illustrates the distribution of the test data (test data only for clarity). We trained a small neural network (with one hidden layer of 5 units) for 500 epochs to classify the data points, achieving an average test accuracy of 95%. Figure 1(d) shows the corresponding confusion matrix. We considered all data points from *class-1* as our unlearn data. We then unlearned this data using the UNSIR [2] algorithm and Fig. 1(b) displays the anti-samples (marked in red) generated by the UNSIR algorithm, along with the confusion matrix for the unlearned model (after 3 epochs) in Fig. 1(e). From Fig. 1(b), we see that the generated anti-samples share similar properties with the retain data, particularly with the *class-3* data points, which negatively influences model performance, as shown in Fig. 1(e).

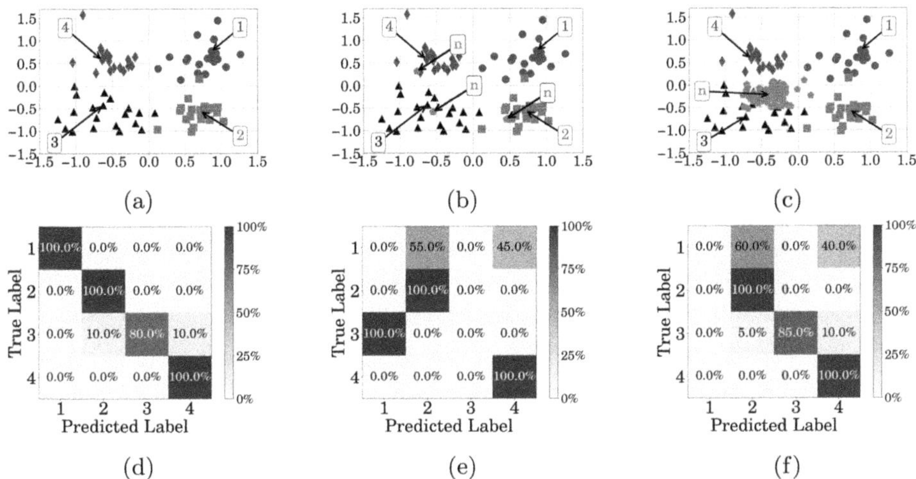

**Fig. 1.** Proof of concept example: (a) Test data. (b) Anti-samples (red color) using UNSIR [2]. (c) Anti-samples (red color) using proposed method. (d) Original model performance. (e) Unlearned using UNSIR [2]. (f) Unlearned using proposed method. (Color figure online)

This paper presents a novel anti-sample generation technique to address this issue for class-unlearning problems. Figure 1(c) shows the anti-samples generated by the proposed method. Using these anti-samples, data were unlearned from a trained neural network model, yielding better performance than the UNSIR algorithm [2]. The anti-samples produced by the proposed method differ from the retained data, as reflected in the model performance shown in Fig. 1(f) (after 1 epoch). The proposed approach generates anti-samples that selectively distort the distribution of the unlearned data. This distortion enables the model to forget knowledge associated with the unlearned data while minimizing negative effects on the retained data. In summary, the contributions are as follows:

- Propose a novel anti-sample generation method that effectively removes the influence of unlearned data from an existing model.
- Demonstrate preservation of model performance through an effective unlearning process that leverages the generated anti-samples.
- Provide an empirical evaluation on *four* public datasets (MNIST [3], CIFAR-10 [7], SVHN [11], and Casia-WebFace [18]) using *four* widely adopted deep learning models (AllCNN [14], ResNet9 [6], ResNet18 [6], and MobileNetV2 [12]).

The rest of the paper is organized as follows. Section 2 presents the proposed methodology. Section 3 reports the experimental evaluation, and Sect. 4 concludes the paper.

## 2    Proposed Methodology

The proposed unlearning process consists of two steps: first, generate anti-samples for the unlearn data; then, the original model is further trained using these generated anti-samples along with the retain dataset (or a subset of it) for a few epochs.

### 2.1    Anti-Sample Generation

The proposed anti-sample generation technique is inspired by a non-parametric distribution approximation method known as MUNGE [1]. In [1], Bucilă et al. proposed an oversampling approach that focuses on the nearest neighbour of a given data point to approximate its distribution. However, the purpose of our anti-samples is to distort the distribution of the data to be unlearned. Therefore, instead of selecting the nearest neighbor, the farthest neighbor from the retained data is identified to construct anti-samples. A pseudocode of the proposed anti-sample generation technique is presented in Algorithm 1.

---

**Algorithm 1:** Proposed algorithm for anti-sample generation

---

**Input:** Unlearn data $D_u$, retain data $D_r$, local variance scaling factor $\rho$, acceptance probability $p$, tail randomizer $t$, number of generated anti-samples $k$, $\epsilon > 0$.

**Output:** A set $D_a$ of generated anti-samples.

1  $Z \leftarrow \phi$;
2  **forall** *datapoint* $x_u$ *in* $D_u$ **do**
3  $\quad$ $z \leftarrow \mathbf{0}$;
4  $\quad$ $q \leftarrow$ a random integer uniformly selected from 1 to $t$;
5  $\quad$ $x_f \leftarrow q^{th}$ farthest neighbour of $x_u$ from $D_r$;
6  $\quad$ **forall** *attribute* $i$ *in* $x_u$ **do**
7  $\quad\quad$ $std \leftarrow \rho(|x_f^i - x_u^i| + \epsilon)$; $x_f^i$ *and* $x_u^i$ *be the* $i^{th}$ *attribute of* $x_f$ *and* $x_u$ *respectively.* $\beta \sim \mathcal{U}(0,1)$; $\mathcal{U}(0,1)$: *Uniform distribution over the interval* $(0,1)$.
8  $\quad\quad$ **if** $\beta \leq p$ **then**
9  $\quad\quad\quad$ $z^i \leftarrow x \sim \mathcal{N}(x_f^i, std)$; $\mathcal{N}(\mu, \sigma)$: *Normal distribution with mean* $\mu$ *and variance* $\sigma$
10  $\quad\quad$ **else**
11  $\quad\quad\quad$ $z^i \leftarrow x_f^i$
12  $\quad\quad$ **end if**
13  $\quad$ **end forall**
14  $\quad$ $Z \leftarrow Z \cup z$;
15  **end forall**
16  $D_a \leftarrow k$ random convex combinations of all the vectors in $Z$ ;
17  **Return** $D_a$

---

Formally, let the original dataset $D = \{(x_1, y_1), (x_2, y_2), ...., (x_n, y_n)\}$ contains $n$ *i.i.d* datapoints, where each $x_i \in \mathbb{R}^d$ and the corresponding class labels $y_i \in \{1, 2, \cdots, c\}$. The dataset is divided into the *retain data* $D_r$ and the *unlearn data* $D_u$ such that $D_r \cap D_u = \Phi$. The task is to remove all the informations about $D_u$ such that the resulting model performed good on $D_r$.

For each data point to be unlearned, $(x_u, y_u) \in D_u$, identify $t$ (referred to as the tail randomizer) farthest neighbours from the retain data $D_r$ ( or subset of $D_r$), denoted as $\{x_{f_1}, x_{f_2}, \cdots, x_{f_t}\}$. Then randomly select one neighbour $x_f$ from $\{x_{f_1}, x_{f_2}, \cdots, x_{f_t}\}$ with uniform probability $Pr(x_f = x_{f_i}) = 1/t$. This randomized selection mitigates the influence of potential outliers, which could otherwise be repeatedly chosen as the farthest points.

Let $z \in \mathbb{R}^d$ be the anti-sample of $x_u$ generated using $x_f$. For the $i$-th coordinate of $z$ (denoted as $z^i$), sample a $\beta$ from a *uniform* distribution over the interval $(0, 1)$. Then $z^i$ is calculated as follows:

$$z^i = \begin{cases} x \sim \mathcal{N}(x_f^i, std^i); std^i = \rho\left(\left|x_u^i - x_f^i\right| + \epsilon\right) \text{ for some } \rho, \epsilon > 0 & \text{if } \beta \leq p \\ x_f^i & \text{if } \beta > p \end{cases}$$

Here, $p$ is the acceptance probability, $\epsilon$ $(> 0)$ ensures a positive local variance $|x_u^i - x_f^i|$. The parameter $\rho$ is a scaling factor of the local variance, related to the local variance defined in [1]. This scaling factor allows the generated anti-samples to vary along each dimension from the farthest neighbour as needed. This adjustment prevents the generation of outliers that could drastically decline the model's performance on the retain data. Using this procedure, we generate a set of anti-samples $\{z_1, z_2, \cdots, z_{|D_u|}\}$ corresponding to each datapoints in the $D_r$. To produce a more substantial set of anti-samples, compute $k$ random convex combinations of $\{z_1, z_2, \cdots, z_{|D_u|}\}$, resulting in the final anti-sample set $\{v_1, v_2, \cdots, v_k\}$.

## 2.2   Train-To-Unlearn

Intuitively, the generated anti-samples are located far from both the unlearn and retain data in the sample space. Merging them with the retain data, the true distribution of the original data is distorted primarily by altering the distribution of the unlearn data. This distortion influences the original model's understanding (i.e., its parameters) regarding the unlearn class. Consequently, the generated anti-samples are used to train the original model alongside the retain data for only a few epochs. We refer to this process as *train-to-unlearn* to distinguish it from the standard learning process. In this step, the anti-samples corrupt the model's learning about the unlearn data by injecting misleading (bad) information into the model. However, since the distribution of the retain data remains unchanged, the model's learning regarding the retain data persists. To accelerate this unlearning, we scale the learning rate during *train-to-unlearn* using a hyper-parameter $\lambda$ (analysed in Subsect. 3.3).

**Table 1.** Performance of the single-class and multi-class unlearning across *four* models on *four* datasets. **#UC:** Number of unlearn classes; **Original & Retrained:** Performance of *original* and *retrained model* on the test data.

| Dataset | #UC | Original (%) $D_r$ | Original (%) $D_u$ | Retrained (%) $D_r$ | Ours (%) $D_r(\uparrow)$ | Ours (%) $D_u(\downarrow)$ |
|---|---|---|---|---|---|---|
| **ResNet9** | | | | | | |
| MNIST | 1 | 99.50 | 99.50 | 99.50 ± 0.10 | 99.01 ± 0.18 | 0.00 ± 0.00 |
| MNIST | 2 | 99.51 | 99.42 | 99.54 ± 0.07 | 99.10 ± 0.22 | 0.00 ± 0.00 |
| MNIST | 4 | 99.49 | 99.51 | 99.57 ± 0.05 | 99.37 ± 0.17 | 0.00 ± 0.00 |
| CIFAR-10 | 1 | 85.52 | 85.52 | 86.63 ± 1.28 | 84.14 ± 1.43 | 0.01 ± 0.03 |
| CIFAR-10 | 2 | 85.75 | 84.59 | 87.41 ± 1.55 | 85.21 ± 2.17 | 0.06 ± 0.10 |
| CIFAR-10 | 4 | 86.91 | 83.43 | 90.35 ± 1.47 | 89.51 ± 2.08 | 0.00 ± 0.00 |
| SVHN | 1 | 94.66 | 94.36 | 94.98 ± 0.36 | 93.21 ± 0.38 | 0.01 ± 0.04 |
| SVHN | 2 | 94.58 | 94.73 | 95.00 ± 0.18 | 93.44 ± 0.78 | 0.05 ± 0.18 |
| SVHN | 4 | 94.24 | 95.11 | 95.38 ± 0.19 | 94.89 ± 0.55 | 0.00 ± 0.00 |
| Casia WebFace | 1 | 82.85 | 82.50 | 82.90 ± 0.30 | 76.46 ± 1.00 | 0.00 ± 0.00 |
| Casia WebFace | 7 | 82.88 | 80.95 | 83.36 ± 0.56 | 76.26 ± 1.27 | 0.00 ± 0.00 |
| Casia WebFace | 10 | 82.77 | 84.52 | 83.71 ± 0.39 | 77.63 ± 2.19 | 0.00 ± 0.00 |
| **AllCNN** | | | | | | |
| MNIST | 1 | 99.31 | 99.31 | 99.55 ± 0.12 | 99.28 ± 0.10 | 0.00 ± 0.00 |
| MNIST | 2 | 99.53 | 99.60 | 99.41 ± 0.14 | 99.32 ± 0.17 | 0.00 ± 0.00 |
| MNIST | 4 | 99.62 | 99.42 | 99.67 ± 0.10 | 99.46 ± 0.06 | 0.00 ± 0.00 |
| CIFAR-10 | 1 | 85.06 | 85.06 | 85.99 ± 1.06 | 84.29 ± 1.52 | 0.19 ± 0.30 |
| CIFAR-10 | 2 | 85.59 | 84.07 | 86.92 ± 1.52 | 86.01 ± 1.79 | 0.06 ± 0.12 |
| CIFAR-10 | 4 | 85.04 | 85.65 | 87.89 ± 1.20 | 86.82 ± 2.74 | 0.02 ± 0.05 |
| SVHN | 1 | 95.16 | 94.64 | 95.43 ± 0.25 | 94.48 ± 0.62 | 0.18 ± 0.22 |
| SVHN | 2 | 95.06 | 95.36 | 95.58 ± 0.91 | 94.75 ± 0.21 | 0.37 ± 0.60 |
| SVHN | 4 | 95.18 | 94.93 | 96.31 ± 0.26 | 96.08 ± 0.18 | 0.43 ± 0.48 |
| Casia WebFace | 1 | 83.83 | 82.67 | 82.56 ± 1.43 | 77.80 ± 1.63 | 0.00 ± 0.00 |
| Casia WebFace | 7 | 83.80 | 84.56 | 83.41 ± 0.96 | 77.89 ± 2.27 | 0.00 ± 0.00 |
| Casia WebFace | 10 | 83.86 | 84.56 | 82.40 ± 1.87 | 77.95 ± 2.06 | 0.00 ± 0.00 |
| **ResNet18** | | | | | | |
| MNIST | 1 | 99.24 | 99.24 | 99.45 ± 0.08 | 98.83 ± 0.35 | 0.00 ± 0.00 |
| MNIST | 2 | 99.28 | 99.03 | 99.51 ± 0.08 | 98.84 ± 0.33 | 0.00 ± 0.00 |
| MNIST | 4 | 99.20 | 99.27 | 99.53 ± 0.13 | 99.01 ± 0.17 | 0.00 ± 0.00 |
| CIFAR-10 | 1 | 81.61 | 81.61 | 82.55 ± 1.23 | 79.44 ± 1.56 | 0.00 ± 0.00 |
| CIFAR-10 | 2 | 81.57 | 81.73 | 84.09 ± 1.65 | 81.20 ± 1.71 | 0.00 ± 0.00 |
| CIFAR-10 | 4 | 81.40 | 81.92 | 86.95 ± 4.19 | 84.61 ± 5.37 | 0.00 ± 0.00 |
| SVHN | 1 | 93.75 | 93.22 | 93.82 ± 0.36 | 91.83 ± 1.13 | 0.00 ± 0.00 |
| SVHN | 2 | 93.74 | 92.93 | 94.19 ± 0.45 | 92.61 ± 1.14 | 0.02 ± 0.07 |
| SVHN | 4 | 93.28 | 93.83 | 94.95 ± 0.88 | 93.78 ± 1.40 | 0.00 ± 0.00 |
| Casia WebFace | 1 | 81.09 | 82.05 | 80.91 ± 1.77 | 74.08 ± 2.37 | 0.00 ± 0.00 |
| Casia WebFace | 7 | 81.08 | 81.50 | 80.92 ± 1.58 | 74.36 ± 1.43 | 0.18 ± 0.27 |
| Casia WebFace | 10 | 81.14 | 79.38 | 80.86 ± 1.89 | 73.46 ± 1.45 | 0.05 ± 0.08 |
| **MobileNet V2** | | | | | | |
| MNIST | 1 | 99.33 | 99.33 | 99.32 ± 0.09 | 98.90 ± 0.43 | 0.00 ± 0.00 |
| MNIST | 2 | 99.30 | 99.42 | 99.34 ± 0.09 | 99.11 ± 0.16 | 0.00 ± 0.00 |
| MNIST | 4 | 99.28 | 99.38 | 99.49 ± 0.19 | 99.46 ± 0.25 | 0.00 ± 0.00 |
| CIFAR-10 | 1 | 81.91 | 81.91 | 82.76 ± 1.98 | 81.51 ± 1.89 | 0.00 ± 0.00 |
| CIFAR-10 | 2 | 81.96 | 81.68 | 84.72 ± 2.08 | 83.27 ± 2.50 | 0.00 ± 0.00 |
| CIFAR-10 | 4 | 81.60 | 82.36 | 88.24 ± 1.53 | 86.16 ± 2.04 | 0.00 ± 0.00 |
| SVHN | 1 | 93.75 | 93.20 | 93.65 ± 0.65 | 91.18 ± 1.16 | 0.00 ± 0.00 |
| SVHN | 2 | 93.71 | 93.35 | 94.00 ± 0.85 | 92.40 ± 1.38 | 0.00 ± 0.00 |
| SVHN | 4 | 94.35 | 92.62 | 95.09 ± 0.27 | 93.14 ± 0.89 | 0.00 ± 0.00 |
| Casia WebFace | 1 | 81.56 | 81.60 | 81.84 ± 1.92 | 75.30 ± 2.19 | 0.00 ± 0.00 |
| Casia WebFace | 7 | 81.54 | 82.46 | 82.14 ± 1.76 | 73.73 ± 1.57 | 0.00 ± 0.00 |
| Casia WebFace | 10 | 81.64 | 79.19 | 81.94 ± 0.91 | 75.82 ± 2.89 | 0.00 ± 0.00 |

# 3    Experimental Evaluation

We experimentally evaluated the unlearning capability of the generated anti-samples on *four* state-of-the-art deep learning models: ResNet9 [6], AllCNN [14], ResNet18 [6], and MobileNetV2 [12], using *four* benchmark datasets: MNIST [3], CIFAR-10 [7], SVHN [11], Casia-WebFace [18]. The ResNet9 and ResNet18 models are specialized deep residual networks, while the AllCNN model consists of only convolutional layers without any pooling layers, and the MobileNetV2 model uses inverted residuals with shortcut connections between the bottleneck layers. The MNIST (handwritten) and SVHN (street-view house numbers) dataset contains grayscale and RGB digit (0–9) images, respectively. The CIFAR-10 datasets contain RGB images of 10 different real-world objects. The Casia-WebFace dataset contains high-resolution RGB face images of $10,000$ individuals; we filter it to the top 300 classes with the highest number of data points to ensure training stability.

## 3.1    Experimental Setup

Each model is trained on all datasets for 30 epochs, and the best-performing instance is considered the *original model*. The *retrained model* is obtained by training the same architecture on the retain data for 30 epochs and selecting the best-performing model. A learning rate of $\alpha = 10^{-3}$ is fixed across all model-dataset pairs. All experiments are conducted on a system equipped with an *NVIDIA 4090 GPU*, a *24-core i9* processor, and *64GB RAM*, running on *Ubuntu 22.04*.

To asses the *effectiveness* [8]( *i.e.* the absolute performance difference between the unlearned and retrained model on the test set) of the proposed method, we perform *two* types of unlearning tasks: *single-class unlearning* and *multi-class unlearning*. For *single-class unlearning*, all data points belonging to a particular class are treated as the unlearn data, while the remaining data points form the retain data. For each dataset, we treat every class as an unlearn class and report the *mean* and *standard deviation* of performance across all classes.

For *multi-class unlearning*, information corresponding to multiple classes is removed. For MNIST, CIFAR-10 and SVHN datasets, we randomly select 2 and 4 classes as unlearning classes; for Casia-WebFace, we select 7 and 10 classes. The unlearning process is repeated 10, 5, 3, and 3 times for the 2, 4, 7, and 10-class settings, respectively, and the *mean* and *standard deviation* are reported across repetitions. For the original model, we report the *mean* accuracy across all classes. For the retrained model, results are reported similar to the unlearning setups. The *train-to-unlearn* step is run for 5 epochs across all dataset-model pairs.

## 3.2    Results and Discussions

The results for all models across all datasets are summarized in Table 1. In this table, the column **"#UC"** denotes the number of unlearned classes: a value of

'**1**' indicates single-class unlearning, while '**2**', '**4**', '**7**' and '**10**' correspond to multi-class unlearning settings.

From Table 1, it can be observed that for single-class unlearning, the proposed method consistently preserves the retain accuracy across MNIST, CIFAR-10, and SVHN datasets for all models, while achieving 0% accuracy on the unlearned data. For the Casia-WebFace dataset, which presents additional challenges due to higher complexity and limited per-class samples, the retain accuracy drops slightly (by approximately 5% to 6%), but the method still attains 0% unlearn accuracy.

In the multi-class unlearning setting, a similar trend is observed. The proposed method maintains competitive retain performance (with the exception of Casia-WebFace) with negligible residual informations (sometimes *zero*) about the unlearn data shown in Table 1. Notably, for certain configurations, the retain accuracy even improves over the original model's performance. For example, on the SVHN dataset with ResNet9, the retain accuracy improves from 86.91% (original) to 89.51% after 4-class unlearning.

**Table 2.** Comparison of single-class unlearning results with state-of-the-art methods for the **ResNet9** model on **MNIST, CIFAR-10,** and **SVHN** datasets.

| Dataset | M-M Method (%) [2] | | GKT (%) [2] | | Ours (%) | |
|---|---|---|---|---|---|---|
| | $D_r(\uparrow)$ | $D_u(\downarrow)$ | $D_r(\uparrow)$ | $D_u(\downarrow)$ | $D_r(\uparrow)$ | $D_u(\downarrow)$ |
| **MNIST** | 12.32 | 0.00 | 94.57 | 0.00 | **99.01** | **0.00** |
| **CIFAR-10** | 10.85 | 0.00 | 56.83 | 0.00 | **84.14** | 0.01 |
| **SVHN** | 53.75 | 49.65 | 39.44 | **0.00** | **93.21** | 0.01 |

We compare the performance of the proposed method with state-of-the-art techniques, as shown in Tables 2, 3 and 4. Table 2 reports single-class unlearning results on the MNIST, CIFAR-10, and SVHN datasets using the ResNet9 model. The proposed method consistently outperforms recent approaches such as M-M [2] (by 40% to 85%) and GKT [2] (by 4% to 54%) in terms of retain accuracy ($D_r$), while maintaining near-zero accuracy on the unlearned data ($D_u$). Table 3 compares both single-class and multi-class unlearning on the CIFAR-10 dataset using AllCNN and ResNet18 models. The proposed method yields significantly better retain performance than NegGrad [4] (by 9% to 64%) and UNSIR [15] (by 6% to 11%). Similarly, Table 4 also presents a comparative study on the Casia-WebFace dataset, where proposed method shows improved retain accuracy over UNSIR [15] across both single and multi-class unlearning scenarios, while keeping the unlearn accuracy very low. These results collectively demonstrate the effectiveness of the proposed method in achieving accurate and efficient unlearning, outperforming existing state-of-the-art techniques across diverse datasets and architectures.

**Table 3.** Comparison with state-of-the-art methods on the **CIFAR-10** dataset for both single-class and multi-class unlearning tasks.

| Model | # UC | NegGrad (%) [4] | | UNSIR (%) [15] | | Ours (%) | |
|---|---|---|---|---|---|---|---|
| | | $D_r(\uparrow)$ | $D_u(\downarrow)$ | $D_r(\uparrow)$ | $D_u(\downarrow)$ | $D_r(\uparrow)$ | $D_u(\downarrow)$ |
| AllCNN | 1 | 42.39 | 13.47 | 73.90 | 0.00 | **84.29** | 0.19 |
| | 2 | 44.25 | 2.20 | 80.76 | 0.00 | **86.01** | 0.06 |
| | 4 | 22.00 | 1.44 | 80.21 | 0.00 | **86.82** | 0.02 |
| ResNet18 | 1 | 66.67 | 7.44 | 71.06 | 0.00 | **79.44** | **0.00** |
| | 2 | 72.12 | 0.05 | 73.61 | 0.00 | **81.20** | **0.00** |
| | 4 | 54.84 | 0.02 | 76.63 | 0.00 | **84.61** | **0.00** |

**Table 4.** Comparison with state-of-the-art methods on the **Casia-Webface** dataset for both single-class and multi-class unlearning tasks.

| Model | # UC | UNSIR (%) [15] | | Ours (%) | |
|---|---|---|---|---|---|
| | | $D_r(\uparrow)$ | $D_u(\downarrow)$ | $D_r(\uparrow)$ | $D_u(\downarrow)$ |
| AllCNN | 1 | 73.90 | 0.00 | **77.80** | **0.00** |
| | 7 | 75.47 | 0.00 | **77.89** | **0.00** |
| | 10 | 73.08 | 0.00 | **77.95** | **0.00** |
| ResNet18 | 1 | 69.70 | 0.00 | **74.08** | **0.00** |
| | 7 | 68.50 | 0.00 | **74.36** | 0.18 |
| | 10 | 67.03 | 0.00 | **73.46** | 0.05 |

## 3.3 Ablation Study

We conduct an ablation study on CIFAR-10 using ResNet18 to assess the impact of *four* hyperparameters: the learning rate scaling factor ($\lambda$), tail randomizer ($t$), local variance scaling factor ($\rho$), and the number of anti-samples ($k$) as shown in Fig. 2. At $\lambda = 2$, the unlearn accuracy drops to 0% while the retain accuracy remains high, but further increasing $\lambda$ leads to a decline in retain accuracy (Fig. 2(a)). An optimal trade-off between unlearning and retention is observed at $t = 20$ (Fig. 2(b)). Unlearning performance enhances while $\rho$ increasing but may reduce retain accuracy if the anti-samples starts resembling with other class samples (Fig. 2(c)). As $k$ increases, unlearning improves and stabilizes around $k = 500$; however, beyond this point, excessive anti-samples begin to degrade retain accuracy (Fig. 2(d)). These findings helps to select optimal hyperparameter values for effective unlearning.

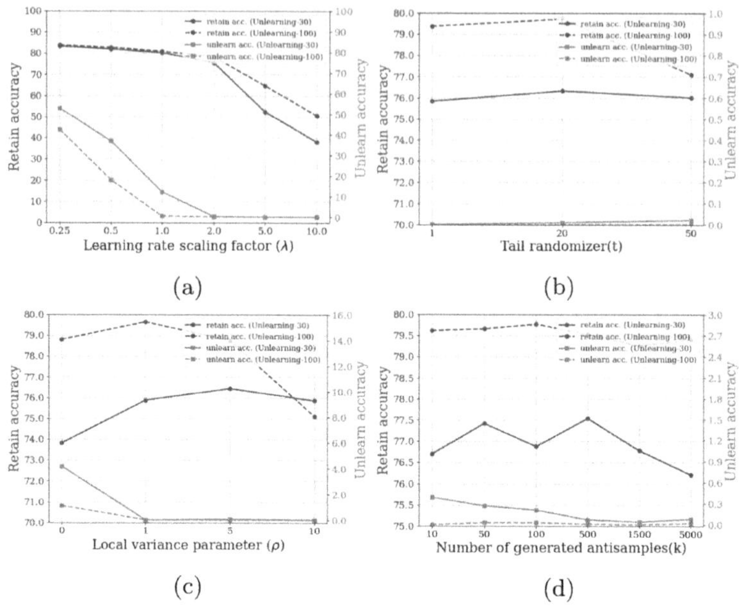

**Fig. 2.** Ablation study of different hyper-parameters.

## 4    Conclusion

This paper introduced an anti-sample generation method for effective machine unlearning. The approach is effective for both single-class and multi-class unlearning tasks. Unlike other anti-sample generation methods, the proposed approach relies on the retain data and does not depend on the model itself. A key distinction of the proposed method is its efficiency in preserving the performance of the retain data. The proposed method empirically evaluated on *four* publicly available datasets using deep learning models of varying sizes and achieved superior results compared to state-of-the-art methods.

## References


1. Buciluă, C., Caruana, R., Niculescu-Mizil, A.: Model compression. In: International Conference on Knowledge Discovery and Data Mining (2006)
2. Chundawat, V.S., Tarun, A.K., Mandal, M., Kankanhalli, M.: Zero-shot machine unlearning. IEEE Trans. Inf. Forensics Secur. (2023)
3. Deng, L.: The mnist database of handwritten digit images for machine learning research. IEEE Signal Process. Mag. (2012)
4. Golatkar, A., Achille, A., Soatto, S.: Eternal sunshine of the spotless net: selective forgetting in deep networks. In: CVPR (2019)
5. Graves, L., Nagisetty, V., Ganesh, V.: Amnesiac machine learning. In: AAAI, pp. 11516–11524 (2021)

6. He, K., Zhang, X., Ren, S., Sun, J.: Deep residual learning for image recognition. In: CVPR, pp. 770–778 (2016)
7. Krizhevsky, A., Nair, V., Hinton, G.: Cifar-10 (Canadian institute for advanced research) (2009). http://www.cs.toronto.edu/~kriz/cifar.html
8. Mercuri, S., et al.: An introduction to machine unlearning. arXiv preprint arXiv:2209.00939 (2022)
9. Minister of innovation, science and industry: Bill c-27 (2022). https://www.parl.ca/DocumentViewer/en/44-1/bill/C-27/first-reading
10. Ministry of law and justice: the digital personal data protection act (2023). https://www.meity.gov.in/data-protection-framework/
11. Netzer, Y., Wang, T., Coates, A., Bissacco, A., Wu, B., Ng, A.Y., et al.: Reading digits in natural images with unsupervised feature learning. In: NIPS Workshop on Deep Learning and Unsupervised Feature Learning (2011)
12. Sandler, M., Howard, A., Zhu, M., Zhmoginov, A., Chen, L.C.: Mobilenetv2: inverted residuals and linear bottlenecks. In: CVPR, pp. 4510–4520 (2018)
13. da Silva, J.: Reddit shares jump after openai chatgpt deal (2024). https://www.bbc.com/news/articles/cxe92v47850o
14. Springenberg, J.T., Dosovitskiy, A., Brox, T., Riedmiller, M.: Striving for simplicity: the all convolutional net (2014). arXiv preprint arXiv:1412.6806
15. Tarun, A.K., Chundawat, V.S., Mandal, M., Kankanhalli, M.: Fast yet effective machine unlearning. IEEE Trans. Neural Netw. Learn. Syst. (2023)
16. Tarun, A.K., Chundawat, V.S., Mandal, M., Kankanhalli, M.: Deep regression unlearning. In: ICML, pp. 33921–33939 (2023)
17. Xu, J., Wu, Z., Wang, C., Jia, X.: Machine unlearning: solutions and challenges (2023). arXiv preprint arXiv:2308.07061
18. Yi, D., Lei, Z., Liao, S., Li, S.Z.: Learning face representation from scratch (2014). arXiv preprint arXiv:1411.7923

# A Graph Neural Network Approach for Parameter Estimation in Bounded Confidence Models


Muhammad Alfas[1]([⊠])[ID], Abhishek Gupta[2][ID], Manoj Kumar[3][ID],
and Sandeep Kumar[2,4][ID]

[1] Department of Mechanical Engineering, Indian Institute of Technology Delhi, New Delhi, India
mez208100@iitd.ac.in
[2] Yardi School of AI, Indian Institute of Technology Delhi, New Delhi, India
{aiz248316,krsandeep}@iitd.ac.in
[3] Indian Institute of Technology (Indian School of Mines), Dhanbad, India
manojkr@iitism.ac.in
[4] Department of Electrical Engineering, Indian Institute of Technology Delhi, New Delhi, India



**Abstract.** Opinion dynamics models are widely used to understand how opinions spread, evolve, and converge within social systems. However, applying these models to real-world data presents a significant challenge: the calibration of empirical observations to fit the underlying theoretical framework. In this work, we introduce a graph neural network-based approach for estimating the parameters in bounded confidence-type opinion dynamics models. In this simulation-based inference framework, graph neural networks are used to encode and summarize the structural and opinion-related features of the data, and a coupling flow network is trained to infer the parameters governing the opinion dynamics model. To enhance the efficiency and scalability of our method, we employ graph sampling techniques that simplify the network structure before passing it to the neural network. We evaluate our approach on synthetic networks and further validate its performance using empirical datasets, demonstrating its effectiveness in recovering meaningful model parameters. We have done comparisons against likelihood methods, and the results indicate the efficacy and efficiency of the proposed model.

**Keywords:** opinion dynamics · simulation-based inference · graph neural networks · bounded confidence models


## 1 Introduction

Opinion dynamics models examine how individual opinions spread within a population and evolve into collective behavior. Understanding the mechanisms underlying this propagation, such as peer influence, conformity, trust, and resistance, has long been a topic of research interest across disciplines like sociology,



S. Mitra et al. (Eds.): PReMI 2025, LNCS 16358, pp. 650–657, 2026.
https://doi.org/10.1007/978-3-032-18480-1_66

psychology, political science, and network theory. The rise of online social networks fundamentally transformed how these models are perceived and applied. Social media platforms quickly became central to marketing strategies and political campaigning, turning opinion dynamics into a powerful tool for influence and engagement.

The foundational work in the field is "A Formal Theory of Social Power" by John R. P. French Jr. [5]. Over the years, a vast body of research has emerged, with models developed to predict how opinions spread through social networks and why they sometimes lead to consensus or polarization. The seminal DeGroot model [4] describes how individuals in a social network iteratively update their beliefs by averaging the opinions of their neighbors over time. Opinion dynamics models can be broadly classified into continuous opinion-space models and discrete opinion-space models. In continuous models, opinions are represented as continuous variables, with DeGroot and bounded confidence models (BCM) being the most widely used. Discrete space models, such as the Galam, Sznajd, and Voter models, represent opinions using integer states [13].

The availability of high computational power and large-scale datasets from social media has enabled researchers to explore these models in real-world settings. However, bridging the gap between empirical data and computational models remains a key challenge. This requires fitting data to models and calibrating parameters that govern opinion change. Parameter estimation in opinion dynamics is typically addressed using simulation-based methods, optimization techniques, or likelihood-based approaches. Simulation-based methods generate data from model simulations and compare them with empirical observations, often using Approximate Bayesian Computation (ABC) or surrogate machine learning models to accelerate estimation. Optimization approaches employ algorithms like gradient descent or meta-heuristics, while likelihood-based approaches leverage probabilistic graphical models to construct likelihood functions for calibration.

Recent simulation-based approaches include works such as [6,15], and [1]. [15] proposes simulation-based distributional calibration using JensenShannon divergence. [6] performs parameter calibration of an agent-based opinion dynamics model via $R^2$ and matrix-distance-based model fitting. [1] develops a data-driven kinetic model with simulation-based calibration. Likelihood-based estimation is explored by [10] and [11], both of which use probabilistic graphical models of the bounded confidence model to design likelihood loss functions, with the latter employing stochastic variational inference. Optimization-based approaches include [3], which uses gradient descent to estimate weighted adjacency matrices, and [16], which applies genetic algorithms for parameter calibration.

In this work, we propose a simulation-based inference (SBI) framework for opinion dynamics parameter estimation. The proposed model builds on the GrepeFlow model [2] and BayesFlow [14]. The remainder of this paper is organized as follows: Sect. 2 describes the methodology in detail, Sect. 3 presents the results, and Sect. 4 concludes the work.

## 2    Methodology

In this work, we extend GrepeFlow from [2] to estimate opinion dynamics parameters using a BCM model. Built on top of the BayesFlow engine [14], GrepeFlow was originally developed for epidemic parameter estimation. Grepe-Flow consists of three main components - a simulator to train the model, a graph reduction module to handle scalability, and a set of neural networks. The major change from the original GrepeFlow is that we deal with continuous data, whereas the epidemic data was categorical. In this work, we employ Hegsel-mannKrause (HK), a BCM model, as the simulator to train data and forest fire sampling for graph reduction. The neural networks are similar to those of Grepe-Flow: GraphSAGE and a coupling flow network. The methodology workflow is shown in Fig. 1.

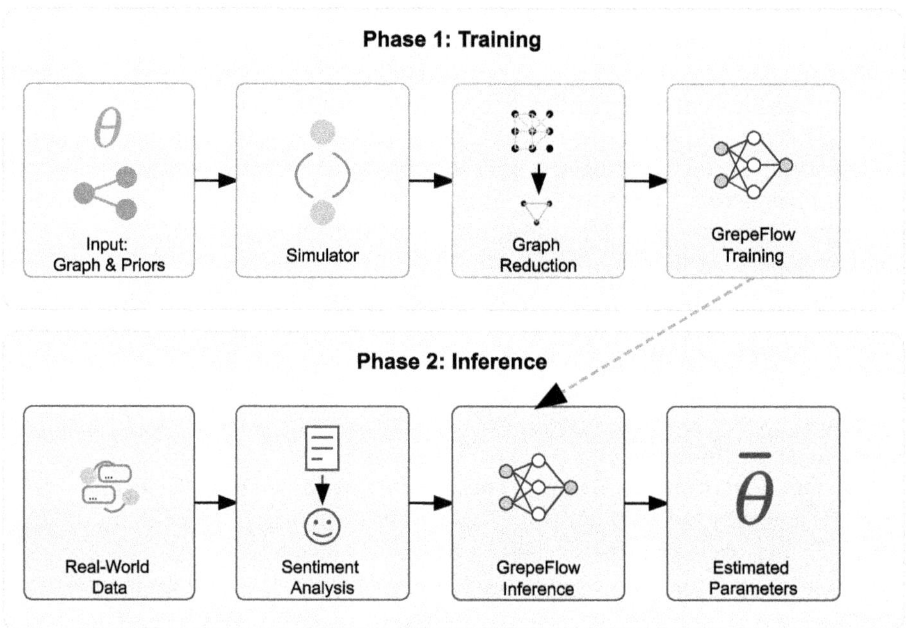



**Fig. 1.** Workflow of the parameter estimation process.

The parameter estimation process consists of two phases - training and inference. In the training phase, a simulator is used to generate data from an input graph and a set of parameters. This data is then passed through a graph reduction module. The reduced graph and data are used to train the GrepeFlow model. In the inference phase, real-world data (a graph and associated text data) is converted into numerical data using a sentiment analyzer. This data is passed through the graph reduction module and then passed into the trained Grepe-Flow model. The GrepeFlow model then provides an estimate for the parameters for the real-world data. The next sections will explain each component of both phases in detail.

## 2.1   Training Phase

In the training phase, we start with a simulator generating data. We use Hegsel-mannKrause (HK), which is a BCM model. BCMs work under the assumption that individuals will ignore ideas that are too far from their own. The maximum allowed opinion difference is called the "bounded confidence," and it is represented using $\epsilon$. The opinions are numerically represented in a range of $(-1, 1)$. Let $G$ be the network where the opinion propagation happens. In the HK model, the opinion of each node is updated by averaging the opinions of all neighbors with the opinion difference less than $\epsilon$. $\epsilon$ is the only parameter we need to estimate in HK models. Let $N(u)$ be the set of neighbours of node $u$ with opinion difference less than $\epsilon$. Then the opinion update in the HK model for the node $u$ is given as follows [8].

$$o_u^{t+1} = \frac{1}{|N(u)|} \sum_{v \in N(u)} o_v^t \tag{1}$$

We generate node-level opinion data using the HK simulator for different values of the parameter $\epsilon$. Training the neural networks with large graphs requires high computational resources. So before training, we reduce the size of the graph and the data. The GrepeFlow framework proposes coarsening and exploratory sampling techniques for graph reduction. However, we focus solely on forest fire sampling (FFS) to achieve faster reduction and better handling of graph sparsity. FFS constructs a representative subgraph by simulating the spread of a fire through the network. It begins from a random node and iteratively "burns" through its neighbors, selectively expanding the subgraph. This process models natural information diffusion and effectively captures local structures and sparsities within the original graph [12].

After graph reduction using FFS, both the sampled graph and node-level opinion data are passed into the GrepeFlow model, which comprises two components: a graph neural network (GNN) as the summary network and a coupling flow network as the inference network. The GNN consists of two GraphSAGE layers, a fully connected layer, and a pooling layer. GraphSAGE (Graph Sample and Aggregate) generates node embeddings by sampling neighbors and aggregating their features through operations such as summation, averaging, or LSTM [7]. The GraphSAGE layers produce node-level embeddings, which the pooling layer averages into a graph-level embedding, referred to as the summary vector, that is then passed to the coupling flow network to predict the input parameter $\epsilon$. The coupling flow network is a normalizing flow neural network built from $D$ invertible blocks as developed in BayesFlow [14], where each block comprises an activation normalization layer, a fixed random permutation to mix information across dimensions, and an affine coupling layer. These coupling layers employ a deep multi-layer perceptron (MLP) subnet to predict the transformation parameters conditioned on the relevant data.

The entire network (summary network and inference network) is trained end-to-end by minimizing the negative log-likelihood of the training samples, which is equivalent to maximizing their probability under the learned model. After training the GrepeFlow model, we evaluate it on the testing data. The next section explains the testing and evaluation process in detail.

## 2.2   Inference Phase

We experiment with two types of testing data - simulated data and real-world social network data. The simulated data is generated using the same HK simulator. To evaluate the efficacy of the model on real-world problems, we conduct experiments with two Reddit datasets. These datasets comprise submissions and comments that were collected for two socio-political topics: Brexit and the Texas Abortion Ban (TAB), for a certain time period. The datasets were preprocessed to handle malformed entries, standardize textual content, and ensure consistent data structures. Relevant submissions were identified through a two-tier keyword filtering approach, where primary and secondary topic-specific terms were applied with a relaxed matching criterion to capture both direct and contextually related discussions.

Comments associated with these filtered submissions were then mapped to their parent posts and transformed into directed useruser interaction pairs, forming the basis for network construction. Then sentiment analyses are conducted using VADER [9] to generate the opinion data of each user over time. Unlike the simulated data, real data don't have continuous data for all users over the entire time period. We have filled the missing value using linear interpolation for individuals who have expressed more than one opinion over the time period. But kept the same opinion score for individuals who expressed only one opinion.

## 3   Results and Discussion

The first set of experiments was conducted using three synthetic networks - BarabásiAlbert (BA), ErdősRényi (ER), and WattsStrogatz (WS). Then we compared the results against the MLE estimator. The MLE estimator is a modified version of the model developed by [10]. We have used $R^2$ and normalized RMSE (NRMSE) as the metrics to evaluate the performance, and the results are provided in Table 1. The recovery plots obtained using GrepeFlow for the three datasets are given in Fig. 2.

From Table 1, it is evident that GrepeFlow consistently outperforms MLE on the BA and WS datasets. Although MLE demonstrates superior performance on the ER dataset, its results are inconsistent overall, as reflected by its comparatively weaker performance on BA and WS. GrepeFlow provides a good fit and lower prediction error for all three networks. The recovery plots show that

**Table 1.** Comparison results for synthetic networks

| Dataset | GrepeFlow | | MLE | |
|---------|-----------|--------|--------|--------|
| | $R^2$ | NRMSE | R2 | NRMSE |
| BA | 0.7368 | 0.1483 | 0.0797 | 0.3397 |
| ER | 0.8170 | 0.1241 | 0.8655 | 0.1128 |
| WS | 0.9594 | 0.0611 | 0.5152 | 0.2576 |

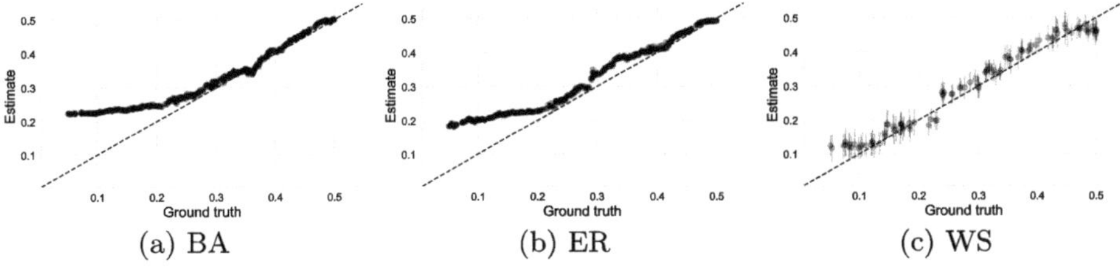

**Fig. 2.** Recovery plots obtained from GrepeFlow.

there is a very low variability in the inference across all three networks. While in lower ranges$(0.01 - 0.2)$, the estimations were not up to the mark.

For the second set of experiments, we use the Reddit datasets: TAB and Brexit. We first generate the network by identifying user interactions. Then, data is generated using the HK simulator for different parameter ranges using the network. The GrepeFlow model is trained with this data. Some inference experiments are done using simulated data to compute $R^2$ and $NRMSE$ values. Then, the actual text dataset is converted into a numerical dataset using VADER, and the inference dataset is built. Finally, the parameters were estimated for the actual data. Since we don't know the true parameter value, we simulate with an estimated parameter and perform the Smirnov (KS) test to compare the simulated data with the actual data. The results are given in Table 2. A comparison of final opinion distribution along the inference samples is visualized using Kernel Density Estimate (KDE) plots in Fig. 3.

**Table 2.** Results from Reddit datasets

| Dataset | $R^2$ | NRMSE | KS p-value |
|---------|-------|-------|------------|
| TAB | 0.7558 | 0.4176 | 0.2723 |
| Brexit | 0.7842 | 0.1322 | 0.0051 |

The $R^2$ results from the Reddit dataset indicate that GrepeFlow is a good fit for both datasets. But when experimented with actual data, the TAB was found to have high p-values, and it was found that the distribution of the model's predictions closely matches the distribution of the actual data. But for the Brexit

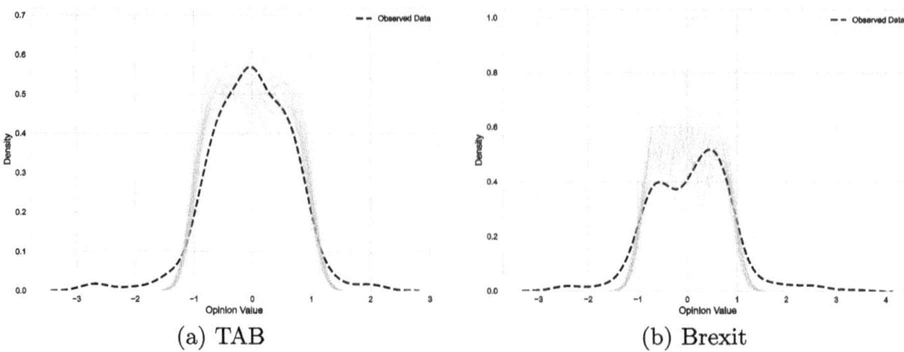

(a) TAB    (b) Brexit

**Fig. 3.** KDE plots of the final opinions from the data with inference samples.

dataset, it yields a low p-value, indicating the model failed to generate a simulation that's similar to actual data. The KDE plots indicate the same result that the TAB final opinion distribution is closer to the actual data, where Brexit data shows significant variation.

The poor performance of the GrepeFlow model on the Brexit dataset may be attributed to several factors. Notably, the network inferred from the Reddit data was overly sparse, potentially leading to significant information loss during the sampling phase. Further investigation using alternative graph reduction techniques and additional datasets is necessary to enhance the model's robustness and generalizability.

## 4    Conclusion

We propose a graph neural network-based approach for opinion dynamics parameter estimation. The framework performs simulation-based inference using a bounded confidence model. To enhance scalability, graph sampling techniques are employed. The results show that the proposed model estimates parameters effectively. We compare the framework against likelihood-based methods and validate its performance. Experiments with real-world data show that the framework's effectiveness needs to be validated before using it for further applications.

The opinion dynamics model we considered—HegselmannKraus—has only one parameter. One future research direction is to explore how this framework performs on more complex models with multiple parameters. Naturally, this would require more training and increased computational resources. Therefore, investigating broader scalability strategies beyond just graph sampling is another promising avenue for future work.

# References


1. Albi, G., Calzola, E., Dimarco, G.: A data-driven kinetic model for opinion dynamics with social network contacts. Eur. J. Appl. Math. **36**(2), 264–290 (2024). https://doi.org/10.1017/s0956792524000068
2. Alfas, M., Kumar, M., Shriyam, S., Kumar, S.: An efficient framework for epidemiological parameter estimation via graph reduction and graph neural networks. ACM Trans. Knowl. Discov. Data **19**(6), 1–29 (2025). https://doi.org/10.1145/3736727
3. De, A., Bhattacharya, S., Bhattacharya, P., Ganguly, N., Chakrabarti, S.: Learning a linear influence model from transient opinion dynamics. In: Proceedings of the 23rd ACM International Conference on Conference on Information and Knowledge Management, CIKM '14, pp. 401–410. ACM (2014). https://doi.org/10.1145/2661829.2662064
4. Degroot, M.H.: Reaching a consensus. J. Am. Stat. Assoc. **69**(345), 118–121 (1974). https://doi.org/10.1080/01621459.1974.10480137
5. French, J.R., Jr.: A formal theory of social power. Psychol. Rev. **63**(3), 181 (1956)
6. Gestefeld, M., Lorenz, J.: Calibrating an opinion dynamics model to empirical opinion distributions and transitions. J. Artif. Soc. Soc. Simul. **26**(4) (2023). https://doi.org/10.18564/jasss.5204
7. Hamilton, W., Ying, Z., Leskovec, J.: Inductive representation learning on large graphs. In: Advances in Neural Information Processing Systems, vol. 30 (2017)
8. Hegselmann, R., Krause, U.: Opinion dynamics and bounded confidence: models, analysis and simulation. J. Artif. Soc. Soc. Simul. (JASSS) **5**(3) (2002)
9. Hutto, C., Gilbert, E.: VADER: a parsimonious rule-based model for sentiment analysis of social media text. In: Proceedings of the International AAAI Conference on Web and Social Media, vol. 8, no. 1, pp. 216–225 (2014). https://doi.org/10.1609/icwsm.v8i1.14550
10. Lenti, J., Monti, C., De Francisci Morales, G.: Likelihood-based methods improve parameter estimation in opinion dynamics models. In: Proceedings of the 17th ACM International Conference on Web Search and Data Mining, WSDM '24, pp. 350–359. ACM (2024). https://doi.org/10.1145/3616855.3635785
11. Lenti, J., Silvestri, F., De Francisci Morales, G.: Variational inference of parameters in opinion dynamics models. In: Proceedings of the International AAAI Conference on Web and Social Media, vol. 19, pp. 2622–2627 (2025). https://doi.org/10.1609/icwsm.v19i1.35963
12. Leskovec, J., Faloutsos, C.: Sampling from large graphs. In: Proceedings of the 12th ACM SIGKDD International Conference on Knowledge Discovery and Data Mining, KDD06, pp. 631–636. ACM (2006). https://doi.org/10.1145/1150402.1150479
13. Noorazar, H.: Recent advances in opinion propagation dynamics: a 2020 survey. Eur. Phys. J. Plus **135**(6) (2020). https://doi.org/10.1140/epjp/s13360-020-00541-2
14. Radev, S.T., Mertens, U.K., Voss, A., Ardizzone, L., Kothe, U.: BayesFlow: learning complex stochastic models with invertible neural networks. IEEE Trans. Neural Netw. Learn. Syst. **33**(4), 1452–1466 (2022). https://doi.org/10.1109/tnnls.2020.3042395
15. Valensise, C.M., Cinelli, M., Quattrociocchi, W.: The drivers of online polarization: fitting models to data. Inf. Sci. **642**, 119152 (2023). https://doi.org/10.1016/j.ins.2023.119152
16. Zhu, J., Yao, Y., Tang, W., Zhang, H.: Dynamic parameter calibration framework for opinion dynamics models. Entropy **24**(8), 1112 (2022). https://doi.org/10.3390/e24081112

# Dynamic Weighted Selective Ensemble Classifier for Radiomics-Based Early Response Prediction in [$^{18}$F]-FDG PET/CT Breast Cancer Imaging


Moumita Dholey[1]([✉]), Shwet Makadiya[1], Ritesh J.M. Santosham[2], Soumendranath Ray[2], Jayanta Das[2], Sanjoy Chatterjee[2], Rosina Ahmed[2], and Jayanta Mukherjee[1]

[1] Indian Institute of Technology Kharagpur, Kharagpur, West Bengal, India
dholey.moumita5@iitkgp.ac.in, jay@cse.iitkgp.ac.in
[2] Tata Medical Center, Kolkata, West Bengal, India
{soumen.ray,jayanta.das,sanjoy.chatterjee,rosina.ahmed}@tmckolkata.com



**Abstract.** This study proposes a novel Dynamic Weighted Selective Ensemble Classifier for robust classification across diverse biomedical datasets. The model integrates bagging with a dual-layer fusion approach–global fusion assigns dynamic weights to base classifiers using a trust evaluation mechanism based on Dempster-Shafer theory and a modified tangent function, while local fusion performs dynamic ensemble selection for context-aware decision refinement. The final prediction is derived through a weighted voting strategy. The efficacy of the proposed model was first validated on 15 publicly available benchmark datasets, where it achieved the best performance in 10 cases, demonstrating strong generalization and adaptability. As a clinical application, the proposed model was evaluated for early response prediction in breast cancer using [$^{18}$F]-FDG PET/CT radiomic features. A total of 81 PET and 66 CT features were extracted per tumor lesion, followed by hybrid feature selection. The proposed model achieved balanced accuracy of 98.72%, 98.38%, 100%, 98.86%, 98.86%, and 100% on the HYPORT PET, HYPORT CT, HYPORT Combined, HYPORT-B PET, HYPORT-B CT, and HYPORT-B Combined datasets, respectively.

**Keywords:** Breast cancer · Ensemble learning · Radiomics · FDG PET/CT


## 1 Introduction

Breast cancer is the fifth leading cause of cancer-related mortality, causing over 685,000 deaths yearly [16]. Forecasts predict a 40.0% increase in breast cancer diagnoses by 2040, with 3 million annual cases. In India, most individuals with breast cancer are in stage 1 (locally progressed or metastatic). Hypofractionated radiotherapy is considered an improved approach to traditional radiotherapy based on breast cancer proliferation dynamics [6]. The HYPORT and HYPORT-B

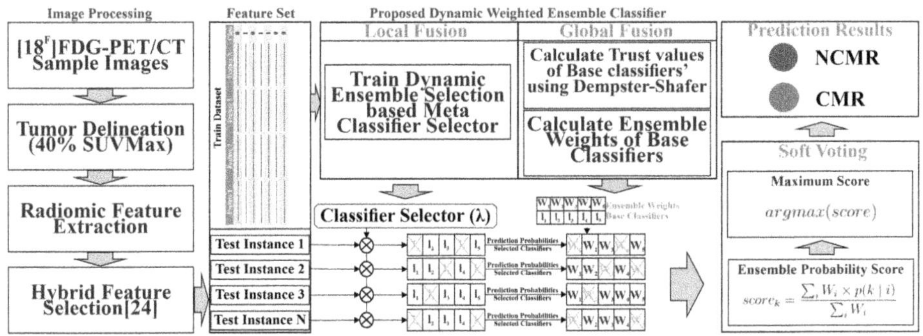


Fig. 1. Abstract workflow diagram of the proposed model.

trials assess the safety and effectiveness of individuals receiving palliative radiation to the breast. The [18F]-fluorodeoxyglucose (FDG) positron emission tomography (PET)/computed tomography (CT) based image features correlate with treatment response, histopathologic markers and prognosis in breast cancer [7]. Radiomic features with machine learning have gained prominence in automated breast cancer response prediction. [18F]-FDG PET/CT is widely used to assess recurrence, treatment response to neoadjuvant therapy, and metastatic disease monitoring [15]. Gomez et al. [5] developed a metabolic response prediction model for metastatic breast cancer using radiomic features from PET/CT scans. Their model combining Lasso feature selection with a Support Vector Machine (SVM) classifier achieved a mean area under the curve (AUC) of 93% with a standard deviation of 6%. Li et al. [10] used a Random Forest (RF) classifier for predicting pathologic complete response, achieving 85.7% accuracy on the training set using radiomics features. In ensemble learning, two strategies,*global fusion* and *local fusion*, aggregate predictions from base classifiers [1]. Global fusion assumes static contributions from base models, while local fusion adjusts each model's influence based on local competence. We propose a hybrid aggregation scheme that combines both fusion strategies to enhance predictive performance. We hypothesize that combining global trust-based weighting with local dynamic ensemble selection improves robustness for small, heterogeneous biomedical datasets. Our primary contributions are (i) proposing a weighted heterogeneous dynamic selective ensemble classification algorithm where base classifiers are selected dynamically with weights based on global performance, and (ii) validating the model on multiple online datasets against state-of-the-art methods [8,11,12,14] and applying it to in-house PET/CT breast cancer data. Figure 1 provides an overview of the proposed model architecture and its major processing components.

## 2  Methodology

### 2.1  Sample Collection

**Online Datasets:** We evaluated the proposed model on a total of 15 publicly available biomedical datasets sourced from the University of California, Irvine (UCI) machine learning repository [4], including *kidney, breast cancer, libras,* *wine, diabetic retinopathy, image segmentation, balance-scale, contraceptive, dermatology, glass, heart-cleveland, statlog-vechile, vertebral-column-3classes, letter recognition,* and *cardiotocography* (Table 1).

**In-house Dataset:** The local samples are collected from Tata Medical Center (TMC), Kolkata. The institutional ethical clearance was taken (EC/TMC/111/17, dated 09/02/2021). Two different single-centre, interventional phase I/II studies, HYPORT and HYPORT B, are conducted at TMC. Patients' de-identified images and clinical data are also archived in a multi-tier web-based medical image bank titled 'CompreHensive Digital ArchiVe of Cancer Imaging - Radiation Oncology (https://chavi.ai)' [9]. In HYPORT, six patients had Complete Metabolic Response (*CMR*) and 14 patients had Non-CMR (*NCMR*), including both Partial and Static metabolic response patients. Meanwhile, in HYPORT-B, 19 patients had *NCMR*, and four patients had *CMR*.

## 2.2  PET/CT Dataset Preparation

Both PET and CT images were resampled to a common resolution with zero origin, unit spacing, and matched dimensions. Tumor volumes were delineated using a fixed SUV thresholding method, with a threshold of 40% $SUV_{max}$, using the LIFEx software. Radiomic features were also extracted in LIFEx from the VOIs: 66 features from CT (9 first-order (histogram), 5 shape, 32 s-order(texture)) and 81 from PET (35 first-order, 5 shape, 32 texture, 9 quantitative). Due to class imbalance in the HYPORT and HYPORT-B datasets, SMOTE and ADASYN were used to generate 200 balanced samples per modality. An iterative hybrid forward feature selection method [3] was applied, resulting in 41, 22, and 72 features for HYPORT PET, CT, and Combined; and 37, 22, and 69 for HYPORT-B PET, CT, and Combined datasets, respectively.

## 2.3  Proposed Weighted Dynamic Ensemble Model

**Heterogeneous Base Classifiers Selection:** In this study, five widely used supervised learning algorithms are selected as base classifiers, denoted as $L = \{l_1, l_2, l_3, l_4, l_5\}$: linear Support Vector Machine (SVM) ($l_1$), Gaussian Naive Bayes (NB) ($l_2$), Decision Tree (DT) ($l_3$), Logistic Regression (LR) ($l_4$), and K-Nearest Neighbors (KNN) ($l_5$). Each classifier is optimized using a grid search strategy to identify the most effective hyper-parameter settings for the training data. The prediction corresponds to the class label associated with the maximum aggregated weighted probability.

The base classifiers are trained individually on the input training set to produce a corresponding set of trained models or hypotheses, denoted by $E = \{T_1, T_2, \ldots, T_5\}$. Each model $T_i \in E$ maps a feature vector $x$ to a posterior probability distribution over the target class space $\mathcal{C} = \{1, 2, \ldots, c\}$ as follows:

$$T(x) = \hat{p} = \{p(y = 1 \mid T, x),\ p(y = 2 \mid T, x),\ \ldots,\ p(y = c \mid T, x)\} \tag{1}$$

where, $\hat{p}$ = predicted posterior probability vector and $y \in \mathcal{C}$ denotes class labels.

---

**Algorithm 1:** Global fusion - Ensemble weight estimation of base classifiers

---

**Input**: Confusion matrix parameters of $i^{th}$ classifier: $tp_i$, $fp_i$, $tn_i$, $fn_i$
**Input**: Training parameters: $\alpha = 1$, $\beta = 1$, $\delta = 0.2$
**Output**: Weights of base classifiers $\{l_1, l_2, l_3, l_4, l_5\}$
1: Updated $\alpha_i$ of classifier $l_i$

$$\alpha_i = \alpha + (tp_i + tn_i) \times \delta \tag{2}$$

2: Updated $\beta_i$ of classifier $l_i$

$$\beta_i = \beta + (fp_i + fn_i) \times \delta \tag{3}$$

3: Uncertainty of classifier $l_i$

$$unc_i = \frac{12 \times \alpha_i \times \beta_i}{(\alpha_i + \beta_i)^2 \times (1 + \alpha_i + \beta_i)} \tag{4}$$

Belief of classifier $l_i$

$$bel_i = \frac{\alpha_i \times (1 - unc_i)}{(\alpha_i + \beta_i)} \tag{5}$$

4: Trust value $(\tau_i)$ of classifier $l_i$

$$\tau_i = bel_i + (0.5 \times unc_i) \tag{6}$$

5: Weighted trust value $(\hat{\tau}_i)$ of classifier $l_i$

$$\hat{\tau}_i = \frac{\tau_i}{\sum \tau_i} \tag{7}$$

6: Transformed trust value of classifier $l_i$

$$W_i = MTanh(\hat{\tau}_i) = \sum \frac{\left(e^{(1+\hat{\tau}_i)^2} - e^{(1-\hat{\tau}_i)^2}\right)}{\left(e^{(1+\hat{\tau}_i)^2} + e^{(1-\hat{\tau}_i)^2}\right)} \tag{8}$$

7: **return** $W = \{W_1, W_2, W_3, W_4, W_5\}$

---

**Global Fusion:** Here, the global fusion works in two stages: probabilistic trust estimation of base classifiers by the DempsterShafer (DS) belief method [13], and classifiers' ensemble weight allocation using a non-linear transformation of measured trust values.

*A. Trust Estimation*: In statistical belief theory, a trust model determines whether or not a classifier's decision is valid. It formed three opinions about the classifier's decision, i.e., Belief (degree of classifier's accuracy), Disbelief (degree of classifier's inaccuracy), and Uncertainty (both belief and disbelief are absent) [13]. For a model, they satisfy the following constraint as mentioned Eq. 9.

$$bel + dbl + unc = 1 \tag{9}$$

where, *bel*, *dbl*, and *unc* indicates belief, disbelief and uncertainty respectively.

In belief theory, *unc* represents a model's intrinsic uncertainty on unknown test data and is defined as:

$$unc = \frac{12 \times \alpha \times \beta}{(\alpha + \beta)^2 \times (1 + \alpha + \beta)} \tag{10}$$

These parameters work as a counter which calculates the correct and incorrect predictions. Finally, the $\alpha, \beta$ parameters are adjusted using a scaling factor $(\delta)$. Furthermore, the belief and disbelief parameters are calculated as follows,

$$bel = \frac{\alpha \times (1 - unc)}{(\alpha + \beta)} \tag{11}$$

$$dbl = \frac{\beta \times (1 - unc)}{(\alpha + \beta)} \tag{12}$$

The classifier's trust, incorporating belief and uncertainty, is computed as:

$$\tau = bel + (0.5 \times unc) \tag{13}$$

Algorithm 1 (lines 1–6) outlines trust value computation using DS. Parameters $\alpha$, $\beta$, and $\delta$ are initialized to 1, 1, and 0.2. Based on the classifier's confusion matrix, $\alpha$ (representing correctness via true positives/negatives) and $\beta$ (representing error via false positives/negatives) are updated using Eqs. 2 and 3, with smoothing factor $\delta$. The belief, uncertainty, and trust are calculated (Eqs. 5 and 6) for each base classifier. The average trust score $\hat{\tau}_i$ for each classifier is computed using Eq. 7.

*B. Ensemble Weight Determination*: To compute ensemble predictions, classifier trust values are transformed into weights and multiplied by prediction scores using maximum average probability. Direct normalization of trust values can cause ambiguity when scores are similar but predictions conflict. To address this, we introduce Modified Hyperbolic Tangent (MTanh), which amplifies small differences in trust. Unlike standard Tanh (output range: [0, 0.762]), MTanh extends the range to [0, 0.96], providing greater discrimination. As a smooth, monotonic, zero-centered function, MTanh enhances strong classifiers and suppresses weaker ones, improving ensemble reliability. It rewards higher trust values

---

**Algorithm 2:** Local fusion - classification steps using DES method and soft-voting

---

**Input**: Query sample $\mathbf{q}_{k,test}$
**Input**: Pool of classifiers $L = \{l_1, ....., l_5\}$
**Input**: Dynamic Selection Dataset $D_{SLC}$
**Output**: Predicted class values of query sample
1: $L' = \emptyset$
2: Find the region of competence $\rho_k$ of $\mathbf{q}_{k,test}$ using $D_{SEL}$
3: Compute the output profile $\tilde{\mathbf{q}}_{k,test}$ of $\mathbf{q}_{k,test}$.
4: Find the $F_p$ similar $\sigma_k$ of $\tilde{\mathbf{q}}_{k,test}$ using $\tilde{D}_{SLC}$
5: **for all** $l_i \in L$ **do**
6:    $v_{i,k} = \text{FeatureExtraction}(\rho_k, \sigma_k, l_i, \mathbf{q}_{k,test})$
7:    input $v_{i,k}$ to $\lambda$
8:    **if** $\alpha_{i,k} = 1$ "$l_i$ is competent for $\mathbf{q}_{k,test}$ " **then**
9:      $L' = L' \cup \{l_i\}$
10:   **end if**
11: **end for**
12: $C_{pred_k} = \text{SoftVoting}(\mathbf{q}_{k,test}, L', [W_i])$
13: **return** $C_{pred_k}$

---

**Table 1.** Performance comparison between classifiers on online UCI datasets

| Dataset | SVM | NB | DT | KNN | LR | DES | VOT | RF | GB | AB | Proposed Ensemble Method | | |
| --- | --- | --- | --- | --- | --- | --- | --- | --- | --- | --- | --- | --- | --- |
| | | | | | | | | | | | DS | DS+Tanh | DS+MTanh |
| kidney | 0.990625 | 0.965 | 0.906875 | 0.958125 | 0.990625 | 0.995625 | 0.99 | 0.98625 | 0.9675 | 0.9825 | 0.99375 | 0.996875 | 0.998125 |
| breast cancer | 0.97193 | 0.943421 | 0.928509 | 0.96886 | 0.978509 | 0.982456 | 0.96886 | 0.956579 | 0.926316 | 0.961842 | 0.98114 | 0.979825 | 0.983772 |
| libras | 0.729861 | 0.632639 | 0.355556 | 0.660417 | 0.7125 | 0.872917 | 0.720139 | 0.729167 | 0.540972 | 0.104861 | 0.878472 | 0.863889 | 0.873194 |
| wine | 0.983333 | 0.966667 | 0.831944 | 0.961111 | 0.979167 | 0.986111 | 0.980556 | 0.980556 | 0.909722 | 0.875 | 0.988889 | 0.984722 | 0.994444 |
| diabetic retinopathy | 0.698698 | 0.633623 | 0.62256 | 0.638178 | 0.71692 | 0.811714 | 0.695011 | 0.675705 | 0.674837 | 0.672668 | 0.803905 | 0.77462 | 0.788308 |
| image segmentation | 0.934524 | 0.804221 | 0.796104 | 0.950433 | 0.928896 | 0.974026 | 0.939827 | 0.972186 | 0.968939 | 0.447186 | 0.978463 | 0.976299 | 0.981169 |
| balance-scale | 0.8964 | 0.8856 | 0.7388 | 0.8212 | 0.8684 | 0.898 | 0.8868 | 0.8264 | 0.7868 | 0.8944 | 0.898 | 0.9068 | 0.9132 |
| contraceptive | 0.543898 | 0.468644 | 0.523559 | 0.481356 | 0.517119 | 0.735763 | 0.534746 | 0.515932 | 0.502203 | 0.54 | 0.731525 | 0.684915 | 0.722203 |
| dermatology | 0.970068 | 0.861905 | 0.871429 | 0.961905 | 0.970748 | 0.983673 | 0.971429 | 0.97551 | 0.929252 | 0.541497 | 0.985714 | 0.976871 | 0.990476 |
| glass | 0.641196 | 0.420266 | 0.631229 | 0.652824 | 0.607973 | 0.77907 | 0.656146 | 0.760797 | 0.667774 | 0.377076 | 0.799003 | 0.820598 | 0.827243 |
| heart-cleveland | 0.568852 | 0.480328 | 0.527049 | 0.57541 | 0.563115 | 0.602459 | 0.567213 | 0.572131 | 0.52459 | 0.506557 | 0.605738 | 0.659016 | 0.647541 |
| statlog-vechile | 0.748378 | 0.457522 | 0.644543 | 0.70531 | 0.781711 | 0.831563 | 0.730088 | 0.739233 | 0.732448 | 0.575221 | 0.835103 | 0.830678 | 0.842773 |
| vertebral-column-3classes | 0.837097 | 0.83629 | 0.816935 | 0.775806 | 0.856452 | 0.894355 | 0.829032 | 0.848387 | 0.782258 | 0.602419 | 0.88629 | 0.862097 | 0.891129 |
| letter recognition | 0.93615 | 0.641387 | 0.254025 | 0.937413 | 0.774363 | 0.94885 | 0.923275 | 0.955288 | 0.944013 | 0.235125 | 0.965213 | 0.96475 | 0.965125 |
| cardiotocography | 0.987192 | 0.952174 | 0.917274 | 0.987192 | 0.988719 | 0.990834 | 0.989307 | 0.987309 | 0.986369 | 0.964277 | 0.990717 | 0.991657 | 0.992597 |
| Multi-Classifiers Multi-Dataset Comparisons | | | | | | | | | | | | | |
| Average Accuracy | 0.829213 | 0.729979 | 0.691093 | 0.802369 | 0.815681 | 0.885828 | 0.825495 | 0.832095 | 0.7896 | 0.618709 | 0.888128 | 0.884907 | 0.894087 |
| Friedman's Rank | 6.666667 | 11.06667 | 11.53333 | 9.266667 | 7.5 | 2.9 | 7.333333 | 6.9 | 9.666667 | 11 | 2.5 | 3.133333 | 1.533333 |
| Standard Deviation | 0.160369 | 0.205636 | 0.207816 | 0.171436 | 0.163538 | 0.115523 | 0.1611 | 0.159767 | 0.174229 | 0.272551 | 0.115394 | 0.112692 | 0.110193 |
| Coefficient of Variation | 0.193399 | 0.281701 | 0.300706 | 0.213662 | 0.200493 | 0.130413 | 0.195156 | 0.192006 | 0.220655 | 0.440516 | 0.12993 | 0.127349 | 0.123246 |
| Borda Score | 110 | 44 | 37 | 71 | 97.5 | 166.5 | 100 | 106.5 | 65 | 45 | 172.5 | 163 | 187 |
| Coverage (%) | 0 | 0 | 0 | 0 | 0 | 20 | 0 | 0 | 0 | 0 | 13.33333 | 6.666667 | 60 |
| Cohen's d vs DS+MTanh | 1.04516 | 1.238834 | 1.141822 | 1.202712 | 1.019787 | 0.442744 | 1.104509 | 1.037174 | 1.210949 | 1.078557 | 0.423281 | 0.782205 | - |

more than *Tanh*, improving decisive predictions. The *Tanh* and *MTanh* function is mathematically expressed as,

$$Tanh(z) = \frac{(e^z - e^{-z})}{(e^z + e^{-z})} \quad , \quad W_i = MTanh(\hat{\tau}_i) = \sum \frac{\left(e^{(1+\hat{\tau}_i)^2} - e^{(1-\hat{\tau}_i)^2}\right)}{\left(e^{(1+\hat{\tau}_i)^2} + e^{(1-\hat{\tau}_i)^2}\right)} \quad (14)$$

where, $z$ is a real integer value, $W_i$ is the $i^{th}$ classifier's ensemble weight.

**Table 2.** Performance comparison between proposed model and prior studies

| Dataset | Prior art | Prior Acc | Prior Methodology | Proposed |
|---|---|---|---|---|
| Kidney | Pal [12] | 0.9723 | Logistic Regression, Decision Tree, SVM, and bagging ensemble | **0.998125** |
| | Krishna.. et al. [12] | 0.782 | A custom CNN model was introduced | |
| | Rehman et al. [12] | 0.883 | Random Forest, SVM, etc. | |
| | Rady & Anwar [12] | 0.7729 | PNN, MLP, SVM, and RBF algorithms | |
| | Han et al. [12] | 0.8779 | Random Forest, SVM, ANN, DT, KNN, and LR | |
| | Dong et al. [12] | 0.768 | LightGBM | |
| | Hu et al. [12] | 0.579 | Multi-task multi-modality Support Vector Machine | |
| Breast Cancer | Kim and Lee [8] | 0.9701 | Weighted Naïve Bayes classifier+exponential loss minimize | **0.983772** |
| | Memis et al. [11] | 0.9504 | Comparison Matrix-Based Fuzzy Parameterized Fuzzy Soft Classifier (FPFS-CMC) | |
| Libras | Tanveer et al. [14] | 0.875 | Ensemble of Random Vector Functional Link (RVFL) networks combined with twin SVM variants | 0.873194 |
| | Memis et al. [11] | **0.9781** | FPFS-CMC | |
| Wine | Tanveer et al. [14] | 0.9888 | Ensemble models combining RVFL + twin SVM variants | **0.994444** |
| | Memis et al. [11] | 0.9724 | FPFS-CMC | |
| Diabetic Retino. | Memis et al. [11] | 0.6597 | FPFS-CMC | **0.788308** |
| Image Segm. | Memis et al. [11] | **0.993** | FPFS-CMC | 0.981169 |
| | Kim and Lee [8] | 0.9874 | Weighted Naïve Bayes classifier+exponential loss minimize | |
| Balance-Scale | Tanveer et al. [14] | **0.957415** | Ensemble models combining RVFL + twin SVM variants | 0.9132 |
| Contraceptive | Tanveer et al. [14] | 0.564172 | Ensemble models combining RVFL + twin SVM variants | **0.722203** |
| Dermatology | Tanveer et al. [14] | 0.986323 | Ensemble models combining RVFL + twin SVM variants | **0.990476** |
| Glass | Tanveer et al. [14] | 0.691595 | Ensemble models combining RVFL + twin SVM variants | **0.827243** |
| | Kim and Lee [8] | 0.7785 | Weighted Naïve Bayes classifier+exponential loss minimize | |
| Heart Cleveland | Tanveer et al. [14] | 0.597436 | Ensemble models combining RVFL + twin SVM variants | **0.647541** |
| Statlog Vehicle | Tanveer et al. [14] | **0.860601** | Ensemble models combining RVFL + twin SVM variants | 0.842773 |
| Vertebral Column | Tanveer et al. [14] | 0.864952 | Ensemble models combining RVFL + twin SVM variants | **0.891129** |
| Letter Recog. | Kim and Lee [8] | **0.9911** | Weighted Naïve Bayes classifier+exponential loss minimize | 0.965125 |
| Cardiotocography | Kim and Lee [8] | 0.9403 | Weighted Naïve Bayes classifier+exponential loss minimize | **0.992597** |

**Local Fusion:** We do not enforce all five base classifiers in every ensemble decision, instead assuming varying competence levels and selecting only the most capable ones per test sample. We employ the META-DES model [2], a meta-learning-based dynamic ensemble selection framework, detailed in Algorithm 2. First, the meta-classifier $\lambda$ is trained offline. For each test instance $q_{k,\text{test}}$, its region of competence $\rho_k$ is identified using samples from the dynamic selection dataset $D_{\text{SLC}}$. The output profile $\tilde{q}_{k,\text{test}}$ is compared to $\tilde{D}_{\text{SLC}}$ using Euclidean distance to obtain the $F_p$ most similar profiles $\sigma_k$. For each base classifier $l_i \in L$, meta-feature vectors $v_{i,j}$ are extracted and fed into $\lambda$. If the predicted class attribute $\alpha_{i,k} = 1$, $l_i$ is included in the final set of dynamically selected classifiers $L'$ for that test sample.

**Final Prediction with Soft Voting:** The ensemble integrates global and local fusion strategies. META-DES performs local fusion by selecting competent base classifiers for each test instance, while global fusion assigns weights to classifiers based on trust values. For test sample $x_k$, only locally selected classifiers contribute to prediction, with outputs weighted by global trust. A soft voting mechanism computes class-wise probability scores, as shown in Algorithm 2. The predicted class label is:

$$C_{pred_k} = \underset{k}{argmax} \frac{\sum_i W_i \times \hat{p}(T_i, x_k)}{\sum_i W_i} \tag{15}$$

where, $\hat{p}$ is the posterior probability scores of classifier model $T_i$ with sample $x_k$, the $k^{th}$ sample of $q_{k,test}$.

# 3    Results and Discussion

The proposed ensemble uses a dynamic bagging framework combining global and local fusion. Global importance is estimated via a DempsterShafer trust-based scheme, transformed using the MTanh function to enhance discriminability. Locally, META-DES dynamically selects competent classifiers per test sample. Final predictions use weighted soft voting, reducing the impact of weak classifiers and enabling sample-specific decisions. The ensemble incorporates five base classifiers SVM, NB, DT, LR, and KNN, each optimized via grid search with 10-fold cross-validation. Common hyper-parameters included: NB (1e-11), DT (entropy, depth = 4), KNN (neighbors = 4, power = 1), SVC (linear, gamma = auto), and LR (L2, C = 1.0, solver = liblinear). The proposed ensemble model was evaluated on 15 publicly available datasets from the UCI Machine Learning Repository, split into 60% training and 40% testing. It was compared against five base classifiers and ensemble methods—Voting (VOT), Random Forest (RF), Gradient Boosting (GB), and Adaptive Boosting (AB). Table 1 presents accuracy comparisons, showing three variants of the proposed model: DS, DS+Tanh, and DS+MTanh. DS uses the trust-based scheme [13]; DS+Tanh applies the hyperbolic tangent function to transform trust values, while DS+MTanh uses the proposed modified Tanh function for dynamic scaling. Other functions were tested but omitted due to lower performance. Seven ensemble metrics evaluated performance: Average Accuracy (AA), Friedman's Rank (FR), Standard Deviation (SD), Coefficient of Variation (CV), Borda Score (BS), Coverage (%), and Cohen's $d$ relative to DS+MTanh. The DS+MTanh model outperformed others, achieving highest AA (0.8941) and lowest FR (1.533), indicating top consistency. It had the lowest SD (0.1102) and CV (0.1232), with highest BS (187.0) and Coverage (60%), confirming its dominance. Large positive Cohen's $d$ values highlight its statistical advantage. Table 2 shows DS+MTanh outperformed existing methods on 10 of 15 datasets, with marginal differences on the remaining five demonstrating strong generalizability.

We demonstrated the effectiveness of radiomic feature-based ensemble models for predicting therapy response in breast cancer patients using a locally collected dataset. Due to the limited sample size, SMOTE and ADASYN were applied to generate synthetic data, producing 200 samples per modality. Each PET/CT modality yielded two datasets—original (imbalanced) and synthetic (balanced) resulting in 12 datasets: HYPORT and HYPORT-B PET, CT, and Combined (each with original and synthetic versions). Data similarity between real and synthetic sets was evaluated using Chi-square and Inverted KolmogorovSmirnov D statistics, with high scores indicating strong alignment (0.797 for HYPORT PET, 0.745 for CT, 0.771 for HYPORT-B PET, and 0.739 for CT). For model evaluation, synthetic datasets were used for training and original ones for testing. Table 3 presents the performance of DS+MTanh, which consistently outperformed all baselines. Five metrics balanced accuracy (BA), precision (PR), recall (RE), F1-score (F1), and AUC were used. The model achieved BA of 98.72%, 98.38%, 100%, 98.86%, 98.86%, and 100% on HYPORT and HYPORT-B PET, CT, and Combined datasets, respectively. Performance improved with

**Table 3.** Performance analysis of classifiers on in-house datasets

| Datasets | Metrics | SVM | NB | DT | KNN | LR | DES | VOT | BAG | GB | AB | Proposed Ensemble Model | | |
| --- | --- | --- | --- | --- | --- | --- | --- | --- | --- | --- | --- | --- | --- | --- |
| | | | | | | | | | | | | DS | DS+Tanh | DS+MTanh |
| HYPORT PET | BA | 0.894127 | 0.855666 | 0.775021 | 0.919768 | 0.92928 | 0.945409 | 0.945409 | 0.932589 | 0.819686 | 0.884202 | 0.945409 | 0.945409 | 0.987179 |
| | F1 | 0.888889 | 0.84058 | 0.783784 | 0.918919 | 0.935065 | 0.947368 | 0.973684 | 0.96 | 0.878049 | 0.923077 | 0.987368 | 0.947368 | 0.987013 |
| | PR | 0.969697 | 0.966667 | 0.828571 | 0.971429 | 0.947368 | 0.972973 | 0.972973 | 0.972222 | 0.813953 | 0.897436 | 0.972973 | 0.98568 | 1.0 |
| | RE | 0.820513 | 0.74359 | 0.74359 | 0.871795 | 0.923077 | 0.923077 | 0.923077 | 0.897436 | 0.897436 | 0.897436 | 0.923077 | 0.923077 | 0.948718 |
| | AUC | 0.950372 | 0.898677 | 0.796526 | 0.940033 | 0.92225 | 0.946237 | 0.945409 | 0.931348 | 0.873449 | 0.918941 | 1.0 | 1.0 | 0.944582 |
| HYPORT CT | BA | 0.933871 | 0.5 | 0.756452 | 0.946371 | 0.901613 | 0.971371 | 0.971371 | 0.95 | 0.939113 | 0.933871 | 0.967742 | 0.983871 | 0.983871 |
| | F1 | 0.935065 | 0.720721 | 0.818182 | 0.948718 | 0.911392 | 0.975 | 0.975 | 0.947368 | 0.95122 | 0.935065 | 0.98 | 0.97561 | 0.987654 |
| | PR | 0.972973 | 0.56338 | 0.75 | 0.973684 | 0.923077 | 0.975 | 0.975 | 1.0 | 0.928571 | 0.972973 | 0.95 | 0.952381 | 0.97561 |
| | RE | 0.9 | 1.0 | 0.9 | 0.925 | 0.9 | 0.975 | 0.975 | 0.9 | 0.975 | 0.9 | 1.0 | 1.0 | 1.0 |
| | AUC | 0.978226 | 0.5 | 0.818145 | 0.994355 | 0.979032 | 0.99879 | 0.987903 | 0.997177 | 0.970968 | 0.977419 | 0.996935 | 0.999 | 0.999597 |
| HYPORT Combined | BA | 0.942101 | 0.906948 | 0.655914 | 1.0 | 1.0 | 1.0 | 1.0 | 0.974359 | 0.764682 | 0.909843 | 1.0 | 1.0 | 1.0 |
| | F1 | 0.948718 | 0.90411 | 0.684211 | 1.0 | 1.0 | 1.0 | 1.0 | 0.973684 | 0.831461 | 0.925 | .99 | 1.0 | 1.0 |
| | PR | 0.948718 | 0.970588 | 0.702703 | 1.0 | 1.0 | 1.0 | 1.0 | 1.0 | 1.0 | 0.74 | 0.99 | 0.99 | 0.99896 |
| | RE | 0.948718 | 0.846154 | 0.666667 | 1.0 | 1.0 | 1.0 | 1.0 | 0.948718 | 0.948718 | 0.948718 | .98995 | 0.99 | 0.99 |
| | AUC | 0.93383 | 0.963606 | 0.734905 | 1.0 | 1.0 | 1.0 | 1.0 | 0.990074 | 0.782878 | 0.974359 | 1.0 | 1.0 | 1.0 |
| HYPORT-B PET | BA | 0.988636 | 0.697884 | 0.818182 | 0.977273 | 0.931818 | 0.965909 | 0.954545 | 0.954545 | 0.896944 | 0.873824 | 0.9789 | 0.98195 | 0.988636 |
| | F1 | 0.988506 | 0.675676 | 0.777778 | 0.976744 | 0.926829 | 0.964706 | 0.952381 | 0.952381 | 0.921348 | 0.913043 | 0.988 | 0.988429 | 0.988506 |
| | PR | 1 | 0.833333 | 1.0 | 1.0 | 1.0 | 1.0 | 1.0 | 1.0 | 0.911111 | 0.875 | 1.0 | 1.0 | 1.0 |
| | RE | 0.977273 | 0.568182 | 0.636364 | 0.954545 | 0.863636 | 0.931818 | 0.909091 | 0.909091 | 0.931818 | 0.954545 | 0.977273 | 0.97 | 0.977273 |
| | AUC | 0.997649 | 0.847962 | 0.818182 | 0.999608 | 0.981975 | 0.9689 | 0.98885 | 0.992947 | 0.92163 | 0.973354 | 1.0 | 0.9988 | 1.0 |
| HYPORT-B CT | BA | 0.94279 | 0.568182 | 0.5 | 0.948668 | 0.94279 | 0.960031 | 0.545455 | 0.5 | 0.44279 | 0.98551 | 0.977273 | 0.98 | 0.988636 |
| | F1 | 0.954545 | 0.24 | 0.5 | 0.953488 | 0.954545 | 0.965517 | 0.965517 | 0.566667 | 0.5 | 0.954545 | 0.966 | 0.957 | 0.956895 |
| | PR | 0.954545 | 0.4489 | 0.56 | 0.97619 | 0.954545 | 0.976744 | 0.976744 | 0.6 | 0.58112 | 0.954545 | 0.96589 | 0.954545 | 0.954545 |
| | RE | 0.954545 | 0.136364 | 0.589 | 0.931818 | 0.954545 | 0.954545 | 0.954545 | 0.590909 | 0.511 | 0.954545 | 0.97 | 0.971 | 0.97732 |
| | AUC | 0.938088 | 0.568182 | 0.5 | 0.956505 | 0.934953 | 0.94906 | 0.956897 | 0.75313 | 0.5 | 0.95768 | 0.94906 | 0.94968 | 0.95 |
| HYPORT-B Combined | BA | 1.0 | 0.559524 | 0.916667 | 0.988095 | 0.97619 | 1.0 | 0.97619 | 0.940476 | 0.952381 | 0.940476 | 1.0 | 1.0 | 1.0 |
| | F1 | 1.0 | 0.212766 | 0.909091 | 0.987952 | 0.97561 | 1.0 | 0.97561 | 0.936709 | 0.95 | 0.936709 | 1.0 | 1.0 | 1.0 |
| | PR | 1.0 | 0.3 | 0.8988 | 0.9968 | 0.989 | 0.99148 | 0.97889 | 0.96555 | 0.9689 | 0.97896 | 0.9969 | 0.99 | 0.99 |
| | RE | 1.0 | 0.119048 | 0.833333 | 0.97619 | 0.952381 | 1.0 | 0.952381 | 0.880952 | 0.904762 | 0.880952 | 0.98889 | 0.99586 | 0.9998 |
| | AUC | 1.0 | 0.559524 | 0.916667 | 1.0 | 1.0 | 1.0 | 1.0 | 1.0 | 0.97619 | 0.964286 | 1.0 | 1.0 | 1.0 |

PET/CT fusion, demonstrating the value of multimodal integration. Lastly, we compared the proposed algorithm with a 3D DenseNet deep learning model. Due to limited data and the need for interpretability, a classical approach was preferred. Table 4 presents the classification results on in-house datasets. Finally, the proposed ensemble shows clear advantages in robustness, adaptability, and interpretability, outperforming standard ensembles and deep networks, particularly on small PET/CT datasets. Its main drawbacks are reliance on limited single-center data, added computational steps, and sensitivity of radiomic features to imaging protocols, underscoring the need for broader validation and optimization.

**Table 4.** Performance of 3D-DenseNet Model on PET/CT Data

| Modality | Study | Acc | PR | RE | F1 |
|---|---|---|---|---|---|
| PET | HYPORT | 66.7% | 44.4% | 66.7% | 53.4% |
| CT | | 83.3% | 88.9% | 83% | 83.81% |
| Combined | | 64.29% | 78.02% | 63.22% | 55.78% |
| PET | HYPORT-B | 77.8% | 60.49% | 77.7% | 68.06% |
| CT | | 77.78% | 60.49% | 77.7% | 68.06% |
| Combined | | 90.0% | 81.08% | 89.55% | 85.26% |

## 4 Conclusion

This study introduced a dynamic weighted selective ensemble classifier that integrates global trust-based weighting with MTanh scaling and local META-DES selection. On 15 UCI datasets, the model achieved the highest average accuracy (0.8941) and the lowest Friedman's rank (1.533), outperforming standard classifiers and ensembles in most cases. For clinical validation, the method attained balanced accuracies of 98.7% (PET), 98.4% (CT), and 100% (PETCT) on HYPORT, and 98.9% (PET), 98.9% (CT), and 100% (PETCT) on HYPORT-B datasets, surpassing both classical baselines and a 3D DenseNet. These results confirm that the proposed ensemble is robust, adaptable, and effective for small, heterogeneous biomedical datasets, with PETCT fusion further boosting predictive power. Future work will extend validation to larger multi-institutional cohorts and explore optimization for clinical deployment.

## References


1. Bonissone, P.P., Xue, F., Subbu, R.: Fast meta-models for local fusion of multiple predictive models. Appl. Soft Comput. **11**(2), 1529–1539 (2011)
2. Cruz, R.M., Sabourin, R., Cavalcanti, G.D., Ren, T.I.: META-DES: a dynamic ensemble selection framework using meta-learning. Pattern Recogn. **48**(5), 1925–1935 (2015)
3. Doe, M., et al.: Ensemble methods with [$^{18}$F]FDG-PET/CT radiomics in breast cancer response prediction. In: Pattern Recognition and Machine Intelligence, pp. 369–379. Springer Nature Switzerland, Cham (2023)
4. Dua, D., Graff, C., et al.: UCI machine learning repository 2017 **7**(1) (2017). http://archive.ics.uci.edu/ml
5. Gómez, O.V., et al.: Analysis of cross-combinations of feature selection and machine-learning classification methods based on [18F] F-FDG PET/CT radiomic features for metabolic response prediction of metastatic breast cancer lesions. Cancers **14**(12), 2922 (2022)
6. Gu, L., et al.: Comparing hypofractionated with conventional fractionated radiotherapy after breast-conserving surgery for early breast cancer: a meta-analysis of randomized controlled trials. Front. Oncol. **11** (2021). https://doi.org/10.3389/fonc.2021.753209

7. Ha, S., Park, S., Bang, J.I., Kim, E.K., Lee, H.Y.: Metabolic radiomics for pre-treatment 18F-FDG PET/CT to characterize locally advanced breast cancer: histopathologic characteristics, response to neoadjuvant chemotherapy, and prognosis. Sci. Rep. **7**(1), 1–11 (2017)

8. Kim, T., Lee, J.S.: Exponential loss minimization for learning weighted naive bayes classifiers. IEEE Access **10**, 22724–22736 (2022)

9. Kundu, S., et al.: Design and development of a medical image databank for assisting studies in radiomics. J. Digit. Imaging **35**(3), 408–423 (2022)

10. Li, P., et al.: 18 F-FDG PET/CT radiomic predictors of pathologic complete response (PCR) to neoadjuvant chemotherapy in breast cancer patients. Eur. J. Nucl. Med. Mol. Imaging **47**, 1116–1126 (2020)

11. Memiş, S., Enginoğlu, S., Erkan, U.: A classification method in machine learning based on soft decision-making via fuzzy parameterized fuzzy soft matrices. Soft. Comput. **26**(3), 1165–1180 (2022)

12. Pal, S.: Chronic kidney disease prediction using machine learning techniques. Biomed. Mater. Devices, 1–7 (2022)

13. Roy, P., Chowdhury, C., Kundu, M., Ghosh, D., Bandyopadhyay, S.: Novel weighted ensemble classifier for smartphone based indoor localization. Expert Syst. Appl. **164**, 113758 (2021)

14. Tanveer, M., Ganaie, M., Suganthan, P.N.: Ensemble of classification models with weighted functional link network. Appl. Soft Comput. **107**, 107322 (2021)

15. Ulaner, G.A.: PET/CT for patients with breast cancer: where is the clinical impact? Am. J. Roentgenol. **213**(2), 254–265 (2019)

16. Zhang, J., et al.: Natural products and derivatives for breast cancer treatment: from drug discovery to molecular mechanism. Phytomedicine, 155600 (2024)

# Chemically-Informed Transformer Architecture for VOC Identification from Multi-sensor Time-Series Data

Sagnik Jana[1(✉)] [ID], Snehraj Gaur[2] [ID], Ritu Gupta[2] [ID],
and Santanu Chaudhury[3] [ID]

[1] Department of Computer Science, Indraprastha Institute of Information
Technology Delhi, New Delhi 110020, India
sagnikjana60@gmail.com

[2] Department of Chemistry, Indian Institute of Technology Delhi,
New Delhi 110016, India
ritugupta@iitd.ac.in

[3] Department of Electrical Engineering, Indian Institute of Technology Delhi, New
Delhi 110016, India
santanuc@ee.iitd.ac.in

**Abstract.** Gas sensor arrays generate time-series responses to volatile organic compounds (VOCs), but traditional ML models ignore chemically relevant information of analytes and sensor functional group sensitivities. We propose a chemically-informed Transformer framework, combining molecular fingerprints (via RDKit), sensor functional group embeddings, and tubelet-based spatio-temporal patching in a ViViT-inspired architecture. The representation space encodes the structure and chemical nature of gases and sensor surfaces for VOC classification. Tested on methanol, propanol, butanone, formaldehyde, and their mixtures, the model captures signal patterns effectively and achieves 96.95% accuracy. This approach is interpretable and generalizable to other sensor datasets.

**Keywords:** Video Vision Transformer · Multi-Sensor ·
Chemically-informed embeddings

## 1 Introduction

The Electronic Nose (e-nose) mimics the biological olfactory mechanism using an array of gas sensors and machine learning (ML) models to identify complex odors [5,6]. Traditional ML approaches such as Support Vector Machines, Random Forests, and CNNs analyze sensor responses but rely heavily on manually extracted features from time-series data [2,3,9,11,12]. However, these methods often overlook the underlying chemical interactions and structural correlations between gases and sensor materials.


S. Mitra et al. (Eds.): PReMI 2025, LNCS 16358, pp. 669–678, 2026.
https://doi.org/10.1007/978-3-032-18480-1_68

Recent transformer-based approaches have shown promise for modeling temporal dependencies in gas sensing data [7,14], yet they still treat sensor outputs as raw numerical sequences, neglecting chemical information.

To overcome these limitations, we propose a chemically-informed video-vision transformer that integrates both sensing dynamics and chemical structure. Using Morgan fingerprints derived via RDKit, our model encodes molecular structures of volatile organic compounds (VOCs) and functional characteristics of sensor materials into a shared embedding space. This enables the network to learn gassensor interactions such as hydrogen bonding, dipole affinity, and $\pi\pi$ stacking directly from data. By combining spatiotemporal embeddings of sensor responses with chemically meaningful representations, the proposed model provides a generalized and interpretable framework for gas mixture classification—to our knowledge, the first of its kind.

## 2   The Problem

The dataset comprises four VOCs—methanol, propanol, butanone, and formaldehyde—including four pure gases, three binary mixtures, and one quaternary mixture. Each VOC was measured at 5, 10, and 25 ppm, with three repetitions per experiment. A sensor array of four chemiresistive sensors with distinct chemical functionalities was used in a dynamic sensing chamber, recording the current response during exposure, equilibrium, and recovery. The sensing mechanism follows a chemiresistive principle, where reducing VOCs donate electrons to the p-type sensor surface, decreasing current due to reduced majority carriers. The response (R) is defined as:

$$\mathbf{R} = \frac{\mathbf{I_a} - \mathbf{I_g}}{\mathbf{I}_a} \times \mathbf{100} \tag{1}$$

where $\mathbf{I_a}$ is the current in ambient air and $\mathbf{I_g}$ is the current in the presence of gas exposure.

**Ethics of Experiments:** All VOC experiments were conducted safely with strict leakage prevention measures.

## 3   Methodology

The proposed method employs RDKit to generate Morgan fingerprints—128-dimensional molecular descriptors representing both VOC analytes and sensor functional groups [4,8]. These fingerprints capture chemical similarities based on molecular topology and are projected to a 64-dimensional embedding space for integration with sensor response features. RDKit's Chem and AllChem modules enable SMILES parsing, substructure analysis, conformer generation, and fingerprint computation, supporting seamless incorporation of chemical information into deep learning workflows.

## 3.1  Embedding Spaces

***Molecular Fingerprint Embedding (Gas-Level Encoding).*** Each gas (pure or mixed) is encoded using its canonical SMILES string [15]. SMILES are converted into 128-dimensional Morgan fingerprints, where each bit indicates the presence of chemical substructures. For mixtures, constituent fingerprints are averaged, yielding chemically rich embeddings that preserve structural similarities (e.g., MethanolPropanol) in vector space:

$$\mathbf{f_g} = \mathbf{Morgan}(\mathbf{SMILES}(\mathbf{g}); \mathbf{r} = \mathbf{2}, \mathbf{d} = \mathbf{128}) \tag{2}$$

For a mixture of gases:

$$\mathbf{f_{g_{mix}}} = \frac{1}{\mathbf{k}} \sum_{i=1}^{k} \mathbf{f_{g_i}} \tag{3}$$

where $\mathbf{g_{mix}} = (\mathbf{g_1}, \mathbf{g_2}, ..., \mathbf{g_k})$

***Sensor-Specific Functional Group Embedding.*** Each sensor $(S_1!-!S_4)$ has surface groups ($e.g., NH_2, SH, COOH$) enabling diverse VOC interactions. Each sensor is assigned functional groups $F_s$, whose Morgan fingerprints $f_{f_g}$ are averaged to form a 128-dimensional embedding:

$$\mathbf{e_s} = \frac{1}{|\mathbf{F_s}|} \sum_{\mathbf{f_g} \in \mathbf{F_s}} \mathbf{f_{f_g}} \tag{4}$$

The resulting [4 × 128] matrix encodes the sensor array's chemical selectivity and is input alongside the signal data.

***Similarity Structure and Regularization.*** A cosine similarity matrix is computed between all fingerprint-derived class vectors to obtain semantic consistency in the embedding space. During training, the learned class embeddings (one per gas) are regularized to align their pairwise similarity matrix with that of the molecular fingerprint vectors. This regularization ensures that learned representations reflect chemical similarity, making the model more generalizable and interpretable.

## 3.2  Signal Processing and Spatiotemporal Embeddings

***Raw Sensor Input Format.*** Each sample is a multivariate time series of shape [S=4 sensors × T=25 time steps], representing current measurements over time. These signals contain both temporal and cross-sensor correlations.

***Tubelet Construction (Sensor-Time Patch Embedding).*** Instead of processing this 2D signal directly, we adopt a spatiotemporal tubelet strategy inspired by video vision transformers. The signal is partitioned into non-overlapping patches (tubelets) of shape [2 sensors × 5 time steps], resulting in 10 patches per sample. Each patch is flattened into a vector of 10 dimension, and projected into a 64-dimensional latent space using a shared linear projection layer. These patch embeddings form the primary input tokens to the transformer. This allows the model to localize and attend to structured events like signal spikes, correlations across sensors, or transient gas features within specific time intervals. Given a sensor matrix $X \in R^{S \times T}$ with $S = 4$ and $T = 25$, we divide it into tubelets of shape $p_s \times p_t = 2 \times 5$. Each tubelet $X_i$ is flattened:

$$\mathbf{z_i} = \text{Flatten}(\mathbf{X_i}) \in \mathbf{R^{P_s \cdot P_t}} \tag{5}$$

The number of tubelets is:

$$\mathbf{N} = \frac{\mathbf{S}}{\mathbf{p_s}} \cdot \frac{\mathbf{T}}{\mathbf{p_t}} = \mathbf{2 \cdot 5 = 10} \tag{6}$$

Each token is linearly projected:

$$\mathbf{h}_i = \mathbf{W}_z \mathbf{z}_i + \mathbf{b}_z, \quad \mathbf{W}_z \in R^{(p_s p_t) \times d_h} \tag{7}$$

***Molecular Fingerprint Conditioning of Patches.*** Each gas's molecular fingerprint (128-dim) is linearly projected to a 64-dimensional vector and concatenated with each patch token, effectively conditioning all spatiotemporal patches on the chemical identity of the analyte. This enables gas-aware representation learning, where the transformer learns not just from the sensor signals, but how these signals are expected to behave given the chemical structure of the gas. Gas fingerprint projection:

$$\mathbf{c}_g = \mathbf{W}_f \mathbf{f}_g + \mathbf{b}_f, \quad \mathbf{W}_f \in R^{128 \times d} \tag{8}$$

Each token is concatenated with cg:

$$\mathbf{h}'_\mathbf{i} = \mathbf{h_i} \oplus \mathbf{c_g} \in \mathbf{R^{2d}} \tag{9}$$

### 3.3   Positional Encoding and Token Design

***Learnable Positional Encoding.*** To retain information about the relative position of each patch in the original 2D sensor-time grid, we use learnable positional encodings. A matrix of shape [1, N+2, D] is initialized and learned during training, where N is the number of tubelets (10), +2 accounts for the CLS token and the sensor token, and D=128 is the total embedding dimension after concatenation. These positional encodings are added to each token in the sequence before feeding them to the transformer processing allowing the model to understand the order and position of signals across sensors and time. Learnable positional embeddings:

$$\mathbf{P} = [\mathbf{p_0}, \dots, \mathbf{p_{N+1}}] \in R^{(N+2) \times 2d} \tag{10}$$

Combined Input:

$$\mathbf{H}_{\text{input}} = [\mathbf{t}_{\text{cls}}, \mathbf{t}_{\text{sensor}}, \mathbf{h}'_1, \dots, \mathbf{h}'_N] + \mathbf{P} \tag{11}$$

***Class Token ([CLS]).*** A learnable classification token (CLS) is added at the beginning of the sequence. The final embedding of this token after transformer process is used for classification. This token gets information from all other tokens through self-attention and acts as the overall representation of the input sample. A learnable classification token:

$$\mathbf{t}_{\mathrm{cls}} \in R^d \tag{12}$$

***Sensor Token.*** A sensor token is also added to the token sequence after the CLS token. This token is derived by averaging all sensor embeddings (from their functional group profiles), projecting the resulting vector into a 64-dimensional space, and concatenating it with itself to match the patch embedding size (64 + 64 = 128). This sensor token tells the transformer about the sensitivity of the sensor array, providing contextual bias that improves selectivity and interpretability. Sensor embeddings are averaged:

$$\mathbf{e}_{\mathrm{sensor}} = \frac{1}{4} \sum_{s=1}^{4} \mathbf{e}_s \tag{13}$$

### 3.4 Transformer Architecture

The core model is a Transformer Encoder with the following design:
Depth: 4 layers
Heads: 4 attention heads per layer
Hidden dimension: 128
Dropout and normalization: Applied within the encoder layers The input to the transformer is a sequence of 12 tokens: [CLS] + [Sensor] + 10 patch tokens. Each token is of dimension 128. The transformer learns to attend across this spatiotemporal token space, capturing both long-range dependencies across time and cross-sensor interactions modulated by chemical conditioning (see Fig. 1).

$$\mathbf{H}_{\mathrm{output}} = \mathrm{TransformerEncoder}(\mathbf{H}_{\mathrm{input}}) \tag{14}$$

Classification Head:

$$\hat{\mathbf{y}} = \mathrm{Softmax}(\mathbf{W}_c \cdot \mathbf{H}_{\mathrm{output}}^{[0]} + \mathbf{b}_c) \tag{15}$$

### 3.5 Classification and Cosine Similarity Regularization

The output of the [CLS] token is fed through a classification head consisting of a layer normalization followed by a linear classifier projecting into 8 class logits. To enhance semantic interpretability, each class is also associated with a learnable embedding vector, which is optimized not only through cross-entropy loss but also regularized using a cosine similarity loss against the fixed chemical

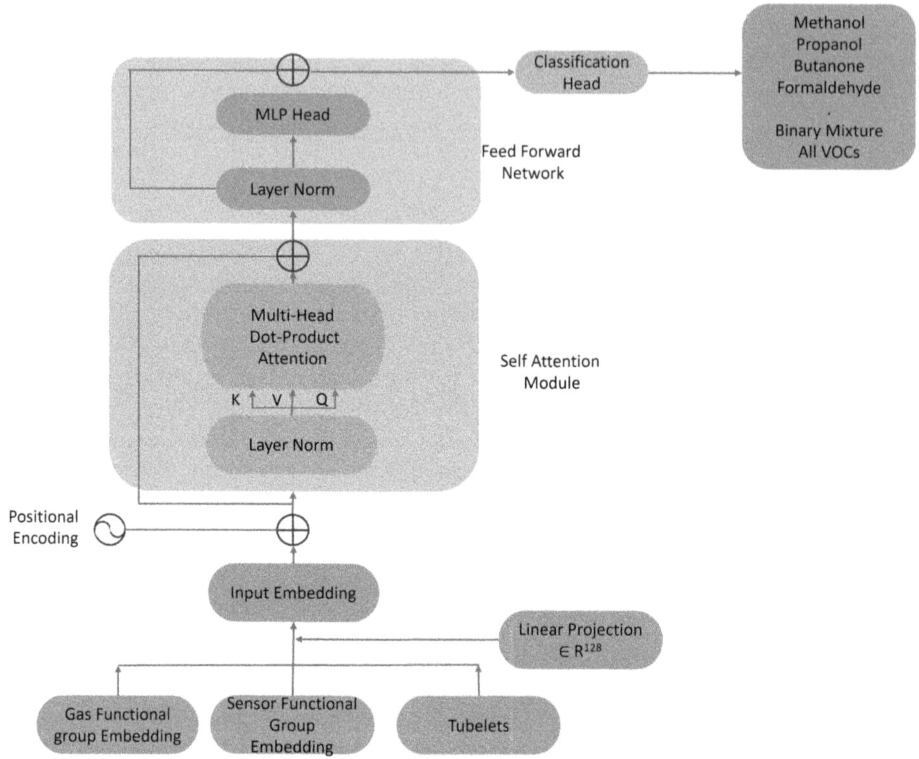


**Fig. 1.** The network structure of gas classification using Video Vision Transformer Model.

fingerprint matrix. This forces class embeddings to show the underlying molecular semantics, so that classes with similar chemical structure have more aligned embeddings.

Cross-Entropy Loss:

$$\mathcal{L}_{\mathrm{CE}} = -\sum_{i=1}^{\mathbf{C}} \mathbf{y_i} \log(\hat{\mathbf{y}}_{\mathbf{i}}) \tag{16}$$

Class and Fingerprint Similarity:

$$\mathbf{S}_{\mathrm{pred}} = \frac{\mathbf{E}_c \mathbf{E}_c^T}{\|\mathbf{E}_c\| \cdot \|\mathbf{E}_c\|^T}, \quad \mathbf{S}_{\mathrm{target}} = \frac{\mathbf{F}_c \mathbf{F}_c^T}{\|\mathbf{F}_c\| \cdot \|\mathbf{F}_c\|^T} \tag{17}$$

Loss:

$$\mathcal{L}_{\mathrm{sim}} = \|\mathbf{S}_{\mathrm{pred}} - \mathbf{S}_{\mathrm{target}}\|_{\mathbf{F}}^{\mathbf{2}} \tag{18}$$

Total Loss:

$$\mathcal{L}_{\mathrm{total}} = \mathcal{L}_{\mathrm{CE}} + \lambda_{\mathrm{sim}} \cdot \mathcal{L}_{\mathrm{sim}} \tag{19}$$

## 3.6   Data Augmentation via Diffusion Model

In order to generate synthetic data for training the model a 1D convolutional diffusion is trained. Noisy data is filtered for clean signals. At inference, Gaussian noise $\epsilon \sim N(0,1)$ is passed through the diffusion network:

$$\hat{\mathbf{X}} = \mathbf{f}_{\text{diff}}(\epsilon) \tag{20}$$

The output $\hat{\mathbf{X}} \in \mathbf{R}^{4 \times 25}$ augmented the training data.

## 3.7   Training Procedure

Training is conducted using a combination of:

1. Cross-entropy loss for classification.
2. Cosine similarity loss to regularize class embeddings against fingerprint similarity.
3. AdamW optimizer with a cosine annealing learning rate scheduler.
4. Gradient clipping for stability.

A batch size of 16 and sequence length of 25 are used. Data is split 80:20 into train and validation sets, and evaluation metrics include accuracy, F1-score, precision, and recall.

AdamW Optimizer:

$$\theta_t = \theta_{t-1} - \eta \cdot \left( \frac{\mathbf{m}_t}{\sqrt{\mathbf{v}_t} + \epsilon} + \lambda \cdot \theta_{t-1} \right) \tag{21}$$

Cosine Annealing Scheduler:

$$\eta_t = \eta_{\min} + \frac{1}{2}(\eta_{\max} - \eta_{\min}) \left( 1 + \cos \left( \frac{t\pi}{T} \right) \right) \tag{22}$$

## 3.8   Results and Their Interpretation

Chemically-informed class embeddings improve interpretability and generalization by incorporating chemical priors. Tubelet and positional embeddings capture spatio-temporal structure, while functional group conditioning integrates domain knowledge. The ViViT model (4 layers, 4 heads, 128 units) achieved 98.16% training and 100% validation accuracy (losses: 0.1301, 0.002) after 100 epochs (Fig. 2). In another setup with time-series data (seq. length $= 25$) and 80/20 split, the model reached 77.49% training and 96.95% validation accuracy (losses: 0.7472, 0.2943) after early stopping (Fig. 3). Figure 4 shows epoch-wise precision, recall, and F1 scores (final $= 1$), while Fig. 5 depicts methanol sensor response at 5 ppm. Table 1 compares model accuracies with existing frameworks.

**Note:** The datasets and sensors used in our work differ from those cited in the table.

**Table 1.** Comparative Analysis of Models

| Model | Accuracy | Gases | Ref |
|---|---|---|---|
| GraphCapsNet | 0.990 | 3 gases | [13] |
| ViT | 0.966 | 3 gases, 3 Mixtures | [1] |
| TC-Sniffer | 0.9295 | 4 gases | [7] |
| Trans-CNN | 0.9935 | 3 gases, 1 Mixture | [10] |
| Gas-ViViT | 0.9695 | 4 gases, 4 Mixtures | This Work |

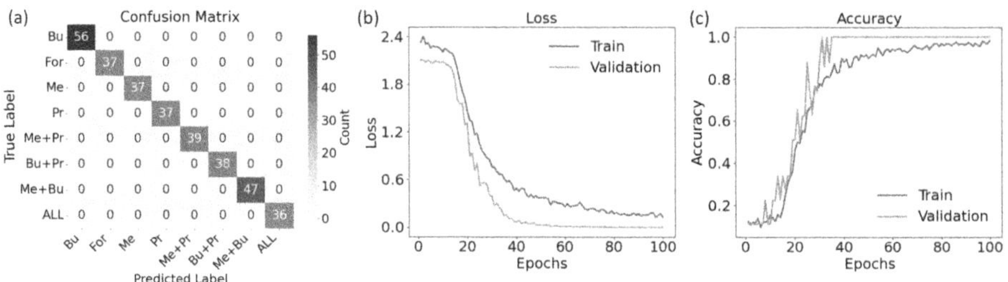

**Fig. 2.** (a) Confusion matrix for VOCs and binary mixtures (80% train, 20% validation). (b) Loss. (c) Accuracy over 100 epochs.

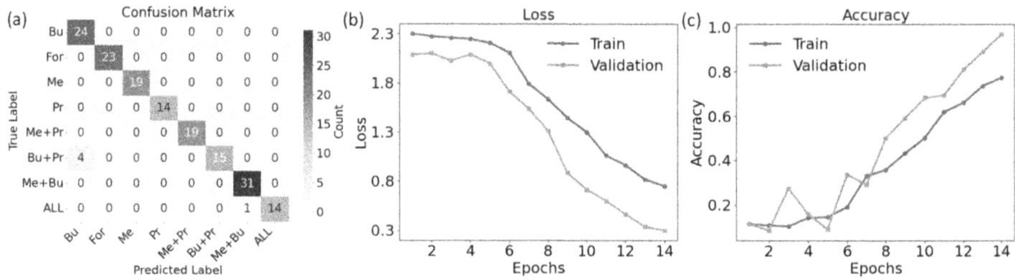

**Fig. 3.** (a) Confusion Matrix for classification of individual VOCs and their binary mixture with Training = 80% and Validation = 20% of the dataset. (b) Loss over epochs (Early Stopping at 96.95% validation). (c) Accuracy over epochs (Early Stopping at 96.95% validation). **Note:** In Figs. 2 & 3 Bu: Butanone, For: Formaldehyde, Me: Methanol, Pr: Propanol and ALL: All VOC Mixture.

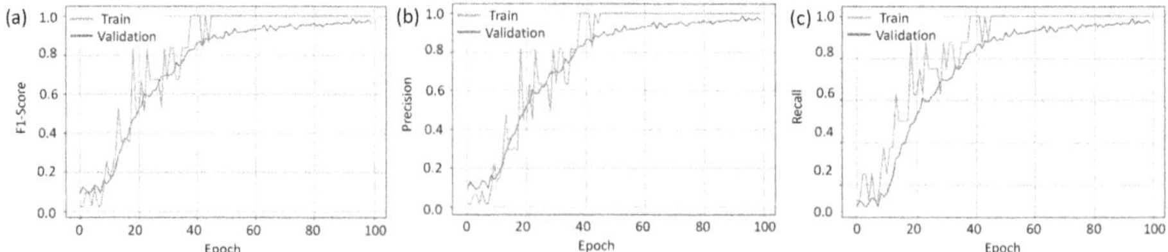

**Fig. 4.** (a) F1-Score, (b) Precision and (c) Recall curves respectively for the 80% training and 20% validation split experiment.

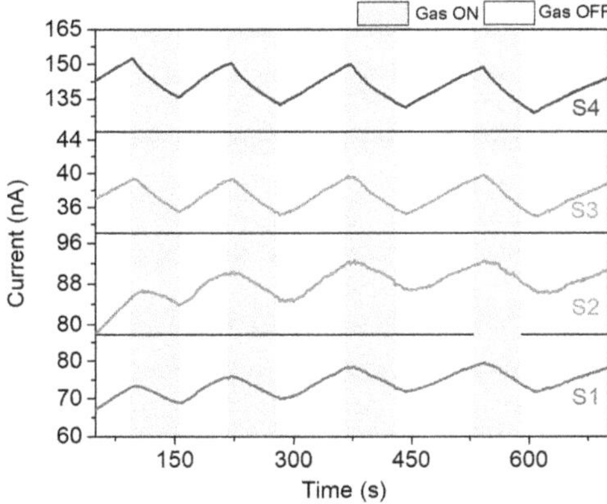


**Fig. 5.** Sensor current responses for methanol for 25ppm (in microampere) over time.

# 4   Conclusion

This work presents a chemically-aware Transformer that integrates molecular fingerprints, sensor functional groups, and positional tubelet embeddings to model spatio-temporal and chemical dependencies. Using similarity regularization and chemical conditioning, it fuses deep learning with domain chemistry for robust, generalizable gas recognition. The domain-informed framework unifies sensor responses, chemical structure, and functional selectivity, outperforming data-driven approaches in mixture, low-data, and noisy scenarios—offering a novel direction for intelligent gas sensing systems.

**Acknowledgments.** The authors acknowledge the research facilities from the Central Research Facility (CRF), IIT Delhi, the Department of Chemistry and the Department of Electrical Engineering, IIT Delhi. SG thanks MHRD (GOI) for the Prime Minister Research Fellowship.

**Disclosure of Interests.** The authors declare no conflict of interest.

# References

1. Du, H., et al.: Vision transformer-based electronic nose for enhanced mixed gases classification. Meas. Sci. Technol. **35**(6), 066008 (2024)
2. Gaur, S., Jat, B.S., Sharma, V., et al.: Machine learning-driven ultrasensitive WSe2/MWCNT hybrid-based E-Nose sensor array for volatiles amines mixture. Adv. Func. Mater. **35**(12), 2417729 (2024)
3. Gaur, S., Sharma, V., Jat, B.S., et al.: Site-selective MoS2-based sensor for detection and discrimination of triethylamine from volatile amines using kinetic analysis and machine learning. Adv. Func. Mater. **34**(39), 2405232 (2024)
4. Gobbi, A., Poppinger, D.: Genetic optimization of combinatorial libraries. Biotechnol. Bioeng. **61**(1), 47–54 (1998)

5. Hu, W., Yin, F., Wang, C., et al.: Electronic noses: from advanced materials to sensors aided with data processing. Adv. Mater. Technol. **4**(2), 1800488 (2019)
6. Jeong, S.Y., Kim, J.S., Lee, J.H.: Rational design of semiconductor-based chemiresistors and their libraries for next-generation artificial olfaction. Adv. Mater. **32**(51) (2020)
7. Jian, Y., Huang, M., Liu, Y., et al.: TC-Sniffer: a transformer-CNN Bibranch framework leveraging auxiliary VOCs for few-shot UBC diagnosis via electronic noses. ACS Sens. **10**(1), 213–224 (2025)
8. Landrum, G.L., et al.: RDKit: a software suite for cheminformatics, computational chemistry, and predictive modeling (2025). https://www.rdkit.org/
9. Lee, B., Kim, S., Choi, H., et al.: Breath analysis system with convolutional neural network (CNN) for early detection of lung cancer. Sens. Actuators, B Chem. **409**, 135578 (2024)
10. Li, L., et al.: Qualitative and quantitative transformer-CNN algorithm models for the screening of exhale biomarkers of early lung cancer patients. Anal. Chem. **97**(12), 6651–6660 (2025)
11. Li, X., Guo, J., Xu, W., Cao, J.: Optimization of the mixed gas detection method based on neural network algorithm. ACS Sens. **8**(2), 822–828 (2023)
12. Nam, Y., Lee, S., Cho, Y., et al.: Synergistic integration of machine learning with microstructure/composition-designed $SnO_2$ and $WO_3$ breath sensors. ACS Sens. **9**(1), 182–194 (2024)
13. Wang, D., Wang, L., Yin, H., Gu, G., Lin, Z., Zhang, W.: Graph-driven models for gas mixture identification and concentration estimation on heterogeneous sensor array signals. IEEE Trans. Instrum. Measur. (2025)
14. Wang, D., Xia, Z., Wang, L., Yan, J., Yin, H.: Gas graph convolutional transformer for robust generalization in adaptive gas mixture concentration estimation. ACS Sens. **9**(4), 1927–1937 (2024)
15. Weininger, D.: Smiles, a chemical language and information system. 1. introduction to methodology and encoding rules. J. Chem. Inf. Comput. Sci. **28**(1), 31–36 (1988)

# Multi-label Granular Ball Twin Support Vector Machine

Amisha Bharti[(✉)], Vikas Kumar, and Vasudha Bhatnagar

Department of Computer Science, University of Delhi, Delhi, India
{abharti,vikas,vbhatnagar}@cs.du.ac.in

**Abstract.** Multi-label classification (MLC) is a common task across diverse real-world applications, including document tagging, disease gene prediction, and multimedia content annotation. However, the traditional MLC approaches struggle to balance classification accuracy with computational efficiency, especially when handling high-dimensional and intrinsically complex data. To resolve this, we propose a multi-label classification model, namely Multi-Label Granular Ball Twin Support Vector Machine (MLGBTSVM) by combining granular ball computing with multi-label twin support vector machine. Our model improves classification accuracy by combining granular ball abstraction with Twin Support Vector Machine's (TSVM) dual non-parallel partitioning hyperplanes to effectively model multi-label data. It uses the Structural Risk Minimization principle, incorporating regularization terms, which effectively mitigate the problem of overfitting. MLGBTSVM also constructs classifiers based on the coarse-to-fine structure of granular balls, thereby reducing dependence on specific data instances and efficiently addressing the optimization problem. A comprehensive evaluation on benchmark datasets reveals that the proposed algorithm exhibits superior generalization performance compared to existing baseline methods.

**Keywords:** Multi-Label Classification · Granular Ball Computing · Structural Risk Minimization · Twin Support Vector Machine

## 1 Introduction

Multi-label classification is an important task in machine learning, especially in applications such as image annotation [10], bioinformatics [9], text categorization [15], and legal judgment analysis [5], where each instance may be associated with multiple labels at the same time. Despite the growing popularity of deep learning methods, traditional classifiers remain relevant due to their efficiency, lower data requirements, and enhanced interpretability. As a result, extending single-label classifiers to the multi-label setting has become an active research area. Among these traditional classifiers, SVM [8] has been widely extended for multi-label scenarios due to its strong generalization capabilities. Its variants have gained prominence due to their solid theoretical foundations and empirical success in various domains. SVM-based multi-label methods, such as Binary Relevance


S. Mitra et al. (Eds.): PReMI 2025, LNCS 16358, pp. 679–686, 2026.
https://doi.org/10.1007/978-3-032-18480-1_69

SVMs, Ranking SVMs, and Label Powerset SVMs, offer effective large-margin separation and generalization [14]. However, their performance can deteriorate in the presence of overlapping classes, label imbalance, and outliers. To address these limitations, recent developments have integrated granular computing with SVM-based models, leading to more adaptive and noise-tolerant classifiers.

Nowadays, the Granular Ball (GB) [12] method has emerged as a technique for simplifying data representation and gaining popularity in single-label classification. A granular ball represents a group of similar data points using a center and a radius, giving a simple summary of local data patterns. Building on this concept, a model called Granular Ball Support Vector Machine (GBSVM) [11] was introduced, which integrates granular ball representation with the traditional SVM framework. Instead of using all individual data points, GBSVM utilizes the centers of granular balls, resulting in faster training and improved robustness to noisy labels. Following this idea, the granular ball concept was also combined with TSVM, leading to the development of Granular Ball Twin Support Vector Machine (GBTSVM) [6] for binary classification. Motivated by the success of GBSVM and GBTSVM in single-label settings, this paper extends the approach to the multi-label domain and proposes a novel model that leverages both granular ball abstraction and the dual-hyperplane structure of TSVM [4].

In this paper, we propose the Multi-label Granular Ball Twin Support Vector Machine (MLGBTSVM). It integrates the granular ball representation into the TSVM framework for MLC. Unlike conventional SVMs, TSVM solves two smaller quadratic programming problems, each constructing a hyperplane closer to one class and farther from the other. When used for multi-label learning with granular balls, this method becomes faster and creates clearer decision boundaries, making it a better choice for large and noisy datasets than MLTSVM [2]. Experiments conducted on multi-label benchmark datasets demonstrate that MLGBTSVM outperforms baseline methods, including Rank SVM [3], Multi-label K-Nearest Label (MLKNN) [13], Multi-label Twin Support Vector Machine (MLTSVM) [2], Multi-label Structural Least Squares Twin SVM (MLSLSTSVM) [1], and an extended version of Rank SVM that incorporates the Granular Ball framework in the multi-label setting. These results show that using granular ball computing for MLC improves generalization accuracy.

The remainder of this paper is organized as follows: Sect. 2 reviews related work, Sect. 4 presents the proposed approach along with experimental results, and Sect. 5 concludes the paper, outlining directions for future research.

## 2    Related Works

This section briefly introduces the foundational concepts underpinning the Multi-Label Support Vector Machine (MLSVM) and Twin Support Vector Machine (TWSVM) paradigms.

**Problem Definition:** Consider a training dataset consisting of $N$ instances, denoted as $\{(\mathbf{x}_i, \mathbf{y}_i)\}_{i=1}^{N}$. Each instance includes a feature vector $\mathbf{x}_i \in \mathbb{R}^d$ and a corresponding multi-label vector $\mathbf{y}_i \in \{-1, +1\}^{\mathcal{K}}$. Here, $d$ represents the dimensionality of the feature space, and $\mathcal{K}$ denotes the total number of distinct labels. Each component of $\mathbf{y}_i$ indicates the relevance of a label, where $+1$ signifies that the $k$-th label is associated with the $i$-th instance, and $-1$ denotes its irrelevance.

The primary goal of these multi-label classification frameworks is to learn a scoring function $f : \mathbb{R}^d \to \mathbb{R}^{\mathcal{K}}$. This function produces a vector of scores, one for each of the $\mathcal{K}$ labels, such that the scores corresponding to relevant labels $(+1)$ are higher than those assigned to irrelevant labels $(-1)$ for any given input feature vector $\mathbf{x}$. The learned function facilitates predicting all relevant labels for new, previously unseen instances.

**Rank-SVM**: Support vector machines is extended to multi-label problems in *Ranking SVM* (MLSVM) formulation [3], which models the multi-label problem as a ranking task. Instead of predicting labels independently, Rank-SVM learns a scoring function to rank relevant labels higher than irrelevant ones, effectively capturing label dependencies. The Rank-SVM optimization problem is formulated as follows:

$$\min_{\{W_k, b_k, \xi_{kpq}\}} \quad \frac{1}{2} \sum_{k=1}^{K} \|W_k\|^2 + d_k \sum_{i=1}^{N} \left( \frac{1}{l_i} \sum_{(p,q) \in (y_i * \bar{y}_i)} \xi_{ipq} \right)$$

$$\text{subject to} \quad (W_p^\top x_i + b_k) - (W_q^\top x_i + b_q) \geq 1 - \xi_{ipq},$$

$$\xi_{ipq} \geq 0, i = 1, 2, ..., N. \tag{1}$$

Wolf Dual of 1 is written in Eq. 2

$$\max_{\alpha} \quad \frac{1}{2} \sum_{i,j=1}^{m} \alpha_i^\top (H_i^\top H_j)(x_i^\top x_j)\alpha_j + \sum_{i=1}^{m} \mathbf{e}^\top \alpha_i$$

$$\text{s.t.} \quad \sum_{i=1}^{m} H_i \alpha_i = 0, \quad 0 \leq \alpha_i \leq \frac{c}{l_i}\mathbf{e}. \tag{2}$$

**MLTSVM**: The MLTSVM [2], use the principle of constructing hyperplanes for only $k-$ label independently with the aim of ensuring computational efficiency. It uses a binary relevance based method independently for each label $k$. It create two sets of complementary index sets $\mathcal{I}_k$ and $\bar{\mathcal{I}}_k$, which contain indexes of positive and negative instances, respectively, for the $k^{th}$ label. Note that $|\mathcal{I}_k \cup \bar{\mathcal{I}}_k| = N$. The mathematical formulation is written as:

$$\min_{\mathbf{w}_k, b_k}, \xi_j \quad \frac{1}{2} \left\| w_k^T x_i + b_k \right\|^2 + d_k \sum_{j \in \bar{\mathcal{I}}} \xi_j + \frac{1}{2}\lambda_k(\|w_k\|^2 + b_k^2)$$

$$\text{s.t.} \quad -(w_k^T x_j + b_k) \geq 1 - \xi_j, \quad \xi_j \geq 0, \forall j \in \bar{\mathcal{I}}_k. \tag{3}$$

The dual of 3, is written in the following:

$$\max_{\alpha} \quad -\frac{1}{2}\alpha^\top G\alpha + \alpha^\top$$

$$\text{s.t.} \quad 0 \leq \alpha \leq d_k. \tag{4}$$

## 3    MLGBTSVM: Multi-label Granular Ball Twin Support Vector Machine

This section introduces the Multi-Label Granular Ball Twin Support Vector Machine (MLGBTSVM), a novel hybrid framework specifically designed to address the challenges of the multi-label classification (MLC) problem. Our proposed model integrates the efficiency of the Twin Support Vector Machine (TWSVM) with the representational power of granular computing, specifically utilizing the Granular Ball concept as previously established in the literature [7].

Let the collection of granular balls be represented as $G = \{gn_i\}_{i=1}^{P}$, where each granular ball $gn_i$ is characterized by its center $c_i$, radius $r_i$, and corresponding label $y_i$. For the multi-label classification task, let $C_i \in \mathbb{R}^{P_1 \times m}$ and $C_j \in \mathbb{R}^{P_2 \times m}$ denote the sets of centers belonging to the positive and negative classes, respectively, such that $P_1 + P_2 = P$ and $C_i \cap C_j = \varnothing$. In a multi-label scenario with $\mathcal{K}$ possible labels, the proposed linear MLGBTSVM framework aims to learn $\mathcal{K}$ proximal hyperplanes. Each hyperplane corresponding to the $k^{\text{th}}$ label is formulated as: $f_k(\mathbf{x}) : C_i W_k^T + b_k = 0$, for $1 \le k \le \mathcal{K}$, where $W_k$ and $b_k$ represent the weight vector and bias term associated with the $k^{\text{th}}$ label, respectively. The empirical risk is minimized through the following loss function:

$$\min_{W_k, b_k} \; \frac{1}{2} \sum_{i=1}^{P_1} ||C_i W_k + b_k||^2 + d_k \sum_{j=1}^{P_2} \xi_k + \frac{\lambda_k}{2}(||W_k||^2 + b_k^2) \tag{5}$$

$$s.t - (C_j W_k + b_k) + \xi_j \ge 1 + r_j, \quad \xi_j \ge 0, \quad \forall j \in \bar{k},$$

Here, $d_k > 0$ denotes the penalty parameter, $\lambda_k$ represents the regularization coefficient, and $\xi$ is the slack variable. The first term in the objective function (5) aims to minimize the squared distance between the hyperplane and the centers of positive-class granular balls, thereby drawing the hyperplane closer to the positive region. The imposed constraints ensure that the hyperplane maintains a minimum unit distance from the negative-class boundaries. The second term penalizes misclassification errors associated with negative samples, while the final term regulates model complexity through the RKHS norm, helping to avoid overfitting. The optimization problem in (5) is solved by formulating its Wolfe dual, which is derived by incorporating the Lagrange multipliers $\alpha_j$ and $\gamma_j$ into the primal problem.

$$L(W_k, b_k, \xi_j, \alpha_j, \gamma_j) = \frac{1}{2} \sum_{i=1}^{P_1} ||C_i W_k + b_k||^2 + d_k \sum_{j=1}^{P_2} \xi_j$$

$$+ \frac{\lambda_k}{2}(||W_k||^2 + b_k^2) + \sum_{j=1}^{P_2} \alpha_j \left( C_j W_k + b_k - \xi_j - 1 - r_j \right) - \sum_{j=1}^{P_2} \gamma_j \xi_j \tag{6}$$

Setting the derivatives of the Lagrangian function of Eq. (6) with respect to $W_k$, $b_k$, $\xi_j$, $\alpha_j$, and $\beta_j$ equal to zero by calculating the following Karush-Kuhn-Tucker

(KKT) as necessary and sufficient optimality conditions.

$$\frac{\partial L}{\partial W_k} \implies \sum_{i=1}^{P_1} C_i^T (C_i W_k + b_k) + \lambda_k I + \sum_{j=1}^{P_2} C_j^T \alpha_j = 0 \tag{7}$$

$$\frac{\partial L}{\partial b_k} = \sum_{i=1}^{P_1} (C_i W_k + b_k) + \lambda_k I + \sum_{j=1}^{P_2} \alpha_j = 0 \tag{8}$$

$$\frac{\partial L}{\partial \xi_j} \implies d_k - \alpha_j - \gamma_j = 0 \tag{9}$$

$$\sum_{j=1}^{P_2} \alpha_j \left( C_j W_k + b_k - \xi_j - 1 - r_j \right) = 0, \alpha_j \geq 0, \tag{10}$$

$$\sum_{j=1}^{P_2} \gamma_j \xi_j = 0, \quad \gamma_j \geq 0. \tag{11}$$

using Eqs. (7) and (8) leads to

$$\sum_{i=1}^{P_1} \binom{C_i^T}{1} (C_i \; 1) \binom{W_k}{b_k} + \lambda_k \binom{W_k}{b_k} + \sum_{j=1}^{P_2} \binom{C_j^T}{1} \alpha_j = 0 \tag{12}$$

Let $U = (C_i \; 1)$, $V = (C_j \; 1)$ and $\eta = \binom{W_k}{b_k}$, then Eq. (7) can be written as:

$$U^T U \eta + V^T \alpha = 0 \implies \eta = -(U^T U + \lambda I) - 1 V^T \alpha \tag{13}$$

The wolfe dual for Eq. (5) can be written as:

$$\max_{\alpha_j} \quad \frac{1}{2} \alpha_j^T V (U^T U + \mathbf{I}\lambda)^{-1} V^T \alpha_j + \alpha_j (1 + r_j) \tag{14}$$
$$\text{s.t.} \quad 0 \leq \alpha_j \leq d_k$$

We calculate optimal value of $\eta = \binom{W_k}{b_k}$. For a new instance $\mathbf{x}$, the assignment of label $k$ is determined by its proximity to the $k^{th}$ hyperplane. The proximity $dist_k(\mathbf{x})$ is calculated as:

$$dist_k(\mathbf{x}) = \frac{|\mathbf{W_k}^T x + b_k)|}{||\mathbf{W_k}||} \tag{15}$$

If $dist_k(\mathbf{x})$ is sufficiently small, specifically $dist_k(\mathbf{x}) \leq \delta$, for a positive threshold $\delta$, then label $k$ is associated with instance $\mathbf{x}$. Following the approach suggested by Chen et al. [2], the threshold $\delta = \min_{\mathbf{W_k}} (\frac{1}{||\mathbf{W_k}||}), 1 \leq k \leq \mathcal{K}$, remains same on all labels.

## 4    Experimental Results and Discussions

In this section, we present the experimental results used to evaluate the performance of the proposed algorithm. Seven publicly available multi-label benchmark datasets are employed for comparative evaluation, with their detailed characteristics summarized in Table 1. We use multi-label evaluation metrics like Hamming Loss (HL), Coverage Error(CE), Ranking Loss (RL), and Average Precision (AP). For the experiments, the regularization parameter $\lambda_k$ and penalty parameter $c_k$ are varied in the range $[2^{-6}, \dots, 2^6]$, while the Gaussian kernel parameter $\sigma$ is selected from $[2^{-3}, \dots, 2^3]$. For granular ball construction using the Gaussian kernel, we vary the number of granular balls ($num$) in $\{2, 3, 4, 5\}$ and the purity threshold ($pur$) in $\{1.00, 0.97, 0.94, \dots, 0.79\}$. After selecting the optimal parameters by solving the Quadratic Programming Problem (QPP), they are used to train the final decision function, following the approach in [2,7,11]. We employ 5-fold cross-validation and report the results as $mean \pm standard\ deviation$ of the evaluation metrics.

**Table 1.** Multi-label benchmark dataset description

| Dataset | Domain | Instances | Labels | Cardinality | Density |
|---|---|---|---|---|---|
| Emotions | music | 593 | 6 | 1.869 | 0.311 |
| Scene | image | 2407 | 6 | 1.074 | 0.179 |
| Yeast | biology | 2417 | 14 | 4.237 | 0.303 |
| Flags | image | 194 | 7 | 3.392 | 0.485 |
| Human | biology | 3106 | 14 | 5.073 | 0.362 |
| Plant | biology | 948 | 12 | 1.080 | 0.090 |
| Medical | text | 978 | 45 | 1.245 | 0.028 |

In MLGBTSVM, increasing the number of granular balls ($num$) captures finer label patterns, while higher purity ($pur$) ensures label consistency within each ball. However, excessively high values may lead to overfitting or overlook rare labels, requiring careful tuning.

Table 2 presents a comprehensive comparison of the proposed $MLGBTSVM$ against the baseline algorithms across four evaluation metrics. For Coverage Error, where lower values signify better performance, MLGBTSVM achieves superior results on five datasets. Similarly, in terms of Ranking Loss and Hamming Loss—both of which favor lower values—the proposed method consistently outperforms the baselines, with the best results emphasized in bold. For Average Precision, higher values correspond to better performance, and MLGBTSVM attains the best scores in five out of seven datasets. These findings demonstrate that MLGBTSVM is a robust and effective approach for multi-label classification, consistently surpassing existing baseline methods across diverse performance metrics.

**Table 2.** Comparison of the proposed $MLGBTSVM$ (mean $\pm$ std) with baseline algorithms $MLSVM$ [3], $MLKNN$ [13], $MLTSVM$ [2], and $MLSLSTSVM$ [1] in terms of Coverage Error, Ranking Loss, Hamming Loss, and Average Precision.

Coverage Error

| Dataset | MLSVM | MLKNN | MLTSVM | MLSLSTSVM | MLGBSVM | MLGBTSVM |
|---|---|---|---|---|---|---|
| Emotions | 0.45 $\pm$ 0.13 | 0.45 $\pm$ 0.13 | 0.38 $\pm$ 0.07 | 0.37 $\pm$ 0.06 | 0.35 $\pm$ 0.09 | **0.32 $\pm$ 0.19** |
| Scene | 0.13 $\pm$ 0.11 | 0.14 $\pm$ 0.16 | 0.15 $\pm$ 0.19 | 0.19 $\pm$ 0.04 | 0.11 $\pm$ 0.02 | **0.09 $\pm$ 0.07** |
| Yeast | 0.51 $\pm$ 0.19 | 0.51 $\pm$ 0.12 | 0.48 $\pm$ 0.13 | 0.47 $\pm$ 0.09 | 0.51 $\pm$ 0.11 | **0.45 $\pm$ 0.03** |
| Flags | 0.54 $\pm$ 0.07 | 0.59 $\pm$ 0.15 | 0.51 $\pm$ 0.17 | 0.51 $\pm$ 0.09 | **0.49 $\pm$ 0.11** | 0.46 $\pm$ 0.06 |
| Human | 0.35 $\pm$ 0.15 | 0.41 $\pm$ 0.19 | 0.31 $\pm$ 0.15 | 0.31 $\pm$ 0.19 | **0.23 $\pm$ 0.19** | 0.26 $\pm$ 0.11 |
| Plant | 0.25 $\pm$ 0.12 | 0.26 $\pm$ 0.11 | 0.20 $\pm$ 0.14 | 0.19 $\pm$ 0.21 | 0.18 $\pm$ 0.05 | **0.16 $\pm$ 0.19** |
| Medical | 0.35 $\pm$ 0.07 | 0.34 $\pm$ 0.14 | 0.26 $\pm$ 0.01 | 0.26 $\pm$ 0.04 | 0.14 $\pm$ 0.06 | **0.12 $\pm$ 0.04** |

Ranking Loss

| Dataset | MLSVM | MLKNN | MLTSVM | MLSLSTSVM | MLGBSVM | MLGBTSVM |
|---|---|---|---|---|---|---|
| Emotions | 0.21 $\pm$ 0.09 | 0.23 $\pm$ 0.09 | 0.21 $\pm$ 0.15 | 0.21 $\pm$ 0.02 | 0.19 $\pm$ 0.08 | **0.17 $\pm$ 0.07** |
| Scene | 0.13 $\pm$ 0.07 | 0.17 $\pm$ 0.11 | 0.12 $\pm$ 0.04 | 0.01 $\pm$ 0.29 | 0.07 $\pm$ 0.02 | **0.05 $\pm$ 0.02** |
| Yeast | 0.17 $\pm$ 0.08 | 0.19 $\pm$ 0.07 | 0.19 $\pm$ 0.07 | 0.18 $\pm$ 0.03 | 0.17 $\pm$ 0.09 | **0.16 $\pm$ 0.06** |
| Flags | 0.29 $\pm$ 0.09 | 0.29 $\pm$ 0.08 | 0.21 $\pm$ 0.10 | 0.21 $\pm$ 0.17 | 0.20 $\pm$ 0.11 | **0.19 $\pm$ 0.15** |
| Human | 0.13 $\pm$ 0.09 | 0.13 $\pm$ 0.13 | 0.11 $\pm$ 0.09 | 0.10 $\pm$ 0.07 | 0.08 $\pm$ 0.07 | **0.08 $\pm$ 0.09** |
| Plant | 0.44 $\pm$ 0.01 | 0.45 $\pm$ 0.15 | 0.23 $\pm$ 0.09 | 0.25 $\pm$ 0.08 | **0.21 $\pm$ 0.12** | 0.29 $\pm$ 0.04 |
| Medical | 0.04 $\pm$ 0.06 | 0.04 $\pm$ 0.01 | 0.03 $\pm$ 0.01 | 0.03 $\pm$ 0.01 | 0.03 $\pm$ 0.01 | **0.02 $\pm$ 0.01** |

Hamming Loss

| Dataset | MLSVM | MLKNN | MLTSVM | MLSLSTSVM | MLGBSVM | MLGBTSVM |
|---|---|---|---|---|---|---|
| Emotions | 0.27 $\pm$ 0.05 | 0.25 $\pm$ 0.09 | 0.21 $\pm$ 0.05 | 0.20 $\pm$ 0.06 | 0.21 $\pm$ 0.08 | **0.19 $\pm$ 0.03** |
| Scene | 0.11 $\pm$ 0.02 | 0.10 $\pm$ 0.07 | 0.09 $\pm$ 0.04 | 0.09 $\pm$ 0.06 | **0.06 $\pm$ 0.09** | 0.07 $\pm$ 0.09 |
| Yeast | 0.21 $\pm$ 0.08 | 0.22 $\pm$ 0.09 | 0.21 $\pm$ 0.09 | 0.21 $\pm$ 0.05 | 0.20 $\pm$ 0.04 | **0.19 $\pm$ 0.03** |
| Flags | 0.27 $\pm$ 0.07 | 0.28 $\pm$ 0.06 | 0.38 $\pm$ 0.04 | 0.39 $\pm$ 0.07 | **0.22 $\pm$ 0.09** | 0.23 $\pm$ 0.12 |
| Human | 0.15 $\pm$ 0.10 | 0.16 $\pm$ 0.11 | 0.14 $\pm$ 0.08 | 0.14 $\pm$ 0.05 | 0.13 $\pm$ 0.11 | **0.11 $\pm$ 0.08** |
| Plant | 0.16 $\pm$ 0.12 | 0.18 $\pm$ 0.09 | 0.20 $\pm$ 0.17 | 0.12 $\pm$ 0.09 | 0.13 $\pm$ 0.07 | **0.13 $\pm$ 0.05** |
| Medical | 0.07 $\pm$ 0.01 | 0.07 $\pm$ 0.03 | 0.06 $\pm$ 0.02 | 0.06 $\pm$ 0.01 | 0.05 $\pm$ 0.03 | **0.04 $\pm$ 0.01** |

Average Precision

| Dataset | MLSVM | MLKNN | MLTSVM | MLSLSTSVM | MLGBSVM | MLGBTSVM |
|---|---|---|---|---|---|---|
| Emotions | 0.73 $\pm$ 0.19 | 0.73 $\pm$ 0.05 | 0.73 $\pm$ 0.06 | 0.73 $\pm$ 0.11 | 0.88 $\pm$ 0.15 | **0.85 $\pm$ 0.09** |
| Scene | 0.81 $\pm$ 0.022 | 0.75 $\pm$ 0.09 | 0.81 $\pm$ 0.22 | 0.84 $\pm$ 0.16 | 0.87 $\pm$ 0.06 | **0.89 $\pm$ 0.01** |
| Yeast | 0.73 $\pm$ 0.024 | 0.74 $\pm$ 0.08 | 0.74 $\pm$ 0.07 | 0.72 $\pm$ 0.08 | 0.76 $\pm$ 0.08 | **0.79 $\pm$ 0.09** |
| Flags | 0.73 $\pm$ 0.018 | 0.73 $\pm$ 0.07 | 0.78 $\pm$ 0.03 | 0.77 $\pm$ 0.07 | 0.80 $\pm$ 0.15 | **0.83 $\pm$ 0.08** |
| Human | 0.68 $\pm$ 0.021 | 0.70 $\pm$ 0.09 | **0.78 $\pm$ 0.03** | 0.71 $\pm$ 0.13 | 0.75 $\pm$ 0.07 | 0.75 $\pm$ 0.10 |
| Plant | 0.63 $\pm$ 0.013 | 0.70 $\pm$ 0.08 | 0.75 $\pm$ 0.09 | 0.72 $\pm$ 0.10 | **0.75 $\pm$ 0.09** | 0.72 $\pm$ 0.11 |
| Medical | 0.76 $\pm$ 0.015 | 0.78 $\pm$ 0.09 | 0.83 $\pm$ 0.14 | 0.81 $\pm$ 0.25 | 0.92 $\pm$ 0.11 | **0.91 $\pm$ 0.15** |

## 5    Conclusions and Future Work

MLGBTSVM combines granular computing with multi-label TSVM methods. The idea is to reduce data complexity by grouping similar data points into granular balls, which helps improve learning efficiency and model strength. The model showed good performance on different multi-label matrices, gave good efficiency. Future plan is to further extend the proposed models on a larger dataset of multi-label datasets, and the addition of label noise will help evaluate the model's robustness and comparison with existing baseline models. Additionally, we will explore alternative loss functions to further optimize its performance.

## References


1. Azad-Manjiri, M., Amiri, A., Saleh Sedghpour, A.: ML-SLSTSVM: a new structural least square twin support vector machine for multi-label learning. Pattern Anal. Appl. **23**, 295–308 (2020)
2. Chen, W.J., Shao, Y.H., Li, C.N., Deng, N.Y.: MLTSVM: a novel twin support vector machine to multi-label learning. Pattern Recogn. **52**, 61–74 (2016)
3. Elisseeff, A., Weston, J.: A kernel method for multi-labelled classification. In: Advances in Neural Information Processing Systems, vol. 14 (2001)
4. Khemchandani, R., Chandra, S., et al.: Twin support vector machines for pattern classification. IEEE Trans. Pattern Anal. Mach. Intell. **29**(5), 905–910 (2007)
5. Meng, C., Todo, Y., Tang, C., Luan, L., Tang, Z.: MFLSCI: multi-granularity fusion and label semantic correlation information for multi-label legal text classification. Eng. Appl. Artif. Intell. **139**, 109604 (2025)
6. Quadir, A., Sajid, M., Tanveer, M.: Granular ball twin support vector machine. IEEE Trans. Neural Netw. Learn. Syst. **36**(7), 12444–12453 (2024)
7. Quadir, A., Tanveer, M.: Granular ball twin support vector machine with pinball loss function. IEEE Trans. Comput. Soc. Syst. (2024)
8. Stitson, M., Weston, J., Gammerman, A., Vovk, V., Vapnik, V.: Theory of support vector machines. Univ. London **117**(827), 188–191 (1996)
9. Tang, T., Zhang, X., Li, W., Wang, Q., Liu, Y., Cao, X.: Co-training based prediction of multi-label protein-protein interactions. Comput. Biol. Med. **177**, 108623 (2024)
10. Wang, X., Pu, T., Zhang, D., Lin, L.: Semantic correlation adaptation for union-set multi-label image recognition. In: International Conference on Pattern Recognition, pp. 210–225. Springer (2025)
11. Xia, S., Lian, X., Wang, G., Gao, X., Chen, J., Peng, X.: GBSVM: granular-ball support vector machine. arXiv preprint: arXiv:2210.03120 (2022)
12. Xia, S., Liu, Y., Ding, X., Wang, G., Yu, H., Luo, Y.: Granular ball computing classifiers for efficient, scalable and robust learning. Inf. Sci. **483**, 136–152 (2019)
13. Zhang, M.L., Zhou, Z.H.: A k-nearest neighbor based algorithm for multi-label classification. In: 2005 IEEE International Conference on Granular Computing, vol. 2, pp. 718–721. IEEE (2005)
14. Zhang, M.L., Zhou, Z.H.: A review on multi-label learning algorithms. IEEE Trans. Knowl. Data Eng. **26**(8), 1819–1837 (2013)
15. Zhao, C., et al.: Multi-label text categorization model based on semanteme and label knowledge guidance. In: 2024 5th International Conference on Artificial Intelligence and Computer Engineering (ICAICE), pp. 197–202. IEEE (2024)

# Word-Level Hindi OCR Correction Using Confusion-Aware Candidates and RoBERTa Re-ranking


Samiksha Sain[(✉)]

I. K. Gujral Punjab Technical University, Main Campus, Kapurthala, Punjab, India
samikshasain03@gmail.com



**Abstract.** Optical Character Recognition (OCR) systems for Hindi script continue to produce significant word-level errors, despite high character-level accuracy largely due to visually similar glyphs and ligature complexity which makes segmentation of characters challenging. Post-processing can address this, but most existing correction modules are either context-free or black-box generative models, limiting precision and control. In this paper, we propose a hybrid model that combines confusion-aware candidate generation with a RoBERTa-based reranker for post-OCR word correction. Given a word-level OCR output from a CRNN model, we generate the top-10 candidate corrections using a Levenshtein search enhanced with a handcrafted confusion map. A binary RoBERTa classifier is then fine-tuned to re-rank these candidates using over 100k confusion-simulated word pairs. We evaluated the model on a set of 2,699 real OCR errors, achieving 59.54% Top-1 Re-ranking accuracy and correcting the 1,607 errors, thereby improving overall OCR accuracy from 97.70% to 99.07%. To our knowledge, this is the first system to apply confusion-aware reranking to Hindi OCR, demonstrating that lightweight language models can significantly improve OCR reliability for low-resource scripts.

**Keywords:** Hindi OCR · RoBERTa · Post-OCR correction · Confusion-aware · Levenshtein search


## 1  Introduction

The digitization of Indic language content is vital for expanding knowledge access and preserving cultural heritage. As per the 2024 IAMAI-Kantar report, India has over 886 million internet users, with 98% (870 million) consuming content in Indic languages. Hindi leads this growth, with an estimated 705 million users, particularly in urban areas where 81% of Indic-language users prefer Hindi [4].

The exponential rise in regional-language internet use has created a strong demand for accurate text recognition systems for scripts like Devanagari, used in Hindi. Since most such content exists as scanned images, manual transcription is slow and impractical. OCR systems address this by converting images to




S. Mitra et al. (Eds.): PReMI 2025, LNCS 16358, pp. 687–696, 2026.
https://doi.org/10.1007/978-3-032-18480-1_70

machine-readable text. However, despite advances in deep learning, Hindi OCR still struggles at the word level due to: (a) large vocabulary size, (b) visually similar characters, (c) limited annotated data, and (d) complex character structures with matras, conjuncts, and diacritics [16].

To address these limitations, we propose a hybrid post-OCR correction system for Hindi text that includes:

- A **confusion-aware candidate generator**, using Levenshtein distance guided by a handcrafted Hindi character confusion map to generate Top-10 plausible correction candidates.
- A **RoBERTa-based reranker**, fine-tuned as a binary classifier to select the most contextually appropriate correction.

To train the reranker, we constructed a dataset of over 100,000 confusion-simulated word pairs. Importantly, the system is evaluated on 2,699 real OCR errors extracted from a CRNN-based OCR model, which were excluded from training.

## 2    Related Work

Several methods have been proposed to detect and correct misspelt words in OCR output, especially for Indic scripts. For handwritten Hindi, Omayio et al. [10] proposed an IHOD-based descriptor for effective word spotting and character recognition. Vinitha and Jawahar [16] conducted an early analysis of error patterns in Indic OCR systems. They identified key sources of noise such as visual similarities between characters (e.g., क vs. ख), encoding issues, and segmentation failures. Their findings emphasized the need for post-processing layers to correct errors that persist despite high character-level accuracy.

Traditional post-OCR correction modules relied on Levenshtein edit distance, dictionary matching, and rule-based substitution techniques. These methods focused primarily on surface similarity between noisy OCR outputs and valid dictionary words. For instance, Abdulkudhur [1] enhanced the Levenshtein algorithm with weighted edit operations and phonetic similarity, which better modeled common misspelling patterns at the character level.

With the rise of deep learning, both RNN-based and transformer-based encoder-decoder architectures, such as TrOCR [6], have enabled more context-aware OCR and post-correction models. HINDIA [13], a Hindi spell-checking system, used a BiRNN-based encoder-decoder with attention trained on synthetic noisy-clean sentence pairs. This architecture effectively captured contextual dependencies via its BiLSTM encoder, while the decoder focused attention on relevant parts of the input sequence during correction. However, these models depend heavily on high-quality parallel training data and may suffer when trained on noisy or poorly corrupted synthetic samples.

Recent years have seen transformer-based models applied to post-OCR correction. Vartani Spellcheck [11] combined Levenshtein-based candidate generation with a BERT-based reranker. Their dataset, derived from Tesseract

OCR on Hindi literary texts like the Ramayana, focused on detecting Out-of-Vocabulary (OOV) words. To improve precision, they integrated a Named Entity Recognition (NER) module from Haptik.ai to exclude valid entities (e.g., names, dates, currencies). Words flagged as misspelt were replaced with [MASK] tokens, whose positions were recorded and then corrected using BERT's masked language modeling. The final prediction was chosen based on the ranking of Levenshtein among the top 10 candidate substitutions.

In the Sanskrit domain, Maheshwari et al. [7] proposed a benchmark dataset for post-OCR correction using transformer models such as T5 and BART. These models were trained to correct synthetically corrupted OCR outputs at the sentence level, advancing evaluation and correction resources for low-resource scripts.

## 3    Methodology

Our correction system uses a two-stage pipeline. First, the CRNN OCR output is passed to a Levenshtein-based candidate generator enhanced with a confusion map, prioritizing common OCR character substitutions. Then, a RoBERTa-based reranker scores the candidates using subword-level embeddings and selects the most likely correction. This combines the precision of edit-distance methods with the contextual learning ability of transformers, improving correction accuracy for Hindi OCR.

### 3.1    CRNN Baseline Model

We adopted a Convolutional Recurrent Neural Network (CRNN) as our base OCR model. It was trained on the ILOCR Hindi Dataset [17], which contains 726,750 synthetic word images and annotations. Word images exceeding 128 pixels in width were excluded to standardize input dimensions.

The CRNN architecture consists of convolutional layers for feature extraction, followed by BiLSTM layers for sequence modeling. Final decoding is done using Connectionist Temporal Classification (CTC) loss. CRNN was originally introduced by Shi et al. [12], and it remains a strong candidate for low-latency OCR tasks. It has previously been used in Indic scripts [5,14,15] with promising results.

Our CRNN model achieved 97.70% character-level accuracy on a held-out test set of 100,000 samples. Despite this, word-level errors due to visual confusions remain, which are targeted by our post-OCR correction pipeline.

### 3.2    Dataset Construction

**Real OCR Errors.** We evaluated the CRNN model on 100k test samples and extracted 2,699 real OCR errors by comparing predictions to ground truth. Each error pair consists of (i) prediction from CRNN (ii) ground truth label. These examples were held out from reranker training and reserved solely for evaluation.

**Synthetic Confusion-Based Dataset.** To train the reranker, we generated a synthetic dataset mimicking real OCR confusion (i) Collected over 100,000 Hindi words from Hindi WordNet [18] (ii) Designed a character-level confusion map using real OCR confusion counts. (iii) applied a 30% per-character corruption rate to simulate OCR noise while preserving word readability. Substitutions used a confusion map built from real CRNN errors, capturing common matra and glyph confusions. The specific character confusion pairs are illustrated in Table 1 (iv) Produced [ocr_output, correct_word] pairs for reranker training.

**Table 1.** Common Hindi Character and Matra Confusions Observed in OCR

| Source | Confused With | Source | Confused With |
| --- | --- | --- | --- |
| क | ख | ख | क |
| ग | घ | घ | ग |
| च | छ | छ | च |
| ज | झ | झ | ज |
| ट | ठ | ठ | ट |
| ड | ढ | ढ | ड |
| त | थ | थ | त |
| द | ध | ध | द |
| प | फ | फ | प |
| ब | भ | भ | ब |
| म | न | न | म |
| र | ल | ल | र |
| स | श | श | स |
| ष | श | ा | ि |
| ि | ा | ी | ि |
| ु | ू | ू | ु |
| ो | ौ | ो | ो |
| ं | ँ | ँ | ं |
| ः | । | । | ः |

## 3.3 Levenshtein Candidate Generation

Levenshtein distance measures the number of single-character edits required to convert one word to another. It is widely used in spell correction systems [1,11]. However, standard Levenshtein scoring treats all edits equally, ignoring OCR-specific confusion (e.g., ब vs. व).

We introduced a confusion-aware Levenshtein search. It uses a handcrafted character confusion map to weigh substitutions differently based on OCR confusion probabilities. For example, substitutions between 'क' and 'ख', or ' ि' and 'ी', receive higher likelihood.

**Motivation for Expanding to Top-K Candidates.** Initially, we generated Top-5 correction candidates. However, the correct word often fell outside this range. Expanding to Top-10 candidates increased recall significantly (Table 2):

$$\text{Recall@10} = \frac{97443}{100090} \approx 97.36\%$$

**Table 2.** Top-k Candidate Recall Accuracy

| Top-k | Recall@k (%) | Correct Present in List |
|---|---|---|
| 5 | 95.74% | 95,829 / 100,090 |
| 10 | 97.36% | 97,443 / 100,090 |

**Confusion-Aware Scoring.** The confusion map was derived from a CSV of real OCR character confusions and normalized into probabilities. Table 3 visualizes the matrix of frequent misrecognitions.

**Table 3.** Sample Confusion Probabilities for Hindi Characters

| Wrong Character | Correct Character | Probability |
|---|---|---|
| ल | र | 0.998 |
| ल | <extra> | 0.0016 |
| ल | ाॊ | 0.0001 |

**Candidate Scoring Function.** For each candidate word $w_{cand}$ and OCR word $w_{ocr}$, we calculate:

$$\text{score}(w_{ocr}, w_{cand}) = \text{LD}(w_{ocr}, w_{cand}) - \text{bonus}$$

The bonus is derived from matching characters via the confusion map.

**Final Candidate List Generation.** All vocabulary words are ranked using the above score, and the Top-10 candidates are selected. The output CSV includes:

```
ocr_output, correct_word, candidate_1, ..., candidate_10
```

This file feeds directly into the RoBERTa reranker as training data.

### 3.4  RoBERTa Reranker Model

RoBERTa (Robustly Optimized BERT Pretraining) is a transformer-based language model that has outperformed BERT on many NLP tasks. We used a Hindi-specific pretrained model (`flax-community/roberta-hindi`) from HuggingFace.

Rather than generating corrections, we model correction as a binary classification task: Given an OCR word and a candidate, the model predicts whether the candidate is correct.

**Training Data Format.** From the candidate CSV, we construct training samples:

- Input: `ocr_output </s> candidate`
- Label: 1 if `candidate` = `correct_word`, else 0

Rows where the correct word was missing from the candidate list were excluded to avoid imbalance.

### 3.5  Model Architecture

We fine-tuned RoBERTa as a binary classifier with:

- WordPiece tokenizer (Devanagari)
- Max input length: 128 tokens
- Loss: Cross-entropy on binary logits

**Training Configuration**

The reranker was fine-tuned using HuggingFace Transformers for three epochs with a training batch size of 16 and evaluation batch size of 32. Model selection was based on the best checkpoint by F1 score, with evaluation performed after each epoch. Mixed precision (fp16) training was enabled to improve efficiency.

## 4  Evaluation and Results

### 4.1  Evaluation Setup

We evaluated the effectiveness of the RoBERTa-based reranker using a held-out test set of 2,699 real OCR errors from a total of 100,000 word images processed by our CRNN baseline. For each erroneous OCR prediction, we generated a Top-10 candidate list using the confusion-aware Levenshtein-based retrieval method. The reranker was then tasked with selecting the most likely correction.

A test instance was counted as successful if the correct word appeared in the Top-1 position of the reranked list. The following metrics were used for evaluation results are visualized in Table 4 and 5 (Fig. 1):

- **Accuracy:** The proportion of samples where the reranker selected the correct word.
- **Precision:** The fraction of predicted corrections that were correct.
- **Recall:** The fraction of all actual corrections correctly predicted.
- **F1 Score:** The harmonic mean of precision and recall.

**Table 4.** Reranker Evaluation on Validation Set

| Metric | Value |
| --- | --- |
| Precision | 1.00 |
| Recall | 0.5883 |
| F1 Score | 0.7408 |

**Table 5.** Real OCR Correction Results

| Metric | Value |
| --- | --- |
| Top-1 Accuracy | 59.54% |
| Total Errors | 2,699 |
| Corrected Errors | 1,607 |
| Final OCR Accuracy | 99.07% |

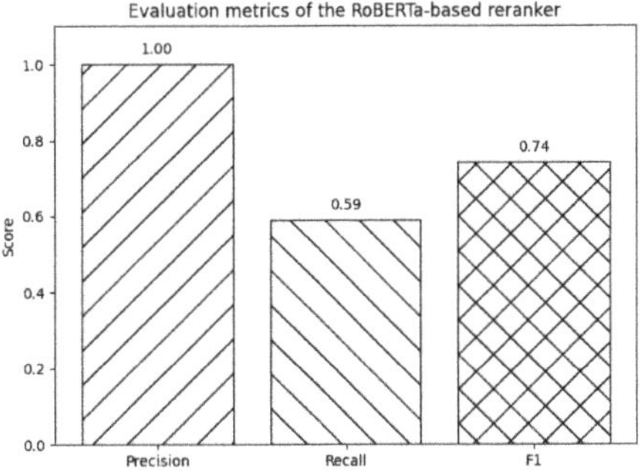

(a) Evaluation metrics of the RoBERTa-based reranker.

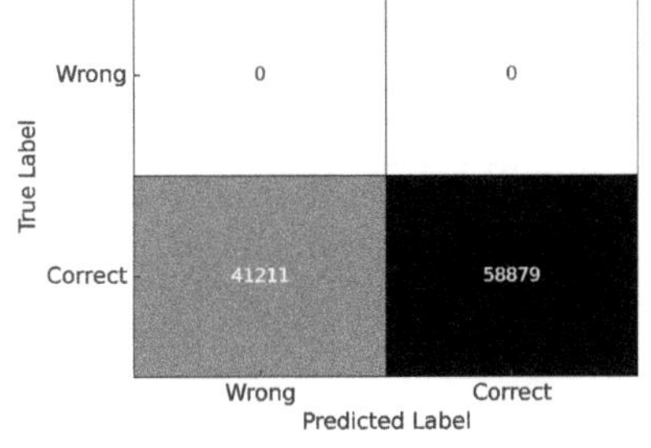

(b) Character confusion matrix.

**Fig. 1.** Performance evaluation of the proposed RoBERTa-based post-OCR correction system.

The RoBERTa reranker achieved a Top-1 accuracy of 59.54% on 2,699 real OCR errors, successfully correcting 1,607 errors and improving overall OCR accuracy from 97.70% to 99.07%. On synthetic validation data, the model achieved perfect precision (1.0), a recall of 0.5883, and an F1 score of 0.7408, demonstrating its ability to distinguish correct corrections during training (Table 6).

### 4.2   Qualitative Examples Table

**Table 6.** Example cases where RoBERTa succeeds but confusion-aware Levenshtein fails.

| OCR | Levenshtein | RoBERTa (Correct) | Ground Truth |
|---|---|---|---|
| झीलवाड | भीलवाड़ा | झीलवाड़ा | झीलवाड़ा |
| छोडड़ेंगे। | छोडड़ेंगे | छोड़ेंगे। | छोड़ेंगे। |

### 4.3   Comparison with Baselines

We benchmark our reranking approach against three baselines: (i) the raw CRNN output, (ii) plain Levenshtein Top-1, and (iii) confusion-aware Levenshtein Top-1. The plain Levenshtein baseline achieved 87.70% Top-1 accuracy on 2,699 OCR errors, improving overall OCR accuracy to 99.60%. Our confusion-aware variant further increased accuracy to 99.82%. In comparison, the RoBERTa-based reranker corrected 1,607 errors (59.54% Top-1), raising overall OCR accuracy to 99.07%. While edit-distance baselines slightly outperform the reranker on isolated words, the reranker succeeds on harder cases where Levenshtein fails, highlighting its value for context-sensitive corrections and future sentence-level tasks (Table 7).

**Table 7.** Comparison of OCR Accuracy Across Methods

| Method | Accuracy (%) |
|---|---|
| CRNN Baseline | 97.70 |
| Plain Levenshtein | 99.60 |
| Levenshtein Top-1 | 99.82 |
| Proposed Reranker | 99.07 |

## 5   Conclusion

This paper presented a hybrid post-OCR correction system for Hindi, combining confusion-aware candidate generation with a RoBERTa-based reranker. Tested on 2,699 OCR errors, it corrected 1,607 cases, raising overall accuracy from 97.70% to 99.07%. While Levenshtein achieved higher Top-1 accuracy on short words through surface similarity, it failed in ambiguous cases where the reranker used contextual cues to succeed. With richer training data and sentence-level extensions, lightweight transformer rerankers show strong potential for improving OCR reliability in low-resource Indic scripts.

**Acknowledgments.** The author sincerely thanks Dr. Neeraj Goel, Assistant Professor at IIT Ropar, for his invaluable guidance and support. His mentorship greatly shaped the direction and quality of this work.

**Disclosure of Interests.** The author has no competing interests to declare that are relevant to the content of this article.

# References


1. Abdulkudhur, H.: An Improved Levenshtein Algorithm for Spelling Correction. Master's thesis, Universiti Utara Malaysia (2017)
2. Arora, S., Malik, L., Bhattacharjee, D.: Handwritten Hindi character recognition: a review. In: Proceedings of the IEEE International Conference on Computer Vision and Image Processing (2024)
3. Gupta, P.: A breadth-first catalog of text processing, speech processing, and multimodal research in South Asian languages. arXiv preprint arXiv:2501.00029 (2024)
4. IAMAI & Kantar: Internet in India Report 2024. Internet and Mobile Association of India (2024)
5. Kukade, J., Pawar, R., Rai, I., Patidar, M.: Optical character recognition for Hindi language using a neural network approach. In: Proceedings of the International Conference on Data Science and Intelligent Applications (2024)
6. Li, M., et al.: TrOCR: transformer-based optical character recognition with pretrained models. arXiv preprint arXiv:2109.10282 (2021)
7. Maheshwari, A., Singh, N., Kulkarni, A.: A benchmark and dataset for post-OCR text correction in Sanskrit. arXiv preprint arXiv:2205.07829 (2022)
8. Malakar, S., Sarkar, R., Basu, S., Kundu, M.: An image database of handwritten Bangla words with automatic benchmarking facilities for character segmentation algorithms. Neural Comput. Appl. **33**(12), 7095–7113 (2021)
9. Naosekpam, V., Sahu, N.: Text detection, recognition and script identification in natural scene images: a review. Int. J. Multimedia Inf. Retrieval **11**, 237–251 (2022)
10. Omayio, E., Indu, S., Panda, J.: Word spotting and character recognition of handwritten Hindi scripts by integral histogram of oriented displacement (IHOD) descriptor. Multimed. Tools Appl. (2024). https://doi.org/10.1007/s11042-023-15219-x
11. Pal, S., Mustafi, S.: Vartani Spellcheck: a context sensitive spell checker for Hindi OCR text using Levenshtein distance and BERT. arXiv preprint arXiv:2011.09894 (2020)
12. Shi, B., Bai, X., Yao, C.: An end-to-end trainable neural network for image-based sequence recognition and its application to scene text recognition. IEEE Trans. Pattern Anal. Mach. Intell. **39**(11), 2298–2304 (2017). https://doi.org/10.1109/TPAMI.2016.2646371
13. Singh, S., Singh, S.: Hindia: a deep learning based model for spell checking of Hindi language. Neural Comput. Appl. **33**, 16035–16049 (2021)
14. Tyagi, S., Dutta, C., Singh, M.: Comparative analysis of different machine learning models on Hindi OCR task. In: Proceedings of IEEE International Conference on Artificial Intelligence and Data Science (2024)
15. Ul-Hasan, A.: Generic Text Recognition Using Long Short-Term Memory Networks. Ph.D. thesis, Technical University of Kaiserslautern (2016)

16. Vinitha, V.S., Jawahar, C.V.: Error detection in Indic OCRs. In: 12th IAPR Workshop on Document Analysis Systems (DAS), pp. 180–185 (2016). https://doi.org/10.1109/DAS.2016.31
17. IIT Hyderabad: ILOCR Hindi Dataset. Internal release, 2019. Dataset of 726,750 synthetic word images.https://ilocr.iiit.ac.in/dataset/49/
18. CFILT, IIT Bombay: Hindi WordNet.https://www.cfilt.iitb.ac.in/wordnet/webhwn/

# Quantum AI

# Quantum Enhanced LSTM for Day Level Parcel Count Forecasting

Rahul Rana[1(✉)] [iD], Kuntal Adak[1], Sakshi Kaushik[1], Suman Kumar Roy[1] [iD], André Siggesjö[2], Frida Nellros[2], Amrit Singh[2], Christian Mejlvang[2], Sudhakara Poojary[1], C. V. Sridhar[1], and Godfrey Claudin Mathais[1]

[1] TCS Incubation, Mumbai, India
{rahul.rana2,adak.kuntal,sakshi.kaushik,suman.r2,sudhakara.poojary,
sridhar.cv,godfrey.mathais}@tcs.com
[2] PostNord, Stockholm, Sweden
{andre.siggesjo,frida.nellros,amrit.singh,
christian.mejlvang}@postnord.com

**Abstract.** Accurate forecasting of day level parcel count is crucial in the logistics industry as it is directly linked to staffing systems help in resource planning. However, it is challenging to forecast over extended periods due to data variability and the unpredictability of future events, often leading to reduced model accuracy. Although classical Long-Short-Term-Memory (LSTM) models, are effective for time series forecasting, they encounter challenges due to computational complexity and large trainable parameters. To address these limitations, we propose a Quantum Enhanced Long-Short-Term-Memory (QELSTM), a deep learning-based approach to solve the time series forecasting problem of one of the largest logistics companies in Europe. Leveraging quantum properties such as superposition and entanglement, QELSTM achieves $\sim 3\%$ better accuracy than classical LSTM, with $\sim 3.78$ times fewer trainable parameters and $\sim 3.66$ times smaller number of computations during training. QELSTM's constant circuit depth enhances scalability for Noisy Intermediate-Scale Quantum (NISQ) computers, unlike existing Quantum Long-Short-Term-Memory (QLSTM) models, which exhibit increasing circuit depths with qubit count. The proposed model is also validated on Apple (AAPL) daily stock price data, showing faster convergence than existing QLSTMs and LSTM with comparable accuracy.

**Keywords:** Quantum Computing · Quantum Machine Learning · Time Series Forecasting · Quantum Long Short Term Memory

## 1 Introduction

Accurate day-level parcel count forecasting is a critical task in the logistics industry for optimizing staffing, route planning, vehicle allocations, and network planning to enhance customer satisfaction [1,2]. Time series forecasting predicts future values based on past observations, requiring careful modeling


S. Mitra et al. (Eds.): PReMI 2025, LNCS 16358, pp. 699–707, 2026.
https://doi.org/10.1007/978-3-032-18480-1_71

of underlying data patterns [3]. Different statistical and machine learning techniques have been developed to address time series forecasting challenges. Out of these, Long Short-Term Memory (LSTM) models, a specialized form of recurrent neural networks (RNNs) have proven particularly effective for multivariate forecasting by capturing long-term dependencies [4,5]. However, LSTMs face issues such as large trainable parameters, high computational cost, and convergence difficulties in long-term prediction tasks. These challenges necessitate the exploration of more advanced and efficient models. In recent research, quantum machine learning shows significant potential to address time series forecasting problems by leveraging the unique properties of quantum computing. Quantum algorithms, such as quantum support vector machines (QSVMs) and quantum neural networks (QNNs), have shown potential in time series forecasting. We propose the Quantum-Enhanced LSTM (QELSTM), a novel approach designed to handle sequential data while capturing intricate long-term dependencies. QELSTM harnesses quantum properties, such as entanglement and superposition, to represent and encode complex correlations within time series data more effectively than classical LSTMs. By exploring large solution spaces more efficiently, quantum computing could provide computational speedups for time series forecasting tasks [6]. This transition from LSTM to QELSTM bridges the gap between traditional and quantum approaches, offering a pathway to overcome the limitations of classical models while unlocking new possibilities for enhanced forecasting accuracy. Previous works have demonstrated the advantages of hybrid Quantum LSTM (QLSTM) models in domains such as carbon price forecasting, solar irradiance prediction, solar power production forecasting [7–9] and chemical tetrosynthesis [10]. While QLSTM works well compared to classical models, their scalability remains constrained due to increasing circuit depth and qubit requirements in Noisy Intermediate-Scale Quantum (NISQ) devices. This paper focuses on optimizing quantum circuit execution for scalability. The proposed QELSTM model maintains constant circuit depth, improving scalability for NISQ systems despite requiring higher qubit counts for extensive features. Its applicability is validated on parcel count forecasting for a Nordic logistics provider and on Apple (AAPL) daily stock data, highlighting its versatility across logistics and financial domains. The rest of the paper is organized as follows: Sect. 2 details the proposed workflow, Sect. 3 presents experimental results and observations, and Sect. 4 discusses the conclusion and future scope.

## 2   Proposed Workflow

The proposed approach begins with feature creation and normalization of the input data, followed by splitting it into training and testing sets. The QELSTM model is then developed and trained on the training data using a gradient based optimizer to minimize the Mean Squared Error (MSE). When the model converges, performance is evaluated on the test set and compared with the classical LSTM to check for improvements. Finally, the trained QELSTM is employed to forecast future parcel counts. The overall process is described in Fig. 1.

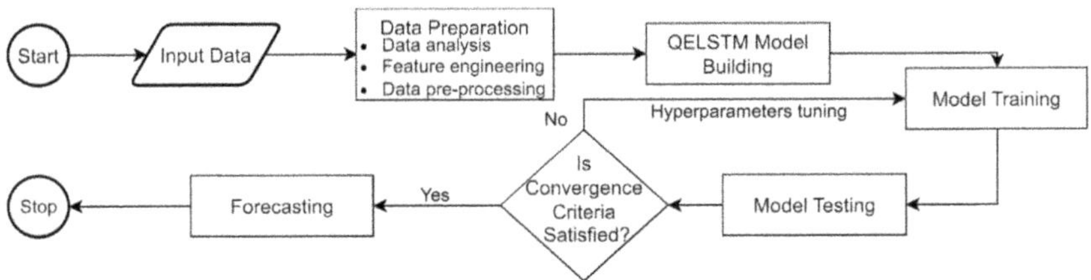

**Fig. 1.** Flowchart of the proposed workflow.

## 2.1 Proposed Methodology

The LSTM, a specialized RNN, addresses the vanishing gradient problem by using memory cells to capture long-term dependencies in sequential data. It features three gates, the input gate, which controls information storage; the forget gate, which discards irrelevant data; and the output gate, which regulates information flow to subsequent layers. The cell state serves as the long-term memory, while the hidden state, derived from it, represents the current sequence understanding. LSTMs are trained using backpropagation to optimize weights and effectively learn sequential patterns [11]. The classical LSTM architecture is illustrated in Fig. 2.

The QELSTM architecture as shown in Fig. 3, includes defining the structure of the quantum gates, qubits, and encoding techniques for the input time series data. Learnable parameters $W$ and $b$ in classical LSTM are replaced by variational quantum circuits for each of the gates with cell, enabling faster learning and convergence. A linear mapping technique is used to reduce the feature dimension before encoding the data into quantum state, which reduces the required qubit counts. The VQC is responsible for optimizing the parameters in the QELSTM model to ensure the model performance. Details of the used VQC is shown in Fig. 4.

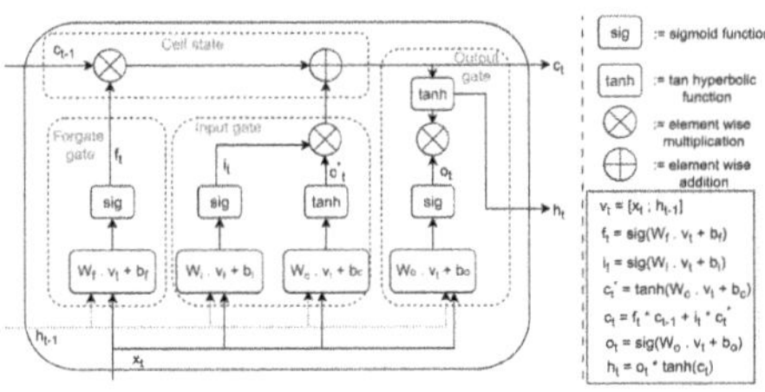

**Fig. 2.** LSTM cell.

## Difference Between Proposed QELSTM and Existing QLSTMs.

In the proposed approach, the VQC employs an odd even patterned CNOT gate arrangement, where qubits interact alternately between odd and even indices

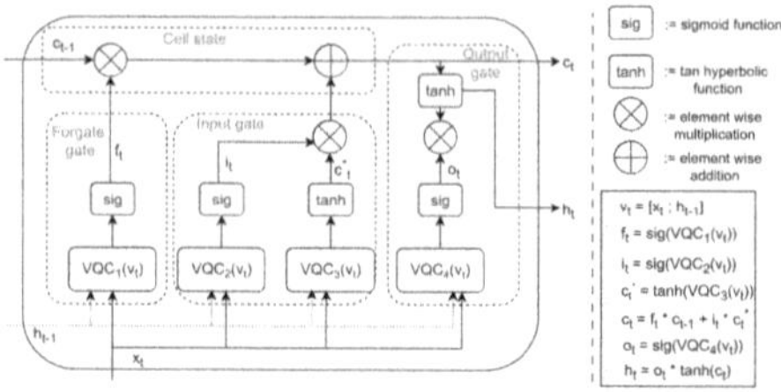

**Fig. 3.** QELSTM cell.

to form a structured entanglement pattern. This design achieves constant circuit depth regardless of qubits count, improving processing efficiency. Whereas, existing QLSTM models exhibit circuit depth that scales linearly with qubits, limiting scalability and suitability on current quantum hardware. The novel VQC architecture is shown in Fig. 4.

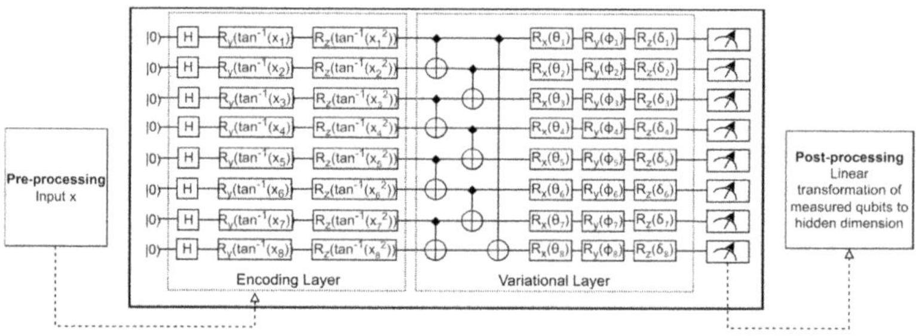

**Fig. 4.** Proposed Variational Quantum Circuit Architecture.

## 2.2 Computational Advantages of QELSTM over LSTM

We have analyzed the computational complexity with respect to trainable parameters and computational steps for a single call of LSTM and QELSTM. The total number of trainable parameters in a LSTM cell is given by $4(d+h)h+4h$, and for QELSTM is $12 \times Q \times S$, where, $d$ is number of features, $h$ is hidden size, $Q$ is number of qubits and $S$ is sequence length (we consider sequence length when calculating the number of parameters of QLSTM because the number of circuits created in each run depends upon the sequence length), where sequence length represents the number of previous days' data used to predict the output. For parcel count data, $d = 20$, $h = 64$, $Q = 8$ and $S = 60$. So the number of trainable parameters in classical LSTM is $4 \times (20 + 64) \times 64 + (4 \times 64) = 21760$ and $12 \times 8 \times 60 = 5760$ for QELSTM. Here, QELSTM has 3.78 times less trainable parameters than classical LSTM.

Further, the total number of computations for each cell in LSTM is $8h(d+h)$ and for QELSTM is $4S(2P+1)$, Where $S$ is sequence length $=$ number of circuits, and $P$ is the number of parameters for each qubit (for our case 3 parameters per qubits). For parcel count data, the number of computations in classical LSTM is $8 \times 64 \times (20+64)) = 43008$ and for QELSTM is $4 \times 60 \times [(2 \times 3 \times 8)+1] = 11760$. The number of computations of QELSTM is 3.66 times less than classical LSTM.

**Advantages of Less parameters**

- Less number of trainable parameters directly impact the number of computations during training.
- A deep learning model with less parameters may converge faster, is less likely to overfit the training data, and can generalize more quickly.

## 3   Results and Observations

### 3.1   System Setup

The hybrid quantum-classical model combines PennyLane [12] with PyTorch to enabling the training of VQCs as neural network layers. PennyLane's Default-Qubit simulator is used in our experiments. It supports quantum circuit design with rotational and CNOT gates, encapsulated in a QNode and interfaced via a TorchLayer. For hardware execution, IonQ's Aria-1 (25-qubit QPU with error mitigation) is accessed through Amazon Braket [13]. The classical environment comprises an 11th Gen Intel® Core$^{\text{TM}}$ i5-1145G7 @ 2.60 GHz $\times$ 8 with 16 GB RAM.

The following evaluation metrics have been used to evaluate the models.

$$Mean\ Absolute\ Percentage\ Error\ (MAPE) = \frac{|y_i - \hat{y}_i|}{y_i},$$
$$MSE = \frac{1}{n}\sum_{i=1}^{n}(y_i - \hat{y}_i)^2,\ \text{and}\ Accuracy = 1 - MAPE$$

Where, $y_i$ is actual data and $\hat{y}_i$ is the forecasted data for $i$th day and $n$ is the total number of days.

### 3.2   Result: Apple (AAPL) Daily Stock Data

This study utilizes Apple (AAPL) daily stock data from the past ten years, using Open, High, Low, and Volume as input features, with Close/Last as the target. The performance of the Classical LSTM, existing QLSTM models [8,11], and the proposed QELSTM is compared.

**Comparison Study of QELSTM with Existing Work:**
As shown in Fig. 5, all models use a hidden dimension of 64, and the proposed QELSTM is performing well in terms of accuracy. Figure 6 presents training and test losses, indicating QELSTM converges faster than the other models.

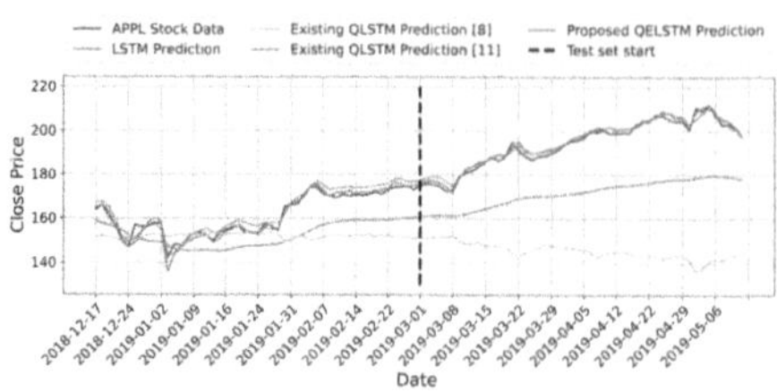

**Fig. 5.** Comparison Study on Apple Stock Data.

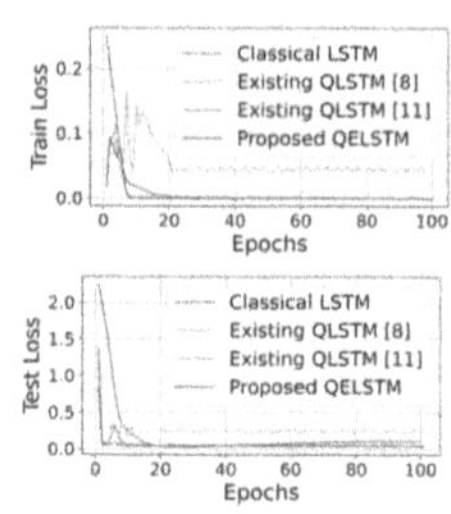

**Fig. 6.** Loss Comparison.

## 3.3 Result: Parcel Count Dataset

This work uses day level parcel count data (2020–2023) from a leading Nordic logistic provider. For all models we used sequence length $= 60$. In Fig. 7, the dotted vertical line separates training and test data. The QELSTM model effectively captures data patterns even with fewer epochs, outperforming the classical LSTM. Table 1 reports approximately $\sim 3\%$ better accuracy for QELSTM. Figure 8 shows QESTM converge faster than LSTM. The proposed quantum circuit design also demonstrates significant improvements in efficiency, maintaining constant circuit depth and a lower gate count compared to existing QLSTM architectures (Fig. 9). These enhancements reduce computational complexity and noise, improving suitability for real time quantum hardware.

**Table 1.** QELSTM vs LSTM: Accuracy comparison

| #Epochs | LSTM | QELSTM |
|---|---|---|
| 10 | 38.97% | **52.82%** |
| 30 | 61.23% | **75.31%** |
| 50 | 75.44% | **80.93%** |
| 100 | 83.57% | **86.56%** |

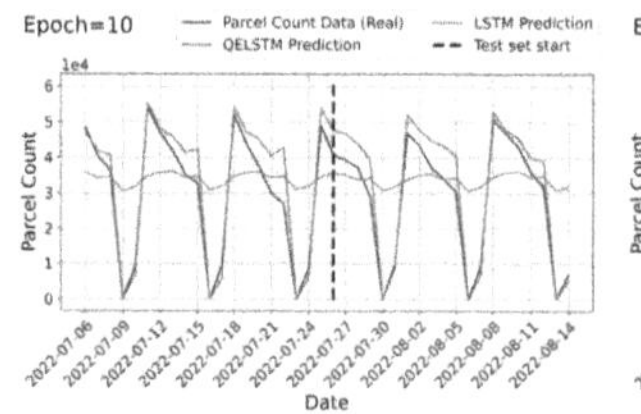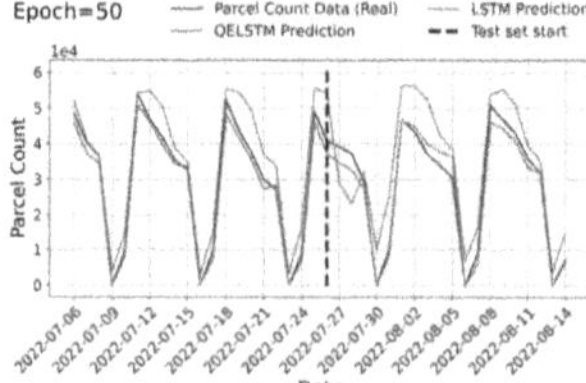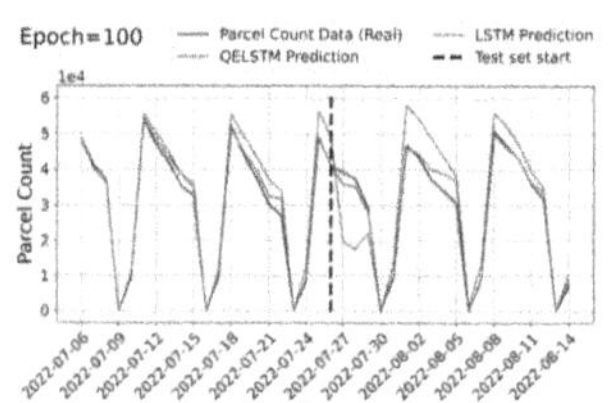

**Fig. 7.** Visualisation of performance of both the model with epochs 10, 50 and 100.

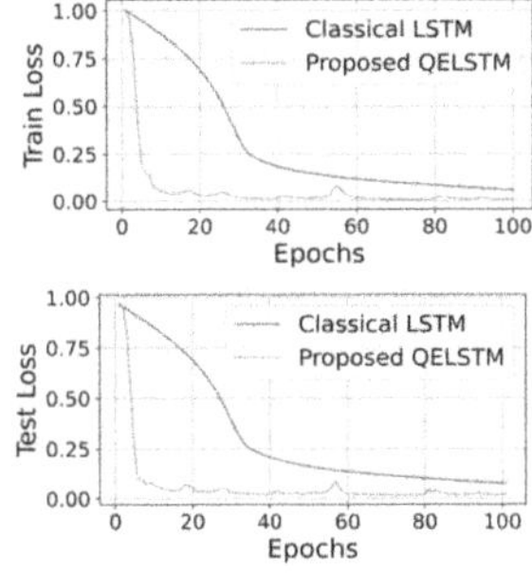

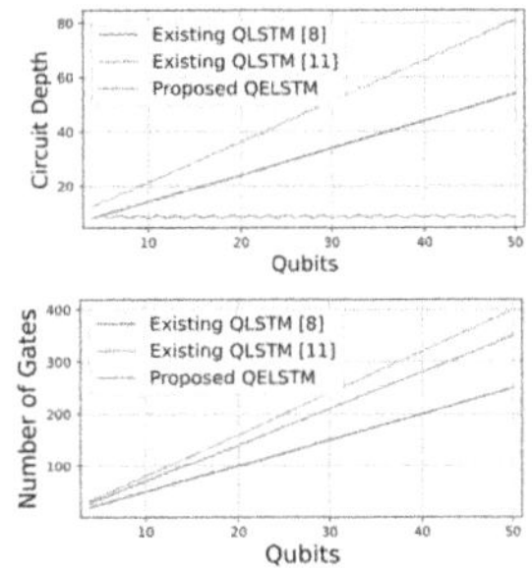

**Fig. 8.** LSTM vs QELSTM: Loss comparison.

**Fig. 9.** LSTM vs QELSTM: Circuit depth and number of gates w.r.t qubits.

## 90 Days Forecast Results by LSTM and QELSTM:

Figure 10 shows the 90 days forecast (02-09-2023 to 30-11-2023) generated by LSTM and proposed QELSTM models. The preceding 30 days of actual data (up to 01-09-2023) are included to provide continuity and facilitate comparison between observed and forecasted trends.

## QELSTM Model Execution on IonQ Aria-1 Quantum Hardware:

The full QELSTM model for parcel count forecasting requires approximately 1.8 million quantum tasks per epoch on IonQ Aria-1, making direct execution impractical due to hardware costs and availability. A simplified QELSTM with a sequence length of 1 (vs. optimal 10) was trained on a simulator and tested on IonQ Aria-1 for a 10-day forecast. Figure 11 shows while accuracy is reduced due to the shorter sequence, results on the simulator and hardware are closely aligned. With optimal hyperparameters and adequate resources, QELSTM could potentially outperform classical LSTM models on quantum hardware, as indicated by simulations.

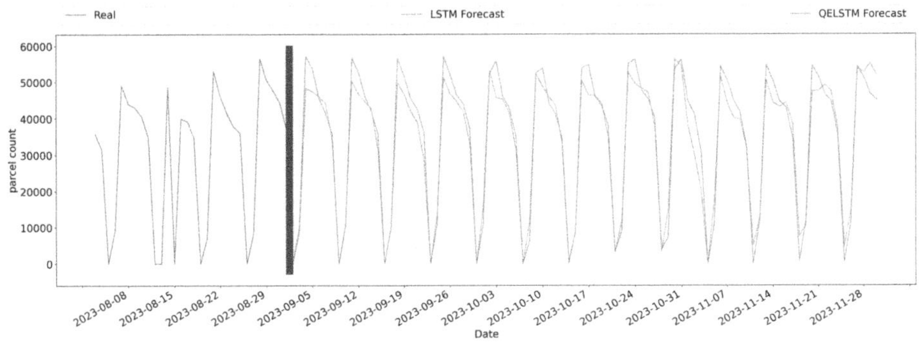

**Fig. 10.** Forecasted Results for 90 days on both LSTM and QELSTM Model.

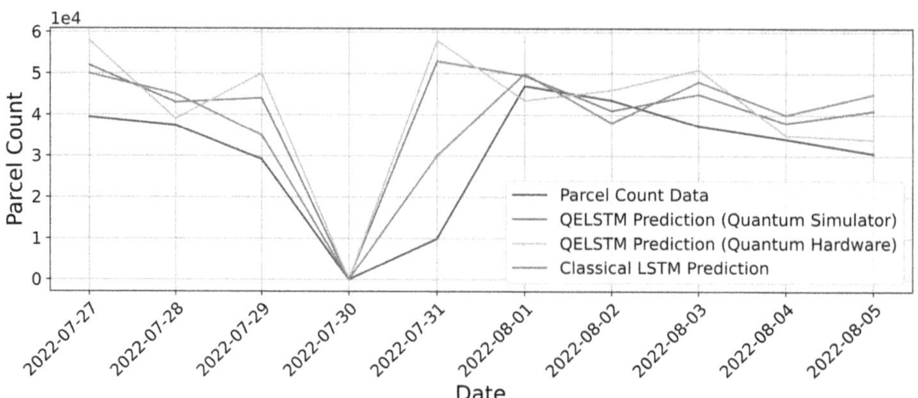


**Fig. 11.** Simplified version of the QELSTM model's performance on IonQ Aria-1.

## 4 Conclusion and Future Scope

The proposed QELSTM model achieves $\sim$ 3% higher accuracy than LSTM in parcel forecasting with $\sim$ 3.78 times fewer parameters and $\sim$ 3.66 times fewer computations. This leads to faster processing, lower costs, and better handling of complex time series patterns. Its successful application to Apple stock data further demonstrates its adaptability across domains. Additionally, QELSTM is more suitable for NISQ devices, maintaining constant circuit depth and requiring fewer gates than existing QLSTMs.

The current model employs a modified angle encoding technique, demanding n qubits for n features—resulting in high qubit usage for 84-dimensional data. Feature dimension reduction mitigated this issue in simulations. Future work will focus on developing qubit-efficient encoding and further reducing circuit depth and gate counts to minimize noise impacts and enhance scalability on real quantum hardware.

**Acknowledgement.** Authors are grateful to M Girish Chandra, Manoj Nambiar and Anil Sharma for their guidance.

## References

1. Karakatsani, N.V., Bunn, D.W.: Forecasting electricity prices: the impact of fundamentals and time-varying coefficients. Int. J. Forecast. **24**(4), 764–785 (2008)
2. Shah, I., Lisi, F.: Forecasting of electricity price through a functional prediction of sale and purchase curves. J. Forecast. **39**(2), 242–259 (2020)
3. Raiyani, A., Lathigara, A., Mehta, H.: Usage of time series forecasting model in supply chain sales prediction. In: IOP Conference Series: Materials Science and Engineering. vol. 1042. no. 1. IOP Publishing (2021)

4. Ghanbari, R., Borna, K.: Multivariate time-series prediction using LSTM neural networks. In: 2021 26th International Computer Conference, Computer Society of Iran (CSICC), IEEE (2021)
5. Van Houdt, G., Mosquera, C., Nápoles, G.: A review on the long short-term memory model. Artif. Intell. Rev. **53**(8), 5929–5955 (2020)
6. Tychola, K.A., Kalampokas, T., Papakostas, G.A.: Quantum machine learning–an overview. Electronics **12**(11), 2379 (2023)
7. Cao, Y., et al.: Linear-layer-enhanced quantum long short-term memory for carbon price forecasting. Quantum Mach. Intell. **5**(2), 26 (2023)
8. Yu, Y., et al.: Prediction of solar irradiance one hour ahead based on quantum long short-term memory network. IEEE Trans. Quantum Eng. **4**, 1–15 (2023)
9. Zafar Khan, S., et al.: Quantum long short-term memory (QLSTM) vs classical LSTM in time series forecasting: a comparative study in solar power forecasting. arXiv e-prints: arXiv-2310 (2023)
10. Beaudoin, C., et al.: Quantum machine learning for material synthesis and hardware security. In: Proceedings of the 41st IEEE/ACM International Conference on Computer-Aided Design (2022)
11. Chen, S.Y.C., Yoo, S., Fang, Y.L.L.: Quantum long short-term memory. In: ICASSP 2022-2022 IEEE International Conference on Acoustics, Speech and Signal Processing (ICASSP). IEEE (2022)
12. Bergholm, V., et al.: Pennylane: Automatic differentiation of hybrid quantum-classical computations. arXiv preprint arXiv:1811.04968 (2018)
13. Amazon Web Services. Amazon Braket (2020)

# Verifiable $(k, l)$-Threshold Quantum Secret Sharing Using Multivariate Polynomials


Darshana Yadav[(✉)]

Department of Mathematics, Indian Institute of Technology, Jodhpur 342030,
Rajasthan, India
`p22ma001@iitj.ac.in`



**Abstract.** We propose a verifiable $(k, l)$-threshold quantum secret sharing (QSS) scheme using symmetric multivariate polynomials and mutually unbiased bases. The scheme enables secure quantum state distribution with identity authentication and dishonest participant detection. Classical and quantum shares are combined to ensure integrity and verifiability. It resists standard quantum attacks including intercept-resend, collusion, entangle measure attack and participant attack. The design is efficient, scalable, and suitable for practical quantum networks.

**Keywords:** Quantum Secret Sharing · mutually unbiased bases · collusion attack


## 1  Introduction

Quantum Secret Sharing (QSS) has emerged as a cornerstone of quantum cryptography, enabling a dealer to divide a secret whether classical or quantum and securely distribute it among multiple participants such that only authorized subsets can reconstruct the original secret [1,2]. Traditional $(k, n)$-threshold QSS schemes require that any $k$ out of $n$ participants collaborate to reconstruct the secret, ensuring that fewer than $k$ participants gain no useful information [1].

The foundational QSS protocol by Hillery, Bužek, and Berthiaume [2] demonstrated how an unknown quantum state could be shared using entangled GHZ states. Since then, numerous QSS protocols have been developed, including those utilizing single-photon states [3], product-state strategies for scalability [4], and schemes supporting sequential communication [5]. However, many existing protocols face practical limitations such as difficulty scaling, lack of internal verification, and vulnerability to impersonation or internal attacks. For instance, attackers may impersonate the dealer during distribution or inject false data during reconstruction, compromising security. Verifiable Secret Sharing (VSS), first proposed by Chor et al. [6], addresses these issues by allowing participants to confirm the integrity and origin of their shares. Recent studies have incorporated quantum VSS approaches using identity-based cryptography, mutually



S. Mitra et al. (Eds.): PReMI 2025, LNCS 16358, pp. 708–715, 2026.
https://doi.org/10.1007/978-3-032-18480-1_72

unbiased bases [7], and bivariate polynomials [8–10], which improve robustness and authentication. However, bivariate approaches can be restrictive in large networks or dynamic systems. In this work, we present a novel verifiable $(k, l)$-threshold quantum secret sharing scheme using multivariate polynomials and mutually unbiased bases (MUBs) [11,12] to enhance flexibility, participant authentication, and resistance to malicious behavior.

The core of our approach involves encoding the secret into a symmetric multivariate polynomial, from which each participant's unitary transformation is derived. These transformations are monitored by the dealer to ensure honesty during the distribution phase. Through polynomial evaluation at unique coordinates, participants receive secure shares embedded in quantum states. This enables lightweight but effective verification, with minimal reliance on external authentication channels. Moreover, participants can authenticate one another using derived protected keys, significantly enhancing mutual trust and security. This scheme provides multiple advantages. It allows early detection and exclusion of dishonest participants, with the dealer able to regenerate the polynomial and quantum state to continue secure communication. It supports mutual authentication using polynomial-derived keys, preventing impersonation attacks. Lastly, it minimizes authentication overhead by integrating verification directly into the structure of the scheme, ensuring practical deployment in real-world quantum communication scenarios.

The rest of the paper is organized as follows. Section 2 introduces the proposed verifiable $(k, l)$-threshold QSS scheme in detail. Section 3 analyzes the security properties of the protocol, highlighting its resilience to internal and external threats. Finally, Sect. 4 concludes the paper and outlines future research directions, including dynamic threshold schemes and decentralized quantum networks.

## 2 $(k, l)$-TQSS Using Symmetric Multivariate Polynomial

This section presents a verifiable $(k, l)$-threshold quantum secret sharing (QSS) scheme involving a trusted dealer, Alice, and $l$ participants labeled $\mathrm{Bob}_1, \mathrm{Bob}_2, \ldots, \mathrm{Bob}_l$. The scheme uses a symmetric multivariate polynomial to generate authenticated shares and employs sequential unitary transformations on quantum states for secret reconstruction and participant authentication.

### 2.1 Share Generation Phase

1. **Polynomial Selection:**
   Alice selects a symmetric multivariate polynomial over a finite field $\mathbb{F}_p$, defined as:

$$G(y_1, y_2, \ldots, y_k) = \sum_{i_1 + \cdots + i_k \leq d} g_{i_1, i_2, \ldots, i_k} y_1^{i_1} y_2^{i_2} \cdots y_k^{i_k} \mod d,$$

   where $g_{i_1, \ldots, i_k} \in \mathbb{F}_d$ and the polynomial is symmetric in all its variables.

2. **Share Computation:**
   For each participant $\text{Bob}_j$, Alice computes:

$$G(y_{1j}, y_2, \ldots, y_k),$$

   where $y_{1j}$ is the public identity of $\text{Bob}_j$. These values form the classical shares.
3. **Quantum State Preparation:**
   Alice prepares a $d$-dimensional quantum state:

$$|\Psi\rangle = \frac{1}{\sqrt{d}} \sum_{i=0}^{d-1} |i\rangle,$$

   and applies a unitary transformation $U_{w_0, v_0}$ where:

$$w_0 = s = G(0, 0, \ldots, 0), \quad v_0 = d - s.$$

   The transformed state becomes:

$$|\Psi\rangle_0 = U_{w_0, v_0} |\Psi\rangle = |\psi_{w_0}^{v_0}\rangle.$$

4. **Hash Publication:**
   Alice computes a hash value $H = h(s)$ and publishes it for verification purposes.

## 2.2  Share Distribution Phase

1. **Classical Share Transmission:**
   Alice securely transmits $G(y_{1j}, y_2, \ldots, y_l)$, to each participant $\text{Bob}_j$.
2. **Quantum State Transmission and Sequential Unitary Operations:**
   Alice sends $|\Psi\rangle_0$ to $\text{Bob}_1$, who applies:

$$w_1 = G(0, 0, \ldots, y_1), \quad v_1 = G(y_1, 0, \ldots, 0) \prod_{t=2}^{p} \frac{y_t}{y_t - y_1} \quad \text{mod } d,$$

   and performs $U_{w_1, v_1}$ on $|\Psi\rangle_0$ to obtain:

$$|\Psi\rangle_1 = U_{w_1, v_1} |\Psi\rangle_0 = |\psi_{w_0 + w_1}^{v_0 + v_1}\rangle.$$

   Each subsequent $\text{Bob}_j$ applies:

$$w_j = G(0, 0, \ldots, y_j), \quad v_j = E(y_j, 0, \ldots, 0) \prod_{\substack{t=1 \\ t \neq j}}^{p} \frac{y_t}{y_t - y_j} \quad \text{mod } d,$$

   resulting in the cumulative transformation:

$$|\Psi\rangle_j = U_{w_j, v_j} |\Psi\rangle_{j-1} = |\psi_{\sum_{i=0}^{j} w_i}^{\sum_{i=0}^{j} v_i}\rangle.$$

   The process continues until $\text{Bob}_p$ receives:

$$|\Psi\rangle_p = |\psi_{\sum_{i=0}^{p} w_i}^{\sum_{i=0}^{p} v_i}\rangle.$$

3. **Pairwise Authentication:**
   Each pair $(\text{Bob}_1, \text{Bob}_2)$ computes a symmetric key:

   $$R_{12} = G(y_1, y_2, \ldots, y_n) = G(y_2, y_1, \ldots, y_n).$$

   Participant $\text{Bob}_j$ sends encrypted values:

   $$p'_j = ER_{ij}(w_j), \quad p''_j = ER_{ij}(v_j),$$

   from which $\text{Bob}_i$ recovers:

   $$w_j = DR_{ij}(p'_j), \quad v_j = DR_{ij}(p''_j).$$

   This process provides mutual identity authentication.
4. **Measurement Basis Computation:**
   $\text{Bob}_p$ computes:

   $$S' = \left( \sum_{i=1}^{p} G(y_i, 0, \ldots, 0) \prod_{\substack{t=1 \\ t \neq i}}^{p} \frac{y_t}{y_t - y_i} \right) \mod d = \sum_{i=1}^{p} v_i.$$

   If $S' = S = G(0, 0, \ldots, 0)$ and $\sum v_i \mod d = 0$, then the participant measures $|\Psi\rangle_p$ in the basis $|u_0^n\rangle$ and obtains measurement result $W$.
5. **Final Sharing and Verification:**
   $\text{Bob}_p$ computes: $C = G_{R_{pj}}(W)$, and sends $C$ to the others. Each $\text{Bob}_j$ verifies: $W = DR_{j_p}(C)$, thus confirming the final participant's integrity.


## 2.3  Verification

To ensure the integrity of the protocol, the dealer Alice compares the measurement outcome $W$ received from the final participant $\text{Bob}_p$ against the expected value. The verification condition is:

$$W = w_0 + w_1 + \cdots + w_p = s + G(0, 0, \ldots, x_1) + \cdots + G(0, 0, \ldots, x_p).$$

If the condition is satisfied, the protocol continues. If not, it suggests that $\text{Bob}_p$ may be dishonest, in which case the protocol is aborted and $\text{Bob}_p$ is excluded from future executions of the scheme.


## 2.4  Secret Reconstruction

When the threshold condition $l \geq p \geq k$ is satisfied, any group of $k$ or more participants $\text{Bob}_j \in \{\text{Bob}_1, \ldots, \text{Bob}_k\}$ can collaboratively reconstruct the secret $w_0 = s$ using the following relation:

$$w_0 = W - \sum_{j=1}^{k} w_j.$$

To ensure the correctness of the reconstruction, the recovered secret is hashed and compared with the previously published value $H = h(s)$.

## 2.5  Validity

Once all $k$ authorized participants complete their sequential operations, the resulting quantum state becomes:

$$|\Psi\rangle_p = \left(\prod_{t=0}^{k} U_{w_t, v_t}\right) |\Psi\rangle = |\psi_{\sum_{t=0}^{k} w_t}^{\sum_{t=0}^{k} v_t}\rangle.$$

The final participant, $\text{Bob}_k$, determines the measurement basis using multivariate Lagrange interpolation and measures the final state in the basis $|u_0^n\rangle$. The measurement yields:

$$W = \sum_{j=0}^{k} w_j.$$

This value is then encrypted with a shared key and distributed to other participants. Using this value, each participant computes the secret:

$$w_0 = W - \sum_{j=1}^{k} r_j.$$

# 3  Security

This section provides a security analysis of the proposed quantum secret sharing (QSS) scheme under different attacks.

## 3.1  Intercept Resend Attacks

An intercept-and-resend attack assumes that an eavesdropper, Eve, captures the quantum state transmitted from participant $\text{Bob}_j$ to $\text{Bob}_{j+1}$. However, without knowledge of the correct measurement basis used by the protocol, Eve has only a $\frac{1}{d}$ chance of selecting the correct basis.

If she measures the state without knowing the correct basis, the outcome she obtains corresponds to:

$$s + \sum_{i=1}^{j-1} w_i.$$

Due to this lack of knowledge, her probability of accurately determining the secret is bounded above by $\frac{1}{d}$. Consequently, the scheme effectively resists intercept-and-resend attacks.

## 3.2  Collision Attacks

Internal collusion among participants poses a more significant threat than external attacks. In the worst-case scenario, only the dealer (Alice) and one participant are honest, while the remaining $k - 1$ participants collude by sharing their values $w_j$ to compute:

$$\sum_{j=1}^{k-1} w_j.$$

Even in this situation, the colluding participants are unable to reconstruct the original secret $w_0$, as they lack the complete information required. Thus, the scheme is resistant to collusion attacks and ensures that fewer than $k$ dishonest participants cannot compromise the secret.

## 3.3  Entangle-And-Measure Attacks

In this type of attack, an eavesdropper Eve attempts to entangle an auxiliary quantum state $|e\rangle$ with the transmitted state using a unitary transformation $U_e$. Her objective is to extract secret information by delaying her measurement until after communication has occurred.

Assume the transmitted state is in the basis $|u_0^n\rangle$ defined as:

$$|u_0^n\rangle = \frac{1}{\sqrt{d}} \sum_{j=0}^{d-1} |j\rangle,$$

Eve applies $U_e$ such that:

$$U_e|j\rangle|e\rangle = \sum_{a=0}^{d-1} b_{ja}|a\rangle|G_{ja}\rangle,$$

where the ancillary states $|G_{ja}\rangle$ satisfy:

$$\sum_{a=0}^{d-1} |b_{ja}|^2 = 1 \quad \text{for all } j, a \in \{0, 1, \ldots, p-1\}.$$

Applying $U_e$ to the total state:

$$U_e(|u_0^n\rangle|e\rangle) = \frac{1}{\sqrt{d}} \sum_{j=0}^{d-1} \omega^{jn} U_e|j\rangle|e\rangle$$

$$= \frac{1}{\sqrt{d}} \sum_{j=0}^{d-1} \omega^{jn} \sum_{a=0}^{p-1} b_{ja}|a\rangle|G_{ja}\rangle$$

$$= \frac{1}{d} \sum_{j=0}^{d-1} \sum_{a=0}^{d-1} \sum_{t=0}^{d-1} \omega^{jn-at} |u_0^n\rangle|G_{ja}\rangle.$$

To avoid detection, Eve must ensure $b_{ja} = 0$ for all $j \neq a$, reducing the transformation to:

$$U_e|j\rangle|e\rangle = b_{jj}|j\rangle|E_{jj}\rangle.$$

$$U_e(|u_0^n\rangle|e\rangle) = \frac{1}{d} \sum_{j=0}^{d-1} \sum_{t=0}^{d-1} \omega^{j(n-t)} b_{jj} |u_0^n\rangle|G_{jj}\rangle.$$

To remain undetected, Eve must also satisfy:

$$\sum_{j=0}^{d-1} \omega^{j(n-t)} b_{jj} |G_{jj}\rangle = 0 \quad \text{for } t \neq n.$$

This leads to:

$$b_{00}|G_{00}\rangle = b_{11}|G_{11}\rangle = \cdots = b_{d-1,d-1}|G_{p-1,p-1}\rangle.$$

Hence, Eve cannot extract meaningful information from the entangled auxiliary system. The same result holds for other bases of the form:

$$|u_i^n\rangle = \frac{1}{\sqrt{d}} \sum_{j=0}^{d-1} \omega^{(n+ij)}|j\rangle,$$

thereby demonstrating the resistance of the proposed QSS scheme to entangle-and-measure attacks.

### 3.4 Dishonest Participant Attack

In this type of attack, one or more participants deliberately substitute random values in place of their legitimate inputs during the execution of the unitary transformations. During the verification phase, each participant independently verifies whether their computed value $S'$ satisfies the expected condition $S' = S = G(0, 0, \ldots, 0)$. Additionally, the dealer, Alice, compares the values $w_i$ and $w_j$, as transmitted by participant $Bob_i$ and received by $Bob_j$, respectively, using the designated measurement basis. This verification mechanism enables Alice to identify any dishonest participant attempting to disrupt the protocol and to exclude them from subsequent rounds of the secret sharing process.

## 4    Conclusion

In this paper, we presented a verifiable $(k, l)$-threshold quantum secret sharing scheme that integrates symmetric multivariate polynomials and mutually unbiased bases to enhance security and scalability. The protocol enables both secure quantum state distribution and mutual identity authentication among participants. By employing classical verification techniques and quantum operations, the scheme successfully detects dishonest behavior and withstands various quantum attacks, including intercept-resend, entangle-measure, and collusion. The use of shared polynomial evaluations for pairwise key generation provides robust identity verification while maintaining low communication overhead. Overall, the proposed scheme offers a practical and reliable solution for secure multi-party quantum communication in future quantum networks.

**Declaration**

**Conflicts of Interest.** This work is free of conflicts of interest, as disclosed by the author.

**Data Availability Statement.** This manuscript does not contain any data.

# References


1. Shamir, A.: How to share a secret. Commun. ACM **22**(11), 612–613 (1979)
2. Hillery, M., Bužek, V., Berthiaume, A.: Quantum secret sharing. Phys. Rev. A **59**(3), 1829 (1999)
3. Zhang, Z.-J., Li, Y., Man, Z.-X.: Multiparty quantum secret sharing. Phys. Rev. A-Atomic Mol. Opt. Phys. **71**(4), 044301 (2005)
4. Guo, G.-P., Guo, G.-C.: Quantum secret sharing without entanglement. Phys. Lett. A **310**(4), 247–251 (2003)
5. Yang, Y.-G., Jia, X., Wang, H.-Y., Zhang, H.: Verifiable quantum (k, n)-threshold secret sharing. Quantum Inf. Process. **11**(6), 1619–1625 (2012)
6. Chor, B., Goldwasser, S., Micali, S., Awerbuch, B.: Verifiable secret sharing and achieving simultaneity in the presence of faults. In: 26th Annual Symposium on Foundations of Computer Science (SFCS 1985), pp. 383–395. IEEE (1985)
7. Lu, C., Miao, F., Hou, J., Meng, K.: Verifiable threshold quantum secret sharing with sequential communication: C. Lu et al. Quantum Inf. Process. **17**(11), 310 (2018)
8. Kumaresan, R., Patra, A., Rangan, C.P.: The round complexity of verifiable secret sharing: the statistical case. In: Abe, M. (eds.) ASIACRYPT 2010. LNCS, vol. 6477, pp. 431–447. Springer, Heidelberg (2010). https://doi.org/10.1007/978-3-642-17373-8_25
9. Nikov, V., Nikova, S.: On proactive secret sharing schemes. In: Handschuh, H., Hasan, M.A. (eds.) SAC 2004. LNCS, vol. 3357, pp. 308–325. Springer, Heidelberg (2004)
10. Ivonovic, I.D.: Geometrical description of quantal state determination. J. Phys. A: Math. Gen. **14**(12), 3241 (1981)
11. Tavakoli, A., Herbauts, I., Żukowski, M., Bourennane, M.: Secret sharing with a single d-level quantum system. Phys. Rev. A **92**(3), 030302 (2015)
12. Wootters, W.K., Fields, B.D.: Optimal state-determination by mutually unbiased measurements. Ann. Phys. **191**(2), 363–381 (1989)

# Superpixel Segmentation Using Quantum Approximate Optimization Algorithm for Binary Labelling

Bidisha Dhara$^{(\boxtimes)}$, Monika Agrawal, and Sumantra Dutta Roy

Indian Institute of Technology Delhi, New Delhi, India
`bidishadhara1@gmail.com`, `maggarwal@care.iitd.ac.in`,
`sumantra@ee.iitd.ac.in`

**Abstract.** We investigate the use of Quantum Approximate Optimization Algorithm (QAOA) for image segmentation and compare its performance against traditional Spectral Clustering. Both methods are applied to segment images into binary labels, using superpixel representations. We employ Adjusted Rand Index (ARI) and Normalized Mutual Information (NMI) to evaluate segmentation quality quantitatively. Our results show that QAOA consistently outperforms Spectral Clustering in terms of both metrics, highlighting its potential as a competitive approach for quantum-assisted image segmentation.

## 1 Introduction

Image Segmentation involves partitioning images into multiple segments or objects and serves as a focal point in image processing and image analysis techniques [1]. The main goal of image segmentation is domain independent partitioning of an image into a set of disjoint regions that are visually different, homogeneous and meaningful with respect to some characteristics or computed properties [2]. It plays a central role in a broad range of applications, including medical image analysis, autonomous vehicles, video surveillance, and augmented reality to count a few [3].

A common approach to segmentation involves using superpixels, which combine perceptually similar pixels to form visually significant entities, lowering the amount of primitives required for future processing stages [4]. These are small image regions with a uniform appearance that are created when the original image is over-segmented and are commonly employed as a pre-processing step in computer vision applications [5]. It has several benefits, such as reducing the workload (e.g., reducing millions of pixels to thousands/hundreds of superpixels) and providing higher-level content information than pixels [6].

Spectral Clustering has been widely used in the literature for image segmentation with superpixels due to its ability to capture complex structures and relationships within the image [7]. However, Spectral Clustering, which builds global structure from local similarities via eigenvectors of a similarity matrix,


S. Mitra et al. (Eds.): PReMI 2025, LNCS 16358, pp. 716–723, 2026.
https://doi.org/10.1007/978-3-032-18480-1_73

faces fundamental limitations [8], particularly in the presence of background noise and multiscale data [9]. Also, this clustering process can be computationally expensive for larger images. These limitations motivate the exploration of alternative approaches, such as quantum algorithms, to improve segmentation performances.

Superpixel-based segmentation can be formulated as a combinatorial optimization problem, necessitating the selection of certain superpixels from a vast set of potential arrangements. Quantum computers promise to solve these problems by offering solutions that may be exponentially faster than the classical equivalent [10]. Current quantum devices have serious constraints, including limited numbers of qubits and noise processes that limit circuit depth. Variational quantum algorithms (VQAs), which use a classical optimizer to train a parameterized quantum circuit, have emerged as a leading strategy to address these constraints [11].

The Quantum Approximate Optimization Algorithm (QAOA) [12] is a hybrid quantum-classical algorithm designed to address combinatorial optimization problems. It has been applied to a variety of combinatorial optimization problems including the Max-Cut [12], Traveling Salesman Problem (TSP) [13], Max-Independent Set (MIS) [14] and graph coloring [5].

In this work, we model the image segmentation task as a combinatorial optimization problem and investigate the application of QAOA to this problem, specifically in the context of superpixel-based segmentation. Image segmentation can be viewed as a Max-Cut problem, where the objective is to maximize the cut between different regions. Our goal is to optimize the partitioning of superpixels into two distinct segments, enabling the identification of optimal boundaries between superpixels.

We present the segmentation results of both QAOA and traditional Spectral Clustering on several images. To evaluate segmentation quality, we use two standard metrics: Adjusted Rand Index (ARI) and Normalized Mutual Information (NMI). Our results show that QAOA consistently outperforms Spectral Clustering in terms of both ARI and NMI.

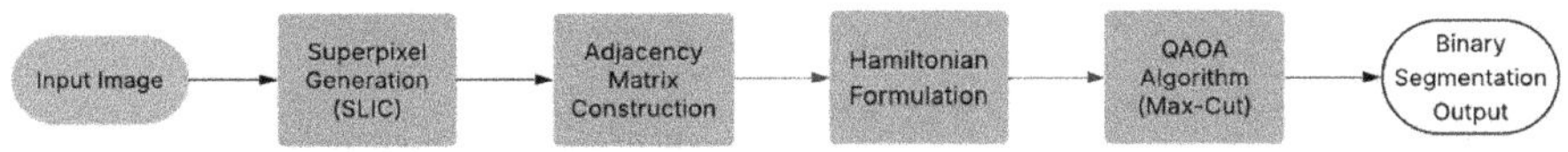


**Fig. 1.** Flowchart illustrating the step-by-step process of the algorithm, from superpixel generation of the input image to binary segmentation via QAOA as the final output. The adjacency matrix is generated using the color distance between the superpixels and the Max-Cut Hamiltonian is formulated using this matrix.

## 2   Problem Formulation

In this work, we address the task of binary image segmentation, where the objective is to divide an image into two distinct regions – typically foreground and background. The image segmentation task can be formulated as a combinatorial optimization problem, where the superpixels are represented as graph nodes. This graph can then be partitioned using the Max-Cut problem, which performs a binary labelling of the nodes, aiming to divide the image into meaningful segments by maximizing the cut between different regions. As image size increases, the corresponding graph grows significantly, making it increasingly challenging for classical methods to handle; this motivates the exploration of quantum approaches to address the computational complexity.

Thus, we apply the Quantum Approximate Optimization Algorithm (QAOA), which uses a hybrid approach to efficiently find an approximate solution to the Max-Cut problem, which in turn can be interpreted as the image segmentation solution, where the image is divided into two distinct regions based on the optimal cut between superpixels.

## 3   Methodology

Figure 1 illustrates the flowchart depicting the step-by-step process of the algorithm. We elaborate the steps here:

### 3.1   Superpixel Generation

Many popular state-of-the-art superpixel generation methods are pixel-based [15]. Many of these clustering methods employ clustering algorithms refining the clusterings until a convergence criterion is satisfied. SLIC (Simple Linear Iterative Clustering) [16] is one such algorithm that segments an image into superpixels by clustering pixels based on color similarity and spatial proximity in the Lab color space. It is an iterative method based on k-means whose superpixel centers start with a simple grid sampling and its distance measurement, which is based only on color, spatial position, and superpixel area, gives better control over the size and compactness of the superpixels.

We first apply SLIC to decompose the image into a certain number of superpixels. Each superpixel is treated as a node in a graph, and edges are constructed between adjacent superpixels to capture local relationships.

### 3.2   Adjacency Graph Construction

Graph theory has a very significant part for performance in image processing in particular image segmentation [17]. To construct the graph representation of the image, we first compute the mean Lab color for each superpixel by averaging the pixel values within each superpixel region. Next, we construct a weighted adjacency matrix where each node represents a superpixel and edges are formed between adjacent superpixels (i.e., those that share a border in the image). For every pair of neighboring superpixels, we calculate the Euclidean distance between their mean Lab color vectors. This color distance is then converted into a similarity weight using a Gaussian kernel: $w_{ij} = exp(\frac{-||c_i - c_j||^2}{2\sigma^2})$ where $c_i$ and $c_j$ are the mean color vectors of superpixels $i$ and $j$, and $\sigma$ controls the sensitivity to color differences.

**Table 1.** Comparison of image segmentation results, including the original image, superpixel boundaries, ground truth, spectral clustering, and QAOA results. The table also presents the performance evaluation using Adjusted Rand Index (ari) and Normalized Mutual Information (NMI) percentages for each image. These images are taken from the BSDS500 dataset.

| Original Image | Superpixel Boundaries | Ground Truth | Spectral Clustering | QAOA Outcome | Accuracy |
|---|---|---|---|---|---|
|  |  |  |  |  | Spectral<br>ARI =0.0409<br>NMI= 0.1512<br><br>QAOA<br>ARI = 0.0957<br>NMI =0.2036 |
|  |  |  |  |  | Spectral<br>ARI =−0.0789<br>NMI= 0.0595<br><br>QAOA<br>ARI = 0.0019<br>NMI =0.0925 |
|  |  |  |  |  | Spectral<br>ARI =0.0408<br>NMI= 0.1084<br><br>QAOA<br>ARI = 0.0850<br>NMI =0.2149 |

## 3.3   Max-Cut Formulation: Hamiltonian

Once the weighted adjacency matrix corresponding to the image is constructed, it is formulated as a Max-Cut problem which partitions the graph's nodes into two disjoint sets such that the sum of the weights of edges crossing the partition is maximized. The intuition is that this would separate the superpixels that look very different from each other, often matching the actual edges of objects in the image.

The Cost Hamiltonian for Max-Cut is given by:

$$H_C = \frac{1}{2} \sum_{\{i,j\}} w_{ij}(1 - Z_i Z_j) \tag{1}$$

where, $w_{ij}$ is the weight of edge between vertex $i$ and $j$ , and $Z_k$ is the Pauli-$Z$ matrix acting on $k-th$ qubit. Here, we use the adjacency matrix generated from superpixels in the previous step, where each edge weight $w_{ij}$ reflects the color similarity between neighboring superpixels.

## 3.4   QAOA

Once the problem is encoded as a Hamiltonian, QAOA performs a hybrid quantum-classical optimization to approximate the optimal solution. The algorithm alternates between two quantum operations applied $p$ times:

- Cost Operator: $U_C(\gamma) = e^{-i\gamma H_C}$ where $H_c$ is the cost Hamiltonian derived from the Max-Cut objective as shown in Eq. 1, and $\gamma$ is the associated parameter to be trained.
- Mixer Operator: $U_B(\beta) = e^{-i\beta H_B}$ where $H_B$ Mixer Hamiltonian and $\beta$ is the associated parameter to be trained.

The final state produced,

$$|\psi(\boldsymbol{\gamma}, \boldsymbol{\beta})\rangle = U_B(\beta_p)U_C(\gamma_p)\cdots U_B(\beta_1)U_C(\gamma_1)|+\rangle^{\otimes n}$$

depends on the $2p$ variational parameters $\boldsymbol{\gamma} = (\gamma_1, \gamma_2, ...\gamma_p)$ and $\boldsymbol{\beta} = (\beta_1, \beta_2, ...\beta_p)$ which are optimized using a classical optimizer to maximize the expected value of the cost function: $\max_{\gamma,\beta} \langle\psi(\boldsymbol{\gamma}, \boldsymbol{\beta})|H_C|\psi(\boldsymbol{\gamma}, \boldsymbol{\beta})\rangle$. The optimized parameters $\boldsymbol{\gamma}$ and $\boldsymbol{\beta}$ give the final quantum state, which approximates the solution by maximizing the cost function.

## 3.5   Interpreting QAOA Output

The output of QAOA is a probability distribution over possible solutions, and we take the output with the highest probability by measuring the final quantum state repeatedly. Since this problem was formulated over superpixels and each superpixel corresponded to a qubit, the output can be interpreted as a binary label for each superpixel.

The binary label from QAOA is used to create a segmentation mask, this label is then applied to all the pixels in the superpixel, resulting in a binary segmented image. This binary labelling effectively separates the image into two distinct regions.

## 3.6   Label Matching: Hungarian Algorithm

Since the ground truth segmentation consists of multiple labels for multiple object classes or regions, but QAOA produces a binary segmentation, we need to map the binary labels from the QAOA output to the multi-label ground truth in an optimal way. This is done by applying the Hungarian algorithm [18], which is used to solve the optimal assignment problem.

The confusion matrix is computed by comparing ground truth labels with the predicted labels. The Hungarian algorithm is applied to the confusion matrix to find the optimal assignment of predicted labels to ground truth labels. This ensures the best alignment between the binary segmentation and the multi-label ground truth, which enables fair comparison and evaluation.

# 4    Results and Simulations

In this work, we formulate binary image segmentation task as an optimization problem and investigate the use of a hybrid quantum-classical algorithm, QAOA, for solving it . Specifically, we explore how QAOA can be applied to partition an image into distinct regions by assigning binary labels to superpixels.

We evaluate our method on images from the BSDS500 dataset [19], a widely used benchmark for image segmentation. We generate superpixels using the SLIC algorithm, implemented via the scikit-image [20] library.

SLIC was configured with a maximum of 20 superpixels and a compactness value of 9. Each superpixel was treated as a node in a graph, and pairwise similarities (as discussed in Sect. 3) were used to define edge weights.

This graph served as the input for the QAOA, where each superpixel was mapped to a qubit. The choice of 20 superpixels corresponds directly to a 20-qubit problem instance, which represents a practical upper limit given the current state of quantum hardware and classical quantum simulation tools. We employed the COBYLA algorithm as the classical optimizer within the QAOA framework, using a circuit depth of $p = 2$, i.e., the quantum circuit consists of two alternating layers: one layer for the mixed Hamiltonian followed by one layer for the cost Hamiltonian, and this sequence is repeated twice. We chose a simple Mixer Hamiltonian, $H_B = \sum X_i$ and $X_i$ is the Pauli-$X$ operator acting on $i-th$ qubit. We used Qiskit [21] and Pennylane [22] for the simulations of the algorithm. To execute the quantum circuit, QAOA leveraged the $default.qubit$ backend [23].

As shown in Table 1, we present a comparison of the segmentation results for both Spectral Clustering and QAOA for specific initial parameters. The table displays the original image alongside the boundaries of the superpixels, the ground truth, the segmentation results obtained using Spectral Clustering, and the segmentation results from the QAOA. Additionally, we provide the performance metrics for each method, namely the Adjusted Rand Index (ARI) and Normalized Mutual Information (NMI), expressed as percentages. Since we perform binary segmentation, but the ground truth contains multiple labels, ARI and NMI are more suitable metrics than pixel accuracy.

$ARI \in [-1, 1]$, where 1 indicates perfect agreement, 0 corresponds to random labeling, and negative values imply worse than random. $NMI \in [0, 1]$, with 1 indicating perfect alignment and 0 meaning no mutual information between segments. These metrics are better at capturing the relationships between different regions or clusters in the ground truth, offering a more meaningful comparison than pixel-level accuracy. Our results demonstrate that QAOA, for specific initial parameters, consistently achieves better performance than spectral clustering, as measured by both ARI and NMI.

# 5    Conclusion

In this study, we explored the use of the Quantum Approximate Optimization Algorithm (QAOA) for binary image segmentation and compared its performance with classical Spectral Clustering. Both methods operated on superpixel-reduced image representations. QAOA consistently outperforms spectral clustering in terms of segmentation quality. These findings highlight the potential of quantum algorithms like QAOA in practical computer vision tasks, particularly in scenarios where perceptual accuracy is critical.

# References


1. Ramesh, K., Kumar, G.K., Swapna, K., Datta, D., Rajest, S.S.: A review of medical image segmentation algorithms. EAI Endorsed Trans. Pervasive Health Technol. (2021)
2. Zuva, T., Olugbara, O.O., Ojo, S.O., Ngwira, S.M.: Image segmentation, available techniques, developments and open issues. Can. J. Image Process. Comput. Vis. (2011)
3. Minaee, S., Boykov, Y., Porikli, F., Plaza, A., Kehtarnavaz, N., Terzopoulos, D.: Image segmentation using deep learning: a survey (2020)
4. J. Prakash, Kumar, B.V.: An extensive survey on superpixel segmentation: a research perspective. Arch. Comput. Meth. Eng. (2023)
5. Tabi, Z., et al.: Quantum optimization for the graph coloring problem with space-efficient embedding. arXiv preprint arXiv:2105.04648 (2021)
6. Barcelos, I.B., et al.: A comprehensive review and new taxonomy on superpixel segmentation. ACM Comput. Surv. (2024)
7. Li, Z., Chen, J., Superpixel segmentation using linear spectral clustering. In: 2015 IEEE Conference on Computer Vision and Pattern Recognition (CVPR) (2015)
8. Nadler, B., Galun, M.: Fundamental limitations of spectral clustering. In: Proceedings of the 20th International Conference on Neural Information Processing Systems, MIT Press (2006)
9. Schölkopf, B., Platt, J., Hofmann, T.: Fundamental Limitations of Spectral Clustering (2007)
10. McClean, J.R., Romero, J., Babbush, R., Aspuru-Guzik, A.: The theory of variational hybrid quantum-classical algorithms. New J. Phys. (2016)
11. Cerezo, M., et al.: Variational quantum algorithms (2021)
12. Farhi, E., Goldstone, J., Gutmann, S.: A quantum approximate optimization algorithm. arXiv preprint arXiv:1411.4028 (2014)
13. Qian, W., et al.: Comparative study of variations in quantum approximate optimization algorithms for the traveling salesman problem. Entropy (2023)
14. Choi, J., Kim, J.: A tutorial on quantum approximate optimization algorithm (QAOA): fundamentals and applications. In: 2019 International Conference on Information and Communication Technology Convergence (ICTC) (2019)
15. Fiedler, M., Alpers, A.: Power-SLIC: fast superpixel segmentations by diagrams (2021)
16. Achanta, R., Shaji, A., Smith, K., Lucchi, A., Fua, P., Süsstrunk, S.: Slic superpixels compared to state-of-the-art superpixel methods. IEEE Trans. Pattern Anal. Mach. Intell. (2012)
17. Basavaprasad, B., Hegadi, R.S.: Graph theory and its application to image segmentation. In: 2017 International Conference on Energy, Communication, Data Analytics and Soft Computing (ICECDS) (2017)
18. Kuhn, H.W.: The hungarian method for the assignment problem. Naval Res. Logistics Quart. (1955)

19. Martin, D., Fowlkes, C., Tal, D., Malik, J.: A database of human segmented natural images and its application to evaluating segmentation algorithms and measuring ecological statistics. In: Proceedings of the 8th International Conference on Computer Vision (2001)
20. https://scikit-image.org/docs/stable/api/skimage.html
21. Qiskit: An open-source quantum computing framework, IBM quantum (2021)
22. https://pennylane.ai/
23. https://docs.pennylane.ai/en/stable/code/api/pennylane.device.html

# Signal Processing

# A Hard Thresholding Based Deep Unrolled Network for Nonnegative Sparse Inverse Problems

Akash Sen$^{(\boxtimes)}$ and C. S. Sastry

Indian Institute of Technology, Hyderabad, India
{ma22resch11003,csastry}@iith.ac.in

**Abstract.** Recovering signals, from their linear measurements, that are sparse and nonnegative plays a pivotal role in numerous applications. Recent advancements in model-based deep learning, particularly deep unrolling techniques, have emerged as powerful alternatives to traditional iterative solvers, offering a balance between interpretability and computational efficiency. In this paper, we introduce a novel unrolled network architecture inspired by the ReLU-based hard thresholding (RHT) algorithm, tailored for sparse and nonnegative signal recovery. An advantage of this unrolling approach lies in providing a faster inference. Unlike conventional hard thresholding used in RHT, we incorporate a differentiable hard thresholding operator as an activation function within the unrolled iterations, which yields improved gradient flow and learning dynamics during training. The resulting framework, termed learned ReLU-based hard thresholding (LRHT), preserves the structural advantages of RHT while enhancing adaptability through learnable parameters. From the experiments we show that the LRHT network shows effective reconstruction results for solving the stated inverse problem.

**Keywords:** Deep unrolling · Linear inverse problem · Non-negative sparse signal recovery

## 1 Introduction

*Nonnegative sparse signal recovery* (NNSSR) is a fundamental problem arising in multiple applications including image reconstruction [1,2], wireless communications [3], computed tomography [4], electrical impedance tomography [5] etc. Here, the goal is to recover a target signal $\mathbf{s} \in \mathbb{R}^m$ with nonnegative components from the linear measurements captured in $\mathbf{x} \in \mathbb{R}^n$ via a sensing matrix $H \in \mathbb{R}^{n \times m}$, with $n \ll m$. Mathematically, the NNSSR problem can be formulated as

$$\min_{\mathbf{s} \geq 0} \|H\mathbf{s} - \mathbf{x}\|_2^2 + \lambda\|\mathbf{s}\|_0, \tag{1}$$

where the $\|.\|_0$ penalty promotes sparsity in the recovered signal and $\lambda > 0$ controls the regularization. Numerous iterative methods have been proposed


S. Mitra et al. (Eds.): PReMI 2025, LNCS 16358, pp. 727–734, 2026.
https://doi.org/10.1007/978-3-032-18480-1_74

to approximate the solution of the above-stated problem, including Nonnegative Orthogonal Matching Pursuit (NOMP) [6], Fast NOMP (FNOMP) [6], and ReLU-based hard thresholding (RHT) [7]. While effective in many cases, existing iterative approaches often suffer from high computational cost. For instance, NOMP and FNOMP require solving a linear system at each iteration, which becomes impractical for large-scale problems. On the other hand, RHT is sensitive to step size selection, which complicates its deployment in real-world scenarios.

In recent years, deep learning-based approaches [8,9] have shown promising results in solving real-world applications. However, conventional deep neural networks (DNNs) lack interpretability and require huge amounts of data for good approximation results. Primarily due to the heuristic and arbitrary nature of their architectural design choices, the DNN approximation is black-box in nature. This lack of interpretability is particularly undesirable in critical applications such as medical imaging [4]. Recently, deep unrolled networks [10,11] have gained attention due to their interpretability and requirement of a moderate amount of data. The unrolled networks are derived from traditional iterative algorithms, and are based on the underlying optimization problems.

In this work, we propose a novel deep unrolled network, *learned ReLU based hard thresholding* (LRHT) for solving the nonnegative sparse signal recovery (NNSSR) problem in a data-driven setup. Specifically, we design the network architecture by unrolling the ReLU-based hard thresholding (RHT) algorithm. Our empirical results demonstrate that LRHT provides promising results in the inverse problem of recovering the conductivity profile [12] in electrical impedance tomography (EIT).

We adopt the following notational conventions throughout the paper. The set of real numbers is denoted by $\mathbb{R}$, and the $n$-dimensional real vector space is denoted by $\mathbb{R}^n$. Scalars are represented by lowercase letters, vectors by bold lowercase letters, and matrices by uppercase letters. The gradient of a function $f$ is denoted by $\nabla f$. The $\ell_1$ and $\ell_2$ norms of a vector $\mathbf{x}$ are written as $\|\mathbf{x}\|_1$ and $\|\mathbf{x}\|_2$, respectively. The notation $\|\cdot\|_0$ refers to the number of non-zero entries in a vector. The composition of two functions is denoted by the symbol "$\circ$". The zero vector is denoted by $\mathbf{0}$.

We organize the paper as follows. In Sect. 2, we revisit the RHT algorithm, and then in Sect. 3, we provide details of the proposed algorithm, LRHT, along with the pseudo-code. We provide the basics of EIT in Sect. 4. The paper ends with simulation results and conclusions in Sects. 5 and 6, respectively.

## 2    ReLU Based Hard Thresholding Algorithm

The authors of [7] have proposed a novel *ReLU based hard thresholding* (RHT) algorithm which solves the NNSSR problem, stated in (1). The RHT algorithm integrates the *ReLU* activation function to enforce nonnegativity and the hard thresholding operator $\mathcal{H}_t$ to promote sparsity. The function *ReLU* is defined as

$ReLU(z) = \max\{0, z\}$ and $\mathcal{H}_\rho$ is defined as

$$\mathcal{H}_\rho(z) = \begin{cases} z, & \text{if } |z| > \rho, \\ 0, & \text{otherwise.} \end{cases} \tag{2}$$

applied component-wise on a vector. At each iteration, the algorithm performs a $ReLU$ activated gradient descent update followed by the hard thresholding operator, $\mathcal{H}_\rho$, ensuring that the intermediate estimates remain nonnegative and $\rho$ sparse. The $k^{th}$ iteration of the RHT algorithm is given by

$$\mathbf{s}_{n+1} = \mathcal{H}_\rho \circ ReLU\left[(I - \eta H^\top H)\mathbf{s}_n + \eta H^\top \mathbf{x}\right]. \tag{3}$$

## 3  Learned ReLU-Based Soft Thresholding

In this section, we discuss the notion of algorithm unrolling and present the proposed learned algorithm meant for nonnegative sparse signal recovery.

### 3.1  Algorithm Unrolling

In recent years, deep neural networks (DNNs) have become popular due to their impressive success across a broad spectrum of applications [8,9]. DNNs typically require substantial volumes of data and act as an opaque 'black-box' approximator and limit the interpretability of the network. Recently, the paradigm of algorithm unrolling has emerged [10,11], which is interpretable in nature and requires a moderate amount of data. In algorithm unrolling, one constructs the neural network architecture by translating the iterations of a classical optimization algorithm into individual neural network layers and stacking $L$ such layers together forms a learnable and interpretable deep unrolled network. The foundational work introducing this idea is in [10], where the authors have proposed the *learned iterative soft-thresholding algorithm* (LISTA), an unrolled version of ISTA. Their results have demonstrated that LISTA outperforms its original counterpart in sparse signal recovery. Drawing inspiration from such advances, we adopt an unrolling-based strategy for solving the NNSSR problem formulated in (1), as detailed in the following subsection.

### 3.2  Proposed LRHT

As stated earlier, our objective is to address the NNSSR problem stated in (1) within an algorithm unrolling framework. To this end, we aim to construct a neural network, whose architecture is inspired by the RHT algorithm. Our goal is to train this network such that, for a given observed signal $\mathbf{x}$, it produces an accurate approximation of the true non-negative sparse signal $\mathbf{s}$. To enable gradient-based learning, we replace the non-differentiable hard thresholding operator, $\mathcal{H}_\rho$, with a smooth approximation [13], defined by

$$\mathcal{H}_{\rho,\mu}^{smooth}(x) = \left(\frac{1}{1 + e^{\left(\frac{-x+\rho}{\mu}\right)}} - \frac{1}{1 + e^{\left(\frac{-x-\rho}{\mu}\right)}} + 1\right) x, \tag{4}$$

where $\mu > 0$ is a parameter defined by the user. We construct the proposed LRHT network by mapping each iteration of RHT algorithm into a corresponding network layer. Specifically, we define $U \equiv (I - \eta H^\top H)$ and $V \equiv \eta H^\top$, and represent the update rule for the $l^{\text{th}}$ layer as:

$$\mathbf{s}_{l+1} = \mathcal{H}^{smooth}_{\rho,\mu} \circ ReLU\left(U^l \mathbf{s}_l + V^l \mathbf{x}\right), \tag{5}$$

where the parameters in $U^l$ and $V^l$ are learnable and layer-specific.

### 3.3   Deep LRHT Model

We now present a concise mathematical formulation of the proposed deep LRHT network. Let the dataset be defined as $\mathcal{D} = \{(\mathbf{x}_i \in \mathbb{R}^n, \mathbf{s}_i \in \mathbb{R}^m)\}_{i=1}^N$. We arrange the inputs and outputs into matrices as $S = \begin{bmatrix} \mathbf{s}_1 \dots \mathbf{s}_N \end{bmatrix} \in \mathbb{R}^{m \times N}$ and $X = \begin{bmatrix} \mathbf{x}_1 \dots \mathbf{x}_N \end{bmatrix} \in \mathbb{R}^{n \times N}$. The LRHT model is defined mathematically as follows:

$$\mathcal{U}_{n,L,\Phi_{\rho,\mu},m} = \Big\{ \mathcal{M}(\mathbf{x};\mathbf{\Theta}) = \Phi_{\rho,\mu}(U^L \mathbf{s}_{L-1} + V^L \mathbf{x}) \mid \mathbf{s}^l = \Phi_{\rho,\mu}(U^l \mathbf{s}^{l-1} + V^l \mathbf{x}),$$

$$U^l \in \mathbb{R}^{m \times m}, V^l \in \mathbb{R}^{m \times n}, \forall l \in \{1,2,\dots,L\} \Big\}, \tag{6}$$

where $\Phi_{\rho,\mu}$ is the per-layer activation function. For $P = L(n^2 + mn)$, the model parameters in vector form are given by $\mathbf{\Theta} = vec\left( \begin{bmatrix} U^1 \dots U^L \end{bmatrix}, \begin{bmatrix} V^1 \dots V^L \end{bmatrix} \right) \in \mathbb{R}^P$, with $\mathbf{s}_0 \in \mathbb{R}^n$ being the initialized vector, $\mathbf{x} \in \mathbb{R}^n$ being the input of the model. If $L > 2$, then any $\mathcal{M} \in \mathcal{U}_{n,L,\Phi_{\rho,\mu},m}$ is known as the Deep LRHT network. Given the data set $\mathcal{D}$, our objective is to find $\mathbf{\Theta}^*$ such that $\mathcal{M}(\mathbf{x}_i;\mathbf{\Theta}^*) \approx \mathbf{s}_i \ \forall i \in \{1,2,\dots,N\}$, which can be found by solving the optimization problem

$$\min_{\mathbf{\Theta} \in \mathbb{R}^P} \left[ \mathcal{L}(\mathbf{\Theta}) := \frac{1}{2}\|\mathcal{M}(X;\mathbf{\Theta}) - S\|_F^2 \right], \tag{7}$$

Algorithm 1 summarizes the LRHT network.

---

**Algorithm 1.** End-to-end inference in an LRHT network

---

1: **Input:** $\mathbf{x} \in \mathbb{R}^n$
2: **Initialize:** $\mathbf{s}_0 \leftarrow \mathbf{0}$, residual $\mathbf{r}_0 \leftarrow \mathbf{s}$
3: **for** $l = 0$ to $L - 1$ **do**
4:     $\mathbf{s}_{l+1} \leftarrow \Phi_{\rho,\mu}(U^l \mathbf{s}_l + V^l \mathbf{x})$
5: **end for**
6: **Output:** Estimated nonnegative sparse signal $\hat{\mathbf{s}} \leftarrow \mathbf{s}_L$

---

# 4    Electrical Impedance Tomography

In Electrical Impedance Tomography (EIT) one reconstructs the internal conductivity distribution of an object by injecting electrical currents and recording the resulting voltages on its boundary. EIT has attracted significant attention in various fields, including imaging in healthcare [14], geophysics [15], due to its ability to provide real-time, low-cost, and portable imaging solutions [16].

The mathematical foundations of EIT are rooted in Maxwell's equations, which provide the behavior of electromagnetic fields in conductive media. Maxwell's equations [17] describe the fundamental interactions of electric and magnetic fields. Given the internal conductivity distribution $\sigma$, the potential inside is related by the following fundamental equation governing electrical impedance tomography,

$$\nabla \cdot (\sigma \nabla u) = 0. \tag{8}$$

As for the boundary conditions, one aims at deriving a relation both for current injection and voltage measurements. In a practical EIT setup, one attaches a finite number of electrodes to the boundary of the object, and injects currents through pairs of electrodes while recording the resulting voltages.

## 4.1    Linearized Inverse Problem in EIT

In EIT, the inverse problem reconstructs the conductivity inside a domain from boundary voltage and current measurements [12,17,18]. In the adjacent stimulation pattern used in practice in CEM, one uses the measurement patterns with currents injected through the adjacent electrodes, and measures differences of voltages of adjacent electrodes. The $i^{th}$ current pattern injects current of $+1$ through the $i^{th}$ electrode and current of $-1$ through the $(i+1)^{th}$ electrode. Therefore, $L_v \times L_v$ voltage measurements are obtained for different current patterns $i = 1, 2, \cdots, L_v$.

Suppose the forward map is given by $\mathcal{E} : L^\infty(\Omega) \to \mathbb{R}^{L_v \times L_v}$, that is, $\mathcal{E}(\sigma) = U$ links the conductivity profile to the voltage measurements. Then from the definition of the Frechet derivative [12], we have

$$\mathcal{E}(\sigma) \approx \mathcal{E}(\sigma_0) + \mathcal{E}'(\sigma_0)(\sigma - \sigma_0),$$

where,

$$\mathcal{E}'(\sigma_0) = \left( \int_\Omega \nabla u_{\sigma_0}^p \cdot \nabla u_{\sigma_0}^q \right)_{p,q=1,2,\cdots,L_v}.$$

In the above equation, $u_{\sigma_0}^j$ is the voltage solution vector for the current pattern $j$ and conductivity $\sigma_0$. In general, one represents the conductivity using finite elements, which leads to a linear system of equations of type

$$J(\sigma - \sigma_0) = \Delta V (:= \mathcal{E}(\sigma) - \mathcal{E}(\sigma_0)), \tag{9}$$

where, for a given number, $N_{mesh}$, of mesh cells, the sizes of the matrix $J$ (the Jacobian or sensitivity matrix given by $\mathcal{E}'(\sigma_0)$) and the vector $(\sigma - \sigma_0)$ are $L_v^2 \times N_{mesh}$ and $N_{mesh} \times 1$ respectively. With a few electrodes put in place, the sensitivity matrix in (9) remains under-determined, and the vector $(\sigma - \sigma_0)$ possesses a few nonzero components. The EIDORS software [19] provides a popular way of generating the discrete system in (9).

## 5    Simulation Results

In this section, we provide an empirical demonstration of our LRHT network and give an account of our experimental setup. We have run our simulation on 2D synthetic data over a square grid with $L_v = 16$ equidistant electrodes located along the edges. We have obtained the data $\{(\mathbf{s}_i \in \mathbb{R}^{1024}, \mathbf{x}_i \in \mathbb{R}^{4096})\}_{i=1}^{10000}$ by using the finite element method [20] through the Julia programming language. We have considered a 6-layered LRHT network, $\mathcal{M}(X; \mathbf{\Theta})$. For the purpose of training, we have used Adam optimizer [21] to minimize the mean squared error (MSE) loss function defined in (7) by setting $N$ to 10000. The number of epochs that we have taken is 1000, with a learning rate of 0.01 and a batch size of 150.

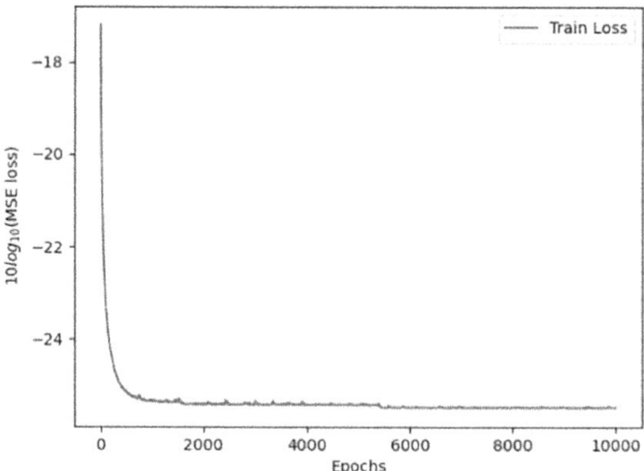


**Fig. 1.** Training Loss vs Epochs for LRHT. This plot implies the successful training of the network.

Figure 1 shows the decay of error with respect to the number of epochs and Fig. 2 shows the reconstruction results obtained from the LRHT network.

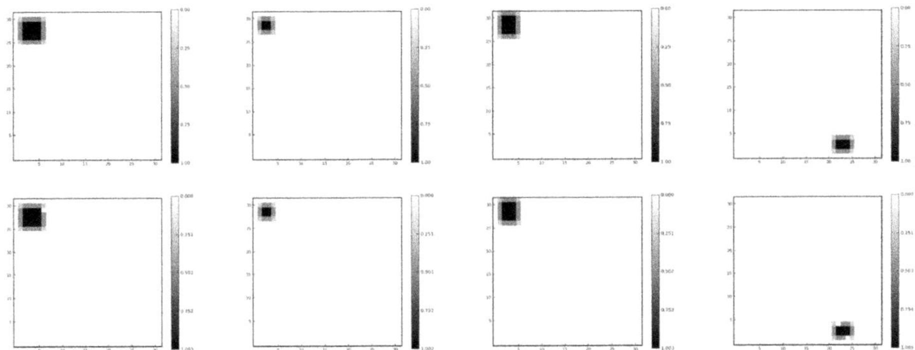

**Fig. 2.** Top row: Target (Ground Truth) signals. Bottom row: Corresponding predictions obtained by the LRHT algorithm.

# 6   Conclusions

We have developed in this paper an unrolled deep neural network, called LRHT, that aims at addressing the nonnegative sparse recovery problem. Specifically, we have designed the network architecture from the classical RHT algorithm. We have taken a smooth approximation of the hard thresholding operator to apply the gradient-based algorithm. Further, we have numerically illustrated the performance of deep LRHT for identifying square-shaped objects in EIT. In our future work, we will attempt to establish the analytical guarantees of the LRHT network along with the extensive simulation results on different applications.

# References


1. Javaheri, A., Zayyani, H., Marvasti, F.: Sparse recovery of missing image samples using a convex similarity index. Signal Process. **152**, 90–103 (2018)
2. Chen, B., Zhang, J.: Content-aware scalable deep compressed sensing. IEEE Trans. Image Process. **31**, 5412–5426 (2022)
3. Li, S., Da Xu, L., Wang, X.: Compressed sensing signal and data acquisition in wireless sensor networks and internet of things. IEEE Trans. Industr. Inf. **9**(4), 2177–2186 (2012)
4. Sonkar, M., Sasmal, P., Theeda, P., Sastry, C.S.: Sparsity-driven deterministic sampling strategy for coded aperture x-ray computed tomography. Meas. Sci. Technol. **33**(3), 034003 (2021). https://dx.doi.org/10.1088/1361-6501/ac39d2
5. Gulati, S., Jampana, P., Sastry, C.S.: A comparative study on performances of adaptive and nonadaptive sparse solvers for electrical impedance tomography. In: Kaur, H., Jakhetiya, V., Goyal, P., Khanna, P., Raman, B., Kumar, S. (eds.) CVIP 2023. CCIS, vol. 2011, pp. 458–467. Springer, Cham (2024). https://doi.org/10.1007/978-3-031-58535-7_38
6. Yaghoobi, M., Wu, D., Davies, M.E.: Fast non-negative orthogonal matching pursuit. IEEE Signal Process. Lett. **22**(9), 1229–1233 (2015)

7. He, Z., Shu, Q., Wang, Y., Wen, J.: A relu-based hard-thresholding algorithm for non-negative sparse signal recovery. Signal Process. **215**, 109260 (2024). https://www.sciencedirect.com/science/article/pii/S0165168423003341
8. Zhang, K., Zuo, W., Zhang, L.: FFDNet: toward a fast and flexible solution for CNN-based image denoising. IEEE Trans. Image Process. **27**(9), 4608–4622 (2018)
9. Nah, S., Hyun Kim, T., Mu Lee, K.: Deep multi-scale convolutional neural network for dynamic scene deblurring. In: Proceedings of the IEEE Conference on Computer Vision and Pattern Recognition, pp. 3883–3891 (2017)
10. Gregor, K., LeCun, Y.: Learning fast approximations of sparse coding. In Proceedings of the 27th International Conference on International Conference on Machine Learning, ser. ICML'10. Madison, WI, USA, pp. 399–406. Omnipress (2010)
11. Monga, V., Li, Y., Eldar, Y.C.: Algorithm unrolling: interpretable, efficient deep learning for signal and image processing. IEEE Signal Process. Mag. **38**(2), 18–44 (2021)
12. Harrach, B.: Interpolation of missing electrode data in electrical impedance tomography. Inverse Prob. **31**(11), 115008 (2015)
13. Zhang, X.-P.: Thresholding neural network for adaptive noise reduction. IEEE Trans. Neural Networks **12**(3), 567–584 (2001)
14. Ke, X.-Y., et al.: Advances in electrical impedance tomography-based brain imaging. Mil. Med. Res. **9**(1), 10 (2022)
15. Wang, H., Zimmermann, E., Weigand, M., Vereecken, H., Huisman, J.A.: Comparison of different inversion strategies for electrical impedance tomography (EIT) measurements. Geophys. J. Int. **235**(3), 2888–2899 (2023)
16. Durdevic, P., Hansen, L., Mai, C., Pedersen, S., Yang, Z.: Cost-effective ERT technique for oil-in-water measurement for offshore hydrocyclone installations. Ifac-papersonline **48**(6), 147–153 (2015)
17. Gulati, S., Jampana, P., Sastry, C.: Series solution and sensitivity analysis of central disc-shaped objects in electrical impedance tomography. Phys. Scr. **99**(11), 115206 (2024)
18. Gulati, S., Jampana, P., Sastry, C.: A comparative study on performances of adaptive and nonadaptive sparse solvers for electrical impedance tomography. In: Computer Vision and Image Processing, Part-3, Springer, CVIP Conf. Proceedings, 202 (2023)
19. Diddi, S., Jampana, P.V., Mangadoddy, N.: Evaluation of two noniterative electrical resistance tomography (ERT) reconstruction algorithms for air-core measurements in hydrocyclone. Ind. Eng. Chem. Res. **61**(49), 18 017–18 029 (2022)
20. Vauhkonen, P.J., Vauhkonen, M., Savolainen, T., Kaipio, J.P.: Three-dimensional electrical impedance tomography based on the complete electrode model. IEEE Trans. Biomed. Eng. **46**(9), 1150–1160 (1999)
21. Kingma, D.P., Ba, J.: Adam: a method for stochastic optimization. arXiv preprint arXiv:1412.6980 (2014)

# Soft Computing/Computational Intelligence

# A Hybrid Bayesian-Monte Carlo Approach for Inventory Management

Sarit Maitra[1(✉)] and Vivek Mishra[2]

[1] Alliance School of Business, Alliance University, Bengaluru, India
sarit.maitra@gmail.com
[2] Alliance School of Engineering, Alliance University, Bengaluru, India

**Abstract.** This study offers a hybrid Simulation-Optimization approach combining Monte Carlo simulation (for demand uncertainty) with Bayesian optimization (for policy tuning), an efficient way to optimize inventory decisions compared to brute-force methods like grid search. It compares two key inventory policies, (1) periodic review (p, Q), and (2) continuous review (r, Q) on historical demand data. While both (r, Q) and (p, Q) policies are well-known, there is a lack of empirical studies comparing their performance under real-world demand variability and lead time uncertainty using advanced simulation-optimization techniques. The results show that the (r, Q) policy performs better, increasing expected profit (18.64%) by dynamically adjusting inventory based on daily demand and lead times.

**Keywords:** Decision making · Demand uncertainty · Inventory management · Monte-Carlo simulations · Optimization

## 1   Introduction

Effective inventory management is critical to organizational performance [1]. In the context of tactical supply chain management, traditional operations research approaches continue to face significant challenges [2]. While traditional analytical models are computationally efficient, they often fail in real-world supply chains due to highly unpredictable business dynamics [3]. In contrast, empirical studies found that simulation models accommodate uncertainty and real-world complexities without oversimplifying assumptions, which makes them increasingly popular in applied arena [4, 5]. Historically, inventory models focused on deterministic demand [6] but their applicability has diminished due to rising demand volatility. Recent studies (e.g., [7]) integrated demand forecasting model for robust optimization while others emphasize the role of advanced optimization techniques in inventory systems [8]. Empirical studies have highlighted the importance of simulation modeling, which is the primary motivation for this work. [9, 10]. The effective optimization involves structural exploitation, theoretical foundations, and algorithm development, whereas the simulation involves probabilistic modeling. This study combined the strengths of both, to develop a hybrid method which allows for an inclusive exploration of the solution space to enhance the effectiveness of decision


S. Mitra et al. (Eds.): PReMI 2025, LNCS 16358, pp. 737–744, 2026.
https://doi.org/10.1007/978-3-032-18480-1_75

making. Monte Carlo simulation (MCS) is used to generate demand and lead time distributions for various products based on historical demands and estimate potential profit maximization under different inventory policies.

Empirical work with case studies on stochastic demand in the context of inventory management is limited [11]. However, simulation-based optimization presents three key challenges: (1) computational expense due to the many iterations required to overcome stochastic noise, (2) the lack of gradient information that limits optimization efficiency, and (3) the what-if nature that provides scenario analysis but not automatic optimization. While specialized metaheuristic optimization techniques, such as Simulated Annealing (SA) and Genetic Algorithms (GA), empirical studies have highlighted that they cannot ensure the quality of the solution [12]. Our hybrid simulation-optimization method overcomes three key limitations of traditional simulation. First, it reduces computational expense by using Bayesian optimization as a surrogate model, requiring fewer simulation runs to converge to near-optimal solutions compared to brute-force Monte Carlo. Second, it addresses the lack of gradient information by modeling the profit function probabilistically, enabling efficient search even in noisy, black-box environments. Third, it transforms passive "what-if" scenario analysis into active optimization by iteratively refining policy parameters based on simulation feedback. Empirical studies found that by modeling the profit function as a Gaussian process, Bayesian optimization intelligently selects the most informative simulation runs, cutting iterations by ~90% in some cases [13].

## 2   Theoretical Model

Figure 1 presents the theoretical framework which is further improved to meet this study's goals and the work's complexity. For each day t (t ranges from 1 to 365), the inventory and sales are updated as in $S_t = min(I_{t-1}, D_t)$. Here, $min(I_{t-1}, D_t) \rightarrow$ the number of units sold on day $t$ ($S_t$), this is based on available inventory from the previous day ($I_{t-1}$) and the demand on the current day ($D_t$).

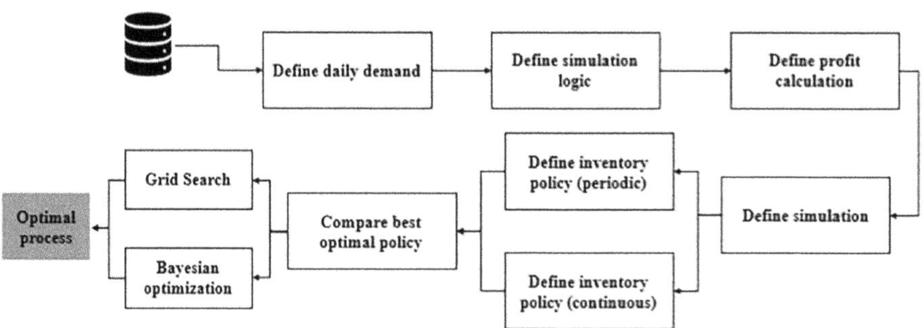


**Fig. 1.** Conceptual framework.

The logic behind this is, if the demand $D_t \leq I_{t-1}$, then $S_t = D_t$ which means all the demand can be satisfied. If the demand $D_t \geq I_{t-1}$, then, $S_t = I_{t-1}$ which means only as much inventory as is available can be sold. This ensures that sales never exceed the available inventory, and that demand is fulfilled as much as possible given the constraints. After fulfilling the demand for the day, the remaining inventory is updated by subtracting the units sold from the inventory level of the previous day $I_t = I_{t-1} - S_t$.

Orders were placed at regular intervals during the review period (p). The immediate inventory update can be presented as $I_t = I_t + Q$ where inventory is updated immediately with the reorder quantity (Q). However, in a realistic scenario, orders placed do not arrive instantly but after a lead time (LT).

Under the above conditions, our proposed system simulates inventory levels, sales, and reorder quantity over 365 days to calculate profit based on sales revenue and costs (holding, ordering, and purchase costs). Equations (1), (2), (3), and (4) formulate revenue, holding, ordering, and purchase costs.

$$revenue = P_s \sum_{t=1}^{365} S_t = \sum (units_{sold}) * (sellingprice) \tag{1}$$

$$holdingcost = C_H \sum_{t=1}^{365} I_t \tag{2}$$

$$Orderingcost = numberoforders \times orderingcostperorder(C_O) \tag{3}$$

$$purchasecostorcostofgoods(COGS) = C_P \sum_{twheretmodulop=0} Q \tag{4}$$

$$total\ costs = holding\ cost + cost\ of\ goods\ sold + ordering\ cost$$

$$profit = revenue - total\ costs$$

The objective function for maximizing profit, considering all costs and revenues, is shown in Eq. (5).

$$= P_s \sum_{t=1}^{365} S_t - \left\{ \left( C_H \sum_{t=1}^{365} I_t \right) + (C_O * n) + \left( C_P * \sum_{twheretmodulop=0} Q \right) \right\} \tag{5}$$

### 2.1 Data Exploration

To verify the applicability, empirical evaluation was conducted using a case study of four highly customized products, where demands are unique to every customer. One year (365 days) sales information was collected for each product. Table 1 presents statistical summary of the demand data.

**Table 1.** Statistical summary.

|  | Pr1 | Pr2 | Pr3 | Pr4 |
|---|---|---|---|---|
| Purchase Cost ($C_p$) | € 12 | € 7 | € 6 | € 37 |
| Lead Time (LT) | 9 days | 6 days | 15 days | 12 days |
| Size | 0.57 | 0.05 | 0.53 | 1.05 |
| Selling Price ($P_s$) | € 16.10 | € 8.60 | € 10.20 | € 68 |
| Starting Stock ($S_t$) | 2750 | 22500 | 5200 | 1400 |
| Mean demand over lead time ($mu$) | 103.50 | 648.55 | 201.68 | 150.06 |
| Std. Dev. of demand ($\sigma_D$) | 37.32 | 26.45 | 31.08 | 3.21 |
| Probability (Probability of demand on any day) | 0.76 | 1.00 | 0.70 | 0.23 |
| Order Cost ($C_o$) | € 1000 | € 1200 | € 1000 | € 1200 |
| Holding Cost ($C_h$) → 20% of unit cost | 20% | 20% | 20% | 20% |
| Expected demand (lead time) | 705 | 3891 | 2266 | 785 |
| Std. Dev. ($\sigma_{leadtime}$) | 165.01 | 64.78 | 383.33 | 299.92 |
| Annual demand | 28,670 | 237,370 | 51,831 | 13,056 |

## 2.2 Bayesian Inference and Monte Carlo Method

Assuming we have a random variable X representing daily demand. The distribution of X is normally distributed with PDF ((f(x))). During the simulation, X was conditionally sampled based on whether an order was placed on the previous day.

If C = 1: Use demand from the previous day ($X_{prev}$) and if C = 0: sample X from the usual distribution. For simplicity, we assume f(x|C = 1) is a Dirac delta ($\delta$) function and f(x|C = 0) is a normal distribution of f(x). The integral representation considering these conditions is $E(x|C) = \int_{-\infty}^{\infty} x * f(x|C) dx$. We model daily demand X as a lognormal random variable (to ensure positivity and skewness) with mean $\mu$ and volatility $\sigma$ derived from historical data. Conditional sampling is introduced to capture order dependencies: if an order occurred the previous day ($C = 1$), demand is fixed to $X_{prev}$; otherwise, X is sampled from $lnN(\mu, \sigma^2)$. Weighted sampling corrects for bias via weights $w(x) = f(x)/f(x \mid C)$. The simulation evaluates inventory dynamics over 365 days, triggering replenishment when stock falls below the reorder point $r = \mu L + k\sigma \sqrt{L}$ (where k is the service-level factor).

## 2.3 Demand Modeling

Demand per period is expressed as $demand per period \sim \aleph(\mu_d, \sigma_d^2)$. The parameters for the log-normal distribution were derived from the $\mu_D$ and $\sigma_D$ during the lead-time. The expected demand, $E(D)$ over the period shown in $E(D_R) = \int_0^R D * f(d) * d(D)$. Over lead time (LT), demand has expectation $E(D_{LT}) = LT * \mu_d$ and variance $\sigma_{DLT}^2 = LT * \sigma_d^2$. Safety stock is $SS = z * \sigma_D * \sqrt{LT}$, and the order-up-to level is $OUP = R * \mu_d + SS$. At each review, order $Q = max(0, OUP - inventory)$. For nonstationary demand, $E(D_R)$ generalizes to $\int_O^R D * f(d)dD$.

## 2.4  Constraints and Assumptions

We have considered the following assumptions, The demand for products follows a log-normal distribution, The lead time for replenishment is deterministic and known in advance, The model considers the various costs associated with inventory management, including purchase, holding, and ordering costs, These costs are assumed to be known and constant over time without considering factors such as inflation or economies of scale, The model assumes that stockouts are not allowed, implying that demand is always met without delay, The demand for each product is assumed to be independent and identically distributed across periods, The demand and the lead time are continuous random variables.

# 3  Empirical Analysis

It starts with the expected demand and updates it based on the actual demand observed on the day that the order is triggered. If an order is triggered, the demand for subsequent days is set as the last high demand. If an order is not triggered, the model samples daily demand using a normal distribution. Table 2 reports the outputs of both sampling approaches using the (p, Q) policy.

**Table 2.** Periodic review - Random vs. Conditional sampling for stochastic demand.

| Product | Reorder quantity | $\mu_{profit}$ | $\sigma_{profit}$ |
|---|---|---|---|
| Pr1 | 4120 | 189543.97 | 4927.64 |
| Pr2 | 33730 | 577530.97 | 5935.75 |
| Pr3 | 7770 | 422764.87 | 22731.94 |
| Pr4 | 2010 | 514094.89 | 72598.22 |

**Total profit → 1,703,934.7 | Time to run: 4527.05 secs**

| Product | Reorder quantity | $\mu_{profit}$ | $\sigma_{profit}$ |
|---|---|---|---|
| Pr1 | 4120 | 189694.80 | 4802.71 |
| Pr2 | 33740 | 577356.19 | 2646.94 |
| Pr3 | 7790 | 420784.23 | 24457.91 |
| Pr4 | 2080 | 429674.36 | 86558.09 |

**Total profit → 1,615,108.92 | Time to run: 3656.68 secs**

This suggests, under simulated conditions, conditional sampling may lead to slightly lower profits overall. In the (r, Q) logic, the reorder point (ROP) is estimated as ROP $=$ SS $+D_{LT}$, where $D_{LT}$ is the demand during the lead time. The inventory level is checked daily, if the INV $\leq$ ROP and no order is in hand, an order is triggered. Thus, the (r, Q) system ensures that inventory levels are managed dynamically based on daily demand and lead-time considerations, allowing for effective inventory control while meeting customer demand and minimizing costs. Table 3 reports the output of the (r, Q) policy.

**Table 3.** Continuous review of stochastic demand.

| Product | r | $\mu_{profit}$ | $\sigma_{profit}$ |
|---|---|---|---|
| Pr1 | 4095 | 447626.66 | 20366.69 |
| Pr2 | 33940 | 1633884.81 | 53635.00 |
| Pr3 | 7710 | 504179.23 | 4608.83 |
| Pr4 | 2370 | 688613.93 | 122741.87 |

**Total profit $\rightarrow$ 3,274,304.64 | Time to run: 4693.92 secs**

The output indicates a significant increase ($>100\%$) in the expected profit (3,274,304.64) compared with previous simulations. A comparative analysis of the optimization approaches employing grid search and Bayesian optimization was employed over a range of Q and r values (incremented by 10). Empirical studies have found that Bayesian optimization is a powerful approach for the global derivative-free optimization of non-convex expensive functions [14]. Table 4 displays consolidated output, which shows an approximate growth of 18.08% (approximately) growth post-grid search optimization.

Because MCS is versatile and popular at the same time in real-life business environments [15], a wide range of outcomes can be predicted by changing the assumptions and constraints of the proposed mode across all parameters.

**Table 4.** Performance optimization.

| Products | $\mu_{profit}$ | r | Q | $\mu_{SS}$ | $\sigma_{profit}$ |
|---|---|---|---|---|---|
| **Grid search** | | | | | |
| Pr1 | 455298.75 | 500 | 3200 | 422 | 18893.89 |
| Pr2 | 2028436.29 | 1000 | 32500 | 352 | 4024.65 |
| Pr3 | 521983.34 | 500 | 7160 | 359 | 13082.08 |
| Pr4 | 860626.65 | 500 | 1620 | 465 | 85071.92 |
| **Total Profit: 3,866,345.03** | | | | | |
| **Bayesian optimization** | | | | | |
| Pr1 | 521836.49 | 4439 | 3845 | 3687 | 34849.75 |

*(continued)*

**Table 4.** (*continued*)

| Products | $\mu_{profit}$ | r | Q | $\mu_{SS}$ | $\sigma_{profit}$ |
|---|---|---|---|---|---|
| Pr2 | 1958021.72 | 35000 | 25000 | 27906 | 109806.55 |
| Pr3 | 771964.35 | 7956 | 10000 | 6647 | 48815.27 |
| Pr4 | 632979.93 | 2848 | 1912 | 2782 | 125500.15 |
| | **Total profit: 3,884,802.49** | | | | |

## 4 Conclusion

This study explores optimization of inventory management strategies using a Monte Carlo Simulation (MCS) and applying both (p, Q) and (r, Q) inventory policies. The goal was to determine the optimal reorder quantities (Q) that maximize profit while minimizing stockout risks and excessive inventory holdings. The results showed that the (r, Q) policy significantly increased expected profit compared to the (p, Q) policy. This is because of its dynamic adaptation to fluctuating demand, resulting in better inventory control and higher profitability. The study also found that conditional sampling in MCS resulted in faster execution times, but slightly lower overall profits. Combining Monte Carlo simulation with Bayesian Optimization significantly reduces computation, achieving optimized inventory policies in approximately 300 runs versus 10,000+. This demonstrates that dynamic inventory management can reduce stockout risks and excess inventory, thereby leading to higher profitability.

## References


1. Atnafu, D., Balda, A.: The impact of inventory management practice on firms' competitiveness and organizational performance: empirical evidence from micro and small enterprises in Ethiopia. Cogent Bus. Manag. **5**(1), 1503219 (2018). https://doi.org/10.1080/23311975.2018.1503219
2. Wu, G., de Carvalho Servia, M.Á., Mowbray, M.: Distributional reinforcement learning for inventory management in multi-echelon supply chains. Digit. Chem. Eng. **6**, 100073 (2023). https://doi.org/10.1016/j.dche.2022.100073
3. Arisha, A., Abo-Hamad, W.: Simulation optimisation methods in supply chain applications: a review. Irish J. Manag. (2010)
4. Heikkinen, R., Sipilä, J., Ojalehto, V., Miettinen, K.: Flexible data driven inventory management with interactive multi-objective lot size optimisation. Int. J. Logist. Syst. Manag. **46**(2), 206–235 (2023). https://doi.org/10.1504/IJLSM.2023.134404
5. Li, T., Fang, W., Baykal-Gürsoy, M.: Two-stage inventory management with financing under demand updates. Int. J. Prod. Econ. **232**, 107915 (2021). https://doi.org/10.1016/j.ijpe.2020.107915
6. Babiloni, E., Guijarro, E.: Fill rate: from its definition to its calculation for the continuous (s, Q) inventory system with discrete demands and lost sales. Cent. Eur. J. Oper. Res. **28**(1), 35–43 (2020). https://doi.org/10.1007/s10100-018-0546-7

7. Ekren, B.Y., Stylos, N., Zwiegelaar, J., Turhanlar, E.E., Kumar, V.: Additive manufacturing integration in E-commerce supply chain network to improve resilience and competitiveness. Simul. Model. Pract. Theory **122**, 102676 (2023). https://doi.org/10.1016/j.simpat.2022.102676

8. Wu, J., Frazier, P.: Practical two-step lookahead Bayesian optimization. In: Advances in Neural Information Processing Systems, vol. 32 (NeurIPS 2019) (2019)

9. Oliveira, J.B., Lima, R.S., Montevechi, J.A.B.: Perspectives and relationships in supply chain simulation: a systematic literature review. Simul. Model. Pract. Theory **62**, 166–191 (2016). https://doi.org/10.1016/j.simpat.2016.02.001

10. Tsai, S.C., Chen, S.T.: A simulation-based multi-objective optimization framework: a case study on inventory management. Omega (Westport) **70**, 148–159 (2017). https://doi.org/10.1016/j.omega.2016.09.007

11. Nasr, W.W., Elshar, I.J.: Continuous inventory control with stochastic and non-stationary Markovian demand. Eur. J. Oper. Res. **270**(1), 198–217 (2018). https://doi.org/10.1016/j.ejor.2018.03.023

12. Abdel-Basset, M., Abdel-Fatah, L., Sangaiah, A.K.: Metaheuristic algorithms: a comprehensive review. In: Computational Intelligence for Multimedia Big Data on the Cloud with Engineering Applications, pp. 185–231. Elsevier (2018). https://doi.org/10.1016/B978-0-12-813314-9.00010-4

13. Shahriari, B., Swersky, K., Wang, Z., Adams, R.P., de Freitas, N.: Taking the human out of the loop: a review of Bayesian optimization. Proc. IEEE **104**(1), 148–175 (2016). https://doi.org/10.1109/JPROC.2015.2494218

14. Kroese, D.P., Brereton, T., Taimre, T., Botev, Z.I.: Why the Monte Carlo method is so important today. WIREs Comput. Stat. **6**(6), 386–392 (2014). https://doi.org/10.1002/wics.1314

15. Klein, A., Falkner, S., Mansur, N., Hutter, F.: Robo: a flexible and robust Bayesian optimization framework in python. In: 31st Conference on Neural Information Processing Systems (NIPS 2017), Long Beach, CA, USA (2017)

# Decentralized Bilevel Optimization for Real-Time V2V Coordination and Collision Avoidance


Somnath Mukhopadhyay[1], Sunita Sarkar[1]($\boxtimes$), Ankur Sinha[2], Prabhakar Kumar[1], and Sabbir Ahmed[1]

[1] Department of Computer Science and Engineering, Assam University, Silchar, India
sarkarsunita2601@gmail.com
[2] Department of Operations and Decision Sciences, Indian Institute of Management Ahmedabad, Ahmedabad, India
asinha@iima.ac.in



**Abstract.** This paper proposes a decentralized bilevel optimization framework for real-time vehicle-to-vehicle (V2V) collision avoidance. To balance collision risk, velocity consensus, and speed efficiency, the upper level uses Particle Swarm Optimization (PSO) to adaptively adjust risk-weight parameters. The lower level solves a constrained Quadratic Programming (QP) problem to compute safe and efficient velocities while satisfying physical and safety constraints. Each vehicle autonomously identifies its neighbors using local sensing and adjusts its trajectory based on a composite risk function. This two-tier structure enables context-aware real-time coordination without the need for centralized control. The simulation results demonstrate that the proposed method achieves smooth velocity alignment and significantly reduces the risk of collisions over time between multiple autonomous vehicles. The decentralized architecture provides scalability and resilience, making it suitable for dense and dynamic traffic environments. In general, this work presents a practical, flexible, and computationally efficient solution for collaborative vehicle motion planning under uncertainty.

**Keywords:** Vehicle-to-Vehicle (V2V) Communication · Bilevel Optimization · Quadratic Programming (QP) · Collision Avoidance · Decentralized Control · Real-Time Coordination


## 1 Introduction

The rapid increase in vehicular traffic in modern urban environments has increased the demand for intelligent, adaptive, and scalable coordination mechanisms. Traditional centralized traffic management systems face challenges in scalability and real-time responsiveness due to communication delays and computational bottlenecks. To overcome these issues, decentralized control strategies such as vehicle platooning, where each vehicle autonomously adapts its motion based on local conditions, have gained significant attention.



S. Mitra et al. (Eds.): PReMI 2025, LNCS 16358, pp. 745–758, 2026.
https://doi.org/10.1007/978-3-032-18480-1_76

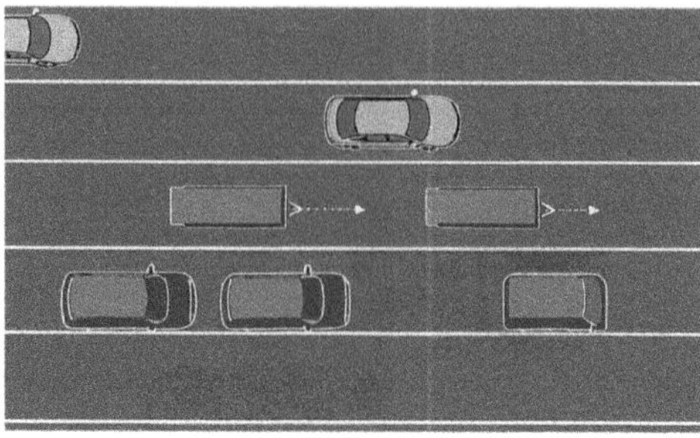

**Fig. 1.** Typical traffic scenario with multiple vehicles traveling in the same direction on a multi-lane road.

Figure 1 illustrates a typical traffic scenario that forms the basis of our study: multiple vehicles traveling in the same direction on a multilane road. In such dynamic and dense environments, each vehicle must continuously adjust its speed while maintaining safe distances from surrounding vehicles, particularly its immediate neighbors. This scenario reflects the core challenges addressed in this research: collision avoidance, velocity consensus, and adaptive coordination under the constraints of decentralized decision making. Current approaches, such as decentralized RL (reinforcement learning), IDM-based rules (Intelligent Driver Model), and fixed-weight bilevel models, frequently lack scalability, adaptability, and neighbor-risk handling. Hence, we propose a bilevel framework to fill these gaps, with the lower level solving a convex Quadratic Programming to determine optimal velocities and the upper level adaptively tuning risk weights using Particle Swarm Optimization. This enables autonomous traffic systems to coordinate in a scalable, risk-aware, and real-time manner. The primary contribution of this paper lies in formulating the vehicle coordination problem as a bilevel optimization problem. Unlike prior works that often fix upper-level parameters or rely on centralized control schemes, this approach dynamically tunes coordination weights in a fully distributed manner. Typically, a Bilevel Optimization problem consists of two levels of problems. The optimizers in each level optimize their objective functions without considering the objective functions of the other level. However, the results of each of them affect the objective value of the other and the decision space [3]. Mathematically, a general bilevel problem is defined in Eq. (1):

$$\min_{x \in X} F(x, y^*(x)) \quad \text{subject to } y^*(x) = \arg \min_{y \in Y(x)} f(x, y) \tag{1}$$

Here, $x$ represents the upper-level decision variables, $y$ are the lower-level decision variables, $F$ is the upper-level objective function, and $f$ is the lower-level objective. The feasible region $Y(x)$ may itself be constrained by $x$. The state-of-the-art methods often use centralized control and fixed weights, which limit adaptability and scalability. The proposed work introduces a decentralized framework that dynamically adjusts risk weights and optimizes velocities, making it robust in dense traffic.

The remainder of this paper is organized as follows. Section 2 details the related works corresponding to our problem. Section 3 details the mathematical formulation and the proposed bilevel optimization methodology. Section 4 presents the simulation results and evaluates the effectiveness of the framework. Finally, Sect. 5 concludes the paper and proposes directions for future research.

## 2   Literature Review

In this section, we review prior work related to our problem across three major categories: (i) bilevel optimization methods, including classical and meta-heuristic strategies for hierarchical decision-making; (ii) practical applications of bilevel models in traffic coordination and multi-agent systems; and (iii) risk-aware motion planning, with a focus on decentralized collision avoidance under uncertainty. We also highlight the limitations of existing V2V coordination approaches, such as static interaction models and the reliance on centralized or communication-dependent strategies. This review motivates the need for our proposed decentralized bilevel framework, which addresses these challenges in a scalable and adaptive manner. Bilevel approaches are broadly classified into evolutionary and classical methods, as highlighted in the foundational review by Sinha et al. [9]. Although mathematically rigorous, classical methods often struggle with nonconvexity, lack of gradient information, and the need for closed-form solutions in the lower-level problem, limiting their applicability to complex or real-time scenarios. To overcome these challenges, Ochs et al. [6] proposed the Enhanced Barrier Smoothing Algorithm (EBSA), which improves tractability by reformulating non-smooth bilevel problems using smoothing functions and augmented Lagrangian techniques. Xu and Ye [16] introduced the DRC-BLEA (Dynamic Resource Competition-Based Bilevel Evolutionary Algorithm) framework, which improves the efficiency of evolutionary algorithms by focusing computational resources on promising regions of the search space.

Beyond theory, bilevel approaches have been used to solve practical issues such as multi-agent reinforcement learning and traffic coordination. Stoilova and Stoilov [10] combine predictive control of the model and bilevel optimization to synchronize traffic signals. Zhang et al. [19] suggest a bilevel actor-critic approach that uses hierarchical learning to enhance policy coordination. Peng et al. [8] combine vehicle routing and signal control to increase urban traffic throughput. These works demonstrate that bilevel structures can successfully coordinate distributed decisions under uncertainty, even though many rely on centralized planning or fixed upper levels. Risk-aware motion planning is necessary for autonomous vehicles operating in unpredictable environments. By anticipating collisions or steering clear of high-risk areas, probabilistic and potential field approaches incorporate risk. A quick risk assessment using real-time reachable sets was proposed by Otte and Pavone [7]; however, its applicability in dynamic, decentralized scenarios is limited due to its reliance on static maps. Using deep reinforcement learning, Chen et al. [1] presented a decentralized, non-communicating multi-agent navigation policy in which agents learn to avoid collisions by using local sensing. The method produces less than ideal group behavior in highly interactive settings because it lacks explicit risk modeling and coordination, despite being scalable and adaptable. Despite progress, current decentralized vehicle coordination methods face key limitations. Safety models like IDM [4,11,13] and MOBIL [12,14] rely on static interaction ranges, lacking adaptability to dynamic traffic. Bilevel frameworks [9] often require centralized updates or offline tuning, reducing real-time responsiveness. Platooning algorithms [2,18] typically assume uniform vehicle dynamics, overlooking mixed traffic challenges. Many V2V systems [1,15] depend on continuous communication, making them vulnerable to network failures. Additionally, most existing approaches struggle to maintain performance under sensing noise or sudden topology changes in dense traffic scenarios. These issues underscore the need for an adaptive, and communication-efficient framework capable of handling real-time topology changes and vehicle heterogeneity with computational efficiency.

The proposed research addresses these challenges by introducing a decentralized PSO-QP bilevel framework for V2V coordination. The upper level employs PSO to adaptively tune per-vehicle risk weights $[b_1, b_2, \lambda]$ in real time, accounting for safety, velocity consensus, and efficiency. Under safety and dynamic constraints, the lower level minimizes a composite risk function by solving a convex Quadratic Program (QP) [5]. Vehicles can cooperatively optimize their trajectories in a fully decentralized manner by leveraging a risk model that combines individual and neighbor-based components. Our model applies this concept to traffic systems, drawing inspiration from Halter and Mostaghim's [3] bilevel decomposition, in which the lower-level manages physical feasibility and the PSO optimizes abstract thermodynamic parameters. We also use decentralized PSO applications, like the ones in Yang et al. [17], where agents use local sensing to coordinate independently. This effort combines convex velocity planning and PSO-based decentralized weight tuning in a real-time bilevel architecture designed for cooperative vehicle platoons.

## 3   Proposed Methodology

This section presents the proposed decentralized bilevel optimization framework for vehicle-to-vehicle (V2V) collision avoidance and coordination. The framework integrates a Particle Swarm Optimization algorithm at the upper level with a constrained Quadratic Programming formulation at the lower level. Each vehicle optimizes its motion autonomously based on interactions with its neighbors. The general workflow of the proposed bilevel optimization framework is illustrated in Fig. 2, which shows the interaction between the upper-level and lower-level optimization stages within the simulation loop. The flow chart begins with the initialization of vehicle positions and velocities. At each iteration, every vehicle detects its nearest neighbors and enters the PSO-based upper-level optimization block to tune the weights influencing risk components. The particle with the lowest local risk defines the optimal weight vector, which is then passed to the lower-level quadratic programming module to compute a safe and efficient velocity. After that, vehicles compute their optimal actions, their states are updated, and the loop continues until the end of the simulation horizon. This decentralized control loop supports parallel execution, enabling scalable and real-time collision avoidance in dense multi-agent V2V traffic scenarios. The steps of the proposed algorithm are shown in Algorithm 1. At each time step, every vehicle operates independently in a decentralized fashion. First, it detects its nearest neighbors using a Euclidean distance-based method. For each vehicle $i$, the Euclidean distance to all other vehicles $j$ is calculated using the Eq. (2), where $(x_i, y_i)$ and $(x_j, y_j)$ denote the 2D positions of vehicles $i$ and $j$, respectively.

$$d_{ij} = \sqrt{(x_j - x_i)^2 + (y_j - y_i)^2} \tag{2}$$

---

**Algorithm 1.** Decentralized PSO–QP Optimization for Vehicle Platooning

---

1: **for** each vehicle $i = 1$ to $N$ **do**
2:     Initialize position $(x_i, y_i)$ and velocity $v_i$
3: **end for**
4: **for** each time step $t = 1$ to $T$ **do**
5:     **for** each vehicle $i$ **do**
6:         Identify neighbors $\mathcal{N}(i)$ using Euclidean distance
7:         Initialize PSO particles for $[b_1, b_2, \lambda]$
8:         **for** each PSO iteration **do**
9:             **for** each particle **do**
10:                 Solve QP to compute $v_i$ using particle's weights.
11:                 Compute individual risk $R_i$.
12:                 Compute local total risk $R_{1,i} = R_i + \sum_{j \in \mathcal{N}(i)} R_j$
13:             **end for**
14:             Update personal and global best particles.
15:         **end for**
16:         Select best weights and solve QP to get final $v_i$.
17:     **end for**
18:     **for** each vehicle $i$ **do**
19:         Update position: $x_i = x_i + v_i \cdot \Delta t$.
20:     **end for**
21: **end for**

---

These distances are then sorted, and the closest neighbors $\mathcal{N}(i)$ are selected based on the smallest non-zero distances. Each vehicle uses these neighbors to run a PSO where particles represent candidate risk-weight vectors. A QP is solved for each particle to obtain a velocity, which is then used to compute risk values. After convergence, the best particle is used to finalize the velocity of the vehicle. Finally, all vehicles update their positions accordingly. The proposed methodology is decentralized because each vehicle here detects its neighbors locally, tunes

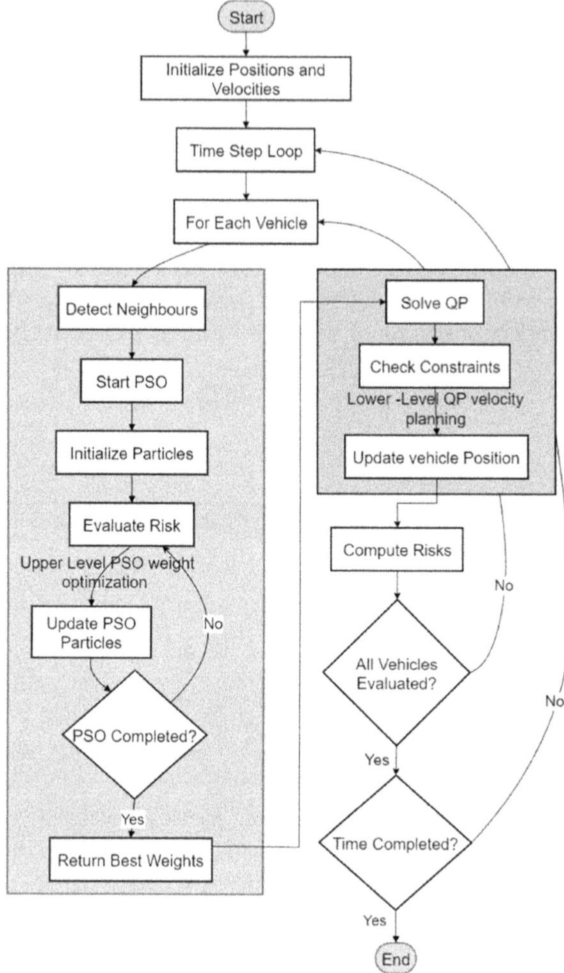



**Fig. 2.** Proposed bilevel optimization framework flowchart.

risk weights and runs its own QP for determining safe velocity. No central controller is required because coordination emerges from local interactions, which ensures scalability and resilience even after communication failures or topology changes.

## 3.1  Upper-Level Optimization for Risk Tuning

At the upper level, each vehicle runs a PSO to tune its risk weight vector $\mathbf{w}_i = [b_{1,i}, b_{2,i}, \lambda_i]$. The goal is to minimize the local total risk, which is defined as the sum of the vehicle with the highest risk and those of its neighbors as defined in Eq. (3), subject to constraints defined in (4).

$$\min_{\mathbf{w}_i} \; R_{1,i}(\mathbf{w}_i) = R_i(\mathbf{w}_i, v_i) + \sum_{j \in \mathcal{N}(i)} R_j(\mathbf{w}_j, v_j) \tag{3}$$

$$0.1 \leq b_{1,i}, \; b_{2,i}, \; \lambda_i \leq 5 \tag{4}$$

Here, $\mathcal{N}(i)$ denotes the set of dynamically detected neighbors of vehicle $i$. The weights $b_{1,i}$, $b_{2,i}$, and $\lambda_i$ control the importance of velocity consensus, collision avoidance, and speed efficiency, respectively. PSO consists of a population of particles that search the search space by moving with a particular velocity toward the best global particle using their experience from past generations [3]. The objective is to find a set of weights that minimizes the total risk $R_{1,i}$, guiding the particles toward the best performing solutions. The Algorithm 2 describes the particle swarm optimization (PSO) process used at the upper level. Each vehicle maintains a swarm of candidate weight vectors $\mathbf{w} = [b_1, b_2, \lambda]$ representing the relative importance of collision risk, velocity consensus, and speed efficiency. At each iteration, the particles update their positions on the basis of their personal best experience and the global best found so far. The cost function $f(\mathbf{w})$ corresponds to the total local risk, which includes the individual risk of the vehicle and the risk of its neighboring vehicles. After $K$ iterations, the particle that reaches the lowest cost provides the optimal weight vector $\mathbf{w}^*$, which is then passed to the lower-level QP to calculate the final velocity.

---

**Algorithm 2.** Particle Swarm Optimization (PSO) for Weight Tuning

---

1: **Input:** Cost function $f(\mathbf{w})$, swarm size $S$, iterations $K$, inertia weights $w_0, w_f$, coefficients $c_1, c_2$, bounds $[l_b, u_b]$
2: Initialize positions $\mathbf{w}_p \sim U(l_b, u_b)$ and velocities $\mathbf{v}_p = 0$ for each particle $p = 1, \ldots, S$
3: Set personal best $\mathbf{p}_p = \mathbf{w}_p$ and global best $\mathbf{g} = \arg\min f(\mathbf{p}_p)$
4: **for** iteration $k = 1$ to $K$ **do**
5:     Compute inertia: $w = w_0 + \dfrac{(w_f - w_0)k}{K}$
6:     **for** each particle $p$ **do**
7:         Update velocity:

$$\mathbf{v}_p \leftarrow w\mathbf{v}_p + c_1 r_1(\mathbf{p}_p - \mathbf{w}_p) + c_2 r_2(\mathbf{g} - \mathbf{w}_p)$$

8:         Update position: $\mathbf{w}_p \leftarrow \mathbf{w}_p + \mathbf{v}_p$
9:         Apply bounds: $\mathbf{w}_p \in [l_b, u_b]$
10:         Evaluate $f(\mathbf{w}_p)$ and update $\mathbf{p}_p$ if improved
11:     **end for**
12:     Update global best $\mathbf{g}$
13: **end for**

---

### 3.2   Lower-Level Optimization for Optimal Velocity

At the lower level, each vehicle computes its optimal velocity using the optimal weight vector $\mathbf{w}_i^* = [b_{1,i}^*, b_{2,i}^*, \lambda_i^*]$. The objective is to minimize the weighted individual risk as defined in Eq. (5), subject to constraints given in Eq. (6), (7), and (8). The cost function components are derived from Eqs. (9), (10), and (11).

$$\min_{\mathbf{v}} \ \mathcal{R}_i(k) = b_{1,i}(k)\, r_i^{\text{col}}(k) + b_{2,i}(k)\, r_i^{\text{con}}(k) + \lambda_i(k)\, r_i^{\text{vel}}(k) \tag{5}$$

$$v_{\min} \leq v_i \leq v_{\max}, \tag{6}$$

$$a_{\min} \cdot \Delta t \leq v_i - v_i^{\text{prev}} \leq a_{\max} \cdot \Delta t, \tag{7}$$

$$d_{ij}^{\text{cur}} + (v_j - v_i)\Delta t \geq d_{\text{safe}}, \quad \forall j \in \mathcal{N}(i). \tag{8}$$

$$\text{Speed deviation:} r_i^{\text{vel}}(k) = \big(v_i(k) - v_{\text{ref}}\big)^2, \tag{9}$$

$$\text{Velocity consensus:} r_i^{\text{con}}(k) = \sum_{j \in \mathcal{N}_i(k)} \big(v_i(k) - v_j(k)\big)^2. \tag{10}$$

$$\text{Collision risk:} r_i^{\text{col}}(k) = \sum_{j \in \mathcal{N}_i(k)} \phi\big(d_{ij}(k) - d_{\text{safe}}\big), \tag{11}$$

Each term enforces a specific behavior: $r_i^{\text{vel}}$ penalizes deviations from the reference speed, $r_i^{\text{con}}$ promotes velocity alignment with neighbors, and $r_i^{\text{col}}$ discourages unsafe gaps. Constraints ((6)) to ((8)) maintain physical limits on velocity and acceleration while ensuring minimum safety distance. This problem is formulated as a standard Quadratic Programming (QP) given in Eq. (12), where $\mathbf{z} = [v_i, s_1, \ldots, s_{|\mathcal{N}(i)|}]^T$, $H$ is positive definite, and the constraints are linear, guaranteeing a unique global optimum.

$$\min_{\mathbf{z}} \ \frac{1}{2}\mathbf{z}^T H \mathbf{z} + f^T \mathbf{z} \qquad \text{subject to: } A\mathbf{z} \leq \mathbf{b}. \tag{12}$$

---

**Algorithm 3.** Lower-Level Quadratic Programming (QP) for Velocity Computation

---

1: **Input:** Optimal weights $\mathbf{w}^* = [b_1, b_2, \lambda]$, vehicle $i$, neighbor set $\mathcal{N}(i)$, positions $(x, y)$, previous velocities $v_j$, parameters $P$.
2: Define decision vector $\mathbf{z} = [v_i, s_1, \ldots, s_{|\mathcal{N}(i)|}]$.
3: Formulate objective function as in (5).
4: Apply constraints (6) to (8).
5: Build QP matrices $(H, f, A, b)$ and solve:

$$\min_{\mathbf{z}} \frac{1}{2}\mathbf{z}^T H \mathbf{z} + f^T \mathbf{z}$$

6: Extract optimal velocity: $v_i^* = z_1^*$.

---

Algorithm 3 summarizes the QP process for computing each vehicle's optimal velocity $v_i^*$. Given the tuned weights $\mathbf{w}^*$ from PSO, the QP minimizes the composite risk while ensuring safety, velocity bounds, and acceleration limits. The solver guarantees a unique and computationally efficient solution because the objective function is convex and the constraints are linear.

## 4   Results and Discussion

In this section, we evaluate the performance of the proposed decentralized PSO-QP bilevel optimization framework through extensive simulation studies. The proposed framework was implemented in MATLAB R2024b (student Version) on a system with 16 GB RAM and a 12th Gen Intel(R) Core(TM) i5-12500H processor (2.00 GHz). Each vehicle performed the PSO-QP cycle independently at each time step, confirming the computational feasibility of decentralized operation in real time. We begin by analyzing the evolution of the states of the vehicle, including velocity, individual risk, and local total risk, along with the convergence behavior of the PSO optimizer in Subsect. 4.1. This unified analysis demonstrates how the controller enables each vehicle to adjust its motion safely and flexibly while adaptively minimizing risk through iterative weight tuning. Next, we provide a combined evaluation of performance and scalability in Subsect. 4.2, including runtime statistics, benchmarking against baseline controllers, and the system responsiveness under varying platoon sizes. Together, these results confirm the effectiveness, responsiveness, and scalability of the proposed framework for real-time vehicle-to-vehicle coordination. To evaluate the proposed PSO-QP coordination framework, simulations were conducted for a platoon of 20 autonomous vehicles navigating a bounded $50\,\mathrm{m} \times 20\,\mathrm{m}$ 2D road. Each vehicle optimizes its local total risk, which includes its own risk and that of its nearest neighbors, dynamically identified at every time step. At the upper level, each vehicle uses 20 particles and 15 iterations per time step. The cognitive and social coefficients are set as $c_1 = c_2 = 1.5$. The inertia weight $w$ follows a linearly decaying schedule as defined in Eq. (13).

$$w(t) = w_0 - \left( \frac{w_0 - w_f}{T_{\mathrm{PSO}}} \right) \cdot t. \tag{13}$$

where $w_0 = 0.9$, $w_f = 0.4$, and $T_{\mathrm{PSO}} = 15$ denotes the number of iterations. At the lower level, a convex Quadratic Program (QP) computes the optimal safe velocity $v$ subject to physical and safety constraints, including the velocity range $v \in [5, 30]\,\mathrm{m/s}$ and a minimum headway of $d_{\mathrm{safe}} = 10\,\mathrm{m}$. The simulation runs for a total duration of $T_{\mathrm{end}} = 20\,\mathrm{s}$ with a step size $\Delta t = 0.1\,\mathrm{s}$. Vehicles are initialized with random velocities within the allowed bounds and placed without overlap. At every time step, the system logs each vehicle's velocity, individual risk $R_i$, and local total risk $R_{l,i}$.

### 4.1   Trajectory Evolution and PSO Convergence Analysis

In this section, we present the evolution of key vehicle states, including individual risk, local-total risk, convergence trends, and velocity profiles, to evaluate the effectiveness of the proposed PSO-QP coordination strategy. Figure 3 provides a consolidated visualization for three representative vehicles. Subfigures (a) to (c) depict the evolution of individual risk over time, demonstrating consistent reduction and dynamic adaptation, even under dense-start conditions. Subfigures (d) to (f) illustrate the corresponding local-total risk, which captures the cumulative influence of neighboring vehicles. The steady downward trends reflect the ability to promote cooperative risk-aware behavior across the platoon. Subfigures (g) to (i) display the velocity profiles, highlighting how vehicles gradually stabilize at desired cruising speeds despite initial disturbances. Finally, subfigures (j) to (l) show PSO convergence behavior, where risk values decline across iterations, confirming the effectiveness of the optimizer in discovering improved weight configurations. These results collectively validate the framework's capability to ensure individual safety, maintain velocity consensus, and enable efficient, decentralized coordination. Table 1 reports a statistical summary including mean, minimum, maximum, and standard deviation of speed, individual risk, and local-total risk across all 20 vehicles to complement the visual analysis. Zero-valued minimum risks further confirm the ability to guide vehicles into conflict-free states under certain conditions.

**Table 1.** Combined per-vehicle statistics: Speed, individual risk, and local total risk (0–20 s).

| Vehicle | Speed (m/s) | | | | Individual Risk $R_i(t)$ | | | | Local Total Risk | | | |
|---|---|---|---|---|---|---|---|---|---|---|---|---|
| | Mean | Min | Max | Std Dev | Mean | Min | Max | Std Dev | Mean | Min | Max | Std Dev |
| Veh01 | 19.53 | 13.66 | 28.99 | 4.56 | 21.48 | 0.00 | 70.15 | 14.51 | 181.13 | 0.00 | 391.21 | 110.84 |
| Veh02 | 26.43 | 17.50 | 30.00 | 4.38 | 13.89 | 0.00 | 44.27 | 9.30 | 78.14 | 0.00 | 253.37 | 60.99 |
| Veh03 | 27.06 | 17.50 | 30.00 | 3.42 | 12.49 | 0.00 | 25.19 | 3.87 | 53.15 | 0.00 | 171.18 | 39.29 |
| Veh04 | 26.92 | 16.60 | 30.00 | 3.78 | 13.70 | 0.00 | 39.55 | 7.09 | 57.92 | 0.00 | 184.05 | 47.09 |
| Veh05 | 17.86 | 11.19 | 28.09 | 5.11 | 37.64 | 0.00 | 71.78 | 22.28 | 210.37 | 0.00 | 388.85 | 106.30 |
| Veh06 | 24.25 | 17.50 | 30.00 | 3.77 | 4.57 | 0.00 | 26.09 | 5.12 | 64.18 | 0.00 | 168.35 | 44.16 |
| Veh07 | 18.49 | 16.68 | 28.36 | 2.89 | 37.14 | 0.00 | 71.44 | 17.14 | 209.11 | 0.00 | 388.85 | 106.03 |
| Veh08 | 24.71 | 17.50 | 29.93 | 3.68 | 26.21 | 0.00 | 68.66 | 19.65 | 192.87 | 0.00 | 388.85 | 103.89 |
| Veh09 | 24.71 | 17.43 | 29.87 | 3.56 | 15.78 | 0.00 | 64.72 | 14.70 | 103.20 | 0.00 | 204.96 | 63.38 |
| Veh10 | 25.73 | 17.50 | 29.99 | 4.08 | 20.13 | 0.00 | 40.40 | 10.32 | 185.25 | 0.00 | 388.85 | 100.85 |
| Veh11 | 25.24 | 17.50 | 30.00 | 4.03 | 15.03 | 0.00 | 48.64 | 11.94 | 117.13 | 0.00 | 227.63 | 74.41 |
| Veh12 | 23.94 | 17.50 | 30.00 | 4.04 | 2.41 | 0.00 | 31.42 | 5.65 | 44.86 | 0.00 | 178.24 | 31.82 |
| Veh13 | 22.43 | 17.50 | 30.00 | 3.20 | 39.01 | 0.00 | 68.99 | 19.56 | 210.62 | 0.00 | 388.85 | 106.57 |
| Veh14 | 24.23 | 17.50 | 30.00 | 3.72 | 39.82 | 0.00 | 70.89 | 17.60 | 211.03 | 0.00 | 388.85 | 106.83 |
| Veh15 | 25.28 | 17.50 | 30.00 | 4.40 | 11.37 | 0.00 | 26.63 | 4.96 | 84.45 | 0.00 | 180.55 | 51.04 |
| Veh16 | 24.79 | 17.50 | 30.00 | 3.80 | 5.10 | 0.00 | 19.94 | 3.22 | 44.96 | 0.00 | 155.30 | 30.62 |
| Veh17 | 24.42 | 17.50 | 30.00 | 3.26 | 6.86 | 0.00 | 42.70 | 11.94 | 74.91 | 0.00 | 222.18 | 59.85 |
| Veh18 | 16.94 | 12.78 | 24.35 | 2.26 | 23.21 | 0.00 | 61.70 | 19.29 | 196.82 | 0.00 | 323.85 | 120.67 |
| Veh19 | 24.55 | 17.50 | 30.00 | 3.90 | 12.29 | 0.00 | 28.40 | 8.08 | 76.89 | 0.00 | 204.38 | 61.02 |
| Veh20 | 24.97 | 17.50 | 30.00 | 3.82 | 5.00 | 0.00 | 19.40 | 2.97 | 44.01 | 0.00 | 155.30 | 28.59 |

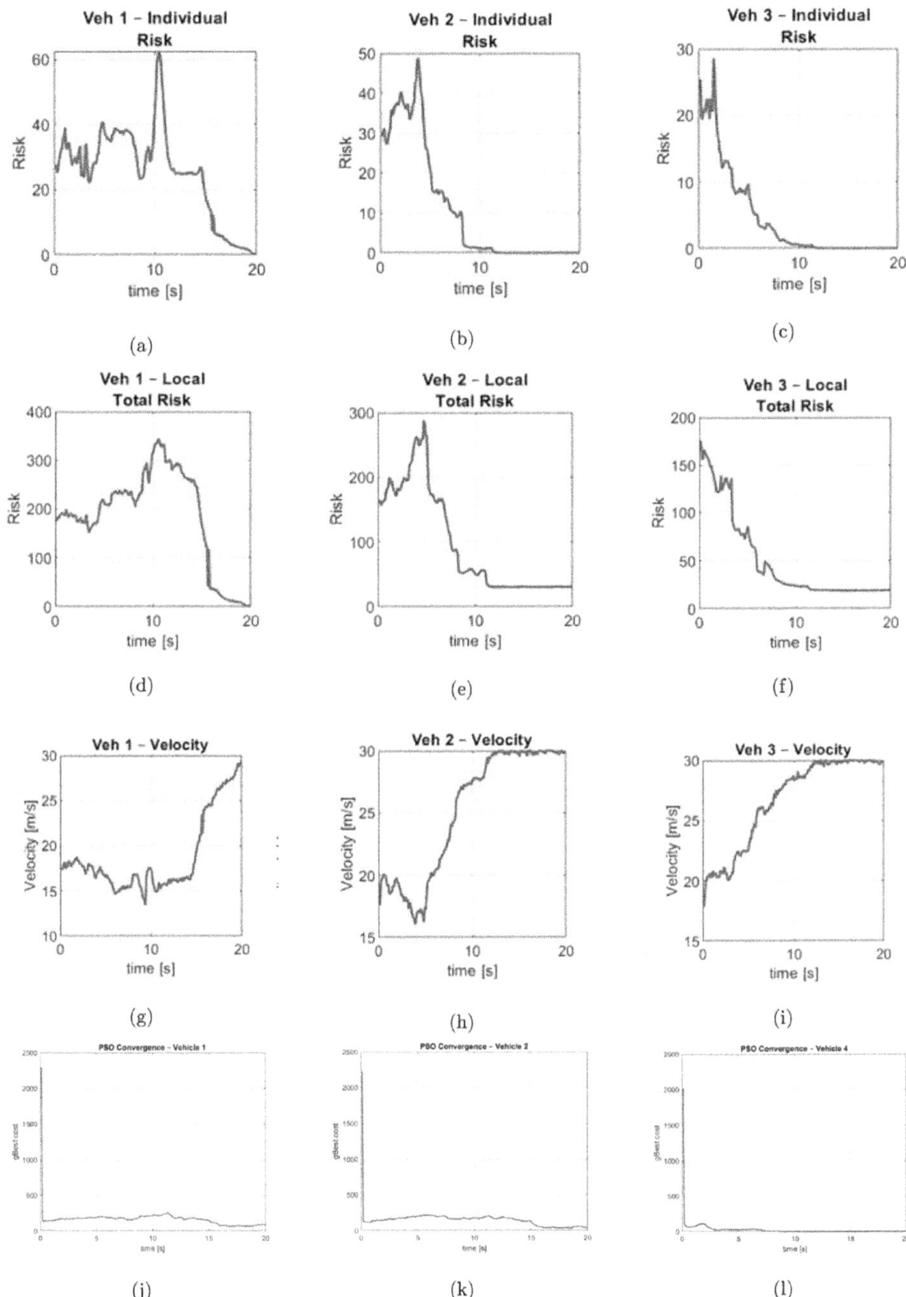

**Fig. 3.** (a-c) individual risk curves, (d-f) total local risk curves, (g-i) velocity curves, (j-l) convergence curves of different vehicles over time.

## 4.2   Performance and Scalability Analysis

Table 2 presents a comprehensive summary of runtime, performance, comparison, and scalability metrics associated with the proposed PSO–QP framework. The top portion of the table reports the computational performance over a 20-second simulation involving 20 autonomous vehicles. The controller maintains an average execution time of 3.8 ms per control cycle, with the worst-case time never exceeding 4.7 ms comfortably within the 10 ms real-time control budget (100 Hz frequency). The PSO layer typically converges within 10 iterations per step, and no QP infeasibility events were recorded throughout the simulation, which means the Quadratic Programming (QP) solver could find a valid solution at every control step throughout the simulation. Additionally, only a small number of acceleration clipping events were observed (mean: 0.6), indicating that the controller adheres well to physical feasibility constraints. The second section of the table presents final performance statistics for the vehicle platoon. The final velocity distribution exhibits strong consensus (mean: 28.56 m/s), while individual and local-total risks remain within acceptable ranges across all vehicles. The average convergence time is 16.16 s, reflecting the ability of the system to stabilize from dense initial conditions. The third section compares the proposed PSO–QP controller against three baseline methods under a dense-start scenario: Fixed-Weight Quadratic Programming (FW–QP), Pure PSO, and the Intelligent Driver Model (IDM). The PSO–QP approach outperforms all alternatives in terms of average and worst-case risk values, velocity tracking accuracy, and controller runtime. Specifically, it reduces average risk by approximately 34% compared to FW-QP and by over 50% relative to IDM while maintaining real-time execution capabilities. Finally, the table includes a scalability analysis based on neighbor detection time for varying platoon sizes. The results confirm that the decentralized architecture scales efficiently, as the detection time remains negligible even when the number of vehicles increases fivefold. This highlights

**Table 2.** Summary of runtime, performance, comparison, and scalability metrics.

| Category | Metric | Min | Max | Mean | Std Dev |
| --- | --- | --- | --- | --- | --- |
| Runtime (PSO-QP) | CPU time per step [ms] | 3.8 | 4.7 | 3.8 | 0.5 |
| | PSO iterations per step | 10.4 | 12 | 10.4 | 1.3 |
| | QP infeasibilities (count) | 0 | 0 | 0 | 0 |
| | Acceleration clipping events | 0.6 | 1 | 0.6 | 0.2 |
| Final Vehicle Performance | Final velocity [m/s] | 25.32 | 30.00 | 28.56 | 1.80 |
| | Final individual risk | 0.0033 | 16.57 | 4.89 | 5.86 |
| | Final total risk | 0.046 | 62.36 | 28.39 | 24.19 |
| | Time to converge [s] | 11.5 | 20.0 | 16.16 | 3.69 |
| Comparison (Dense-start) | Avg risk $\overline{\mathcal{R}}$ | PSO-QP: 241, Fixed-Weight QP: 365, Pure PSO: 419, IDM: 487 | | | |
| | Max risk $\mathcal{R}_{\max}$ | PSO-QP: 398, Fixed-Weight QP: 560, Pure PSO: 598, IDM: 714 | | | |
| | Velocity error $\varepsilon_v$ [m/s] | PSO-QP: 0.62, Fixed-Weight QP: 0.94, Pure PSO: 1.13, IDM: 1.67 | | | |
| | Runtime per step $t_{\text{CPU}}$ [ms] | PSO-QP: 3.8, Fixed-Weight QP: 1.7, Pure PSO: 7.5, IDM: 0.4 | | | |
| Scalability Analysis | Vehicles $= 10$ | Neighbor detection time: 0.000003 s | | | |
| | Vehicles $= 20$ | Neighbor detection time: 0.000055 s | | | |
| | Vehicles $= 50$ | Neighbor detection time: 0.000240 s | | | |

the potential of the framework for deployment in large-scale, real-time traffic coordination systems.

## 5    Conclusion and Future Work

We proposed a decentralized V2V collision avoidance framework based on bilevel optimization, combining PSO and QP, where each vehicle minimizes a local risk function that balances safety, velocity consensus, and efficiency. Simulations show smooth and safe velocity convergence with real-time feasibility and decentralized operation. Future work will focus on real-world applicability, including multi-lane overtaking, complex road networks, and heterogeneous vehicle dynamics. Key challenges such as sensor noise, actuator delays, hardware failures, communication latency, and mixed human-autonomy traffic will be addressed through robust optimization, adaptive calibration, and hybrid sensing-communication strategies. Integration with traffic signals, legal compliance, and validation through field experiments or high-fidelity simulators like *SUMO* and *CARLA* will be essential for deployment.

## References


1. Chen, Y., Everett, M., Liu, M., How, J.P.: Decentralized non-communicating multiagent collision avoidance with deep reinforcement learning. In: Proceedings of the IEEE International Conference on Robotics and Automation (ICRA), pp. 285–292 (2017)
2. Chien, S., Ding, B., Wei, C.: Dynamic safety distance model for proactive collision avoidance in truck platooning. IEEE Trans. Intell. Transp. Syst. **22**(5), 2872–2882 (2021)
3. Halter, W., Mostaghim, S.: Bilevel optimization of multi-component chemical systems using particle swarm optimization. In: 2006 IEEE International Conference on Evolutionary Computation, pp. 1240–1247 (2006). https://doi.org/10.1109/CEC.2006.1688451
4. Holley, D., et al.: MR-IDM: merge reactive intelligent driver model for realistic lane-merging behavior. arXiv preprint arXiv:2305.12014 (2023). https://arxiv.org/abs/2305.12014
5. Nocedal, J., Wright, S.J.: Numerical Optimization. Springer Series in Operations Research and Financial Engineering, 2nd edn. Springer, Heidelbeg (2006). https://doi.org/10.1007/978-0-387-40065-5
6. Ochs, P., Ranftl, R., Brox, T., Pock, T.: Bilevel optimization with nonsmooth lower level problems. IEEE Trans. Evol. Comput. **22**(2), 276–295 (2015)
7. Otte, M., Pavone, M.: Safe motion planning in unknown environments: optimality benchmarks and tractable policies. IEEE Trans. Rob. **34**(5), 1242–1257 (2018)
8. Peng, X., Gao, H., Han, G., Wang, H., Zhang, M.: Joint optimization of traffic signal control and vehicle routing in signalized road networks using multi-agent deep reinforcement learning (2023). https://arxiv.org/abs/2310.10856
9. Sinha, A., Malo, P., Deb, K.: A review on bilevel optimization: from classical to evolutionary approaches and applications. IEEE Trans. Evol. Comput. **22**(2), 276–295 (2018)

10. Stoilova, K., Stoilov, T.: Model predictive traffic control by bi-level optimization. Appl. Sci. **12**(9), 4147 (2022)
11. Treiber, M., Hennecke, A., Helbing, D.: Congested traffic states in empirical observations and microscopic simulations. Phys. Rev. E **62**(2), 1805–1824 (2000)
12. Treiber, M., Kesting, A., Helbing, D.: General lane-changing model mobil for car-following models. Transp. Res. Record J. Transp. Res. Board **1999**(1), 86–94 (2007)
13. Treiber, M., Hennecke, A., Helbing, D.: Congested traffic states in empirical observations and microscopic simulations. Phys. Rev. E **62**(2), 1805–1824 (2000). https://doi.org/10.1103/PhysRevE.62.1805
14. Treiber, M., Kesting, A.: Modeling lane-changing decisions with mobil. In: Appert-Rolland, C., Chevoir, F., Gondret, P., Lassarre, S., Lebacque, J., Schreckenberg, M. (eds.) Traffic and Granular Flow '07, pp. 211–221. Springer, Heidelberg (2007). https://doi.org/10.1007/978-3-540-77074-9_19
15. Wei, Z., Xie, L., Zhang, J.: Adaptive inter-vehicle distance control using v2v communication and radar fusion. IEEE Access **8**, 89390–89400 (2020)
16. Xu, D., Ye, K., Zheng, Z., Zhou, T., Yen, G.G., Jiang, M.: An efficient dynamic resource allocation framework for evolutionary bilevel optimization. IEEE Trans. Cybernet. **55**(2), 726–739 (2025). https://doi.org/10.1109/TCYB.2024.3492075
17. Yang, J., Ji, H., Liu, J.: Particle swarm optimization algorithm for passive multi-target tracking. Appl. Soft Comput. **15**, 2398–2402 (2011)
18. Yang, X., Zheng, N.: An adaptive safe distance control algorithm for autonomous vehicles in curved roads. IEEE Trans. Intell. Veh. **5**(4), 579–589 (2020)
19. Zhang, H., et al.: Bi-level actor-critic for multi-agent coordination. In: Proceedings of the AAAI Conference on Artificial Intelligence, vol. 34, pp. 7325–7332 (2020)

# Speech and Audio Processing

# Audio Deepfake Detection Using Fusion of Fractal and MFCCs Features

Daksh Arvindbhai Patel$^{(\boxtimes)}$ and Hemant A. Patil

Speech Research Lab, Dhirubhai Ambani University (formerly DA-IICT),
Gandhinagar, Gujarat, India
{202411091,hemant_patil}@dau.ac.in

**Abstract.** Deepfake audio is growing so convincing that it threatens our ability to trust phone calls, voice notes, and news broadcasts. To counter this, we combine state-of-the-art features, such as Mel Frequency Cepstral Coefficients (MFCCs) with lightweight signal descriptors–spectral centroid, bandwidth, roll-off, and zero-crossing rate–and three Fractal Dimension measures: Hurst R/S exponent, Katz fractal dimension (FD), and Higuchi FD. These fractal features capture subtle self-similar patterns in genuine speech that synthetic voices still struggle to replicate.

**Keywords:** Deepfake detection · Fractal dimension · MFCC · Hurst exponent · Katz algorithm · Higuchi algorithm

## 1 Introduction

Artificial Intelligence voice generators have become so good that they can now spin up speech that sounds almost indistinguishable from a real person. That is great for dubbing movies, building accessible voice assistants, and other creative uses. However, it also opens the door to scams, misinformation, and identity theft. A realistic fake clip of a public figure can tank markets or sway opinions before anyone spots the ruse. Old-school defences–checking file metadata or running basic speaker verification tools no longer cut it. Today's neural networks (think WaveNet, Tacotron, and their descendants) synthesize speech so cleanly that humans and many conventional algorithms are fooled [2].

### Motivation

We aimed to build a practical deepfake audio detector that can run with minimal computational resources, so we deliberately avoided large deep learning architectures. Instead, we construct models using classical machine learning algorithms, which are faster to train and lighter to deploy. To provide a simple neural baseline, we include a shallow MLP (with only a minimal hidden structure) purely for comparison, demonstrating that even without deep models, the fused *Fractal* and *Spectral* features yield strong separability between *real* and *synthetic* audio.

© The Author(s), under exclusive license to Springer Nature Switzerland AG 2026
S. Mitra et al. (Eds.): PReMI 2025, LNCS 16358, pp. 761–769, 2026.
https://doi.org/10.1007/978-3-032-18480-1_77

Researchers have tried several countermeasures: looking at spectrogram quirks, modeling timing patterns, or feeding classic features, such as Mel Frequency Cepstral Coefficients (MFCCs) into machine learning classifiers [1]. Those tactics help, but they often miss the faint fingerprints that separate a genuine voice from a synthetic one. We need features that can pick up those deeper, subtle clues hidden in the signal.

1. Captures multi-scale signal complexity and patterns of regularity/irregularity in natural speech that deepfake generators often fail to reproduce
2. Sensitive to self-similarity and roughness, revealing subtle artifacts beyond what MFCCs can detect.
3. When merged with MFCC features, provides complementary structure *vs.* spectral information, boosting feature discriminative power, and improving classification accuracy.
4. Aggregates over windows, tolerates moderate noise, and enables effective detection without heavy deep models.

The remainder of the paper is structured as follows: Sect. 2 reviews related work and highlights key challenges. Section 3 outlines the experimental setup and evaluation measures. Section 4 presents the results and analysis, followed by conclusions in Sect. 5.

## 2    Related Work

Prior approaches in audio deepfake detection rely on spectral features, such as MFCCs combined with classical ML classifiers (e.g., SVM, GMM), establishing baselines but lacking robustness to unseen attacks [1]. Surveys highlight challenges, such as generalization across datasets, domain shifts, and evolving synthesis methods [Khanjani *et al..*, 2023 [2]]. Deep learning advancements include CNNs (ResNet, RawNet2), graph networks (AASIST), and self-supervised models (wav2vec 2.0), improving detection on dataset, such as ASVspoof and FoR. Fractal dimensions (Hurst, Katz, and Higuchi) have been used in speech pathology for capturing complexity [5], but not yet in deepfakes–our novelty lies in fusing them with MFCCs to detect subtle irregularities in the natural/real audio missed by spectral features alone.

## 3    Proposed Method

### 3.1    Fractal Dimension Algorithm

Fractal Dimension (FD) analysis quantifies the complexity and self-similarity of a time-series signal–properties that differ subtly between genuine *vs.* synthetic speech. We employ three complementary FD measures: the Hurst R/S exponent, Katz FD, and Higuchi FD. Each captures a different facet of signal structure and, together with MFCC and spectral descriptors, forms a rich feature set for deepfake audio detection [5].

**Hurst R/S Exponent Method:** Initially, introduced by H. E. Hurst to study Nile River levels, the Hurst exponent $H$ measures long-range dependence [5]. For audio, it reflects how strongly a signal's short-term fluctuations persist (or anti-persist) over time. The Hurst exponent measures the long-term memory of a time series. It is estimated using the rescaled range $(R/S)$ analysis. For a region of size $n$, the cumulative deviation is stored in a vector, $X(t)$. The range $R_n$ is calculated as [5]:

$$R_n = \max\{X(t)\} - \min\{X(t)\}, \tag{1}$$

where $n$ is the number of samples. The standard deviation $S_n$ for the same region is [5]:

$$S_n = \sqrt{\frac{1}{n}\sum_{t=1}^{n}(x(t) - \mu)^2}, \tag{2}$$

where $x(t)$ is the signal, and $\mu$ is its mean. The ratio $R/S$ is computed for different window sizes $n$, and a graph of $\log_2(R/S)$ *vs.* $\log_2(n)$ is plotted. The slope of the resulting line gives the Hurst exponent, $H$. The FD is computed as [5]:

$$D = 2 - H. \tag{3}$$

The Hurst exponent $H$ characterizes signal behavior: $H \approx 0.5$ indicates a random walk, $H > 0.5$ suggests persistent (positively correlated) trends, while $H < 0.5$ reflects anti-persistent (negatively correlated) dynamics.

**Katz Fractal Dimension:** Katz describes FD $D$ as the extra length a waveform accumulates beyond its straight-line span. Let $L$ be the total curve length (sum of distances between successive samples), $d$ the maximum Euclidean distance from the first sample to any other, and $\bar{a}$ the average step between consecutive samples. The Katz FD is given by [5]:

$$D = \frac{\log_{10}(L/\bar{a})}{\log_{10}(d/\bar{a})}, \tag{4}$$

where $L$ reflects waveform roughness, $d$ captures its overall extent, and $\bar{a}$ normalises for sampling frequency.

**Higuchi Algorithm:** The Higuchi method forms new waveforms by subsampling the signal with varying delay factors $k$ (from 1 to $k_{\max}$). For each delay $k$ and starting point $m\,(= 1,\ldots,k)$, the sub-sampled series is given by:

$$x_m^k = \{x(m),\, x(m+k),\, x(m+2k),\, x(m + \lfloor (N-m)/k \rfloor k)\}, \tag{5}$$

where $N$ is the window length. The length of this waveform is then given by [5]:

$$L(m,k) = \frac{\displaystyle\sum_{i=1}^{\lfloor (N-m)/k \rfloor} |x(m+ik) - x(m+(i-1)k)|}{\lfloor (N-m)/k \rfloor \cdot \dfrac{k}{N-1}}, \tag{3}$$

$$L(k) = \sum_{m=1}^{k} L(m,k). \tag{4}$$

The FD is the slope of the least-squares line fitted $\ln L(k)$ *vs.* $\ln(1/k)$; a steeper slope indicates more transients and hence, a higher FD.

### 3.2  Dataset Used

We used the Fake-or-Real dataset to perform the ADD experiments. FoR contains multiple subsets as shown in Table 1. Corpus contains 1,31,926 wav files in the dev set, 26,680 in the valid set, and 11,184 in the test set [7].

**Table 1.** Summary of the *Fake-or-Real* Corpus. After [7].

| Subset | Size | Description |
| --- | --- | --- |
| For-original | 7.7 GB | Raw, unprocessed real and synthetic clips |
| For-norm | 5.8 GB | Resampled, normalized, and gender-balanced |
| For-2 s | 1.0 GB | 2-s excerpts from *for-norm* |
| For-rerec | 1.5 GB | *for-2 s* replayed to simulate telephone channels |

**Preprocessing:** Duplicates removed, 16 kHz mono PCM conversion, silence trimming, and z-score normalization

### 3.3  Mel Frequency Cepstral Coefficients (MFCCs)

We extract *40*-dimensional MFCCs per speech frame, augment them with first- and second-order derivatives, and pool mean and standard deviation to get fixed-length descriptors that capture spectral content and temporal dynamics. MFCC features were extracted using 128 ms frames with 96 ms overlap at a 16 kHz sampling rate. A total of 40 MFCC coefficients were computed from each frame to capture the spectral characteristics necessary for deepfake detection. These are fused with fractal dimension (FD) features to add multi-scale complexity information, improving deepfake separability. In addition, we compute spectral centroid, bandwidth, rolloff, zero-crossing rate, and RMS energy–each summarized by mean and standard deviation–to provide complementary shape and energy cues. This compact, hybrid feature set balances discriminative power and robustness [10].

### 3.4  Machine Learning (ML) Classifiers

Several classical ML algorithms were selected based on their robust performance and interpretability:

**Support Vector Machine:** SVM uses hyperplane optimization to maximize the margin between audio classes. The decision boundary is defined as:

$$\mathbf{w} \cdot \mathbf{x} + b = 0, \text{ and the optimisation minimises:} \tag{6}$$

$$\frac{1}{2}\|\mathbf{w}\|^2 \quad \text{subject to:} \tag{7}$$

$$y_i(\mathbf{w} \cdot \mathbf{x}_i + b) \geq 1, \tag{8}$$

for all samples, efficiently managing high-dimensional feature spaces. In our experiments, we use the Radial Basis Function (RBF) kernel with a regularisation parameter $C = 4$ to allow a soft margin, enabling better generalization on noisy or overlapping deepfake *vs.* real audio feature distributions.

**Random Forest (RF):** An ensemble classifier of decision trees, providing resilience to overfitting and clear interpretation of feature importance. Predictions are made by majority voting across trees.

**Decision Tree (DT)/Binary Tree:** A non-parametric supervised learning method that builds a tree by recursively splitting data to minimize impurity, such as the *Gini index*:

$$G = 1 - \sum_{k=1}^{K} p_k^2, \tag{9}$$

where $p_k$ is the probability of class, $k$. Known for simplicity, interpretability, and fast inference.

**Multi-layer Perceptron (MLP) Classifier**[1]: A feedforward neural network, where each neuron computes [5]:

$$\sigma(\mathbf{w} \cdot \mathbf{x} + b), \tag{10}$$

with activation function $\sigma$ (e.g., sigmoid or ReLU), trained via backpropagation to minimize loss.

**XGBoost:** An optimized gradient boosting framework that minimizes a regularized objective function [5]:

$$\mathcal{L} = \sum_{i=1}^{n} l(\hat{y}_i, y_i) + \sum_{k=1}^{K} \Omega(f_k), \tag{11}$$

where $l$ is the loss, and $\Omega$ is regularization on trees, $f_k$.

---

[1] We used the MLP classifier to compare across feature sets.

## 3.5   Exprimental Setup

All the experiments were carried out using the cloud-based instance, which runs on the NVIDIA GTX 1080 (8 GB, 8.9 teraFLOPs). We used the PyTorch 2.5.1, Numpy 1.21.0 and Librosa 0.9.0.

## 4   Experimental Results

The results in Table 2 show that fusing MFCC-40 with FD features significantly enhances deepfake detection, with the combination of Hurst and MFCC-40 providing the best overall trade-off. Gradient Boosting achieves the highest accuracy at 90.79%, while SVM reaches the lowest EER of 2.97%, highlighting the complementary role of the Hurst exponent in adding long-range complexity cues to the spectral MFCCs. While Katz and Higuchi features also contribute, they are less effective than Hurst. SVM excels in terms of well-ranked scores and sharp class separability, whereas Gradient Boosting captures more intricate feature interactions and could benefit from threshold tuning to optimize its error

**Table 2.** Comparison of Test Results Across Different Feature Sets

| Model | Accuracy (%) | AUC | EER (%) | Features |
|---|---|---|---|---|
| SVM | 87.35 | 0.9507 | **3.41** | Higuchi FD + MFCC-40 |
| MLP Classifier | **88.67** | 0.9045 | 4.40 | |
| Decision Tree | 82.02 | 0.7933 | 18.45 | |
| XGBoost | 81.87 | **0.9524** | 11.91 | |
| Gradient Boosting | 81.74 | 0.8957 | 18.23 | |
| SVM | **88.00** | **0.9962** | 3.19 | Katz FD + MFCC-40 |
| MLP Classifier | 87.10 | 0.9201 | 4.38 | |
| Decision Tree | 79.72 | 0.7875 | 20.08 | |
| XGBoost | 81.81 | 0.9574 | 10.44 | |
| Gradient Boosting | 81.74 | 0.8957 | 18.23 | |
| SVM | **88.45** | **0.9609** | 3.02 | MFCC-40 |
| MLP Classifier | 87.81 | 0.9164 | 4.23 | |
| Decision Tree | 79.39 | 0.7849 | 24.17 | |
| XGBoost | 80.79 | 0.9510 | 11.61 | |
| Gradient Boosting | 81.74 | 0.8957 | 18.23 | |
| SVM | 89.95 | 0.9477 | **2.97** | Hurst FD + MFCC-40 |
| MLP Classifier | 86.30 | 0.9416 | 3.91 | |
| Decision Tree | 73.48 | 0.7366 | 27.96 | |
| XGBoost | 78.05 | 0.9522 | 11.78 | |
| Gradient Boosting | **90.79** | **0.9676** | 8.87 | |

trade-off. Combining the two models through an ensemble or calibrated scoring scheme could lead to a more robust and reliable detector. The proposed fusion approach remains computationally efficient, avoiding the need for heavy deep learning models. The RBF kernel was chosen for SVM due to its ability to handle non-linear separability in high-dimensional audio feature spaces, outperforming linear and polynomial kernels in capturing complex patterns that distinguish deepfake from real audio. The selection of a soft margin parameter, $C = 4$, strikes a balance, allowing for tolerance to noise and overlaps while minimizing overfitting, thereby enhancing generalization compared to lower (e.g., $C = 1$) or higher (e.g., $C = 10$) values in our dataset experiments.

Katz+MFCC-40 and Higuchi+MFCC-40 also outperform the MFCC-40 baseline in most cases, though their gains vary by classifier: ensemble methods (SVM, XGBoost, Gradient Boosting) consistently extract benefit, whereas decision trees suffer on some fractal-enhanced inputs. Incorporating fractal complexity–particularly via the Hurst exponent- adds complementary structure to spectral MFCC information, improving accuracy and more reliable discrimination between real *vs.* synthetic audio (Table 3).

Table 3. Features and Models with Accuracy

| Features | Models | Accuracy (%) |
|---|---|---|
| MFCC-20 [8] | SVM | 67 |
| | RF | 62 |
| | KNN | 62 |
| | XGB | 59 |
| | NB | 67.27 |
| Timbre Model Analysis [7] | NB | 67.27 |
| | SVM | 73.46 |
| | DT (J48) | 70.26 |
| | RF | 71.47 |
| STFT, Mel Spectrograms, MFCC and CQT [1] | VGG19 | 89.79 |
| MFCC-40, centroid, contrast, bandwidth [1] | LSTM | 91 |
| | VGG16 | 93 |
| FD, MFCC-40 contrast [Proposed Approach] | SVM | 89.95 |
| | MLP Classifier | 88.67 |
| | Decision Tree | 82.02 |
| | XGBoost | 81.87 |
| | **Gradient Boosting** | **90.79** |

## 5    Conclusions and Discussions

In this work, we demonstrated that combining fractal dimension features (Hurst R/S, Katz, and Higuchi) with traditional audio descriptors (MFCC-40 and spectral features) significantly improves deepfake audio detection. The fusion of complexity-aware and frequency-based features enhanced model separability and provided stable performance across classical machine learning classifiers. Our evaluation is limited to specific types of synthetic audio generation techniques. The rapidly evolving landscape of neural vocoder architectures (WaveNet, HiFi-GAN, BigVGAN) may introduce novel artifacts that our current feature set may not adequately capture. Additionally, a key flaw in our approach is the challenge of developing algorithms capable of processing streaming audio with minimal *latency*, which is critical for live applications, such as video calls or broadcast monitoring, while maintaining detection accuracy. Future work will focus on addressing these limitations by introducing new features, such as the fractal density graph, and evaluating our approach on more diverse and recent datasets, including those with varying languages, accents, and recording conditions. We will also explore methods for real-time deepfake detection and model integration with low-latency systems.

## References


1. Hamza, A., et al.: Deepfake audio detection via MFCC features using machine learning. IEEE Access **10**, 134018–134028 (2022)
2. Yi, J., Wang, C., Tao, J., Zhang, X., Zhang, C. Y., Zhao, Y.: Audio deepfake detection: a survey (2023c). https://doi.org/10.48550/arXiv.2308.14970. Accessed 31 July 2025
3. Gomez-Garcia, J. A., et al. On the use of automatic voice pathology detection algorithms in telemonitoring of patients with Parkinson's disease. In: Proceedings of the $20^{th}$ European Signal Processing Conference (EUSIPCO), Bucharest, Romania, pp. 724–728. IEEE (2012)
4. The Fake-or-Real (FoR) Dataset (deepfake audio). Kaggle (2024). https://www.kaggle.com/datasets/mohammedabdeldayem/the-fake-or-real-dataset/code. Accessed 31 July 2025
5. Baljekar, P.N., Patil, H.A.: A comparison of waveform fractal dimension techniques for voice pathology classification. In: 2012 IEEE International Conference on Acoustics, Speech and Signal Processing (ICASSP), Kyoto, Japan, pp. 4461–4464. IEEE (2012)
6. Khochare, J., Joshi, C., Yenarkar, B., Suratkar, S., Kazi, F.: A deep learning framework for audio deepfake detection. Arabian J. Sci. Eng. **47**, 1–12 (2021)
7. Reimao, R., Tzerpos, V.: FoR: a dataset for synthetic speech detection. In: Proceeding of International Conference on Speech Technology Human-Computer Dialogue (SpeD), pp. 1–10 (2019)
8. Khochare, J., Joshi, C., Yenarkar, B., Suratkar, S., Kazi, F.: A deep learning framework for audio deepfake detection. Arab. J. Sci. Eng. **47**, 1–12 (2021)

9. Reimao, R., Tzerpos, V.: FoR: a dataset for synthetic speech detection. In: Proceedings of the International Conference on Speech Technology and Human-Computer Dialogue (SpeD), pp. 1–10 (2019)
10. Abdul, Z.K., Al-Talabani, A.K.: Mel frequency cepstral coefficient and its application: a review. IEEE Access **10**, 122136–122158 (2022)

# Whisper-Based Multilingual ASR For Indic Languages

Saroj Pandit[(✉)], Ravindrakumar M. Purohit, and Hemant A. Patil

Speech Research Lab, Dhirubhai Ambani University (formerly DA-IICT),
Gandhinagar, Gujarat, India
`{202418048,202321002,hemant_patil}@dau.ac.in`

**Abstract.** This study conducts a comprehensive comparison of Whisper Automatic Speech Recognition (ASR) models–medium, turbo, and large–across 15 Indic languages. We have taken the dataset from IndicTTS. For each language, we evaluated model performance, measuring Word Error Rate (WER), Character Error Rate (CER), and Phoneme Error Rate (PER). Significantly, all whisper variants struggled to recognise specific low-resource languages, including Dogri, Maithili, Manipuri, and Rajasthani, underscoring existing gaps in multilingual coverage for the ASR task. Consistent with expectations, the larger whisper models demonstrated superior accuracy over their smaller models. Most languages, such as Hindi and Tamil, are the best-performing languages among all 15 Indic languages. Our findings offer actionable insights into the strengths and current limitations of whisper models, reinforcing the need for further research in supporting underrepresented languages.

**Keywords:** Automatic Speech Recognization · Pre-trained Model · Whisper · Indic Languages · Language Identification(LI)

## 1 Introduction

Automatic Speech Recognition (ASR) has witnessed significant advancements in recent years, driven by the availability of large-scale datasets, self-supervised learning, and transformer-based architectures. These improvements have led to remarkable reductions in error rates across multiple languages and domains. ASR systems find widespread applications in voice assistants, transcription services, customer service automation, and real-time captioning for accessibility, with the rise of multilingual environments. ASR systems can be broadly categorized into traditional signal processing-based approaches and modern deep learning-based systems. Early ASR models relied heavily on acoustic modelling, Hidden Markov Models [8], and Gaussian Mixture Models [10], while recent systems leverage neural architectures for end-to-end(E2E) ASR. Neural ASR

---

S. Pandit and R. M. Purohit—These authors contributed equally.


S. Mitra et al. (Eds.): PReMI 2025, LNCS 16358, pp. 770–778, 2026.
https://doi.org/10.1007/978-3-032-18480-1_78

models such as DeepSpeech [5], wav2vec 2.0 [2], and Whisper [9], utilize large-scale training and transformer-based architectures to capture both *phonetic* and *linguistic* patterns effectively. These models have significantly outperformed classical approaches in terms of *robustness* and *adaptability*. Despite these advancements, challenges persist–particularly for low-resource languages, where data scarcity, dialectal variation, and limited pretraining cause elevated error rates. Indic languages exemplify this challenge with their script diversity and phonetic complexity. The key contributions of this paper are as follows:

1. We evaluate the Whisper models, e.g., medium (M), turbo (T), and large (L) on 15 Indic languages using a balanced gender dataset from IndicTTS.
2. We identify languages that whisper fails to recognize effectively (Dogri, Maithili, Manipuri, and Rajasthani), highlighting limitations in language detection.
3. We compare model performance using Word Error Rate (WER), Character Error Rate (CER), and Phoneme Error Rate (PER).
4. Hindi and Tamil are the best performing across whisper models.

The structure of the remaining paper is as follows: Sect. 2 presents related work, and Sects. 3 and 4 experiment on the Indic language using a whisper model and show the results with language-specific discussion(s), respectively. Section 5 completes the paper with a conclusion.

## 2   Related Work

Traditional ASR systems were built using a pipeline of acoustic models, language models, and pronunciation dictionaries [6]. These systems required domain-specific feature engineering and struggled with generalization across diverse linguistic domains. Recent developments in E2E neural ASR have simplified this pipeline. OpenAI's Whisper model [9] represents a significant leap in multilingual ASR. Trained on 680,000 h of labeled audio, it supports over 90 languages and exhibits strong robustness across domains. However, its performance on low-resource languages, especially many Indic languages, remains unexplored. Prior research on Indic ASR includes the MUCS shared task [3], which focused on benchmarking ASR systems for Indian languages using the ULCA dataset[1]. Other studies like emphasize better language models, pronunciation lexicons, and robust audio corpora tailored to Indic scripts and phonetics [7]. In this context, our work contributes a comparative evaluation of Whisper's ASR models(medium, turbo and large) on 15 Indic languages, we used dataset from IndicTTS, providing new insights into model strengths and limitations in handling low-resource languages.

---

[1] https://bhashini.gov.in/ulca/model/benchmark-datasets {Last Access Date: July $28^{th}$, 2025}.

## 2.1    Whisper Model

Whisper is a multilingual, multitask ASR system developed by OpenAI [9]. it supports tasks, such as transcription, translation, and language identification. The whisper architecture follows a simple encoder-decoder transformer framework. The encoder processes log-Mel spectrogram features from audio into a sequence of hidden representations, capturing the audio's features, and the decoder generates transcriptions tokens one at a time conditioned on the encoder's output and previously generated tokens using sequence-to-sequence (seq2seq) approach, and the model outputs a probability distribution over the text for the next token where used an activation function such as Softmax for multiple-distribution. Whisper models are released in multiple parameter sizes as shown in Table 1, ranging from `tiny` to `large-v2`, with varying numbers of parameters: `medium` (769M), `large` (1550M), and `turbo` (based on optimized large version via OpenAI API) (Fig. 1).

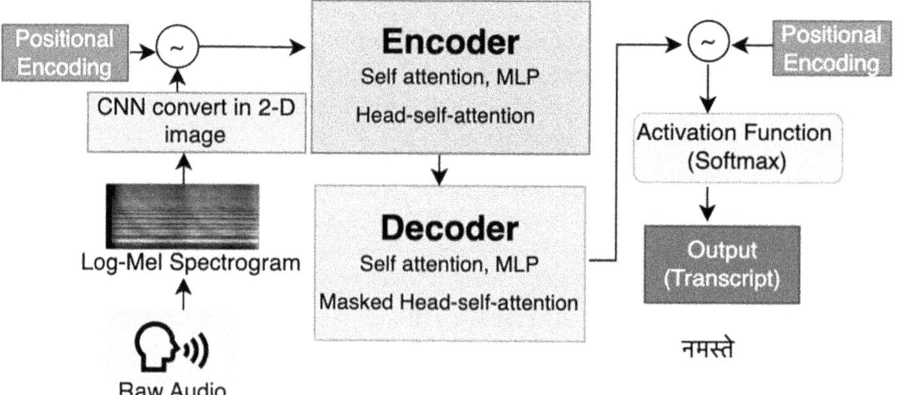


**Fig. 1.** Simplified Whisper Encoder-Decoder Architecture.

## 2.2    Evaluation Plan

**Language Identification** We observed that all Whisper models failed to detect or transcribe the speech content meaningfully for four languages: Dogri, Maithili, Manipuri, and Rajasthani. This aligns with prior studies indicating that these languages are either unsupported or severely underrepresented in whisper's training data. These cases were logged separately and excluded from metric aggregation in performance plots.

**Table 1.** Whisper model comparison: architecture, resource requirements, and speed. Adapted from [9].

| Model | Layers | Width | Heads | VRAM | Speed | Evaluated |
|---|---|---|---|---|---|---|
| Tiny | 4 | 384 | 6 | $\sim$1 GB | $\sim$10$\times$ | |
| Base | 6 | 512 | 8 | $\sim$1 GB | $\sim$7$\times$ | |
| Small | 12 | 768 | 12 | $\sim$2 GB | $\sim$4$\times$ | |
| Medium (M) | 24 | 1024 | 16 | $\sim$5 GB | $\sim$2$\times$ | ✓ |
| Large (L) | 32 | 1280 | 20 | $\sim$10 GB | 1$\times$ | ✓ |
| Turbo (T) | – | – | – | $\sim$6 GB | $\sim$8$\times$ | ✓ |

---

**Algorithm 1.** Compute WER, CER, and PER for Whisper Models Across Languages

---

1: **Input:** Dataset $\mathcal{D} = \{(x_i, y_i)\}_{i=1}^{N}$, Models $\mathcal{M}$, Languages $\mathcal{L}$
2: **Output:** Metrics $\mathrm{WER}_{m,l}, \mathrm{CER}_{m,l}, \mathrm{PER}_{m,l}$ for each $m \in \mathcal{M}, l \in \mathcal{L}$
3: **for all** $l \in \mathcal{L}$ **do**
4:     **for all** $m \in \mathcal{M}$ **do**
5:         Initialize $W, C, P \leftarrow 0$
6:         Initialize $W_{ref}, C_{ref}, P_{ref} \leftarrow 0$
7:         **for all** $(x_i, y_i) \in \mathcal{D}_l$ **do**
8:             $\hat{y}_i \leftarrow \mathrm{ASR}_m(x_i)$
9:             $W \leftarrow W + \mathrm{EditDist}_{\mathrm{word}}(\hat{y}_i, y_i)$
10:            $W_{ref} \leftarrow W_{ref} + \mathrm{WordCount}(y_i)$
11:            $C \leftarrow C + \mathrm{EditDist}_{\mathrm{char}}(\hat{y}_i, y_i)$
12:            $C_{ref} \leftarrow C_{ref} + \mathrm{CharCount}(y_i)$
13:            $P \leftarrow P + \mathrm{EditDist}_{\mathrm{phoneme}}(\hat{y}_i, y_i)$
14:            $P_{ref} \leftarrow P_{ref} + \mathrm{PhonemeCount}(y_i)$
15:         **end for**
16:         $\mathrm{WER}_{m,l} \leftarrow \frac{W}{W_{ref}}$
17:         $\mathrm{CER}_{m,l} \leftarrow \frac{C}{C_{ref}}$
18:         $\mathrm{PER}_{m,l} \leftarrow \frac{P}{P_{ref}}$
19:     **end for**
20: **end for**

---

## 3 Experiments

### 3.1 Dataset Used

We used the publicly available dataset from IndicTTS[2] For each of the 15 Indic languages (in particular e.g., Assamese (As), Bengali (Bn), Gujarati (Gu), Hindi (Hi), Kannada (Kn), Malayalam (Ml), Nepali (Ne), Punjabi (Pa), Sanskrit (Sa), Tamil (Ta), Telugu (Te), Dogri (Do), Maithili (Mi), Manipuri (Ma), and Rajasthani (Ra), we selected 200 audio samples–100 male and 100 female

---

[2] https://www.iitm.ac.in/donlab/indictts/database {Last Access Date: July $28^{th}$, 2025}.

recordings–ensuring gender balance. All audio files were manually reviewed to exclude noise, silence, or recording artifacts. The recordings were converted to the 16 kHz sampling rate as whisper's preprocessing pipeline required. Transcripts were pre-cleaned to match whisper's expected text normalization format.

### 3.2  Evaluation Metrics

1. WER [4]: It is calculated as:

$$\text{WER} = \frac{S + D + I}{N},$$

   where $S$ is the number of substitutions, $D$ is deletions, $I$ is insertions, and $N$ is the total number of words in the reference transcript. CER and PER follow the same formula, computed at the character and phoneme levels, respectively.
2. CER: It is used to evaluate text transcription systems' accuracy by measuring the character-level error rate. The calculation for this metric follows the same method as WER.
3. PER: It assesses the performance of speech recognition systems by calculating the rate of errors at the phoneme-level. PER can be calculated using the same method as WER.

## 4  Results

We evaluated three versions of OpenAI's Whisper ASR system: `medium` (M) (769M parameters), `turbo` (T) (an optimised version of `large` (L) accessible via the OpenAI API), and `significant` (1.55B parameters). Each model was used without fine-tuning and was applied directly to transcribe the audio samples. We explicitly set the target language in order to ensure fair comparison across all the models' performance. Our study comprehensively evaluates Whisper's medium, turbo, and large models on 15 Indic languages, analysing their transcription quality using WER, CER, and PER. The results reveal several important trends and model behaviours that affect ASR in multilingual, low-resource settings. Whisper Large consistently outperforms the medium and turbo versions across most tested Indic languages. This improvement can be attributed to its larger parameter size (1.55B), allowing for a deeper understanding of linguistic features. Large achieves lower WER, CER, and PER scores on average, indicating more accurate transcriptions. Whisper Large demonstrates high transcription accuracy in languages, such as Hi, Bn, Ta, and Kn, where digital resources are relatively abundant. For instance, WER and CER for Hi are significantly lower compared to less-resourced languages. In most cases, Whisper turbo performs better than medium but is still outperformed by large. Turbo-speed-optimised architecture slightly compromises accuracy for efficiency. While turbo might be helpful for low-latency applications, the large model is more appropriate when transcription quality is the priority. We notice that all three whisper models cannot detect languages, such as Do, Mi, Ma, and Ra. These languages consistently return empty. This pattern highlights a critical gap in whisper's training: low-resource languages with limited digital presence are not adequately supported, resulting in practical usability challenges (Fig. 2).

**Table 2.** WER, CER, and PER (in %) of Whisper models across Indic languages. Where Do, Ma, Mi, and Ra were not identified by Whisper architecture.

| Lang. | Measures | Type | As | Bn | Gu | Hi | Kn | Ml | Ne | Pa | Sa | Ta | Te | Do | Mi | Ma | Ra |
|---|---|---|---|---|---|---|---|---|---|---|---|---|---|---|---|---|---|
| [9] | WER | M | 1.25 | 0.11 | 1.03 | 0.14 | 0.48 | 1.04 | 0.32 | 0.15 | 0.18 | 0.60 | 0.28 | – | – | – | – |
| | | T | 1.14 | 1.07 | 1.04 | 0.15 | 0.49 | 1.03 | 0.29 | 0.18 | 0.19 | 0.59 | 0.24 | – | – | – | – |
| | | L | 1.02 | 0.45 | 0.94 | 0.12 | 0.36 | 0.92 | 0.18 | 0.10 | 0.09 | 0.48 | 0.18 | – | – | – | – |
| | CER | M | 0.58 | 0.05 | 0.48 | 0.06 | 0.23 | 0.53 | 0.15 | 0.07 | 0.08 | 0.29 | 0.12 | – | – | – | – |
| | | T | 0.52 | 0.49 | 0.51 | 0.07 | 0.22 | 0.49 | 0.13 | 0.08 | 0.08 | 0.26 | 0.10 | – | – | – | – |
| | | L | 0.47 | 0.22 | 0.42 | 0.06 | 0.18 | 0.40 | 0.08 | 0.04 | 0.04 | 0.21 | 0.08 | – | – | – | – |
| | PER | M | 0.62 | 0.06 | 0.50 | 0.07 | 0.26 | 0.56 | 0.17 | 0.08 | 0.09 | 0.32 | 0.14 | – | – | – | – |
| | | T | 0.56 | 0.52 | 0.54 | 0.08 | 0.25 | 0.52 | 0.14 | 0.09 | 0.09 | 0.29 | 0.11 | – | – | – | – |
| | | L | 0.50 | 0.23 | 0.44 | 0.07 | 0.20 | 0.43 | 0.09 | 0.05 | 0.05 | 0.23 | 0.09 | – | – | – | – |
| [1] | WER | – | 0.31 | 0.66 | 0.26 | 0.18 | 0.25 | 0.43 | 0.30 | 0.28 | 0.26 | 0.31 | 0.28 | 0.41 | 0.46 | 1.01 | – |
| | CER | – | 0.10 | 0.48 | 0.07 | 0.07 | 0.07 | 0.12 | 0.08 | 0.10 | 0.06 | 0.07 | 0.06 | 0.16 | 0.13 | 0.88 | – |
| | PER | – | 0.31 | 0.66 | 0.26 | 0.18 | 0.25 | 0.43 | 0.30 | 0.28 | 0.26 | 0.31 | 0.28 | 0.41 | 0.46 | 1.01 | – |

As shown in Table 2, A comparative evaluation reveals a complex performance landscape between Whisper models and the IndicConformer baseline across 15 Indic languages, with complementary strengths that challenge the notion of universal superiority in multilingual ASR. [3]

Whisper-large demonstrates superior performance on six languages–Bn (0.45 vs 0.66), Hi (0.12 vs 0.18), Ne (0.18 vs 0.30), Pa (0.10 vs 0.28), Sa (0.09 vs 0.26), and Te (0.18 vs 0.28)–achieving particularly impressive results on Sa (2.9× reduction) and Pa (2.8× reduction). Conversely, IndicConformer achieves substantially lower error rates on five languages: As (0.31 vs 1.02), Gu (0.26 vs 0.94), Ka (0.25 vs 0.36), Ml (0.43 vs 0.92), and Ta (0.31 vs 0.48), with the most dramatic improvements observed in As (3.3× reduction) and Gu (3.6× reduction). The consistent hierarchical performance pattern across Whisper variants (large > turbo > medium) indicates that model capacity directly impacts ASR quality, with similar trends reflected across WER, CER, and PER metrics. However, language coverage emerges as a critical differentiator: IndicConformer successfully processes 14 of 15 languages, failing only on Ra, whereas Whisper models fail to identify four extremely low-resource languages–Do, Mi, Ma, and Ra. This 27

---

[3] https://iamshreeji-copy2.github.io/Evaluating_Whisper/.

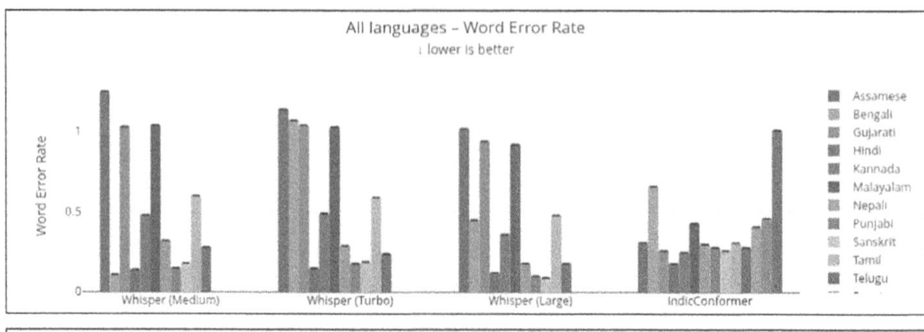

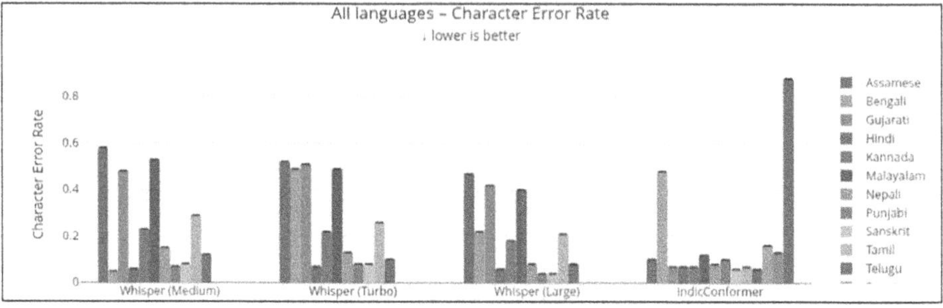

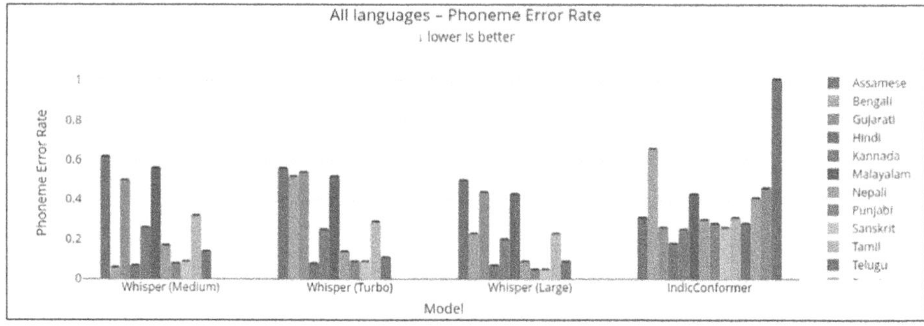

**Fig. 2.** WER, CER, PER comparison of Whisper models across Indic languages.

coverage gap is particularly significant given that IndicConformer maintains reasonable performance on these challenging languages (WER: 0.41–1.01), demonstrating that specialized architectures trained on language-family-specific data can provide more robust coverage for underrepresented varieties.

## 5    Conclusion

This study provides a comprehensive analysis of the performance of whisper medium, turbo, and large models and the IndicConformer model across 15 Indic languages, using standard ASR evaluation metrics, WER, CER, and PER. Among the evaluated models, Whisper-large consistently achieved the best performance across most high-resource languages such as Hi, Bn, Ne, Pa, Sa, and

Te. This reaffirms the advantage of scaling model size for improved transcription accuracy in a multilingual ASR task. However, a notable observation was the consistent underperformance of all whisper variants on low-resource Indic languages, including Do, Mi, Ma, and Ra. However, IndicConformer successfully processes. This suggests that even the most advanced ASR systems today are inadequately equipped to handle the linguistic diversity of low-resource languages–despite being trained on vast multilingual datasets. These findings not only highlight the *scalability* and *effectiveness* of Whisper for high-resource languages but also expose a critical limitation in current ASR systems when it comes to low-resource languages. For practical deployment in Indic language contexts, our results suggest that a hybrid approach leveraging Whisper's strengths on well-resourced languages (Hi, Bn, Sa, Pa, Ne, Te) while relying on IndicConformer for languages where it demonstrates superior performance (As, Gu, Ka, Ml, Ta) and critical coverage (Do, Mi, Ma) would provide optimal results.

In essence, our results serve as both a benchmark and a wake-up call: the journey toward universal and equitable speech recognition must go beyond size and speed–it must embrace linguistic diversity at its core. Future work will involve evaluating other open-source ASR frameworks (e.g., ESPnet[4], SpeechBrain[5], AI4Bharat[6]), exploring data augmentation techniques, and should investigate whether targeted fine-tuning of Whisper on low-resource Indic languages can bridge this coverage gap while maintaining its competitive performance on well-represented languages.

**Acknowledgment.** The authors sincerely thank the Staff and Administration of Dhirubhai Ambani University (formerly DA-IICT), Gandhinagar, India, for their support and cooperation to carry out this research work.

# References


1. AI4Bharat: Indicconformer: Conformer-based hybrid rnnt-ctc asr models for Indian languages (2024). https://github.com/AI4Bharat/IndicConformerASR, gitHub repository for IndicConformer ASR models covering 22 Indian languages. Released under the MIT license
2. Baevski, A., Zhou, Y., Mohamed, A., Auli, M.: wav2vec 2.0: a framework for self-supervised learning of speech representations. In: Advances in Neural Information Processing Systems (NeurIPS), pp. 12449–12460 (2020)
3. Bhat, R.A., et al.: Overview of the second workshop on multilingual and indic language natural language processing (milnlp). In: Proceedings of the $2^{nd}$ Workshop on International Conference on Machine Learning Techniques and NLP (MLNLP) (2021)
4. Goldwater, S., Johnson, M.: Words worth: how robust automatic speech recognition is to speech variations. In: IEEE Workshop on Spoken Language Technology (SLT), Berkeley, California, USA, pp. 248–253 (2010)


---

[4] https://espnet.github.io/espnet/ {Last Access Date: $28^{th}$, 2025}.
[5] https://github.com/speechbrain/speechbrain {Last Access Date: July $28^{th}$, 2025}.
[6] https://ai4bharat.iitm.ac.in/areas/asr {Last Access Date: July $28^{th}$, 2025}.

5. Hannun, A., et al.: Deep speech: scaling up end-to-end speech recognition. arXiv preprint arXiv:1412.5567 (2014). Accessed 28 July 2025
6. Jurafsky, D., Martin, J.H.: Speech and Language Processing. Pearson, Boston (2009)
7. Kakwani, D., et al.: Indicnlpsuite: monolingual corpora, evaluation benchmarks and pre-trained multilingual language models for Indian languages. arXiv preprint arXiv:2005.00085 (2020). Accessed 28 July 2025
8. Rabiner, L., Juang, B.: An introduction to hidden Markov models. IEEE ASSP Mag. **3**(1), 4–16 (1986)
9. Radford, A., et al.: Robust speech recognition via large-scale weak supervision. arXiv preprint arXiv:2212.04356 (2023). Accessed 28 July 2025
10. Wan, H., Wang, H., Scotney, B., Liu, J.: A novel Gaussian mixture model for classification. In: IEEE International Conference on Systems, Man and Cybernetics (SMC), Bari, Italy, pp. 3298–3303 (2019)

# Hybrid Audio Fingerprinting of Human Voice Under Distortion

Aakash Mourya, Bittu Kumari, and Anjali Diwan[(⊠)]

Marwadi University, Rajkot, India
`anjali.diwan@ieee.org`

**Abstract.** One of the most important tasks in audio signal processing is accurately identifying audio signals when they contain distortions from the real world. In this work, we suggest a scalable and lightweight framework for audio fingerprinting and matching that can recognize signals that have undergone different acoustic changes. The system uses a peak-based hashing mechanism to extract reliable time-frequency features from audio recordings. The spectral energy peaks and their temporal correlations are compactly represented by these fingerprints. Spectral statistics are used to create a low-dimensional embedding that further captures audio characteristics. We present a distortion augmentation pipeline that creates audio variations via dynamic range clipping, gain modification, additive noise, and equalization in order to evaluate robustness. Every version is fingerprinted separately and compared to a reference database made from the original audio files. Hash-set intersections and frequency-based score calculation are used for matching. The suggested fingerprinting technique is suitable for real-time media verification, speaker matching, and audio retrieval systems, as demonstrated by experimental results that show it maintains high identification accuracy under a variety of distortion conditions.

**Keywords:** Audio Fingerprinting · Peak Hashing · Time-Frequency Features · Robust Matching · Distortion Invariance · Audio Retrieval

## 1 Introduction

The ability of effectively identify and retrieve the audio samples from large audio clips is a key requirement in countless real world applications, including media verification, copyright protection, forensics analysis and security monitoring. Earlier audio fingerprinting techniques such as Shazam [12], Audfprint [2], Chroma print and Panako were basically designed and optimized for music retrieval and song identification, which was relatively focused on working on clean and studio recorded audio content. However using these techniques on human voice including conversational speech, field recording and noisy environment creates more and more challenges due to timbre, intonation, noise and multiple kind of background changes a lot which degrades the recording quality.


S. Mitra et al. (Eds.): PReMI 2025, LNCS 16358, pp. 779–786, 2026.
https://doi.org/10.1007/978-3-032-18480-1_79

In this research work, we are proposing an effective and understandable audio fingerprinting system designed specifically for audio data from humans. Moreover, we clearly model a vast range of distortions which can be encountered in a voice recording in real life operating conditions. This comes in contrast to neural systems.

We compared our work with the some of the state of the art from which one is [5] Kamuni et al. (2024) which uses contrastive training method which improves distortion tolerance in audio fingerprinting as well as to traditional fingerprinting technique. Their work lack interpret-ability and it mainly focuses on musical notes. This approach effectively handles time-scale changes and performs consistently under compression, noise, and audio editing. Because of its resilience and scalability, it is ideal for content identification and anti-piracy applications. The method also looks into the trade-offs between bitrate and robustness and offers suggestions for possible improvements for real-world use [11].

Analyzing Audio Characteristics to Identify Deepfake [9] Singing Voices This study evaluated a range of audio features, such as MFCC, Log-Spectrogram, and Wav2Vec 2.0, using CNN-based classifiers (ResNet-18 and LCNN) to detect singing voice deepfakes. The findings demonstrated that while log-spectrograms perform better for singing, Wav2Vec 2.0 performs well for both speech and singing.

A Multi-Stage Framework for Audio Deepfake Detection: This all-inclusive framework combines pretrained models (such as XLS-R, Whisper, and WavLM) for feature extraction for classifying real versus fake [4]. This work improves the DejaVu audio fingerprinting algorithm (FFT and peak hashing) using ML techniques to increase accuracy in noisy and distorted environments [5].

Deepfake Audio Neural Stitching Detection System (ADD 2022) This system improved detection accuracy and noise resistance by combining neural stitching with handcrafted and pre-trained features using ResNet-34, building on previous research. It encourages the use of different models for speaking and singing voices and emphasizes the importance of advanced models such as Wav2Vec 2.0 for dependable feature extraction [17]. This approach is very necessary for applications like media verification with low cost settings where music systems like Shazam [?] are unsuitable. Our proposed methodology is a light weight and interpretable fingerprinting framework especially made for human speech signal. The proposed method achieves reliable and scalable speech matching under real world distortions like clipping, noise and gain variation by integrating matching spectral embeddings with spectral peak hashing. In order to ensure real life robustness we also present a distortion spectral pipeline for testing and comparing under various audio circumstances.

## 2   Proposed Methodology

In this project we present a very lightweight audio fingerprinting methodology which has been optimized for human voice recordings under real world distortions such as noise, loudness, background noise, clipping, gain variation and equalization artefacts. Unlike music oriented fingerprinting technique, our method is completely based on human voice integrating spectral hashing along with complementary embedding based speech descriptors. The method ensures very significant accuracy for matching the audio fingerprint even when the voice is so much deteriorated. The complete system pipeline is divided in six different stages and they are: pre-processing, spectrogram analysis, spectral peak detection mentioned by Keum et al. [6], fingerprint hash generation [7], embedding extraction, and matching.

These all 6 steps come together to make a complete pipeline also shown in Fig. 1 which visually shows the complete working of our proposed method.

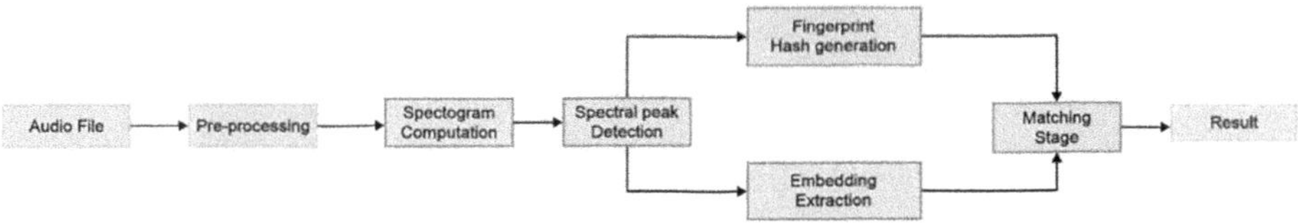


**Fig. 1.** Overview of the complete pipeline of the proposed audio fingerprinting method.

This complete process begins with feeding the audio waveforms $x(t)$ in .wav format. It is then passed to pre-processing stage. Since the frequency of human voice falls under a small range of 300 Hz to 8000 Hz, we use a bandpass filter which can be defined as:

$$H(f) = \begin{cases} 1, & \text{if } 300 \leq f \leq 8000 \text{ Hz,} \\ 0, & \text{otherwise.} \end{cases}$$

where $H(f)$ is the frequency response of the bandpass filter, and $f$ is the frequency in Hz. By using the band-pass filtering, high frequency noise and low frequency hums which nowhere contribute to usable speech content. After applied filtering, amplitude normalization is applied which can be helpful in lessening the impact of fluctuation in recording level.

$$\tilde{x}(t) = \frac{x(t)}{\max(|x(t)|)}$$

This stage ensures multiple dynamic variations between recording and the actual voice won't distort subsequent spectral analysis. The normalized signal from the pre-processing part $\tilde{x}(t)$ is exposed to Short-Time Fourier Transform (STFT) analysis to get STFT representation, which can also be represented mathematically as :

$$S(t, f) = \sum_{n=-\infty}^{\infty} \tilde{x}(n) \cdot w(t - n) \cdot e^{-j2\pi f n}$$

In the above mentioned formula w(t) denotes a Hann window function which balances time and frequency resolution. After that a logarithmic decible scale is formed from the magnitude spectogram using:

$$S_{\mathrm{dB}}(t, f) = 20 \log_{10} |S(t, f)|$$

It provides a clear representation of signal energy across frequencies and time that is visually so much relevant. As shown in Fig. 2 mentioned below also shows the spectogram for a representative human voice embedding. The primary patterns which are used for extracting the fingerprint from a voice signal are highlighted in the below figure, which can show the distribution of spectral energy with respect to time and frequency.

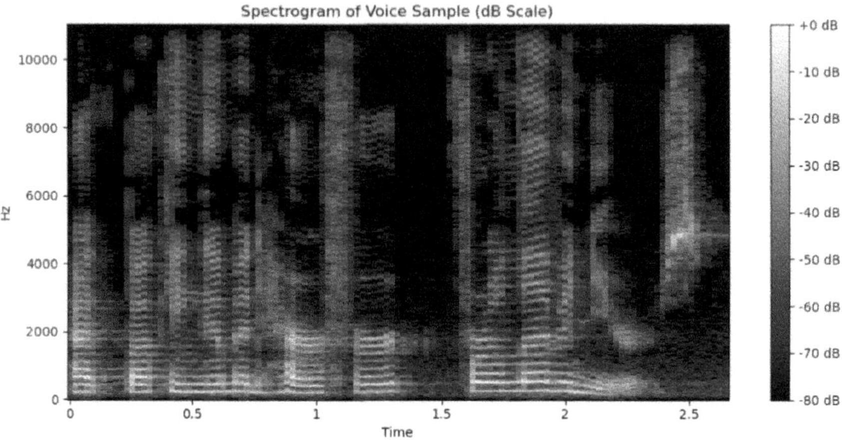


**Fig. 2.** Spectrogram of a human voice sample used for spectral peak detection.

To precisely define the spectrum we have applied spectral peak identification and structure of speech on the decible scaled spectogram. Local maxima can be identified using the two dimension maximum filter technique which is bounded in a configuration window, which extracts important time-frequency peaks $(t_i, f_i)$. After this process a global threshold is applied $\theta_{\mathrm{dB}} = -5\,\mathrm{dB}$ which is applied for rejecting the spurious low energy peaks:

$$P = \{(t_i, f_i) \mid S_{\mathrm{dB}}(t_i, f_i) > \theta_{\mathrm{dB}}, \text{ local maximum}\}.$$

As shown in Fig. 3 further illustrates the further steps of process where detected spectral peaks are paired using anchor target relationship to generate robust hash codes.

Peaks which are below the defined minimum frequency are removed from the signal to prevent artifact. Using spectral hashing, these identified spectral peaks form a base to create a very strong audio fingerprint. After this whole process peak pairs are created one as an anchor(t1, f1) and another as a goal(t2, f2) within a predetermined frame. We compute the quantized frequency indices:

$$q_{f_1} = \left\lfloor \frac{\Delta f}{f_1} \right\rfloor, \quad q_{f_2} = \left\lfloor \frac{\Delta f}{f_2} \right\rfloor$$

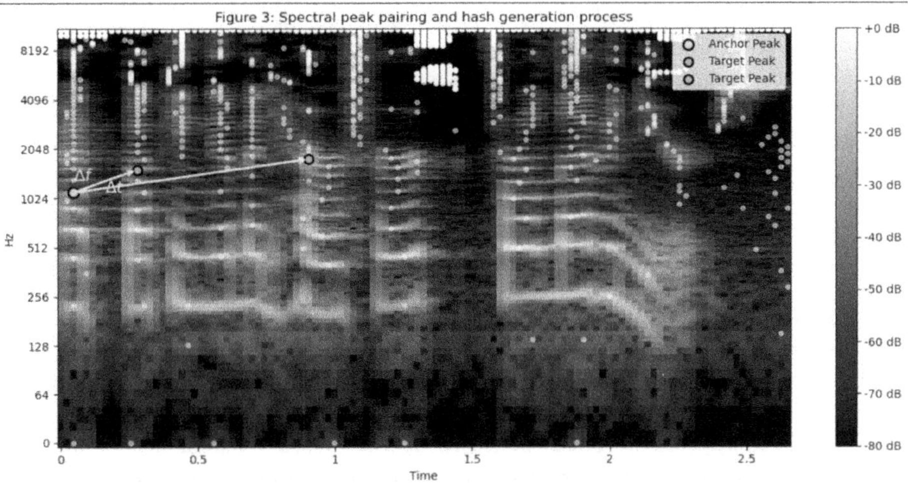


**Fig. 3.** Spectrogram with anchor-target peak pairing and hash generation arrows.

These quantized values are concatenated and encoded into a SHA-1 hash:

$$h = \text{SHA1}(q_{f_1} \mid q_{f_2} \mid \Delta t).$$

To further when we have to differentiate between 2 similar voice signals and improve robustness under severe distortion conditions, along with that we also extract a complementary low-dimensional spectral embedding vector for each single audio file. For each signal, these five features are especially computed: Zero Crossing Rate (ZCR), Spectral Centroid, Spectral Bandwidth, Spectral Rolloff, and Spectral Flatness can be summarised up as follow:

$$\mathbf{e} = [\text{ZCR, Centroid, Bandwidth, Rolloff, Flatness}]$$

Each feature captures different aspects of spectral shape and energy distribution. For instance, the "centre of mass" of the spectral energy is represented by the Spectral Centroid, which is determined by:

$$\text{Centroid} = \frac{\sum_f f \cdot |S(t,f)|}{\sum_f |S(t,f)|}$$

When there is a severe deterioration in audio fingerprint due to massive distortion in the audio then we use embedding vector which further helps in recognizing the audio even when there is a extreme distortion.

During the query matching we use the same process which was being used for fingerprint generation. The overlap cardinality between query and database hashes is used to get the primary matching score:

$$\text{Score}_{\text{hash}}(x_q, x_i) = |H_q \cap H_i|$$

The $H_i$ denotes the stored hash for data generated for all audio tracks. The candidate with maximum overlap is selected. In addition embedding vectors are also compared using euclidean distance which increase the matching accuracy when there is a extensive distortion in the signal.

The proposed methodology was completely tested on Macbook M1 showing faster and reliable hash generation and matching for distorted and clean audio. The applications are like speaker verification and audio forensics because of low latency.

## 3   Result

We carried out extensive evaluation on speech recordings both in clean and pure settings and also with real world acoustic degradation to be occurred. In order to check the effectiveness of the proposed system which is hybrid audio fingerprinting is compared with the State of the art fingerprinting techniques and also with some other techniques with multiple datasets such as [1,10,13]. We used the real audio from the dataset and added the distortion manually such as background noise, equalization boost and gain variation.

Matching accuracy was calculated on common and identical datasets for a perfect fair comparision.

**Table 1.** Fingerprint matching results: Accuracy comparison with state-of-the-art with proposed work

| No. of Seconds | Accuracy for SOTA [5] | without distortion | With Distortion |
| --- | --- | --- | --- |
| 1 s | 60.00% | 68.89% | 75.56% |
| 2 s | 95.60% | 91.11% | 91.11% |
| 3 s | 97.80% | 93.33% | 91.11% |
| 4 s | 97.80% | 95.56% | 95.56% |
| 5 s | 100% | 99.17% | 97.78% |
| **6 s** | **100%** | **99.17%** | **98.12%** |

The Table 1 is a clear comparison between the proposed method with state-of-the-art by Kamuni et al. [5]. Here we can clearly see that even at minimum time as well our system was able to beat state-of-the-art even with and without distortion. The accuracy increased for both with and without distortion when time increases. In the state-of-the-art the outcome was on a clean audio without distortion dataset. Our model was comparable for both with and without distortion.

The Table 2 shows the comparison of the audio signals while additive noise and without additive noise was added to it. In the paper by Zahid et al. [8] has carried out multiple methods but we are clealry taking the best accuracy they have achieved. they have used multiple methods like PRH [15], RARE [3], MLH

**Table 2.** Fingerprint matching results: Best Accuracy of fingerprint matching with and without distortion against state-of-the-art

| Method/Author | Year | With Distortion | Without Distortion |
| --- | --- | --- | --- |
| Zahid et al. [8] | 2020 | 79.9% | 91.23% |
| Tarun et al. [16] | 2022 | 86% | 98% |
| **Proposed Method** | 2025 | **98.12%** | **99.17** |

[14] and SHAZAM. From all of 4 Shazam worked best for without noise and MLH for with noise. In another paper by Tarun et al. [16] there is a clear comparison between the actual audio file and down sampled files. The best accuracy is taken for comparison on random 50 songs which is less than our proposed work.

**Table 3.** Comparison of the proposed method across different datasets.

| Dataset | With Distortion (%) | Without Distortion (%) |
| --- | --- | --- |
| GTZAN [10] | 98.12 | 99.17 |
| VoxCeleb [13] | 96.34 | 97.19 |
| FOR dataset [1] | 94.34 | 96.18 |
| Custom dataset [1] [13] | 93.40 | 95.71 |

The Table 3 shows a clear outcome of our proposed algorithm on different datasets. Our main motive was to design it for human voice but for comparison with state-of-the-art we also ran it on musical signals and it was clearly comparable when it comes to distortion based accuracy. The outcomes are effective even when dataset is large and is of human voice. The custom dataset is created with matching two different datasets and then they are being tested further.

## 4   Conclusion

In this work we have proposed a robust hybrid audio fingerprinting system which combines spectral hashing with complementary spectral embedding which was able to increase the accuracy under distortion. Our system was able to give an accuracy of 98.12% on a distorted audio and accuracy of 99.17% on clean audio which outperforms all the previous methods during distortion. The hybrid design is perfect combination of low computation and high accuracy output in real life distortion such as background noise, clipping, gain variations, and equalization artifacts. Future work will explore Deep learning based embedding to increase the distortion accuracy with much better outcomes.

# References


1. Abdeldayem, M.: The fake or real dataset (2022). https://www.kaggle.com/datasets/mohammedabdeldayem/the-fake-or-real-dataset
2. Ansori, M., et al.: Hades: hash-based audio copy detection system for copyright protection in decentralized music sharing. IEEE Trans. Netw. Serv. Manag. **20**, 2845–2853 (2023). https://doi.org/10.1109/TNSM.2023.3241610
3. Bertin-Mahieux, T., Ellis, D.: Large-scale cover song recognition using hashed chroma landmarks. In: WASPAA 2011, pp. 117–120 (2011). https://doi.org/10.1109/ASPAA.2011.6082307
4. Gohari, M., et al.: Audio features investigation for singing voice deepfake detection. In: ICASSP 2025, pp. 1–5 (2025). https://doi.org/10.1109/ICASSP49660.2025.10888452
5. Kamuni, N., et al.: Advancing audio fingerprinting accuracy with ai and ml: addressing background noise and distortion challenges. In: ICSC, pp. 341–345 (2024). https://doi.org/10.1109/ICSC59802.2024.00064
6. Keum, J., Lee, H.S.: Speaker change detection based on spectral peak track analysis for Korean broadcast news. In: ICICS 2005, pp. 724–728 (2005). https://doi.org/10.1109/ICICS.2005.1689143
7. Liu, L., et al.: Voice source tracking technology based on perceptual hash of fingerprint image. In: IC-NIDC 2021, pp. 349–353 (2021). https://doi.org/10.1109/IC-NIDC54101.2021.9660452
8. Mehmood, Z., et al.: Potential barriers to music fingerprinting algorithms in the presence of background noise. In: CDMA 2020, pp. 25–30 (2020). https://doi.org/10.1109/CDMA47397.2020.00010
9. Modak, S., et al.: Specvit: a custom vision-transformer based approach for audio deepfake detection. In: ICASSP 2025, pp. 1–5 (2025). https://doi.org/10.1109/ICASSP49660.2025.10889022
10. Olteanu, A.: Gtzan dataset - music genre classification (2021). https://www.kaggle.com/datasets/andradaolteanu/gtzan-dataset-music-genre-classification
11. Radhakrishnan, R., et al.: Audio signature extraction based on projections of spectrograms. In: ICME, pp. 2110–2113 (2007). https://doi.org/10.1109/ICME.2007.4285099
12. Rasmusson, A.: Audio Fingerprinting and Identification in Streaming Environments. Master's thesis, Chalmers University of Technology (2022). https://odr.chalmers.se/items/730f333b-7312-46b0-9260-b348ee2916c6
13. Sabahesaraki: Voxceleb 1 dataset (2023). https://www.kaggle.com/datasets/sabahesaraki/voxceleb-1-dataset
14. Son, W., et al.: Sub-fingerprint masking for a robust audio fingerprinting system in a real-noise environment for portable consumer devices. IEEE Trans. Consum. Electron. **56**, 156–160 (2010). https://doi.org/10.1109/TCE.2010.5439139
15. Su, J., et al.: Empirical analysis of content-based music retrieval for music identification. In: ICMT 2011, pp. 3516–3519 (2011). https://doi.org/10.1109/ICMT.2011.6002145
16. Yadav, T., et al.: Real time audio synchronization using audio fingerprinting techniques. In: PCEMS 2022, pp. 16–20 (2022). https://doi.org/10.1109/PCEMS55161.2022.9808050
17. Yan, R., et al.: Audio deepfake detection system with neural stitching for add 2022. In: ICASSP 2022, pp. 9226–9230 (2022). https://doi.org/10.1109/ICASSP43922.2022.9746820

# Adaptive Multi-scale Speaker Diarization on DISPLACE 2024 Challenge Task


Ravindrakumar M. Purohit[1]($\boxtimes$) (iD), Vijay Hothi[2] (iD), and Hemant A. Patil[1] (iD)

[1] Speech Research Lab, Dhirubhai Ambani University (formerly DA-IICT),
Gandhinagar, India
{202321002,hemant_patil}@dau.ac.in
[2] Research Scholar, Gujarat Technological University (GTU), Ahmedabad, India



**Abstract.** Recent advancements in neural networks have significantly improved speaker segmentation and identification across diverse scenarios. Performance of speaker diarization (SD) remains challenging in far-field environments due to background noise, reverberation, and overlapping speech. To address these challenges, this study introduces an adaptive multi-scale SD system designed for the DISPLACE 2024 dataset (Track 1). Building upon an existing speaker embedding techniques, our proposed system use a Multi-Scale Diarization Decoder (MSDD) with overlapping windows at various temporal scales to capture *local* and *global* contextual dependencies effectively. A novel scale-weighting mechanism enhances robustness by dynamically adjusting multi-scale feature contributions during inference. Additionally, a sliding window inference approach enables processing of continuous audio streams. Evaluated on the DISPLACE 2024 dataset, our method achieved a Diarization Error Rate (DER) of 9.22%, marking a 69.22% improvement over the baseline DER of 29.96%.

**Keywords:** Speaker Diarization (SD) · Feature Extraction · Speaker Embeddings · Multi-Scale Diarization Decoder


## 1 Introduction

Speaker Diarization (SD) addresses the problem of "who spoke when" by segmenting and attributing speech segments to individual speakers using robust, real-time deep learning techniques [1]. Recent advances are underpinned by neural speaker embeddings, which provide compact, discriminative representations resilient to diverse acoustic conditions, as illustrated in Fig. 1. Early methods, such as $d$-vectors, utilised deep networks for direct speaker-discriminative embedding extraction, establishing the neural embedding paradigm. This evolved with x-vectors, which employed Time Delay Neural Network (TDNN) and statistical pooling to model long-range temporal dependencies became a state of the art architecture for the SD task. Subsequent innovations, such as $c$-vectors,

R. M. Purohit and V. Hothi—Contributed equally.

leveraged contrastive self-supervised learning for enhanced inter-speaker discrimination and intra-speaker compactness, boosting generalisation in low-resource, and noisy conditions [10].

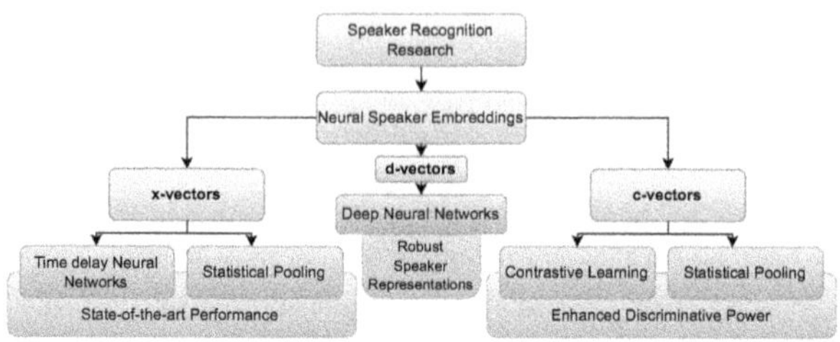


**Fig. 1.** Recent advancements in Speaker Diarization. After [10].

The ECAPA-TDNN architecture further improved discriminative power by integrating channel attention, residual connections, and squeeze-excitation blocks [3]. Collectively, these developments have driven significant reductions in Diarization Error Rate (DER) and speaker confusion when incorporated into end-to-end pipelines.

1. To the best of our knowledge, this is the first study of its kind to enhance speaker diarization by addressing technologically challenging overlapping speech scenarios, using the Multi-Scale Diarization Decoder (MSDD) architecture, which employs overlapping windows at multiple scales to maximize temporal context.
2. To perform SD experiments, we utilised the DISPLACE dataset, which features conversational recordings of 3 to 5 fluent participants in Indian accents [7].
3. The proposed system achieved a DER of 9.22%, using a sliding window inference mechanism. This represents a 65.5% relative improvement over the TalTech-IRIT-LIS system (DER of 26.70%), which was the winning submission at INTERSPEECH 2024 [13].

The remainder of the paper is organized as follows: Sect. 2 discusses the related work in the domain. Sections 3 and 4 mention the proposed architecture and results. Finally, Sect. 5 concludes with a summary and highlights key open research problems that require the attention of the research community.

## 2 Related Work

The DISPLACE 2023 and 2024 Challenges, Track 1, evaluates speaker diarization on far-field conversational recordings, as outlined in the official guidelines[1] [2,7] (Fig. 2).

---

[1] Challenge website: https://displace2024.github.io/.

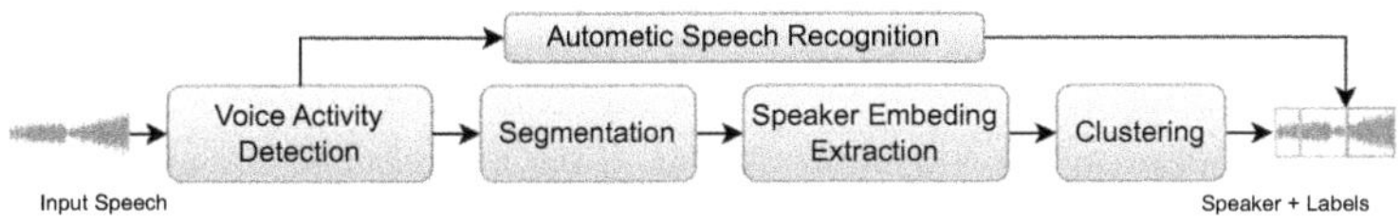


**Fig. 2.** Existing neural speaker diarization pipeline.

These conditions, characterised by reverberation, background noise, and overlapping speech, pose significant challenges for conventional speaker diarization systems. Such systems often assume clean, non-overlapping audio, making them less effective in handling the spatial ambiguity and acoustic distortions inherent in far-field data, which complicates accurate speaker segmentation and clustering. Team TalTech-IRIT-LIS secured first place in the 2024 DISPLACE Challenge SD track with an ensemble system based on the *pyannote*[2]. audio pipeline, enhanced by their PixIT method for joint diarization and speech separation. They improved PixIT by using separation outputs for speaker embedding extraction, achieving a DER of 27.1% on the evaluation dataset [13].

Traditional diarization pipelines follow a sequential approach involving VAD, embedding extraction, and clustering but struggle with overlapping speech. Overlap-aware methods like PixIT [13] jointly optimize separation and diarization using Permutation and Mixture Invariant Training, effectively disentangling concurrent speakers and improving downstream tasks such as ASR. However, this approach requires supervised diarization labels and may exhibit limited generalization due to reliance on synthetic mixtures. Alternatively, multi-scale methods such as the Multi-Scale Diarization Decoder (MSDD) [5] operate directly on audio mixtures at multiple temporal resolutions, capturing local and global context through dynamic scale weighting and overlap-aware label estimation without explicit separation or clustering. While MSDD demonstrates strong domain adaptability and lower DER (3.92% on CALLHOME), its performance may degrade in high-overlap scenarios. Our proposed adaptive multi-scale system enhances MSDD with efficient VAD and embeddings, achieving superior diarization accuracy without explicit separation. This highlights a fundamental trade-off: separation-based methods offer robust overlap resolution with increased complexity, whereas multi-scale approaches provide efficient scalability, suggesting hybrid frameworks as a promising direction.

## 3    Proposed Architecture SD System

Our proposed adaptive multi-scale SD system builds on the work of Park *et al.* [9] by incorporating an innovative acoustic-context-driven scale weighting mechanism. MarbleNet, an efficient neural network, is employed to separate speech from non-speech segments for voice activity detection (VAD). By employing 1D

---

[2] https://www.pyannote.ai/.

depth-wise separable convolutions, MarbleNet ensures low computational overhead while delivering robust performance in noisy conditions, making it well-suited for pre-processing in SD systems [4]. TitaNet-Large, an advanced neural architecture, generates high-fidelity speaker embeddings ($t$-vectors) through 1D depth-wise separable convolutions, augmented with Squeeze-and-Excitation layers and global context attention mechanisms [8] (Figs. 3 and 4).

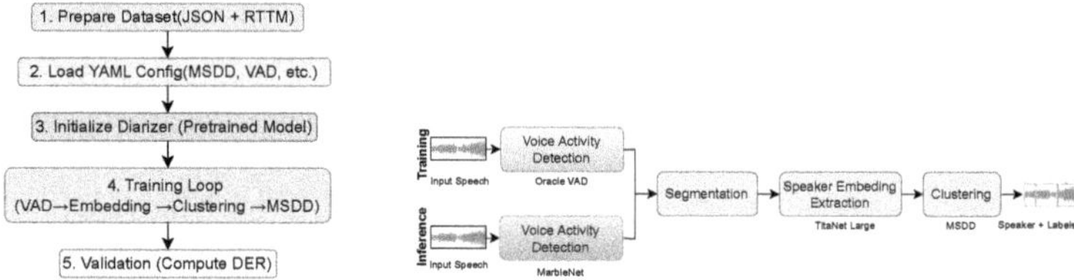


**Fig. 3.** Proposed Architecture: Adaptive Multi-Scale Diarization Decoder.

**Fig. 4.** Proposed training and inference pipeline of the Multi-Scale Diarization Decoder, After [4,8].

The MSDD framework enhances SD by processing audio across multiple temporal resolutions (e.g., 0.5 s to 1.5 s segments). It leverages TitaNet-Large for multi-scale speaker embedding extraction, followed by normalised maximum eigengap spectral clustering (NME-SC) in order to assign initial speaker labels. MSDD dynamically adjusts weights across scales to optimise label estimation, supporting overlap-aware diarization, and accommodating varying speaker counts.

**Training:** It accepts the $< wavs, rttm >$ pairwise and performs the VAD in the first stage to detect the speech regions. The speech region identified by VAD is divided into smaller segments in order to ensure that each segment contains speech from a single speaker. We used the TitaNet Large [8] in order to extract the speaker-specific features from speech and MSDD to predict the speaker labels for each segment using a clustering approach.

**Inference:** The inference workflow is similar to training, except for stage 1. It uses MarbleNet to detect speech and non-speech regions. Unlike Oracle VAD, which requires reference annotations, MarbleNet[3] can detect speech regions without relying on ground truth labels.

**Database Details:** The DISPLACE 2024[4] The meeting corpus comprises 32 h of multilingual, multi-party conversational recordings (3–5 participants 30–60

---

[3] Pretrained weights available at: https://huggingface.co/nvidia/Frame_VAD_Multi lingual_MarbleNet_v2.0.

[4] Corpus available at: https://zenodo.org/records/12166687.

---

**Algorithm 1.** Pseudocode for Training and Inference. After [5]

---

**Require:** Speech $x$, Config $C$, Mode $m \in \{\text{Training, Inference}\}$
1: Initialize MSDD model $M$ and parameters $\Theta$ from $C$
2: // Dataset Split: 70% training, 20% validation, 10% test from DISPLACE 2024
3: // Augmentation: Add noise (SNR 10-20dB), speed perturbation (0.9x-1.1x)
4: **for** each audio sample $x_i \in D$ **do**
5:     // Extract VAD segments using MarbleNet with overlap tolerance of 0.3s
6:     Extract VAD segments: $S_i \leftarrow \text{VAD}(x_i)$
7:     // Extract speaker embeddings using TitaNet-Large with 192-dim output
8:     Extract speaker embeddings: $E_i \leftarrow \text{Embed}(x_i; C_{\text{embed}})$
9:     **if** $m = \text{Infer}$ **then**
10:         // Clustering: Normalized Maximum Eigengap Spectral Clustering (NME-SC)
11:         // Hyperparameters: k=5 clusters, tolerance=0.01, max iterations=100
12:         Cluster Initialization: $C_i \leftarrow \text{Cluster}(E_i)$
13:         Predict logits, $\hat{Y}_i \leftarrow M(E_i, C_i)$
14:         // Thresholding with adaptive cutoff (0.5 default, fine-tuned to 0.6)
15:         Thresholding, $\tilde{Y}_i \leftarrow T(\hat{Y}_i)$
16:         Predictions, $\bar{Y}_i \leftarrow \text{Smooth}(\tilde{Y}_i)$
17:         Convert to RTTM, $R_i \leftarrow \text{Postprocess}(\bar{Y}_i)$
18:         **if** ASR is enabled **then**
19:             Transcribe, $T_i \leftarrow \text{ASR}(x_i)$
20:             Align, $T_i \leftarrow \text{Align}(T_i, R_i)$
21:         **end if**
22:     **else**
23:         // Load ground-truth labels with 80% RTTM overlap tolerance
24:         Load ground-truth labels, $Y_i$
25:         Predict logits, $\hat{Y}_i \leftarrow M(E_i)$
26:         // Fine-tuning: Use Adam optimizer, learning rate 1e-3, cosine annealing
27:         Compute loss, $L_i \leftarrow \text{LBCE}(\hat{Y}_i, Y_i)$
28:         // Pretrained weights (MarbleNet, TitaNet-Large) reduce training time by 40%
29:         // vs. from-scratch; fine-tuning boosts DER by 2% over pretrained baseline
30:         Update model, $\Theta \leftarrow \Theta - \eta \cdot \nabla_\Theta L_i$
31:     **end if**
32: **end for**

---

minutes per session). That dataset comprises a development set containing 35 audio recordings totaling approximately 20 h of speech, and an evaluation set comprising 32 recordings spanning around 18 h. Which were recorded at IISc Bengaluru and NITK using far-field (omnidirectional and unidirectional) and close-field (lapel) microphones at 16 kHz sampling frequency. The corpus includes overlapping speech, making it suitable for robust diarization benchmarking [7].

**Model Parameters:** The model parameters used in experiments are mentioned in Table 1.

**Table 1.** MSDD Model Configuration Parameters

| Parameter | Value |
|---|---|
| Scales | 5 |
| Window Length (s) | [1.5, 1.25, 1.0, 0.75, 0.5] |
| Shift Length (s) | [0.75, 0.625, 0.5, 0.375, 0.25] |
| Overlap (%) | 50 |
| Multiscale Weights | [1, 1, 1, 1, 1] |
| No. of LSTM Layers | 3 |
| CNN o/p Channels | 32 |
| Conv Layer Repetitions | 2 |
| Embed. Dimension | 192 |
| Loss Function | $\mathcal{L}_{\mathrm{BCE}}$ |
| Learning Rate | $1 \times 10^{-3}$ |
| Scheduler | Cosine Annealing |
| Dropout Rate | $5 \times 10^{-1}$ |
| Sampling Rate | 16000 |

**Experimental Setup:** All the experiments were performed using the Ubuntu 24.04 LTS-based workstation, equipped with an Intel Core i7-12700 processor, 16GB of RAM, and an NVIDIA GTX 1080 GPU (8GB VRAM, 8.9 Teraflops).

### 3.1   Performance Evaluation Metric Used

The proposed system is evaluated using the standard measures, such as the DER metric, with no forgiveness collar (a short time window applied around speaker change point during evaluation).

**DER** [12]: It quantifies aggregate error in speaker segmentation and clustering as per Eq. 1, by representing the proportion of time misattributed to speakers, i.e.,

$$\mathrm{DER}(\%) = \left( \frac{\text{Missed Detection} + \text{False Alarm} + \text{Speaker Confusion}}{\text{Total Reference Duration}} \right) \times 100 \tag{1}$$

## 4   Results and Discussion

In this section, we validated the proposed system with baseline and SOTA methods of DISPLACE 2024 on both development and evaluation sets. As shown in Table 2, DISPLACE-2023 baseline system achieves a DER of 27.33%

on the development set, with higher error rates in the evaluation set of 32.18%. In DISPLACE 2024, organizers set the baseline DER to 25.45% and 29.96% on the development set and evaluation set, respectively, where `pyannote-diarization-3.1` system achieved the DERs of 29.53% and 34.96% on the development and evaluation set, respectively, using the ECAPA-TDNN [3], AHC.

**Table 2.** Comparison of the DER (%) on the Baseline System(s) and SOTA of the DISPLACE 2024 Challenge. '–' denotes that the result is disclosed by the authors.

| Submission | Dev% | Eval% |
|---|---|---|
| DISPLACE-2023 Baseline [2] | 27.33 | 32.18 |
| DISPLACE-2024 Baseline [7] | 25.45 | 29.96 |
| Pyannote Diarization 3.1 [11] | 29.53 | 34.96 |
| Hybrid-Diarization System [11] | 26.37 | 28.04 |
| #1TalTech-IRIT-LIS [6] | – | 27.15 |
| #2TalTech-IRIT-LIS (#1 + 10 s Sliding Windows) [6] | – | 26.70 |
| Proposed System | – | 9.22 |

Other systems presented in [11] show competitive results, with evaluation DERs of 26.37% and 28.04%, respectively. Notably, the *winner* system at DISPLACE 2024, the TalTech-IRIT-LIS system, uses a combination of advanced neural architectures, such as PixIT, DPTNet, and sliding window mechanisms, and reported improved VADwith DERs of 27.15% and 26.70%. Our proposed DAU-GTU system, integrating MarbleNet, TitaNet-Large, and MSDD modules, outperforms all SOTA models by achieving a significant reduction in evaluation DER to 9.22%, by demonstrating the effectiveness of the proposed method in speaker diarization tasks.

## 4.1 Computational Complexity and Real-Time Feasibility

The proposed system leverages efficient neural architectures to balance performance and computational demands. The MarbleNet VAD model is lightweight with approximately 310,000 parameters, enabling fast processing. The TitaNet-Large for speaker embeddings has about 23 million parameters, optimized for efficiency through 1D depth-wise separable convolutions. The MSDD component, with 3 LSTM layers and 192-dimensional embeddings, adds roughly 1.5 million parameters.

The proposed model was trained for 20 h on the development set, which required approximately 5 h on the NVIDIA GTX 1080 GPU. We used a sample of about 20 min from the 18-hour evaluation set for inference.

## 5  Summary and Conclusions

In this paper, we used an adaptive multi-scale SD system for the DISPLACE 2024 dataset (Track 1) task. The proposed system achieves a DER of 9.22% through a novel MarbleNet VAD and TitaNet Large speaker embedding extraction model, where clustering is performed using the MSDD, and an ensemble system reaches the DER of 9.22% on the eval set. Our approach outperforms the challenge baseline, demonstrating robustness to far-field conversational audio. Open research challenges include minimising dependence on manually annotated speech data (e.g., RTTM files), optimising the SD pipeline for real-time applications, and improving the SD in challenging, acoustically noisy environments. Future work will involve extensive testing on wider demographic and acoustic variance datasets to systematically assess and mitigate any potential biases due to the imbalanced training data (e.g., varying microphone distances, accent diversity).

## References


1. Anguera, X., Bozonnet, S., Evans, N., Fredouille, C., Friedland, G., Vinyals, O.: Speaker diarization: a review of recent research. IEEE Trans. Audio Speech Lang. Process. **20**(2), 356–370 (2012)
2. Baghel, S., et al.: Summary of the displace challenge 2023–diarization of speaker and language in conversational environments. arXiv preprint arXiv:2311.12564 (2023). Accessed 28 July 2025
3. Dawalatabad, N., Ravanelli, M., Grondin, F., Thienpondt, J., Desplanques, B., Na, H.: Ecapa-tdnn embeddings for speaker diarization. arXiv preprint arXiv:2104.01466 (2021). Accessed 28 July 2025
4. Jia, F., Majumdar, S., Ginsburg, B.: Marblenet: deep 1d time-channel separable convolutional neural network for voice activity detection. In: IEEE International Conference on Acoustics, Speech and Signal Processing (ICASSP), Toronto, Ontario, Canada, pp. 6818–6822 (2021))
5. Jones, A., Brown, B.: Multi-scale diarization decoder for speaker segmentation. IEEE Trans. Audio Speech Lang. Process. **32**, 456–465 (2024)
6. Kalda, J., Alumäe, T., Lebourdais, M., Bredin, H., Baroudi, S., Marxer, R.: Taltech-irit-lis speaker and language diarization systems for displace 2024. arXiv preprint arXiv:2407.12743 (2024). Accessed 28 July 2025
7. Kalluri, S.B., et al.: The second displace challenge: diarization of speaker and language in conversational environments. arXiv preprint arXiv:2406.09494 (2024). Accessed 28 July 2025
8. Koluguri, N.R., Park, T., Ginsburg, B.: Titanet: neural model for speaker representation with 1d depth-wise separable convolutions and global context. In: IEEE International Conference on Acoustics, Speech and Signal Processing (ICASSP), Singapore (2022)
9. Park, T.J., et al.: Multi-scale speaker diarization with dynamic scale weighting. In: INTERSPEECH, Dublin, Ireland, pp. 5080–5084 (2023)
10. Park, T.J., Kanda, N., Dimitriadis, D., Han, K.J., Watanabe, S., Narayanan, S.: A review of speaker diarization: recent advances with deep learning. Comput. Speech Lang. **72**, 101317 (2022)

11. Pîrlogeanu, G., Pascu, O., Georgescu, A.L., Cucu, H.: Hybrid-diarization system with overlap post-processing for the displace 2024 challenge. In: INTERSPEECH, Kos Island, Greece, pp. 1625–1629 (2024)
12. Ryant, N., et al.: First dihard challenge evaluation plan. In: Technical Report. Linguistic Data Consortium, University of Pennsylvania (2018)
13. Team TalTech-IRIT-LIS: Submissions to the DISPLACE 2024 Challenge. Technical report, DISPLACE 2024 Challenge. Team TalTech-IRIT-LIS (2024)

# Evaluating Pretrained General-Purpose Audio Representations for Music Genre Classification

Kashish Rai[1(✉)] and Mrinmoy Bhattacharjee[2]

[1] Department of Mathematics, Indian Institute of Technology Patna, Patna, India
`kashish_2302mc04@iitp.ac.in`
[2] Department of CSE, Indian Institute of Technology Jammu, Jammu, India

**Abstract.** This study investigates the use of self-supervised learning embeddings, particularly BYOL-A, in conjunction with a deep neural network classifier for Music Genre Classification. Our experiments demonstrate that BYOL-A embeddings outperform other pre-trained models, such as PANNs and VGGish, achieving an accuracy of 81.5% on the GTZAN dataset and 64.3% on FMA-Small. The proposed DNN classifier improved performance by 10–16% over linear classifiers. We explore the effects of contrastive and triplet loss and multitask training with optimized loss weights, achieving the highest accuracy. To address cross-dataset challenges, we combined GTZAN and FMA-Small into a unified 18-class label space for joint training, resulting in slight performance drops on GTZAN but comparable results on FMA-Small. The scripts developed in this work are publicly available (https://github.com/ kashishrai12/musicgenre-classification).

**Keywords:** music genre · semi-supervised learning · classification · gtzan

## 1 Introduction

Music, a universally appealing art form, is often categorized into genres like jazz, pop and others. Music Genre Classification (MGC) helps in efficient music archiving and retrieval. Researchers have used audio feature engineering to create discriminative representations for training classifiers for MGC [8,9,11]. Recent studies show that deep audio foundation models, trained on large datasets via Self-Supervised Learning (SSL), are highly effective at generating discriminating feature embeddings for MGC [5–7,13,15]. This work explores the impact of carefully designed classifiers using SSL embeddings for MGC.

Singh et al. [11] compare the effectiveness of standard audio feature representations like Chromagram, Mel-Frequency Cepstral Coefficients (MFCC), and Swaragram [12] with deep learning models like Convolutional Neural Networks (CNN) and Recurrent Neural Networks (RNN) for the MGC task. Their results indicate that Mel-scale features and Swaragram features are the most generic

© The Author(s), under exclusive license to Springer Nature Switzerland AG 2026
S. Mitra et al. (Eds.): PReMI 2025, LNCS 16358, pp. 796–804, 2026.
https://doi.org/10.1007/978-3-032-18480-1_81

representations across datasets. Other researchers have also utilized music spectrograms as input features for training classifiers for MGC [8]. Ru et al. [9] proposed a multi-modal and multi-label MGC approach by leveraging the inter-genre correlations and the relationship between parallel music and lyrics data.

Recent MGC research has shifted from signal processing-based features to deep SSL embeddings. Zhao et al. [15] introduced the S3T model, trained with a momentum-based contrastive learning approach using the Swin Transformer backbone for MGC and music tagging tasks. Spijkervet et al. [13] developed the CLMR framework, based on SimCLR, for music classification from raw audio waveforms, utilizing data augmentation techniques. Niizumi et al. [7] proposed BYOL-A, an SSL framework for audio, extending BYOL with audio-specific augmentations and a novel encoder. Kong et al. [6] introduced Pretrained Audio Neural Networks (PANNs), large-scale pre-trained convolutional networks for audio classification and MGC tasks. Hershey et al. [5] proposed the VGGish model, a CNN architecture pre-trained on YouTube data and established a baseline for audio embedding extraction in music information retrieval.

Previous work has mainly focused on extracting generalizable SSL embeddings , often using a simple linear layer to map embeddings to target labels of the downstream task. However, limited attention has been given to designing classifier architectures or learning frameworks to improve MGC performance using SSL embeddings. This work explores the impact of carefully designed classifiers trained on SSL embeddings to enhance MGC. The paper is structured as follows. Section 2 presents the methodology for designing a better MGC classifier with SSL embeddings, Sect. 3 covers experiments and results, and Sect. 4 concludes the paper.

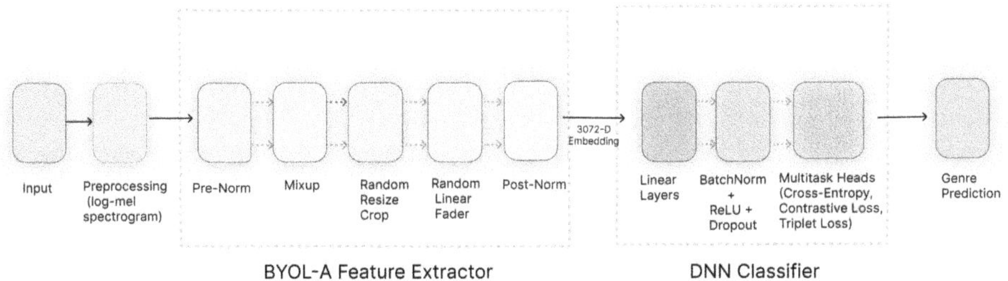


**Fig. 1.** Diagram representing the proposed MGC system. The system consists of SSL embedding extractor followed by an DNN classifier for music genre prediction.

## 2   Methodology

This work uses general-purpose audio SSL models to extract feature embeddings and train carefully designed classifiers to improve MGC performance. A block diagram of the proposed system is illustrated in Fig. 1. The feature extraction approach used in this work is described below.

### 2.1  Feature Extraction

This work compares three different pre-trained SSL models for extracting feature representations, viz., BYOL-A [7], PANNs [6], and VGGish [5]. Each of these models is briefly described next.

In BYOL-A [7], raw audio is converted to log-mel spectrograms and fed into a dual-network architecture with an online and target network. Augmentations like Mixup, Random Resize Crop, and Random Linear Fader are applied to ensure robustness to common audio perturbations. The encoder combines convolutional feature maps and temporal pooling to capture both local and global features. This results in a 3072-dimensional embedding for each 30-second audio track, encoding both temporal and spectral characteristics.

We use the CNN14 model from the PANNs framework [6] to extract audio embeddings. Pretrained on the large-scale AudioSet dataset [3], PANNs capture rich acoustic patterns. The input waveform is converted to a log-mel spectrogram and processed by a deep CNN with convolutional blocks and global pooling. The model outputs a 2048-dimensional embedding per segment, summarizing spectral and temporal information. The embeddings are averaged over time to form a compact representation for each 30s audio clip.

Hershey et al. [5] introduced VGGish, a compact audio feature extractor based on the VGG architecture [10] and pretrained on AudioSet [3]. Audio is resampled to 16kHz and converted into 0.96s log-mel spectrogram patches, which are processed by a VGG-like network to produce 128-dimensional embeddings. For our experiments, embeddings from a 30s audio track are averaged to create a fixed-length feature vector for MGC tasks. The next subsection discusses the classifier training details.

### 2.2  Classifier Training

Our approach centers on designing and training a DNN classifier to map SSL embeddings to music genre labels. The architecture is tailored to utilize the high-dimensional feature space and prevent overfitting. The input layer receives the SSL embedding, followed by hidden layers with linear transformations, Batch Normalization, ReLU activation, and Dropout regularization. These layers progressively reduce dimensions, ensuring effective feature abstraction and regularization. The final architecture was determined empirically.

In the initial experiments for the MGC task, the classifiers are trained using the cross-entropy loss, as defined below.

$$L_{CE} = -\frac{1}{N} \sum_{i=1}^{N} log(p_i) \tag{1}$$

where, $p_i$ is the predicted probability of true class for the $i^{th}$ sample and $N$ is the number of samples in the batch. To further enhance the discriminative capacity of the learned representations, we explored advanced loss functions, viz., contrastive loss and triplet loss. Some previous works have also explored contrastive loss for the classification of music genres [1,9,13]. The contrastive loss is defined as follows [4].

$$L_{CL} = \frac{1}{N} \sum_{i=1}^{N} \left\{ (1 - y_i) \cdot \max \left( m - D_w \left( z_i^{(1)}, z_i^{(2)} \right), 0 \right)^2 + y \cdot D_w \left( z_i^{(1)}, z_i^{(2)} \right)^2 \right\} \tag{2}$$

where, $D_w \left( z_i^{(1)}, z_i^{(2)} \right) = \sqrt{\sum_{k=1}^{n} \left( z_i^{(1)}[k] - z_i^{(2)}[k] + \epsilon \right)^2}$ is the Euclidean distance, $\epsilon = 1e^{-6}$ is used for numerical stability, $z_i^{(1)}$ and $z_i^{(2)}$ are the model outputs for the $i^{th}$ input $x_i$, $y$ is a binary label indicating similar ($y = 0$) or dissimilar ($y = 1$) pairs, and $m = 1.0$ is the loss margin. We have also explored the Triplet loss, which is described below.

$$L_{TL} = D_w \left( \mathcal{F} \left( x_i^{(a)} \right), \mathcal{F} \left( x_i^{(p)} \right) \right) - D_w \left( \mathcal{F} \left( x_i^{(a)} \right), \mathcal{F} \left( x_i^{(n)} \right) \right) + \epsilon \tag{3}$$

where, $\mathcal{F}$ is the model that takes the $i^{th}$ input $x_i$ and produces a $d$-dimensional output $\mathcal{F}(x_i)$, and $\epsilon$ is the bias term. Superscripts $(a)$, $(p)$, and $(n)$ denote the anchor, positive, and negative samples, respectively. These losses were incorporated into the training regime as single-task and multi-task setups alongside the standard cross-entropy loss. The multi-task setup involved multiple output heads, each optimized for a specific loss component, with carefully adjusted weighting parameters. For example, the total loss in the multi-task training, with separate output heads for cross-entropy, contrastive, and triplet losses, is computed as $L = \alpha \cdot L_{CE} + \beta \cdot L_{CL} + (1 - \alpha - \beta) \cdot L_{TL}$. Details of the various configurations explored are provided in Subsect. 3.3.

## 3  Experiments and Results

To evaluate the proposed approach, we conducted experiments to assess the impact of architectural choices, feature extraction methods, and training strategies on MGC performance. Embeddings from BYOL-A [7], PANNs [6], and VGGish [5] were used as input features for the classifier. Two datasets were used for benchmarking: GTZAN [14], consisting of 1000 half-minute music excerpts labeled in 10 categories, and the FMA Small subset [2], with 8000 30s tracks labeled into 8 genres. A consistent feature extraction pipeline was applied to both datasets, and embeddings from different models were compared. The experiments and results are detailed in the following subsections.

### 3.1  Selection of DNN Architecture

The impact of hidden layer depth in the DNN classifier was tested with one to four hidden layers (Fig. 2(a)) using a learning rate of $5e^{-4}$ and batch size of 64. A three-hidden-layer configuration yielded the best performance, with a test accuracy of 78.5%. The effect of node count in this configuration (128, 64, and 32 nodes) was also explored (Fig. 2(b)), with doubling the node count achieving the best accuracy of 76.5%. No other configurations led to significant improvements.

Dropout regularization was tested at various rates (Fig. 2(c)), with the best performance at a rate of 0.3, enhancing generalization. Different activation functions, viz. LeakyReLU, ELU, and Swish were also evaluated (Fig. 2(d)), with ReLU yielding the highest accuracy of 79%. Swish and ELU performed similarly

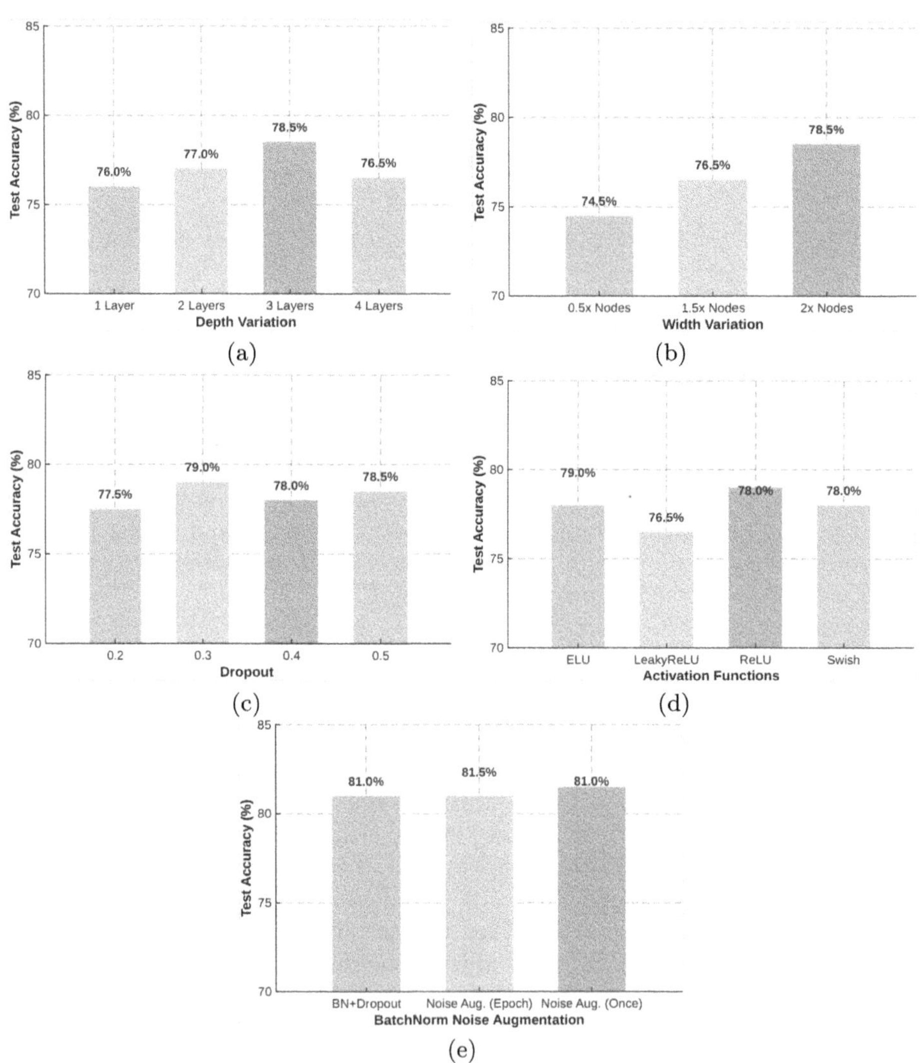

**Fig. 2.** Performance of various model architecture tuning experiments performed on the GTZAN dataset using *BYOL-A* embeddings as model input feature. The test accuracy (%) for different parameter variations is reported.

but did not surpass ReLU. After each linear transformation, applying batch normalization was found to stabilize training and improve convergence, achieving a test accuracy of around 81% when combined with a dropout rate of 0.3.

**Table 1.** Test Accuracy (%) of using different feature extractors on GTZAN and FMA-Small datasets. Results are reported for our best DNN classifier trained on embeddings from each feature extractor.

| Feature Extractor | GTZAN (%) | FMA-Small (%) |
| --- | --- | --- |
| Niizumi et al. [7] | 70.1 | – |
| Defferrard et al. [2] | – | 58.0 |
| Ours + BYOL-A embeddings | 81.5 | 64.3 |
| Ours + PANNs embeddings | 77.0 | 58.0 |
| Ours + VGGish embeddings | 79.5 | 58.04 |

A series of experiments assessed the impact of noise augmentation on model robustness (Fig. 2(e)). Gaussian noise was added to input embeddings with varied Signal-to-Noise Ratios (SNR) and positions in time. Applying around 20dB of Gaussian noise at the start of training yielded the best test accuracy of 81.5%. Noise augmentation also reduced the number of epochs for convergence from 50 to about 35 and helped prevent overfitting.

## 3.2   Comparison of Feature Extraction Models

A comparison of BYOL-A embeddings with other pre-trained audio models is shown in Table 1. On the GTZAN dataset, BYOL-A achieved 81.5% accuracy, outperforming PANNs (77%) and VGGish (79.5%). BYOL-A also performed better on the FMA-Small dataset with 64.3% accuracy. The proposed DNN classifier provided a relative accuracy improvement of $10 - 16\%$ on the GTZAN dataset for all feature extractors and 11% on FMA-Small using BYOL-A. These results demonstrate the superior discriminative power of BYOL-A embeddings for MGC and the impact of designing a customized classifier compared to a linear classifier layer.

## 3.3   Multitask Training

To improve the discriminative power of embeddings, contrastive and triplet loss functions were tested in multitask learning setups with cross-entropy loss. The classifier was extended with multiple output heads, each corresponding to a different loss (e.g., cross-entropy, contrastive, or triplet). Three multitask configurations were explored. First, a 2-head setup having contrastive or triplet loss plus an auxiliary cross-entropy head for the anchor sample. Second, a 3-head setup has two auxiliary cross-entropy losses for anchor and non-anchor samples besides

**Table 2.** Multitask training results with different loss configurations. Cross-entropy (CE) weights are shown for each classification head, with only one of Contrastive or Triplet used per setup. A ✓ indicates the active loss head, with the weight in brackets.

| | Cross-Entropy ($\alpha$) | | | Contrastive ($\beta$) | Triplet ($(1-\alpha-\beta)$) | Acc (%) |
|---|---|---|---|---|---|---|
| 2 Heads | ✓(0.5) | – | – | ✓ (0.5) | – | 79.0 |
| | ✓(0.5) | – | – | – | ✓ (0.5) | 77.0 |
| 3 Heads | ✓(0.45) | ✓(0.45) | – | ✓ (0.1) | – | 80.0 |
| | ✓(0.40) | ✓(0.40) | – | ✓ (0.2) | – | 79.5 |
| | ✓(0.35) | ✓(0.35) | – | ✓ (0.3) | - | **81.5** |
| | ✓(0.30) | ✓(0.30) | – | ✓ (0.4) | – | 77.5 |
| | ✓(0.25) | ✓(0.25) | – | ✓ (0.5) | – | 81.0 |
| | ✓(0.20) | ✓(0.20) | – | ✓ (0.6) | – | 78.5 |
| | ✓(0.15) | ✓(0.15) | – | ✓ (0.7) | – | 79.5 |
| | ✓(0.10) | ✓(0.10) | – | ✓ (0.8) | – | 78.0 |
| | ✓(0.05) | ✓(0.05) | – | ✓ (0.9) | – | 77.5 |
| | ✓(0.07) | ✓(0.63) | – | ✓ (0.3) | – | 80.0 |
| | ✓(0.21) | ✓(0.49) | – | ✓ (0.3) | – | 79.5 |
| | ✓(0.49) | ✓(0.21) | – | ✓ (0.3) | – | 78.5 |
| | ✓(0.63) | ✓(0.07) | – | ✓ (0.3) | – | 81.0 |
| | ✓(0.35) | ✓(0.35) | – | – | ✓ (0.3) | 80.0 |
| 4 Heads | ✓(0.23) | ✓(0.23) | ✓(0.23) | – | ✓ (0.3) | 79.5 |

the main loss function (contrastive or triplet). Finally, a 4-head setup was used only for the main loss function as triplet loss with auxiliary cross-entropy heads for anchor, positive, and negative samples. By optimizing a weighted combination of these losses, the model learned representations that were discriminative for genre classification and robust to intra-class variability.

As shown in Table 2, contrastive loss in a 2-head setup achieved up to 79% accuracy, while triplet loss ranged from 77% to 80.5%. Multitask training with contrastive and cross-entropy loss achieved the best accuracy of 81.5% when loss weights were optimized.

### 3.4 Domain Normalization

The GTZAN and FMA-Small datasets have 10 and 8 non-overlapping genres, respectively. Such a scenario makes cross-dataset evaluation difficult. We combined both datasets into a unified label space of 18 classes for joint training to address this. Using the best DNN architecture with BYOL-A feature extraction, the model was trained to predict one of these 18 classes. As shown in Table 3, models trained on the combined dataset performed slightly worse on GTZAN but similarly on FMA-Small. While learning MGC on an augmented label space is more challenging, the BYOL-A embeddings with the designed DNN classifier

**Table 3.** Test Accuracy (%) on GTZAN and FMA-Small using BYOL-A Features

| Training Dataset | GTZAN (%) | FMA-Small (%) |
| --- | --- | --- |
| Niizumi et al. [7] | 70.1 | – |
| Defferrard et al. [2] | – | 58.0 |
| Ours (trained on *GTZAN*) | **81.5** | – |
| Ours (trained on *FMA-Small*) | – | **64.3** |
| Ours (trained on *GTZAN + FMA-Small*) | 78.0 | 64.25 |

still performed well. Such results highlight the need for domain adaptation to improve generalization.

## 4 Conclusion

This study investigates the effectiveness of SSL embeddings combined with a well-designed DNN classifier for MGC. The approach achieved competitive accuracies on the GTZAN and FMA-Small datasets, with BYOL-A embeddings outperforming PANNs and VGGish in both datasets. Fine-tuning with contrastive and triplet losses provided marginal improvements, while multitask training with contrastive and cross-entropy losses yielded the best accuracy of 81.5%. Training on a combined dataset of 18 genres revealed challenges in domain adaptation. These results emphasize the superior discriminative power of BYOL-A embeddings and the importance of a customized classifier over simple linear layers. Future work will explore embeddings from different SSL model depths and apply domain adaptation techniques to improve cross-dataset performance.

## References


1. Costanzi, G.H., Teixeira, L.O., Felipe, G.Z., Cavalcanti, G.D., Costa, Y.M.: Music genre classification using contrastive dissimilarity. In: Proceedings of 31st International Conference on Systems, Signals and Image Processing (IWSSIP), pp. 1–8 (2024)
2. Defferrard, M., Benzi, K., Vandergheynst, P., Bresson, X.: FMA: a dataset for music analysis. In: Proceedings of 18th International Society for Music Information Retrieval Conference (ISMIR) (2017)
3. Gemmeke, J.F., et al.: Audio Set: an ontology and human-labeled dataset for audio events. In: Proceedings of IEEE International Conference on Acoustics, Speech and Signal Processing (ICASSP), New Orleans, LA, pp. 776–780 (2017)
4. Hadsell, R., Chopra, S., LeCun, Y.: Dimensionality reduction by learning an invariant mapping. In: Proceedings of IEEE Computer Society Conference on Computer Vision and Pattern Recognition (CVPR'06), vol. 2, pp. 1735–1742 (2006)
5. Hershey, S., et al.: Cnn architectures for large-scale audio classification. In: Proceedings of IEEE International Conference on Acoustics, Speech and Signal Processing (ICASSP), pp. 131–135 (2017)

6. Kong, Q., Cao, Y., Iqbal, T., Wang, Y., Wang, W., Plumbley, M.D.: PANNs: large-scale pretrained audio neural networks for audio pattern recognition. IEEE/ACM Trans. Audio Speech Lang. Process. **28**, 2880–2894 (2020)
7. Niizumi, D., Takeuchi, D., Ohishi, Y., Harada, N., Kashino, K.: BYOL for audio: exploring pre-trained general-purpose audio representations. IEEE/ACM Trans. Audio Speech Lang. Process. **31**, 137–151 (2022)
8. Pelchat, N., Gelowitz, C.M.: Neural network music genre classification. Can. J. Electr. Comput. Eng. **43**(3), 170–173 (2020)
9. Ru, G., Zhang, X., Wang, J., Cheng, N., Xiao, J.: Improving music genre classification from multi-modal properties of music and genre correlations perspective. In: Proceedings of IEEE International Conference on Acoustics, Speech and Signal Processing (ICASSP), pp. 1–5 (2023)
10. Simonyan, K., Zisserman, A.: Very deep convolutional networks for large-scale image recognition. arXiv preprint arXiv:1409.1556 (2014)
11. Singh, Y., Biswas, A.: Robustness of musical features on deep learning models for music genre classification. Expert Syst. Appl. **199**, 116879 (2022)
12. Singh, Y., Kumar, R., Biswas, A.: Swaragram: Shruti-based chromagram for Indian classical music. In: Proceedings of 25th International Symposium on Frontiers of Research in Speech and Music (FRSM), pp. 109–118. Springer, Heidelberg (2021)
13. Spijkervet, J., Burgoyne, J.A.: Contrastive learning of musical representations. In: Proceedings of 22nd International Society for Music Information Retrieval Conference, pp. 673–681. ISMIR (2021)
14. Tzanetakis, G., Cook, P.: Musical genre classification of audio signals. IEEE Trans. Speech Audio Process. **10**(5), 293–302 (2002)
15. Zhao, H., Zhang, C., Zhu, B., Ma, Z., Zhang, K.: S3T: self-supervised pre-training with swin transformer for music classification. In: Proceedings of IEEE International Conference on Acoustics, Speech and Signal Processing (ICASSP), pp. 606–610 (2022)

# Detection of Cloned Voice in Marathi Using Acoustic and Spectral-Temporal Features


Mahesh Thor[iD] and Rajesh Kumar[(✉)][iD]

Goverment Institute of Forensic Science, Chhatrapati Sambhajinagar 431004,
Maharashtra, India
`maheshthor007@gmail.com`, `rajeshkumar512@gmail.com`



**Abstract.** The increasing sophistication of voice cloning technologies has led to serious challenges in voice-based authentication and forensic analysis, particularly for regional languages such as Marathi. This study presents a system for detecting cloned versus original speech using acoustic as well as spectral-temporal features. While features such as formant frequencies, pitch, jitter, and shimmer were also explored, these voice quality measures exhibited limited discriminative power when used independently, particularly against advanced synthetic voices. Therefore, the system emphasizes Mel-Frequency Cepstral Coefficients (MFCC) and its dynamic derivatives (delta and delta-delta), which provide a more robust representation of speech patterns. A Gaussian Mixture Model (GMM) classifier is used to distinguish between original and cloned Marathi voice samples based on MFCC features. The system demonstrates high accuracy and reliability, validating the effectiveness of spectral-based analysis combined with GMM modeling in detecting voice spoofing.

**Keywords:** Cloned voice · Pitch · Formants · jitter · shimmer · GMM · MFCC · Marathi


## 1 Introduction

The rise of voice cloning and synthetic speech generation technologies has opened a new frontier in speech synthesis, characterized by improved quality, accurate speaker identity replication, and enhanced emotional control. While this represents a technological milestone, it has simultaneously introduced critical challenges in security, forensics, and privacy, particularly in voice-based biometric authentication. The misuse of cloned voices for impersonation, misinformation, financial fraud, and cybercrimes has grown significantly, raising the urgent need for effective cloned voice detection systems.

Conventional speaker verification methods, largely based on Hidden Markov Models (HMMs) [1] or GMM-UBM frameworks, were initially designed to withstand human vocal mimicry. However, these systems are now highly vulnerable to text-to-speech (TTS) and voice conversion (VC) attacks [2], especially those



S. Mitra et al. (Eds.): PReMI 2025, LNCS 16358, pp. 805–812, 2026.
https://doi.org/10.1007/978-3-032-18480-1_82

based on deep learning architectures such as WaveNet, Tacotron, and GAN-based vocoders [3,4]. Features like pitch (F0), formants, jitter, and shimmer, though useful for analyzing voice quality, often exhibit minimal variation in cloned voices, limiting their standalone discriminative ability [1,5].

Instead, spectral features, particularly MFCCs [6], have shown greater robustness in detecting spoofed speech. MFCCs simulate the human auditory system and can capture the subtle spectral cues often lost or distorted in synthetic speech. When combined with delta and delta-delta features, MFCCs provide a more comprehensive representation of temporal dynamics. Constant Q Cepstral Coefficients (CQCCs) [7]and modulation-based features such as instantaneous amplitude and frequency (IA/IF) [8] have shown promise in replay and synthetic attack detection.

More recent approaches employ deep learning, including CNNs, ResNets, and transformer-based models, which automatically learn hierarchical representations of real vs. cloned speech. For example, Abdulla and Moosa [9] developed a CNN-based model capable of distinguishing cloned voices using spectrogram inputs, achieving high accuracy across clean and noisy conditions. Other work, like AASIST (Audio Anti-Spoofing using Integrated Spectro-Temporal Features) [10]and RawNet2 [11], uses raw waveform inputs and attention modules to further improve detection performance, especially under real-world conditions and unseen attack types [12].

Despite various reported works, there is a notable lack of research addressing Indian languages in the area of voice cloning detection is concerned. This study develops and evaluates a system specifically tailored for Marathi, an Indian language that remains underexplored in this domain. The system combines MFCC-based spectral analysis with GMM for classification. While exploratory features such as pitch and formants are considered for comparative analysis, the emphasis is placed on MFCC due to its proven effectiveness in capturing spectral patterns relevant to speaker identity. Additionally, voice quality features like jitter and shimmer were investigated to distinguish cloned from original voices

## 2   Methodology

The proposed study outlines a structured framework for detecting cloned voices in the Marathi language by integrating acoustic signal processing with statistical pattern recognition methods. As illustrated in Fig. 1, the methodology comprises four main stages: data collection, voice cloning, signal preprocessing, and acoustic-computational analysis.

### 2.1   Data Acquisition and Generation of Cloned Voice

Voice samples were collected from 50 student participants at the Government Institute of Forensic Science, Chhatrapati Sambhajinagar (MS), India, following informed consent. Each participant provided a read speech by reading a predefined paragraph in Marathi. Audio was captured using the Zoom R8 multitrack

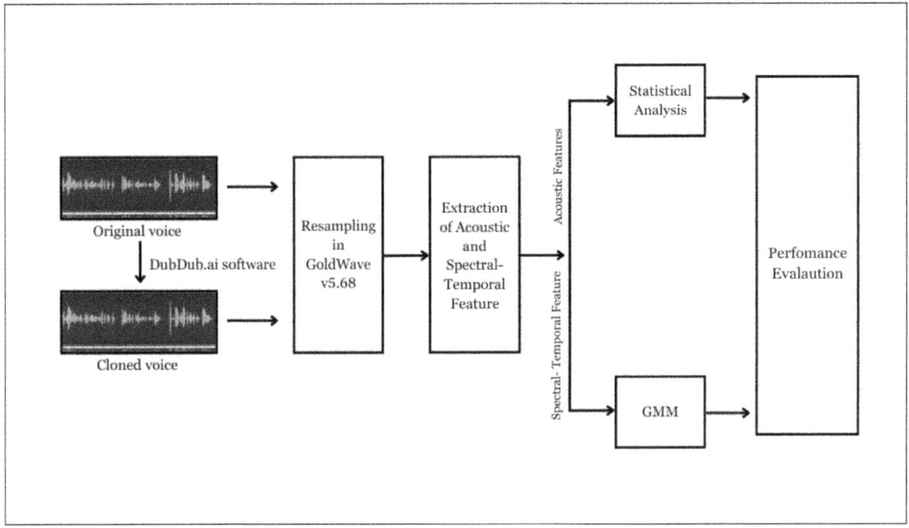


**Fig. 1.** Schematic diagram of proposed methodology.

recorder at a sampling rate of 44.1 kHz. Original voice samples were uploaded to DubDub.ai [13] to generate their corresponding cloned versions.

To ensure consistency in subsequent acoustic analysis, both original and cloned speech samples were resampled to a common rate of 11.025 kHz using GoldWave v5.68. [14] Additional preprocessing procedures such as noise reduction, band-pass filtering, equalization, and manual amplitude normalization were applied to minimize background noise and improve the clarity of the speech signals.

## 2.2   Features Extraction

For this study, to explore the efficiency of acoustic features for cloned voice detection, pitch, formants, jitter, and shimmer was considered for this study while MFCC was considered as spectral-temporal features.

The OT-Expert software (version 1.9.2) was used to extract the fundamental frequency (F0) to examine natural pitch variations. Praat version 6.3.12 [15] was used to extract formant frequencies F1 to F4, as well as jitter and shimmer. These acoustic features reflect the articulatory and physiological mechanisms of human speech, which are often inadequately modeled in cloned voices.

For this study, we consider MFCC and their derivatives (delta and delta-delta) as spectral-temporal features. 13 MFCC coefficients per frame was extracted. In addition to static MFCCs, dynamic derivatives such as delta ($\Delta$) and delta-delta ($\Delta \Delta$) coefficients were computed to capture temporal variations in speech patterns, which may be smoothed or absent in synthetic voices.

### 2.3 GMM Classification

Gaussian Mixture Models (GMMs) were employed as statistical classifiers to model the feature distributions of the original and cloned voices. Separate GMMs were trained on 30 original and 30 cloned samples, each using 64 components and full covariance matrices to better capture speaker variability. Test samples (40 in total) were classified using log-likelihood scores from each GMM, and a SoftMax-based confidence measure was computed.

### 2.4 Statistical Analysis

To validate acoustic differences, statistical testing was conducted. Violin plots were generated using the DATA Tab Calculator. One-way ANOVA and independent t-tests were used to determine the statistical significance of variations in pitch, formants, jitter, shimmer, and MFCC-based features using SYSTAT statistical software (version 13.2) [16] (significance level: $p < 0.05$).

### 2.5 Experimental Setup

All experiments were performed on a standard desktop machine (Intel Core i3-1115G4 @ 3.00 GHz, 8 GB RAM, Windows 64-bit). Feature extraction was implemented using Python (Librosa and SciPy). OTExpert and Praat [15] were used independently due to compatibility constraints.

## 3 Results and Discussion

A comprehensive set of acoustic and spectral-temporal features was extracted from original and cloned Marathi speech samples to detect synthetic voice characteristics. The analyzed parameters included pitch, formant frequencies (F1–F4), jitter, shimmer, and MFCC-based features (including delta and delta-delta derivatives). The results indicate that while cloned voices effectively replicate superficial prosodic cues, deeper spectral and temporal parameters reveal consistent and measurable deviations from natural speech, which can be exploited for forensic detection.

The mean and median pitch values were computed separately for male and female speakers. For female voices, the mean pitch yielded a p-value of 0.7022 and the median pitch 0.9837, while for male voices, the mean and median pitch values produced p-values of 0.5399 and 0.9837, respectively. These results indicate no statistically significant differences between original and cloned voices across genders. This suggests that pitch alone cannot reliably discriminate between genuine and synthetic speech. The findings align with prior studies by Ogihara et al. (2005) [1] and Wu et al. (2015) [17], which reported that modern voice synthesis systems can reproduce natural pitch patterns, making it an ineffective standalone marker in forensic applications. While pitch provides a coarse prosodic cue, it lacks sensitivity to fine temporal and spectral irregularities that are often introduced during cloning.

Formant frequencies (F1–F4) were extracted using Praat to analyze resonance characteristics of the vocal tract. F1 exhibited statistically significant shifts for both male (p = 0.0008) and female (p = 0.00004) voices, highlighting its reliability as a gender-independent discriminator. F2 and F4 were significant for female voices (p = 0.0027 and p = 0.0394, respectively), while F3 did not show significant differences (p= 0.120015). These results suggest that F1 captures key spectral changes due to synthesis artifacts, such as resonance flattening or over smoothing. The selective significance of F2 and F4 in female voices indicates that synthesis may differentially affect higher formants depending on vocal characteristics, emphasizing the importance of multi-formant analysis in forensic investigations. Overall, formant analysis provides an interpretable and statistically validated cue for detecting synthetic speech, complementing other acoustic parameters.

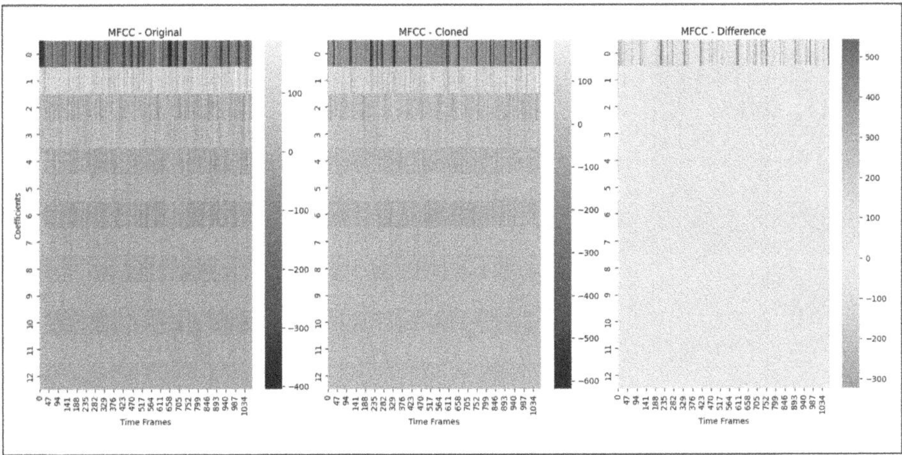

**Fig. 2.** MFCC heatmap showing natural variation in original voice vs. smoothed patterns in cloned voice.

Jitter and shimmer quantify short-term variations in Pitch and amplitude, reflecting voice stability and natural variability. For female speakers, both jitter (p = 3.15 $\times 10^{-7}$) and shimmer (p = 0.00129) were significantly different between the original and cloned voices, with synthetic voices exhibiting smoother and more regular patterns. In male voices, however, these parameters were not statistically significant (jitter: p = 0.1367, shimmer: p = 0.105), suggesting that perturbation features may be less sensitive to cloned male voices. The differences in female voices are consistent with the notion that synthetic systems often impose artificial regularity, reducing micro-variations in amplitude and frequency. Therefore, jitter and shimmer remain valuable complementary features for voice clone detection, particularly in female speech.

### 3.1   MFCC and Temporal Derivative Features

For evaluation, the system was tested on 40 previously unseen speech samples (20 original and 20 cloned). Of these, 32 samples were correctly classified, yielding an overall accuracy of 80%. The confidence scores observed during classification ranged between 65% and 85%.

MFCCs were computed to capture the spectral envelope and timbral structure of the speech samples. Original voices exhibited rich, irregular spectral transitions, while cloned voices displayed flattened and overly smoothed patterns, with darker regions in the heatmaps indicating lower spectral energy. These differences, as seen in Fig. 2, suggest that MFCCs effectively capture fine-grained spectral variations present in natural speech but often lost in vocoder-based synthesis, making them a reliable feature for distinguishing between genuine and cloned voices.

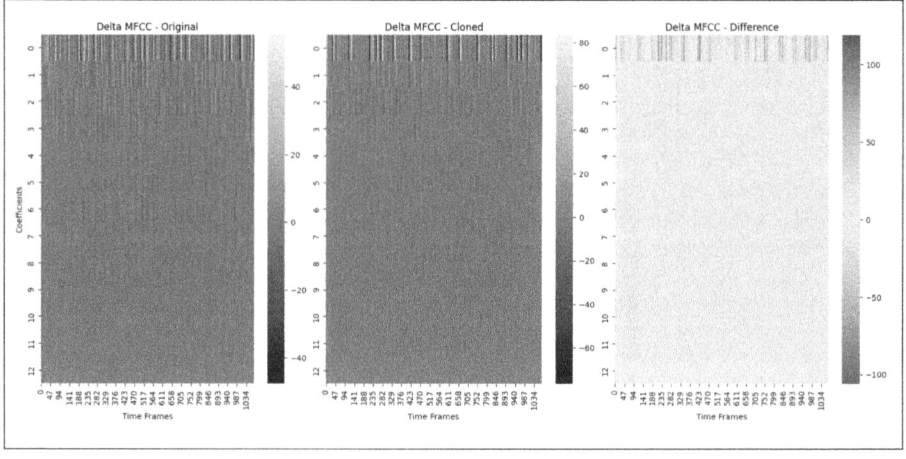

**Fig. 3.** Delta MFCC highlighting dynamic transitions in the original and uniform changes in the cloned voice.

Delta MFCCs, representing the rate of change of spectral coefficients over time, revealed sharp and dynamic transitions in original speech, reflecting natural phoneme articulation and coarticulation. In contrast, cloned voices showed smoother, more uniform trajectories, indicating reduced temporal variation. These patterns, as seen in Fig. 3, demonstrate that delta features are sensitive to temporal dynamics, providing complementary discriminatory power to static MFCCs and highlighting the limitations of synthetic voice generation in reproducing natural speech dynamics.

Delta-delta MFCCs, which measure the acceleration of spectral changes, showed nonlinear and unpredictable patterns in original voices, consistent with natural prosody and expressive modulation. Cloned voices, however, exhibited

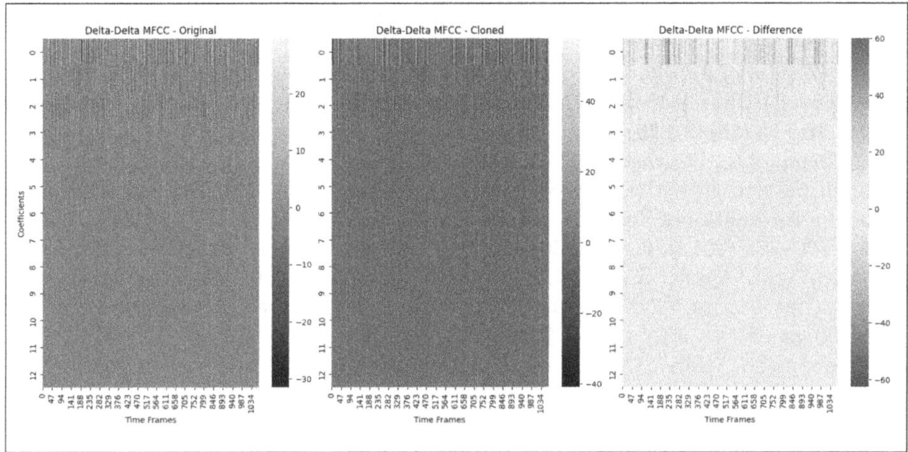

**Fig. 4.** Delta-Delta MFCC showing irregular acceleration in original vs. flat pattern in cloned voice.

flat and repetitive acceleration patterns, reflecting synthesis artifacts and a lack of natural temporal expressiveness. These differences, as seen in Fig. 4, confirm that delta-delta features provide additional robustness for detecting synthetic speech, capturing higher-order temporal variations that static and delta MFCCs alone may not reveal.

## 4    Conclusion and Future Work

This study presents a comprehensive and explainable framework for detecting cloned speech in the Marathi language using acoustic and spectral-temporal features. By integrating MFCC, their delta and delta-delta derivatives, and GMM-based classification, the system effectively identified cloned voices. Acoustic features such as formants, jitter, and shimmer provided supportive cues, with the F1 formant showing consistent significance across genders. However, it was the dynamic behavior of MFCC-based features captured through visual heatmaps and statistical differences that offered the most reliable distinction between genuine and synthetic speech samples.

Future work focus on expanding the dataset with more diverse and real-world voice samples, and to apply deep learning based methods.

## References


1. Ogihara, A., Shiozaki, A.: Discrimination Method of Synthetic Speech Using Pitch Frequency Against Synthetic Speech Falsification (2005)
2. Li, M., Ahmadiadli, Y., Zhang, X.-P.: Audio anti-spoofing detection: a survey (2024)

3. Van Den Oord, A., et al.: WaveNet: A Generative Model for Raw Audio. London, UK (2016)

4. Qiu, Z., Tang, J., Zhang, Y., Li, J., Bai, X.: A voice cloning method based on the improved HiFi-GAN model. Comput. Intell. Neurosci. 2022 (2022). https://doi.org/10.1155/2022/6707304

5. De Leon, P.L., Stewart, B., Yamagishi, J.: Synthetic speech discrimination using pitch pattern statistics derived from image analysis. In: 13th Annual Conference of the International Speech Communication Association (INTERSPEECH 2012), pp. 370–373 (2012). https://doi.org/10.21437/interspeech.2012-135

6. Wani, T.M., Qadri, S.A.A., Comminiello, D., Amerini, I.: Detecting audio deepfakes: integrating CNN and BiLSTM with multi-feature concatenation. In: Proceedings of the 2024 ACM Workshop on Information Hiding and Multimedia Security (IH MMSec 2024), pp. 271–276. ACM (2024). https://doi.org/10.1145/3658664.3659647

7. Jia, Y., et al.: Transfer Learning from Speaker Verification to Multispeaker Text-to-Speech Synthesis (2019)

8. Kamble, M.R., Patil, H.A.: Novel variable length energy separation algorithm using instantaneous amplitude features for replay detection. In: Proceedings of INTERSPEECH 2018, pp. 646–650. International Speech Communication Association (2018). https://doi.org/10.21437/Interspeech.2018-1687

9. Abdulla, H.A., Abdulla, A.I., Moosa, J.: Voice cloning detection using deep learning. In: 2024 International Conference on IT Innovation and Knowledge Discovery (ITIKD), pp. 1–6 (2025). https://doi.org/10.1109/ITIKD63574.2025.11005188

10. Jung, J.-W., et al.: AASIST: audio anti-spoofing using integrated spectro-temporal graph attention networks. In: ICASSP 2022 - IEEE International Conference on Acoustics, Speech and Signal Processing, pp. 2367–6371. IEEE, Singapore (2022). https://doi.org/10.1109/ICASSP43922.2022.9747766

11. Tak, H., Patino, J., Todisco, M., Nautsch, A., Evans, N., Larcher, A.: End-to-end anti-spoofing with RawNet2. In: ICASSP 2021 - IEEE International Conference on Acoustics, Speech and Signal Processing (ICASSP), p. 6369. EURECOM, Sophia Antipolis, France; LIUM - Université du Maine, Le Mans, France (2021). https://doi.org/10.48550/arXiv.2011.01108

12. Jung, J., et al.: AASIST: audio anti-spoofing using integrated spectro-temporal graph attention networks. In: ICASSP 2022 - IEEE International Conference on Acoustics, Speech and Signal Processing, pp. 6367–6371 (2022). https://doi.org/10.1109/ICASSP43922.2022.9747766

13. DubDub.AI: AI Dubbing and Voice Cloning Platform. https://dubdub.ai/, last Accessed 07 Oct 2025

14. GoldWave Inc.: GoldWave. https://goldwave.com/, last Accessed 07 Oct 2025

15. Boersma, P., Weenink, D.: Praat: Doing Phonetics by Computer. http://www.praat.org/, last Accessed 07 Oct 2025

16. Systat Software Inc.: SYSTAT 13.2. https://grafiti.com/product/systat-v13-2/, last Accessed 08 Oct 2025

17. Wu, Z., Evans, N., Kinnunen, T., Yamagishi, J., Alegre, F., Li, H.: Spoofing and countermeasures for speaker verification: a survey. Speech Commun. 66, 130–153 (2015). https://doi.org/10.1016/j.specom.2014.10.005

# A Low-Cost, Language-Independent Framework for Mild Cognitive Impairment Detection Using Speech Signals

Rishabh[1]($\boxtimes$) iD, Dhirendra Kumar[2] iD, Yogendra Meena[3] iD, and Kuldeep Singh[1] iD

[1] Department of Computer Science, University of Delhi, New Delhi, India
{rishabh,ksingh}@cs.du.ac.in
[2] Department of Applied Mathematics, Delhi Technological University, New Delhi, India
dhirendrakumar@dtu.ac.in
[3] School of Computer and Systems Sciences, Jawaharlal Nehru University, New Delhi, India
yogendra@mail.jnu.ac.in

**Abstract.** Mild Cognitive Impairment (MCI), an early stage of dementia including Alzheimer's disease, is often marked by memory deficits, speech impairments, and reduced reasoning ability. Speech analysis offers a promising, non-invasive tool for early detection of cognitive decline. However, existing approaches typically rely on pre-trained models, language-specific models, or transcription-based features, limiting their applicability in multilingual and low-resource settings. In this study, we introduce a novel, low-cost framework that eliminates the need for transcriptions or pre-trained language models by leveraging only 14 carefully selected, language-independent acoustic features. These features capture prosodic, phonatory, and temporal speech characteristics known to correlate with cognitive decline and are consistent across both English and Chinese speech. The proposed model trained using traditional machine learning algorithms is highly efficient, requiring approximately 14 s for training, making it well-suited for scalable deployment. Evaluated on the bilingual TAUKADIAL dataset, our framework achieves an unweighted average recall (UAR) of 68.36% for MCI classification and a root mean squared error (RMSE) of 2.59 for MMSE score prediction. The results highlight the framework's cross-linguistic generalizability, computational efficiency, and clinical potential for accessible cognitive assessment.

**Keywords:** Mild Cognitive Impairment · Speech Analysis · Acoustic Features · Language-Independent Features · Cognitive Assessment · TAUKADIAL

## 1 Introduction

Alzheimer's disease (AD) is an irreversible neurodegenerative disorder that leads to progressive brain deterioration. In addition to memory impairment, it is characterized by a decline in various cognitive functions. Without the development of an effective cure or preventive measures, it is projected that approximately 14 million individuals in the United States will be affected by AD by the year 2050 [16]. Mild Cognitive

© The Author(s), under exclusive license to Springer Nature Switzerland AG 2026
S. Mitra et al. (Eds.): PReMI 2025, LNCS 16358, pp. 813–821, 2026.
https://doi.org/10.1007/978-3-032-18480-1_83

Impairment (MCI) is an early stage of dementia, including AD, characterized by minor problems with memory loss, speech, language impairment, and reasoning difficulties. Early detection of MCI is critical, allowing for timely intervention and improvements in quality of life and enabling cohort enrichment towards the understanding of pathology and the development of therapeutical approaches.

The detection of MCI and AD via speech recordings has drawn growing research interest, focusing on linguistic, acoustic, and cognitive aspects. A key approach involves domain adaptation (DA) to enhance cross-domain generalization. Farzana et al. [6] showed DA's effectiveness by leveraging linguistic features from diverse spoken datasets. Similarly, the ADReSS-M Challenge [22] explored acoustic and linguistic features by integrating pre-trained multilingual Automatic Speech Recognition (ASR) to address language variability in dementia detection. Hajjar et al. [12] applied digital voice biomarkers to detect cognitive decline and track AD progression. Multimodal and ensemble methods further improved outcomes. Sarawgi et al. [26] developed an ensemble model combining acoustic, cognitive, and linguistic features through neural networks with temporal modeling, achieving strong results in AD classification and Mini-Mental State Examination (MMSE) prediction. Gosztolya et al. [11] used ASR-derived acoustic and linguistic features with a Support Vector Machine, showing the value of traditional ML in dementia diagnostics.

Current clinical assessments of MCI rely on brain imaging, cognitive and neurological exams [3], genetic testing, and biomarker analysis [2]. MRI-based studies use convolutional neural networks [27] and extract features like voxel and vertex details [15]. However, such methods are costly and often impractical for wide deployment, prompting a need for scalable, low-cost diagnostic alternatives [19]. Given dementia's rising prevalence and economic impact, early cognitive impairment detection is now a major healthcare priority. Speech, as an accessible behavioral marker of cognition, offers promise for scalable diagnosis [9]. While recent work [6, 11, 22, 26] has focused on multimodal models using language-dependent features. However, these approaches may be constrained by linguistic variability and dataset limitations.

To address these challenges, we propose a language-independent framework for MCI detection, aiming to enhance cross-linguistic adaptability and broaden the applicability of speech-based cognitive assessment methods. In this study, we make the following key contributions:

1. We propose a low-cost, language-independent framework for classifying MCI with Normal Cognition (NC), as well as predicting MMSE scores using only acoustic features.
2. We conduct a detailed analysis of 14 handcrafted features encompassing acoustic, prosodic, voice quality, temporal, and phonetic features relevant to MCI.
3. We demonstrate the cross-linguistic generalizability of the proposed method through cross-language evaluation, wherein models trained on one language (English or Chinese) are tested on the other.

## 2  Methodology

The proposed methodology comprises three key stages: Dataset Selection, Feature Extraction, and Model Selection. We employ the TAUKADIAL dataset [20], which includes both English and Chinese speech samples. To build a low-cost, language-independent model, we manually curated 14 cognitively and clinically relevant non-linguistic features covering acoustic, prosodic, voice quality, temporal, and phonetic aspects without relying on transcriptions, all of which are known to be impacted by MCI. This compact, interpretable, and domain-informed feature set supports scalable deployment in multilingual and resource-limited settings. The extracted features are then used to train machine learning models for MCI classification and MMSE score prediction. Figure 1 illustrates the overall architecture.

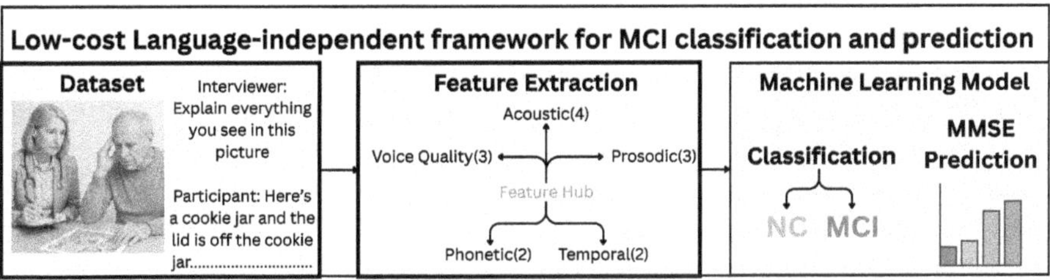


**Fig. 1.** Architectural diagram of the proposed low-cost, language-independent framework for MCI diagnosis and MMSE score prediction.

### 2.1 Dataset

This study uses the TAUKADIAL dataset [20], comprising 507 English and Chinese speech samples from picture description tasks by participants aged 60–90. They are classified as MCI or NC. The dataset is age- and gender-balanced and includes 246 English and 261 Chinese samples, totaling 528 min.

### 2.2 Feature Extraction

Language-independent features were extracted from raw speech, including acoustic, prosodic, voice quality, temporal, and phonetic features. These audio-based markers are chosen for their cognitive relevance and cost-effectiveness. A summary of the features is provided below:

1. **Acoustic Features**
   (a) Mean Pitch ($F_0$): It represents vocal cord vibration rate, linked to vocal tension and identity; averaged over voiced segments.
   (b) Jitter: It measures pitch instability using relative differences in consecutive pitch periods [18].
   (c) Shimmer: It quantifies amplitude fluctuations via RMS energy differences across glottal cycles [18].
   (d) Harmonic to Noise Ratio (HNR): It indicates voice clarity by comparing harmonic to noise energy [18].

2. **Prosodic Features**
   (a) Speech Rate: It calculated as total duration divided by number of pauses; lower rates suggest cognitive difficulty [7].
   (b) Number of Pauses: Silent regions >0.5 sec detected via amplitude threshold; increased pauses imply impaired fluency [7].
   (c) Average Pause Duration: Mean pause length, where longer pauses reflect cognitive load or hesitation [7].
3. **Voice Quality Features**
   (a) Tremor: Normalized pitch variation, indicative of neuromuscular or vocal control issues [23].
   (b) Breathiness: Approximated as the inverse of HNR; signals inefficient vocal fold closure and airflow issues.
   (c) Vocal Fry: Low-frequency, irregular phonation (20–75 Hz); may reflect relaxed or pathological speech.
4. **Temporal Features**
   (a) Segment Duration: Total duration based on sample count and sampling rate; used to normalize speech metrics.
   (b) Speech to Pause Ratio: It indicates the duration of spoken content relative to pauses.
5. **Phonetic Features**
   (a) Vowel Space Area (VSA): It is the product of $F_1$ and $F_2$ formants; assesses articulatory precision [17].
   (b) Phoneme Duration Variability: It captures rhythmic consistency through variability in phoneme length.

### 2.3   Machine Learning Model

In this study, we are addressing the classification of MCI with NC, and the prediction of MMSE score. Classification experiments were conducted using six distinct classification algorithms from scikit-learn library, i.e., Logistic Regression (LR) [5], Naive Bayes (NB) [25], Decision Tree (DT) [25], Random Forest (RF) [4], Gradient Boosting (GB) [4], and AdaBoost (AB) [8]. Prediction experiments were conducted by using five distinct regression algorithms, namely Linear Regression (Lin-R) [13], DT, RF, GB, and AB.

## 3   Experiments

In this section, we outline the evaluation metrics, experimental setup and results obtained. Additionally, we emperically investigate the following scenarios:

1. Investigate into determining the relevent language independent features.
2. Training on data of one language and testing on another to validate language independent model.

### 3.1  Experimental Setup and Metrics

We evaluated our classification and prediction model on TAUKADIAL dataset. 10-fold cross-validation was applied on training data, and model was evaluated on testing data, with 80-20 train-test split. The experiments were conducted using scikit-learn on a machine equipped with an AMD Ryzen 9 6000HX processor @3.30GHz CPU with 16 GB RAM, and an NVIDIA graphics RTX 3080. Following the TAUKADIAL challenge, we evaluated our model using unweighted average recall (UAR) and F1-score for classification, and root mean square energy (RMSE) and $R^2$ for MMSE score prediction

### 3.2  Ablation Study

We conducted two key experiments to evaluate the effectiveness and generalizability of the proposed framework.

First, Table 1 presents the results of the MCI vs. NC classification task using 14 carefully selected language-independent acoustic features across multiple machine learning algorithms. Among these, the Random Forest classifier achieved the best classification performance with a UAR of 68.36%, demonstrating the strong discriminative capability of the audio-based feature set for cognitive impairment detection. For MMSE score prediction, gradient boosting achieved the lowest RMSE of 2.59, highlighting the predictive strength of the same feature set. The relative contribution of individual features is visualized in Fig. 2, where shimmer, vowel space area, and average pause duration emerged as the most influential features. This ranking aligns with prior evidence that vocal instability, articulatory undershoot, and prolonged pausing are early indicators of cognitive decline, reflecting deficits in motor control and speech planning.

Second, to assess the framework's language independence, we performed a cross-lingual ablation study. As shown in Table 2, models were trained on one language (English or Chinese) and tested on the other. The AdaBoost classifier achieved a UAR of 55.03% when trained on English and tested on Chinese, and 55.27% when trained on Chinese and tested on English. These consistent cross-language results validate the robustness and generalizability of the proposed feature set and framework, confirming its suitability for multilingual and low-resource settings.

Together, these evaluations confirm that the proposed language-independent acoustic features not only perform competitively in within-language scenarios but also generalize well across languages, supporting scalable deployment for speech-based cognitive assessment.

### 3.3  Results and Discussion

We evaluated the proposed framework on the TAUKADIAL dataset, which includes 506 bilingual speech samples (English and Chinese). A set of 14 handcrafted, language-independent features spanning acoustic, prosodic, temporal, phonetic, and voice quality domains was extracted to capture speech markers relevant to cognitive decline. These features were used to train several traditional machine learning models for both classification (MCI vs. NC) and regression (MMSE score prediction) tasks. For MCI classification, the best-performing model achieved an UAR of 68.36%, F1-score of 62.65%,

**Table 1.** Classification (UAR, F1-score) and MMSE prediction (RMSE, $R^2$) results using language-independent acoustic features on the 80-20 train-test split.

| Algorithm | UAR | F1-score | RMSE | $R^2$ |
|---|---|---|---|---|
| LR / Lin-R [5, 13] | 63.33% | 59.34% | 3.27 | 0.06 |
| NB [25] | 49.12% | 52.63% | – | – |
| DT [25] | 51.40% | 46.15% | 3.36 | 0.01 |
| RF [4] | **68.36%** | **62.65%** | 2.66 | 0.37 |
| GB [4] | 60.00% | 54.54% | **2.59** | **0.41** |
| AB [8] | 60.93% | 58.33% | 2.62 | 0.40 |

**Table 2.** Validation of the language-independent model through cross-linguistic evaluation by training on English data and testing on Chinese data, and vice versa. Additionally, the model was evaluated within the same language by training and testing on English data as well as on Chinese data.

| Algorithm | Split | UAR | F1-score | RMSE | $R^2$ |
|---|---|---|---|---|---|
| LR / Lin-R [5, 13] | Train English, Test Chinese | 50.96% | 27.42% | 0.54 | -0.01 |
| | Train Chinese, Test English | 50.96% | 44.23% | 0.54 | -0.27 |
| | Train English, Test English | 56.66% | 31.57% | 0.51 | -0.07 |
| | Train Chinese, Test Chinese | 56.90% | 55.17% | 0.53 | -0.14 |
| NB [25] | Train English, Test Chinese | 51.06% | **54.92%** | – | – |
| | Train Chinese, Test English | 47.65% | 44.44% | – | – |
| | Train English, Test English | **65.00%** | **65.57%** | – | – |
| | Train Chinese, Test Chinese | 62.45% | 62.29% | – | – |
| DT [25] | Train English, Test Chinese | 51.76% | 52.98% | 0.69 | -0.90 |
| | Train Chinese, Test English | 47.53% | 39.23% | 0.71 | -1.19 |
| | Train English, Test English | 53.33% | 50.00% | 0.68 | -0.86 |
| | Train Chinese, Test Chinese | 52.35% | 52.45% | 0.69 | -0.95 |
| RF [4] | Train English, Test Chinese | 53.69% | 35.48% | **0.52** | -0.01 |
| | Train Chinese, Test English | 52.37% | 45.87% | 0.52 | -0.19 |
| | Train English, Test English | 60.00% | 42.85% | 0.53 | -0.13 |
| | Train Chinese, Test Chinese | 56.22% | 51.85% | 0.52 | -0.10 |
| **GB** [4] | Train English, Test Chinese | 51.11% | 39.23% | 0.55 | -0.01 |
| | Train Chinese, Test English | 53.00% | 47.32% | 0.56 | -0.35 |
| | Train English, Test English | 56.66% | 48.00% | 0.54 | -0.18 |
| | Train Chinese, Test Chinese | 61.78% | 59.64% | **0.40** | -0.15 |
| **AB** [8] | Train English, Test Chinese | **55.03%** | 48.45% | **0.52** | 0.02 |
| | Train Chinese, Test English | **55.27%** | **49.77%** | **0.50** | -0.08 |
| | Train English, Test English | 56.66% | 51.85% | **0.50** | -0.02 |
| | Train Chinese, Test Chinese | **65.15%** | **63.15%** | 0.51 | -0.09 |

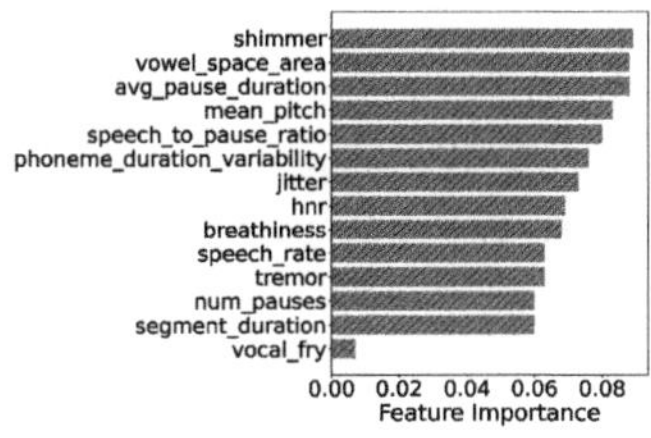


**Fig. 2.** Feature importance for Mild Cognitive Impairment diagnosis with language-independent features.

accuracy of 69.60%, sensitivity of 57.78%, and specificity of 78.94%. For MMSE prediction, the model attained a RMSE of 2.59 and an $R^2$ score of 0.41, indicating reasonable predictive capability from speech alone. Cross-language evaluations further validated the framework's language independence. Since the feature set is compact (14 dimensions) and was deliberately curated for clinical interpretability, we did not apply dimensionality reduction techniques (e.g., PCA, LASSO), which could obscure the contribution of individual features and add unnecessary complexity. The 10-fold cross-validation using Random Forest completed in just 14.88 s on a standard CPU, highlighting the framework's computational efficiency and suitability for real-time, low-resource deployment. Table 3 presents a comparative summary against existing state-of-the-art methods.

**Table 3.** Performance comparison of the proposed method with existing approaches for MCI classification and MMSE score prediction on the TAUKADIAL dataset.

| Reference | Method | Accuracy | Sensitivity | Specificity | UAR | F1-score | RMSE |
|---|---|---|---|---|---|---|---|
| Baseline [21] | w2v + eGeMAPs | 59.20% | 58.7% | 59.7% | 59.18% | 60.20% | 2.89 |
| [24] | Multimodal | – | – | – | 56.18% | – | **2.50** |
| [14] | Multimodals | 45.1% | – | – | – | – | 2.57 |
| [10] | wav2vec2 | – | – | – | 49.4% | 56.5% | 2.60 |
| [1] | Language Agnostic | 61.2% | 62.0% | 61.2% | 61.6% | 56.6% | 2.58 |
| **Proposed  Method** | Acoustic + Random Forest | **69.60%** | 57.78% | **78.94%** | **68.36%** | **62.65%** | 2.59 |

## 4   Conclusion

This study introduces a low-cost, language-independent framework for MCI detection and MMSE score prediction using 14 handcrafted acoustic features capturing prosodic, phonetic, voice quality, and temporal characteristics. The Random Forest achieved a UAR of 68.36% for MCI classification. MMSE prediction with gradient boosting achieved an RMSE of 2.59, demonstrating the effectiveness of the proposed feature set. Cross-linguistic evaluations further confirmed the framework's generalizability, with

UARs of 55.03% and 55.27% when training and testing across English and Chinese. Although cross-language performance is lower, the results highlight the robustness and potential of this approach for multilingual and low-resource scenarios. Future work will focus on expanding the dataset to enhance performance and facilitate broader deployment.

# References


1. Agbavor, F., Liang, H.: Multilingual prediction of cognitive impairment with large language models and speech analysis. Brain Sci. **14**(12), 1292 (2024). https://doi.org/10.3390/brainsci14121292
2. Alberdi, A., Aztiria, A., Basarab, A.: On the early diagnosis of alzheimer's disease from multimodal signals: a survey. Artif. Intell. Med. **71**, 1–29 (2016). https://doi.org/10.1016/j.artmed.2016.06.003
3. Anderson, N.D.: State of the science on mild cognitive impairment (MCI). CNS Spectr. **24**(1), 78–87 (2019). https://doi.org/10.1017/S1092852918001347
4. Breiman, L.: Random forests. Mach. Learn. **45**(1), 5–32 (2001). https://doi.org/10.1023/A:1010933404324
5. Cessie, S.l., Houwelingen, J.V.: Ridge estimators in logistic regression. J. Roy. Stat. Soc. Ser. C (Appl. Stat.) **41**(1), 191–201 (1992)
6. Farzana, S., Parde, N.: Towards domain-agnostic and domain-adaptive dementia detection from spoken language, pp. 11965–11978. Association for Computational Linguistics, Toronto, Canada (Jul 2023). https://doi.org/10.18653/v1/2023.acl-long.668
7. Frederique Gayraud, H.R.L., Barkat-Defradas, M.: Syntactic and lexical context of pauses and hesitations in the discourse of alzheimer patients and healthy elderly subjects. Clin. Linguist. Phonetics **25**(3), 198–209 (2011). https://doi.org/10.3109/02699206.2010.521612
8. Freund, Y., et al.: Experiments with a new boosting algorithm. In: ICML. vol. 96, pp. 148–156. Citeseer (1996)
9. de la Fuente Garcia, S., Ritchie, C.W., Luz, S.: Artificial intelligence, speech, and language processing approaches to monitoring alzheimer's disease: a systematic review. J. Alzheimer's Dis. **78**(4), 1547–1574 (2020). https://doi.org/10.3233/JAD-200888
10. Gosztolya, G., Tóth, L.: Combining acoustic feature sets for detecting mild cognitive impairment in the interspeech'24 taukadial challenge. In: Interspeech 2024, pp. 957–961 (2024).https://doi.org/10.21437/Interspeech.2024-984
11. Gosztolya, G., Vincze, V., Tóth, L., Pákáski, M., Kálmán, J., Hoffmann, I.: Identifying mild cognitive impairment and mild Alzheimer's disease based on spontaneous speech using ASR and linguistic features. Comput. Speech Lang. **53**, 181–197 (2019). https://doi.org/10.1016/j.csl.2018.07.007
12. Hajjar, I., et al.: Development of digital voice biomarkers and associations with cognition, cerebrospinal biomarkers, and neural representation in early Alzheimer's disease. Alzheimer's Dement: Diagn. Assess. Dis. Monit. **15**(1), e12393 (2023). https://doi.org/10.1002/dad2.12393
13. Han, J., Pei, J., Tong, H.: Data mining: concepts and techniques. Morgan kaufmann (2022)
14. Hoang, B., Pang, Y., Dodge, H., Zhou, J.: Translingual language markers for cognitive assessment from spontaneous speech. In: Interspeech 2024, pp. 977–981 (2024). https://doi.org/10.21437/Interspeech.2024-1422
15. Hämäläinen, A., et al.: Voxel-based morphometry to detect brain atrophy in progressive mild cognitive impairment. Neuroimage **37**(4), 1122–1131 (2007). https://doi.org/10.1016/j.neuroimage.2007.06.016

16. Illinois Department of Public Health: Top 10 causes of death among men. Accessed 19 Jan 2025
17. Kent, R.D., Kim, Y.: Toward an acoustic typology of motor speech disorders. Clin. Linguist. Phonetics **17**(6), 427–445 (2003). https://doi.org/10.1080/0269920031000086248, pMID: 14564830
18. Lee, J., et al.: Exploring voice acoustic features associated with cognitive status in Korean speakers: a preliminary machine learning study. Diagnostics **14**(24) (2024). https://doi.org/10.3390/diagnostics14242837
19. Li, R., Wang, X., Lawler, K., Garg, S., Bai, Q., Alty, J.: Applications of artificial intelligence to aid early detection of dementia: a scoping review on current capabilities and future directions. J. Biomed. Inform. **127**, 104030 (2022). https://doi.org/10.1016/j.jbi.2022.104030
20. Luz, S., et al.: Connected speech-based cognitive assessment in Chinese and English (2024)
21. Luz, S., et al.: Connected speech-based cognitive assessment in Chinese and English (2024). https://arxiv.org/abs/2406.10272
22. Luz, S., Haider, F., Fromm, D., Lazarou, I., Kompatsiaris, I., MacWhinney, B.: An overview of the address-m signal processing grand challenge on multilingual Alzheimer's dementia recognition through spontaneous speech. IEEE Open J. Signal Process. **5**, 738–749 (2024). https://doi.org/10.1109/OJSP.2024.3378595
23. Mahon, E., Lachman, M.E.: Voice biomarkers as indicators of cognitive changes in middle and later adulthood. Neurobiol. Aging **119**, 22–35 (2022). https://doi.org/10.1016/j.neurobiolaging.2022.06.010
24. Ortiz-Perez, D., Garcia-Rodriguez, J., Tomás, D.: Cognitive insights across languages: enhancing multimodal interview analysis. In: Interspeech 2024. pp. 952–956 (2024). https://doi.org/10.21437/Interspeech.2024-914
25. Salzberg, S.L.: C4.5: programs for machine learning by J. Ross Quinlan. Morgan Kaufmann Publishers, Inc., 1993. Machine Learning **16**(3), 235–240 (1994). https://doi.org/10.1007/BF00993309
26. Sarawgi, U., Zulfikar, W., Soliman, N., Maes, P.: Multimodal inductive transfer learning for detection of Alzheimer's dementia and its severity (2020)
27. Zheng, C., Xia, Y., Pan, Y., Chen, J.: Automated identification of dementia using medical imaging: a survey from a pattern classification perspective. Brain Inform. **3**(1), 17–27 (2016). https://doi.org/10.1007/s40708-015-0027-x

# Affective Profiling in Indian Speech Using Analytic Signal-Matched Filter Bank Features and Valence–Arousal–Dominance Mapping


Geetanjali Srivastava[✉], Girish Wamanrao Sursakar, and Priyanka Jain

Neurocognitive AI and XR Group, CDAC Delhi, New Delhi, India
dr.geetanjali@outlook.com, {girishs,priyankaj}@cdac.in



**Abstract.** This study presents a multi-view learning framework for speech emotion recognition (SER) based affective profiling in Indian speech data by introducing analytic signal matched filter bank (ASMFB) features. We explore categorical emotion classification and dimensional emotion representation using the valencearousaldominance (VAD) model. A lightweight convolutional neural network (CNN) is trained on features extracted using ASMFB, which captures timefrequency information relevant for emotional expression in speech. The model predicts one of five emotion classes–happy, sad, fear, surprise, and neutral, and these are then mapped to fixed VAD values derived from standardized psychological resources.

To ensure cultural and acoustic relevance, we use the Indian Emotional Speech Corpus, a dataset where speakers express different emotions using the same utterances. The framework supports both discrete and continuous affect modeling and includes visualizations such as 2D and 3D VAD scatter plots and emotional trajectory curves over time. By integrating emotion classification and VAD mapping in a single pipeline, this work offers a practical and interpretable approach to SER for Indian speech, with potential applications in affective computing, emotion-aware systems, and real-world audio analytics.

Our model achieved a classification accuracy of 89.87% and an average VAD distance (error) of 0.0308, showing a strong ability to accurately recognize the emotional tone of speech based on arousal, valence and dominance. Compared to previous studies, this result marks a clear improvement over earlier studies. These findings suggest that our approach is not only reliable but also more precise in modeling the subtle emotional dimensions present in human speech.

**Keywords:** Convolution neural networks · Audio analysis · SER · Valence arousal dominance · Multirate Filter Banks




S. Mitra et al. (Eds.): PReMI 2025, LNCS 16358, pp. 822–831, 2026.
https://doi.org/10.1007/978-3-032-18480-1_84

# 1   Introduction

The ability to recognize emotions and sentiments from speech has garnered significant attention across diverse fields like computer vision, speech processing, natural language processing, etc., for many decades. Traditionally, emotion recognition in speech has often focused on classifying discrete emotional states such as happiness, sadness, or anger. Sentiment analysis, a related task, typically categorizes spoken expressions into positive, negative, or neutral polarities. While these categorical approaches have proven useful, they often fail to capture the inherent complexity and continuous nature of human emotional experience [1,2].

To address this limitation, researchers have also explored representing emotions in a continuous dimensional space. The Valence-Arousal-Dominance (VAD) model, particularly Russell's circumplex model of affect [4], posits that emotional states can be effectively described along dimensions of pleasantness (valence) and activation level (arousal). The dominance dimension, indicating the degree of control, is often considered highly correlated with arousal and thus sometimes omitted. Psychological studies have long supported the notion that discrete emotion categories can be mapped onto specific regions within this continuous valence arousal space [1–3,5,6,12,13].

Contemporary Speech Emotion Recognition (SER) systems often treat the prediction of discrete emotions, sentiment, and continuous emotional dimensions as separate tasks [1,3,10,11,14,18,22]. A common paradigm involves utilizing pretrained audio encoders, typically trained on large-scale speech corpora, and subsequently fine-tuning these encoders on specific emotion datasets. Prior work has demonstrated the effectiveness of initializing SER models with weights from speaker recognition tasks, particularly for smaller datasets like IEMOCAP [5]. Interestingly, traditional data augmentation techniques have shown limited benefits for SER, especially on larger and more diverse datasets. Recent advancements in transformer architectures have led to improved performance, particularly in predicting continuous emotion dimensions.

Despite the progress in independently modeling discrete and continuous aspects of emotion in speech, there remains a relative lack of research explicitly bridging these two perspectives [3]. The established psychological link between the continuous dimensional space of emotions and discrete emotional labels suggests a potential for synergistic learning. This paper investigates the relationship between predicted continuous emotional dimensions and their correspondence to categorical emotions and sentiments in Indian publicly available speech emotion datasets. Furthermore, we propose a novel feature based on analytic signal matched filter bank for multi-view training framework that leverages the complementary information present in dimensional scores, discrete emotion categories, and sentiment labels within speech emotion corpora. While prior research has explored the relationship between continuous dimensional representations and discrete emotion labels in speech, and multi-view methodology have been demonstrated in the context of SER [6], the novelty of this work lies in two key aspects. First, this paper introduces filter bank-based feature specifically designed to enhance the joint learning of VAD mappings and speaker's emotion classification. Second, this work focuses on the Indian Emotional Speech Corpora (IESC) [3], applying the proposed approach to Indian speakers, a domain that has received less attention in previous research. This focus on the Indian corpora, combined with the introduction of a tailored filter bank feature [7], distinguishes our approach from existing literature, which has predominantly focused on non-Indian datasets.

## 2    Database

IESC is a collection of emotional speech recordings contributed by eight individuals from northern India–five men and three women. The dataset includes a total of 600 audio clips, each reflecting one of five emotions: neutral, happy, angry, sad, and fearful [3].

All recordings were made in quiet indoor settings using a mobile phone with a speech recorder application. To ensure clarity and minimize background noise, the speakers used headphones equipped with built-in microphones. The recordings were saved in .wav format for consistent audio quality.

## 3    Methodology

This study demonstrates a deep learning-based method for recognizing emotions from speech using features derived from a analytic signal decomposition technique-ASMFB combined with a custom convolutional neural network (CNN). The methodology consists of three main stages: preprocessing, feature extraction using a matched filter bank [7,9], and emotion classification using a deep CNN and emotion-to VAD vector mapping. The flow of the methodology is summarized in Fig. 1.

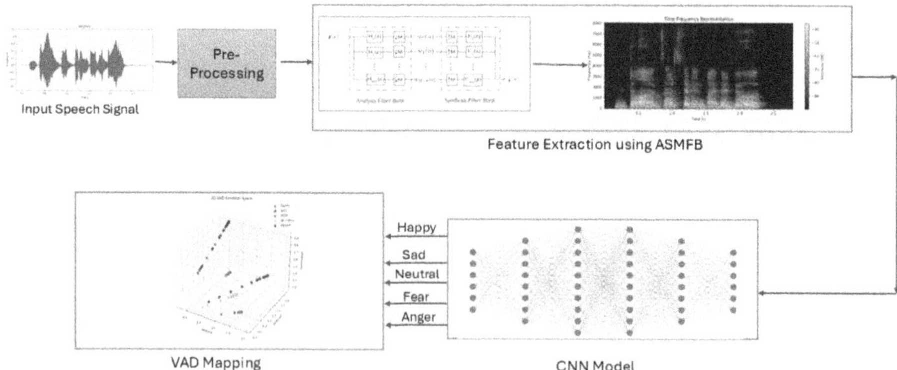


**Fig. 1.** Methodology: Process Flow of the End-to-End Emotion Recognition and VAD Mapping Framework from Speech.

## 3.1   Audio Preprocessing and Feature Extraction

In speech recognition systems, one of the crucial tasks is segmentation. To process any spoken speech, it is essential to first divide the signal into stationary components, each of which typically corresponds to a phoneme. The ASMFB, as proposed in [7], offers an effective solution for this segmentation task. This method decomposes a quasi-stationary speech signal into multiple sub-bands. The ASMFB is a real-time signal decomposition technique that is adaptive to the characteristics of the input signal. It decomposes input signals into non-overlapping narrow frequency bands. The ASMFB is a multirate filter bank that is M-band, uniformly decimated, and derived by integrating the signal matched analysis and synthesis filter banks within the context of analytic signals [7,9].

Each audio file was first preprocessed by resampling to a consistent sampling rate of 16,000 Hz, followed by min-max normalization to scale the audio signal into the [0, 1] range. For feature extraction, we employed an analytic signal matched filter bank, a technique designed to decompose the raw speech signal into multiple narrow frequency bands. This decomposition enhances the resolution of frequency components and better preserves the temporal characteristics of emotional cues in speech. The matched filter approach is conceptually similar to traditional filter banks used in MFCC extraction but offers improved time-frequency localization [3,7,9].

Once decomposed, the output of the filter bank was used to compute a Mel spectrogram for each audio signal as shown in Fig. 2. We used 128 Mel bands, and each spectrogram was padded or truncated to a fixed length of 128 frames along the time axis. These processed Mel-spectrograms served as the input feature representations for the CNN model.

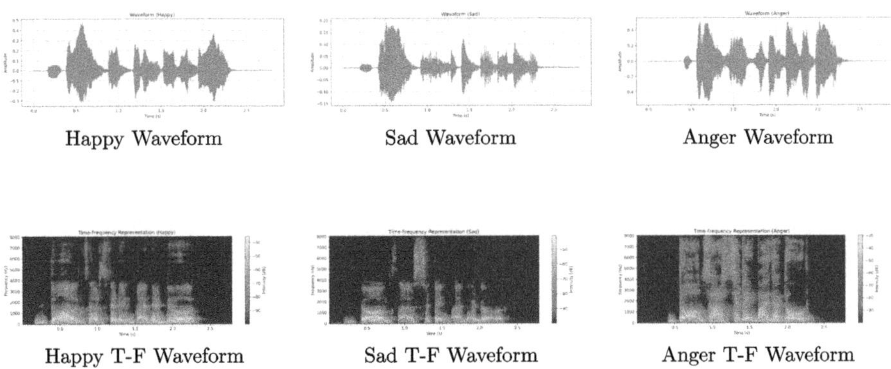

| | | |
|:---:|:---:|:---:|
| Happy Waveform | Sad Waveform | Anger Waveform |
| Happy T-F Waveform | Sad T-F Waveform | Anger T-F Waveform |

**Fig. 2.** Waveform and corresponding Time-Frequency (spectrogram) representations for Happy, Sad, and Angry emotional speech.

## 3.2   CNN Model Architecture

We developed a custom deep CNN of five convolutional blocks with each block comprising a Conv2D layer, succedded by batch normalization, ReLU activation, and dropout. Dropout was used to improve generalization, with a rate of 0.2 in the convolutional layers (Fig. 3).

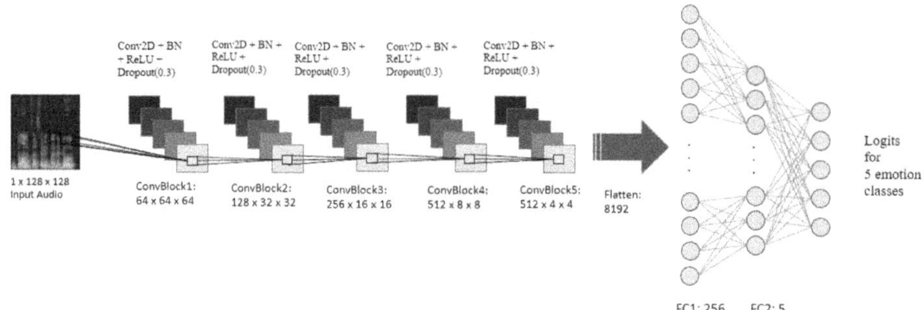


**Fig. 3.** CNN Architecture used for Training the Classification Model.

The output from the last convolutional block was flattened and sent through a fully connected layer reducing the dimensionality from 8192 to 256, succeeded by a ReLU activation and a final fully connected layer to 5 output classes. A dropout rate of 0.5 was applied before the fully connected stage to further mitigate overfitting. The network was trained using the CrossEntropyLoss function.

## 3.3   Training Configuration

The model was trained and evaluated on the IESC [3], which comprises 600 audio recordings of emotional speech from 8 Indian speakers (5 male, 3 female). The dataset covers five emotion categories: Anger, Fear, Happy, Neutral, and Sad. Two fixed English sentences were spoken under different emotional states. To maintain speaker and class balance, four speakers contributed 10 samples per emotion, and four contributed 20 samples per emotion. The data set was divided into 80% for training (480 files) and 20% for testing (120 files).

Model training was performed over 100 epochs (37 epoch on early stopping) with a learning rate of 0.001 using the Adam-optimizer and a batch size of 16. The model achieved a test accuracy of 89.87%, demonstrating its effectiveness in learning discriminative emotional representations from decomposed spectral features (Table 1).

## 3.4   Emotion to VAD Mapping

In this study, we used a predefined VAD dictionary sourced from a [6] for mapping emotional categories to VAD values. This dictionary provides continuous

**Table 1.** Mapping discrete emotion categories onto the VAD scale

| Emotion | Valence(V) | Arousal(A) | Dominance(D) |
| --- | --- | --- | --- |
| Happy | 0.987 | 0.529 | 0.596 |
| Neutral | 0.883 | 0.170 | 0.304 |
| Sad | 0.736 | 0.305 | 0.401 |
| Angry | 0.235 | 0.863 | 0.918 |
| Fear | 0.431 | 0.607 | 0.415 |

numerical representations of emotions based on these three psychological dimensions, all scaled between 0 and 1 shown in Table 2.

The methodology used in the paper [6] for generating this VAD dictionary involved three different pre-trained models. Each of these models predicts the VAD values based on speech signals, using deep learning techniques.

For our study, we leveraged this predefined VAD dictionary from [6]. When our model predicts an emotion, we map it to the corresponding VAD values from this dictionary, ensuring a more continuous and detailed representation of emotions, rather than relying solely on discrete emotion labels.

This VAD dictionary allows us to analyze and visualize emotions in a more dynamic way by plotting them in the VAD space. It also opens the door for additional analyses, such as calculating the Euclidean distance between predicted and actual VAD values to assess the model's accuracy. Furthermore, the VAD values can be used in future applications, like emotion regulation systems or affective dialogue systems, to better understand and respond to emotional states.

Using the established VAD dictionary from the [6], our objective is to ensure that our emotion predictions align with the widely accepted understanding of emotions in the research community, enhancing the quality and interpretability of our results.

## 4   Experimental Results

To evaluate the usefulness of the proposed methodology, we carried out extensive experiments on the dataset IESC [3]. The dataset consists of 600 audio samples distributed across five emotion classes: Anger, Fear, Happy, Neutral, and Sad, recorded by 8 native North Indian speakers. The data was split into 80% training (480 samples) and 20% testing (120 samples).

### 4.1   Model Performance

The deep learning model developed for this task is a custom 5-layer Convolutional Neural Network (CNN) that receives Mel spectrograms derived from analytically decomposed signals using a matched filter bank. This architecture was designed to effectively capture both temporal and spectral emotional features from speech (Fig. 4).

(a) Training Loss

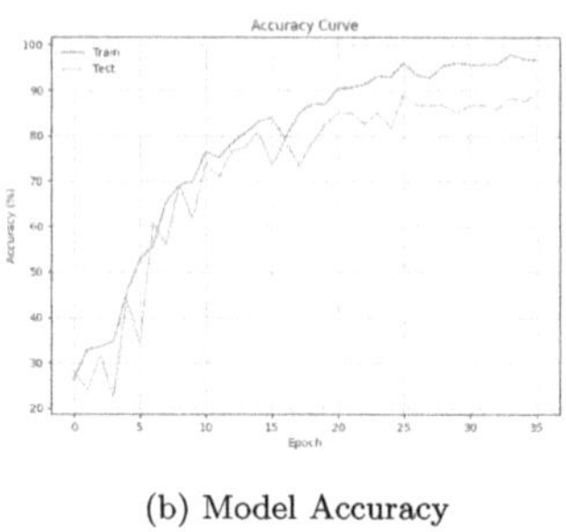

(b) Model Accuracy

**Fig. 4.** Model Performance: Training Loss and Model Accuracy.

The model attained a classification accuracy of 89.87% in the test audio dataset. This performance reflects the model's capability to learn discriminative patterns across the different emotion classes, even with a relatively modest-sized dataset (Fig. 5).

## 4.2  VAD Mapping and Visualization

In addition to class prediction, each output emotion label was mapped to a corresponding VAD vector using a predefined dictionary. This mapping enabled the transformation of categorical outputs into continuous emotional coordinates. The mapped VAD values were then used for:

1. Visualizing emotional trajectories in 3D and 2D projections of VAD space.
2. Computing Euclidean distances between true and predicted emotional coordinates (useful for evaluating the expressiveness of the model).
3. Supporting downstream applications, such as emotion-aware systems and affective computing models.
4. The integration of VAD analysis provided a richer representation of emotional states, moving beyond simple classification to more nuanced emotional modeling.

## 4.3  Average VAD Distance (Error)

To quantify the similarity between the true and predicted emotional representations in the VAD space, the Euclidean distance metric is calculated. In a 3-dimensional VAD space, each emotion is marked as a point, and the distance between the true vector $(v_1, a_1, d_1)$ and the predicted vector $(v_2, a_2, d_2)$ is calculated using the formula:

$$\text{Distance} = \sqrt{(v_1 - v_2)^2 + (a_1 - a_2)^2 + (d_1 - d_2)^2}$$

This measure provides an interpretable estimate of how closely the predicted emotion aligns with the ground truth in terms of its affective characteristics. Average VAD Distance (Error) is 0.0308. This result shows our model's VAD mapping accuracy is strong, with a low average error.

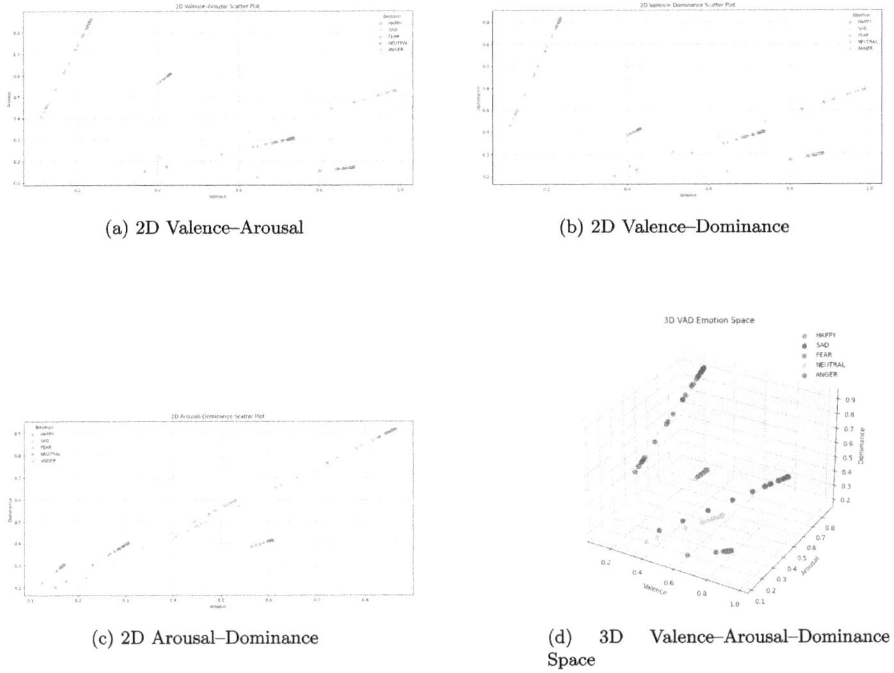

(a) 2D Valence–Arousal

(b) 2D Valence–Dominance

(c) 2D Arousal–Dominance

(d)   3D   Valence–Arousal–Dominance Space

**Fig. 5.** VAD scatter plots showing emotional clustering across dimensions.

**Table 2.** VAD distance analysis for predicted emotions, comparing true and predicted VAD vectors along with Euclidean distance

| Emotion | True VAD | Predicted VAD | Distance |
|---|---|---|---|
| Happy | (0.89, 0.79, 0.74) | (0.88, 0.77, 0.72) | 0.0300 |
| Surprise | (0.68, 0.91, 0.58) | (0.67, 0.90, 0.60) | 0.0245 |
| Neutral | (0.50, 0.50, 0.50) | (0.52, 0.49, 0.53) | 0.0374 |
| Sad | (0.18, 0.32, 0.35) | (0.21, 0.33, 0.37) | 0.0374 |
| Fear | (0.15, 0.84, 0.30) | (0.14, 0.83, 0.28) | 0.0245 |

## 5   Conclusion

The combination of signal decomposition using ASMFB, time-frequency features, and a deep CNN resulted in a reliable framework for SER. The model performed well, achieving 89.87% accuracy in classifying five emotion categories and a low average VAD error of 0.0308, showing that it can closely match the emotional tone of speech with high precision. The results demonstrate the capability of the system to effectively interpret emotion from voice signals, not only in categorical form but also in continuous affective dimensions via VAD mapping.

# References


1. Khare, S.K., Blanes-Vidal, V., Nadimi, E.S., Acharya, U.R.: Emotion recognition and artificial intelligence: a systematic review (2014–2023) and research recommendations. Inf. Fusion **102**, 102019 (2024)
2. Gobl, C., Ní Chasaide, A.: The role of voice quality in communicating emotion, mood and attitude. Speech Commun. **40**(1), pp. 189–212 (2003)
3. Singh, Y., Goel, S.: A lightweight 2D CNN based approach for speaker-independent emotion recognition from speech with new Indian emotional speech corpora. Multimed. Tools Appl. **82**, 1–19 (2023)
4. Russell, J.A.: A circumplex model of affect. J. Pers. Soc. Psychol. **39**(6), 1161–1178 (1980)
5. Busso, C., et al.: IEMOCAP: Interactive emotional dyadic motion capture database. Lang. Resour. Eval. **42**(4), 335–359 (2008)
6. Rizhinashvili, D., Sham, A.H., Anbarjafari, G.: Enhanced speech emotion recognition using averaged valence arousal dominance mapping and deep neural networks. SIViP **18**, 7445–7454 (2024)
7. Srivastava, G., Joshi, S.D.: Time frequency analysis of analytic signal using signal matched filter bank. In: Proceedings of the 2018 International Conference on Signals and Systems (ICSigSys), Bali, Indonesia, pp. 181–184 (2018)
8. Cowie, R., et al.: Emotion recognition in human-computer interaction. IEEE Signal Process. Mag. **18**(1), 32–80 (2001)
9. Srivastava, G., Joshi, S.D.: Harmonic decomposition of ECG signal using analytic signal matched filter bank. In: Proceedings of the 2019 Second International Conference on Advanced Computational and Communication Paradigms (ICACCP), Gangtok, India, pp. 1–4 (2019)
10. Zhou, Y., Sun, Y., Zhang, J., Yan, Y.: Speech emotion recognition using both spectral and prosodic features. In: International Conference on Information Engineering and Computer Science, pp. 1–4 (2009)
11. Schneider, S., Baevski, A., Collobert, R., Auli, M.: wav2vec: Unsupervised pretraining for speech recognition (2019). arXiv preprint arXiv:1904.05862
12. Verma, G.K., Tiwary, U.S.: Affect representation and recognition in 3D continuous valence-arousal-dominance space. Multimed. Tools Appl. **76**, 2159–2183 (2017)
13. Warriner, A.B., Kuperman, V., Brysbaert, M.: Norms of valence, arousal, and dominance for 13,915 English lemmas. Behav. Res. Methods **45**, 1191–1207 (2013)
14. Baevski, A., Zhou, Y., Mohamed, A., Auli, M.: wav2vec 2.0: a framework for self-supervised learning of speech representations. NeurIPS **33**, pp. 449–460 (2020)
15. Sobin, C., Alpert, M.: Emotion in speech: the acoustic attributes of fear, anger, sadness, and joy. J. Psycholinguist. Res. **28**, 347–365 (1999)
16. Banse, R., Scherer, K.R.: Acoustic profiles in vocal emotion expression. J. Pers. Soc. Psychol. **70**(3), 614 (1996)
17. Anagnostopoulos, C., Iliou, T., Giannoukos, I.: Features and classifiers for emotion recognition from speech: a survey from 2000 to 2011. Artif. Intell. Rev. **43**, 155–177 (2015)
18. Khalil, R.A., et al.: Speech emotion recognition using deep learning techniques: a review. IEEE Access **7**, 117327–117345 (2019)
19. Bharti, D., Kukana, P.: A hybrid machine learning model for emotion recognition from speech signals. In: ICOSEC, pp. 491–496 (2020)
20. Noroozi, F., et al.: Vocal-based emotion recognition using random forests and decision tree. Int. J. Speech Technol. **20**, 239–246 (2017)

21. Anand, N., Verma, P.: Convoluted feelings: convolutional and recurrent nets for detecting emotion from audio data (2015)
22. Chen, M., et al.: 3-D convolutional recurrent neural networks with attention model for speech emotion recognition. IEEE Signal Process. Lett. **25**(10), 1440–1444 (2018)

# LaghuVani: How Clearly Can Tiny Vocoders Speak Bengali and Maithili?

Kaustubh S. Wade[ID], Ravindrakumar M. Purohit[(✉)][ID], and Hemant A. Patil[ID]

Speech Research Lab, Dhirubhai Ambani University (formerly DA-IICT),
Gandhinagar, India
{202418024,202321002,hemant_patil}@dau.ac.in

**Abstract.** Recent advancements in deep learning have improved the quality and naturalness of SS. However, these improvements were achieved at the cost of increased model complexity. This work explored and tried to build a scalable framework by proposing a 0.02M parameter vocoder architecture to serve low-resource Indic languages, particularly Bengali and Maithili. We systematically scaled down a 112M architecture, with five parameters: 6M, 1M, 0.5M, 0.1M, and 0.02M parameters, to analyse the trade-off between model *compactness* and synthesis *quality*. We used subjective (e.g., MOS, NISQA) and objective metrics (e.g., PESQ, STOI, SNR, MCD, MSD, FAD, PCC). Quantitatively, the LaghuVani-V1 (6M) achieves 4.14 and 2.80 on the 5-scale MOS for Bengali and Maithili, respectively. The compact model LaghuVani-V5 (0.02M, with parameter reduction of 7000×) achieved the remarkable faster RTF, that is 388× faster on an NVIDIA GTX 1080 8GB GPU with notable MOS of the range of 1.3-1.8 after $1\times 10^5$ after (batch size of 8) steps only. Furthermore, we conducted the human-centric evaluation instead of relying on the MOS to assess "How clearly tiny vocoders can articulate speech?". We found that, for models below 1M, the noise power is greater than the speech power. So it is difficult to hear and recognise the words.

**Keywords:** Neural vocoder · Low-resource TTS · Model compression · Indic Languages · Speech quality evaluation

## 1 Introduction

Recent state-of-the-art (SOTA) models in neural speech synthesis (SS), such as WaveNet, HiFi-GAN [4], and BigVGAN [5], significantly improved SS quality over previous rule-based and statistical-based methods. However, the complexity and computational demands make them difficult for real-time SS settings, due to limited hardware availability/capabilities or constrained memory footprints. To minimise these limitations, our work focuses on developing and testing a highly

K. S. Wade and R. M. Purohit—Equal contribution.

compact vocoder model to balance between synthesis quality and efficiency, particularly for resource-constrained settings. In this work, our contributions are as follows:

1. We compress a state-of-the-art 112M-parameter vocoder down to just 0.0M parameters, by compressing it 7000×, resulting in a reduction in model size, while retaining intelligibility and basic perceptual quality.
2. We designed and compared five compact models (LaghuVani V1-V5, all variants remain under 10M parameters) with parameter sizes of 6M, 1M, 0.5M, 0.1M, and 0.02M, providing the trade-off between the synthesis quality and model compactness.
3. All model variants are trained and evaluated on Bengali and Maithili, two low-resourced Indic languages.
4. We evaluated the generated samples using the two subjective (MOS, NISQA-MOS) and seven objective metrics (PESQ, STOI, SNR [dB], MCD, FAD, PCC, MSD). Generated samples made publicly available at[1].

The structure of the remaining paper is as follows: Sect. 2 presents related work, and Sects. 3 and 4 discuss the proposed framework of the LaghuVani and experimental details, respectively. Section 5 shows the results with language-specific discussion(s) and observations. Section 6 completes the paper with a conclusion.

## 2   Related Work

WaveNet [12] established a high-quality baseline for neural vocoders but incurred prohibitive inference latency. Later architectures, such as UnivNet [3] and BigV-GAN [5], leveraged multi-resolution (spectral/period) discriminators and alias-free components to enhance fidelity further. However, most were trained in high-resource languages, and the number remains comparatively large. Furthermore, a few works [8–11] developed the language-wise (e.g., Gujarati, Hindi, Marathi) vocoder for the best-suited performance. However, exploring the number of parameters vs. the speech quality for the Bengali and Maithili remained unexplored. The closest work to ours is Chaudhary *et al.* [1], who pursue parameter-efficient, on-device vocoders. However, the evaluation was done only for English and Hindi. In contrast, we address low-resource Indic languages (Bengali, Maithili) and push compression much further (down to 0.02M parameters), systematically exploring qualityâĂŞsize trade-offs across five variants w.r.t. the number of parameters.

## 3   Proposed Framework

In this section, we present the overall architecture: the Generator in Sect. 3.1, and the Discriminators are described in Sect. 3.3. Figure 1 shows the complete

---

[1] https://speech-lab-qx7rma9p.github.io/LaghuVani/.

framework, which consists of one Generator and two Discriminators: the Multi-Period Discriminator (MPD), which operates on time-domain features, and the Multi-Resolution Discriminator (MRD), which analyzes frequency-domain representations.

## 3.1 LaghuVani-Generator

The LaghuVani-Generator is derived from BigVGAN [5], a high-capacity neural vocoder originally designed for universal SS. Generator contains 1D convolution layer and transposed 1D convolution blocks for upsampling. Each upsampling stage is connected with an Anti-aliased Multi-Periodicity (AMP) module by aggregating input features from residual blocks exhibiting channel-wise periodicities. Within the AMP module, upsampling and downsampling operations are performed with low-pass filtering, followed by dilated 1D convolutions to capture long-range *temporal* dependencies. This is succeeded by a nonlinear transformation block consisting of a Snake1D activation function, a 1D convolution, and a *tanh* activation, introducing smooth and periodic nonlinearities essential for SS.

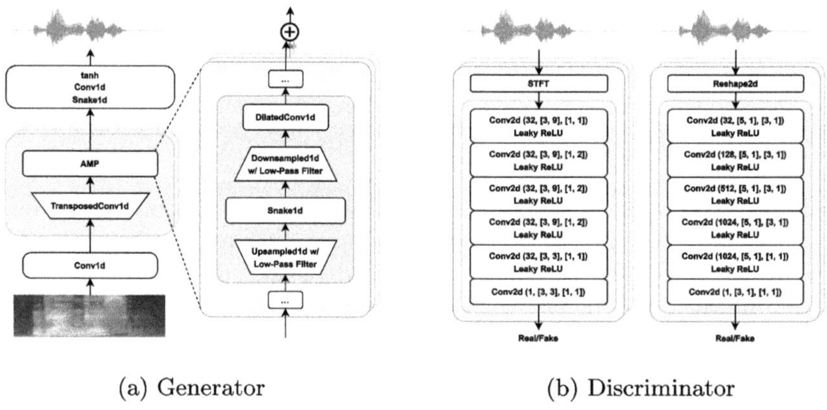


(a) Generator          (b) Discriminator

**Fig. 1.** Architectural overview of the Generator and Discriminator.

## 3.2 Model Configurations

We design five scaled variants of the LaghuVani Generator (V1âĂŞV5), progressively reducing parameters from 6M to $2\times10^4$. While retaining key components, such as, transposed convolutions and AMP blocks [5], we downscale initial channels, upsampling depth, and kernel sizes to suit low-resource settings. Inspired by compact vocoders, e.g., HiFi-GAN [4] and UnivNet [3], smaller variants use a fewer residual blocks and shorter hop sizes (e.g., 32 samples). Detailed configurations are shown in Table 1.

## 3.3   LaghuVani-Discriminator

The discriminator consists of two parts: Multi-Scale Discriminator (MSD) and Multi-Resolution Discriminator (MRD). MSD captures audio features at different resolutions by downsampling the input waveform, while MRD uses multiple convolutional branches with varying kernel sizes and dilations to capture diverse temporal patterns. Together, they help improve adversarial feedback and enhance audio realism.

**Table 1.** Comparison of Parameter Configurations for the Proposed LaghuVani Models

| Parameter | V1 | V2 | V3 | V4 | V5 |
|---|---|---|---|---|---|
| $\alpha$ | | | $1 \times 10^{-4}$ | | |
| $\beta_1$ | | | 0.8 | | |
| $\beta_2$ | | | 0.99 | | |
| LR decay | | | 0.9999996 | | |
| Upsample rates | [4,4,2,2] | [4,4,2] | [4,4] | [4,2] | [1] |
| Init. channel | 256 | 128 | 96 | 64 | 48 |
| # kernels | 3 | 2 | | 1 | |
| Kernel sizes | [3,5,7] | [3,5] | | [3] | |
| Upsample layers | 4 | 4 | 3 | 2 | 1 |
| Upsample k-sizes | [8,8,4,4] | | | [8,8,4] | |
| Dilation sizes | [1,2]×3 | [1,2]×2 | | [1] | |
| num_mels | | | 80 | | |
| FFT points | | | 1024 | | |
| Hop size | | 64 | | 32 | |
| Window size | | | 1024 | | |
| Batch Size | | | 8 | | |
| Trained steps | 100K | 100K | 100K | 200K | 200K |

## 3.4   Loss Function Employed

We used adversarial, feature-matching, and L1 loss without additional changes. This combination provided training stability and perceptual quality across model sizes.

1. **Adversarial loss:** It encourages the generator to produce outputs indistinguishable from real speech by fooling the discriminators. In particular,

$$\mathcal{L}_{adv}(G; D_k) = \mathbb{E}_s \left[ (D_k(G(s)) - 1)^2 \right], \tag{1}$$

$$\mathcal{L}_{adv}(D_k; G) = \mathbb{E}_{(x,s)} \left[ (D_k(x) - 1)^2 + (D_k(G(s)))^2 \right]. \tag{2}$$

2. **Feature matching loss (FM)**: It ensures the generator matches intermediate activations of the discriminator, in order to improve stability and realism. i.e.,

$$\mathcal{L}_{fm}(G; D_k) = \mathbb{E}_{(x,s)}\left[\sum_{i=1}^{T}\frac{1}{N}||D_k^i(x) - D_k^i(G(s))||_1\right]. \tag{3}$$

3. **L1 loss**: It minimises the absolute difference between predicted and target Mel spectrograms to preserve acoustic structure. i.e.,

$$\mathcal{L}_{mel}(G) = \mathbb{E}_{(x,s)}\left[||\phi(x) - \phi(G(s))||_1\right]. \tag{4}$$

## 4   Experimental Setup

**Dataset used at setup:**

We used publicly available datasets from the SYSPIN initiative [2] for Maithili and Bengali, which include recordings of male and female speakers, at 48 kHz, 24-bits resolution, and mono-channel. Each dataset is monolingual and validated at sampling frequency, which makes it suitable for TTS research. We downsampled to 24,050 Hz in the preprocessing stage and took the 8:1:1 for training, testing, and validation.

**Experimental Setup:**

All experiments were conducted on a Windows machine with an AMD Ryzen 5 5600X CPU, 16GB RAM, NVIDIA RTX 3060 Ti (8GB) for training and NVIDIA GTX 1080 (8GB) for inference.

## 5   Results and Discussion

Fig. 2 visually corroborates these trends: harmonic structure remains clear and sharply defined through LaghuVani-V2 but blurs and collapses from LaghuVani-V3 onward. For the complete set of audio samples, extended metrics tables (including standard deviations), and interactive plots, please visit our demo website at[2].

---

[2] https://speech-lab-qx7rma9p.github.io/LaghuVani/.

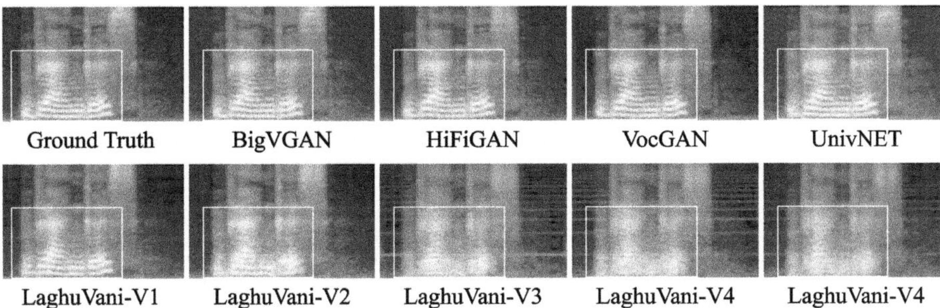

| Ground Truth | BigVGAN | HiFiGAN | VocGAN | UnivNET |
|---|---|---|---|---|

| LaghuVani-V1 | LaghuVani-V2 | LaghuVani-V3 | LaghuVani-V4 | LaghuVani-V4 |
|---|---|---|---|---|

**Fig. 2.** Mel spectrogram comparison of an utterance across Ground-Truth, four SOTA vocoders, and five proposed LaghuVani models.

**Inference Speed (Real-Time Factor (RTF)):** LaghuVani-V1 runs 33.82× faster than real-time on CPU and 108.38× on GPU, offering strong inference efficiency despite being the largest among the proposed models. It is faster than BigVGAN [5](44.72× GPU) while being much smaller (6M *vs.* 112M). Although HiFi-GAN [4] is quicker on GPU (167.9×), it uses over twice the parameters. The smaller LaghuVani models (V2âĂŞV5) achieve even higher speeds—up to 253.59× (CPU) and 368.89× (GPU), making them ideal for ultra-low-latency and edge deployments (as shown in Table 2).

**Table 2.** Inference Speeds (RTF) on CPU and GPU for both the Datasets ('-' indicates speed has not been disclosed by the author or is not publicly available online)

| Architecture | Param(s) (M) | CPU (↑) | GPU (↑) | GPU Used (VRAM) | TFLOPs (↑) |
|---|---|---|---|---|---|
| VocGAN [13] | 6.8 | 3.24× | 416.7× | NVIDIA GTX 1080TI (11 GB) | 11.3 |
| UnivNET [3] | 10.5 | - | 200× | NVIDIA Tesla V100 (80 GB) | 125 |
| HiFi-GAN [4] | 14.01 | 13.4× | 167.9× | NVIDIA Tesla V100 (80 GB) | 125 |
| BigVGAN [5] | 112 | - | 44.72× | NVIDIA RTX 8000 (48 GB) | 16.3 |
| LaghuVani-V1 | 6 | 33.82× | 108.38× | NVIDIA GTX 1080 (8 GB) | 8.87 |
| LaghuVani-V2 | 1 | 66.28× | 196.48× | NVIDIA GTX 1080 (8 GB) | 8.87 |
| LaghuVani-V3 | 0.5 | 200.8× | 388.87× | NVIDIA GTX 1080 (8 GB) | 8.87 |
| LaghuVani-V4 | 0.1 | 240.89× | 387.83× | NVIDIA GTX 1080 (8 GB) | 8.87 |
| LaghuVani-V5 | 0.02 | 253.59× | 368.89× | NVIDIA GTX 1080 (8 GB) | 8.87 |

Bengali proves more challenging to model: under LaghuVani-V1 the MCD for Bengali is 25.9 dB versus 21.5 dB for Maithili, and its STOI is about 0.015 points lower. The steeper performance curves for Bengali imply that scaling thresholds must be adjusted per language.under LaghuVani-V1 the MCD for Bengali is 25.9

**Table 3.** Subjective and Objective evaluation on the Bengali and Maithili test sets (↑ higher is better, ↓ lower is better).

| Model | MOS (↑) | NISQA (↑) | PESQ (↑) | STOI (↑) | SNR (↑) [dB] | MCD (aℰ§) | FAD (↓) | PCC (↑) | MSD (↓) |
|---|---|---|---|---|---|---|---|---|---|
| Maithili | | | | | | | | | |
| VocGAN [13] | 4.202±0.081 | 4.211±0.531 | 2.765±0.217 | 0.951±0.009 | -2.880±0.543 | 30.591±2.965 | 15.624±0.058 | -0.035±0.123 | 0.548±0.145 |
| Univnet [3] | 3.930±0.090 | 4.254±0.502 | 3.249±0.215 | 0.973±0.006 | -2.440±0.770 | 20.457±1.732 | 30.970±0.099 | 0.072±0.160 | 0.559±0.129 |
| HiFiGAN [4] | 4.100±0.050 | 4.568±0.365 | 3.088±0.257 | 0.967±0.005 | -2.530±0.530 | 19.190±2.592 | 8.322±0.055 | 0.017±0.105 | 0.338±0.075 |
| BigVGAN [5] | 4.110±0.090 | 4.563±0.402 | 4.450±0.106 | 0.997±0.001 | 5.259±3.171 | 4.271±0.776 | 9.870±0.047 | 0.805±0.141 | 0.134±0.040 |
| LaghuVani-V1 | 2.800±0.768 | 3.256±0.538 | 1.894±0.142 | 0.916±0.013 | -1.366±1.242 | 21.469±1.965 | 15.107±0.129 | 0.195±0.218 | 0.652±0.156 |
| LaghuVani-V2 | 2.050±0.605 | 1.675±0.327 | 1.196±0.044 | 0.818±0.040 | -1.409±0.431 | 32.917±4.325 | 78.653±0.372 | 0.047±0.±67 | 0.857±0.204 |
| LaghuVani-V3 | 1.250±0.444 | 0.890±0.156 | 1.058±0.011 | 0.683±0.051 | -1.006±0.596 | 52.179±5.183 | 158.491±0.458 | -0.023±0.039 | 1.556±0.561 |
| LaghuVani-V4 | 1.400±0.503 | 0.847±0.132 | 1.061±0.013 | 0.704±0.051 | -0.560±0.244 | 47.178±5.117 | 158.671±0.452 | 0.065±0.068 | 1.509±0.619 |
| LaghuVani-V5 | 1.300±0.470 | 0.843±0.144 | 1.057±0.011 | 0.693±0.053 | -0.662±0.275 | 49.103±5.189 | 163.573±0.480 | 0.054±0.071 | 1.511±0.621 |
| Bengali | | | | | | | | | |
| VocGAN [13] | 4.202±0.081 | 4.621±0.292 | 2.676±0.289 | 0.947±0.018 | -3.031±0.460 | 35.979±6.023 | 23.645±0.121 | -0.023±0.108 | 0.209±0.085 |
| Univnet [3] | 3.930±0.090 | 4.654±0.427 | 3.259±0.192 | 0.973±0.009 | -2.797±0.491 | 17.696±3.298 | 26.985±0.069 | 0.021±0.105 | 0.191±0.102 |
| HiFiGAN [4] | 4.100±0.050 | 4.740±0.331 | 3.024±0.147 | 0.964±0.006 | -2.663±0.505 | 18.181±2.330 | 11.726±0.061 | -0.006±0.109 | 0.215±0.077 |
| BigVGAN [5] | 4.110±0.090 | 4.794±0.431 | 4.427±0.123 | 0.997±0.001 | 4.110±3.679 | 4.130±1.016 | 14.595±0.055 | 0.727±0.210 | 0.053±0.031 |
| LaghuVani-V1 | 4.140±1.069 | 2.834±0.577 | 1.748±0.111 | 0.901±0.014 | -2.092±0.329 | 25.862±3.314 | 23.527±0.135 | 0.044±0.081 | 0.409±0.201 |
| LaghuVani-V2 | 3.180±1.190 | 1.278±0.210 | 1.206±0.054 | 0.797±0.053 | -1.028±0.432 | 37.492±7.803 | 87.772±0.299 | 0.044±0.057 | 0.776±0.483 |
| LaghuVani-V3 | 1.760±0.894 | 0.679±0.122 | 1.047±0.009 | 0.684±0.059 | -0.708±0.417 | 59.083±5.098 | 163.024±0.360 | 0.004±0.018 | 1.173±0.625 |
| LaghuVani-V4 | 1.900±1.165 | 0.705±0.099 | 1.062±0.014 | 0.691±0.064 | -0.525±0.234 | 55.891±6.017 | 158.404±0.361 | 0.002±0.018 | 1.193±0.576 |
| LaghuVani-V5 | 1.880±1.062 | 0.659±0.088 | 1.055±0.011 | 0.688±0.062 | -0.599±0.300 | 65.229±8.208 | 159.768±0.377 | 0.012±0.021 | 1.110±0.603 |

dB versus 21.5 dB for Maithili, and its STOI is about 0.015 points lower. The steeper performance curves for Bengali imply that scaling thresholds must be adjusted per language(Table 3).

Furthermore, we noticed four main reasons why Bengali is more complex for speech synthesis as compared to the Maithili (e.g., Indo-Aryan family) language from subjective evaluation, as follows [7] [6].

1. Bengali contains a non-transparent orthography (e.g., a single grapheme can correspond to multiple phonemes), unlike Maithili, where the written and spoken forms closely match, which leads to the complicated grapheme-to-phoneme conversion.
2. Bengali uses subject-object-verb order, lacks auxiliary verbs, and attaches prepositions to nouns, making word segmentation and syntactic modelling harder for speech synthesis.
3. There are approx. 118 consonants/conjuncts and uses extensive diacritics, where a single character can represent multiple consonants; dialects and regional variations further complicate pronunciation.
4. Bengali dictionary contains borrowed words from Persian, Arabic, and English, silent letters, and phonetically similar words challenge speech recognition systems, requiring advanced models to resolve ambiguities.

**Deployment Implications:** LaghuVani-V1 is the smallest model that maintains high intelligibility, with STOI above 0.90 and NISQA above 3, offering the best trade-off between *size* and *quality*. LaghuVani-V2 retains usable intelligibility (STOI ≈ 0.79–0.82), but NISQA drops below 2, indicating perceptual artefacts. LaghuVani-V3 to V5 show diminishing returns—PESQ saturates, MCD, and MSD rise sharply, and PCC turns negative. These trends have clear deployment implications: LaghuVani-V1 is compact enough to run on low-resource or edge devices while maintaining quality. Further compression below 1M parameters may enable lighter deployment but would require additional processing to preserve speech fidelity.

## 6    Closing Remarks and Discussion

This study presented a methodology to reduce the size of the baseline vocoder from 112 M to 0.02 M parameters, creating five versions (LaghuVani V1–V5), and tested them on Bengali and Maithili. LaghuVani-V1 (6 M) maintains good intelligibility (STOI $\approx$ 0.90–0.92) and reasonable perceptual quality. From LaghuVani-V2 (1 M) onward, quality drops sharply. PESQ levels off around 1.05–1.20, MCD and MSD increase significantly, and PCC approaches zero, indicating a loss of speech signal quality. MOS for Bengali drops from 4.14 (V1) to 1.88 (V5), while Maithili shows a slower decline in MOS, suggesting it handles compression better. FAD scores follow a similar pattern; furthermore, we observed a drop in audio quality. We plan to expand the MOS study and incorporate CLAP to better capture human perceptual judgments. **LaghuVani-V1** (6 M) achieves STOI $\geq 0.90$ (0.916 for Maithili / 0.901 for Bengali), PESQ $\approx 1.9$, and MCD $\sim 21$–$26$ dB— intelligibility is good, though fidelity drops. Below 1 M, STOI falls ($\sim 0.82/0.80$) and MCD exceeds 37 dB, leading to audible artefacts. **LaghuVani-V1** shows a sharper degradation on Bengali: its MCD climbs to 25.9 dB versus 21.5 dB for Maithili, with similar gaps in other metrics—implying that Bengali vocoder demands greater model capacity.

## References


1. Chaudhary, V., Sharma, R., Agrawal, A., Patil, H.A.: Efficient TTs for indian languages using lightweight neural vocoders. In: Proc. Interspeech (2024)
2. Group, I.S.: Syspin: speech corpus for indian languages (2024). https://syspin.iisc.ac.in/datasets, Accessed 15 May 2025
3. Jang, Y., Kim, J., Kim, M.J.: Univnet: a neural vocoder with multi-resolution spectrogram discriminators for high-fidelity waveform generation. In: Proc. Interspeech (2021)
4. Kong, J., Kim, J., Bae, J.: HIFI-GAN: generative adversarial networks for efficient and high fidelity speech synthesis. In: Proc. NeurIPS (2020)
5. Lee, J., Kim, J.M., Kim, D., Kim, S.h., Yoon, S., Kim, M.J.: Bigvgan: a universal neural vocoder with large-scale training. In: Proc. Advances in Neural Information Processing Systems (NeurIPS) (2023)
6. Mridha, M.F., Ohi, A.Q., Hamid, M.A., Monowar, M.M.: A study on the challenges and opportunities of speech recognition for bengali language. Artif. Intell. Rev. **55**(4), 3431–3455 (2022). https://doi.org/10.1007/s10462-021-10083-3
7. Narendra, N.P., Rao, K.S., Ghosh, K., Vempada, R.R., Maity, S.: Development of syllable-based text to speech synthesis system in bengali. Int. J. Speech Technol. **14**(3), 167–181 (2011). https://doi.org/10.1007/s10772-011-9094-4

8. Purohit, R.M., Kumar, S., Patil, H.A.: Vaachika: A gan-based neural vocoder for marathi language. In: International Conference on Asian Language Processing (IALP), pp. 129-134 (2025, Sarawak, Malaysia)
9. Purohit, R.M., Patil, H.A.: Whether to use pretrain neural vocoders or not?: an empirical analysis for indic speech synthesis. In: 2025 International Conference on Asian Language Processing (IALP), pp. 123–128 (2025).https://doi.org/10.1109/IALP68296.2024.11156270
10. Purohit, R.M., Patil, H.A.: Swar: a longformer-based gan vocoder for gujarati language. In: Proceedings of the European Signal Processing Conference (EUSIPCO), pp. 516–520 (2025, Palermo, Italy)
11. Purohit, R.M., Patil, H.A.: Swar (hindi): a speaker-aware vocoder for low-resource speech synthesis. In: International Conference on Asian Language Processing (IALP), pp. 141–146 (2025, Sarawak, Malaysia)
12. Van Den Oord, A., et al.: Wavenet: a generative model for raw audio. arXiv preprint arXiv:1609.03499 (2016)
13. Yang, J., Lee, J., Kim, Y., Cho, H., Kim, I.: Vocgan: a high-fidelity real-time vocoder with a hierarchically-nested adversarial network. In: Interspeech 2020. pp. 200–204 (2020). https://doi.org/10.21437/Interspeech.2020-1238

# MHTVDD: Multilingual Half-Truth Voices for Audio Deepfake Detection

Satyam R. Tiwari[1]([⊠])[iD], Jayraj S. Lakkad[2][iD], and Hemant A. Patil[3][iD]

[1] Sarvajanik College of Engineering and Technology, Surat, India
satyamtiwari.co22d2@scet.ac.in
[2] Charotar University of Science and Technology (CHARUSAT), Anand, India
22CS033@charusat.edu.in
[3] DAU (formerly DA-IICT), Gandhinagar, India
hemant_patil@dau.ac.in

**Abstract.** With the rapid progress in neural speech synthesis and voice conversion, audio deepfakes have become a growing concern. Most existing research focuses on detecting clips that are either fully real or fully fake. However, real-world threats are often more subtle, where fake segments are quietly inserted into real audio, making them much harder to detect. To tackle this, we present a new multilingual dataset that simulates these realistic "half-truth" scenarios. By alternating short segments of real speech from the VCTK corpus with deepfake audio generated using YourTTS and X-TTS, we create interleaved clips that better reflect how deepfakes might be used in practice. We evaluate three deep learning models CNN, Bi-LSTM, and ResNet-18 across four versions of our dataset, each increasing in complexity. On the simpler versions ($V_1$ and $V_2$), CNN performs the best, achieving up to 84% accuracy when detecting fully real or fake clips. But in the more challenging interleaved versions ($V_3$ and $V_4$), ResNet-18 shows stronger performance, handling mixed audio more effectively. These results highlight the limits of standard binary classifiers and the need for more advanced, segment-aware detection systems. Our dataset and benchmarks aim to push forward research in building practical and robust solutions for detecting deepfake audio in the wild.

**Keywords:** Audio Deepfake Detection (ADD) · Speech Synthesis · Audio Forensics · Fake Detection

## 1 Introduction

In recent years, AI tools have made it incredibly easy to generate fake human voices that sound almost real. Advanced models like YourTTS [1] can produce speech that not only conveys a message but also mimics a person's natural tone, rhythm, and speaking style with impressive accuracy. While these technologies have many positive applications such as enabling voice assistants, assisting people with speech impairments, or enabling personalized voice synthesis, they


S. Mitra et al. (Eds.): PReMI 2025, LNCS 16358, pp. 841–849, 2026.
https://doi.org/10.1007/978-3-032-18480-1_86

also come with serious risks. Deepfake audio [2] is increasingly being used to spread misinformation, impersonate individuals, and manipulate public opinion, all while being difficult to detect with the human ear or traditional systems. So far, most research efforts have focused on detecting audio clips that are either fully real or fully fake. However, the real world is far more nuanced. Attackers may take an authentic audio recording and subtly insert short segments of fake speech to distort the message creating what we refer to as "half-truth" audio. These hybrid clips are particularly dangerous because they retain the natural flow and credibility of real speech while embedding false or misleading content. Despite their growing relevance and potential for harm, this type of deepfake audio has received surprisingly little attention from the research community.

To tackle this growing challenge, we created a new dataset that mimics real-world deepfake scenarios where both real and fake speech are mixed together. We began with real English speech from the VCTK dataset [3] and generated fake versions using YourTTS [1]. Then, we stitched them together alternating between short real and fake segments so the final audio sounds smooth and natural but is secretly tampered with. This makes it much harder for traditional detection systems to catch the fakes. To see how well current models handle this more realistic type of deepfake, we tested three deep learning models: Bi-LSTM, which is good at recognizing time-based patterns; ResNet-18, which treats audio like an image to analyze spectrograms; and CNN, which excels at detecting local patterns in audio. We used common metrics like accuracy, precision, and $F_1$ score to compare their performance. Our findings show that these models struggle more with our mixed real-fake clips than with completely real or fake ones. Through this work, we hope to raise awareness about the dangers of segment-level deepfakes and offer a benchmark dataset to help researchers build stronger, more realistic detection tools.

1. Instead of using clips that are fully real or fake, our dataset mixes short segments of both within the same audio. This "half-truth" setup makes detection harder, as shown by a drop in model accuracy from 84% on V1 to 60% on V3.
2. Our dataset includes English, Hindi, and Hindi-English mixed audio. This helps test how well models handle cross-language and code-switched deepfakes. Accuracy dropped from 78.5% on clean Hindi (V2) to 57% on mixed Hindi (V4).
3. We compare CNN, Bi-LSTM, and ResNet-18 across all versions. CNN worked best on clean data (84% on V1), while ResNet-18 handled mixed audio better (60% on V3, 57% on V4), showing it's more robust to subtle changes. Here, The Implemented work is present publicly at github[1] and Hugging face[2] too.

We start by exploring research in Sect. 2, highlighting key advances relevant to our work. Section 3 describes the experimental design and implementation details. Our results and their interpretation are discussed in Sect. 4. Finally,

---

[1] https://github.com/Jayrajsl001/MHTVDD.
[2] https://huggingface.co/datasets/thesatyam12/MHTVDD.

Sect. 5 concludes the paper by summarizing our contributions and suggesting directions for future research.

## 2    Related Works

Recent advances in speech synthesis and voice conversion have made it easier than ever to create deepfake audio that mimics real human voices. This has led to growing interest in developing effective detection methods. So far, most research frames the task as a binary classification problem, where audio is labeled as either fully real or fully fake. Datasets like ASVspoof 2019 [4] and ASVspoof 2021 [5] are commonly used, but they typically focus on single-language speech and assume fully synthesized clips, which does not reflect real-world complexity. To address this, recent work has begun to explore partial manipulations, where only parts of an utterance such as a few wordsâĂŤare fake. Efforts like the PartialSpoof challenge [6] and the HAD dataset [7] show that current models often struggle with these more subtle cases. At the same time, multilingual deepfake detection is gaining attention. Datasets such as SpeechFake [8], MLAADC [9], and GGMDDC [10] support cross-lingual evaluation, but still rely on clip-level labels and lack examples with mixed real and fake segments. The challenge of detecting deepfakes in code-switched speech also remains largely unaddressed.

From the modeling perspective, architectures such as Bi-LSTM, ResNet-18, and various convolutional neural networks (CNNs) have demonstrated strong performance in detecting deepfake audio, particularly when applied to spectrograms or time-series features. However, these models are typically tested on clean datasets where clips are entirely real or entirely fake. As a result, it remains unclear how well they perform when manipulation is more subtle such as when real and fake segments are mixed within a single utterance. In short, while significant progress has been made in the field of audio deepfake detection, several important challenges remain. These include detecting segment-level edits, handling multilingual and translated speech, and identifying deepfakes embedded within otherwise genuine audio. These are the specific gaps our work seeks to address.

## 3    Experimental Setup

To test how well deepfake detection works in different language and audio mixing scenarios, we set up four experiments. Each one follows the same basic process cleaning and translating text, generating speech using TTS models, keeping the speaker's voice consistent with embeddings, converting audio into spectrograms, and then training deep learning models to classify the results.

### 3.1    V1 (English Real and Deepfake)

In version V1, we begin with real English speech samples taken from the VCTK dataset [3]. To generate corresponding deepfake audio, we employ the YourTTS model [1], which supports multilingual and multi-speaker voice synthesis. For each speaker, we extract voice characteristics, known as speaker embeddings, from their original recordings and input them into the model. This allows the synthetic speech to closely resemble the original speaker's voice. The result is a set of real-fake audio pairs in English, where both clips share the same content and speaker identity, but one is genuine and the other is artificially generated.

### 3.2   V2 (Hindi Real and Deepfake)

In version $V_2$, we create a Hindi deepfake dataset by generating both real and synthetic Hindi speech from the English audio in the VCTK corpus. We begin by translating the English transcripts into Hindi using the deep_translator library, which uses the Google Translate API for efficient batch processing [11]. To produce real Hindi audio, we pair the translated text with speaker embeddings from the original recordings and use the X-TTS model [12] to generate speech that retains the original speaker's voice and style.

For the synthetic Hindi speech, we first generate deepfake English audio using YourTTS, then pair it with the same Hindi translation and speaker embeddings. This input is passed through X-TTS to synthesize fake Hindi speech that mimics the original speaker. The result is a set of real and fake Hindi clips identical in content and voice, but differing in authenticity (Fig. 1).

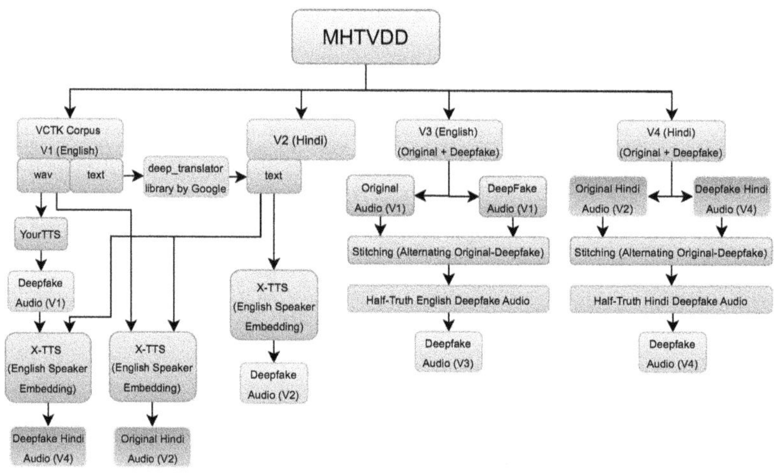


**Fig. 1.** MHTVDD Dataset Preparation architecture for $V_1$, $V_2$, $V_3$, and $V_4$.

### 3.3   V3 (English Real and Real-Deepfake Interleaved)

In version $V_3$, we design a specialized dataset that blends real and fake English speech within a single audio clip. This is done by alternating short segments one from the original VCTK recordings, followed by another generated using the YourTTS model [1]. To ensure the speaker's voice stays consistent, we use the original speaker embeddings when synthesizing the fake parts. This setup reflects a more realistic scenario, where deepfake audio might be subtly inserted into a genuine conversation. Although the entire clip is in English, the switching between real and synthetic speech makes it significantly more challenging for detection systems to identify which parts are authentic.

### 3.4   V4 (Hindi Real and Real-Deepfake Interleaved)

In version $V_4$, we develop a Hindi dataset where each audio clip contains a blend of real and deepfake speech, arranged by alternating between the two. The process starts by translating English transcripts from the VCTK dataset into Hindi using the deep_translator library, which leverages the Google Translate API for efficient batch processing [11]. To generate real Hindi speech, we combine the translated text with speaker embeddings derived from the original English audio and feed them into the X-TTS model [12], resulting in natural-sounding Hindi speech that preserves the original speaker's voice.

For the synthetic component, we first use YourTTS to create deepfake English speech from the original recordings. This audio is paired with the Hindi translation and passed through X-TTS, generating fake Hindi speech that closely mimics the speaker's vocal traits. Because both real and fake segments share the same content and voice characteristics, the difference lies in their authenticity. We then interleave short real and fake segments within each clip to produce subtle, mixed-content samples designed to reflect realistic deepfake scenarios, where manipulated audio may be hidden within genuine speech.

Each of the four datasets $V_1$, $V_2$, $V_3$, and $V_4$ is split into three subsets: 80% for training, 10% for validation during model tuning, and the final 10% for testing. To evaluate the datasets, we use three classification models: ResNet-18, Bi-LSTM, and a standard 1D CNN. These models are trained to distinguish between real and fake audio using Mel-spectrogram features, which help capture subtle artifacts introduced by synthetic speech generation.

The Bi-LSTM model treats the spectrogram as a sequence of time-series data, allowing it to learn long-term temporal and phonetic dependencies that are often disrupted in deepfake audio. ResNet-18, by contrast, processes the spectrograms as 2D images and uses residual connections to extract deep spectral features making it effective at identifying fine-grained signal artifacts. The 1D CNN focuses on local acoustic patterns, enabling it to detect abrupt or unnatural transitions in the speech waveform. All models are trained with a binary classification objective using cross-entropy loss and optimized via the Adam algorithm.

We assess model performance using standard metrics: accuracy, precision, recall, F1-score, and ROC-AUC. This setup allows for a direct comparison between time-based models (Bi-LSTM, 1D CNN) and frequency-based models (ResNet-18) across both monolingual datasets ($V_1$, $V_2$) and more complex, mixed-content datasets ($V_3$, $V_4$).

## 3.5  Dataset Details

Our dataset is built upon the VCTK corpus [3], which provides high-quality, studio-recorded English speech. Its clean and consistent recordings make it well-suited for developing and evaluating deepfake detection models. Prior to use, we preprocess the text by converting it to lowercase, removing punctuation, and performing sentence tokenization. For the audio, we apply global mean and variance normalization to the extracted features, ensuring consistency across all samples during training and evaluation (Table 1).

**Table 1.** Dataset Specifications

| Feature | Value / Description |
| --- | --- |
| Source Corpus | VCTK Corpus (Version 0.92) |
| Total Speakers Used | 30 speakers (15 male, 15 female) |
| Total Utterances | 12,000 utterances ($\approx 400$ per speaker) |
| Total Audio Duration | 12 h ($\approx 43,200$ seconds) |
| Avg. Duration per File | 3.6 s |
| Original Sampling Rate | 48,000 Hz |
| Processed Sampling Rate | 16,000 Hz |
| Audio Format | WAV, 16-bit PCM, mono channel |
| Languages (Original) | 1 language (English) |
| Transcription Format | .txt and .json (aligned per utterance) |
| Text Files Available | 12,000 transcripts (1 per utterance) |
| Speaker Embedding Size | 512 dimensions (extracted using ECAPA-TDNN) |
| Channel Type | Mono (converted if needed) |
| Mel Feature Dimensions | 80-dimensional log-mel spectrograms |
| Feature Extraction Params | FFT=1024, Win Length=25ms, Hop Length=10 ms |
| Approx. Storage Size | 10.2 GB (after trimming/resampling) |

## 3.6  Training Setup

For model training, we utilize Kaggle's cloud environment, which offers a dual NVIDIA T4 GPU setup (T4×2), with each GPU providing 16 GB of VRAM. All models are implemented in Python using the PyTorch framework, with CUDA acceleration enabled to ensure efficient training. To maintain fairness and reproducibility, all datasets are trained and evaluated under identical hardware conditions.

# 4   Experimental Results

The results from datasets $V_1$ and $V_2$ show that the CNN model consistently performs better than BiLSTM and ResNet. It achieves higher accuracy, AUC, precision, and recall, while also maintaining a much lower loss. For instance, on $V_1$, CNN reaches 83.1% accuracy and 82.3% AUC, showing it handles the task effectively. Even though performance slightly drops on $V_2$, CNN still proves to be the most reliable, suggesting it can handle moderate variations in data. These results show that CNN is especially good at capturing spatial features and offers a solid balance of simplicity and performance. In contrast, more complex models like BiLSTM and ResNet do not show clear advantages here, especially when the task involves limited or structured data.

| Performance of $V_1$ Dataset on different models | | | | | | | | | |
|---|---|---|---|---|---|---|---|---|---|
| Model | Accuracy | AUC | Loss | Precision | Recall | Val. Accuracy | Val. AUC | Val. Loss | Val. Precision | Val. Recall |
| CNN | **0.84** | **0.831** | **0.00116** | **0.831** | **0.840** | **0.831** | **0.823** | **0.00231** | **0.823** | **0.831** |
| BiLSTM | 0.77 | 0.795 | 0.499 | 0.758 | 0.807 | 0.758 | 0.782 | 0.506 | 0.745 | 0.795 |
| ResNet | 0.78 | 0.805 | 0.492 | 0.768 | 0.792 | 0.768 | 0.792 | 0.501 | 0.755 | 0.780 |

| Performance of $V_2$ Dataset on different models | | | | | | | | | |
|---|---|---|---|---|---|---|---|---|---|
| Model | Accuracy | AUC | Loss | Precision | Recall | Val. Accuracy | Val. AUC | Val. Loss | Val. Precision | Val. Recall |
| CNN | **0.785** | **0.777** | **0.00124** | **0.777** | 0.785 | **0.777** | **0.769** | **0.00247** | **0.769** | **0.777** |
| BiLSTM | 0.75 | 0.774 | 0.512 | 0.738 | **0.786** | 0.738 | 0.762 | 0.520 | 0.726 | 0.774 |
| ResNet | 0.76 | 0.784 | 0.505 | 0.748 | 0.772 | 0.748 | 0.772 | 0.514 | 0.736 | 0.760 |

| Performance of $V_3$ Dataset on different models | | | | | | | | | |
|---|---|---|---|---|---|---|---|---|---|
| Model | Accuracy | AUC | Loss | Precision | Recall | Val. Accuracy | Val. AUC | Val. Loss | Val. Precision | Val. Recall |
| CNN | 0.59 | 0.62 | **0.65** | 0.58 | 0.61 | 0.58 | 0.61 | 0.66 | 0.57 | 0.60 |
| BiLSTM | 0.58 | 0.60 | 0.66 | 0.57 | **0.63** | 0.57 | 0.59 | 0.66 | 0.56 | **0.62** |
| ResNet | **0.60** | **0.63** | **0.65** | **0.59** | 0.60 | **0.59** | **0.62** | **0.65** | **0.58** | 0.61 |

| Performance of $V_4$ Dataset on different models | | | | | | | | | |
|---|---|---|---|---|---|---|---|---|---|
| Model | Accuracy | AUC | Loss | Precision | Recall | Val. Accuracy | Val. AUC | Val. Loss | Val. Precision | Val. Recall |
| CNN | 0.56 | **0.58** | 0.67 | 0.55 | 0.60 | 0.55 | 0.57 | 0.68 | 0.54 | 0.58 |
| BiLSTM | 0.55 | 0.57 | 0.68 | 0.54 | **0.62** | 0.54 | 0.56 | 0.68 | 0.53 | **0.60** |
| ResNet | **0.57** | **0.58** | **0.67** | **0.56** | 0.55 | **0.56** | **0.58** | **0.67** | **0.55** | 0.57 |

The sharp drop in performance on datasets $V_3$ and $V_4$ makes it clear that model accuracy depends heavily on the quality and structure of the data. Even with advanced architectures, all models struggled most likely due to issues like noisy labels, imbalance between real and fake segments, or the lack of clearly separable features. Interestingly, BiLSTM shows higher recall but low precision on $V_4$, meaning it is flagging more positives but with many false alarms. This does not necessarily indicate poor model quality rather, it points to the dataset being ambiguous or confusing. Also, since training and validation results are similar, we can infer that this is not simply a case of overfitting. The real issue lies in the models lacking access to sufficiently reliable patterns to learn from. This leads to an important insight: improving the dataset through better labeling, noise reduction, or data augmentation is likely to have a greater impact than increasing model complexity. In fact, even the best-performing model (CNN) falls short when the dataset itself lacks clarity. Ultimately, this reinforces a core principle in AI: better data beats bigger models.

## 5    Summary

When we look at the results across all four dataset versions ($V_1$ to $V_4$), it clearly highlights the value and uniqueness of the dataset we have created for deepfake detection. In the simpler cases like $V_1$ with clean English audio and $V_2$ with translated Hindi models such as CNN performed quite well, with accuracy reaching up to 84% and 78.5%. However, performance drops significantly in the more challenging scenarios presented in $V_3$ and $V_4$, where real and fake segments are mixed within the same clip. This makes it evident that most deepfake detection models struggle when the manipulation is more subtle and realistic similar to what might be encountered in practical, real-world settings. Our dataset pushes beyond basic, clear-cut cases and introduces more complex challenges, particularly with multilingual and mixed-content audio. It helps reveal the limitations of current models and points toward the need for smarter, more reliable detection systems.

## References

1. Casanova, E., Weber, J., Shulby, C.D., Junior, A.C., Gölge, E., Ponti, M.A.: YourTTS: towards zero-shot multi-speaker TTS and zero-shot voice conversion for everyone. In: Proceedings of the 39th International Conference on Machine Learning (ICML). Baltimore, Maryland, USA: PMLR, 2022, pp. 2709–2720 (2022)
2. Pei, G., et al.:Deepfake generation and detection: A benchmark and survey. arXiv preprint arXiv:2403.17881 (2024)
3. Veaux, C., Yamagishi, J., MacDonald, K.: The voice cloning toolkit (vctk) corpus. https://datashare.ed.ac.uk/handle/10283/2651, Edinburgh, Scotland, UK, 2017, university of Edinburgh. Centre for Speech Technology Research (CSTR) (2017)
4. Todisco, M., Delgado, H., Evans, N., Yamagishi, J., Kinnunen, T., et al.: Asvspoof 2019: Future horizons in spoofed and fake audio detection. In: Proceedings of Interspeech, Graz, Austria, 2019, pp. 1008–1012 (2019)
5. Yamagishi, J., et al.: Asvspoof 2021: accelerating progress in spoofed and deepfake speech detection. In: Proceedings of Interspeech, Brno, Czech Republic, 2021, pp. 3660–3664 (2021)
6. Zhang, L., Wang, X., Cooper, E., Evans, N., Yamagishi, J.: The Partialspoof Database and Countermeasures for the Detection of Short Fake Speech Segments Embedded in an Utterance. Speech, and Language Processing, IEEE/ACM Transactions on Audio (2022)
7. Yi, J., et al.: Half-truth: A partially fake audio detection dataset. arXiv preprint arXiv:2104.03617 (2021)
8. Huang, W., Gu, Y., Wang, Z., Zhu, H., Qian, Y.: Speechfake: A large-scale multilingual speech deepfake dataset toward cutting-edge speech generation methods,. 2025, preprint; DOI unavailable (2025)
9. Shah, A.J., Purohit, R.M., Vaghera, D.H., Patil, H.: Mladdc: multi-lingual audio deepfake detection corpus. In: Audio Imagination: NeurIPS 2024 Workshop on AI-Driven Speech, Music, and Sound Generation. Vancouver, British Columbia, Canada (2024)
10. Purohit, R.M., Shah, A.J., Patil, H.A.: GGMDDC: a GAN-guided multilingual audio deepfake detection dataset (2024), DOI unavailable

11. Tabei, N.:"deep-translator: a flexible free and unlimited python translator library," https://github.com/nidhaloff/deep-translator, Munich, Germany (2020). Accessed 30 July 2025
12. Castro, P.S., Gölge, E., Meyer, J., Schüldt, C.: X-TTS: a massively multilingual zero-shot text-to-speech model. arXiv preprint arXiv:2309.15547, Ithaca, New York, USA, 2023, last accessed: August 7, (2025). https://arxiv.org/abs/2309.15547

# Swarm Intelligence

# Quantum Swarm Intelligence Combined with Kapur Entropy for Optimized Retinal Image Segmentation

Sajad Ahmad Rather$^{(\boxtimes)}$ , Mohd Yasir Arafat, and Partha Pratim Roy

Indian Institute of Technology Roorkee, Roorkee, India
{sajad.pd,partha}@cs.iitr.ac.in, my_arafat@ph.iitr.ac.in

**Abstract.** The segmentation of retinal images into multiple meaningful regions is a critical step in medical image interpretation, directly impacting diagnostic accuracy and clinical decision support. Conventional thresholding techniques, while foundational, often suffer from limitations in handling complex pixel distributions, particularly in high-dimensional search spaces where the risk of premature convergence and local stagnation increases with the number of thresholds. In response to these challenges, this work implements the Quantum-behaved Particle Swarm Optimization (QPSO) algorithm tailored for multilevel threshold-based segmentation. Distinct from classical PSO, QPSO integrates probabilistic modeling rooted in quantum theory, enabling a superior balance between global exploration and local exploitation. The segmentation framework is guided by Kapur's entropy, which serves as a fitness criterion to optimize the selection of threshold values by maximizing inter-region information content. The QPSO is systematically applied to publicly available retinal image datasets, and its performance is benchmarked against a suite of seven contemporary metaheuristic algorithms. Quantitative evaluation is conducted using standard metrics, including PSNR, SSIM, FSIM, and MSE, while statistical robustness is established through non-parametric Wilcoxon signed-rank and Friedman tests. Experimental results consistently indicate the superiority of QPSO, achieving an SSIM of 0.88, FSIM of 0.89, and PSNR of 24.77, underscoring its potential as an effective and computationally efficient solution for complex medical image segmentation tasks.

**Keywords:** Medical Imaging · Quantum Computing · Metaheuristics · Kapur's Entropy Criterion · Particle Swarm Optimization (PSO) · Multilevel Thresholding

## 1 Introduction

The integration of medical imaging technologies into clinical workflows has revolutionized diagnostic and therapeutic paradigms by enabling high-resolution, non-invasive visualization of internal anatomical and pathological structures [1]. These modalities are indispensable in modern medicine, underpinning the detection, assessment, and longitudinal monitoring of a wide range of diseases,


S. Mitra et al. (Eds.): PReMI 2025, LNCS 16358, pp. 853–863, 2026.
https://doi.org/10.1007/978-3-032-18480-1_87

including malignancies, neurodegenerative conditions, and cardiovascular abnormalities [2]. Central to the analytical processing of such imaging data is the task of image segmentation–an essential computational procedure that delineates regions of interest by clustering pixels based on intensity profiles and spatial coherence [3]. This step is foundational across imaging modalities, including Magnetic Resonance Imaging (MRI), Computed Tomography (CT), and ultrasonography, where it facilitates automated interpretation and extraction of critical anatomical features [4]. In oncological imaging, for instance, precise segmentation enables accurate localization of tumor margins, supports radiation dose planning, and assists in monitoring therapeutic response [5]. Similarly, in cardiovascular imaging, segmentation aids in the demarcation of vascular territories and myocardial regions, contributing to the diagnosis of conditions such as stenosis and aneurysms [6]. In neurological contexts, the ability to segment cortical and subcortical brain structures enhances the identification of pathological hallmarks associated with disorders like Alzheimer's disease and multiple sclerosis [7].

Metaheuristic algorithms are advanced stochastic optimization techniques designed to efficiently tackle complex, nonlinear, and high-dimensional problems where traditional methods often underperform, especially in non-convex search spaces [8]. Inspired by natural and evolutionary processes, these algorithms–such as Genetic Algorithms (GA), Particle Swarm Optimization (PSO), Ant Colony Optimization (ACO), and Simulated Annealing (SA)–employ a strategic balance between exploration and exploitation to identify near-optimal solutions [9]. In medical image analysis, particularly in segmentation tasks involving modalities like MRI, CT, and retinal imaging, metaheuristics have demonstrated significant robustness in handling issues like noise, low contrast, and ambiguous anatomical boundaries that hinder classical approaches [10]. Retinal image analysis benefits greatly from metaheuristic algorithms, which excel at segmenting complex anatomical features such as the optic disc, macula, and vascular networks, where traditional methods often struggle [11]. These structures are essential for early diagnosis and monitoring of ocular diseases including diabetic retinopathy, glaucoma, and age-related macular degeneration [12]. By effectively avoiding local minima and enabling global search, metaheuristics achieve precise segmentation even in low-contrast or degraded images, surpassing classical thresholding and edge-detection approaches [13]. Additionally, they facilitate systemic disease diagnosis by detecting subtle retinal vascular changes associated with hypertension, diabetes, and cardiovascular disorders [14]. This work applies Quantum-behaved Particle Swarm Optimization (QPSO) for multilevel segmentation to enhance vascular structure extraction, aiming to improve diagnostic accuracy in retinal pathology. The core contributions of this research are summarized as follows: (1) A novel multilevel image segmentation methodology is proposed based on Quantum-behaved Particle Swarm Optimization (QPSO), which leverages quantum-inspired probabilistic modeling to enhance global optimization efficiency. (2) Kapur's entropy is employed as the fitness criterion to determine optimal threshold levels, enabling precise partitioning of retinal images by maximizing informational content across grayscale distributions. (3) The QPSO-based segmentation framework is validated on high-resolution retinal fundus datasets, demonstrating accurate delineation of critical anatomical features such as blood vessels, the optic disc, and macular region for early pathology detection. (4) Quantitative evaluation is performed using PSNR, SSIM, FSIM, and MSE to assess segmentation quality and reconstruction fidelity. (5) Comparative experiments with seven state-of-the-art metaheuristic algorithms reveal that QPSO outperforms peers in terms of segmentation accuracy, convergence behavior, robustness, and computational cost, establishing its practical relevance in ophthalmic image analysis.

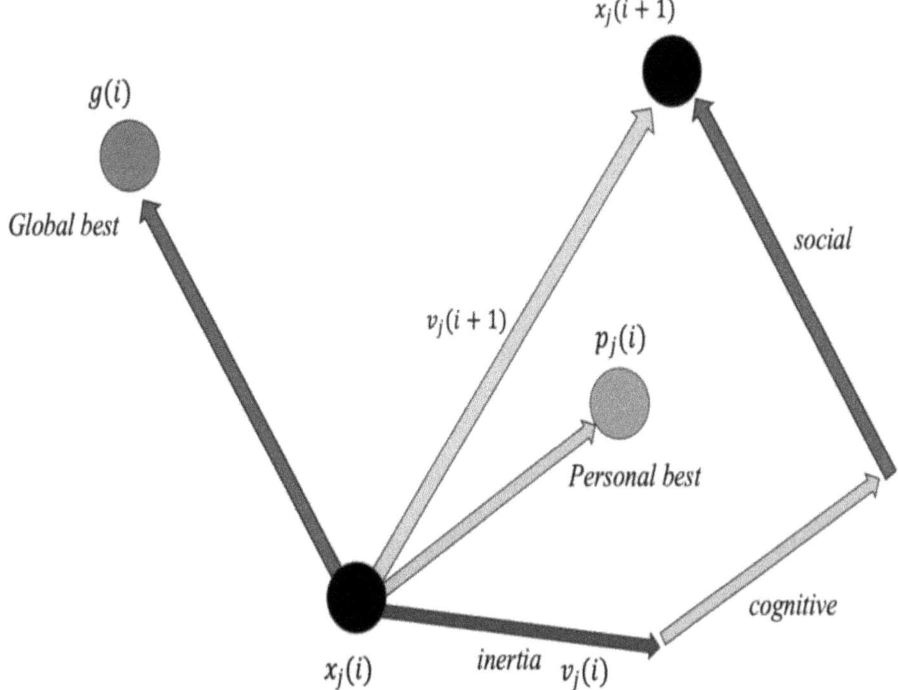



**Fig. 1.** Particle update mechanism in Particle Swarm Optimization (PSO). The particle's new position $x_j(i+1)$ is influenced by inertia, cognitive (personal best $p_j(i)$), and social (global best $g(i)$) components, resulting in the updated velocity $v_j(i+1)$.

## 2   Methodology

### 2.1   Particle Swarm Optimization

Particle Swarm Optimization (PSO) [15] is a population-based optimization technique inspired by the collective behavior of biological swarms, such as flocks of birds or schools of fish. In this algorithm, each particle represents a potential solution and navigates the search space by updating its velocity and position based on both individual experience and social collaboration within the swarm, as shown in Fig. 1. The velocity of each particle is updated according to the following equation:

$$v_i^{t+1} = w \cdot v_i^t + c_1 \cdot r_1 \cdot (p_i^t - x_i^t) + c_2 \cdot r_2 \cdot (g^t - x_i^t) \tag{1}$$

where $w$ denotes the inertia weight, $c_1$ and $c_2$ are cognitive and social acceleration coefficients respectively, $r_1$ and $r_2$ are uniformly distributed random numbers in the range $[0, 1]$, $p_i^t$ is the best-known position of the particle, and $g^t$ is the best-known global position found by the swarm. Subsequently, the position of each particle is updated as:

$$x_i^{t+1} = x_i^t + v_i^{t+1} \tag{2}$$

This iterative process guides the particles toward the optimal solution by balancing exploration and exploitation, making PSO effective for solving various complex optimization problems.

## 2.2   Kapur's Entropy Criterion

Kapur's entropy-based segmentation is a widely adopted approach that focuses on maximizing the information gained from segmenting an image's histogram into multiple meaningful classes [16]. By partitioning the histogram according to optimal threshold values, the method aims to maximize the sum of entropies from all segmented regions, ensuring that each class retains significant discriminatory information.

Let an image consist of $L$ discrete gray levels and be segmented using a set of $m - 1$ thresholds $\{t_1, t_2, \ldots, t_{m-1}\}$. The probability associated with class $i$, spanning the interval $[t_{i-1} + 1, t_i]$, is calculated as:

$$P_i = \sum_{j=t_{i-1}+1}^{t_i} p(j) \tag{3}$$

where $p(j)$ represents the normalized probability of gray level $j$. The entropy for class $i$ is then computed using the following relation:

$$E_i = - \sum_{j=t_{i-1}+1}^{t_i} \left( \frac{p(j)}{P_i} \right) \log \left( \frac{p(j)}{P_i} \right) \tag{4}$$

The global objective is to maximize the total entropy across all $m$ classes, which is given by:

$$E = \sum_{i=1}^{m} E_i \tag{5}$$

The optimal threshold set is the one that maximizes this total entropy $E$, ensuring that the segmented regions capture the most informative characteristics of the image.

## 2.3  Image Segmentation Leveraging Quantum Dynamics in Particle Swarm Optimization

The standard formulation of Particle Swarm Optimization (PSO) is hindered by inherent structural limitations that impact its scalability and solution robustness. Chief among these is its predisposition to early convergence, where particles aggregate around local optima due to insufficient exploratory dynamics. This issue is compounded by the algorithm's sensitivity to hyperparameter calibration–specifically the inertia weight and cognitive-social acceleration constants–which govern swarm behavior but often require meticulous tuning. Additionally, PSO's deterministic update mechanism restricts dynamic adaptability, thereby impeding its ability to effectively explore complex or high-dimensional search spaces. As the dimensionality of the problem increases, the algorithm's computational overhead grows substantially, further deteriorating its convergence performance and solution diversity.

Quantum-behaved Particle Swarm Optimization (QPSO) represents a paradigm shift from classical PSO by embedding quantum mechanics into the swarm intelligence framework. Unlike conventional PSO, which updates particle trajectories using deterministic velocity rules, QPSO employs a quantum delta potential well model wherein particle positions are governed by probabilistic wave functions. This probabilistic behavior significantly enhances the algorithm's exploratory dynamics and alleviates issues such as stagnation in local optima. A distinctive advantage of QPSO is its simplified control structure. Its optimization behavior is primarily regulated by a single contraction-expansion coefficient, thereby eliminating the need for multiple parameter settings and facilitating a more adaptive trade-off between diversification and intensification during the search process. The particle position in QPSO is updated using the following expression:

$$x_i(t+1) = p_i \pm \beta \cdot |\varphi_i - x_i(t)| \cdot \ln\left(\frac{1}{u}\right) \tag{6}$$

Here, $x_i(t)$ is the current position of the $i$-th particle, $p_i$ represents the local attractor derived from the particle's personal and global best, $\varphi_i$ denotes the center of the quantum potential field, $\beta$ is the contraction-expansion coefficient, and $u \in (0,1)$ is a uniformly distributed random variable. This stochastic update strategy not only improves global search capability but also enhances convergence speed and robustness in solving high-dimensional and nonlinear optimization problems. The operational framework of the multilevel thresholding method using QPSO is demonstrated in Fig. 2.

## 3  Experimental Results and Discussion

This section describes the experimental configuration, including the datasets used, the evaluation metrics adopted, and the baseline algorithms selected for comparison.

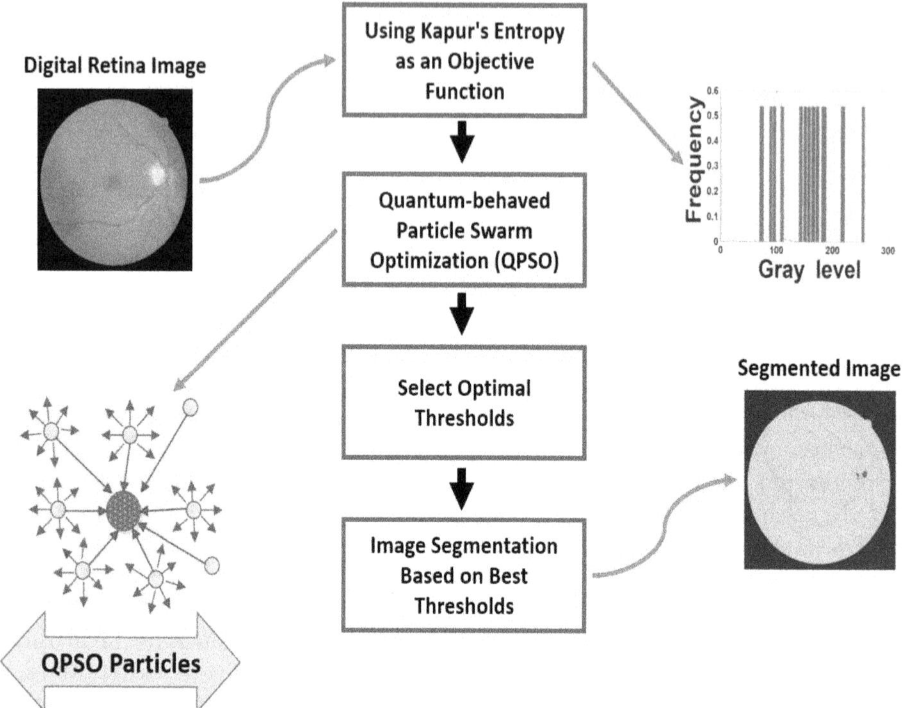



**Fig. 2.** Flowchart of the QPSO-based multilevel thresholding approach for retinal image segmentation. The method uses Kapur's entropy as the objective function and applies QPSO to select optimal thresholds for accurate segmentation.

## 3.1   Experimental Setup

This study assesses the QPSO method for retinal image segmentation using datasets from the Kaggle repository[1], where pixel intensities range from 0 to 255. The DRIVE dataset, sourced from a diabetic retinopathy screening program in the Netherlands, contains images mostly free of retinopathy, with some exhibiting early mild signs. Images were captured with a Canon CR5 camera featuring a 45° field of view and a resolution of 768 × 584 pixels. For benchmarking, multiple heuristic algorithms–including PSO [17], GSA [18], PSOGSA [19], SSA [20], CPSOGSA [21], GWO [22], and GJO [23]–were implemented with their original parameter settings. Each algorithm ran with 30 agents over 300 iterations, stopping when 10% of runs converged. Experiments were performed on MATLAB R2024a using a 2.00 GHz Intel i7 Xeon processor. Segmentation quality was evaluated using MSE, PSNR, SSIM, and FSIM metrics.

---

[1] https://www.kaggle.com/datasets/andrewmvd/drive-digital-retinal-images-for-vessel-extraction.

## 3.2   Simulation Results

The results in Table 1 affirm the strong performance of QPSO in determining optimal thresholds for multilevel image segmentation. It consistently outperforms competing algorithms across key metrics, including PSNR, SSIM, FSIM, and Kapur's fitness values, indicating high-quality segmentation with preserved structural integrity. Notably, the QPSO variant demonstrates excellent computational efficiency, completing the thresholding process in just 23.42 s, which is significantly faster than its counterparts. The statistical analysis further reinforces QPSO's superiority, with p-values less than 0.05 across all comparison methods, indicating significant performance gains. This is further supported by its leading position in the Friedman mean rank evaluation, highlighting the algorithm's robustness, precision, and consistency in handling complex segmentation tasks as shown in Fig. 3.

**Table 1.** Benchmarking of heuristic algorithms for multilevel thresholding at $k = 10$.

| Method | Optimal Thresholds | STD ↓ | MSE ↓ | PSNR ↑ | SSIM ↑ | FSIM ↑ | Kapur's Fitness Values ↑ | Run Time ↓ | $p$-Values ↓ |
|---|---|---|---|---|---|---|---|---|---|
| GSA | 121,156,120,129,122,155,158,124,151,176 | 0.38 | 4726.57 | 11.38 | 0.21 | 0.72 | 32.42 | 31.27 | 1.95E-03 |
| PSO | 6,7,10,20,25,27,38,40,53,54 | 0.87 | 2914.68 | 13.48 | 0.70 | 0.77 | 27.80 | 27.24 | 1.95E-03 |
| PSOGSA | 10,12,14,17,18,26,78,82,86,107 | 1.13 | 274.02 | 23.75 | 0.68 | 0.87 | 28.38 | 26.15 | 1.95E-03 |
| CPSOGSA | 5,31,34,34,37,59,69,82,85,106 | 0.84 | 270.13 | 23.81 | 0.86 | 0.88 | 28.94 | 25.85 | 1.95E-03 |
| SSA | 135,182,155,160,169,84,167,70,175,183 | 3.19 | 678.50 | 19.81 | 0.61 | 0.80 | 29.39 | 33.17 | 1.95E-03 |
| GWO | 42,51,83,69,60,18,37,78,35,40 | 2.27 | 989.05 | 18.17 | 0.61 | 0.75 | 28.13 | 31.72 | 1.95E-03 |
| GJO | 216,178,191,225,119,226,192,173,228,112 | 2.55 | 2994.99 | 13.36 | 0.33 | 0.68 | 32.41 | 32.69 | 1.95E-03 |
| **QPSO** | **118,161,255,193,246,142,242,189,255,72** | **0.19** | **250.53** | **24.77** | **0.88** | **0.89** | **38.25** | **23.42** | **0000001** |

The effectiveness of QPSO is evident in Fig. 4, where both the convergence curves and boxplots demonstrate its superior optimization behavior compared to other algorithms. QPSO not only reaches the highest fitness values but also converges rapidly, indicating efficient exploration and exploitation within the pixel intensity search space. The boxplots further validate its robustness, displaying low variance, compact interquartile ranges, and fewer outliers, all of which suggest consistent performance across independent runs. This reliability, combined with its computational efficiency, highlights QPSO's dominance in both accuracy and speed. Moreover, as shown in Fig. 5, QPSO exhibits exceptional performance in retinal image segmentation, accurately extracting blood vessels at various threshold levels ($k = 10, 15, 20$).

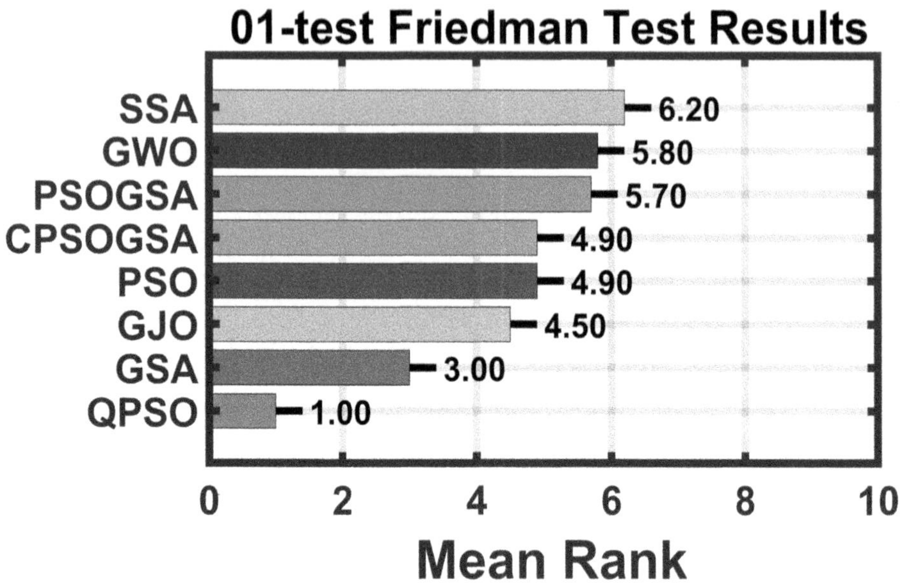



**Fig. 3.** Friedman test results for the 01-test case show that QPSO achieved the best mean rank (1.00), indicating superior performance compared to other algorithms.

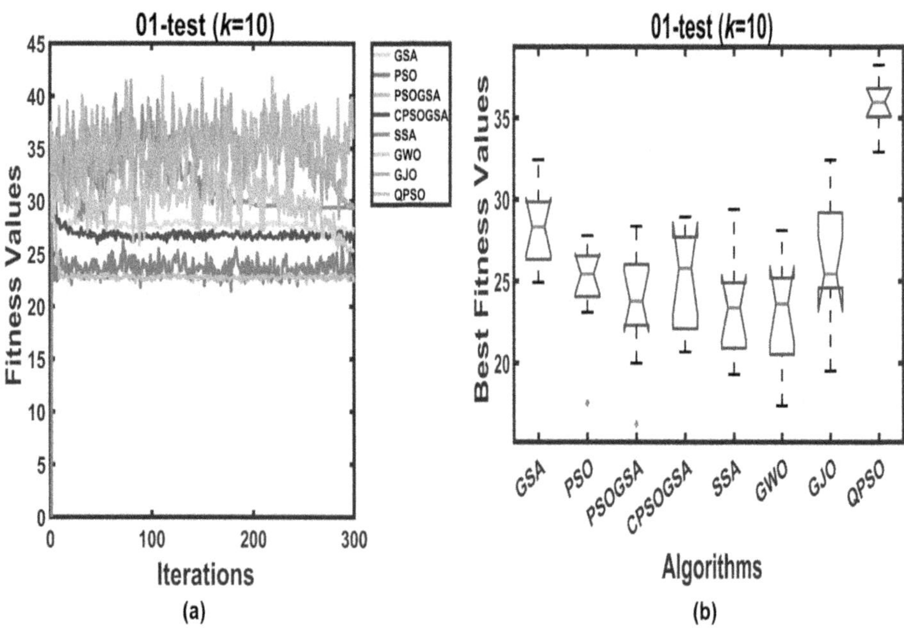



**Fig. 4.** Convergence curves (a) and boxplots (b) for the 01-test image at $k = 10$, illustrating QPSO's superior performance with the highest fitness values, fastest convergence, and minimal variance across runs.

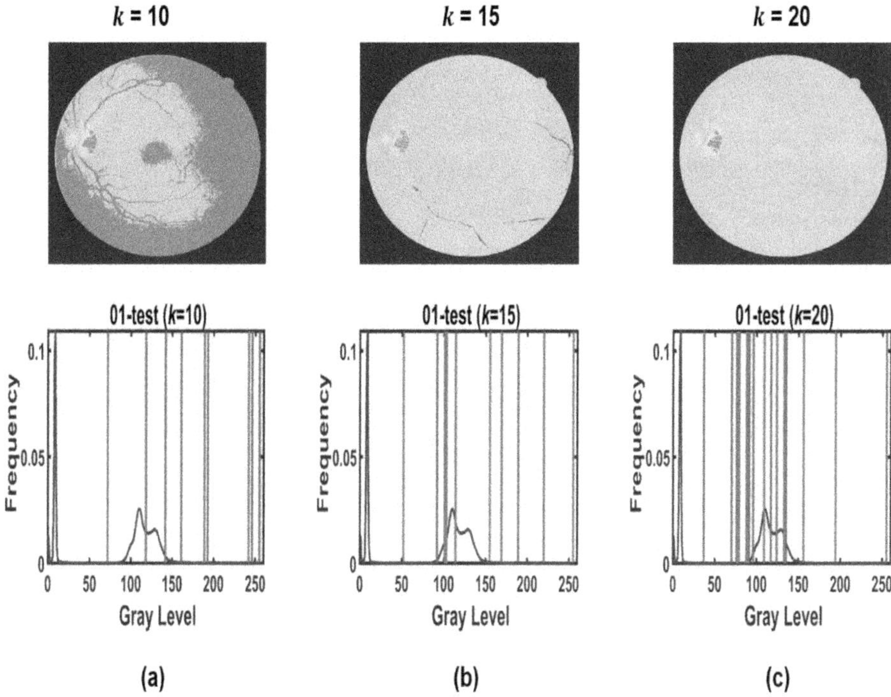



**Fig. 5.** Retinal segmentation results and histogram entropy plots using QPSO with jet colormap at $k = 10, 15, 20$, illustrating its efficiency in multilevel thresholding and vascular structure enhancement.

## 4    Conclusion

Retinal image segmentation has greatly benefited from the application of Quantum-behaved Particle Swarm Optimization (QPSO), particularly when combined with Kapur's entropy-based objective function. This integration enables QPSO to effectively determine optimal threshold values across multiple intensity levels, resulting in accurate segmentation with rapid convergence and low computational cost. Its superior performance is reflected in key evaluation metrics–SSIM, FSIM, PSNR, MSE, and runtime–demonstrating robustness in delineating retinal blood vessels, which is vital for the early diagnosis of ocular diseases such as diabetic retinopathy and glaucoma. Given its clinical relevance, QPSO holds significant potential as a diagnostic aid in ophthalmology and endocrinology. Future enhancements may involve extending the approach to multimodal imaging, integrating strategies like opposition-based learning or Lévy flight, and exploring advanced entropy models such as Masi, Tsallis, and Renyi to further boost segmentation accuracy and optimization efficiency.

**Acknowledgements.** The authors gratefully acknowledge the financial support received from the Anusandhan National Research Foundation (ANRF)-National Post Doctoral Fellowship (N-PDF) (File No. PDF/2023/000567), Government of India.

# References


1. Hussain, S., et al.: Modern diagnostic imaging technique applications and risk factors in the medical field: a review. Biomed. Res. Int. **2022**(1), 1–16 (2022)
2. Wang, Y.R., et al.: Screening and diagnosis of cardiovascular disease using artificial intelligence-enabled cardiac magnetic resonance imaging. Nat. Med. **2024**, 1–10 (2024)
3. Rayed, M.E., Islam, S.S., Niha, S.I., Jim, J.R., Kabir, M.M., Mridha, M.F.: Deep learning for medical image segmentation: State-of-the-art advancements and challenges. Inform. Med. Unlocked **2024**(101504), 1–12 (2024)
4. Ma, J., He, Y., Li, F., Han, L., You, C., Wang, B.: Segment anything in medical images. Nat. Commun. **15**(1), 654 (2024)
5. Jalalifar, S.A., Soliman, H., Sahgal, A., Sadeghi-Naini, A.: Impact of Tumour segmentation accuracy on efficacy of quantitative MRI biomarkers of radiotherapy outcome in brain metastasis. Cancers **14**(20), 5133 (2022)
6. Counseller, Q., Aboelkassem, Y.: Recent technologies in cardiac imaging. Front. Med. Technol. **4**, 984492 (2023)
7. Kim, J., Jeong, M., Stiles, W.R., Choi, H.S.: Neuroimaging modalities in Alzheimer's disease: diagnosis and clinical features. Int. J. Mol. Sci. **23**(11), 6079 (2022)
8. Rajwar, K., Deep, K., Das, S.: An exhaustive review of the metaheuristic algorithms for search and optimization: taxonomy, applications, and open challenges. Artif. Intell. Rev. **56**(11), 13187–13257 (2023)
9. Rani, R., Jain, S., Garg, H.: A review of nature-inspired algorithms on single-objective optimization problems from 2019 to 2023. Artif. Intell. Rev. **57**(5), 1–51 (2024)
10. Li, M., Jiang, Y., Zhang, Y., Zhu, H.: Medical image analysis using deep learning algorithms. Front. Public Health **11**, 1273253 (2023)
11. Grzybowski, A., Jin, K., Zhou, J., Pan, X., Wang, M., Ye, J., Wong, T.Y.: Retina fundus photograph-based artificial intelligence algorithms in medicine: a systematic review. Ophthalmol. Ther. **2024**, 1–25 (2024)
12. Zang, P., Hormel, T.T., Hwang, T.S., Bailey, S.T., Huang, D., Jia, Y.: Deep-learning–aided diagnosis of diabetic retinopathy, age-related macular degeneration, and glaucoma based on structural and angiographic OCT. Ophthalmol. Sci. **3**(1), 100245 (2023)
13. Kavitha, K.V.N., Shanmugam, A., Imoize, A.L.: Optimized deep knowledge-based no-reference image quality index for denoised MRI images. Sci. Afr. **20**, e01680 (2023)
14. Soltani, A., Battikh, T., Jabri, I., Lakhoua, N.: A new expert system based on fuzzy logic and image processing algorithms for early glaucoma diagnosis. Biomed. Signal Process. Control **40**, 366–377 (2018)
15. Gad, A.G.: Particle swarm optimization algorithm and its applications: a systematic review. Arch. Comput. Methods Eng. **29**(5), 2531–2561 (2022)

16. Abdel-Basset, M., Mohamed, R., Abouhawwash, M.: A new fusion of whale optimizer algorithm with Kapur's entropy for multi-threshold image segmentation: analysis and validations. Artif. Intell. Rev. **55**(8), 6389–6459 (2022)
17. Kennedy, J., Eberhart, R.: Particle swarm optimization. In: Proceedings of the ICNN'95 - International Conference Neural Network, vol. 4, pp. 1942–1948. IEEE (1995)
18. Rashedi, E., Nezamabadi-Pour, H., Saryazdi, S.: GSA: a gravitational search algorithm. Inf. Sci. **179**(13), 2232–2248 (2009)
19. Chaudhari, S., Thakare, A., Anter, A.M.: PSOGSA: a parallel implementation model for data clustering using new hybrid swarm intelligence and improved machine learning technique. Sustain. Comput. Inform. Syst. **41**, 100953 (2024)
20. Abualigah, L., Shehab, M., Alshinwan, M., Alabool, H.: Salp swarm algorithm: a comprehensive survey. Neural Comput. Appl. **32**(15), 11195–11215 (2020)
21. Rather, S.A., Bala, P.S.: Levy flight and chaos theory-based gravitational search algorithm for global optimization: LCGSA for global optimization. Int. J. Appl. Metaheurist. Comput. **13**(1), 1–58 (2022)
22. Mirjalili, S., Mirjalili, S.M., Lewis, A.: Grey wolf optimizer. Adv. Eng. Softw. **69**, 46–61 (2014)
23. Chopra, N., Ansari, M.M.: Golden jackal optimization: a novel nature-inspired optimizer for engineering applications. Expert Syst. Appl. **198**, 116924 (2022)

# Video Processing

# Automated Tracking of Ocular Movements of Fish Using a Semi-supervised Algorithm: A Laboratory Study on Optokinetic Response of Adult Zebrafish


Barnini Bhattacharya[1]([✉]) [iD], Shibsankar Roy[1] [iD], Sanmoy Bandyopadhyay[2] [iD], Bijay Bal[3] [iD], Shankarashis Mukherjee[4] [iD], Anuradha Bhat[5] [iD], and Kuntal Ghosh[1]([✉]) [iD]

[1] Indian Statistical Institute, 203, B.T. Road, Kolkata 700108, India
barnibhattacharya@gmail.com, kuntalghos@gmail.com
[2] Aryabhatta Research Institute of Observational Sciences, Manora Peak, Nainital 263001, India
[3] Saha Institute of Nuclear Physics (Retired), AF Block, Bidhan Nagar, Kolkata 700064, India
[4] West Bengal State University, Kolkata, West Bengal 700126, India
[5] Indian Institutes of Science Education and Research, Kolkata, West Bengal 741246, India



**Abstract.** Optokinetic Response or OKR is a reflexive visuomotor response of vertebrates to a surrounding visual stimulus in motion. The eye movements during OKR can be divided into two phases – the slow SPEM (smooth pursuit eye movement) phase, along the same direction of the moving stimulus and the fast nystagmus phase (corrective saccadic movements), in the opposite direction. OKR is considered to be a crucial indicator of several fundamental and pathological aspects of visual functioning. Zebrafish, a freshwater fish, is an emerging animal model for vision research. However, in the context of national scenario, there remains a dearth of quantitative OKR studies in zebrafish. Moreover, globally, only a few commercially available instruments for recording OKR in zebrafish are available. Thus, OKR recording and computerized tracking of the ocular movement in response to the visual stimulus from videographic data remains a challenging area of research. The present study thus, aimed at automated tracking of the ocular movements of zebrafish, using a semi-supervised computerized tracking algorithm, in response to the visual stimulus, through development of a customized and cost-effective OKR apparatus, in the laboratory. The eye movement was quantified in terms of the frequency of the ocular movement of the fish, as computed from the nystagmus frequency. The results obtained from the proposed algorithm was standardized using the manually computed values (the actual count method) and was also compared with that of the classical methods of Optical Flow and FlowNet. The proposed technique outperformed the classical methods by offering the best balance between accuracy and stability.

**Keywords:** Semi-supervised Tracking · Ocular Movements · Adult Zebrafish · Optokinetic Response



© The Author(s), under exclusive license to Springer Nature Switzerland AG 2026
S. Mitra et al. (Eds.): PReMI 2025, LNCS 16358, pp. 867–876, 2026.
https://doi.org/10.1007/978-3-032-18480-1_88

# 1  Introduction

Among the several visuomotor reflexes, the optokinetic response (OKR) is one of the most studied responses across vertebrates, ranging from rodents to fish. The OKR involves reflexive tracking of the surrounding objects in motion in order to stabilize the image on the retina [1]. It mainly consists of two phases – a slow phase termed as smooth pursuit eye movement (SPEM) that occurs in the same direction of the surrounding stimulus in motion and the other is the fast nystagmus phase that involves corrective eye movements in the opposite direction to that of the moving stimulus [2]. OKR is considered as an important motion stabilization reflex. It is a highly conserved response across the animal kingdom because motion stabilization and maintenance of visual acuity is of vital importance for orientation in space, hunting for prey, or escaping from predators [3]. The response is used for diagnosing visual defects (like lesions in the visual pathway) and other diseases associated with visuomotor deficits like Parkinson's disease, for assessing conscious perception and also for objectively measuring visual acuity (the resolving power of eyes) in both children and adults [4–6]. The first ever recorded application of OKR (1950) in research was that of the pigeon model [7]. Since then, several animal models have been used for studying vertebrate OKR. Among them, in recent times, Zebrafish is considered to be an ideal animal model to study visual physiology owing to the similarity of their retina to other vertebrates [8, 9].

In the laboratory, OKR is induced through a visual stimulus consisting of alternate black and white striped drum that revolves around the subject [10]. In humans, to record OKR in a laboratory, the subject must be seated in an examination chair, wearing goggles where the visual stimulus is displayed while the surrounding light is turned off. The pupils must be clearly visible in order to record the saccadic eye movement through the examination monitor. The subject is then instructed to fixate the gaze on the target point (around 1 m away). The eye position is then calibrated by instructing the patient to follow the target point as rapidly as possible using only ocular motion; that is, while keeping the head motionless [11].

Despite the use of zebrafish for visual research, there exist a dearth of commercially available instruments that can record OKR in adult and larval zebrafish. Till date probably, there is only one Europe-based company that is known to manufacture OKR instrument (VisioBox 2.0, manufactured by Viewpoint Behavior Technology) [12]. As a result, most of the studies conducted on OKR assessment of zebrafish have developed laboratory-based OKR instruments. Till date some research works have developed software to automatically record the OKR of mostly larval fish in terms of change in visual angle before and after stimulus presentation [13–15]. The presence of tracking software to count the no. of ocular movements of adult zebrafish is comparatively less [16, 17].

In view of this, in the present study, a semi-supervised computerized tracking algorithm has been proposed for automated tracking of the ocular movements of adult zebrafish, in response to the optokinetic stimulus, through development of a customized and cost-effective OKR apparatus, in the laboratory. The novel semi-supervised object tracing technique was used to quantify the frequency of the oscillatory eye movement of the fish. The proposed tracking method involved both, region-based segmentation, and edge-based segmentation. The region-based segmentation was used to identify the region of interest based on pixel similarities and the edge-based segmentation was used to detect the boundaries of the ocular region by analyzing the changes in pixel intensity. Once the ocular region of the zebrafish was accurately identified, detailed statistical analysis was performed to quantify the frequency of the fish's oscillatory eye movement.

## 2  Methodology

### 2.1  Evoking OKR in Adult Zebrafish Using the Lab-Built OKR Apparatus

For the study to induce OKR the lab-built OKR recorder was used (see Fig. 1). The apparatus consisted of a center-fixed surround rotating drum, a fixed platform for placing the mounted fish to be used in experimentation, a stimulus display region for presenting the visual stimulus consisting of alternate black and white stripes (see Fig. 1) and an electrical unit for controlling the speed and direction of the rotating visual stimulus. Adult zebrafish were procured from registered fish breeder and maintained in the institutional Animal House Facility (registration no. 2146/GO/Re/S/22/CPCSEA). After a 10 days acclimatization period 5 adult zebrafish were used for the study.

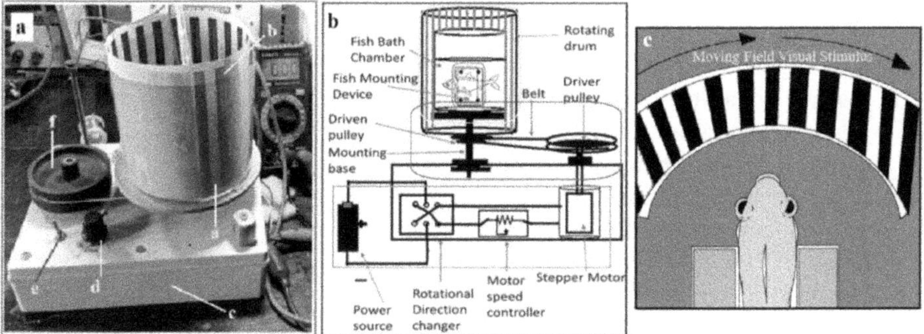


**Fig. 1.** **a)** The lab-built OKR Recorder a - rotating drum, b - interchangeable grating pattern, c - electrical unit, d - speed controller, e - direction modulator, f – pulley; **b)** Schematic Diagram of the Customized OKR Apparatus; **c)** Top view of the internal segment of the recording unit of the apparatus with the mounted fish and OKR stimulus in the surrounding

For mounting the fish, hypothermia induced anaesthesia was used and the fish were securely placed inside a glass cylindrical chamber that allowed the fish to have a clear visual field of the stimulus. Following this the surrounding wall of the drum was rotated using the electrical unit of the apparatus to induce the characteristic ocular movement in the fish. The visual stimulus was presented for a period of 10 s. The experimental results were digitally recorded using a mobile phone camera (resolution $1080 \times 1920$ pixels and around 30 frames per second). The experimental protocol was designed by following the CCSEA guidelines for experimentation on fish. The whole experimental protocol was approved by the Institutional Animal Ethics Committee of Indian Statistical Institute (proposal no. ISI-IAEC/2022/01/01).

## 2.2   Tracking of the Frequency of the Ocular Movement

The frequency of the ocular movement was calculated in terms of the nystagmus frequency during the smooth pursuit eye movement phase of OKR [18]. In order to carry out the task of quantifying the frequency of the oscillatory eye movement of the fish a novel semi-supervised object tracking technique has been applied. The overall technique is assembled in two parts. The first part consists of computer vision techniques, which deals with the identification of the ocular region of the zebrafish, and the later part deals with the statistical analysis which targets in calculating the total number of oscillatory eye movement. For the first part of the tracking process, both region-based as-well-as edge-based segmentation techniques have been applied for proper identification of the boundary of the region of interest (RoI). The boundary identification of RoI has been carried out in six steps. In the very first step, human interpretation has been incorporated to crop out the region from video containing the zebrafish. Basically, this step has been implemented in the work in order to avoid the computational complexity and to reduce the computational time. In the later step, simple threshold-based segmentation given by,

$$g_i(x, y) = \{1 \ if \ I_i(x, y) \ \leq \ Th \ 0 \ if I_i(x, y) > Th, \tag{1}$$

has been applied on each and every frame extracted out from the cropped video with a view to segment out the zebrafish from the extracted frames. Here, in Eq. 1, the term $I_i(x, y)$ denotes the pixel intensity of the $i$-$th$ frame at $(x, y)$ coordinates, the term $g_i(x, y)$ denotes the segmented output and $Th$ indicates the threshold value. Followed by this thresholding technique, area - based image morphological operation has been applied, where image-disconnected component was analyzed to remove the redundant regions from the segmented image [19, 20]. That is, if a segmented image component does not satisfy the specified area threshold criterion, that component is removed from the segmented image. In the next stage, the filtered segmented image is divided into four quadrants, and the quadrant with no changes is labeled as zero, to reduce the computational complexity. At the final stage of ocular region's edge detection, binary quadrant with label one is extracted out and the edge of the retained region is detected using canny edge detection technique [21]. Now, at the final phase of tracking of the frequency of the ocular movement, a two-dimensional graph is generated based on the coordinate points of the detected canny edge for each frame of the cropped video, in such a way that x-axis of the graph replicates the pixel coordinate location along x-axis in binary quadrant with label one, similarly, y-axis of the graph replicates the pixel coordinate location along y-axis in the same quadrant image. Then after statistical data analysis has been carried out based on the plotted graph, where variance in the $y$ data for each x-coordinate has been calculated using the formulation,

$$s^2 = \frac{\sum_{i=1}^{n}(y_i - \bar{y})^2}{n - 1}, \tag{2}$$

where, n denotes the total number of extracted frames. Based on these variance values, the x-coordinate with maximum variance is located. This particular x-coordinate with maximum variance value in turn resembles the point in zebrafish ocular which is having maximum number of movement frequency. Followed by this, Gaussian filter has been applied over the y data for corresponding x-coordinate to eliminate the small fluctuation in $y$ value that occurs due to surrounding conditions of the experimental setup, like, movement of water, lighting condition during capturing of video, etc. Thereafter, the frequency of ocular movement has been calculated based on the number of detected peaks in the filtered $y$ data using the formulation given by,

$$P = \sum_{i=1}^{n} \mathbb{I}(f(i, y_i) > f(i-1, y_{i-1}) \wedge f(i, y_i) > f(i+1, y_{i+1}), \tag{3}$$

where, the notion II resembles the indicator function that is 1 if the condition is true and 0 otherwise. The results obtained using the developed algorithm were validated by comparing the ocular frequency with those obtained through manual counting using the frame-by-frame option (total 300 frames) of the VLC media player. The overall block diagram of the proposed technique of ocular movement frequency tracking is shown in Fig. 2. And the algorithmic structure used to implement the ocular tracking process is described in Table 1, which provides the corresponding pseudocode representation.

## 3  Results

In the present study the speed of the rotating drum was kept fixed at 1.05 rad.s$^{-1}$ (10 rpm). The spatial frequency of the visual stimulus was computed to be as 0.2 cpd. In the study the frequency of the ocular movement of the three fish tracked and quantified using the developed algorithm has been graphically represented in Fig. 3 below. In the graph the no. of peaks represents the smooth pursuit eye movement along the same direction of the rotating drum (visual stimulus) and the no. of valleys represents the corrective saccadic movement in the opposite direction (Table 2).

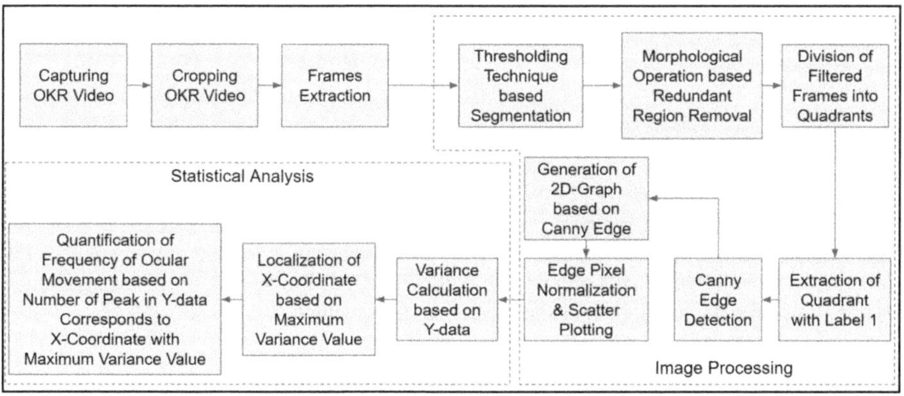


**Fig. 2.** Block diagram of the proposed technique

The results have been compared with the output obtained using the classical method (Fig. 3) of optical flow [21] and FlowNet [22]. Considering the Actual Count as ground truth, it reports an average frequency of 15.20 ± 5.36 events. The Proposed Method

**Table 1.** The pseudocode representing the core steps of the proposed method

```
 1: procedure Ocular_Movement_Tracking(OKR_Video)
 2:   video ← LOAD_VIDEO(OKR_Video)
 3:   rotated_video ← ROTATE(video, −90)
 4:   roi_video ← CROP(rotated_video, region_of_interest)
 5:   frames ← EXTRACT_FRAMES(roi_video)
 6:   for each frame in frames do
 7:     gray ← CONVERT_TO_GRAYSCALE(frame)
 8:     segmented ← THRESHOLD(gray)
 9:     cleaned ← REMOVE_SMALL_OBJECTS(segmented, size_threshold)
10:     edge_map ← CANNY_EDGE_DETECTION(cleaned)
11:     (x, y) ← EXTRACT_EDGE_COORDINATES(edge_map)
12:     y_norm ← NORMALIZE(y)
13:     STORE(y_norm, corresponding_to = x)
14:   end for
15:   var_y[x] ← CALCULATE_VARIANCE(y_norm[x])
16:   x_max ← ARGMAX(var_y[x])
17:   y_smooth ← GAUSSIAN_SMOOTH(y_norm[x_max])
18:   peaks ← DETECT_PEAKS(y_smooth)
19:   frequency ← COUNT(peaks) / VIDEO_DURATION(OKR_Video)
20: end procedure
```

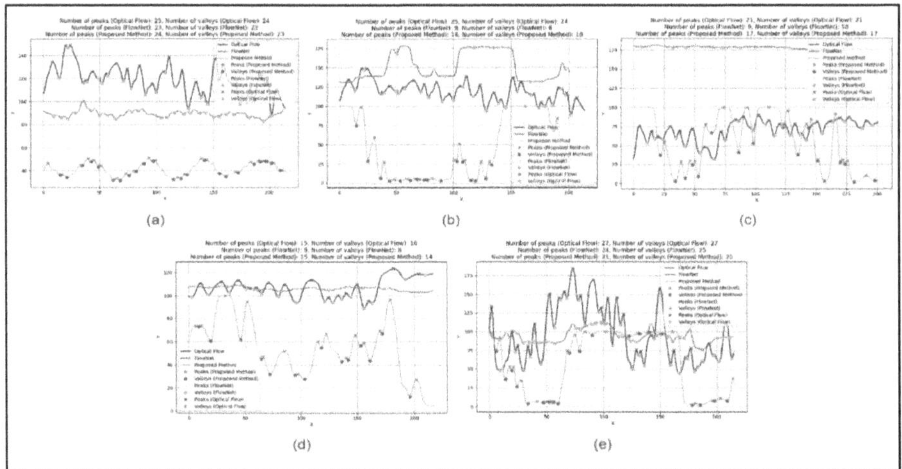

**Fig. 3.** Comparative graphical representation of the frequency of the ocular movement of a) Fish 1, b) Fish 2, c) Fish 3, d) Fish 4 and e) Fish 5 eliciting OKR in presence of the visual stimulus obtained using the proposed method and the optical flow method

shows the closest overall match, detecting 19.00 ± 3.54 peaks and 18.40 ± 3.36 valleys with lower variability, indicating stable and consistent performance. Although the FlowNet Method reports average values (14.60 ± 8.14 peaks and 14.80 ± 8.46 valleys) numerically closer to the actual count, its high standard deviation reflects poor consistency across trials. The Optical Flow Method overestimates both peaks and valleys (22.20 ± 4.60 and 22.20 ± 4.09), likely due to sensitivity to minor motion changes.

**Table 2.** Tabular Representation of the number of peaks and valleys, and related MSE obtained from the computerized tracking data of the ocular movement

| Sl. No. | Actual Count | Proposed Method | | Optical Flow Method | | FlowNet Method | |
|---|---|---|---|---|---|---|---|
| | *Frequency* | *No. of Peaks* | *No. of Valleys* | *No. of Peaks* | *No. of Valleys* | *No. of Peaks* | *No. of Valleys* |
| 1 | 23 | 24 | 23 | 25 | 24 | 23 | 23 |
| 2 | 8 | 18 | 18 | 23 | 23 | 9 | 8 |
| 3 | 14 | 17 | 17 | 21 | 21 | 9 | 10 |
| 4 | 15 | 15 | 14 | 15 | 16 | 8 | 8 |
| 5 | 16 | 21 | 20 | 27 | 27 | 24 | 25 |
| AM ± SD | 15.20 ± 5.36 | 19.00 ± 3.54 | 18.40 ± 3.36 | 22.20 ± 4.60 | 22.20 ± 4.09 | 14.60 ± 8.14 | 14.80 ± 8.46 |
| Bias | – | 3.80 | 3.20 | 7.00 | 7.00 | −0.60 | −0.40 |
| Variance | – | 12.53 | 11.29 | 21.16 | 16.72 | 66.26 | 71.55 |
| MSE | – | 26.96 | 21.53 | 70.16 | 65.72 | 66.62 | 71.71 |
| Average MSE | – | 24.25 | | 67.94 | | 69.17 | |

From a statistical standpoint, the Mean Squared Error (MSE) - which combines both bias and variance serves as a more comprehensive indicator of performance. Mathematically, it is expressed as

$$MSE = \left( \mathbb{E}\left[ \hat{\theta} \right] - \theta \right)^2 + \sigma^2 \tag{4}$$

where $\hat{\theta}$ denotes the estimated value (detected event count), $\theta$ is the ground truth, and represents the expectation over multiple trials. In the Eq. (5) the first term $\left( \mathbb{E}\left[ \hat{\theta} \right] - \theta \right)^2$ represents the squared bias, measuring the systematic error between the average estimate and the true value, and $\sigma^2$ denotes the variance of the estimator, quantifying the variability of the estimates across trials. Although the proposed method introduces a modest positive bias, its significantly lower variance minimizes the overall MSE (as seen in Table 2), offering a better balance between accuracy and reliability. As such, it yields the closest overall match by minimizing variability.

## 4  Discussion

The proposed tracking method used in the study involved both, region-based segmentation, and edge-based segmentation. The region-based segmentation was used to identify the region of interest based on pixel similarities and the edge-based segmentation was used to detect the boundaries of the ocular region by analyzing the changes in pixel intensity. Once the ocular region of the zebrafish was accurately identified, detailed statistical analysis was performed to quantify the frequency of the fish's oscillatory eye movement. To standardize the findings the computed values were compared with other classical tracking methods like optical flow and FlowNet [22, 23]. The results indicated that the initial attempt to track and quantify the ocular movement frequency using the proposed method was effective in automatically tracking the oscillatory eye movements of zebrafish in presence of the optokinetic stimulus. It may be further used for understanding how different stimuli influence the OKR in adult zebrafish by noting the variation in frequency (no. of peaks and valleys) of the ocular movement. Increasing the sample size in order to improve the tracking accuracy and to further develop the algorithm remains the future goal of the present study. In the present study the frequency of ocular movement computed using the proposed method was validated using the data obtained from manual counting (frame by frame) and was then compared with the classical optical flow method as well as with FlowNet method. Some of the recent works have also developed eye tracking algorithms based on similar techniques [16]. Some other works have used deep learning-based algorithms like DeepLabCut for measuring visual function in zebrafish [24]. From our results it may be found that the proposed algorithm provides quite reliable computed values of the ocular movement frequency. The comparative results have been represented in Table 1 above. From the resultant graphs it is evident that the proposed technique for ocular movement detection outperforms the existing classical optical flow method and the FlowNet method by offering the best balance between accuracy and stability. The system enables non-invasive, scalable tracking of attention and behavior across biology, robotics, environmental monitoring, and astronomy, supporting tasks from species identification to robotic navigation. Additionally, it may be applied for analyzing solar Coronal Mass Ejection (CME) events. However, performance may be limited by morphological differences, environmental noise, and sensor quality. Moreover, fully interpreting complex cognition leads to the requirement of integration with additional data sources. In future, the present study may aid in modelling of vision-related pathological conditions like light-induced retinal degeneration [24], lesion of visual pathway [1, 25], for studying neurological diseases associated with visuomotor deficits like cerebellar ataxia [26] and for testing the efficacy of novel drugs for treatment or control of visual or neurological disorders [27], using adult zebrafish model.

## 5   Conclusion

From the study it may thus be concluded that the proposed approach to quantify the ocular movement of zebrafish, generated in response to the visual stimulus may prove to be effective in quantitatively studying the OKR of small-sized fish in terms of frequency of the angular eye movement. The future objective is to implement the convolutional neural network (CNN) based optical flow method for further improvements in quantification of the fish ocular movements.

**Acknowledgments.** The authors acknowledge DST-CSRI, GoI for funding the project.

**Data Availability.**   The videos used for the study have been uploaded to a repository (https://git hub.com/barninibiophysics/Zebrafish.git) for future use.

**Disclosure of Interests.**   The authors declare no conflicts of interest.

# References


1. Huang, Y.Y., Neuhauss, S.C.: The optokinetic response in zebrafish and its applications. Front. Biosci.-Landmark **13**(5), 1899–1916 (2008)
2. Schlegel, D.K., Neuhauss, S.C.: The larval visual system and behavioral responses to visual stimuli. In: Behavioral and Neural Genetics of Zebrafish, pp. 35–48. Academic Press, United States (2020)
3. Takhmazyan, T., Cameron, D.J.: Comparing the visual acuity of zebrafish using analog and digital systems. Invest. Ophthalmol. Vis. Sci. **63**(7), 2562 (2022)
4. Thomas, B.B., Seiler, M.J., Sadda, S.R., Coffey, P.J., Aramant, R.B.: Optokinetic test to evaluate visual acuity of each eye independently. J. Neurosci. Methods **138**(1–2), 7–13 (2004)
5. Miura, K., Takemura, A., Taki, M., Kawano, K.: Model of optokinetic responses involving two different visual motion processing pathways. Prog. Brain Res. **248**, 329–340 (2019)
6. Fujiwara, M., Ding, C., Kaunitz, L., Stout, J.C., Thyagarajan, D., Tsuchiya, N.: Optokinetic nystagmus reflects perceptual directions in the onset binocular rivalry in Parkinson's disease. PLoS ONE **12**(3), 0173707 (2017)
7. Fulton, A.B., Manning, K.A., Dobson, V.: A behavioral method for efficient screening of visual acuity in young infants. II. Clinical application. Investig. Ophthalmol. Vis. Sci. **17**(12), 1151–1157 (1978)
8. Chhetri, J., Jacobson, G., Gueven, N.: Zebrafish—on the move towards ophthalmological research. Eye **28**(4), 367–380 (2014)
9. Avanesov, A., Malicki, J.: Analysis of the retina in the zebrafish model. In: Methods in Cell Biology, pp. 153–204. Academic Press, United States (2010)
10. Cameron, D.J., et al.: The optokinetic response as a quantitative measure of visual acuity in zebrafish. J. Visual. Exp. **9**(80), 50832 (2013)
11. Kang, J.J., Lee, S.U., Kim, J.M., Oh, S.Y.: Recording and interpretation of ocular movements: saccades, smooth pursuit, and optokinetic nystagmus. Ann. Clin. Neurophysiol. **25**(2), 55–65 (2023)
12. VisioBox Homepage. https://www.viewpoint.fr/product/zebrafish/visual-function/visiobox. Accessed 08 Sept 2024
13. Scheetz, S.D., Shao, E., Zhou, Y., Cario, C.L., Bai, Q., Burton, E.A.: An open-source method to analyze optokinetic reflex responses in larval zebrafish. J. Neurosci. Methods **1**(293), 329–337 (2018)
14. Straumann, D., Ying-Yu Huang, M.: Velocity storage mechanism in zebrafish larvae. J. Physiol. **592**(1), 203–214 (2014)
15. Rodwell, V., Birchall, A., Yoon, H.J., Kuht, H.J., Norton, W.H., Thomas, M.G.: A novel portable flip-phone based visual behaviour assay for zebrafish. Sci. Rep. **14**(1), 236 (2024)
16. Dehmelt, F.A., von Daranyi, A., Leyden, C., Arrenberg, A.B.: Evoking and tracking zebrafish eye movement in multiple larvae with ZebEyeTrack. Nat. Protoc. **13**(7), 1539–1568 (2018)
17. Sánchez, A.G., Álvarez, Y., Colligris, B., Kennedy, B.N.: Affordable and effective optokinetic response methods to assess visual acuity and contrast sensitivity in larval to juvenile zebrafish. Open Res. Europe **1** (2021)
18. Bhattacharya, B., Roy, S., Bal, B., Mukherjee, S., Bhat, A., Ghosh, K.: Effect of Variation of Spatial and Temporal Frequencies of the Moving Field Visual Stimulus on Optokinetic Response of Adult Zebrafish. Zebrafish (2025)
19. Abbott, R., Williams, L.: Multiple target tracking with lazy background subtraction and connected components analysis. Mach. Vis. Appl. **20**(2), 93–101 (2009)
20. Bandyopadhyay, S., Das, S., Datta, A.: Fuzzy energy-based dual contours model for automated coronal hole detection in SDO/AIA solar disk images. Adv. Space Res. **65**(10), 2435–2455 (2020)

21. Canny, J.: A computational approach to edge detection. IEEE Trans. Pattern Anal. Mach. Intell. **6**, 679–698 (1986)
22. Lucas, B.D., Kanade, T.: An iterative image registration technique with an application to stereo vision. In: IJCAI'81: 7th International Joint Conference on Artificial Intelligence, vol. 2, pp. 674–679 (1981)
23. Dosovitskiy, A., et al.: Flownet: learning optical flow with convolutional networks. In: Proceedings of the IEEE International Conference on Computer Vision, pp. 2758–2766 (2015)
24. Patil, M., et al.: A deep learning approach to measure visual function in zebrafish. Biology **14**(6), 663 (2025)
25. Gunaseelan, A., Narenthiran, K.R., Tantry, M.A., Santhakumar, K.: A Simple and Cost-Effective Setup to Analyze Optokinetic Response in Adult Zebrafish. Zebrafish (2025)
26. Sarasamma, S., Karim, A., Orengo, J.P.: Zebrafish models of rare neurological diseases like Spinocerebellar Ataxias (SCAs): advantages and limitations. Biology **2**(10), 1322 (2023)
27. Shao, E., Scheetz, S.D., Xie, W., Burton, E.A.: Modulation of the zebrafish optokinetic reflex by pharmacologic agents targeting GABAA receptors. Neurosci. Lett. **671**, 33–37 (2018)

# Author Index





S. Mitra et al. (Eds.): PReMI 2025, LNCS 16358, pp. 877–880, 2026.
https://doi.org/10.1007/978-3-032-18480-1

GPSR Compliance
The European Union's (EU) General Product Safety Regulation (GPSR) is a set
of rules that requires consumer products to be safe and our obligations to
ensure this.

If you have any concerns about our products, you can contact us on

ProductSafety@springernature.com

In case Publisher is established outside the EU, the EU authorized
representative is:

Springer Nature Customer Service Center GmbH
Europaplatz 3
69115 Heidelberg, Germany